Adobe® Photoshop® CS4
Complete Concepts and Techniques

Gary B. Shelly
Joy L. Starks
Indiana University Purdue University Indianapolis (IUPUI)

COURSE TECHNOLOGY
CENGAGE Learning

Australia • Brazil • Japan • Korea • Mexico • Singapore • Spain • United Kingdom • United States

COURSE TECHNOLOGY
CENGAGE Learning™

Adobe® Photoshop® CS4
Complete Concepts and Techniques,
Gary B. Shelly, Joy L. Starks

Executive Editor: Kathleen McMahon

Product Manager: Crystal Parenteau

Associate Product Manager: Jon Farnham

Editorial Assistant: Lauren Brody

Director of Marketing: Cheryl Costantini

Marketing Manager: Tristen Kendall

Marketing Coordinator: Julie Schuster

Print Buyer: Julio Esperas

Director of Production: Patty Stephan

Senior Content Project Manager: Jill Braiewa

Developmental Editor: Amanda Brodkin

QA Manuscript Reviewers: Susan Whalen and Danielle Shaw

Copyeditor: Troy Lilly

Proofreader: Kim Kosmatka

Indexer: Liz Cunningham

Art Director: Marissa Falco

Cover and Text Design: Joel Sadagursky

Cover Photo: Jon Chomitz

Compositor: GEX Publishing Services

© 2010 Course Technology, Cengage Learning

ALL RIGHTS RESERVED. No part of this work covered by the copyright herein may be reproduced, transmitted, stored or used in any form or by any means graphic, electronic, or mechanical, including but not limited to photocopying, recording, scanning, digitizing, taping, Web distribution, information networks, or information storage and retrieval systems, except as permitted under Section 107 or 108 of the 1976 United States Copyright Act, without the prior written permission of the publisher.

For product information and technology assistance, contact us at
Cengage Learning Customer & Sales Support, 1-800-354-9706

For permission to use material from this text or product, submit all requests online at **cengage.com/permissions**
Further permissions questions can be emailed to
permissionrequest@cengage.com

Library of Congress Control Number: 2009930826

ISBN-13: 978-1-4390-7930-0

ISBN-10: 1-4390-7930-7

Course Technology
20 Channel Center Street
Boston, Massachusetts 02210
USA

Cengage Learning is a leading provider of customized learning solutions with office locations around the globe, including Singapore, the United Kingdom, Australia, Mexico, Brazil, and Japan. Locate your local office at:
www.cengage.com/global

Cengage Learning products are represented in Canada by Nelson Education, Ltd.

To learn more about Course Technology, visit **www.cengage.com/coursetechnology**

Purchase any of our products at your local college bookstore or at our preferred online store **www.ichapters.com**

Printed in the United States of America
1 2 3 4 5 6 7 15 14 13 12 11 10 09

Adobe Photoshop® CS4
Complete Concepts and Techniques

Contents

Preface	viii

CHAPTER ONE
Editing a Photo

Objectives	**PS 1**
What Is Photoshop CS4?	**PS 2**
Project — Postcard Graphic	**PS 3**
Overview	PS 4
Starting Photoshop	**PS 5**
To Start Photoshop	PS 5
Customizing the Photoshop Workspace	**PS 6**
To Restore the Default Workspace	PS 7
To Reset the Tools Panel	PS 8
To Reset the Options Bar	PS 8
Opening a Photo	**PS 10**
To Open a Photo	PS 10
The Photoshop Workspace	**PS 12**
The Application Bar	PS 12
The Menu Bar	PS 13
The Options Bar	PS 14
The Tools Panel	PS 14
The Document Window	PS 15
Panels	PS 16
File Types	**PS 18**
Saving a Photo	**PS 19**
To Save a Photo in the PSD Format	PS 20
Viewing Photos	**PS 24**
Zooming	PS 24
To Use the Zoom Tool	PS 25
The Navigator Panel	PS 27
To View and Use the Navigator Panel	PS 28
To Collapse the Navigator Panel	PS 29
The Hand Tool	PS 30
To Use the Hand Tool	PS 30
To Change the Screen Mode	PS 31
Rulers	PS 33
To Display Rulers	PS 33
Editing the Photo	**PS 34**
Cropping	PS 35
To Crop a Photo	PS 37
Creating a Blended Border	**PS 39**
Making Selections	PS 40
To Select All	PS 40
Modifying Selections	PS 41
To Create a Border Using the Modify Submenu	PS 42
Filling a Selection	PS 43
To Fill a Selection	PS 44
To Deselect	PS 46
Saving a Photo with the Same File Name	**PS 46**
Changing Image Sizes	**PS 47**
To Resize the Image	PS 47
To Save a Photo with a Different Name	PS 49
Printing a Photo	**PS 49**
To Print a Photo	PS 50
To Close a Photo	PS 51
Saving a Photo for Use on the Web	**PS 52**
Using the Save for Web & Devices Command	PS 53
To Preview Using the Save for Web & Devices Dialog Box	PS 53
To Choose a Download Speed	PS 55
Options in the Save for Web & Devices Dialog Box	PS 56
To Set Other Options in the Save for Web & Devices Dialog Box	PS 57
To Preview the Photo on the Web	PS 59
To Save the Photo for the Web	PS 60
Adobe Bridge	**PS 60**
To Use Bridge to View Files	PS 61
To Close Bridge	PS 63
Photoshop Help	**PS 63**
To Access Photoshop Help	PS 64
Using the Search Box	PS 65
To Use the Help Search Box	PS 65
To Quit Photoshop	PS 66
Chapter Summary	**PS 67**
Learn It Online	**PS 68**
Apply Your Knowledge	**PS 68**
Extend Your Knowledge	**PS 70**
Make It Right	**PS 71**
In the Lab	**PS 71**
Cases and Places	**PS 76**

CHAPTER TWO
Using Selection Tools and Shortcut Keys

Objectives	**PS 77**
Introduction	**PS 78**
Project — Advertisement Graphic	**PS 78**
Overview	PS 78
Creating an Advertising Piece	**PS 80**
Starting and Customizing Photoshop	PS 81
The Save As Dialog Box	PS 83
The Marquee Tools	**PS 85**
To Use the Rectangular Marquee Tool	PS 89
The Move Tool	**PS 90**
To Use the Move Tool	PS 91
The Magic Wand Tool	**PS 92**
To Subtract from a Selection Using the Magic Wand Tool	PS 93
To Duplicate the Selection	PS 94
The Transformation Commands	**PS 95**
To Scale a Selection	PS 98
To Flip a Selection	PS 99
Warping	PS 101
To Warp a Selection	PS 101
To Deselect Using Shortcut Keys	PS 103
The History Panel	**PS 103**
To Display the History Panel	PS 105
Using the History Panel	PS 105
To Use the History Panel	PS 106
To Collapse the History Panel	PS 107
Grids and Guides	**PS 108**
To Display a Grid	PS 109
To Create Guides	PS 110
The Quick Selection Tool	**PS 112**
To Use the Quick Selection Tool	PS 113
To Undo Using the History Panel	PS 115
The Refine Edge Dialog Box	PS 115
To Refine Edges	PS 117
The Lasso Tools	**PS 119**
To Select Using the Lasso Tool	PS 121
To Select Using the Magnetic Lasso Tool	PS 123
To Rotate a Selection	PS 126
Using the Polygonal Lasso Tool	PS 127
To Select Using the Polygonal Lasso Tool	PS 128
The Grow Command	PS 131
To Grow the Selection	PS 133
Finishing the Advertisement	PS 134
Creating PDF Files	**PS 138**
To Create a PDF File Using the Print Command	PS 138
To View the PDF File	PS 141
Keyboard Shortcuts	**PS 142**
Creating a Keyboard Shortcut	PS 142
To Create a New Keyboard Shortcut	PS 143
To Test a New Keyboard Shortcut	PS 146
To Return to the Default Settings for Keyboard Shortcuts	PS 147
Chapter Summary	**PS 149**
Learn It Online	**PS 149**
Apply Your Knowledge	**PS 150**
Extend Your Knowledge	**PS 151**
Make It Right	**PS 153**
In the Lab	**PS 154**
Cases and Places	**PS 158**

CHAPTER THREE
Working with Layers

Objectives	**PS 159**
Introduction	**PS 160**
Project — Landscape Design	**PS 160**
Overview	PS 162
Creating a Composite	**PS 162**
Starting and Customizing Photoshop	PS 163
To Reset the Default Colors	PS 164
Creating a Composite Image Using Layers	**PS 167**
Layers	PS 167
To Display the Layers Panel	PS 169
To Change Layer Panel Options	PS 169
Creating a Layer Via Cut	**PS 171**
To Create a Layer Via Cut	PS 172
To Name and Color a Layer	PS 173
To Hide and Show a Layer	PS 174
Creating a Layer from Another Image	**PS 175**
To Open a Second Image	PS 176
Displaying Multiple Files	PS 176
To Arrange the Document Windows	PS 177
To Create a Layer by Dragging an Entire Image	PS 178
To Set Layer Properties Using the Context Menu	PS 179
Creating a Layer by Dragging a Selection	**PS 180**
To Create a Layer by Dragging a Selection	PS 182
The Eraser Tools	**PS 185**
Using the Magic Eraser Tool	PS 186
To Erase Using the Magic Eraser Tool	PS 186
Using the Eraser Tool	PS 188
To Erase Using the Eraser Tool	PS 189
Using the Background Eraser Tool	PS 191
To Erase Using the Background Eraser Tool	PS 191
To Consolidate the Windows	PS 195
Layer Masks	**PS 196**
To Create a Layer Mask	PS 197
To Correct a Masking Error	PS 199
The Masks Panel	PS 200
To Use the Masks Panel	PS 202
Fine-Tuning Layers	**PS 205**
Making an Opacity Change to a Layer	PS 206
To Make an Opacity Change to a Layer	PS 206
The Adjustments Panel	PS 207
Level Adjustments	PS 208
To Make a Level Adjustment	PS 209
To Adjust the Hue and Saturation	PS 210

Brightness and Contrast	PS 211
To Change the Brightness and Contrast	PS 212
Layer Styles	**PS 213**
To Add a Layer Style	PS 214
To Hide Layer Effects in the Layers Panel	PS 215
Applying a Render Filter	PS 216
To Apply a Render Filter	PS 216
The Clone Stamp Tool	**PS 218**
To Create a Clone	PS 220
Flattening a Composite Image	**PS 224**
To Flatten a Composite Image	PS 225
To Save a File in the TIF Format	PS 226
Chapter Summary	**PS 228**
Learn It Online	**PS 228**
Apply Your Knowledge	**PS 229**
Extend Your Knowledge	**PS 231**
Make It Right	**PS 234**
In the Lab	**PS 235**
Cases and Places	**PS 239**

CHAPTER FOUR
Drawing and Painting with Color

Objectives	PS 241
Introduction	PS 242
Project — Menu Front Cover	PS 242
Overview	PS 242
Creating a New File	**PS 244**
Starting and Customizing Photoshop	PS 245
To Create a Photoshop File from Scratch	PS 247
The Color Panel	**PS 250**
To Change the Color Panel	PS 250
Gradients	**PS 251**
To Create a Gradient	PS 253
Gradient Presets	PS 254
To Select a Gradient Preset	PS 255
The Select Stop Color Dialog Box	PS 256
To Select a Stop Color	PS 256
To Draw the Gradient	PS 258
Sampling Colors	**PS 259**
To Use the Eyedropper Tool	PS 260
Inserting Text	**PS 261**
To Select the Horizontal Type Tool	PS 262
To Set Font Options	PS 262
To Insert Text	PS 264
Stroking Text	PS 266
To Stroke the Text	PS 266
Shapes	**PS 268**
To Create a Shape	PS 270
To Skew a Shape	PS 271
To Add a Drop Shadow	PS 272
To Add New Shapes Using the Shape Picker	PS 274
The Paint Bucket Tool	**PS 279**
To Create a New Layer	PS 280
To Create a Polygonal Selection	PS 281
Editing Default Colors	PS 282
To Edit the Foreground Color	PS 282
To Fill Using the Paint Bucket Tool	PS 283

Painting with Brushes	**PS 284**
The Brush Tool	PS 286
To Select the Brush Tool	PS 286
To Use the Brush Preset Picker	PS 287
To Draw Using the Brush Tool	PS 287
To Draw Straight Lines with the Brush Tool	PS 288
The Brushes Panel	PS 291
Brush Options	PS 292
To Display the Brushes Panel	PS 293
To Append a New Brush Set to the Brushes Panel	PS 294
To Select the Brush Tip and Settings	PS 295
To Paint Using the 50s_Star Brush Tip	PS 295
Finishing the Menu Cover	PS 296
To Use the Ornament Brush Tip	PS 298
Chapter Summary	**PS 300**
Learn It Online	**PS 301**
Apply Your Knowledge	**PS 301**
Extend Your Knowledge	**PS 302**
Make It Right	**PS 304**
In the Lab	**PS 305**
Cases and Places	**PS 310**

CHAPTER FIVE
Enhancing and Repairing Photos

Objectives	PS 311
Introduction	PS 312
Project — Enhancing and Repairing Photos	PS 312
Overview	PS 314
Gathering Images	**PS 314**
Scanners	PS 315
Digital Cameras	PS 316
Web Graphics	PS 317
Starting and Customizing Photoshop	PS 317
Restoring Documents	**PS 318**
To Correct Yellowed Portions of the Document	PS 320
Blending Modes	**PS 321**
To Set the Blending Mode	PS 323
To Set Levels	PS 324
Sharpening Images	**PS 325**
To Apply the Unsharp Mask Filter	PS 326
To Recreate Missing Portions of the Document	PS 327
To Use the Eraser Tool	PS 329
Retouching Tools	**PS 330**
The Spot Healing Brush Tool	PS 331
To Duplicate a Layer for Corrections	PS 332
To Repair Damage with the Spot Healing Brush Tool	PS 333
The Healing Brush Tool	PS 335
To Sample and Paint with the Healing Brush Tool	PS 335
The Patch Tool	PS 337
To Patch Areas	PS 338
To View the Corrections	PS 340
The Red Eye Tool	PS 342
To Correct Red-Eye	PS 342
The Dodge, Burn, and Sponge Tools	**PS 345**
To Lighten Using the Dodge Tool	PS 345
Vignetting	PS 346
To Darken Using the Burn Tool	PS 347

Lens Correction Tools	PS 348
Angle and Perspective Errors	PS 349
To Correct Angle and Perspective Errors	PS 351
The Blur, Sharpen, and Smudge Tools	PS 356
To Blur	PS 357
Chapter Summary	PS 360
Learn It Online	PS 360
Apply Your Knowledge	PS 361
Extend Your Knowledge	PS 362
Make It Right	PS 364
In the Lab	PS 365
Cases and Places	PS 368

CHAPTER SIX
Creating Color Channels and Actions

Objectives	PS 369
Introduction	PS 370
Project — Candy Shop Advertising	PS 370
Overview	PS 372
Starting and Customizing Photoshop	PS 372
Using Channels	PS 376
The Channels Panel	PS 376
To View Channels	PS 377
To Select Using a Channel	PS 379
Alpha Channels	PS 380
To Create an Alpha Channel	PS 380
To Edit the Alpha Channel	PS 382
To Delete a Background Using an Alpha Channel	PS 383
Color Toning and Conversions	PS 385
Black and White	PS 386
To Desaturate	PS 386
To Create a Black-and-White Adjustment	PS 387
Sepia	PS 389
To Create a Sepia Image Using Selective Color	PS 390
Duotone	PS 391
To Convert an Image to Duotone	PS 391
Logos	PS 395
To Warp Text	PS 398
Actions	PS 401
The Actions Panel	PS 402
To Display the Actions Panel	PS 403
To Append Action Sets	PS 404
To Play an Action	PS 405
To Create a New Action Set	PS 407
To Create a New Action	PS 408
To Record an Action	PS 409
To Test the Action	PS 412
To Save an Action Set	PS 412
Completing the Advertisement	PS 413
Preparing for Four-Color Processing	PS 415
Using LAB Color	PS 416
To Convert to LAB Color	PS 417
Resizing, Resampling, and Interpolation	PS 417
The Image Size Dialog Box	PS 419
To Resize a File with Resampling	PS 419

Printing Color Separations	PS 421
To Print Color Separations	PS 421
Chapter Summary	PS 422
Learn It Online	PS 423
Apply Your Knowledge	PS 423
Extend Your Knowledge	PS 426
Make It Right	PS 427
In the Lab	PS 428
Cases and Places	PS 432

Appendices

APPENDIX A
Project Planning Guidelines

Using Project Planning Guidelines	APP 1
Determine the Project's Purpose	APP 1
Analyze Your Audience	APP 1
Gather Possible Content	APP 2
Determine What Content to Present to Your Audience	APP 2
Summary	APP 2

APPENDIX B
Graphic Design Overview

Understanding Design Principles	APP 3
Balance	APP 4
Contrast	APP 5
Dominance	APP 5
Proximity	APP 6
Repetition	APP 6
Closure	APP 7
Continuance	APP 7
Negative Space	APP 8
Unity	APP 8
Layout Grids	APP 8
Color Theory	APP 9
Color Properties	APP 9
Color Models	APP 10
Psychological Considerations of Color	APP 11
Print Considerations for Color	APP 11
Web Considerations for Color	APP 11
Relativity	APP 12
Color Schemes and Matching	APP 12
Typography	APP 15
Readability	APP 15
Typeface Categories	APP 16
Designing for Web vs. Print	APP 16
Device Dependency and Fluidity	APP 16
Pixels, Dimensions, and Resolution	APP 17
Working as a Graphic Designer	APP 19
Jobs in Graphic Design	APP 19
Design Projects	APP 20
Client and Designer Roles	APP 20

Defining the Project	APP 21
Specifying Project Details	APP 21
Collecting Materials	APP 21
Summary	**APP 22**

APPENDIX C
Changing Screen Resolution and Editing Preferences

Screen Resolution	**APP 23**
To Change Screen Resolution	APP 23
Editing Photoshop Preferences	**APP 27**
Editing General Preferences	APP 27
To Edit General Preferences	APP 27
Menu Command Preferences	**APP 29**
Hiding and Showing Menu Commands	APP 29
To Hide and Show Menu Commands	APP 30
To Add Color to Menu Commands	APP 33
Resetting the Panels, Keyboard Shortcuts, and Menus	APP 35
To Reset Tool Presets	APP 35
Resetting Panel Components	APP 36
To Reset the Brushes	APP 36
Changing Preferences	**APP 37**
Resetting Styles	**APP 38**
Searching the Web	**APP 38**

APPENDIX D
Using Photoshop Help

Photoshop Help	**APP 39**
Searching for Help Using Words and Phrases	**APP 39**
To Obtain Help Using the Search Box	APP 41
Using the Topics List	**APP 43**
To Use the Topics List	APP 43
To View a Video	APP 44
Using Photoshop Help PDF	**APP 45**
To Open Photoshop Help PDF	APP 45
To Navigate the Documentation by Chapter	APP 46
To Use the Find Box	APP 47
Use Help	**APP 48**

APPENDIX E
Using Adobe Bridge CS4

Adobe Bridge	**APP 49**
To Start Bridge Using Windows	APP 49
To Reset the Workspace	APP 50
The Adobe Bridge Window	**APP 51**
The Panels	APP 51
Toolbars and Buttons	APP 52
Bridge Navigation and File Viewing	APP 53
To Navigate and View Files Using Bridge	APP 54
Managing Files	APP 54
To Copy a File	APP 55
Metadata	**APP 56**
To Assign and View Metadata	APP 56
To Enter a New Keyword	APP 58
To Rate a Photo	APP 59
To Label a Photo with Color-Coding	APP 59
Searching Bridge	APP 61
Using the Find Command	APP 61
To Use the Find Command	APP 61
Using Bridge	**APP 64**
Quick Reference Summary	**QR 1**
Index	**IND 1**
Credits	**CRE 1**

Preface

The Shelly Cashman Series® offers the finest textbooks in computer education. We are proud of the fact that our previous Photoshop books have been so well received. With each new edition of our Photoshop books, we have made significant improvements based on the comments made by instructors and students. The Adobe Photoshop CS4 books continue with the innovation, quality, and reliability you have come to expect from the Shelly Cashman Series.

In 2006 and 2007, the Shelly Cashman Series development team carefully reviewed our pedagogy and analyzed its effectiveness in teaching today's student. An extensive customer survey produced results confirming what the series is best known for: its step-by-step, screen-by-screen instructions, its project-oriented approach, and the quality of its content.

We learned, though, that students entering computer courses today are different than students taking these classes just a few years ago. Students today read less, but need to retain more. They need not only to be able to perform skills, but to retain those skills and know how to apply them to different settings. Today's students need to be continually engaged and challenged to retain what they're learning.

As a result, we've renewed our commitment to focusing on the user and how they learn best. This commitment is reflected in every change we've made to our Photoshop book.

Objectives of This Textbook

Adobe Photoshop CS4: Complete Concepts and Techniques is intended for a course that offers an introduction to Photoshop and image editing. No previous experience with Adobe Photoshop CS4 is assumed, and no mathematics beyond the high school freshman level is required.

The objectives of this book are:

- To teach the fundamentals and more advanced features of Adobe Photoshop CS4
- To expose students to image editing and graphic design fundamentals
- To develop an exercise-oriented approach that promotes learning by doing
- To encourage independent study and to help those who are working alone
- To show how to use effective graphics in both business and personal situations
- To assist students in designing successful graphical documents from scratch and from components

Distinguishing Features

A Proven Pedagogy with an Emphasis on Project Planning Each chapter presents a practical problem to be solved, within a project planning framework. The project orientation is strengthened by the use of Plan Ahead boxes, that encourage critical thinking about how to proceed at various points in the project. Step-by-step instructions with supporting screens guide students through the steps. Instructional steps are supported by the Q&A, Experimental Step, and BTW features.

A Visually Engaging Book that Maintains Student Interest The step-by-step tasks, with supporting figures, provide a rich visual experience for the student. Call-outs on the screens that present both explanatory and navigational information provide students with information they need when they need to know it.

Supporting Reference Materials (Quick Reference, Appendices) The appendices provide additional information about the Application at hand, such as the Help Feature and customizing the application. With the Quick Reference, students can quickly look up information about a single task, such as keyboard shortcuts, and find page references of where in the book the task is illustrated.

Integration of the World Wide Web The World Wide Web is integrated into the Photoshop CS4 learning experience by (1) BTW annotations; (2) a Quick Reference Summary Web page; and (3) the Learn It Online section for each chapter.

End-of-Chapter Student Activities Extensive end of chapter activities provide a variety of reinforcement opportunities for students where they can apply and expand their skills through individual and group work.

Instructor Resources CD-ROM

The Instructor Resources include both teaching and testing aids.

INSTRUCTOR'S MANUAL Includes lecture notes summarizing the chapter sections, figures and boxed elements found in every chapter, teacher tips, classroom activities, lab activities, and quick quizzes in Microsoft Word files.

SYLLABUS Easily customizable sample syllabi that cover policies, assignments, exams, and other course information.

FIGURE FILES Illustrations for every figure in the textbook in electronic form.

POWERPOINT PRESENTATIONS A multimedia lecture presentation system that provides slides for each chapter. Presentations are based on chapter objectives.

SOLUTIONS TO EXERCISES Includes solutions for all end-of-chapter and chapter reinforcement exercises.

TEST BANK & TEST ENGINE Test Banks include 112 questions for every chapter, featuring objective-based and critical thinking question types, and including page number references and figure references, when appropriate. Also included is the test engine, ExamView, the ultimate tool for your objective-based testing needs.

DATA FILES FOR STUDENTS Includes all the files that are required by students to complete the exercises.

ADDITIONAL ACTIVITIES FOR STUDENTS Consists of Chapter Reinforcement Exercises, which are true/false, multiple-choice, and short answer questions that help students gain confidence in the material learned.

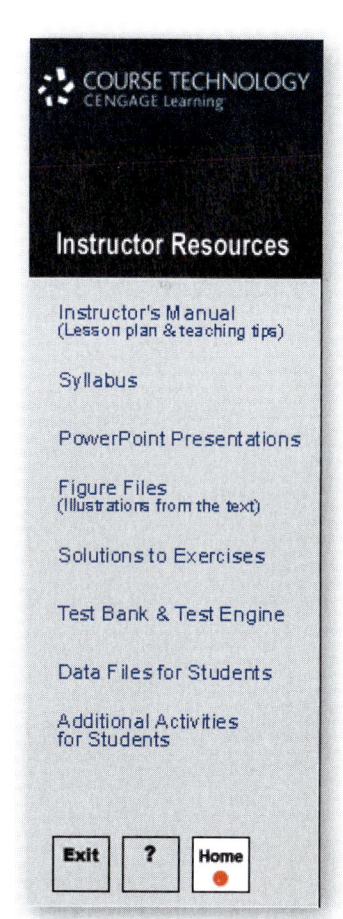

Content for Online Learning
Course Technology has partnered with Blackboard, the leading distance learning solution provider and class-management platform today. The resources available for download with this title are the test banks in Blackboard- and WebCT-compatible formats. To access this material, simply visit our password-protected instructor resources available at www.cengage.com/coursetechnology. For additional information or for an instructor username and password, please contact your sales representative.

CourseCasts Learning on the Go. Always Available…Always Relevant.
Our fast-paced world is driven by technology. You know because you are an active participant — always on the go, always keeping up with technological trends, and always learning new ways to embrace technology to power your life. Let CourseCasts, hosted by Ken Baldauf of Florida State University, be your guide into weekly updates in this ever-changing space. These timely, relevant podcasts are produced weekly and are available for download at http://coursecasts.course.com or directly from iTunes (search by CourseCasts). CourseCasts are a perfect solution to getting students (and even instructors) to learn on the go!

CourseNotes
Course Technology's CourseNotes are six-panel quick reference cards that reinforce the most important and widely used features of a software application in a visual and user-friendly format. CourseNotes serve as a great reference tool during and after the student completes the course. CourseNotes for Microsoft Office 2007, Word 2007, Excel 2007, Access 2007, PowerPoint 2007, Windows Vista, and more are available now!

Adobe Photoshop CS4 30-Day Trial Edition
A copy of the Photoshop CS4 30-Day trial edition can be downloaded from the Adobe Web site (www.adobe.com). Point to Downloads in the top navigation bar, click Trial Downloads, and then follow the on-screen instructions. When you activate the software, you will receive a license that allows you to use the software for 30 days. Course Technology and Adobe provide no product support for this trial edition. When the trial period ends, you can purchase a copy of Adobe Photoshop CS4, or uninstall the trial edition and reinstall your previous version. The minimum system requirements for the 30-day trial edition is a 1.8GHz or faster processor; Microsoft® Windows® XP with Service Pack 2 (Service Pack 3 recommended) or Windows Vista® Home Premium, Business, Ultimate, or Enterprise with Service Pack 1 (certified for 32-bit Windows XP and 32-bit and 64-bit Windows Vista); 512MB of RAM (1GB recommended); 1GB of available hard-disk space for installation; 1,024×768 display (1,280×800 recommended) with 16-bit video card; DVD-ROM drive; QuickTime 7.2 software required for multimedia features; and Broadband Internet connection required for online services.

Textbook Walk-Through

Plan Ahead boxes prepare students to create successful projects by encouraging them to think strategically about what they are trying to accomplish before they begin working.

Step-by-step instructions now provide a context beyond the point-and-click. Each step provides information on why students are performing each task, or what will occur as a result.

PS 4 Photoshop Chapter 1 Editing a Photo

Overview

As you read this chapter, you will learn how to edit the photo shown in Figure 1–1 by performing these general tasks:

- Customize the workspace.
- Display and navigate a photo at various magnifications.
- Crop a photo effectively.
- Create a blended border.
- Fill a selection.
- Resize and print a photo.
- Save, close, and then reopen a photo.
- Save a photo for the Web.
- Use Adobe Bridge.
- Use Photoshop Help.

Plan Ahead

General Project Guidelines

When editing a photo, the actions you perform and decisions you make will affect the appearance and characteristics of the finished product. As you edit a photo, such as the one shown in Figure 1–1a, you should follow these general guidelines:

1. **Find an appropriate image or photo.** Keep in mind the purpose and the graphic needs of the project when choosing an image or photo. Decide ahead of time on the file type and whether the image will be used on the Web. An eye-catching graphic image should convey a universal theme. The photo should grab the attention of viewers and draw them into the picture, whether in print or on the Web.

2. **Keep design principles in mind.** As you edit, keep in mind your subject, your audience, the required size and shape of the graphic, color decisions, the rule of thirds, the golden rectangle, and other design principles.

3. **Determine how to edit the photo to highlight the theme.** Decide which parts of the photo portray your message and which parts are visual clutter. Crop and resize the photo as needed.

4. **Identify finishing touches that will further enhance the photo.** The overall appearance of a photo significantly affects its ability to communicate clearly. You might want to add text or a border.

5. **Prepare for publication.** Resize the photo as needed to fit the allotted space. Save the photo on a storage media, such as a hard disk, USB flash drive, or CD. Print the photo or publish it to the Web.

When necessary, more specific details concerning the above guidelines are presented at appropriate points in the chapter. The chapter also will identify the actions performed and decisions made regarding these guidelines during the creation of the edited photo shown in Figure 1–1b.

PS 10 Photoshop Chapter 1 Editing a Photo

Opening a Photo

To open a photo in Photoshop, it must be [...] system or on an external storage device. [...] from the storage location to the screen wh[...] The changes do not become permanent, [...] file on a storage device. The photos used [...] back of the book. Your instructor may des[...]

To Open a Photo

The following steps open the file, Bison, from a DVD located [...] might differ.

1
- Insert the DVD containing the Data Files for Students that accompanies this book into your DVD drive. After a few seconds, if Windows displays a dialog box, click its Close button.

  Q&A What if I don't have the DVD?
  You will need the Data Files for Students to complete the activities and exercises in this book. See your instructor for information on how to acquire the necessary files.

- With the Photoshop window open, click File on the menu bar to display the File menu (Figure 1–9).

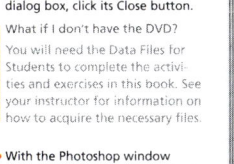

Figure 1–9

2
- Click Open on the File menu to display the Open dialog box.
- Click the Look in box arrow to display a list of the available storage locations on your system (Figure 1–10).

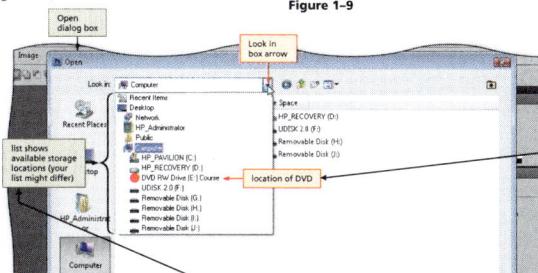

Figure 1–10

BTW

Screen Shots

Callouts in screenshots give students information they need, when they need to know it. The Series has always used plenty of callouts to ensure that students don't get lost. Now, color distinguishes the content in the callouts to make them more meaningful.

Navigational callouts in red show students where to click.

Explanatory callouts summarize what is happening on screen.

Textbook Walk-Through

Q&A boxes offer questions students may have when working through the steps and provide additional information about what they are doing right where they need it.

Experiment Steps within our step-by-step instructions, encourage students to explore, experiment, and take advantage of the features of Adobe Photoshop CS4. These steps are not necessary to complete the projects, but are designed to increase the confidence with the software and build problem-solving skills.

PS 48 Photoshop Chapter 1 Editing a Photo

2
- Click Image Size to display the Image Size dialog box.
- In the Document Size area, double-click the value in the Width box and then type 6 to replace the previous value (Figure 1–58).

Q&A Why did the height change?
When you change the width, Photoshop automatically adjusts the height to maintain the proportions of the photo. Your exact height might differ slightly depending on how closely you cropped the original photo.

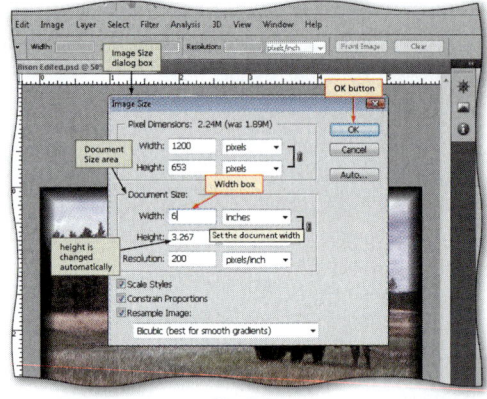

Figure 1–58

3
- Click the OK button to finish resizing the image (Figure 1–59).

Experiment
- Click the status bar menu button, point to Show, and then

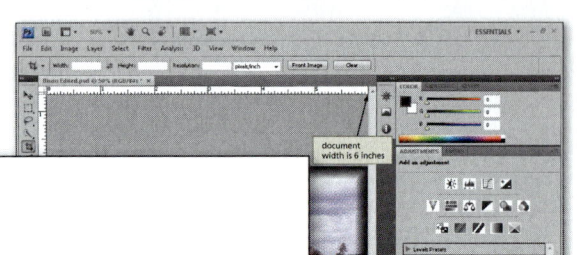

PS 38 Photoshop Chapter 1 Editing a Photo

2
- Scroll to the upper-left corner of the photo, if necessary.
- Using the rulers as guides, drag a rectangle beginning at the upper-left corner of the photo. Continue dragging right to approximately 5.5 inches on the horizontal ruler, and then down to approximately 3 inches on the vertical ruler. Do not release the mouse button (Figure 1–44).

Experiment
- If you want to practice cropping, press the ESC key and drag again. Press the SHIFT key down while you crop to constrain the proportions. When you are done experimenting, crop to 5.5 by 3 inches.

Figure 1–44

3
- Release the mouse button to display the crop selection (Figure 1–45).

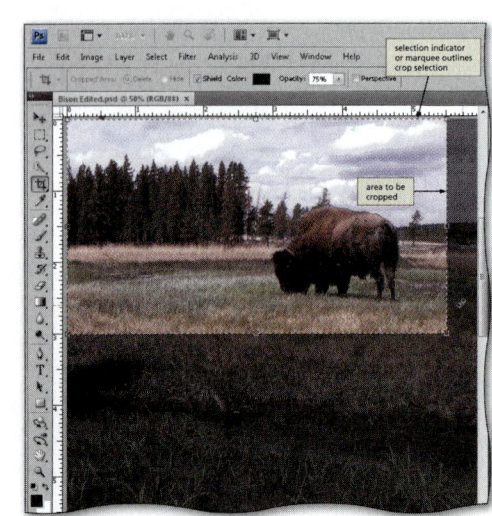

Figure 1–45

Textbook Walk-Through

Other Ways boxes that follow many of the step sequences explain the other ways to complete the task presented.

PS 6 Photoshop Chapter 1 Editing a Photo

2
- Click Adobe Photoshop CS4 to start Photoshop (Figure 1–3).
- After a few moments, when the Photoshop window is displayed, if the window is not maximized, click the Maximize button to maximize the window.

Q&A What is a maximized window?

A maximized window fills the entire screen. When you maximize a window, the Maximize button changes to a Restore Down button.

Figure 1–3

Other Ways
1. Double-click Photoshop icon on desktop, if one is present
2. Click Adobe Photoshop CS4 on Start menu

Customizing the Photoshop Workspace

The screen in Figure 1–3 shows how the Photoshop workspace looks the first time you start Photoshop after installation on most computers. Photoshop does not open a blank or default [document auto]matically; rather, the Application bar, a menu bar, and the options bar — also [called the] Control panel — appear across the top of the screen with a gray work area below [the options] bar. The Tools panel is displayed on the left; other panels are displayed on the [right. The] gray work area and panels are referred to collectively as the **workspace**. [As y]ou work in Photoshop, the panels, the selected tool, and the options bar settings [may cha]nge. Therefore, if you want your screen to match the figures in this book, you [must res]tore the default workspace, select the default tool, and reset the options bar. For [more infor]mation about how to change other, advanced Photoshop settings, see Appendix C. [Beca]use of a default preference setting, each time you start Photoshop, the [worksho]p workspace is displayed the same way it was the last time you used Photoshop. [If pane]ls are relocated, then they will appear in their new locations the next time [you start P]hotoshop. You can create and save your own workspaces, or use Photoshop's [default wor]kspaces that show a group of panels used for certain tasks. For example, the [the man]y workspace displays the Character panel, the Paragraph panel, and the Styles [panel, all] of which you would need for working with text. You will learn more about [workspaces lat]er in this chapter. Similarly, if values on the options bar are changed or a

---

PS 70 Photoshop Chapter 1 Editing a Photo

Extend Your Knowledge

Extend the skills you learned in this chapter and experiment with new skills. You may need to use Help to complete the assignment.

Exploring Border Width and Fill Options

Instructions: Start Photoshop and perform the customization steps found on pages PS 7 through PS 9. Open the Extend 1-1 Wood Turtle file in the Chapter01 folder from the Data Files for Students and save it as Extend 1-1 Wood Turtle Edited in the PSD file format. You can access the Data Files for Students on the DVD that accompanies this book. See the inside back cover of this book for instructions on downloading the Data Files for Students, or contact your instructor for information on accessing the required files.

The wood turtle photo (Figure 1–88) is to be added to a middle school science handout about amphibians and reptiles. Before the photo is inserted in the handout document, you must add a complementary border to the photo. The only requirement is that the border not be black or white.

Figure 1–88

Before you save the photo with a border, you need to explore different border widths and fill options to find the right combination. As you experiment with border options, you can press the CTRL+ALT+Z keys to quickly step back through the current editing history, returning the photo to a previous state.

Perform the following tasks:
1. Select the entire photo.
2. Specify a border width.
3. Set the border fill contents, blending, and opacity options of your choice and apply them to the photo. Make a note of your width and fill settings for future reference.
4. After viewing the resulting border, press the CTRL+ALT+Z keys enough times to step back to the photo's original unedited state.
5. Repeat Steps 1–4 several times to experiment with different border widths and fills; then apply the border that best complements the photo and save the changes to the photo.
6. Close the photo and close Photoshop.

Extend Your Knowledge projects at the end of each chapter allow students to extend and expand on the skills learned within the chapter. Students use critical thinking to experiment with new skills to complete each project.

Textbook Walk-Through

Make It Right projects call on students to analyze a file, discover errors in it, and fix them using the skills they learned in the chapter.

Make It Right

Analyze a project and correct all errors and/or improve the design.

Changing a Photo's Focus and Optimizing It for the Web

Instructions: Start Photoshop and perform the customization steps found on pages PS 7 through PS 9. Open the Make It Right 1-1 Young Stars file in the Chapter01 folder from the Data Files for Students and save it as Make It Right 1-1 Young Stars Edited in the PSD file format. You can access the Data Files for Students on the DVD that accompanies this book. See the inside back cover of this book for instructions on downloading the Data Files for Students, or contact your instructor for information about accessing the required files.

Members of your Astronomy Club have selected the Young Stars photo (Figure 1–89) for the club's Web site. You are tasked with editing the photo to more clearly focus on the cluster of stars and their trailing dust blanket, and then optimizing the photo for the Web.

Keeping the rule of thirds and the golden rectangle 5:8 ratio concepts in mind, crop the photo to change its focal point and resave it. Then save the photo for the Web as Make-It-Right-1-1-Young-Stars-for-Web using the optimal settings for a GIF file with maximum colors and 250 pixels in width.

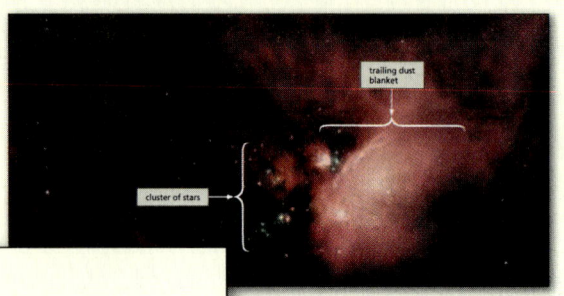

Figure 1–89

Cases and Places

Apply your creative thinking and problem-solving skills to design and implement a solution.

- • Easier   • • More Difficult

• 1: Cropping a Photo for a Social Networking Site
You would like to place a photo of your recent tubing adventure on your social networking site. The photo you have is of two people. You need to crop out the other person who is tubing. After starting Photoshop and resetting the workspace, you select the photo, Case 1-1 Tubing, from the Chapter01 folder of the Data Files for Students. Save the photo on your USB flash drive storage device as Case 1-1 Tubing Edited, using the PSD format. Crop the photo to remove one of the inner tubes, keeping in mind the rule of thirds, the golden rectangle, and the direction of the action. Save the photo again and print a copy for your instructor.

• 2: Creating a Rack Card Graphic with a Border
You are an intern with a tour company. They are planning a bus tour that follows the original Lewis and Clark trail and want to produce a rack card advertising the trip. On the back of the rack card, they would like a photo of one of the sites along the trail. The photo named Case 1-2 Monument is located in the Chapter01 folder of the Data Files for Students. Save the photo on your USB flash drive storage device as Case 1-2 Monument Edited, using the PSD format. Rack cards typically measure 4 × 9 inches; the photo needs to fit in the upper half. Resize the photo to be 3.75 inches wide. Create a border of 100 pixels. Do not use smoothing. Fill the border with 50% black opacity.

• • 3: Planning for Cropping
Look through magazines or newspapers for color photos that might be cropped. If possible, cut out three photos and mark them by hand with cropping lines. Write a short paragraph for each one describing why you think the photo could benefit from cropping. If the cropped photo needs to be resized, give the exact dimensions. List at least two uses for the photo, other than the one in which it was displayed. Attach the photos to the descriptions and submit them to your instructor.

• • 4: Scanning, Resizing, and Adding a Border to a Photo
Make It Personal
Use a scanner to scan a favorite action photo. Using the scanner's software, save the photo in the highest possible resolution, using the most color settings. Bring the picture into Photoshop and save it on your storage device. Crop it to remove extra background images. Use the rule of thirds to focus on the main point of interest. Recall that in the case of moving objects, you generally should leave space in front of them into which they can move. Resize the photo to fit your favorite frame. Add a blended border if it will not detract from the images in the photo. Send the edited photo by e-mail to a friend or use it in a page layout program to create a greeting card.

• • 5: Optimizing a Digital Photo
Working Together
Your school would like to display a picture of the main building or student center on the Web site's home page. Your team has been assigned to take the photo and optimize it for the Web. Using a digital camera or camera phone, each team member should take a picture of the building from various angles. As a team, open each digital file and choose one or two that best incorporate the styles and suggestions in this chapter. Choose a border that highlights the color and dynamic of the photo. Resize the photo to less than 500 × 500 pixels. As a group, make decisions in the Save for Web & Devices dialog box on the 4-Up tab as to which optimization would best suit the school's needs. Show the final products to another person or group in your class for suggestions. Submit the best one to your instructor.

Found within the Cases & Places exercises, the **Make It Personal** activities call on students to create an open-ended project that relates to their personal lives.

About Our New Cover Look

Learning styles of students have changed, but the Shelly Cashman Series' dedication to their success has remained steadfast for over 30 years. We are committed to continually updating our approach and content to reflect the way today's students learn and experience new technology.

This focus on the user is reflected in our bold new cover design, which features photographs of real students using the Shelly Cashman Series in their courses. Each book features a different user, reflecting the many ages, experiences, and backgrounds of all of the students learning with our books. When you use the Shelly Cashman Series, you can be assured that you are learning computer skills using the most effective courseware available.

We would like to thank the administration and faculty at the participating schools for their help in making our vision a reality. Most of all, we'd like to thank the wonderful students from all over the world who learn

1 Editing a Photo

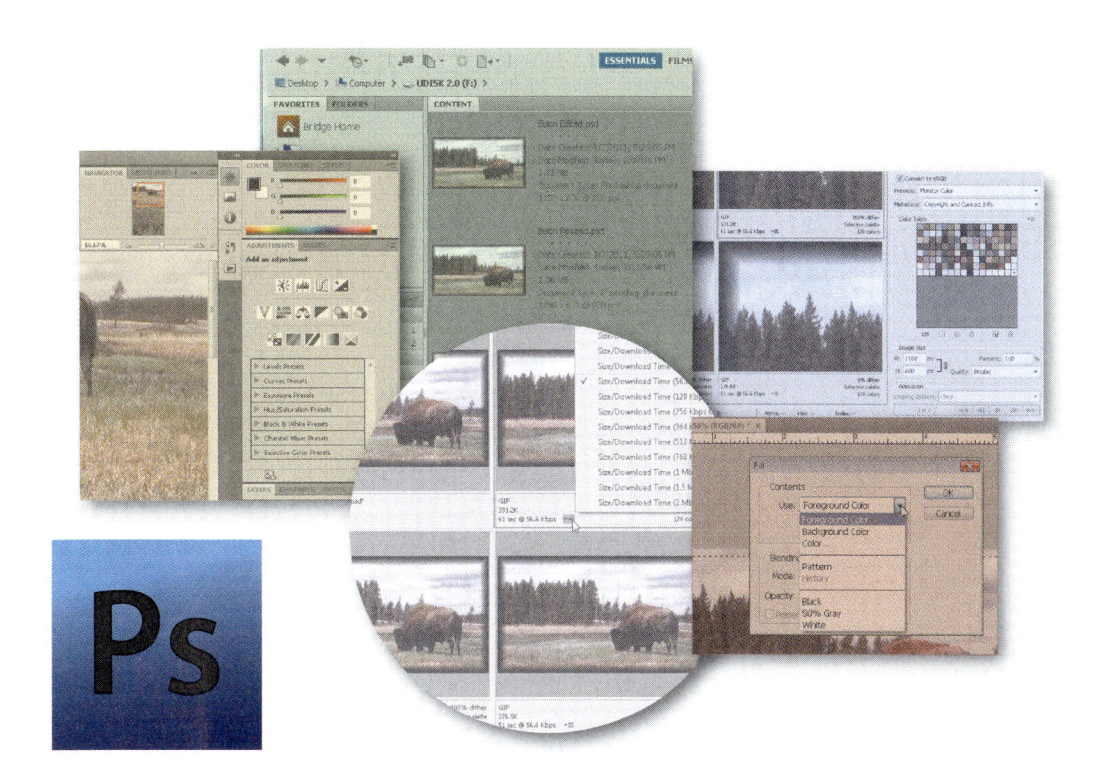

Objectives

You will have mastered the material in this chapter when you can:

- Start Photoshop and customize the Photoshop workspace
- Open a photo
- Identify parts of the Photoshop workspace
- Explain file types
- Save a photo for both print and the Web
- View a photo using the Navigator panel, Zoom tool, Hand tool, and screen modes
- Display rulers
- Crop a photo
- Create a blended border
- Resize a photo
- Print a photo
- View files in Adobe Bridge
- Access Photoshop Help
- Close a photo and quit Photoshop

1 | Editing a Photo

What Is Photoshop CS4?

Photoshop CS4 is a popular image editing software program produced by Adobe Systems Incorporated. Image editing software refers to computer programs that allow you to create and modify **digital images**, or pictures in electronic form. One type of digital image is a digital **photograph** or **photo**, which is a photograph taken with a camera and stored as a digitized array. The photo then is converted into a print, a slide, or used in another file. Other types of digital images include scanned images or electronic forms of original artwork created from scratch. Digital images are used in graphic applications, advertising, print publishing, and on the Web. Personal uses include personal photos, online photo sharing, scrapbooking, blogging, and social networking, among others. Image editing software, such as Photoshop, can be used for basic adjustments such as rotating, cropping, or resizing, as well as for more advanced manipulations, such as airbrushing, retouching, removing red-eye, changing the contrast of an image, balancing, or combining elements of different images. Because Photoshop allows you to save multilayered composite images and then return later to extract parts of those images, it works well for repurposing a wide variety of graphic-related files.

Photoshop CS4 is part of the Adobe Creative Suite 4 and comes packaged with most of the suite versions. It also is sold and used independently as a stand-alone application. Photoshop CS4 is available for both the PC and Macintosh computer platforms. Photoshop CS4 Extended includes all of the features of Photoshop CS4 and some new features for working with 3D imagery, motion-based content, and advanced image analysis. The chapters in this book are described using Photoshop CS4 on the PC platform, running the Windows Vista operating system.

To illustrate the features of Photoshop CS4, this book presents a series of chapters that use Photoshop to edit photos similar to those you will encounter in academic and business environments, as well as photos for personal use.

Project Planning Guidelines

> The process of editing a photo requires careful analysis and planning. As a starting point, choose a photo that correctly expresses your desired subject or theme. Once the theme is determined, analyze the intended audience. Define a plan for editing that enhances the photo, eliminates visual clutter, improves color and contrast, and corrects defects. Always work on a duplicate of an original image. Finally, determine the file format and print style that will be most successful at delivering the message. Details of these guidelines are provided in Appendix A. In addition, each chapter in this book provides practical applications of these planning considerations.

Project — Postcard Graphic

A **postcard** is a rectangular piece of mail intended for writing and sending without an envelope. People use postcards for greetings, announcements, reminders, and business contacts. Many times, a postcard is an effective marketing tool used to generate prospective leads at a relatively low cost. One of the most popular uses for postcards involves pictures. Businesses and organizations produce a postcard with a photo or graphic on one side and a short description with room to write a brief correspondence on the other. People purchase picture postcards to mail to friends or to serve as reminders of their vacation. Sometimes a picture postcard is mailed to attract attention and direct people to Web sites or business locations. A postcard graphic must portray its message or theme clearly, in an eye-catching manner, keeping in mind the relevant audience.

The project in this chapter uses Photoshop to enhance a photograph of a bison to be used on a postcard produced by a wildlife park. The original photo is displayed in Figure 1–1a. The edited photo is displayed in Figure 1–1b. The enhancements will emphasize the bison by positioning the scene to make the layout appear more visually appealing and to crop some of the background. A dark border color will make the bison stand out. Finally, the photo will be resized to fit on a postcard and then optimized for the park's Web site.

Figure 1–1

Overview

As you read this chapter, you will learn how to edit the photo shown in Figure 1–1 by performing these general tasks:

- Customize the workspace.
- Display and navigate a photo at various magnifications.
- Crop a photo effectively.
- Create a blended border.
- Fill a selection.
- Resize and print a photo.
- Save, close, and then reopen a photo.
- Save a photo for the Web.
- Use Adobe Bridge.
- Use Photoshop Help.

Plan Ahead

General Project Guidelines

When editing a photo, the actions you perform and decisions you make will affect the appearance and characteristics of the finished product. As you edit a photo, such as the one shown in Figure 1–1a, you should follow these general guidelines:

1. **Find an appropriate image or photo.** Keep in mind the purpose and the graphic needs of the project when choosing an image or photo. Decide ahead of time on the file type and whether the image will be used on the Web. An eye-catching graphic image should convey a universal theme. The photo should grab the attention of viewers and draw them into the picture, whether in print or on the Web.

2. **Keep design principles in mind.** As you edit, keep in mind your subject, your audience, the required size and shape of the graphic, color decisions, the rule of thirds, the golden rectangle, and other design principles.

3. **Determine how to edit the photo to highlight the theme.** Decide which parts of the photo portray your message and which parts are visual clutter. Crop and resize the photo as needed.

4. **Identify finishing touches that will further enhance the photo.** The overall appearance of a photo significantly affects its ability to communicate clearly. You might want to add text or a border.

5. **Prepare for publication.** Resize the photo as needed to fit the allotted space. Save the photo on a storage media, such as a hard disk, USB flash drive, or CD. Print the photo or publish it to the Web.

When necessary, more specific details concerning the above guidelines are presented at appropriate points in the chapter. The chapter also will identify the actions performed and decisions made regarding these guidelines during the creation of the edited photo shown in Figure 1–1b.

Starting Photoshop

If you are using a computer to step through the project in this chapter, and you want your screen to match the figures in this book, you should change your screen's resolution to 1024 × 768. For information about how to change a computer's resolution, read Appendix C.

BTW

Screen Resolution
If your system has a high-resolution monitor with a screen resolution of 1280 × 800 or higher, lowering that resolution to 1024 × 768 may cause some images to be distorted because of a difference in the aspect ratio. If you want to keep your high-resolution setting, be aware that the location of on-screen tools might vary slightly from the book.

To Start Photoshop

The following steps, which assume Windows Vista is running, start Photoshop, based on a typical installation. You may need to ask your instructor how to start Photoshop for your computer.

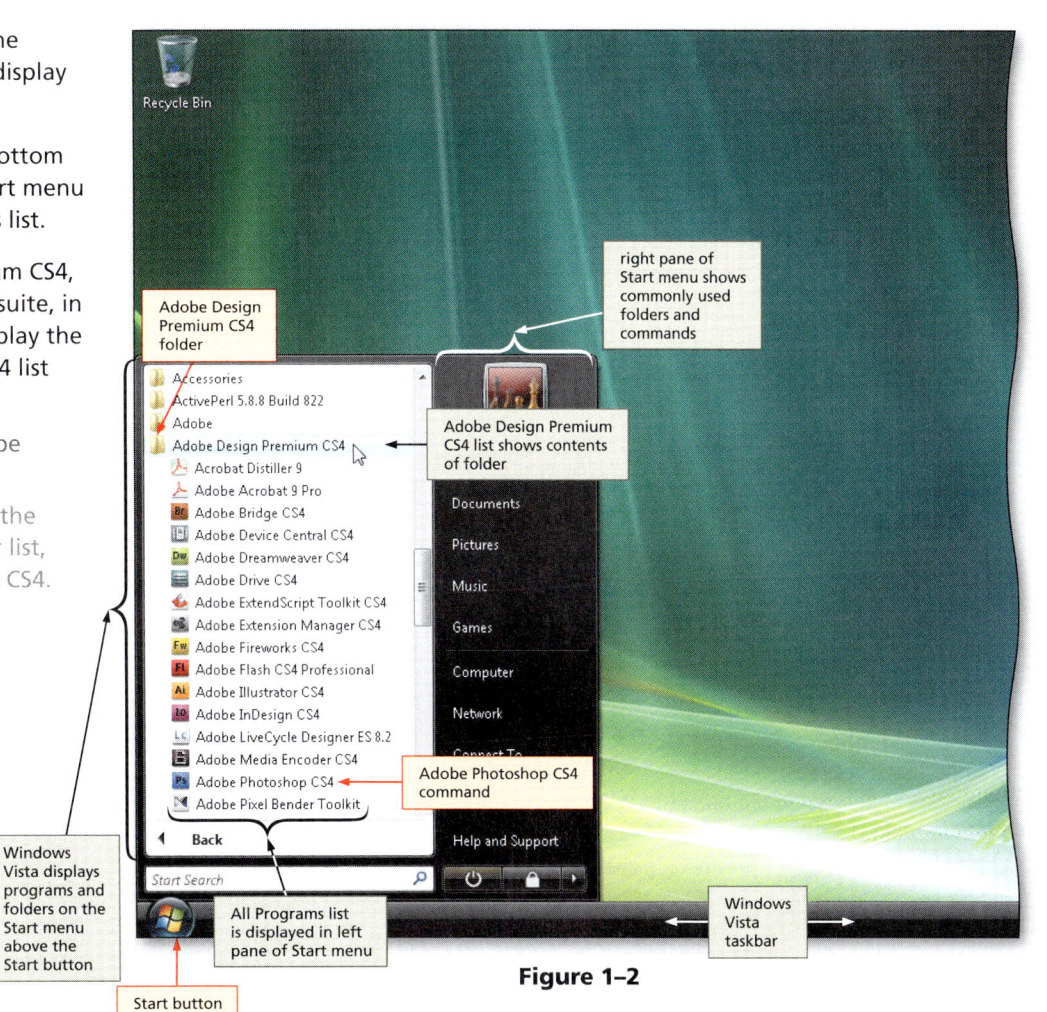

1
- Click the Start button on the Windows Vista taskbar to display the Start menu.
- Click All Programs at the bottom of the left pane on the Start menu to display the All Programs list.
- Click Adobe Design Premium CS4, or your version of the CS4 suite, in the All Programs list to display the Adobe Design Premium CS4 list (Figure 1–2).

Q&A What if I do not have Adobe Design Premium CS4?

You do not need access to the entire Adobe suite. In your list, look for Adobe Photoshop CS4.

Figure 1–2

2
- Click Adobe Photoshop CS4 to start Photoshop (Figure 1–3).

- After a few moments, when the Photoshop window is displayed, if the window is not maximized, click the Maximize button to maximize the window.

Q&A What is a maximized window?

A maximized window fills the entire screen. When you maximize a window, the Maximize button changes to a Restore Down button.

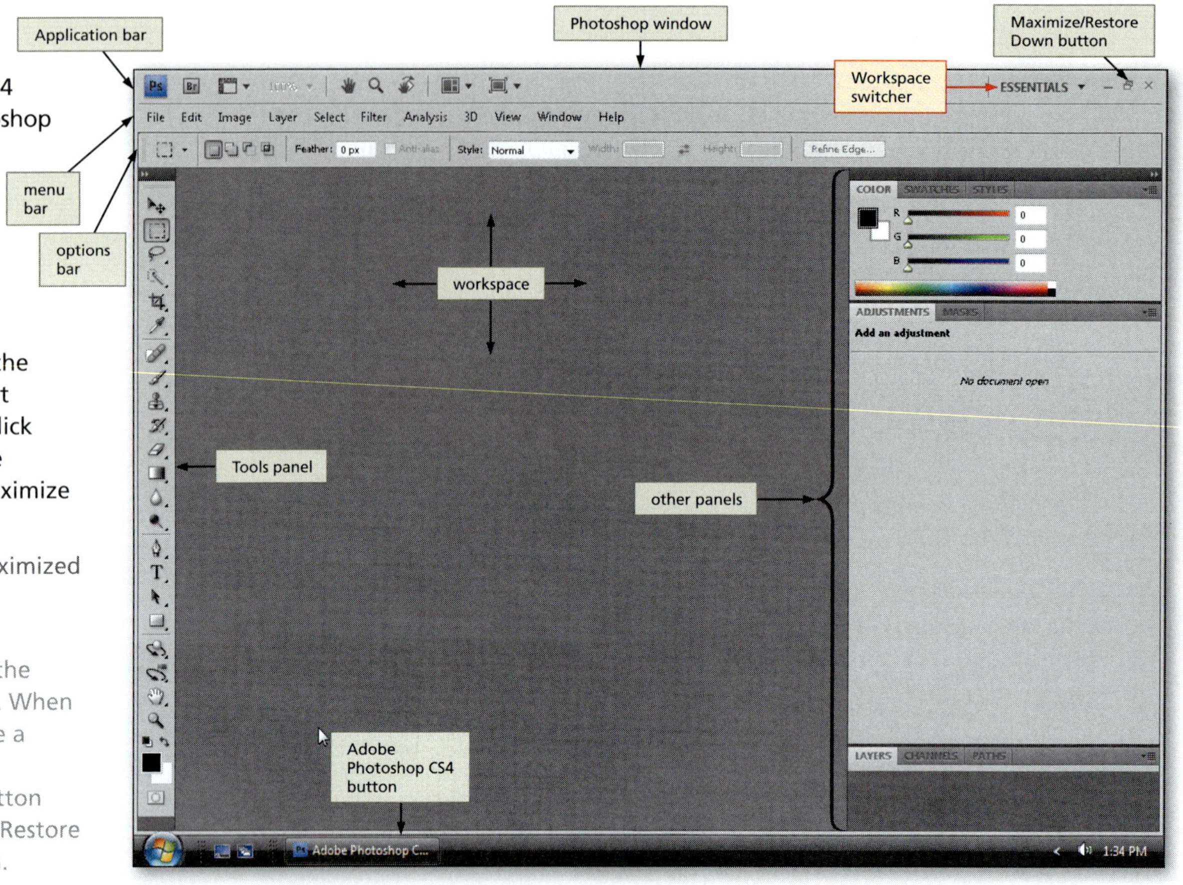

Figure 1–3

Other Ways
1. Double-click Photoshop icon on desktop, if one is present
2. Click Adobe Photoshop CS4 on Start menu

BTW
Adobe Suite Workspaces
The workspaces of the various applications in Adobe Creative Suite 4 share the same appearance to make it easy to move between applications.

Customizing the Photoshop Workspace

The screen in Figure 1–3 shows how the Photoshop workspace looks the first time you start Photoshop after installation on most computers. Photoshop does not open a blank or default photo automatically; rather, the Application bar, a menu bar, and the options bar — also called the Control panel — appear across the top of the screen with a gray work area below the options bar. The Tools panel is displayed on the left; other panels are displayed on the right. The gray work area and panels are referred to collectively as the **workspace**.

As you work in Photoshop, the panels, the selected tool, and the options bar settings might change. Therefore, if you want your screen to match the figures in this book, you should restore the default workspace, select the default tool, and reset the options bar. For more information about how to change other, advanced Photoshop settings, see Appendix C.

Because of a default preference setting, each time you start Photoshop, the Photoshop workspace is displayed the same way it was the last time you used Photoshop. If the panels are relocated, then they will appear in their new locations the next time you start Photoshop. You can create and save your own workspaces, or use Photoshop's saved workspaces that show a group of panels used for certain tasks. For example, the Typography workspace displays the Character panel, the Paragraph panel, and the Styles panel, all of which you would need for working with text. You will learn more about panels later in this chapter. Similarly, if values on the options bar are changed or a different tool is selected, they will remain changed the next time you start Photoshop. If you wish to return the workspace to its default settings, follow these steps each time you start Photoshop.

To Restore the Default Workspace

The **Workspace switcher** is a button on the Application bar that allows you to choose a stored or saved workspace. Photoshop displays the name of the selected workspace on the Workspace switcher. The default workspace, called Essentials, displays commonly used panels. The following steps restore the workspace to the Essentials setting.

1
- Click the Workspace switcher on the Application bar to display the names of saved workspaces (Figure 1–4).

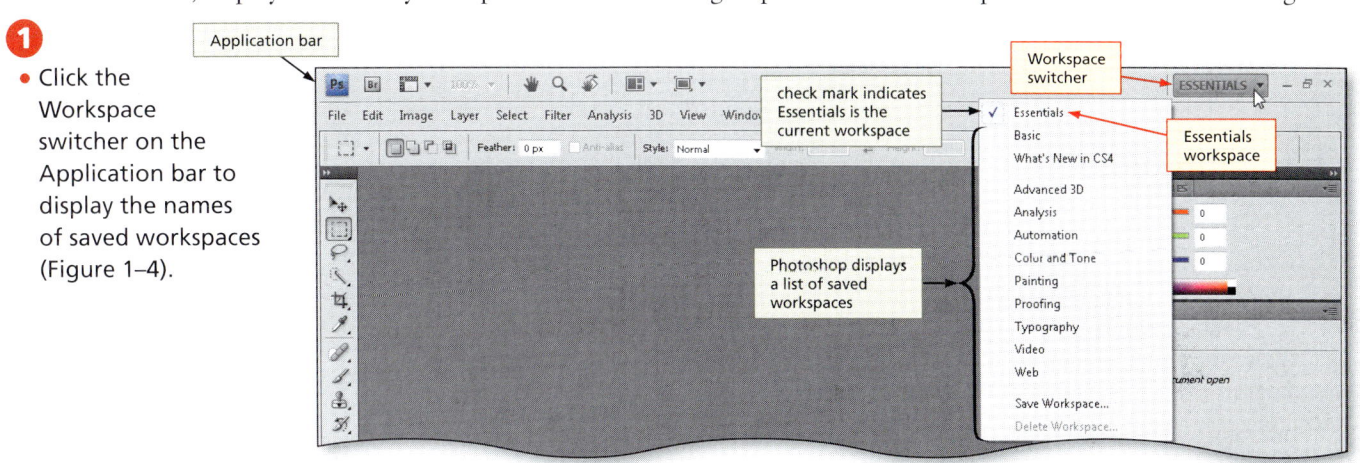

Figure 1–4

2
- Click Essentials to restore the workspace to its default settings (Figure 1–5).

Q&A My screen did not change. Did I do something wrong?

If Photoshop is a new installation on your system, you might notice few changes on your screen.

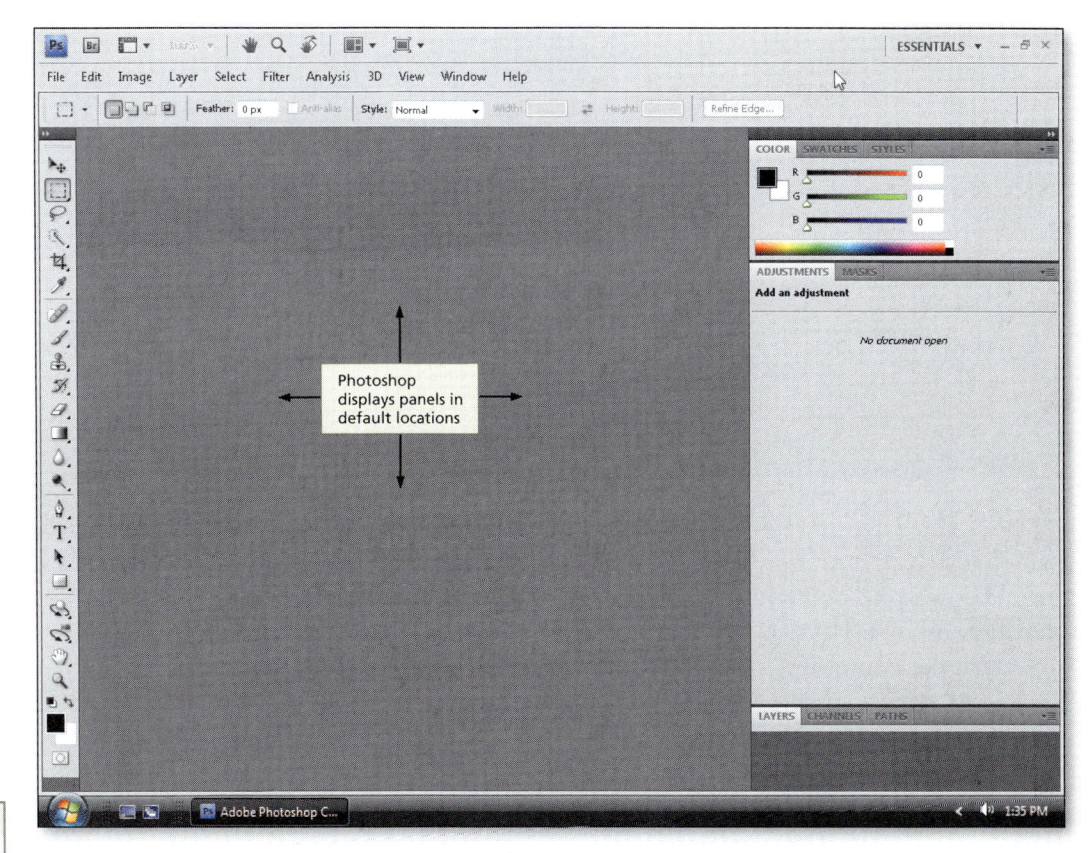

Other Ways
1. On Window menu, point to Workspace, click Essentials (Default)

Figure 1–5

To Reset the Tools Panel

The following steps reset the Tools panel to its default setting.

1
- Click the Rectangular Marquee Tool (M) button on the Tools panel to select it (Figure 1–6).

Q&A What appeared when I pointed to the button?

When you point to many objects in the Photoshop workspace, such as a tool or button, Photoshop displays a tool tip. A **tool tip** is a short, on-screen note associated with the object to which you are pointing, which helps you identify the button.

2
- If the tools in the Tools panel appear in two columns, click the double arrow at the top of the Tools panel.

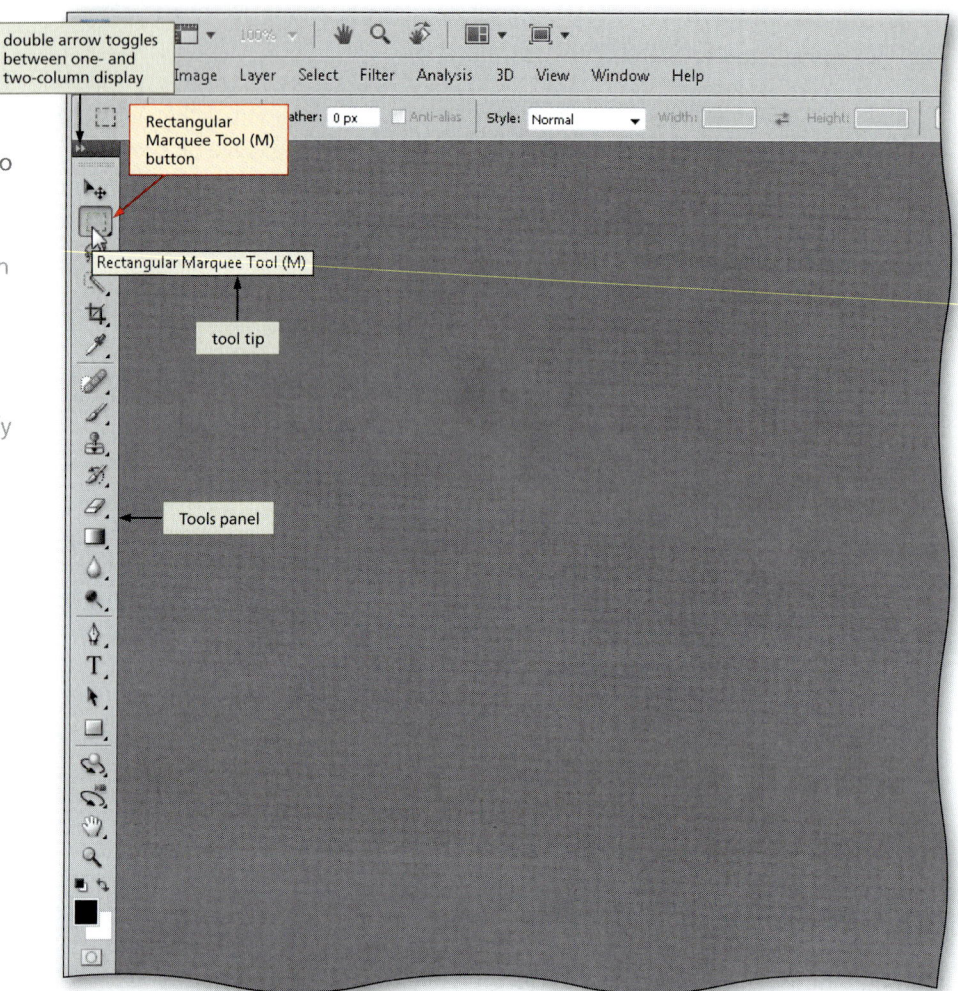

Figure 1–6

Other Ways
1. Press M

To Reset the Options Bar

As you work through the chapters, editing and creating photos, you will find that the options bar is **context sensitive**, which means it changes as you select different tools. In addition, the options and settings are retained for the next time you use Photoshop. To match the figures in this book, you should reset the options bar each time you start Photoshop using a context menu. A **context menu**, or **shortcut menu**, appears when you right-click some objects in the Photoshop workspace. The menu displays commands relevant to the active tool, selection, or panel.

The steps on the next page reset all tool settings in the options bar using a context menu.

Customizing the Photoshop Workspace **PS 9**

1
- Right-click the Rectangular Marquee tool icon on the options bar to display its context menu (Figure 1–7).

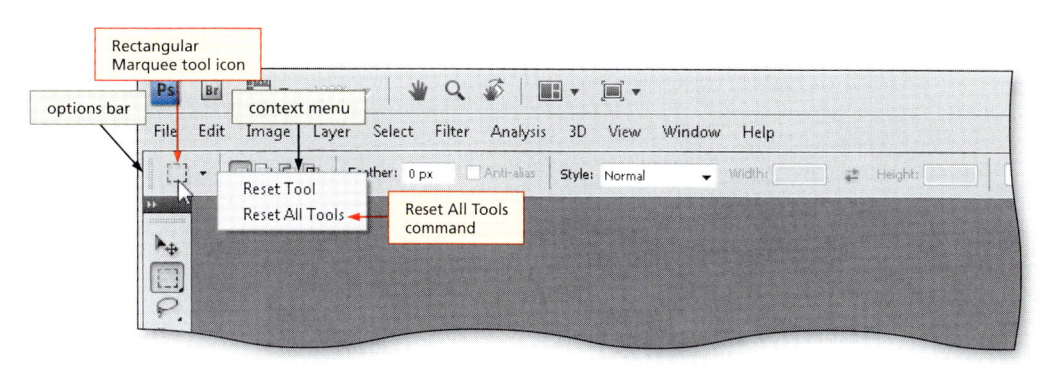

Figure 1–7

2
- Click Reset All Tools to display a confirmation dialog box (Figure 1–8).

3
- Click the OK button to restore the tools to their default settings.

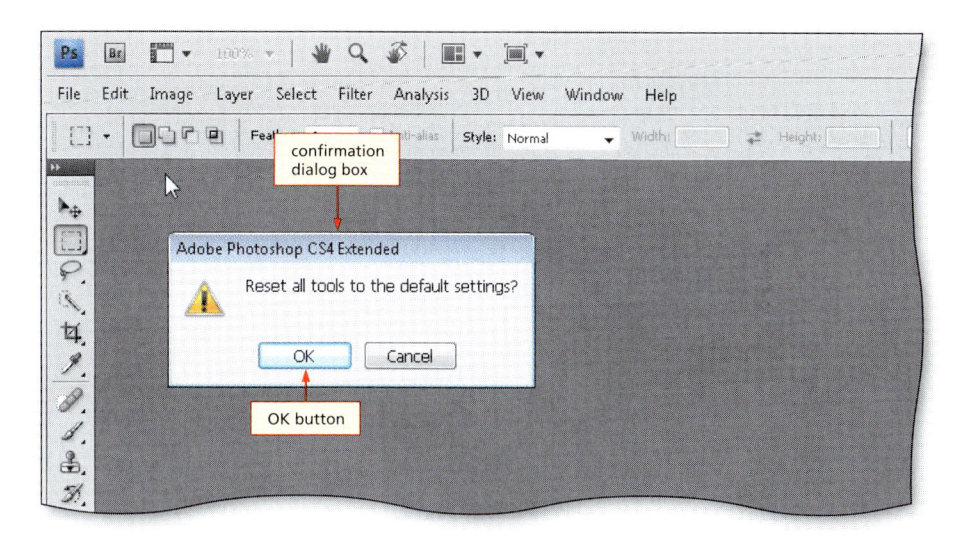

Figure 1–8

Find the appropriate image or photo.
Sometimes a person or business gives you a specific photo for use in a project. Other times, you are assigned a theme and asked to find or take the photo. An eye-catching graphic image should convey a universal theme or visually convey a message that is not expressed easily with words. Keep the audience in mind as you choose a photo. Photos generally fall into one of four categories:

- In advertising, a photo might show a product, service, result, model, or benefit.
- In a public service setting, a photo might represent a topic of interest, nature, signage, buildings, or a photo of historical importance.
- In industry, a photo might display a process, product, work organization, employee, facility, layout, equipment, safety, result, or culture.
- For personal or journalistic use, a photo might be a portrait, scenery, action shot, or event.

The images used in postcards must fit into a small space. Most postcards are rectangular, at least 3.5 inches high and 5 inches long — some are larger. A common size is 4 inches by 6 inches. A picture postcard might contain text printed over the picture or a border to attract attention. A graphic designed for a postcard should be of high quality, use strong color, and must deliver a message in the clearest, most attractive, and most effective way possible.

Plan Ahead

BTW

Context Menus
Photoshop uses the term, context menu, for any short menu that appears when you right-click. Other applications may call it a shortcut menu. The two terms are synonomous.

Opening a Photo

To open a photo in Photoshop, it must be stored as a digital file on your computer system or on an external storage device. To **open** a photo, you bring a copy of the file from the storage location to the screen where you can **edit** or make changes to the photo. The changes do not become permanent, however, until you **save** or store the changed file on a storage device. The photos used in this book are stored on a DVD located in the back of the book. Your instructor may designate a different location for the photos.

To Open a Photo

The following steps open the file, Bison, from a DVD located in drive E. The drive letter of your DVD drive might differ.

1

- Insert the DVD containing the Data Files for Students that accompanies this book into your DVD drive. After a few seconds, if Windows displays a dialog box, click its Close button.

Q&A What if I don't have the DVD?

You will need the Data Files for Students to complete the activities and exercises in this book. See your instructor for information on how to acquire the necessary files.

- With the Photoshop window open, click File on the menu bar to display the File menu (Figure 1–9).

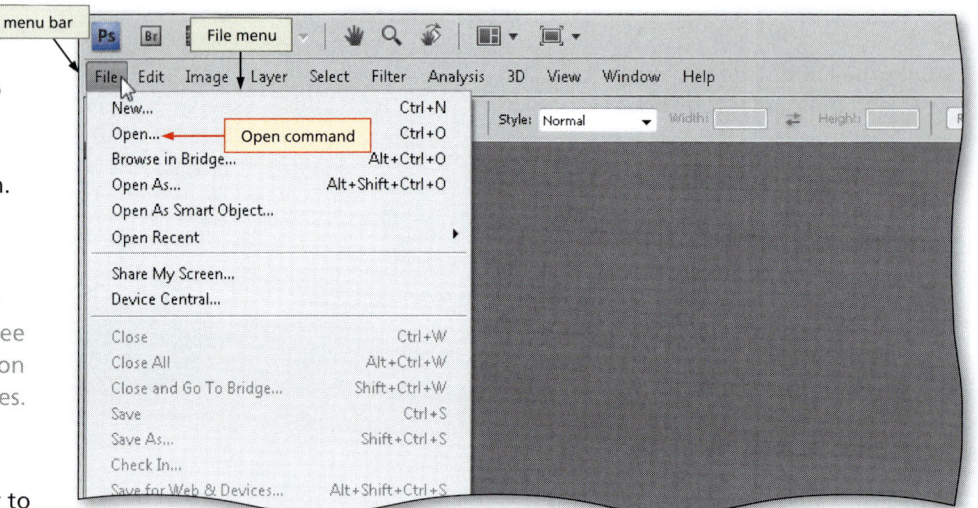

Figure 1–9

2

- Click Open on the File menu to display the Open dialog box.
- Click the Look in box arrow to display a list of the available storage locations on your system (Figure 1–10).

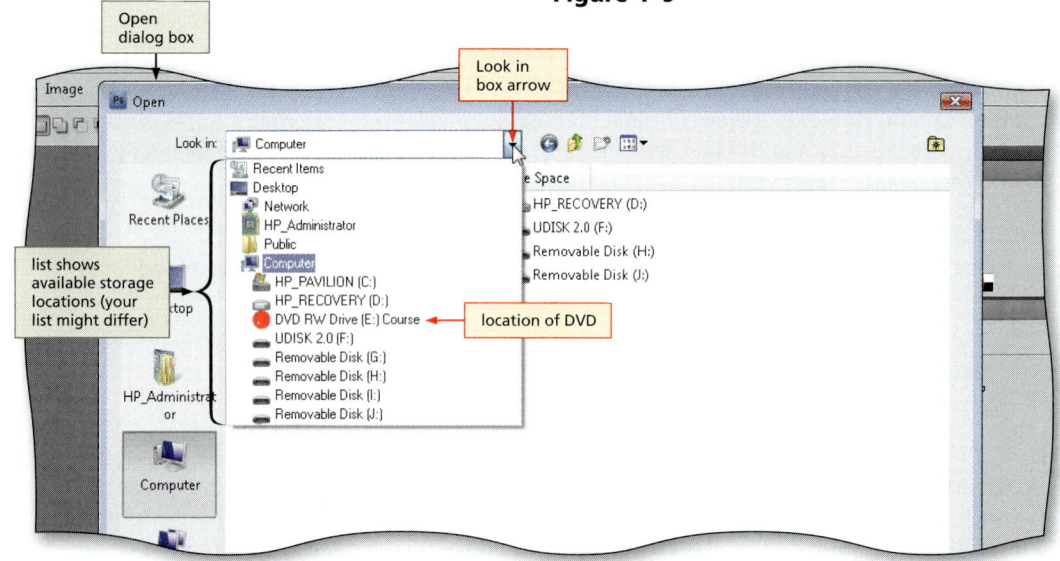

Figure 1–10

Opening a Photo **PS 11**

3
- Click drive E, or the drive associated with your DVD, to display its contents (Figure 1–11).

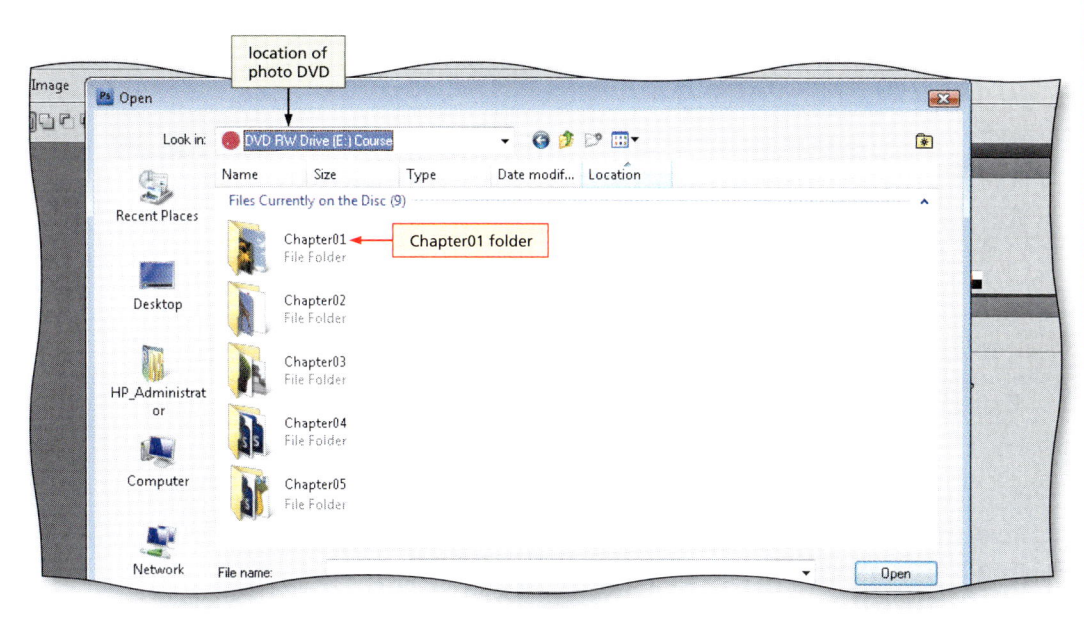

Figure 1–11

4
- Double-click the Chapter01 folder and then click the file, Bison, to select it (Figure 1–12).

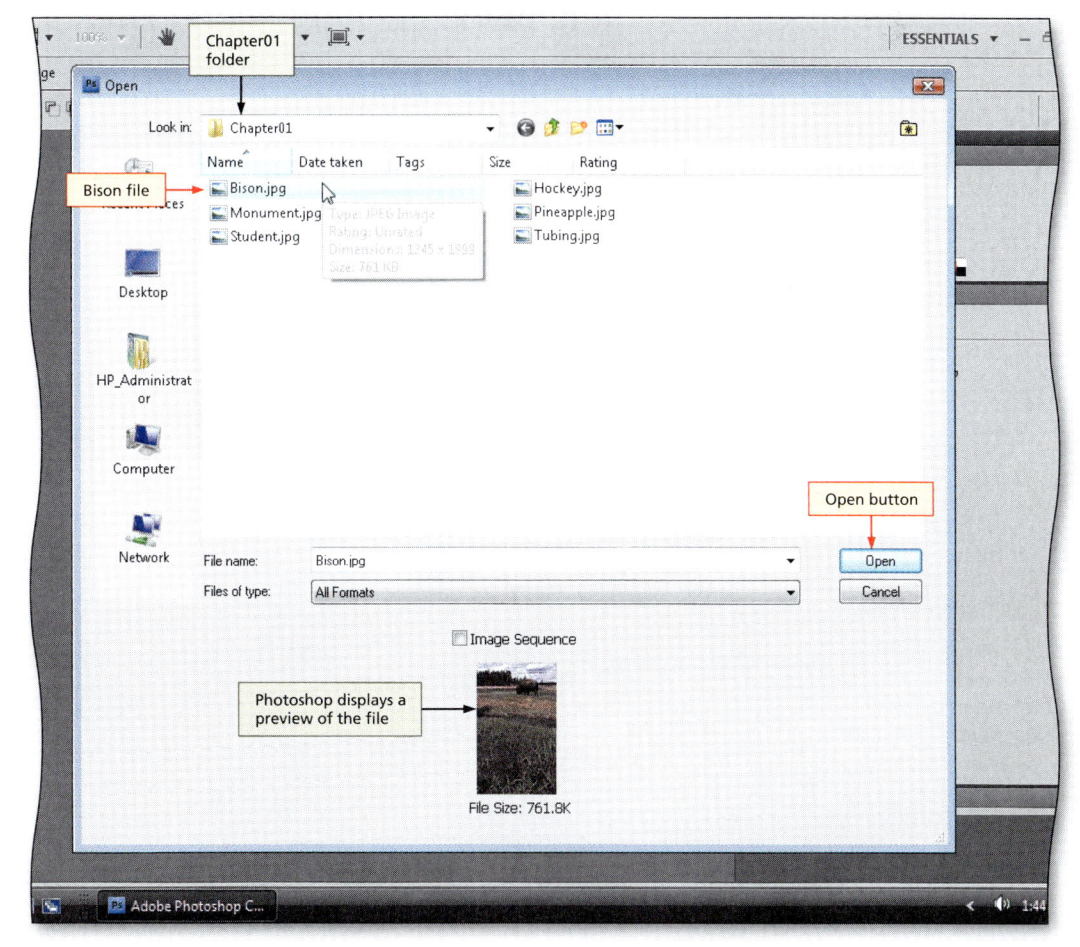

Figure 1–12

5
- Click the Open button to open the file (Figure 1–13).

Q&A How do I edit a printed photo?

Most of the images you will use in this book already are stored in digital format; however, when you have a print copy of a picture, rather than a digital file stored on your system, that you wish to use in Photoshop, it sometimes is necessary to scan the picture using a scanner. A **scanner** is a device used to convert a hard copy into a digital form for storage, retrieval, or other electronic purposes. Photoshop allows you to bring a copy from the scanner, directly into the workspace.

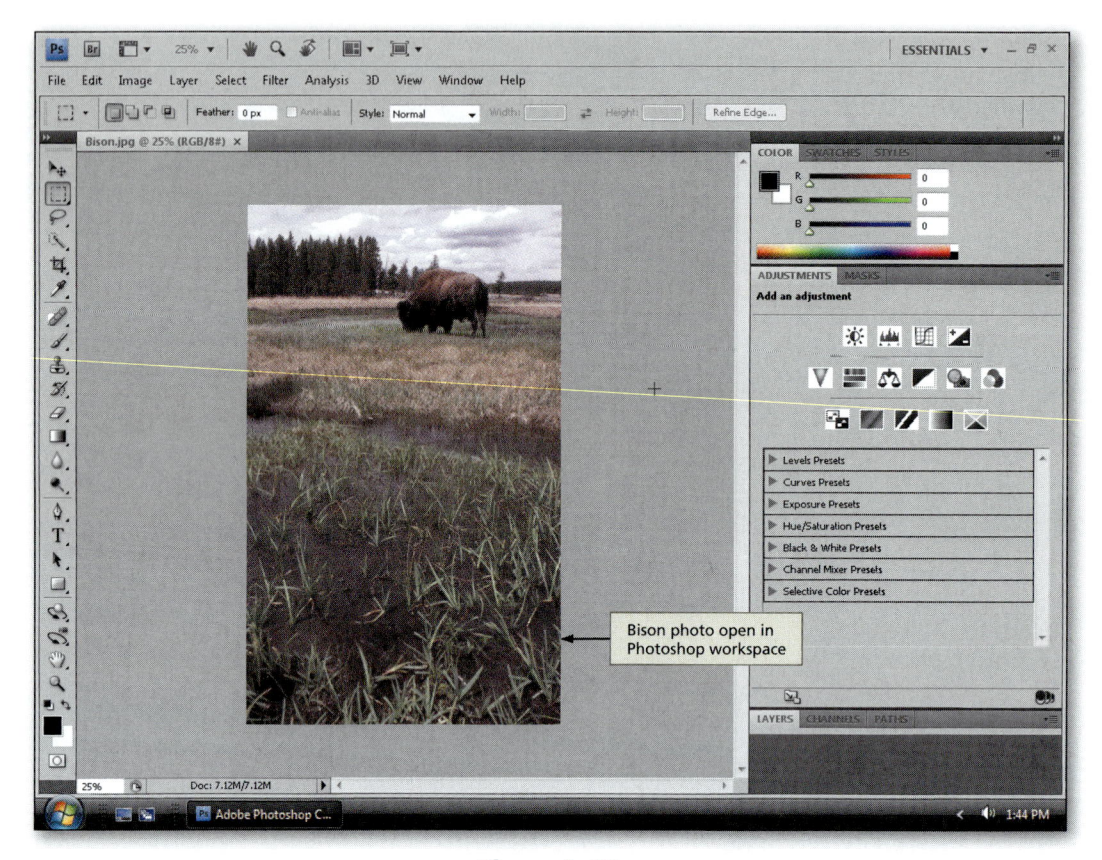

Figure 1–13

Other Ways
1. Press CTRL+O, select File, click Open
2. In Windows, right-click file, click Open With, click Adobe Photoshop CS4

The Photoshop Workspace

The Photoshop workspace consists of a variety of components to make your work more efficient and to make your photo documents look more professional. The following sections discuss these components.

BTW **Panels vs. Palettes**
In previous versions of the Adobe Creative Suite, the panels were called palettes. In all of the CS4 applications, panels can be grouped, stacked, or docked in the workspace, just as palettes were.

The Application Bar

The **Application bar** appears at the top of the workspace (Figure 1–14). The Application bar contains the application icon button, the Launch Bridge button, and commonly used controls related to document manipulation. On the right side of the Application bar are the Workspace switcher and common window clip controls. Your Application bar might contain different controls depending on the chosen saved workspace.

Figure 1–14

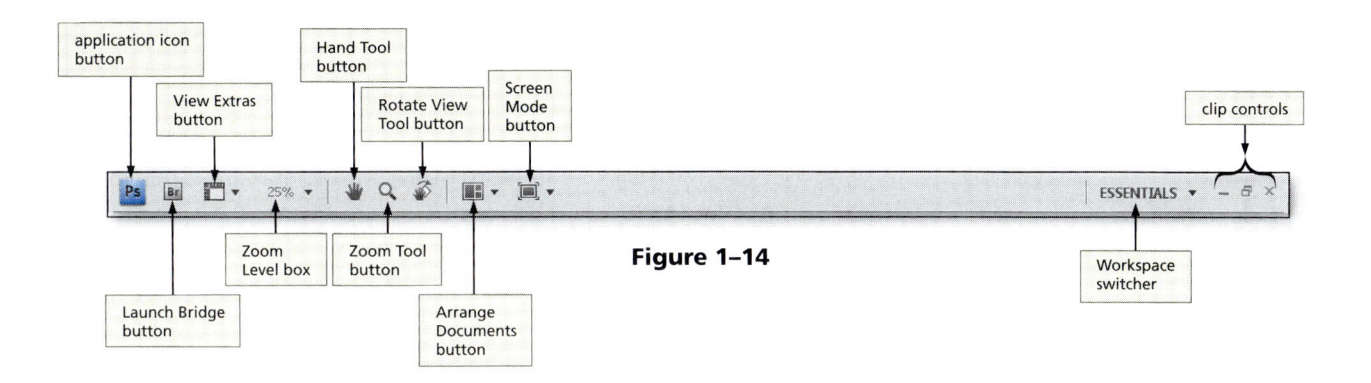

The Menu Bar

The menu bar appears at the top of the screen just below the Application bar (Figure 1–15). The **menu bar** is a toolbar that displays the Photoshop menu names. Each **menu** contains a list of commands you can use to perform tasks such as opening, saving, printing, and editing photos. To display a menu, such as the Edit menu, click the Edit menu name on the menu bar. If you point to a command on a menu that has an arrow on its right edge, as shown in Figure 1–15, a **submenu**, or secondary menu, displays another list of commands.

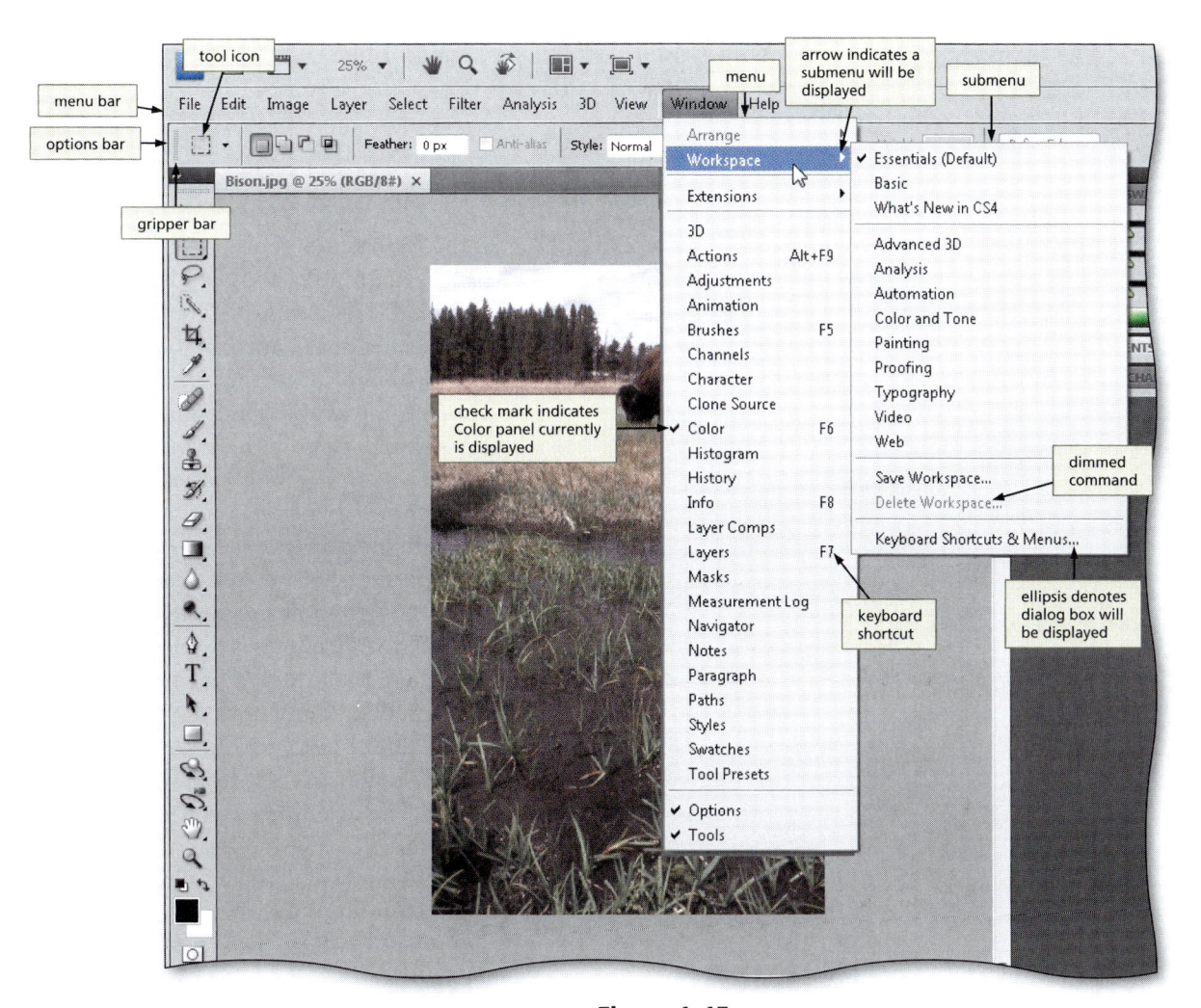

Figure 1–15

When Photoshop first is installed, all of the menu commands within a menu appear when you click the menu name. To hide seldom-used menu commands, you can click the Menus command on the Edit menu and follow the on-screen instructions. A **hidden command** does not immediately appear on a menu. If menu commands have been hidden, a Show All Menu Items command will appear at the bottom of the menu list. Click the Show All Menu Items command, or press and hold the CTRL key when you click the menu name to display all menu commands, including hidden ones.

The Options Bar

The **options bar** (Figure 1–15 on the previous page) is displayed below the menu bar. Sometimes called the **Control panel**, the options bar contains buttons and boxes that allow you to perform tasks more quickly than when using the menu bar and related menus. Most buttons on the options bar display words or images to help you remember their functions. When you point to a button or box on the options bar, a tool tip is displayed below the mouse pointer. The options bar changes to reflect the tool currently selected on the Tools panel. For example, a tool related to text might display a font box on the options bar, whereas a tool related to painting will display a brush button. The selected tool always appears as an icon on the left side of the options bar. As each tool is discussed, the associated options bar will be explained in more detail.

You can move the options bar in the workspace by using the gray **gripper bar** on the left side of the options bar. You can **dock** or attach the options bar at the top or bottom of the screen, or **float** it in any other location in the workspace.

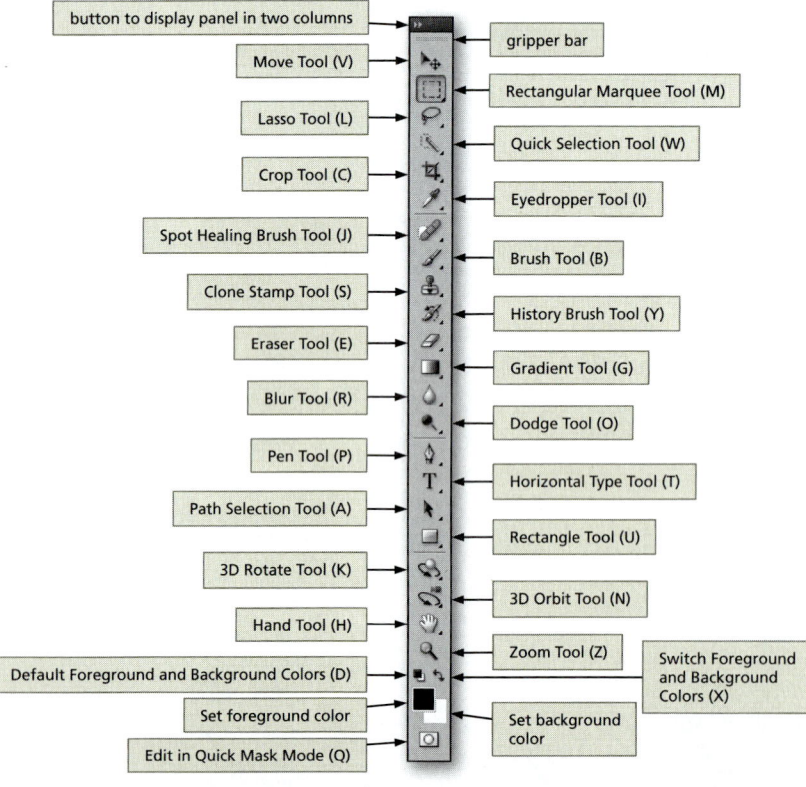

Figure 1–16

The Tools Panel

On the left side of the workspace is the Photoshop Tools panel. The Tools panel is a group of **tools,** or buttons, organized into a movable toolbar. The Tools panel floats. You can move the Tools panel by dragging its gripper bar. You also can show or hide the Tools panel by clicking Tools on the Window menu. Each tool on the Tools panel displays a **tool icon**. When you point to the tool, a tool tip displays the name of the tool including its shortcut key. You can expand some tools to show hidden tools beneath them. Expandable tools display a small triangle in the lower-right corner of the tool icon. Click and hold the tool button or right-click a tool to see or select one of its hidden tools from the context menu. The default tool names are listed in Figure 1–16.

When you click a tool on the Tools panel to use it, Photoshop selects the button and changes the options bar as necessary. When using a tool from the Tools panel, the mouse pointer changes to reflect the selected tool.

The Tools panel is organized by purpose. At the very top of the panel is a button to display the panel in two columns, followed underneath by the gripper bar. Below that, the selection tools appear, then the crop and slice tools, followed by retouching, painting, drawing and type, annotation, measuring, and navigation tools. At the bottom of the Tools panel are buttons to set colors and create a quick mask.

The Document Window

The **document window** is the light gray area within the workspace that displays the active file or image. The document window contains the title bar, display area, scroll bars, and status bar (Figure 1–17).

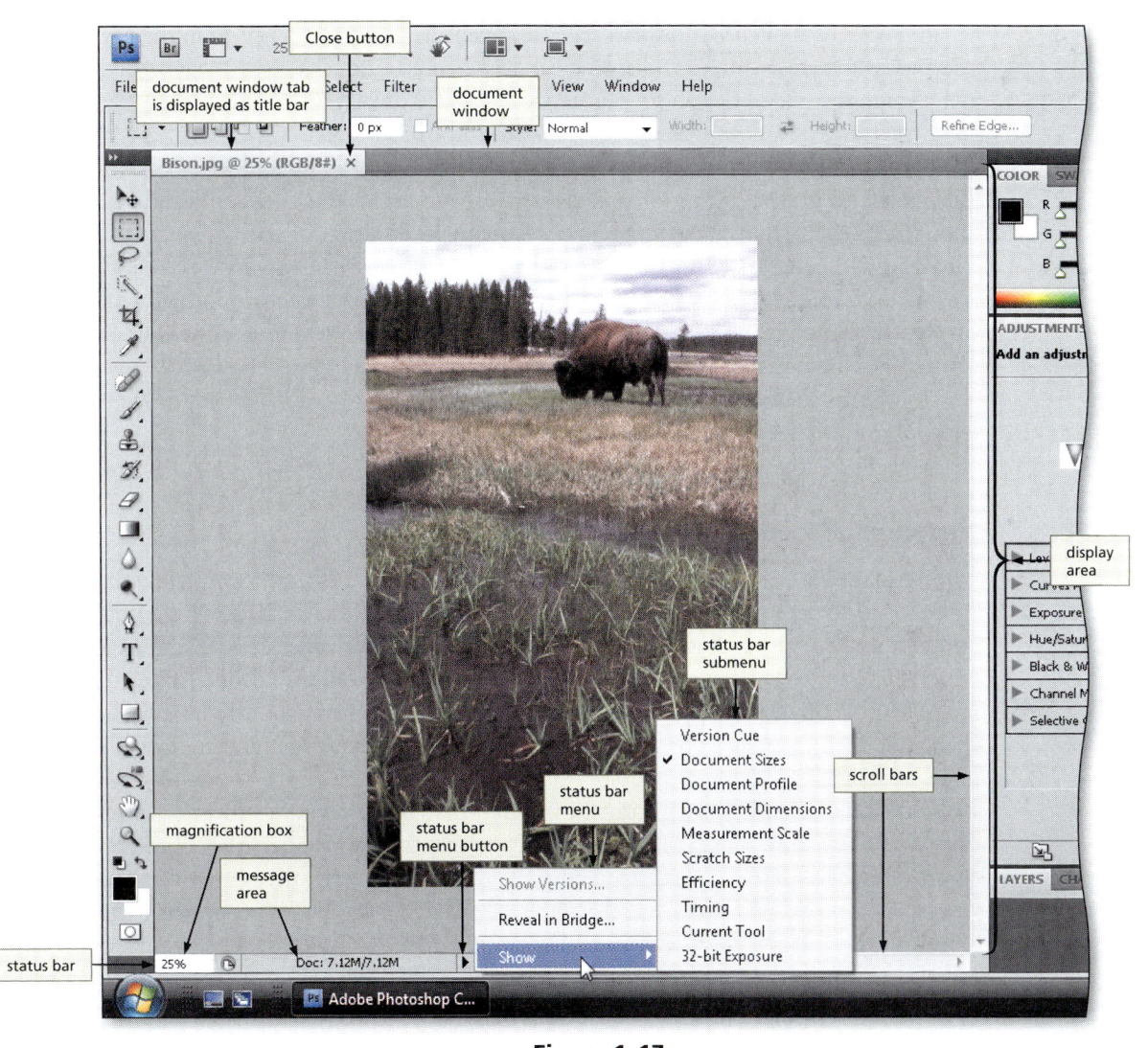

Figure 1–17

Title Bar Photoshop displays a light gray **title bar** at the top of the document window. The title bar displays the name of the file, the magnification, and the color mode. When the title bar is docked, the file information is displayed in a **document window tab**, along with a Close button (Figure 1–17). When undocked, the title bar expands across the top of the document window and displays Minimize, Restore Down, and Close buttons. If you have multiple files open, each has its own document window tab. You can move the document window by dragging the document window tab, or dock it again by dragging the title bar close to the options bar.

Display Area The **display area** is the portion of the document window that displays the photo or image. You perform most tool tasks and edit the photo in the display area.

Scroll Bars **Scroll bars** appear on the right and bottom of the document window. When the photo is bigger than the document window, the scroll bars become active and display scroll arrows and scroll boxes to move the image up, down, left, and right.

Status Bar Across the bottom of the document window, Photoshop displays the **status bar**. The status bar contains a magnification box. **Magnification** refers to the percentage of enlargement or reduction on the screen. For example, a 50% indication in the magnification box means the entire photo is displayed at 50 percent of its actual size. Magnification does not change the size of the photo physically; it merely displays it on the screen at a different size. You can type a new percentage in the magnification box to display a different view of the photo.

Next to the magnification box is the **message area**. Messages can display information about the file size, the current tool, or the document dimensions. When you first start Photoshop, the message area displays information about the document size.

On the right side of the status bar is the status bar menu button, that, when clicked, displays a status bar menu. You use the status bar menu to change the message area or to change to other versions of the document.

Your installation of Photoshop might display rulers at the top and left of the document window. You will learn about rulers later in this chapter.

Panels

A **panel** is a collection of graphically displayed choices and commands, such as those involving colors, brushes, actions, or layers (Figure 1–18). Panels help you monitor and modify your work. Each panel displays a panel tab with the name of the panel and a panel menu button. When you click the panel menu button, also called the panel menu icon, Photoshop displays a context-sensitive menu that allows you to make changes to the panel. Some panels have a status bar across the bottom. A panel can display buttons, boxes, sliders, scroll bars, or drop-down lists.

By default, panels are grouped by general purpose. A panel **group** or **tab group** displays several panels horizontally in a group joined by a title bar. When you first start Photoshop, several panels are grouped and then docked vertically on the right side of the workspace. As you add other panels to the workspace, each panel group has a title bar with a button that collapses the panels. Panels are **collapsed** when they display only an icon. Panels are **minimized** when they display only their name. Panels are **expanded** when they display their contents. Right-clicking a group title bar displays a menu with choices for panel placement and docking.

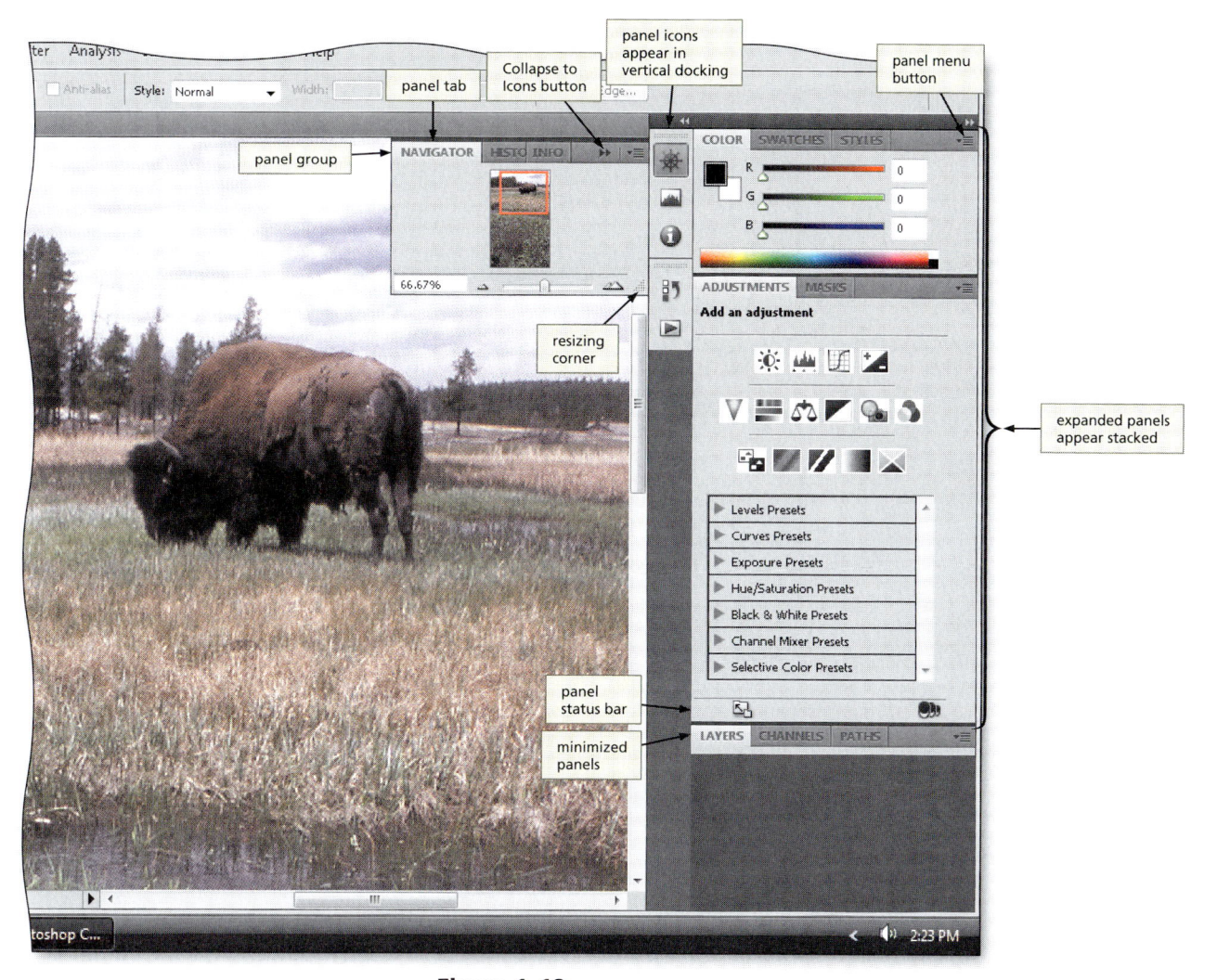

Figure 1–18

When you close a panel by clicking Close on the panel menu, it no longer is displayed. You can redisplay the panel by clicking the panel name on the Window menu or by a using shortcut key. If you choose to display a new panel that is not part of the current workspace, it appears to the left of the vertical docking; however, panels may be added to the vertical docking by dragging the panel tab onto the docking title bar.

You can arrange and reposition panels either individually or in groups. To move them individually, drag their tabs; to move a group, drag the area to the right of the tabs. To float a panel in the workspace, drag its tab outside of the vertical docking. You can create a **stack** of floating panels by dragging a panel tab to a location below another floating panel and docking it.

Sometimes you might want to hide all the panels to display more of the document window. To hide all panels, press the TAB key. Press the TAB key again to display the panels.

Photoshop comes with 25 panels, described in Table 1–1 on the next page. As each panel is introduced throughout this book, its function and characteristics will be explained further.

Table 1–1 Photoshop Panels	
Panel Name	**Purpose**
3D	to show the 3D layer components, settings, and options of the associated 3D file — available in Photoshop Extended only
Actions	to record, play, edit, and delete individual actions
Adjustments	to create nondestructive adjustment layers with color and tonal adjustments
Animation	to create a sequence of images or frames, displayed as motion over time
Brushes	to select preset brushes and design custom brushes
Channels	to create and manage channels
Character	to provide options for formatting characters
Clone Source	to set up and manipulate sample sources for the Clone Stamp tools or Healing Brush tools
Color	to display the color values for the current foreground and background colors
Histogram	to view tonal and color information about an image
History	to jump to any recent state of the image created during the current working session
Info	to display color values and document status information
Layer Comps	to display multiple compositions of a page layout
Layers	to show and hide layers, create new layers, and work with groups of layers
Masks	to create precise, editable pixel- and vector-based masks
Measurement Log	to record measurement data about a measured object — available in Photoshop Extended only
Navigator	to change the view or magnification of the photo using a thumbnail display
Notes	to insert, edit, and delete notes attached to files
Options	to display options and settings for the currently selected tool
Paragraph	to change the formatting of columns and paragraphs
Paths	to list the name and a thumbnail image of each saved path, the current work path, and the current vector mask
Styles	to view and select preset styles
Swatches	to store colors that you need to use often
Tools	to select tools
Tool Presets	to save and reuse tool settings

File Types

A **file type** refers to the internal characteristics of digital files; it designates the operational or structural characteristics of a file. Each digital file, graphic or otherwise, is stored with specific kinds of formatting related to how the file is displayed on the screen, how it prints, and the software it uses to do so. Computer systems use the file type to help users open the file with the appropriate software. File types are distinguished by a special file extension. **File extensions**, in most computer systems, are identified by a three- or four-letter suffix after the file name. For example, Bison.jpg refers to a file named Bison with the extension and file type JPG. A period separates the file name and its extension. When you are exploring files on your system, you might see the file extensions as part of the file name, or you might see a column of information about file types.

Graphic files are created and stored using many different file types and extensions. The type of file sometimes is determined by the hardware or software used to create the file. Other times, the user has a choice in applying a file type and makes the decision based on the file size, the intended purpose of the graphic file — such as whether the file is to be used on the Web — or the desired color mode.

A few common graphic file types are listed in Table 1–2.

Table 1–2 Graphic File Types		
File Extension	**File Type**	**Description**
BMP	Bitmap	BMP is a standard Windows image format used on DOS and Windows-compatible computers. BMP format supports many different color modes.
EPS	Encapsulated PostScript	EPS files can contain both bitmap and vector graphics. Almost all graphics, illustration, and page-layout programs support the EPS format, which can be used to transfer PostScript artwork between applications.
GIF	Graphics Interchange Format	GIF commonly is used to display graphics and images on Web pages. It is a compressed format designed to minimize file size and electronic transfer time.
JPG or JPEG	Joint Photographic Experts Group	JPG files commonly are used to display photographs on Web pages. JPG format supports many different color modes. JPG retains all color information in an RGB image, unlike GIF format. Most digital cameras produce JPG files.
PDF	Portable Document Format	PDF is a flexible file format based on the PostScript imaging model that is cross-platform and cross-application. PDF files accurately display and preserve fonts, page layouts, and graphics. PDF files can contain electronic document search and navigation features such as hyperlinks.
PSD	Photoshop Document	PSD format is the default file format in Photoshop and the only format that supports all Photoshop features. Other Adobe applications can import PSD files directly and preserve many Photoshop features due to the tight integration between Adobe products.
RAW	Photoshop Raw	RAW format is a flexible file format used for transferring images between applications and computer platforms. There are no pixel or file size restrictions in this format. Documents saved in the Photoshop Raw format cannot contain layers.
TIF or TIFF	Tagged Image File Format	TIF is a flexible bitmap image format supported by almost all paint, image-editing, and page-layout applications. This format often is used for files that are to be exchanged between applications or computer platforms. Most desktop scanners can produce TIF images.

BTW

File Extensions
The default setting for file extensions in Photoshop is to use a lowercase three-letter extension. If you wish to change the extension, do the following: Press SHIFT+CTRL+S to access the Save As dialog box. In the File name text box, type the file name, period, and extension within quotation marks. Click the Save button.

Saving a Photo

As you make changes to a file in Photoshop, the computer stores it in memory. If you turn off the computer or if you lose electrical power, the file in memory is lost. If you plan to use the photo later, you must save it on a storage device such as a USB flash drive or hard disk.

While you are editing, to preserve the most features such as layers, effects, masks, and styles, Photoshop recommends that you save photos in the **PSD format**. PSD, which stands for Photoshop Document Format, is the default file format for files created from scratch and supports files up to 2 gigabytes (GB) in size. The PSD format also maximizes portability among other Adobe versions and applications.

In addition to saving in the PSD format, you will save the photo with a new file name and in a new location, so that the original photo is preserved in case you need to start again. Even though you have yet to edit the photo, it is a good practice to save a copy of the file on your personal storage device early in the process.

BTW

Saving Photos
When you save a photo on a storage device, it also remains in main memory and is displayed on the screen.

To Save a Photo in the PSD Format

The following steps use the Save As command to save a photo on a USB flash drive using the file name, Bison Edited.

1
- With your USB flash drive connected to one of the computer's USB ports, click File on the menu bar to display the File menu (Figure 1–19).

Q&A Do I have to save to a USB flash drive?

No. You can save to any device or folder. A **folder** is a specific location on a storage medium. You can save to the default folder or a different folder.

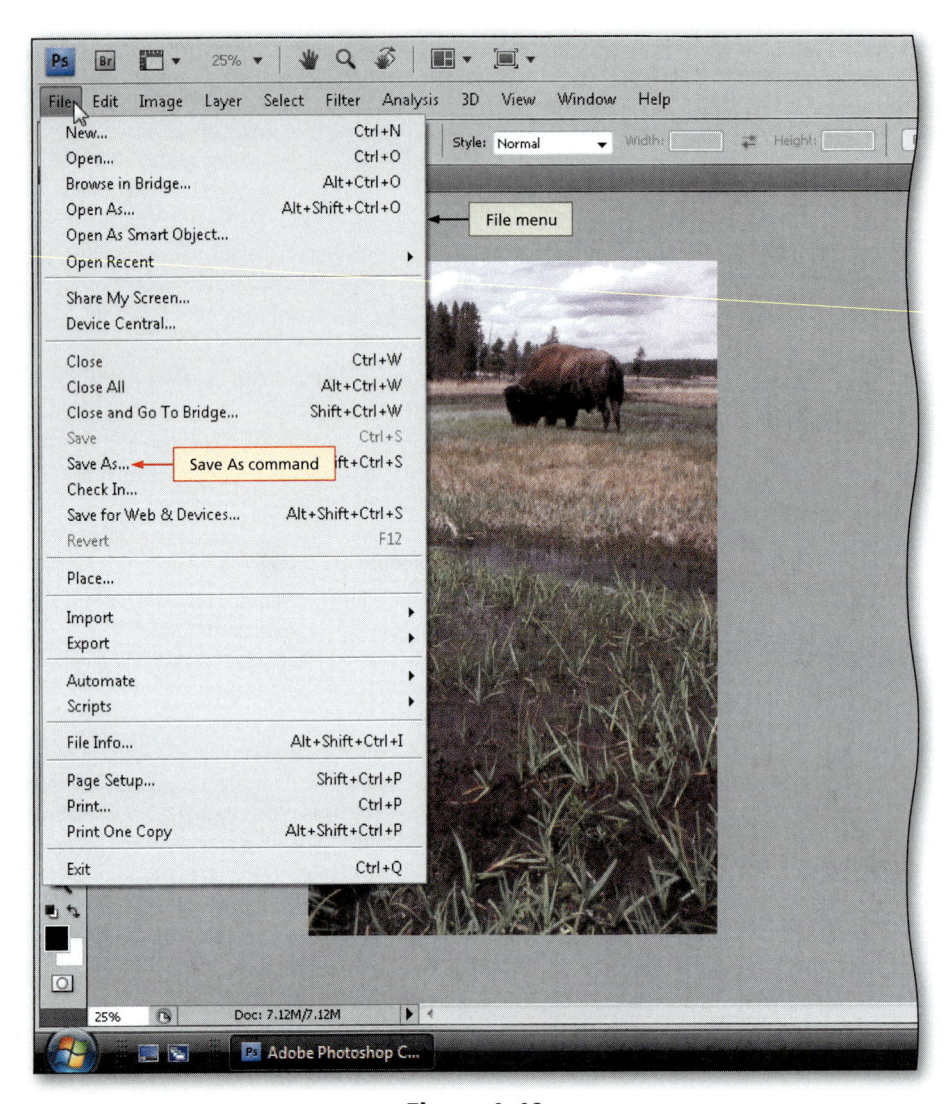

Figure 1–19

Saving a Photo **PS** 21

2

- Click Save As to display the Save As dialog box.

- Type `Bison Edited` in the File name text box to change the file name. Do not press the ENTER key after typing the file name (Figure 1–20).

Q&A Do I have to use that file name?

It is good practice to identify the relationship of this photo to the original by using at least part of the original file name with some notation about its status.

Q&A What characters can I use in a file name?

A file name can have a maximum of 260 characters, including spaces. The only invalid characters are the backslash (\), slash (/), colon (:), asterisk (*), question mark (?), quotation mark ("), less than symbol (<), greater than symbol (>), and vertical bar (|).

Figure 1–20

3

- Click the Save in box arrow to display the list of available drives (Figure 1–21).

- If necessary, scroll until UDISK 2.0 (F:) appears in the list of available drives.

Q&A Why is my list of drives arranged and named differently?

The size of the Save As dialog box and your computer's configuration determine how the list is displayed and how the drives are named.

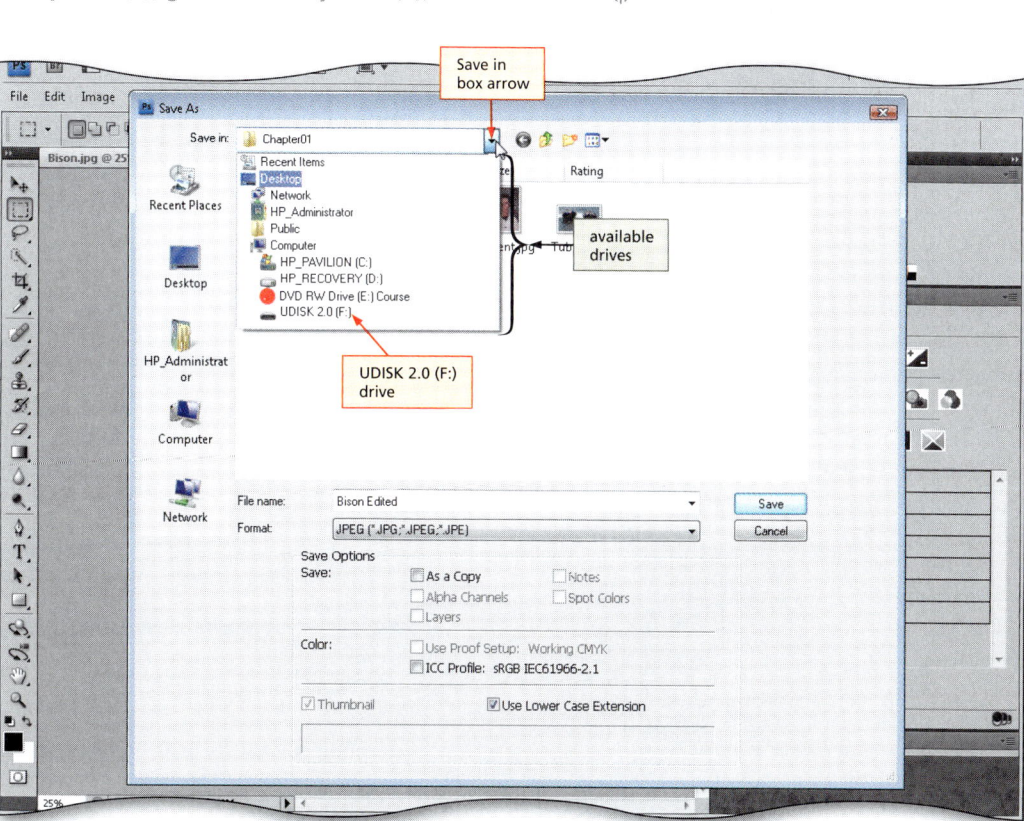

Figure 1–21

4
- Click UDISK 2.0 (F:), or the location of your USB flash drive in the list, as the new save location (Figure 1–22).

Q&A | What if my USB flash drive has a different name or letter?

It is very likely that your USB flash drive will have a different name and drive letter and be connected to a different port. Verify that the device in your Computer list is correct.

Q&A | How do I save the file if I am not using a USB flash drive?

Use the same process, but select your desired save location in the Save in list.

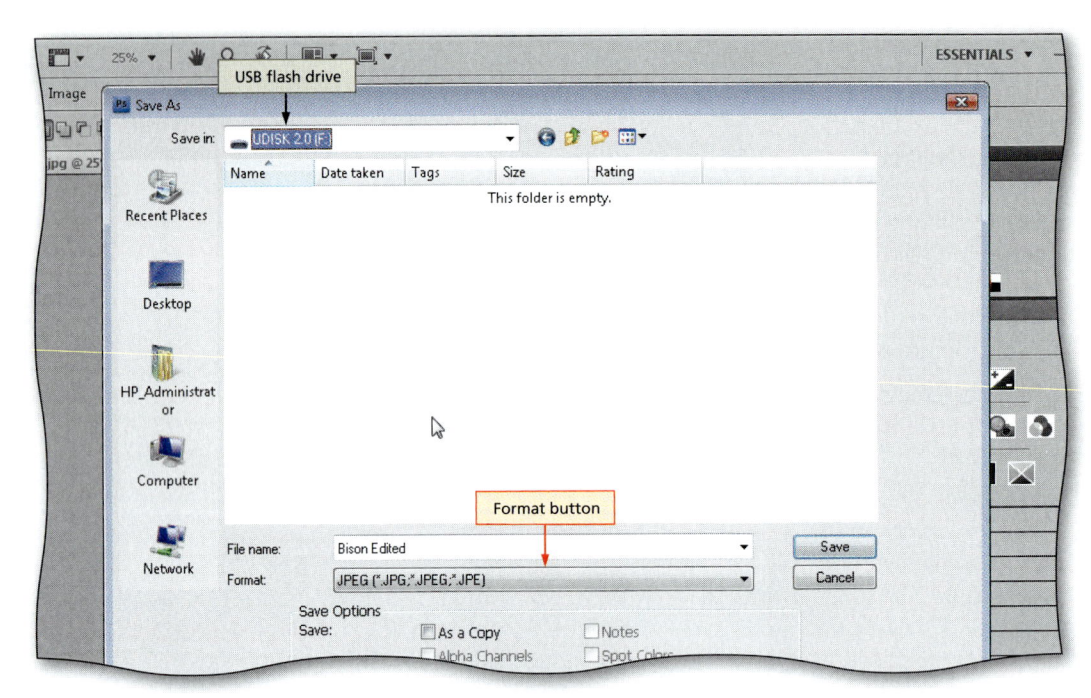

Figure 1–22

5
- Click the Format button to display the list of available file formats (Figure 1–23).

Q&A | Should I make a special folder for my photos?

You might want to create a folder for each chapter in this book. If so, click the Create New Folder button in the Save As dialog box. When the new folder is displayed, type a chapter name such as `Chapter01` and then press the ENTER key.

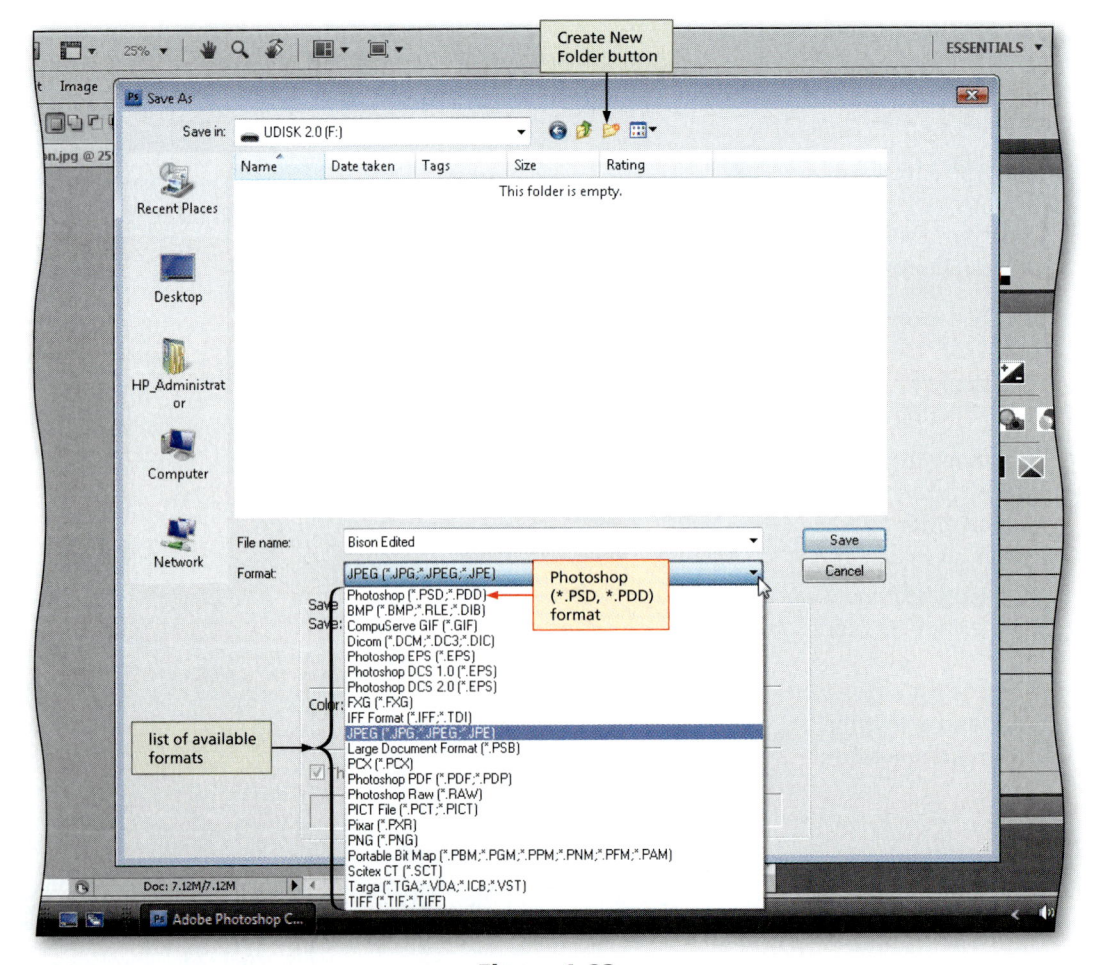

Figure 1–23

Saving a Photo **PS 23**

6
- Click Photoshop (*.PSD, *.PDD) to select it (Figure 1–24).

Q&A What is PDD?

The **PDD format** is used with images created by Photo Deluxe and other software packages. Some older digital cameras produce files with a PDD extension as well.

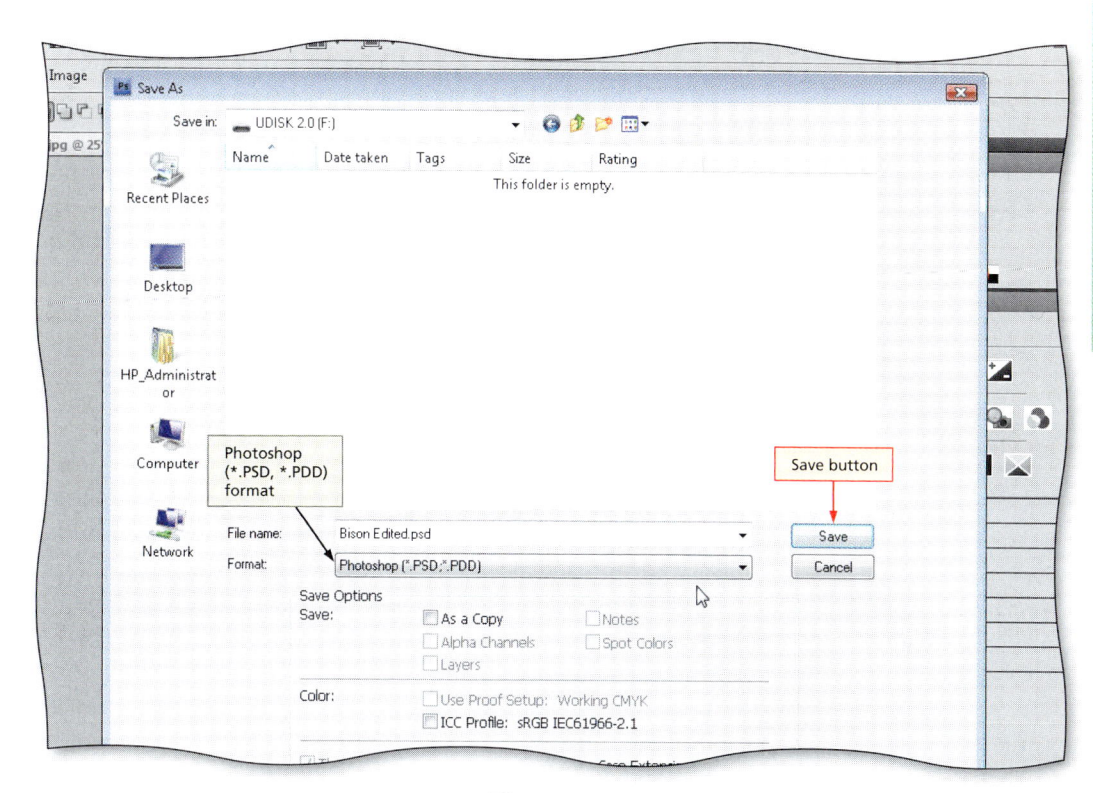

Figure 1–24

7
- Click the Save button in the Save As dialog box to save the photo on the USB flash drive in the PSD format with the file name, Bison Edited (Figure 1–25).

Q&A How do I know that the project is saved?

While Photoshop is saving your file, it briefly displays a Working in Background shape. In addition, your USB drive might have a light that flashes during the save process. The new file name appears on the document window tab.

Figure 1–25

Other Ways
1. Press SHIFT+CTRL+S, choose settings, click Save button

Viewing Photos

Photoshop allows you to view photos in many different ways, by adjusting the document window and by using different tools and panels. Using good navigation techniques to view images can help you edit the details of a photo or check for problems. For example, you might want to zoom in on a specific portion of the photo or move to a different location in a large photo. You might want to use a ruler to measure certain portions of the photo. Or you might want to view the image without the distraction of the panels and menu. Zooming, navigating, scrolling, and changing the screen mode are some ways to view the document window and its photo.

Zooming

To make careful edits in a photo, you sometimes need to change the magnification or **zoom**. Zooming allows you to focus on certain parts of the photo, such as a specific person in a crowd scene or details in a complicated picture. A magnification of 100% means the photo is displayed at its actual size. Zooming in enlarges the magnification and percentage of the photo; zooming out reduces the magnification. Note that zooming does not change the size of the photo; it merely changes the appearance of the photo in the document window.

The Zoom Tool (Z) button displays a magnifying glass icon on the Photoshop Tools panel. The Z in parentheses indicates that you can press the Z key to access the tool. Another way to access the Zoom tool is to use the Zoom Tool button located on the Application bar. Both of the buttons and the shortcut key perform the exact same function. Choosing one over the other is a matter of personal choice. Most people use the shortcut key. Others choose a button because of its proximity to the mouse pointer at the time.

When you use the Zoom tool, each click magnifies the image to the next preset percentage. When positioned in the photo, the Zoom tool mouse pointer displays a magnifying glass, with either a plus sign, indicating an increase in magnification, or a minus sign, indicating a decrease in magnification. Right-clicking with the Zoom tool in the photo displays a shortcut menu with options to zoom in or zoom out, among others.

Figure 1–26 displays the Zoom tool's options bar, with buttons to zoom in and out. Other options include check boxes used when working with multiple photos, displaying the actual pixels, fitting the entire photo on the screen, filling the screen, and displaying the photo at its print size.

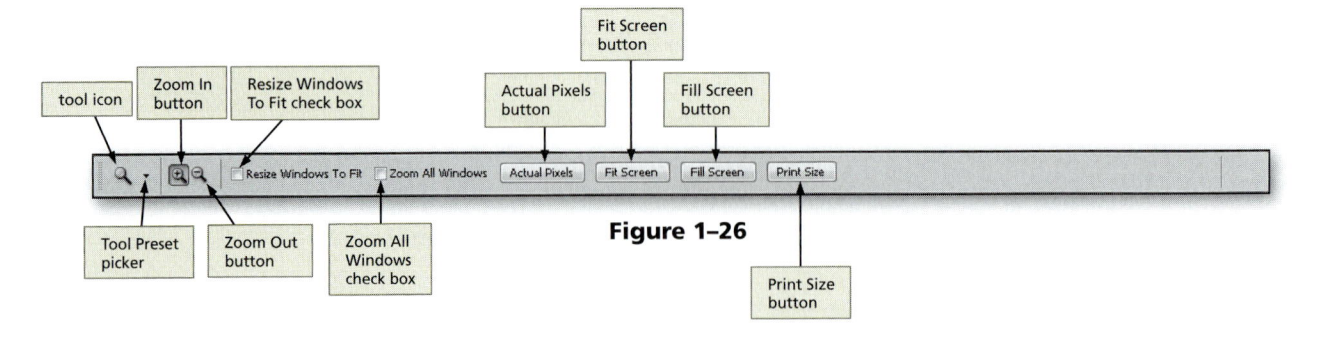

Figure 1–26

To Use the Zoom Tool

The following steps use the Zoom Tool button on the Application bar to zoom in on the bison for careful editing later in the chapter.

1
- Click the Zoom Tool button on the Application bar to select it.

- Move the mouse pointer into the document window to display the magnifying glass mouse pointer (Figure 1–27).

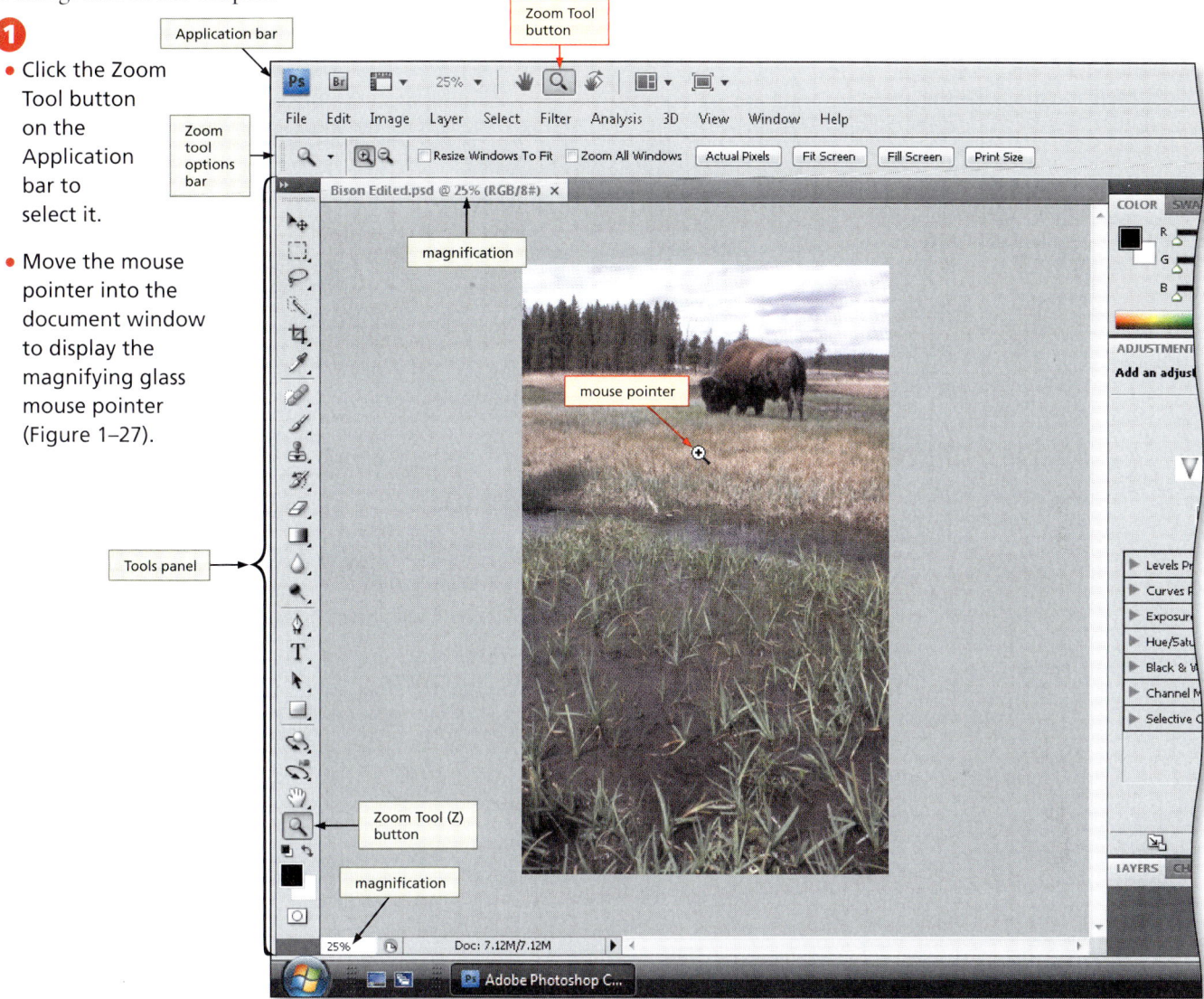

Figure 1–27

2

- Click the bison twice to zoom in (Figure 1–28).

🔍 **Experiment**

- On the options bar, click the Zoom In button and then click the photo. Click the Zoom Out button and then click the photo. ALT+click the photo to zoom in the opposite direction from the options bar setting. Zoom to 50% magnification.

3

- If necessary, zoom to 50% magnification.

Figure 1–28

Other Ways

1. To select Zoom tool, click Zoom Tool (Z) button
2. To select Zoom tool, press Z
3. Select Zoom tool, press ALT+click
4. Select Zoom tool, press CTRL+PLUS SIGN (+) or CTRL+MINUS SIGN (-)
5. On View menu, click Zoom In or Zoom Out
6. On document window status bar, type percentage in magnification box

The Navigator Panel

Another convenient way to zoom and move around the photo is to use the Navigator panel. The Navigator panel (Figure 1–29) is used to change the view of your document window using a thumbnail display. To display the Navigator panel, choose Navigator from the Window menu.

BTW

Ways to Zoom
There are many ways to zoom, including the Zoom tool, the Zoom buttons, the magnification box, and the Navigator panel. You also can use the Zoom Level list on the Application bar or shortcut keys. How you zoom depends on your personal preference and whether you wish to change the current tool.

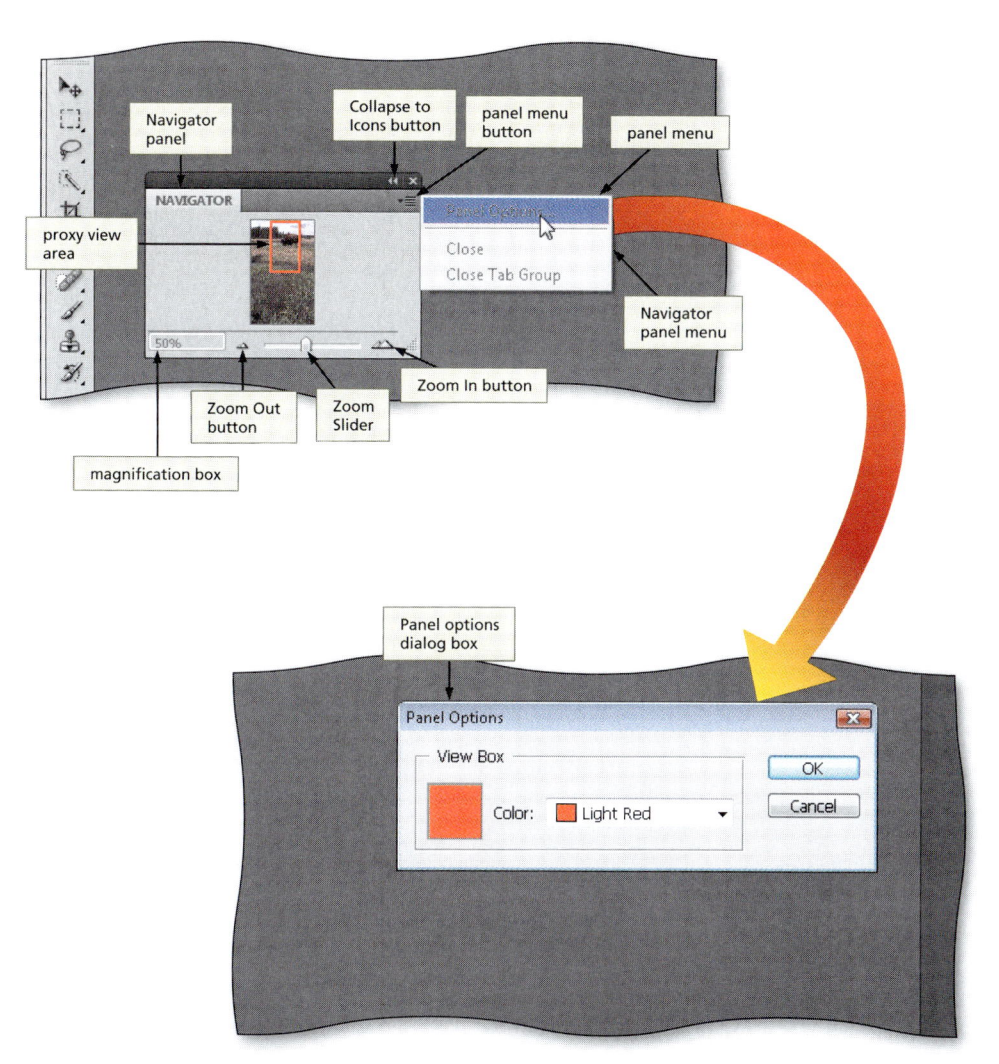

Figure 1–29

The rectangle with the red border in the Navigator panel is called the **proxy view area** or **view box**, which outlines the currently viewable area in the window. Dragging the proxy view area changes the portion of the photo that is displayed in the document window. In the lower portion of the Navigator panel, you can type in the desired magnification, or you can use the slider or buttons to increase or decrease the magnification.

In Figure 1–29 on the previous page, the Navigator panel menu appears when you click the panel menu button. The Panel Options command displays the Panel Options dialog box.

To move the panel, drag the panel tab. To collapse the panel, click the Collapse to Icons button. To close the panel, click the panel's Close button or click Close on the panel menu.

When you are using a different tool on the Tools panel, such as a text tool or brush tool, it is easier to use the Navigator panel to zoom and move around in the photo. That way, you do not have to change to the Zoom tool, perform the zoom, and then change back to your editing tool.

To View and Use the Navigator Panel

The following steps use the Navigator panel to position the view in the document window.

1
- Click Window on the menu bar to display the Window menu (Figure 1–30).

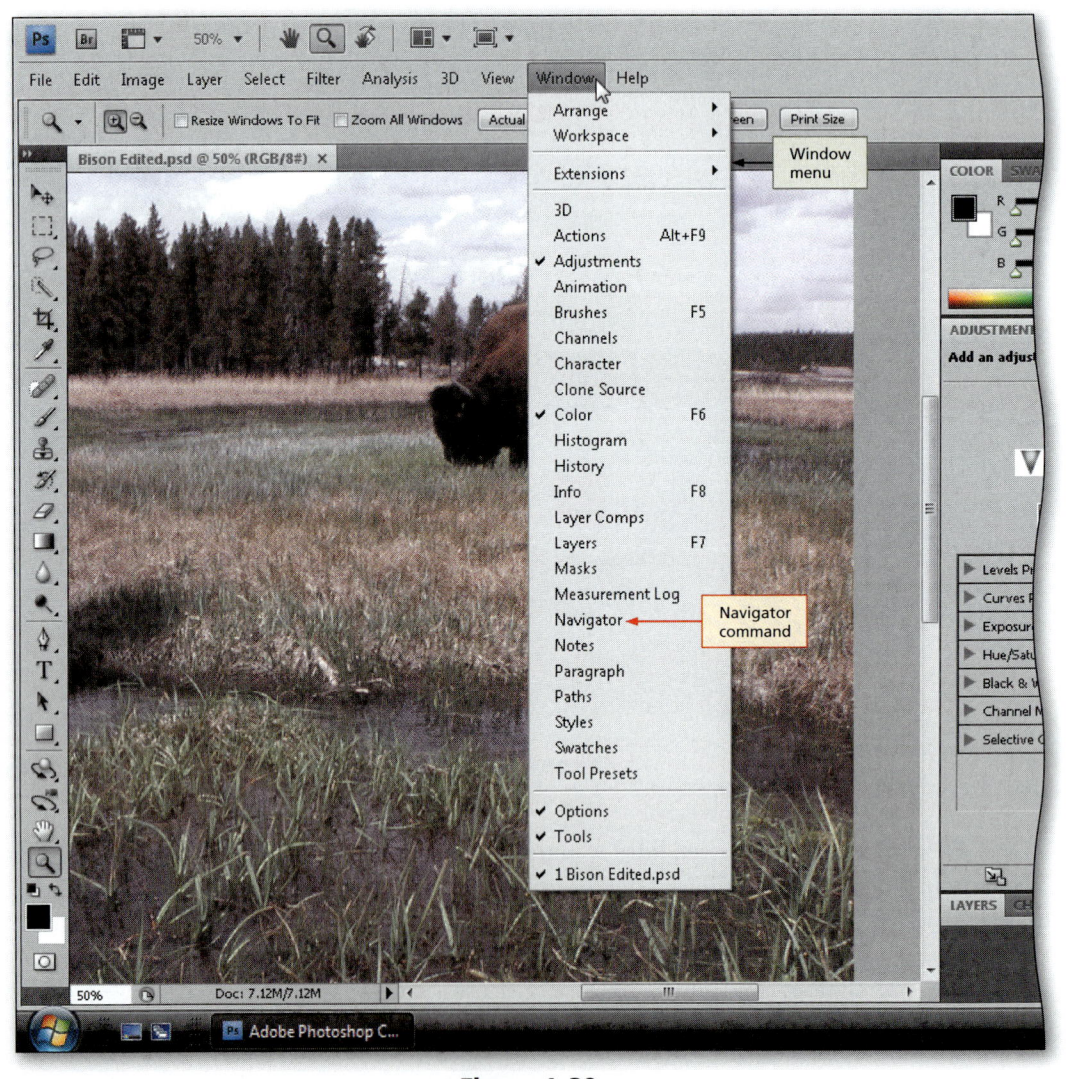

Figure 1–30

Viewing Photos **PS 29**

2

- Click Navigator to display the Navigator panel.

- Drag the proxy view area to display the lower portion of the photo (Figure 1–31).

  🔍 **Experiment**

- Drag the proxy view area to display different portions of the photo, and then drag to display the lower portion of the photo.

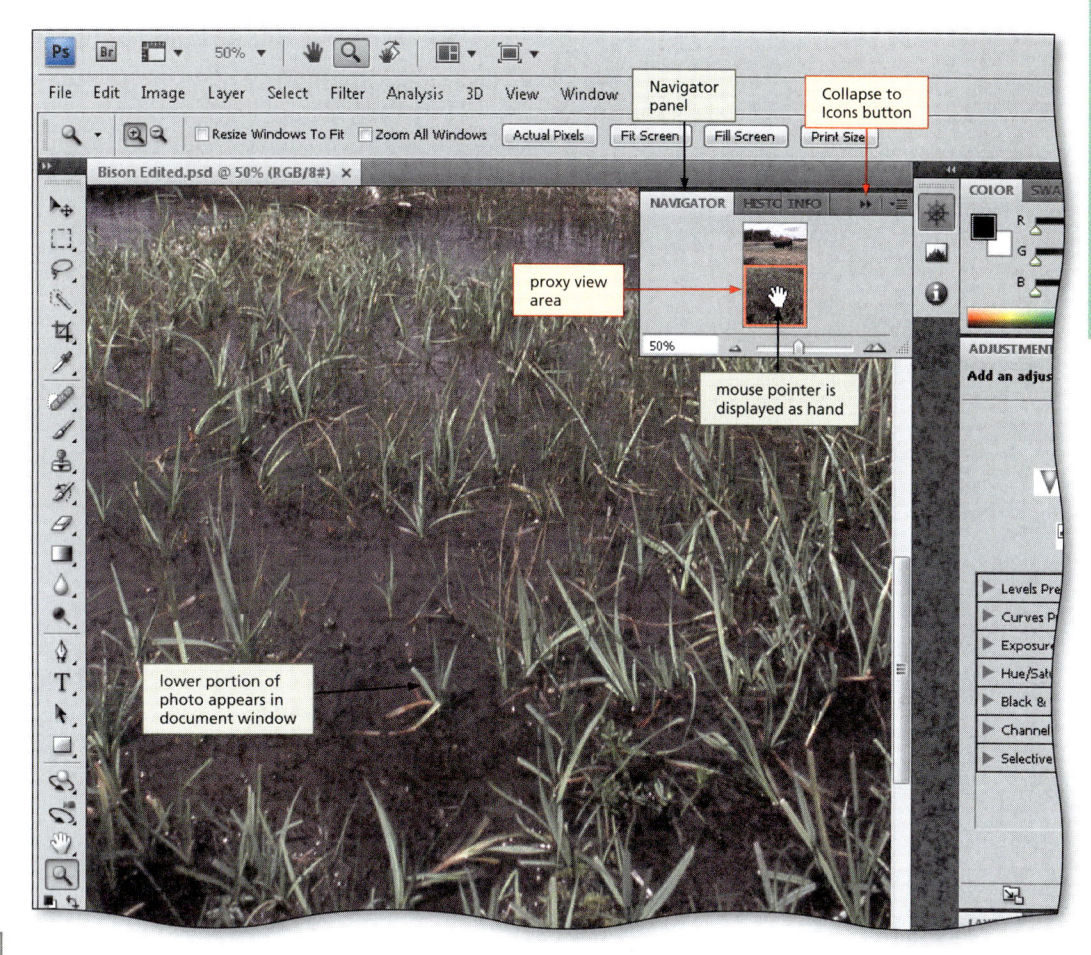

Figure 1–31

Other Ways

1. If panel is minimized, click Navigator button

To Collapse the Navigator Panel

The following step collapses the Navigator panel and its tab group.

1

- In the Navigator panel, click the Collapse to Icons button to display only the panel icons in a vertical docking (Figure 1–32).

Figure 1–32

Other Ways

1. Click Navigator panel icon in vertical docking

The Hand Tool

The Hand tool also can be used to move around in the photo if the photo has been magnified to be larger than the document window. To use the Hand tool, click the Hand Tool (H) button on the Tools panel or the Hand Tool button on the Application bar. Then, drag in the display area of the document window.

The Hand tool options bar (Figure 1–33) displays boxes and buttons to assist you in scrolling and manipulating the document window.

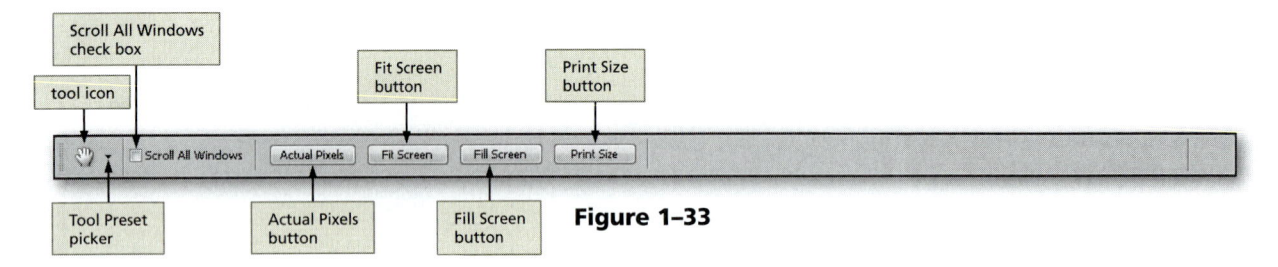

Figure 1–33

To Use the Hand Tool

The following step uses the Hand tool to view a different part of the photo.

1
- On the Application bar, click the Hand Tool button to select the Hand tool.
- Drag in the document window to display the upper portion of the photo (Figure 1–34).

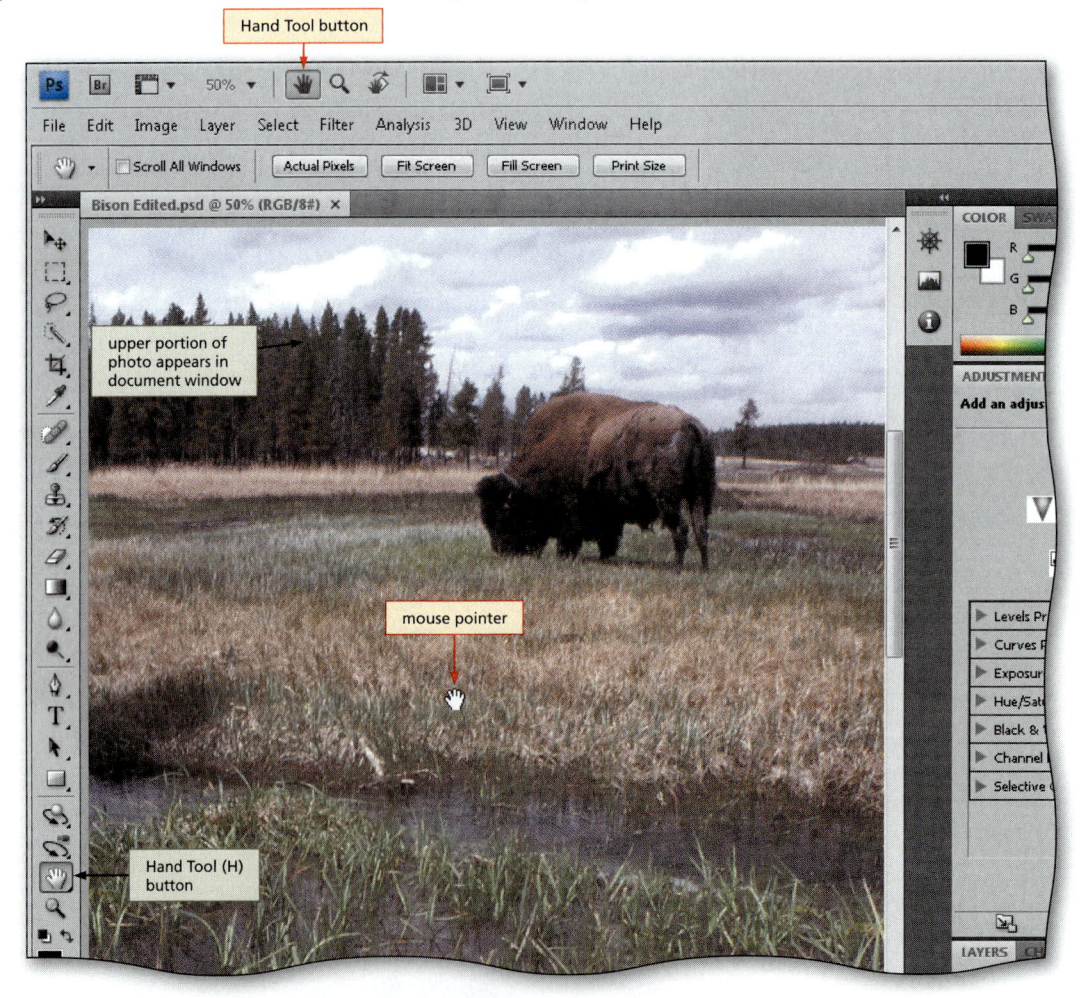

Other Ways
1. On Tools panel, click Hand Tool (H) button, drag photo
2. Press H, drag photo

Figure 1–34

To Change the Screen Mode

To change the way the panels, bars, and document window appear, Photoshop includes three **screen modes**, or ways to view the document window. **Standard screen mode** displays the Application bar, menu bar, document window, scroll bars, and visible panels. **Full screen mode** displays only the image and rulers, if they are visible, on a black background. **Full screen mode with menu** enlarges the document window to fill the workspace and combines the Application bar and menu bar. To switch between the three screen modes, you can use the Screen Mode button on the Application bar, choose commands on the View menu, or press the F key, as performed in the following steps.

1
- On the Application bar, click the Screen Mode button to display its menu (Figure 1–35).

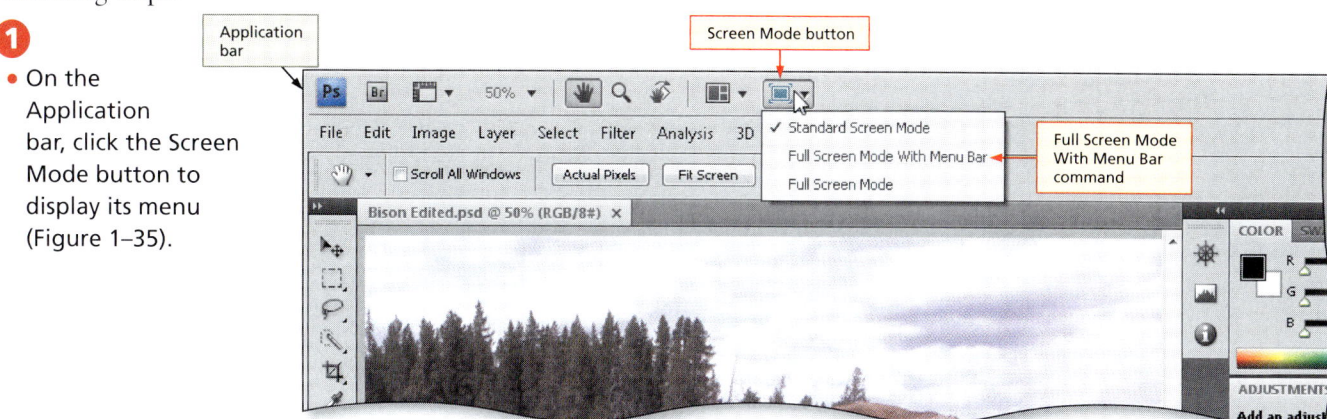

Figure 1–35

2
- Click Full Screen Mode With Menu Bar to view a larger image (Figure 1–36).

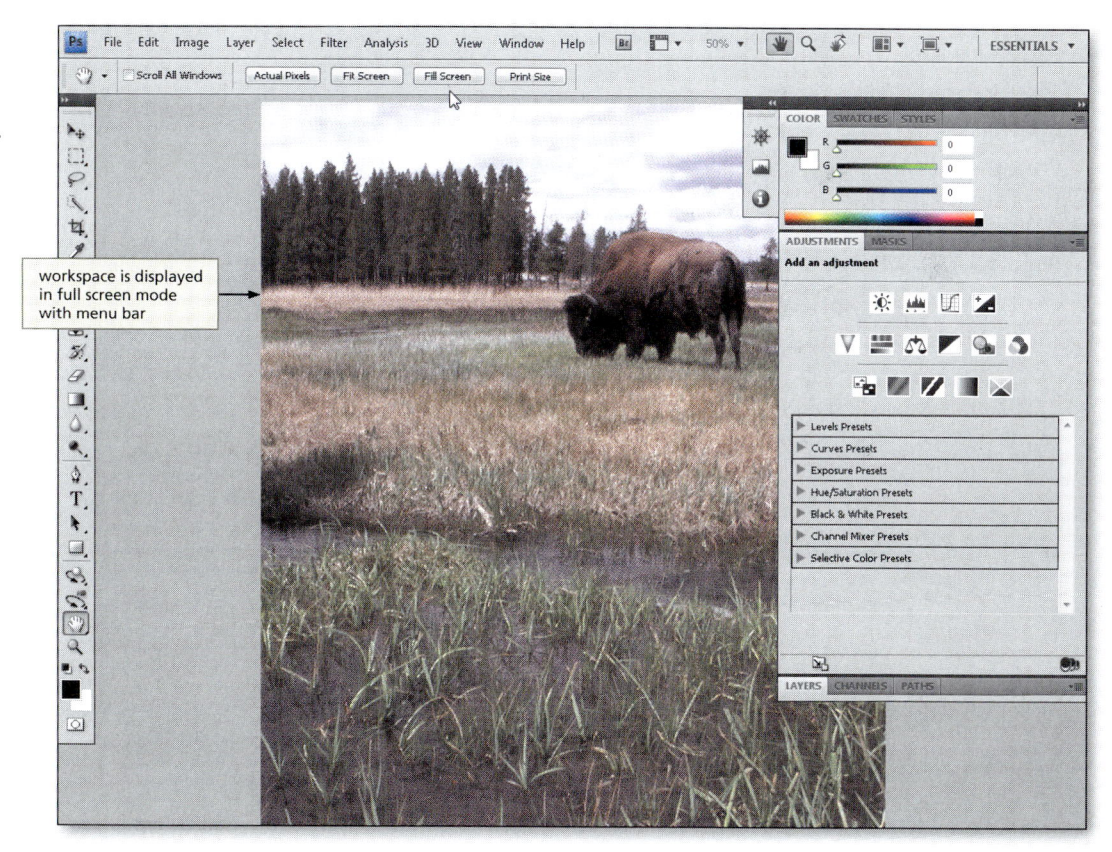

Figure 1–36

Photoshop Chapter 1 Editing a Photo

3
- Press the F key to change to the full screen mode (Figure 1–37).

workspace is displayed in full screen mode

Figure 1–37

4
- Press the F key again to return to the standard screen mode (Figure 1–38).

workspace is displayed in standard screen mode

Other Ways
1. On View menu, point to Screen Mode, click desired mode

Figure 1–38

Rulers

To make careful edits in a photo, sometimes it is necessary to use precise measurements in addition to zooming and navigating. In these cases, it is necessary to change the Photoshop document window to view the rulers. **Rulers** appear on the top and left sides of the document window. Rulers help you position images or elements precisely. As you move your mouse over a photo, markers on the ruler display the mouse pointer's position.

Rulers display inches by default, but you can right-click a ruler to change the increment to pixels, centimeters, or other measurements. You can drag the mouse from a ruler to any position in the photo to display a **ruler guide**, or green line, that helps you straighten or align objects by providing a visual cue. Ruler guides do not print. You will learn more about ruler guides in Chapter 2.

To Display Rulers

The following steps display the rulers in the document window.

1
- On the Application bar, click the View Extras button to display its menu (Figure 1–39).

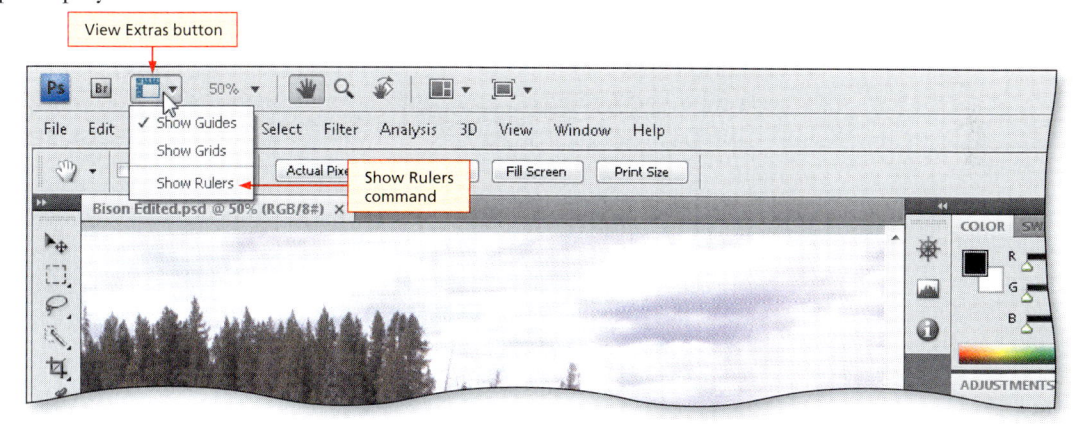

Figure 1–39

2
- Click Show Rulers to display the rulers in the document window (Figure 1–40).

Experiment

- Click the View Extras button. If the Show Guides command does not display a check mark, then click Show Guides. Drag down from the horizontal ruler to create a ruler guide in the photo. Drag right from the vertical ruler to create a vertical ruler guide in the photo. Click the View Extras button and then click Show Guides to turn off the check mark.

Other Ways
1. Press CTRL+R
2. On View menu, click Rulers

Figure 1–40

Plan Ahead

> **Keep design principles in mind.**
> You always should perform editing with design principles in mind. If you want to emphasize a single object on a fairly solid background, you might need to **crop**, or trim, extraneous space around the object. Adding a border or decorative frame around a photo sometimes can be an effective way to highlight or make the photo stand out on the page. Using a border color that complements one of the colors already in the photo creates a strong, visually connected image. For more information about graphic design concepts, read Appendix B.

Editing the Photo

Editing, or making corrections and changes to a photo, involves a wide variety of tasks such as changing the focus of interest, recoloring portions of the photo, correcting defects, adding new artwork, or changing the file type for specific purposes. Editing is also called **post-processing** because it includes actions you take after the picture has been processed by the camera or scanner.

Table 1–3 suggests typical categories and types of edits you might perform on photos; there are many others. These edits commonly overlap; and, when performed in combination, they might create new editing varieties. You will learn more about edits as you work through the chapters in this book.

Table 1–3 Photo Edits

Category	Types of Edits
Resize and Focus	cropping, shrinking, enlarging, slicing, changing the aspect, rotating, leveling, mirroring, collinear editing
Enhancements and Layering	filters, layers, clones, borders, artwork, text, animation, painting, morphing, ordering, styles, masks, cutaways, selections, depth perception, anti-aliasing, move, warp, shapes, rasterizing
Color	correction, contrast, blending, modes and systems, separations, resolution, screening, levels, ruling, trapping, matching, black and white
Correction	sharpening, red-eye, tears, correcting distortion, retouching, reducing noise, blur, dodge, burn
File Type	camera raw, print, Web, animated images

Editing the bison photo will involve three steps. First, you will crop the photo to remove excessive background. Next, you will add a border and fill it with color. Finally, you will resize the photo to fit the intended use and size requirements.

Plan Ahead

> **Determine how to edit the photo to highlight the theme.**
> Look at your photo carefully. Are there parts that detract from the central figure? Would the theme be illustrated better by only displaying a portion of the photo? Decide which parts of the photo portray your message and which parts are visual clutter.
>
> - Use the rule of thirds to position visual lines.
> - Crop the photo to remove excess border.
> - Rotate the photo if necessary.

Cropping

The first step in editing the bison photo is to crop, or trim away, some of the extra grass and visual clutter so the photo focuses on the bison. Photographers try to compose and capture images full-frame, which means the object of interest fills the dimensions of the photo. When that is not possible, photographers and graphic artists crop the photo either to create an illusion of full-frame, to fit unusual shapes in layouts, or to make the image more dramatic. From a design point of view, sometimes it is necessary to crop a photo to straighten an image, remove distracting elements, or simplify the subject. The goal of most cropping is to make the most important feature in the original photo stand out. Cropping is sometimes used to convert a digital photo's proportions to those typical for traditional photos.

Most photographers and graphic artists use the **rule of thirds**, also called the principle of thirds, when placing the focus of interest. Imagine that the scene is divided into thirds both vertically and horizontally. The intersections of these imaginary lines suggest four positions for placing the focus of interest (Figure 1–41). The position you select depends on the subject and how you would like that subject to be presented. For instance, there might be a shadow, path, or visual line you wish to include. In the case of moving objects, you generally should leave space in front of them, into which they theoretically can move. When eyes are involved, it is better to leave space on the side toward which the person or animal is looking, so they do not appear to look directly out of the setting.

BTW

Cropping
To evaluate an image for cropping, make a printout. Using two L shapes cut from paper, form a size and shape rectangle to isolate a portion of the image. Draw lines on the printout to use as a guide when cropping in Photoshop.

BTW

Trimming vs. Cropping
The Trim command also crops an image by removing unwanted portions of the photo, but in a different way than the Crop command. The Trim command, on the Image menu, trims surrounding transparent pixels, or background pixels of the color you specify.

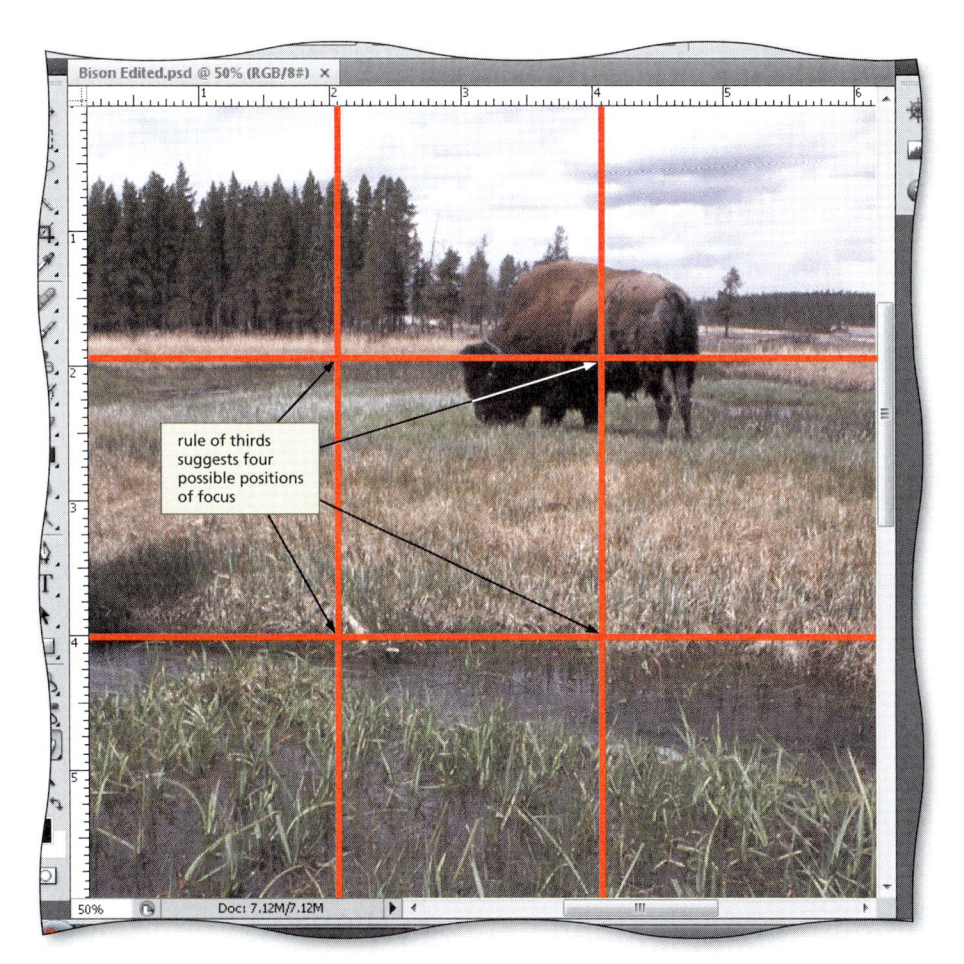

Figure 1–41

BTW

Document Size
Cropping reduces the storage size of the document, which is the size of the saved, flattened file in Adobe Photoshop format. The document window status bar displays the new document size after cropping.

Because the bison photo will be used on a postcard, the photo's orientation should be **landscape**, or horizontal. In most cases, you should try to crop to a rectangular shape with an approximate short-side to long-side ratio of 5:8. Sometimes called the **golden rectangle**, a 5:8 ratio emulates natural geometric forms such as flowers, leaves, shells, and butterflies. Most digital cameras take pictures with a similar ratio.

The Crop Tool (C) button on the Tools panel is used to drag or select the portion of the photo you wish to retain. Photoshop displays handles around the edge of the crop for further adjustments, if necessary. Then, when you press the ENTER key, the rest of the photo is trimmed away or cropped.

When the Crop tool is selected, the options bar displays boxes and buttons to assist cropping activities (Figure 1–42a). You can specify the exact height and width of the crop, as well as the resolution to use if resampling. The Front Image button allows you to crop using the dimensions of another photo. When you make a selection with the Crop tool, the options bar changes to include choices about the background display color of the cropped area and the ability to change the perspective while cropping (Figure 1–42b).

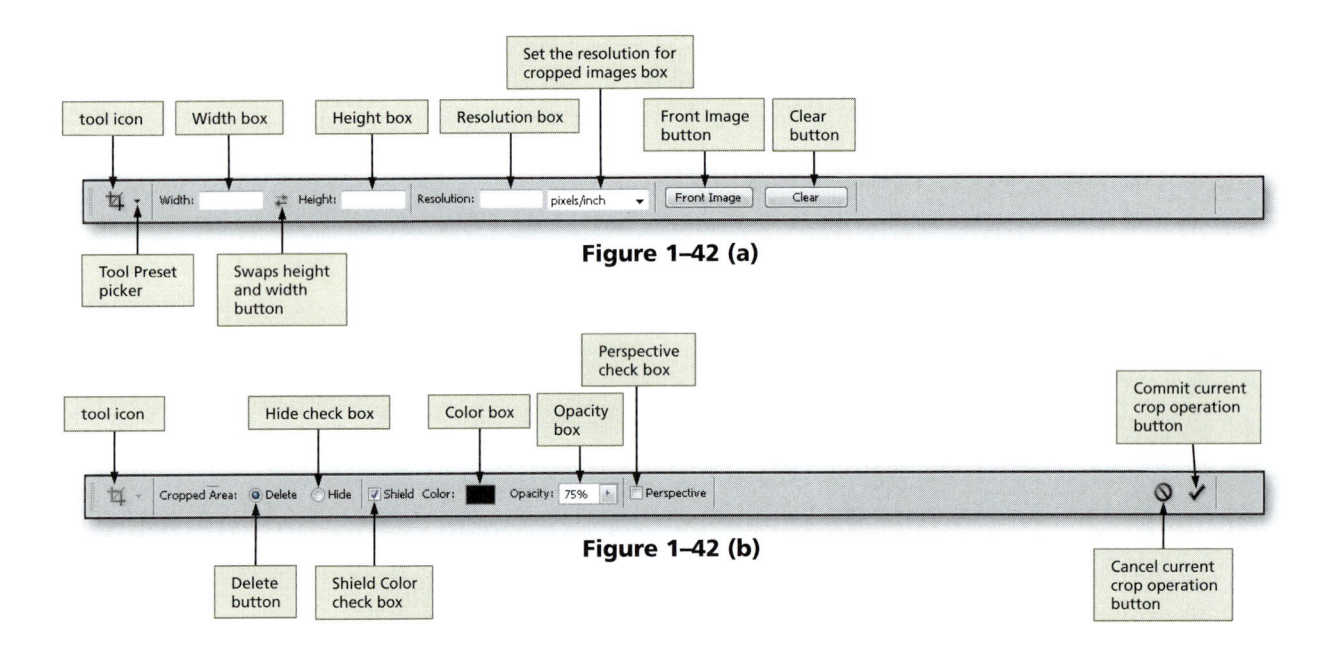

Figure 1–42 (a)

Figure 1–42 (b)

BTW

Reviewing Your Edits
Each edit or state of the photo is recorded sequentially in the History panel. If you want to step back through the edits or go back to a particular state, such as the previous crop, click the state in the History panel. You will learn more about the History panel in a future chapter.

If you make a mistake while dragging the cropping area and want to start over, you can click the Cancel current crop operation button (Figure 1–42b) or press the ESC key, which cancels the selection. If you already have performed the crop and then change your mind, you have several choices. You can click the Undo command on the Edit menu, or you can press CTRL+Z to undo the last edit.

To Crop a Photo

To make the bison the focus of the photo, the extra foreground will be cropped, as well as the background clutter of the building. Using the rule of thirds, the bison will be positioned on the right to provide a line of sight to the left. The following steps crop the photo of the bison using the rule of thirds and the golden rectangle ratio.

1
- To select the Crop tool, click the Crop Tool (C) button on the Tools panel (Figure 1–43).

Figure 1–43

2

- Scroll to the upper-left corner of the photo, if necessary.

- Using the rulers as guides, drag a rectangle beginning at the upper-left corner of the photo. Continue dragging right to approximately 5.5 inches on the horizontal ruler, and then down to approximately 3 inches on the vertical ruler. Do not release the mouse button (Figure 1–44).

🔎 **Experiment**

- If you want to practice cropping, press the ESC key and drag again. Press the SHIFT key down while you crop to constrain the proportions. When you are done experimenting, crop to 5.5 by 3 inches.

Figure 1–44

3

- Release the mouse button to display the crop selection (Figure 1–45).

Figure 1–45

4
- Press the ENTER key to complete the crop (Figure 1–46).

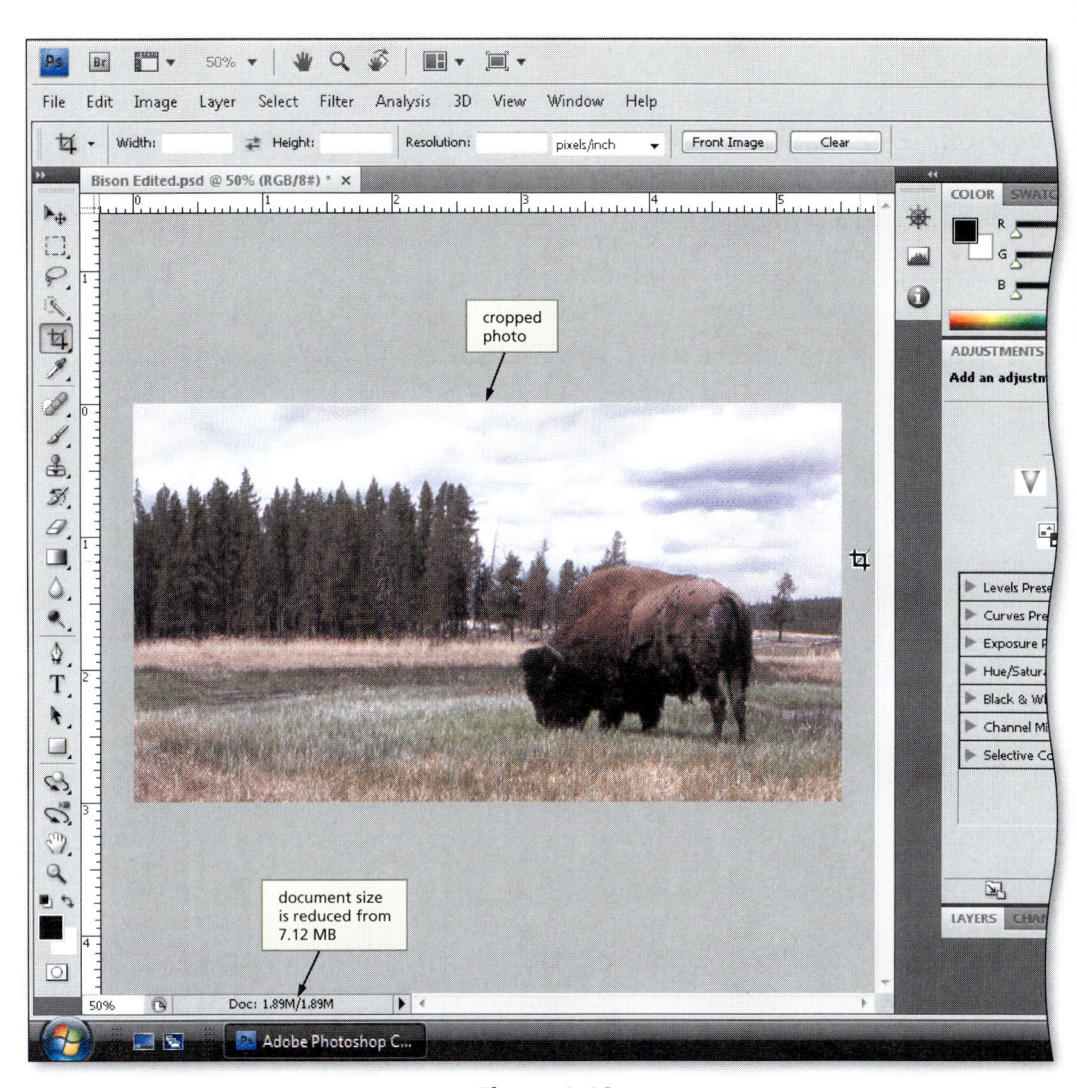

Figure 1–46

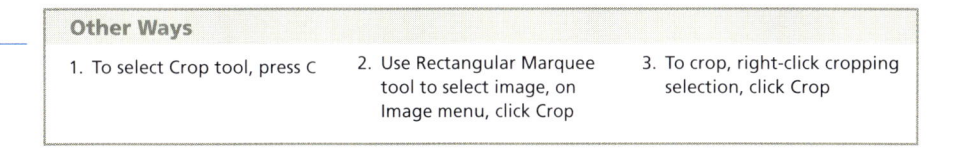

Other Ways		
1. To select Crop tool, press C	2. Use Rectangular Marquee tool to select image, on Image menu, click Crop	3. To crop, right-click cropping selection, click Crop

Plan Ahead

Add finishing touches.
If a border is required by the customer or needed for layout placement, choose a color and width that neither overwhelms nor overlaps any detail in the photo. A border should frame the subject, rather than become the subject.

Creating a Blended Border

A **border** is a decorative edge on a photo or a portion of a photo. Photoshop provides many ways to create a border, ranging from simple color transformations around the edge of the photo, to predefined decorated layers, to stylized photo frames.

A border helps define the edge of the photo, especially when the photo might be placed on colored paper or on a Web page with a background texture. A border visually

BTW

Resolution
Resolution refers to the number of pixels per linear inch. Graphics for print purposes are usually higher resolution than those for use on the Web. Images designed for the Web are limited by the resolution of the computer screen, which usually varies from 72 to 96 pixels per inch.

separates the photo from the rest of the page, while focusing the viewer's attention. Rounded borders soften the images in a photo. Square borders are more formal. Decorative borders on a static photo can add interest and amusement, but easily can detract from the focus on a busier photo. **Blended borders** are not a solid fill; rather, they blend a fill color from the outer edge toward the middle, sometimes providing a three-dimensional effect. A border that complements the photo in style, color, and juxtaposition is best.

To add a border to the bison photo, you first will select pixels along the edge of the image. A **pixel** is an individual dot of light that is the basic unit used to create digital images. Then you will fill the color black into the border pixels, using a normal blending mode, to create an appropriate frame for the photo.

Making Selections

Specifying or isolating an area of your photo for editing is called making a **selection**. By selecting specific areas, you can edit and apply special effects to portions of your image while leaving the unselected areas untouched.

Selections can be simple shapes such as rectangles or ovals, or unusually shaped areas of a photo, outlining specific objects. Selections can be the entire photo or as small a portion as one pixel. A selection displays a marquee in Photoshop. A **marquee** is a flashing or pulsating border, sometimes called marching ants.

To Select All

In the case of the bison photo, you will select the entire photo in order to create a border. The following steps use the Select menu to select all of the photo.

1
- On the menu bar, click Select to display its menu (Figure 1–47).

Figure 1–47

2
- On the Select menu, click All to select the entire photo and display the marquee (Figure 1–48).

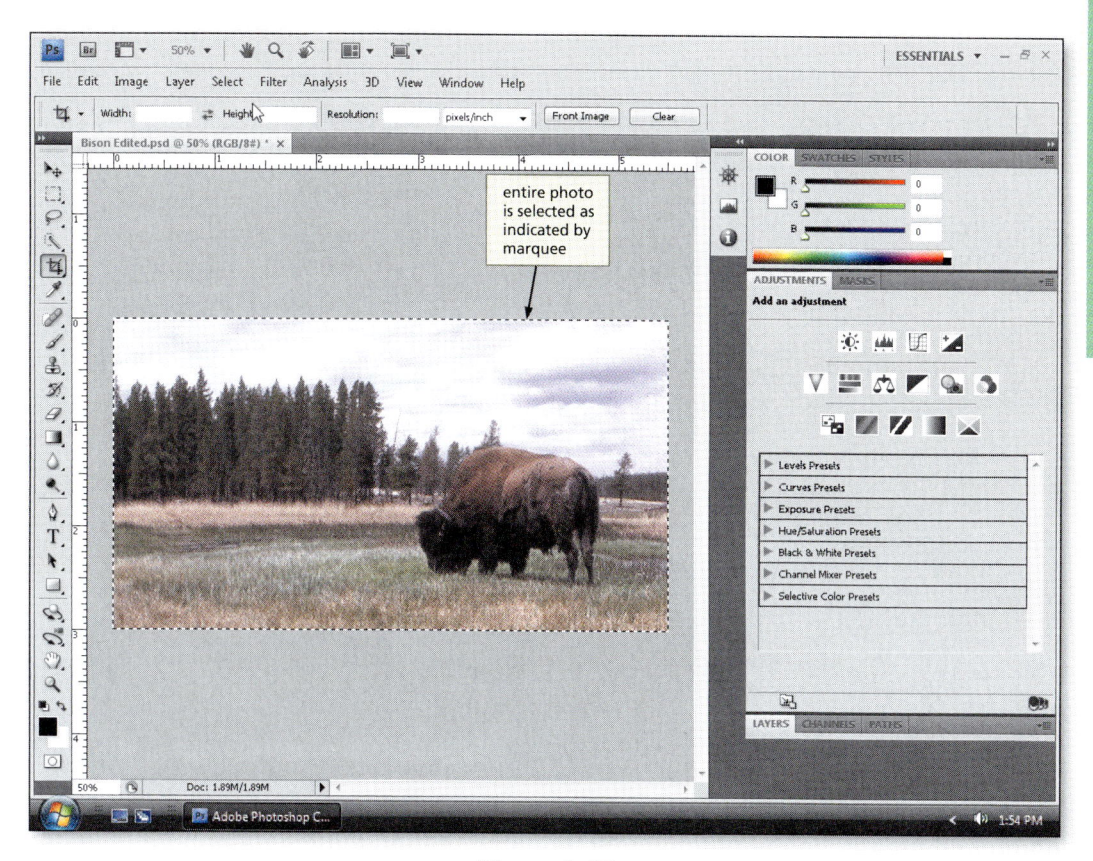

Figure 1–48

> **Other Ways**
> 1. To select all, press CTRL+A
> 2. To select areas, use selection tools

Modifying Selections

After creating the selection, you might wish to modify it to change the border. On the Select menu, Photoshop displays a Modify command and a submenu. First, you enter how many pixels you wish to include in the border. Then you can customize the border with the commands on the Modify submenu, as described in Table 1–4.

> **BTW**
>
> **Selections**
> When you select all, Photoshop displays the photo with a marquee around all four edges. The selection tools on the Tools panel also can help you make selections in the photo. The Rectangular Marquee, Lasso, Quick Selection, and Magic Wand tools will be discussed in Chapter 2.

Table 1–4 Commands on the Modify Submenu

Type of Modification	Result
Border	This command allows you to select a width of pixels, from 1 to 200, to be split evenly on either side of the existing selection border. If the selection is already on the edge, then half of the entered value will be included in the border.
Smooth	Photoshop examines the number of pixels in a radius around the selection. To smooth the selection, if more than half of the pixels already were selected, Photoshop adds the rest within the radius. If less than half were selected, the pixels are removed. The overall effect is to smooth sharp corners and jagged lines, reducing patchiness.
Expand	The border is increased by a number of pixels from 1 to 100. Any portion of the selection border running along the canvas's edge is unaffected.
Contract	The border is decreased by a number of pixels from 1 to 100. Any portion of the selection border running along the canvas's edge is unaffected.
Feather	This command creates a feather edge with a width from 0 to 250 pixels.

To Create a Border Using the Modify Submenu

The following steps use the Modify submenu to select the Border command and enter a width.

1
- On the menu bar, click Select, and then point to Modify to display the Modify submenu (Figure 1–49).

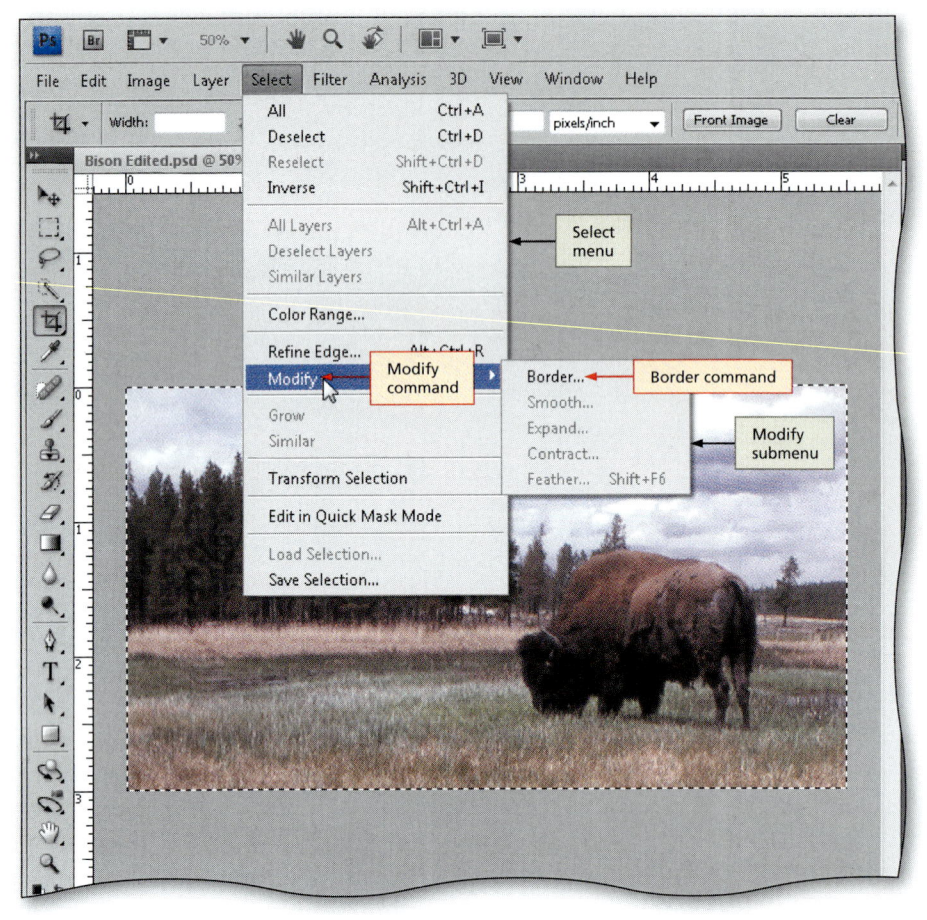

Figure 1–49

2
- Click Border on the Modify submenu to display the Border Selection dialog box.
- Type 50 in the Width box to create a border on each side of the photo (Figure 1–50).

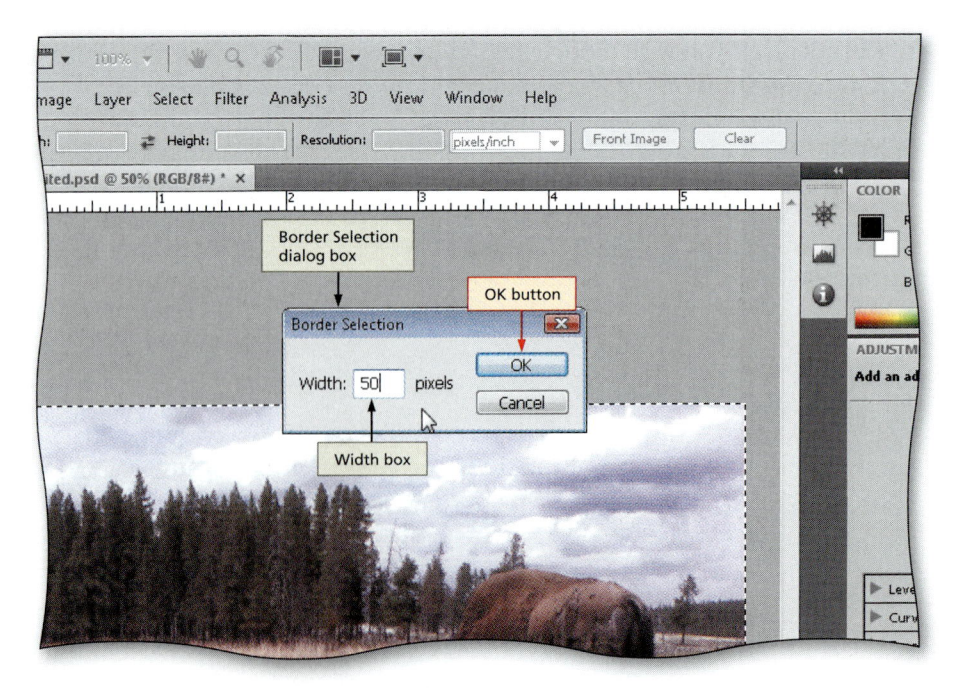

Figure 1–50

3
- Click the OK button in the Border Selection dialog box to define the selection (Figure 1–51).

Q&A Is the border 50 pixels wide?

No. Photoshop adds half of those pixels to either side of the selection. Because the selection was already on the edge of the photo, only 25 inner pixels were added.

Experiment
- To practice smoothing the border, click the Select menu, point to Modify, and then click Smooth. Enter a value in the Sample Radius box and then click the OK button. Notice the rounded rectangle in the border marquee. Press CTRL+Z to undo the Smooth command.

25 pixels are selected on edge of photo

Figure 1–51

Filling a Selection

When you **fill** a selection, you blend a color or a pattern into the selection area. Photoshop allows you to choose a color, a blending mode, and a percentage of opacity. **Blending modes** are the ways in which pixels in the image are affected by a color. Examples of blending modes include normal, lighten, darken, and other color manipulations. **Opacity** refers to the level at which you can see through the color to reveal the paper or layer beneath it. For example, 1% opacity appears nearly transparent, whereas 100% opacity appears completely opaque.

PS 44 Photoshop Chapter 1 Editing a Photo

To Fill a Selection

The following steps fill the border selection with 100% black, using a Normal blending mode, which paints each pixel to make it the result color.

1
- On the menu bar, click Edit to display the Edit menu (Figure 1–52).

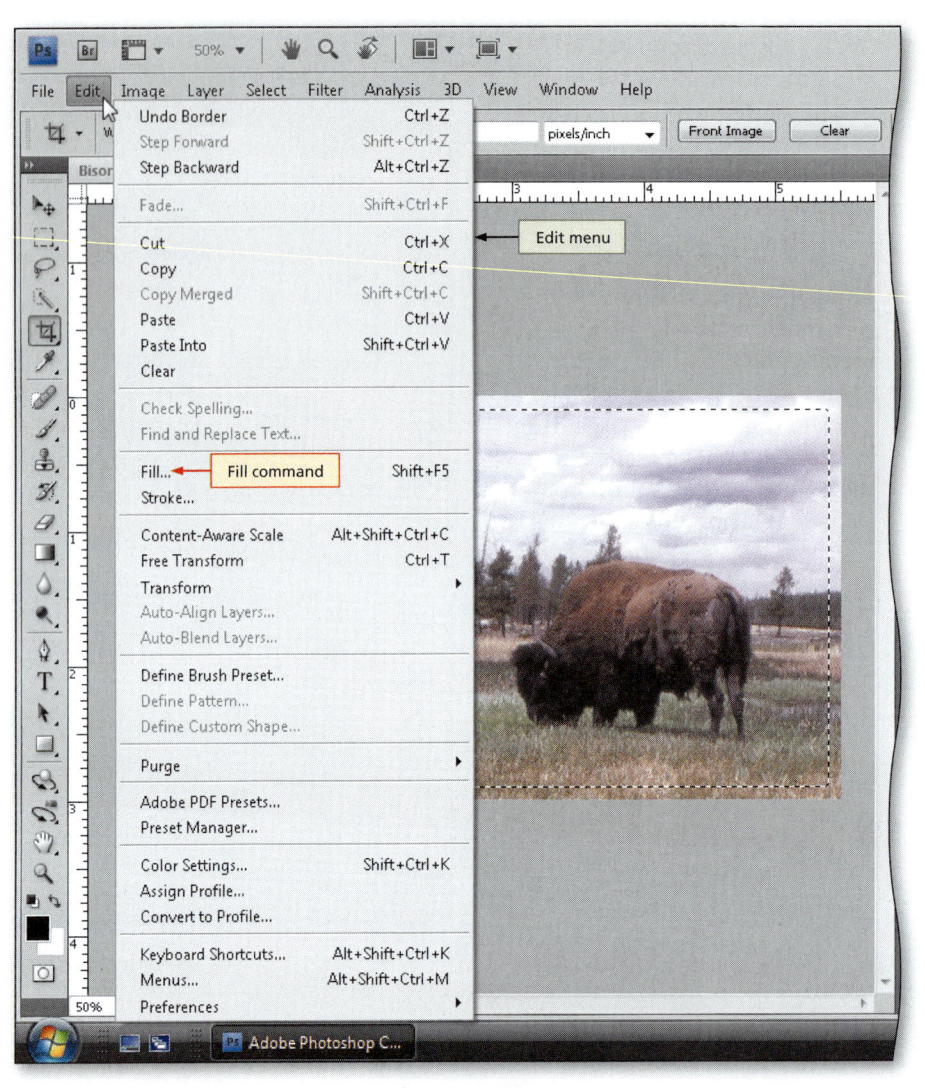

Figure 1–52

2
- Click Fill to display the Fill dialog box.
- Click the Use box arrow to display a list of colors or patterns (Figure 1–53).

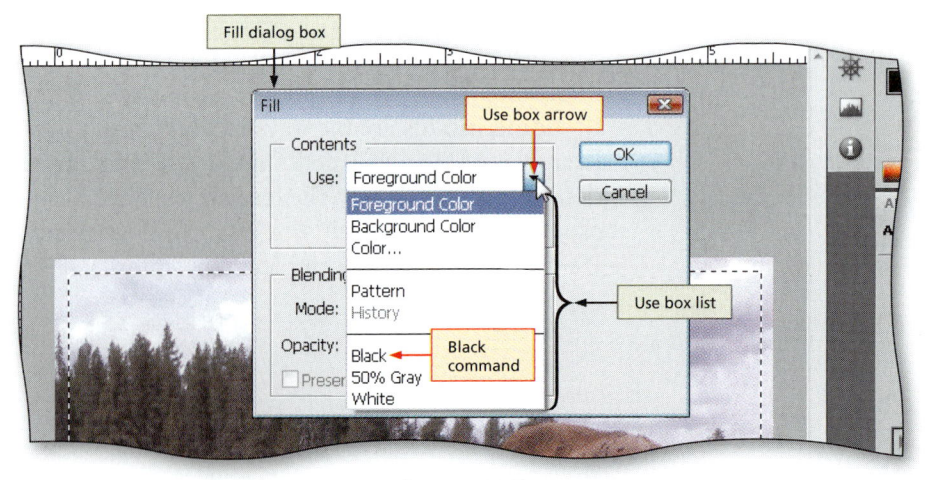

Figure 1–53

Creating a Blended Border **PS 45**

3
- In the Use box list, click Black to use black as the color of the border selection.
- If necessary, click the Mode box arrow and then click Normal to choose normal blending.
- If necessary, double-click the value in the Opacity box and then type `100` to define the opacity (Figure 1–54).

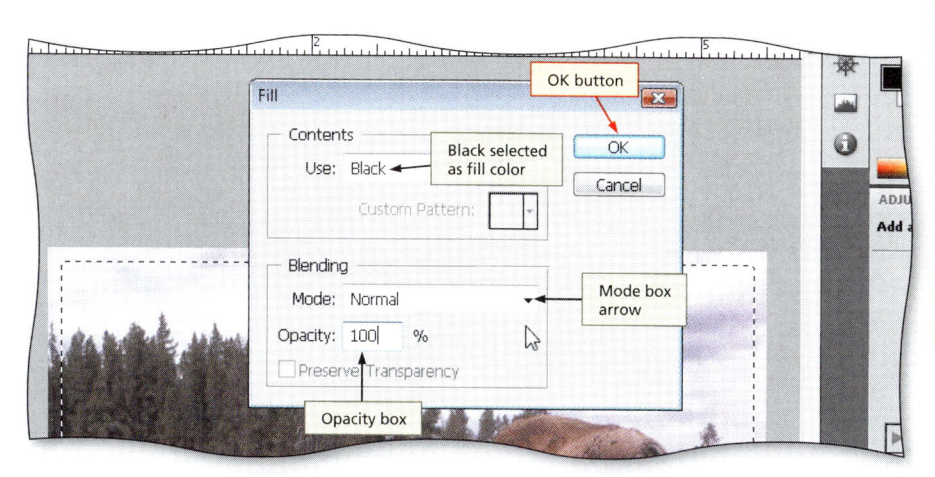

Figure 1–54

4
- Click the OK button to close the Fill dialog box and apply the black border (Figure 1–55).

Figure 1–55

Other Ways
1. To display the Fill dialog box, press SHIFT+F5

To Deselect

When you are done editing a selection, you should remove the selection indicator so it no longer is displayed. To **deselect** a previous selection, click Deselect on the Select menu or press CTRL+D. Depending on the currently selected tool, you might be able to click the document window to deselect. The following step removes the selection.

1

- Click Select on the menu bar and then click Deselect to remove the selection (Figure 1–56).

Q&A Why does my mouse pointer still display the Crop tool mouse pointer?

Deselecting does not change the current tool on the Tools panel. Whichever tool you used previous to the deselecting process will display its own mouse pointer.

Figure 1–56

Other Ways
1. Press CTRL+D

Saving a Photo with the Same File Name

Because you have made many edits to the photo, it is a good idea to save the photo again. When you saved the document the first time, you assigned a file name to it (Bison Edited). When you use the following procedure, Photoshop automatically assigns the same file name to the photo, and it is stored in the same location.

To Save a Photo with the Same File Name

The following step saves the Bison Edited file with the changes you made.

1

- Click File on the menu bar and then click Save to save the photo with the same file name.

Other Ways
1. Press CTRL+S

> **Prepare for publication.**
> Keep in mind the 5:8 ratio of well-designed photos and the limitations of your space. Resize the photo. Print a copy and evaluate its visual appeal. If you are going to publish the photo to the Web, determine the following:
> - Typical download speed of your audience
> - Browser considerations
> - Number of colors
> - File type
>
>   Finally, save the photo with a descriptive name indicating its completion.

Plan Ahead

Changing Image Sizes

Sometimes it is necessary to resize an image to fit within certain space limitations. **Resize** means to scale or change the dimensions of the photo. Zooming in or dragging a corner of the document window to change the size is not the same as actually changing the dimensions of the photo. Resizing in a page layout program, such as Publisher, QuarkXPress, or InDesign, merely stretches the pixels. In Photoshop, resizing means adding to or subtracting from the number of pixels.

Photoshop uses a mathematical process called **interpolation**, or **resampling**, when it changes the number of pixels. The program interpolates or calculates how to add new pixels to the photo to match those already there. Photoshop samples the pixels and reproduces them to determine where and how to enlarge or reduce the photo.

When you resize a photo, you must consider many things, such as the type of file, the width, the height, and the resolution. **Resolution** refers to the number of pixels per inch, printed on a page or displayed on a monitor. Not all photos lend themselves to resizing. Some file types lose quality and sharpness when resized. Fine details cannot be interpolated from low-resolution photos. Resizing works best for small changes where exact dimensions are critical. If possible, it usually is better to take a photo at the highest feasible resolution or rescan the image at a higher resolution rather than resize it later.

In those cases where it is impossible to create the photo at the proper size, Photoshop helps you resize or scale your photos for print or online media. Because the bison photo will be printed on a postcard at a specific size, you will change the width to 6 inches wide.

To Resize the Image

The following steps resize the image to create a custom-sized photo for printing.

1
- Click Image on the menu bar to display the Image menu (Figure 1–57).

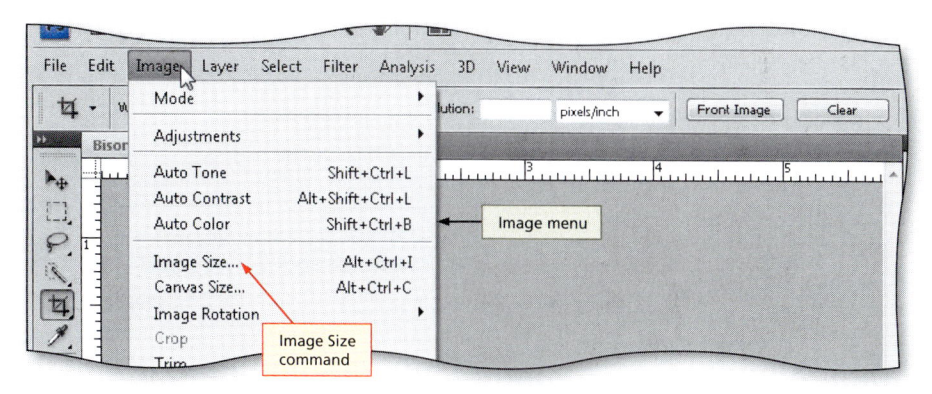

Figure 1–57

PS 48 Photoshop Chapter 1 Editing a Photo

2
- Click Image Size to display the Image Size dialog box.
- In the Document Size area, double-click the value in the Width box and then type 6 to replace the previous value (Figure 1–58).

Q&A Why did the height change?

When you change the width, Photoshop automatically adjusts the height to maintain the proportions of the photo. Your exact height might differ slightly depending on how closely you cropped the original photo.

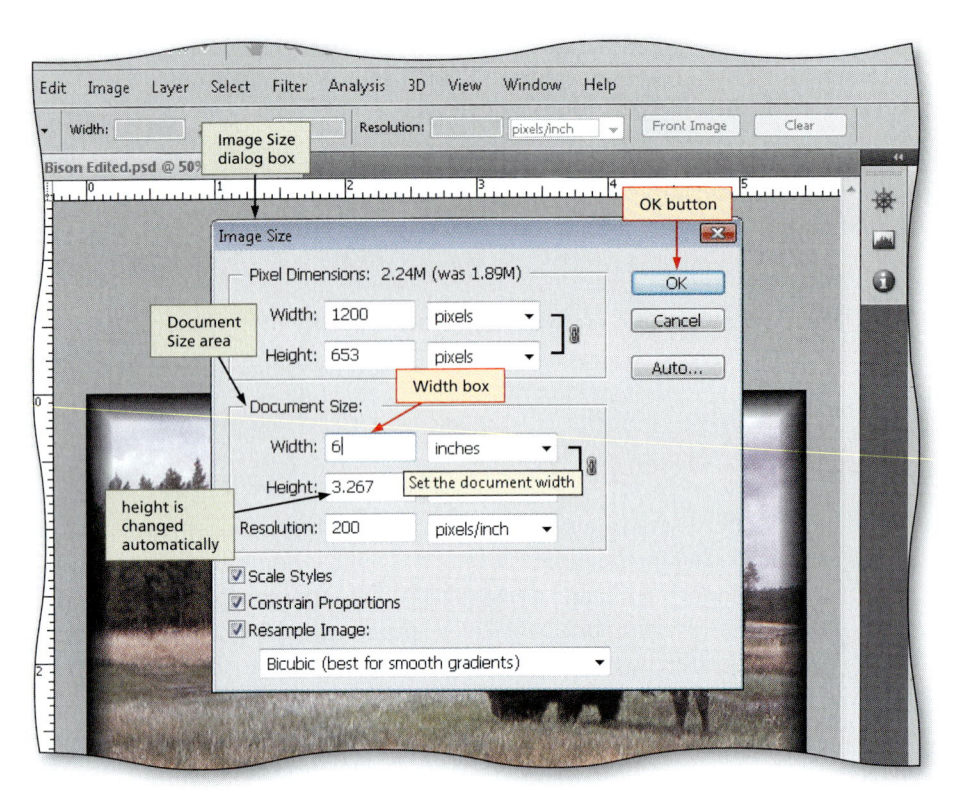

Figure 1–58

3
- Click the OK button to finish resizing the image (Figure 1–59).

🔍 **Experiment**

- Click the status bar menu button, point to Show, and then click Document Dimensions to verify that the image size has been changed. Then, click the status bar menu button again, point to Show and then click Document Sizes to redisplay the document size.

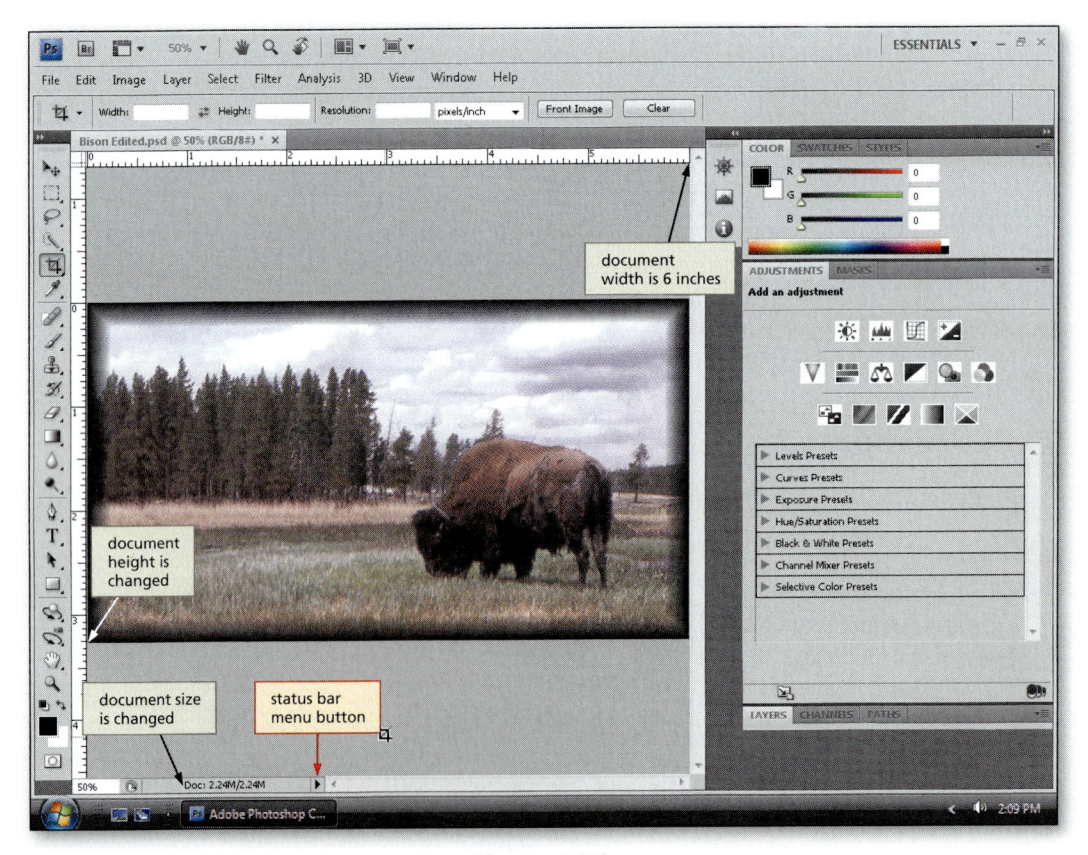

Figure 1–59

To Save a Photo with a Different Name

Many graphic designers will save multiple copies of the same photo with various edits. Because this photo has been resized to print properly, you need to save it with a different name as performed in the following steps.

❶
- Click File on the menu bar and then click Save As to display the Save As dialog box.

- In the Save As dialog box, type `Bison Resized` in the File name text box.

- If necessary, click the Save in box arrow and then click UDISK 2.0 (F:), or the location of your USB flash drive and appropriate folder in the list (Figure 1–60).

❷
- Click the Save button to save the image with the new name.

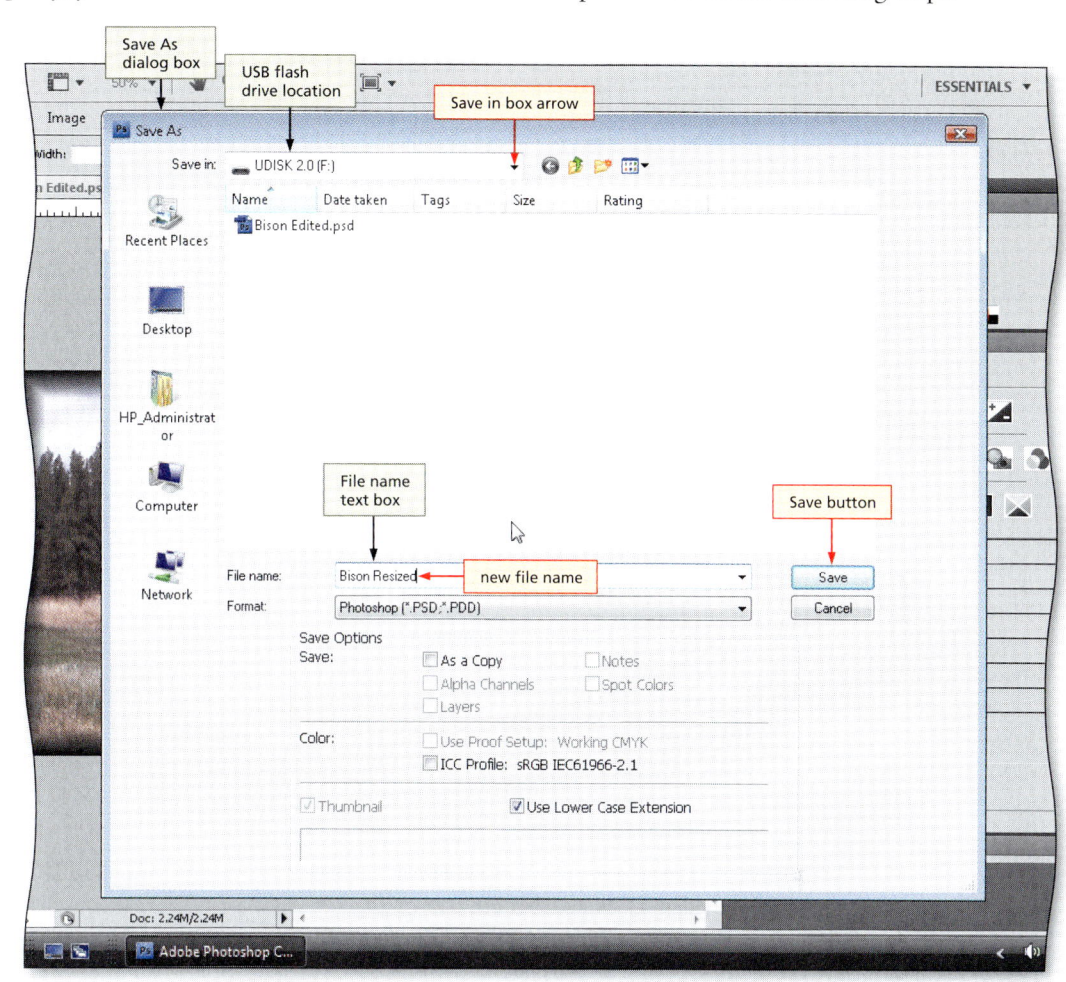

Figure 1–60

Other Ways
1. Press SHIFT+CTRL+S

Printing a Photo

The photo now can be printed, saved, taken to a professional print shop, or sent online to a printing service. A printed version of the photo is called a **hard copy** or **printout**. You can print one copy using the Print One Copy command on the File menu, or to display the Print dialog box, you can click Print on the File menu.

The Print One Copy command sends the printout to the default printer. If you are not sure which printer is your default printer, choose the Print command. In the Print dialog box, click the Printer box arrow and choose your current printer. You will learn more about the Print dialog box in Chapter 2.

After printing a copy of the photo, you will close the photo. Then, you will return to the version of the photo before resizing to prepare a Web version.

To Print a Photo

The following steps print the photo created in this chapter.

1
- Ready the printer according to the printer instructions.
- Click File on the menu bar and then click Print to display the Print dialog box.
- If necessary, click the Printer box arrow and then select your printer from the list. Do not change any other settings (Figure 1–61).

Q&A Does Photoshop have a Print button?

Photoshop's Print commands are available on the menu or by using shortcut keys. There is no Print button on the options bar.

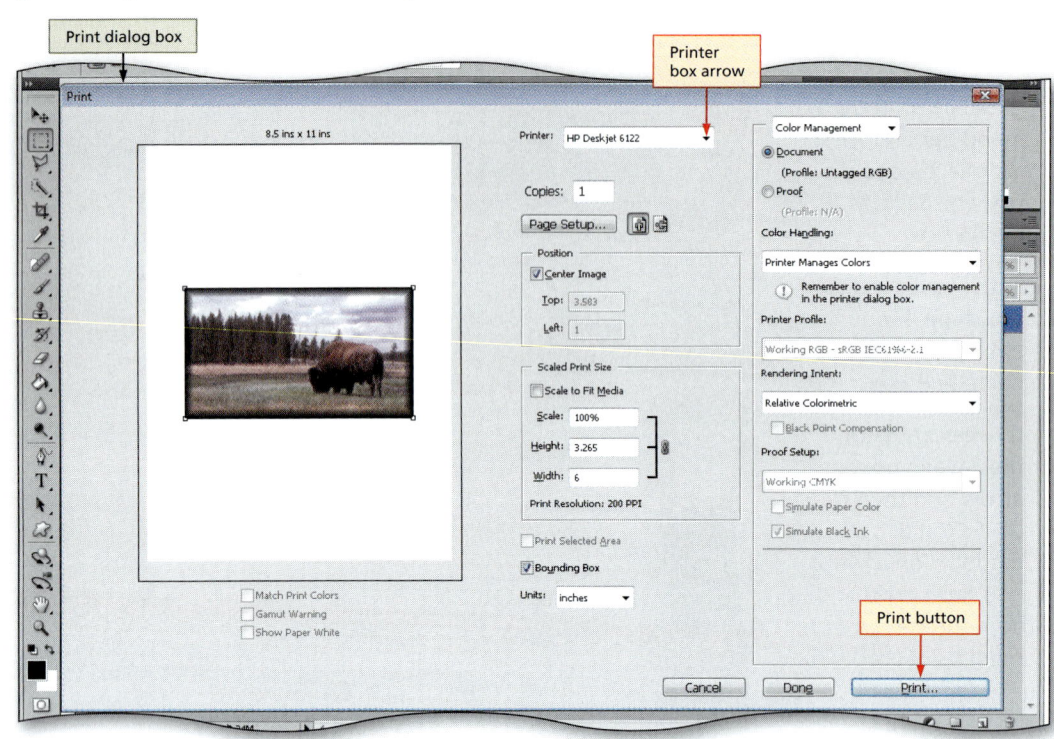

Figure 1–61

2
- In the Print dialog box, click the Print button to start the printing process. If your system displays a second Print dialog box, unique to your printer, click its Print button.
- When the printer stops, retrieve the hard copy of the photo (Figure 1–62).

Other Ways
1. To print one copy, press ALT+SHIFT+CTRL+P
2. To display Print dialog box, press CTRL+P

Figure 1–62

To Close a Photo

The following steps close the Bison Resized document window without quitting Photoshop.

1
- Position the mouse pointer over the Close button on the tab at the top of the document window (Figure 1–63).

2
- Click the Close button to close the document window and the image file.

Figure 1–63

To Open the Bison Edited File

The following steps open the Bison Edited file.

1 Press CTRL+O to display the Open dialog box.

2 If necessary, click the Look in box arrow and navigate to the storage location on your system where you saved the Bison Edited file.

3 Double-click the Bison Edited file to open it (Figure 1–64 on the following page).

Figure 1–64

Saving a Photo for Use on the Web

When preparing photos for the Web, you often need to compromise between the quality of the display and file size. Web users do not want to wait while large photos load from the Web to their individual computer systems. To solve this problem, Photoshop provides several commands to compress the file size of an image while optimizing its online display quality. Additionally, Photoshop allows you to save the photo in a variety of formats such as **GIF**, which is a compressed graphic format designed to minimize file size and electronic transfer time, or as an **HTML** (Hypertext Markup Language) file, which contains all the necessary information to display your photo in a Web browser.

Therefore, you have two choices in Photoshop CS4 for creating Web images: the Zoomify command and the Save for Web & Devices command. The Zoomify command allows you to create a high-resolution image for the Web, complete with a background and tools for navigation, panning, and zooming. To **zoomify**, click Export on the File menu and then click Zoomify. In the Zoomify Export dialog box, you set various Web and export options. Photoshop creates the HTML code and accompanying files for you to upload to a Web server.

If you do not want the extra HTML files for the background, navigation, and zooming, you can create a single graphic file using the Save for Web & Devices command. The resulting graphic can be used on the Web or on a variety of mobile devices.

Optimization is the process of changing the photo to make it most effective for its purpose. The Save for Web & Devices command allows you to preview optimized images in different file formats, and with different file attributes, for precise optimization. You can view multiple versions of a photo simultaneously and modify settings as you preview the image.

BTW

Printing
When you use the Print One Copy command to print a document, Photoshop prints the photo automatically using preset options. To print multiple copies, display the Print dialog box by clicking File on the menu bar, clicking Print, and then entering the number of copies you want to print.

Using the Save for Web & Devices Command

To optimize the bison photo for use on the Web, you need to make decisions about the file size and how long it might take to load on a Web page. These kinds of decisions must take into consideration the audience and the nature of the Web page. For example, Web pages geared for college campuses probably could assume a faster download time than those who target a wide range of home users. An e-commerce site that needs high-quality photography to sell its product will make certain choices in color and resolution.

The hardware and software of Web users also is taken into consideration. For instance, if a Web photo contains more colors than the user's monitor can display, most browsers will **dither**, or approximate, the colors that it cannot display, by blending colors that it can. Dithering might not be appropriate for some Web pages, because it increases the file size and therefore causes the page to load more slowly.

Many other appearance settings play a role in the quality of Web graphics, some of which are subjective in nature. As you become more experienced in Photoshop, you will learn how to make choices about dithering, colors, texture, image size, and other settings.

To Preview Using the Save for Web & Devices Dialog Box

The followings steps use the Save for Web & Devices command to display previews for four possible Web formats.

1
- With the Bison Edited photo open, click File on the menu bar to display the File menu (Figure 1–65).

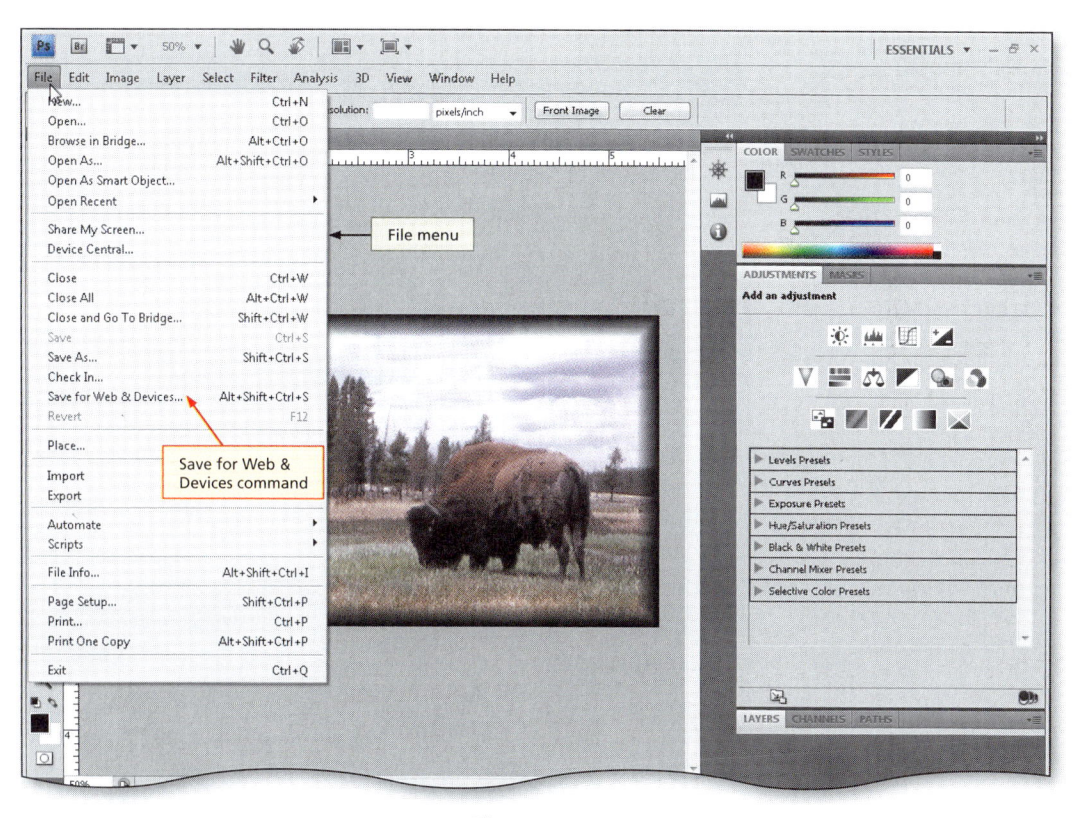

Figure 1–65

PS 54 Photoshop Chapter 1 Editing a Photo

2

- Click Save for Web & Devices to display the Save for Web & Devices dialog box.

- Click the 4-Up tab, if necessary, to display four versions of the photo.

- Click the Zoom Level box arrow to display the possible magnifications (Figure 1–66).

Q&A Why are there four frames?

Photoshop displays four previews — the original photo and three others that are converted to different resolutions to optimize download times on the Web.

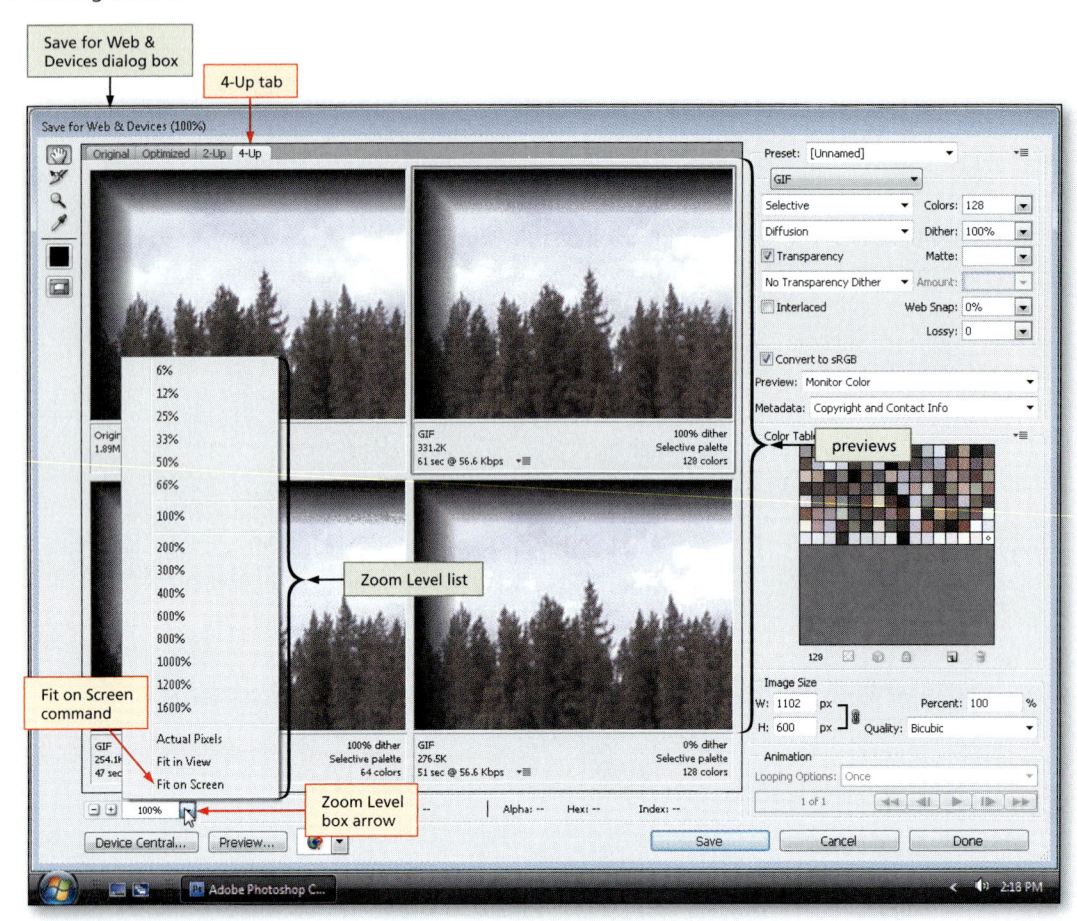

Figure 1–66

3

- Click Fit on Screen in the list to display the entire picture in each frame.

- Click the upper-right preview, if necessary, to choose a high-quality, fast-loading version of the photo (Figure 1–67).

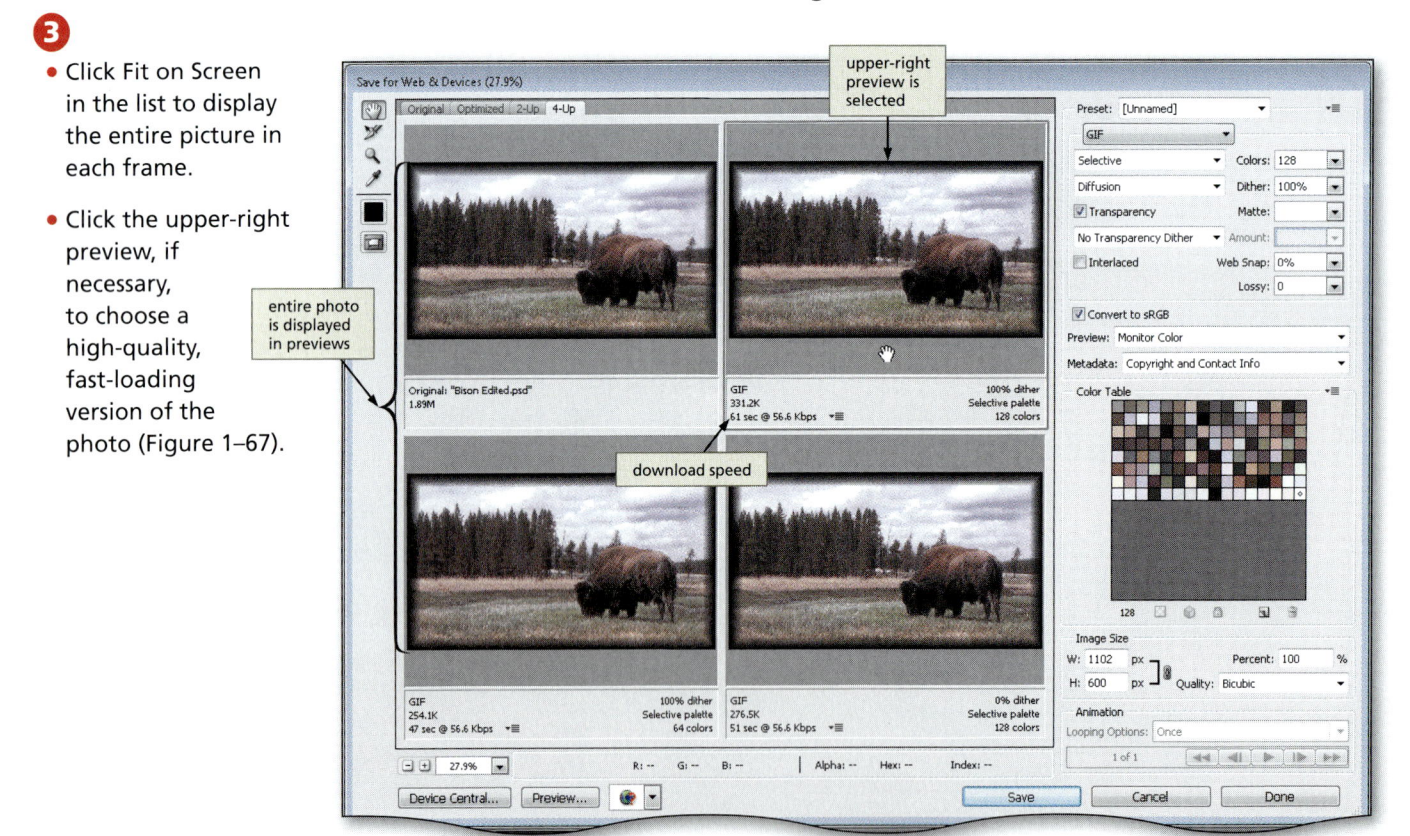

Figure 1–67

To Choose a Download Speed

For even faster downloads when the photo is displayed as a Web graphic, you can choose a download speed that will be similar to that of your target audience. The **annotation area** below each image in the Save for Web & Devices dialog box provides optimization information such as the size of the optimized file and the estimated download time using the selected modem speed.

The following steps change the download speed to 512 kilobytes per second (Kbps).

1
- In the annotation area below the upper-right preview, click the Select download speed button to display the list of connection speeds (Figure 1–68).

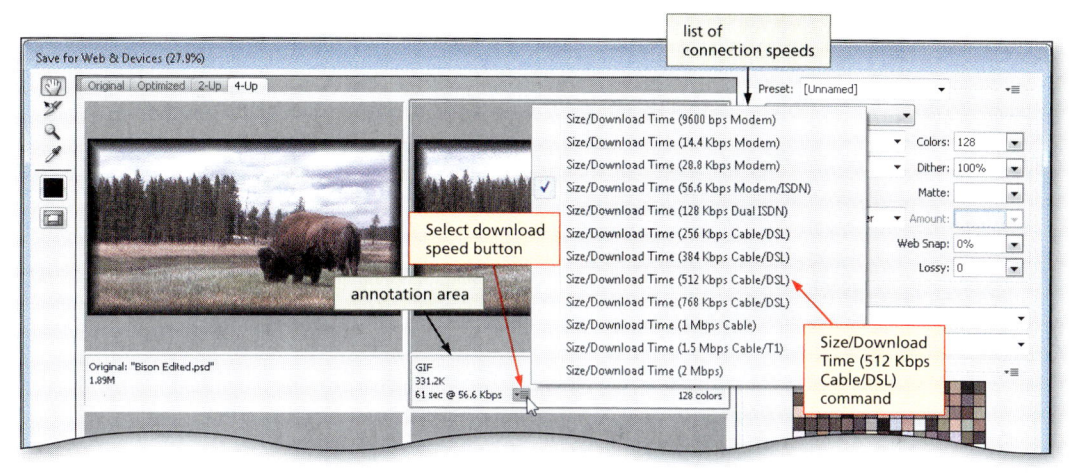

Figure 1–68

2
- In the list, click Size/Download Time (512 Kbps Cable/DSL) or an appropriate speed (Figure 1–69).

Q&A How fast will the picture download?

In Figure 1–67, the speed was 61 seconds at 56.6 Kbps. At 512 Kbps, the photo will download in 8 seconds, as shown in Figure 1–69. Your download times might differ slightly.

Experiment
- Click the Select download speed button to display the list of connection speeds and then click various connection speeds to see how the download times are affected. When finished, click Size/Download Time (512 Kbps Cable/DSL) in the list.

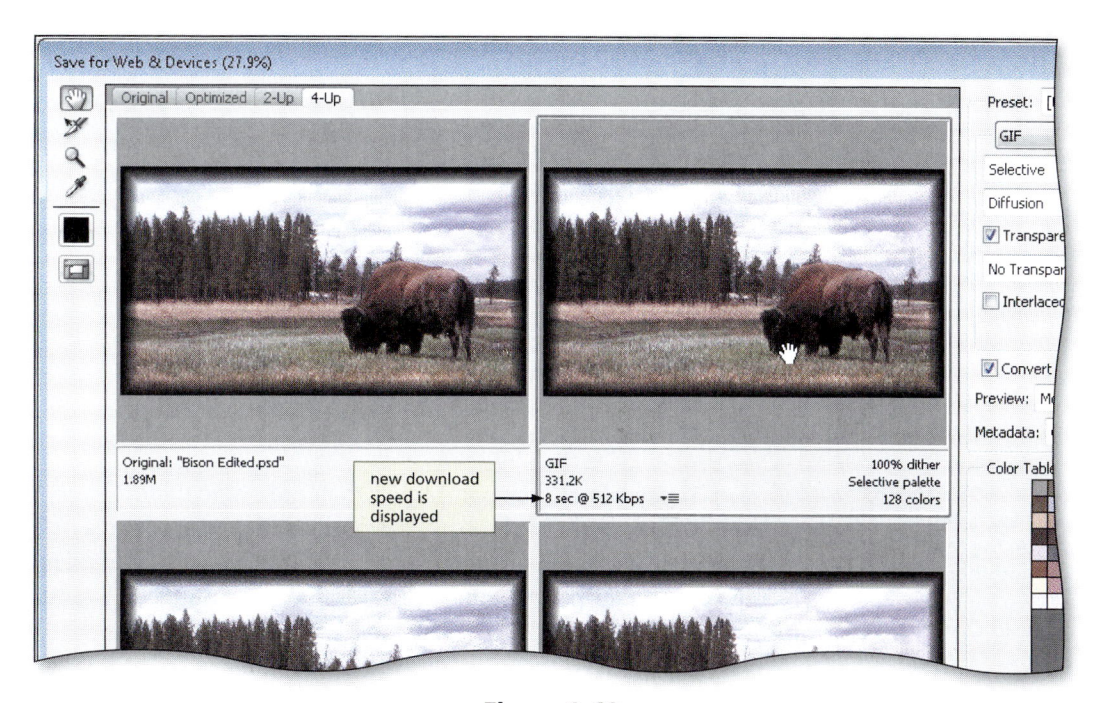

Figure 1–69

Other Ways
1. Right-click annotation area, select download speed

Options in the Save for Web & Devices Dialog Box

On the left side of the Save for Web & Devices dialog box, Photoshop provides several tools to move, zoom, select colors, and slice a portion of the selected preview (Figure 1–70). Along the bottom of the Save for Web & Devices dialog box are buttons to preview the image and perform file functions.

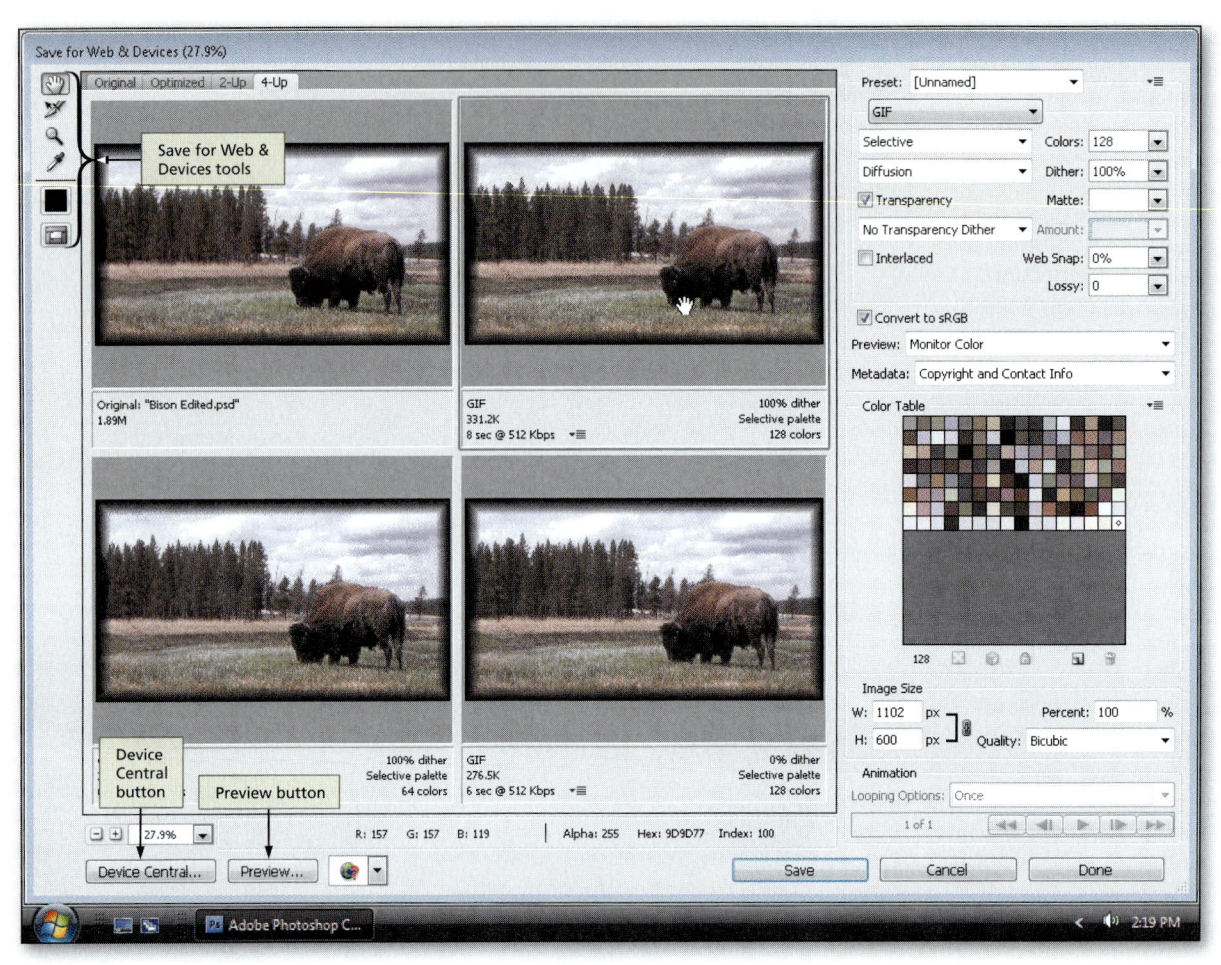

Figure 1–70

BTW

CS4 Device Central
Device Central enables you to preview how Photoshop files will look on a variety of mobile devices. An emulator or mock-up displays the device and preview. Photoshop supports most cell phone displays, portable electronic devices, and MP3 players with video. In the Device Central window, you can adjust settings for lighting, scaling, and alignment.

If you choose a preview other than the original located on the upper left, the Save for Web & Devices dialog box displays options in the Preset area on the right. The Preset area lets you make changes to the selected preview such as the file type, the number of colors, transparency, dithering, and photo finishes. Fine-tuning these kinds of optimization settings allows you to balance the image quality and file size.

Below the Preset area are the Color Table and Image Size areas. The Color Table area and its buttons and menu display different options based on the choices you made in the Preset area. The colors used in the selected preview can be locked, deleted, set to transparent, or adjusted for standard Web palettes. The Image Size area allows you to make changes to the size of the image similar to those changes you made using the Image Size command earlier in the chapter. Changing the image size affects all four previews. The settings are not permanent until you click the Save button.

Saving a Photo for Use on the Web **PS 57**

To Set Other Options in the Save for Web & Devices Dialog Box

In the following steps, you will set the type of file to use and the number of colors. Recall that GIF commonly is used to display graphics and images on Web pages. It is a compressed format designed to minimize file size and electronic transfer time. You will choose the most colors possible for the GIF format, which is 256.

1
- In the Preset area, click the Optimized file format button to display the list of file types (Figure 1–71).

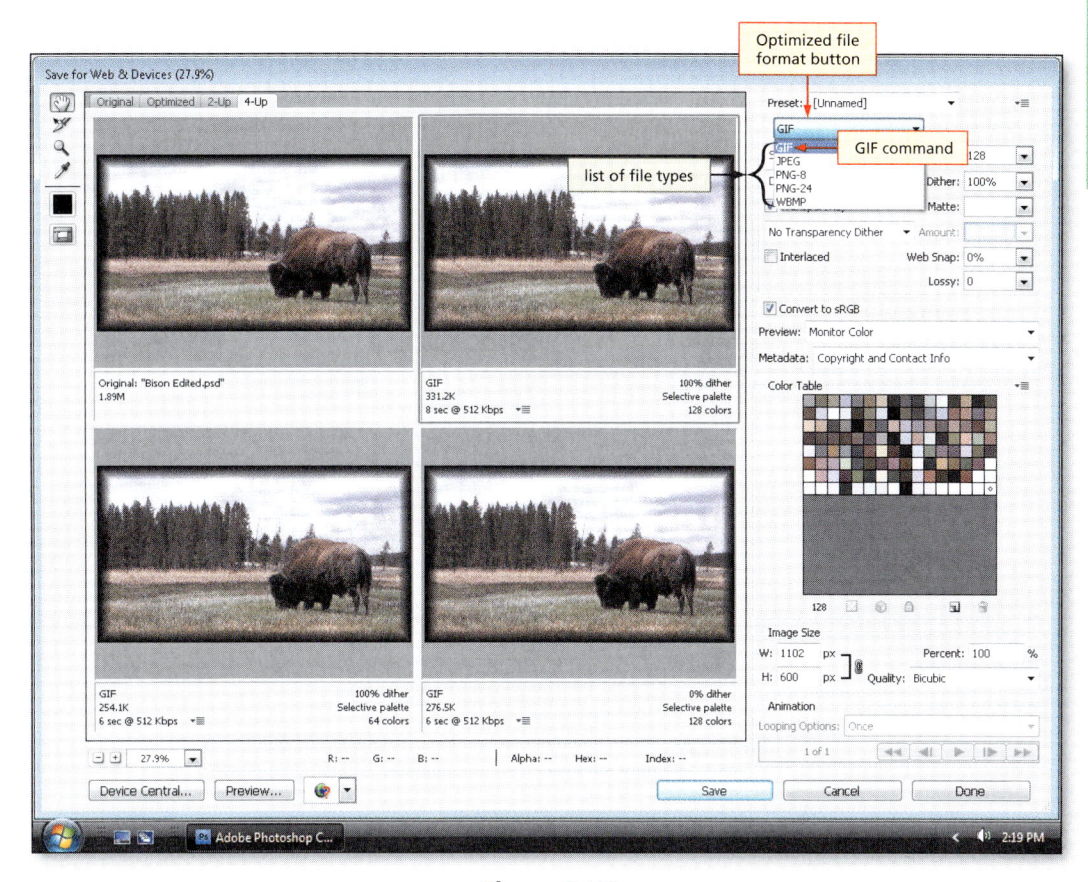

Figure 1–71

2
- If necessary, click GIF in the list to select the format.
- Click the Colors box arrow to display the list of possible number of colors (Figure 1–72).

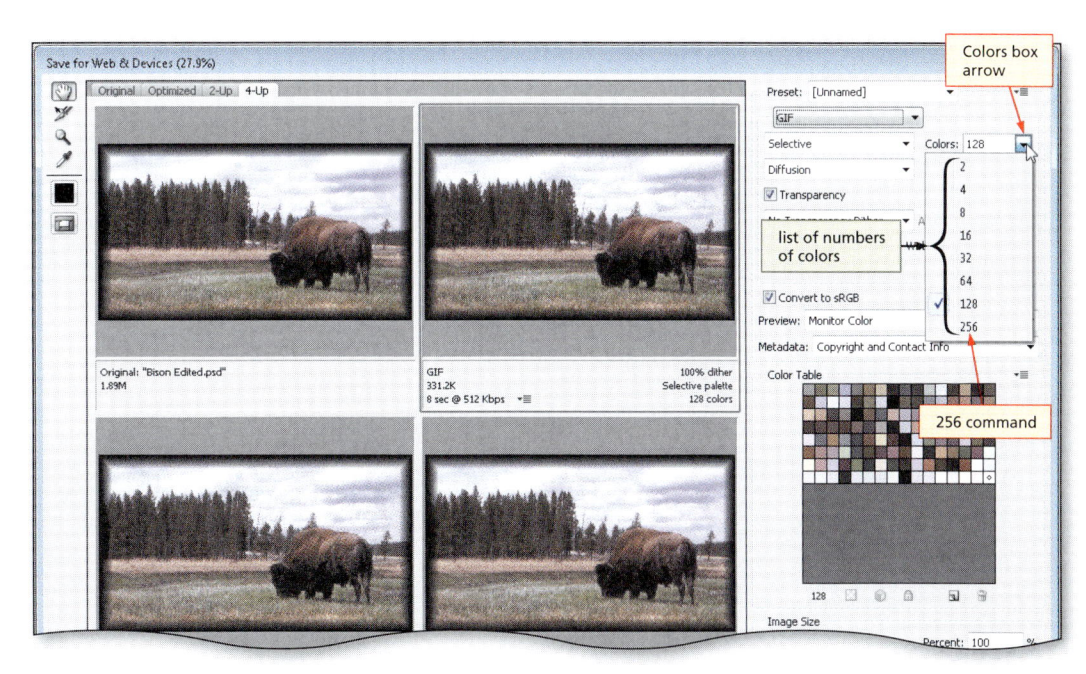

Figure 1–72

3

- If necessary, click 256 in the list to select 256 colors.

- In the Image Size area, double-click the number in the width box, and then type 500 to change the width (Figure 1–73).

Q&A What if the picture is too big for the Web page?

You can use the Image size area to set a height and/or width for large Web graphics; however, many Web developers prefer to set the size using HTML code so the graphic fits appropriately in their layout.

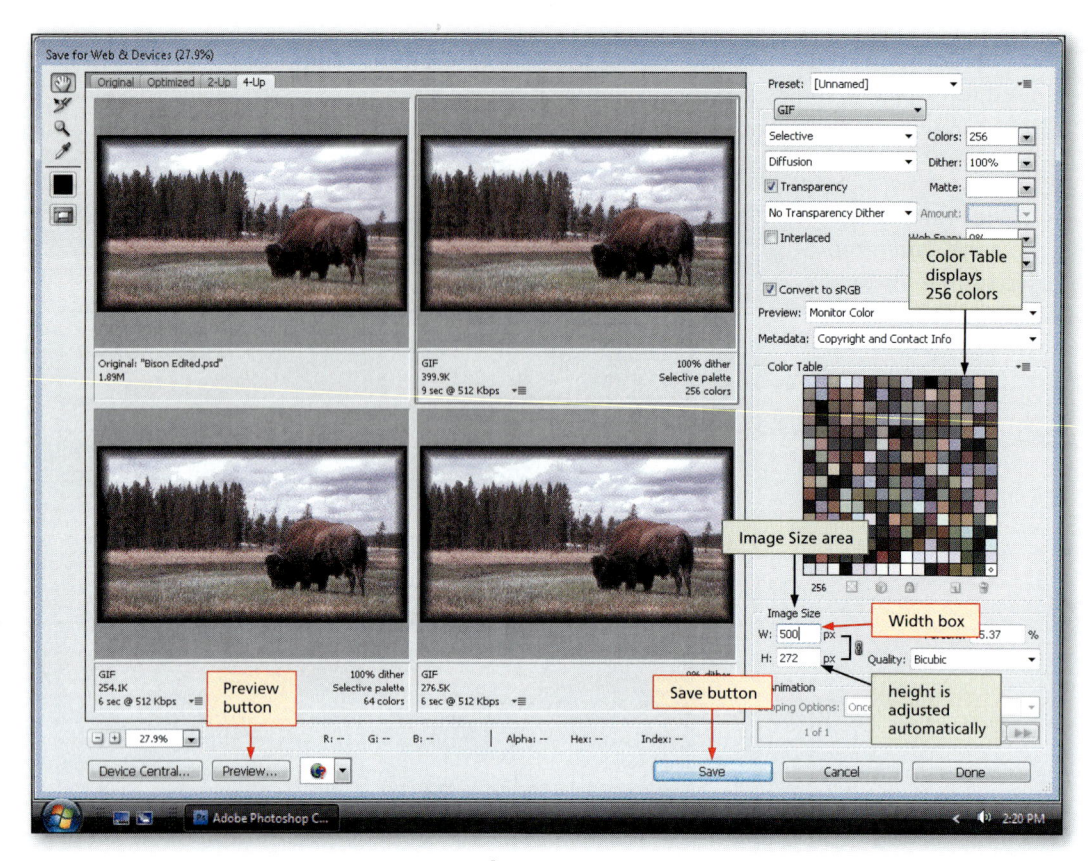

Figure 1–73

To Preview the Photo on the Web

It is always a good idea to preview a photo before uploading it to the Web to check for errors. When Photoshop displays a Web preview of any photo, it also displays the characteristics of the file and the HTML code used to create the preview. The following steps preview the image in a browser.

1

- Click the Preview button to display the photo in a Web browser (Figure 1–74).

Q&A When I clicked the Preview button, the HTML code displayed in Notepad. Should it open in a browser?

If Photoshop cannot detect a default browser on your system, you may have to click the box arrow next to the Preview button (Figure 1–73), and then click Edit List to add your browser.

Q&A How would I use the HTML code?

As a Web designer, you might copy and paste the code into a text editor or Web creation software, replacing BrowserPreview with the name of the file. After saving the code, the HTML file and the photo would be uploaded to a server.

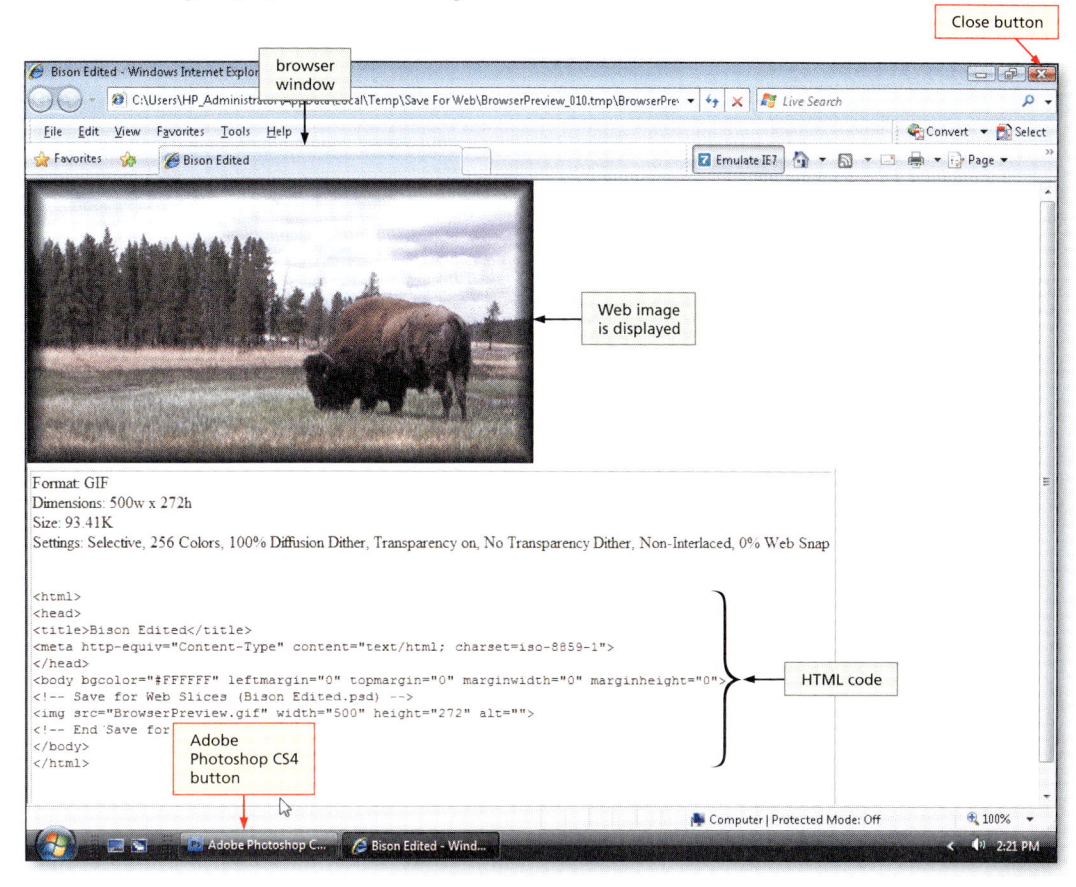

Figure 1–74

2

- Click the Close button on the browser's title bar to close the browser window. If necessary, click the Adobe Photoshop CS4 button on the taskbar to return to the Save for Web & Devices dialog box.

Q&A What else can I do in the Save for Web & Devices dialog box?

In the upper-left corner is a group of tools (Figure 1–71) that allows you to save and display Web slices, pick up certain colors out of the previews, and navigate larger pictures.

To Save the Photo for the Web

When you click the Save button in the Save for Web & Devices dialog box, you will name the Web graphic and save it in a location of your choice, as performed in the following steps.

1
- Click the Save button to display the Save Optimized As dialog box.
- Type `Bison-for-Web` in the File name text box.
- If necessary, click the Save in box arrow and then click UDISK 2.0 (F:), or the location of your USB flash drive and appropriate folder in the list (Figure 1–75).

Q&A Why are the words in the file name hyphenated?

For ease of use, it is standard for Web graphics to have no spaces in their file names.

2
- Click the Save button to complete the saving process.

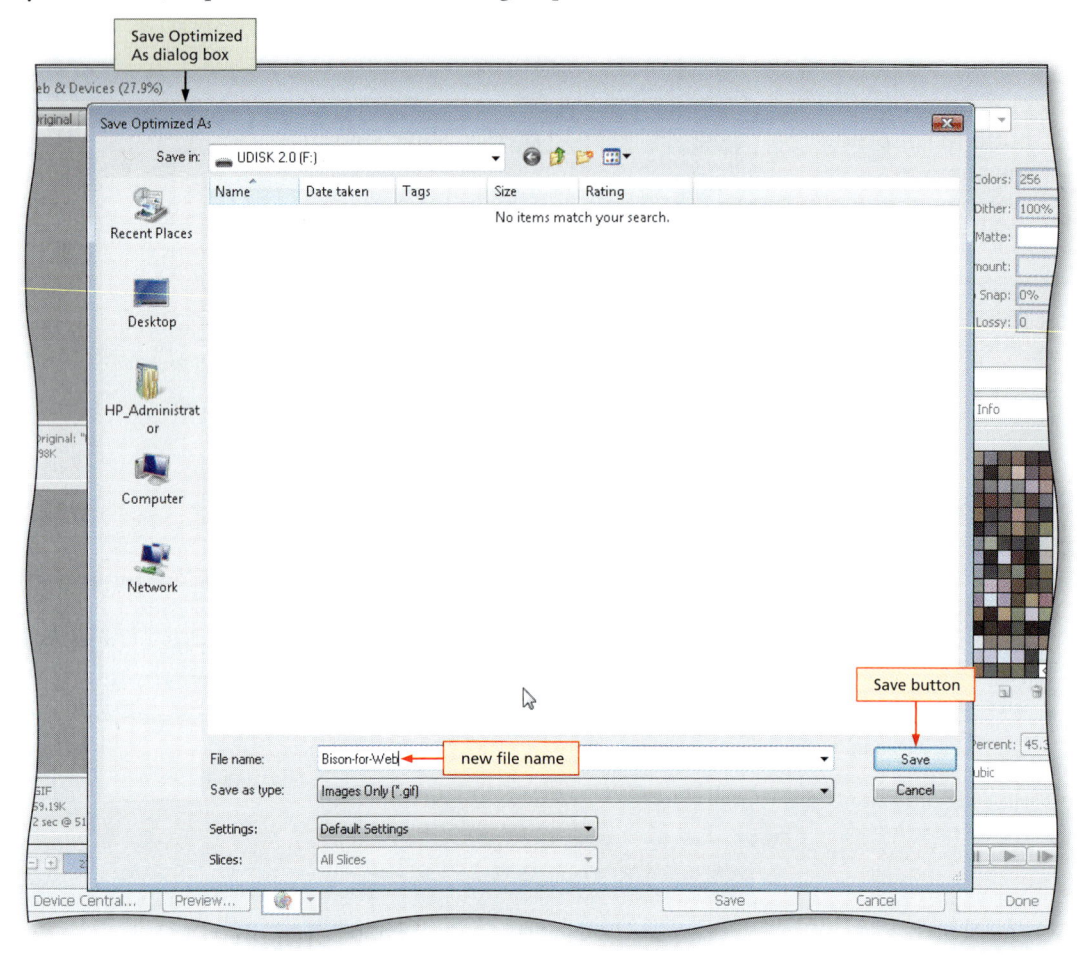

Figure 1–75

Adobe Bridge

BTW

Opening Files in Adobe Bridge
When working with multiple photos, or organizing your photos, it might be more convenient to use the Bridge tool to open files. In other cases, use the Open command on the Photoshop File menu if you only want to open a single photo for editing.

Adobe Bridge is a file exploration tool similar to Windows Explorer. Bridge can be used with any of the software programs in the Adobe Creative Suite. Using Bridge, you can locate, drag, organize, browse, and standardize color settings across your content for use in print, on the Web, and on mobile devices. A useful Bridge tool allows you to attach or assign keywords, or **metadata**, used for searching and categorizing photos. Metadata is divided into three categories: file information, image usage, and image creation data. The Bridge interface is explained in detail in Appendix E.

You can use Bridge to organize your photos into folders, set keywords for future searching, or simply open a file by double-clicking the **thumbnail** or small picture. You also can view the files in a list, in a grid, or with details by using the buttons in the lower-right corner of the Bridge window. Bridge is similar to a database for your photos.

To Use Bridge to View Files

So far in this chapter, you have saved the edited bison photo, a version for printing, and a version for the Web. The following steps open Bridge and view those files as thumbnails and then with details.

1
- Point to the Launch Bridge button on the Application bar (Figure 1–76).

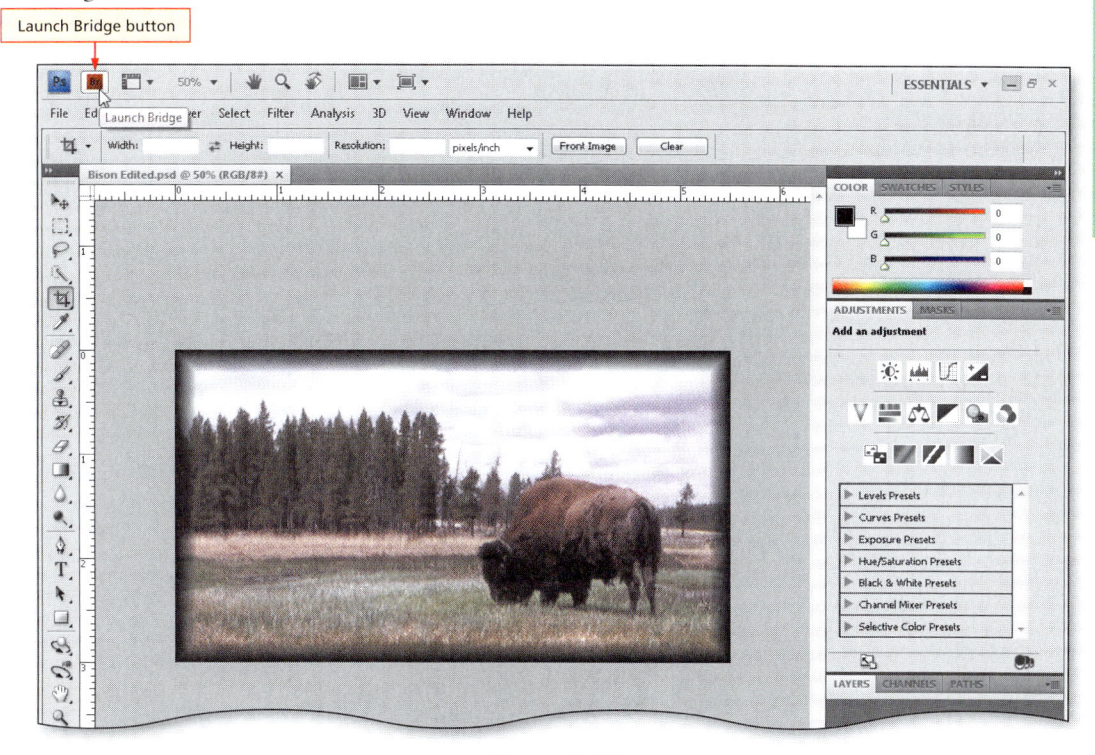

Figure 1–76

2
- Click the Launch Bridge button to open Adobe Bridge in a new window.
- If Bridge displays a dialog box, click the No button.
- If necessary, click Computer in the Favorites pane to display the locations.
- In the lower-right corner, click the View content as thumbnails button (Figure 1–77).

Q&A Why does my screen look different?

Your computer might have different storage locations, or the locations might display icons at a different size.

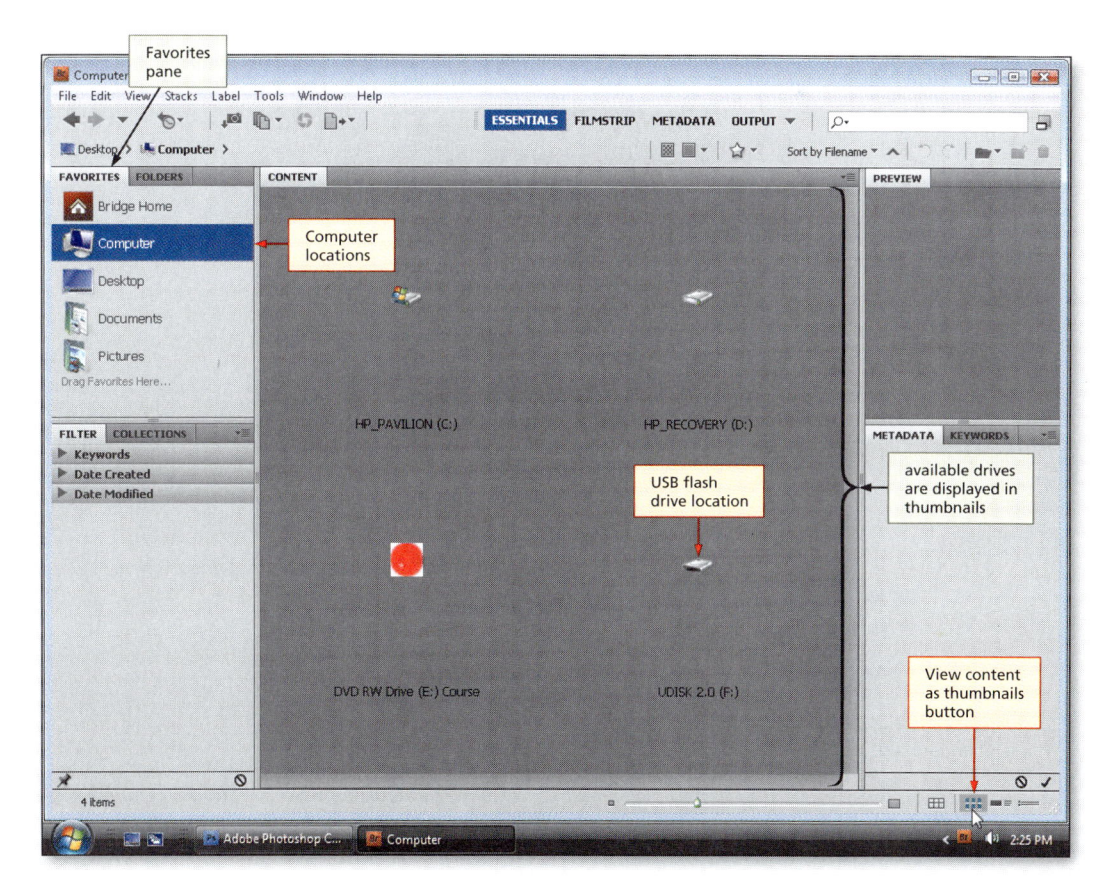

Figure 1–77

PS 62 Photoshop Chapter 1 Editing a Photo

3
- Double-click your USB flash drive location to display its contents (Figure 1–78).
- If you created a Chapter01 folder, double-click the Chapter01 folder.

🔍 **Experiment**
- Drag the slider to display the thumbnails at different sizes.

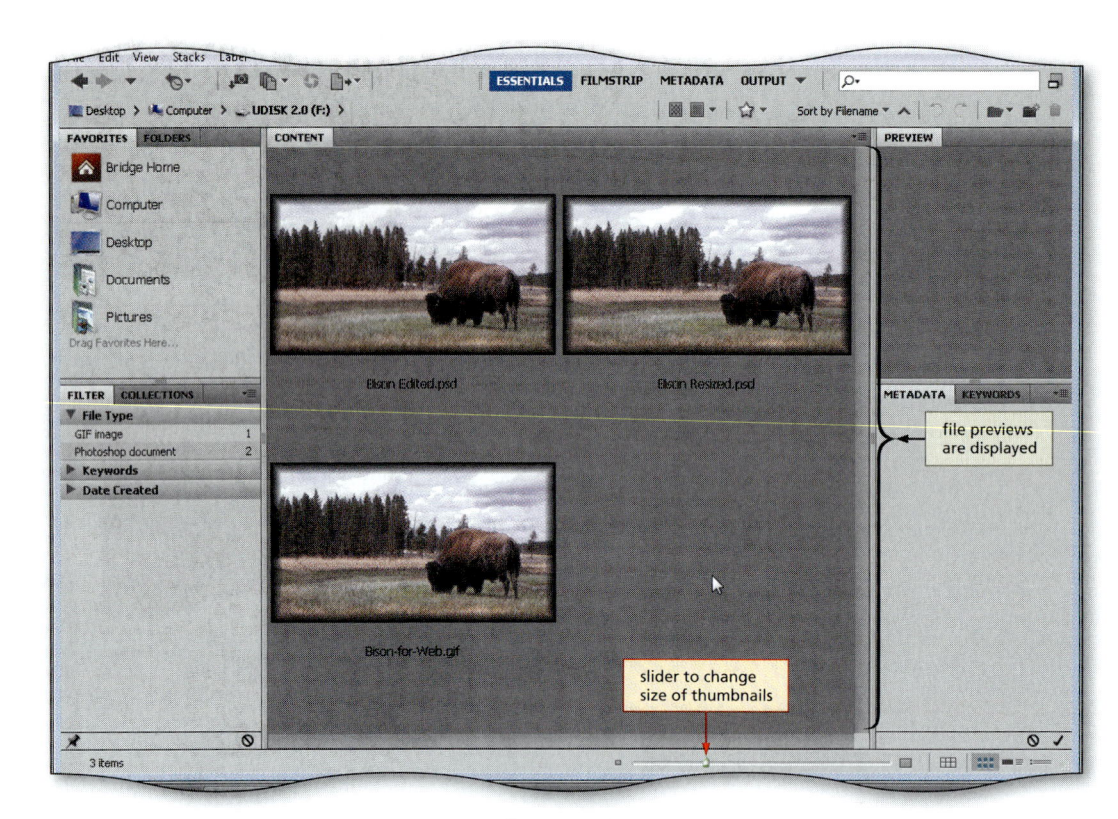

Figure 1–78

4
- In the lower-right corner of the Bridge window, click the View content as details button to display details about the files (Figure 1–79).

Other Ways
1. To open Bridge, press ALT+CTRL+O
2. To open Bridge, on File menu, click Browse in Bridge
3. In Windows Vista, to open Bridge, click Start button, point to All Programs, click Adobe Bridge CS4
4. To view details, on View menu, click As Details

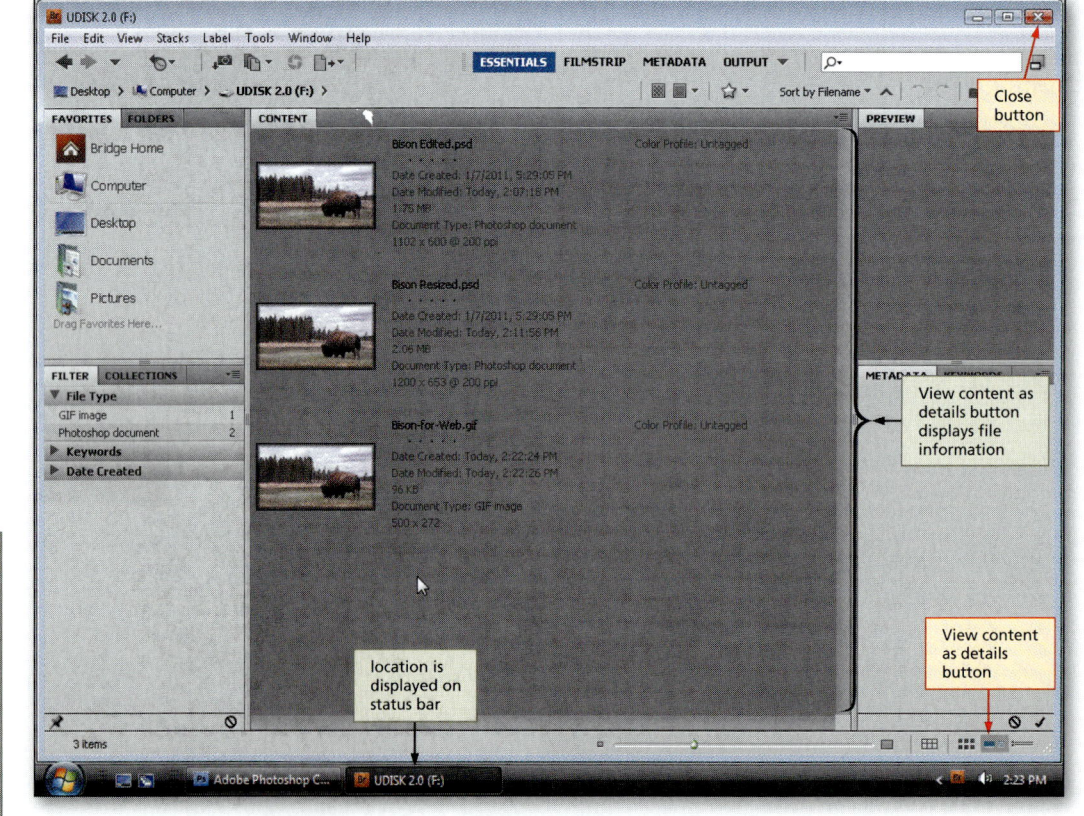

Figure 1–79

To Close Bridge

The following step closes Bridge.

1
- Click the Close button on the Bridge title bar to close Bridge and return to Photoshop (Figure 1–80).

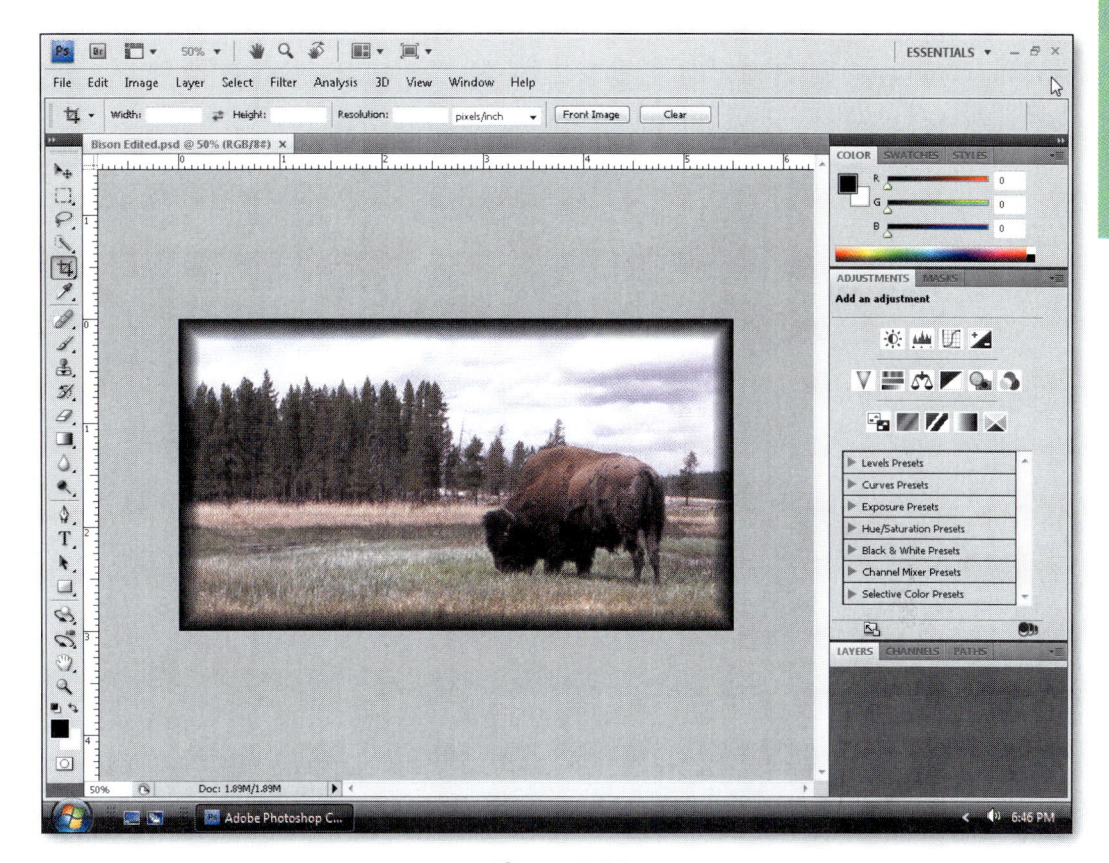

Figure 1–80

Other Ways
1. On File menu, click Exit
2. Press CTRL+Q

Photoshop Help

At anytime while you are using Photoshop, you can get answers to questions using **Photoshop Help**. You activate Photoshop Help either by clicking Help on the menu bar or by pressing the F1 key. The Help menu includes commands to display more information about your copy of Photoshop as well as a list of how-to guides for common tasks. The Photoshop Help command connects you, through the Adobe Photoshop Support Center on the Web, to a wealth of assistance, including tutorials with detailed instructions accompanied by illustrations and videos. Used properly, this form of online assistance can increase your productivity and reduce your frustration by minimizing the time you spend learning how to use Photoshop. Additional information about using Photoshop Help is available in Appendix D.

BTW

Community Help
Community Help is an integrated Web environment that includes Photoshop Help and gives you access to community-generated content moderated by Adobe and industry experts. Comments from users help guide you to an answer.

To Access Photoshop Help

The following steps display Photoshop Help and then obtain information using the Search box. You must be connected to the Web if you plan to perform these steps on a computer.

1
- With Photoshop open on your system, press the F1 key to access the Adobe Photoshop Support Center online (Figure 1–81).

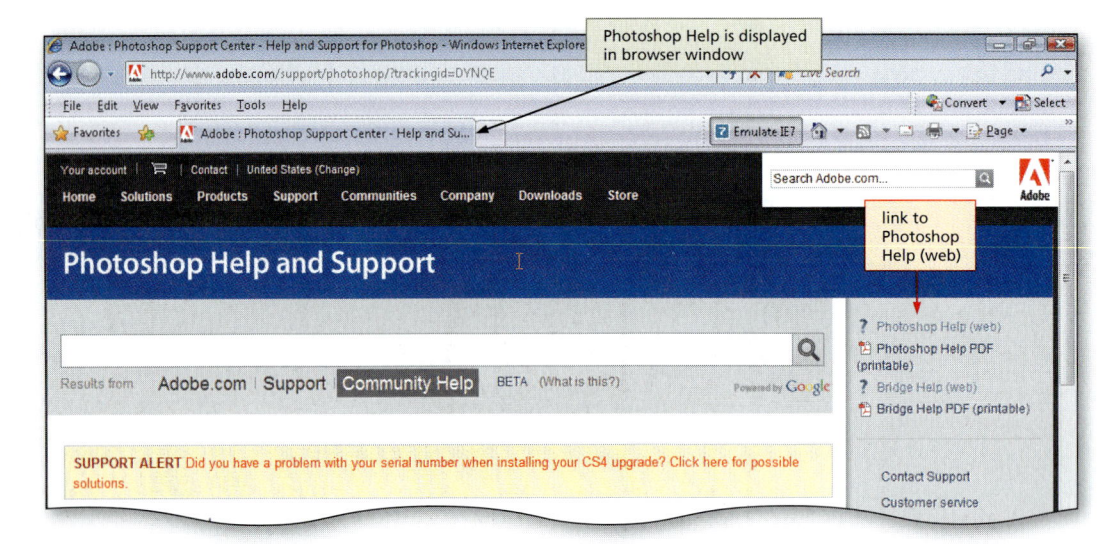

Figure 1–81

2
- On the right side of the window, click the link to Photoshop Help (web) to display the Using Adobe Photoshop CS4 window.

- If necessary, double-click the title bar to maximize the window (Figure 1–82).

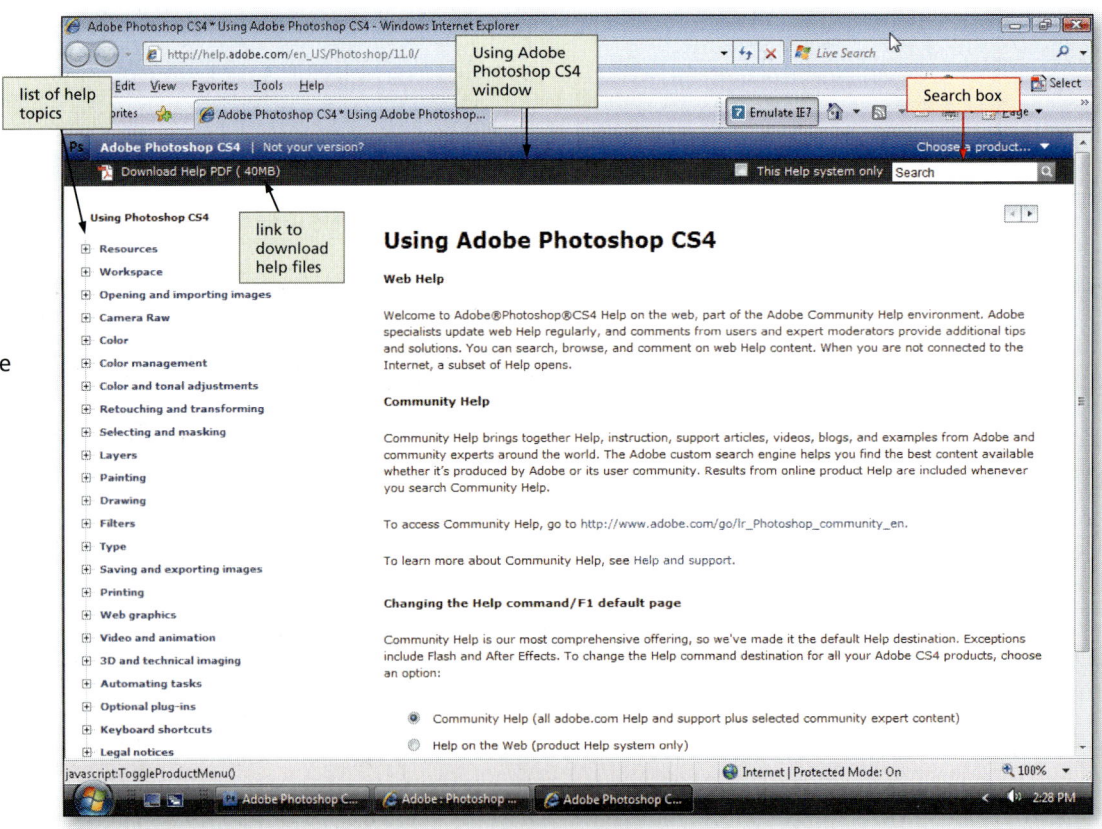

Figure 1–82

Other Ways

1. On Help menu, click Photoshop Help

Using the Search Box

The Search box, located on the upper-right side of the Photoshop Help window (Figure 1–82), allows you to type words or phrases about which you want additional information and help, such as cropping or printing images. When you press the ENTER key, Photoshop Help responds by displaying a list of topics related to the word or phrase you typed.

To Use the Help Search Box

The following steps use the Search box to obtain information about the Tools panel.

1
- Click the Search box and then type About Tools to enter the search topic (Figure 1–83).

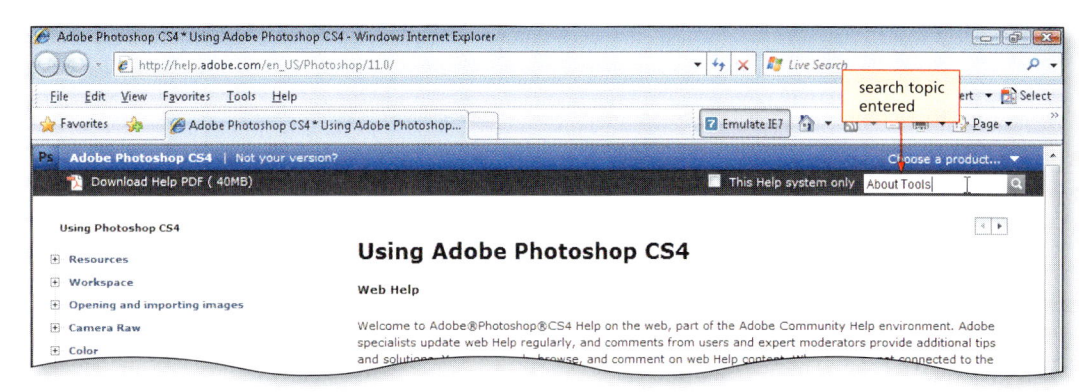

Figure 1–83

2
- Press the ENTER key to display the relevant links (Figure 1–84).

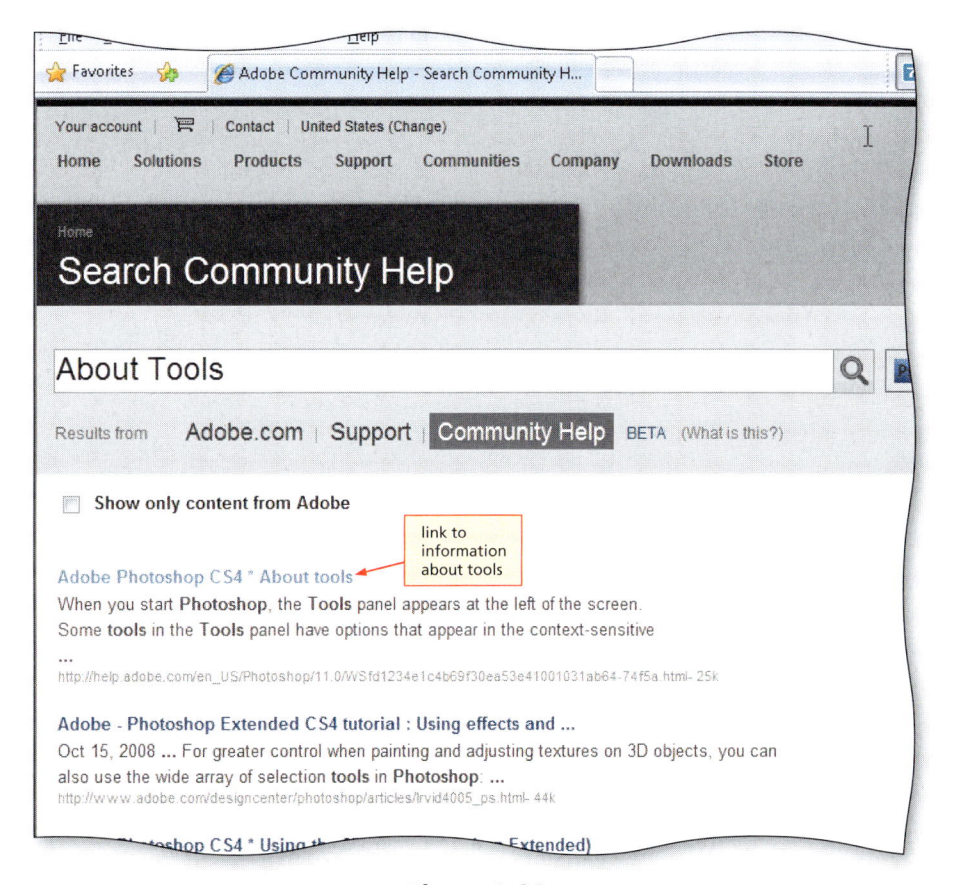

Figure 1–84

3

- Click the first link, About Photoshop CS4 * About tools, to display the contents (Figure 1–85).

- Read the information about tools.

🔎 **Experiment**

- Click other links to view more information, or search for other topics using the Search Box.

4

- In the browser title bar, click the Close button to close the window.

- If necessary, also close the Adobe Product Center window, and then click the Adobe Photoshop CS4 button on the taskbar to return to Photoshop.

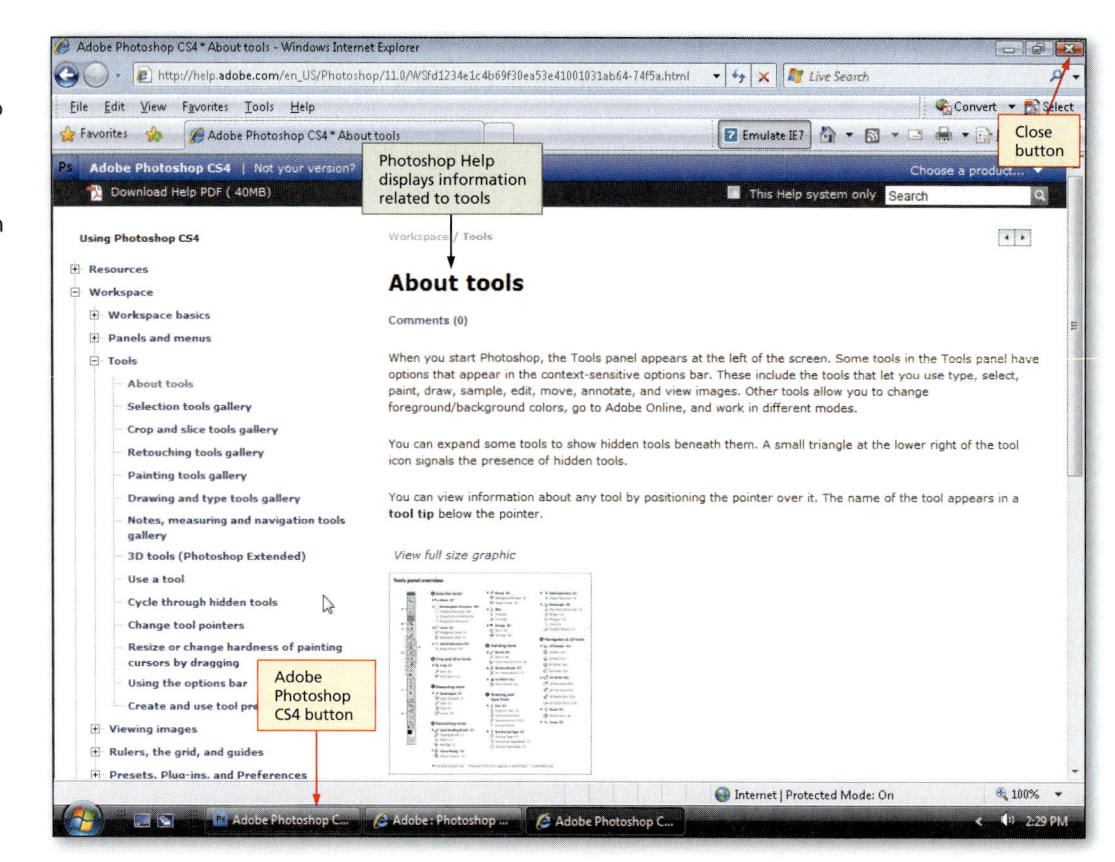

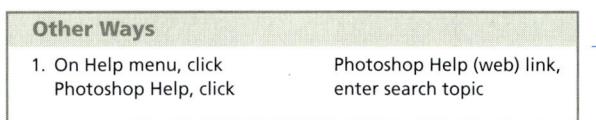

Figure 1–85

Other Ways	
1. On Help menu, click Photoshop Help, click	Photoshop Help (web) link, enter search topic

To Quit Photoshop

The following steps quit Photoshop and return control to Windows.

1

- Point to the Close button on the right side of the Application bar (Figure 1–86).

2

- Click the Close button to close the window.

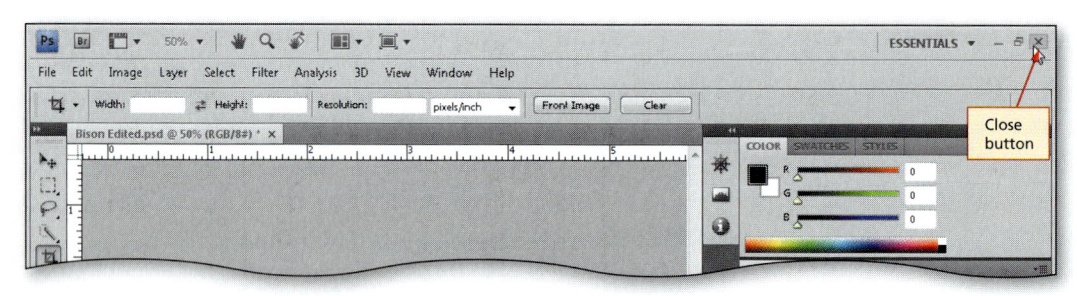

Figure 1–86

- If Photoshop displays a dialog box asking you to save changes, click the No button.

Other Ways	
1. On File menu, click Exit	2. Press CTRL+Q

Chapter Summary

In this chapter, you gained a broad knowledge of Photoshop. First, you learned how to start Photoshop. You were introduced to the Photoshop workspace. You learned how to open a photo and zoom in. You learned about design issues related to the placement of visual points of interest. You then learned how to crop a photo to eliminate extraneous background. After you added a blended border, you resized the image.

Once you saved the photo, you learned how to print it. You used the Save for Web & Devices command to optimize and save a Web version. You learned how to use Adobe Bridge to view files and Adobe Help to research specific help topics. Finally, you learned how to quit Photoshop.

The items listed below include all the new Photoshop skills you have learned in this chapter:

1. Start Photoshop (PS 5)
2. Restore the Default Workspace (PS 7)
3. Reset the Tools Panel (PS 8)
4. Reset the Options Bar (PS 8)
5. Open a Photo (PS 10)
6. Save a Photo in the PSD Format (PS 20)
7. Use the Zoom Tool (PS 25)
8. View and Use the Navigator Panel (PS 28)
9. Collapse the Navigator Panel (PS 29)
10. Use the Hand Tool (PS 30)
11. Change the Screen Mode (PS 31)
12. Display Rulers (PS 33)
13. Crop a Photo (PS 37)
14. Select All (PS 40)
15. Create a Border Using the Modify Submenu (PS 42)
16. Fill a Selection (PS 44)
17. Deselect (PS 46)
18. Save a Photo with the Same File Name (PS 46)
19. Resize the Image (PS 47)
20. Save a Photo with a Different Name (PS 49)
21. Print a Photo (PS 50)
22. Close a Photo (PS 51)
23. Open the Bison Edited File (PS 51)
24. Preview Using the Save for Web & Devices Dialog Box (PS 53)
25. Choose a Download Speed (PS 55)
26. Set Other Options in the Save for Web & Devices Dialog Box (PS 57)
27. Preview the Photo on the Web (PS 59)
28. Save the Photo for the Web (PS 60)
29. Use Bridge to View Files (PS 61)
30. Close Bridge (PS 63)
31. Access Photoshop Help (PS 64)
32. Use the Help Search Box (PS 65)
33. Quit Photoshop (PS 66)

Learn It Online

Test your knowledge of chapter content and key terms.

Instructions: To complete the Learn It Online exercises, start your browser, click the Address bar, and then enter the Web address scsite.com/pscs4/learn. When the Photoshop CS4 Learn It Online page is displayed, click the link for the exercise you want to complete and then read the instructions.

Chapter Reinforcement TF, MC, and SA
A series of true/false, multiple choice, and short answer questions that test your knowledge of the chapter content.

Flash Cards
An interactive learning environment where you identify chapter key terms associated with displayed definitions.

Practice Test
A series of multiple choice questions that test your knowledge of chapter content and key terms.

Who Wants to Be a Computer Genius?
An interactive game that challenges your knowledge of chapter content in the style of a television quiz show.

Wheel of Terms
An interactive game that challenges your knowledge of chapter key terms in the style of the television show *Wheel of Fortune*.

Crossword Puzzle Challenge
A crossword puzzle that challenges your knowledge of key terms presented in the chapter.

Apply Your Knowledge

Reinforce the skills and apply the concepts you learned in this chapter.

Editing a Photo in the Photoshop Workspace
Instructions: Start Photoshop and perform the customization steps found on pages PS 7 through PS 9. Open the Apply 1-1 White Asters file in the Chapter01 folder from the Data Files for Students and save it as Apply 1-1 White Asters Edited in the PSD file format. You can access the Data Files for Students on the DVD that accompanies this book. See the inside back cover of this book for instructions on downloading the Data Files for Students, or contact your instructor for information about accessing the required files.

First, you will crop the photo, add a black border, and save the edited photo, as shown in Figure 1–87. Next, you will resize the photo for printing and print one copy. Finally, you will reopen your edited photo, and then you will optimize it for the Web, save, and close it.

Perform the following tasks:
1. Use the Zoom tool to zoom the photo to 50% magnification, if necessary.
2. Use the Hand tool to reposition the photo in the workspace to view different areas of the zoomed photo.
3. Press CTRL+MINUS SIGN (-) to zoom the photo out to 16.67%.
4. Press CTRL+R, if necessary, to display the rulers. Click the View Extras Button on the Application bar. If Show Guides does not display a check mark, click Show Guides.
5. Move the mouse pointer to the vertical ruler and drag a ruler guide to the 2-inch position on the horizontal ruler. Move the mouse pointer to the horizontal ruler and drag a ruler guide to the 5.5-inch position on the vertical ruler. (*Hint*: If you have a problem positioning the ruler guides, click View on the menu bar, click Clear Guides, and try again.)

black, 10-pixel border

photo is cropped to 5.5 inches by 8 inches

Figure 1–87

6. Use the Crop tool to crop the photo, retaining the portion to the right of the vertical ruler guide and above the horizontal ruler guide. (*Hint*: If your cropping selection does not look correct, you can press the ESC key to clear the selection before you press the ENTER key. Immediately after cropping the photo, you can click Undo on the Edit menu to undo the crop action.) Click View on the menu bar and then click Clear Guides when finished cropping the photo.

7. Select the photo and add a 10-pixel, black border to the photo. (*Hint*: Remember that you are adding 10 pixels to each side of the photo's width; for a total of 20 pixels.) Press CTRL+D to clear your selection when finished creating the border.

8. Press CTRL+S to save the Apply 1-1 White Asters Edited photo with the same file name in the same location.

9. Resize the photo width to 5 inches to create a custom-sized photo for printing.

10. Save the resized file as Apply 1-1 White Asters for Print.

11. With your instructor's permission, print one copy of the photo and then close it. If Photoshop displays a dialog box about saving again, click the No button.

12. Open the Apply 1-1 White Asters Edited file.

13. Save the photo for the Web, displaying it in the 4-Up tab and zoomed to fit on the screen. Select the preview that has been optimized for the GIF file format with 256 colors. Adjust the download speed to 512 Kbps, if necessary, and change the photo width to 400 pixels.

14. Preview the optimized photo in your browser, and print the browser page. Close the browser.

15. Save the photo as Apply-1-1-White-Asters-for-Web.

16. Close the Apply 1-1 White Asters Edited file without saving it and close Photoshop.

Extend Your Knowledge

Extend the skills you learned in this chapter and experiment with new skills. You may need to use Help to complete the assignment.

Exploring Border Width and Fill Options

Instructions: Start Photoshop and perform the customization steps found on pages PS 7 through PS 9. Open the Extend 1-1 Wood Turtle file in the Chapter01 folder from the Data Files for Students and save it as Extend 1-1 Wood Turtle Edited in the PSD file format. You can access the Data Files for Students on the DVD that accompanies this book. See the inside back cover of this book for instructions on downloading the Data Files for Students, or contact your instructor for information about accessing the required files.

The wood turtle photo (Figure 1–88) is to be added to a middle school science handout about amphibians and reptiles. Before the photo is inserted in the handout document, you must add a complementary border to the photo. The only requirement is that the border not be black or white.

Figure 1–88

Before you save the photo with a border, you need to explore different border widths and fill options to find the right combination. As you experiment with border options, you can press the CTRL+ALT+Z keys to quickly step back through the current editing history, returning the photo to a previous state.

Perform the following tasks:
1. Select the entire photo.
2. Specify a border width.
3. Set the border fill contents, blending, and opacity options of your choice and apply them to the photo. Make a note of your width and fill settings for future reference.
4. After viewing the resulting border, press the CTRL+ALT+Z keys enough times to step back to the photo's original unedited state.
5. Repeat Steps 1–4 several times to experiment with different border widths and fills; then apply the border that best complements the photo and save the changes to the photo.
6. Close the photo and close Photoshop.

Make It Right

Analyze a project and correct all errors and/or improve the design.

Changing a Photo's Focus and Optimizing It for the Web

Instructions: Start Photoshop and perform the customization steps found on pages PS 7 through PS 9. Open the Make It Right 1-1 Young Stars file in the Chapter01 folder from the Data Files for Students and save it as Make It Right 1-1 Young Stars Edited in the PSD file format. You can access the Data Files for Students on the DVD that accompanies this book. See the inside back cover of this book for instructions on downloading the Data Files for Students, or contact your instructor for information about accessing the required files.

Members of your Astronomy Club have selected the Young Stars photo (Figure 1–89) for the club's Web site. You are tasked with editing the photo to more clearly focus on the cluster of stars and their trailing dust blanket, and then optimizing the photo for the Web.

Keeping the rule of thirds and the golden rectangle 5:8 ratio concepts in mind, crop the photo to change its focal point and resave it. Then save the photo for the Web as Make-It-Right-1-1-Young-Stars-for-Web using the optimal settings for a GIF file with maximum colors and 250 pixels in width.

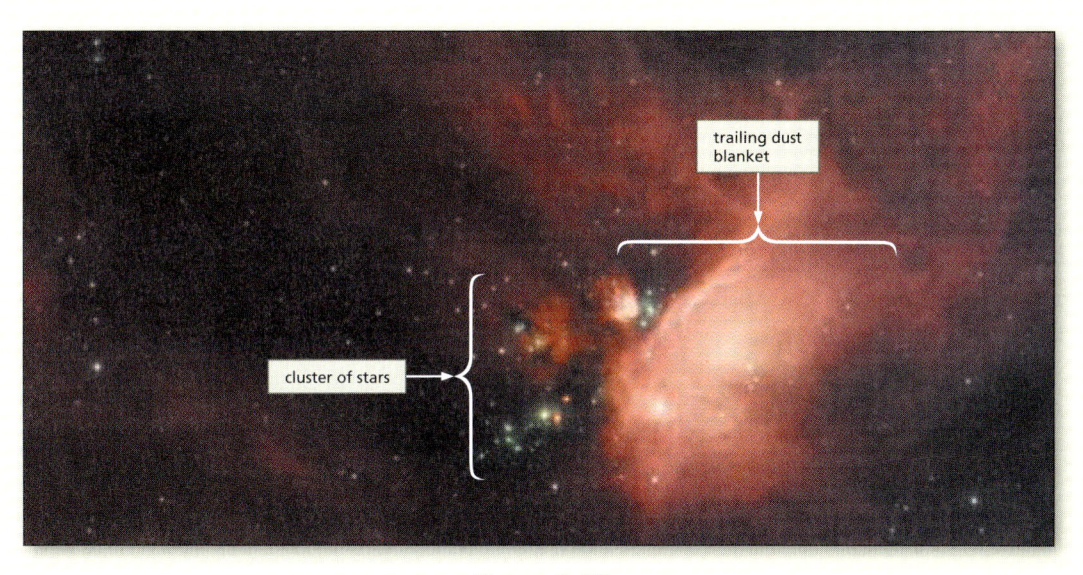

Figure 1–89

In the Lab

Design and/or create a project using the guidelines, concepts, and skills presented in this chapter. Labs are listed in order of increasing difficulty.

Lab 1: Using Precise Measurements to Crop and Resize a Photo

Problem: As a member of your high school reunion committee, it is your task to assemble the class photo directory. You are to edit a high school student photo and prepare it for print in the reunion directory. The photo needs to fit in a space 1.75 inches high and 1.33 inches wide. Each photo needs to have approximately the same amount of space above the headshot .25 inches. The publisher wants the photo saved in a JPG format. The edited photo is displayed in Figure 1–90 on the following page.

Continued >

In the Lab *continued*

Figure 1–90

Instructions:

1. Start Photoshop and perform the customization steps found on pages PS 7 through PS 9.
2. Click the Workspace switcher on the Application bar and then click Essentials to restore the workspace to its default settings.
3. Right-click the Rectangular Marquee Tool (M) button on the Tools panel and then click Rectangular Marquee Tool.
4. Right-click the Rectangular Marquee tool icon on the options bar and then click Reset All Tools. When Photoshop displays a confirmation dialog box, click the OK button.
5. Open the file, Lab 1-1 Student, from the Chapter01 folder of the Data Files for Students or from a location specified by your instructor.
6. Use the Save As command on the File menu to save the file on your storage device with the name, Lab 1-1 Student Edited. Click the Save button. If Photoshop displays a JPEG Options dialog box, click the OK button.
7. Use the Navigator panel to zoom the photo to 50% magnification, if necessary.
8. If the rulers do not appear, press CTRL+R to view the rulers.
9. Drag from the horizontal ruler down into the photo until the green ruler guide touches the top of the student's head. Drag a second ruler guide to a position .25 inches above the first one as measured on the vertical ruler. If you make a mistake while dragging a ruler guide, click Undo New Guide on the Edit menu.
10. Select the Crop tool. Drag from the left margin at the upper green line, down and to the right to include all of the lower portion of the photo. *Hint*: If your selection is not perfect, press the ESC key and then drag again.
11. Press the ENTER key. If your crop does not seem correct, click the Undo command on the Edit menu and repeat Steps 9 and 10.
12. Once your photo has .25 inches of space above the student's head, save the photo again.
13. Click the Image Size command on the Image menu. When the Image Size dialog box is displayed in the Document Size area, type 1.75 in the Height box. Click the OK button.

14. Save the resized file with a new file name, Lab 1-1 Student for Print. If a JPEG Options dialog box is displayed, click the OK button.
15. Use the Print One Copy command on the File menu to print a copy of the photo.
16. Quit Photoshop.
17. Send the photo as an e-mail attachment to your instructor, or follow your instructor's directions for submitting the lab assignment.

In the Lab

Lab 2: Creating a Border

Problem: The local hockey team is preparing a flyer to advertise their next game. The marketing department would like you to take one of the pictures from the last game and crop it to show just the face-off players and the official. Because the flyer will be printed on white paper, you should create a white border so the photo blends into the background and adds to the ice rink effect. The edited photo is displayed in Figure 1–91.

Figure 1–91

Instructions:
1. Start Photoshop. Perform the customization steps found on pages PS 7 through PS 9.
2. Open the file, Lab 1-2 Hockey, from the Chapter01 folder of the Data Files for Students or from a location specified by your instructor.
3. Use the Save As command on the File menu to save the file on your storage device with the name, Lab 1-2 Hockey Edited, in the PSD format.
4. Click the Zoom Tool (Z) button on the Tools panel. Click the official to center the photo in the display. Zoom as necessary so you can make precise edits.

Continued >

In the Lab *continued*

5. Crop the picture to display only the official and the two hockey players ready for the face-off. Use the golden rectangle ratio of approximately 5:8. The vertical line of the hockey stick and the visual line of the official should be positioned using the rule of thirds.
6. Press CTRL+S to save the photo again.
7. Press CTRL+A to select all of the photo.
8. To create the border, do the following:
    a. On the Select menu, point to Modify, and then click Border.
    b. When the Border Selection dialog box is displayed, type 100 in the Width Box. Click the OK button.
    c. On the Select menu, point to Modify, and then click Smooth.
    d. When the Smooth Selection dialog box is displayed, type 50 in the Sample Radius box to smooth the corners. Click the OK button.
    e. Press SHIFT+F5 to access the Fill command.
    f. When the Fill dialog box is displayed, click the Use box arrow and then click White in the list.
    g. Click the Mode box arrow and then click Normal in the list, if necessary.
    h. If necessary, type 100 in the Opacity box. Click the OK button.
    i. Press CTRL+D to deselect the border.
9. Save the photo again.
10. Use the Print One Copy command on the File menu to print a copy of the photo.
11. Close the document window.
12. Quit Photoshop.
13. Send the photo as an e-mail attachment to your instructor, or follow your instructor's directions for submitting the lab assignment.

In the Lab

Lab 3: Preparing a Photo for the Web

Problem: As an independent consultant in Web site design, you have been hired by the Pineapple Growers Association to prepare a photo of an exotic pineapple growing in a field for use on the association's Web site. The edited photo is displayed in Figure 1–92.

Instructions:
1. Start Photoshop. Perform the customization steps found on pages PS 7 through PS 9.
2. Open the file, Lab 1-3 Pineapple, from the Chapter01 folder of the Data Files for Students or from a location specified by your instructor.
3. Use the Save As command on the File menu to save the file on your storage device with the name, Lab 1-3 Pineapple Edited, in the PSD format.
4. Resize the photo to 500 pixels wide.
5. On the Help menu, click Photoshop Help. Search for the word, Optimization. Read about optimizing for the Web. Print a copy of the help topic and then close the Adobe Help window.
6. When the Photoshop window again is displayed, click Save for Web & Devices on the File menu.
7. When the Save for Web & Devices dialog box is displayed, click the 4-Up tab.
8. Click the Zoom Level box arrow in the lower-left corner of the dialog box and then click Fit on Screen.

Figure 1–92

9. Right-click in the annotation area and then choose the connection speed of your Internet connection. See your instructor if you are not sure of your connection speed.
10. Click the preview that looks the best on the screen.
11. Make the following changes to the Save for Web & Devices settings at the right side of the Save for Web & Devices dialog box. Some of the settings might be set correctly already. If you are unsure of a setting, point to the setting to display its tool tip.
    a. Click the Color reduction algorithm box arrow and then click Selective in the list. The Selective command produces images with the greatest color integrity.
    b. Click the Specify the dither algorithm box arrow, and then click Noise in the list. The Noise command randomly diffuses the color across adjacent pixels without creating seams.
    c. Click the Maximum number of colors in the Color Table box arrow, and then click 256 in the list. While most monitors can display millions of colors, choosing 256 colors ensures that older monitors can display realistic colors in your photo on the Web.
12. For extra credit, create a Web page by doing the following lettered steps. Otherwise, skip to Step 13.
    a. Click the Preview button.
    b. The Web preview will open a browser window. In the lower portion of the window, the browser will display the HTML code necessary to display the picture as a Web page. Drag the code to select it. Press CTRL+C to copy it.
    c. Open a text editor program such as Notepad or TextPad and press CTRL+V to paste the code into the editing window. Replace the words, BrowserPreview, with the words, Lab-1-3-Pineapple-for-Web in the code. Save the file as Lab-3-1-Pineapple.html in the same folder as your photo. Close the text editor.
    d. Click the Close button in the browser window.
13. Click the Save button in the Save for Web & Devices dialog box. When the Save Optimized As dialog box is displayed, type Lab-1-3-Pineapple-for-Web as the file name. Click the Save button.
14. Close the document window and quit Photoshop.
15. Send the GIF file to your instructor.
16. If you did the extra credit, view your HTML file as a Web page. See your instructor for instructions on uploading the GIF and HTML files to a server or other ways to submit your assignment.

Cases and Places

Apply your creative thinking and problem-solving skills to design and implement a solution.

• Easier   •• More Difficult

• 1: Cropping a Photo for a Social Networking Site

You would like to place a photo of your recent tubing adventure on your social networking site. The photo you have is of two people. You need to crop out the other person who is tubing. After starting Photoshop and resetting the workspace, you select the photo, Case 1-1 Tubing, from the Chapter01 folder of the Data Files for Students. Save the photo on your USB flash drive storage device as Case 1-1 Tubing Edited, using the PSD format. Crop the photo to remove one of the inner tubes, keeping in mind the rule of thirds, the golden rectangle, and the direction of the action. Save the photo again and print a copy for your instructor.

• 2: Creating a Rack Card Graphic with a Border

You are an intern with a tour company. They are planning a bus tour that follows the original Lewis and Clark trail and want to produce a rack card advertising the trip. On the back of the rack card, they would like a photo of one of the sites along the trail. The photo named Case 1-2 Monument is located in the Chapter01 folder of the Data Files for Students. Save the photo on your USB flash drive storage device as Case 1-2 Monument Edited, using the PSD format. Rack cards typically measure 4 × 9 inches; the photo needs to fit in the upper half. Resize the photo to be 3.75 inches wide. Create a border of 100 pixels. Do not use smoothing. Fill the border with 50% black opacity.

•• 3: Planning for Cropping

Look through magazines or newspapers for color photos that might be cropped. If possible, cut out three photos and mark them by hand with cropping lines. Write a short paragraph for each one describing why you think the photo could benefit from cropping. If the cropped photo needs to be resized, give the exact dimensions. List at least two uses for the photo, other than the one in which it was displayed. Attach the photos to the descriptions and submit them to your instructor.

•• 4: Scanning, Resizing, and Adding a Border to a Photo

Make It Personal

Use a scanner to scan a favorite action photo. Using the scanner's software, save the photo in the highest possible resolution, using the most color settings. Bring the picture into Photoshop and save it on your storage device. Crop it to remove extra background images. Use the rule of thirds to focus on the main point of interest. Recall that in the case of moving objects, you generally should leave space in front of them into which they can move. Resize the photo to fit your favorite frame. Add a blended border if it will not detract from the images in the photo. Send the edited photo by e-mail to a friend or use it in a page layout program to create a greeting card.

•• 5: Optimizing a Digital Photo

Working Together

Your school would like to display a picture of the main building or student center on the Web site's home page. Your team has been assigned to take the photo and optimize it for the Web. Using a digital camera or camera phone, each team member should take a picture of the building from various angles. As a team, open each digital file and choose one or two that best incorporate the styles and suggestions in this chapter. Choose a border that highlights the color and dynamic of the photo. Resize the photo to less than 500 × 500 pixels. As a group, make decisions in the Save for Web & Devices dialog box on the 4-Up tab as to which optimization would best suit the school's needs. Show the final products to another person or group in your class for suggestions. Submit the best one to your instructor.

2 Using Selection Tools and Shortcut Keys

Objectives

You will have mastered the material in this chapter when you can:

- Explain the terms perspective, layout, and storyboard
- Describe selection tools
- Select objects in a photo
- Use all the marquee tools
- Move a selection
- Make transformation edits
- View states in the History panel
- Employ the lasso tools
- Use the Grow command and Refine Edges to adjust selections
- Add and subtract areas from selections
- Use ruler grids and guides
- Select objects using the Quick Selection and Magic Wand tools
- Print to a PDF file
- Create new keyboard shortcuts

2 | Using Selection Tools and Shortcut Keys

Introduction

In Chapter 1, you learned about the Photoshop interface as well as navigation and zooming techniques. You cropped and resized a photo, added a border, and saved the photo for both Web and print media. You learned about online Help, along with opening, saving, and printing photos. This chapter continues to emphasize those topics, and presents some new ones.

Recall that specifying or isolating an area of your photo for editing is called making a selection. By selecting specific areas, you can edit and apply special effects to portions of your image, while leaving the unselected areas untouched. The new topics covered in this chapter include the marquee tools used to select rectangular or elliptical areas, the lasso tools used to select free-form segments or shapes, and the Quick Selection and Magic Wand tools used to select consistently colored areas. You will learn how to use the Move tool and transformation tools to duplicate, move, scale, skew, and warp those selections. Finally, you will print to a PDF file and create a new keyboard shortcut.

Project — Advertisement Graphic

An **advertisement**, or **ad**, is a form of communication that promotes a product or service to a potential customer. An advertisement tries to persuade consumers to purchase the product or service. An advertisement typically has a single message directed toward a target audience.

A graphic designed for advertising, sometimes called an **advertising piece**, needs to catch the customer's eye and entice him or her to purchase the product. A clear graphic with strong contrast, item repetition, and visual lines will tell the story, while enhancing text that might be added later. Chapter 2 illustrates the creation of an advertising piece to be used in a grocery store's newspaper ad. You will begin with the image in Figure 2–1a that shows a selection of peppers. You then will manipulate the image by selecting, editing, and moving the objects to produce a more attractive layout, creating Figure 2–1b that will be displayed in the newspaper.

Overview

As you read this chapter, you will learn how to create the advertisement graphic shown in Figure 2–1b by performing these general tasks:

- Select portions of the photo.
- Copy, move, rotate, and flip selections.
- Use the transformation commands to edit, scale, warp, and skew selections.
- Eliminate white space in and among objects in selected areas.
- Retrace editing steps using the History panel.
- Refine edges of selections.
- Print to a PDF file.
- Create a new shortcut key.

(a)

(b)

Figure 2–1

General Project Guidelines

When editing a photo, the actions you perform and decisions you make will affect the appearance and characteristics of the finished product. As you edit a photo, such as the one shown in Figure 2–1a, you should follow these general guidelines:

1. **Choose the correct tool.** When you need to copy and paste portions of your photo, consider carefully which Photoshop selection tool to use. You want the procedure to be efficient and produce a clear image. Keep in mind the shape, background, purpose, and your expertise with various tools.

2. **Plan your duplications.** Use a storyboard or make a list of the items you plan to duplicate. Then decide whether it will be an exact duplication or one that is manipulated, called a transformed copy. The decision depends on the visual effect you want to achieve and the customer requirements.

3. **Use grids and guides.** When you are working with exact measurements, close cropping and moving, or just want to align things easily, use grids and guides to display non-printing lines across the document window. With Photoshop snapping, selections can be brought into line. Visual estimations of size and location are easier to perceive.

4. **Create files in portable formats.** You might have to distribute your artwork in a variety of formats depending on how it will be used. Portability is an important consideration. It usually is safe to begin work in the Photoshop PSD format and then use the Save as command or Print command to convert to the PDF format, which can be read by anyone on the Web with a free reader. PDF files are platform and software independent.

When necessary, more specific details concerning the above guidelines are presented at appropriate points in the chapter. The chapter also will identify the actions performed and decisions made regarding these guidelines during the creation of the edited photo shown in Figure 2–1b.

Plan Ahead

Photoshop Help
The best way to become familiar with Photoshop Help is to use it. Appendix D includes detailed information about Photoshop Help and exercises that will help you gain confidence in using it.

Creating an Advertising Piece

Figure 2–2 illustrates the design decisions made to create the final advertising piece. An attractive layout using multiple objects is a good marketing strategy, visually and subconsciously, encouraging the viewer to purchase more than one item. **Layout** refers to placing visual elements into a pleasing and understandable arrangement; in the grocery advertisement, the layout is suggestive of how the product or products might look in a buyer's home. Advertising artists and product designers try to determine how the target consumer will use the product and group objects accordingly in the layout.

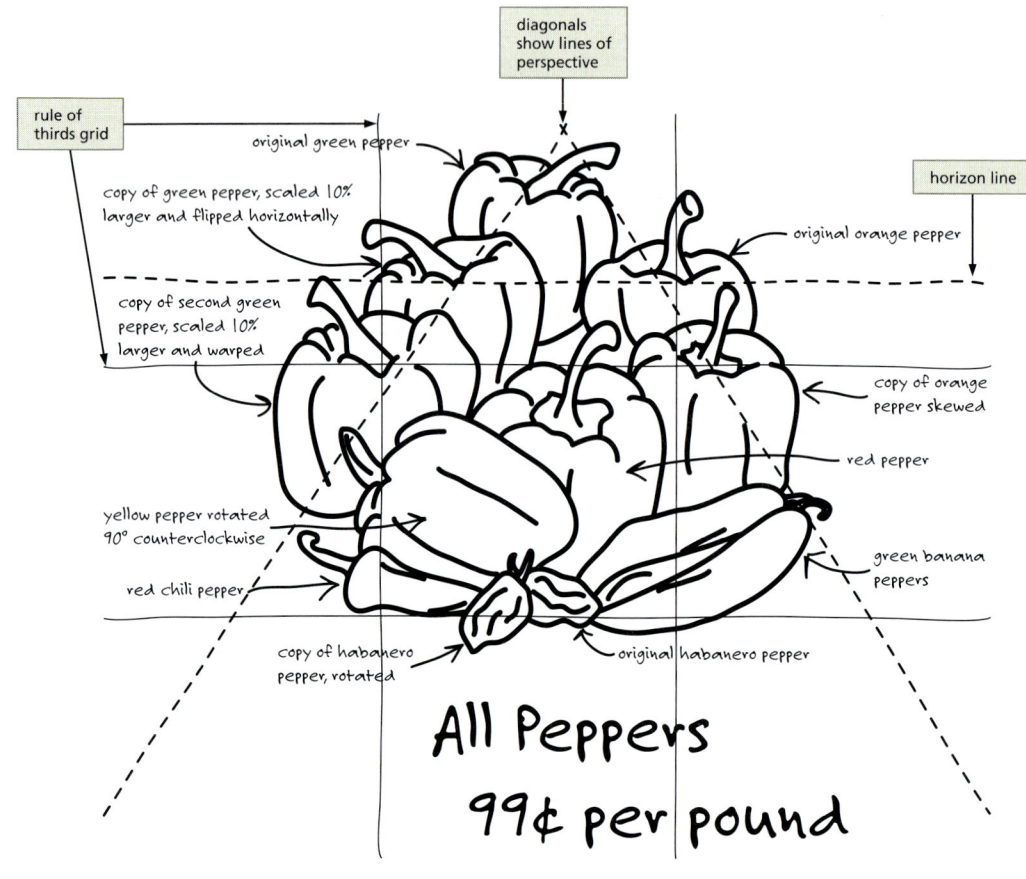

Figure 2–2

From a design point of view, creating visual diagonal lines creates perspective. **Perspective** is the technique photographers, designers, and artists use to create the illusion of three dimensions on a flat or two-dimensional surface. Perspective is a means of fooling the eye by making it appear as if there is depth or receding space in the image. Adjusting the sizes and juxtaposing the objects creates asymmetrical balance and visual tension between the featured products. The diagonal alignment of the peppers leads the viewer's eye to the background, as does the placement of smaller peppers in front of the larger ones.

The **horizon line** in perspective drawing is a virtual horizontal line across the picture. The placement of the horizon line determines from where the viewer seems to be looking, such as down from a high place or up from close to the ground. In the peppers advertisement, the horizon line runs across the middle of the drawing, just above the center. The viewer is high enough to see the top of the peppers, as if the peppers are sitting on a kitchen counter.

Using white space, or the nonimage area, is effective in directing the viewer to notice what is important. The products grouped this way are, in a sense, framed by the white space.

This product layout also helps other members of the design team when it is time to make decisions about type placement. The group of products can be shifted up or down, as one image, to accommodate the layout and text, including the font sizes, placement, title, description, and price information. Recall that the rule of thirds offers a useful means to make effective layouts for images and text.

Designing a preliminary layout sketch, similar to Figure 2–2, to help you make choices about placement, size, perspective, and spacing, is referred to as creating a **storyboard**, **thumbnail**, or **rough**.

> **BTW**
>
> **Quick Reference**
> For a table that lists how to complete the tasks covered in this book using the mouse, shortcut menu, and keyboard, see the Quick Reference Summary at the back of this book or visit the Photoshop CS4 Quick Reference Web page (scsite.com/pscs4/qr).

Starting and Customizing Photoshop

The following steps start Photoshop, reset the default workspace, and reset tools. After opening a photo, the rulers are displayed, and the file is saved with a new file name to begin editing.

To Start Photoshop

If you are stepping through this project on a computer and you want your screen to match the figures in this book, then you should change your computer's resolution to 1024 × 768 and reset the tools and panels. For more information about how to change the resolution on your computer, and other advanced Photoshop settings, read Appendix C.

The following steps, which assume Windows Vista is running, start Photoshop based on a typical installation. You may need to ask your instructor how to start Photoshop for your system.

1 Click the Start button on the Windows Vista taskbar to display the Start menu and then click All Programs at the bottom of the left pane on the Start menu to display the All Programs list.

2 Click Adobe Design Premium CS4, or your version of the Adobe suite, in the All Programs list, if necessary, and then click Adobe Photoshop CS4 to start Photoshop.

3 If the Photoshop window is not maximized, click the Maximize button next to the Close button on the Application bar to maximize the window.

To Reset the Workspace

As discussed in Chapter 1, it is helpful to reset the workspace so that the tools and panels appear in their default positions. The following steps use the Workspace switcher to select the Essentials workspace.

1. Click the Workspace switcher on the Application bar to display the names of saved workspaces.

2. Click Essentials to restore the workspace to its default settings.

To Reset the Tools and the Options Bar

Recall that the Tools panel and the options bar retain their settings from previous Photoshop sessions. The following steps select the Rectangular Marquee tool and reset all tool settings in the options bar.

1. Click the Rectangular Marquee Tool (M) button on the Tools panel to select it.

2. If the tools in the Tools panel are displayed in two columns, click the double arrow at the top of the Tools panel to change the panel to one column.

3. Right-click the Rectangular Marquee tool icon on the options bar to display the context menu and then click Reset All Tools. When Photoshop displays a confirmation dialog box, click the OK button to restore the tools to their default settings.

To Open a Photo

To open a photo in Photoshop it must be stored as a digital file on your computer system or on an external storage device. The photos used in this book are stored in the Data Files for Students. You can access the Data Files for Students on the DVD that accompanies this book. See the inside back cover of this book for instructions on downloading the Data Files for Students, or contact your instructor for information about accessing the required files.

The following steps open the file, Peppers, from a DVD located in drive E.

1. Insert the DVD that accompanies this book into your DVD drive. After a few seconds, if Windows displays a dialog box, click its Close button.

2. With the Photoshop window open, click File on the menu bar, and then click Open to display the Open dialog box.

3. In the Open dialog box, click the Look in box arrow to display the list of available locations, and then click drive E or the drive associated with your DVD.

4. Double-click the Chapter02 folder to open it, and then double-click the file, Peppers, to open it.

5. When Photoshop displays the image in the document window, if the magnification shown on the status bar is not 50%, double-click the magnification box on the document window status bar, type 50, and then press the ENTER key to change the magnification (Figure 2–3).

Creating an Advertising Piece **PS 83**

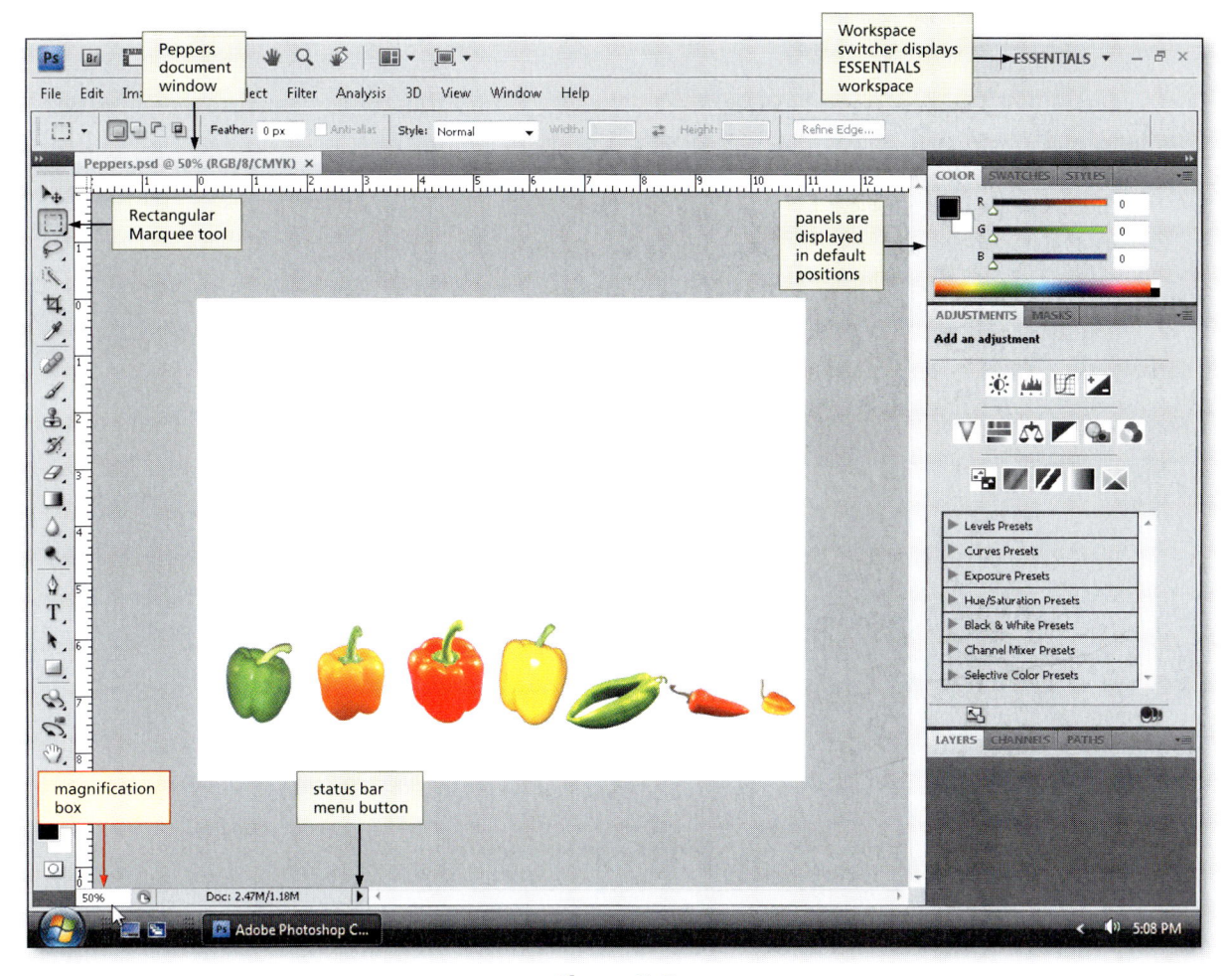

Figure 2–3

To View Rulers

The following steps display the rulers in the document window to facilitate making precise measurements.

1. If the rulers do not appear on the top and left sides of the document window, click the View Extras button on the Application bar to display its menu.

2. Click Show Rulers on the menu to display rulers in the workspace.

3. If necessary, right-click the horizontal ruler and then click Inches on the context menu to display the rulers in inches.

The Save As Dialog Box

In Chapter 1 you learned that the Save As dialog box allows you to name a file, specify a location, and assign a file type. There are other buttons to assist you in saving (Figure 2–4 on the next page). On the left side of the Save As dialog box is a locations bar that contains commonly used storage locations. To the right of the Save in box are buttons to move up and down in the folder hierarchy, create new folders, and change the way the files are displayed.

Document Window Status Bar
The status bar of the document window in Figure 2–3 shows the current document size. To display the document dimensions, click the status bar menu button, point to Show, and then click Document Dimensions.

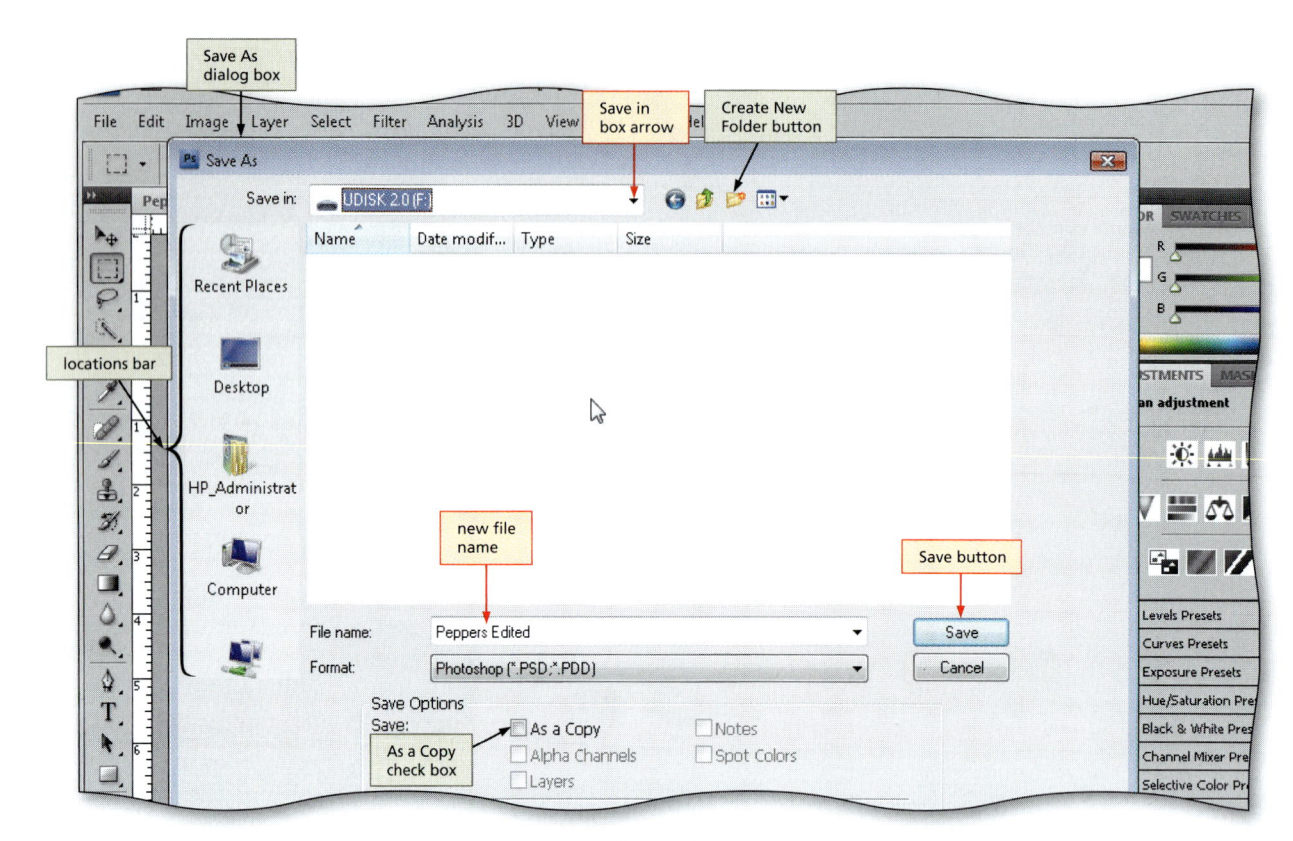

Figure 2–4

In the lower part of the Save As dialog box are Save options, including the As a Copy check box. When checked, Photoshop automatically appends the word, copy, to the file name, thus allowing you to save a second version of the file in the same location. A copy file has the same attributes, and can be edited in the same manner, as the original file. Making multiple copies of an original file also is useful if you want to make and save several different versions of a layout.

To Save a Photo

Even though you have yet to edit the photo, it is a good practice to save the file on your personal storage device early in the process. The following steps save the photo with the name Peppers Edited.

1. With your USB flash drive connected to one of the computer's USB ports, click File on the menu bar to display the File menu and then click Save As to display the Save As dialog box.

2. In the file name text box, type Peppers Edited to rename the file. Do not press the ENTER key after typing the file name.

3. Click the Save in box arrow and then click UDISK 2.0 (F:), or the location associated with your USB flash drive, in the list, if necessary (Figure 2–4).

4. Click the Save button in the Save As dialog box to save the file.

Plan Ahead

Choose the correct tool.
When you need to copy and paste portions of your photo, consider carefully which selection tool to use. You want the procedure to be efficient and produce a clear image. Keep in mind the following as you choose a selection tool:

- the shape of the selection
- the background around the selection
- the contrast between the selection and its surroundings
- the proximity of the selection to other objects
- your expertise in using the tool
- the availability of other pointing devices, such as a graphics tablet
- the destination of the paste

The Marquee Tools

The **marquee tools** allow you to draw a marquee that selects a portion of the document window. Marquee tools are useful when the part of an image or photo that you wish to select fits into a rectangular or an elliptical shape. Photoshop has four marquee tools (Figure 2–5) that appear in a context menu when you click the tool and hold down the mouse button, or when you right-click the tool. You can select any of the marquee tools from this context menu. Recall that Photoshop offers the added flexibility of selecting a tool with a single letter shortcut key. Pressing the M key activates the current marquee tool.

BTW

Marquee Tool Selection
If you are using a different tool, and want to activate the marquee tools, you can click the Rectangular Marquee Tool (M) button on the Tools panel or press the M key on the keyboard to select the tool. Once the tool is selected, pressing SHIFT+M toggles between the Rectangular and Elliptical Marquee tools. You must choose the Row and Column Marquee tools from the context menu — there are no keyboard shortcuts.

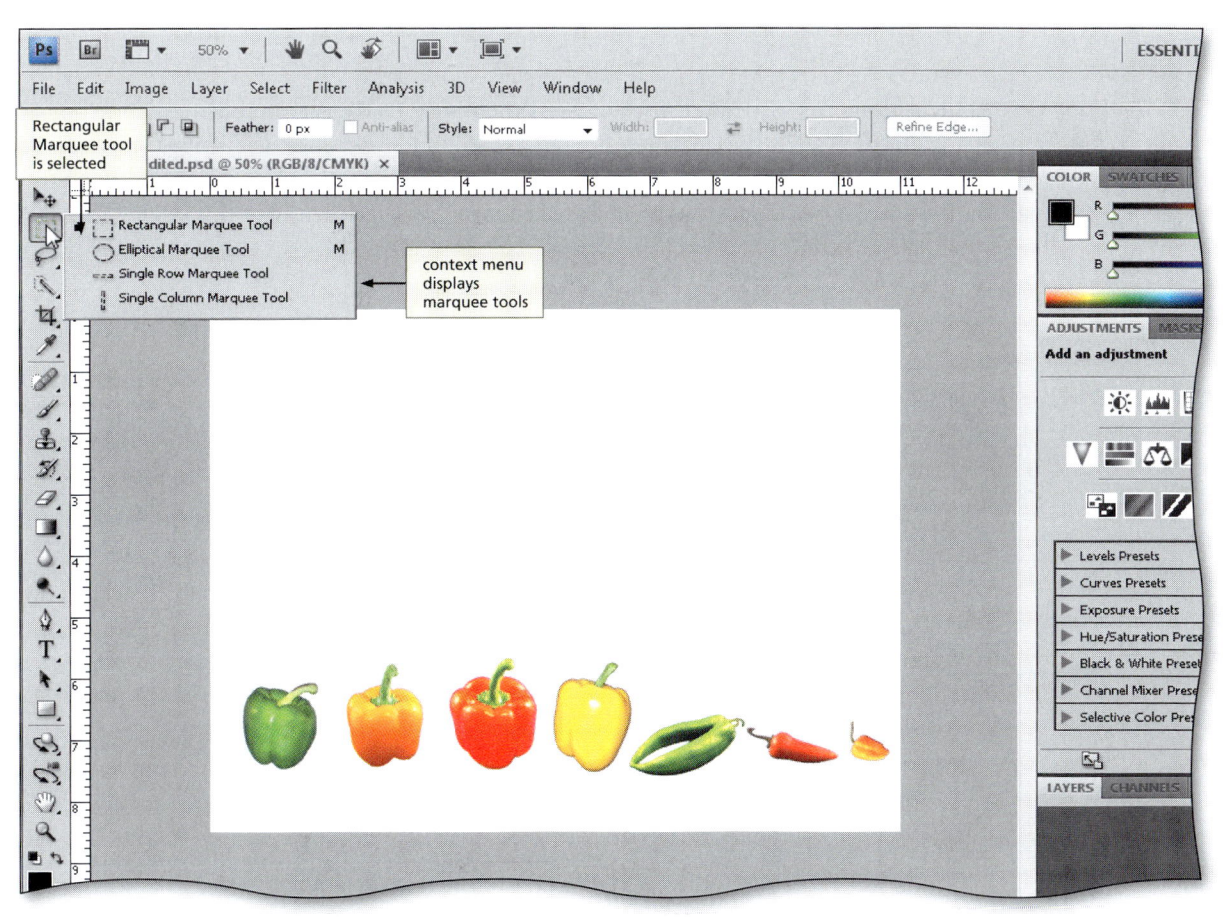

Figure 2–5

BTW

Single Row and Single Column Marquee Tools
To create interesting backgrounds, wallpapers, and color ribbons using the Single Row or Single Column Marquee tools, choose a colorful photo and create a single row or single column marquee. Press CTRL+T to display the bounding box. Then drag the sizing handles until the selection fills the document window.

The Rectangular Marquee tool is the default marquee tool that selects a rectangular or square portion of the image or photo. The Elliptical Marquee tool allows you to select an ellipsis, oval, or circular area.

Dragging with the Rectangular or Elliptical Marquee tools creates a marquee drawn from a corner. If you press the SHIFT key while dragging a marquee, Photoshop **constrains** the proportions of the shape, creating a perfect square or circle. If you press the ALT key while drawing a selection, the marquee is created from the center. Pressing SHIFT+ALT starts from the center and constrains the proportions.

The Single Row Marquee tool allows you to select a single row of pixels. The Single Column Marquee tool allows you to select a single column of pixels. A single click in the document window then creates the selection. Because a single row or column of pixels is so small, it is easier to use these two marquee tools at higher magnifications.

Table 2–1 describes the four marquee tools.

Table 2–1 The Marquee Tools			
Tool	**Purpose**	**Shortcut**	**Button**
Rectangular Marquee	selects a rectangular or square portion of the document window	M SHIFT+M toggles to Elliptical Marquee	
Elliptical Marquee	selects an elliptical, oval, or circular portion of the document window	M SHIFT+M toggles to Rectangular Marquee	
Single Row Marquee	selects a single row of pixels in the document window	(none)	
Single Column Marquee	selects a single column of pixels in the document window	(none)	

The options bar associated with each of the marquee tools contains many buttons and settings to draw effective marquees (Figure 2–6). The options bar displays an icon for the chosen marquee on the left, followed by the Tool Preset picker. The Tool Preset picker allows you to save and reuse toolbar settings. You will learn how to use the Tool Preset picker in a later chapter.

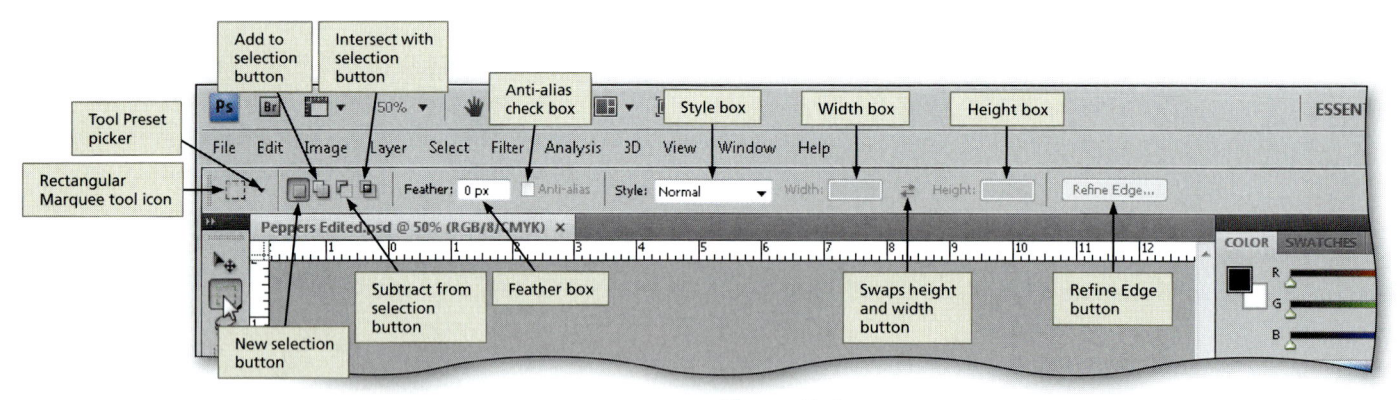

Figure 2–6

The next four buttons to the right adjust the selection (Figure 2–6). When selected, the New selection button allows you to start a new marquee.

The Add to selection button draws a rectangle or ellipsis and adds it to any current selection. The Add to selection button is useful for selecting the extra corners of an L-shaped object or for shapes that do not fit within a single rectangle or ellipsis. To activate the Add to selection button, you can click it on the options bar or hold down the SHIFT key while dragging a second selection. When adding to a selection, the mouse pointer changes to a crosshair with a plus sign.

The Subtract from selection button allows you to deselect or remove a portion of an existing selection. The new rectangle or ellipsis is removed from the original selection. It is useful for removing block portions of the background around oddly shaped images, or for deselecting ornamentation in an object. To activate the Subtract from selection button, you can click it on the options bar or hold down the ALT key while dragging. When subtracting from a selection, the mouse pointer changes to a crosshair with a minus sign.

The Intersect with selection button allows you to draw a second rectangle or ellipsis across a portion of the previously selected area, resulting in a selection border only around the area in which the two selections overlap. To activate the Intersect with selection button, you click it on the options bar, or hold down the SHIFT and ALT keys while dragging. When creating an intersection, the mouse pointer changes to a crosshair with an X.

To the right of the selection buttons, the options bar displays a Feather box. **Feathering** softens the edges of the selection. In traditional photography, feathering is called **vignetting,** which creates a soft-edged border around an image that blends into the background. Feathering sometimes is used in wedding photos or when a haloed effect is desired. The width of the feather is measured in pixels. When using the Elliptical Marquee tool, you can further specify blending by selecting the Anti-alias check box. **Anti-aliasing** softens the block-like, staircase look of rounded corners. Figure 2–7 shows a rectangle with no feathering, one with five pixels of feathering, an ellipsis with no anti-aliasing, and one created with a check mark in the Anti-alias, check box.

BTW

The Tool Preset Picker
The Tool Preset picker is displayed on the options bar of most tools. When you click the button, Photoshop displays a list of settings used during the current Photoshop session or previously saved options bar settings. The list makes it easier to save and reuse tool settings. You can load, edit, and create libraries of tool presets in conjunction with the Tool Presets panel. To choose a tool preset, click the Tool Preset picker in the options bar, and then select a preset from the list.

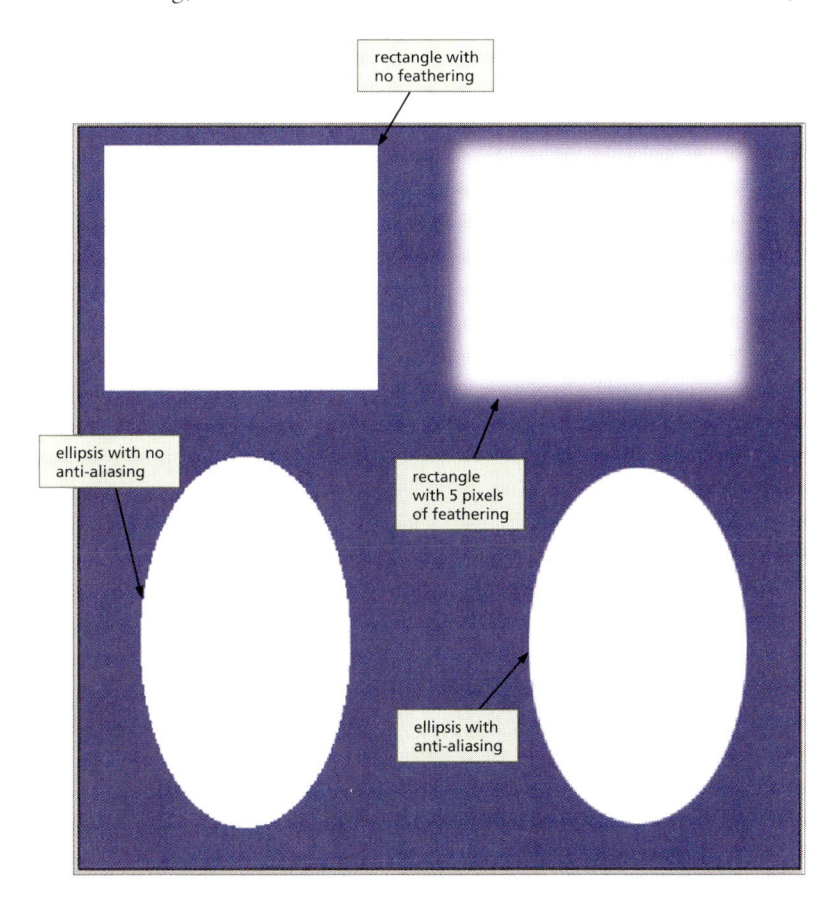

Figure 2–7

> **BTW**
>
> **Anti-Aliasing**
> Anti-aliasing is available for the Elliptical Marquee tool, the Lasso tool, the Polygonal Lasso tool, the Magnetic Lasso tool, and the Magic Wand tool. You must specify this option before using these tools. Once a selection is made, you cannot add anti-aliasing.

When using the Rectangular Marquee tool or the Elliptical Marquee tool, you can click the Style box arrow (Figure 2–6) to choose how the size of the marquee selection is determined. A Normal style sets the selection marquee proportions by dragging. A Fixed Ratio style sets a height-to-width ratio using decimal values. For example, to draw a marquee twice as wide as it is high, enter 2 for the width and 1 for the height, and then drag in the photo. A Fixed Size style allows you to specify exact pixel values for the marquee's height and width. The Width box and Height box become enabled when you choose a style other than Normal. A button between the two boxes swaps the values, if desired.

Sometimes you need to make subtle changes to a selection marquee. For example, if the border or edge of a selection seems to be jagged or hazy, or if the colors at the edge of a selection bleed slightly across the marquee, you can use the Refine Edge button. When clicked, it opens a dialog box in which you can increase or decrease the radius of the marquee, change the contrast, and smooth the selection border.

Once you have drawn a marquee, you can choose from other options for further manipulation of the selected area. Right-clicking a selection displays a context menu that provides access to many other useful commands such as deselecting, reselecting, or selecting the **inverse**, which means selecting everything in the image outside of the current selection. Right-clicking a selection also enables you to create layers, apply color fills and strokes, and make other changes that you will learn about in future chapters.

If you make a mistake or change your mind when drawing a marquee, you can do one of three things:

1. If you want to start over, and the New selection button is selected on the options bar, you can click somewhere else in the document window to deselect the marquee; then simply draw a new marquee. Deselecting also is available as a command on the Select menu and on the context menu.
2. If you have already drawn the marquee but wish to move or reposition it, and the New selection button is selected on the options bar, you can drag the selection to the new location.
3. If you want to reposition while you are creating the marquee, do not release the mouse button. Press and hold the SPACEBAR, drag the marquee to the new location, and then release the SPACEBAR. At that point, you can continue dragging to finish drawing the marquee. Repositioning in this manner can be done while using any of the four selection adjustment buttons on the options bar.

To Use the Rectangular Marquee Tool

The following steps select the green bell pepper in the Peppers Edited image using the Rectangular Marquee tool.

1
- Right-click the Rectangular Marquee Tool (M) button on the Tools panel to display its context menu (Figure 2–8).

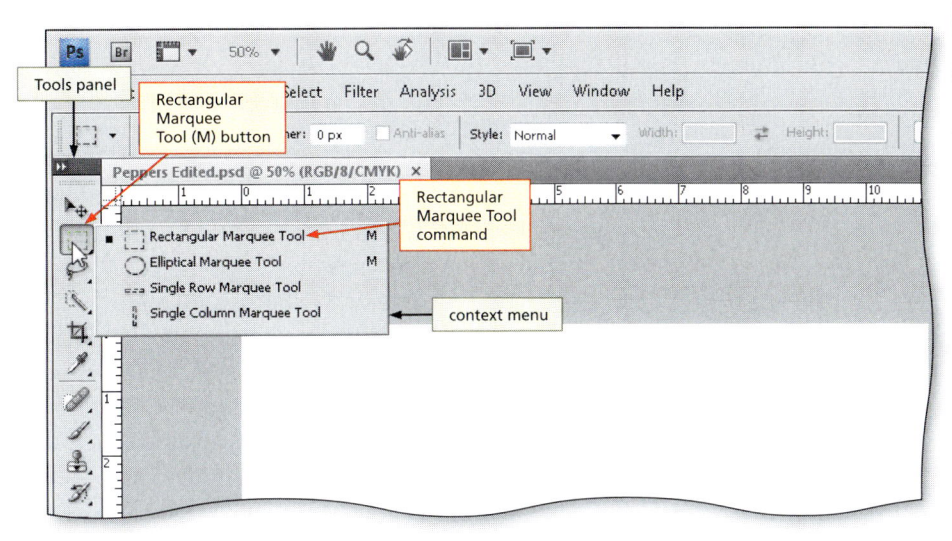

Figure 2–8

2
- Click Rectangular Marquee Tool to select it. If the New selection button is not selected on the options bar, click to select it.
- In the photo, drag to draw a rectangle as close as possible around the green bell pepper to create a marquee selection (Figure 2–9).

Experiment
- Practice drawing rectangular and elliptical marquees. Press SHIFT+M to switch between the two. SHIFT+drag to look at the effects. When you are finished, redraw a rectangle around the green bell pepper.

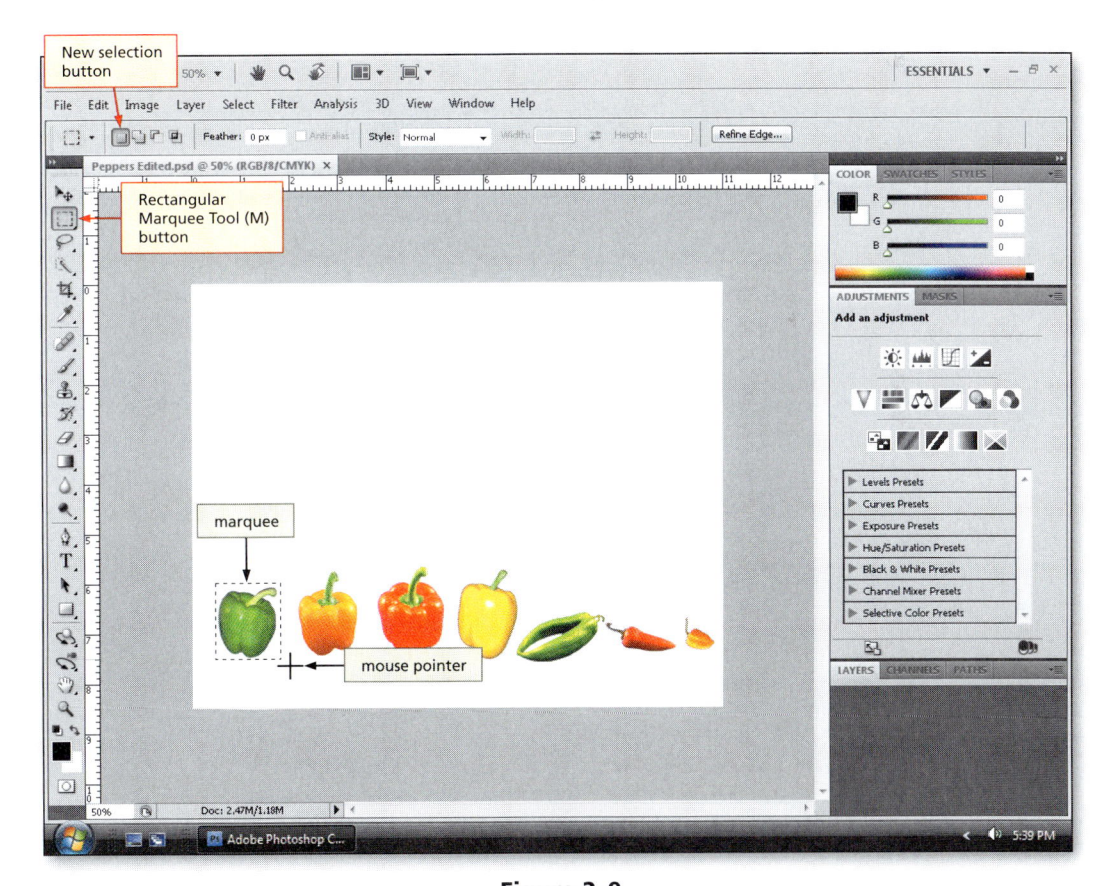

Figure 2–9

Other Ways
1. Press M key or SHIFT+M until Rectangular Marquee tool is active, drag selection

The Move Tool

BTW

Deleting Selections
You can delete a selection by pressing the delete key on the keyboard. If you delete by accident, press CTRL+Z to bring the selection back.

BTW

Layers
A layer is a portion of the image that is superimposed or separated from other parts of the document. Think of layers as sheets of clear film stacked one on top of the other. In Chapter 3 you will learn how to change the composition of an image by changing the order and attributes of layers.

The Move tool on the Photoshop Tools panel is used to move or make other changes to selections. Activating the Move tool by clicking the Move Tool (V) button, or by pressing the V key on the keyboard, enables you to move the selection border and its contents by dragging in the document window. When you first use the Move tool, the mouse pointer displays a black arrowhead with scissors. To move the selection in a straight line, press and hold the SHIFT key while dragging. If you press and hold the ALT key while dragging, you **duplicate** or move only a copy of the selected area, effectively copying and pasting the selection. While duplicating, the mouse pointer changes to a black arrowhead with a white arrowhead behind it.

When you move selections, you need to be careful about overlapping images. As you will learn in Chapter 3, Photoshop might layer or overlap portions of images when you move them. While that sometimes is preferred when creating collages or composite images, it is undesirable if an important object is obscured. Close tracing while creating selections and careful placement of moved selections will prevent unwanted layering.

The Move tool options bar displays tools to help define the scope of the move (Figure 2–10). Later, as you learn about layers, you will use the Auto-Select check box to select layer groupings or single layers. The align and distribute buttons and the Auto-Align Layers button also are used with layers. The Show Transform Controls check box causes Photoshop to display sizing handles on the selection border and adds a centered reference point to the selection.

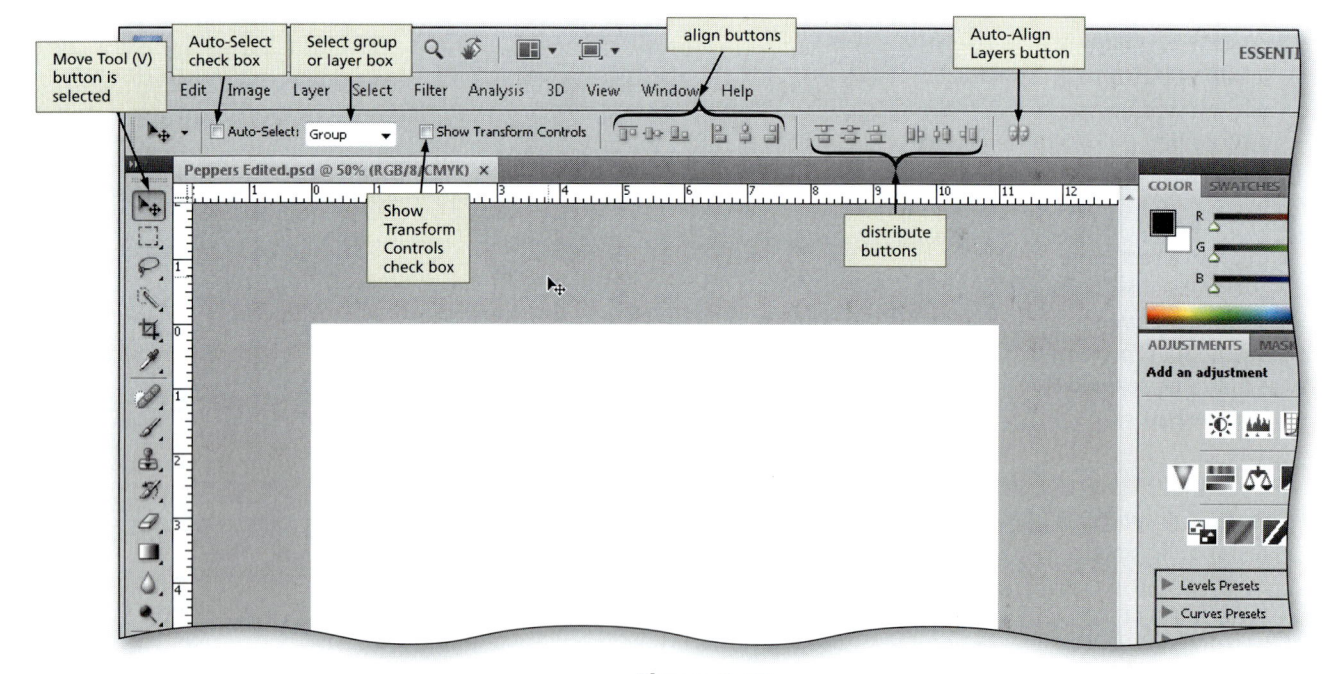

Figure 2–10

BTW

Nudging Selections
Nudging Selections Instead of dragging to move a selection, you can use the arrow keys on the keyboard to move in small increments. The process is called **nudging**.

As you use the Move tool throughout this chapter, be careful to position your mouse inside the selection before moving. Do not try to move a selection by dragging its border. Do not drag any sizing handles or center reference points that may be displayed, unless instructed to do so. If you drag one by mistake, press the ESC key.

To Use the Move Tool

The next steps in preparing the layout for the advertisement involve rearranging the components of the original image. Using the Move tool, you will move the green bell pepper up and to the right.

1

- With the green bell pepper still selected, click the Move Tool (V) button on the Tools panel to select it.

- If necessary, on the options bar, click the Auto-Select check box so it does not display a check mark. If necessary, click the Show Transform Controls check box so it does not display a check mark (Figure 2–11).

Q&A Are there any other tools nested with the Move tool?

No, the Move tool does not have a context menu. Tools with a context menu display a small black rectangle in the lower-right corner.

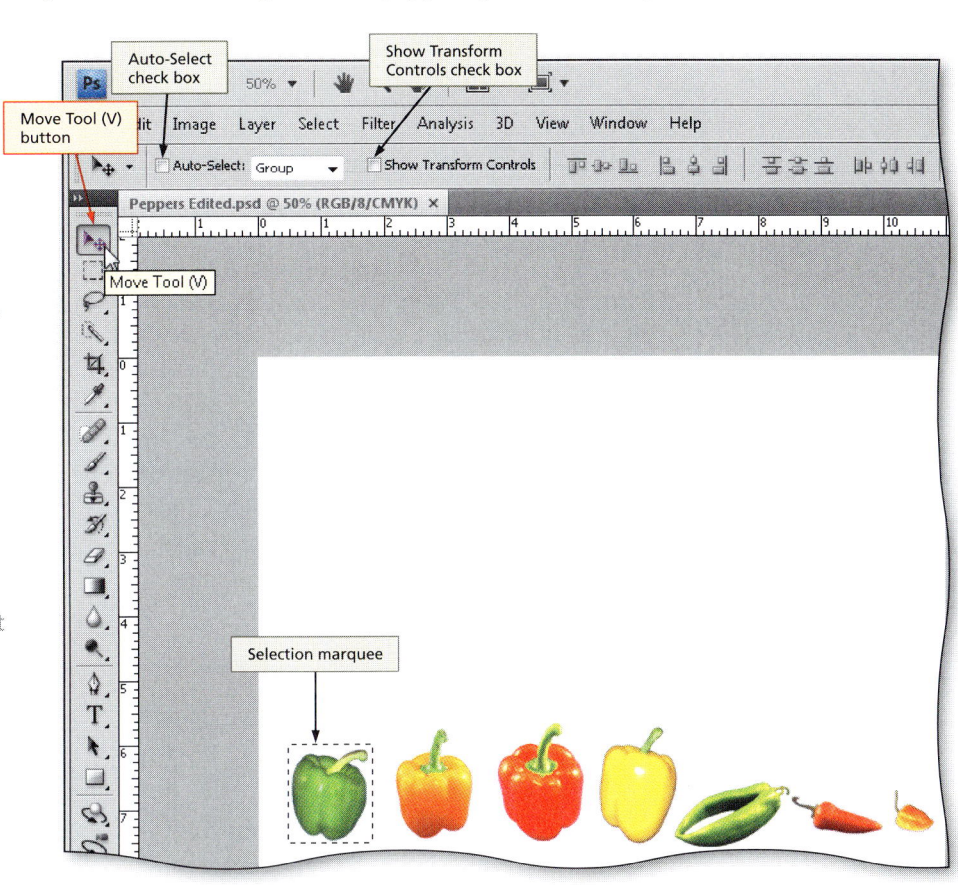

Figure 2–11

2

- Drag the selection to a position above the red and yellow bell peppers, near the top margin and approximately centered (Figure 2–12). Do not press any other keys.

Q&A My document window shows a black square. What did I do wrong?

It is possible that the default colors on your system were changed by another user. Press CTRL+Z to undo the move. Press the D key to select the default foreground and background colors. If black is not on top at the bottom of the Tools panel, press the X key to exchange the black and white colors.

Figure 2–12

Other Ways

1. Press V, drag selection

The Magic Wand Tool

The **Magic Wand tool** lets you select a consistently colored area with a single click. For example, if you wanted to select the blue sky in an image, clicking with the Magic Wand tool would automatically select it, no matter what the shape of the blue area. To use the Magic Wand tool, you click the Magic Wand Tool (W) button on the Tools panel or press SHIFT+W on the keyboard. When you use the Magic Wand tool and click in the image, Photoshop selects every pixel that contains the same or similar colors as the location you clicked. The default setting is to select contiguous pixels only; but Photoshop allows you to change that setting to select all pixels of the same color. The Magic Wand tool mouse pointer appears as a small line with a starburst, or magic wand, on the end.

The Magic Wand tool options bar (Figure 2–13) contains the same selection adjustment buttons as the marquee tools, including the ability to create a new selection, add to or subtract from a selection, and intersect selections. The Magic Wand tool options bar also has a Tolerance box that allows you to enter a value that determines the similarity or difference in the color of the selected pixels. A low value selects the few colors very similar to the pixel you click. A higher value selects a broader range of colors. As with the marquee tools, the Anti-alias check box smooths the jagged edges of a selection by softening the color transition between edge pixels and background pixels. While anti-aliasing is useful when cutting, copying, and pasting selections to create composite images, it might leave behind a trace shadow when a selection is cut or moved.

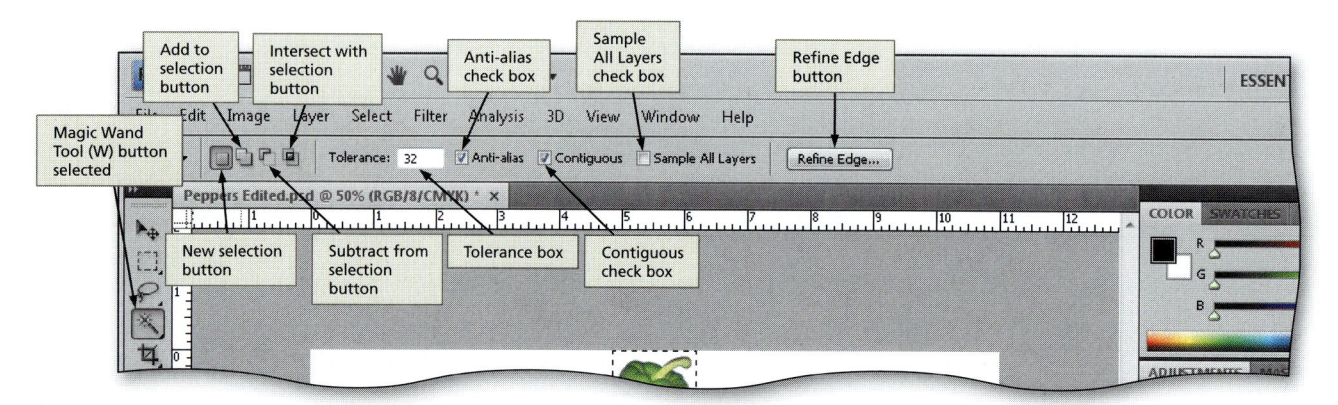

Figure 2–13

When checked, the Contiguous check box selects only adjacent areas using the same colors. Otherwise, all pixels in the entire image that use the same colors are selected. Finally, the Sample All Layers check box selects colors using data from all visible layers. Otherwise, the Magic Wand tool selects colors from the active layer only.

Besides using the options bar, the Magic Wand tool can be used with many shortcut keys. Holding down the SHIFT key while clicking adds to a Magic Wand tool selection. Holding down the ALT key while clicking subtracts from the selection. Holding down the CTRL key while dragging with the Magic Wand tool moves the selection.

To Subtract from a Selection Using the Magic Wand Tool

The following steps use the Magic Wand tool to eliminate the white background in the selection, leaving only the green bell pepper inside the marquee.

1

- With the green bell pepper still selected, right-click the Quick Selection Tool (W) button on the Tools panel to display the context menu (Figure 2–14).

Q&A Could I press the W key to choose the Magic Wand tool?

If the Quick Selection tool is displayed on the Tools panel, you would have to press SHIFT+W. If the Magic Wand tool is displayed on the Tools panel, you can press the W key.

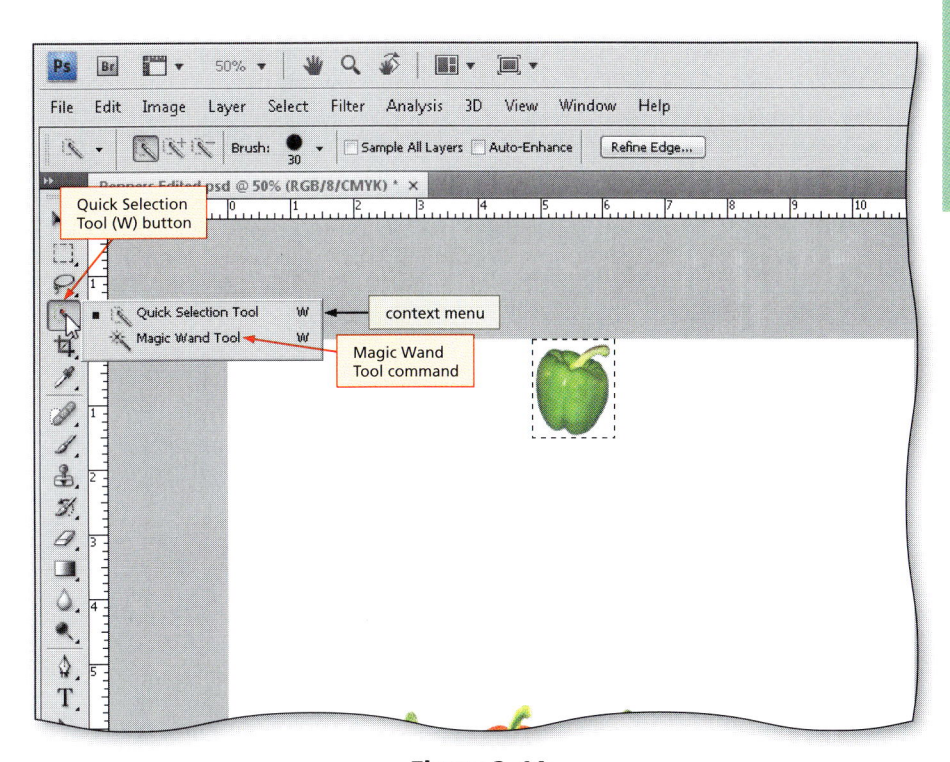

Figure 2–14

2

- Click Magic Wand Tool to select it.

- On the options bar, click the Subtract from selection button. Click the Anti-alias check box so it does not display a check mark. If necessary, click to display a check mark in the Contiguous check box.

- Move the mouse pointer to a location within the selection marquee, positioned over a white area (Figure 2–15).

Q&A What is the minus sign beside the mouse pointer?

The minus sign appears whenever you choose to subtract from a selection. A plus sign would indicate an addition to the selection, and an X indicates an intersection. Photoshop displays these signs so you do not have to glance up at the options bar to see which button is selected while you drag the selection.

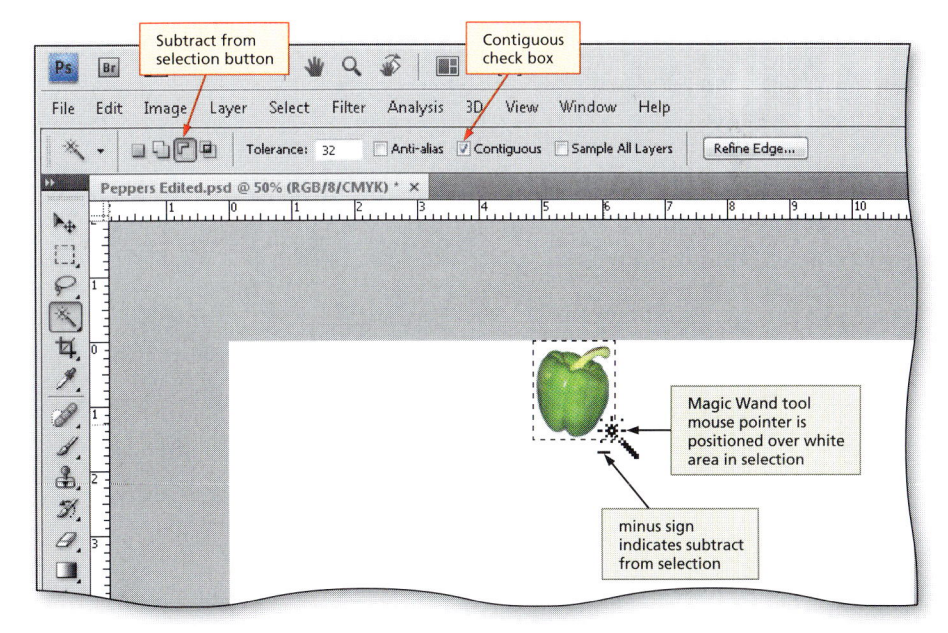

Figure 2–15

3

- Using the tip of the Magic Wand tool mouse pointer, click the white space inside the selection marquee to remove the white color from the selection (Figure 2–16). Do not press any other keys.

Q&A What if I make a mistake and click the wrong color?

You can undo the latest edit by pressing CTRL+Z.

Other Ways

1. To select Magic Wand tool, press W or SHIFT+W until Magic Wand tool is active
2. Select Magic Wand tool, ALT+click selection
3. Select Magic Wand tool, right-click photo, click Subtract From Selection

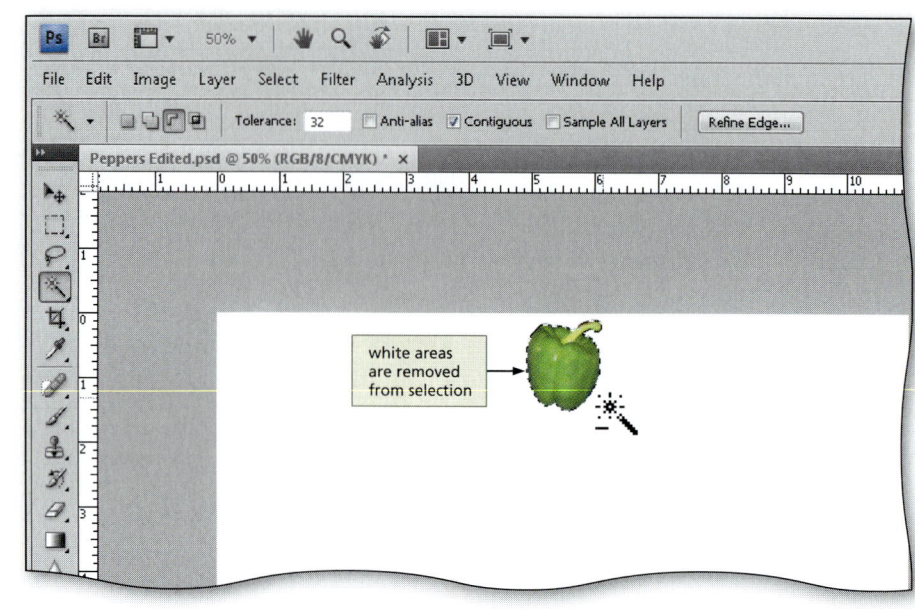

Figure 2–16

To Duplicate the Selection

Recall that pressing and holding the ALT key while dragging with the Move tool creates a copy, or duplicates, the selection. The following step accesses the Move tool and creates a copy of the selected green bell pepper.

1

- On the Tools panel, click the Move Tool (V) button to select the Move tool.
- Press and hold the ALT key while dragging the selection to a location slightly down and left of the original, as shown in Figure 2–17. The copy will overlap the original.

Other Ways

1. Press CTRL+C, press CTRL+V, press V, drag selection
2. Press V, ALT+drag selection
3. Select Magic Wand tool, CTRL+drag selection

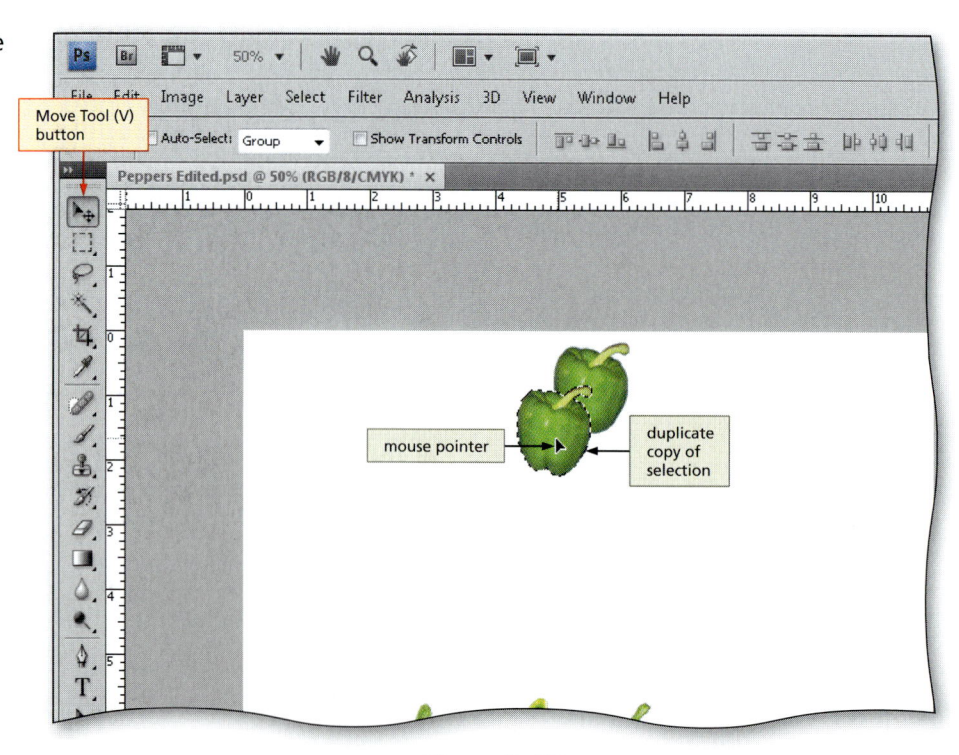

Figure 2–17

> **Plan Ahead**
>
> **Plan your duplications.**
> Creating a storyboard, either by hand or by using software, allows you to plan your image and make decisions about copies and placement. Some graphic artists annotate each copy in the storyboard with information about size, shape, location, and the tool they plan to use (Figure 2–2 on page PS 80). For example, when you paste or drag a new copy of an image into a photo, you have two choices. You can keep the copy as an exact duplicate, or you can transform the copy. The choice depends on the visual effect you want to achieve and the customer requirements. Notating those requirements on your storyboard ahead of time will facilitate creating your image.
>
> An exact copy might be used for duplication of a logo or a border; or you might want to create a tiled background. In commercial applications, duplication might be used to represent growth; or several copies might be placed beside each other in the same photo to emphasize a brand. Sometimes artists will duplicate an item several times when creating a quick sketch or a rough draft. Across photos, exact duplicates maintain consistency and product identification.
>
> Transforming a copy or section provides additional flexibility and diversity. You might want to create the illusion of multiple, different items to promote sales. Scaling, skewing, warping, and distorting provide interest and differentiation, and sometimes can correct lens errors. Flipping, rotating, or changing the perspective of the copy avoids unexciting reproductions and creates the illusion of three dimensions.

The Transformation Commands

In Photoshop, the word **transform** refers to making physical changes to a selection. To choose a transformation command, click the Edit menu, point to Transform, and then click the desired transformation. Alternatively, you can click Transform Selection on the context menu that is displayed when you right-click a selection.

When you choose to transform, or when you click the Show Transform Controls check box on the Move tool options bar, Photoshop displays a **bounding box**, or border with six sizing handles around the selection (Figure 2–18). A small **reference point**, a fixed pivot point around which transformations are performed, is displayed in the center of the selection as a small circle with a crosshair symbol. Reference points can be moved by dragging.

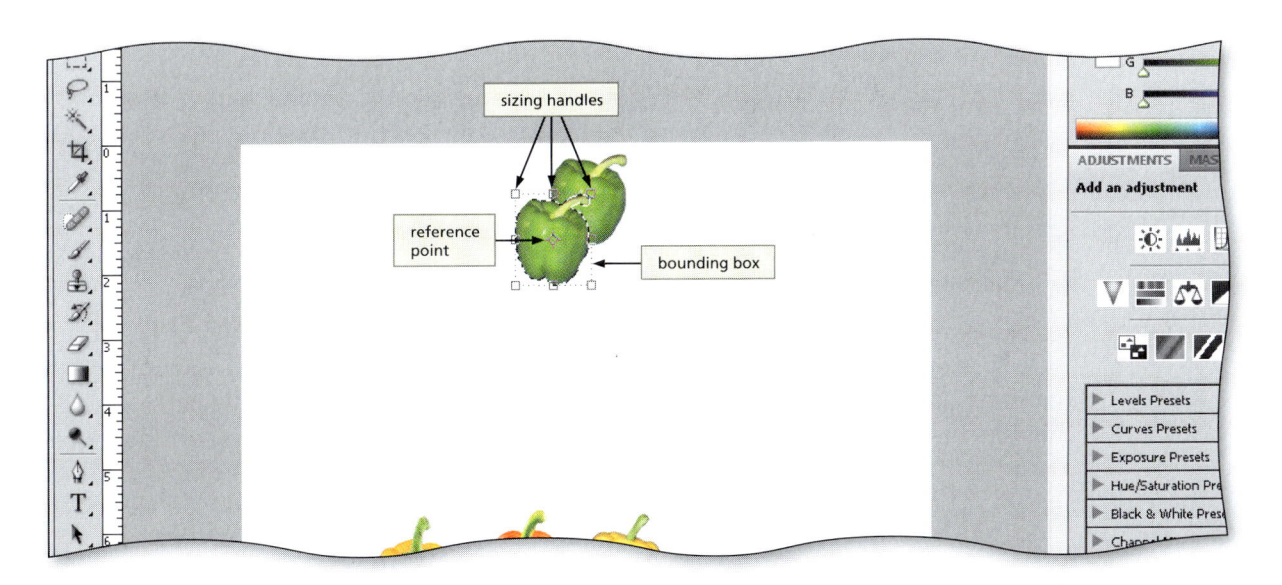

Figure 2–18

Table 2–2 lists the types of transformations you can perform on a selection, the techniques used to perform a particular transformation, and the result of the transformation. Many of the commands also are on the context menu when you right-click the bounding box. If you choose **free transform**, you must use the mouse techniques to perform the transformation.

Table 2–2 Transformation Commands			
Using the Menu	**Using the Mouse (Free Transform)**	**Using the Transform Options Bar**	**Result**
Scale	Drag a sizing handle on the bounding box. SHIFT+drag to scale proportionately. ALT+drag to scale opposite sides at the same time.	To scale numerically, enter percentages in the Width and Height boxes, shown as W and H, on the options bar. Click the Link icon to maintain the aspect ratio.	Selection is displayed at a different size.
Rotate Rotate 180° Rotate 90° CW Rotate 90° CCW (CW stands for clockwise. CCW stands for counterclockwise.)	Move the mouse pointer outside the bounding box border. It becomes a curved, two-headed arrow. Drag in the direction you wish to rotate. SHIFT+drag to constrain the rotation to 15° increments.	In the Set Rotation box, shown as a compass on the options bar, type a positive number for clockwise rotation or a negative number for counterclockwise rotation.	Selection is rotated or revolved around the reference point.
Skew	Right-click selection and then click Skew. Drag a side of the bounding box. ALT+drag to skew both vertically and horizontally.	To skew numerically, enter decimal values in the horizontal skew and vertical skew boxes, shown as H and V on the options bar.	Selection is tilted or slanted either horizontally or vertically.
Distort	Right-click selection and then click Distort. Drag a corner sizing handle to stretch the bounding box.	Enter new numbers in the location, size, rotation, and skew boxes.	Selection is larger on one edge than on the others.
Perspective	Right-click selection and then click Perspective. Drag a corner sizing handle to apply perspective to the bounding box.	Enter new numbers in the size, rotation, and skew boxes.	The selection appears larger on one edge than on the others, giving the larger edge the appearance of being closer to the viewer.
Warp	When the warp mesh is displayed, drag any line or point.	Click the Custom box arrow. Click a custom warp.	Selection is reshaped with bulge, arch, warped corner, or twist.
Flip Horizontal Flip Vertical	Flipping is available only on the menu.	Flipping is available only on the menu.	Selection is turned upside down or mirrored.

To display the Transform options bar, create a selection and then choose Free Transform on the Edit menu, click a sizing handle, or press CTRL+T. Photoshop displays a Transform options bar that contains boxes and buttons to help you with your transformation (Figure 2–19).

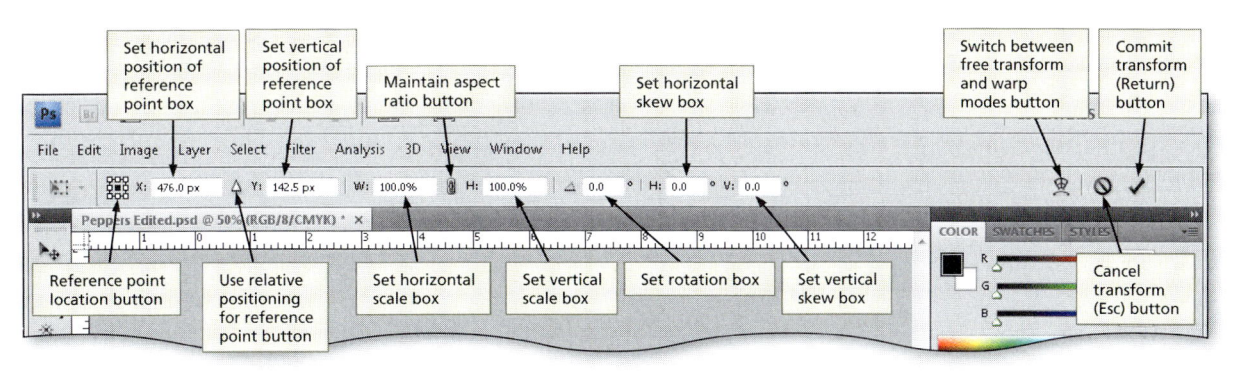

Figure 2–19

On the left side of the Transform options bar, Photoshop displays the Reference point location button. Each of the nine squares on the button corresponds to a point on the bounding box. Transformations applied to the selection are made in relation to the selected reference point. The middle square is selected by default. To select a different reference point, click a different square on the Reference point location button.

The X and Y boxes allow you to place the reference point at an exact pixel location in the document window by entering horizontal and vertical values. When you enter a value in one of those boxes, the entire selection is moved. If you click the Use relative positioning for reference point button, located between the X and Y boxes, the movement of the selection is relative to the current location.

The W and H boxes allow you to scale the width and height of the selection. When you click the Maintain aspect ratio button between the W and H boxes, the aspect ratio of the selection is maintained.

To the right of the scale boxes is a Set rotation box. Entering a positive number **rotates**, or turns, the selection clockwise; a negative number rotates the selection counter-clockwise.

The H and V boxes, to the right of the Set rotation box, set the horizontal and vertical skews of the selection, measured in degrees. A positive number skews the selection to the right; a negative number skews to the left.

A unique feature is the ability to drag labels to change the box values. For example, if you drag the H, Y, W, or other labels, the values in the text boxes change. The labels are called **scrubby sliders** and are hidden until you position the mouse pointer over the label. When you point to any of the scrubby sliders on the Transform options bar, the mouse pointer changes to a hand with a double-headed arrow, indicating the ability to drag. Dragging to the right increases the value; dragging to the left decreases the value. Holding down the SHIFT key while dragging the scrubby slider accelerates the change by a factor of 10. Many options bars also use scrubby sliders.

On the far right of the Transform options bar are three buttons. The first one switches between the Transform options bar and the Warp options bar. After you are finished making transformations, you **commit** changes, or apply the transformations by pressing the ENTER key or by clicking the Commit transform (Return) button. Committing the transformation is the same as saving it. If you do not wish to make the transformation, press the ESC key or click the Cancel transform (Esc) button.

After transforming a selection, you must either commit or cancel the transformation before you can perform any other action in Photoshop.

BTW | **Resizing**
Photoshop allows you to apply some transformations to entire images or photos, rather than just selections. For example, you can change the size of the photo or rotate the image using the Image menu. You then can enter dimensions or rotation percentages on the submenu and subsequent dialog boxes.

To Scale a Selection

As described in Table 2–2, when you **scale** a selection, you resize it by changing its width, height, or both. The following steps use the Show Transform Controls check box to display the bounding box. Then, to enlarge the size of the pepper proportionally, the steps transform freely by SHIFT+dragging a corner sizing handle.

1
- With the Move Tool (V) button still selected, click the Show Transform Controls check box on the options bar to display the bounding box.
- Point to the lower-left sizing handle of the selection border to display the mouse pointer as a two-headed arrow (Figure 2–20).

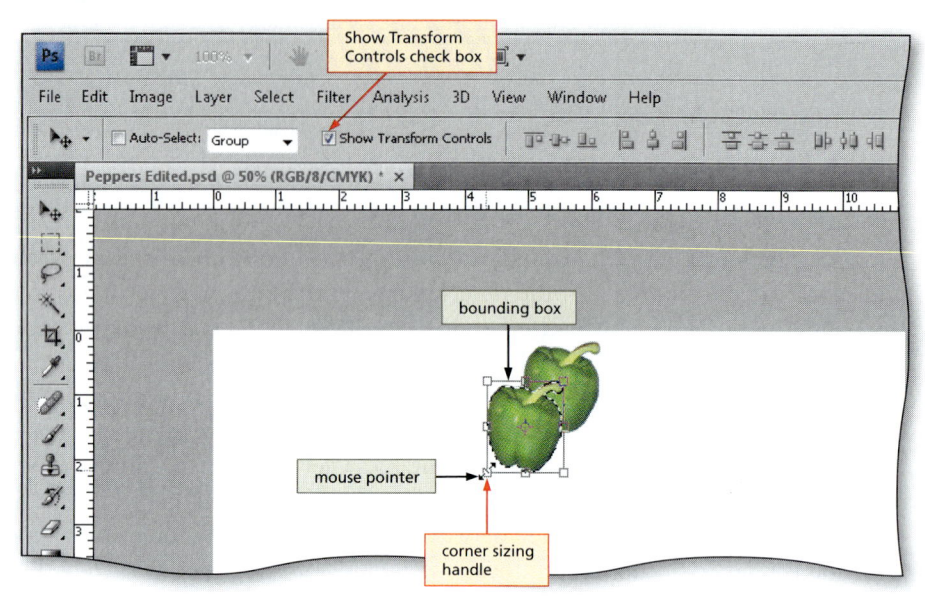

Figure 2–20

2
- SHIFT+drag the lower-left sizing handle away from the center of the pepper until it is resized approximately 10 percent larger than the original (Figure 2–21).

Q&A How can I estimate a 10 percent enlargement in size?

The values in the W: and H: boxes on the options bar change as you scale the image. You can drag until they display approximately 110%.

3
- Press the ENTER key to commit the change. Do not press any other keys.

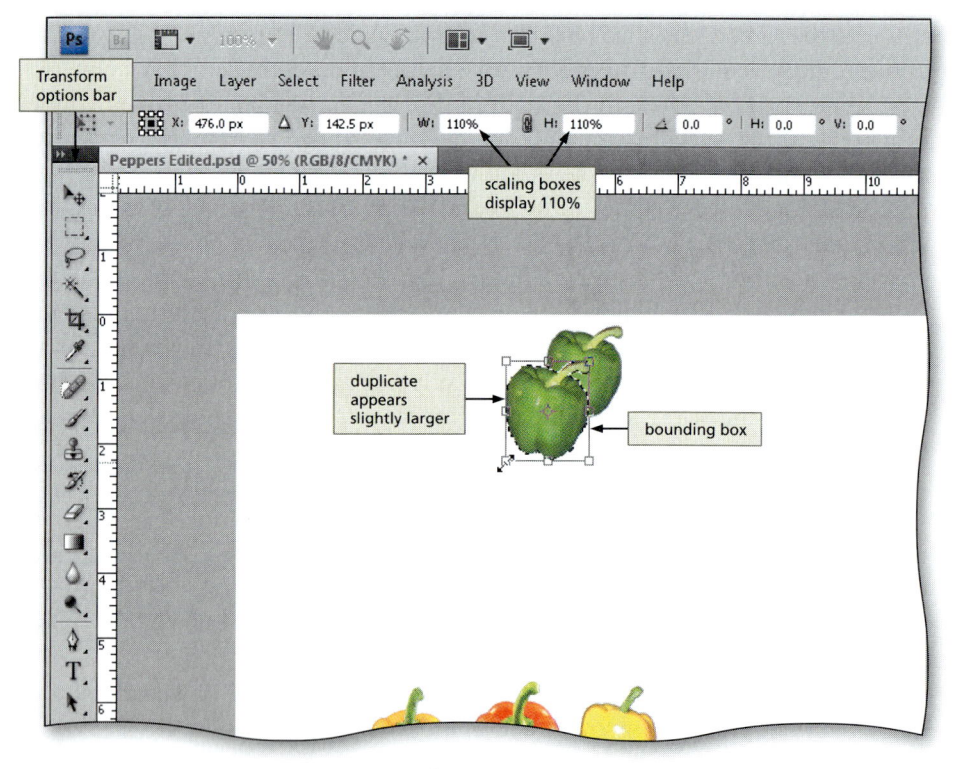

Figure 2–21

Other Ways

1. On Transform options bar, enter new width and height, press ENTER
2. Press CTRL+T, right-click selection, click Scale, drag selection handle
3. On Edit menu point to Transform, click Scale, drag selection handle

The Transformation Commands **PS 99**

To Flip a Selection

Another way to add variety to a duplication of an image is to rotate or flip it. As described in Table 2–2 on page PS 96, when you **flip** a selection, Photoshop creates a mirror image with a horizontal flip, or an upside-down version of the selection with a vertical flip. Flipping is available on the Edit menu and its Transform submenu or on the context menu when you right-click. Flip transformations do not have to be committed.

The following steps flip the selection horizontally.

1
- With the green bell pepper still selected, click Edit on the menu bar and then point to Transform to display the Transform submenu (Figure 2–22).

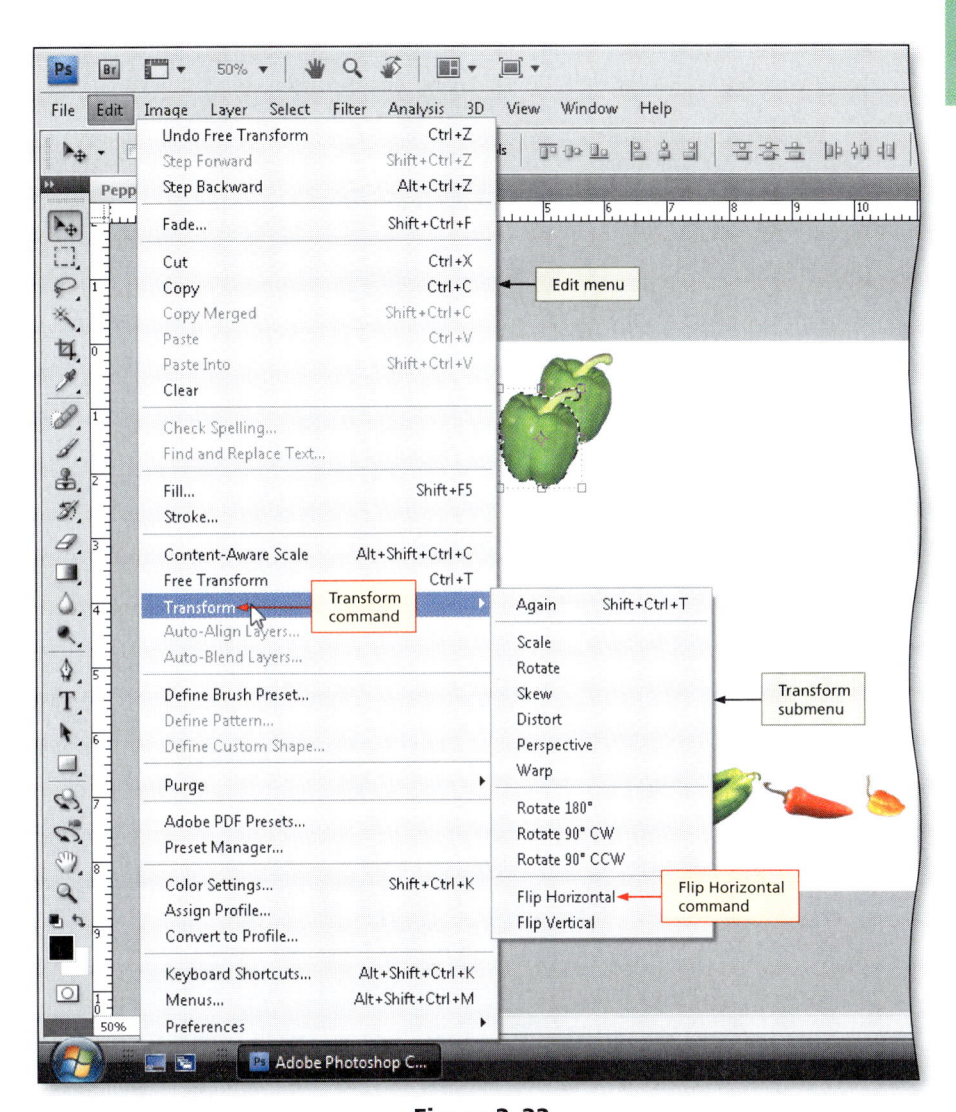

Figure 2–22

2
- Click Flip Horizontal to flip the selection horizontally (Figure 2–23).

Q&A | What if I make a mistake and flip or rotate the wrong way?

You can undo the latest edit by pressing CTRL+Z.

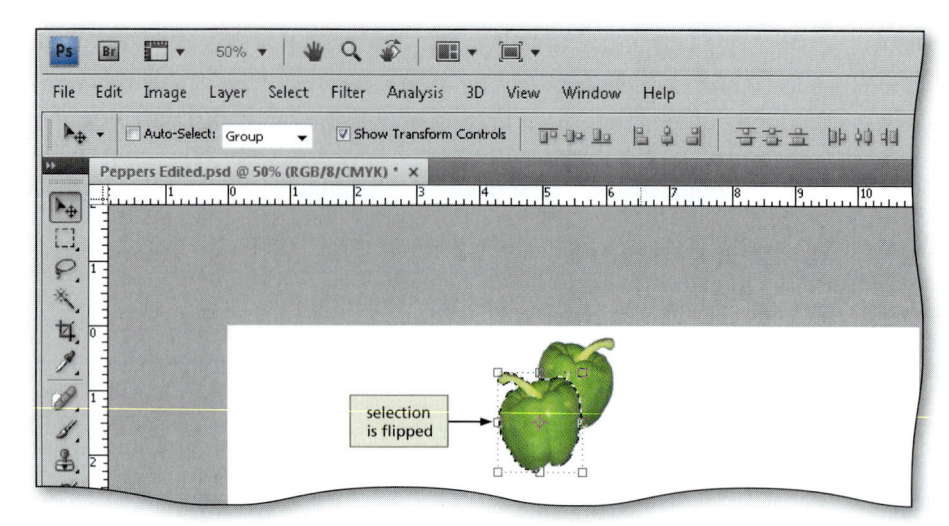

Figure 2–23

Other Ways
1. Right-click selection, click desired flip command

To Duplicate and Resize a Selection

The following steps create another copy of the selected green bell pepper.

1 Click the Move Tool (V) button on the Tools panel.

2 ALT+drag the selection to a location slightly down and left of the previous copy. The copy will overlap the previous copy.

3 SHIFT+drag the lower-left sizing handle of the selection to scale or enlarge the copy to approximately 110% of the previous copy (Figure 2–24).

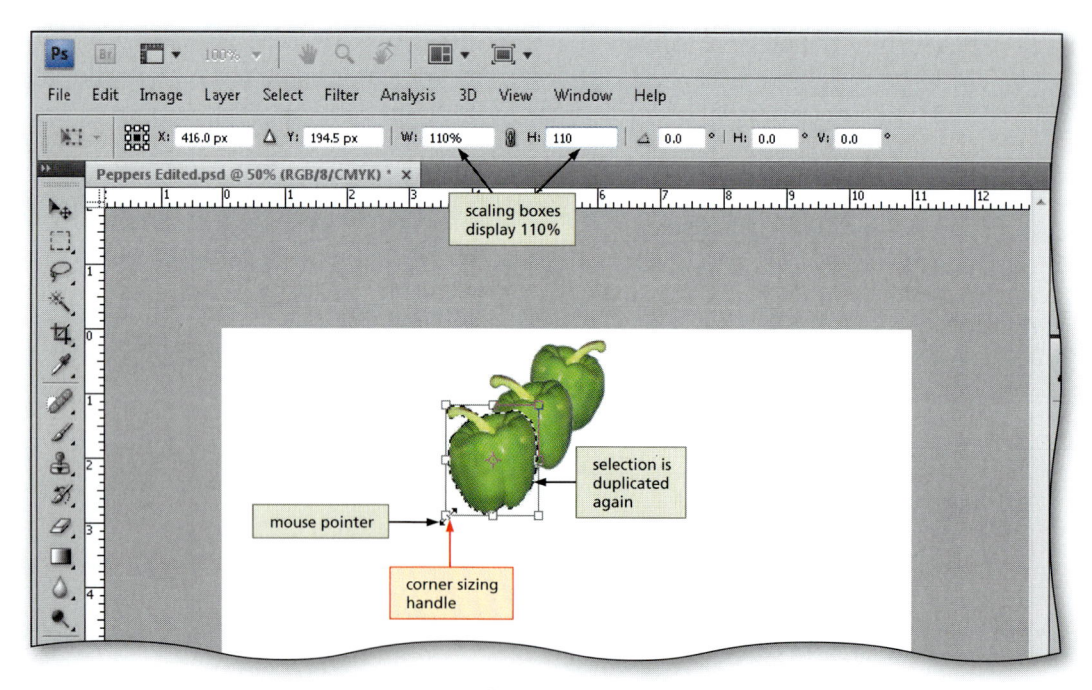

Figure 2–24

Warping

When you **warp**, you turn or twist the selection out of shape. Photoshop displays a grid, or mesh of intersected lines, with extra sizing handles on the border (Figure 2–25). You can drag anywhere in the grid or drag any sizing handle to create a customized warp.

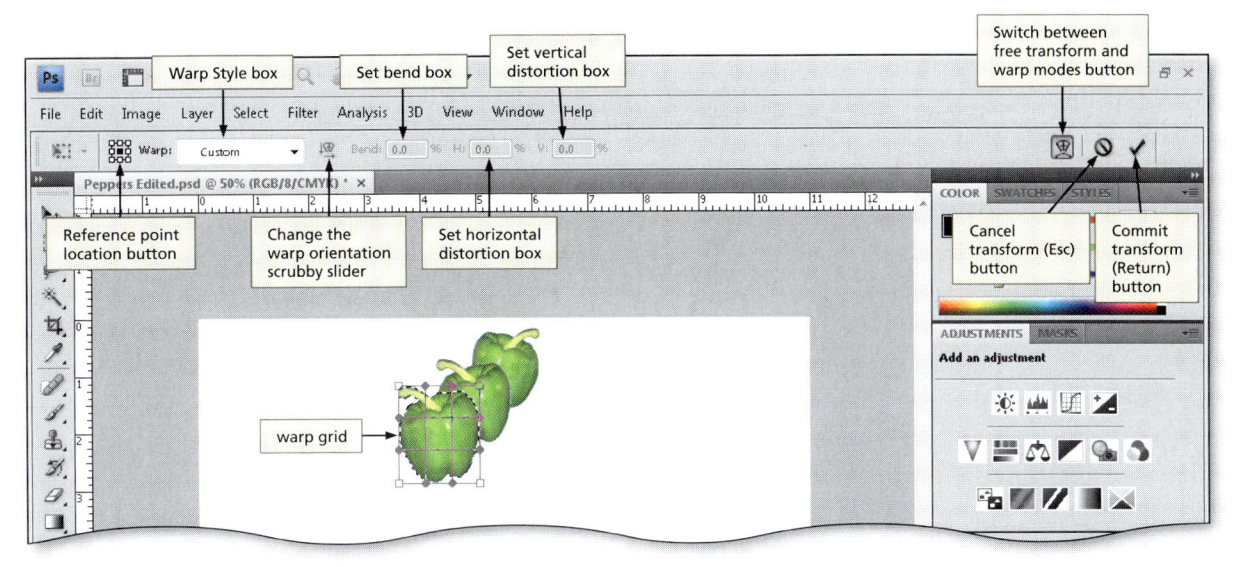

Figure 2–25

On the right side of the Transform options bar is a Switch between free transform and warp modes button. Clicking the button causes Photoshop to display the Warp options bar. You also can access the Warp options bar by clicking Warp on the Edit menu's Transform submenu and on a selection's context menu.

On the left side of the Warp options bar is the Reference point location button, which works the same way as it does on the Transform options bar, applying the warp in relation to the selected reference point. The Warp Style box arrow displays a list of standard shapes, including arc, wave, shell, and flag. The warp styles are malleable by using the other buttons on the options bar, including the ability to change the orientation of the warp, adjust the amount of bend in the warp, and set the horizontal and vertical skews.

To Warp a Selection

The following steps warp the selection to change it slightly, creating a unique copy.

1
- On the Transform options bar, click the Switch between free transform and warp modes button to display the Warp options bar and the warp grid on the selection (Figure 2–26).

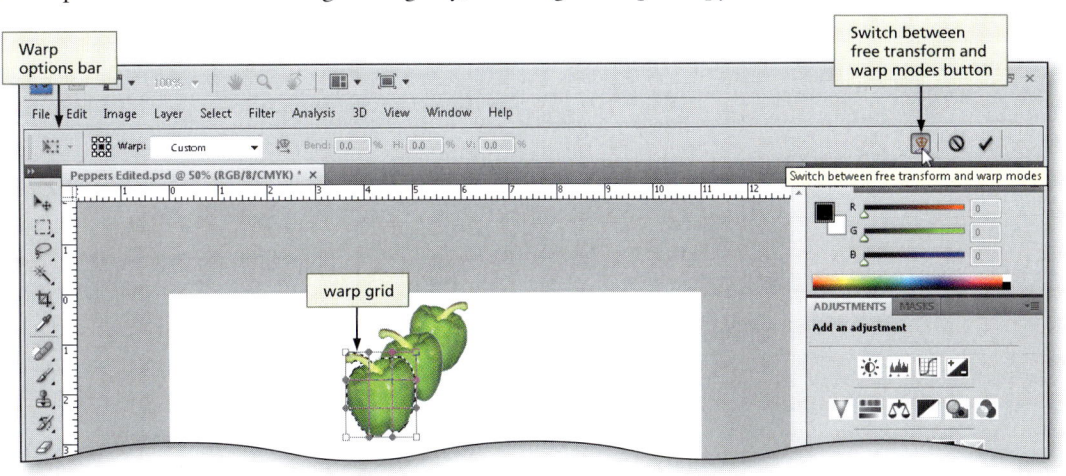

Figure 2–26

2

- In the grid, drag several points to warp the selection (Figure 2–27).

🔍 **Experiment**

- Drag various lines and control points to create different skews and distortions. After each one, press CTRL+Z to undo the warp. Warp the selection so that it looks similar to Figure 2–27.

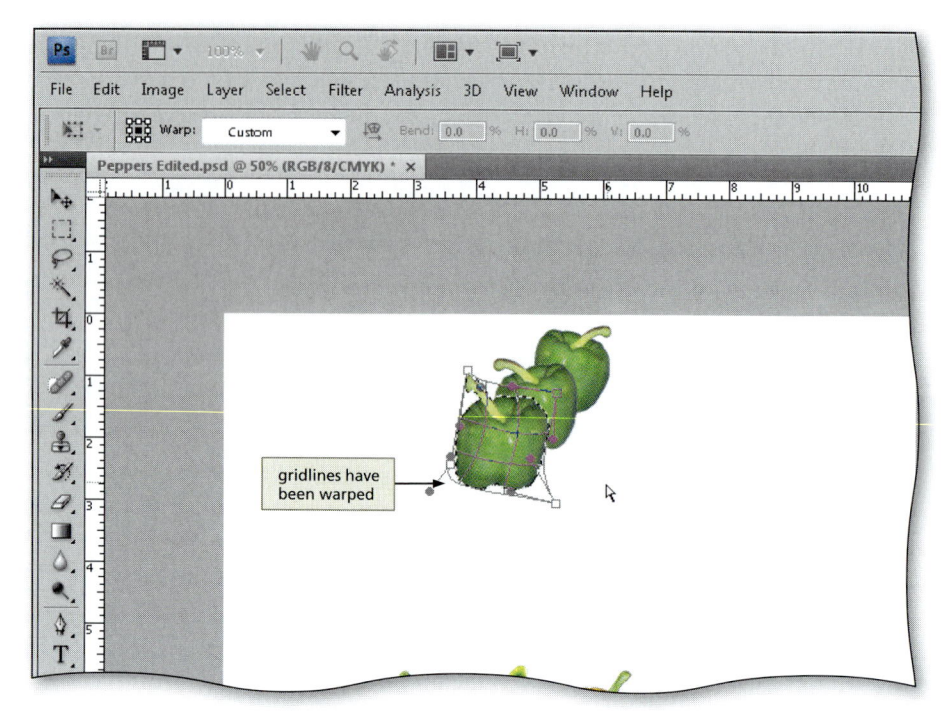

Figure 2–27

3

- Press the ENTER key to commit the transformation (Figure 2–28).

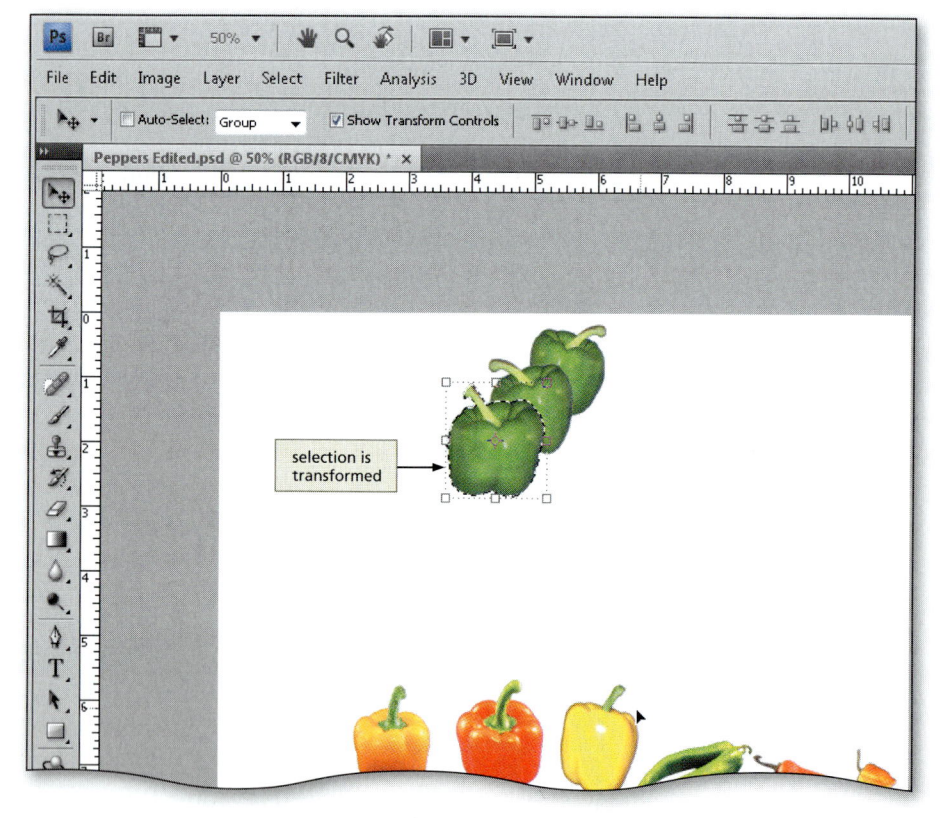

Figure 2–28

Other Ways

1. Press CTRL+T, right-click selection, click Warp, adjust control points

To Deselect Using Shortcut Keys

You are finished with the green bell pepper. The following step deselects the selection.

1. Press CTRL+D to deselect (Figure 2–29).

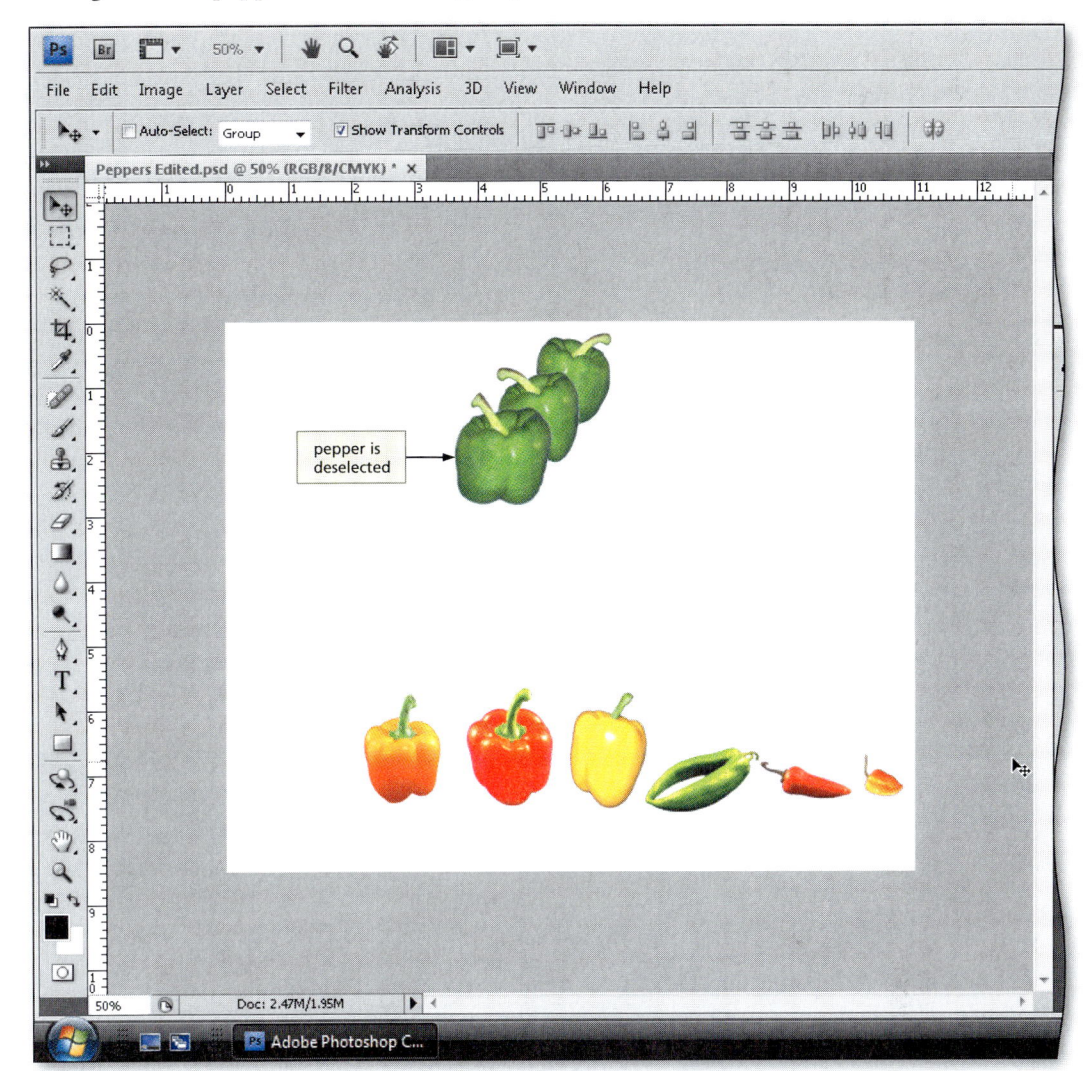

Figure 2–29

The History Panel

The History panel is displayed by clicking History on the Window menu. The History panel records each step, called a **state**, as you edit a photo (Figure 2–30 on the next page). Photoshop displays the initial state of the document at the top of the panel. Each time you apply a change to an image, the new state of that image is added to the bottom of the panel. Each state is listed with the name of the tool or command used to change the image. For example, when you deselected the green bell pepper, the word Deselect was displayed as a step in the history of the file. The step just above Deselect in the History panel denotes the free transformation of the green bell pepper when you warped the selection.

PS 104 Photoshop Chapter 2 Using Selection Tools and Shortcut Keys

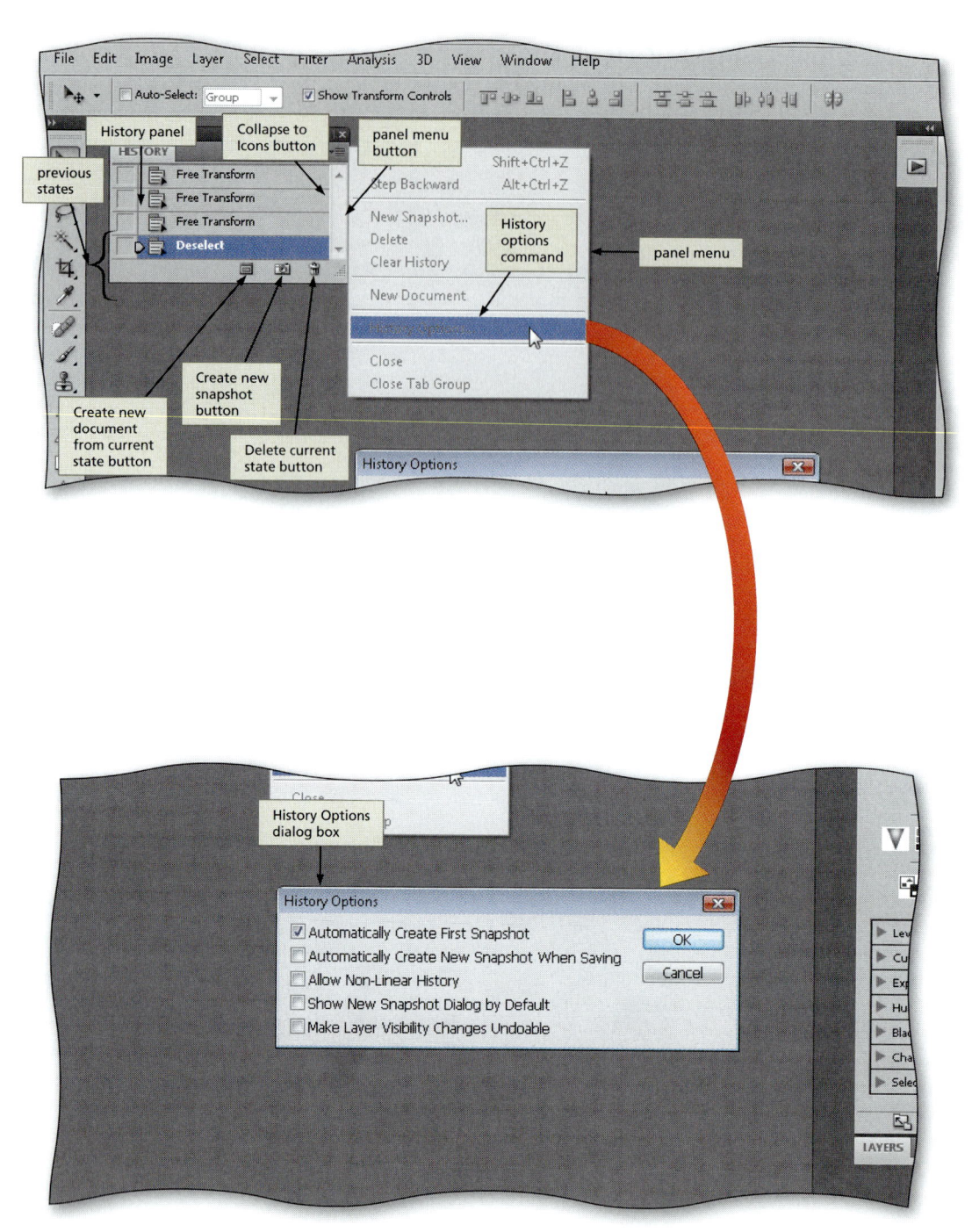

Figure 2–30

When you click History on the Window menu, the History panel appears to the left of the other displayed panels. Like the Navigator panel that you learned about in Chapter 1, the History panel also has a panel menu where you can clear all states, change the history settings, or dock the panel. Buttons on the History panel status bar allow you to create a new document, save the selected state, or delete it. The panel can be collapsed by clicking the History button in the vertical docking or by clicking the Collapse to icons button. To redisplay a collapsed History panel, click the History button in the vertical docking or choose it again from the Window menu.

To Display the History Panel

The following steps display the History panel using the Window menu.

1
- On the menu bar, click Window to display the Window menu (Figure 2–31).

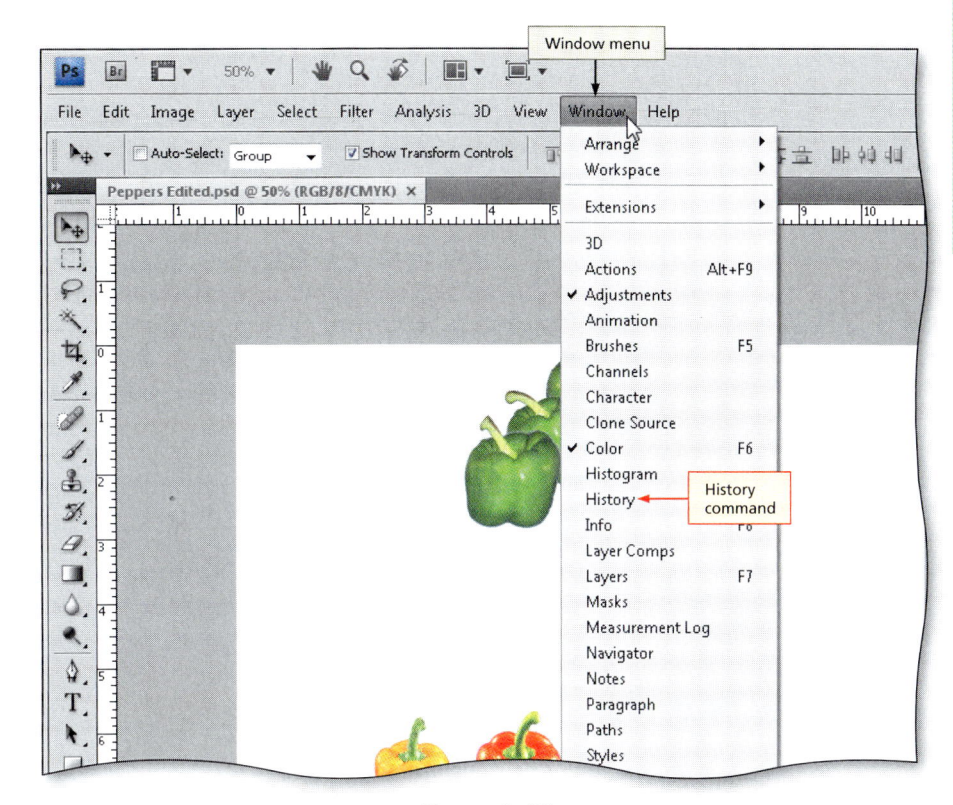

Figure 2–31

2
- Click History to display the History panel (Figure 2–32).

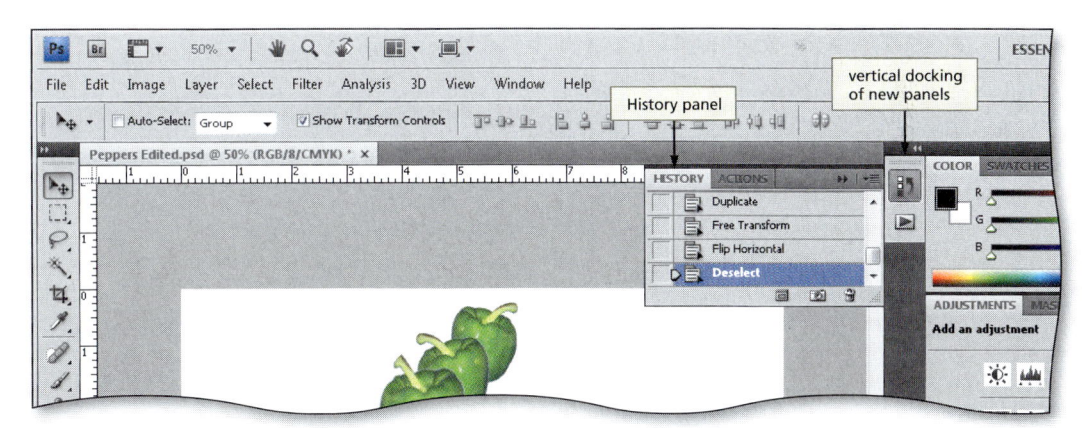

Figure 2–32

Using the History Panel

The History panel is used in several different ways. When you select one of the states, the image reverts to how it looked when that change first was applied. Some users use the History panel to undo mistakes. Others use it to try out or experiment with different edits. By clicking a state, you can view the state temporarily or start working again from that point. You can step forward and backward through the states in the History panel by pressing CTRL+SHIFT+Z or CTRL+ALT+Z respectively.

Selecting a state and then changing the image in any way eliminates all the states in the History panel that came after it; however, if you select a state and change the image by accident, you can use the Undo command or CTRL+Z to restore the eliminated states. If you select the Allow Non-Linear History check box in the History Options dialog box (Figure 2–30 on page PS 104), deleting a state deletes only that state.

You can use the History panel to jump to any recent state of the image created during the current working session by clicking the state. Alternatively, you also can give a state a new name called a **snapshot**. Naming a snapshot makes it easy to identify. Snapshots are stored at the top of the History panel and make it easy to compare effects. For example, you can take a snapshot before and after a series of transformations. Then, by clicking between the two snapshots in the History panel, you can see the total effect, or choose the before snapshot and start over. To create a snapshot, right-click the step and then click New Snapshot on the context menu or click the Create new snapshot button on the History panel status bar. Snapshots are not saved with the image — closing an image deletes its snapshots.

Not all steps are recorded in the History panel. For instance, changes to panels, color settings, actions, and preferences are not reflected in the History panel, because they are not changes to a particular image.

By default, the History panel lists the previous 20 states. You can change the number of remembered states by changing a preference setting (see Appendix C). Older states are deleted automatically to free more memory for Photoshop. Once you close and reopen the document, all states and snapshots from the last working session are cleared from the panel.

To Use the History Panel

The following steps show how to use the History panel to view a previous state.

1
- In the History panel, click the Duplicate state to display the selection before you warped it (Figure 2–33). Do not click anywhere else.

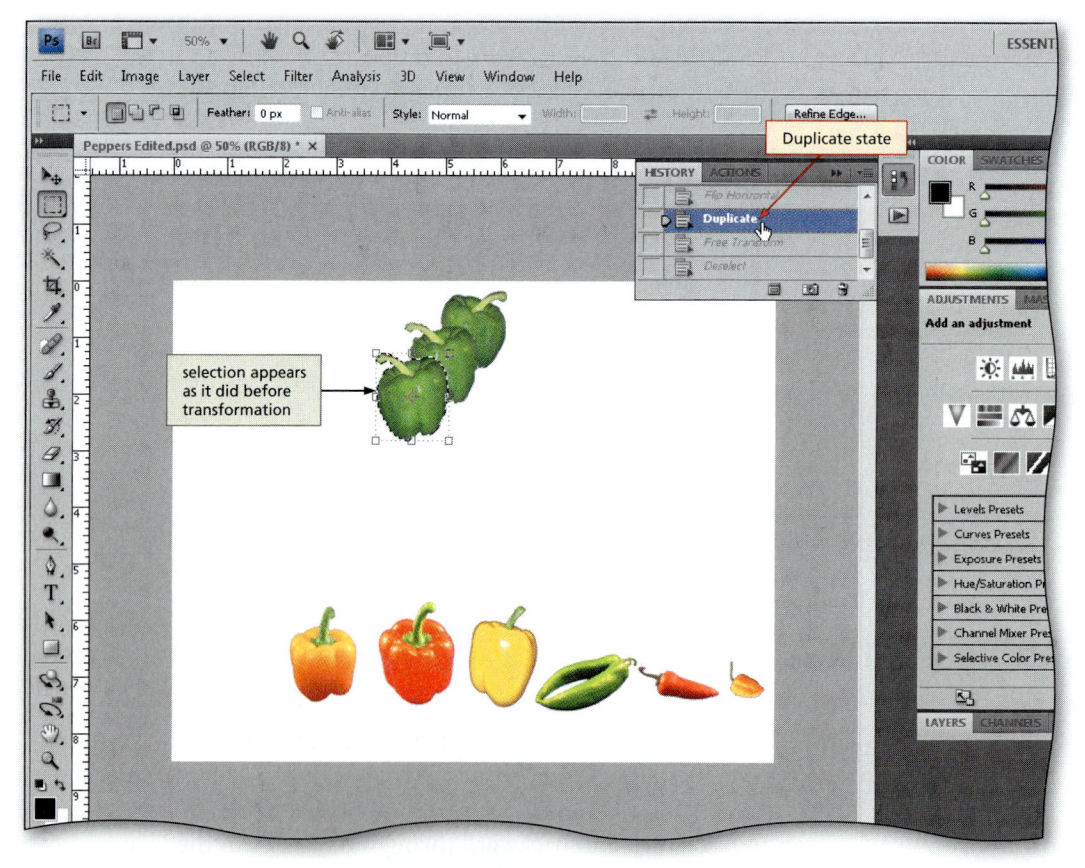

Figure 2–33

2

- In the History panel, click the Deselect state at the bottom of the list to return the image to its most recent state (Figure 2–34).

Other Ways

1. To step forward, press CTRL+SHIFT+Z
2. To step forward, on History panel menu, click Step Forward
3. To step backward, press CTRL+ALT+Z
4. To step backward, on History panel menu, click Step Backward

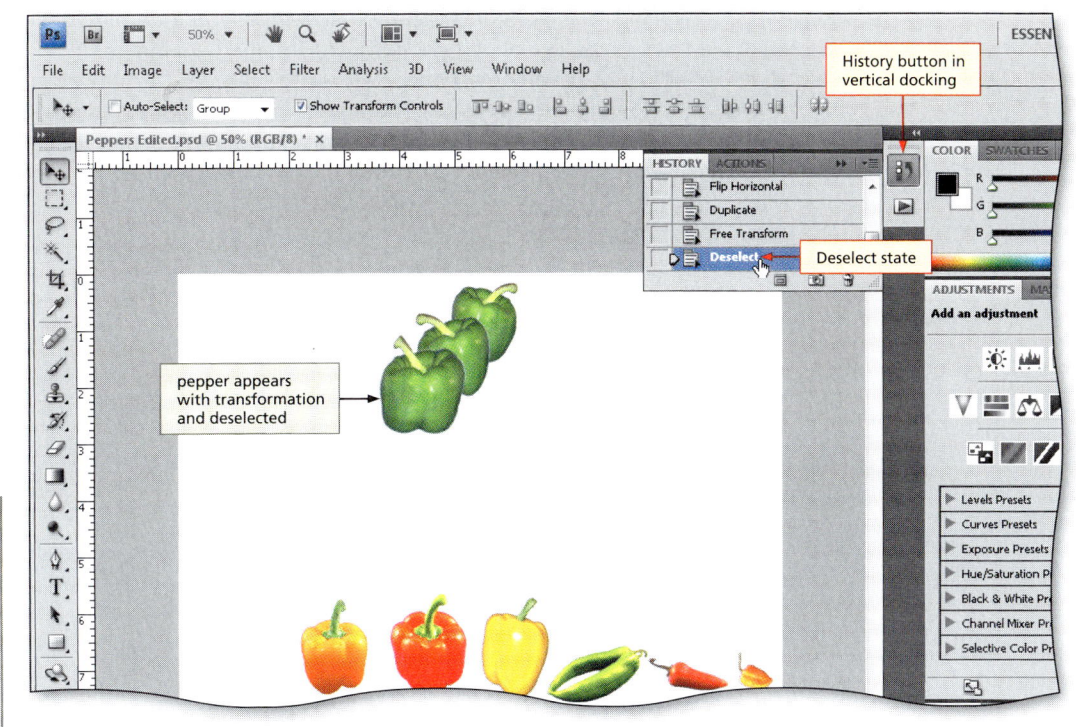

Figure 2–34

To Collapse the History Panel

You can redisplay the History panel whenever you need it; however, the following step collapses the History panel to a button in the vertical docking so you can see more of the document window.

1

- Click the History button to collapse the panel (Figure 2–35).

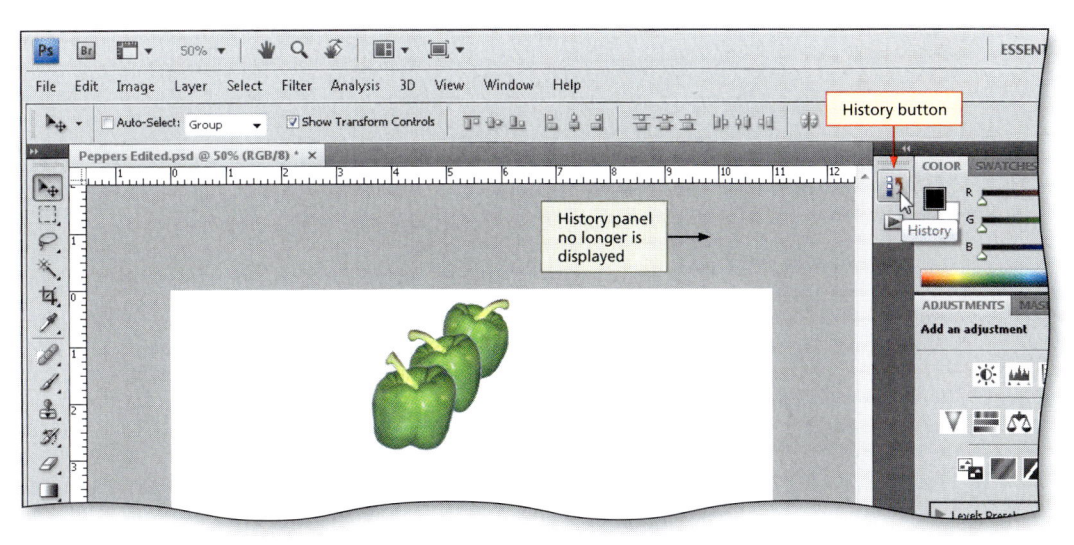

Figure 2–35

Other Ways

1. Click Collapse to Icons button

Plan Ahead

> **Use grids and guides.**
> Showing grids in your document window gives you multiple horizontal and vertical lines with which you can align selections, copies, and new images. Grids also can help you match and adjust sizes and perspective.
>
> Create guides when you have an exact margin, location, or size in mind. Because selections will snap to guides, you easily can create an upper-left corner to use as a boundary when you move and copy. Grids and guides do not print and are turned on and off without difficulty.

Grids and Guides

Photoshop has a **grid** of lines that can be displayed over the top of the image. The grid is useful for laying out elements symmetrically or positioning them precisely. The grid can appear as nonprinting lines or as dots. To display the grid, click the View Extras button on the Application bar and then click Show Grids. Alternately, you can click Show on the View menu and then click Grid.

A **guide** is a nonprinting ruler line or dashed line that graphic designers use to align objects or mark key measurements. Recall that to create a guide, you turn on the ruler display and then drag from the horizontal ruler at the top of the document window or from the vertical ruler at the left side of the document window. When you release the mouse, a light, blue-green line is displayed across the image.

Table 2–3 displays various ways to manipulate guides.

Table 2–3 Manipulating Guides

Action	Steps
Change color and style	Double-click guide.
Clear all guides	On the View menu, click Clear Guides.
Convert between horizontal and vertical guide	Select the Move tool, ALT+click guide.
Create	Drag from ruler into document window; or, on the View menu, click New Guide, and then enter the orientation and position.
Lock in place	On the View menu, click Lock Guides.
Move	Select the Move tool, and then drag the guide to a new location.
Remove	Select the Move tool, and then drag the guide to the ruler.
Snap guide to ruler tick	SHIFT+drag the ruler.
Turn on/off display	On the Application bar, click View Extras, and then click Show Guides; or, on the View menu, point to Show, and then click Guides; or press CTRL+SEMICOLON (;).

The term **snapping** refers to the ability of objects to attach, or automatically align with a grid or guide. For example, if you select an object in your image and begin to move it, as you get close to a guide, the object's selection border will attach itself to the guide. It is not a permanent attachment. If you do not wish to leave the object there, simply keep dragging. To turn on or off snapping, click Snap on the View menu.

In a later chapter, you will learn about smart guides that are displayed automatically when you draw a shape or move a layer. Smart guides further help align shapes, slices, selections, and layers. Appendix C describes how to set guide and grid preferences using the Edit menu.

The next sections illustrate how to display grids and then create both a horizontal and vertical guide.

To Display a Grid

The following steps display the grid.

1
- On the Application bar, click the View Extras button to display its menu (Figure 2–36).

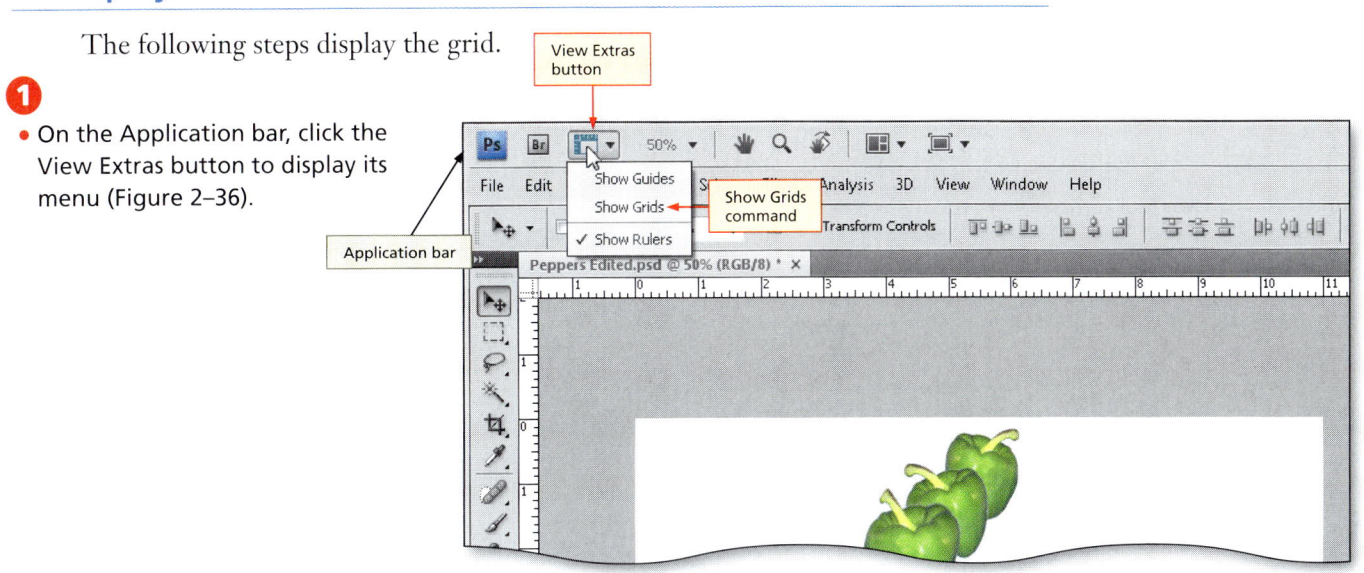

Figure 2–36

2
- If the Show Grids command does not display a check mark, click it to display the grid (Figure 2–37).

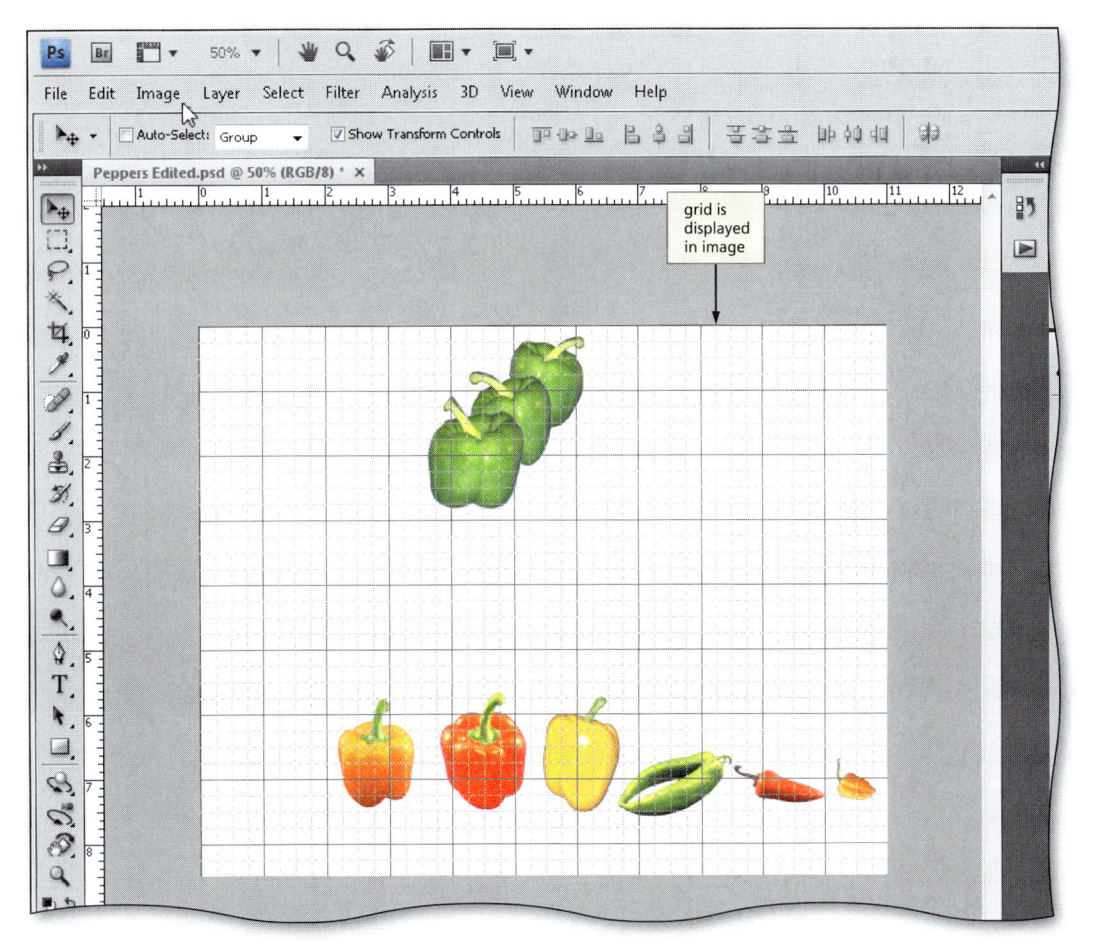

Figure 2–37

Other Ways
1. Press CTRL+APOSTROPHE(')
2. On View menu, point to Show, click Grid

To Turn Off the Grid Display

The display of a grid is a **toggle**, which means that you turn it off in the same manner that you turned it on; in this case, with the same command.

1 On the Application bar, click the View Extras button to display its menu.

2 Click Show Grids to remove the check mark and remove the grid from the display (Figure 2–38).

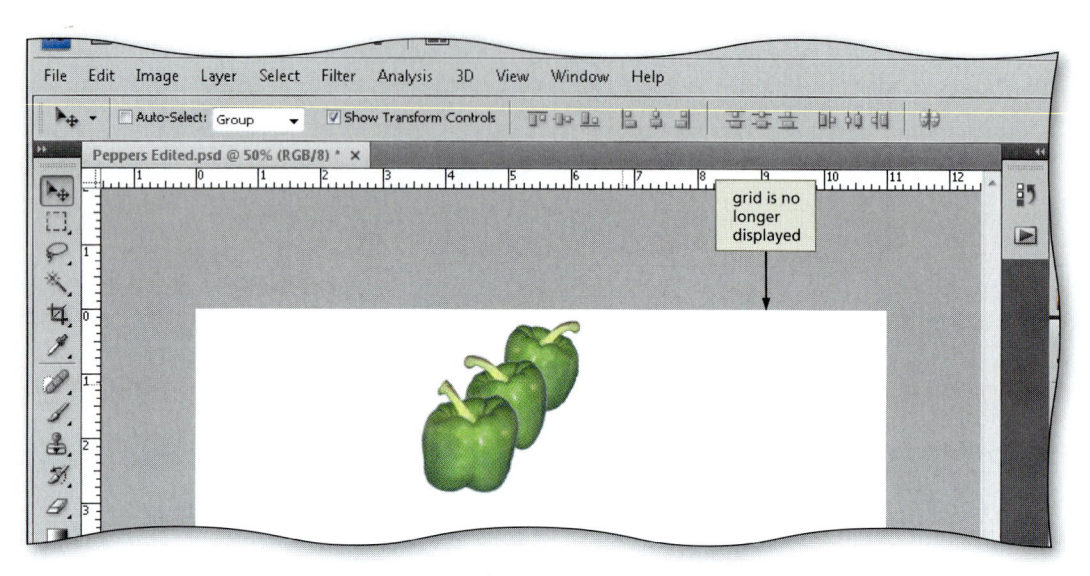

Figure 2–38

To Create Guides

To copy and place the peppers in a way that provides some symmetry in the advertisement, guides will be placed in the image. A horizontal guide will be placed at the top of the second green pepper. Vertical guides will be placed to divide the final advertisement into approximate thirds. When you create a new guide, Photoshop enables the Show Guides command even if it is not on. The following steps create guides.

1
- Click the horizontal ruler at the top of the document window and then drag down into the image until the ruler guide is just below the stem of the second green bell pepper, as shown in Figure 2–39.

- Release the mouse button.

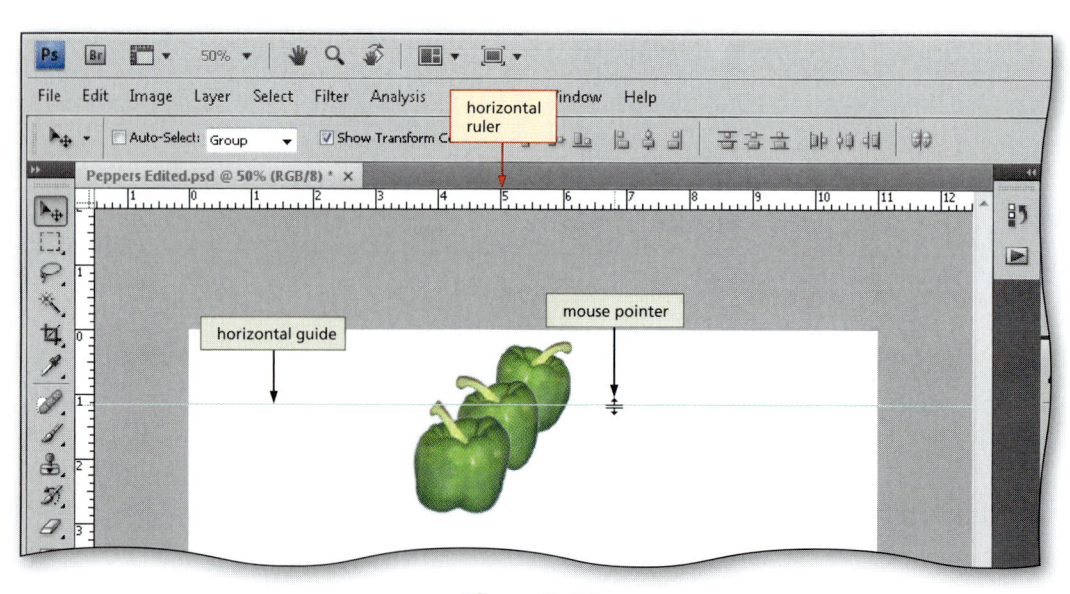

Figure 2–39

Grids and Guides **PS 111**

2
- Click the vertical ruler at the left of the document window and then drag right, into the image, to create a vertical guide even with the bottom of the stem in the second green bell pepper, as shown in Figure 2–40.
- Release the mouse button.

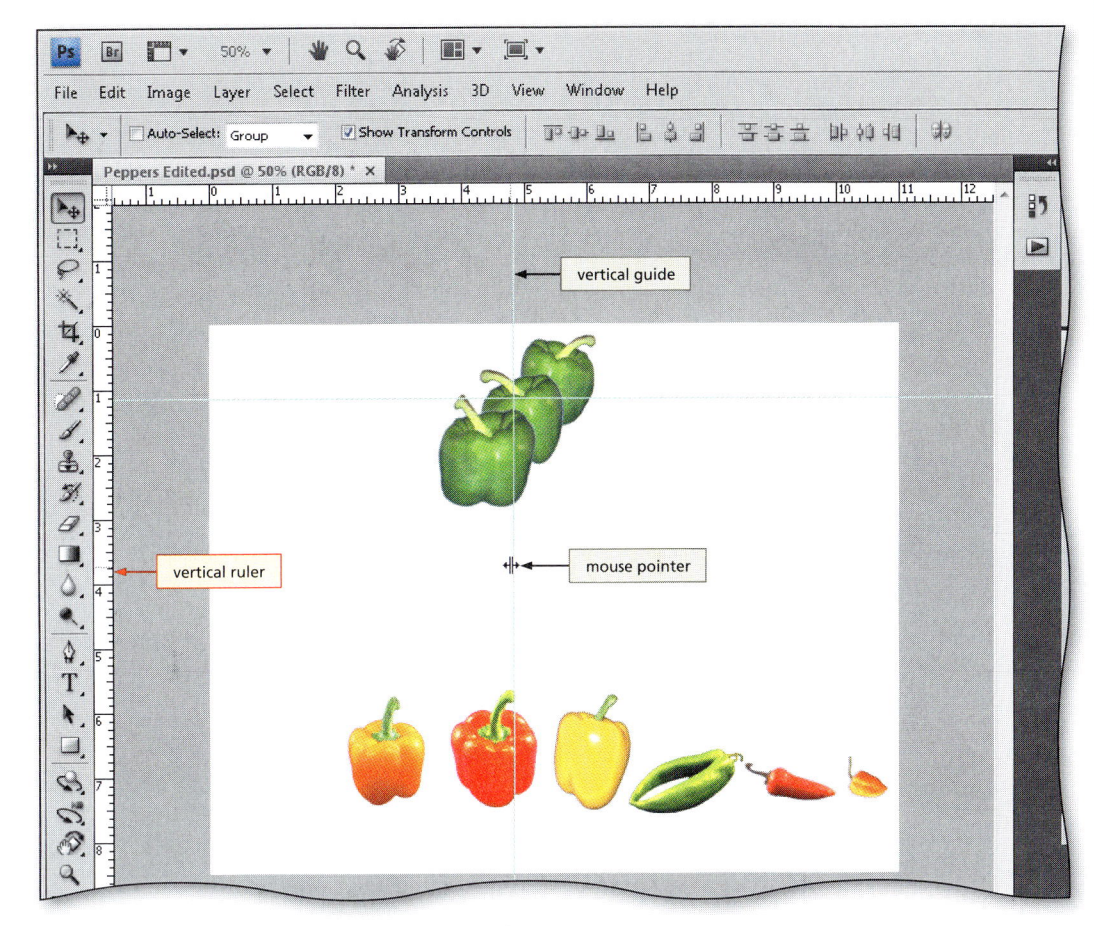

Figure 2–40

3
- Using the same technique, drag another guide from the vertical ruler and release the mouse button at 6.5 inches as measured on the horizontal ruler (Figure 2–41).

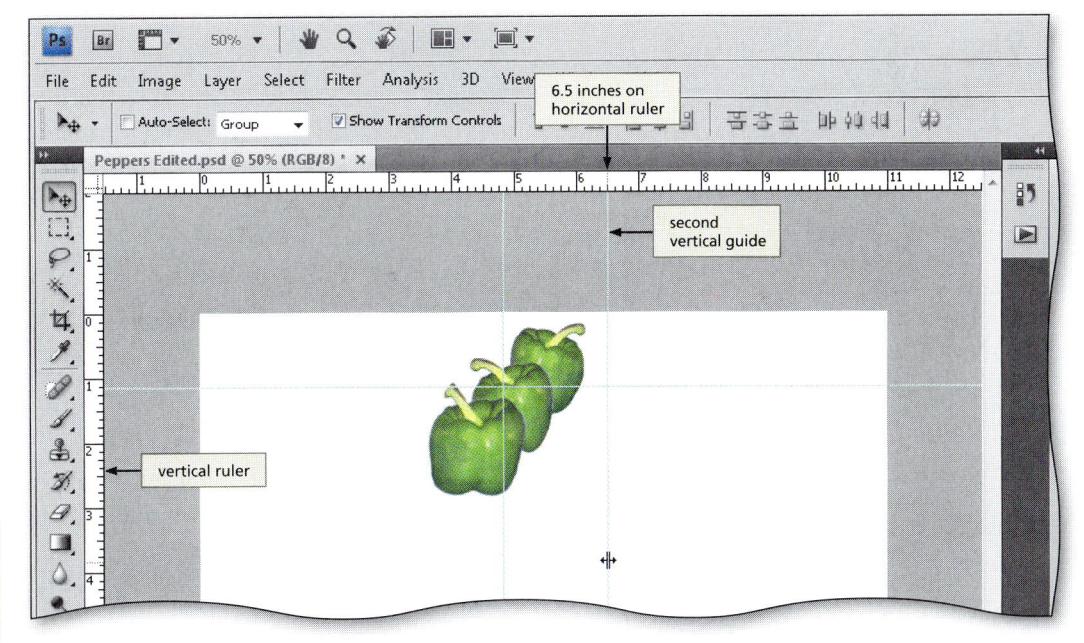

Figure 2–41

Other Ways

1. To show or hide guides, press CTRL+SEMI-COLON (;)
2. To create guide, on View menu click New Guide, enter value, click OK

The Quick Selection Tool

The Quick Selection tool is used to draw a selection quickly using the mouse. As you drag, a selection is created automatically, expanding outward to find and follow the defined edges in the image. Dragging a quick selection is almost like painting a stroke with a brush. The Quick Selection tool does not create a rectangular or oval selection; rather, it looks for a contrast in color and aligns the selection border to that contrast. It is most useful for isolated objects or parts of an image that contain a contrasting background.

The Quick Selection Tool (W) button is nested with the Magic Wand tool on the Tools panel. You can access it from the context menu or by pressing the W key; or if the Magic Wand tool has been used previously, press SHIFT+W. When using the Quick Selection tool, the mouse pointer changes to a brush tip that displays a circle with a centered cross inside. You can decrease or increase the size of the brush tip by using the LEFT BRACKET ([) or RIGHT BRACKET (]) keys respectively, or by using the options bar.

The Quick Selection Tool options bar (Figure 2–42) displays the size of the brush and contains some of the same buttons as other selection tools. It also contains an Auto-Enhance check box that reduces roughness in the selection boundary when the box is checked.

> **BTW**
>
> **Displaying Extras**
> On the View menu is an Extras command with which you can show or hide selection edges, guides, target paths, slices, annotations, layer borders, and smart guides. You also can use CTRL+H to show or hide those items.

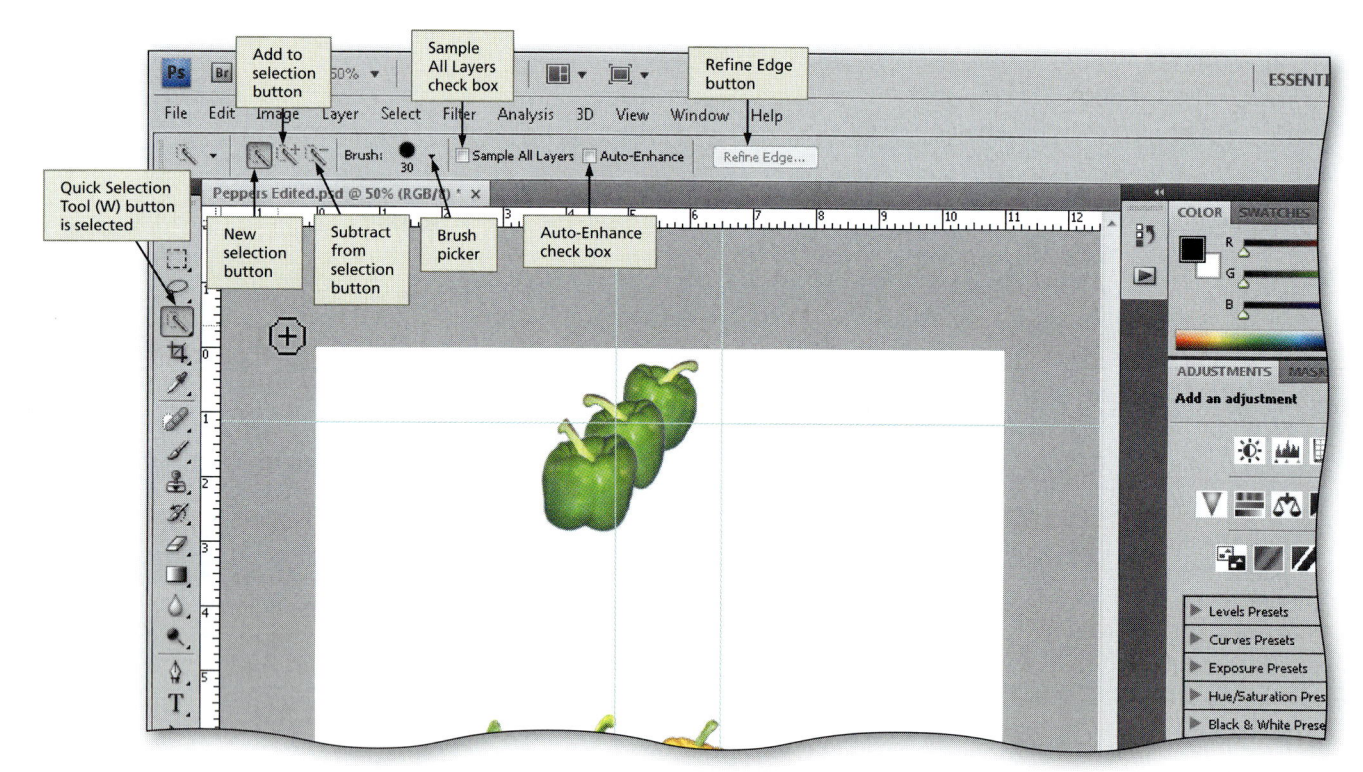

Figure 2–42

You will use the Quick Selection tool to select the orange bell pepper. Then, when moving the pepper leaves a shadow behind, you will undo the move and refine the edges. Finally, you will move the pepper to a location near the others in the advertisement.

As you use the Quick Selection tool, if you make a mistake and want to start over, you can deselect by pressing CTRL+D, and then start again.

> **BTW**
>
> **Guides and Grids**
> You can change the color or style of guides and grids. On the Edit menu, point to Preferences, and then click Guides, Grid, & Slices or Guides, Grid, Slices & Convert.

To Use the Quick Selection Tool

The following steps use the Quick Selection tool to select the orange bell pepper.

1

- Right-click the Magic Wand Tool (W) button on the Tools panel, and then click Quick Selection Tool to select it.

- On the options bar, click the New selection button, if necessary. Click the Auto-Enhance check box so it displays a check mark, if necessary.

- Move the mouse pointer to the location above the stem of the orange bell pepper.

- If necessary, adjust the mouse pointer tip to be approximately the same size as the width of the stem by pressing the [or] key (Figure 2–43).

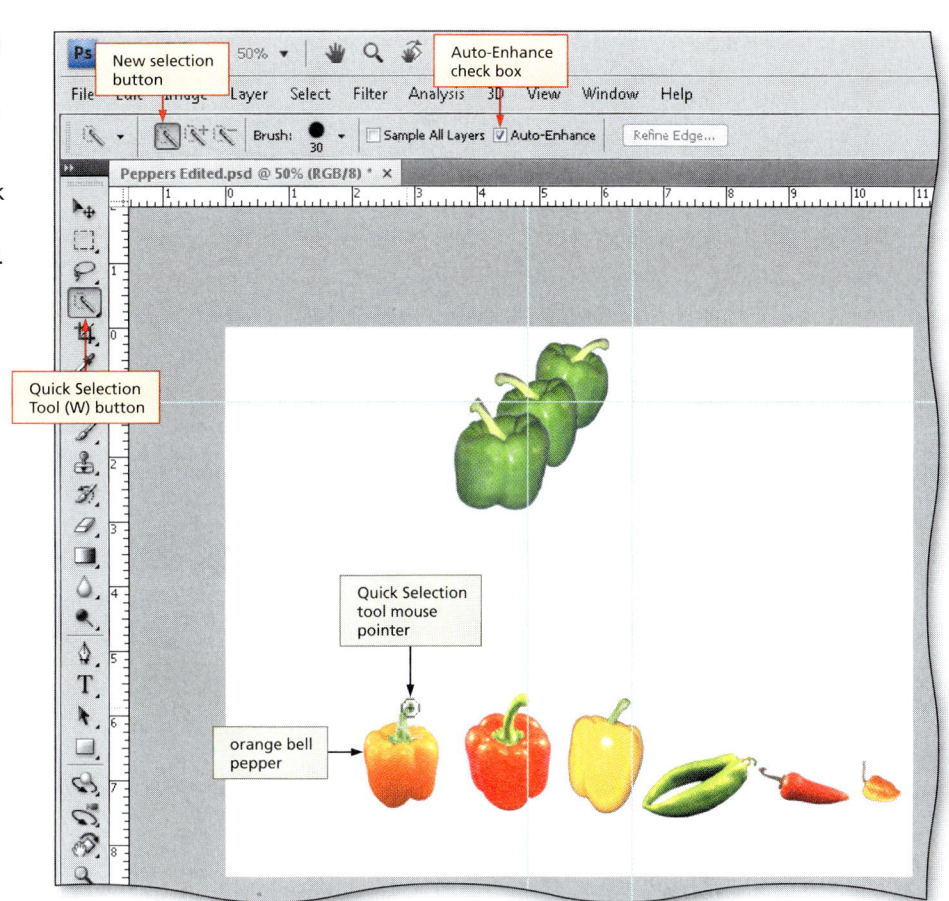

Figure 2–43

2

- Slowly drag down until the selection border is displayed around the pepper (Figure 2–44).

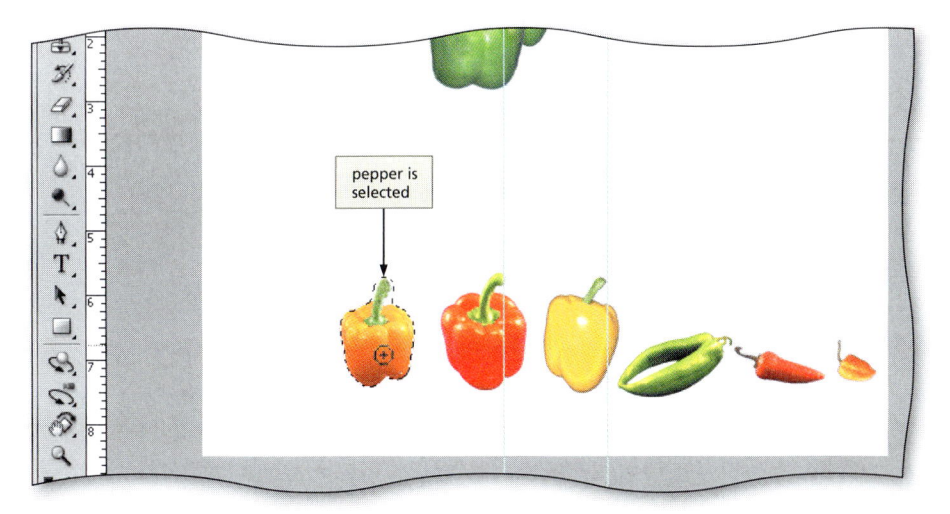

Figure 2–44

> **Other Ways**
>
> 1. Press W or SHIFT+W until Quick Selection tool is active, drag selection

To Move a Selection

The following steps move the orange bell pepper using the Move tool. If you make a mistake while moving, press CTRL+Z and then move again. If you accidentally move a sizing handle or the center reference point, press the ESC key to cancel the transformation.

1 On the Tools panel, click the Move Tool (V) button to select it.

2 Drag the selection up and to the right until the bottom of the stem aligns with the horizontal guide and the right vertical guide (Figure 2–45).

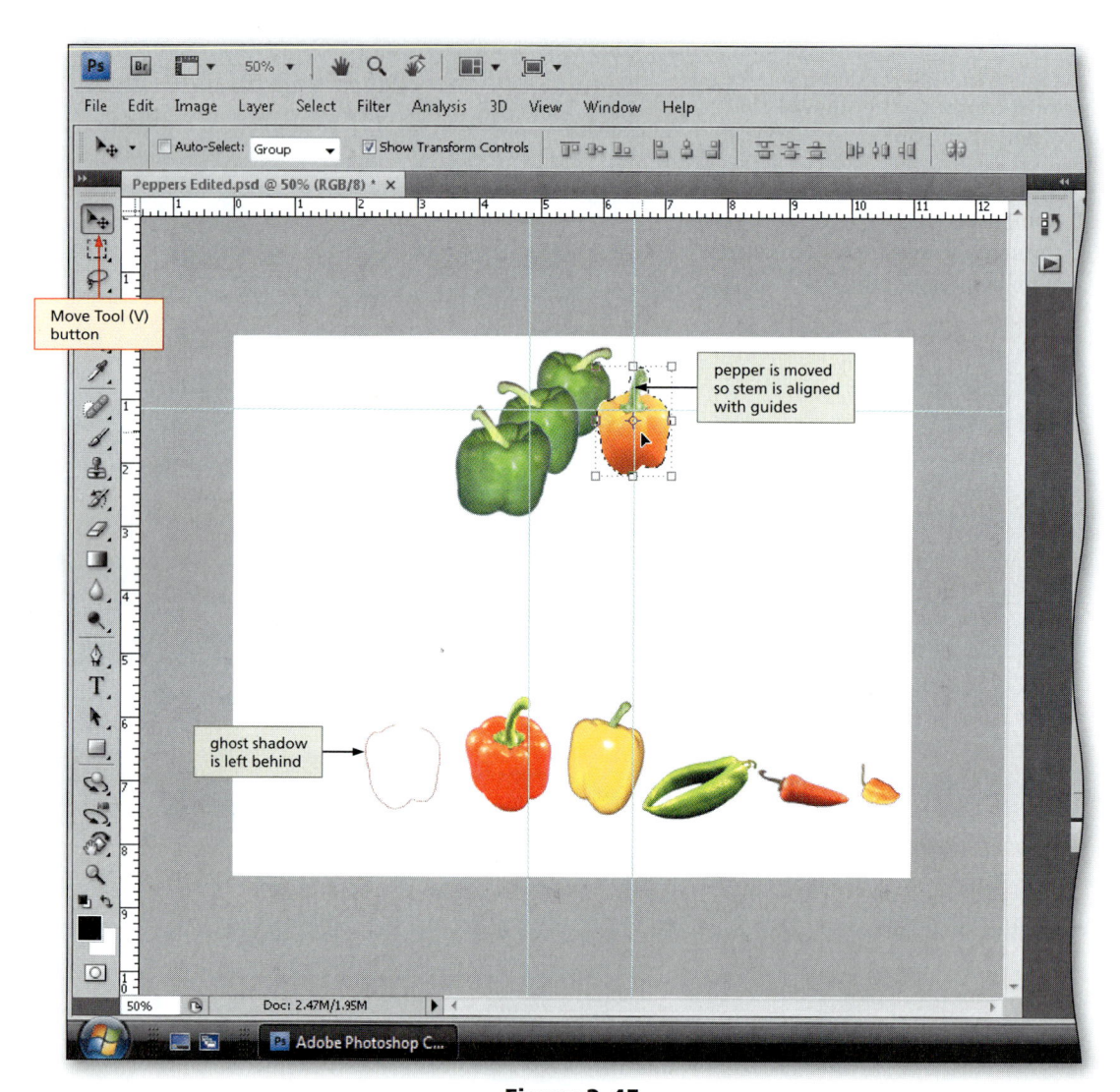

Figure 2–45

To Undo Using the History Panel

Notice in Figure 2–45 that a halo or ghost shadow was left in the previous location of the pepper. That sometimes happens with any of the selection tools, especially when fringe pixels are faded. The following steps undo the Move command so the error can be corrected.

1
- Click the History button in the vertical docking of panels to display the History panel.
- Click the Quick Selection state in the History panel to go back one step (Figure 2–46). Do not press any other keys.

Q&A Could I have pressed CTRL+Z to undo the move?

Yes, if you only need to undo one step, pressing CTRL+Z will work. If you need to go back more than one step, you can press CTRL+ALT+Z or use the History panel.

2
- Click the History button again to collapse the History panel.

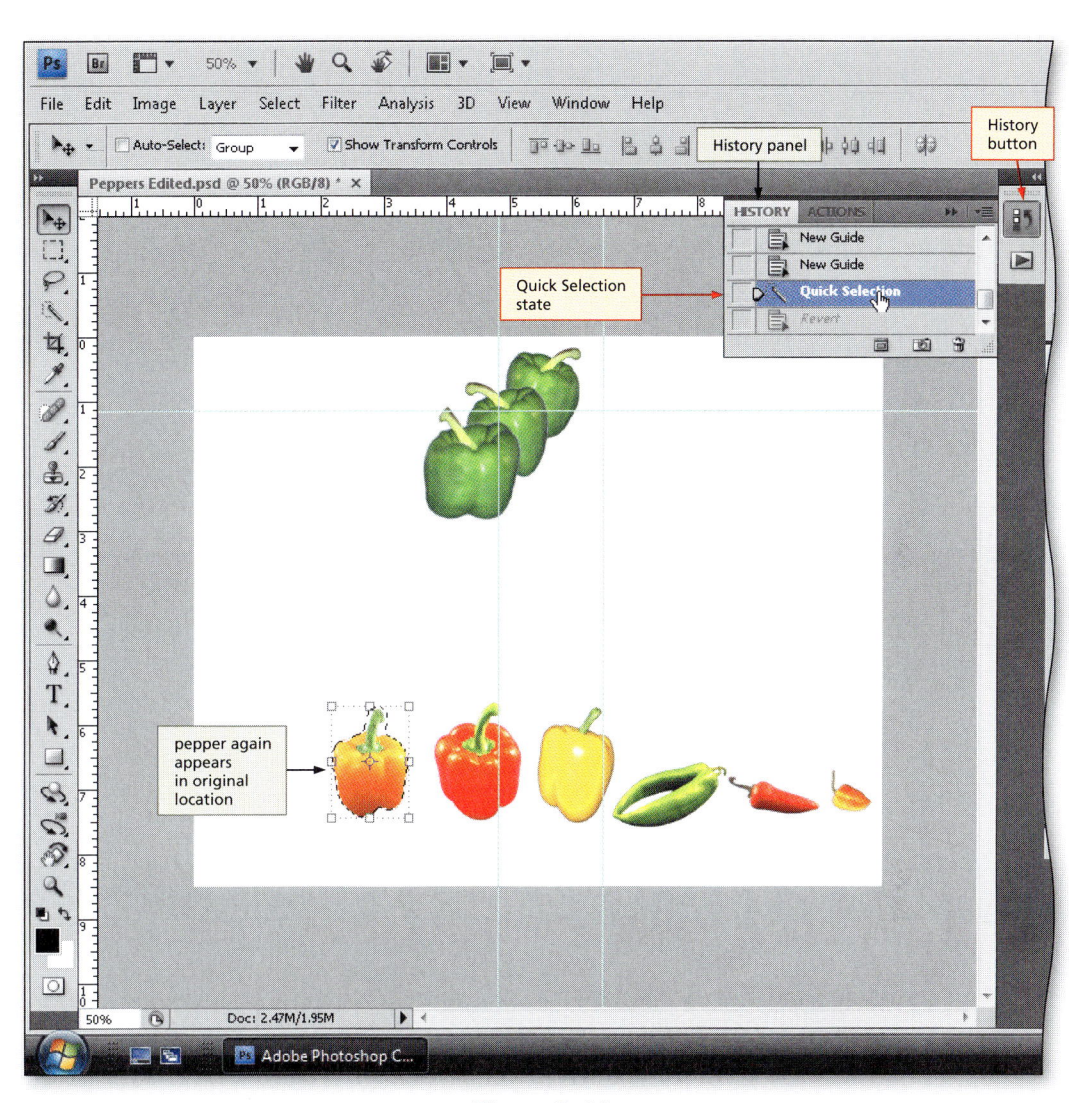

Figure 2–46

Other Ways
1. Press CTRL+ALT+Z

The Refine Edge Dialog Box

Recall that the Refine Edge button displays a dialog box where you can make choices about improving selections with jagged edges, soft transitions, hazy borders, or fine details. The Refine Edge dialog box has controls to improve the quality of a selection's edges and allows you to view the selection against different backgrounds for easy editing (Figure 2–47).

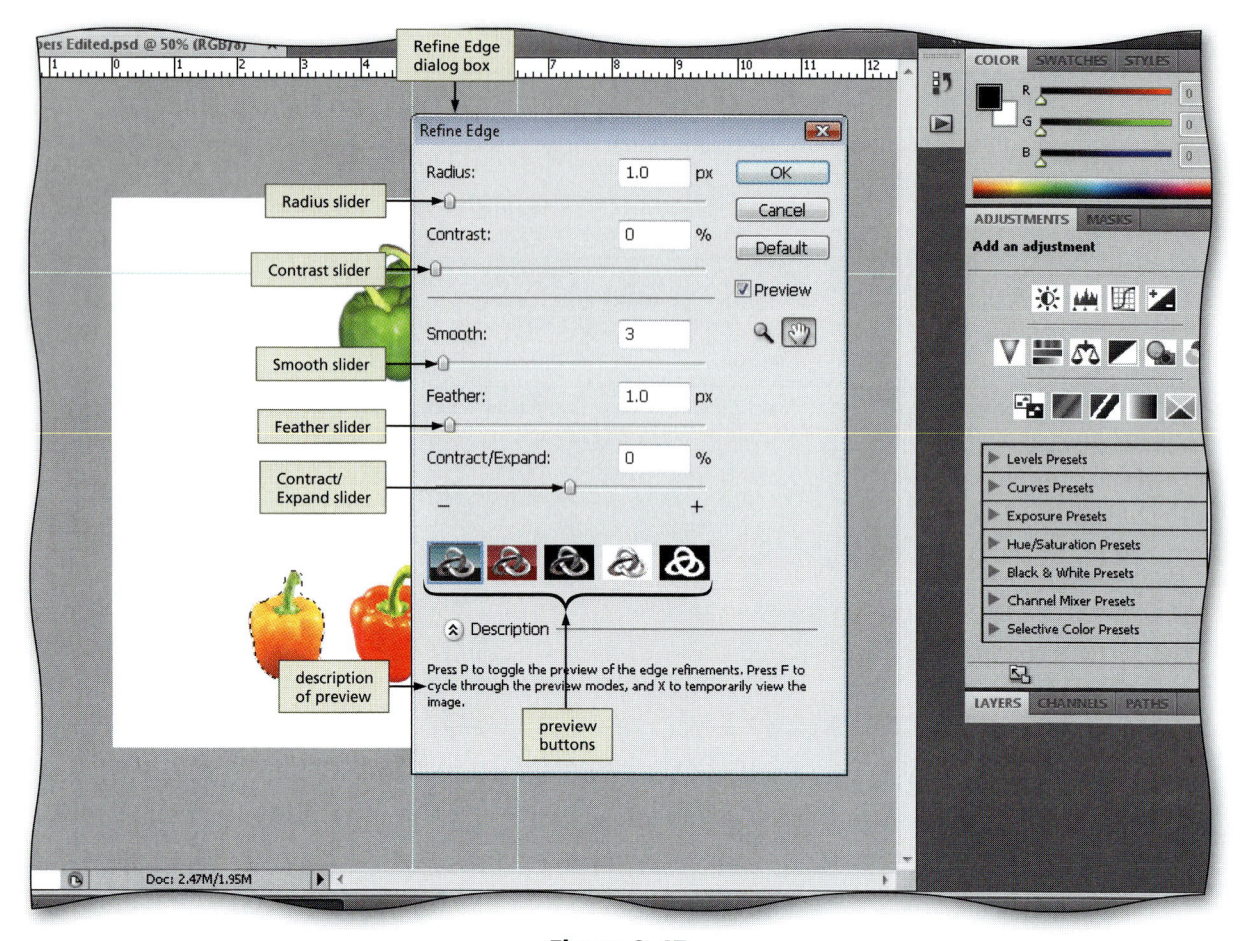

Figure 2–47

Table 2–4 displays the controls in the Refine Edge dialog box and their functions.

Table 2–4 Controls in the Refine Edge Dialog Box	
Control	**Function**
Radius slider	used to adjust the size of the selection boundary by pixels
Contrast slider	sharpens the selection edges to remove any hazy or extraneous pixels, sometimes called fuzzy artifacts or noise; increasing the contrast percentage can remove excessive noise near selection edges caused by a high radius setting
Smooth slider	reduces irregular areas in the selection boundary to create a smoother outline with values from 0 to 100 pixels
Feather slider	softens the edges of the selection for blending into backgrounds using values from 0 to 250 pixels
Contract/Expand slider	shrinks or enlarges the selection border for subtle changes
Preview buttons	used to adjust display to monitor changes

The various settings in the Refine Edge dialog box take practice to use intuitively. The more experience you have adjusting the settings, the more comfortable you will feel with the controls. To improve selections for images on a contrasting background, you should first increase the radius and then increase the contrast to sharpen the edges. For grayscale images or selections where the colors of the object and the background are similar, try smoothing first, then feathering. For all selections, you might need to adjust the Contract/Expand slider.

To Refine Edges

First, you will refine the edges of the selection in the following steps.

1

- On the Tools panel, click the Quick Selection Tool (W) button to return to the Quick Selection tool.

- On the Quick Selection tool options bar, click the Refine Edge button to display the Refine Edge dialog box (Figure 2–48).

2

- Click the Standard preview button to display the entire image in the document window.

- To increase the radius, drag the Radius slider until the Radius box displays 3.

- To increase the contrast, drag the Contrast slider until the Contrast box displays 25.

- Drag the Contract/Expand slider until the percentage is 55% to expand the selection (Figure 2–49).

🔍 **Experiment**

- Drag the Contract/Expand slider to various percentages and watch how the selection changes. Return the slider to 55%.

3

- Click the OK button in the Refine Edge dialog box to apply the changes and close the box.

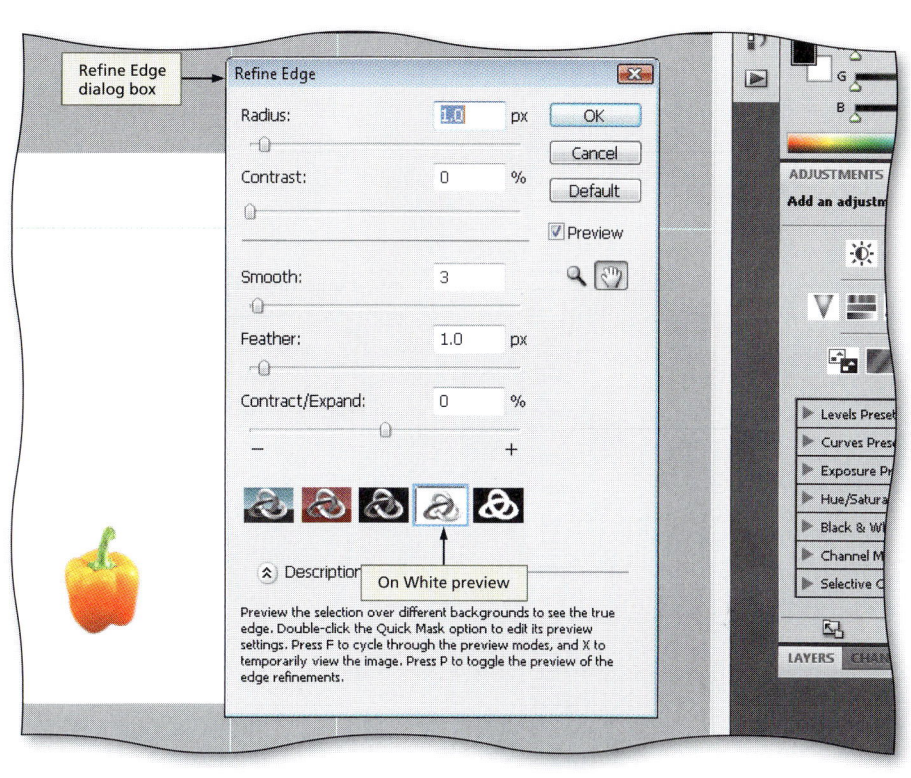

Figure 2–48

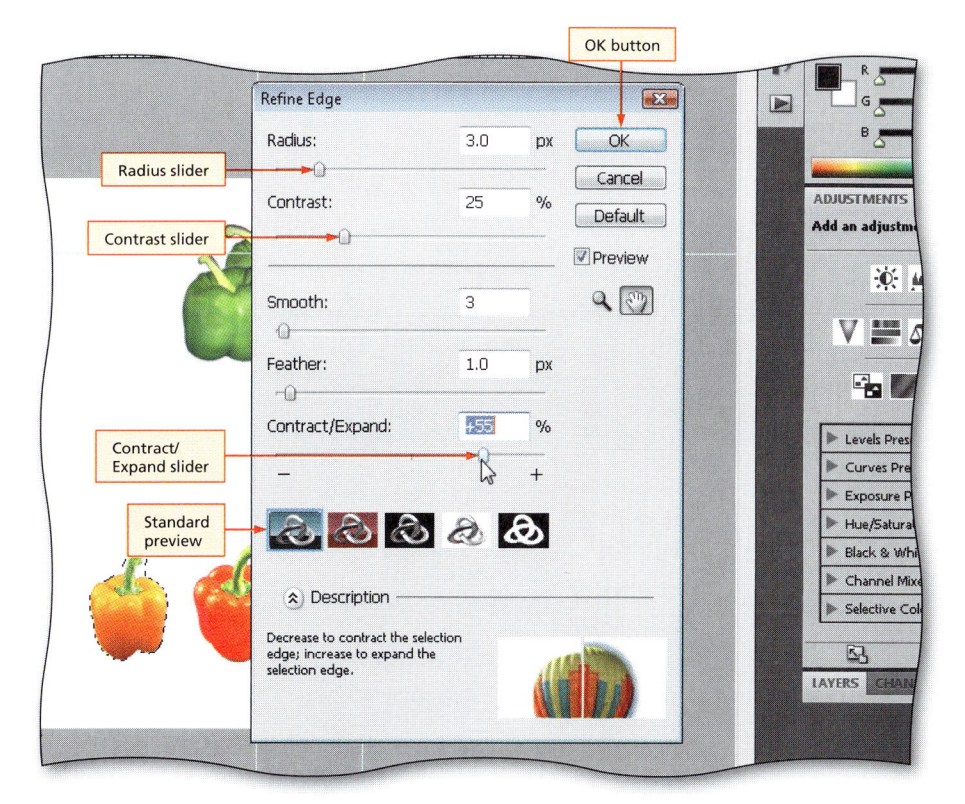

Figure 2–49

Other Ways

1. Right-click selection, click Refine Edge, choose settings, click OK

To Move Again

Next, you will move the orange bell pepper again, this time without leaving behind a ghost border.

① Click the Move Tool (V) button on the Tools panel to select it.

② Drag the selection up and to the right until the bottom of the stem aligns with the horizontal ruler and the right vertical guide. Do not drag the bounding box or center reference point. Do not click or press any other keys (Figure 2–50).

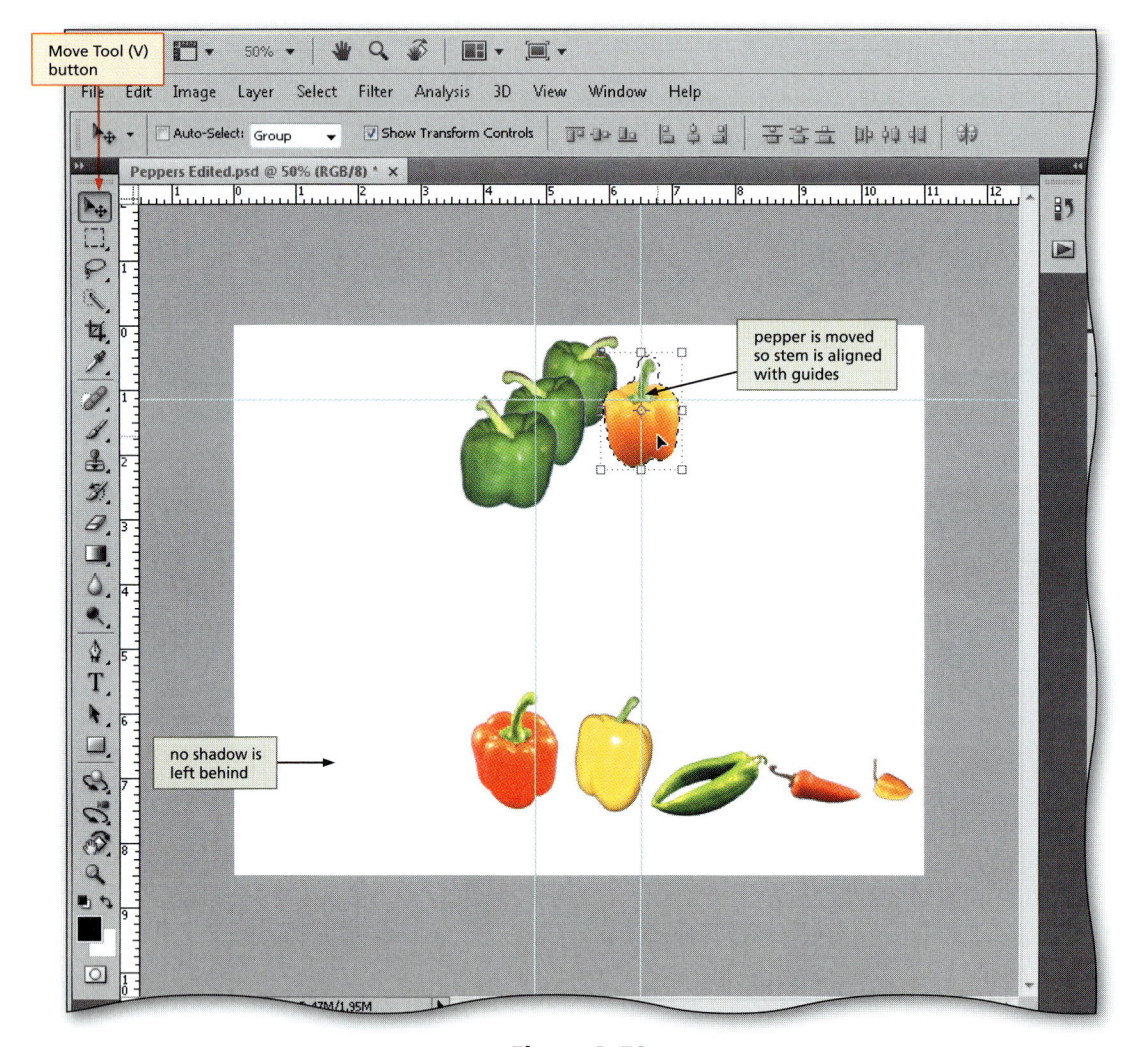

Figure 2–50

To Create a Copy and Skew

Finally, you will create and skew a copy of the orange pepper to create more diversity in the advertisement.

① With the Move tool still selected, ALT+drag the selection down and to the right to create a duplicate.

② Press CTRL+T to display the Transform options bar.

③ Right-click the selection and then click Skew on the context menu.

4 Drag the right sizing handle slightly downward to create a skewed copy similar to the one in Figure 2–51.

5 Press the ENTER key to confirm the transformation.

6 Press CTRL+D to deselect.

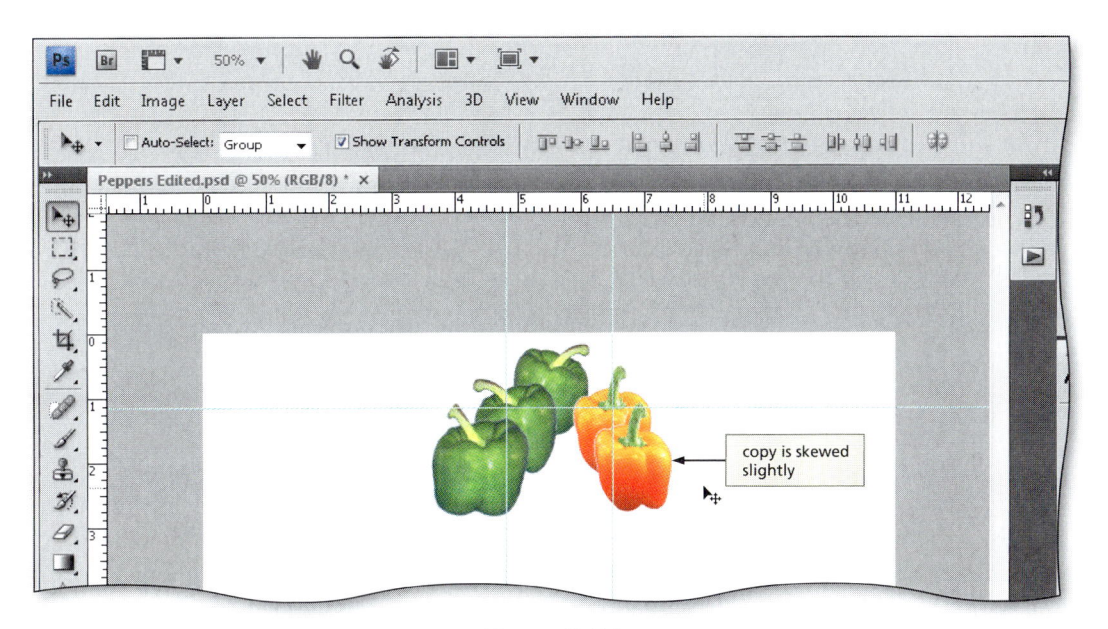

Figure 2–51

The Lasso Tools

The **lasso tools** are used to draw freehand selection borders around objects. The lasso tools provide more flexibility than the marquee tools with their standardized shapes, and might be more suitable than the Quick Selection tool when the object has a non-contrasting background. There are three kinds of lasso tools. The first is the default Lasso tool, which allows you to create a selection by using the mouse to drag around any object in the document window. You select the Lasso Tool (L) button on the Tools panel. You then begin to drag around the desired area. When you release the mouse, Photoshop connects the selection border to the point where you began dragging, finishing the loop. The Lasso tool is useful for a quick, rough selection.

The Polygonal Lasso tool is chosen from the Lasso tool's context menu. It is similar to the Lasso tool in that it draws irregular shapes in the image; however, the Polygonal Lasso tool uses straight line segments. To use the Polygonal Lasso tool, choose the tool, click in the document window, release the mouse button, and then move the mouse in straight lines, clicking each time you turn a corner. When you get back to the beginning of the polygon, double-click to complete the selection.

The Magnetic Lasso tool also can be chosen from the context menu. To use the Magnetic Lasso tool, you click close to the edge of the object you wish to select. The Magnetic Lasso tool tries to find the edge of the object by looking for the closest color change. It then attaches the marquee to the pixel on the edge of the color change. As you move the mouse, the Magnetic Lasso tool follows that change with a magnetic attraction. The Magnetic Lasso tool's marquee displays fastening points on the edge of the object. You can create more fastening points by clicking as you move the mouse, to force a change in direction or to adjust the

BTW

The History Panel
The History panel will list a Duplicate state when the ALT key is used to copy a selection. The word Paste will appear next to the state when the Copy and Paste commands are used from the keyboard or menu. The Copy command alone does not affect how the image looks; it merely sends a copy to the system clipboard. Therefore, it is not saved as a state.

BTW

Lasso Tool Selection
If you are using a different tool, and want to activate the Lasso tool, you can click the Lasso Tool (L) button on the Tools panel or press the L key on the keyboard to select the Lasso tool. Once the Lasso tool is selected, pressing SHIFT+L cycles through the three lasso tools.

magnetic attraction. When you get all the way around the object, you click at the connection point to complete the loop, or double-click to have Photoshop connect the loop for you. Because the Magnetic Lasso tool looks for changes in color to define the edges of an object, it might not be as effective for making selections in images with a busy background or images with low contrast. Each of the lasso tools displays its icon as the mouse pointer.

Table 2–5 describes the three lasso tools.

Table 2–5 The Lasso Tools

Tool	Purpose	Shortcut	Button
Lasso	used to draw freeform loops, creating a selection border	L SHIFT+L toggles through all three lasso tools	
Polygonal Lasso	used to draw straight lines, creating segments of a selection border	L SHIFT+L toggles through all three lasso tools	
Magnetic Lasso	used to draw a selection border that snaps to the edge of contrasting color areas in the image	L SHIFT+L toggles through all three lasso tools	

Each of the lasso tools displays an options bar similar to the marquee options bar, with buttons to add to, subtract from, and intersect with the selection, as well as the ability to feather the border. The Magnetic Lasso tool options bar (Figure 2–52) also includes an Anti-alias check box to smooth the borders of a selection. Unique to the Magnetic Lasso tool options bar, however, is a Contrast box to enter the **contrast**, or sensitivity of color that Photoshop evaluates in making the path selection. A higher value detects only edges that contrast sharply with their surroundings; a lower value detects lower-contrast edges. The Width box causes the Magnetic Lasso tool to detect edges only within the specified distance from the mouse pointer. A Frequency box allows you to specify the rate at which the lasso sets fastening points. A higher value anchors the selection border in place more quickly. A tablet pressure button on the right is used to change the pen width when using a graphic drawing tablet instead of a mouse.

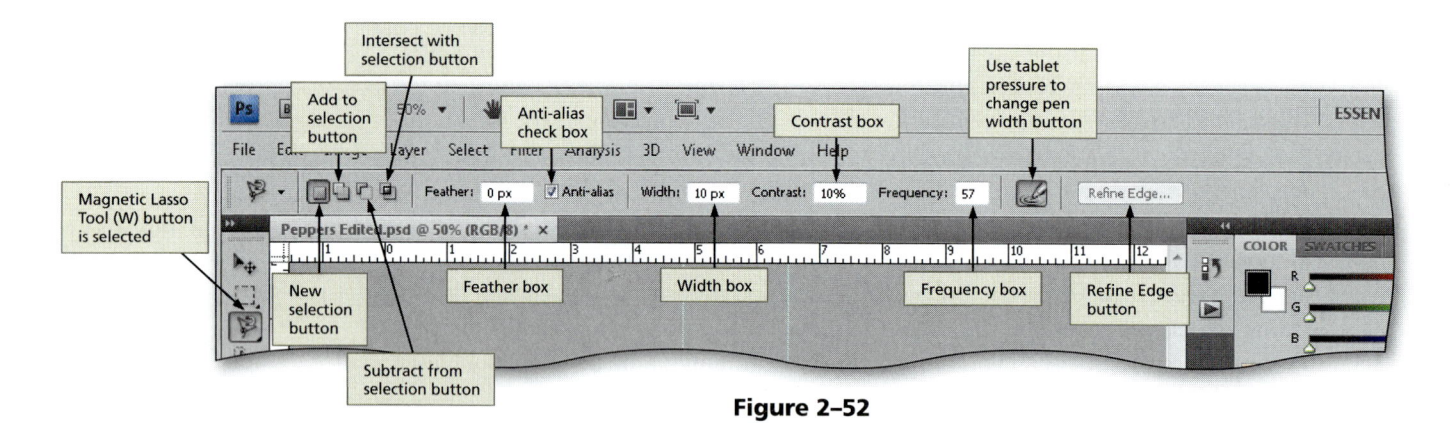

Figure 2–52

You will use the Lasso tool to select the red bell pepper. Then you will subtract or remove any extra white space in the selection using the Magic Wand tool. Finally, you will move the pepper to a location near the others in the advertisement.

As you use the Lasso tool, if you make a mistake and want to start over, you can deselect by pressing CTRL+D, and then start again.

To Select Using the Lasso Tool

The following steps select the red bell pepper by dragging around it.

1
- Right-click the Lasso Tool (L) button on the Tools panel to display the context menu (Figure 2–53).

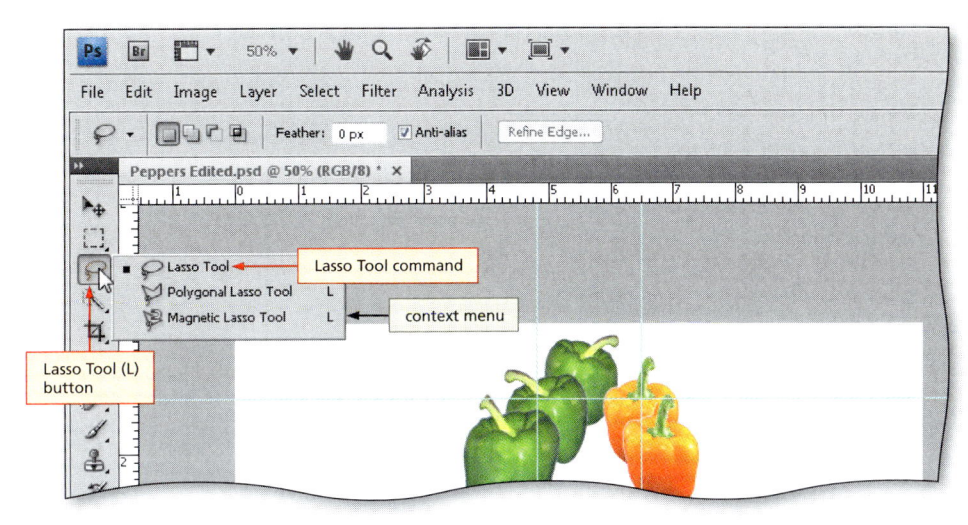

Figure 2–53

2
- Click Lasso Tool to select it.
- If necessary, on the options bar, click the New selection button.
- Drag around the red bell pepper to create a complete circular area, connecting the beginning and end points (Figure 2–54).

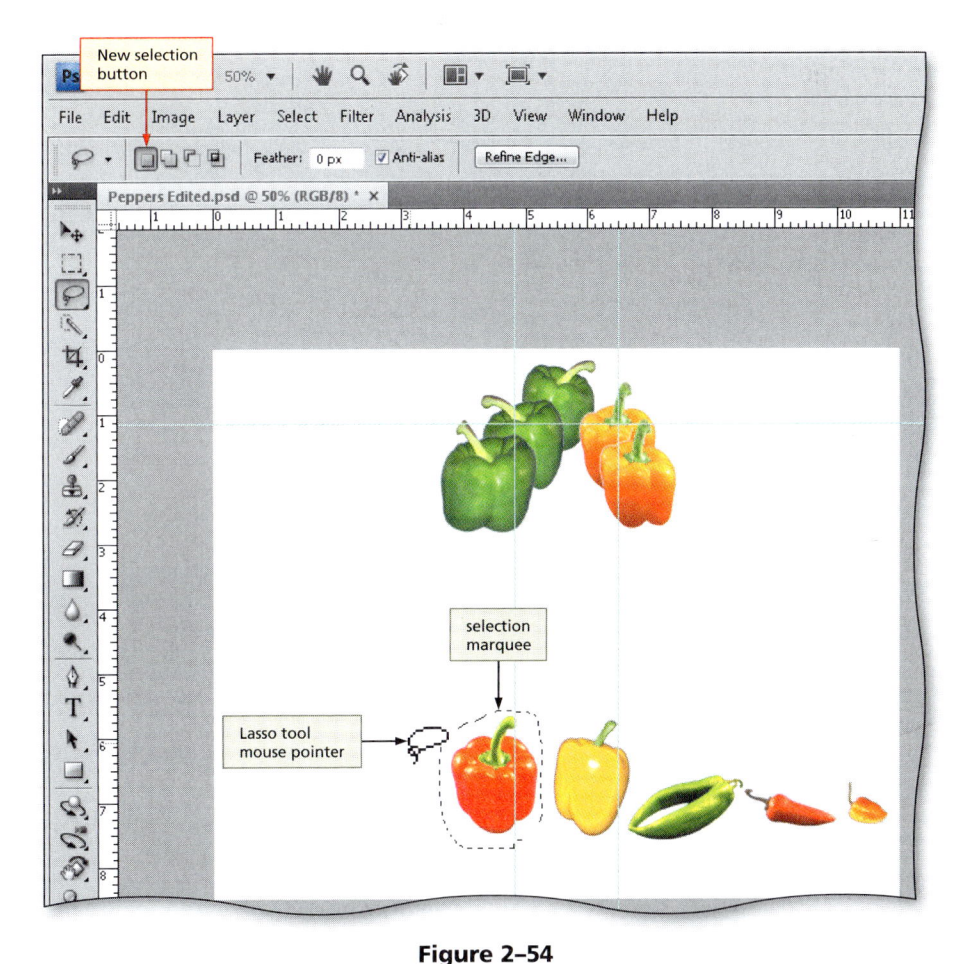

Figure 2–54

Other Ways
1. Press L or SHIFT+L until Lasso tool is active, drag selection

To Remove White Space Using the Magic Wand Tool

The following steps select the Magic Wand tool and then subtract the white space from the selection.

1 Right-click the Quick Selection Tool (W) and then click Magic Wand Tool to select it.

2 On the options bar, click the Subtract from selection button, if necessary.

3 Move the mouse pointer to the white space inside the selection and then click to remove the white space (Figure 2–55).

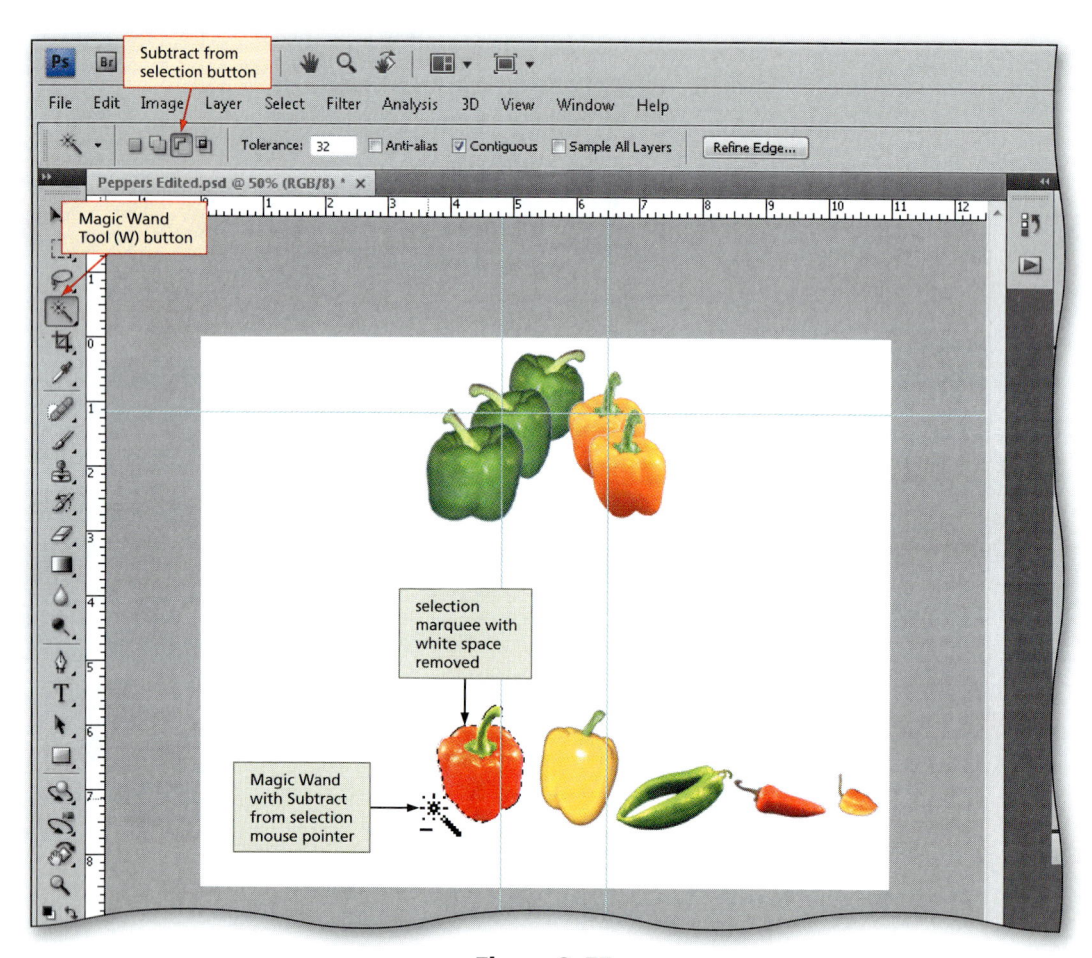

Figure 2–55

To Snap the Red Bell Pepper to a Ruler Guide

The next step moves the selected red bell pepper so that it snaps to the right vertical ruler.

1 Click the Move Tool (V) button on the Tools panel to select it.

2 Slowly drag the selection to a location in the middle of the other peppers. When the selection snaps to the right vertical guide, release the mouse button (Figure 2–56).

3 Press CTRL+D to deselect.

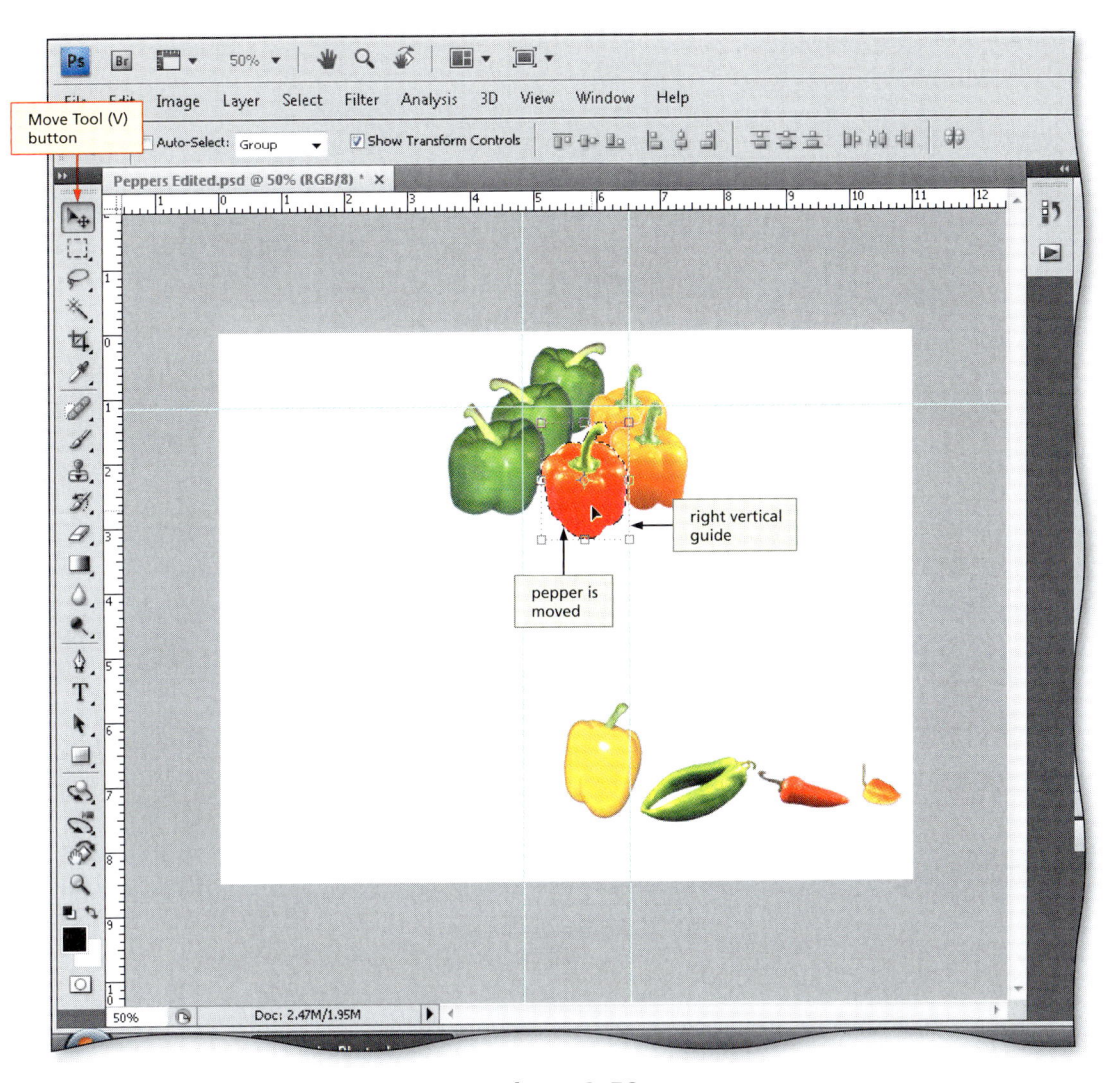

Figure 2–56

To Zoom Using Shortcut Keys

In preparation for selecting the yellow banana peppers, the next steps zoom using shortcut keys.

1. Press the Z key to select the Zoom tool.
2. Click the Zoom In button on the options bar.
3. Click the yellow bell pepper twice to zoom to 100%.

To Select Using the Magnetic Lasso Tool

The steps on the next page use the Magnetic Lasso tool to select the yellow bell pepper. Changing the contrast helps detect the edges, increasing the magnetism of the edge of the peppers. Then you will refine the edges and rotate the selection. Finally, you will move the selection to a location near the other peppers in the advertisement.

As you use the Magnetic Lasso tool, if you make a mistake and want to start over, double-click to complete the lasso, deselect by pressing CTRL+D, and then start again.

1

- Right-click the current lasso tool and then click Magnetic Lasso Tool to select it from the context menu.

- If necessary, on the options bar, click the New selection button.

- Double-click the Contrast box and type 75 to replace the value.

- Move the mouse pointer close to the edge of the yellow bell pepper to display the Magnetic Lasso tool mouse pointer (Figure 2–57).

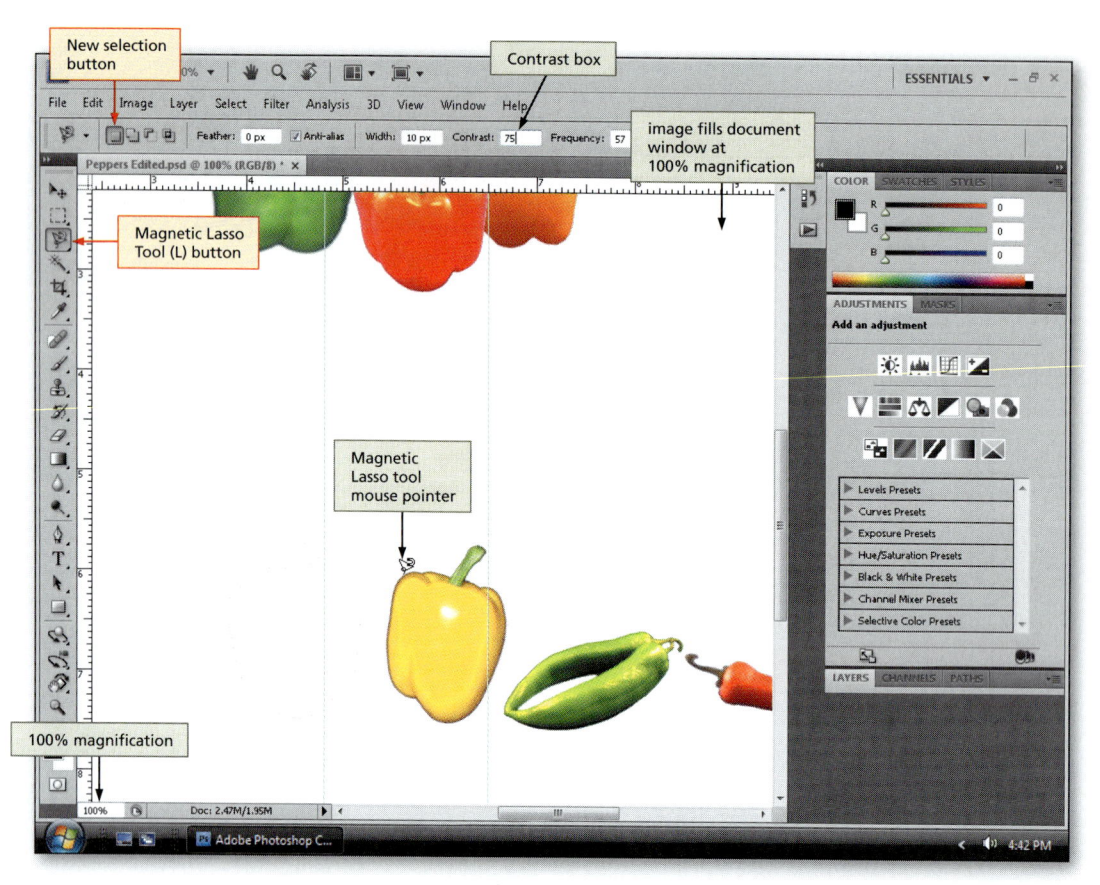

Figure 2–57

2

- Click the edge of the yellow bell pepper to start the selection.

- Move, rather than drag, the mouse pointer slowly along the edge of the pepper to create the selection marquee (Figure 2–58).

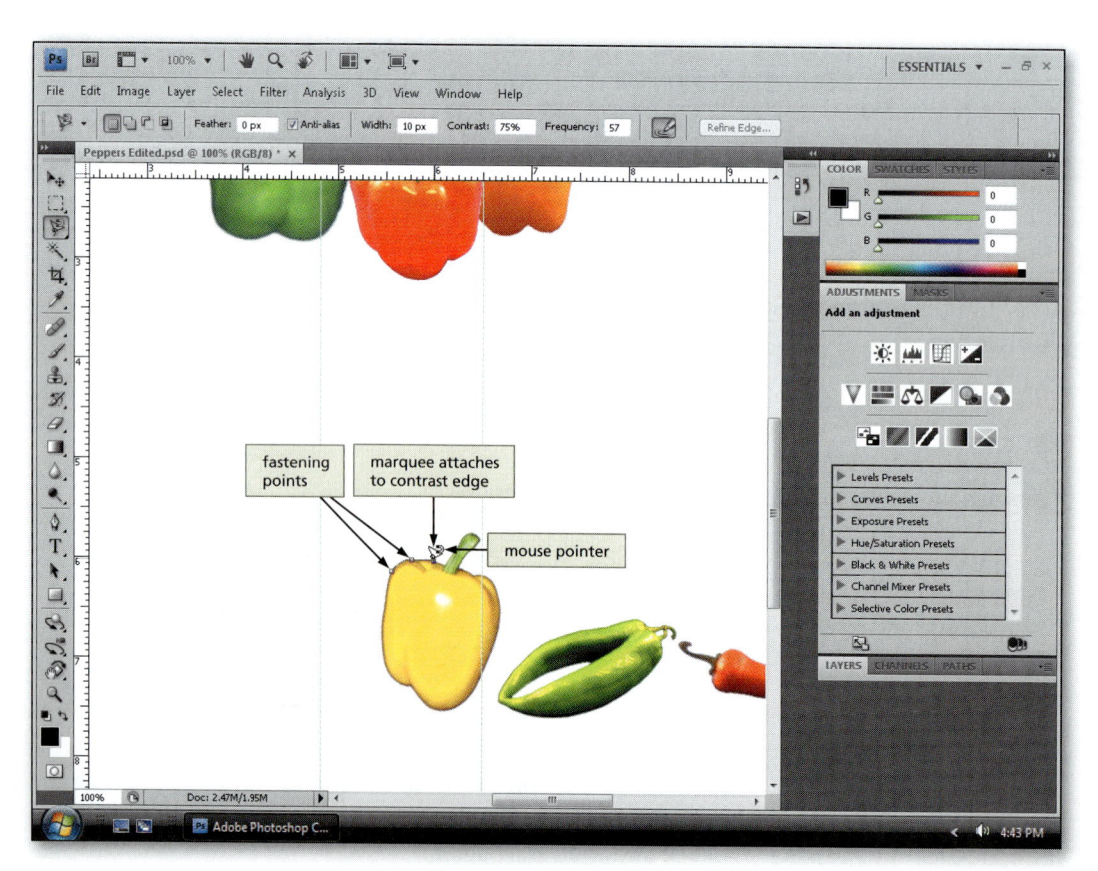

Figure 2–58

3
- Continue moving the mouse pointer around the edge of the pepper. Click the mouse when turning a corner to create an extra fastening point.
- When you get all the way around the pepper, click the first fastening point to complete the selection (Figure 2–59).

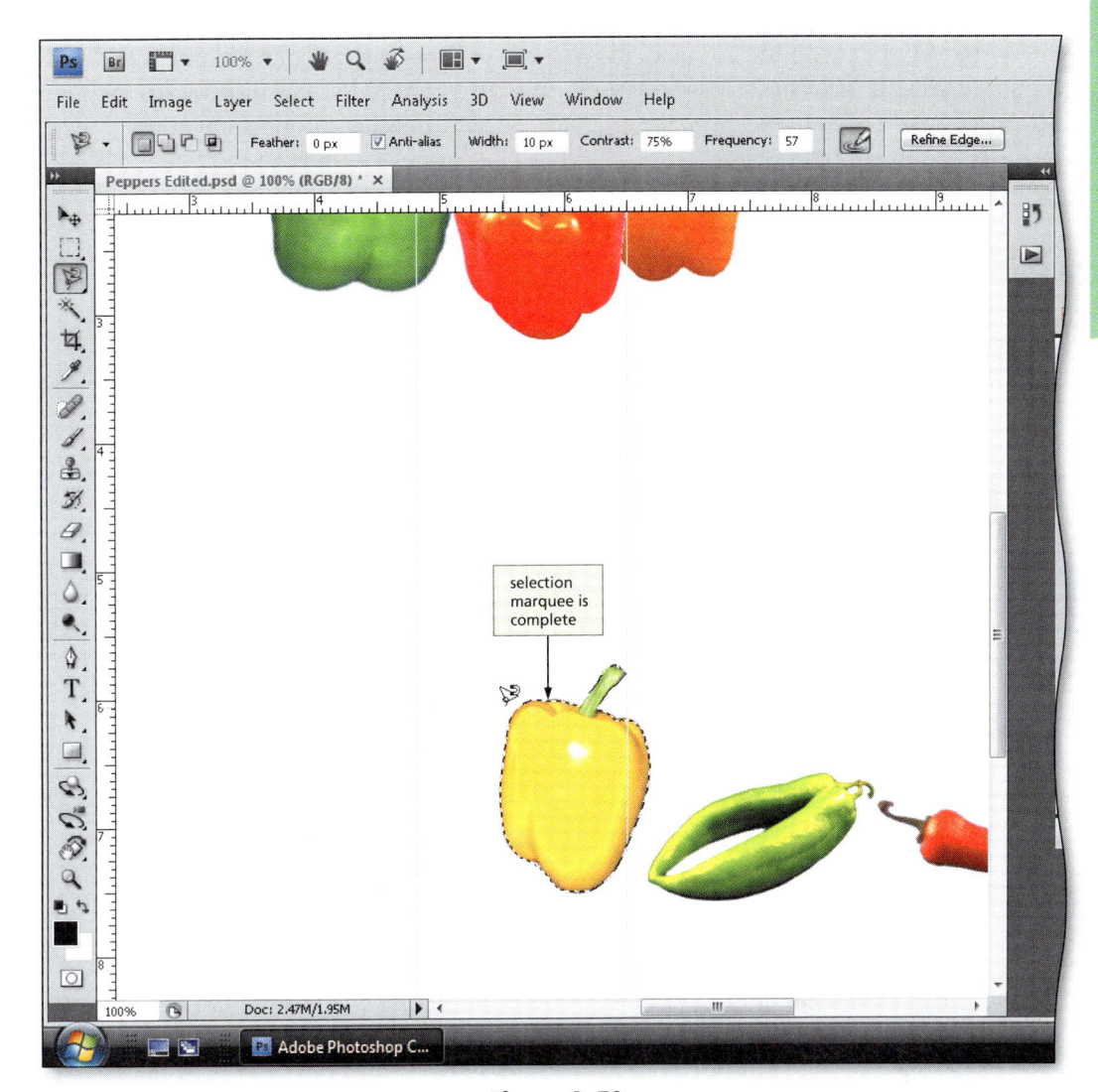

Figure 2–59

Other Ways
1. Press L or SHIFT+L until Magnetic Lasso tool is active, click photo, move mouse

To Refine Edges Using the Context Menu

1 Right-click the selection to display the context menu.

2 Click Refine Edge to display the Refine Edge dialog box.

3 To adjust the settings, type 3 in the Radius box. Type 30 in the Contrast box. Type 50 in the Contract/Expand box. Type 0 in the Smooth and Feather boxes, if necessary.

4 Click the OK button to close the Refine Edge dialog box.

To Rotate a Selection

You will use the mouse to rotate the yellow bell pepper in the following steps. Recall that the reference point, or the small circle at the center of a selection, serves as the pivot point during rotation. The default placement is in the center of the selection. If you drag the reference point to another location, any rotation performed on the selection will pivot around that new location.

1

- Press CTRL+T to display the bounding box and the Transform options bar.

- Move the mouse pointer to the upper-left corner of the yellow pepper, just outside of the bounding box.

- When the mouse pointer displays a double-headed curved arrow, drag to the left and down until the pepper is positioned on its side, as shown in Figure 2–60.

Experiment

- On the options bar, drag the Rotate scrubby slider in either direction to watch the selection rotate. When you are done, press the ESC key to cancel the rotation, and then press CTRL+T again.

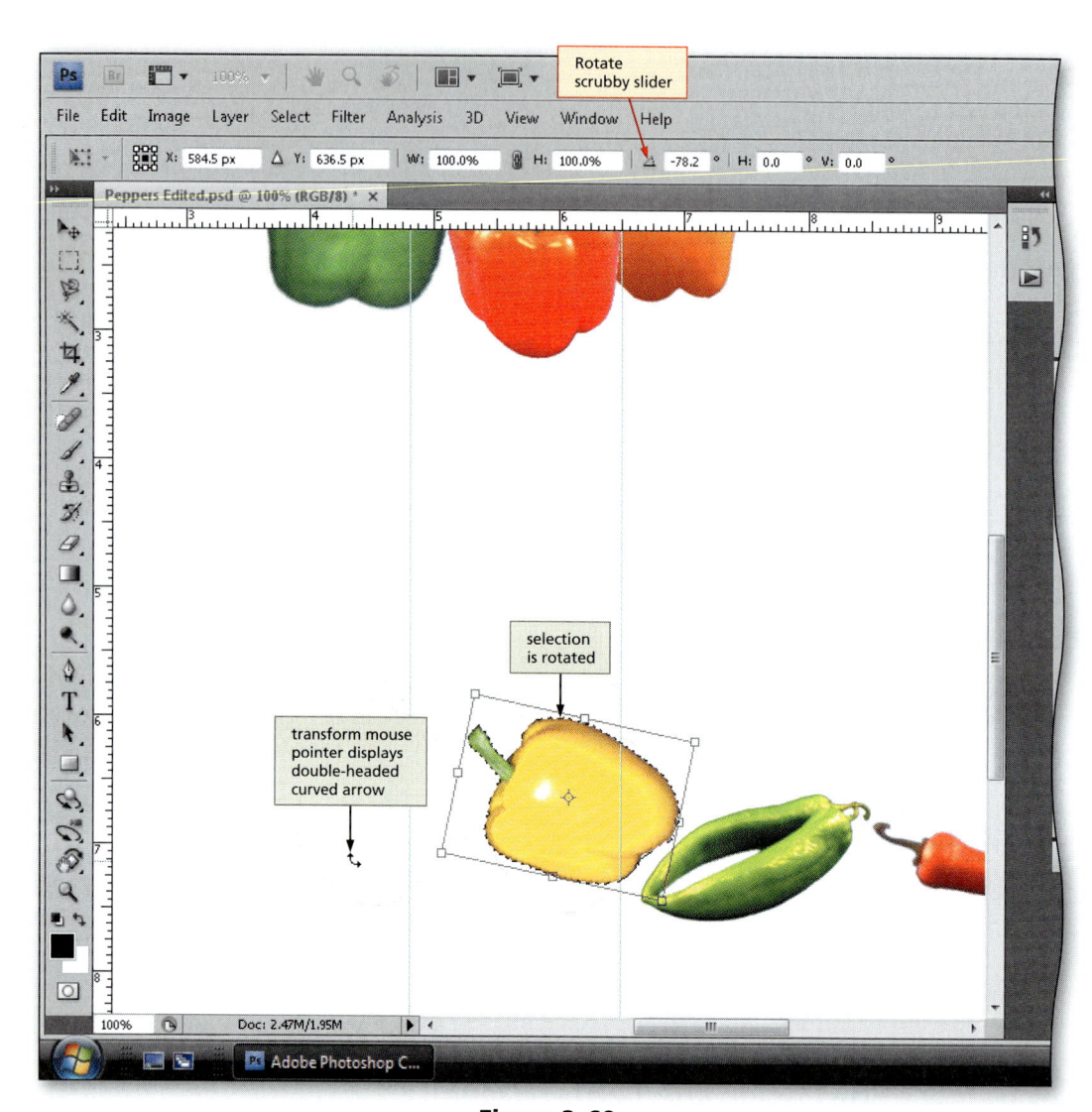

Figure 2–60

2

- Press the ENTER key to confirm the transformation.

Other Ways		
1. On Edit menu, click Free Transform, drag selection	2. On Edit menu, point to Transform, click desired rotate command	3. On options bar, enter degree rotation in Set Rotation box

To Zoom and Move a Selection Using Shortcut Keys

To move the selection, the following steps use shortcut keys.

1. Press the Z key to activate the Zoom tool. Press CTRL + HYPHEN (-) enough times to zoom to 50%.

2. Press the V key to activate the Move tool.

3. Drag the selection to a location in front of the other peppers as shown in Figure 2–61. Do not drag the bounding box or center reference point if they are displayed. Do not click or press any other keys.

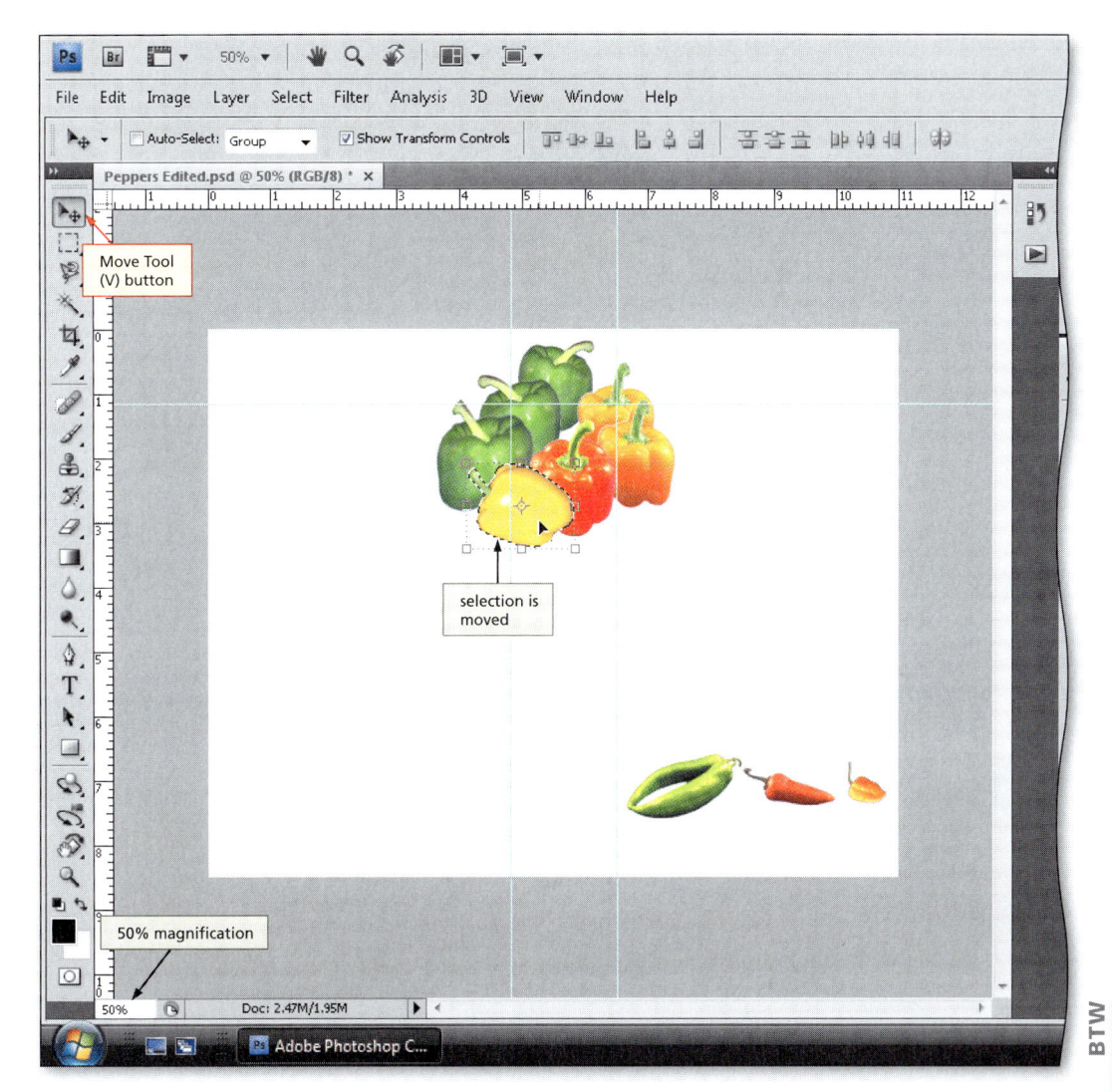

Figure 2–61

Using the Polygonal Lasso Tool

You will use the Polygonal Lasso tool to select the green banana peppers. Then you will remove any extra white space in the selection using the Magic Wand tool. Finally, you will move the selection to a location in front of the other peppers, aligned with the right vertical guide.

As you use the Polygonal Lasso tool, if you make a mistake and want to start over, double-click to finish the lasso, deselect by pressing CTRL+D, and then start again.

BTW

Cutting and Pasting
Just as you do in other applications, you can use the Cut, Copy, and Paste commands from the Edit menu or shortcut keys to make changes to selections. Unless you predefine a selection area by dragging a marquee, the Paste command pastes to the center of the document window. Both the commands and the shortcut keys create a new layer when they copy or paste.

To Select Using the Polygonal Lasso Tool

The following steps select the green banana peppers by drawing lines around them with the Polygonal Lasso tool.

1

- Right-click the Lasso Tool (L) button on the Tools panel to display the context menu and then click Polygonal Lasso to select the tool.

- If necessary, on the options bar, click the New selection button.

🔍 **Experiment**

- Practice using the Polygonal Lasso tool to draw a triangle by doing the following: in a blank area of the photo, click to begin; move the mouse pointer to the right and then click to create one side; move the mouse pointer up and then click to create a second side; move the mouse pointer to the beginning point and then click to complete the lasso.

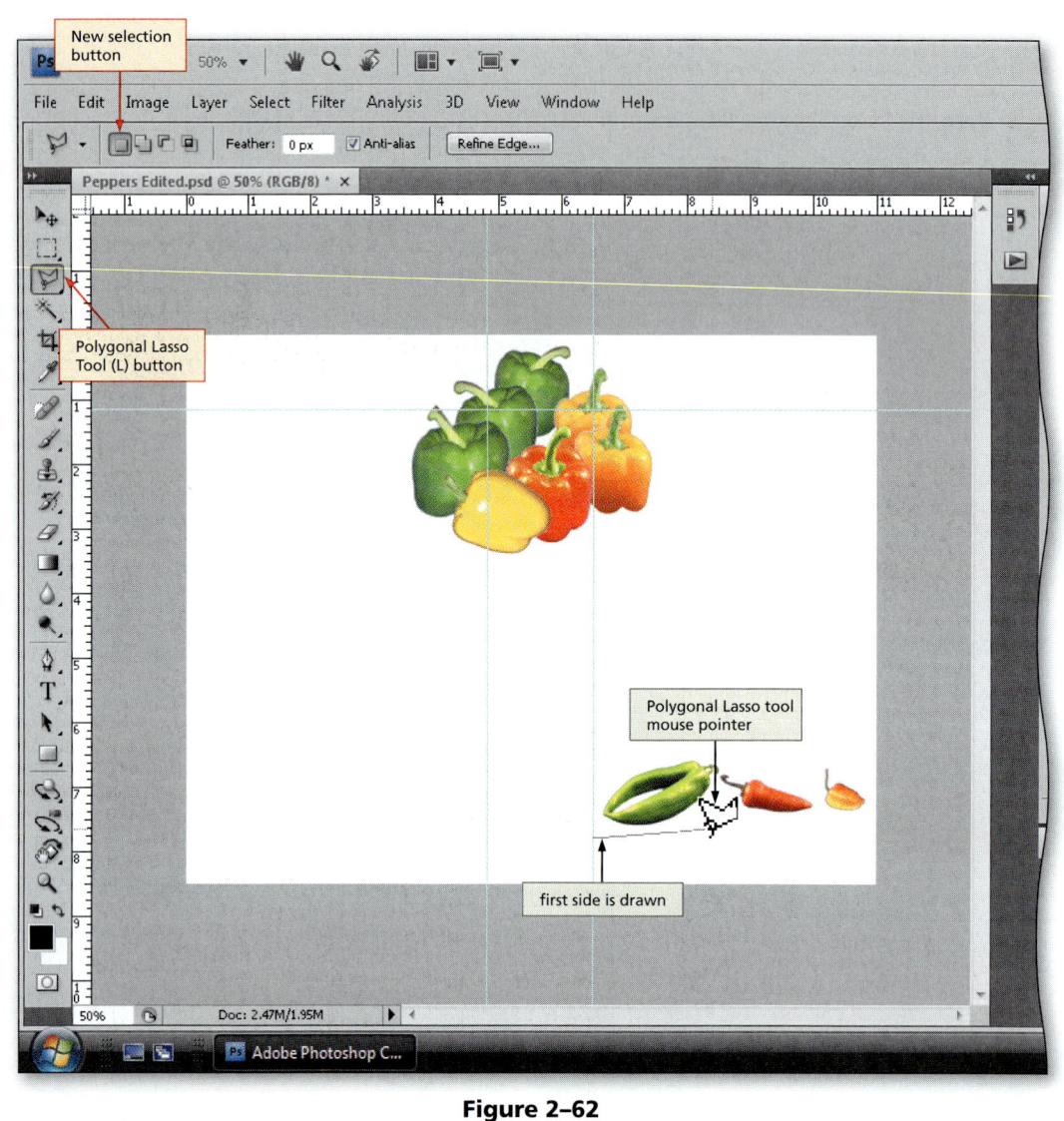

Figure 2–62

2

- Click below the green banana peppers on the lower-left corner to begin the first line.

- Move the mouse pointer to the right to create the first line. Do not drag or click (Figure 2–62).

The Lasso Tools **PS 129**

③
- Move the mouse pointer just past the green banana peppers and then click to create a corner and start a new line.
- Move the mouse pointer up to create the second line segment. Do not overlap any other pepper (Figure 2–63).

④
- Continue creating line segments by moving the mouse pointer and clicking each time you need to change direction.
- When you complete the lines all the way around the pepper, double-click to connect them and complete the selection (Figure 2–64).

Q&A What was the small circle that appeared when I moved close to the beginning of the polygonal lasso?

When the mouse pointer moves close to where you started the polygonal lasso, Photoshop displays a small circle, which means you can click to complete the lasso. Otherwise, you have to double-click.

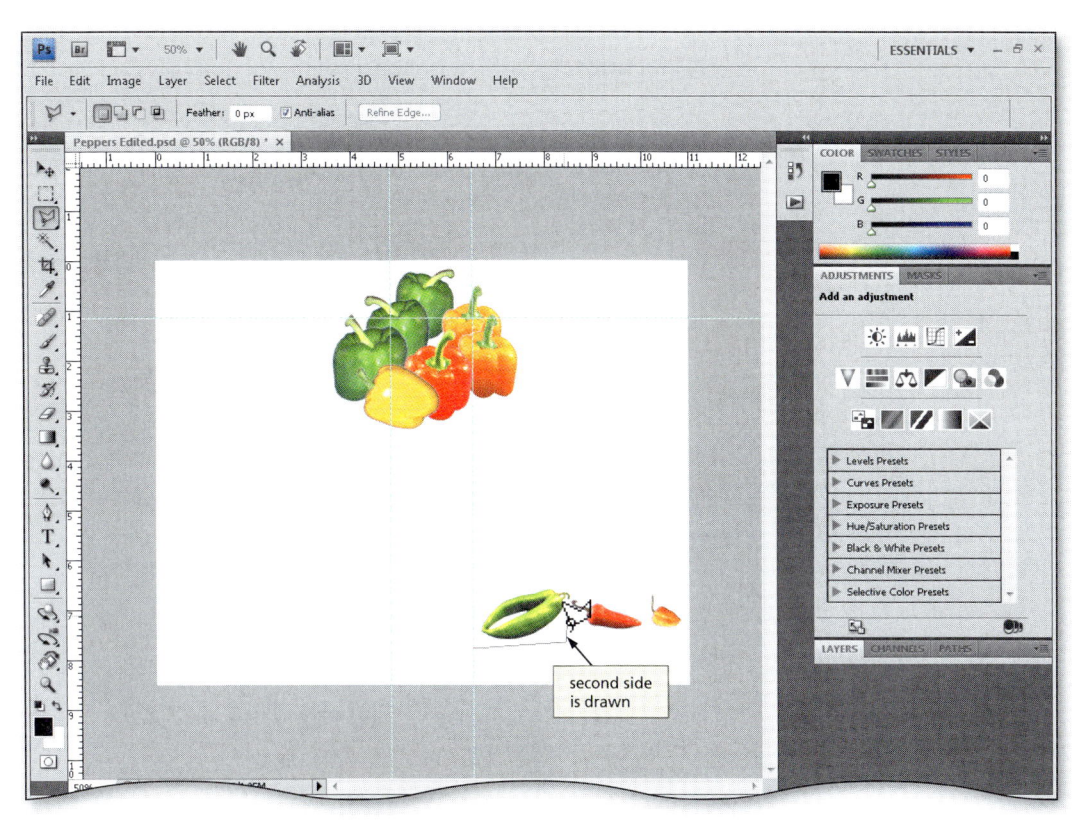

Figure 2–63

Figure 2–64

Other Ways

1. Press L or SHIFT+L until Polygonal Lasso tool is active, click photo, move mouse

To Remove White Space Using Shortcut Keys

To remove the white space in the selection, the following steps use shortcut keys.

1. Press the W key to select the Magic Wand tool.

2. On the options bar, click to remove the check mark in the contiguous check box so the Magic Wand tool will select the white area both around and in between the peppers.

3. ALT+click the white space inside the selection to remove it (Figure 2–65).

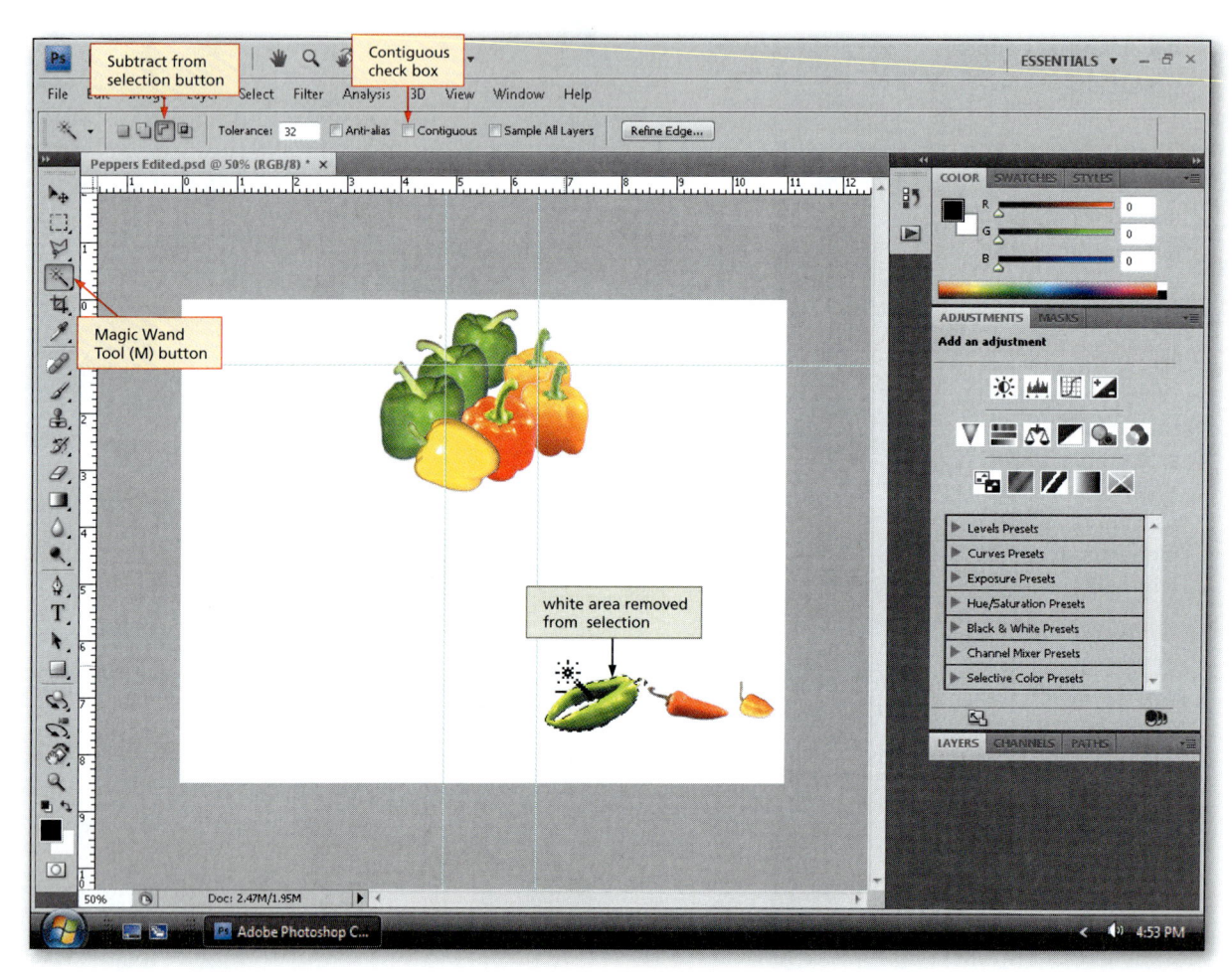

Figure 2–65

To Move Again

The following steps move the green banana peppers.

1. Press the V key to activate the Move tool.

2. Drag the green banana peppers to a location slightly lower than the red and orange bell peppers, and centered on the right vertical guide, as shown in Figure 2–66. Do not drag the bounding box or center reference point if they are displayed.

3. Press CTRL+D to deselect.

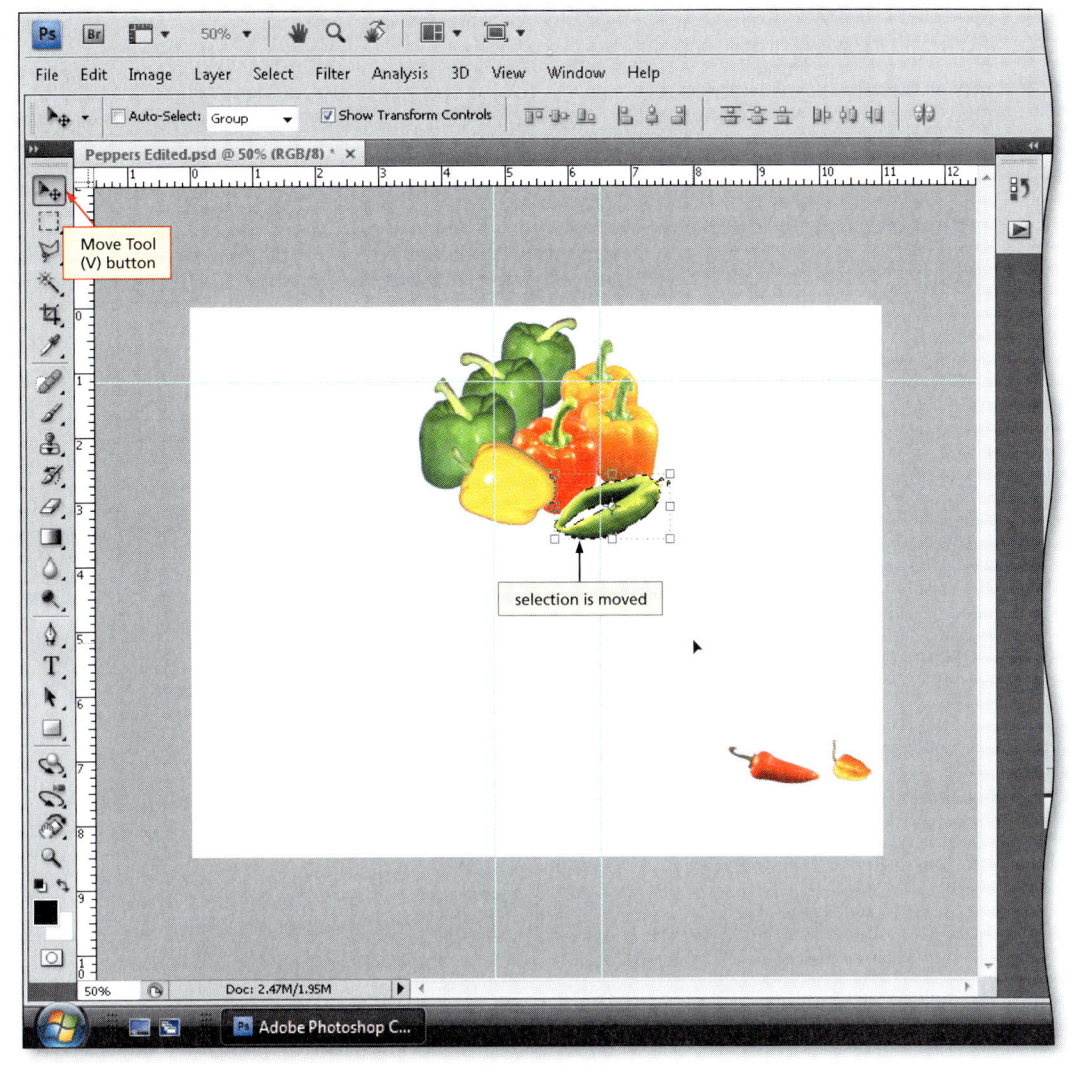

Figure 2–66

The Grow Command

A quick way to increase the size of a selection without using the Refine Edge dialog box is to use the Grow command on the Select menu. The Grow command will increase, or **grow**, the selection border to include all adjacent pixels falling within the tolerance range as specified in the options bar of most selection tools. Choosing the Grow command more than once will increase the selection in increments. Using the Grow command helps to avoid leaving behind a ghost shadow when you move the selection.

In the next sections, you will select the red chili pepper and then grow the selection to avoid leaving a ghost shadow when you move it.

The Similar Command
The Similar command increases the selection to include pixels throughout the selection, not just adjacent ones, which fall within the specified tolerance range. Choosing the Similar command more than once will increase the selection in increments.

To Zoom and Select Using Shortcut Keys

1. Press and hold the CTRL key and then press the PLUS (+) key enough times to zoom to 100%. Scroll the document window as necessary to center the red chili pepper.

2. Press the M key to select the current marquee tool.

3. Drag around the red chili pepper. Do not overlap any other peppers.

4. Press the W key. If the Quick Selection tool is selected on the Tools panel, press SHIFT+W to select the Magic Wand tool.

5. ALT+click the white space inside the selection to subtract from the selection (Figure 2–67).

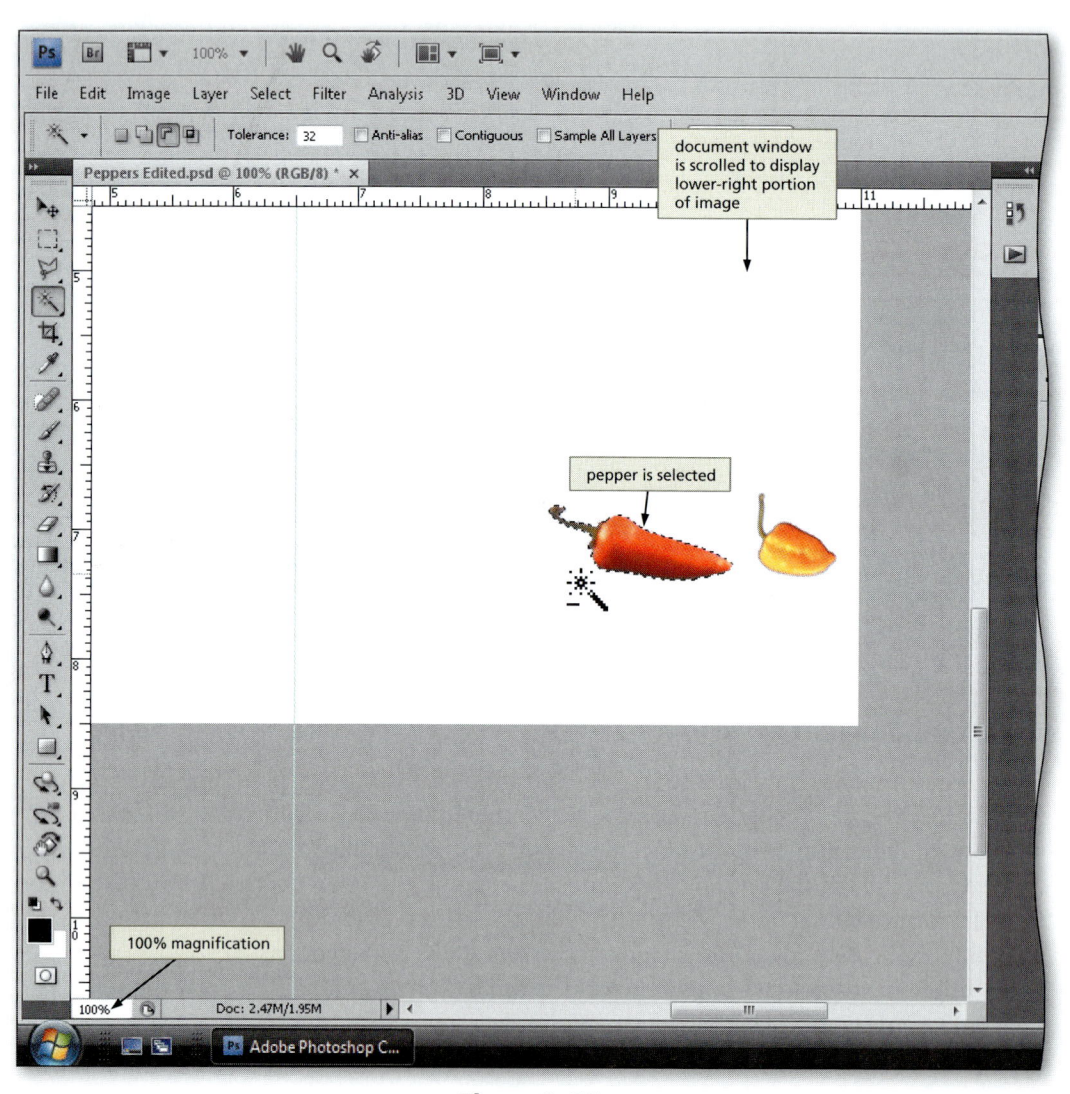

Figure 2–67

To Grow the Selection

1
- Click Select on the menu bar to display the Select menu (Figure 2–68).

Q&A Will I notice a big difference after I use the Grow command?

You might not see the subtle change in the selection marquee; however, growing the border helps ensure that you will not leave behind a ghost shadow when you move the selection.

2
- Click Grow to increase the selection border.

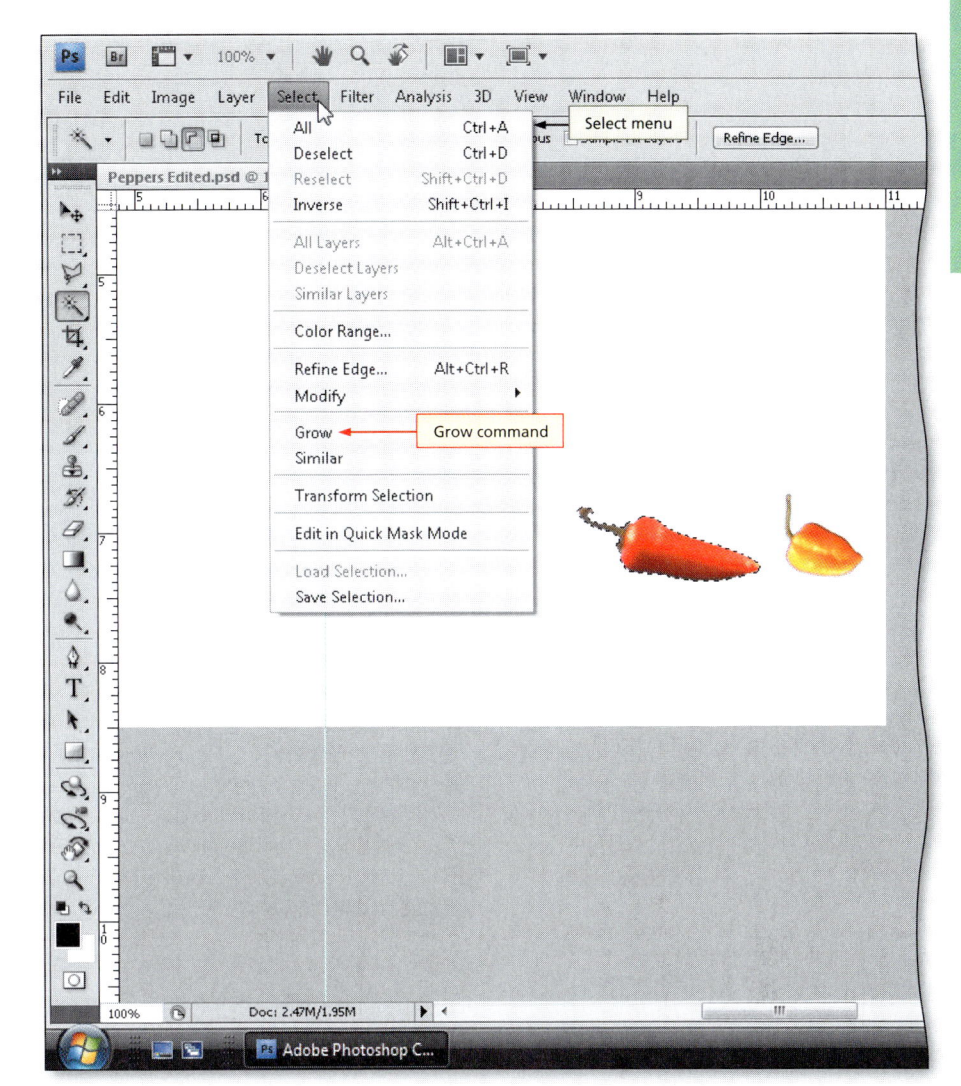

Figure 2–68

To Move the Red Chili Pepper

1 Press the Z key to activate the Zoom tool.

2 Press CTRL+minus sign (–) enough times to zoom out to 50%.

3 Press the V key to activate the Move tool.

4 Drag the red chili pepper to a location in front of the yellow bell pepper, approximately centered on the vertical guide, as shown in Figure 2–69 on the following page.

5 Press CTRL+D to deselect.

Figure 2–69

Finishing the Advertisement

Using the skills you have learned about selecting, moving, duplicating, and rotating, you will finish the advertisement. First, you will select and move the orange habanero pepper. Then, you will create a duplicate, rotating and moving it to its final location in the advertisement. As a final step, you will crop the advertisement to center the peppers.

To Select and Move the Orange Habanero Pepper

1. Use any of the selection tools to select the orange habanero pepper.
2. Use the Magic Wand tool to subtract the white space in the selection, if necessary.
3. Use the Grow command on the Select menu to increase the selection border.
4. Press the V key to activate the Move tool.
5. Drag to move the orange habanero pepper to a location just in front of the other peppers, as shown in Figure 2–70. Do not drag the bounding box or the center reference point if they are displayed. Do not deselect.

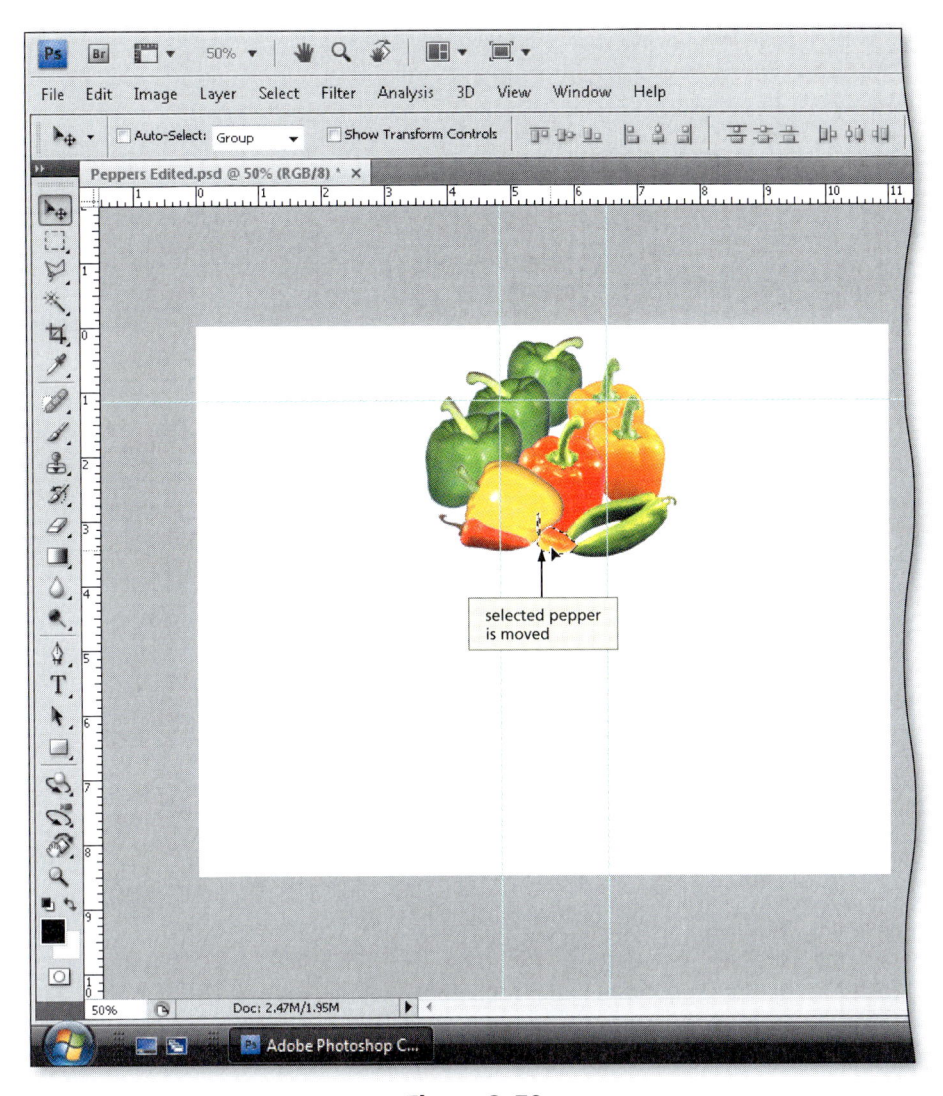

Figure 2–70

To Duplicate the Orange Habanero Pepper

1. With the orange habanero pepper still selected, and with the Move tool still selected, ALT+drag to create a duplicate copy next to the original.

2. Display the bounding box by pressing CTRL+T.

3. Drag outside the selection to rotate the orange habanero pepper until the stem points down. Press the ENTER key to confirm the transformation.

4. Move the copy to the left of the original, as shown in Figure 2–71.

5. Press CTRL+D to deselect.

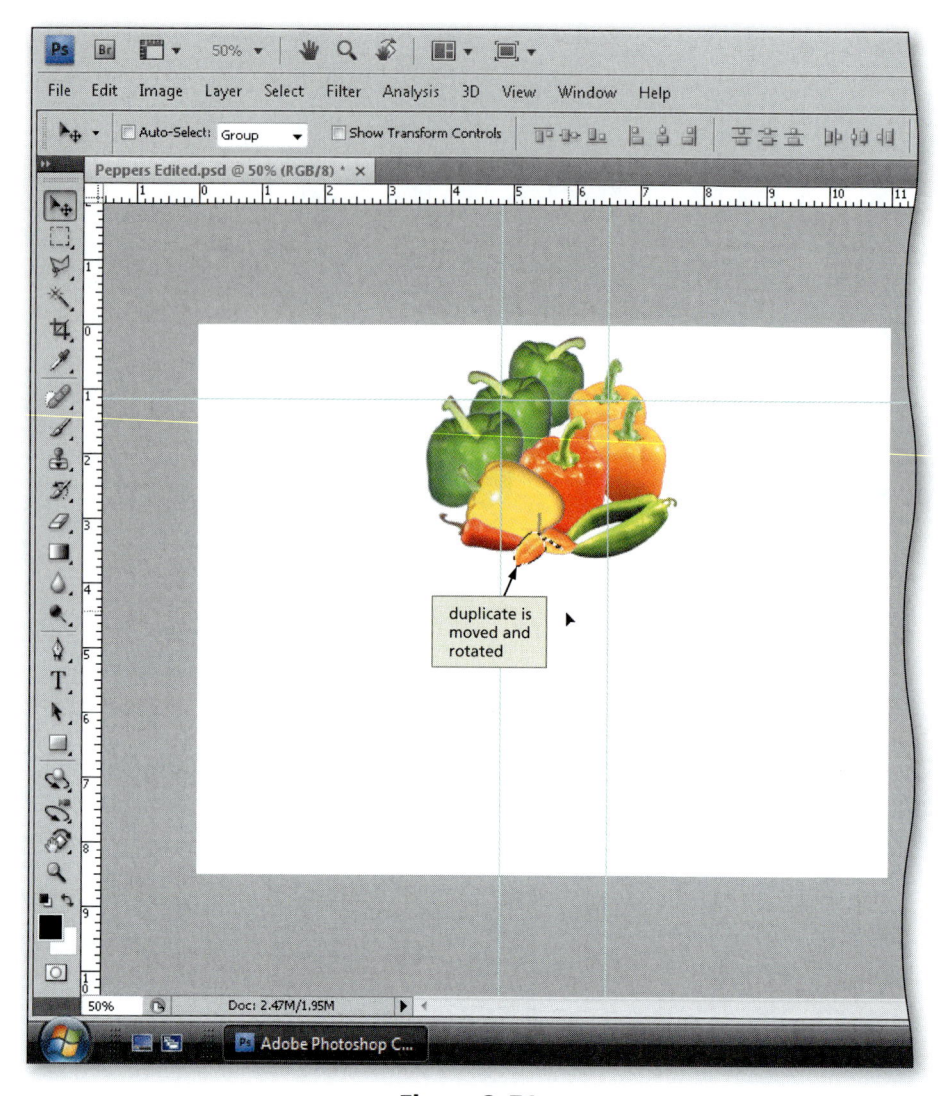

Figure 2–71

To Crop the Advertisement

Finally, you will crop the advertisement to center the peppers, including a minimal amount of border space.

1. Press the C key to access the Crop tool.

2. Drag from the top border to create a crop that leaves an even amount of white space on all four sides of the peppers, as shown in Figure 2–72.

3. Press the ENTER key to complete the crop.

Figure 2–72

To Save Using a Shortcut Key

You will save the image again, with the same file name, using a shortcut key.

1. Press CTRL+S to save the Peppers Edited file with the same name.

Create files in portable formats.
You might have to distribute your artwork in a variety of formats for customers, print shops, Webmasters, and e-mail attachments. The format you choose depends on how the file will be used, but portability is always a consideration. The document might need to be used with various operating systems, monitor resolutions, computing environments, and servers.

It is a good idea to discuss with your customer the types of formats he or she might need. It usually is safe to begin work in the Photoshop PSD format and then use the Save as command or Print command to convert the files. PDF is a portable format that can be read by anyone on the Web with a free reader. The PDF format is platform and software independent. Commonly, PDF files are virus free and safe as e-mail attachments.

Plan Ahead

Creating PDF Files

BTW

Scale to Fit
A special feature of the Print dialog box is the ability to scale the output. The Scale to Fit media check box will adjust the size of the image to fit the output medium or page size. Additionally, you can scale by a percentage. Any entered value that is less than 100% will cause a bounding box to display for free transform scaling.

The final step is to create a PDF file of the advertising image for document exchange. PDF stands for Portable Document Format, a flexible file format based on the PostScript imaging model that is cross-platform and cross-application. PDF files accurately display and preserve fonts, page layouts, and graphics. There are two ways to create a PDF file in Photoshop. First, you can save the file in the PDF format. Alternatively, you can use the Print command to create the PDF format, allowing you to make some changes to the settings before saving, which you will do in the following steps.

Recall that in Chapter 1 you printed using the Print dialog box with printer settings such as scaling, paper size, orientation, color management, and the number of copies. Photoshop's Print dialog box is standard to all output types such as printers, fax machines, One Note software, and PDF format. The dialog box also allows you to convert the photo to a positive or negative image on film. You can use the film to create a master plate for printing by a mechanical press.

To Create a PDF File Using the Print Command

The following steps use the Adobe PDF driver that comes with the Adobe Creative Suite CS4 package. If you do not have the entire suite installed on your system, you may not be able to create and save a PDF file. In that case, see your instructor for ways generate a PDF file.

1
- Click File on the menu bar and then click Print to display the Print dialog box (Figure 2–73).

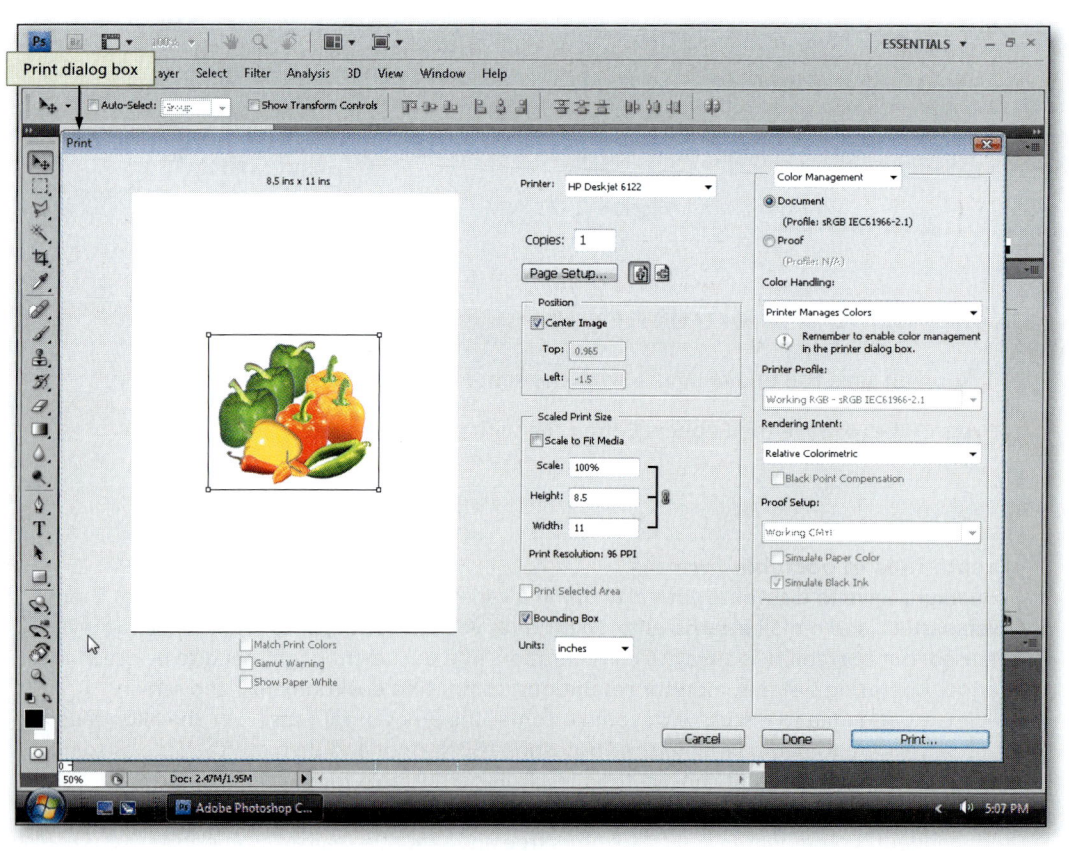

Figure 2–73

Creating PDF Files **PS 139**

2
- In the Print dialog box, click the Printer box arrow to display its list (Figure 2–74).

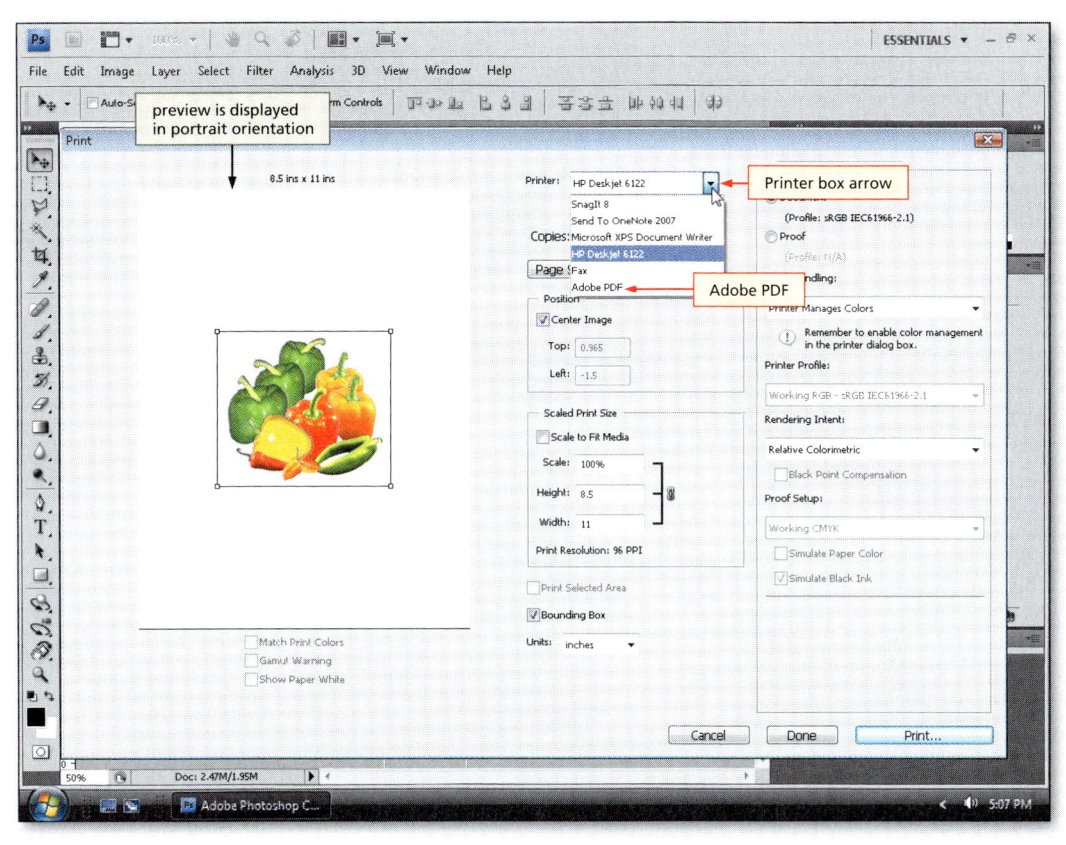

Figure 2–74

3
- Click Adobe PDF in the list to select it.
- Click the Print paper in landscape orientation button to change the orientation (Figure 2–75).

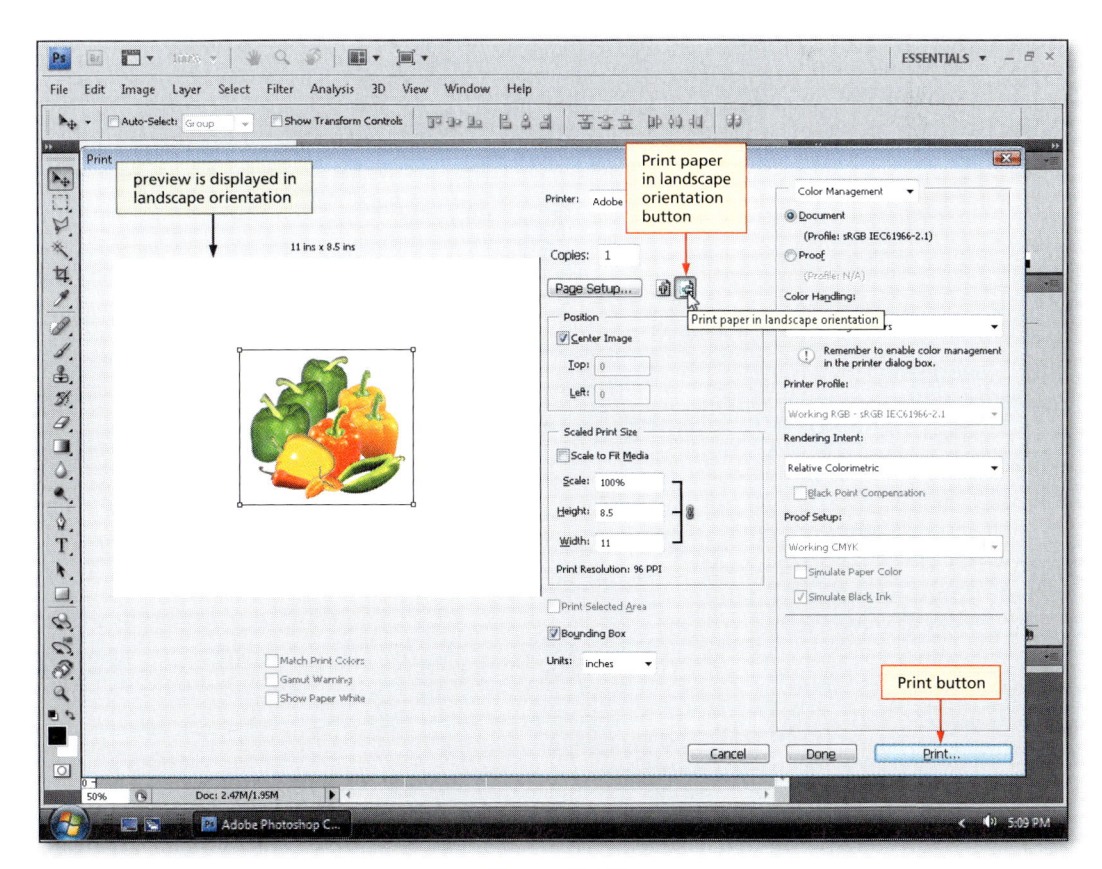

Figure 2–75

PS 140 Photoshop Chapter 2 Using Selection Tools and Shortcut Keys

4

- Click the Print button to display your printer's Print dialog box, and then click its Print button to display Photoshop's Save PDF File As dialog box. If Photoshop displays a Browse Folders button, click the button to display the folders and the Favorite Links area as shown in Figure 2–76.

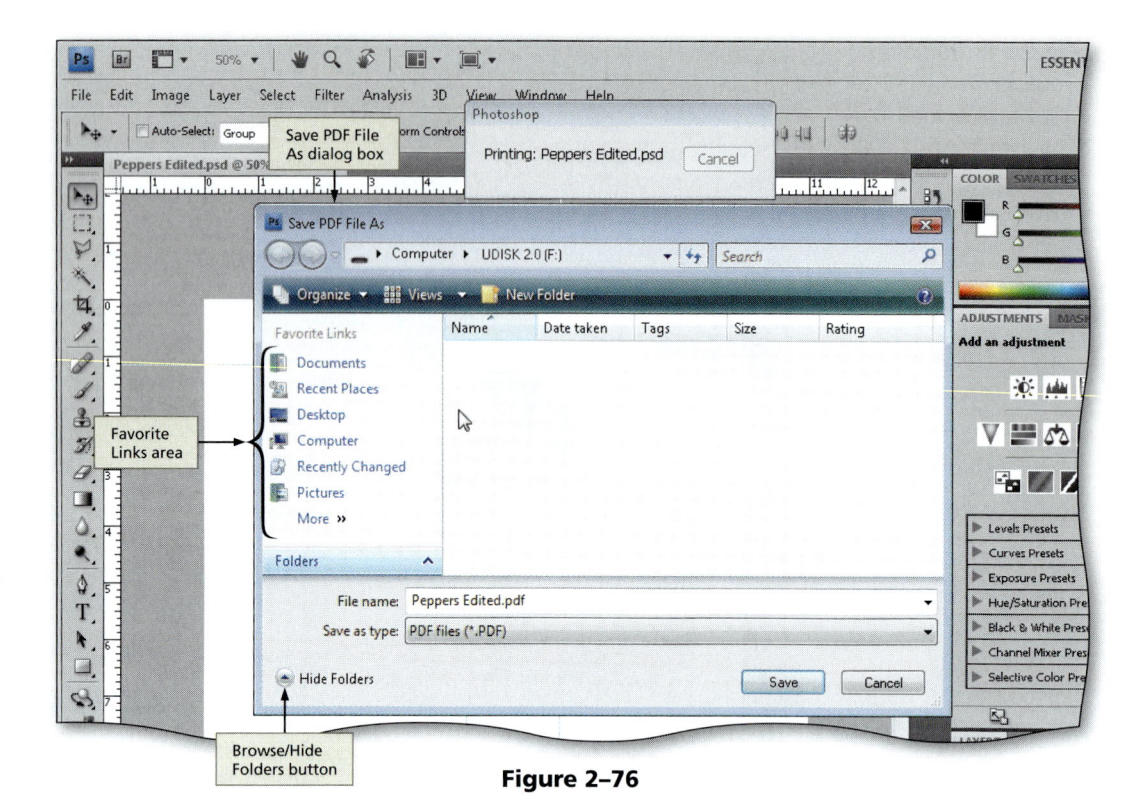

Q&A The Save PDF File As dialog box did not appear. What happened?

If you have multiple windows open on your system, the dialog box might be behind some of the other windows. In that case, minimize the other windows until the dialog box is displayed.

Figure 2–76

5

- In the File name text box, type `Peppers PDF` to rename the file. Do not press the ENTER key.

- If the location of your flash drive does not display in the Save in box, click Computer in the Favorite Links area to display a list of available drives and then scroll until UDISK 2.0 (F:), or the location of your flash drive, appears in the list of available drives. Double-click to select the location of your flash drive (Figure 2–77).

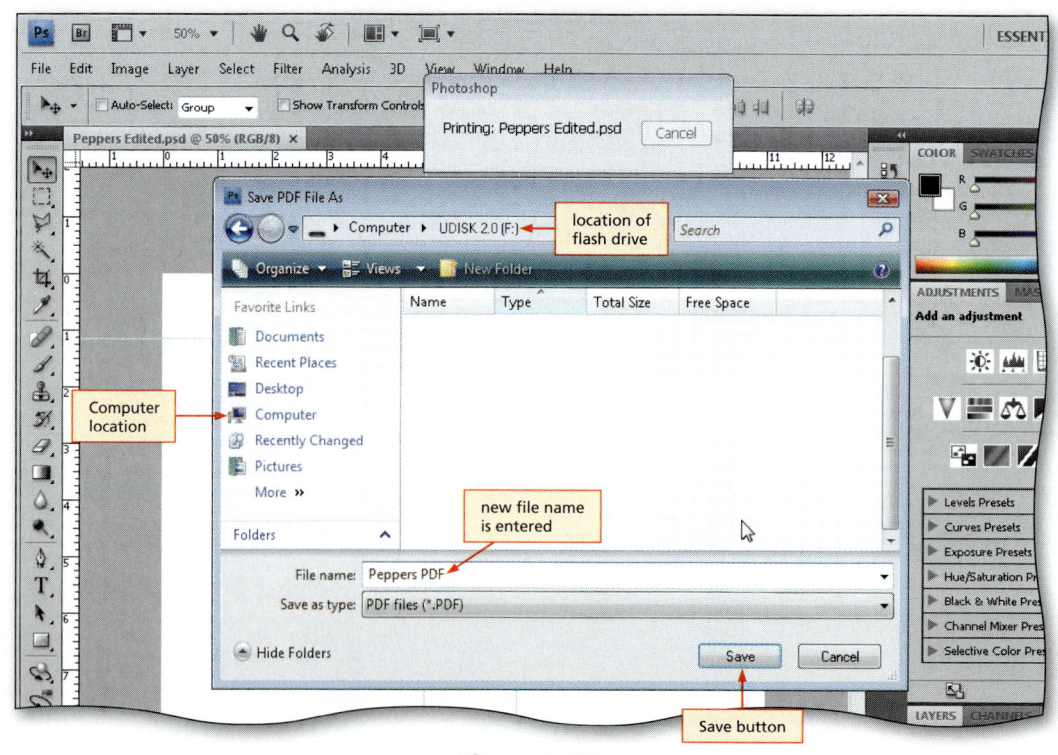

Figure 2–77

6
- Click the Save button in the Save PDF File As dialog box, to save the PDF document on the USB flash drive with the file name, Peppers PDF.

Q&A Why is the Save PDF File As dialog box different from the other Save dialog boxes?

The Save PDF File As dialog box is generated by the operating system — in this case, Windows Vista — rather than by Adobe Photoshop. The dialog box inherits its characteristics, including folder navigation, from the operating system.

Other Ways
1. Press CTRL+P, click Document box arrow, click Adobe PDF, click Print 2. On File menu, click Save As, click Format box arrow, click Photoshop PDF (*.PDF, *.PDP)

To View the PDF File

After a few moments, your system should open the PDF file automatically and display a button on the Windows Vista taskbar. If a PDF reader is not installed on your system, you might encounter a dialog box informing you that your system cannot open the file. In that case, click the OK button and skip the following step.

1
- When your system displays the Peppers PDF button on the task bar, click it to display the PDF version of the photo. Type 75 in the Zoom percentage box and then scroll as necessary to view the entire advertisement (Figure 2–78).

Q&A Why does my screen look different?

The advertisement graphic should open with the version of Adobe Reader or Adobe Acrobat currently installed on your system. Because you only are viewing the file in this format, any version is fine.

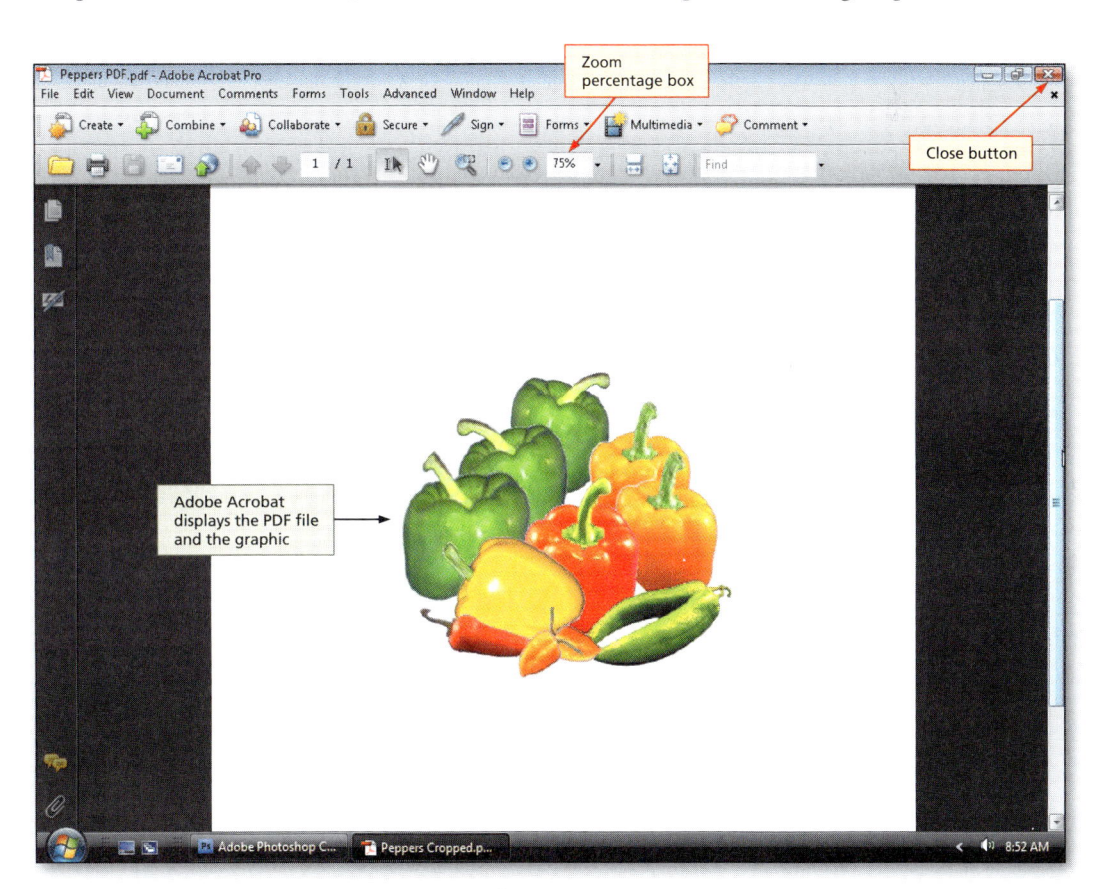

Figure 2–78

To Close the PDF File

1 Click the Close button in the Peppers PDF window. If necessary, click the Adobe Photoshop button on the Windows Vista taskbar to return to Photoshop.

To Close a Photo without Closing Photoshop

Recall that when you are finished editing a photo, you should close it. Closing a photo helps save system resources. You can close a photo after you have saved it and continue working in Photoshop, as the following steps illustrate.

1 With the Peppers Edited document window selected, click the Close button on the document window tab to close the photo.

2 If Photoshop displays a dialog box, click the No button to ignore the changes since the last time you saved the photo.

Keyboard Shortcuts

Recall that a **keyboard shortcut**, or **shortcut key**, is a way to activate menu or tool commands using the keyboard rather than the mouse. For example, pressing the L key on the keyboard immediately selects the current lasso tool without having to move your mouse away from working in the image. Shortcuts with two keystrokes are common as well, such as the use of CTRL+A to select an entire image. Shortcuts are useful when you do not want to take the time to traverse the menu system, or when you are making precise edits and selections with the mouse and do not want to go back to any of the panels to change tools or settings. A Quick Reference Summary describing Photoshop's keyboard shortcuts is included in the back of the book.

While many keyboard shortcuts already exist in Photoshop, there might be times when additional shortcuts would be useful. For instance, the Single Row and Single Column Marquee tools have no shortcut key. If those are tools that you use frequently, adding the Single Row and Single Column Marquee tools to the M keyboard shortcut might be helpful. Photoshop allows users to create, customize, and save keyboard shortcuts in one of three areas: menus, panels, and tools. When you create keyboard shortcuts, you can add them to Photoshop's default settings, save them in a personalized set for retrieval in future editing sessions, or delete them from your system.

Creating a Keyboard Shortcut

To create a new keyboard shortcut, Photoshop provides a dialog box interface, accessible from the Edit menu. Using that dialog box, you can select one of the three shortcut areas. Then you can choose a shortcut key or combination of keys. For menu commands, your shortcut keystrokes must include the CTRL key or a function key. When creating shortcuts for tools, you must use a single alphabetic character. To avoid conflicting duplications, Photoshop immediately warns you if you have chosen a keyboard shortcut used somewhere else in the program.

In the following steps, you will create a shortcut to display the History panel. While that command is accessible on the Window menu, a shortcut would save time when you need to view or edit the states in the History panel. Because the shortcut emulates the command from the menu, the same shortcut would show or hide the panel.

To Create a New Keyboard Shortcut

1
- Click Edit on the menu bar to display the Edit menu (Figure 2–79).

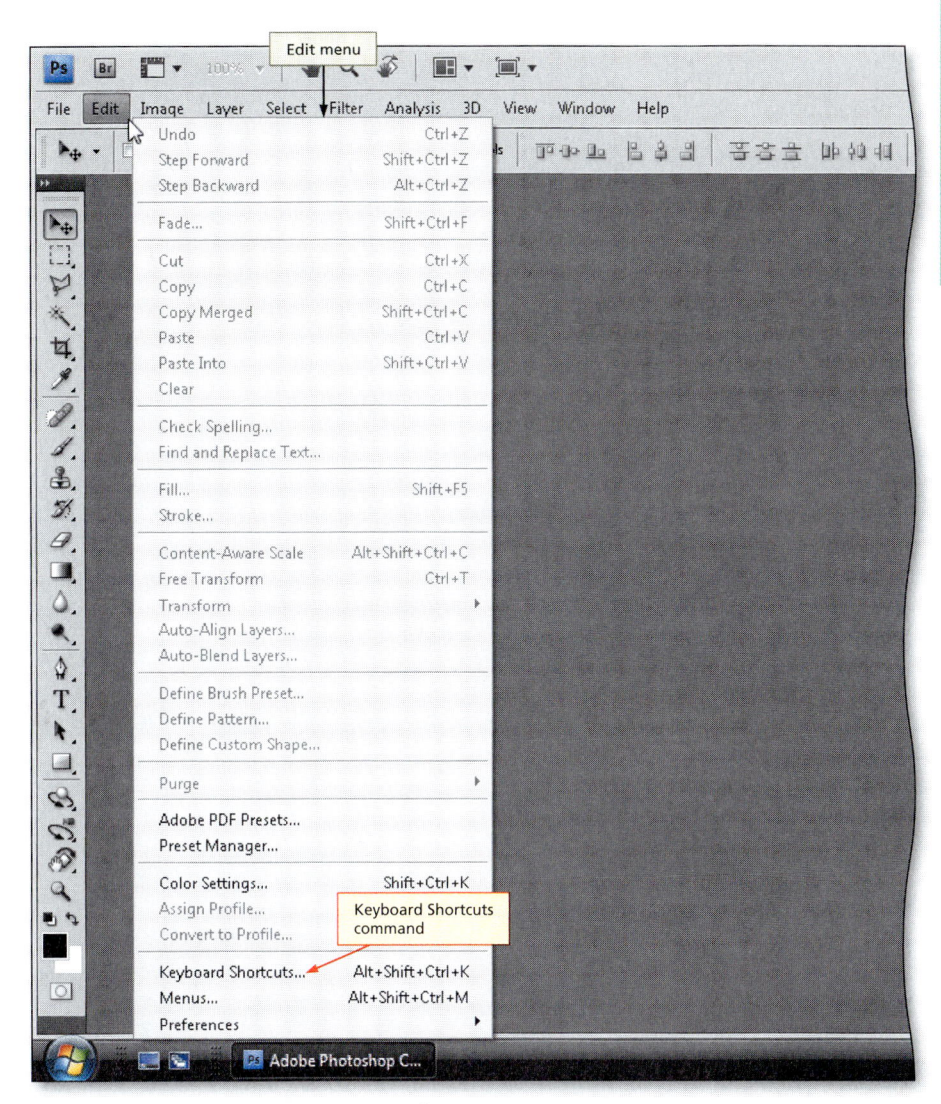

Figure 2–79

2

- Click Keyboard Shortcuts to display the Keyboard Shortcuts and Menus dialog box.

- If necessary, click the Keyboard Shortcuts tab to display its settings.

- If the Set box does not display Photoshop Defaults, click the Set box arrow and then click Photoshop Defaults in the list.

- If the Shortcuts For box does not display Application Menus, click the Shortcuts For box arrow and then click Application Menus in the list (Figure 2–80).

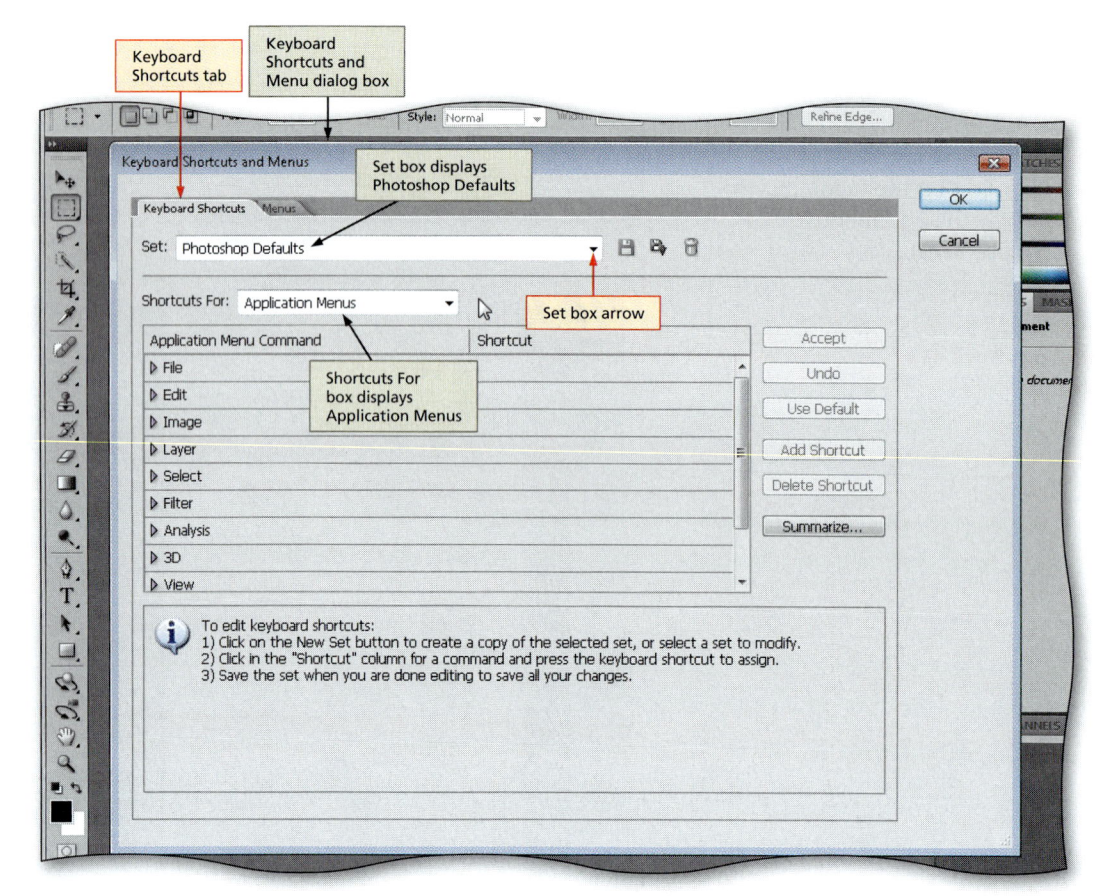

Figure 2–80

3

- In the Application Menu Command list, scroll down and then double-click Window to display the list of Window menu commands.

- Scroll down to display History under the Window menu commands, and then click History to display a shortcut key box (Figure 2–81).

Q&A What are the buttons at the top of the dialog box used for?

The Save all changes to the current set of shortcuts button allows you to name the set for future retrieval. The Create a new set based on the current set of shortcuts button creates a copy of the current keyboard shortcut settings. The Delete the current set of shortcuts button deletes the set.

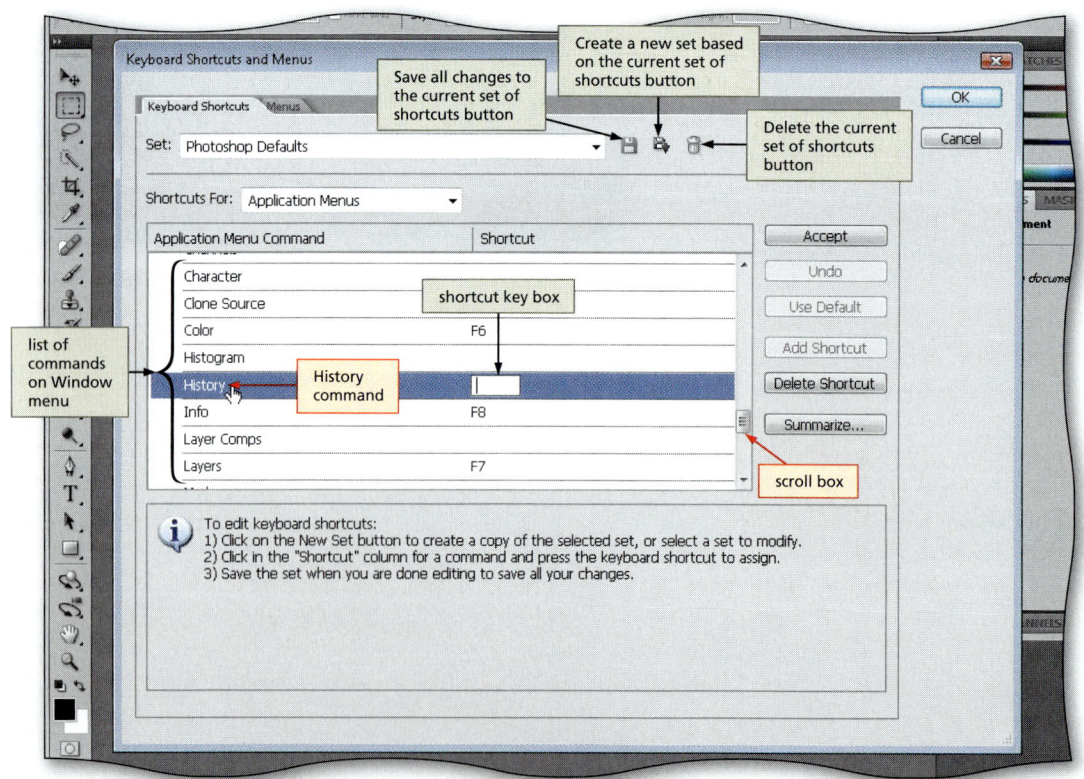

Figure 2–81

④
- Press the F12 key to enter a new shortcut keystroke for the History command (Figure 2–82).

Q&A

How can I find out which shortcuts keys still are available?

When you click the Summarize button, Photoshop creates a Web page with all of the keyboard shortcuts in the set. You can save that file on your system.

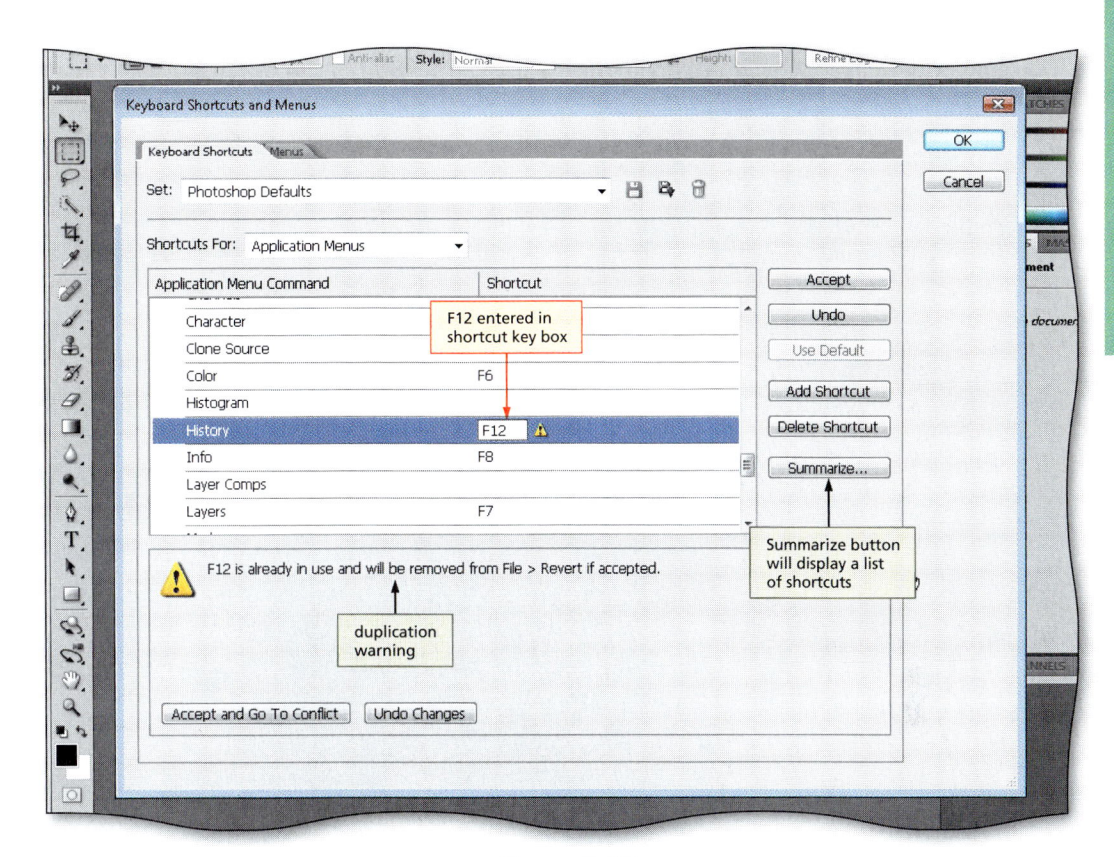

Figure 2–82

⑤
- Because Photoshop warns you that the F12 key already is being used as a shortcut for a different command, press CTRL+COMMA(,) to enter a new shortcut.
- Click the Accept button to set the shortcut key (Figure 2–83).

⑥
- Click the OK button to close the dialog box.

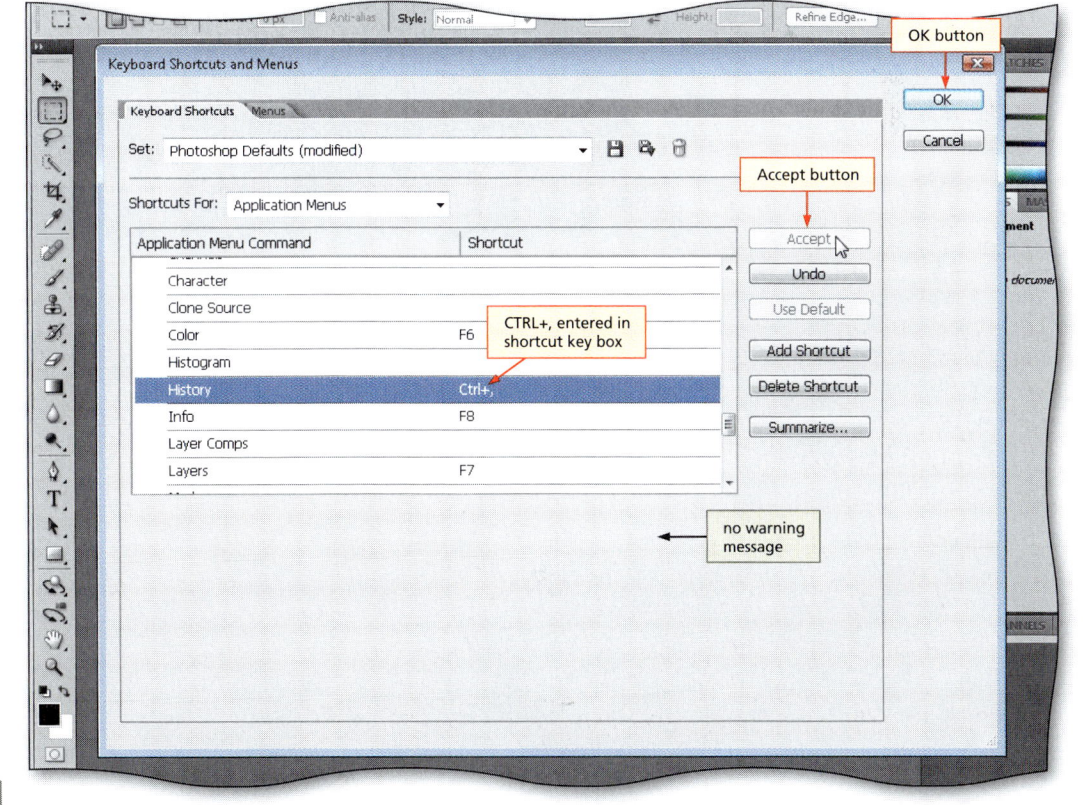

Other Ways

1. Press ALT+SHIFT+CTRL+K, edit settings, click OK

Figure 2–83

To Test a New Keyboard Shortcut

The next steps test the new keyboard shortcut.

1
- Click the Workspace switcher on the Application bar and then click Essentials to reset the workspace.
- Click Window on the menu bar to verify that the shortcut key has been assigned to the History command (Figure 2–84).

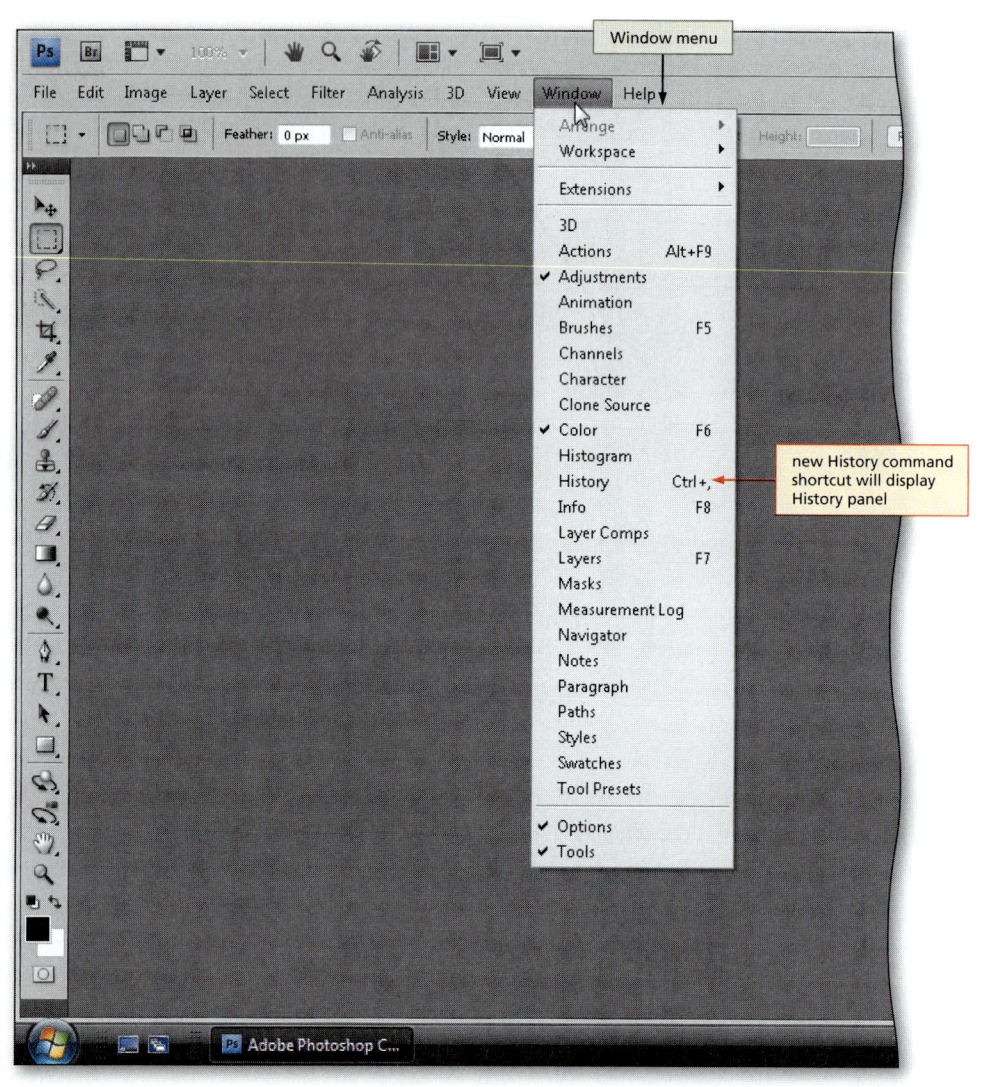

Figure 2–84

2

- Click the workspace away from the Window menu to hide the menu.

- Press CTRL+COMMA(,) to test the shortcut and display the History panel (Figure 2–85).

Q&A | Will the new shortcut be saved permanently?

The new shortcut will be saved on your system in the Photoshop Defaults (modified) set. That set will be in effect the next time you start Photoshop. If you wish to remove it, you can edit that specific shortcut, or delete the set by clicking the Delete the current set of shortcuts button.

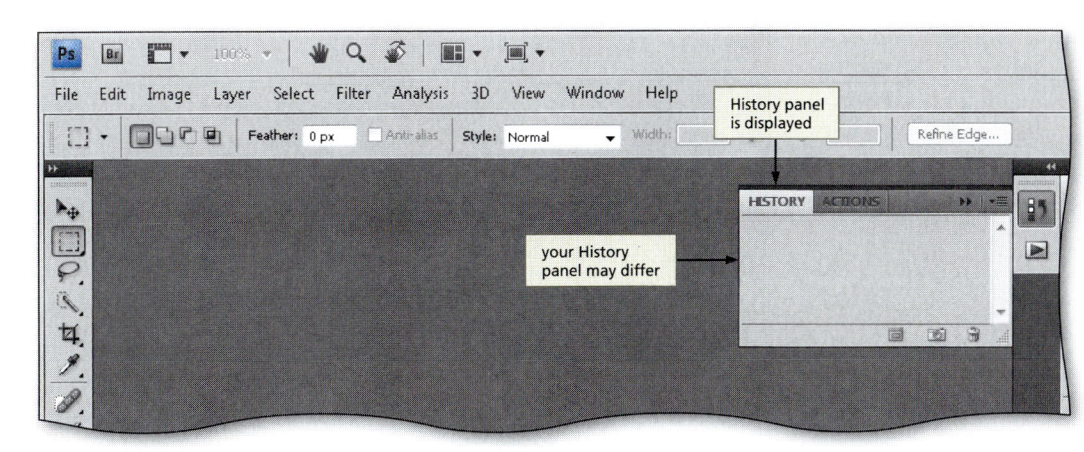

Figure 2–85

To Return to the Default Settings for Keyboard Shortcuts

It is a good idea, especially in a lab situation, to reset the keyboard shortcuts to their default settings. The following steps restore the default shortcut keys.

1

- Click Edit on the menu bar and then click Keyboard Shortcuts to display the Keyboard Shortcuts and Menus dialog box.

- On the Keyboards Shortcuts tab, click the Set box arrow to display the list (Figure 2–86).

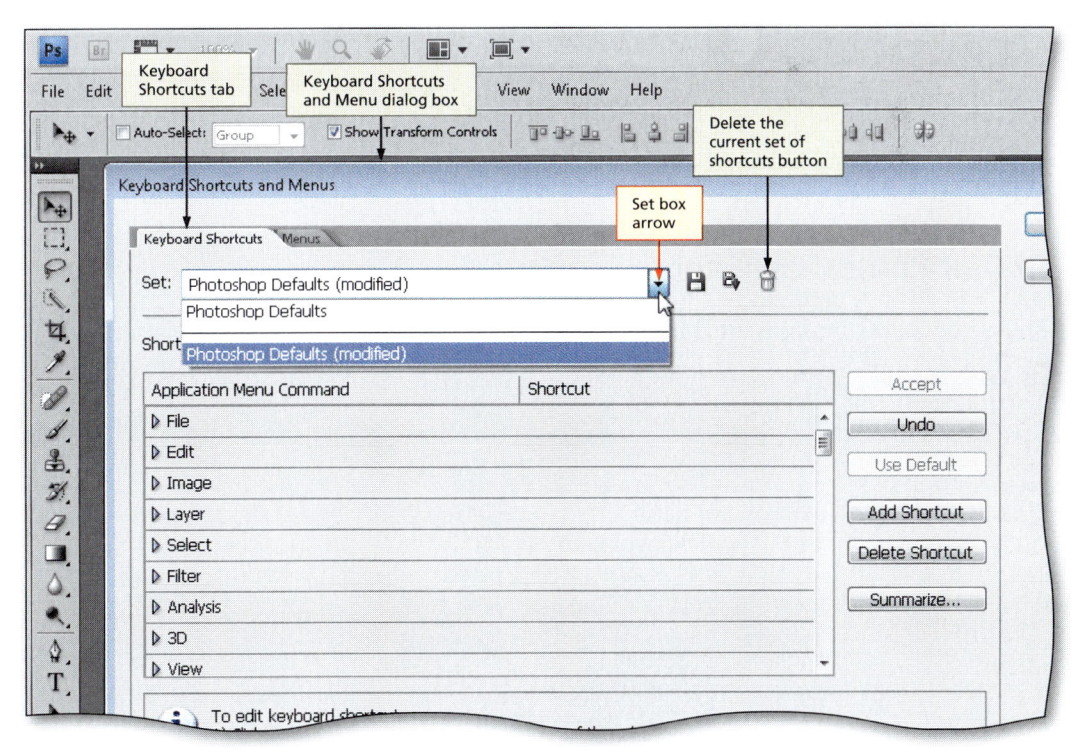

Figure 2–86

2

- Click Photoshop Defaults to choose the default settings for shortcuts.

- When Photoshop displays a message asking if you want to save your changes, click the No button to cancel your changes (Figure 2–87).

3

- In the Keyboards Shortcuts and Menus dialog box, click the OK button to close the dialog box.

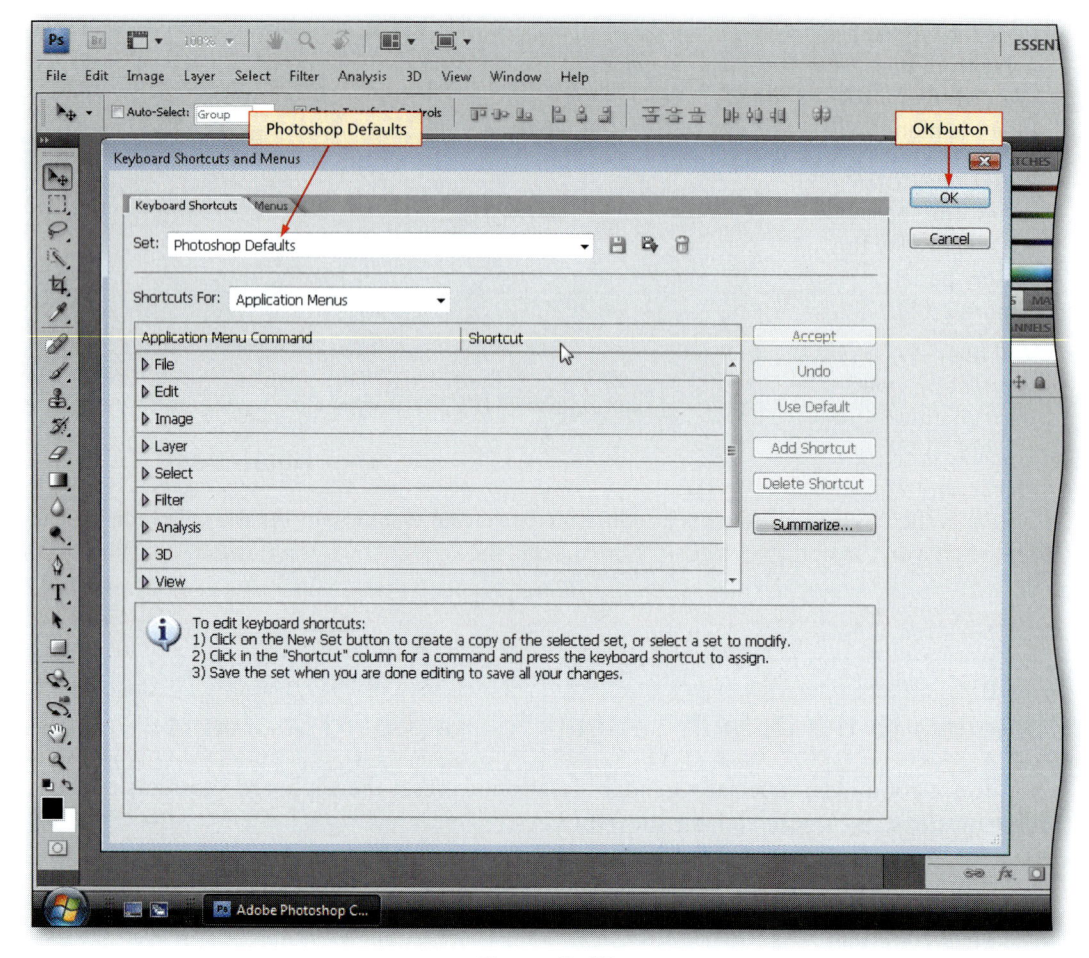

Figure 2–87

To Quit Photoshop Using a Shortcut Key

The following step shows how to quit Photoshop and return control to Windows.

1

- Press CTRL+Q to quit Photoshop.

Chapter Summary

In this chapter, you learned how to use selection tools, including the marquee tools, the lasso tools, the Quick Selection tool, and the Magic Wand tool. You worked with the Subtract from selection command, the Refine Edge dialog box, and the Grow command to edit the selection border. Once the selection was complete, you then learned many of the transformation commands, including scaling and rotating. You used the Move tool to move and copy selections. Each of the tools and commands had its own options bar with settings to control how the tool or command worked. You learned about the History panel and its states. Finally, you learned how to create and test a new keyboard shortcut.

The items listed below include all the new Photoshop skills you have learned in this chapter:

1. Use the Rectangular Marquee Tool (PS 89)
2. Use the Move Tool (PS 91)
3. Subtract from a Selection Using the Magic Wand Tool (PS 93)
4. Duplicate the Selection (PS 94)
5. Scale a Selection (PS 98)
6. Flip a Selection (PS 99)
7. Warp a Selection (PS 101)
8. Deselect Using Shortcut Keys (PS 103)
9. Display the History Panel (PS 105)
10. Use the History Panel (PS 106)
11. Collapse the History Panel (PS 107)
12. Display a Grid (PS 109)
13. Create Guides (PS 110)
14. Use the Quick Selection Tool (PS 113)
15. Undo Using the History Panel (PS 115)
16. Refine Edges (PS 117)
17. Select Using the Lasso Tool (PS 121)
18. Select Using the Magnetic Lasso Tool (PS 123)
19. Rotate a Selection (PS 126)
20. Select Using the Polygonal Lasso Tool (PS 128)
21. Grow the Selection (PS 133)
22. Create a PDF File Using the Print Command (PS 138)
23. View the PDF File (PS 141)
24. Create a New Keyboard Shortcut (PS 143)
25. Test a New Keyboard Shortcut (PS 146)
26. Return to the Default Settings for Keyboard Shortcuts (PS 147)

Learn It Online

Test your knowledge of chapter content and key terms.

Instructions: To complete the Learn It Online exercises, start your browser, click the Address bar, and then enter the Web address scsite.com/pscs4/learn. When the Photoshop CS4 Learn It Online page is displayed, click the link for the exercise you want to complete and then read the instructions.

Chapter Reinforcement TF, MC, and SA
A series of true/false, multiple choice, and short answer questions that test your knowledge of the chapter content.

Flash Cards
An interactive learning environment where you identify chapter key terms associated with displayed definitions.

Practice Test
A series of multiple choice questions that test your knowledge of chapter content and key terms.

Who Wants To Be a Computer Genius?
An interactive game that challenges your knowledge of chapter content in the style of a television quiz show.

Wheel of Terms
An interactive game that challenges your knowledge of chapter key terms in the style of the television show *Wheel of Fortune*.

Crossword Puzzle Challenge
A crossword puzzle that challenges your knowledge of key terms presented in the chapter.

PS 150 Photoshop Chapter 2 Using Selection Tools and Shortcut Keys

Apply Your Knowledge

Reinforce the skills and apply the concepts you learned in this chapter.

Moving and Duplicating Selections

Instructions: Start Photoshop and perform the customization steps found on pages PS 7 through PS 9. Open the Apply 2-1 Bread file in the Chapter02 folder from the Data Files for Students and save it, in the PSD file format, as Apply 2-1 Bread Edited. You can access the Data Files for Students on the DVD that accompanies this book; see the inside back cover of this book for instructions on downloading the Data Files for Students, or contact your instructor for information about accessing the required files.

You will create another grocery advertisement, this one featuring bakery items. First, you will select individual items from within the file, and then you will transform and move them so that the finished design looks like Figure 2–88. You will place the rest of the images from back to front.

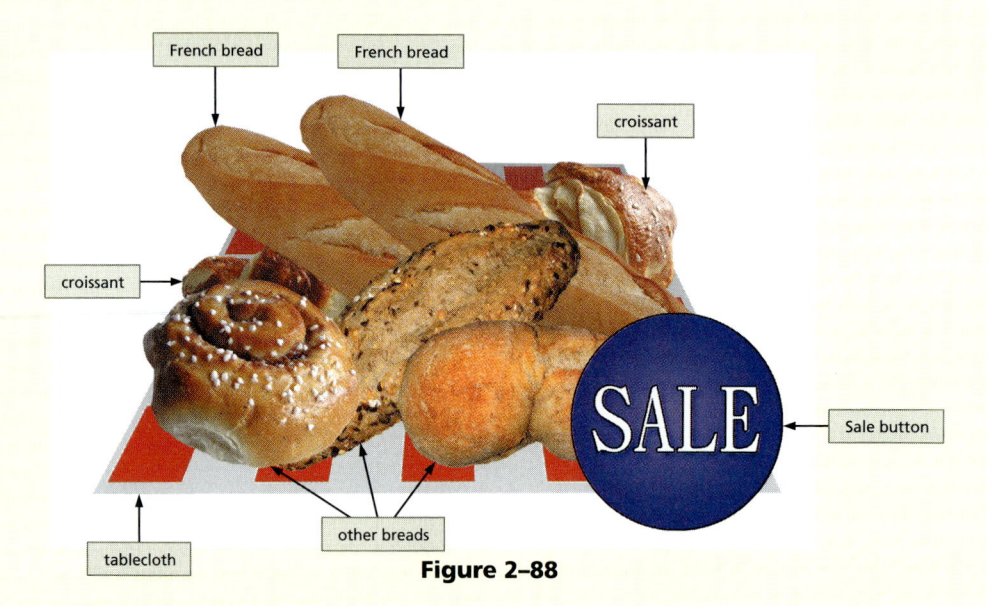

Figure 2–88

Perform the following tasks:
1. Because the checkered tablecloth is in the very back of the arrangement, you will start with it. Use the Rectangular Marquee tool to select the checkered tablecloth.
2. Use the Move tool to move the tablecloth to the top-center of the page. Do not deselect the tablecloth.
3. With the Move tool still selected, click the Show Transform Controls check box on the options bar so it displays a check mark. To distort the tablecloth and make it appear in perspective, CTRL+drag each of the lower corner sizing handles down and outward. Do not overlap any of the bread items. The result should be a trapezoid shape, as shown in Figure 2–88. If you make a mistake, press the ESC key and start again. When you are satisfied with the shape, press the ENTER key to confirm the transformation. Do not deselect.
4. The croissant is the back-most item in the arrangement. Use the Polygonal Lasso tool to select the croissant. (*Hint:* The croissant is the lower-right item in the Apply 2-1 Bread image.) Right-click the Quick Selection Tool (W) button on the Tools panel, and then click Magic Wand Tool. On the options bar, click the Subtract from selection button, then click the white area around the croissant to remove it.

5. Use the Move tool to move the croissant to the upper-right portion of the tablecloth. ALT+drag a second croissant to a location below and to the left of the first, as shown in Figure 2–88. Press CTRL+D to deselect it.
6. Repeat Steps 4 and 5 to select and move the French bread.
7. ALT+drag the French bread to the right to create a duplicate.
8. Select and move the remaining bread items until you are satisfied with the arrangement. For each bread item, use a selection tool that will approximate the shape of the bread. On the options bar, use the Add to selection and Subtract from selection buttons as necessary. Use the Magic Wand tool to remove white space around the selection before moving it.
9. Right-click the Rectangular Marquee Tool (M) button on the Tools panel, then click Elliptical Marquee Tool. Use the Elliptical Marquee tool to select the Sale button. (*Hint*: Press and hold the SHIFT key as you select to maintain a perfect circle.)
10. Move the Sale button to the lower-right portion of the ad.
11. Use the Crop tool to select the portion of the image to use for the final ad. (*Hint:* The remaining white space is not needed.)
12. Save the Apply 2-1 Bread Edited file, and then close Photoshop.
13. Submit the assignment in the format specified by your instructor.

Extend Your Knowledge

Extend the skills you learned in this chapter and experiment with new skills. You may need to use Help to complete the assignment.

Separating Objects from the Background

Instructions: Start Photoshop and perform the customization steps found on pages PS 7 through PS 9. Open the Extend 2-1 Flowers file in the Chapter02 folder from the Data Files for Students and save it, in the PSD format, as Extend 2-1 Flowers Edited. You can access the Data Files for Students on the DVD that accompanies this book; see the inside back cover of this book for instructions on downloading the Data Files for Students, or contact your instructor for information about accessing the required files.

   The original flower image displays the flowers in their natural settings, with various colors in the background. After moving the frame and making a copy, you will select the flowers while preventing background colors from straying into the selection. Finally, you will position each flower in front of a frame.

Perform the following tasks:
1. Use the Elliptical Marquee tool to select the oval frame. (*Hint:* For more careful placement, while dragging to create the selection, you can press the SPACEBAR key to adjust the location of the drag and then release it to continue drawing the marquee.) Be careful to select only the frame, and eliminate any white around the edge of the selection using the Magic Wand tool and the Subtract from selection button.
2. Drag the selection to a location below the left side of the word, Flowers. Do not be concerned if you leave a slight shadow behind. Press CTRL+T to display the Transform options bar. Increase the selection to 110 percent both in width and height. Press the ENTER key to commit the transformation.
3. With the frame still selected, SHIFT+ALT+drag to create a duplicate and place it to the right of the original (Figure 2–89).

Continued >

Extend Your Knowledge *continued*

Figure 2–89

4. Use appropriate selection tools to select the upper flower and its stem. (*Hint:* Use the Magic Wand tool with a tolerance setting of 50 to select the contiguous pink and then add to the selection using other tools.) Click the Intersect with selection button to combine selected areas, if necessary. Do not include the background.

5. To ensure that the selection does not have any stray pixels around its border, use the Refine Edge dialog box to refine the edge by increasing the radius to .7 px.

6. As you create the selection, if necessary, press CTRL+ALT+Z to step back through the editing history and return the image to an earlier state.

7. Move the selected flower onto the left frame.

8. Repeat steps 4 through 7 for the lower flower and the right frame.

9. Crop the image to include only the word, Flowers, and the two framed flowers. Save the changes.

10. Use the Magic Wand tool to select the blue color in the word, Flowers. (*Hint:* To select all of the letters, you will have to remove the check mark in the Contiguous box.) If parts of the image are selected that are not in the word, Flowers, use the Subtract from selection button to remove them.

11. Use Photoshop Help to investigate how to soften the edges of selections. Use the Refine Edge dialog box to soften the edges. Expand the selection and feather the edges.

12. Use Photoshop Help to investigate how to stroke a selection or layer with color. With the letters selected, use the Stroke command on the Edit menu to display the Stroke dialog box. Stroke the selection with a white color, 5 pixels wide, on the outside of the selection.

13. Close the photo and close Photoshop. Send the revised photo to your instructor as an e-mail attachment.

Make It Right

Analyze a project and correct all errors and/or improve the design.

Correcting Item Alignment, Sizing, and Content

Instructions: Start Photoshop and perform the customization steps found on pages PS 7 through PS 9. Open the Make It Right 2-1 Fruit file in the Chapter02 folder from the Data Files for Students and save it, in the PSD file format, as Make It Right 2-1 Fruit Edited. You can access the Data Files for Students on the DVD that accompanies this book; see the inside back cover of this book for instructions on downloading the Data Files for Students, or contact your instructor for information about accessing the required files.

The grocery store advertising team has created a new ad featuring fresh fruit for the produce department, but there are some flaws in the composition, as shown in Figure 2–90, that you must fix. First, you must center the words, FRESH and FRUITS, and improve their rotation so that they fit the circle better. The potato also does not belong in the fruit ad; obscure or remove the potato so that it is not visible. You may replace it using an existing fruit or select the extra pear on the right side. Finally, crop the entire image to match the layout.

Save the project again. Submit the revised document in the format specified by your instructor.

Figure 2–90

In the Lab

Design and/or create a publication using the guidelines, concepts, and skills presented in this chapter. Labs are listed in order of increasing difficulty.

Lab 1: Using the Keyboard with the Magic Wand Tool

Problem: As e-cards gain popularity, the need for good graphics also has increased. A small e-commerce site has hired you as its photo specialist to assist with images and photos used in the greeting cards provided online. Your first assignment is to provide a clean image for a card whose greeting will read, "I'm off my rocker! I forgot your birthday!" A photographer has submitted a photo of a rocker, but the layout artist needs the background removed and the rocker scaled to approximately half of its original size. The layout artist has requested a PDF of your final product. You decide to practice using the function keys to perform most of the editing tasks. The edited photo is displayed in Figure 2–91.

Figure 2–91

Instructions: Perform the following tasks:

1. Start Photoshop. Set the default workspace and reset all tools.
2. Press CTRL+O to open the Lab 2-1 Rocker file from the Chapter02 folder of the Data Files for Students, or from a location specified by your instructor.
3. Press SHIFT+CTRL+S to display the Save As dialog box. Save the file on your storage device with the name, Lab 2-1 Rocker Edited.
4. If the photo does not appear at 16.67% magnification, press CTRL+PLUS SIGN (+) or CTRL+HYPHEN (-) to zoom in or out as necessary.
5. To remove the wallpaper:
   a. Press the W key to choose the Magic Wand tool. If the Quick Selection tool is the active tool, press SHIFT+W to select the Magic Wand tool.
   b. On the options bar, click the Contiguous box so it does not display a check mark.
   c. Click the blue wallpaper and then press CTRL+X to remove it.
6. To remove the floor:
   a. On the options bar, click the Contiguous box so it displays a check mark.
   b. Click the floor. SHIFT+click other parts of the floor to add to the selection. (*Hint*: Be sure to click all of the floor, including the spaces between the chair legs.)
   c. Use the Navigator panel to zoom as necessary, or if your computer's mouse has a wheel, ALT+wheel back and forth to zoom. Press CTRL+X to remove the floor selection.
7. To remove the baseboard:
   a. Repeat Step 6 for the baseboard.
   b. If you make an error or some areas are deleted by mistake, click Window on the menu bar, and then click History to display the History panel. Press CTRL+ALT+Z to step backward through the states in the History panel, or click the first state in the History panel and begin again with Step 5.

8. Using the Magic Wand tool, SHIFT+click any remaining part of the photo that is not the rocker and remove it.
9. To select only the rocker:
   a. On the Magic Wand tool options bar, click the New selection button and then click to remove the check mark in the Contiguous box. Click the white area of the photo.
   b. Press SHIFT+CTRL+I to select the inverse. The rocker now should be selected.
10. To scale the rocker:
    a. Press CTRL+T to free transform the rocker selection. On the options bar, drag the W scrubby slider to 50%. Drag the H scrubby slider to 50%.
    b. Press the ENTER key to commit the transformations.
    c. Press CTRL+D to deselect, if necessary.
11. Press CTRL+S to save the file with the same name. If Photoshop displays a Photoshop Format Options dialog box, click the OK button.
12. To create the PDF file:
    a. Press CTRL+P to display the Print dialog box, and then choose Adobe PDF in the Printer box list. Click the Print button. When your printer's Print dialog box is displayed, click its Print button.
    b. When the Save PDF File As dialog box is displayed, browse to your USB flash drive location. Name the file, Lab 2-1 Rocker PDF. Click the Save button.
    c. When the Adobe Acrobat or Adobe Reader window is displayed, view the file and then press CTRL+Q to close the window.
13. Click the Photoshop button on the Windows taskbar, if necessary. Close the document window by pressing CTRL+W. If Photoshop displays a dialog box asking you to save again, click the No button.
14. Quit Photoshop by pressing CTRL+Q.
15. Send the PDF file as an e-mail attachment to your instructor, or follow your instructor's directions for submitting the lab assignment.

In the Lab

Lab 2: Applying Skew, Perspective, and Warp Transformations

Problem: Hobby Express, a store that specializes in model trains and remote control toys, wants a new logo. They would like to illustrate the concept of a train engine racing to the store. The picture will appear on their letterhead, business cards, and advertising pieces. They would like a digital file so they can use the logo for other graphic purposes. The edited photo is shown in Figure 2–92.

Continued >

In the Lab *continued*

Figure 2–92

Instructions: Perform the following tasks:
1. Start Photoshop. Set the default workspace and reset all tools.
2. Open the file, Lab 2-2 Engine, from the Chapter02 folder of the Data Files for Students, or from a location specified by your instructor.
3. Use the Save As command to save the file on your storage device with the name Lab 2-2 Engine Edited.
4. Click the Magic Wand Tool (W) button on the Tools panel and deselect the Contiguous check box on the options bar. If necessary, type 32 in the Tolerance box. Select all of the blue background.
5. To add the green grass in the lower-right corner of the photo to the selection, on the Magic Wand tool options bar, click the Add to selection button. Type 50 in the Tolerance box, click the Contiguous check box so it displays its check mark, and then click the grass. Press the DELETE key to delete the selected areas.
6. On the Select menu, click Inverse.
7. On the Edit menu, point to Transform, and then click Warp. When Photoshop displays the warp grid, locate the upper-left warp point that appears as a gray circle on the grid. Drag the warp point to the left until the smokestack bends slightly.
8. Right-click the selection and then click Skew on the context menu. Drag the upper-middle sizing handle to the left. Do not drag it off the document window. If you make a mistake, press the ESC key and then skew again.
9. Experiment with the Perspective and Distort commands to make the engine look as if it were moving. The front of the engine should appear closer than the rear. The smokestack should curve backward to simulate motion. Apply any transformations.
10. Save the photo again and print a copy for your instructor.

In the Lab

Lab 3: Creating Shortcuts, Saving Sets, and Viewing the Shortcut Summary

Problem: You have decided to create a new keyboard shortcut to reset all tools, rather than having to move the mouse to the options bar, right-click, and then choose to reset all tools. Because other family members work on your computer system, you would like to save the new shortcut in a separate set for your personal use. You also would like to see a complete listing of the Photoshop shortcuts for your system.

Instructions: Perform the following tasks:

1. Start Photoshop. Set the default workspace and reset all tools.
2. On the Edit menu, click Keyboard Shortcuts. When the Keyboard Shortcuts and Menus dialog box is displayed, if necessary click the Keyboard Shortcuts tab. If necessary, click the Set box arrow and then click Photoshop Defaults in the list.
3. Click the Shortcuts For box arrow and then click Panel Menus in the list.
4. Scroll down and double-click Tool Presets in the list.
5. Scroll down and click Reset All Tools in the list and then press CTRL+/ to choose the shortcut combination. Click the Accept button.
6. Click the Create a new set based on the current set of shortcuts button. When the Save dialog box is displayed, type your name in the File name box. Click the Save button.
7. When the Keyboard Shortcuts and Menus dialog box again is displayed, click the Summarize button. In the Save dialog box, type My Shortcut Summary in the File name box. Click the Save in box arrow and choose your USB flash drive location, if necessary. Click the Save button.
8. The Shortcut Summary should open automatically in your browser (Figure 2–93). If it does not, use a Computer window or an Explore window to navigate to your USB flash drive. Double-click the My Shortcut Summary HTML file. When the summary appears, print the page and turn it in to your instructor.
9. Close the browser. Click the OK button to close the Keyboard Shortcuts and Menus dialog box. Quit Photoshop.

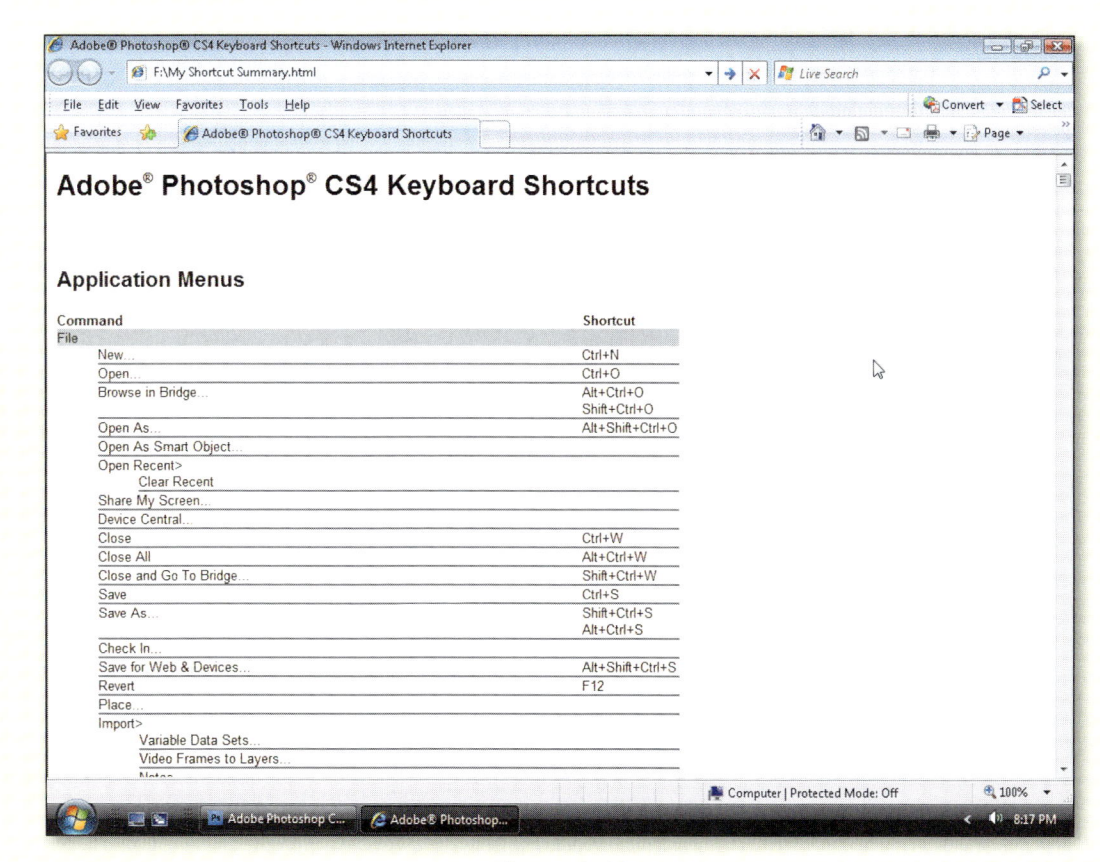

Figure 2–93

Cases and Places

Apply your creative thinking and problem-solving skills to design and implement a solution.

• Easier   •• More Difficult

• 1: Creating a Money Graphic

Your local bank is starting an initiative to encourage children to open a savings account using their loose change. The bank would like a before and after picture showing how money can grow with interest. A file named Case 2-1 Coins is located in the Chapter02 folder of the Data Files for Students. Start Photoshop and use the Elliptical Marquee tool to select each coin and duplicate it several times to fill the image with coins. Rotate and layer some of the coins to make the image look more interesting. Save the photo with the name, Case 2-1 Coins Edited on your USB flash drive storage device.

•• 2: Creating a Poster for the Computer Lab

The computer lab at your school wants a poster reminding students to save their work often. The department chair has asked you to create a graphic of a computer mouse that seems to be eating data. He has taken a picture of a mouse from the lab and started the poster for you. A file named Case 2-2 Poster is located in the Chapter02 folder of the Data Files for Students. Start Photoshop and use the selection tools to select the mouse. Flip the mouse horizontally. Then, using the Subtract from selection button, remove the white part around the selection. Also remove the dark gray bottom portion of the mouse from the selection. With the top portion of the mouse selected, warp the selection up and away from the bottom part of the mouse to simulate an open mouth. Move the selection close to the 0 and 1 data pattern. Save a copy of the poster as a PDF and send it as an e-mail attachment to your instructor.

• 3: Thinking about Transformations

Look through magazines or newspapers for color photos with distinctive transformations such as perspective, skew, or warp. If possible, cut out three photos. Write a short paragraph for each example describing how you think the image was generated. List the tool, the transformation, and the potential problems associated with duplicating the process. Describe the idea being conveyed by the photo and describe a second possible conceptual application for the photo. Attach the photos to the descriptions and submit them to your instructor. If directed by your instructor to do so, recreate the image.

•• 4: Duplicating and Transforming Objects

Make It Personal

Use your digital camera to take a picture of a small object in your home, such as a can of soup or a piece of fruit. Transfer the picture to your computer system and open it with Photoshop. Duplicate the object several times and perform a different transformation technique on each copy, such as scale, rotate, skew, warp, distort, and perspective. Save the photo and send a copy to your instructor.

•• 5: Creating a Group Photo

Working Together

Your group has been assigned to create a collage from individual photos. Using a digital camera or camera phone, each team member should take a picture of their favorite soft drink. Using Photoshop, open each digital file and select only the bottle, can, or glass. Invert the selection and press the DELETE key to eliminate the background. Save each file. Choose the picture with the most white space to be the master photo. In each of the other photos, use the Magnetic Lasso tool to select the individual. Copy the selection and then paste it into the master photo, creating a collage. Scale and move the selections as necessary to make the picture look good. Try to match the proportions for a realistic composition, or exaggerate proportions for more humorous results. Experiment with overlapping selections. Use the History panel to return to previous states when errors are made. Submit the final product to your teacher.

3 | Working with Layers

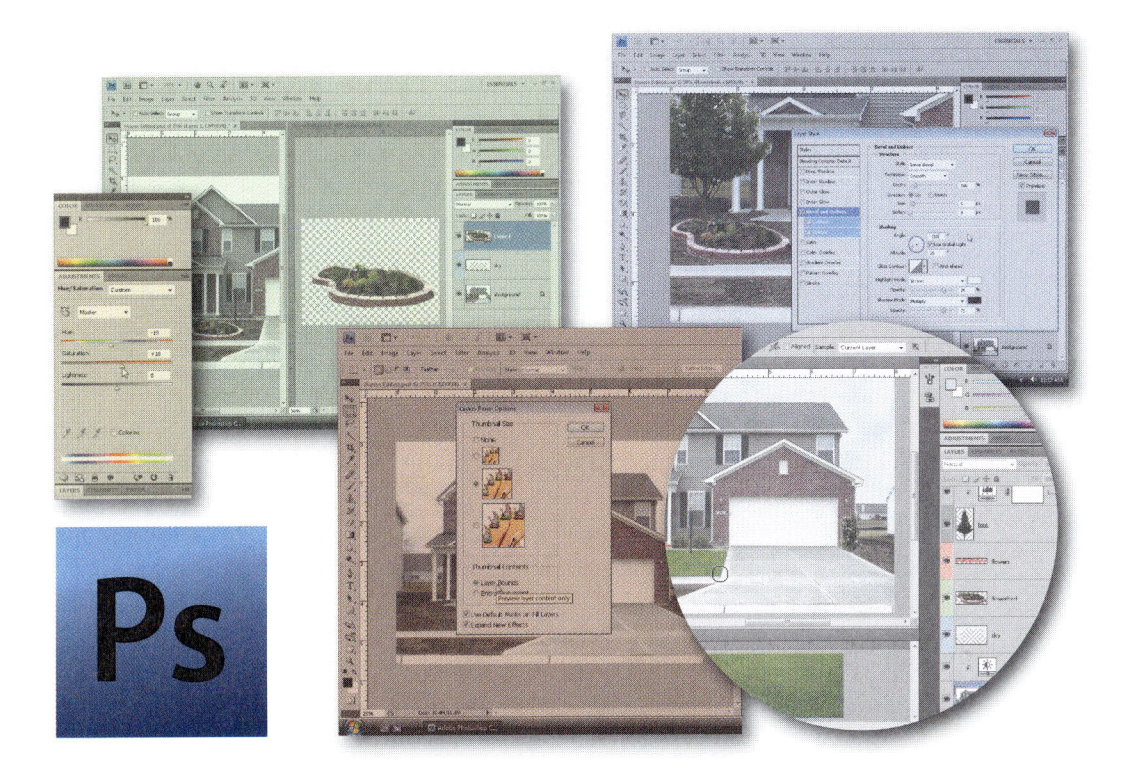

Objectives

You will have mastered the material in this chapter when you can:

- Create a layer via cut and use the Layers panel
- Select, name, color, hide, and view layers
- Create a new layer from another image or selection
- Set layer properties
- Resize a layer
- Erase portions of layers and images
- Use the Eraser, Magic Eraser, and Background Eraser tools
- Create layer masks
- Make level adjustments and opacity changes
- Apply filter adjustments
- Create a layer style
- Add a render filter
- Use the Clone Stamp tool
- Flatten a composite image

3 | Working with Layers

Introduction

Whether it is adding a new person to a photograph, combining artistic effects from different genres, or creating 3D animation, the concept of layers in Photoshop allows you to work on one element of an image without disturbing the others. A **layer** is an image superimposed or separated from other parts of the photograph. You might think of layers as sheets of clear film stacked one on top of one another. You can see through **transparent** areas of a layer to the layers below. The nontransparent, or **opaque,** areas of a layer are solid and obscure lower layers. You can change the composition of an image by changing the order and attributes of layers. In addition, special features, such as adjustment layers, layer masks, fill layers, and layer styles, allow you to create sophisticated effects.

Another tool that graphic designers use when they want to recreate a portion of another photo is the Clone Stamp tool. As you will learn in this chapter, the Clone Stamp tool takes a sample of an image and then applies, as you draw, an exact copy of that image to your document.

Graphic designers use layers and clones along with other tools in Photoshop to create **composite** images that combine or merge multiple images and drawings to create a new image, also referred to as a **montage**. Composite images illustrate the power of Photoshop and are used to prepare documents for businesses, advertising, marketing, and media artwork. Composite images such as navigation bars can be created in Photoshop and used on the Web along with layered buttons, graphics, and background images.

Project — Landscape Design

Chapter 3 uses Photoshop to create a composite image from several photographs by using layers. Specifically, it begins with a photo of a recently constructed house and creates a composite image by inserting layers of flowers, shrubs, trees, and sod to create a complete landscape design. The process is illustrated in Figure 3–1.

The enhancements will show how the home will look after appropriate landscaping has been installed. Sod will replace the dirt; shrubs and trees will be planted. The photo will be edited to display a bright summer day with clouds in the sky. Finally, layers will be adjusted to give the house maximum curb appeal.

Figure 3–1

PS 161

Overview

As you read this chapter, you will learn how to create the composite landscape shown in Figure 3–1 on the previous page by performing these general tasks:

- Create a layer via cut.
- Insert layers from new images.
- Use the eraser tools.
- Add a layer mask.
- Create layer adjustments.
- Apply layer styles and render filters.
- Flatten the image.
- Save the photo in the TIF format.

Plan Ahead

General Project Guidelines

When editing a photo, the actions you perform and decisions you make will affect the appearance and characteristics of the finished product. As you edit a photo, such as the one shown in Figure 3–1, you should follow these general guidelines:

1. **Gather your photos and plan your layers.** The graphics you choose should convey the overall message of your composite image. Choose high-quality photos with similar lighting characteristics. Create an ordered list of the layers you plan to include. Select images that are consistent with the visual effect you want to achieve as well as with customer requirements.

2. **Create Layer Adjustments.** Fine-tune your layers by creating layer adjustments. Look at each layer and evaluate how it fits into the background scene. Experiment with different adjustment tools until the layer looks just right. Decide whether to use destructive or non-destructive edits. Keep in mind the standard tonal dimensions of brightness, saturation, and hue.

3. **Edit Layer Styles.** Add variety to your layers by including layer styles such as shadow, glow, emboss, bevel, overlay, and stroke. Make sure the layer style does not overwhelm the overall image or detract from previous layer adjustments.

When necessary, more specific details concerning the above guidelines are presented at appropriate points in the chapter. The chapter also will identify the actions performed and decisions made regarding these guidelines during the creation of the edited photo shown in Figure 3–1.

Creating a Composite

Creating a composite with visual layers is a powerful effect. Photographers sometimes try to achieve the effect by using a sharp focus on objects in the foreground against an out-of-focus background. Others stage their photos with three layers of visual action. For example, at a baseball game, a person in the stands (foreground) may be observing a close call at first base (middle ground), while outfielders watch from afar (background). When those kinds of photographic techniques cannot be achieved, graphic artists use **composition techniques** to layer images and actions. Not only can you make realistic changes to parts of a photo, but you can add additional images and control their placement, blending, and special effects. In addition, changes to a layer can be edited independently of the layer itself, which is extremely helpful in composite production.

Simple layers are positioned in photos to incorporate new objects or new people. Layer effects may be added to layers to create an adjustment, to add a blending mode, or to edit coloring, fill, and opacity. Masks are used to conceal or reveal part of a layer. All of the layering techniques are **nondestructive**, which means that no pixels are changed in the process; the effect is applied over the image or layer to create the change.

When an image duplication is required and layering a new copy does not achieve the required effect, some graphic artists **clone**, or reproduce, an image by painting a copy into the scene. As with masks, cloning allows you to control exactly how much of the image you want to use — even down to the smallest pixel. Cloning also can be used to remove minor imperfections in a photo or to clone over intricate elements that do not fit into the picture.

The steps on the following pages create a composite image with layers; layer effects; and adjustments, masks, and cloning.

Starting and Customizing Photoshop

The following steps start Photoshop and reset the default workspace, tools, and colors. After opening a photo, the rulers are displayed, and the file is saved with a new file name to begin editing.

To Start Photoshop

If you are stepping through this project on a computer and you want your screen to match the figures in this book, then you should change your computer's resolution to 1024 × 768 and reset the tools and panels. For more information about how to change the resolution on your computer, and other advanced Photoshop settings, read Appendix C.

The following steps, which assume Windows Vista is running, start Photoshop based on a typical installation. You may need to ask your instructor how to start Photoshop for your system.

1. Click the Start button on the Windows Vista taskbar to display the Start menu and then click All Programs at the bottom of the left pane on the Start menu to display the All Programs list.

2. Click Adobe Design Premium CS4, or your version of the Adobe suite, in the All Programs list, and then click Adobe Photoshop CS4 to start Photoshop.

3. If the Photoshop window is not maximized, click the Maximize button next to the Close button on the Application bar to maximize the window.

To Reset the Workspace

As discussed in Chapter 1, it is helpful to reset the workspace so that the tools and panels appear in their default positions. The following steps use the Workspace switcher to select the Essentials workspace.

1. Click the Workspace switcher on the Application bar to display the names of saved workspaces.

2. Click Essentials to restore the workspace to its default settings.

To Reset the Tools and the Options Bar

Recall that the Tools panel and the options bar retain their settings from previous Photoshop sessions. The following steps select the Rectangular Marquee tool and reset all tool settings in the options bar.

1 Click the Rectangular Marquee Tool (M) button on the Tools panel to select it.

2 If the tools in the Tools panel are displayed in two columns, click the double arrow at the top of the Tools panel to change the panel to one column.

3 Right-click the Rectangular Marquee tool icon on the options bar to display the context menu, and then click Reset All Tools. When Photoshop displays a confirmation dialog box, click the OK button to restore the tools to their default settings.

To Reset the Default Colors

The default color settings in Photoshop are a black foreground on a white background and are displayed in the lower portion of the Tools panel. You will learn more about using color in future chapters; however, in preparation for working with layers, and to ensure your layers match the figures in this book, the following step resets the default colors. Color settings carry over from one Photoshop session to the next. In lab situations, it is a good idea to reset the default colors every time you start Photoshop. If white appears on black in the Tools panel, you can either click the Switch Foreground and Background Colors (X) button or press the X key to exchange the colors.

1
- On the Tools panel, click the Default Foreground and Background Colors (D) button to reset the default colors of black and white (Figure 3–2). If black is not the foreground color, press the X key to reverse the colors.

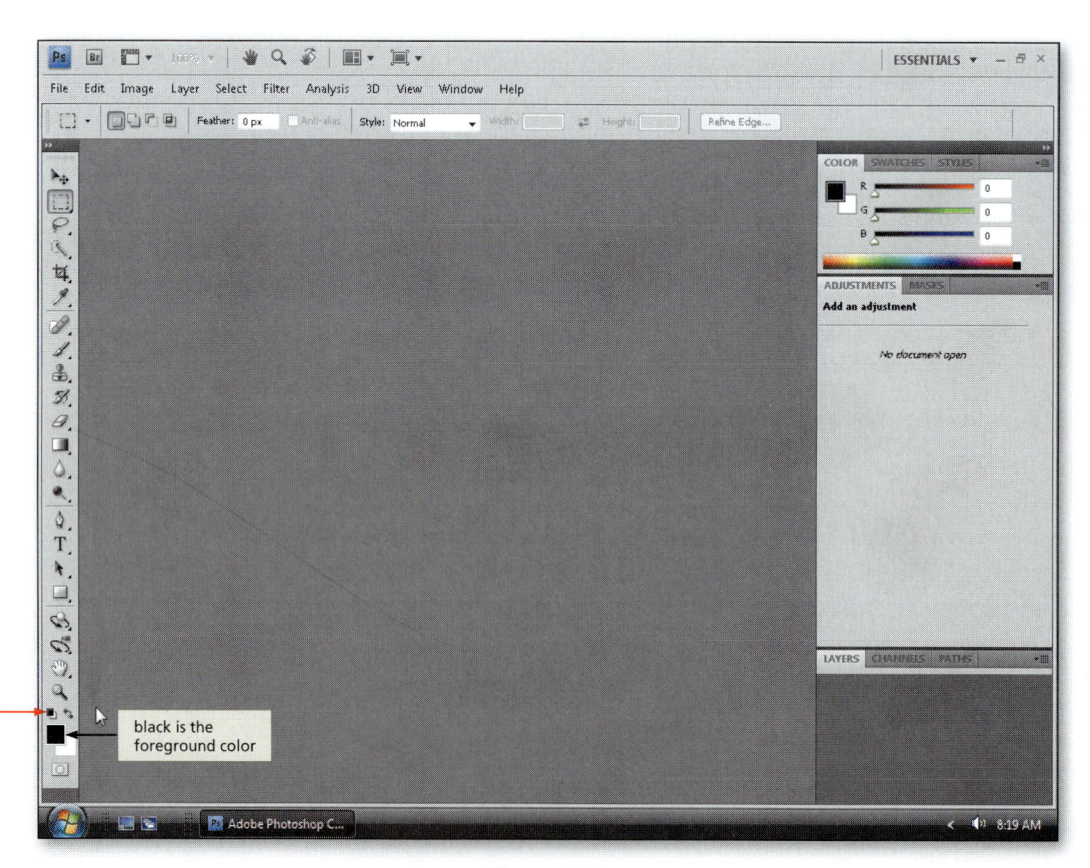

Figure 3–2

Other Ways
1. Press D

To Open a Photo

To open a photo in Photoshop, it must be stored as a digital file on your computer system or on an external storage device. The photos used in this book are stored in the Data Files for Students. You can access the Data Files for Students on the DVD that accompanies this book. See the inside back cover of this book for instructions on downloading the Data Files for Students, or contact your instructor for information about accessing the required files.

The following steps open the file, House, from a DVD located in drive E.

1. Insert the DVD that accompanies this book into your DVD drive. After a few seconds, if Windows displays a dialog box, click its Close button.

2. With the Photoshop window open, click File on the menu bar, and then click Open to display the Open dialog box.

3. In the Open dialog box, click the Look in box arrow to display the list of available locations, and then click drive E or the drive associated with your DVD.

4. Double-click the Chapter03 folder to open it, and then double-click the file, House, to open it.

5. When Photoshop displays the image in the document window, if the magnification is not 25% as shown on the status bar, double-click the magnification box on the document window status bar, type 25, and then press the ENTER key to change the magnification (Figure 3–3).

6. If the rulers do not appear, press CTRL+R. If inches do not appear on the ruler as the unit of measurement, right-click the ruler and then click Inches on the context menu.

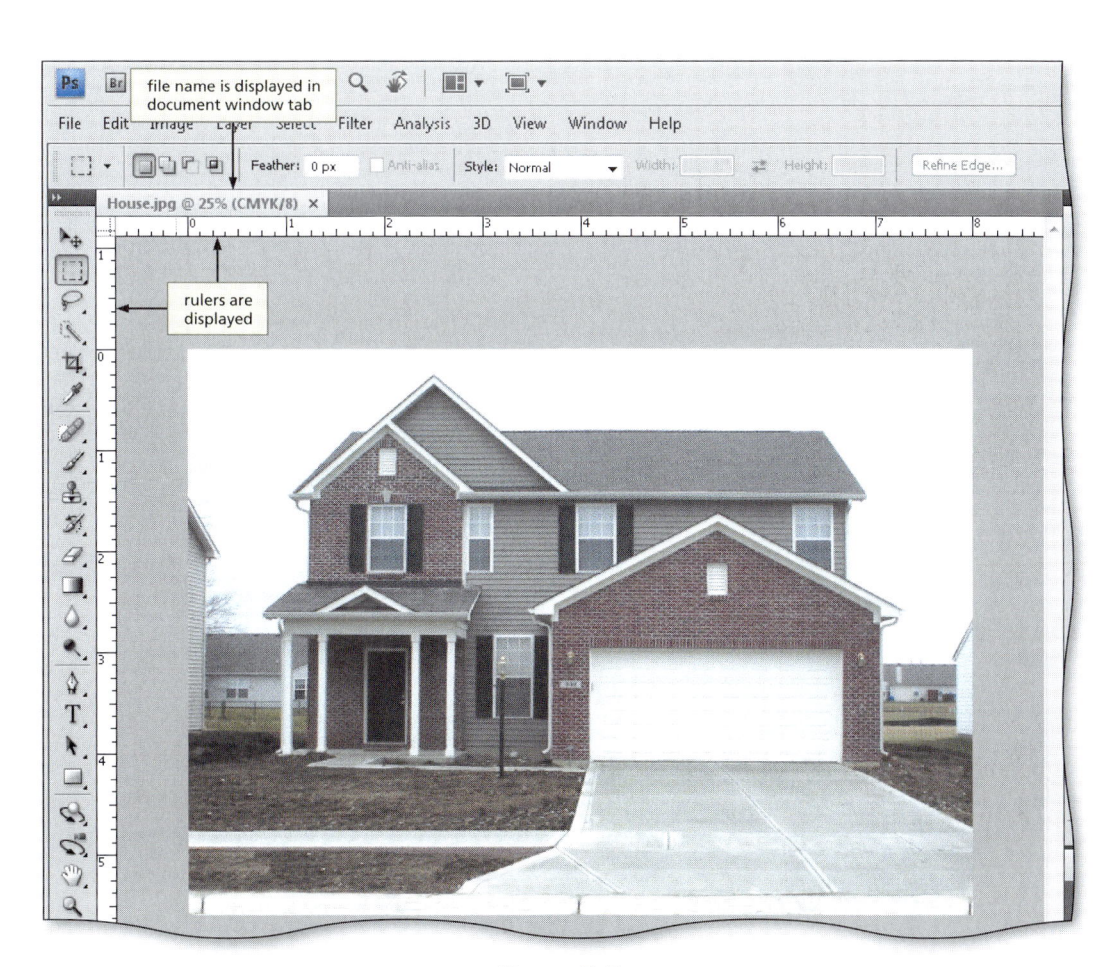

Figure 3–3

To Save a Photo

Even though you have yet to edit the photo, it is a good practice to save the file on your personal storage device early in the process. The photo was taken with a digital camera and was saved in the JPG format. In order to use all of the tools and features in Photoshop, you will save the file in the PSD format with the name, House Edited.

1 With your USB flash drive connected to one of the computer's USB ports, click File on the menu bar to display the File menu, and then click Save As to display the Save As dialog box.

2 In the file name text box, type `House Edited` to rename the file. Do not press the ENTER key after typing the file name.

3 Click the Save in box arrow, and then click UDISK 2.0 (F:), or the location associated with your USB flash drive, in the list. If you want to create a folder for the photos in Chapter 3, click the Create New Folder button. Then when the new folder is displayed, type a chapter name, such as Chapter03, and press the ENTER key.

4 Click the Format button to display the list of available file formats, and then click Photoshop (*.PSD, *.PDD) in the list (Figure 3–4).

5 Click the Save button in the Save As dialog box to save the file.

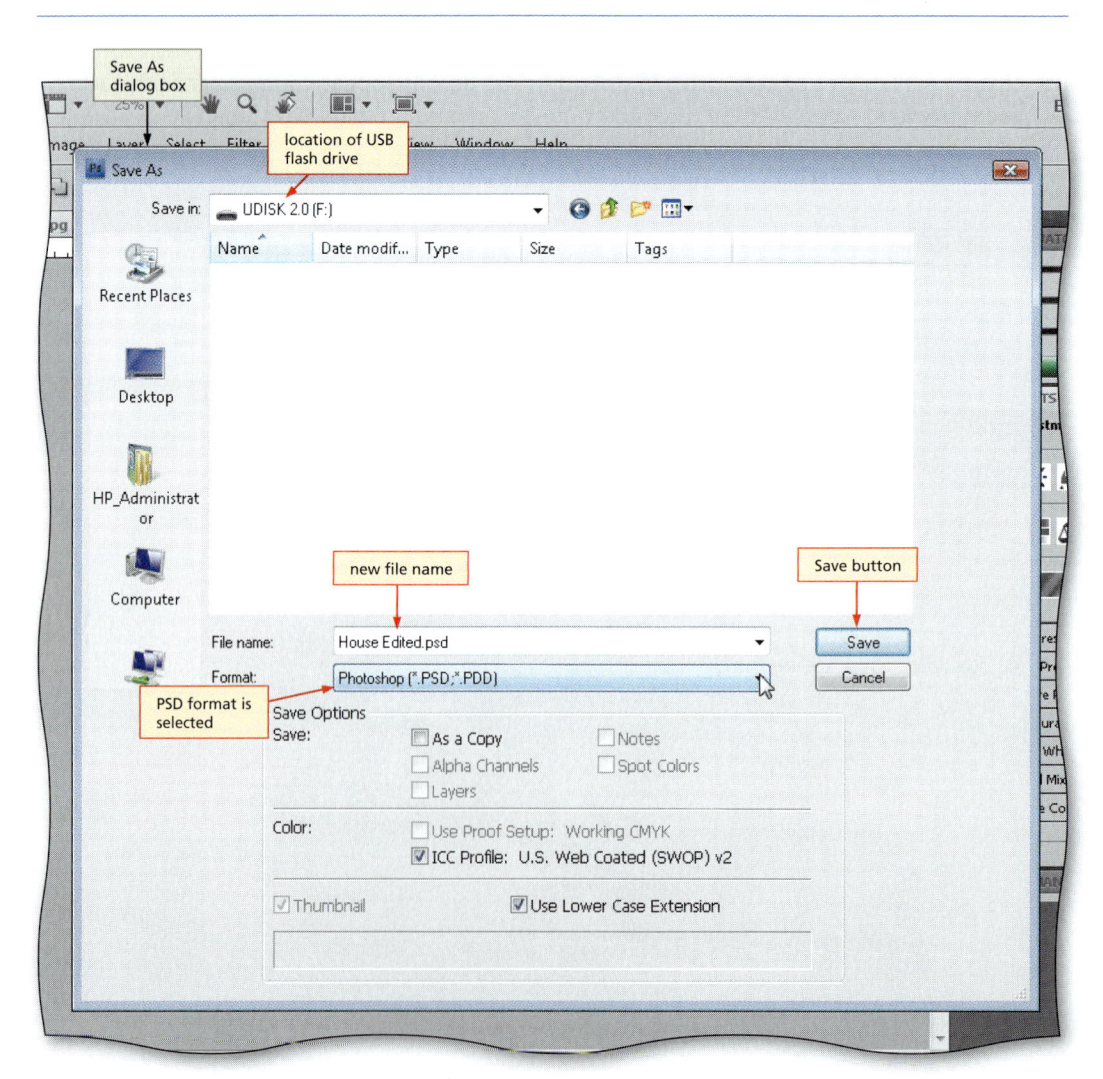

Figure 3–4

Plan Ahead

Gather your photos and plan your layers.
One of the keys to successful image compositions is finding the best source material with similar lighting situations and tonal qualities. Choose high-quality photos and images that convey your overall message. Make sure you have permission to use the images if they are not original photographs taken by you or provided to you by a colleague or client. Obtain several versions of the same photo, if possible, including photos from different angles and with different lighting situations. Make two copies of each photo and store one as a backup. Crop unwanted portions of the photos before adding them as new layers.

Creating a Composite Image Using Layers

Photoshop has many tools to help create composite images, photomontages, and collages. A composite, or composite image, is one that is created by combining multiple photographs or images to display in a single combined file. Graphic artists use the newer term, **photomontage**, to refer to both the process and the result of creating a composite from photos.

Layers

One of the most powerful tools in Photoshop is layering. A layer is a section within a Photoshop document that you can manipulate independently from the rest of the document. Layers can be stacked one on top of the other, resembling sheets of clear film, to form a composite image.

Layers have been used by business and industry for years. Cartoonists create layers of physical transparencies to help with animation. The medical field uses overlays to illustrate anatomical features. Virtual simulations use layers to display processes. With Photoshop, layers are easy to create and export for these kinds of applications.

Recall that you used selections in Chapter 2 to move, copy, transform, and delete portions of a photo. Layers can perform all of the same functions performed by selecting, while providing added features. The most powerful feature of layers is the ability to revisit a portion of the image to make further changes, even after deselecting. Layers can be created, copied, deleted, displayed, hidden, merged, locked, grouped, repositioned, and flattened. Layers can be composed of images, patterns, text, shapes, colors, or filters. You can use layers to apply special effects, correct or colorize pictures, repair damaged photos, or import text elements. In previous chapters, you worked with images in a flat, single layer called the **Background layer**. In this chapter, you will create, name, and manipulate multiple layers on top of the Background layer.

Many layer manipulations are performed using the **Layers panel**, which lists all the layers, groups, and layer effects in an image (Figure 3–5 on the next page). Each time you insert a layer onto an image, the new layer is added to the top of the panel. The default display of a layer on the Layers panel includes a visibility icon, a thumbnail of the layer, and the layer's name. To the right of the layer's name, a locking icon or other manipulations might appear.

Photoshop allows you to lock three different components of layers. Lock transparent pixels confines editing to opaque layer portions. Lock image pixels prevents modification of the layer's pixels using paint tools. Lock position prevents the layer from being moved. The Lock all button enables all of the three ways of locking the layer. When a layer is locked, a lock icon appears to the right of the name on the Layers panel.

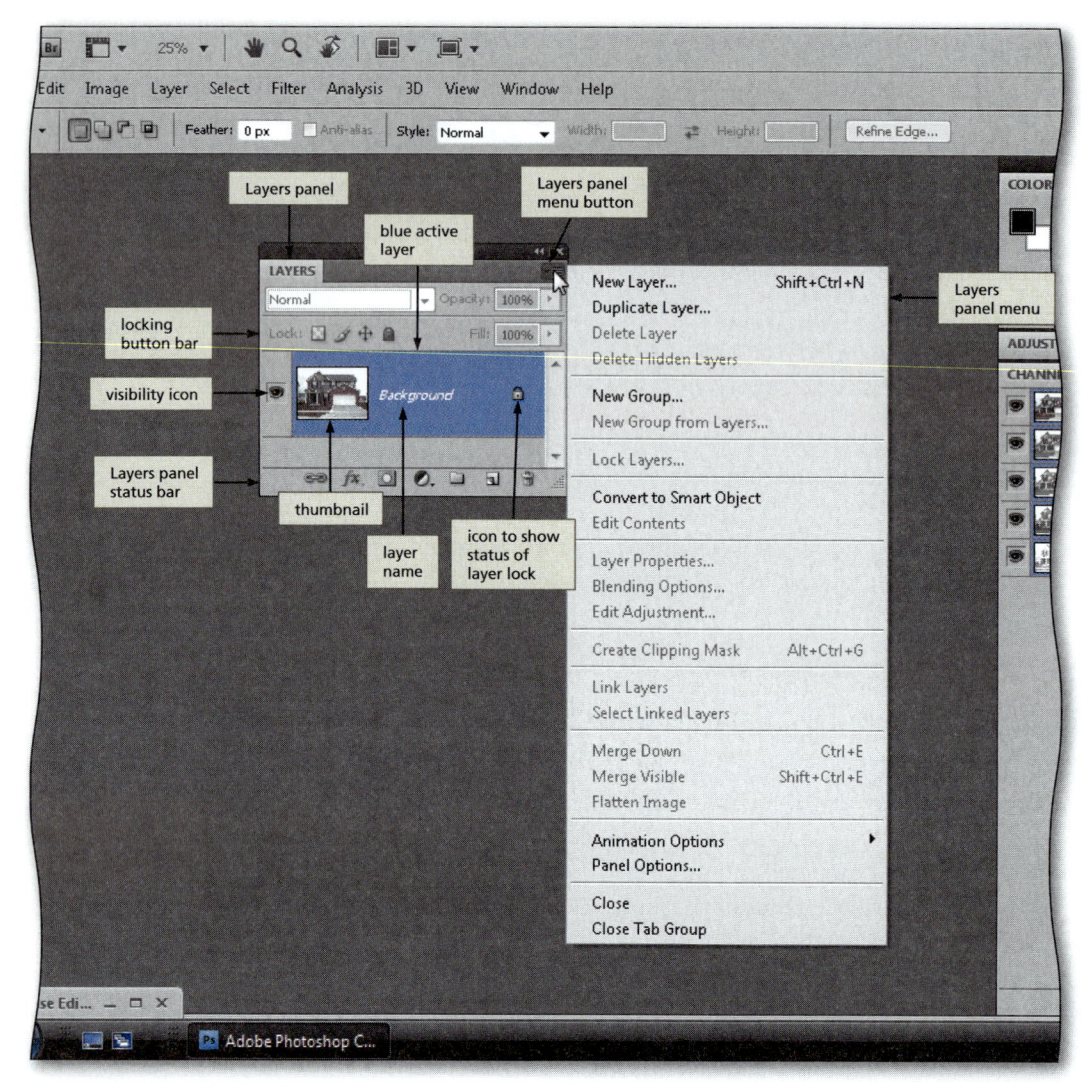

Figure 3–5

The Layers panel is used in several different manners: to show and hide layers, create new layers, and work with groups of layers. You can access additional commands and attributes by clicking the Layers panel menu button or by right-clicking a layer. The Layers panel defines how layers interact. As you use the buttons and boxes on the Layers panel, each will be explained.

While Photoshop allows background editing, as you have done in previous chapters, the Background layer cannot be moved, nor can its transparency be changed. In other words, the Background layer fills the document window, and there is no layer behind the background. It is partially locked by default and displays a hollow lock (Figure 3–5). If you want to convert the Background layer into a fully editable layer, double-click the layer on the Layers panel, and then when the New Layer dialog box is displayed, click the OK button.

When working with layers, it is important to make sure you know which layer you are editing by looking at the active layer on the Layers panel or by looking at the layer name, appended to the file name on the document window tab. Many other layer commands also can be accessed on the Layer menu, including making adjustments to the layer, creating layer masks, grouping layers, and other editing and placement commands.

BTW

Arranging Layers
To rearrange layers, change their visibility, or better organize them, drag the layer up or down on the Layers panel. The top layer on the Layers panel is displayed in front of any other layers in the document window. The Layer menu also contains an Arrange submenu to help you organize your layers.

To Display the Layers Panel

The following step displays the Layers panel.

1
- Double-click the Layers panel tab to display the Layers panel (Figure 3–6).

Figure 3–6

> **Other Ways**
> 1. On Window menu, click Layers
> 2. Press F7

To Change Layer Panel Options

The Panel Options command, accessible from the Layers panel menu, allows you to change the view and size of the thumbnail related to each layer. A **thumbnail** is a small visual preview of the layer on the Layers panel. Displaying thumbnails of each layer allows you to see easily what the layer looks like and helps you to be more efficient when editing a layer. To improve performance and save monitor space, however, some Photoshop users choose not to display thumbnails. The Panel Options dialog box allows you to choose small, medium, large, or no thumbnails. In addition, you can specify thumbnail contents by choosing the Layer Bounds option that causes the Layers panel to display only the layer, restricting the thumbnail to the object's pixels on the layer.

The steps on the next page select a medium-sized thumbnail of each layer and the Layer Bounds option.

PS 170 Photoshop Chapter 3 Working with Layers

1
- Click the Layers panel menu button to display the Layers panel menu if necessary (Figure 3–7).

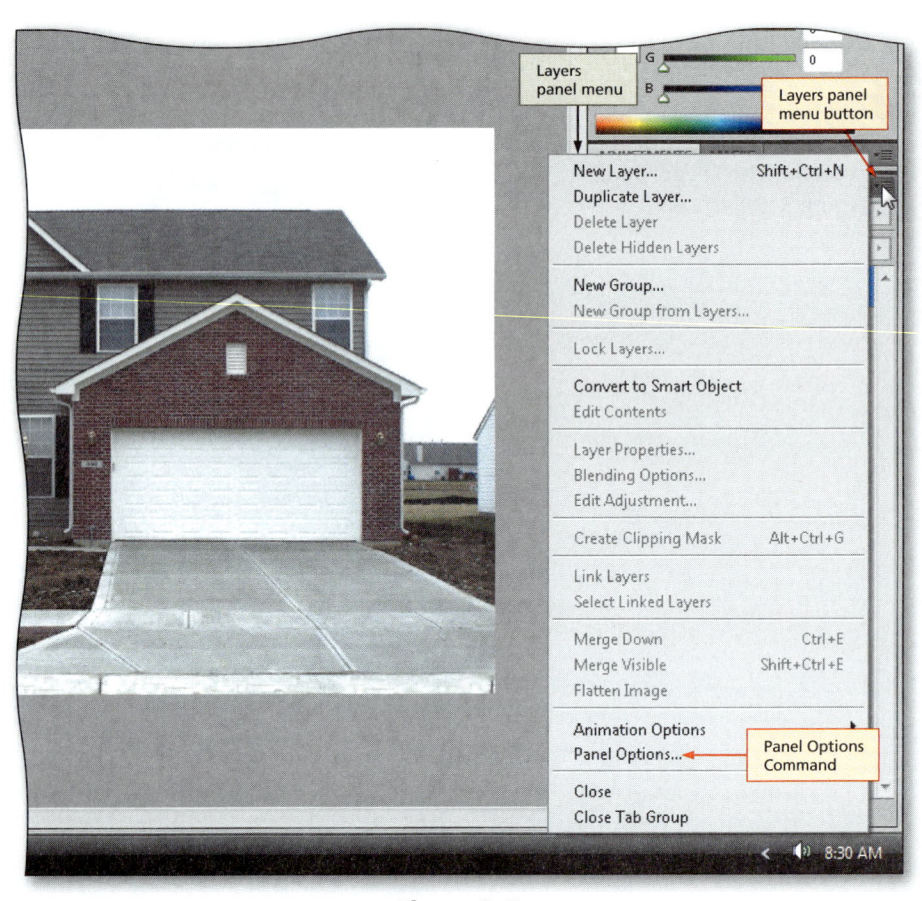

Figure 3–7

2
- Click Panel Options on the menu to display the Layers Panel Options dialog box.
- Click the medium thumbnail to select it.
- Click Layer Bounds to change the look and feel of the Layers panel (Figure 3–8).

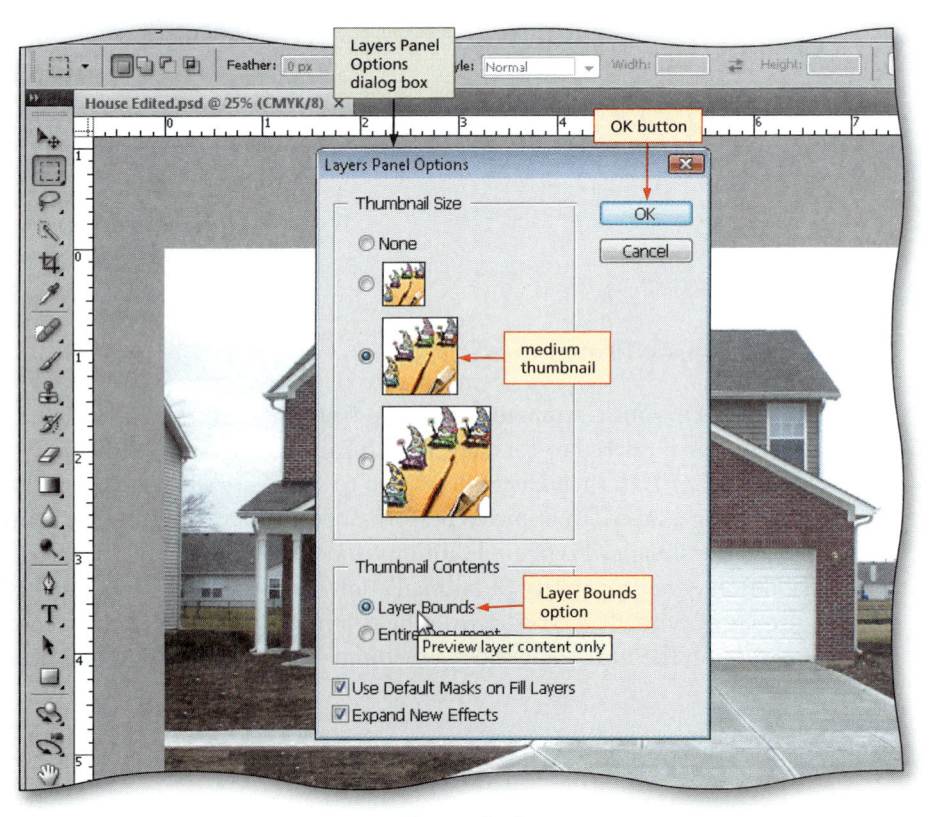

Figure 3–8

3

- Click the OK button to close the Layers Panel Options dialog box (Figure 3–9).

Q&A | Should I see a difference on the Layers panel?

Depending on the previous settings on your system, the size of the thumbnail probably changed on the Layers panel. The Layer Bounds will not appear until you create a layer other than the Background layer.

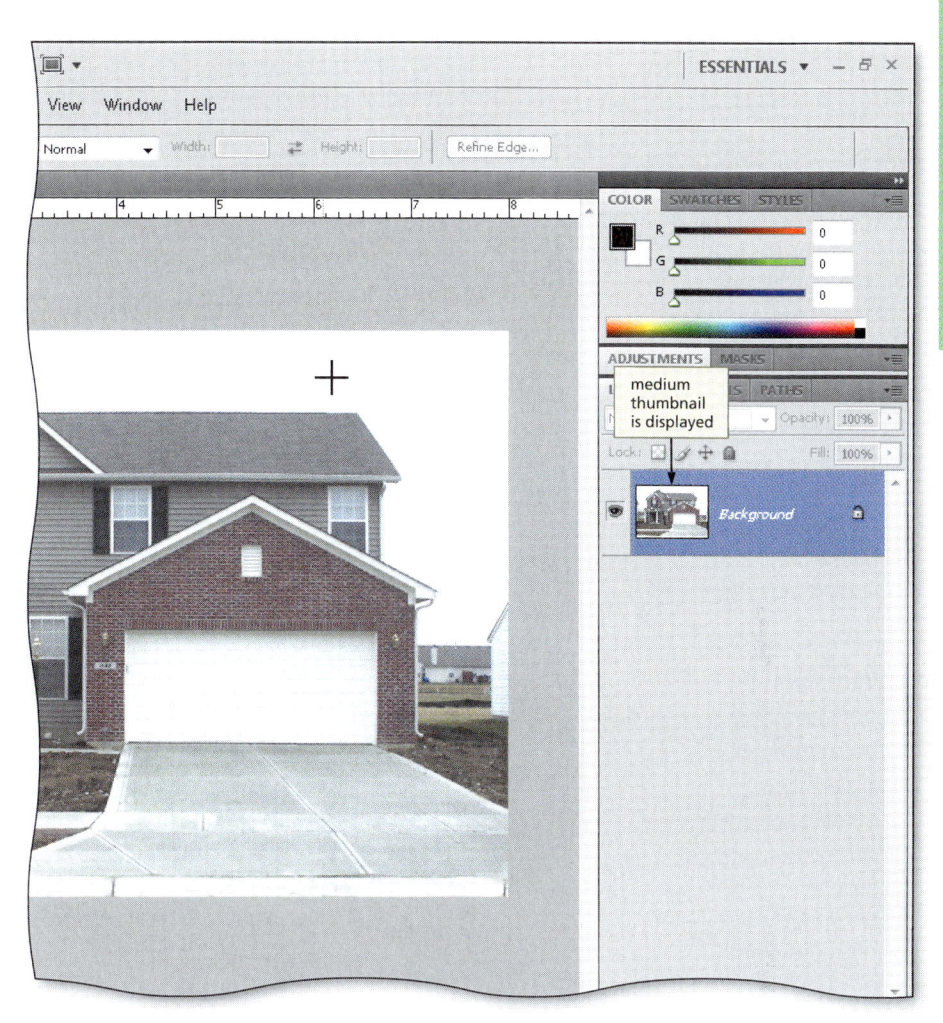

Figure 3–9

Other Ways

1. On Layers panel, right-click any layer thumbnail except background, choose thumbnail size

Creating a Layer Via Cut

There are several ways to create a layer. You can:

- isolate a portion of the image and then cut or make a layer copy
- create a new layer by copying from a different image
- duplicate a layer that already exists
- create a new, blank layer on which you can draw or create text

When you add a layer to an image, a new layer is created above, or on top of, the currently selected layer, creating a **stacking order**. By default, layers are named and numbered sequentially. The stacking order of layers in an image can be rearranged to change the appearance of the image. The final appearance of an edited Photoshop document is a view of the layer stack from the top down.

The Layer via Cut command is used to create a new layer by cutting from the Background layer or cutting from another layer. You then can edit the layer independently from the Background layer. The Layer via Cut command is different from the Layer via Copy command in that it removes the selection from the background. Future edits to the Background, such as changing the color or lighting, will not affect the cut layer.

BTW

Moving Layers
If a layer is partially eclipsed, or overlapped, by another layer, select the layer on the Layers panel, click Layer on the menu bar, point to Arrange, and then click one of the options to bring the layer to the front or send it to the back.

To Create a Layer Via Cut

The following steps create a new layer that includes only the sky. You will use the Magic Wand tool to select the sky and then use the Layer via Cut command to isolate the sky from the rest of the photo, creating a new layer.

1
- On the Tools panel, right-click the Quick Selection tool, and then click Magic Wand Tool on the context menu.
- On the options bar, type 20 in the Tolerance box, and then click the Contiguous check box so it displays a check mark, if necessary.
- In the photo, click the sky (Figure 3–10).

Q&A Why did I change the tolerance?

The tolerance setting determines the range of affected colors. A low value selects colors very similar to the clicked location. A higher value selects a broader range of colors.

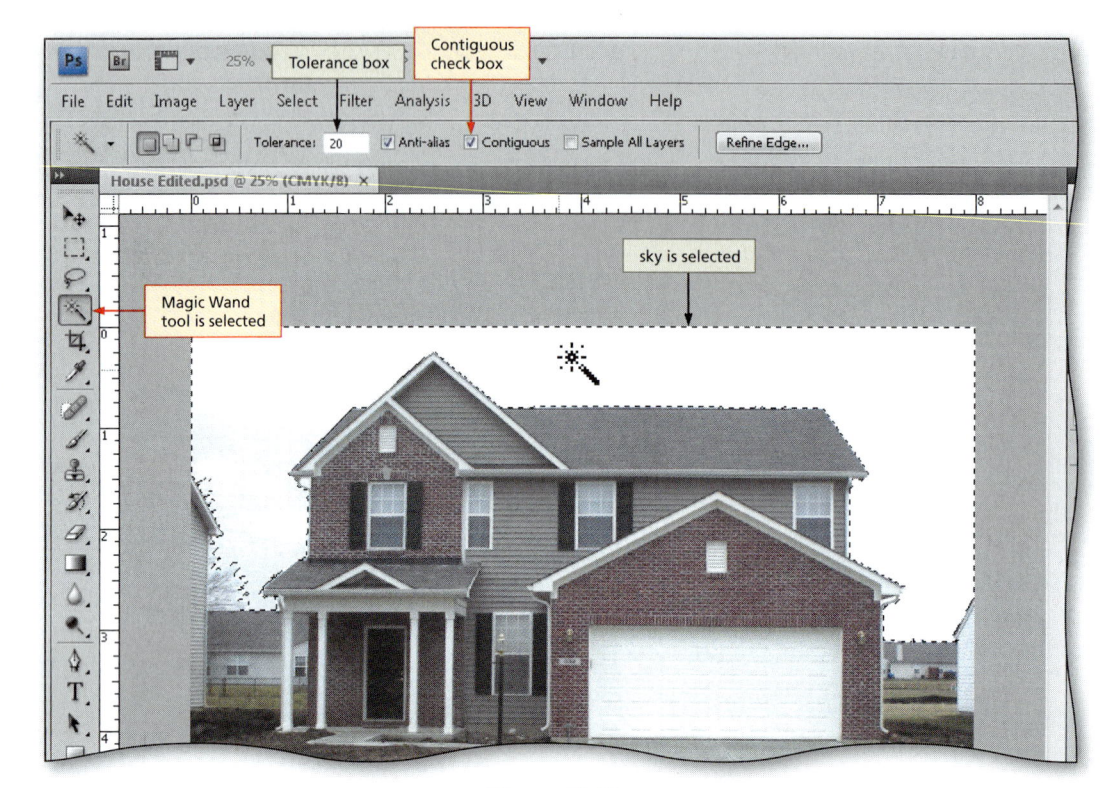

Figure 3–10

2
- Right-click the sky to display the Selection context menu (Figure 3–11).

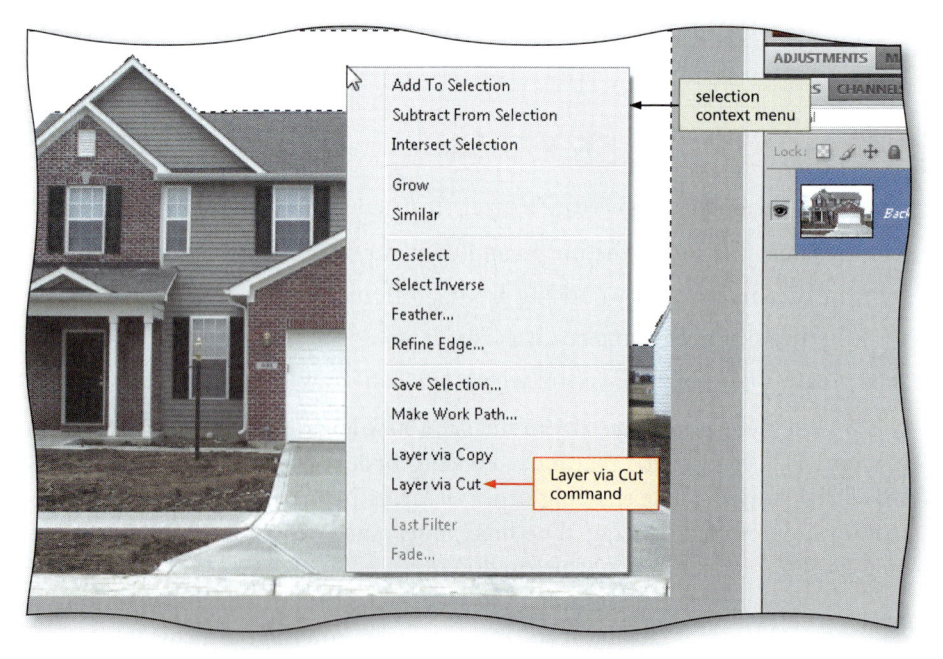

Figure 3–11

Creating a Layer Via Cut **PS 173**

3
- Click Layer via Cut on the context menu to create the new layer (Figure 3–12).

Other Ways
1. Create selection, on Layer menu, point to New, click Layer via Cut
2. Create selection, press SHIFT+CTRL+J

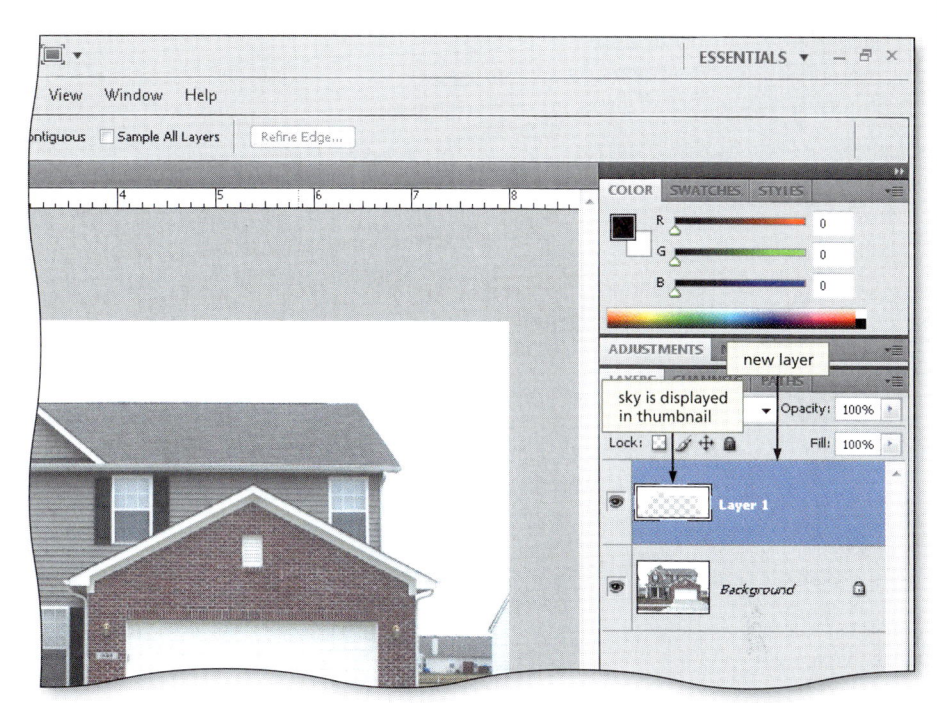

Figure 3–12

To Name and Color a Layer

It is a good practice to give each layer a unique name so you can identify it more easily. The name of the active layer appears on the Layers panel and also on the title bar of the document window. Photoshop allows you to give each layer its own color identification as well. To name and color a layer, you will use the Layers panel menu to display the Layer Properties dialog box in the following steps.

1
- Click the Layers panel menu button and then click Layer Properties to display the Layer Properties dialog box.
- Type sky in the Name box to name the layer, sky.
- Click the Color box arrow and then click Blue in the list to choose a blue identification color (Figure 3–13).

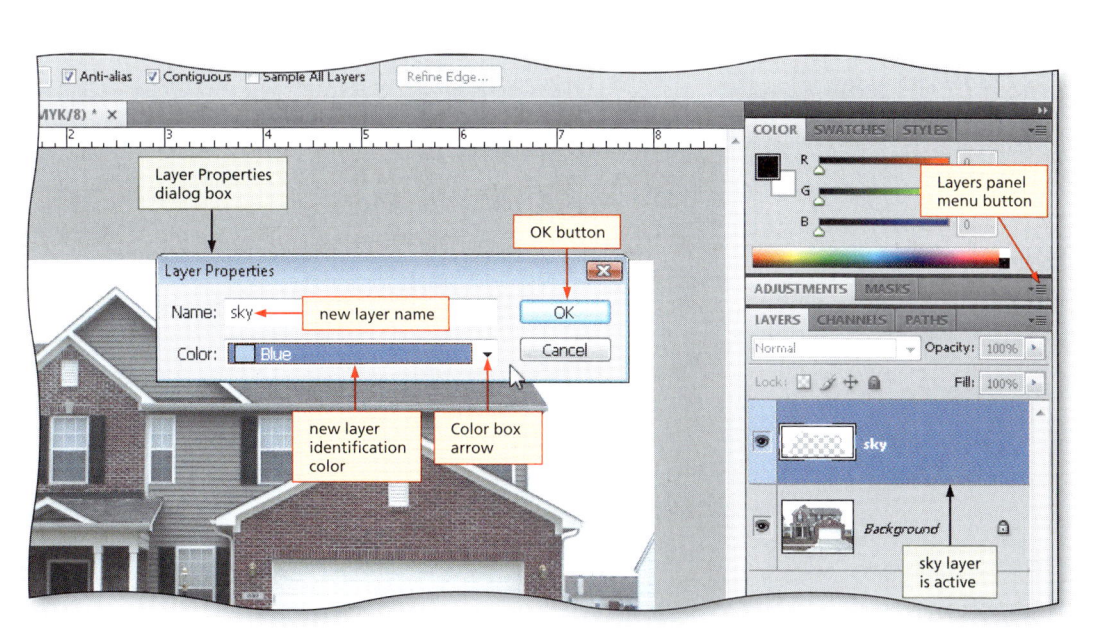

Figure 3–13

2

- Click the OK button to display the new settings on the Layers panel (Figure 3–14).

Q&A

What are the options for layer colors?

Photoshop reserves seven colors for color coding layers: red, orange, yellow, green, blue, violet, and gray. If you have more than seven layers, you can group layers that have similar characteristics with one the same color.

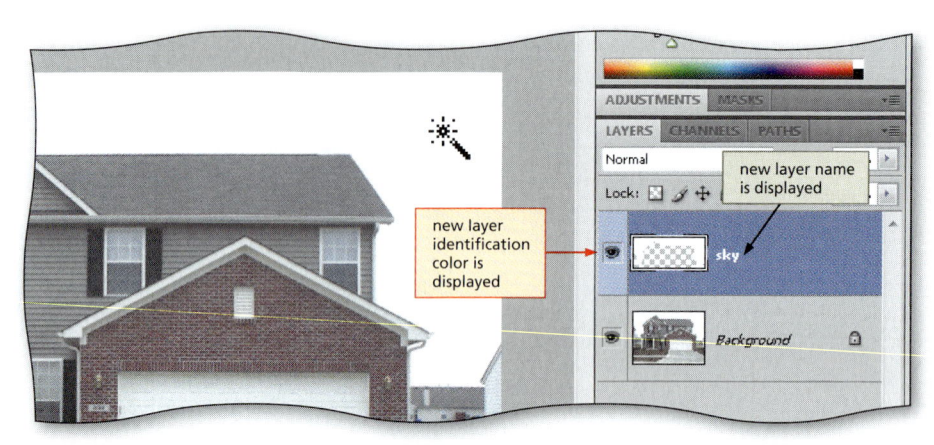

Figure 3–14

Other Ways

1. Right-click layer, click Layer Properties, type new name, choose new color, click OK
2. To name layer, on Layers panel, double-click layer name, type new name, press ENTER
3. To color layer, on Layers panel, right-click visibility area, click color

---

To Hide and Show a Layer

To hide or view a layer, click the Indicates layer visibility button to the left of the thumbnail on the Layers panel. When the layer is visible in the document window, the button displays an eye icon. When the layer is invisible, the button is blank. The following steps hide and show the Background layer.

1

- Click the Indicates layer visibility button to the left of the Background layer to hide the layer in the document window and hide the visibility icon (Figure 3–15).

Q&A

What is the checkerboard effect in the sky layer?

The checkerboard effect represents blank portions of the document window that are transparent.

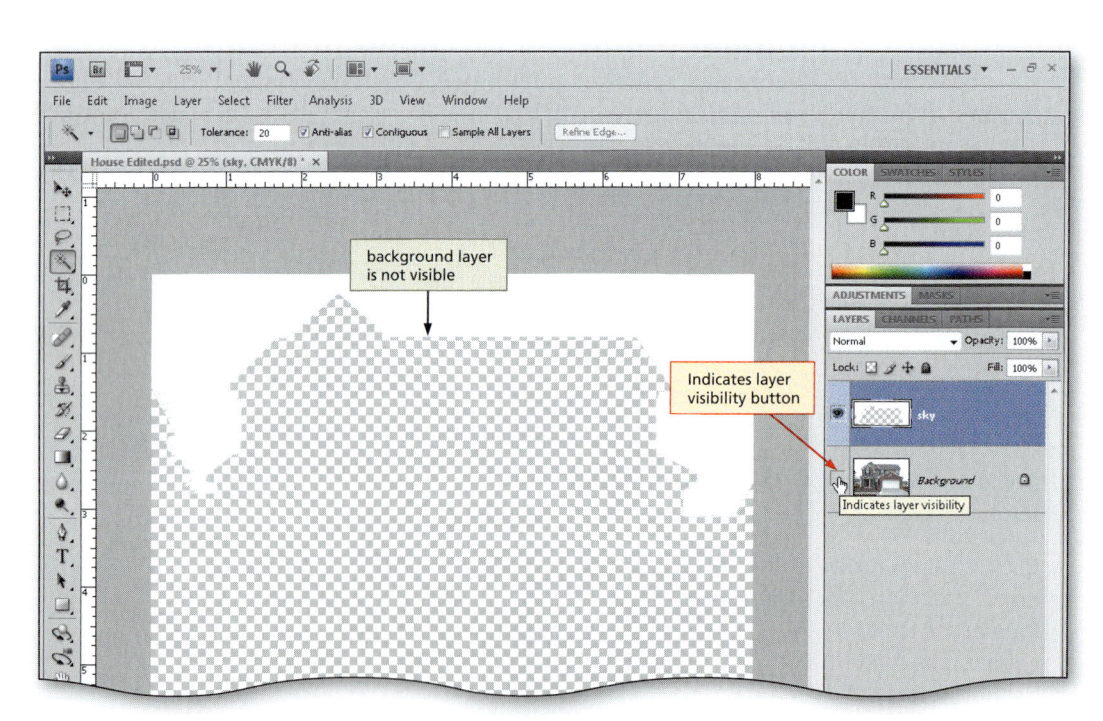

Figure 3–15

❷
- Click the Indicates layer visibility button again to show the Background layer in the document window and display the visibility icon (Figure 3–16).

background layer is visible

Indicates layer visibility button

Indicates layer visibility

Other Ways
1. Right-click visibility icon, click Hide this layer or Show this layer
2. On Layer menu, click Hide Layers or Show Layers

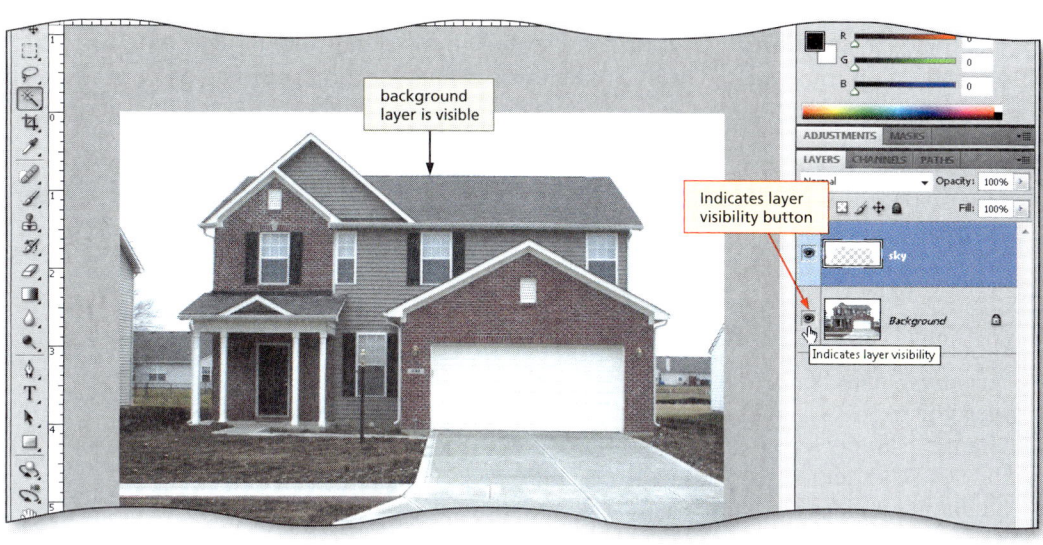

Figure 3–16

Creating a Layer from Another Image

When you create composite images, you might want to create layers from other images. It is important to choose images that closely match or complement color, lighting, size, and perspective if you want your image to look natural. While you can adjust disparate images to improve how well they match, it is easier to start with as close a match as possible, ideally with similar lighting situations and tonal qualities.

Many sources exist for composite images. For example, you can use your own digital photos, scanned images, images from royalty-free Web sites, or you can draw your own. If you use a photo or image from the Web, make sure you have legal rights to use the image. Legal rights include permission from the photographer or artist to use the image, or purchasing these rights, through a contract, from an online store.

The basic process of creating a new layer from another image involves opening a second image, selecting the area you wish to use, and then moving it to the original photo in a drag-and-drop, or cut-and-paste, fashion. Once the layer exists in the destination photo, you might need to do some editing to remove portions of the layer, to resize it, or to make tonal adjustments.

To view only one layer in the document window, ALT+click the visibility icon for the layer you wish to view. All other layers will be hidden. Pressing ALT+click again restores the previous visibility settings. Show or hide all other layers by selecting Show/Hide all other layers from the visibility icon's context menu. To hide or view several contiguous layers, drag through the eye column.

To delete a layer permanently, right-click the layer name and then click Delete Layer on the context menu, or activate the layer and press the del key.

The Layers Panel Context Menus
The Layers panel displays many ways to work with layers. For example, right-clicking the layer name displays a different context menu from the one you see when right-clicking the thumbnail. Double-clicking the layer name allows you to rename the layer; double-clicking the thumbnail opens the Layer Style dialog box.

To Open a Second Image

To add a landscaped flower bed as a layer to the House Edited image, you will need to open a new file, Flowerbed, from the Data Files for Students, or from a location specified by your instructor. The following steps open the Flowerbed file.

1

- Press CTRL+O to display the Open dialog box.

- In the Open dialog box, if necessary, click the Look in box arrow, and then navigate to the Chapter03 folder of the Data Files for Students, or a location specified by your instructor.

- Double-click the file named Flowerbed to open it.

- Change the magnification to 50 percent (Figure 3–17).

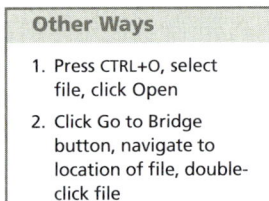

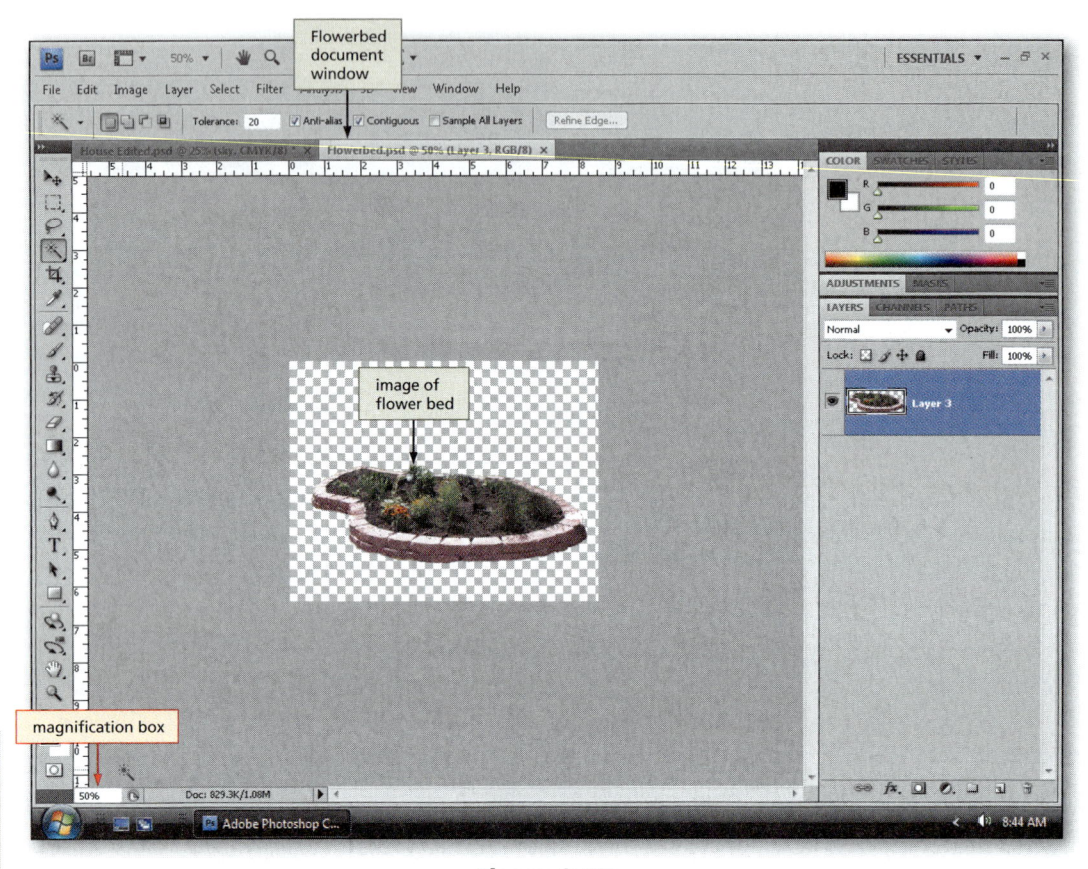

> **Other Ways**
> 1. Press CTRL+O, select file, click Open
> 2. Click Go to Bridge button, navigate to location of file, double-click file

Figure 3–17

BTW

Creating Layer Groups
Layer groups help you manage and organize layers in a logical manner. To create a layer group, click the Create New Group button on the Layers panel. A new layer will appear with a folder icon. You then can drag layers into the folder or use the Layers panel menu to insert a new layer. You can apply attributes and masks to the entire group.

Displaying Multiple Files

Recall that when you open more than one file, the document windows are tabbed by default; however, Photoshop offers more than 25 different ways to **arrange** document windows. These arrangement options are accessible from a list that appears when you click the Arrange Documents button on the Application bar. You also can create a custom workspace by moving and manipulating document windows.

For example, you might want to display two document windows, horizontally or vertically, in order to drag and drop from one image to another. You might want to compare different versions or views of photos, beside each other in the document window. Or when creating a panorama, you might want to preview how certain photos will look, side by side.

When you are done viewing multiple document windows in the workspace, you can **consolidate**, or view only one window at a time, using the Arrange Documents button, or by right-clicking the document tab.

Creating a Layer from Another Image **PS 177**

To Arrange the Document Windows

The following steps display the House Edited and Flowerbed windows beside each other using the Arrange Documents button on the Application bar.

1
- On the Application bar, click the Arrange Documents button to display its list (Figure 3–18).

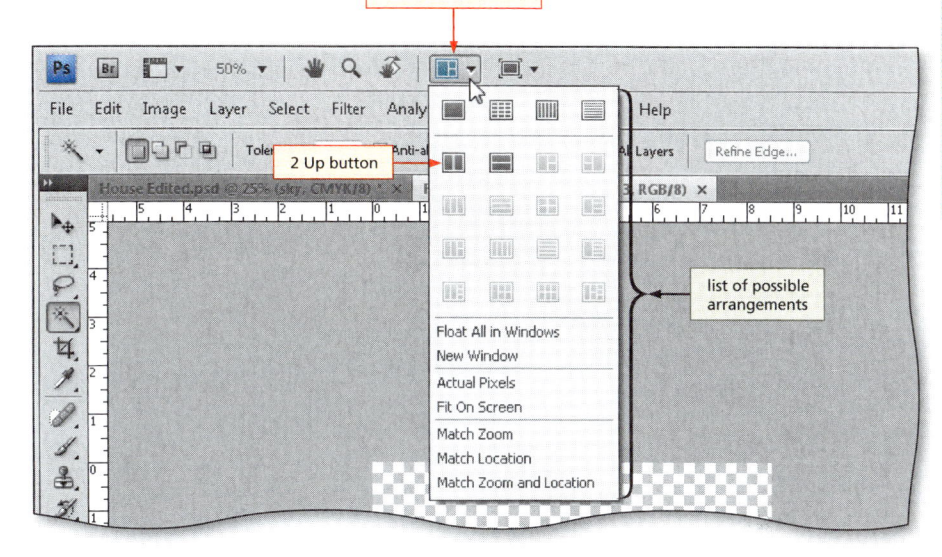

Figure 3–18

2
- Click the first 2 Up button in the list to display the windows beside each other (Figure 3–19).

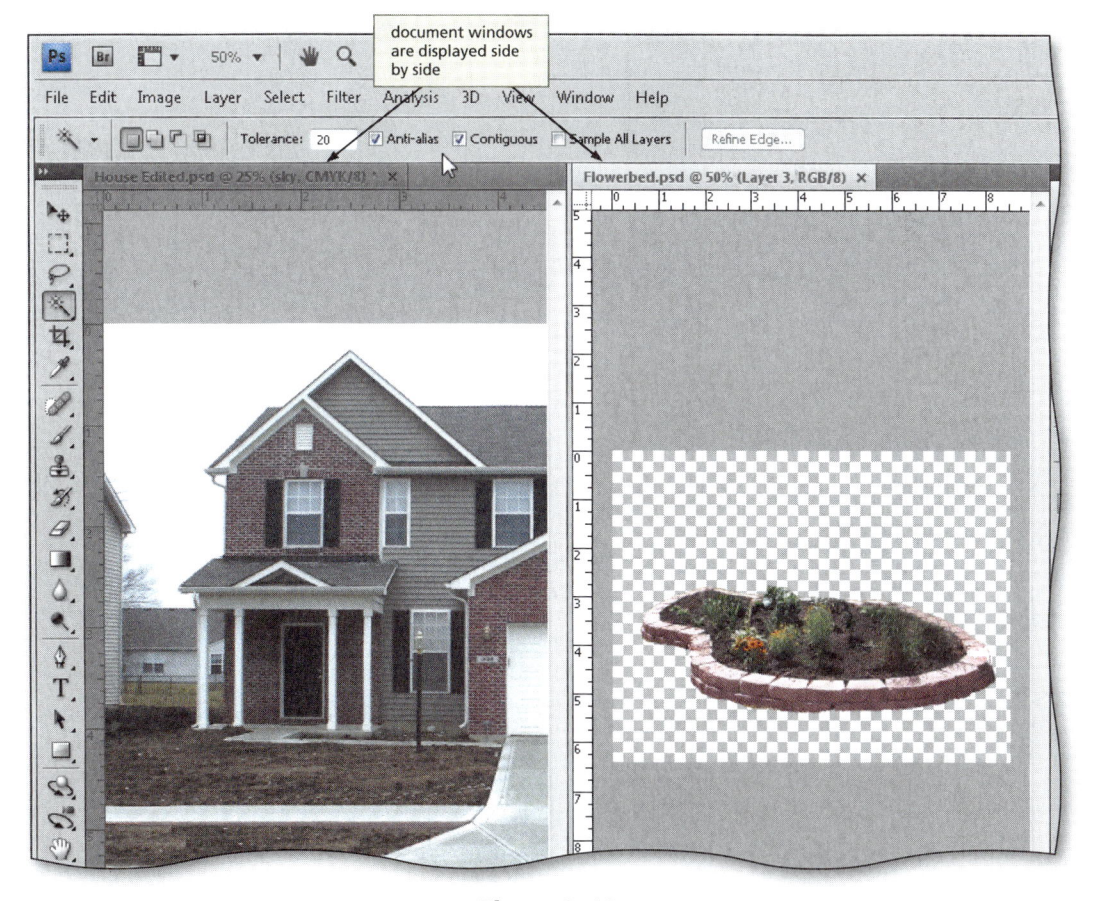

Figure 3–19

To Create a Layer by Dragging an Entire Image

When you drag a selection from one document window to the other, Photoshop creates a new layer in the destination document window. If you want to include the entire image from the source window, use the Move tool to drag from any location in the source window to the destination window. Each new layer is displayed on the Layers panel above the currently selected layer; in this case, the sky. Dragging between document windows is an automatic duplication rather than a true move. The original or source image remains unchanged.

The flower bed image will be used in its entirety as a landscaping feature in the front yard to the left of the driveway. The following step moves the image from the source window, Flowerbed, to the destination window, House Edited.

1
- Press the V key to activate the Move tool.
- Drag the flower bed image into the House Edited window and drop it to the left of the driveway (Figure 3–20).

Other Ways
1. In source window, on Edit menu click Copy, in destination window on Edit menu click Paste

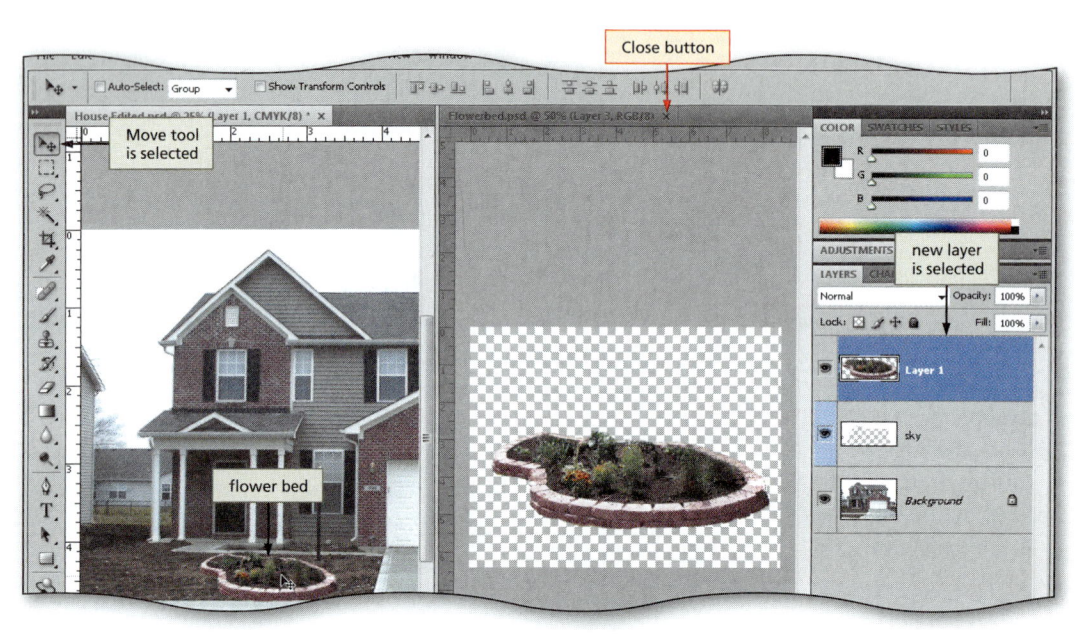

Figure 3–20

BTW
Adobe Stock Images Photoshop offers the option to download low-resolution, complementary versions of many images. You can work with the complementary images until you make your final decision, at which point you can purchase and download a high-resolution image.

To Close the Flowerbed Document Window

Because you are finished with the Flowerbed image the following step closes the Flowerbed window.

1 Click the Close button on the Flowerbed document window tab. If Photoshop asks you to save the file again, click the No button.

To Position a Layer

With the Move tool, the following step drags the flower bed to a new location.

1 With the new layer still selected, drag the layer so its vertical center is approximately even with the far left column on the porch and its horizontal center is between the house and the sidewalk.

Creating a Layer from Another Image **PS 179**

To Set Layer Properties Using the Context Menu

The following steps set the layer properties for the flower bed, this time using the context menu displayed by right-clicking the layer itself.

1
- On the Layers panel, right-click the layer named Layer 1 to display the context menu (Figure 3–21).

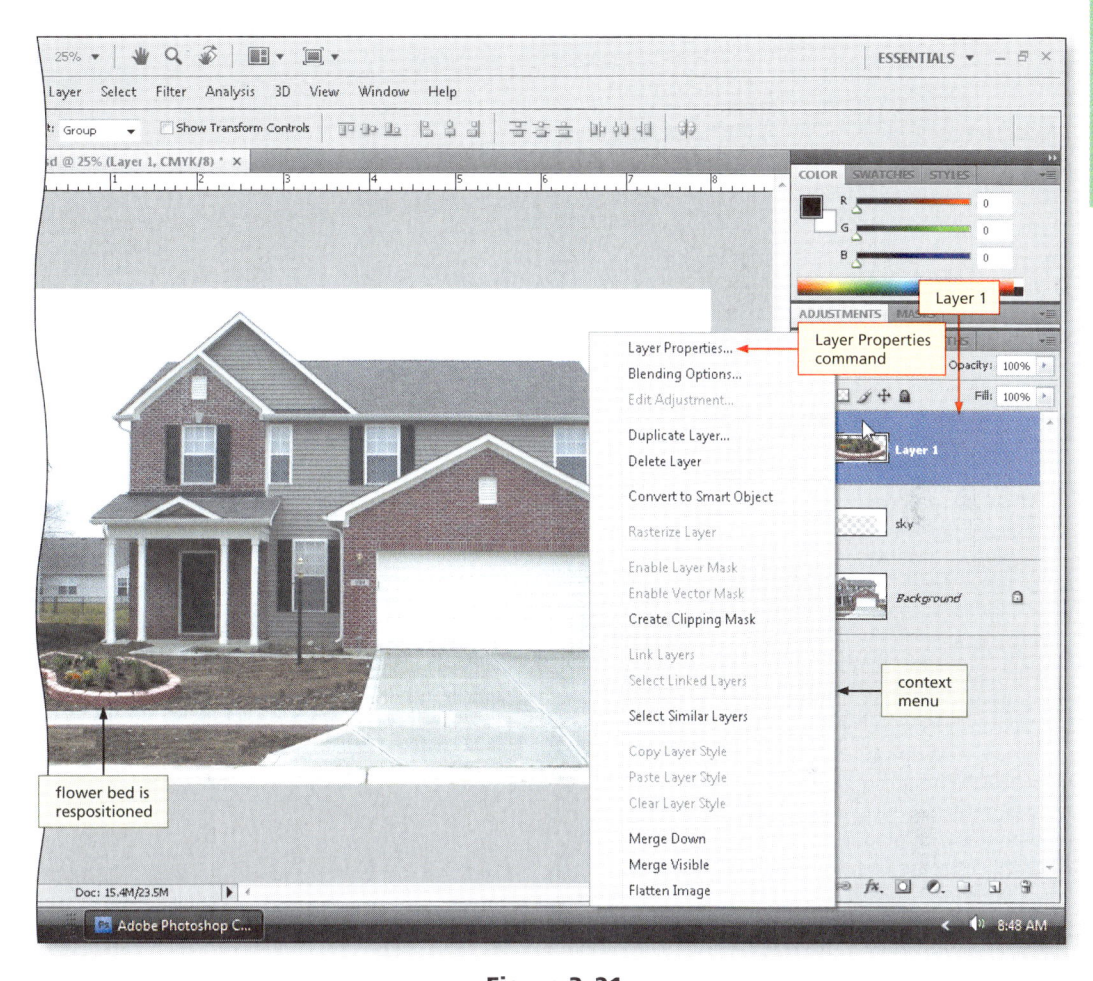

Figure 3–21

2
- Click Layer Properties on the menu to display the Layer Properties dialog box.
- Type flowerbed in the Name box to name the layer.
- Click the Color box arrow, and then click Green in the list to choose a green identification color (Figure 3–22).

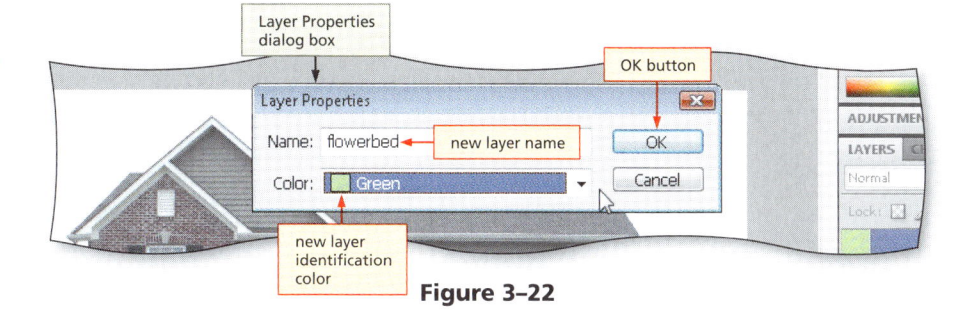

Figure 3–22

③
- Click the OK button to display the new settings on the Layers panel (Figure 3–23).

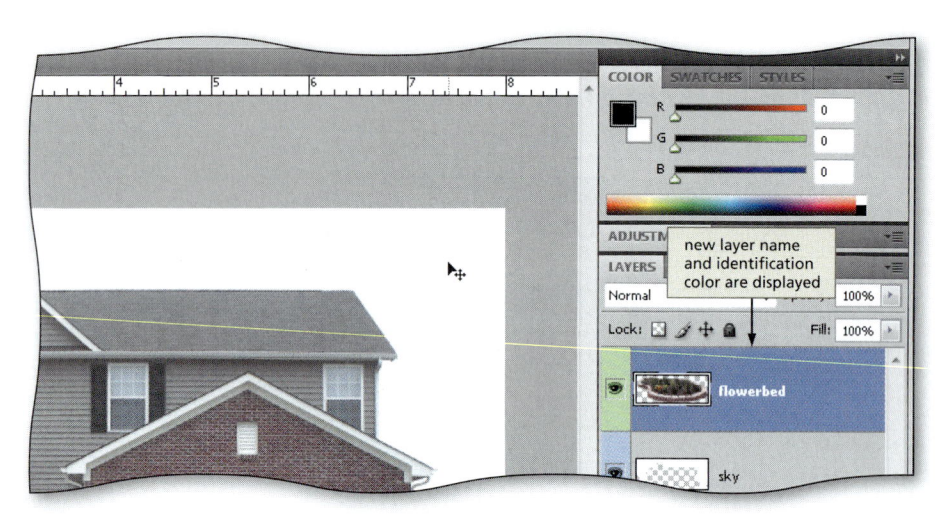

new layer name and identification color are displayed

Figure 3–23

Other Ways
1. Click Layers panel menu button, click Layer Properties, type new name, choose new color, click OK button

BTW

Smart Objects
You can convert a layer into a smart object, which is a nondestructive layer that does not change the original pixels. They are useful for warping, scaling, or rotating both raster and vector graphic layers. To convert a layer into a smart object, right-click the layer, and then click Convert to Smart Object on the context menu.

To Save the File

Because you have created layers and made changes to the image, it is a good idea to save the file again.

① Press CTRL+S to save the House Edited file with the same name. If Photoshop displays a dialog box about compatibility, click the OK button.

Creating a Layer by Dragging a Selection

Sometimes you do not want to move an entire image from one window to another. When you want only a part of an image, you create a selection, as you learned about in Chapter 2. After opening the new image and displaying the windows side by side, graphic artists select the portion of the image they want to use, and then drag the selection from the source window to the destination window to create a layer. Once the selection exists in the destination file, some editing, such as scaling, erasing, or adjusting, commonly is necessary.

To Open the Flowers Image

The flowers that will appear between the porch and sidewalk are a part of a larger image. The following steps open a file named Flowers, in preparation for selecting part of the image.

① To display the Open dialog box, press CTRL+O.

② Click the Look in box arrow, and then navigate to the Chapter03 folder of the Data Files for Students, or a location specified by your instructor, if necessary.

③ Double-click the file named Flowers to open it. Change the magnification to 100% if necessary (Figure 3–24).

To Select the Flowers

When adding the flowers image to the House Edited image, you will not need the surrounding shrubbery or grass. The following steps select the flowers using the Magnetic Lasso tool.

① Right-click the Lasso Tool (L) button and then click Magnetic Lasso Tool on the context menu.

② Drag around the pink flowers. Avoid including greenery in the selection and avoid the ground below the flowers. If you make a mistake while selecting, press the ESC key and then begin again. When you complete the lasso around the flowers, double-click to complete the selection (Figure 3–24).

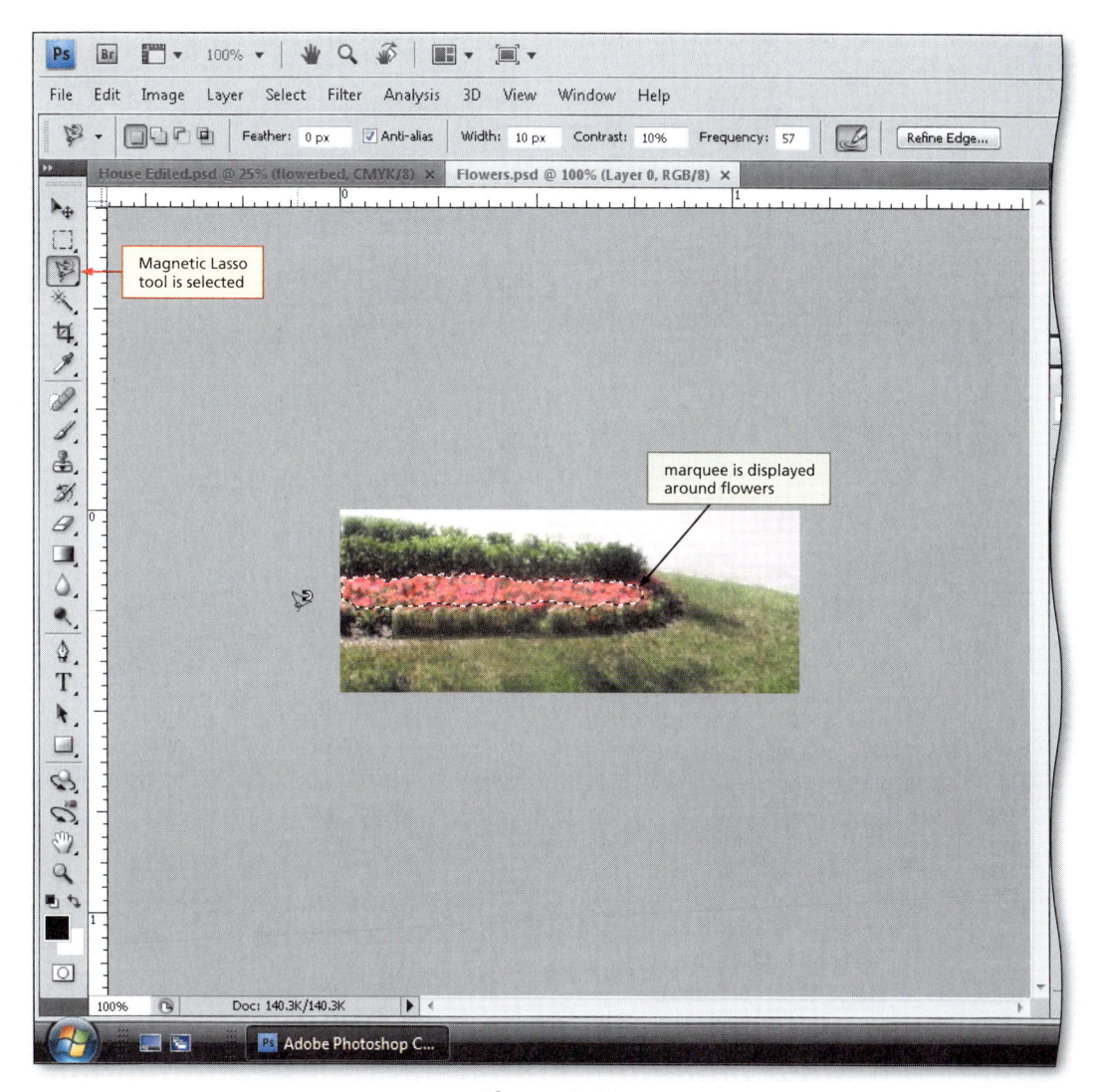

Figure 3–24

To Create a Layer by Dragging a Selection

To facilitate dragging the selection between windows, you will view the windows side by side and then move the selection.

1
- On the Application bar, click the Arrange Documents button to display its list, and then click the first 2 Up button to display the windows beside each other.

🔍 **Experiment**
- Click the Arrange documents button and then click the Tile All Horizontally button. Open a third file and then try some of the other configurations. When you are done, close the third file. Click the Arrange documents button and then click the first 2 Up button.

2
- Click the Move Tool (V) button on the Tools panel.
- Drag the selection and drop it in the House Edited window (Figure 3–25).

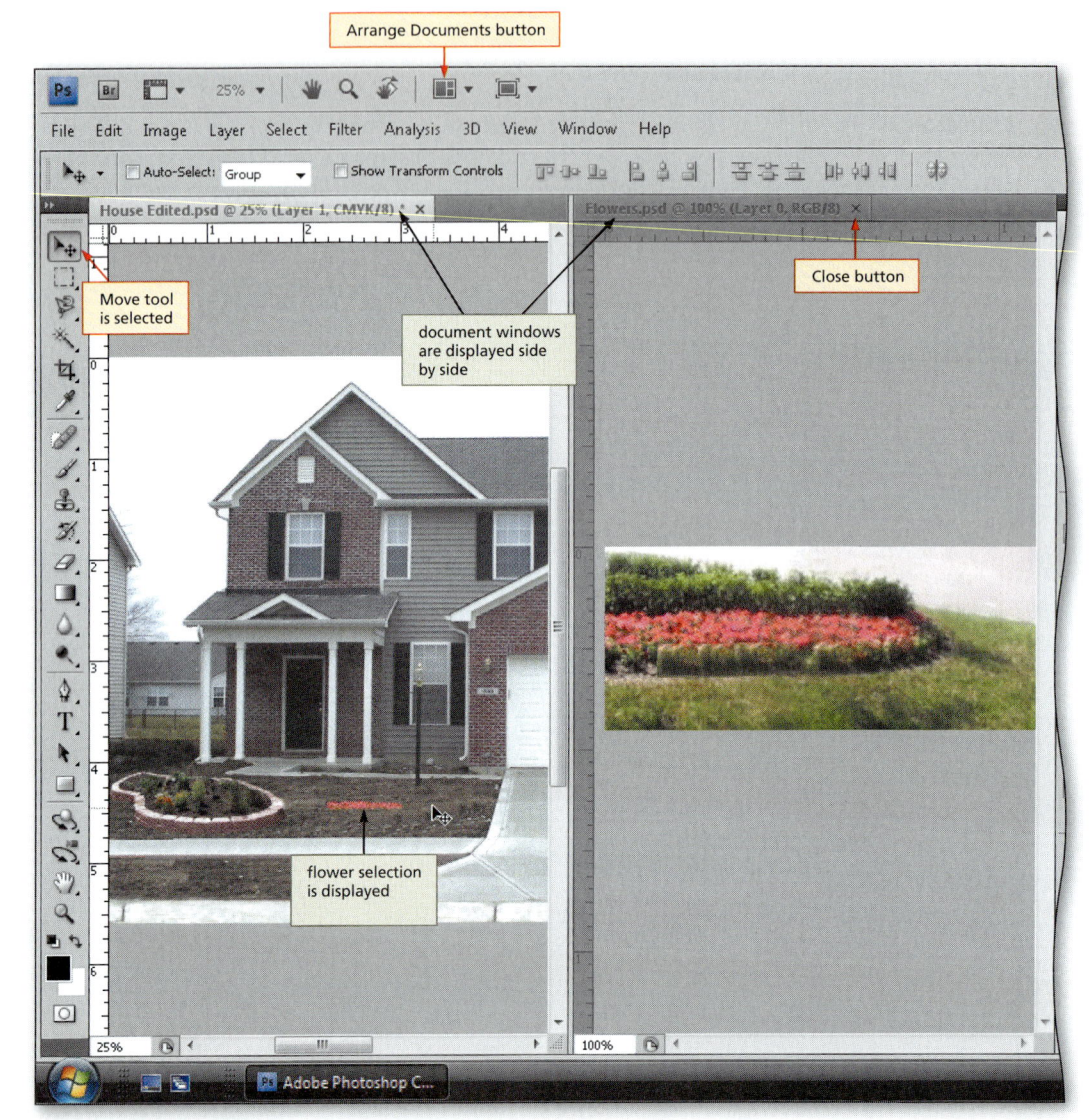

Figure 3–25

Q&A | Why are the flowers so small?

The photos used in composites may come from a variety of sources and camera types, with a variety of different resolutions, and with different physical sizes. Remember that the magnification has nothing to do with the physical size of the photo.

Other Ways
1. In source window, create selection, on Edit menu, click Copy, in destination window, on Edit menu, click Paste

To Close the Flowers Window

The next step closes the Flowers window.

1 Click the Close button in the Flowers window. If Photoshop displays a dialog box asking if you want to save the changes, click the No button.

To Move the Flowers Layer

The following steps move the new layer to a location between the porch and the sidewalk.

1. On the status bar, type 50% in the magnification box and then press the ENTER key to change the magnification.

2. With the new layer still selected, drag the layer to a location between the porch and the sidewalk.

3. Use the arrow keys to nudge the layer into place, as shown in Figure 3–26.

4. Change the magnification back to 25 percent.

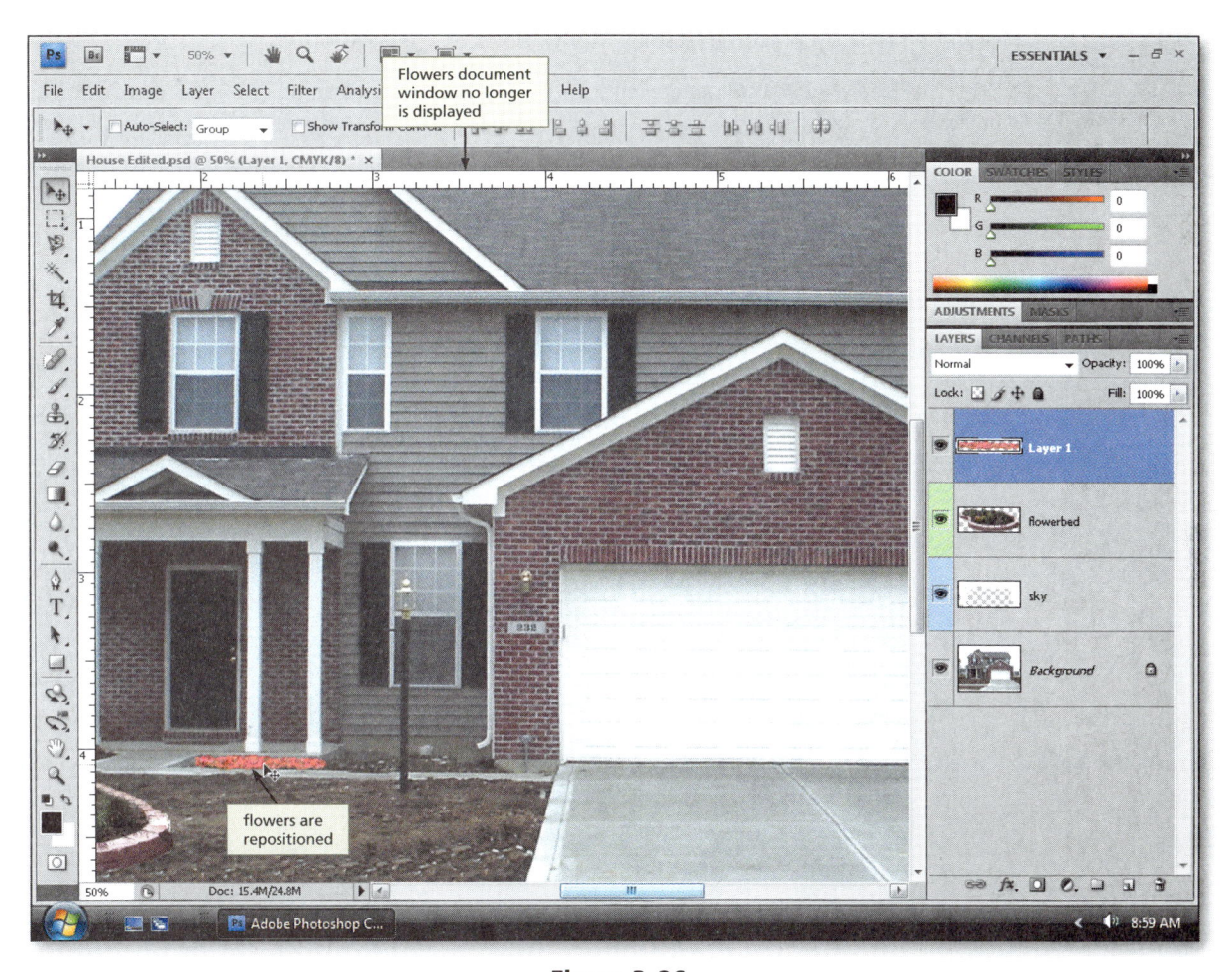

Figure 3–26

To Set the Flowers Layer Properties

The following steps set the flowers layer properties.

1. Right-click Layer 1 on the Layers panel. Click Layer Properties on the context menu.

2. Type flowers in the Name box. Click the Color box arrow, and then click Red.

3. Click the OK button to apply the settings.

To Open the Tree Image

The following steps open a file named Tree in preparation for using the Eraser tools.

1. Open the Tree file from the Chapter03 folder of the Data Files for Students, or a location specified by your instructor, if necessary.

2. Change the magnification to 33.33%, if necessary, to view the entire image.

To Create the Tree Layer

1. On the Application bar, click the Arrange Documents button to display its list, and then click the first 2 Up button to display the windows beside each other.

2. With the Tree window still active, click the Move Tool (V) button on the Tools panel, if necessary.

3. Drag the entire tree image and drop it in the House Edited window (Figure 3–27).

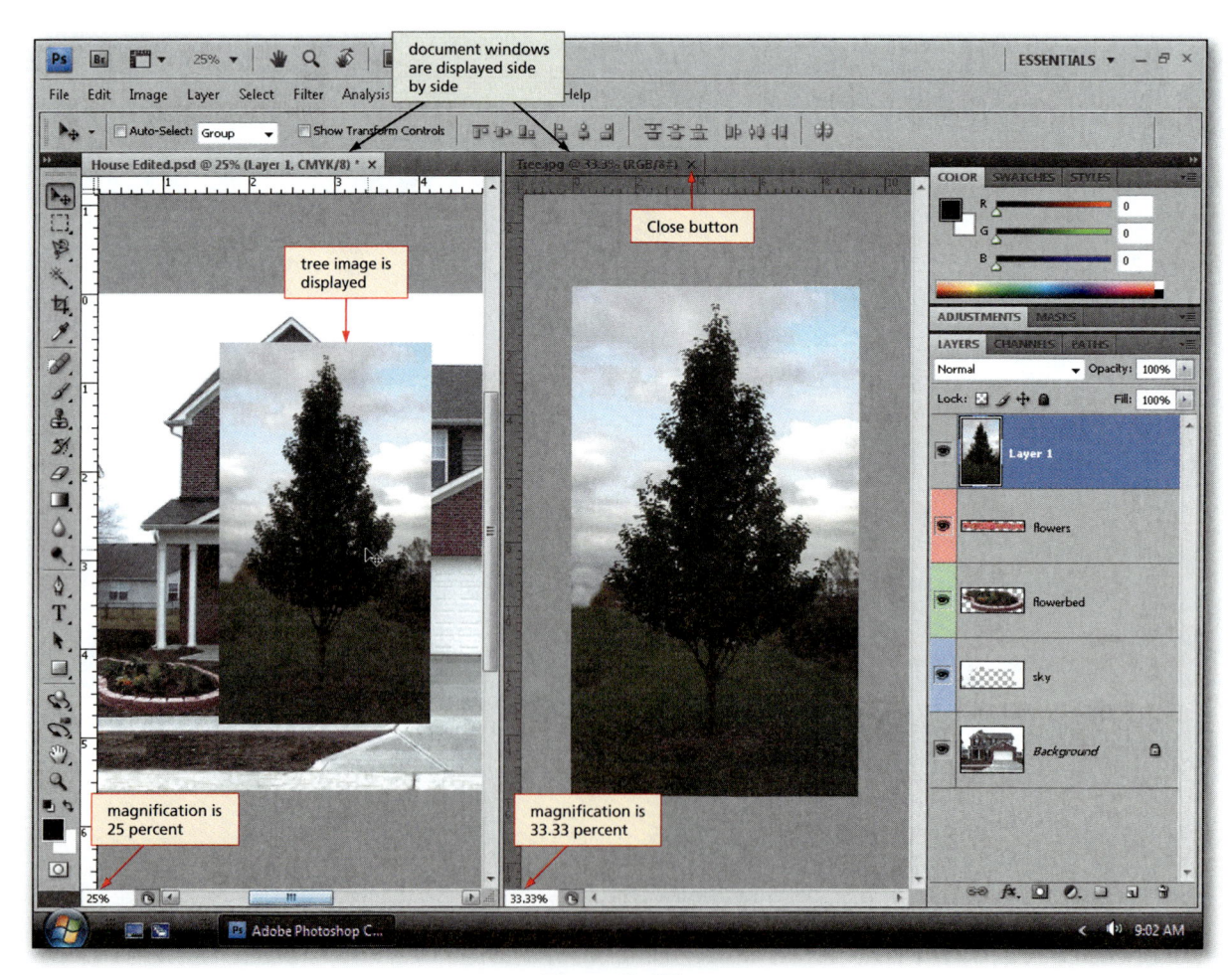

Figure 3–27

To Close the Tree Window

Because you are finished with the original tree image, you will close the Tree window in the following step.

1 Close the Tree document window. If Photoshop displays a dialog box asking if you want to save the changes, click the No button.

To Move the Tree and Set the Layer Properties

The following steps move the tree to a location for easy editing, and then set the layer properties.

1 With the Move tool still selected, drag the tree layer to a location in the driveway for easier editing.

2 Right-click Layer 1 on the Layers panel. Click Layer Properties on the context menu.

3 Type `tree` in the Name box. Click the Color box arrow, and then click Gray.

4 Click the OK button to apply the settings.

The Eraser Tools

When creating a composite image, you can limit the selected area of the source image as you did in the flowers layer, but sometimes a layer still has extra color or objects that are not appropriate for the composite image. The image might be shaped oddly, making selecting tedious, or there might be other images in the background that come along with the selection no matter what you do. In those cases, dragging the image into a layer and then erasing part of that layer gives you more freedom and control in how the layer is displayed.

On the options bar, when you right-click the Eraser Tool (E) button, Photoshop displays the three eraser tools. To alternate among the three eraser tools, press SHIFT+E. To access the eraser tools after using a different tool, press the E key.

The eraser tools are described in Table 3–1.

Table 3–1 Eraser Tools

Tool	Purpose	Shortcut	Button
Eraser tool	erases pixels beneath the cursor or brush tip	E SHIFT+E toggles through all three eraser tools	
Background Eraser tool	erases sample color from the center of the brush	E SHIFT+E toggles through all three eraser tools	
Magic Eraser tool	erases all similarly colored pixels	E SHIFT+E toggles through all three eraser tools	

When using the eraser tools, it is best to erase small portions at a time. That way each erasure is a separate state on the History panel. If you make mistakes, you can click earlier states on the panel. Small erasures also can be undone. To undo an erasure, press CTRL+Z, or click Edit on the menu bar, and then click Undo Eraser.

Using the Magic Eraser Tool

The Magic Eraser tool erases all similarly colored pixels with one click. The Magic Eraser tool options bar (Figure 3–28) gives you the choice of contiguous or non-contiguous pixels and allows you to enter a tolerance value to define the range of colors that can be erased. A lower tolerance erases pixels within a range of color values very similar to the pixel you click. A higher tolerance erases pixels within a broader range. Recall that the Anti-alias check box creates a smooth edge that can apply to both selecting and erasing. Also recall that opacity refers to the level at which you can see through a color to reveal the layer beneath it. When using the eraser tools, an opacity of 100% completely erases pixels. A lower opacity partially erases pixels.

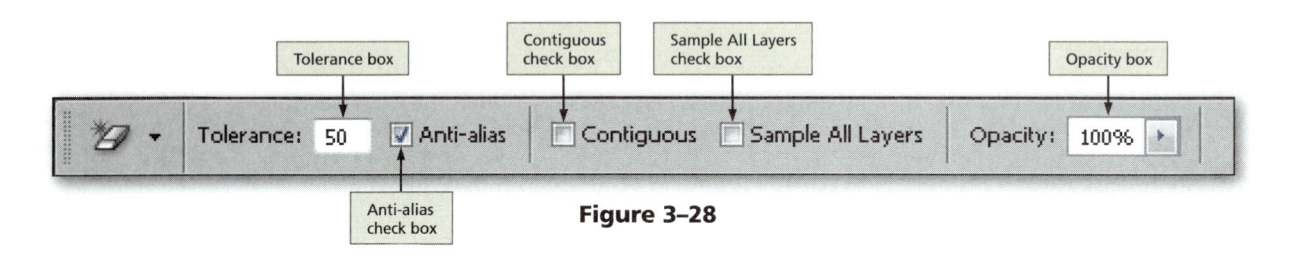

Figure 3–28

To Erase Using the Magic Eraser Tool

The following steps use the Magic Eraser tool to remove the sky around and behind the tree.

1
- With the tree layer still selected, right-click the Eraser Tool (E) button on the Tools panel to display the context menu (Figure 3–29).

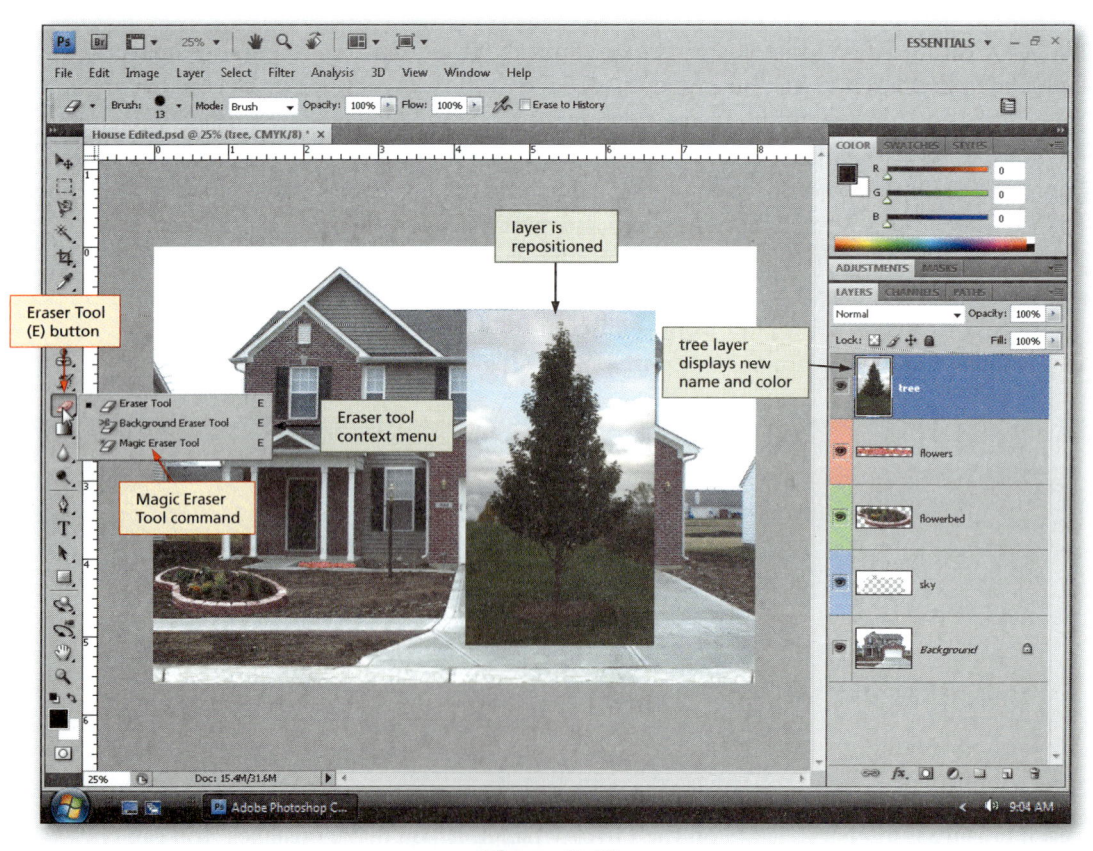

Figure 3–29

The Eraser Tools **PS 187**

2
- Click Magic Eraser Tool to select it.
- On the Magic Eraser options bar, type 50 in the Tolerance box. If necessary, click the Anti-alias check box to display the check mark. If necessary, click the Contiguous check box so it does not display a check mark.
- Move the mouse pointer to a portion of the tree layer containing the sky (Figure 3–30).

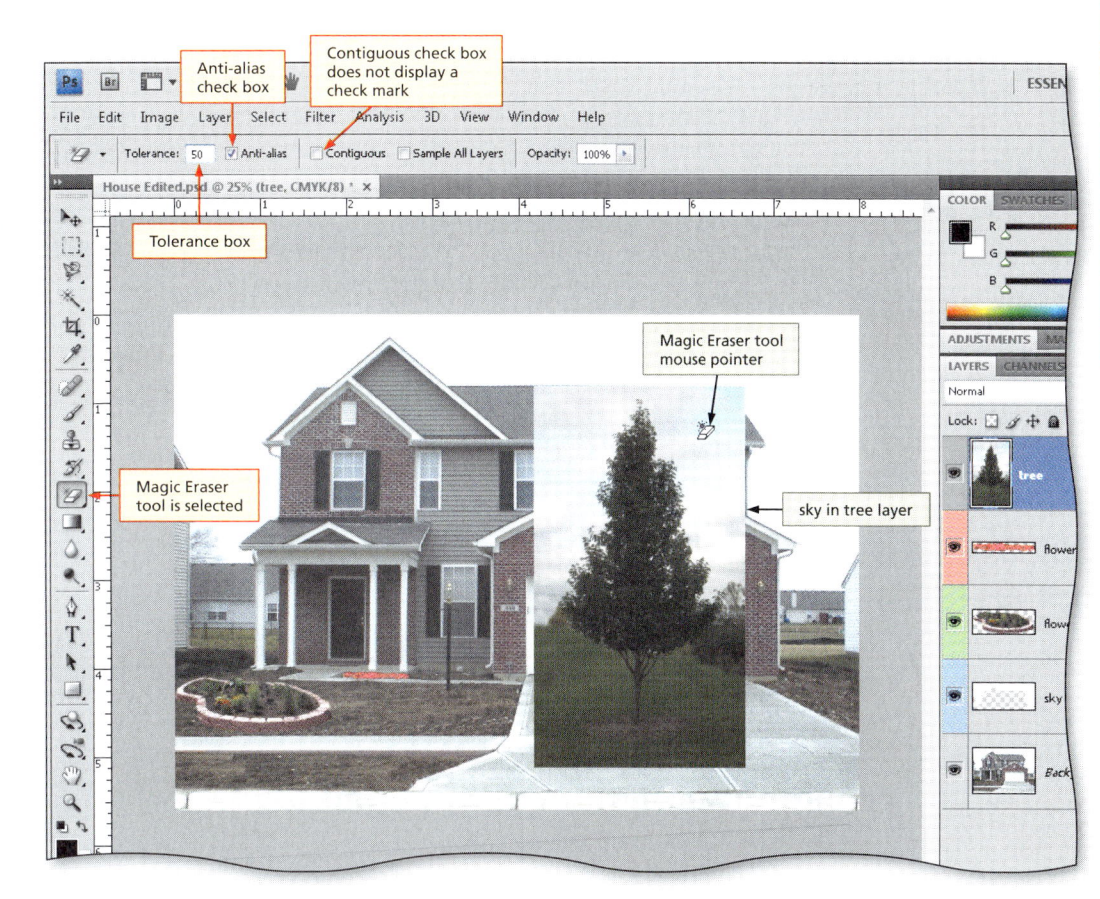

Figure 3–30

3
- Click the sky to delete all of the sky color (Figure 3–31).
- If some sky remains in your layer, click it.

Other Ways

1. Press SHIFT+E until Magic Eraser tool is selected, click document

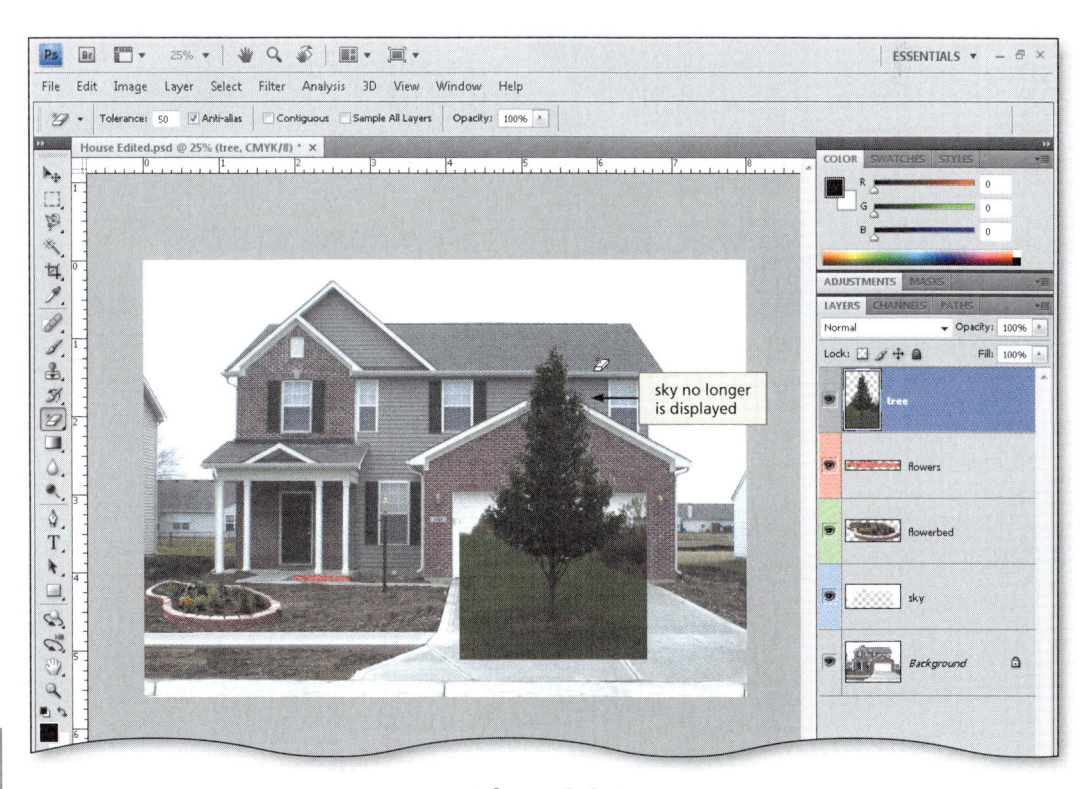

Figure 3–31

Using the Eraser Tool

The Eraser tool changes pixels in the image as you drag through them. On most layers, the Eraser tool simply erases the pixels or changes them to transparent. On the Background layer, the pixels are changed to white. On a locked layer, the Eraser tool changes the pixels to the background color.

The Eraser tool options bar (Figure 3–32) displays a Mode box in which you can choose one of three shapes for erasure: brush, block, and pen. The brush shape gives you the most flexibility in size, and many different brush tips are available. The default brush tip is a circle. Block mode is a hard-edged, fixed-sized square with no options for changing the opacity or flow; however, it does give you quick access to a square to erase straight lines and corners. The pencil mode is similar to the brush mode, except that the pencil does not spread as much into adjacent pixels.

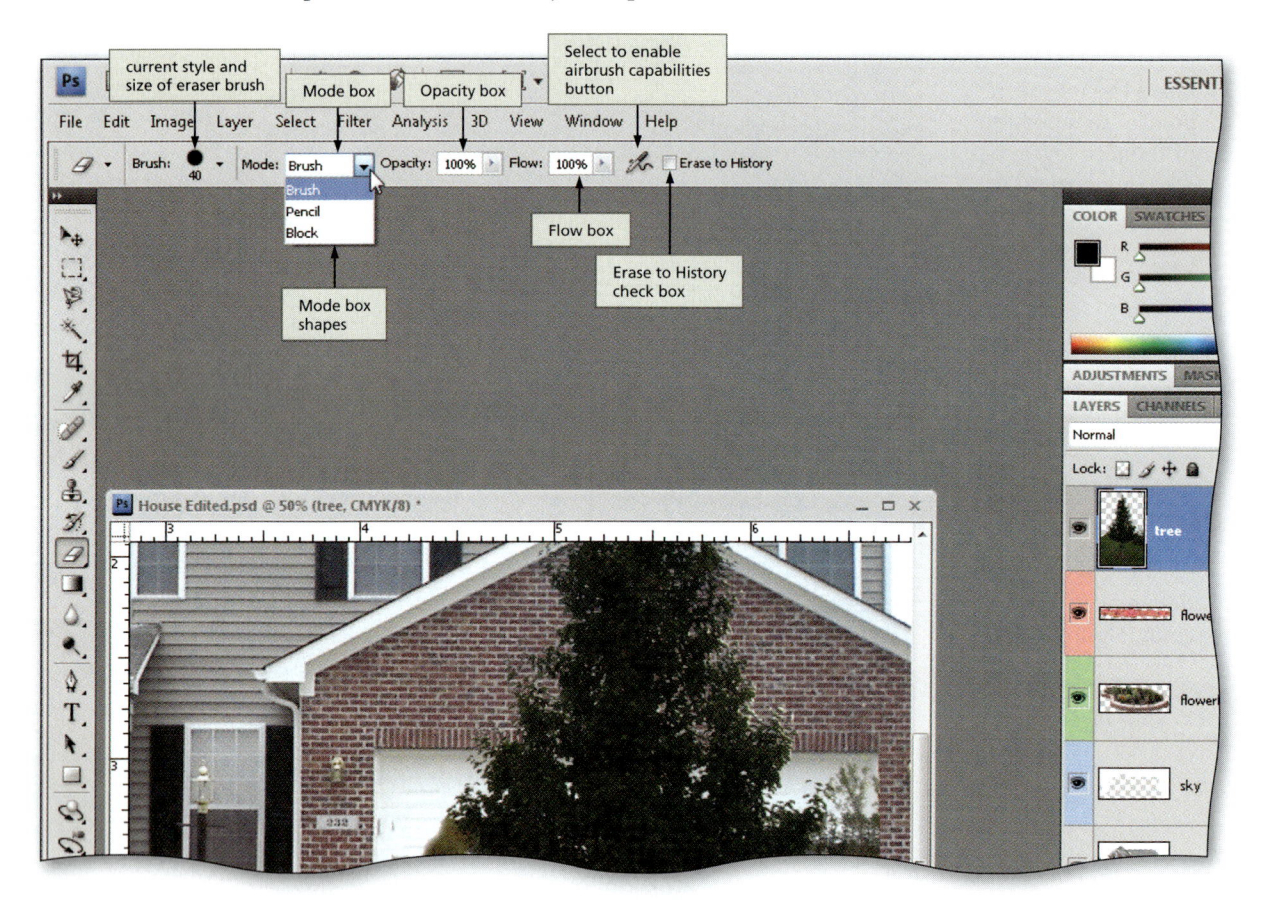

Figure 3–32

As with the Magic Eraser tool options bar, an Opacity box allows you to specify the depth of the erasure. The Flow box specifies how quickly the erasure is performed. In addition, you can erase to a saved state or snapshot in the History panel.

As you erase with the brush shape, the RIGHT BRACKET ( ]) and LEFT BRACKET ([ ) keys increase and decrease the size of the eraser, respectively. Some users find it easier to erase in a layer when only that layer is displayed. Recall that if you want to display only the layer, ALT+click the layer's visibility icon. ALT+click the visibility icon again to re-display the background and other layers.

To Erase Using the Eraser Tool

To erase more of the background in the tree layer, the following steps use the Eraser tool.

1
- Increase the magnification of the document window to 50 percent. Scroll to display the lower portion of the tree layer.
- With the tree layer still selected, right-click the Eraser Tool (E) button on the Tools panel, and then click Eraser Tool on the context menu.
- Move the mouse pointer to a portion of the tree layer containing grass.
- Press the RIGHT BRACKET (]) key several times to resize the eraser until the mouse pointer changes from a dot to a small circle (Figure 3–33).

2
- Drag the mouse across a portion of the grass to erase it. Do not drag across the tree or its trunk (Figure 3–34).

  Experiment
- Drag a short erasure over the tree trunk that creates an error. Then press CTRL+Z to undo the erasure.

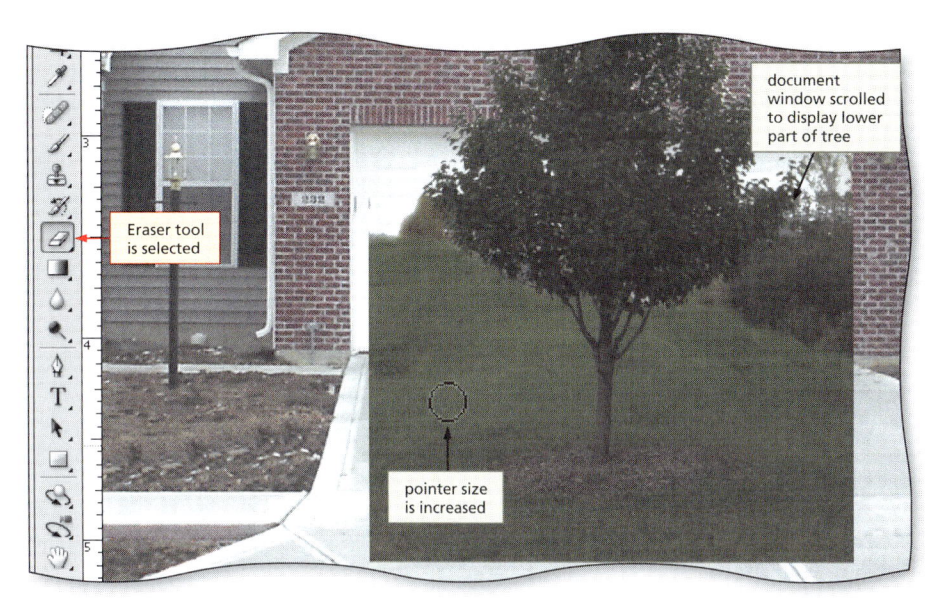

Figure 3–33

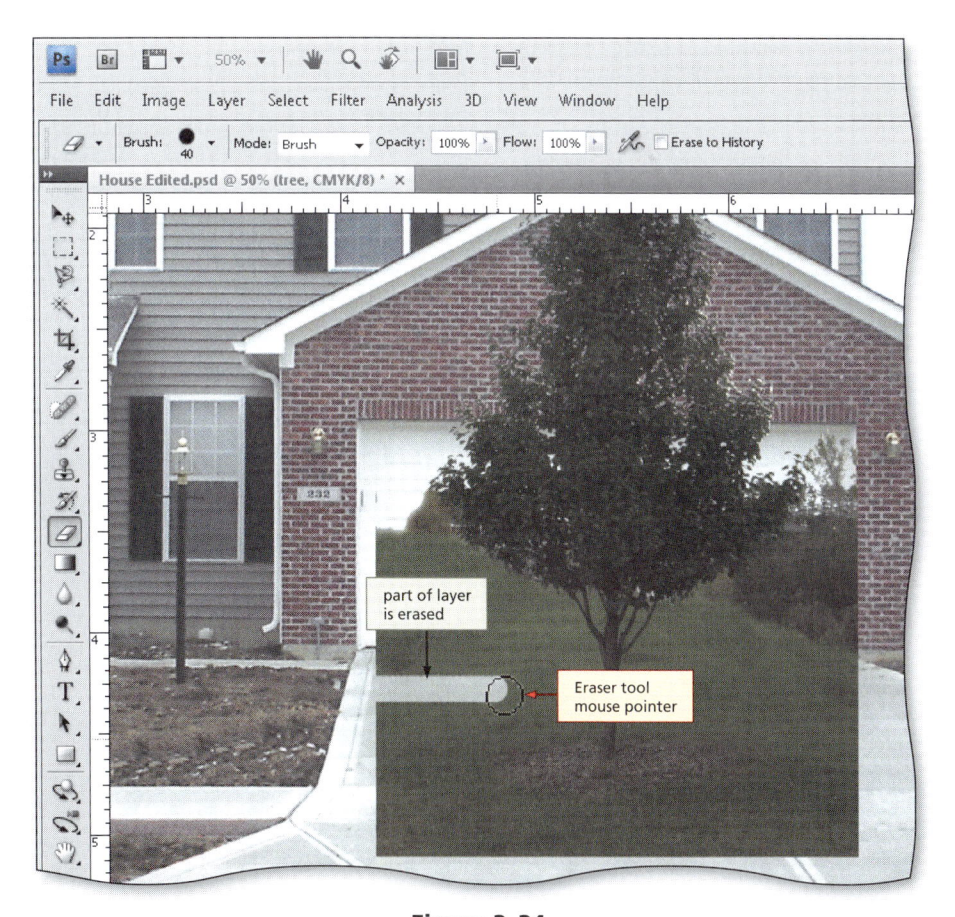

Figure 3–34

3

- Continue dragging, using the LEFT BRACKET ([) and RIGHT BRACKET (]) keys to change the size of your eraser. Zoom in as necessary, to erase the majority of the grass, dirt, and background shrubs. Do not try to erase the grass showing behind the tree limbs (Figure 3–35).

Figure 3–35

4

- To delete close to the tree trunk, click the Mode box arrow on the options bar and then chose Block.

- Increase the magnification and scroll as necessary to view the tree trunk.

- Using the Block shape, drag close to the trunk on each side of the tree to erase more of the grass (Figure 3–36).

Q&A Can I change the size of the block?

No, the block eraser cannot be resized. You can change the magnification, however, to help you erase smaller portions using the block.

5

- If necessary, change the magnification back to 50 percent.

Figure 3–36

Other Ways

1. Press SHIFT+E until Eraser tool is selected, click document

Using the Background Eraser Tool

The Background Eraser tool erases the background while maintaining the edges of an object in the foreground, based on a set color that you choose for the background. The Background Eraser samples the color in the center of the mouse pointer, called the **hot spot**. As you drag, the tool erases that color, leaving the rest of the layer as foreground. You release the mouse and drag again to sample a different color. On the Background Eraser Tool options bar (Figure 3–37) you can use the tolerance setting to control the range of colors that will be erased, sample the color selections, and adjust the sharpness of the boundaries by setting limits. The three sampling buttons on the Background Eraser Tool options bar sample in different ways. Sampling: Continuous samples colors and erases continuously as you drag; Sampling Once: erases only the areas containing the color you first click; and Sampling: Background Swatch erases only areas containing the current color on the Tools panel, Color panel, or Swatches panel.

BTW

The Background Eraser Tool
The Background Eraser tool samples the hot spot and then, as you drag, it deletes that color wherever it appears inside the brush. The Background Eraser tool overrides the lock transparency setting of a layer.

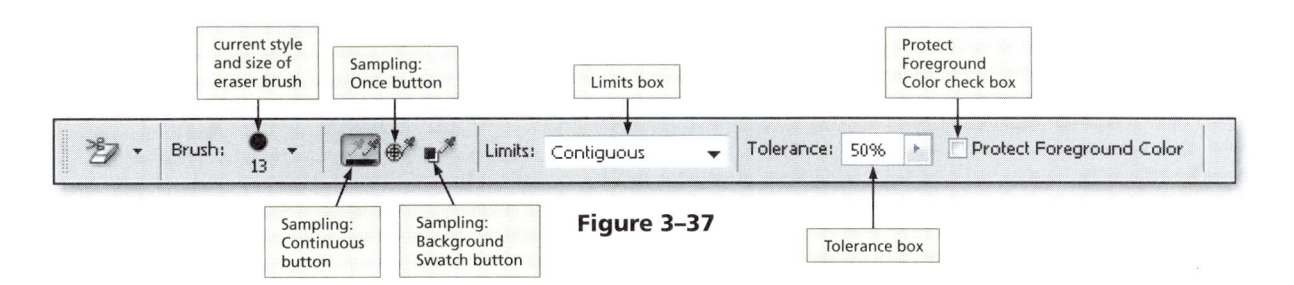

Figure 3–37

To Erase Using the Background Eraser Tool

The following steps show how to use the Background Eraser tool to remove the grass from behind the branches of the tree. If you make a mistake while erasing, click the previous state on the History panel or press CTRL+Z and begin erasing again.

1
- With the tree layer still selected, right-click the Eraser Tool (E) button on the Tools panel and then click Background Eraser Tool on the context menu to select the tool.
- On the options bar, click the Sampling: Once button.
- Click the Limits box arrow to display its list (Figure 3–38).

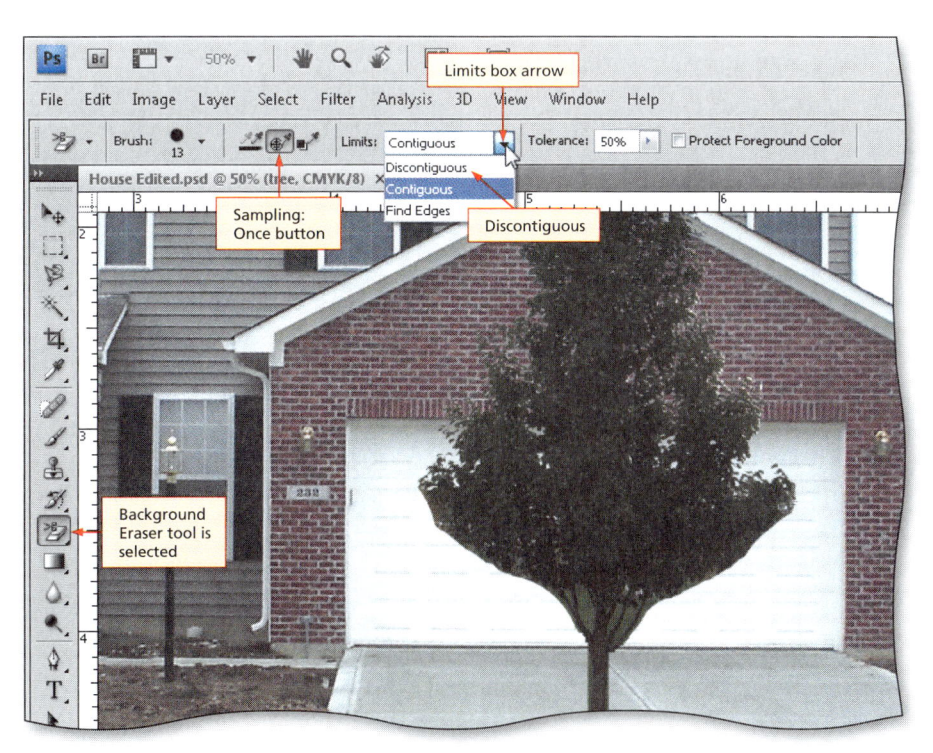

Figure 3–38

PS 192 Photoshop Chapter 3 Working with Layers

2

- Click Discontiguous to choose the setting.
- Type 25 in the Tolerance box, and then press the ENTER key.
- Click the Protect Foreground Color check box so it displays a check mark.
- Move the mouse pointer to the document window and then press the RIGHT BRACKET (]) key several times to increase the size of the eraser (Figure 3–39).

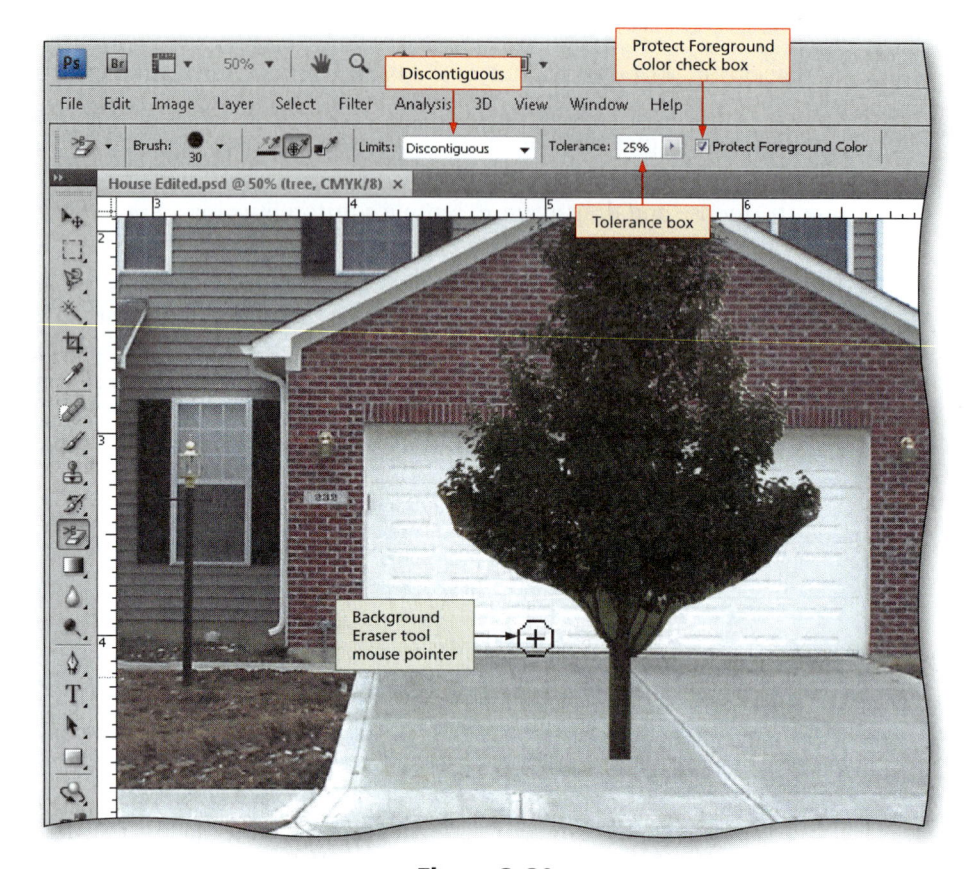

Figure 3–39

3

- Position the mouse pointer directly over a portion of the grass in between the branches of the tree.
- Click and hold the mouse button. Slowly drag across the lower limbs of the tree to erase the grass in the background (Figure 3–40).

Q&A Do I have to erase all of the grass?

No, it does not have to be perfect, because the tree will be moved into an area that ultimately will have grass all around it anyway. If you make a mistake, step backward on the History panel and erase again.

Figure 3–40

4
- If any grass remains, repeat Step 3. Adjust the brush size as necessary with the bracket keys and carefully erase small portions at a time.

Other Ways

1. Press SHIFT+E until Background Eraser tool is selected, set options bar, click document

To Reposition the Tree Layer

The final step in editing the tree layer is to move it to a position in the flower bed.

1. Decrease the magnification to 25%.
2. With the tree layer selected, press the V key to activate the Move tool.
3. Drag the layer so the base of the tree is in the flower bed (Figure 3–41). Part of the tree might be eclipsed by the left margin.

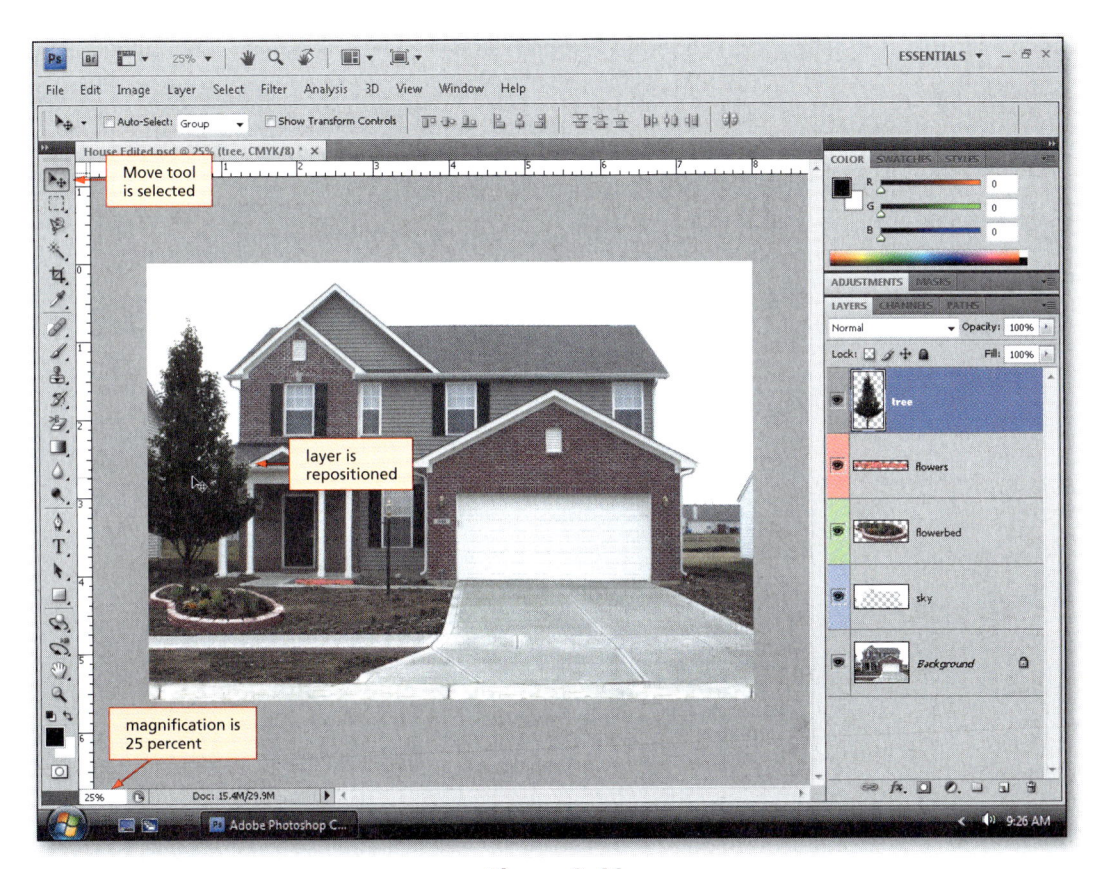

Figure 3–41

To Open the Shrub Image

The following steps open a file named Shrub in preparation for creating a layer mask.

1. Open the Shrub file from the Chapter03 folder of the Data Files for Students, or a location specified by your instructor, if necessary.

2. Change the magnification to 50%, if necessary.

To Create the Shrub Layer

To create the shrub layer, you first will move the entire image into the House Edited document window.

1. On the Application bar, click the Arrange Documents button to display its list, and then click the first 2 Up button to display the windows beside each other.

2. Activate the Move tool, if necessary.

3. Drag the shrub image and drop it in the House Edited window (Figure 3–42).

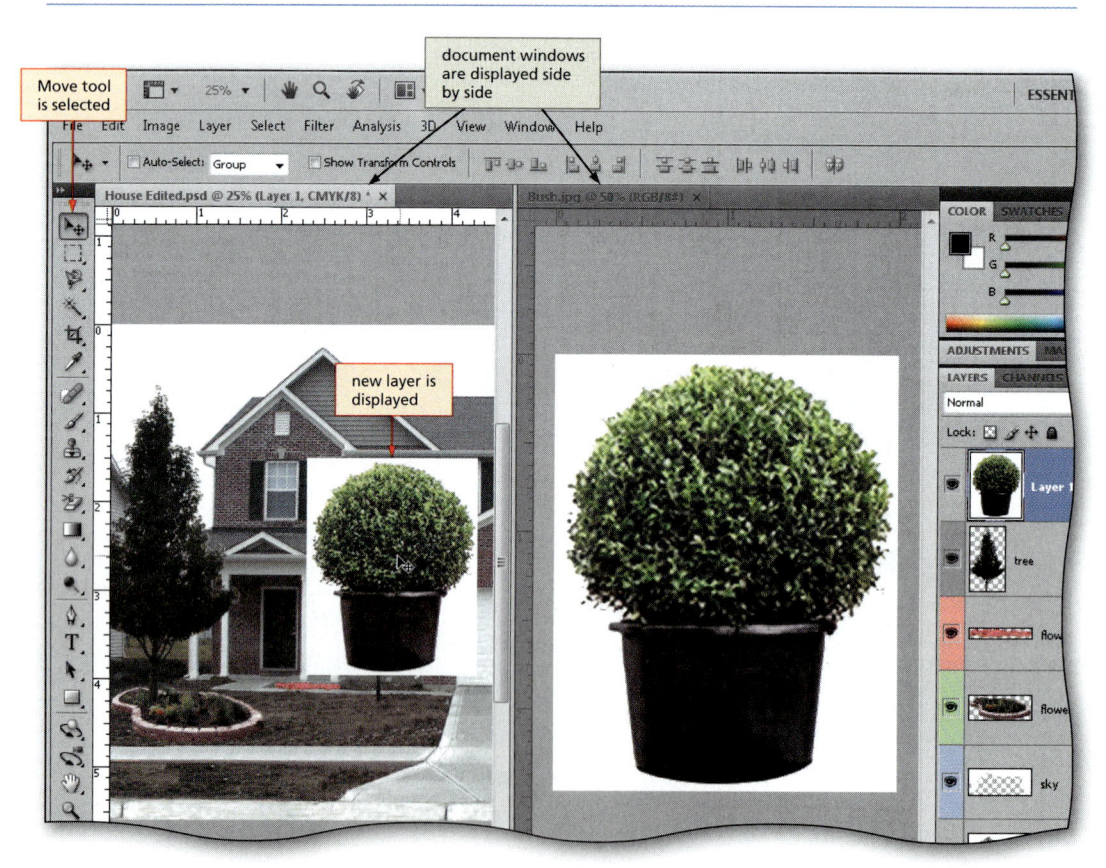

Figure 3–42

The Eraser Tools **PS 195**

To Consolidate the Windows

The following steps return the display to view only one image at a time, by right-clicking the House Edited tab at the top of the document window and choosing to consolidate on the context menu. Because you will use it again later in the chapter, you will not close the Shrub window.

1
- Right-click the tab at the top of the House Edited document window to display the context menu (Figure 3–43).

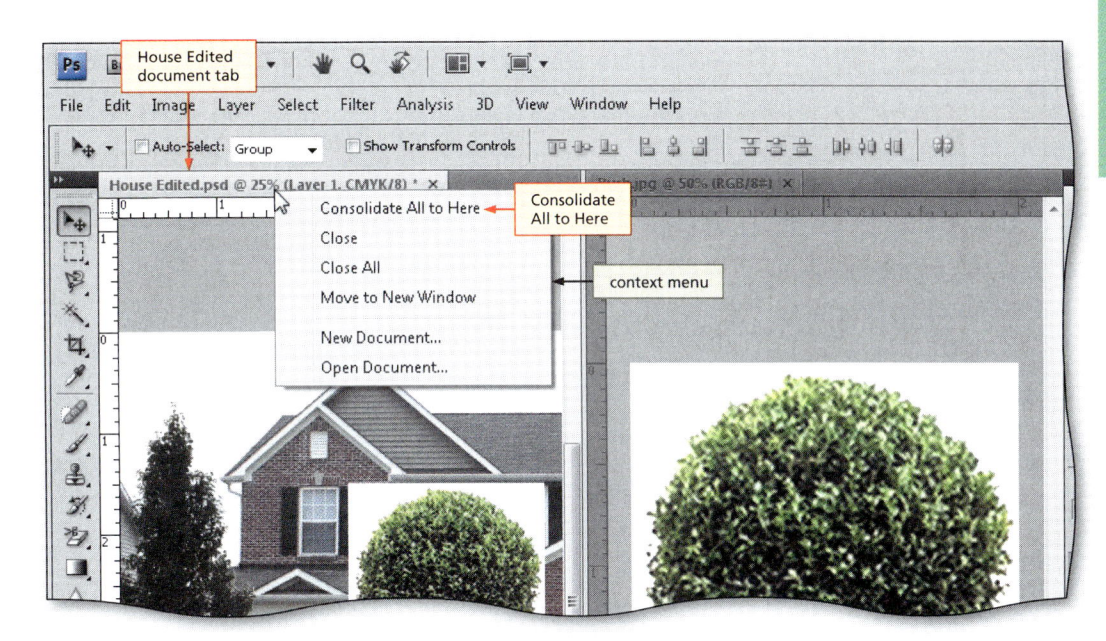

Figure 3–43

2
- Click Consolidate All to Here to view one document at a time (Figure 3–44).

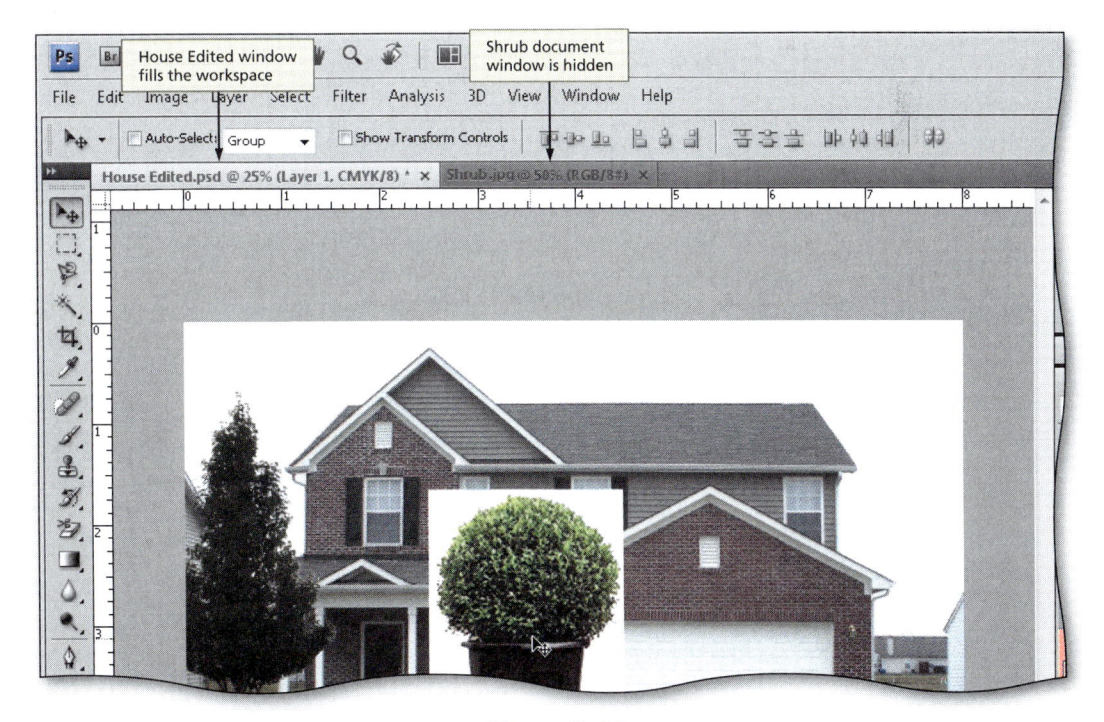

Figure 3–44

Other Ways
1. Click Arrange Documents button, click Consolidate All

To Move the Shrub and Set the Layer Properties

The following steps move the shrub to a location for easy editing, and then set the layer properties.

① With the Move tool still activated, drag the new layer to a location in the driveway for easier editing.

② Rename the new layer, shrub.

③ Change the shrub layer's identification color to Violet.

④ Click the OK button to display the settings on the Layers panel.

To Save the File

Many layers have been added to the composite image. You should save the file again.

① Save the House Edited file with the same name.

Layer Masks

Another way to edit layers is by creating a mask. A **mask** shows or hides portions of a layer; it also can protect areas of the layer from inadvertent editing. For example, in a graphic of an exotic animal, you might want to mask all of the area except the animal, rather than permanently delete the background. Or, if you wanted to layer a musical score over the top of a piano graphic, you might mask the edges of the paper so the notes look like they blend into the piano. A mask does not alter the layer as the Eraser tool did; it merely overlays a template to conceal a portion of the layer. That way, if you change your mind and need to display more of the layer, you can — nothing has been erased permanently. With the Eraser tool, you would have to delete the layer, open a backup copy, recreate the layer, and then begin to edit again. With masks, you simply edit the mask.

Photoshop provides two types of masks. **Layer masks** are resolution-dependent bitmap images that are created with the painting or selection tools. **Vector masks** are resolution independent and are created with a pen or shape tool. In this chapter, you will create a layer mask.

A layer mask is a **grayscale** image, which means each pixel in the mask is represented by a single color on a scale from black to white. Therefore, to create a mask, you paint over the layer with black. If you change your mind and want to unmask, you paint with white. Painting with gray displays various levels of transparency in the layer.

Once you have created a mask, you might want to perform other manipulations on the mask. For example, if you want to unlink a mask to move it independently of its layer, click the link icon on the Layers panel. To unlink a mask temporarily, SHIFT+click the link icon. If you want to mask the entire layer completely, you can ALT+click the Add layer mask button. In that case, you would paint with white in the mask to reveal portions of the mask. To make the mask permanent and reduce overall file size, apply the mask using a command on the mask's context menu.

Layer Masks **PS 197**

To Create a Layer Mask

To create a layer mask, Photoshop provides an Add layer mask button on the status bar of the Layers panel. When clicked, the button adds a second thumbnail to the layer's description on the panel. By default, the mask is **linked,** or connected to, the selected layer. A link icon is displayed between the layer thumbnail and the mask thumbnail. The following steps mask the pot and white border of the shrub layer.

1

- With the shrub layer selected, click the Add layer mask button on the Layers panel status bar to create a layer mask (Figure 3–45).

Q&A What is the new notation on the Layers panel?

Photoshop adds a layer mask thumbnail to the selected layer on the panel. The link icon links the mask to the layer. The mask is selected.

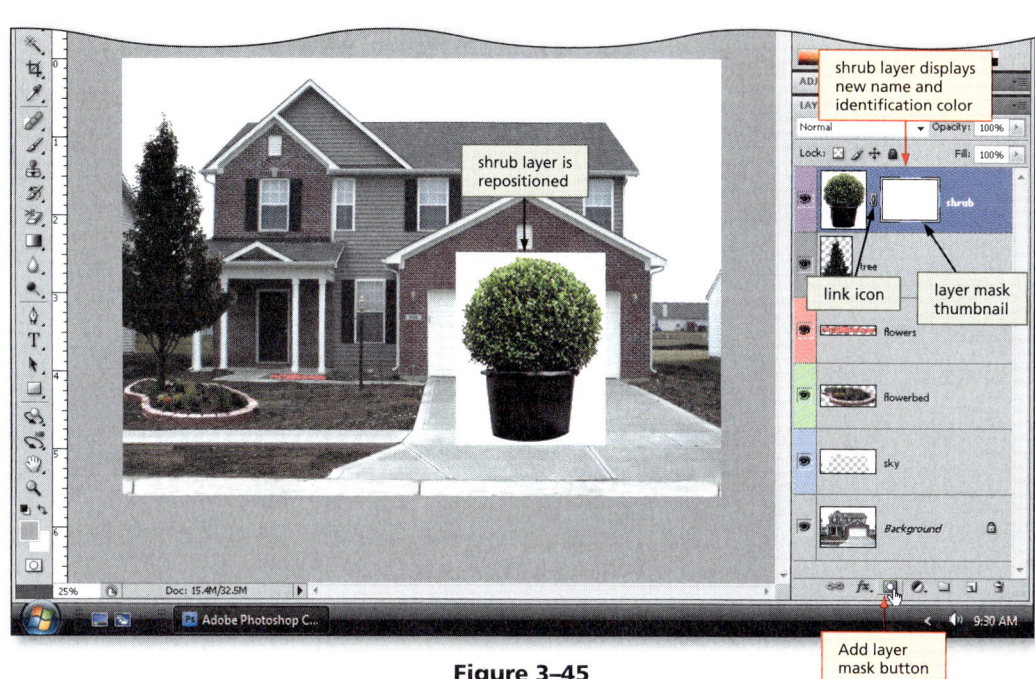

Figure 3–45

2

- Press the D key to activate the default color scheme.
- Press the X key to reverse the colors so black is in the foreground.
- Press the B key to activate the brush and then move the mouse pointer into the document window.
- Press the RIGHT BRACKET (]) key to increase the size of the brush's circle, as necessary (Figure 3–46).

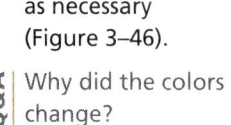

Q&A Why did the colors change?

A mask is a grayscale image. When you added the mask, Photoshop changed the foreground color automatically.

Figure 3–46

PS 198 Photoshop Chapter 3 Working with Layers

3
- Drag the mouse in the layer to reveal the background underneath. Do not drag the shrub itself (Figure 3–47).

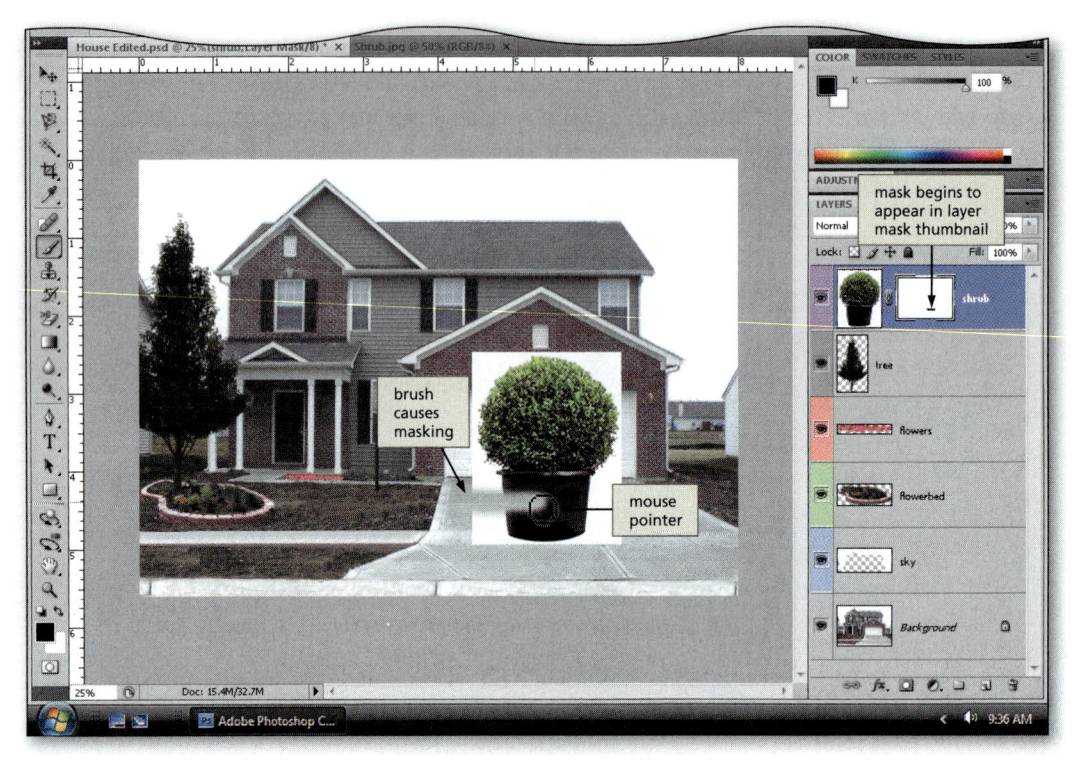

Figure 3–47

4
- Continue dragging through the layer to remove everything except the shrub. Adjust the size of the brush as necessary using the bracket keys until only the shrub is visible (Figure 3–48).

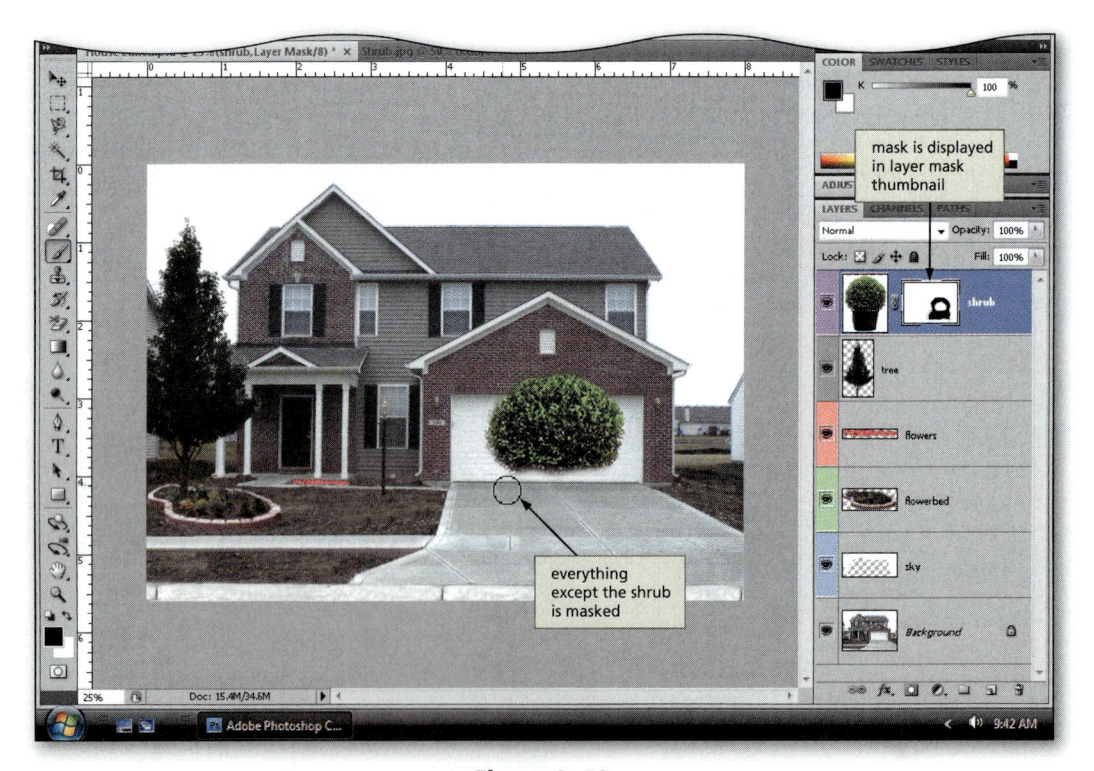

Figure 3–48

Layer Masks **PS 199**

To Correct a Masking Error

The following steps create a masking error and then unmask the area by painting with white.

1
- Drag across the shrub to mask it (Figure 3–49).

Figure 3–49

2
- Press the X key to switch the foreground and background colors.
- Drag across the same portion of the shrub to unmask it (Figure 3–50).

3
- Press the X key again to return to the default foreground and background colors.

Figure 3–50

Other Ways
1. On Layer menu, point to Layer Mask, click Reveal All

To Resize and Move the Shrub Layer

1. With the layer selected, press the V key to activate the Move tool. Click the Show Transform Controls check box to select it, if necessary.

2. Press CTRL+T to display the Transform options bar and the bounding box.

3. SHIFT+drag a corner sizing handle to decrease the size of the layer to approximately 25%, as displayed in the Transform options bar scale boxes.

4. Press the ENTER key to confirm the transformation. On the options bar, click to remove the check mark in the Show Transform Controls check box, if necessary.

5. Drag the layer to a location between the house and sidewalk as shown in Figure 3–51. Nudge the layer into place using the ARROW keys.

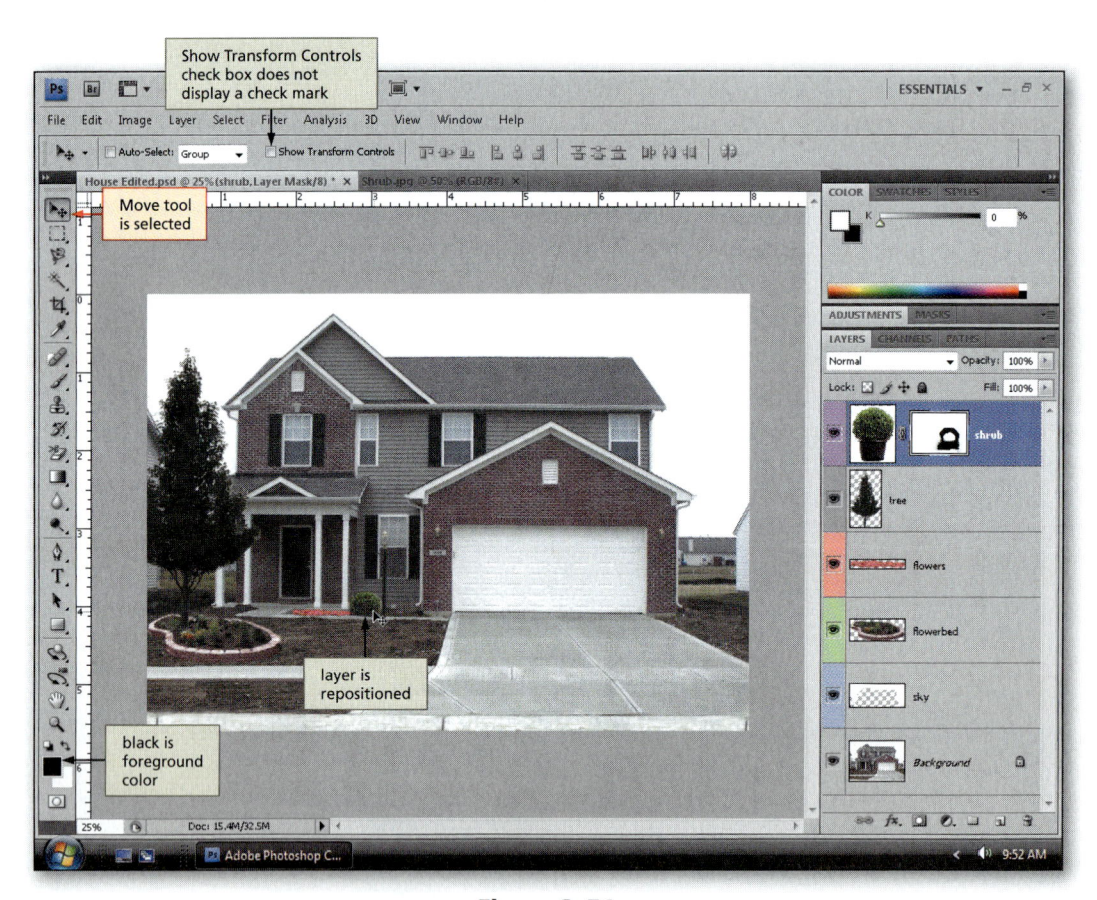

Figure 3–51

The Masks Panel

The Masks panel (Figure 3–52) provides additional controls to adjust a layer mask. You can change the density of the mask to allow more or less of the masked content to show through. For example, if you wanted to create a special effects layer to show a timeline or to animate a process, you could create several layer masks with varying percentages of density. Additionally, you can invert the mask in the same way you can invert a selection. The Masks panel allows you to feather the edges and refine the mask border. When creating a **selection layer mask**, instead of painting in the layer mask, the selection border dictates the transparent portion of the layer.

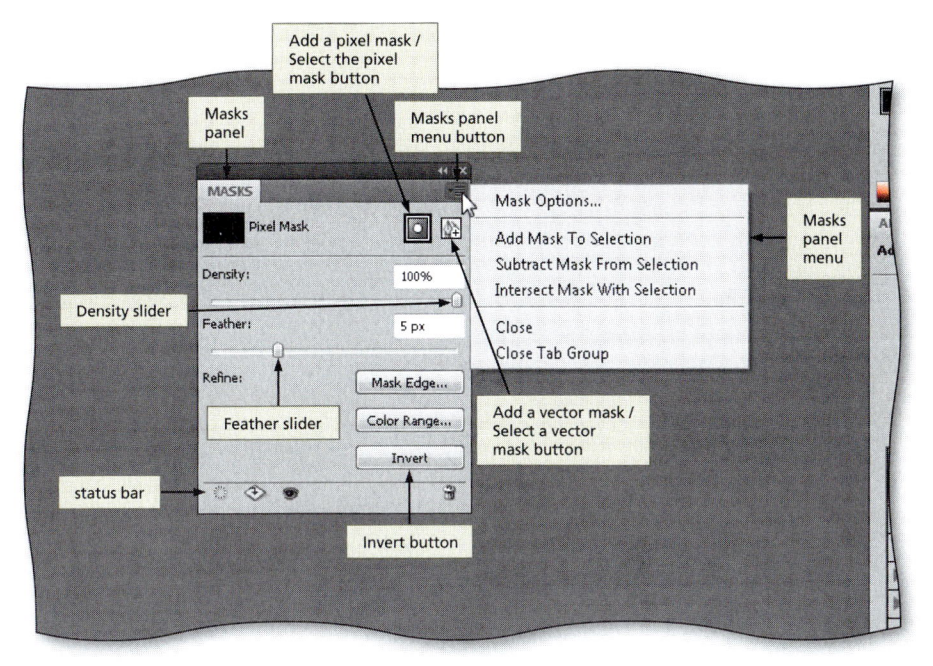

Figure 3–52

You will create a second copy of the shrub and then use the Masks panel to create a selection mask.

To Copy and Paste a Second Shrub

The following steps copy and paste a second shrub into the House Edited image.

① Click the Shrub document window tab to select the Shrub window.

② Press CTRL+A to select the entire image.

③ Press CTRL+C to copy the image.

④ Click the House Edited document window tab to select the House Edited window.

⑤ Press CTRL+V to paste the shrub image.

To Close the Shrub Window

Because you are finished with the original shrub image, you will close the Shrub document window in the following step.

① Close the Shrub document window. If Photoshop displays a dialog box asking if you want to save the changes, click the No button.

To Use the Masks Panel

The following steps create a selection and then use the Masks Panel to create a selection and set mask properties.

1

- Click the Masks panel tab to display the Masks panel.

- On the Tools panel, right-click the Rectangular Marquee Tool (M) button, and then select Elliptical Marquee Tool from the context menu.

- ALT+drag to create a marquee from the center of the shrub. Include as much of the shrub as possible, but not the pot or the white border. Release the mouse button before releasing the ALT key (Figure 3–53).

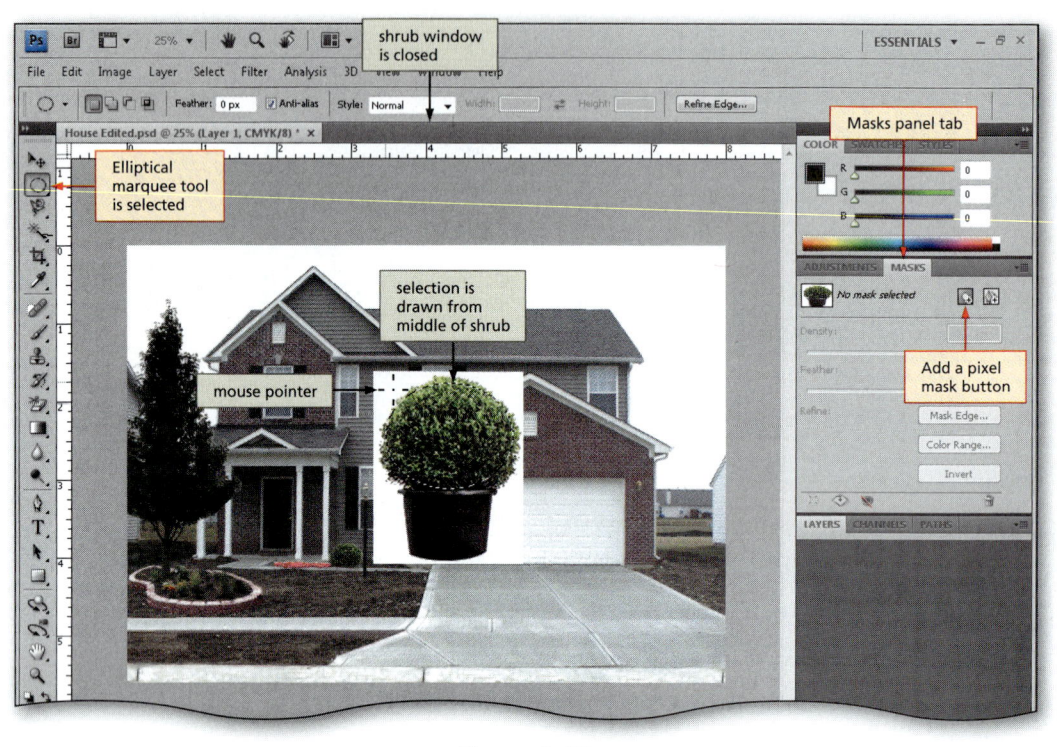

Figure 3–53

2

- On the Masks panel, click the Add a pixel mask button to create the selection layer mask (Figure 3–54).

Experiment

- Click the Invert button to display the inverted mask. Click the Invert button again to return to the shrub. Drag the Density slider to various percentages and watch the mask fade. Drag the Feather slider to various pixels and watch the edge of the mask soften and blend with less contrast.

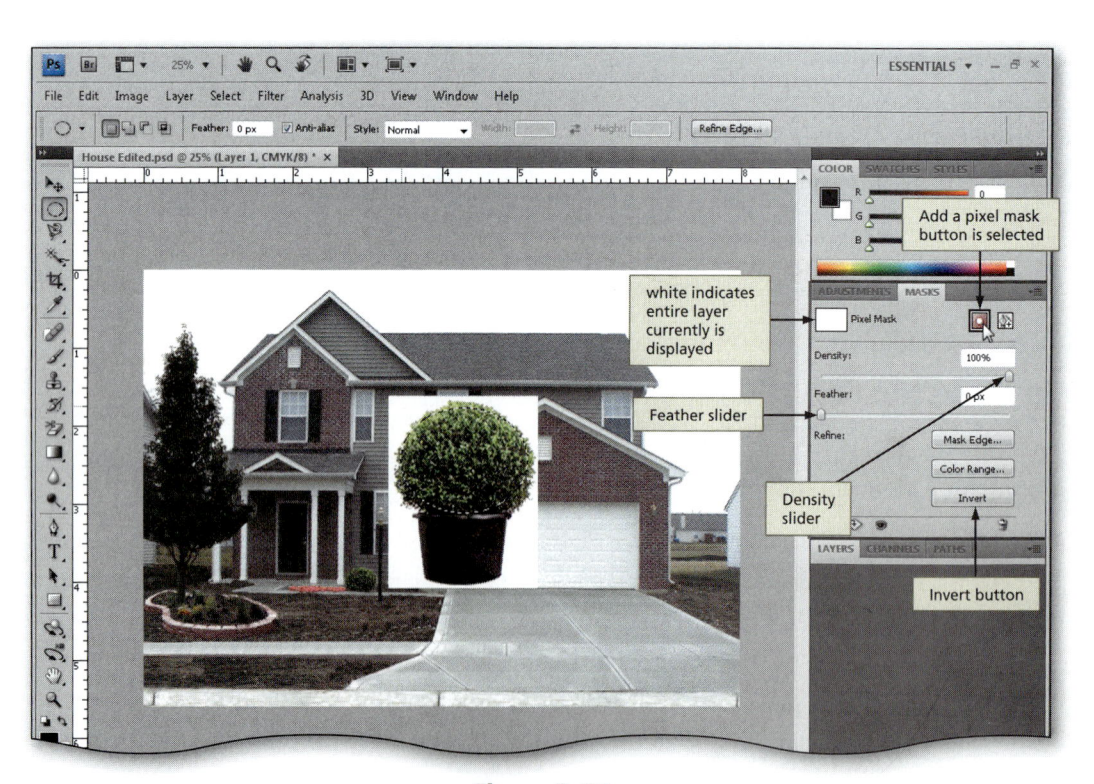

Figure 3–54

❸
- Drag the Density slider to 100%, if necessary, to make the mask opaque.

- Drag the Feather slider to 5 px to create a feathered edge (Figure 3–55).

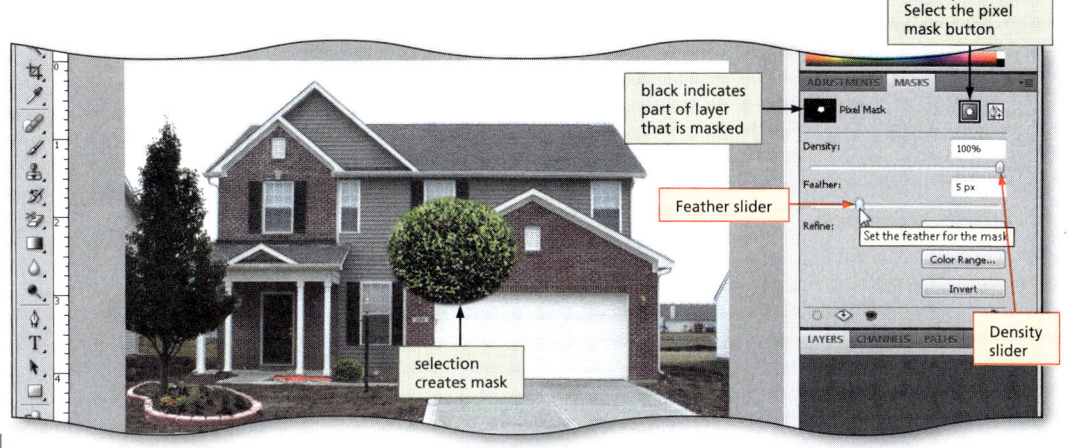

Figure 3–55

Other Ways
1. On Window menu, click Masks, adjust settings

To Resize, Reposition, and Set Layer Properties

To complete the shrub layer, it must be resized, repositioned, and named. The following steps accomplish these modifications.

❶ With the layer selected, press the V key to activate the Move tool, if necessary.

❷ Press CTRL+T to display the Transform options bar and the bounding box.

❸ SHIFT+drag a corner sizing handle to decrease the size of the layer to approximately 25% as displayed in the Transformation options bar scale boxes. Press the ENTER key to apply the transformation.

❹ Drag the layer to a location between the house and sidewalk, on the other size of the lamppost. Nudge as necessary.

❺ Double-click the Layers panel tab to display the Layers panel.

❻ Right-click the selected layer on the Layers panel, and then click Layer Properties. When the Layer Properties dialog box is displayed, type `second shrub` in the Name box. Click the Color box arrow, and then click Violet in the list. Click the OK button.

BTW

Moving Masks
To move the mask, first click the link icon on the Layers panel to unlink the mask from the layer. Select the Move tool. Then, in the document window, drag the layer to reposition it. When the mask is positioned correctly, click between the layer and layer mask on the Layers panel to relink them.

BTW

Layer Comps
Graphic artists often create multiple versions, or **compositions**, of their work. A **layer comp** is a single view of the page layout with specific visible layers and attributes. You can use layer comps to demo versions of your composition to customers or colleagues, or simply to jump back and forth between different views and layers of your document. Similar to the History panel's snapshot, a layer comp takes a picture of the composite, using the Layers panel to show a particular stage of development.

BTW

Layer Comps vs. History Snapshots
Layer comps include the visibility, position, and appearance of layers, not the edited steps. In addition, layer comps are saved with the document, whereas History panel snapshots are not. You can export layer comps to separate graphic or PDF files for easy distribution.

BTW

Layer Comps Panel
The Layer Comps panel is displayed from the Window menu. The panel includes a status bar with buttons to move back and forth through the comps, to update comps from the current view, to create them, and to delete them. The Layer Comps menu has some of those same commands, as well as others to duplicate a layer comp and set its properties.

To Create Another Layer

The final new layer will be a trellis, positioned on the right side of the garage.

1. Open the file, Trellis, from the Chapter03 folder of the Data Files for Students, or from a location specified by your instructor. Change the magnification to 100%, if necessary.

2. Press the L key to activate the Lasso tool. If the Magnetic Lasso tool is not selected, press SHIFT+L to change to the Magnetic Lasso tool. Carefully select the trellis and flowers, minimizing the amount of background fence and dirt.

3. Press CTRL+C to copy the selection.

4. Click the House Edited document window tab to select the House Edited window.

5. Press CTRL+V to paste the selection.

6. Press CTRL+T to display the Transform options bar and the bounding box. Scale the selection down to 75 percent. Press the ENTER key to confirm the transformation.

7. Press the V key to select the Move tool.

8. Drag the selection to a location on the right side of the garage (Figure 3–56).

Figure 3–56

To Set Properties for the Trellis Layer

The following step sets layer properties for the trellis layer.

1. Rename the new layer, trellis, and change its identification color to Orange.

To Close the Trellis Document Window

Because you are finished with the Trellis image, the following step closes the Trellis document window.

1 Close the Trellis document window.

To Save the File

All of the layers have been created; it is a good time to save the file again.

1 Save the House Edited file with the same name.

> **Create layer adjustments.**
> Layer adjustments allow you to fine-tune your layers. Evaluate layers to see if a change in levels, brightness, saturation, or hue would help them to fit into the background scene. Use nondestructive edits when possible, so if the client does not like the adjustment, it can be removed.

BTW

Duplicating Layers
To create two layers, duplicate a layer by right-clicking it on the Layers panel, and then clicking Duplicate Layer on the context menu. Then name the new layer and specify to which open document window the layer should be added. A duplicate layer can be used to create an entirely new document in the same manner.

Plan Ahead

Fine-Tuning Layers

Sometimes layers need special **adjustments** in order to fit into their new surroundings in the document window. This fine-tuning usually involves **tonal adjustments** that affect the range of color, lighting, opacity, level, or fill; **style adjustments** such as special effects or blends; or **filter adjustments** that let you apply predetermined pictures, tiles, or patterns. With the correct adjustment, a layer seems to meld into the image and maintains a consistency of appearance for the overall composite image.

When you do not want to alter the pixels in an image permanently, you can create an extra layer in which to make changes while preserving the original pixels. An **adjustment layer** is a new layer added to the image to affect a large-scale tonal change. You can create adjustment layers for the entire composite image or just a specific layer.

Adjustment layers have several advantages. They are nondestructive, which means you can experiment with various settings and reedit the adjustment layer at any time. Adjustment layers reduce the amount of damage you do to an image by making direct edits. They also can be copied to other images, saving time and maintaining consistency.

If you want to make permanent tonal, style, or filter changes to the pixels themselves, you can edit the layer directly. Features such as opacity, fill, and blending modes can be changed on the Layers panel. These changes can be undone using the History panel, but become permanent when the image is saved.

Making an Opacity Change to a Layer

Some adjustment tools specific to layers are located on the Layers panel. The Opacity box allows you to change the opacity or transparency of a layer. You can control exactly how solid the objects on a specific layer appear. For example, if you wanted to display an American flag superimposed over the top of a memorial or monument, you might change the flag layer's opacity to 50 percent. The monument would be easily visible through the flag.

The Fill box changes the fill of a layer's opacity as well, but **Fill** only changes the pixels in the layer rather than changing any applied layer styles or blending modes. If you have no layer styles or blending modes, you can use either the Opacity or Fill box. When you click either the Opacity box arrow or the Fill box arrow, a slider displays to adjust the percentage. You also can type a percentage in either box.

The Blending mode box arrow displays a list of blending modes that can be applied to the selected layer or layers. **Blending modes** define how an object interacts with other objects, such as the Background layer. You will learn more about blending modes in a later chapter.

To Make an Opacity Change to a Layer

The next steps show how to lighten the color in the shrub layers by lowering the opacity, to make the shrubs fit better into the landscaping design.

1
- If necessary, zoom the document window to 50 percent.
- On the Layers panel, scroll down and then click the shrub layer to select it.
- Point to the word, Opacity, and then drag the scrubby slider to the left until the Opacity box displays 75% to lighten the color of the shrub (Figure 3–57).

2
- On the Layers panel, click the second shrub layer to select it. Point to the word, Opacity, and then drag the scrubby slider to the left until the Opacity box displays 75%.

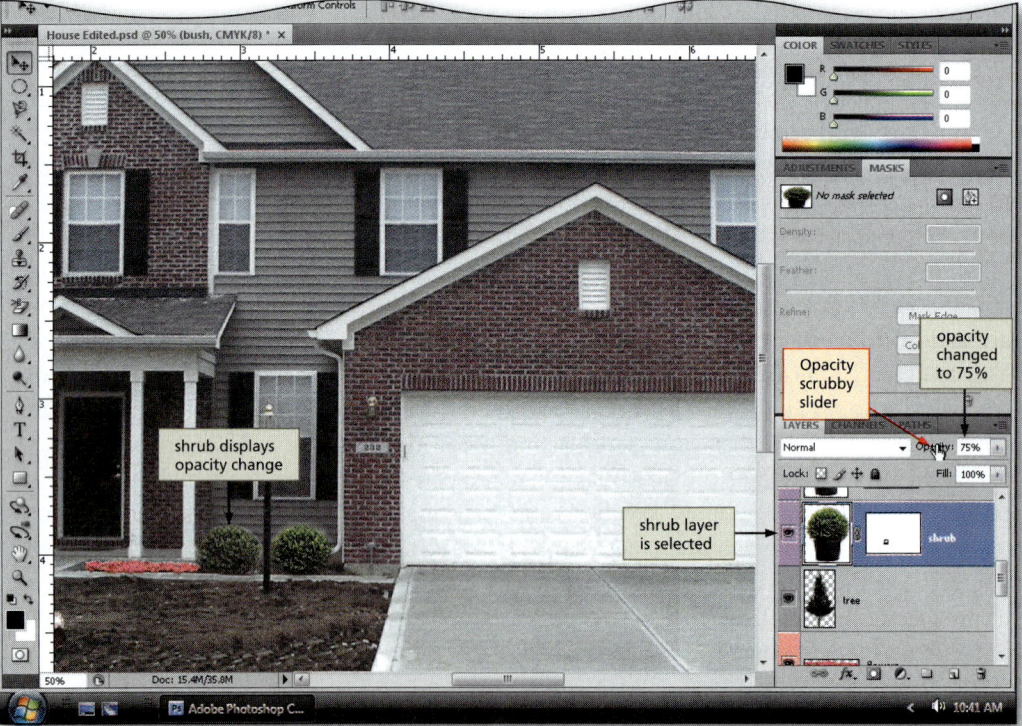

Figure 3–57

The Adjustments Panel

Other tools that nondestructively adjust image lighting and shading are located on the Adjustments panel (Figure 3–58). While you will use some of the adjustment features in this chapter, you will learn more about these commands in future chapters.

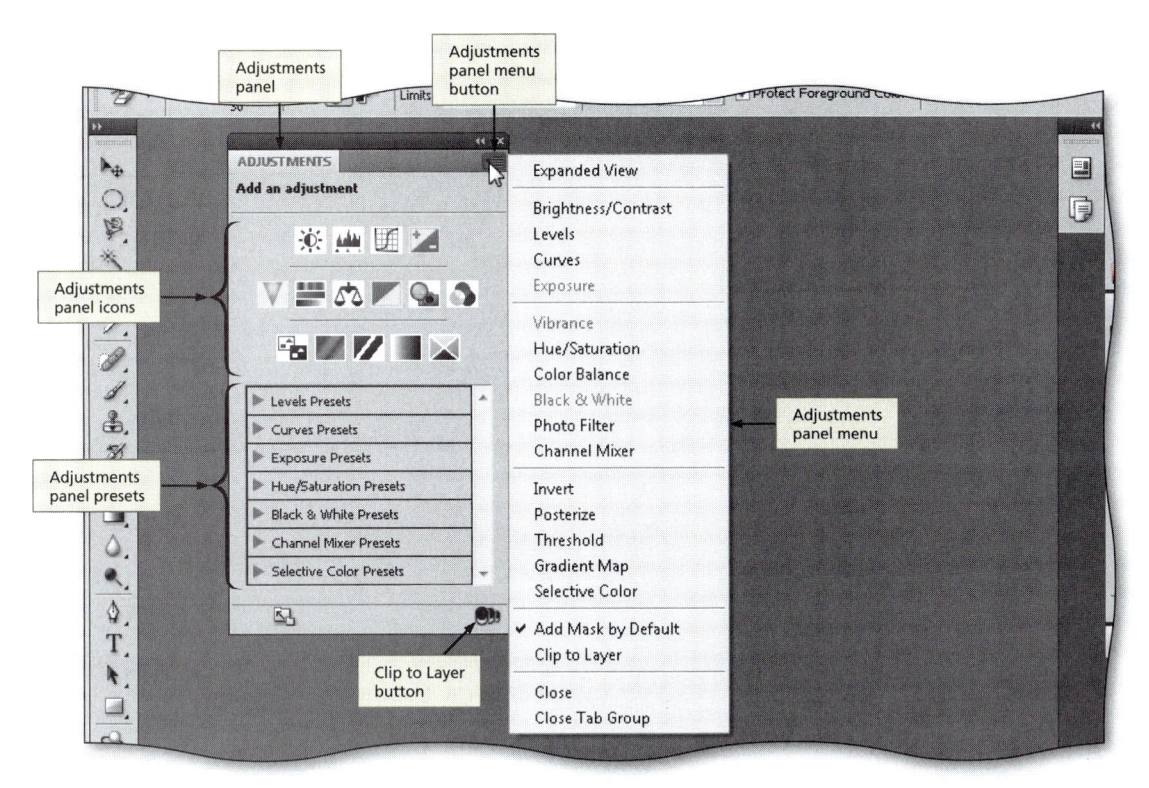

Figure 3–58

Clicking an adjustment icon or a preset displays the settings for the specific adjustment, including channel selectors, eyedroppers, sliders, and input boxes, among others. Buttons on the Adjustments panel status bar allow you to specify visibility, delete the adjustment, return to the main Adjustments panel, or create a **clip** that applies the adjustment to a layer rather than the entire image.

Some adjustments also display their settings using a dialog box, if accessed from outside the Adjustments panel with a shortcut key or a menu command. Table 3–2 on the following page displays a list of the Adjustments available on the Adjustments panel. Many of the adjustments are available using a menu command as well.

Table 3–2 Adjustments Panel Icons

Adjustment	Description	Shortcut (if available)	Icon
Brightness/Contrast	changes general brightness (shadows and highlights) and overall contrast (tonal range)		
Levels	adjusts color balance for shadows, midtones, highlights, and color channels	CTRL+L	
Curves	adjusts individual points in the tonal range of black to white	CTRL+M	
Exposure	changes exposure, which adjusts the highlights; changes offset, which darkens the shadows and midtones; changes gamma, which adjusts the midtones		
Vibrance	adjusts vibrance and color saturation settings so shifting to primary colors, or clipping, is minimized		
Hue/Saturation	changes hue, saturation, and lightness of entire image or specific colors	CTRL+U	
Color Balance	adjusts the overall midtone of colors in an image	CTRL+B	
Black & White	converts a color image to grayscale	ALT+SHIFT+CTRL+B	
Photo Filter	simulates effects of using a filter in front of a camera lens		
Channel Mixer	modifies and adjusts individual color channels		
Invert	converts every color to its inverse or opposite	CTRL+I	
Posterize	specifies the number of tonal levels in each channel		
Threshold	converts images to high-contrast black and white		
Gradient Map	maps colors to a specified gradient fill		
Selective Color	changes the mixture of colors in each of the primary color components		

BTW

Level Sliders
In the Levels dialog box, the Input Level sliders on each end map the black point (on the left) and white point (on the right) to the settings of the Output sliders. The middle Input slider adjusts the gamma or midtone in the image, changing the intensity values of the middle range of gray tones without dramatically altering the highlights and shadows. As you move any of the Input Level sliders, the black point, midtone, and white point change in the Output sliders; all the remaining levels are redistributed.

Level Adjustments

A **level adjustment** is one way to make tonal changes to shadows, midtones, and highlights. A **shadow** is a darkened shade in an image. A **midtone**, also called **gamma**, is the midpoint gray between shadows and highlights. A **highlight** is a portion of an image that is strongly illuminated and may appear as the lightest or whitest part of the image. To change levels, Photoshop uses black, gray, and white sliders to adjust any or all of the three tonal input levels. A **histogram**, or frequency distribution bar chart, indicates the amount of color in the tonal ranges.

A general guideline is to drag the black-and-white sliders to the first indication, or outlier, of color change in the histogram. Then, experiment with the gray slider to change the intensity value of the middle range of gray tones without dramatically altering the highlights and shadows. Becoming proficient at adjusting levels takes practice. Furthermore, adjustments are subjective; the impact of some effects is a matter of opinion.

To Make a Level Adjustment

In the tree layer of the image, you will access the Adjustments panel, and then adjust the levels to make the layer better fit into the picture. The following steps make level adjustments to the tree.

1
- Zoom the document window to 25 percent.
- On the Layers panel, scroll as necessary to select the tree layer.
- Click the Adjustments panel tab to display its icons, buttons, and settings (Figure 3–59).

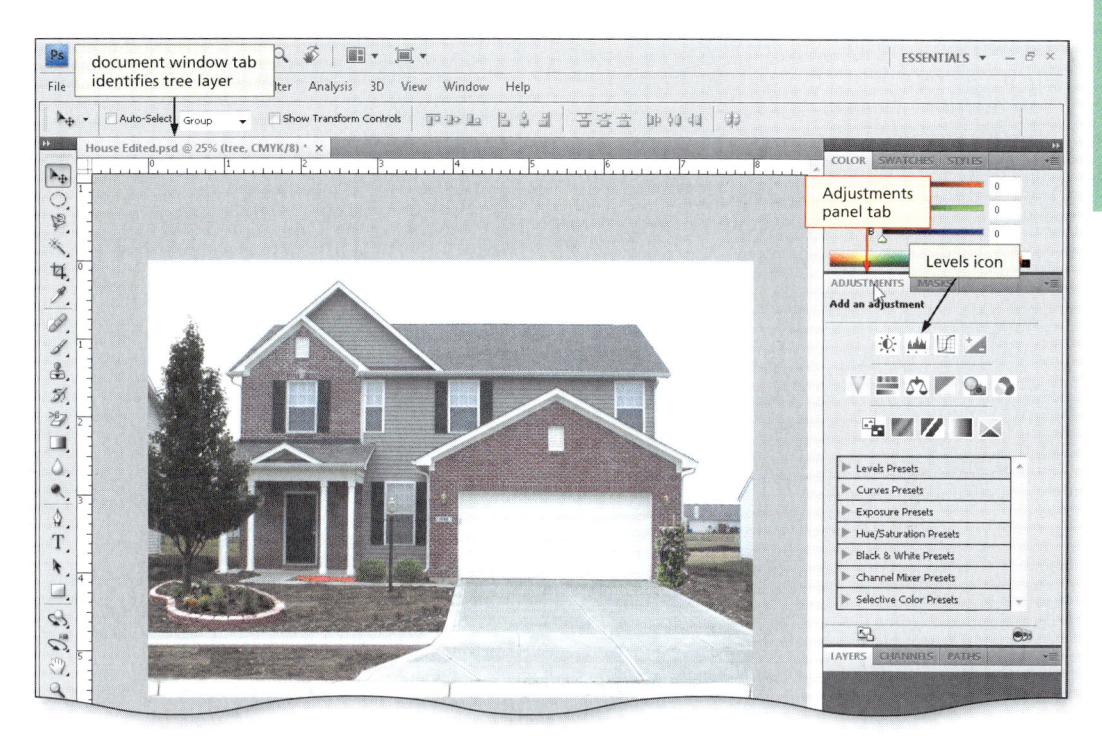

Figure 3–59

2
- Click the Levels icon to display the level settings and options.
- On the Adjustments panel status bar, click the Clip to layer button (Figure 3–60).

  Experiment
- Drag the three sliders to see how they affect the tree layer.

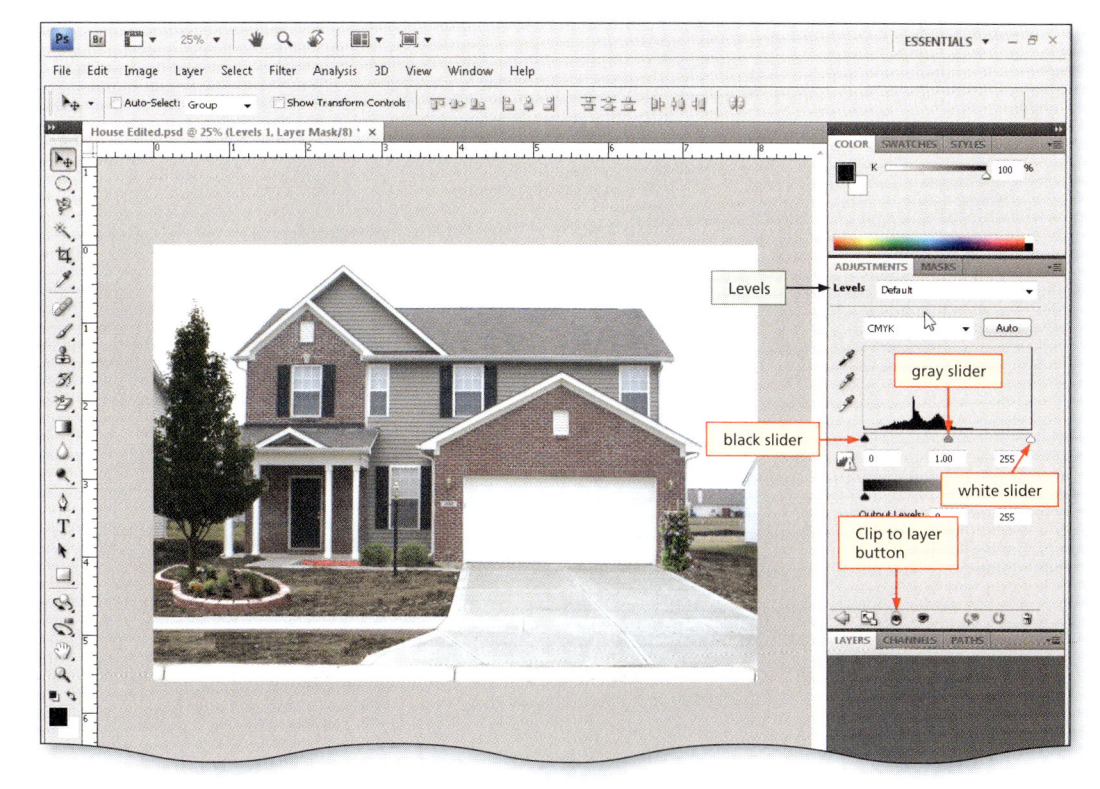

Figure 3–60

3
- In the input area, drag the white highlight slider to approximately 170, aligning it with the first visible change on the right side of the histogram.
- Drag the black shadow slider to approximately 25, again aligning it with the first visible change on the left side of the histogram.
- Drag the gray midtone slider to 1.10 to adjust the midtone colors (Figure 3–61).

Q&A My visible changes were at different levels. Did I do something wrong?

No, your histogram may differ, depending on your previous erasures.

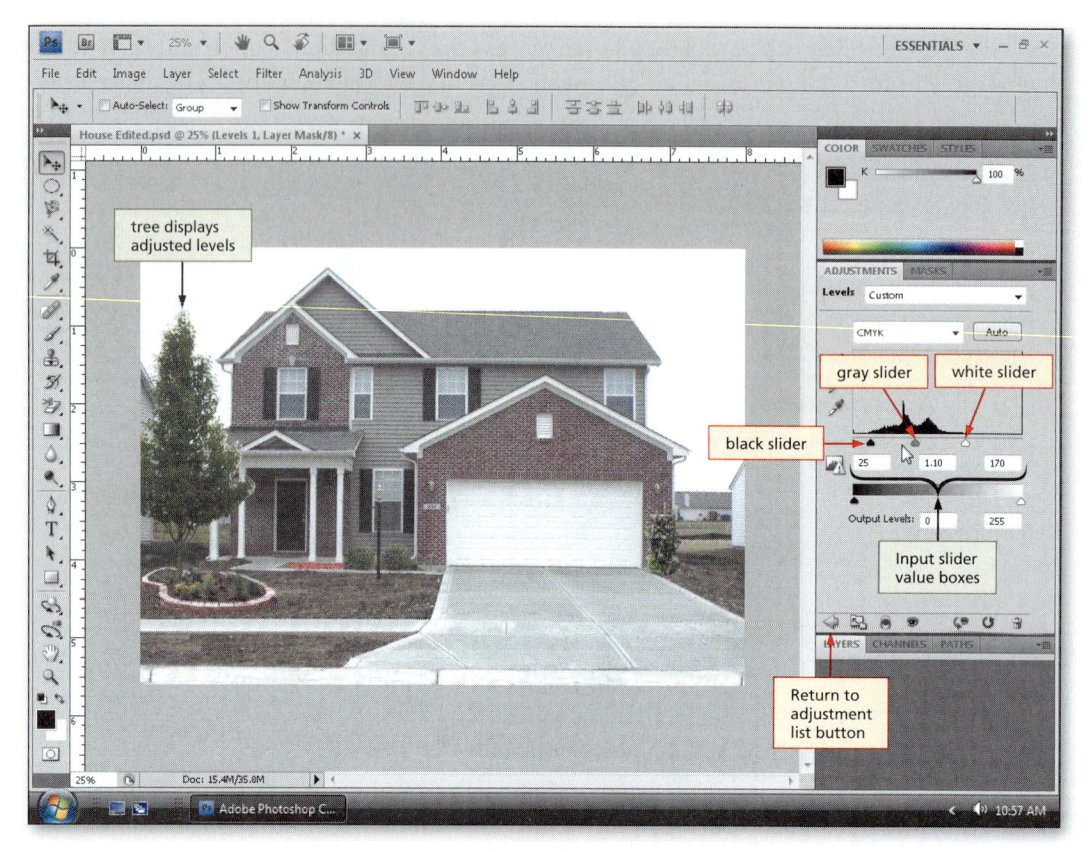

Figure 3–61

4
- Click the Return to adjustment list button to display all of the adjustment icons and settings.

Q&A Did the Layers panel change?

Yes, if you double-click the Layers panel tab, you will see an extra layer created just above the tree layer, with a clipping symbol to imply the relationship.

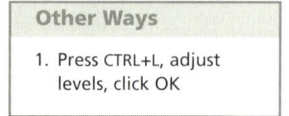

Other Ways
1. Press CTRL+L, adjust levels, click OK

To Adjust the Hue and Saturation

Another way to adjust a layer or image is to change the hue or saturation. **Hue** is the shade of a color in an image. **Saturation** is the intensity of a hue and is highly dependent upon the chosen color model; but in general, pastels have low saturation, and bright colors are highly saturated. Learn more about color models and the color wheel in later chapters and by reading Appendix B.

The following step adjusts the hue and saturation of one of the shrubs so they do not appear identical.

1
- Double-click the Layers panel tab and then select the shrub layer.
- Double-click the Adjustments panel tab and then click the Hue/Saturation icon.
- On the Adjustments panel status bar, click the Clip to layer button.
- Drag the Hue slider to –10. Drag the Saturation slider to +10 (Figure 3–62).

Experiment

- Drag the sliders to view the affect of hue and saturation settings to the layer. When you are done experimenting, drag the Hue slider to –10 and the Saturation slider to +10.

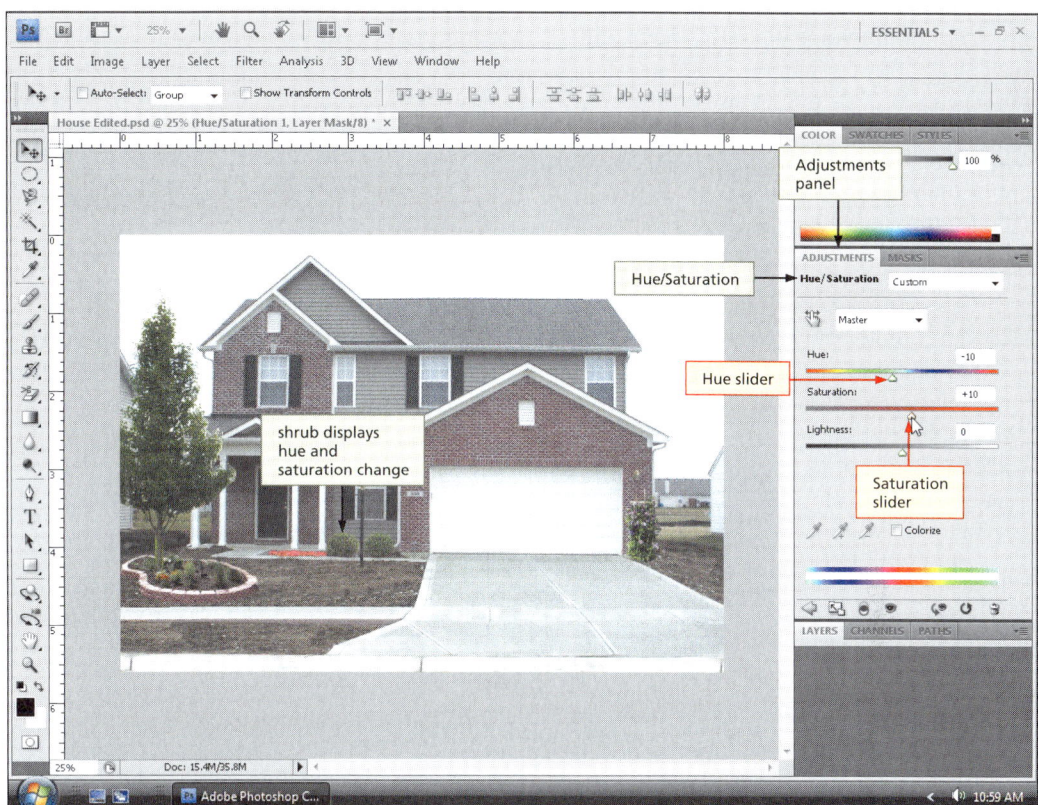

Figure 3–62

Other Ways

1. Select layer, press CTRL+U, drag sliders, right-click layer, click Create Clipping Mask

Brightness and Contrast

Brightness refers to color luminance or intensity of a light source. It is perceived as lightness or darkness in an image. In Photoshop, brightness is measured on a sliding scale from –150 to +150. Negative numbers move the brightness toward black. Positive numbers compress the highlights and expand the shadows. For example, the layer might be an image that was photographed on a cloudy day; conversely, the image might appear overexposed by having been too close to a photographer's flash. Either way, editing the brightness might enhance the image.

Contrast is the difference between the lightest and darkest tones in an image, involving mainly the midtones. When you increase contrast, the middle-to-dark areas become darker, and the middle-to-light areas become lighter. High-contrast images contain few color variations between the lightest and darkest parts of the image; low-contrast images contain more tonal gradations.

BTW

Other Level Adjustments
The three eyedroppers in the Levels area allow you to select the values for shadow, midtone, and highlight from the image itself. To do so, click the eyedropper and then click the location in the image that you want use. Once selected, that color becomes the slider value.

PS 212 Photoshop Chapter 3 Working with Layers

To Change the Brightness and Contrast

The following steps edit the brightness and contrast of the Background by creating an adjustment layer.

1
- Double-click the Layers panel tab, and then scroll down to select the Background layer.
- On the Layers panel, click the Create new fill or adjustment layer button to display the list of adjustments (Figure 3–63).

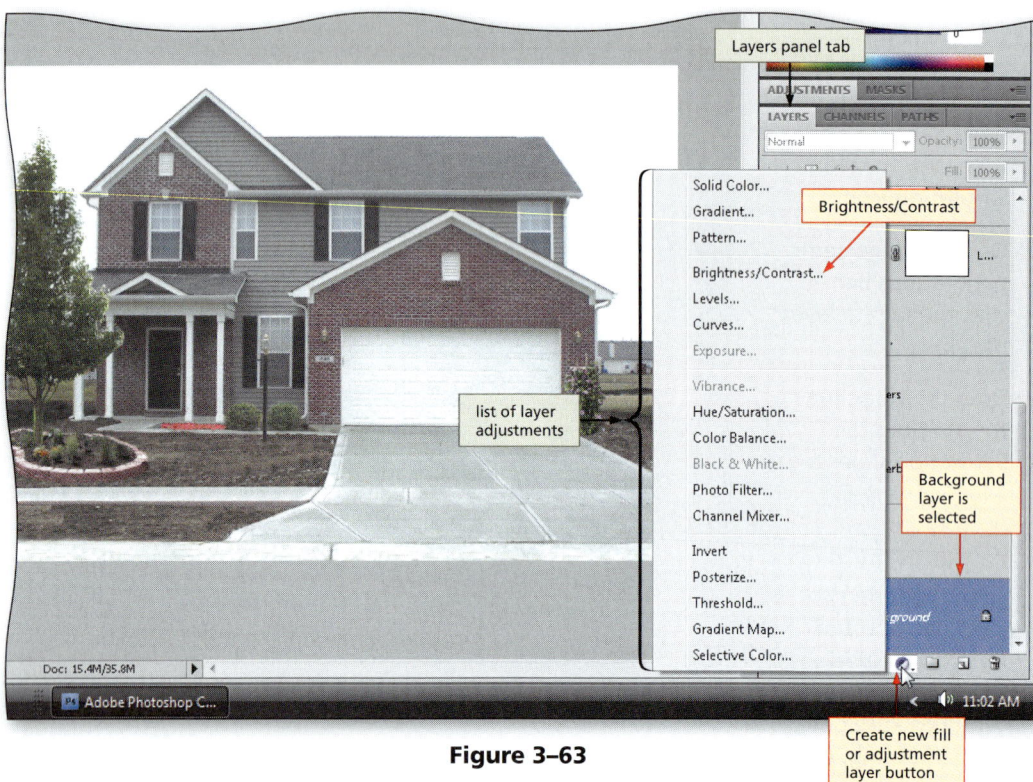

Figure 3–63

2
- Click Brightness/Contrast in the list.
- When the Brightness/Contrast settings appear on the Adjustments panel, on the Adjustments panel status bar, click the Clip to layer button.
- Drag the Brightness slider to +10 and the Contrast slider to -10 to create the illusion of a sunnier day in the image (Figure 3–64).

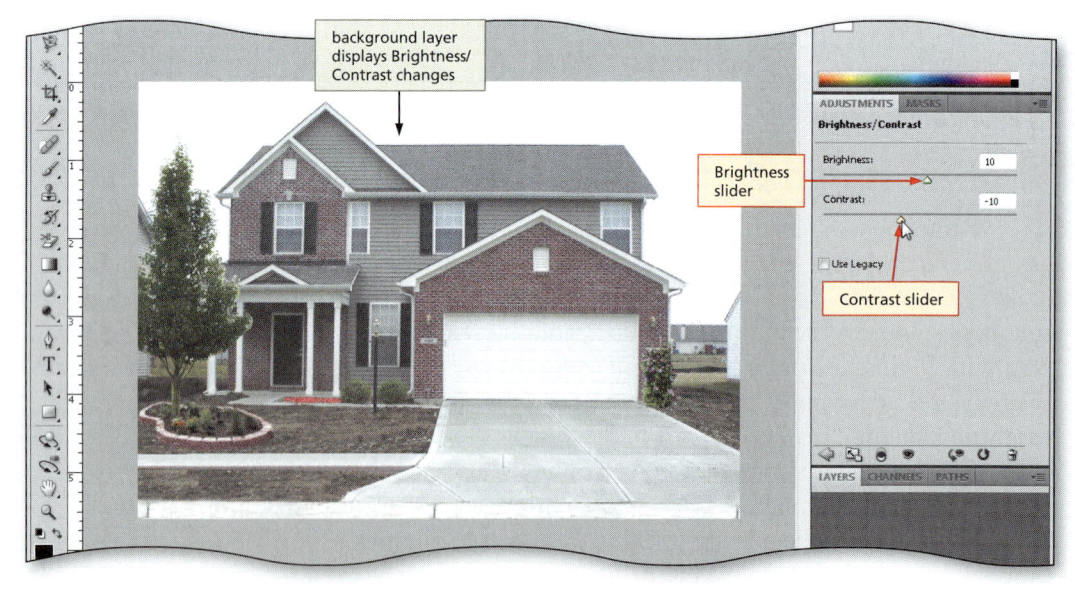

Figure 3–64

Other Ways
1. On Adjustments panel, click Brightness/Contrast icon, click third button on status bar, adjust settings
2. On Layer menu, point to New Adjustment Layer, click Brightness/Contrast, click OK, adjust settings

> **Plan Ahead**
>
> **Edit layer styles.**
> Layer styles add dimension, texture, and definition to your layers. Styles such as shadow, glow, emboss, bevel, overlay, and stroke commonly distinguish the layer rather than making it fit in. Choose the settings carefully and think about direction, angle, distance, and spread. Make sure the layer style does not overwhelm the overall image or detract from previous layer adjustments.

Layer Styles

Similar to a layer adjustment, a **layer style** is applied to a layer rather than changing the layer's actual pixels. Layer styles, or layer effects, affect the appearance of the layer by adding depth, shadow, shading, texture, or overlay. A layer can display multiple styles or effects.

Table 3–3 lists the layer styles.

Table 3–3 Layer Styles

Style	Description
Drop Shadow	creates a shadow behind the layer
Inner Shadow	creates a shadow inside the edges of the layer
Inner Glow	adds a glow around the inside edge of the layer
Outer Glow	adds a glow around the outside edge of the layer
Bevel and Emboss	adds highlights and shading to a layer
Satin	applies interior shading to create a satin finish
Color Overlay	adds a color over the layer
Gradient Overlay	inserts a gradient in front of the layer
Pattern Overlay	fills the layer with a pattern
Stroke	outlines the layer with a color, gradient, or pattern

Each of the layer styles has its own set of options and properties. Table 3–4 describes some of the Layer Style options. The options apply to many of the styles.

Table 3–4 Layer Style Options

Option	Description
Angle	sets a degree value for the lighting angle at which the effect is applied
Anti-alias	blends the edge pixels of a contour or gloss contour
Blend Mode	determines how a layer style blends with its underlying layers
Color	assigns the color of a shadow, glow, or highlight
Contour	allows you to create rings of transparency such as gradients, fades, beveling and embossing, and sculpting
Depth	sets the depth of a bevel or pattern
Distance	specifies the offset distance for a shadow or satin effect
Fill Type	sets the content of a stroke
Global Light	allows you to set an angle to simulate the direction of the light
Gloss Contour	creates a glossy, metallic appearance on a bevel or emboss effect

Table 3–4 Layer Style Options (*continued*)

Option	Description
Gradient	indicates the gradient of a layer effect
Highlight or Shadow Mode	specifies the blending mode of a bevel or emboss highlight or shadow
Jitter	varies the color and opacity of a gradient
Layer Knocks Out Drop Shadow	controls the drop shadow's visibility in a semitransparent layer
Noise	assigns the number of random elements in the opacity of a glow or shadow
Opacity	sets the opacity or transparency
Pattern	specifies the pattern
Position	sets the position of a stroke
Range	controls which portion or range of the glow is targeted for the contour
Size	specifies the amount of blur or the size of the shadow
Soften	blurs the results of shading to reduce unwanted artifacts
Source	specifies the source for an inner glow
Style	specifies the style of a bevel or emboss

When a layer has a style applied to it, an fx icon appears to the right of the layer's name on the Layers panel. You can expand the icon on the Layers panel to view all of the applied effects and edit them when changing the style.

As you can tell from Table 3–3 and Table 3–4, there are a large number of layer styles and settings in Photoshop. As you use them, many of these settings will be explained in future chapters.

To Add a Layer Style

The following steps add a layer style to the flower bed. You will create a shaded bevel to improve the edge of the flower bed and make it fit its surroundings.

1

- Zoom to 50 percent, and then scroll to view the flower bed in the document window.

- On the Layers panel, scroll up and select the flowerbed layer.

- Click the Add a layer style button to display the menu (Figure 3–65).

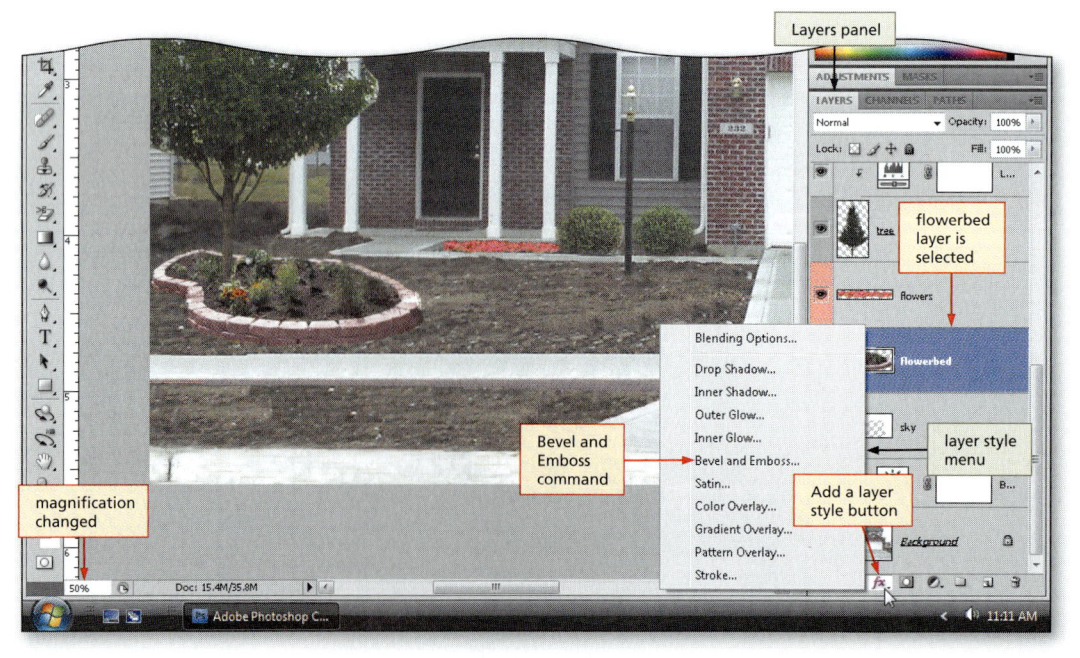

Figure 3–65

Layer Styles **PS 215**

2
- Click Bevel and Emboss to display the Layer Style dialog box. If necessary, drag the title bar of the dialog box to the right so the flower bed is visible.

- In the Layer Style dialog box, type –150 in the Angle box (Figure 3–66).

3
- Click the OK button to close the Layer Style dialog box.

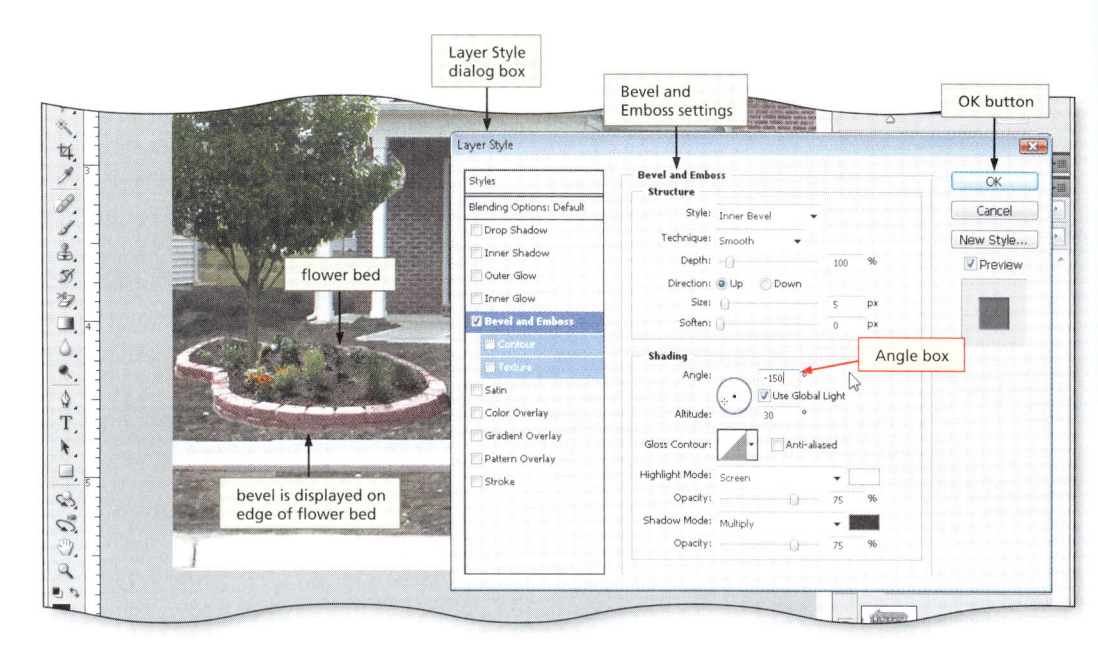

Figure 3–66

To Hide Layer Effects in the Layers Panel

The following step uses the Reveal layer effects button to display the effects in the Layers panel.

1
- On the Layers panel, in the flower bed layer, click the Reveals layer effects in the panel button to hide the added effects on the Layers panel (Figure 3–67).

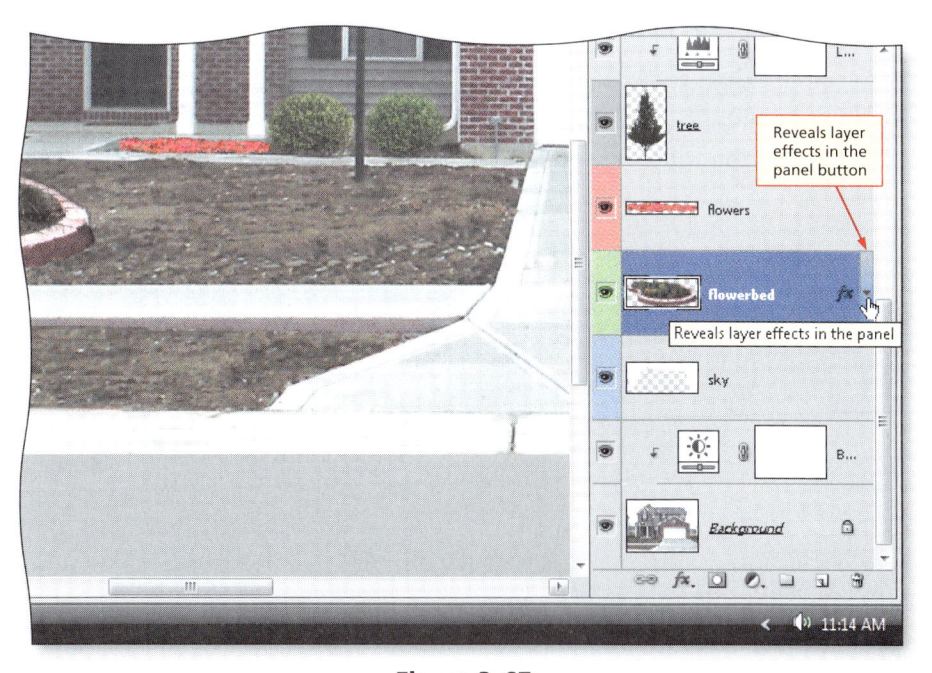

Figure 3–67

Other Ways

1. On Layer menu, point to Layer Style, click Bevel and Emboss, choose settings, click OK

Applying a Render Filter

Photoshop uses many different filters, blends, styles, and color changes to produce special effects in layers. In addition to the previous layer styles and adjustments, one special effect that will be useful in the House Edited image is that of clouds. The Clouds filter is a render filter that purposefully distorts the colors in a layer or mask to simulate clouds in the sky. Among the more than 100 filters that come installed with Photoshop, the **render filters** create specialized patterns. Other examples of filter groups include artistic filters, blurs, textures, and sketches. You will learn more about filters in a later chapter.

Table 3–5 displays the render filters included in an initial installation of Photoshop.

> **BTW**
>
> **The Angle Radius Icon**
> The angle adjusts the direction of the bevel on a 360-degree scale: 180 degrees both clockwise and counter-clockwise. In addition to entering a degree setting, the angle radius icon (Figure 3–66) allows you to drag to the desired direction.

> **BTW**
>
> **Copying and Moving Layer Styles**
> To copy a layer style, right-click the source layer and then click Copy Layer Style on the context menu. Right-click the destination layer and then click Paste Layer Style. To move a layer style, drag the fx icon from one layer to another on the Layers panel.

Table 3–5 Render Filters

Render Filter	Description
Clouds	Filter produces a cloud pattern using the current foreground and background colors. To generate a bolder cloud pattern, hold down the ALT key while creating the filter.
Difference Clouds	Filter produces a softer, hazier cloud pattern using the current foreground and background colors. Applying the filter several times creates marble-like rib and vein patterns.
Fibers	Filter produces a woven fiber pattern using the foreground and background colors. Variance and strength settings control the color, length, and weave of the fibers.
Lens Flare	Filter produces a glare that simulates refraction caused by shining a bright light into a camera lens.
Lighting Effects	Filter produces a lighting effect based on choices made in style, type, property, and channel. It cannot be used with a mask.

To Apply a Render Filter

In the following steps, the sky layer is selected. Because the render filter uses the current foreground and background colors, you will change the colors to light blue and white, creating a stronger cloud pattern in the photograph. You will learn more about colors and the Color panel in a later chapter.

Layer Styles **PS 217**

1
- Zoom to 25 percent magnification.
- On the Layers panel, select the sky layer.
- Press W to activate the Magic Wand tool, and then, in the document window, click the sky.
- In the Color panel, click a very light blue color along the top of the color bar (Figure 3–68).

Q&A How can I choose a lighter blue?

In the Color panel, you can drag the sliders or enter the numbers in the color boxes from Figure 3–68 to get exactly the same color. You will learn more about the Color panel in a later chapter.

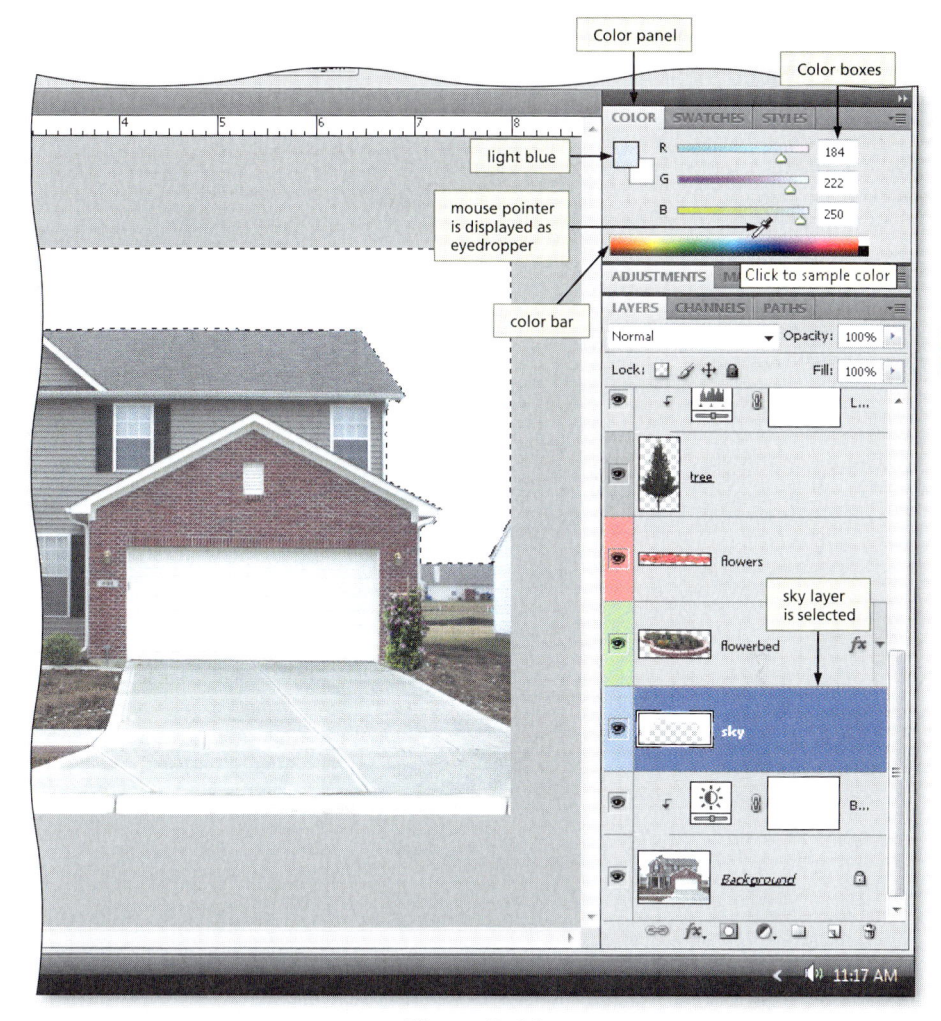

Figure 3–68

2
- Click Filter on the menu bar and then point to Render to display the Render submenu (Figure 3–69).

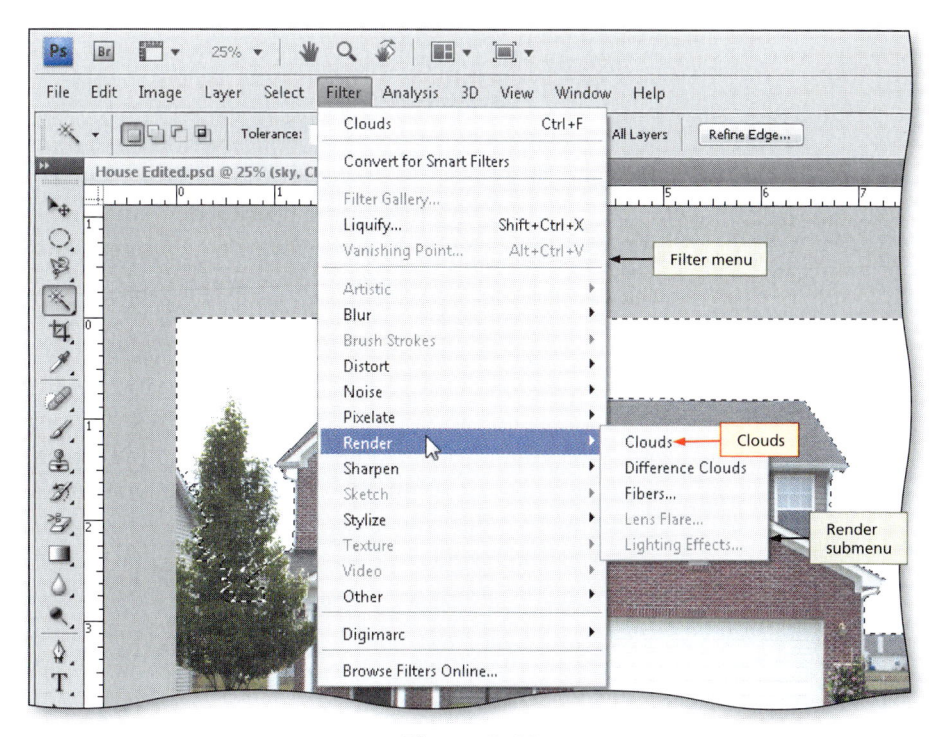

Figure 3–69

3
- Click Clouds on the Render submenu to display the effect.
- Press CTRL+D to remove the selection marquee (Figure 3–70).

Q&A Why do my clouds look different?

Because the cloud filter randomizes colors, your pattern will differ.

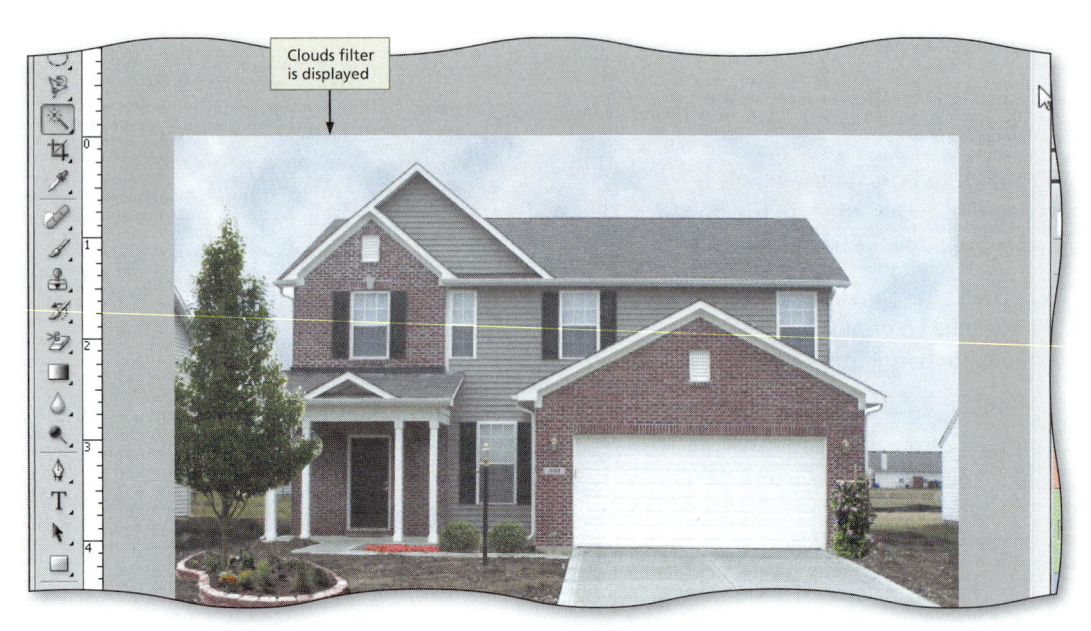

Figure 3–70

To Save Again

Before you add the sod and make a permanent change to the image, you should save the file again. That way, if you make a mistake, you can reopen the file and begin again.

1 Press CTRL+S to save the House Edited file with the same name.

The Clone Stamp Tool

The Clone Stamp tool reproduces portions of an image, changing the pixels in a specific area. After clicking the Clone Stamp Tool (S) button on the Tools panel, you press and hold ALT while clicking the portion of the picture that you wish to copy. Photoshop takes a **sample** of the image, remembering where you clicked. You then move the mouse pointer to the position where you wish to create the copy. As you drag with the brush, the image is applied. Each stroke of the tool paints on more of the sample. The Clone Stamp tool is useful for duplicating specific parts of an object or correcting defects in an image. You can clone from image to image, or clone locations within the same document window.

The Clone Source panel (Figure 3–71) is displayed by clicking Clone Source on the Window menu. The panel has options to rotate or scale the sample, or specify the size and orientation. The Clone Source panel makes it easy to create variegated patterns using multiple sources. You can create up to five different clone sources to select the one you need quickly, without re-sampling each time. For example, if you are using the Clone Stamp tool to repair several minor imperfections in an old photo, you can select your various samples first, and then use the sources as needed. The Clone Source panel also helps you create unique clones positioned at different angles and perspectives from the original.

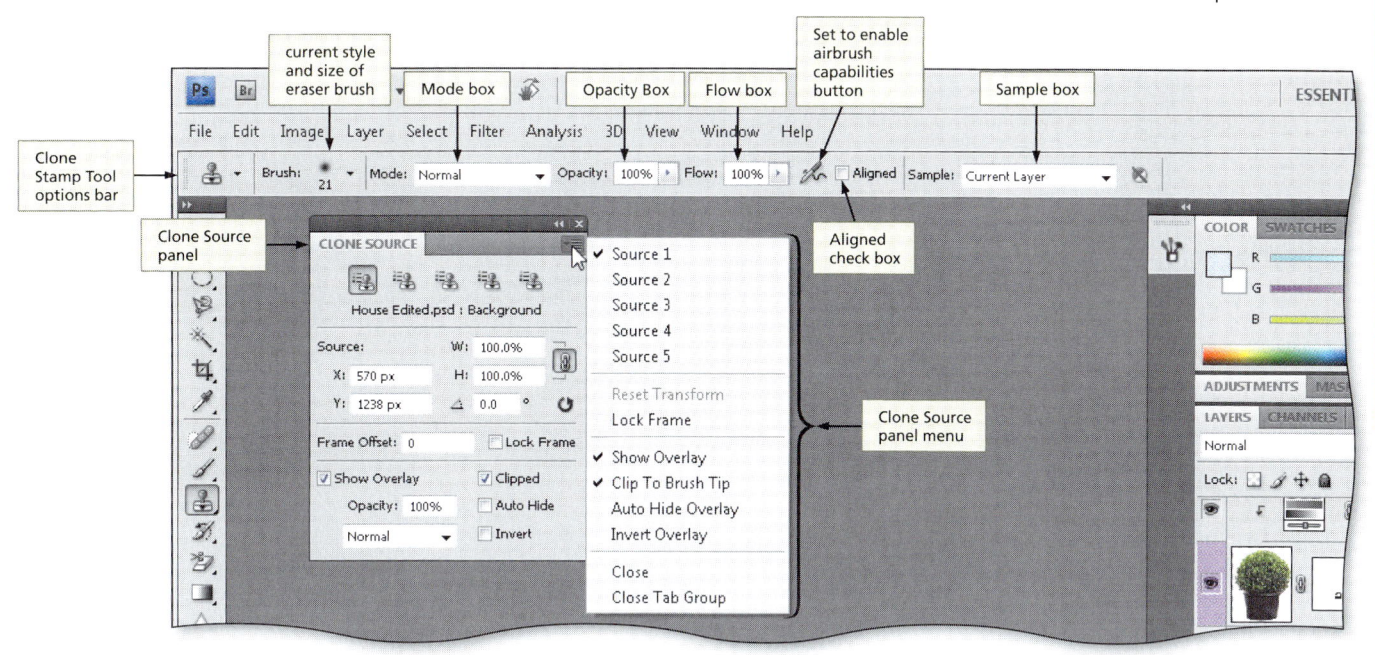

Figure 3-71

The Clone Stamp options bar (Figure 3–71) displays some of the same settings that you used with layer masks, along with an Aligned check box and Sample box. When Aligned is selected, the sample point is not reset if you start dragging in a new location; in other words, the sampling moves to a relative point in the original image. When Aligned is not selected, the sample point begins again as you start a new clone. The default value is to sample only the current layer or background. When All Layers is selected in the Sample box, the clone displays all layers. One restriction when using the Clone Stamp tool from one image to another is that both images have to be in the same color mode, such as RGB or CMYK. The color mode of an image is displayed on the document window tab. You will learn more about color modes in a later chapter.

On the Clone Stamp tool context menu, a second kind of stamp, the Pattern Stamp tool, allows you to paint with a pattern chosen from Photoshop's pattern library. A **pattern** is an image that is repeated, or tiled, when you use it to fill a layer or selection. On the Pattern Stamp options bar, a Pattern Picker box arrow displays installed patterns. You can import additional patterns into the Pattern Picker box.

To Open the Sod File and Arrange the Windows

To finish the composite image of the house and landscaping, you will add sod to the yard. The following steps open the Sod file.

1. Open the Sod file from the Chapter03 folder of the Data Files for Students, or from a location specified by your instructor.

2. Zoom to 25 percent magnification.

3. On the Application bar, click the Arrange Documents button, and then click the second 2 Up button so the windows display above one another.

4. Drag the border between the two document windows down, so more of the House Edited window is displayed, as shown in Figure 3–72.

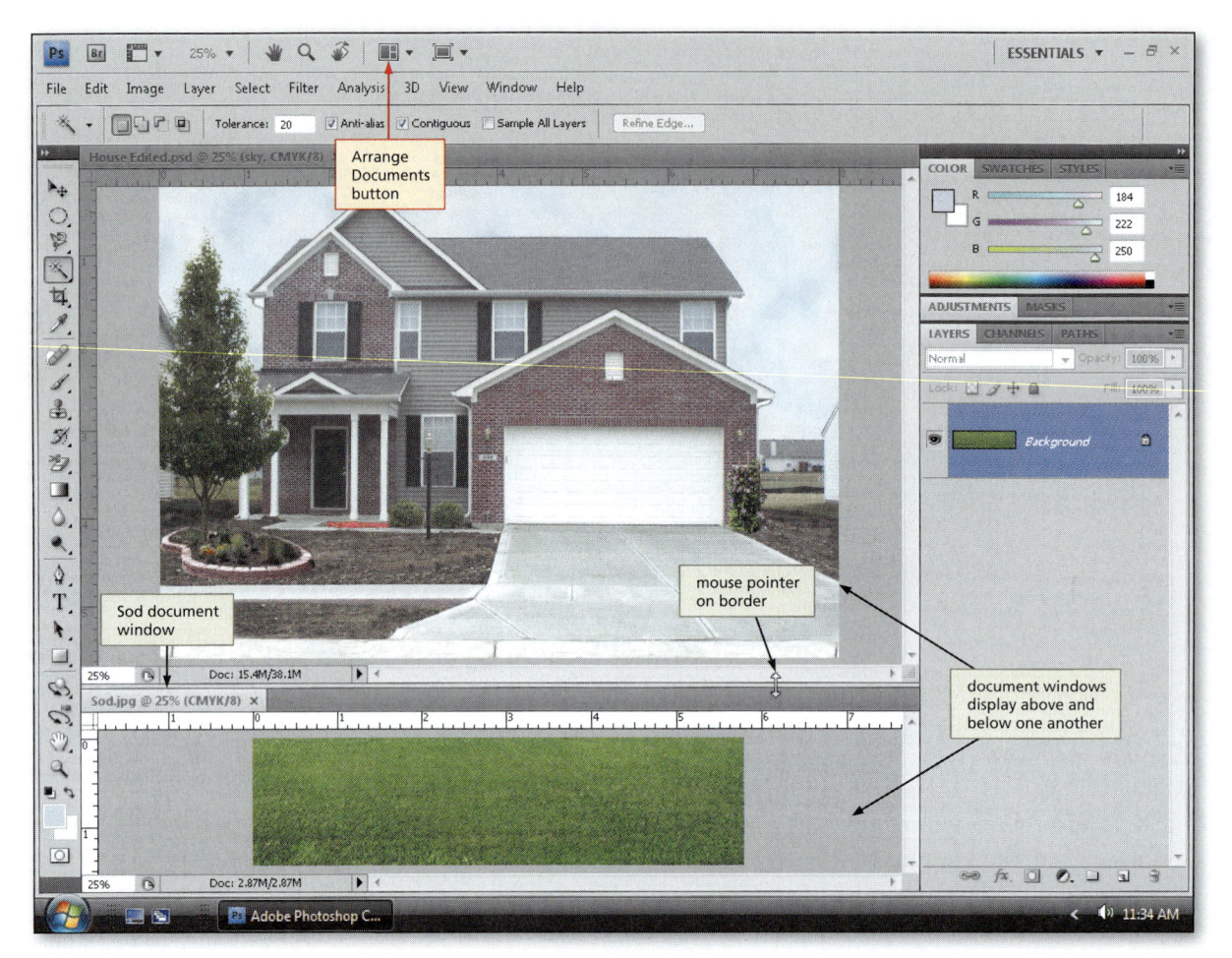

Figure 3–72

To Create a Clone

Using the Clone Stamp tool, you will sample the Sod image and then clone it all around the yard in the House Edited image to add grass, as shown in the following steps. This cloning changes the pixels of the Background layer. If you want to create the clone on its own layer, click the Background layer, and then press SHIFT+CTRL+N to create a new layer.

As you clone the sod, adjust the magnification of the image to view the corners and small areas clearly. If you make a mistake while cloning, press CTRL+Z to undo the most recent clone stroke or access the History panel and click a previous state. Then begin cloning again.

The Clone Stamp Tool   PS 221

1

- With the Sod window active, click Window on the menu bar, and then click Clone Source to display the Clone Source panel.

- On the panel, click the Invert box to remove its check mark, if necessary.

- On the Tools panel, right-click the Clone Stamp Tool (S) button to display its context menu (Figure 3–73).

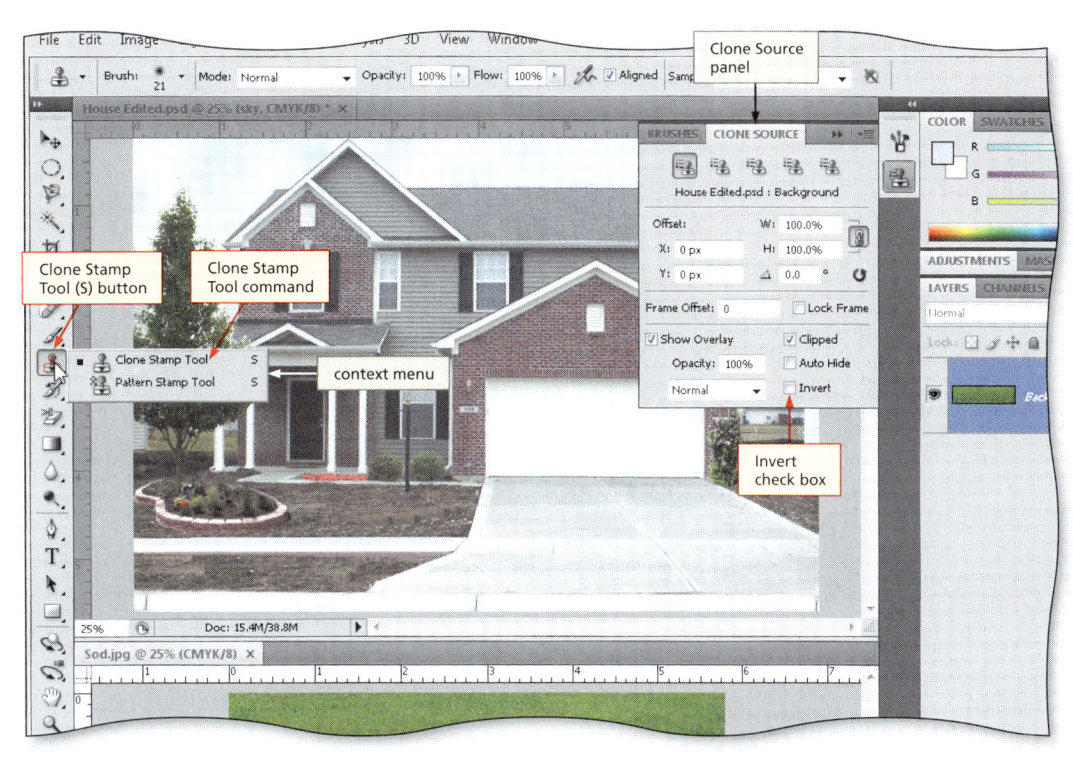

Figure 3–73

2

- Click Clone Stamp Tool on the context menu.

- On the options bar, click the Aligned check box so it does not display a check mark.

- Move the mouse pointer to the Sod window and ALT+click in the upper-left corner of the sod to sample the grass (Figure 3–74).

Q&A How do I know if I indicated the clone source correctly?

As you ALT+click, the Clone Stamp tool displays a crosshair mouse pointer and the Clone Source panel displays the source of the clone.

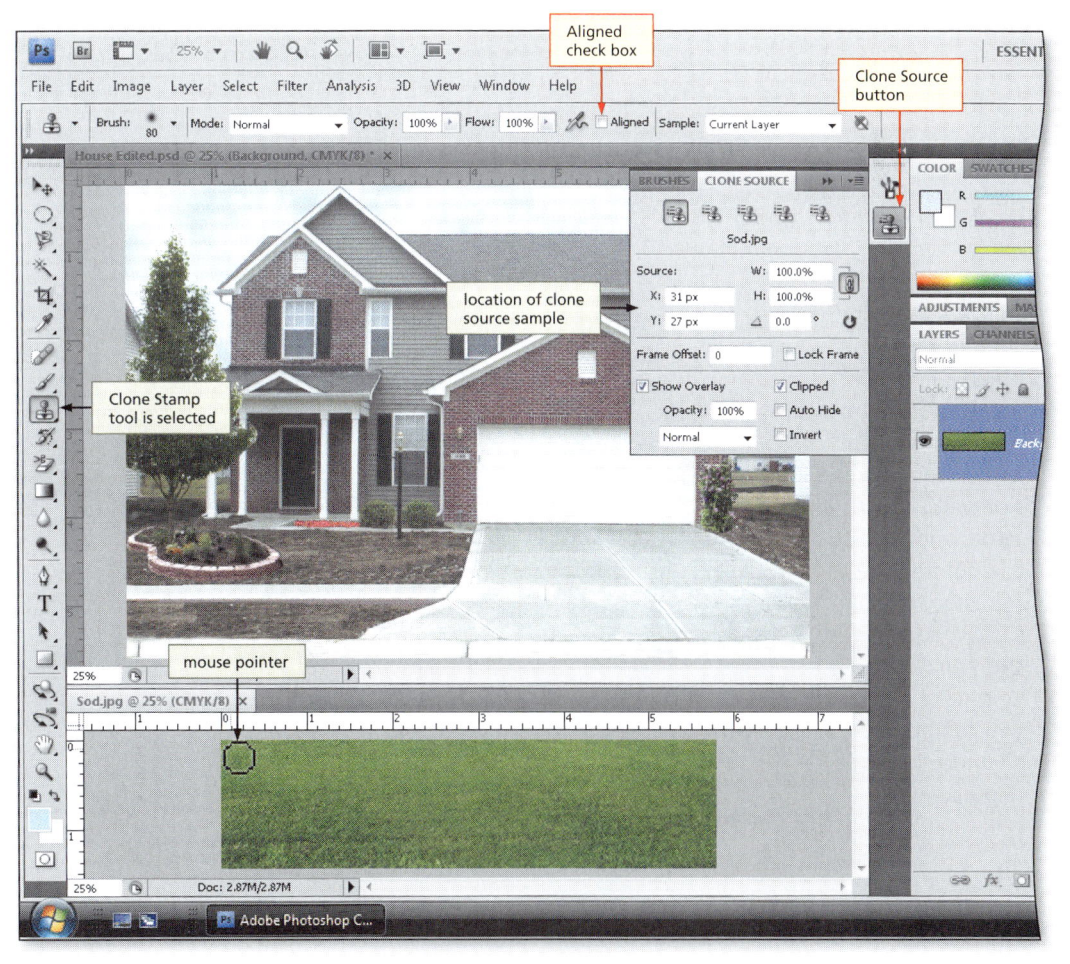

Figure 3–74

3
- Click the Clone Source button in the vertical docking to collapse the panel.
- Click the House Edited document window tab to make it active.
- On the Layers panel, select the Background layer.
- Move the mouse pointer into the document window, and then press the RIGHT BRACKET ( ]) key to increase the size of the mouse pointer as necessary (Figure 3–75).

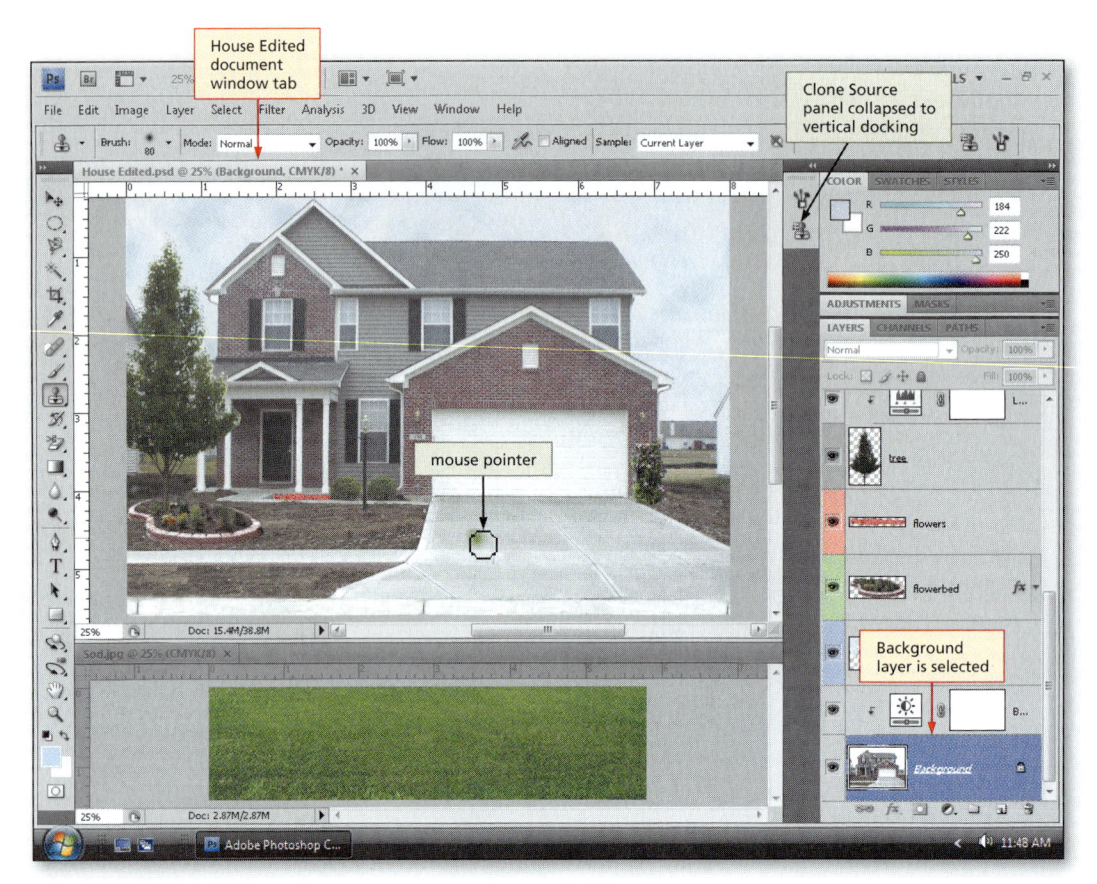

Figure 3–75

4
- Move the mouse pointer to the upper-left corner of the dirt.
- Working from left to right, click and drag to fill in the area from the left margin to the house, and then in front of the house to the sidewalk. Zoom, scroll, and adjust the pointer size as necessary to fill in small areas. Use short strokes, so if you make a mistake, you can press CTRL+Z to undo the error (Figure 3–76).

Q&A | How do I clone around the flower bed?

Because you are dragging in the Background layer, you can drag through any of the other layers, such as the tree or the flower bed. Do not drag through the house, sidewalk, or driveway, however.

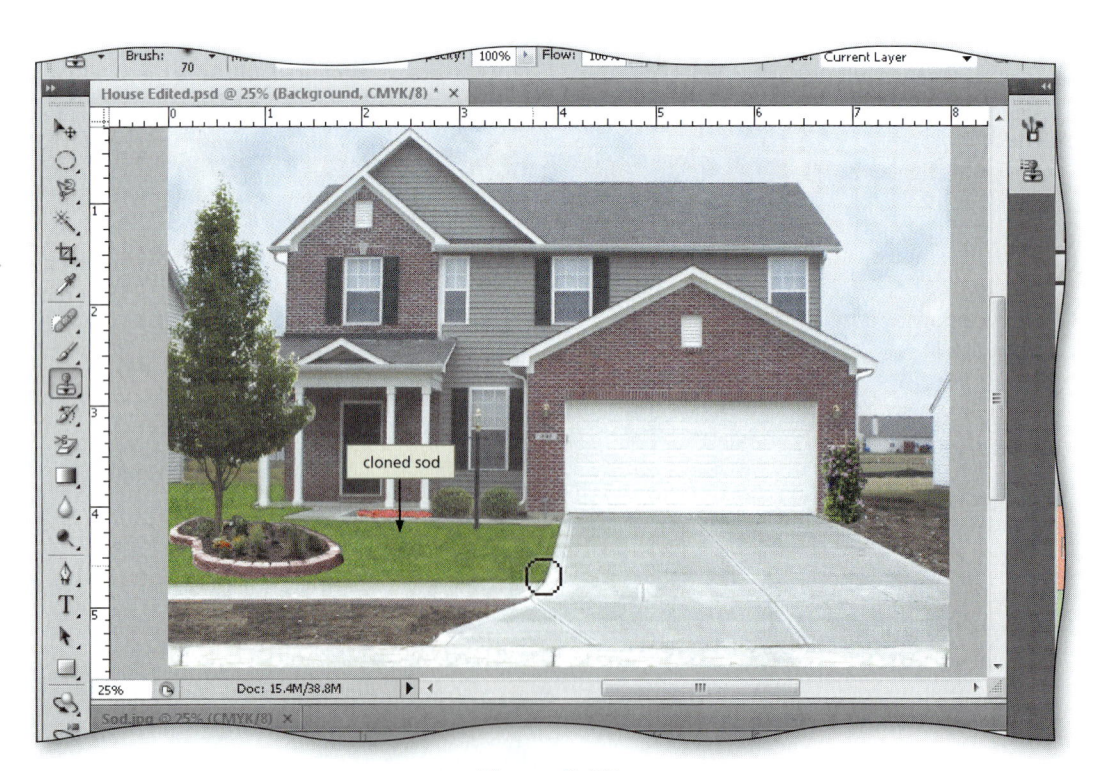

Figure 3–76

The Clone Stamp Tool PS 223

5
- Click the Sod window title bar again.
- To create a more variegated and realistic pattern, resample the sod by ALT+clicking in the lower-left corner of the sod image.
- Click the House Edited window title bar, and then begin dragging to fill the area below the sidewalk.
- Fill in all of the area left of the driveway (Figure 3–77).

Q&A What is the cross mouse pointer in the other window?

The Clone Stamp tool gives you two pointers. The mouse pointer at the destination of the clone points to the area that will receive the clone. The mouse pointer at the source of the clone is for reference, and follows your movement so you can see what is coming next.

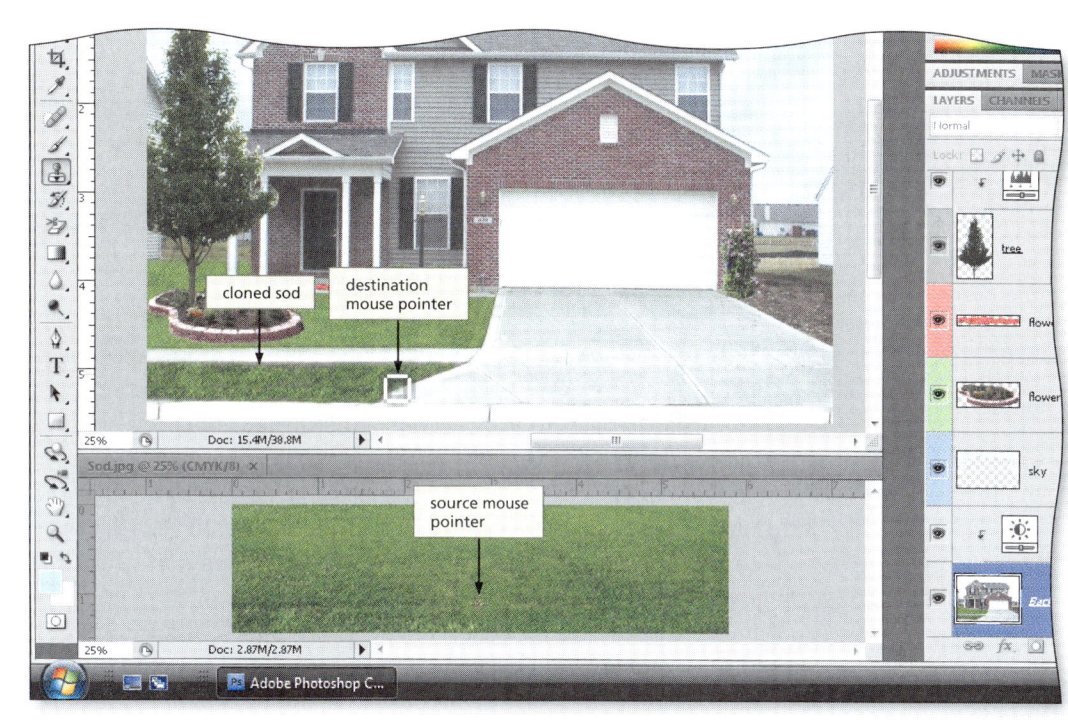

Figure 3–77

6
- Using the techniques in the previous steps, clone as necessary to fill in the grass on the right side of the driveway (Figure 3–78).

Q&A Could I hide the other layers while cloning the grass?
Yes, hiding the layers may make it easier for you to clone.

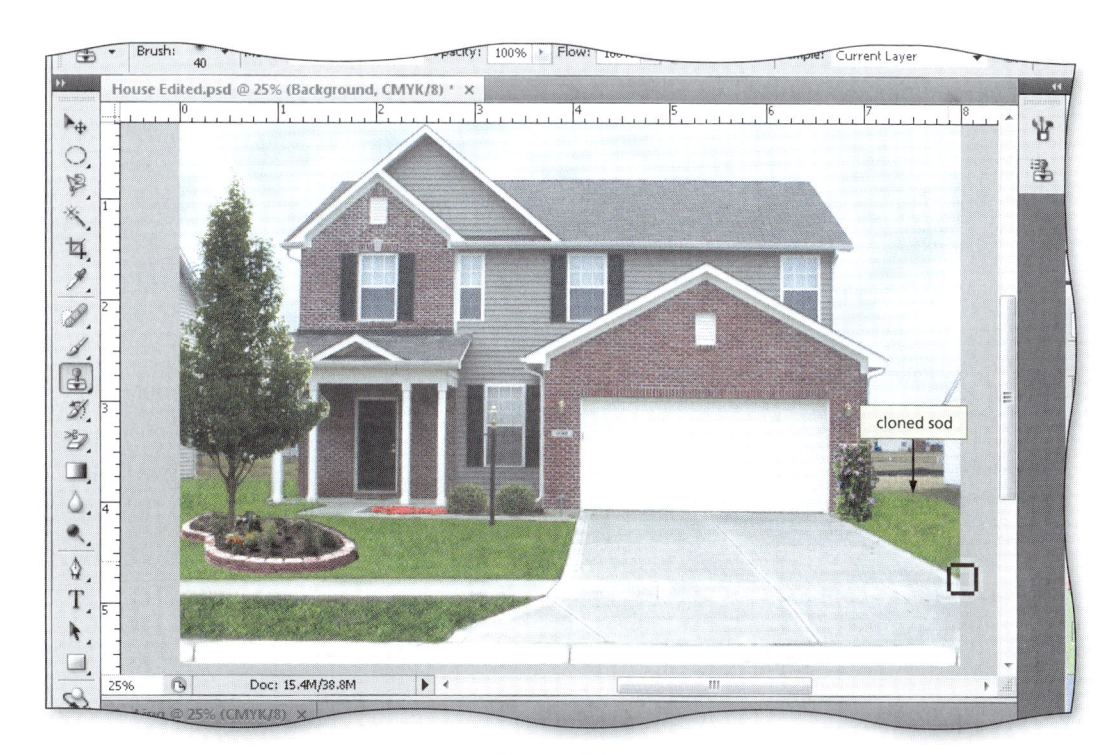

Figure 3–78

Other Ways

1. From another tool, press S key, ALT+click sample, drag clone
2. From Pattern Stamp tool, press SHIFT+S, ALT+click sample, drag clone

To Close the Sod Window

The next step is to close the Sod window.

1 Close the Sod document window. If Photoshop asks if you want to save changes to the document, click the No button.

> **BTW**
>
> **The History Brush**
> The History Brush tool paints a copy of the selected state or snapshot on the History panel into the current image window, similar to the Clone tool. To activate the History Brush tool, click the History Brush Tool (Y) button on the Tools panel, and then click the Set the source icon to the left of any state on the History panel.

Flattening a Composite Image

When you **flatten** a composite image, Photoshop reduces the file size by merging all visible layers into the background, discarding hidden layers, and applying masks. A flattened file is easier to print, export, and display on the Web. It is a good practice, however, to save the layered version in PSD format before flattening in case you want to make further changes to the file. It is very important to remember that once a file is flattened and saved, no changes can be made to individual layers. If you flatten an image and then change your mind, if the file still is open, you can click the previous state on the History panel to restore all of the layers.

If you want to save each layer as a separate file, click File on the menu bar, point to Scripts, and then click Export Layers to Files. This script is useful if you think you might want to use your layers in other composite images.

First, you will save the file, maintaining the layers, in the PSD format with the name, House Composite. Then you will flatten the composite image. Finally, you will save the flattened file in TIF format with the name, House Complete.

To Save the Composite Image

1 With your USB flash drive connected to one of the computer's USB ports, click File on the menu bar and then click Save As.

2 When the Save As dialog box is displayed, type `House Composite` in the File name text box. Do not press the ENTER key after typing the file name.

3 If necessary, click the Format box arrow and then choose Photoshop (*.PSD, *.PDD) in the list.

4 If necessary, click the Save in box arrow and then click UDISK 2.0 (F:), or the location associated with your USB flash drive, in the list.

5 Click the Save button in the Save As dialog box. If Photoshop displays an options dialog box, click the OK button.

To Flatten a Composite Image

1
- Zoom to 25 percent magnification, if necessary.
- Click Layer on the menu bar to display the Layer menu (Figure 3–79).

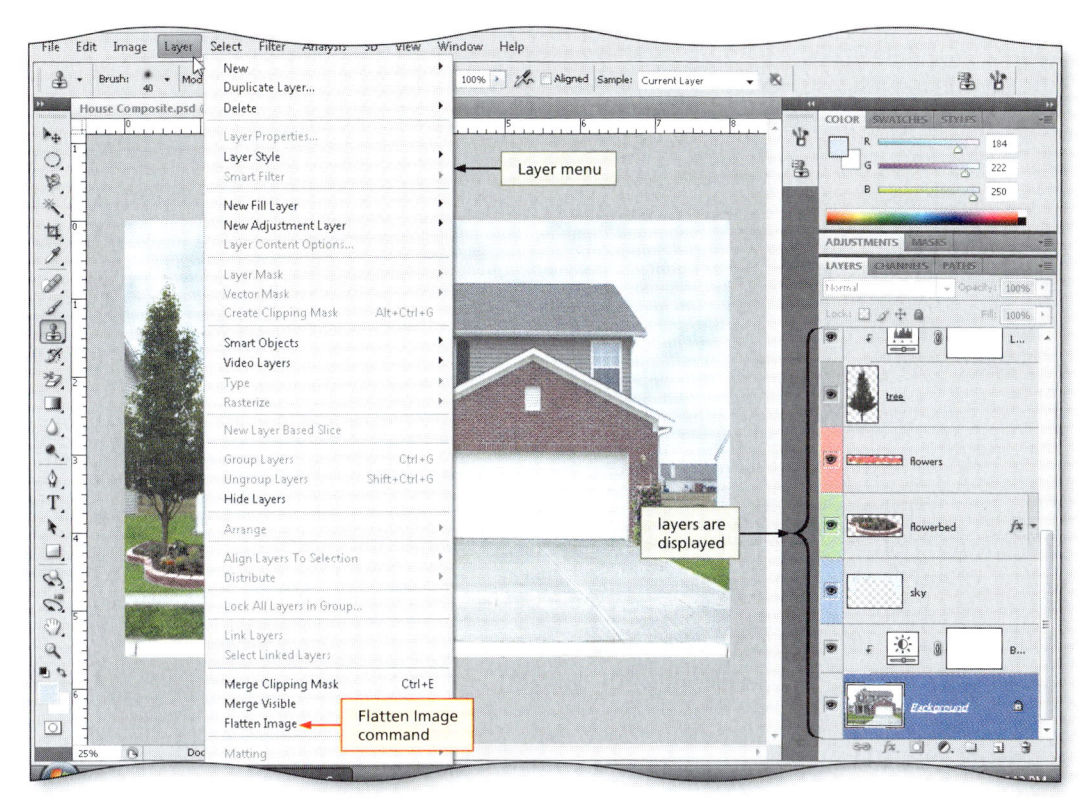

Figure 3–79

2
- Click Flatten Image on the Layer menu. If Photoshop displays a dialog box asking if you want to discard hidden layers, click the OK button (Figure 3–80).

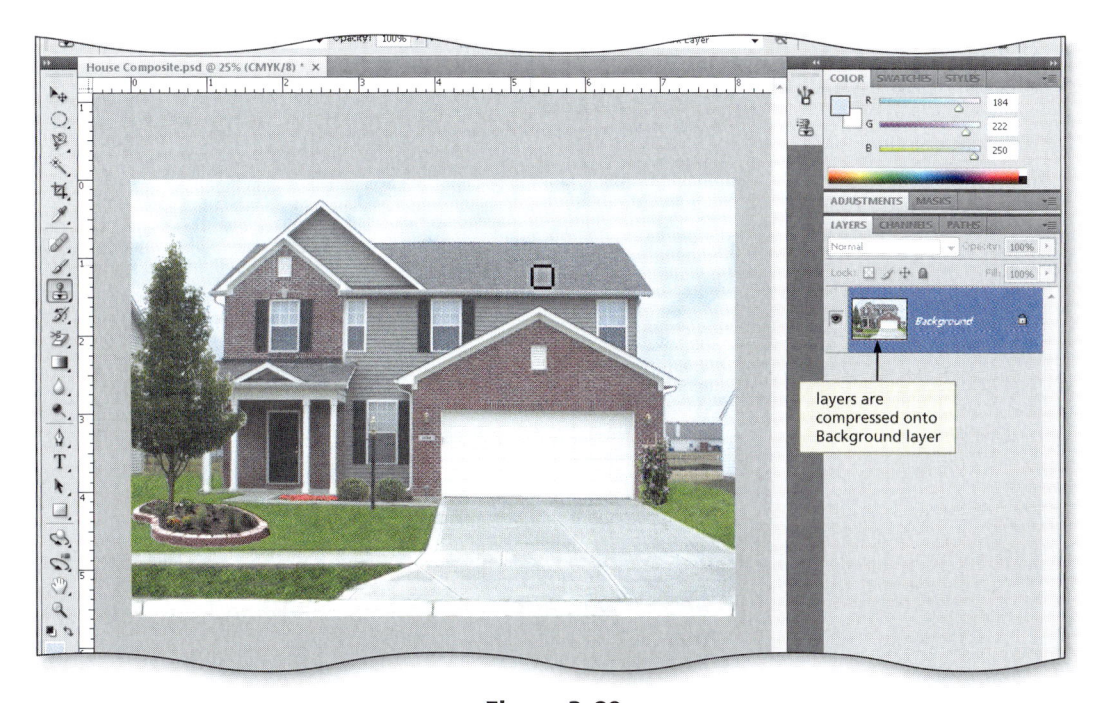

Figure 3–80

Other Ways	
1. Right-click any layer, click Flatten Image	2. Click Layers panel menu button, click Flatten Image

To Save a File in the TIF Format

TIF, or TIFF, is a flexible raster image format. A **raster image** is a digital image represented by a matrix of pixels. **TIFF** stands for Tagged Image File Format and is a common file format for images acquired from scanners and screen capture programs. Because TIF files are supported by virtually all paint, image-editing, and page-layout applications, it also is a versatile format for cross-platform applications.

The following steps save the flattened image as a TIF file.

1

- With your USB flash drive connected to one of the computer's USB ports, click File on the menu bar and then click Save As.

- When the Save As dialog box is displayed, type House TIFF in the File name text box. Do not press the ENTER key after typing the file name.

- Click the Format box arrow and then click TIFF (*.TIF, *.TIFF) in the list.

- Click the Save in box arrow and then click UDISK 2.0 (F:), or the location associated with your USB flash drive, in the list (Figure 3–81).

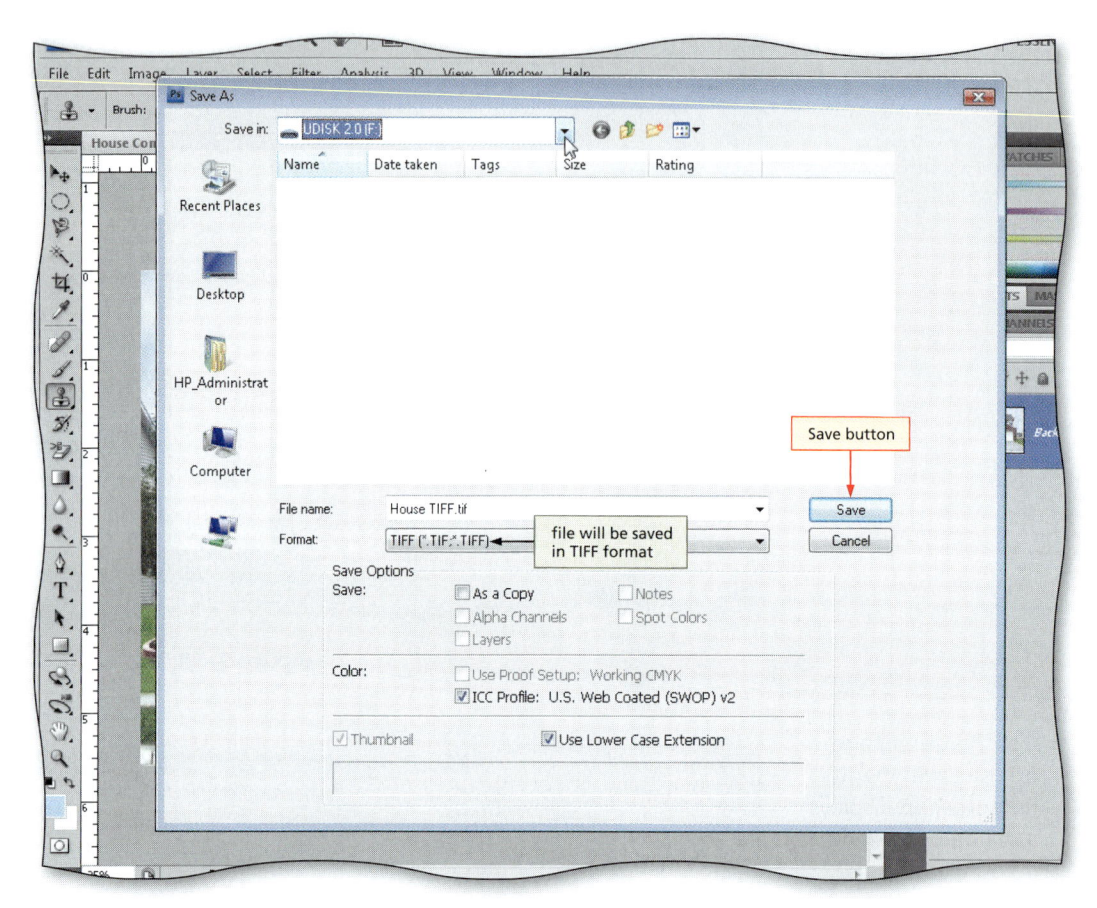

Figure 3–81

2
- Click the Save button in the Save As dialog box (Figure 3–82).

3
- In the TIFF Options dialog box, click the OK button.

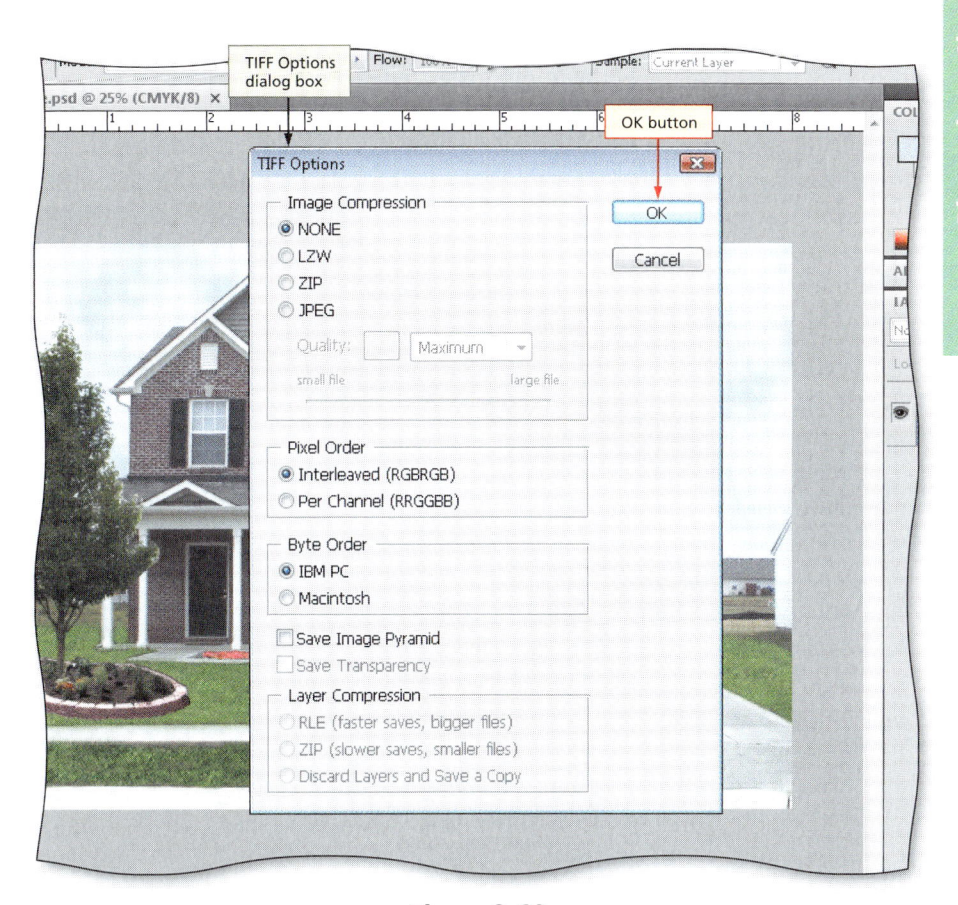

Figure 3–82

Other Ways
1. Press SHIFT+CTRL+S

To Print the House TIFF Image

The following steps print a copy of the House TIFF image on the default printer. If you are not sure which printer is set as your default, use the Print command rather than the Print one Copy command so you can choose your printer.

1 Ready the printer according to the printer instructions.

2 Click File on the menu bar and then click Print One Copy on the File menu to print the image on the default printer.

BTW — Photoshop Help
The best way to become familiar with Photoshop Help is to use it. Appendix D includes detailed information about Photoshop Help and exercises that will help you gain confidence in using it.

To Close the Document Window and Quit Photoshop

The final steps close the document window and quit Photoshop.

1 Click the Close button in the document window.

2 If Photoshop displays a dialog box, click the No button to ignore the changes since the last time you saved the photo.

3 Click the Close button on the right side of the Photoshop title bar.

BTW — Quick Reference
For a table that lists how to complete the tasks covered in this book using the mouse, shortcut menu, and keyboard, see the Quick Reference Summary at the back of this book or visit the Photoshop CS4 Quick Reference Web page (scsite.com/pscs4/qr).

Chapter Summary

In editing the landscape of the house image, you gained a broad knowledge of Photoshop's layering capabilities. First, you were introduced to the concept of layers. You created a layer via cut, a layer from another image, and a layer from a selection, using the Layers panel to set options, select, rename, color, view, and hide layers. Then you used the eraser tools to erase portions of the layer that were not needed in the final composite image.

You learned how to hide portions of layers and fine-tuned layers with layer adjustments, styles, and render filters. Finally, you used the Clone Stamp tool to copy grass into the composite image. The file was flattened and saved in the TIF format.

The items listed below include all the new Photoshop skills you have learned in this chapter:

1. Reset the Default Colors (PS 164)
2. Display the Layers Panel (PS 169)
3. Change Layer Panel Options (PS 169)
4. Create a Layer Via Cut (PS 172)
5. Name and Color a Layer (PS 173)
6. Hide and Show a Layer (PS 174)
7. Open a Second Image (PS 176)
8. Arrange the Document Windows (PS 177)
9. Create a Layer by Dragging an Entire Image (PS 178)
10. Set the Layer Properties Using the Context Menu (PS 179)
11. Create a Layer by Dragging a Selection (PS 182)
12. Erase Using the Magic Eraser Tool (PS 186)
13. Erase Using the Eraser Tool (PS 189)
14. Erase Using the Background Eraser Tool (PS 191)
15. Consolidate the Windows (PS 195)
16. Create a Layer Mask (PS 197)
17. Correct a Masking Error (PS 199)
18. Use the Masks Panel (PS 202)
19. Make an Opacity Change to a Layer (PS 206)
20. Make a Level Adjustment (PS 209)
21. Adjust the Hue and Saturation (PS 210)
22. Change the Brightness and Contrast (PS 212)
23. Add a Layer Style (PS 214)
24. Hide Layer Effects in the Layers Panel (PS 215)
25. Apply a Render Filter (PS 216)
26. Create a Clone (PS 220)
27. Flatten a Composite Image (PS 225)
28. Save a File in the TIF Format (PS 226)

Learn It Online

Test your knowledge of chapter content and key terms.

Instructions: To complete the Learn It Online exercises, start your browser, click the Address bar, and then enter the Web address scsite.com/pscs4/learn. When the Photoshop CS4 Learn It Online page is displayed, click the link for the exercise you want to complete and then read the instructions.

Chapter Reinforcement TF, MC, and SA
A series of true/false, multiple choice, and short answer questions that test your knowledge of the chapter content.

Flash Cards
An interactive learning environment where you identify chapter key terms associated with displayed definitions.

Practice Test
A series of multiple choice questions that test your knowledge of chapter content and key terms.

Who Wants To Be a Computer Genius?
An interactive game that challenges your knowledge of chapter content in the style of a television quiz show.

Wheel of Terms
An interactive game that challenges your knowledge of chapter key terms in the style of the television show *Wheel of Fortune*.

Crossword Puzzle Challenge
A crossword puzzle that challenges your knowledge of key terms presented in the chapter.

Apply Your Knowledge

Reinforce the skills and apply the concepts you learned in this chapter.

Creating Layers Using Shortcut Keys

Instructions: Start Photoshop and perform the customization steps found on pages PS 7 through PS 9. Open the Apply 3-1 Beach file from the Chapter03 folder of the Data Files for Students. You can access the Data Files for Students on the DVD that accompanies this book. See the inside back cover of this book for instructions on downloading the Data Files for Students, or contact your instructor for information about accessing the required files.

The purpose of this exercise is to create a composite photo by creating layers and to create both PSD and TIF versions of the final photo. The edited photo is displayed in Figure 3–83.

Figure 3–83

Perform the following tasks:

1. Change the magnification to 25 percent, if necessary. Press SHIFT+CTRL+S to open the Save As dialog box. Enter the name, `Apply 3-1 Beach Composite`. Do not press the ENTER key. Click the Format box arrow and then select the Photoshop PSD format. Click the Save in box arrow and then select your USB flash drive location. Click the Save button to save the file in the PSD format.

2. Remove the visitors from the beach:
   a. Press the S key to select the Clone Stamp tool. On the options bar, click the Aligned check box so it does not display a check mark. ALT+click the sand to the right of the people on the beach. Drag over the people to erase them from the beach.

Continued >

Apply Your Knowledge *continued*

3. Insert the gull and create a duplicate:
   a. Press CTRL+O and open the Apply 3-1 Gull file from the Chapter03 folder. On the Application bar, click the Arrange Documents buttons, and then click the first 2 Up button to display both of the document windows.
   b. When Photoshop displays the image, use the Magic Wand tool with a tolerance setting of 50 to select the sky around the bird. Press SHIFT+CTRL+I to select the Inverse.
   c. Right-click the selection and then click Grow to increase the selection slightly.
   d. Press the V key to select the Move tool. Drag the gull into the beach scene.
   e. Press CTRL+T to display the bounding box. SHIFT+drag a sizing handle to scale the gull layer. Drag the gull to a position as shown in Figure 3–81 on page PS 226. Press the ENTER key.
   f. Rename the layer, gull, and use a violet identification color.
   g. On the Layers panel, right-click the gull layer and then click Duplicate Layer. Name the duplicate layer, second gull. (*Hint*: The second gull will appear directly over the top of the first gull.)
   h. If necessary, press the V key to activate the Move tool, and then drag the second gull to a position above the first. If necessary, press CTRL+T to display the bounding box. SHIFT+drag a corner sizing handle to make the second gull smaller, thereby giving the composite image a sense of perspective. Press the ENTER key to commit the transformation.
   i. Close the Apply 3-1 Gull window.
4. Group the gull layers. Shift-click the two gull layers and then choose New Group from Layers on the panel menu. Name the group, Birds. When the layer group appears in the Layers panel, change the identification color to violet.
5. Next, insert the large umbrella and add a layer mask:
   a. Press CTRL+O and open the Apply 3-1 Large Umbrella image from the Chapter03 folder. Use the Arrange Documents button to arrange the two windows side by side.
   b. When Photoshop displays the image, if necessary, press the V key to select the Move tool. Drag the umbrella to the beach scene. Press CTRL+T to display the bounding box, then resize the umbrella and position it between the trees. Press the ENTER key to accept the transformation.
   c. On the Layers panel, click the Add layer mask button.
   d. Press the D key to select the default foreground and background colors on the Tools panel. If black is not the foreground color, press the X key to switch the foreground and background colors. Press the B key to activate the brush. Drag to mask any portions of the umbrella that eclipse the trees. (*Hint:* If you make a mistake and mask too much, press the X key to alternate to white and drag over the error.)
   e. Rename the layer, umbrella, and use a blue identification color.
   f. Close the Apply 3-1 Large Umbrella window.
6. Insert the beach ball and add a drop shadow:
   a. Press CTRL+O and open the Apply 3-1 Beach Ball file from the Chapter03 folder. Use the Arrange Documents button to arrange the two windows side by side.
   b. When Photoshop displays the image, press the V key to select the Move tool. Drag from the Beach Ball image to the beach scene.
   c. Press the E key to select the eraser tools and then, if necessary, press SHIFT+E to toggle to the Magic Eraser tool. On the options bar, type 15 in the Tolerance box. Click the Contiguous check box so it displays a check mark, if necessary. Click the white portions around the edge of the beach ball to erase them.

d. Select the Move tool, if necessary, and drag the beach ball to a position in the lower part of the scene.

e. On the Layers panel, click the Add a layer style button and then click Drop Shadow. When the Layer Style dialog box is displayed, type 70 in the Opacity box; drag the Angle radius to 97. Type 8 in the Distance box. Click the OK button.

f. Rename the layer, ball, and use a red identification color.

g. Close the Apply 3-1 Beach Ball window.

7. Finally, insert the beach pail:

a. Press CTRL+O and open the Apply 3-1 Beach Pail file from the Chapter03 folder. Use the Arrange Documents button to arrange the two windows side by side.

b. When Photoshop displays the image, drag a rectangular marquee around the beach pail and its shadow staying as close to the edges of the pail as possible. Press the V key to select the Move tool. Drag the selection into the beach scene.

c. Press the E key to access the current eraser tool. Press SHIFT+E to access the Eraser tool. On the options bar, click the Mode box arrow and then click Brush in the list, if necessary. Erase any areas around the pail that should not appear in the layer. Zoom and resize the size of your eraser, as necessary. Do not erase the shadow beneath the bucket.

d. If necessary, press CTRL+T and then scale the selection to match Figure 3–83 on page PS 229. Press the ENTER key to commit the transformation.

e. Rename the layer, pail, and use a yellow identification color.

f. Close the Apply 3-1 Beach Pail window.

8. Save the file again by pressing CTRL+S.

9. On the Layers panel menu, click Flatten Image.

10. Press SHIFT+CTRL+S to open the Save As dialog box. Type `Apply 3-1 Beach Complete` in the Name box. Click the Format box arrow and then click TIFF in the list. Click the Save button. If Photoshop displays a dialog box, click the OK button.

11. Turn in a hard copy of the photo to your instructor.

12. Quit Photoshop.

Extend Your Knowledge

Extend the skills you learned in this chapter and experiment with new skills. You may need to use Help to complete the assignment.

Creating a Toy Advertisement Graphic

Instructions: Start Photoshop and reset the workspace, default colors, and all tools. Open the Extend 3-1 Robot Background file from the Chapter03 folder of the Data Files for Students and save it as Extend 3-1 Robot Composite. You can access the Data Files for Students on the DVD that accompanies this book. See the inside back cover of this book for instructions on downloading the Data Files for Students, or contact your instructor for information about accessing the required files.

The purpose of this exercise is to create a composite photo for a toy company, starting with a plain background, adding and adjusting layers. You will create both a PSD and TIF version of the final graphic.

Continued >

Extend Your Knowledge *continued*

Perform the following tasks:
1. With the Extend 3-1 Robot Composite file open, use the Clone Stamp tool to clone over the shadow on the right side of the image. To do so:
    a. Select the Clone Stamp tool. On the options bar, click the Aligned check box so it does not display a check mark.
    b. ALT+click the ground approximately one inch below the shadow to create the sample for the clone. Drag over the shadowed area, including any rocks, to create a cloned area and hide the shadow. (*Hint*: Use the LEFT and RIGHT BRACKET keys to adjust the size of the mouse pointer as needed.)
2. To create a sky layer:
    a. Use the Magic Wand tool and the Add to Selection button to select all of the sky.
    b. On the Layer menu, point to New, and then click Layer via Cut.
    c. On the Layers panel, double-click the layer name and type sky to rename the layer. Right-click the visibility icon and choose Blue in the list.
3. To add the robot body:
    a. Open the Extend 3-1 Robot Body file from the Chapter03 folder of the Data Files for Students.
    b. On the Application bar, use the Arrange Documents button to display the windows side by side.
    c. Use the Move tool to drag the robot body from the Robot Body document window to the Robot Composite document window. (*Hint:* Holding down the SHIFT key as you drag automatically centers the image and creates a new layer.)
    d. Name the layer, robot, and use a violet identification color.
    e. Close the Extend 3-1 Robot Body document window.
4. Repeat Step 3 to add the shadow graphic using the file, Extend 3-1 Robot Shadow file from the Chapter03 folder of the Data Files for Students. Position it behind the robot near the feet, as shown in Figure 3–84. Name the layer, shadow, and use a gray identification color. Close the Extend 3-1 Robot Shadow document window.

Figure 3–84

5. To move the layer behind the robot, on the Layers panel, drag the shadow layer just below the robot layer.
6. Repeat Step 3 to add the earth graphic using the file, Extend 3-1 Robot Earth file from the Chapter03 folder of the Data Files for Students. Position it in the upper-right corner of the scene. Name the layer, earth, and use a green identification color. Close the Extend 3-1 Robot Earth document window.
7. Repeat Step 3 to add the title graphic using the file, Extend 3-1 Robot Title file from the Chapter03 folder of the Data Files for Students. Position the words centered above the robot's head. Name the layer, title, and use a yellow identification color. Close the Extend 3-1 Robot Title document window.
8. To create an adjustment layer and make the background appear more like a moonscape:
    a. On the Layers panel, select the Background layer.
    b. Double-click the Adjustments panel tab to show the panel and its controls.
    c. Click the Hue/Saturation button to display the settings.
    d. On the status bar, click the Clip to Layer button to create a new adjustment layer for the background.
    e. Change the Hue to +20 and the Saturation to –80.
    f. On the status bar, click the Return to adjustment list button.
9. To create an adjustment layer and make the sky layer appear black:
    a. Double-click the Layers panel tab to display the Layers panel. Select the sky layer.
    b. Double-click the Adjustments panel tab to show the panel.
    c. Click the Brightness/Contrast button to display the controls.
    d. On the Adjustments panel status bar, click the Clip to Layer button to create a new adjustment layer for the sky. Click the Use Legacy check box to select it, if necessary.
    e. Drag both the Brightness and Contrast sliders to the left to create a black sky.
    f. On the status bar, click the Return to adjustment list button.
10. To add a layer effect to the title layer:
    a. Double-click the Layers panel tab to show the Layers panel. Select the title layer. Click the Add a layer style button on the Layers panel status bar, and then click Stroke to open the Layer Style dialog box. (*Hint:* You may want to read about the Stroke command in Photoshop Help.) Drag the Layer style dialog box title bar so you can view the robot and the dialog box.
    b. In the Layer style dialog box, click the Color box to display the Select stroke color dialog box. Drag the Select stroke color dialog box title bar so you can view the robot and the dialog box.
    c. Click the yellow eyes of the robot to select the yellow color. (*Hint:* The mouse pointer looks like an eyedropper when selecting a color.)
    d. Click the OK button to close the Select stroke color dialog box and then click the OK button to close the Layer style dialog box.
11. Save the composite file again with all the layers.
12. Flatten the image.
13. Press SHIFT+CTRL+S to open the Save As dialog box. Type `Extend 3-1 Robot Complete` in the Name box. Click the Format box arrow and then click TIFF in the list. Click the Save button. If Photoshop displays a dialog box, click the OK button.
14. Quit Photoshop.

PS 234 Photoshop Chapter 3 Working with Layers

Make It Right

Analyze a project and correct all errors and/or improve the design.

Instructions: Start Photoshop and perform the customization steps found on pages PS 7 through PS 9. Open the Make It Right 3-1 Desert file from the Chapter03 folder of the Data Files for Students. You can access the Data Files for Students on the DVD that accompanies this book. See the inside back cover of this book for instructions on downloading the Data Files for Students, or contact your instructor for information about accessing the required files.

The photo has layers that are invisible, layers that need transformation, and layers that need to be moved, trimmed, and adjusted for levels (Figure 3–85).

Instructions: Save the file on your storage device in the PSD format with the name, Make It Right 3-1 Desert Composite. For each invisible layer, reveal the layer, correct any order problem by dragging the layer to an appropriate position in the Layers panel, erase or mask parts of the layer as necessary, and move the layer to a logical position.

Use the Adjustments panel and tools such as Levels, Brightness/Contrast, and Hue/Saturation to create adjustment layers. (*Hint:* Do not forget to click the Clip to layer button in the Adjustments panel status bar, so the adjustment will apply to that layer only.) Make any other adjustments or layer style changes as you deem necessary. Save the file again and submit it in the format specified by your instructor.

Figure 3–85

In the Lab

Design and/or create a project using the guidelines, concepts, and skills presented in this chapter. Labs are listed in order of increasing difficulty.

Lab 1: Making Level Adjustments Using Masks

Problem: A local tourist company has hired you to create its latest brochure about historic homes. You encounter a photo that is too dark to use in the brochure. You decide to try adjusting the levels to lighten the trees, grass, and shrubs in the photo and prepare it for print in the brochure. The edited photo is shown in Figure 3–86.

Figure 3–86

Instructions: Perform the following tasks:
1. Start Photoshop. Set the default workspace, default colors, and reset all tools.
2. Open the file Lab 3-1 Historic Home from the Chapter03 folder of the Data Files for Students. You can access the Data Files for Students on the DVD that accompanies this book. See the inside back cover of this book for instructions on downloading the Data Files for Students, or contact your instructor for information about accessing the required files.
3. Click the Save As command on the File menu. Type `Lab 3-1 Historic Home Edited` as the file name. Click the Format box arrow and click Photoshop in the list. Browse to your USB flash drive storage device. Click the Save button. If Photoshop displays a Format Options dialog box, click the OK button.
4. Zoom to 100 percent magnification, if necessary.
5. On the Tools panel, right-click the current lasso tool. Click Lasso Tool on the context menu. Drag with the Lasso tool to draw around the house. Stay as close to the house itself as possible. Do not include trees, shrubs, or the sky.
6. Press the W key to activate the Magic Wand tool. On the options bar, click the Add to selection button and then, if necessary, click the Contiguous check box so it displays a check mark.

Continued >

In the Lab *continued*

7. In the document window, click the sky.
8. Click Select on the menu bar and then click Inverse to select the inverse of the house and sky, which would be the trees, shrubs, and grounds.
9. Click Layer on the menu bar, point to New, and then click Layer via Cut.
10. On the Layers panel, rename the layer, grounds.
11. With the layer selected, press CTRL+L to open the Levels dialog box. In the Input Levels area, drag the white slider to the left until the grounds are lighter and the features easily discerned, and then click the OK button in the dialog box.
12. On the Layers panel, click the Background layer.
13. On the Color panel, click a light blue color.
14. Press the W key to activate the Magic Wand tool. On the options bar, click the Add to selection button and then, if necessary, click the Contiguous check box so it displays a check mark. In the document window, click the sky in various locations until all of the sky is selected.
15. Click Filter on the menu bar, point to Render, and then click Clouds.
16. Press CTRL+S to save the photo again. If Photoshop displays the Photoshop Format Options dialog box, click the OK button.
17. Press SHIFT+CTRL+S to access the Save As dialog box. Choose the TIFF format and name the file Lab 3-1 Historic Home Complete.
18. Print a copy and turn it in to your instructor.

In the Lab

Lab 2: Creating Layer Comps

Problem: A trophy manufacturing company has hired you to create some layer comps for marketing their new line of baseball trophies. The current graphic has layers for the background, inside, and outside of the box. You are to insert the trophy graphic and scale it to fit the box. Then create layer comps showing the inside and the outside. The edited photo is shown in Figure 3–87.

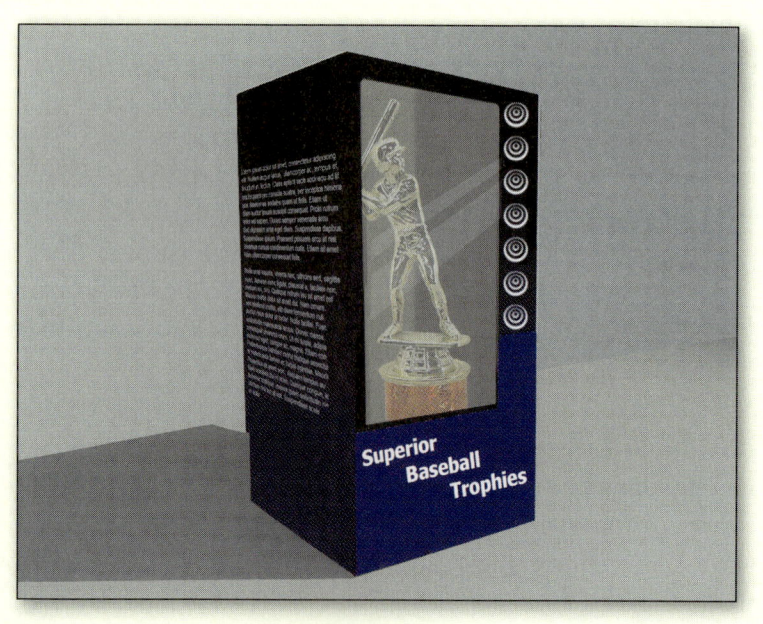

Figure 3–87

Instructions: Perform the following tasks:
1. Start Photoshop. Set the default workspace, default colors, and reset all tools.
2. Open the file Lab 3-2 Marketing Graphic from the Chapter03 folder of the Data Files for Students. You can access the Data Files for Students on the DVD that accompanies this book. See the inside back cover of this book for instructions on downloading the Data Files for Students, or contact your instructor for information about accessing the required files.
3. Save the file with the name, `Lab 3-2 Marketing Graphic Composite`. If necessary, click the Format box arrow and click Photoshop in the list. Browse to your USB flash drive storage device. Click the Save button. If Photoshop displays a Format Options dialog box, click the OK button.
4. Show and hide the various layers using the visibility icon to gain familiarity with the graphic.
5. Make the Background layer and the inside layer visible, and hide all other layers. Select the inside layer.
6. Open the file Lab 3-2 Trophy from the Chapter03 folder of the Data Files for Students. Use the Arrange Documents button to display the windows side by side.
7. Use the Move tool to drag the trophy from its own window into the Lab 3-2 Marketing Graphic Composite document window. Scale the trophy to fit in the box. Make the outside layer visible and make sure the trophy can be seen through the opening in the outer box. Name the layer, trophy.
8. Make the front panel layer visible and select it. Adjust the Opacity setting so the layer looks more transparent, as if it were plastic.
9. Make the gleam layer visible. Adjust the Opacity and Fill settings as necessary. Save the file.
10. Use Help to learn about Layer Comps. Also read the BTW boxes on pages PS 203 and PS 204. Open the Layer Comps panel and create the layer comps described in Table 3–6.

Table 3–6 Marketing Graphic Layer Comps

Layer Comp Name	Visible Layers
Empty Box	Background, inside
Inner Box with Trophy	Background, inside, trophy
Outer Box with Trophy	Background, inside, trophy, outside, shadow
Complete Graphic	All layers

11. Save the file again.
12. For extra credit, copy the trophy layer and scale it to approximately 30 percent of its original size. In the Layers panel, move the layer above the outside layer. Position the trophy in the lower-middle portion of the box. Warp the layer to make it wrap around the corner of the box. Create a layer comp named Complete with Wrapped Logo and include all layers.
13. Submit this assignment in the format specified by your instructor.

In the Lab

Lab 3: Using the Clone Stamp Tool and Creating a Layer with Outer Glow

Problem: The marketing agency that you work for has asked you to edit the latest advertisement for Qintara perfume. You decide to use Photoshop's layering capabilities to insert the image of the perfume bottle. You also decide to clone the Q of their logo multiple times to create a stylistic band of color across the advertisement. A sample of the advertisement is shown in Figure 3–88.

Instructions: Perform the following tasks:

1. Start Photoshop. Set the default workspace, default colors, and reset all tools. Open the file Lab 3-3 Perfume from the Chapter03 folder of the Data Files for Students. Rename the file, `Lab 3-3 Perfume Edited` and save it as a PSD file on your storage device.

2. Select the layer named slogan, if necessary. Move the layer to the lower portion of the image.

3. Open the file Lab 3-3 Bottle. Drag a copy to the Lab 3-3 Perfume Edited window.

   Name the new layer, bottle, and set its layer properties. Close the Lab 3-3 Bottle document window.

4. Create a layer mask in the bottle layer. (*Hint:* In the lower part of the Tools panel, make sure you have black over white for the foreground and background colors.) Use the Brush tool with black to make the area around the bottle transparent. Add an Outer Glow layer style with a size of 25.

5. Click the Background layer. Using the Clone Stamp tool, ALT+click the top of the letter Q in the logo. Move the mouse pointer down and to the right. Drag to create a clone of the Q.

6. Repeat Step 5, creating multiple, overlapped clones of the letter Q as shown in Figure 3–88. Use short strokes. If you make a mistake, click the previous state on the History panel and drag again.

7. When you are satisfied with your clones, flatten the image. Save the file again and submit a copy to your instructor.

Figure 3–88

Cases and Places

Apply your creative thinking and problem-solving skills to design and implement a solution.

• Easier   •• More Difficult

• 1: Cloning within the Same Document
You recently took a photo of a deer at the local forest preserve. To make the picture more interesting, you decide to create a layer and clone the deer. Open the photo named Case 3-1 Deer, located in the Chapter03 folder of the Data Files for Students. Click the Layer command on the menu bar, point to New and then click Layer. Click the Background layer, choose the Clone Stamp tool, and take a sample of the middle of the deer. Click the new layer and clone the deer. On the Edit menu, click Free Transform and resize the cloned deer so it appears to be farther away. Create a layer comp with the second deer and one without it. Save the file as Case 3-1 Deer Edited on your storage device.

• 2: Creating a City Graphic
Earlier in this chapter, a suggestion was made to create a flag with 50 percent opacity superimposed over a memorial. Locate or take a photo of a memorial in your city and a picture of your flag. If necessary, obtain permission to use a digital photo or scan the images. Open the photos. Select only the flag and then drag it as a new layer into the memorial photo. Resize the layer to fit across the memorial. Change the opacity to 50 percent. Make other corrections as necessary. Save the composite photo and print a copy.

•• 3: Thinking about Composites
Look through magazines or newspapers for color photos that display distinctive layering techniques. If possible, cut out three or four photos. Write a paragraph about each one; describe how you think it was generated. Look for cloning, opacity changes, adjustment layers, filters, and layer effects. Attach the photos to the descriptions and submit them to your instructor. If directed to do so by your instructor, scan the image and use the Layer via Cut command to recreate the layers.

•• 4: Designing and Creating a Family Vacation Photo
Make It Personal
You are planning a family reunion at a vacation spot and want to create a photo to advertise the event to your family. Use a scanner to scan photos of the vacation spot and photos of your family members. Using the scanner's software, save the photos in the highest possible resolution, using the most color settings. Bring the vacation photo into Photoshop and save it on your storage device. One at a time, open each of the family member photos and drag the images into layers on top of the vacation spot photo. Use Layer masks to hide the background in the layers and adjust the levels so the family members fit into the picture. Flatten the photo and save it in the TIF format. Send the edited photo by e-mail to members of your family or to your instructor as directed.

•• 5: Creating a Composite Classroom
Working Together
The school is refurbishing room Tech 329 into a state-of-the-art technology lab and teaching center. Your group has been asked to come up with a design for the new lab. Have each member of the team visit existing labs at your school and take pictures of features they would like to see in a new lab. Gather other pictures from catalogs. Have one team member take a picture of an empty classroom if possible. Layer each of the features into the empty classroom. Scale and adjust each layer to fit its surroundings. Use the eraser tools as needed. Clone multiple workstations. Present your composite lab to other groups for discussion and suggestions for improvement.

4 Drawing and Painting with Color

Objectives

You will have mastered the material in this chapter when you can:

- Create a Photoshop document from scratch
- Differentiate between color modes
- Apply gradients using the Gradient tool
- Select colors using color dialog boxes
- Create text with the type tools
- Stroke text
- Sample colors with the Eyedropper tool
- Differentiate among the shape tools, modes, and settings
- Append shapes using the Shape Preset picker
- Paint and draw using Photoshop brushes
- Adjust the hardness and diameter settings of brushes
- Load new brushes in the Brushes panel
- Use the Brush Preset picker
- Apply colors with the Paint Bucket tool

4 Drawing and Painting with Color

Introduction

In both academic and business environments, you will be called upon to create graphics from scratch using the tools and techniques available in Photoshop. While many sources of graphics, such as clip art and stock photos, are widely available, some are copyrighted, rights-controlled, or expensive to buy. Others have to be edited so extensively that it might be easier to start from scratch. Still others simply do not fit the particular circumstances for the required project. By creating the graphic from scratch, you solve many of the problems that result when attempting to use ready-made images. If you have good artistic and drawing skills, and an input device such as a graphics tablet, the kinds of graphics you can create are limitless.

Another way to design graphics is to start from scratch and add images that are digital photographs or scans. That way, your image has the best of both worlds — incorporating the texture and lines of drawing with the realism of actual photographs. In Photoshop, working from scratch to create an image or illustration is better when the subject is conceptual, imaginative, less formal, or open to interpretation. Beginning with a digital photo is better when the subject is living, tangible, for sale, or more formal; photography does not risk loss of meaning through interpretation. Whatever style of imagery you choose, you need to know how to use the drawing and painting tools in Photoshop.

Project — Menu Front Cover

Chapter 4 uses Photoshop to create a graphic for the front of a printed menu. It constructs the gradient, text, brush strokes, and stars from scratch, while using the images of a real projector and pizza to add a sense of reality and detail. The graphic lets the viewer know what to expect at the restaurant. The completed image is displayed in Figure 4–1.

Overview

As you read this chapter, you will learn how to create the composite image shown in Figure 4–1 by performing these general tasks:

- Create a new file, starting with a blank canvas.
- Apply a gradient background.
- Add stroked text that matches a color in the gradient.
- Create a realistic-looking graphic using shapes.
- Choose colors using a variety of tools and dialog boxes.
- Insert real images combined with drawn images.
- Use brushes to draw lines, shapes, and strokes.

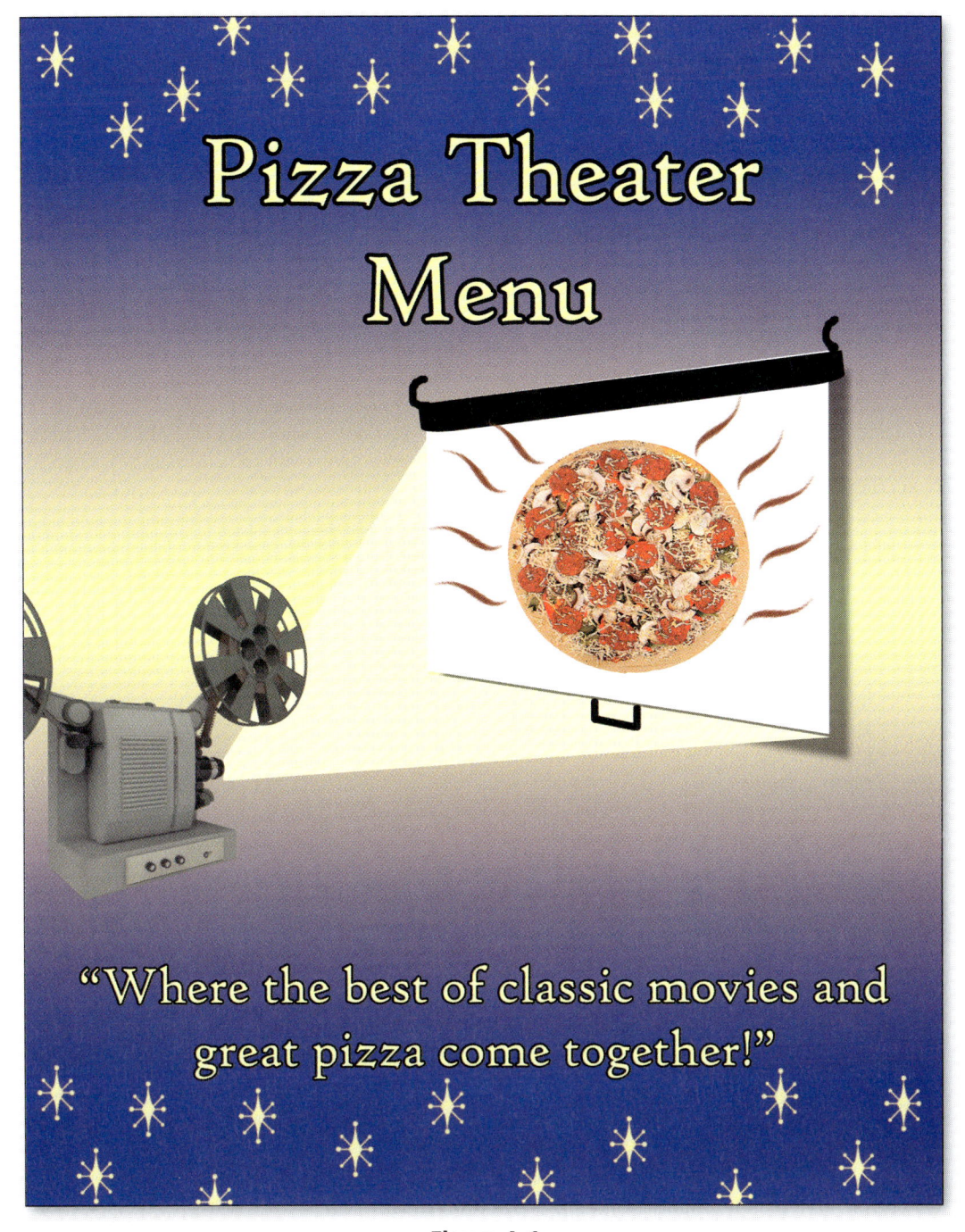

Figure 4–1

Plan Ahead

General Project Guidelines
When editing a photo, the actions you perform and decisions you make will affect the appearance and characteristics of the finished product. As you create a photo, such as the one shown in Figure 4–1 on the previous page, you should follow these general guidelines:

1. **Plan your layout and gather necessary photos.** As you plan your layout of original graphics, create the storyboard and the graphic from the back to the front. Decide on the background first, then layers, followed by foreground objects or text. The graphics you choose should convey the overall message, incorporating high-quality photos with similar lighting characteristics. Keep in mind the customer requirements. For professional-looking graphics, keep in mind the principles of contrast, alignment, repetition, and proximity.

2. **Apply effective text styles and strokes.** It is common to use text to educate and inform, but text often becomes a creative element itself in the design. The first rule of text is to choose a font that is easy to read. No matter how creative the font style is, if the customer cannot make out the words, the text fails. Avoid using more than two different fonts on the same page or graphic. As a second font, use either the same font at a different size, or a highly contrasting font. Keep similar text components in proximity of each other. For example, do not split the address, phone number, and Web page address onto different parts of the page. Use a stroke of color around the text for a more distinctive look that stands out.

3. **Use predefined shapes for tangible objects.** Use shapes rather than freehand drawings when you are trying to create a graphic that represents a tangible object. Shapes allow you to maintain straight lines, even corners, constrained proportions, and even curves. Except when intentionally creating a randomized pattern, try to align shapes with something else in the graphic, or parallel to the edge of the publication.

4. **Choose colors purposefully.** Consider the cost of full color printing, paper, shelf life, and customer requirements when choosing your colors. Try to repeat colors that already exist in incorporated images. Some clients already may have colors that help brand their publications. Consult with the client and print shops for the correct color numbers and the plan for printing. Unless you want a rainbow special effect, limit your colors to two or three on a contrasting background.

5. **Design your brush strokes.** Brushes imitate the actions of artistic paintbrushes. By varying the settings, such as tip shape, hardness, etc., you can add imaginative strokes to your work.

When necessary, more specific details concerning the above guidelines are presented at appropriate points in the chapter. The chapter also will identify the actions performed and decisions made regarding these guidelines during the creation of the edited photo shown in Figure 4–1.

BTW

Color Modes and File Size
Because there are four colors involved in CMYK images, instead of three as in RGB images, CMYK images use 33% more file space than RGB images.

BTW

Converting Between Modes
In Photoshop, you can easily convert from one color mode to another. When you point to Mode on the Image menu, the various color modes can be selected. As you choose a new color mode, Photoshop will inform you of any problems converting the image.

Creating a New File

In this chapter, you will create a new Photoshop document from scratch. Photoshop allows you to customize the attributes of file name, image size, resolution, color mode, and background when creating a new document image. Alternatively, Photoshop provides several groups of attributes that are preset. The new image size can be set in pixels, inches, or centimeters, among others. You can set the width and height independently. When setting the resolution of an image, you specify the number of **pixels per inch** (**ppi**), or **pixels per centimeter**, that are printed on a page.

A **color mode**, or **color method**, determines the number of colors and combinations of colors used to display and print the image. Each color mode uses a numerical method called a **color model**, or **color space**, to describe the color. Photoshop bases its color modes on the color models that commonly are useful when publishing images. Color modes also directly affect the file size of an image. As you will learn in this chapter, choosing a color mode determines which Photoshop tools and file formats are available.

When choosing a color mode, you must take into consideration many factors, including purpose, printing options, file size, number of colors, and layers that may be flattened in later conversions between color modes. Common color modes include RGB, CMYK, LAB, Indexed, and Grayscale, among others. See Appendix B for more details about each of the color modes.

RGB (red, green, blue) is considered an additive color mode because its colors are created by adding together different wavelengths of light in various intensities. Also called **24-bit color**, RGB color mode is used typically for images that are reproduced on monitors, projectors, slides, transparencies, and the Web.

CMYK (cyan, magenta, yellow, black) is considered a subtractive color mode because its colors are created when light strikes an object or image and the wavelengths are absorbed. Also called the **four-color process**, the CMYK color mode is used by most desktop printers and commercial printing businesses.

A **gamut**, or **color gamut**, is the range of colors that can be displayed or printed. The color gamut on your monitor may not be the same as on your printer. For example, the RGB color mode displays a wider range of discernible colors than does CMYK. When you print an RGB image that is displayed on your monitor, it must be reproduced with CMYK inks on your printer. Because the gamut of color that can be reproduced with ink is smaller than what we see with our eyes, any color that cannot be printed is referred to as **out of gamut**. In Photoshop, you will see an out of gamut warning if you select colors that have to be converted from RGB to CMYK. If you plan to send your image to a professional print shop, be sure to get details about color modes, models, and gamuts before the image is printed.

Once you choose a color mode, you also can set a bit depth. The **bit depth**, also called **pixel depth** or **color depth**, measures how much color information is available for displaying or printing each pixel in an image. The word **bit** stands for binary digit. A bit depth of eight means that Photoshop assigns eight binary settings for each color.

Photoshop's **color management system** (**CMS**) translates colors from the color space of one device into a device-independent color space. The process is called **color mapping**, or **gamut mapping**.

> **BTW**
>
> **LAB Color**
> Three basic parameters make up the LAB color mode. First, the lightness of the color is measured from 0 (indicating black) to 100 (indicating white). The second parameter represents the color's position between magenta and green — negative values indicate green while positive values indicate magenta. Finally, the third parameter indicates a color's position between yellow and blue — negative values indicate blue while positive values indicate yellow.

Starting and Customizing Photoshop

The following steps start Photoshop, and reset the default workspace, tools, colors, and Layers panel thumbnails. After opening a blank canvas, the rulers are displayed, and the file is saved to begin editing.

To Start Photoshop

The following steps, which assume Windows Vista is running, start Photoshop based on a typical installation.

1. Click the Start button on the Windows Vista taskbar and then click All Programs to display the All Programs list.

2. Click Adobe Design Premium CS4, or your version of the Adobe suite, in the All Programs list, and then click Adobe Photoshop CS4 to start Photoshop.

3. Maximize the Photoshop window, if necessary.

> **BTW**
>
> **Indexed Color**
> When converting to Indexed color, Photoshop builds a color lookup table (CLUT), which stores and indexes the colors in the image. If a color in the original image does not appear in the table, Photoshop chooses the closest one, or dithers the available colors to simulate the color. Indexed color mode therefore limits the panel of colors to reduce file size yet maintain visual quality.

Colors on the Web
The Web typically uses a six-digit hexadecimal number to represent its color mode. Hexadecimal is a numbering system based on groups of 16, using the numbers 0 through 9 and the letters A through F. In decimal numbers, used for color modes other than the Web, three separate numbers are used for each of the 256 available colors per channel.

Grayscale Printing
Although a grayscale image on a computer screen can display up to 256 levels of gray, a printing press can reproduce only about 50 levels of gray per ink. Therefore, a grayscale image printed with only black ink can look coarse compared to the same image printed with two to four inks, with each individual ink reproducing up to 50 levels of gray.

Image Sizes
For very large publications, reduce the magnification to see the entire image in the document window. The larger the dimensions of your publication, the larger the file size. Photoshop imposes no limit to the size of your publication, except for its ability to fit on your storage device. System resources may be slower in larger documents.

To Reset the Workspace

The following step uses the Workspace switcher to select the Essentials workspace.

1. Click the Workspace switcher and then click Essentials to restore the workspace to its default settings.

To Reset the Tools and the Options Bar

The following steps select the Rectangular Marquee tool and reset all tool settings in the options bar.

1. Activate the Rectangular Marquee Tool (M) button on the Tools panel.
2. Change the Tools panel to one column, if necessary.
3. Right-click the Rectangular Marquee tool icon on the options bar to display the context menu, click Reset All Tools, and then the OK button if necessary.

To Reset the Default Colors

The following step resets the default colors.

1. On the Tools panel, click the Default Foreground and Background Colors (D) button to reset the default colors of black and white. If black is not the foreground color, press the X key to reverse the colors.

To Reset the Layers Panel

The following steps reset the Layers panel to make the thumbnails match the figures shown in this book.

1. Click the Layers panel menu button and then click Panel Options on the list to display the Layers Panel Options dialog box.
2. Click the option button for the smallest of the thumbnail sizes.
3. If necessary, click the Layer Bounds option button to select it.
4. Click the OK button.

To Create a Photoshop File from Scratch

The menu cover graphic will be approximately 8 by 10 inches to accommodate the size of the printed menu. A resolution of 300 ppi will be used to maintain a high-quality printed image. Because the graphic will be printed, rather than used on the Web, the color mode will be CMYK and the bit depth will be 8. The background will be transparent at the beginning.

The following steps use the New command on the File menu and set the attributes for a new document image.

1

- Click File on the menu bar, and then click New to display the New dialog box (Figure 4–2).

Q&A My settings are different. Did I do something wrong?

No, your settings will differ. Photoshop imports the settings from the last copy performed on your system, in case you want to create a new file from something you copied.

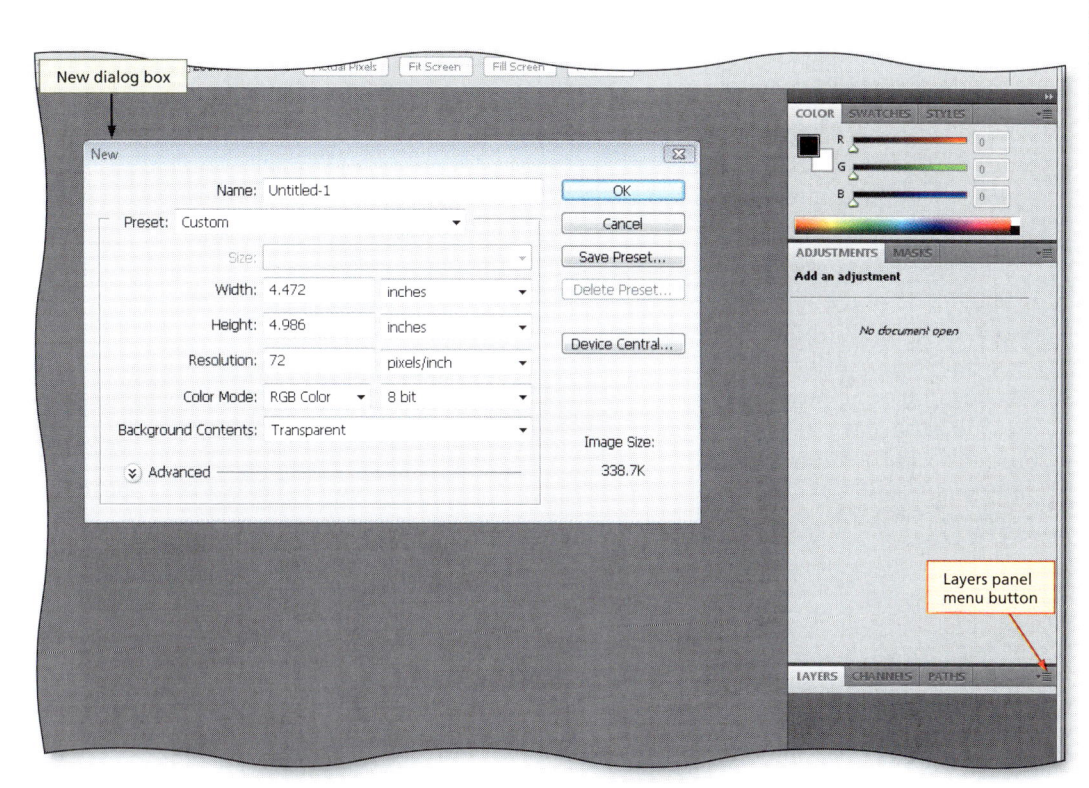

Figure 4–2

2

- Type `Menu Cover` in the Name box to name the graphic.

- If necessary, click the Preset box arrow, and then click Custom in the list.

- If necessary, click the Width unit box arrow, and then click inches in the list.

- Double-click the Width box and then type `8` to enter a value of 8 inches wide.

- Double-click the Height box and then type `10` to enter a value of 10 inches high (Figure 4–3).

Q&A What other measurement units can I use?

Photoshop allows you to choose various scales for new photos, including inches, pixels, centimeters, millimeters, points, and others.

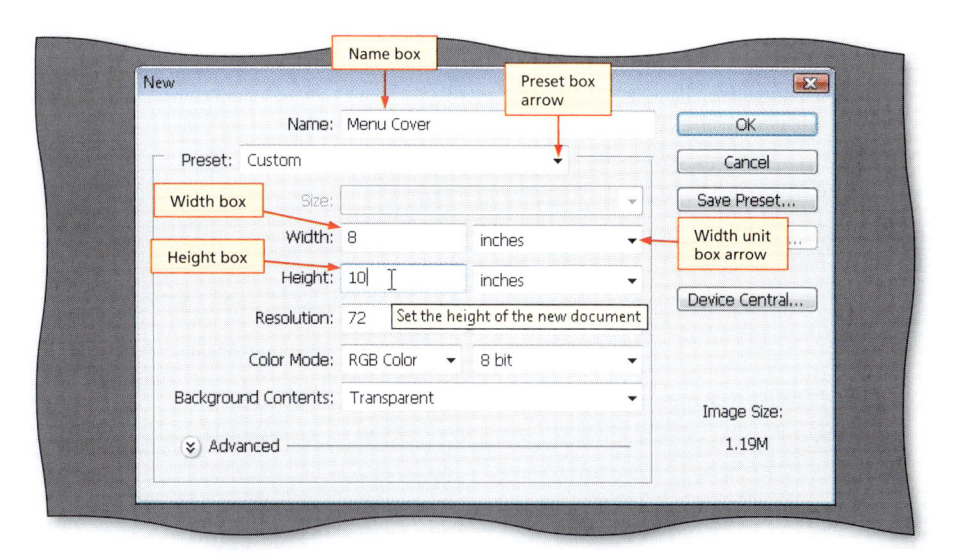

Figure 4–3

3

- Double-click the Resolution box and then type 300 to create 300 pixels per inch.
- If necessary, click the Resolution unit box arrow, and then click pixels/inch in the list.
- Click the Color Mode box arrow to display its list (Figure 4–4).

Q&A What does the Save Preset button do?

Once you choose a color mode, Photoshop displays an approximate image size on the right side of the New dialog box, based on your settings. If you find that you commonly use those specific settings, you could click the Save Preset button and give your attributes a name. In future sessions, you then could choose the preset from a list.

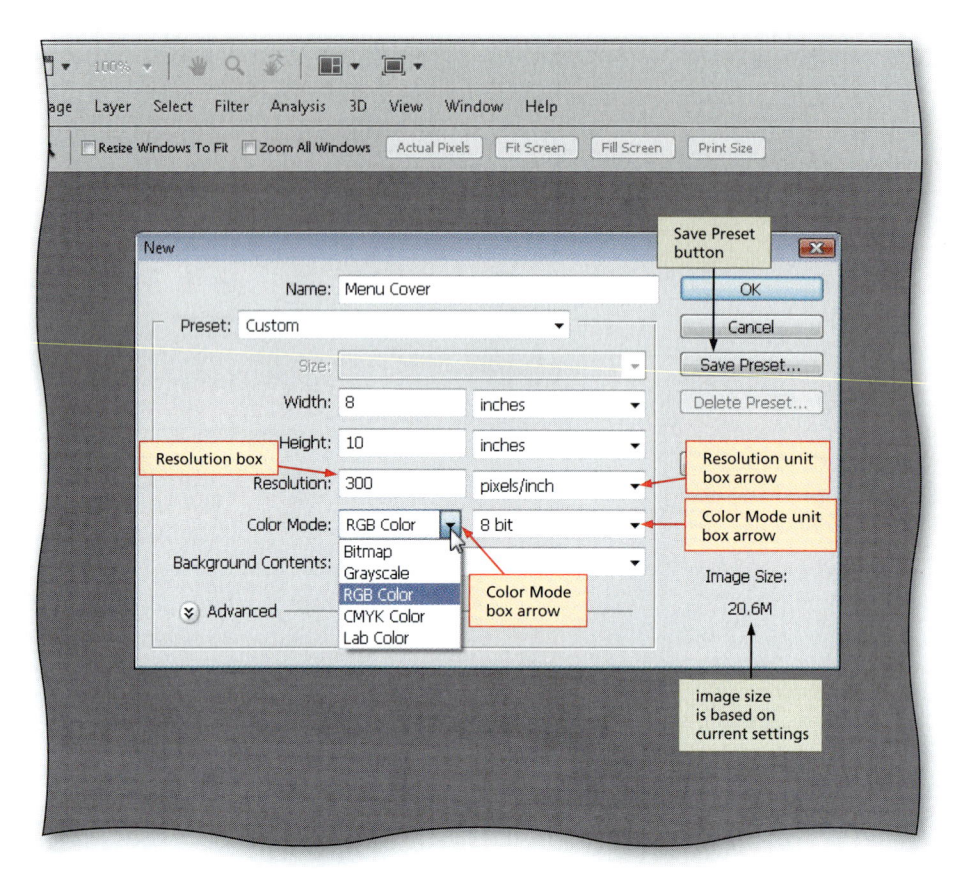

Figure 4–4

4

- Click CMYK Color in the list to choose the CMYK color mode.
- If necessary, click the Color Mode unit box arrow and then click 8 bit in the list.
- If necessary, click the Background Contents box arrow, and then click Transparent in the list to set the color (Figure 4–5).

Q&A What color would display if I chose Background Color?

When you select Background color in the Background Contents list, the current background color, as noted on the Tools panel, becomes the default color of the blank canvas. The other option is white.

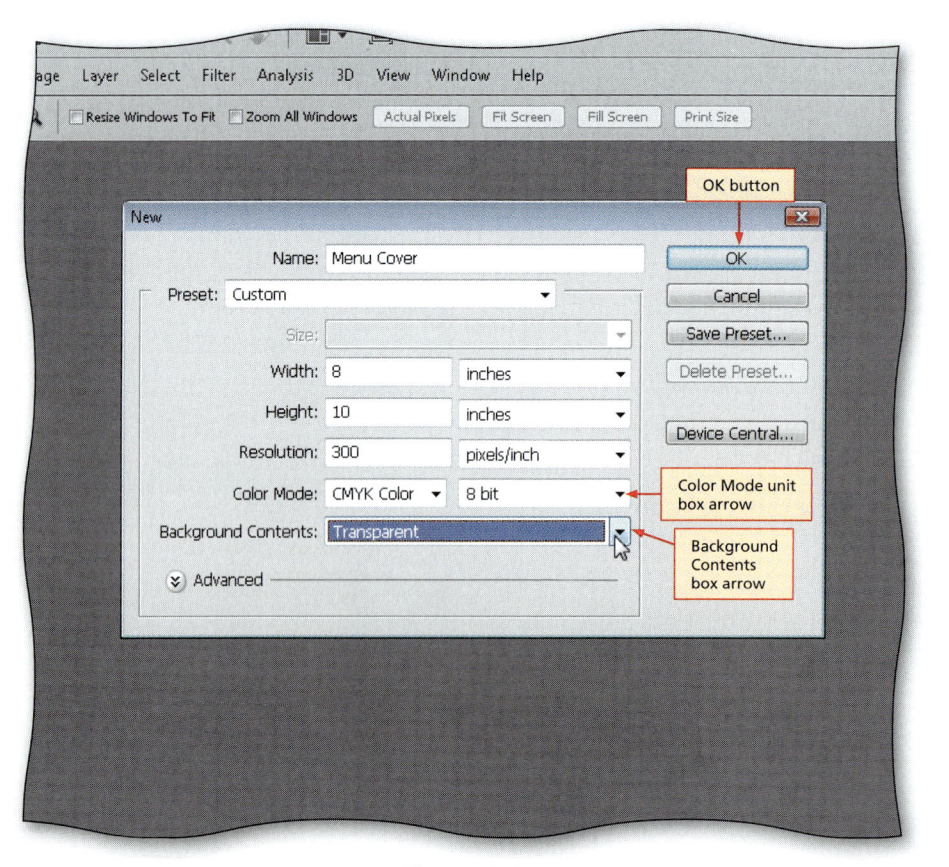

Figure 4–5

5
- Click the OK button to close the dialog box.

- On the document window status bar, double-click the magnification box, type `16.67` if necessary, and then press the ENTER key.

- If the rulers do not appear in the document window, press CTRL+R (Figure 4–6).

Figure 4–6

> **Other Ways**
> 1. Press CTRL+N, set attributes

To Save a Photo

Even though the file has a name in the document window tab, it is not saved on a storage device. The next steps save the file with the name Menu Cover.

1. With your USB flash drive connected to one of the computer's USB ports, click File on the menu bar to display the File menu and then click Save As to display the Save As dialog box.

2. In the file name text box, type `Menu Cover`, if necessary, to rename the file. Do not press the ENTER key after typing the file name.

3. Click the Save in box arrow and then click UDISK 2.0 (F:), or the location associated with your USB flash drive, in the list. If you want to create a folder for the photos in Chapter 4, click the Create New Folder button. Then when the new folder is displayed, type a chapter name, such as Chapter04, and press the ENTER key.

4. Click the Format button to display the list of available file formats and then click Photoshop (*.PSD, *.PDD) in the list, if necessary.

5. Click the Save button in the Save As dialog box to save the file. If Photoshop displays a dialog box, click the OK button.

The Color Panel

Photoshop has many different ways to select or specify colors for use in the document window. You specify colors when you use paint, gradient, or fill tools. Previously in this chapter you used the Color picker dialog box to choose colors. Some other ways include using the Color panel, the Swatches panel, the Eyedropper tool, the Color Sampler tool, and the Info panel.

A convenient way to select and edit colors is to use the Color panel (Figure 4–7), which displays numeric color values for the current foreground and background colors. Using the sliders in the Color panel, you can edit the foreground and background colors using different color modes. Photoshop uses the **foreground color** to paint and fill selections and create text. The **background color** commonly is used with fills and masks. Some special effects filters also use the foreground and background colors. At the bottom of the panel, you can choose a color from the entire color spectrum, by clicking in the Color bar. The Color panel menu allows you to change the color mode, change the displayed sliders, copy the color, or close the panel.

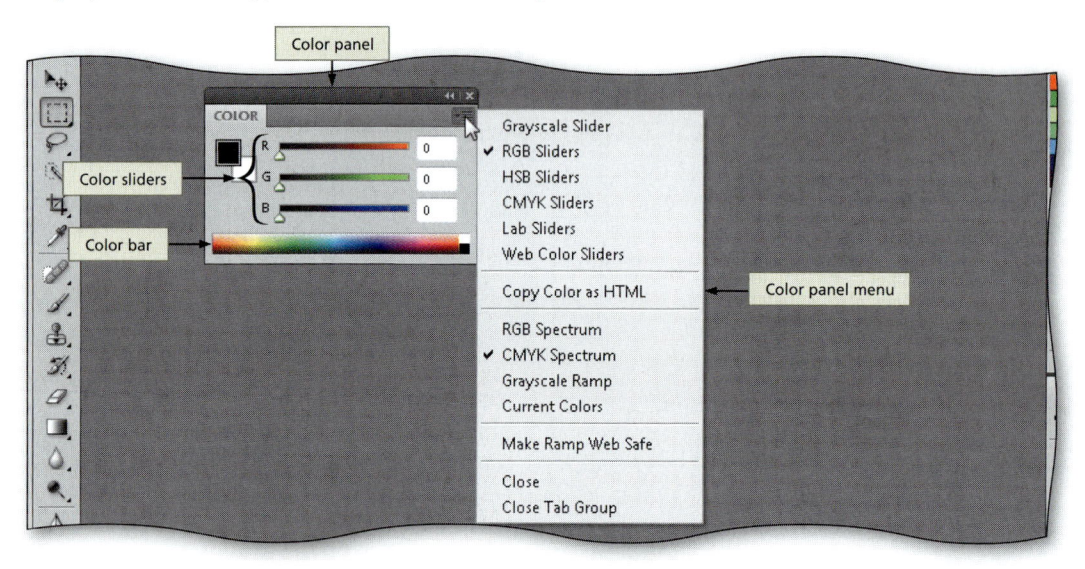

Figure 4–7

To Change the Color Panel

The following steps change the Color panel to reflect CMYK colors in the sliders and on the color bar.

1
- Click the Color panel menu button to display its menu (Figure 4–8).

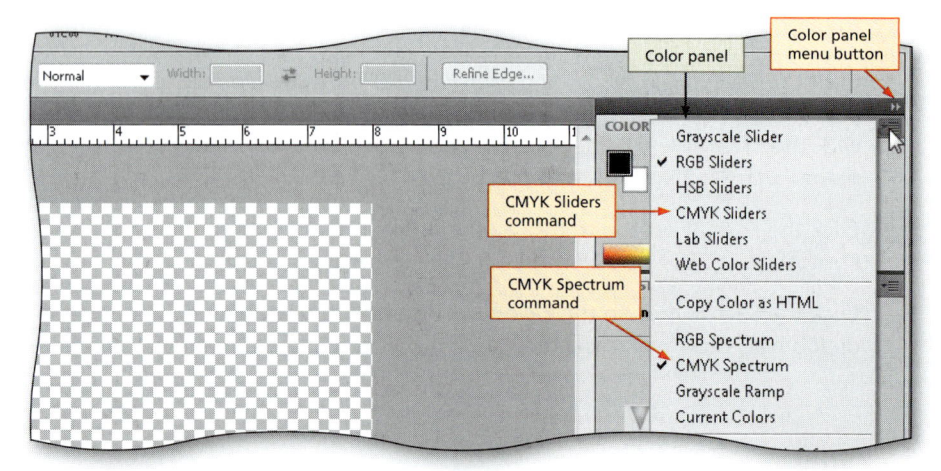

Figure 4–8

2
- Click CMYK Sliders to change the sliders in the Color panel.
- Click the menu button again, and then click CMYK Spectrum to change the color bar, if necessary (Figure 4–9).

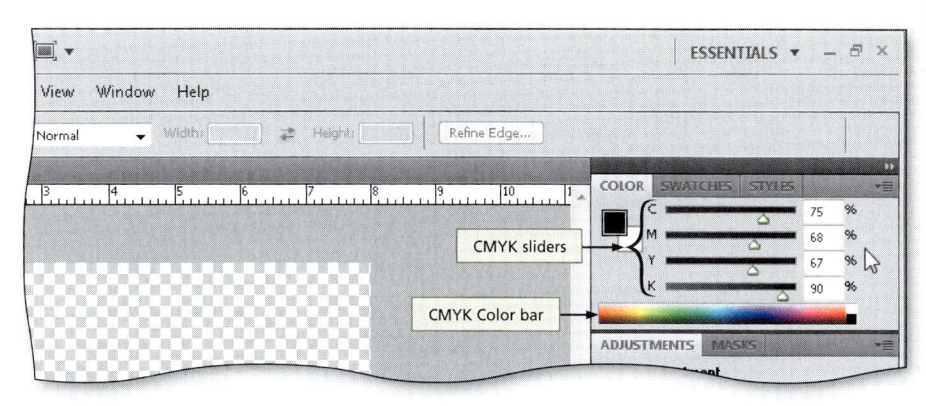

Figure 4–9

> **Plan Ahead**
>
> **Plan your layout and gather necessary photos.**
> Recall that a storyboard is a preliminary layout sketch to help plan graphics placement, size, perspective, and spacing. Using a storyboard allows you to create an original graphic from the back to the front.
>
> - As you start on the graphic, fill the background with color, unless the graphic will become part of another publication.
> - For busy foregrounds, keep the background simple, with perhaps one color. If text will be used, keep in mind that anything in the darker half of the color spectrum will need light color text and vice versa.
> - Use black backgrounds sparingly – they are most effective for starkness and special effects.
> - For extra depth or perspective, consider using a gradient. A gradient can create depth, add visual interest, or highlight a portion of an image. Use colors that will match colors in your graphic or those desired by the customer. The direction of the gradient should either lead viewers toward a specific focal point or entice them to turn the page.

Gradients

A **gradient**, or **gradient fill**, is a graphic effect consisting of a smooth blend, change, or transition from one color to another. While there is potential for overuse with gradients, subtle gradients add depth and texture to a graphic or Web page. Shade-to-shade gradients sometimes seem elegant and emotive. They can emulate how light strikes real-world surfaces. Vertical gradients help the eyes to move further down the page. Graphic artists usually save bright, striped gradients for smaller portions of a page such as a heading, or when they intentionally want to overwhelm the viewer.

Typically used as a graduated blend between two colors, the direction of a gradient transition can be top to bottom, bottom to top, side to side, or a variety of other shapes and diagonals. Gradients can be applied to the entire image or a selected portion of an image. Photoshop offers many preset gradient fills, or you can create your own. Gradients work best with RGB or CMYK colors. The Gradient tool cannot be used with the Bitmap or Index color modes.

> **BTW**
> **Auto Color and Color Balance**
> The Auto Color command adjusts the contrast and color of an image or layer by neutralizing the midtones and clipping the black and white pixels. The Color Balance command displays a dialog box where you can set specific color levels and balance tones.

> **BTW**
> **Match Color**
> The Match Color command matches colors between multiple images, layers, or selections, allowing you to change the luminance, change the color range, or neutralize a colorcast. The Match Color command works only in RGB mode.

To create a gradient, you select an area of an image and then click the Gradient Tool (G) button on the Tools panel. If you right-click the Gradient Tool (G) button, its context menu includes the Gradient tool and the Paint Bucket tool.

The Gradient options bar (Figure 4–10) allows you to set the style, blending mode, and other attributes for the gradient fill. If you do not select a portion of the image, the gradient will be applied to the entire image.

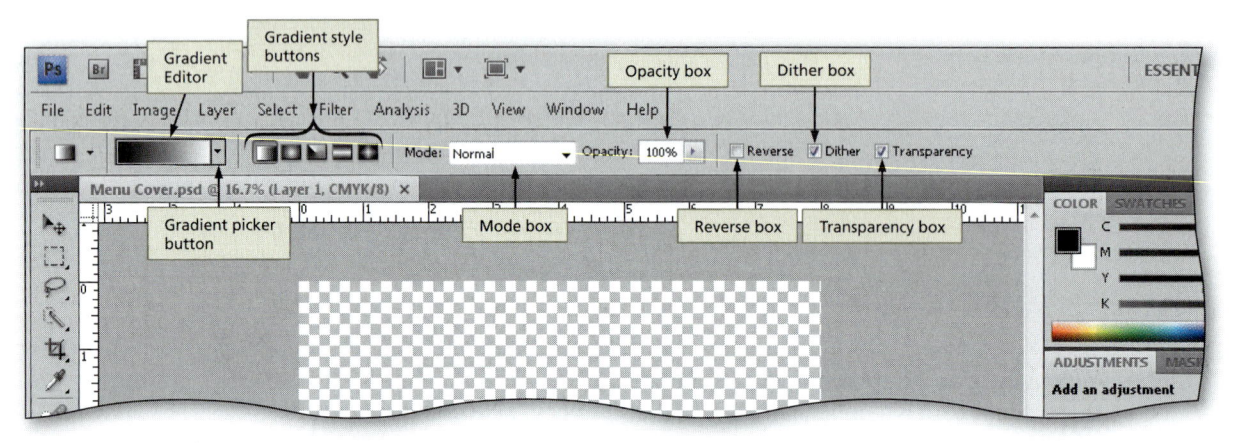

Figure 4–10

BTW

Replace Color
The Replace Color command displays a dialog box to change colors by setting the hue, saturation, and lightness of the selected areas. It also allows you to remove fuzziness.

You can click the Gradient Editor box to display the Gradient Editor dialog box, or you can choose a preset gradient by clicking the Gradient picker button. The Gradient Editor dialog box, also called the **Gradient Editor**, allows you to define a new gradient by modifying a copy of an existing gradient or preset, or by choosing colors to create a new blend.

To the right of the Gradient picker button are the gradient styles or shades. A **gradient style** is the way the colors are arranged with regard to the reflection of light in the gradient. Table 4–1 displays the five gradient styles.

BTW

Removing Color Casts
A **colorcast** is a shade in a photo that should not exist. For example, green grass should not have a red colorcast. To remove a colorcast, use the Match Color dialog box. Click the Neutralize check box and then drag the sliders until the preview displays no colorcast.

Table 4–1 Gradient Styles		
Gradient	**Style**	**Button**
Linear	shades from the starting point to the ending point in a straight line	
Radial	shades from the starting point to the ending point in a circular pattern	
Angle	shades in a counterclockwise sweep around the starting point	
Reflected	shades using symmetric linear gradients on either side of the starting point	
Diamond	shades from the starting point outward in a diamond pattern — the ending point defines one corner of the diamond	

On the right side of the Gradient options bar, Photoshop includes an Opacity box to set the percentage of opacity, a Reverse check box to reverse the order of colors in the gradient fill, a Dither check box to create a smoother blend with less banding, and a Transparency check box to create a transparency mask for the gradient fill.

To Create a Gradient

To create a gradient in the Menu Cover image, you will select the Gradient tool and then access the Gradient Editor from the options bar.

1

- Click the Gradient Tool (G) button on the Tools panel to display the Gradient tool options bar.

- On the Gradient options bar, click the Reflected Gradient button to select the gradient style (Figure 4–11).

Q&A My Tools panel displays a picture of a paint bucket. How do I access the Gradient tool?

You can either right-click the Paint Bucket Tool (G) button and choose Gradient Tool from the context menu, or press SHIFT+G to access the Gradient tool.

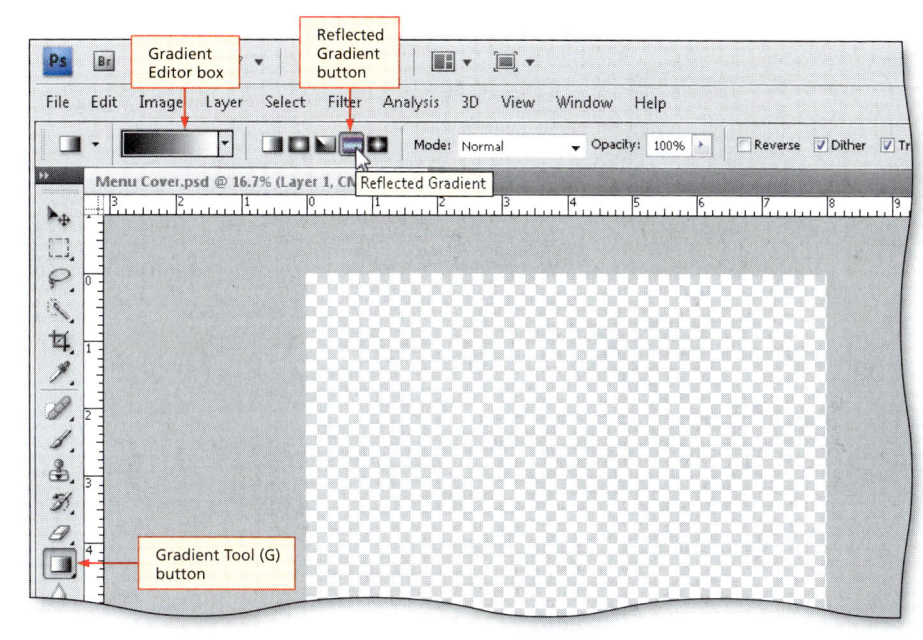

Figure 4–11

2

- Click the Gradient Editor box to display the Gradient Editor dialog box (Figure 4–12).

Experiment

- Click each of the various presets in the Gradient Editor dialog box and watch how the color settings vary.

Other Ways

1. Press SHIFT+G, click Gradient Editor box, choose settings

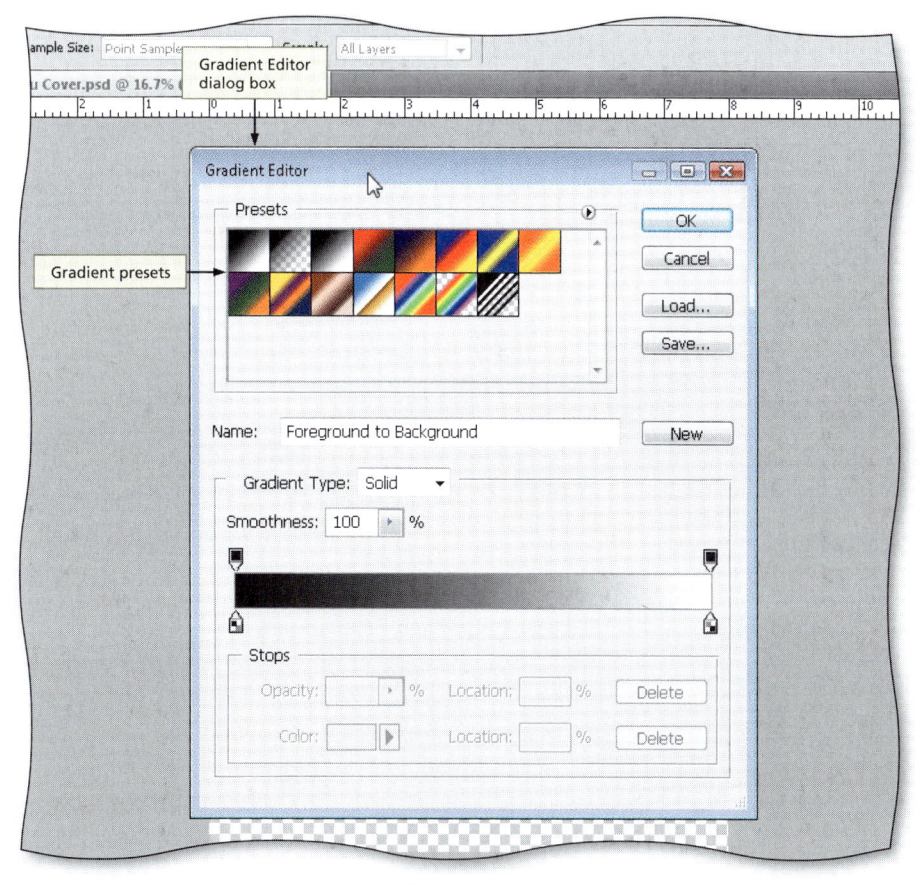

Figure 4–12

Gradient Presets

In the Gradient Editor dialog box, the Presets area contains a menu button. When clicked, the menu button displays choices for thumbnail size and other gradient presets (Figure 4–13). Photoshop has eight sets of gradients that can be used to create a wide variety of special fill effects. When you choose to use one of the additional sets, Photoshop will ask if you want to replace or append the new gradient set. Clicking the Reset Gradients command changes the presets back to the default list.

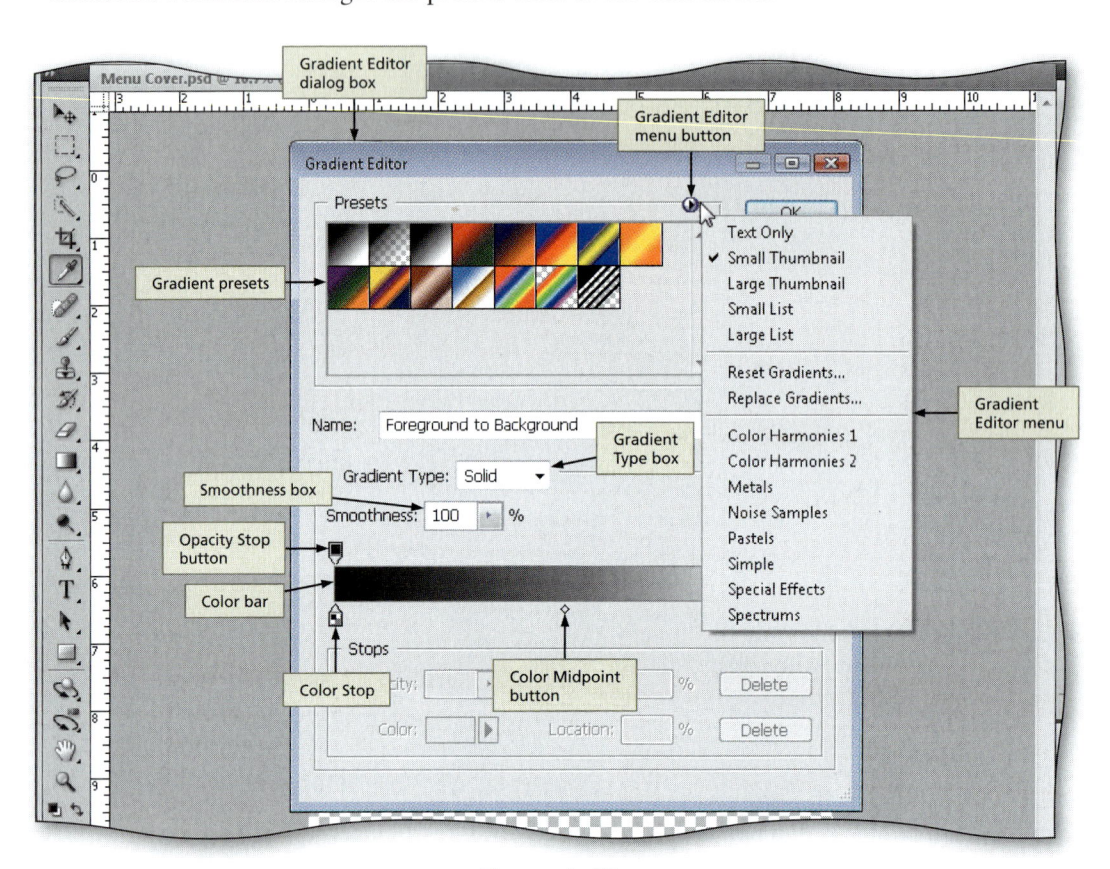

Figure 4–13

Opacity Stops
Clicking an Opacity Stop button allows you to enter a percentage of opacity and a location within the color bar for the opacity to begin. A layer with 1% opacity appears nearly transparent, whereas one with 100% opacity appears completely opaque.

If the gradient you create is one that you plan to use several times, you can name it in the Name box and then click the Save button to save it as a gradient file within Photoshop. In subsequent sessions, you then can load the saved gradient to use it again.

In addition to the **solid gradient** that creates a solid color spectrum transition through the gradient, you alternatively can choose the noise gradient. A **noise gradient** is a gradient that contains randomly distributed color specks within the range of colors that you specify.

The **smoothness** setting is a percentage determining the smoothness of the transition between color bands. One hundred percent indicates an equally weighted transition in color pixels. Using lower transition values, the gradient colors will appear more pixilated, with abrupt transitions in the color bands. This effect is more evident when creating gradients with nonadjacent colors in the color spectrum. When working with a noise gradient, the Smoothness box becomes a Roughness box indicating how vividly the colors transition between one another.

The color bar in the Gradient Editor dialog box has stop buttons for opacity above the bar and stop buttons for color below it. Once the colors are selected, a small diamond is displayed below the color bar. The diamond is called the Color Midpoint button. It indicates the place in the gradient where it displays an even mix of the starting and ending colors. You can drag the diamond to adjust the midpoint location.

By default, Photoshop displays two Color Stop buttons to produce a gradient from one color to a second color, but additional Color Stop buttons can be added by clicking just below the color bar. Color Stop buttons can be dragged to force the transition to begin at an earlier or later point in the resulting gradient. To delete a Color Stop, click the Color Stop button and then click the Delete button. To edit the color, double-click the Color Stop button. By placing Color Stop buttons very close together in the Gradient Editor, you can reduce the gradient effect and produce strong, distinct bands of color for exciting and creative special effects.

To Select a Gradient Preset

The following steps select a two color gradient for the background using contrasting colors. In addition, you will verify the settings for 100 percent smoothness and a solid gradient fill.

1
- In the Gradient Editor dialog box, click the Blue, Yellow, Blue preset to select it.

- If necessary, click the Gradient Type box arrow and then click Solid in the list to create a solid gradient.

- If necessary, type 100 in the Smoothness box (Figure 4–14).

Q&A I do not have the same presets. What should I do?

Click the triangle menu button in the upper-right corner of the Presets area and then click Reset Gradients. When Photoshop displays a dialog box, click the OK button.

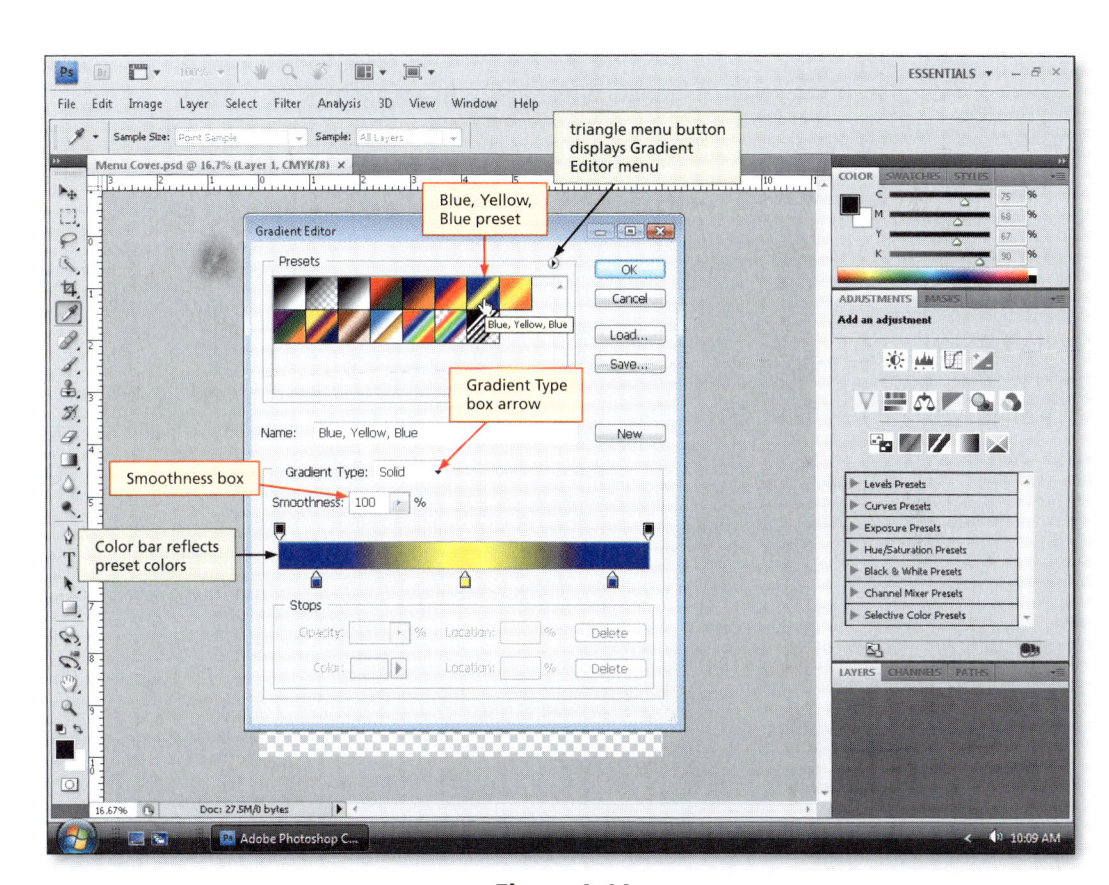

Figure 4–14

The Select Stop Color Dialog Box

The next step is to edit the gradient colors using the Select stop color dialog box (shown in Figure 4–15). This type of dialog box, allows you to choose a color from the color field or define the color numerically. In many of the color dialog boxes, you can set the foreground color, background color, text color, gradient colors, and others. In Photoshop, the Select stop color dialog box is used with various tools to set target colors such as gradients, filters, fill layers, certain layer styles, and shape layers. When you click the color field, the Select stop color dialog box displays the numeric values for HSB, RGB, LAB, CMYK, and hexadecimal color numbers. You also can enter values for the color modes adjusting the color field automatically. A color slider bar allows you to change the color field.

To Select a Stop Color

The following steps access the Select stop color dialog box and change the middle color of the gradient by entering specific values for cyan, magenta, yellow, and black (CMYK).

1
- In the Gradient Editor dialog box, double-click the middle Color Stop button to display the Select stop color dialog box (Figure 4–15).

Q&A When do you use the Only Web Colors check box?

Select the check box when you want to display only Web-safe colors — the 216 colors that appear solid, non-dithered, and consistently on any computer monitor. If an exclamation point appears near the OK button, it means that the chosen color is out of gamut.

Experiment
- Drag the color slider bar and watch the color field change.

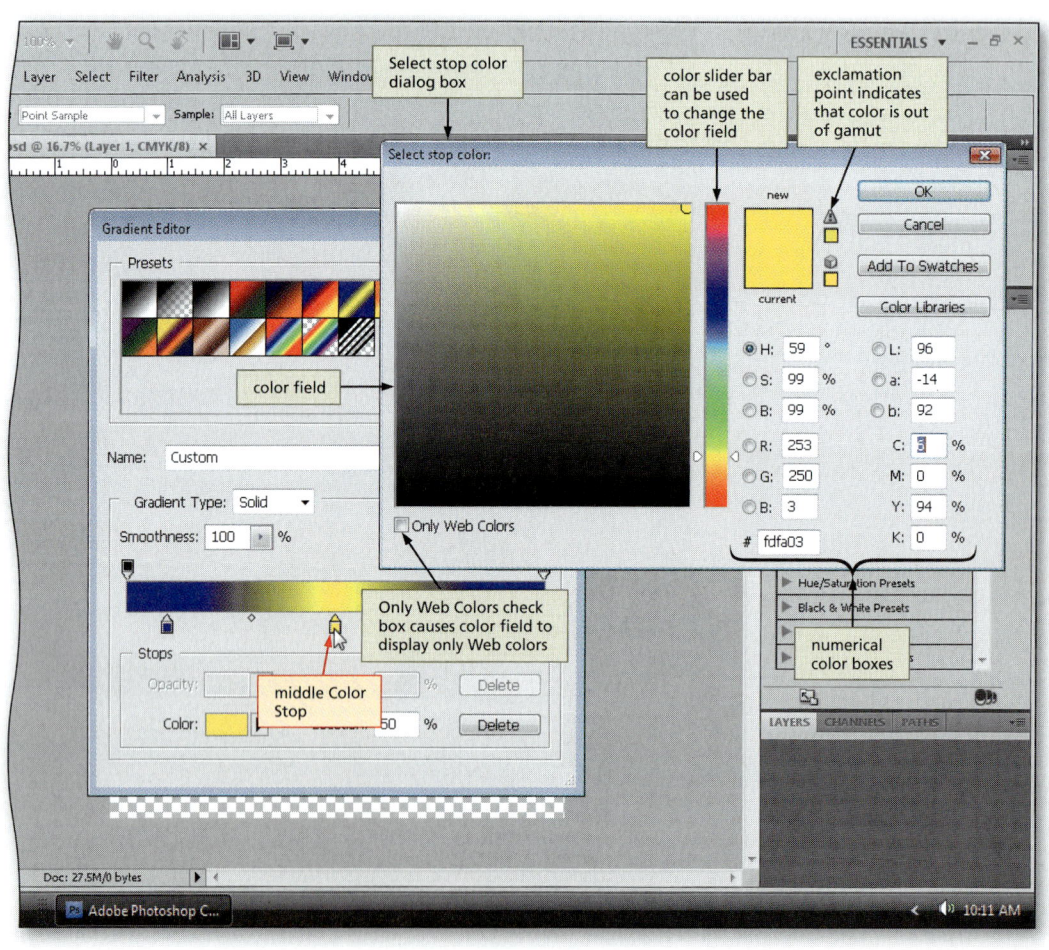

Figure 4–15

Gradients **PS 257**

2
- To create a paler yellow, enter 3 in the C box, 0 in the M box, 48 in the Y box, and 0 in the B box (Figure 4–16).

Q&A Can I also click the color I want?

Yes, you can click a color in the Color box, click an option button to display a different palette, or drag the scrubby slider labels to select a color.

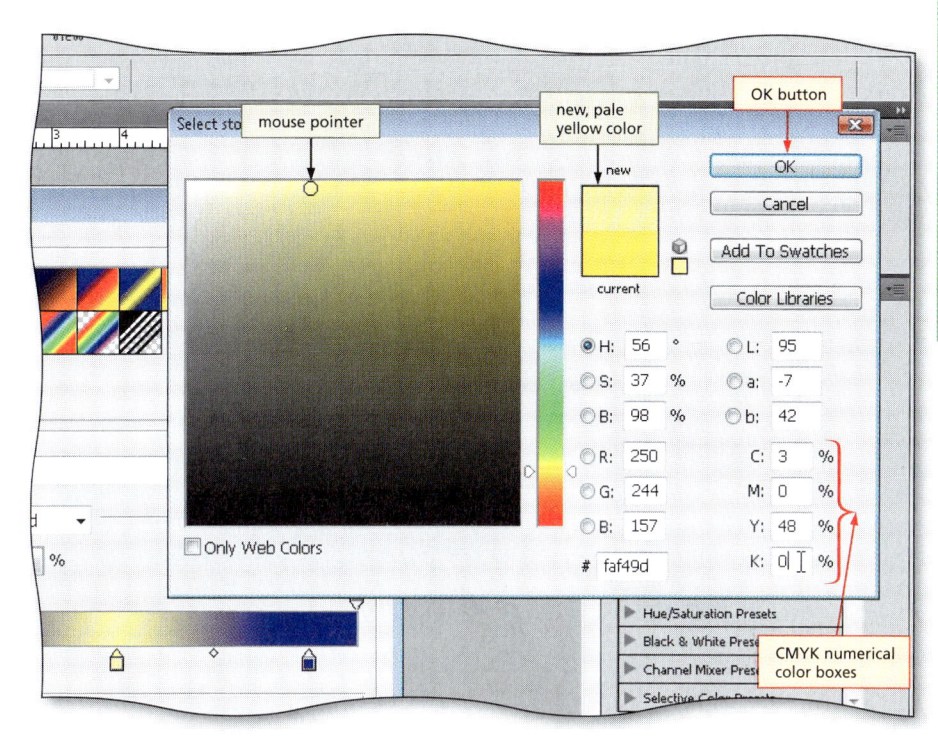

Figure 4–16

3
- Click the OK button to close the Select stop color dialog box (Figure 4–17).

Q&A What do the small diamonds under the color bar do?

The diamonds represent the color midpoint. They can be dragged to force the transition between colors to happen at a different place.

4
- Click the OK button to close the Gradient Editor dialog box.

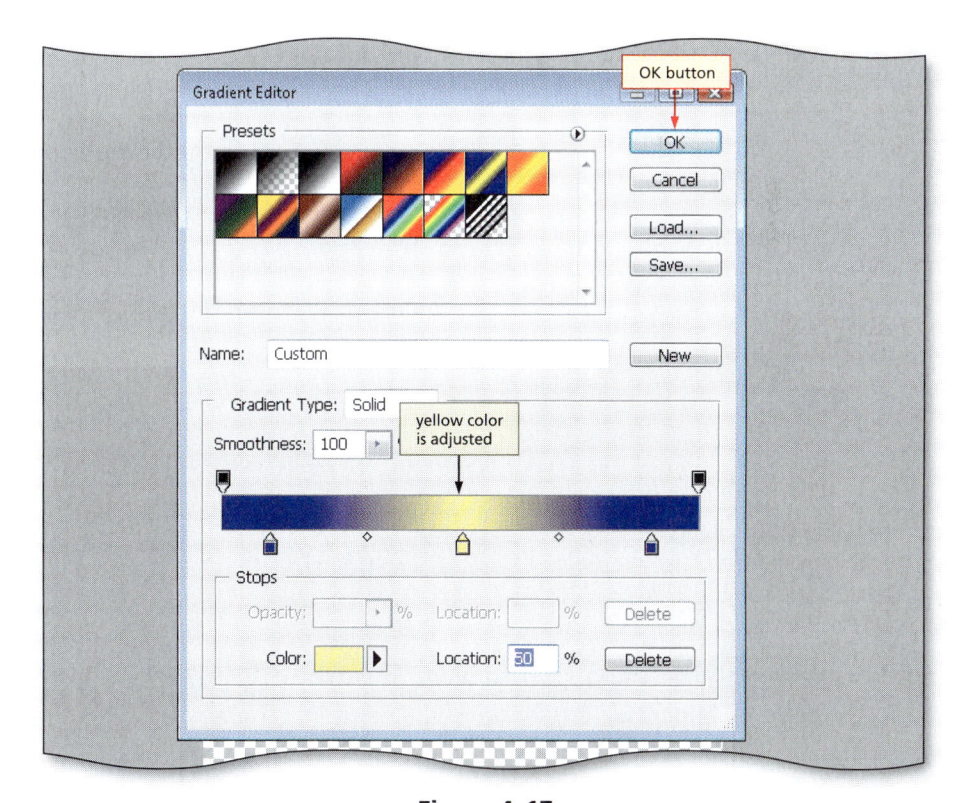

Figure 4–17

Other Ways

1. In Gradient Editor dialog box, click Color box, select color, click OK

To Draw the Gradient

The final step in creating a gradient background for the menu cover is to apply the gradient. To apply the gradient, you drag in the image or selected area at the point where you want the base color to begin. For linear and radial gradients, you drag in the direction of the desired transition. The rate of transition is dependent on the settings in the Gradient Editor dialog box with its color stops and midpoint.

1
- In the document window, SHIFT+drag from the top edge of the canvas to the bottom edge (Figure 4–18).

Q&A Do I have to drag in the center?

No. This linear gradient will be the same from left to right. Pressing and holding the SHIFT key keeps the line straight.

Experiment
- Click another style button on the Gradient options bar. Drag in the document window to display a different style gradient. Press CTRL+Z to return to the gradient shown in Figure 4–18.

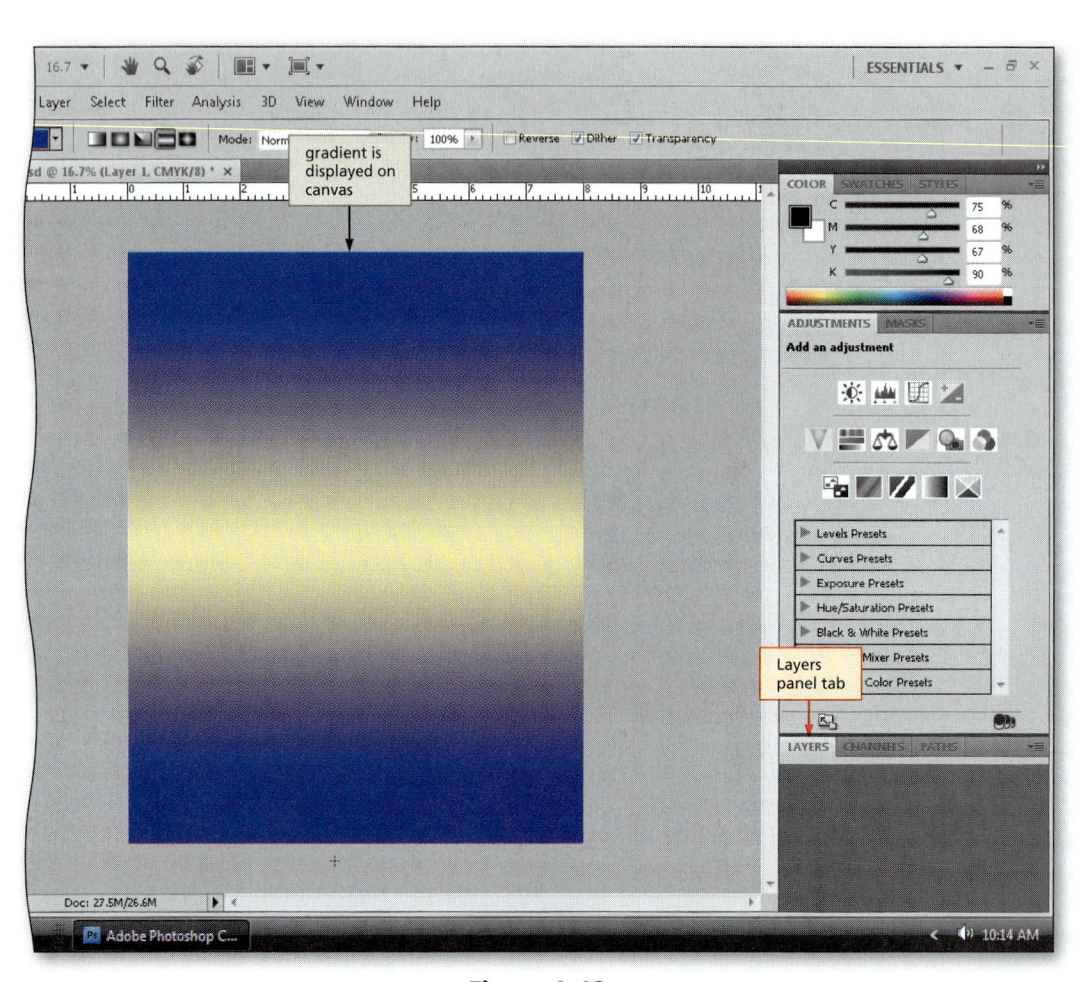

Figure 4–18

BTW

Gradient Directions
You can create a gradient at any straight line, angle, or position. If you start and end in the extreme corners of the frame, the grade is across the entire area. To leave the corners solid and start the grade more toward the center, drag and end closer to the middle of the area. To constrain the line angle to a multiple of 45°, hold down the SHIFT key as you drag.

To Set Layer Properties

The following steps name the layer and set its identification color.

1 Double-click the Layers panel tab to display the Layers panel, if necessary.

2 Double-click the name of the layer, Layer 1, in the Layers panel. Type gradient background and then press the ENTER key to replace the name.

3 Right-click the visibility icon, and then click Blue in the list to change the layer's identification color (Figure 4–19).

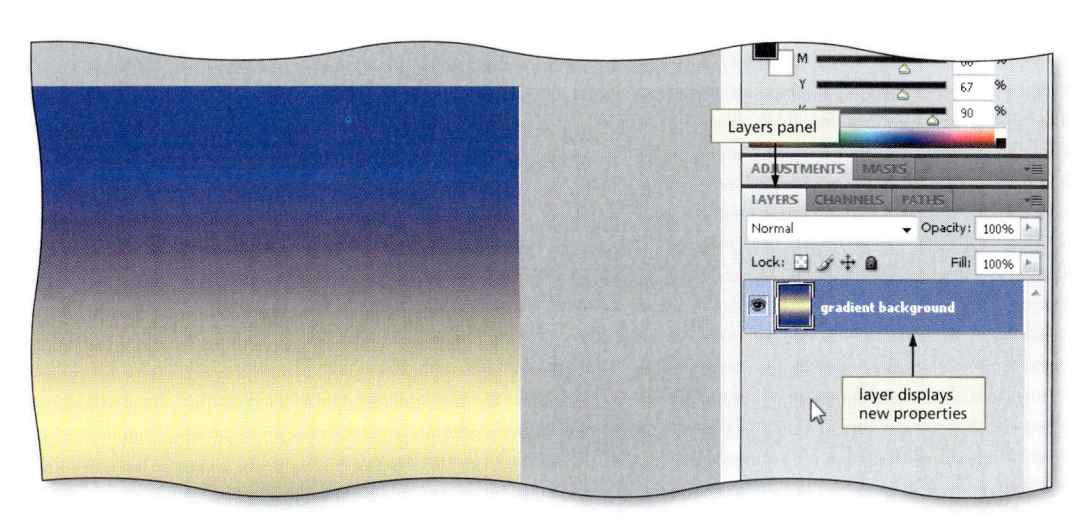

Figure 4-19

To Save the File

Because you have created a gradient and made changes to the image, it is a good idea to save the file again.

1. Press CTRL+S to save the Menu Cover file with the same name.

Sampling Colors

The Eyedropper tool samples an existing color in a graphic or panel to assign a new foreground or background color. When you click a color using the Eyedropper tool, Photoshop sets a new foreground color in the Tools panel and Color Panel. When you ALT+click a color, Photoshop sets a new background color.

The Eyedropper options bar (Figure 4-20) allows you to change the sample size and sample from the active image or from anywhere else in the Photoshop window. The Sample Size box list contains several choices. The default size, Point Sample, samples the precise color of the pixel you click. The other sample sizes, such as 3 by 3 Average and 5 by 5 Average, sample the color of the pixel where you click along with the surrounding pixels, and then calculate an average color value of the area.

BTW

Color Sampler Tool
If you right-click the Eyedropper Tool (I) button on the Tools panel, you can choose the Color Sampler tool from the context menu. Clicking with the Color Sampler tool will display the color mode values in the Info panel. You can click to select up to four color samples per image.

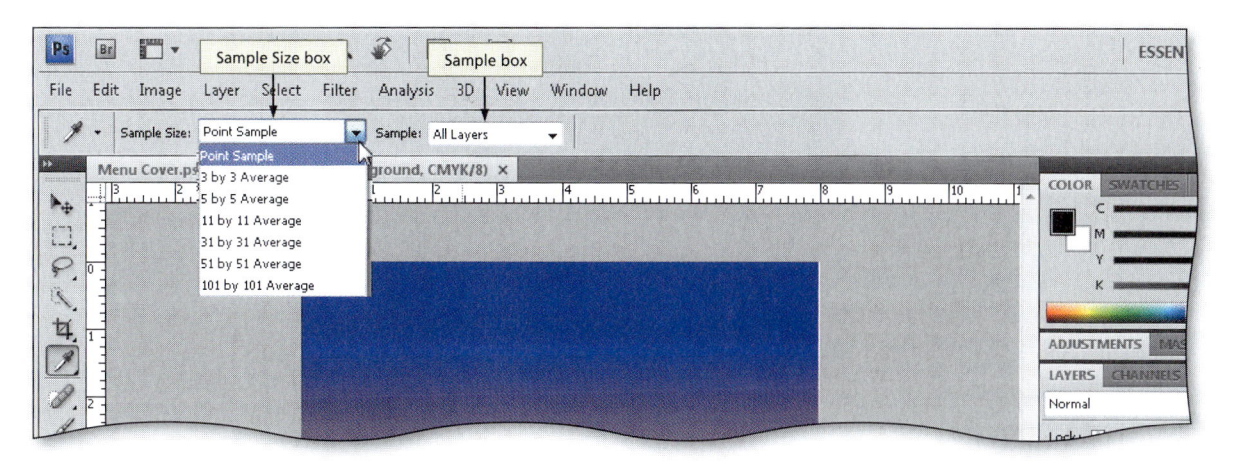

Figure 4-20

PS 260   Photoshop Chapter 4   Drawing and Painting with Color

Sampling a color guarantees that you will match the color without having to reenter color values on the Colors Panel.

To Use the Eyedropper Tool

The following steps select the Eyedropper tool and then sample a yellow color from the middle of the gradient to use as the foreground color for future editing. Using a color from the gradient maintains color consistency in all parts of the menu cover.

1
- On the Tools panel, right-click the Eyedropper Tool (I) button to display its context menu (Figure 4–21).

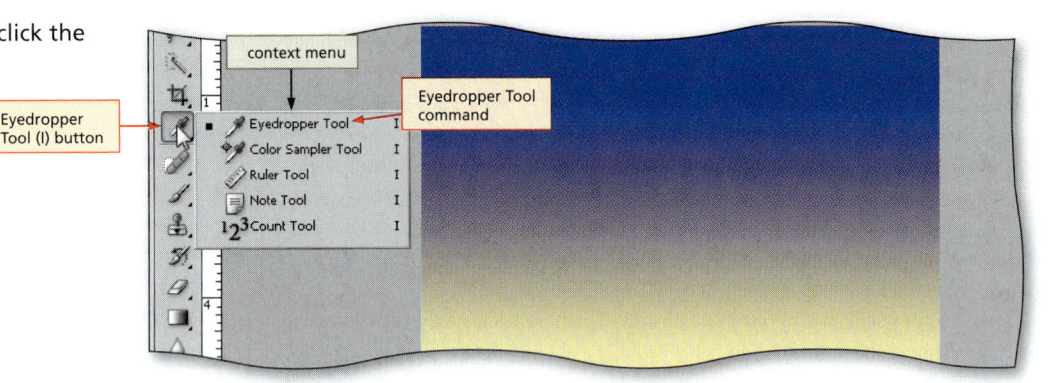

Figure 4–21

2
- Click Eyedropper Tool to select it.
- Move the mouse pointer into the document window and then click in the middle of the yellow color to select it as the foreground color (Figure 4–22).

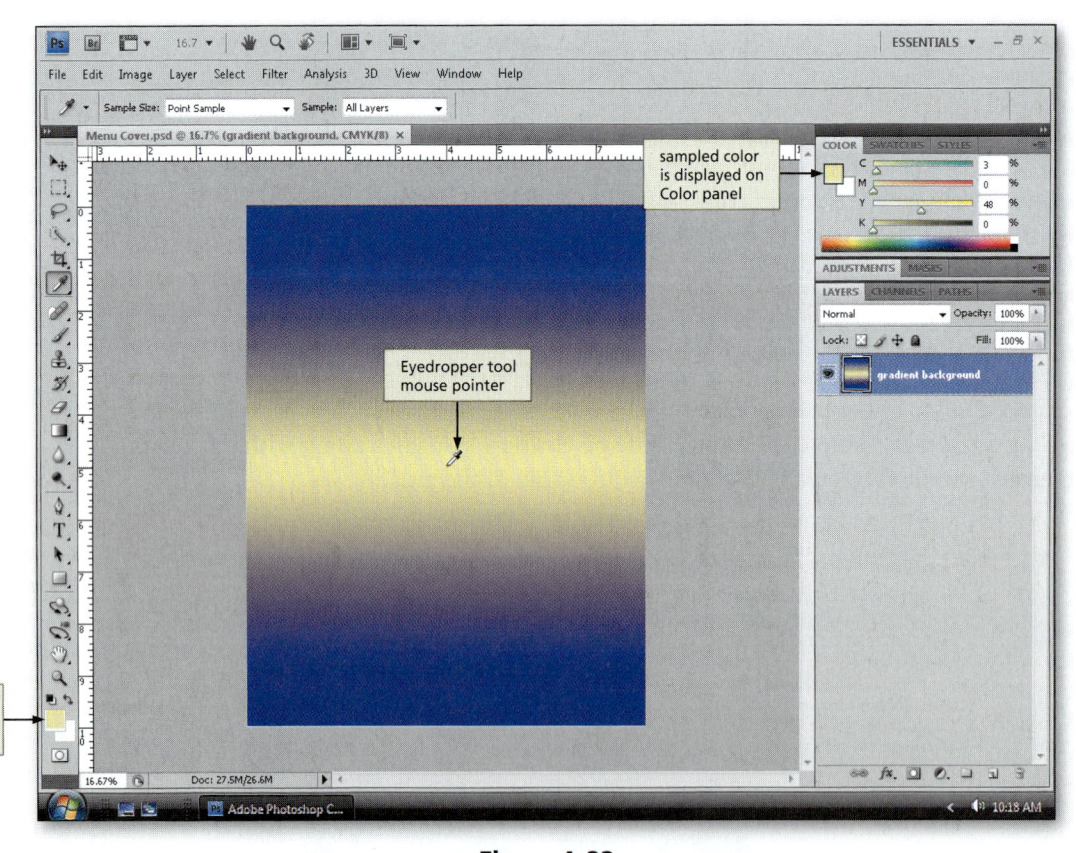

Figure 4–22

Other Ways
1. Press I, click color

> **Apply effective text styles and strokes.**
> A **font** or **typeface** defines the appearance and shape of the letters, numbers, and special characters used in text. The fonts you use create the look, feel, and style of your graphic publications.
>
> - For a more historical, retro, formal, or literary look and feel, use a serif font. **Serif** means flourish, and indicates that the letters will contain small intersecting lines, sometimes called appendages, at the end of characters.
> - For a more modern feel, use **sans-serif**, which means without flourish, and displays in block-like letters without appendages.
> - Use strokes or outlines around the lettering when the text has high priority in the graphic, and you want a distinctive look. White strokes make dark text stand out; conversely, black strokes around light-colored text help delineate the text and make it stand out.

Plan Ahead

Inserting Text

The next steps use a type tool to create text in the upper and lower parts of the menu cover. On the Tools panel, the default type tool is the Horizontal Type tool. When you right-click the tool button, Photoshop displays the Vertical Type tool, the Horizontal Type Mask tool, and the Vertical Type Mask tool on the context menu. When you use the Horizontal or Vertical Type tools, Photoshop automatically creates a new layer in the Layers panel. The mask tools create a selection in the shape of the text on the current layer rather than creating a new one.

The options bar for the type tools (Figure 4–23) includes boxes and buttons typical of those found in a word processing toolbar, including font family, font style, font size, and justification. An additional box is used to control the anti-aliasing. A Create warped text button allows you to create text in specialized formations, similar to the WordArt tool in Microsoft Word. On the right side of the options bar are buttons to cancel and commit editing changes. In a future chapter, you will learn about the Character and Paragraph panels that provide additional tools for manipulating text.

BTW

Adjusting Text
To adjust the size of the text bounding box, drag the sizing handles. Later, if you need to edit the text, you select the layer and select the type tool. The mouse pointer then becomes a cursor when positioned over the text.

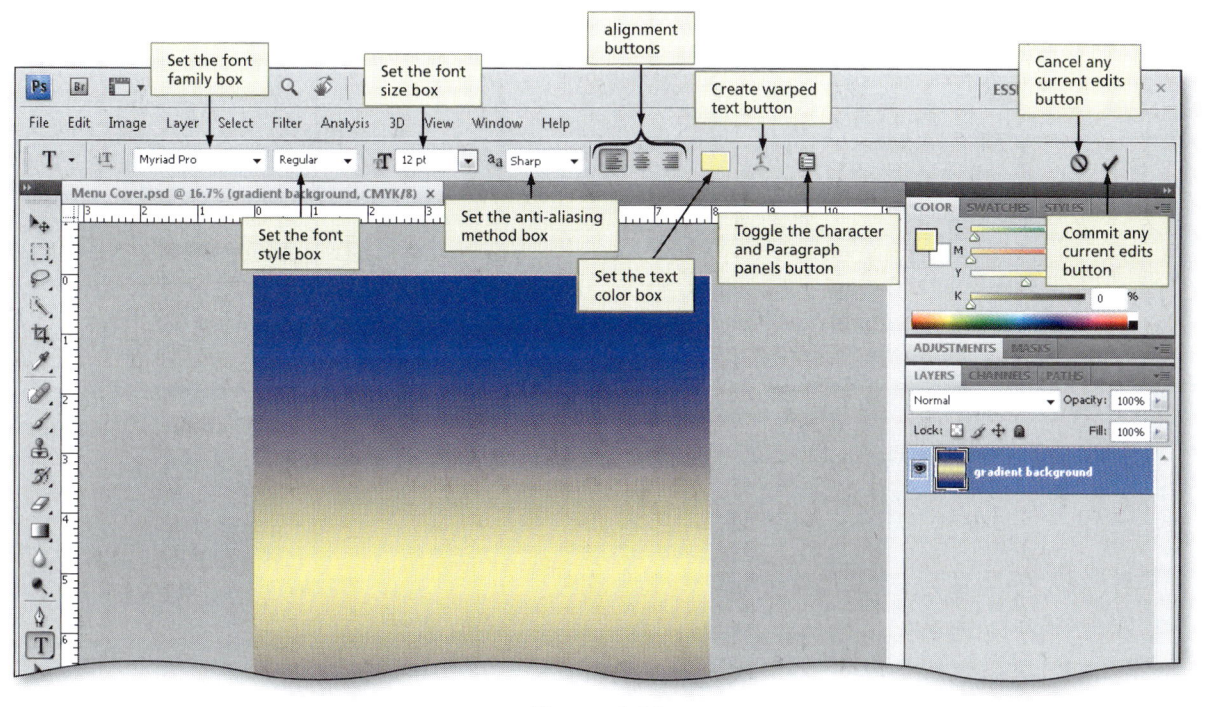

Figure 4–23

PS 262 Photoshop Chapter 4 Drawing and Painting with Color

To Select the Horizontal Type Tool

The following steps select the Horizontal Type tool on the Tools panel.

1
- Right-click the current type tool on the options bar to display the context menu (Figure 4–24).

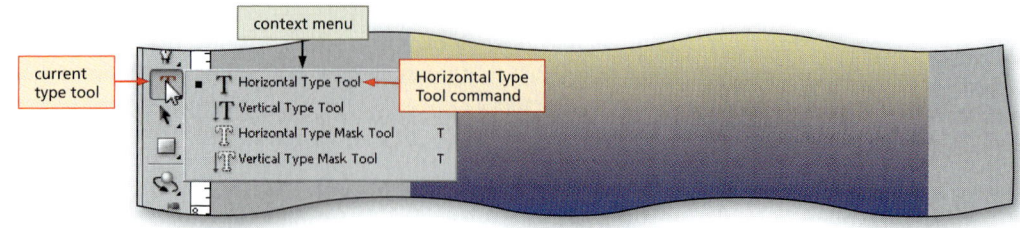

2
- Click Horizontal Type Tool to select it in the list.

Figure 4–24

Other Ways
1. Press T

To Set Font Options

The following steps select font settings on the options bar. You will use center alignment and the same font for both text areas on the menu cover. The upper text will use a font size of 60.

1
- On the options bar, click the Set the font family box arrow to display the list of font families (Figure 4–25).

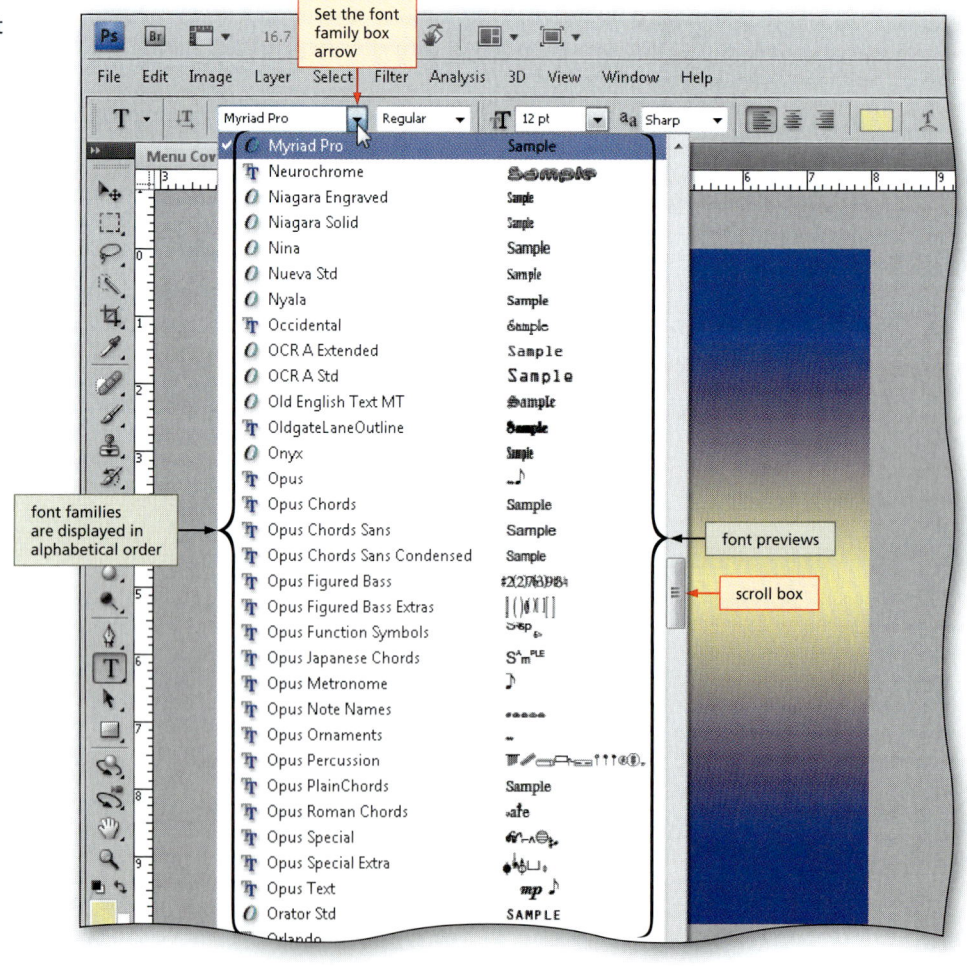

Figure 4–25

Inserting Text **PS 263**

2
- Scroll as necessary, and then click High Tower Text or a similar font in the list.
- Click the Set the font size box arrow to display the list of font sizes (Figure 4–26).

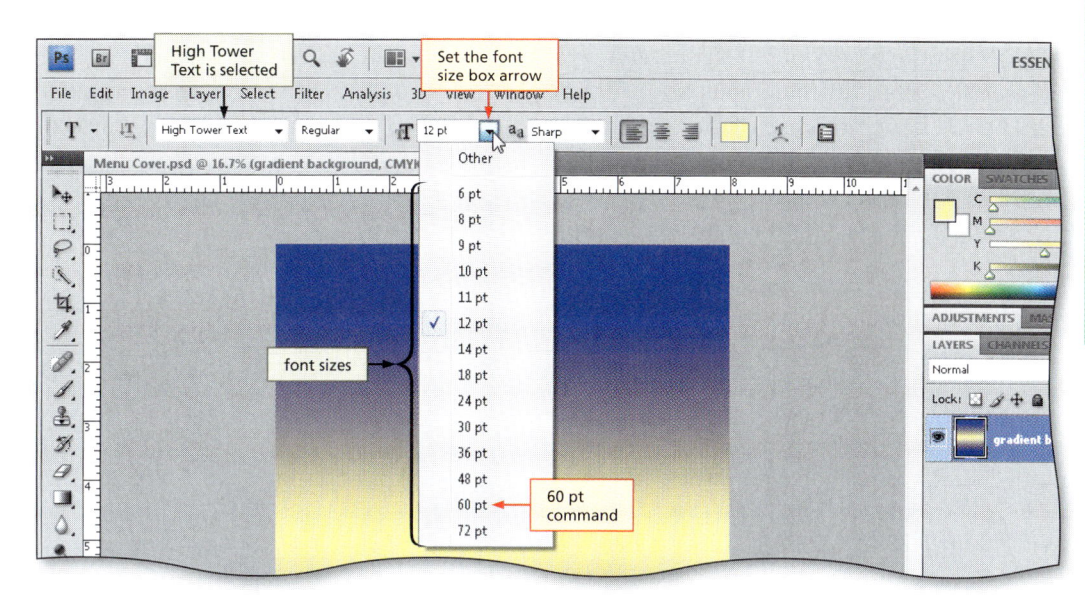

Figure 4–26

3
- Click 60 pt to choose a font size of 60.
- Click the Set the anti-aliasing method box arrow to display the various anti-aliasing methods (Figure 4–27).

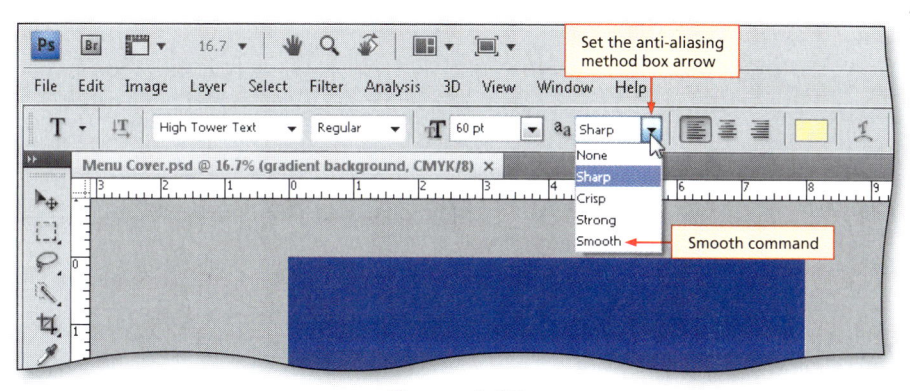

Figure 4–27

4
- Click Smooth to set the anti-aliasing method.
- Click the Center text button to specify that the text will be centered (Figure 4–28).

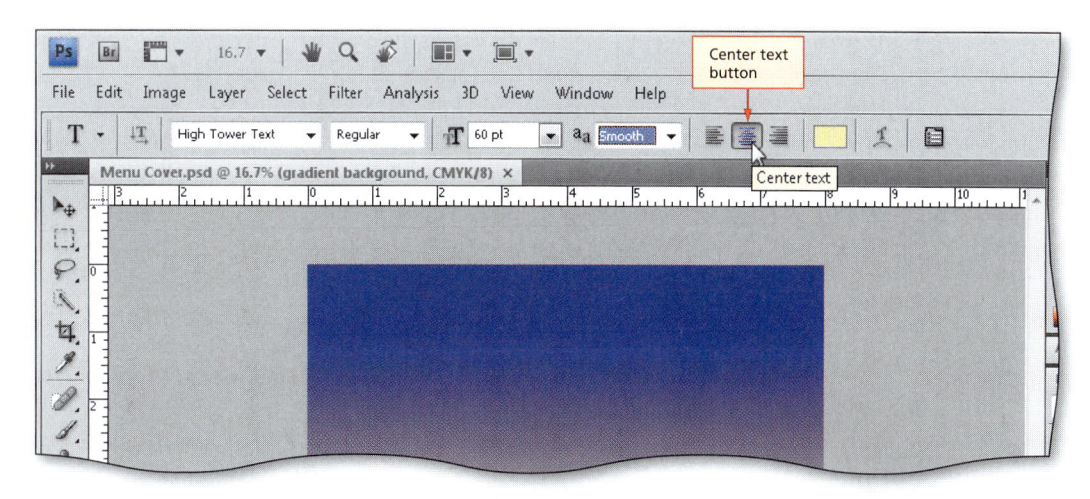

Figure 4–28

To Insert Text

With the type tool selected, you drag a bounding box in the document window to insert text. The mouse pointer changes to a small, open book outline. After typing the text, the Commit any current edits button completes the entry. Then, if the size of the bounding box needs to be adjusted, you can drag the sizing handles. Later, if you need to edit the text, you select the layer and select the type tool. The mouse pointer then becomes a cursor when positioned over the text.

The following steps enter the menu title.

1

- With the Horizontal Type tool still selected, drag a bounding box beginning approximately one inch from the upper-left corner of the layout. Continue dragging until the box is approximately six inches wide and two inches tall, as shown in Figure 4–29.

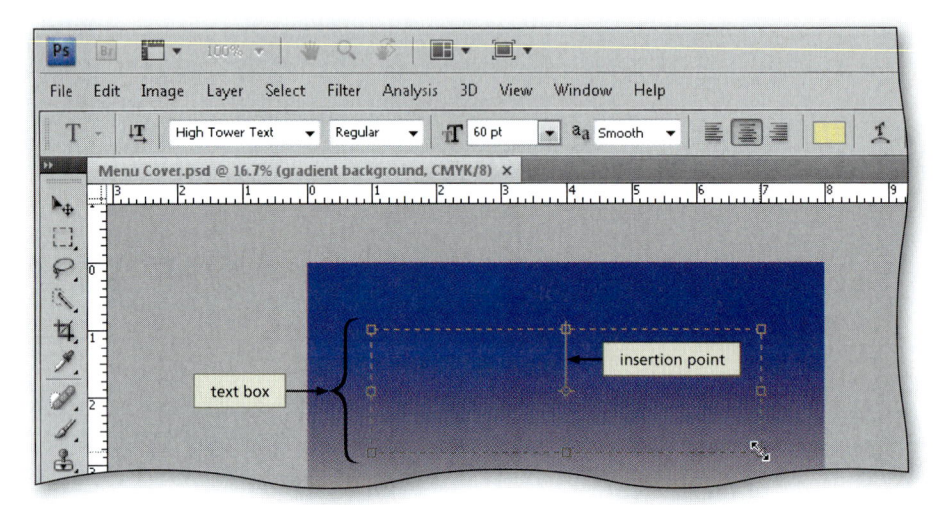

Figure 4–29

2

- Type Pizza Theater and then press the ENTER key.

- Type Menu to complete the text (Figure 4–30).

Q&A Can I make changes and corrections to the text?

Yes, you can click anywhere in the text box, use the ARROW keys, the BACKSPACE key, and the DELETE key just as you do in word processing.

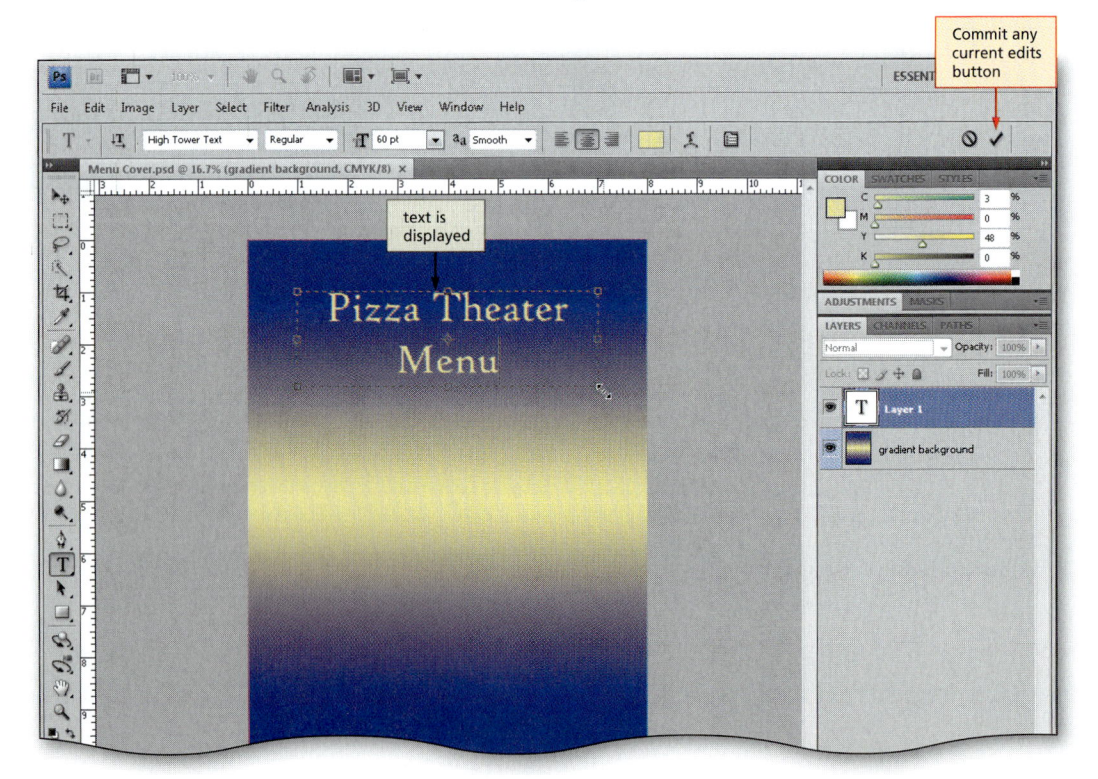

Figure 4–30

3
- On the options bar, click the Commit any current edits button to finish the new layer. If necessary, press the V key to access the Move tool and then reposition the text layer in the document window (Figure 4–31).

Figure 4–31

To Set Layer Properties

The following step sets the identification color for the new text layer. While you can rename text layers, Photoshop uses the words of the text as the layer name, by default.

1 Right-click the visibility icon for the new text layer, and then click Gray in the list to change the layer's identification color.

To Insert More Text

The following steps change the font size to 32 and enter the text for the lower portion of the menu cover. The font family and color are repeated for consistency.

1 With the Horizontal Type tool still selected, in the document window, drag a bounding box beginning at the left edge of the layout, approximately 2.5 inches from the bottom. Continue dragging to the right edge of the layout and down to create a box approximately 1.5 inches tall.

2 On the options bar, drag to select the text in the Set the font size box. Type 32 and then press the ENTER key to change the font size to 32.

3 Type "Where the best of classic movies and great pizza come together!" to complete the text.

4 On the options bar, click the Commit any current edits button to complete the entry and create the new layer. If necessary, press the V key to access the Move tool and then reposition the text layer in the document window.

5 Right-click the visibility icon for the new text layer, and then click Gray in the list to change the layer's identification color.

BTW

Using the ENTER Key with Type Tools
You cannot use the ENTER key to commit the text box as you do with selection transformations, because pressing the ENTER key creates a new line in the text. Use the Commit any current edits button on the options bar.

Stroking Text

Recall that you used layer styles to create a shadow and bevel in Chapter 3. The Stroke layer style commonly is used with text. A **stroke** is an outline on the current layer using a color, gradient, or pattern. Figure 4–32 displays some stroke options such as stroking outside, stroking inside, stroking center, and changing the color and size of the stroke. Combining these settings yields endless possibilities. Additionally, you can change the opacity and blending mode of a stroke. You will learn about blending modes in a later chapter.

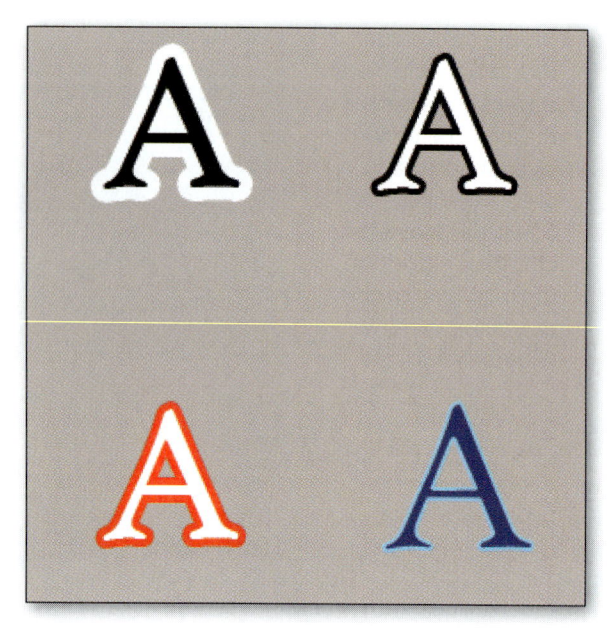

Figure 4–32

To Stroke the Text

The following steps stroke the text with black in both layers. On the larger letters at the top of the menu cover, the stroke will be 10 pixels in width. On the smaller letters at the bottom of the menu cover, you will use a stroke 5 pixels wide.

1
- With the "Where the best…" text layer still selected, click the Add a layer style button on the Layers panel status bar to display the list of layer styles (Figure 4–33).

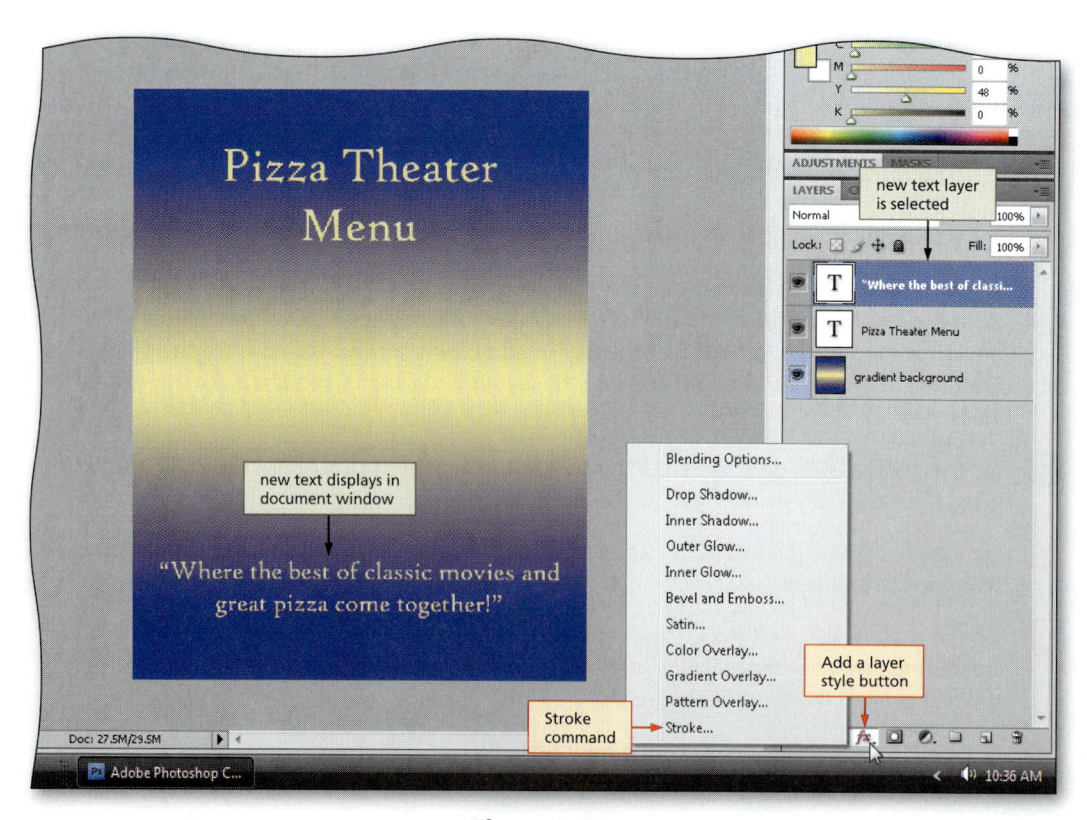

Figure 4–33

Inserting Text **PS 267**

2
- Click Stroke to display the Layer Style dialog box.
- Drag the Size slider to 5 pixels to increase the size of the stroke (Figure 4–34).

🔍 **Experiment**
- Drag the Size slider to various sizes and watch how it affects the text. Drag the opacity slider to various settings and watch the transparency of the stroke change. Reset the Size back to 5 pixels and the Opacity to 100% when you are finished.

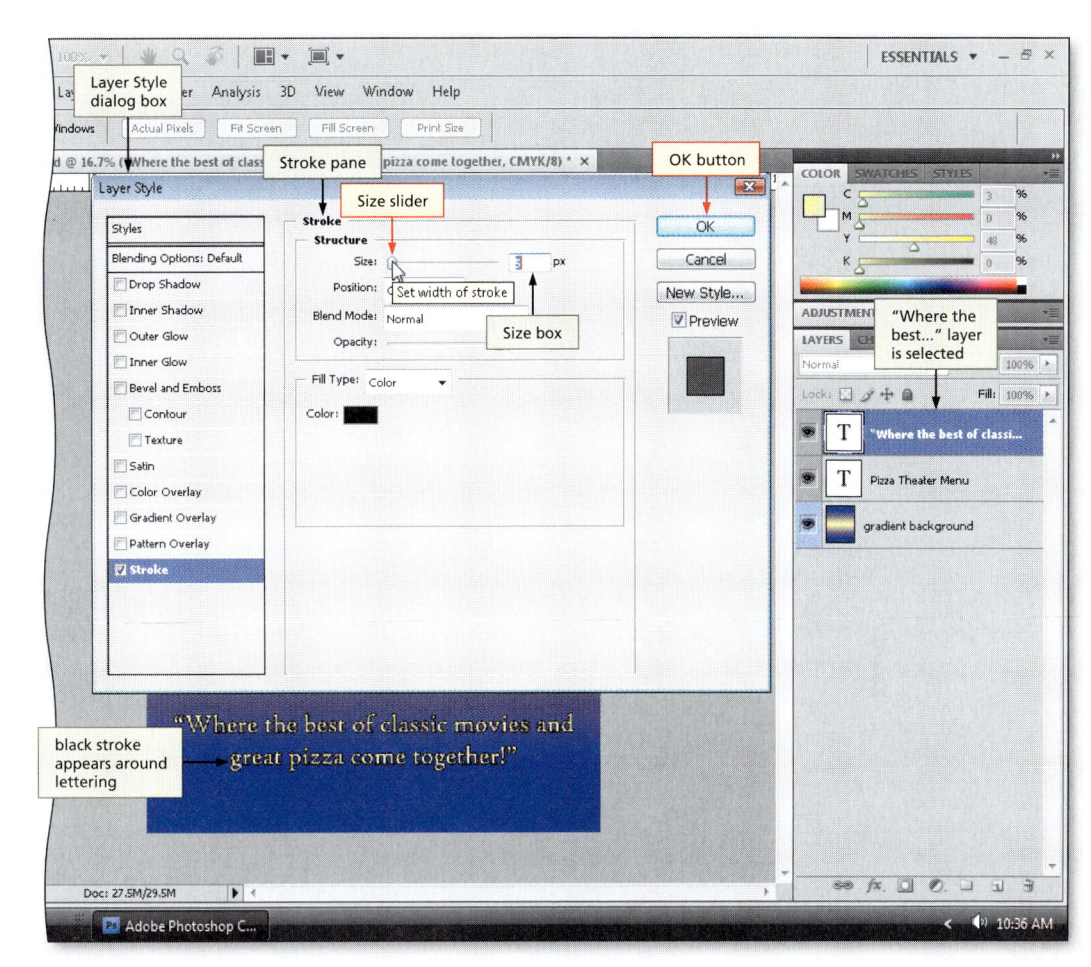

Figure 4–34

3
- Click the OK button to close the dialog box.
- On the Layers panel, click the Pizza Theater Menu layer to select it.
- On the Layers panel status bar, click the Add a layer style button and then click Stroke to display the Layer Style dialog box again.
- Drag the Size slider to 10 pixels to increase the size of the stroke (Figure 4–35).

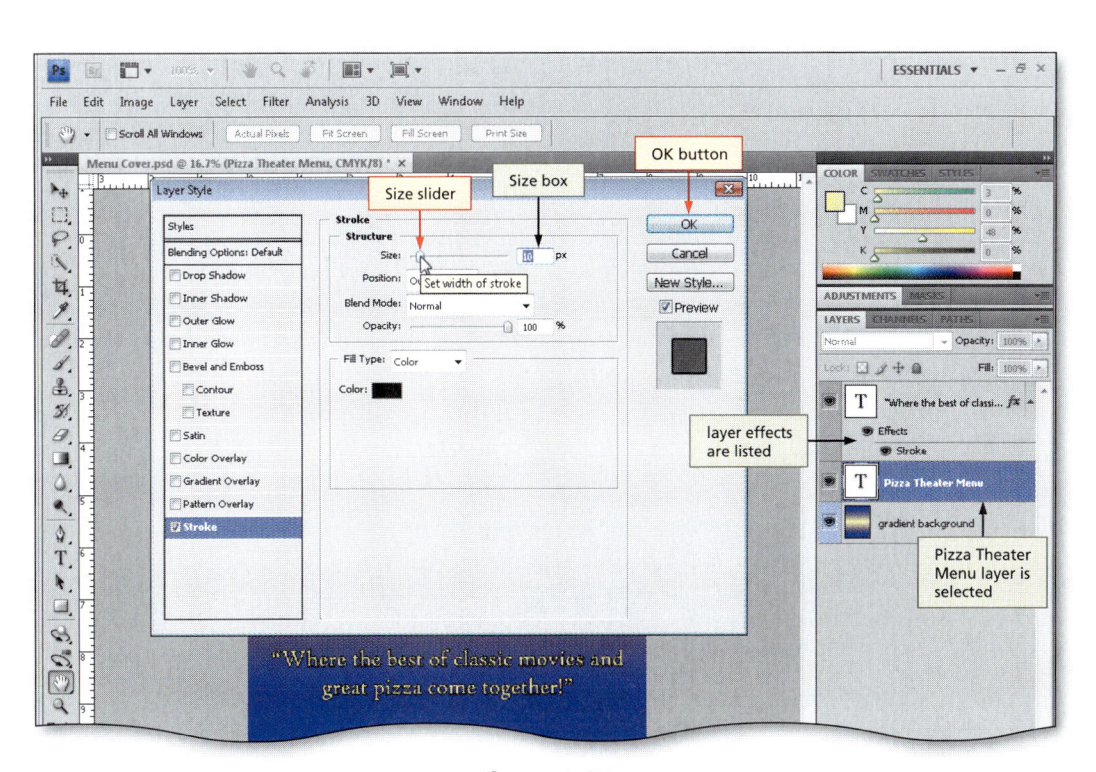

Figure 4–35

4
- Click the OK button to close the dialog box (Figure 4–36).

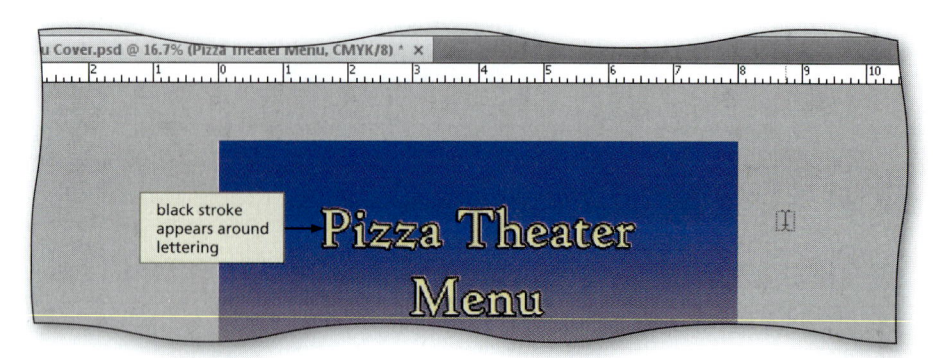

black stroke appears around lettering

Figure 4–36

Plan Ahead

Use predefined shapes for tangible objects.
If you are trying to create a graphic that the viewer will recognize right away, start with a predefined shape. This is especially true if you do not have a drawing tablet or your artistic skills are limited. Shapes allow you to maintain straight lines, even corners, constrained proportions, and consistent curves. To create unique graphics, shapes can be scaled, distorted, skewed, warped, shadowed, and combined in many ways. Using shapes does not limit your creativity, however. Try experimenting with combinations and transformations of shapes to create graphics with perspective, horizon lines, and alignment.

Shapes

One of the more creative uses for Photoshop is drawing shapes. A **shape** is a specific figure or form that can be drawn or inserted into an image. A shape is usually a **vector object** or **vector shape**, which means it does not lose its sharp lines or anti-aliasing if it is resized or reshaped. A vector object is made up of lines and curves defined by mathematical vectors or formulas. Photoshop provides six standard shapes, a variety of custom shapes, and the ability to create new shapes using a path. A path is a special kind of vector shape that you will learn about in a later chapter.

The Shape tool options bar (Figure 4–37) contains buttons to choose shapes; to add, subtract, and intersect shapes; and to choose shape styles, modes, and colors. If you select a custom shape, the options bar displays a Shape box with a Custom Shape picker button, which lets you choose from a panel of customized shapes. Besides the traditional shapes of lines, rectangles, and an ellipse, you can create freeform shapes, equilateral polygons, rounded rectangles and custom shapes when edited.

BTW

Shapes
Additional shapes can be appended using the Shape picker menu button, providing access to shapes ranging from arrows and shields to musical notes, thought bubbles, and more.

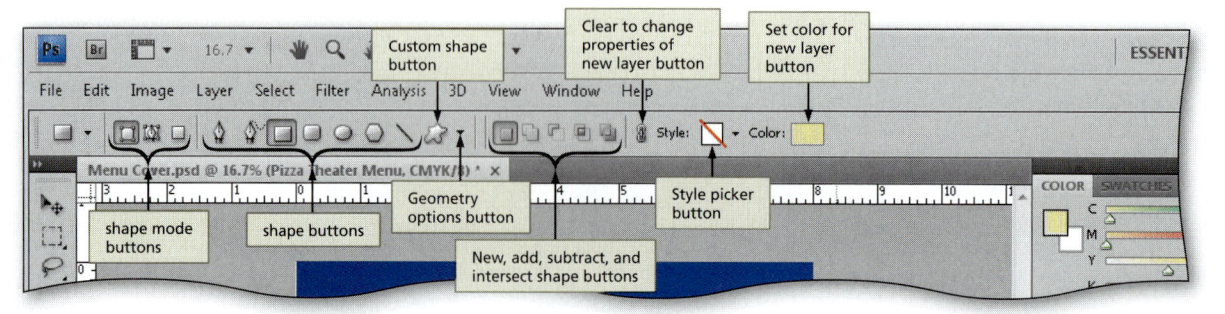

Figure 4–37

When clicked, a Geometry options button displays context sensitive settings for each of the shapes. Table 4–2 displays the geometry options, the shape or shapes with which they are associated, and a description of their functions.

Table 4–2 Geometry Options for Shapes

Shape	Options	Description
Line	Arrowheads, Width, Length, Concavity	adds arrowheads to a line, specifies the proportions of the arrowhead as a percentage of the line width, specifies concavity value defining the amount of curvature on the widest part of the arrowhead
Ellipse	Circle	constrains to a circle
Freeform Pen	Curve Fit	controls how sensitive the final path is to the movement of the mouse or stylus based on a value between 0.5 and 10.0 pixels — a higher value creates a simpler path with fewer anchor points
Rectangle, Rounded Rectangle, Ellipse, Custom Shape	Proportional or Define Proportions	renders proportional shape based on the values you enter in the W (width) and H (height) boxes
Custom Shape	Defined Size	renders a custom shape based on the size specifications
Rectangle, Rounded Rectangle, Ellipse, Custom Shape	Fixed Size	renders a fixed size based on the values you enter in the W (width) and H (height) text boxes
Rectangle, Rounded Rectangle, Ellipse Custom Shape	From Center	renders the shape from the center
Freeform Pen	Magnetic	draws a path that snaps to the edges of defined areas, allowing the user to define the range and sensitivity of the snapping behavior, as well as the complexity of the resulting path
Freeform Pen	Pen Pressure	when working with a stylus tablet, an increase in pen pressure causes the width to decrease
Rounded Rectangle, Polygon	Radius	for rounded rectangles, specifies the corner radius; for polygons, specifies the distance from the center of a polygon to the outer points
Pen	Rubber Band	previews path segments as you draw
Polygon	Sides	specifies the number of sides in a polygon
Polygon	Smooth Corners or Smooth Indents	renders the shape with smooth corners or indents
Rectangle, Rounded Rectangle	Snap to Pixels	snaps edges of a rectangle or rounded rectangle to the pixel boundaries
Rectangle, Rounded Rectangle	Square	constrains to a square
Polygon	Star	creates a star from the specified radius — a 50% setting creates points that are half the total radius of the star; a larger value creates sharper, thinner points; a smaller value creates fuller points
Rectangle, Rounded Rectangle, Ellipse, Custom Shape	Unconstrained	does not constrain shapes

BTW

Shape Modes
Photoshop has three shape modes: shape layers, paths, and fill pixels, which are accessible through the options bar. A **shape layer** is a vector object that occupies its own layer. Because shape layers are moved, resized, aligned, and distributed easily, they are useful for creating Web graphics. You can draw multiple shapes on a single layer

BTW

Resizing Shapes
To resize a shape, press CTRL+T to display the shape's bounding box. Resize the shape by dragging the sizing handles, then press the ENTER key.

BTW

The Polygon Shape
You can specify the number of sides a polygon shape has. For example, to create a triangle, enter 3 in the Sides box on the options bar. If you click the Geometry options button, you can change the polygon to a star. The number of sides then becomes the number of points on the star.

To Create a Shape

The following steps draw a rectangle shape to create the white projector screen on the menu cover. While you easily can drag to create shapes in the document window, you will use the geometry options to create a rectangle with specific dimensions.

1
- Press the X key to switch foreground and background colors.
- On the Layers panel, click the "Where the best…" layer.
- On the Tools panel, click the current shape tool.
- On the options bar, click the Shape layers button and then click the Rectangle Tool button to select them, if necessary.
- Click the Geometry options button to display the Geometry options panel (Figure 4–38).

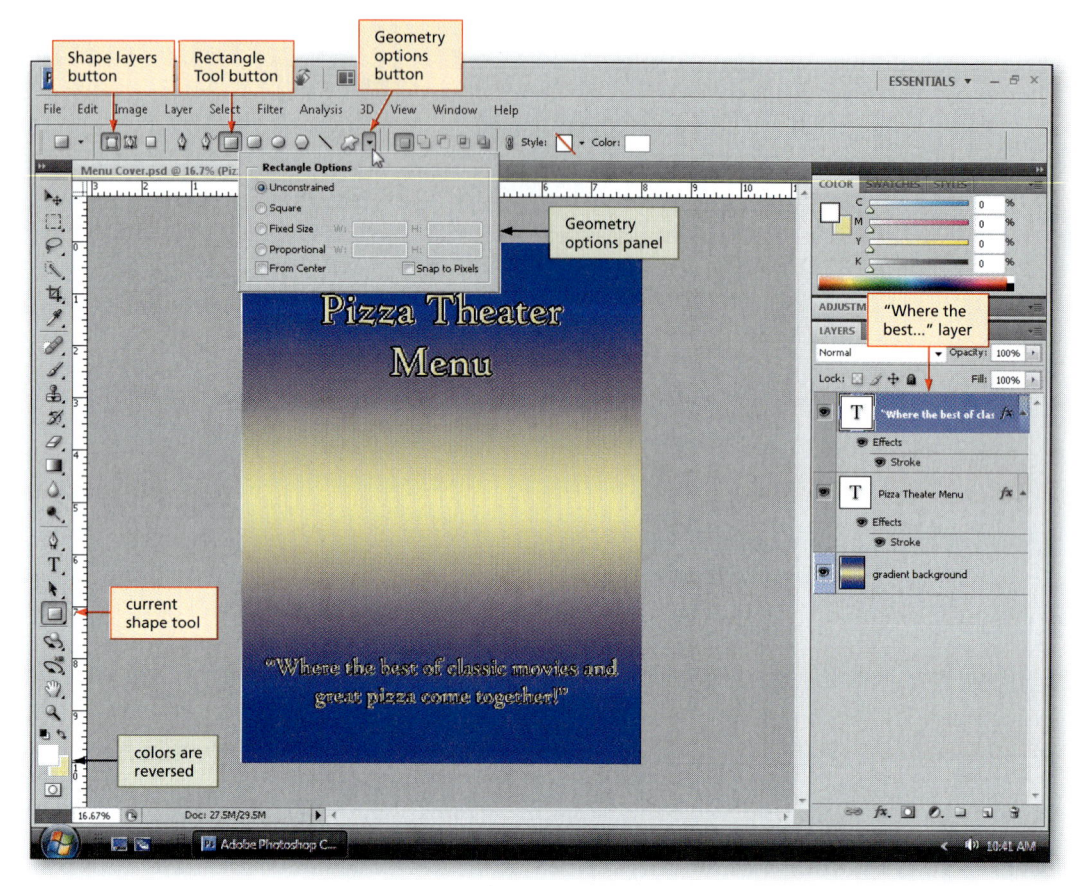

Figure 4–38

2
- Click the Fixed Size option button and then enter 3.5 in the W box and 2.25 in the H box to set the dimensions (Figure 4–39).

Figure 4–39

Shapes **PS 271**

3

- Click the document window to create the rectangle.
- Press the V key to activate the Move tool and then drag the new rectangle to a location in the center right of the document window, as shown in Figure 4–40.

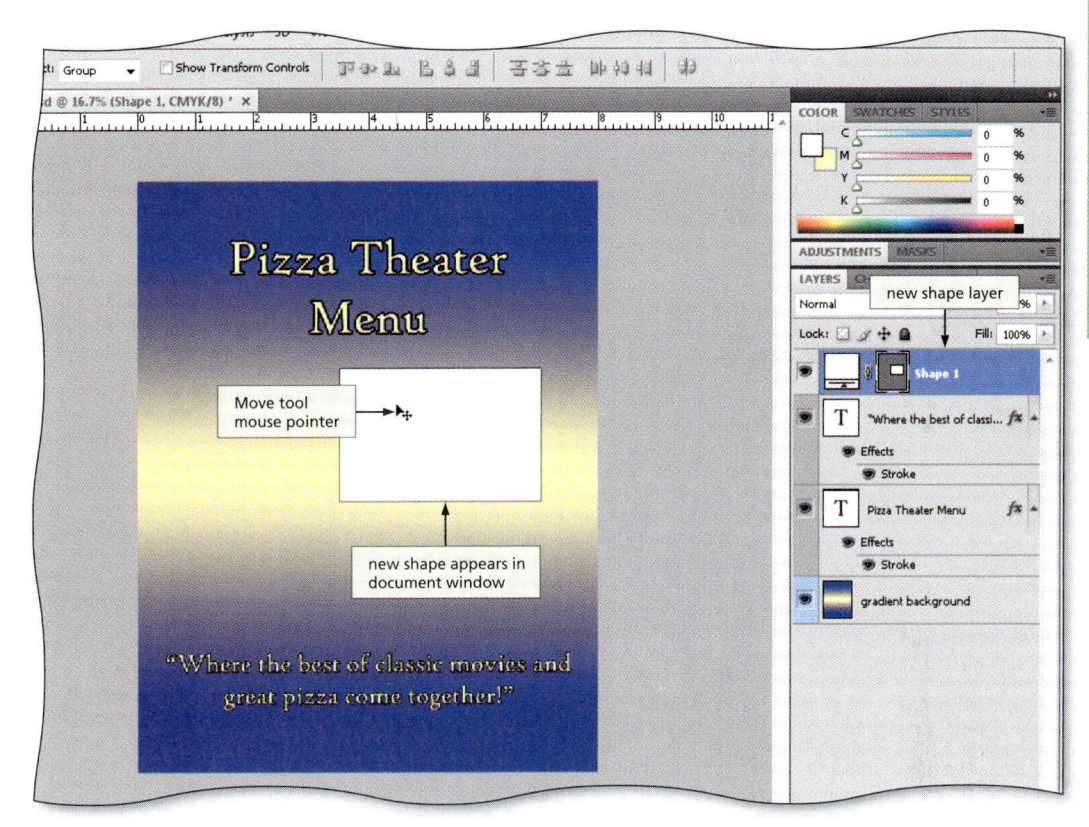

Figure 4–40

To Skew a Shape

The following steps skew the rectangle shape to create a sense of perspective.

1

- Press CTRL+T to display the bounding box and the Transform options bar.
- Right-click the rectangle to display the context menu (Figure 4–41).

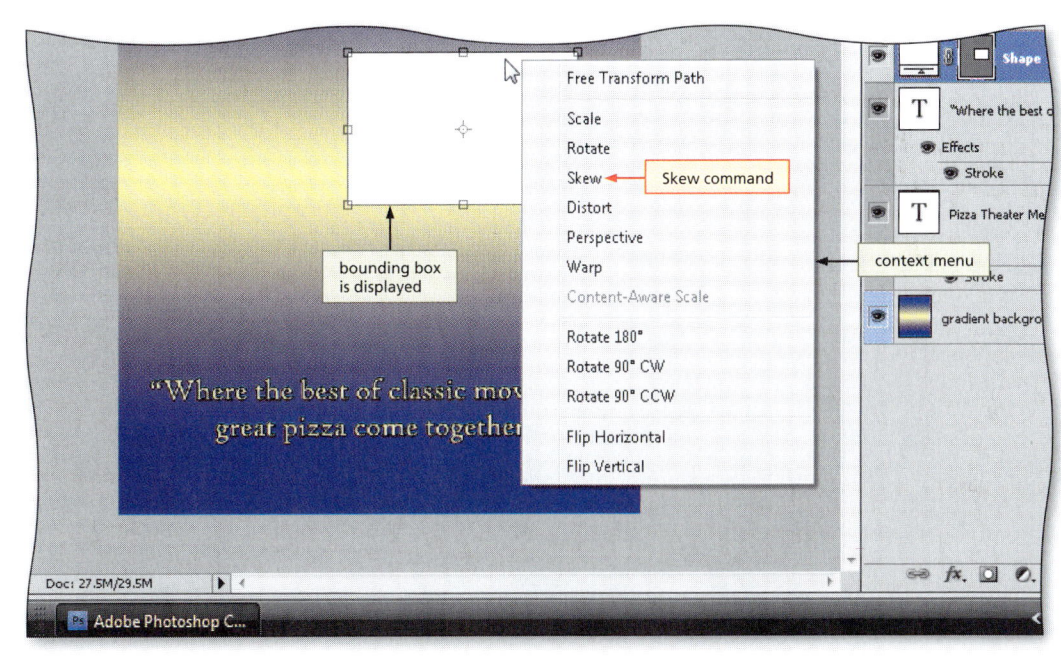

Figure 4–41

2

- Click Skew to skew the shape.

- Drag the upper-right sizing handle upward, approximately .25 inches, and then drag the lower-right sizing handle downward, approximately .5 inches to create a sense of perspective (Figure 4–42).

3

- Press the ENTER key to commit the transformation.

Figure 4–42

To Add a Drop Shadow

The next step adds a drop shadow to the rectangle, using the Layer Style dialog box. A **drop shadow** is a gray border that appears along one or two sides of an image to create the illusion of light shining on the object. A drop shadow adds to the three-dimensional effect by creating depth and giving the impression that the object is raised above the background.

1

- With the Shape 1 layer still selected, click the Add a layer style button on the Layers panel status bar to display the list of layer styles.

- Click Drop Shadow to display the Layer Style dialog box (Figure 4–43).

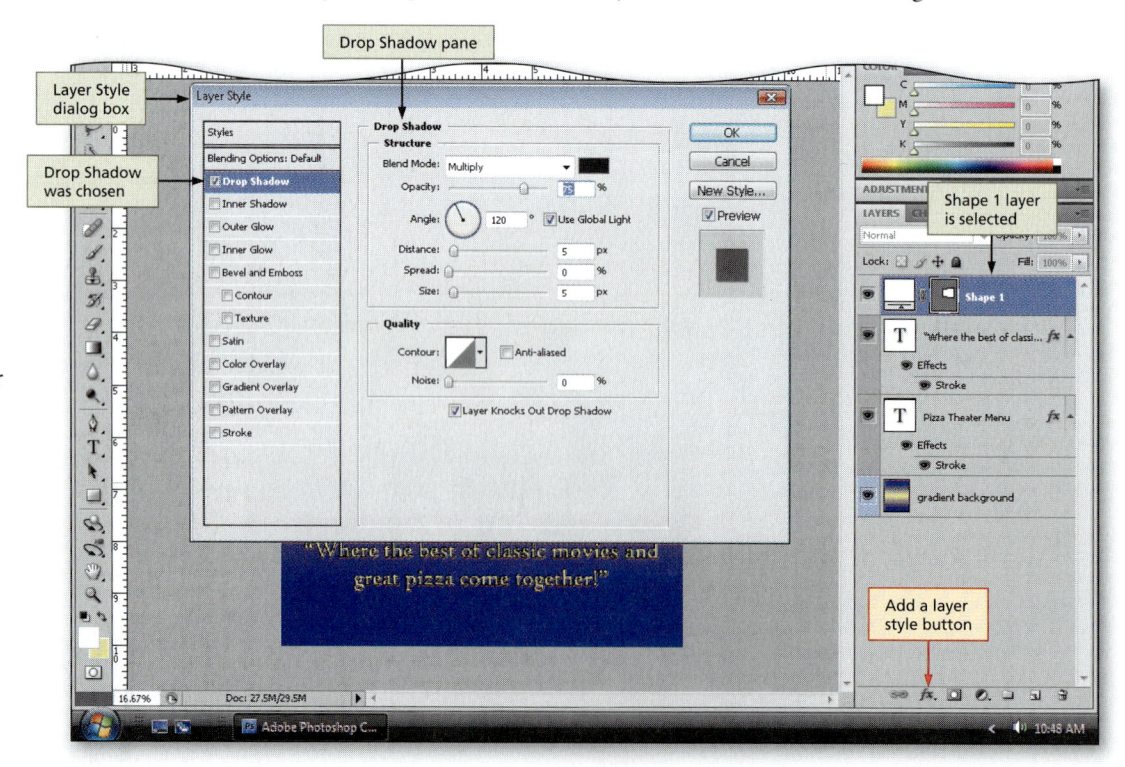

Figure 4–43

2

- Drag the Opacity slider to 50% to create a shadow that is 50 percent transparent.
- Type 130 in the Angle box. Click to display a check mark in the Use Global Light check box, if necessary.
- Drag the Distance slider to 75px to specify the offset distance for the shadow.
- Drag the Spread slider to 20% to expand the boundaries of the shadow.
- Type 32 in the Size box to set the size of the shadow (Figure 4–44).

🔍 **Experiment**

- Practice adjusting the shadow by dragging the distance, spread, and size sliders. Watch the changes in the document window. When you are finished, return the three settings to 75, 20, and 32 respectively.

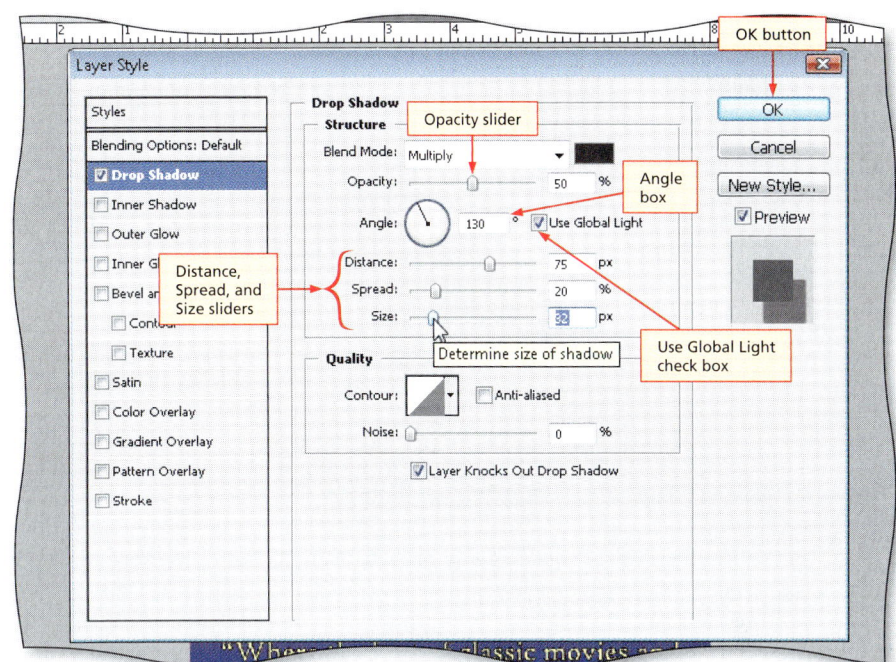

Figure 4–44

3

- Click the OK button to close the Layer Style dialog box and apply the drop shadow (Figure 4–45).

Q&A | Could I have dragged the Angle radius itself, instead of typing in the Angle box?

Yes, in any panel or dialog box that an Angle radius is displayed, you can drag the radius clockwise or counterclockwise to adjust the angle by how it looks, rather than by entering a number.

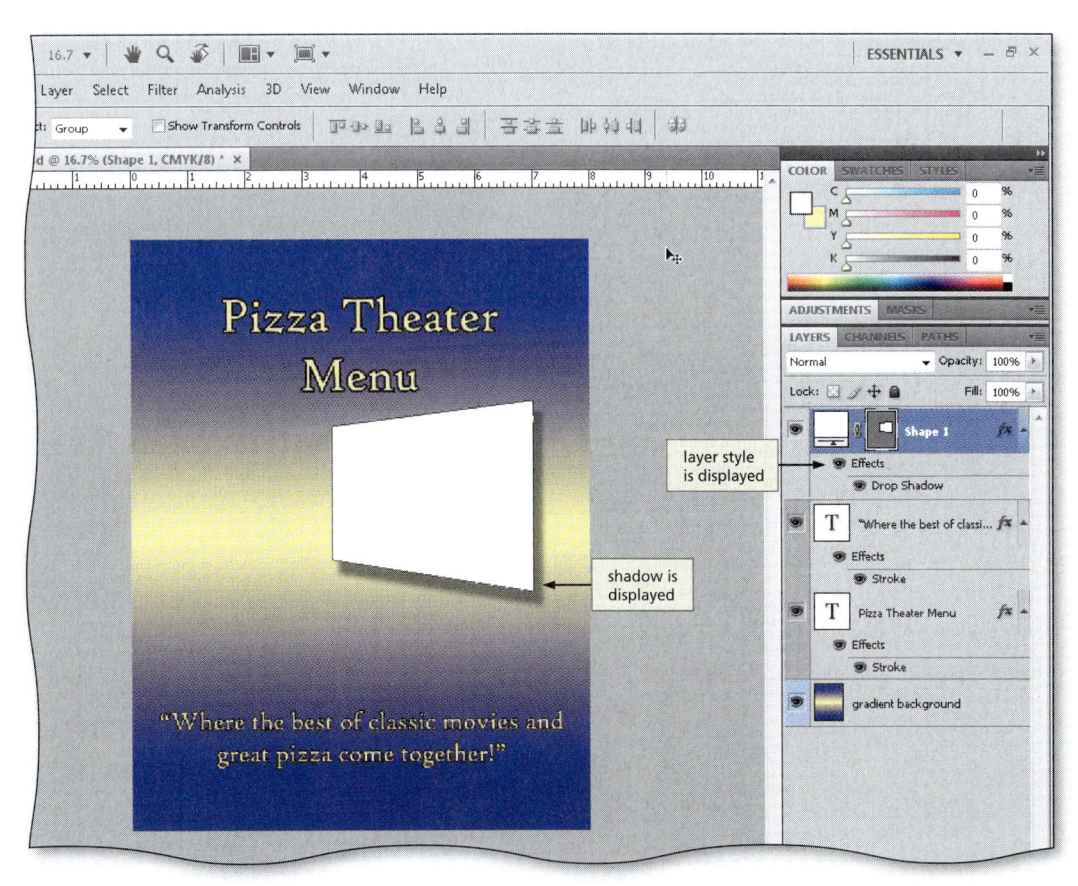

Figure 4–45

BTW

Info Panel
The Info panel displays information about the color values beneath the mouse pointer and other useful information depending on the tool that you use. For example, the Info panel can tell you if the color you are using will not print in certain color modes. To view the Info panel, click Info on the Window menu, or press the F8 key on the keyboard.

To Set Layer Properties

The following steps name the projector screen layer and set its identification color.

1 Double-click the name, Shape 1, in the Layers panel. Type `screen` to replace the name and press the ENTER key.

2 Right-click the visibility icon, and then click Orange in the list to change the layer's identification color.

To Add New Shapes Using the Shape Picker

The following steps use a custom shape to create the black screen housing at the top of the screen. First, you will choose the Custom Shape tool on the options bar. Then, you will append additional shapes to the Custom Shape picker panel and choose one to use for the screen housing.

1
- Press the D key to choose the default colors. If the Tools panel does not display black over white, press the X key to switch background and foreground colors.

- Press the U key to access the current shape tool.

- On the options bar, click the Shape layers button and the Custom Shape Tool button to select both buttons.

- Click the Shape picker button to display its list.

- Click the Shape picker menu button to display the Shape picker menu (Figure 4–46).

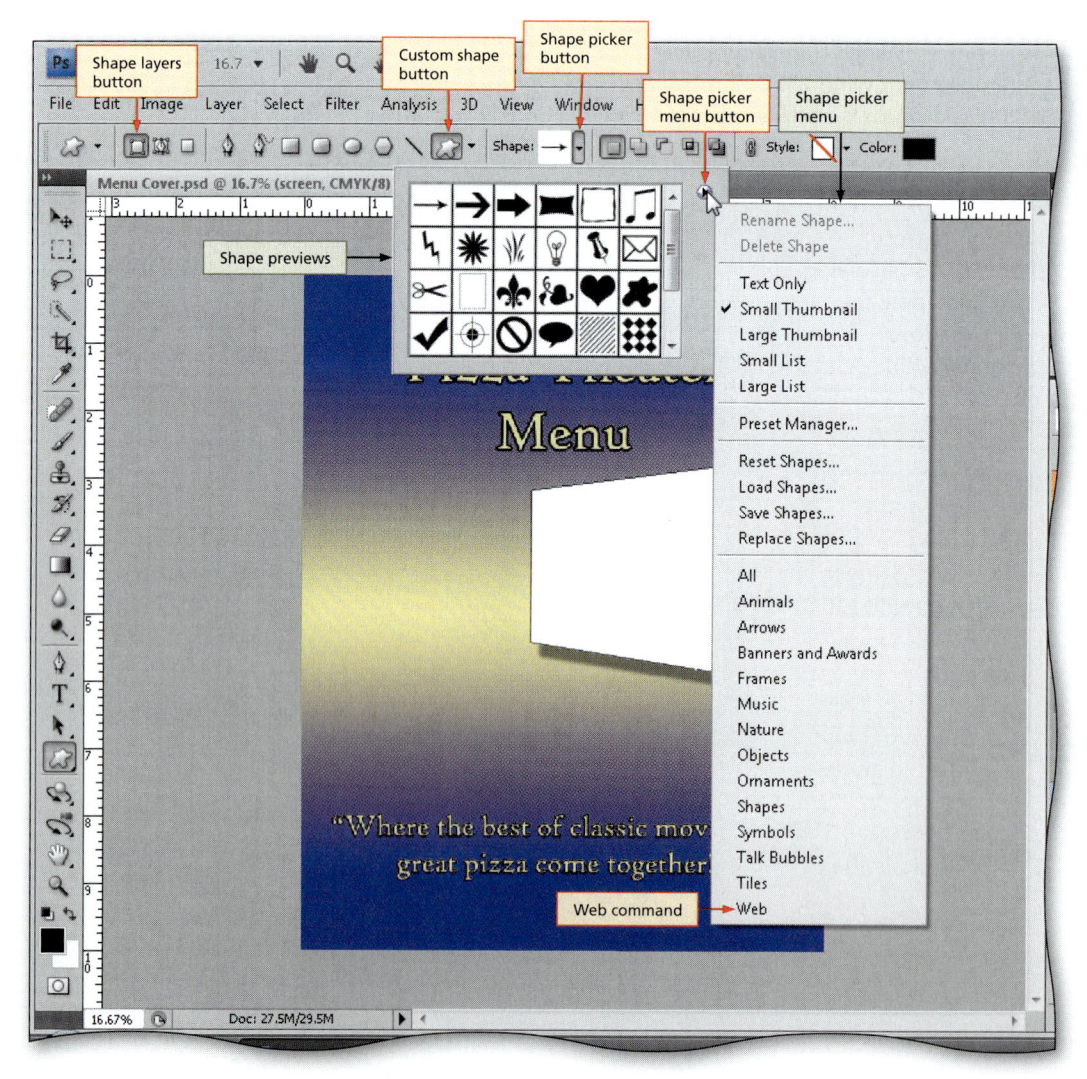

Figure 4–46

2
- Click Web to select Web shapes and to display a confirmation dialog box (Figure 4–47).

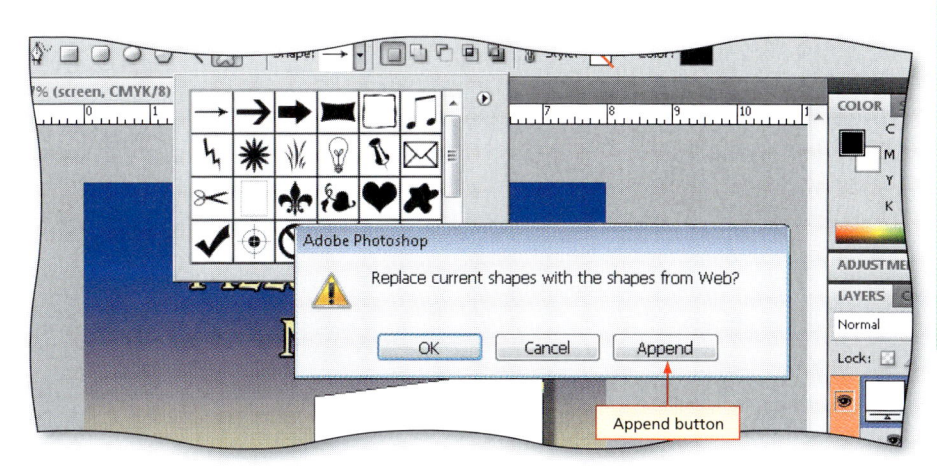

Figure 4–47

3
- Click the Append button to add the Web shapes to the end of the current list of custom shapes.
- Scroll down in the list to display the new shapes.
- Point to the Tabbed Button preview to display the tool tip (Figure 4–48).

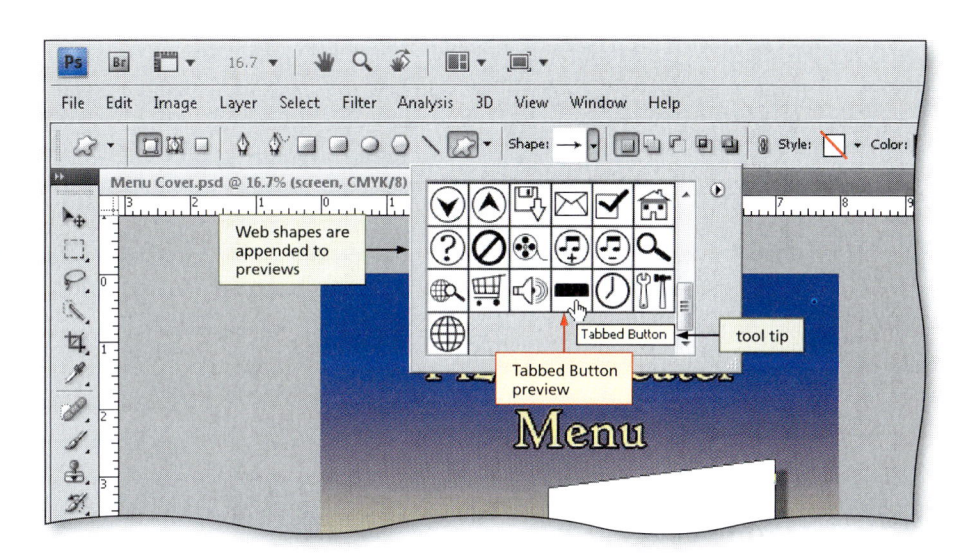

Figure 4–48

4
- Double-click the Tabbed Button shape to choose it and to close the panel (Figure 4–49).
- Click the Clear to change properties of new layer button so it is not selected, if necessary.

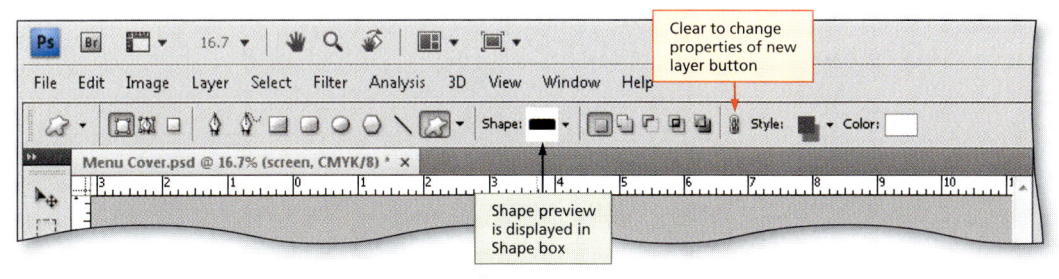

Figure 4–49

Q&A What is the purpose of the Clear to change properties button?

That button clears the settings from the previous shape layer; specifically, it resets the color back to the default foreground color and removes the layer effects that were created for the previous shape layer.

PS 276 Photoshop Chapter 4 Drawing and Painting with Color

5
- Click the Style picker button and then point to the Default Style (None) preview to display the tool tip (Figure 4–50).

6
- Double-click the Default Style (None) preview to choose it and to close the panel.

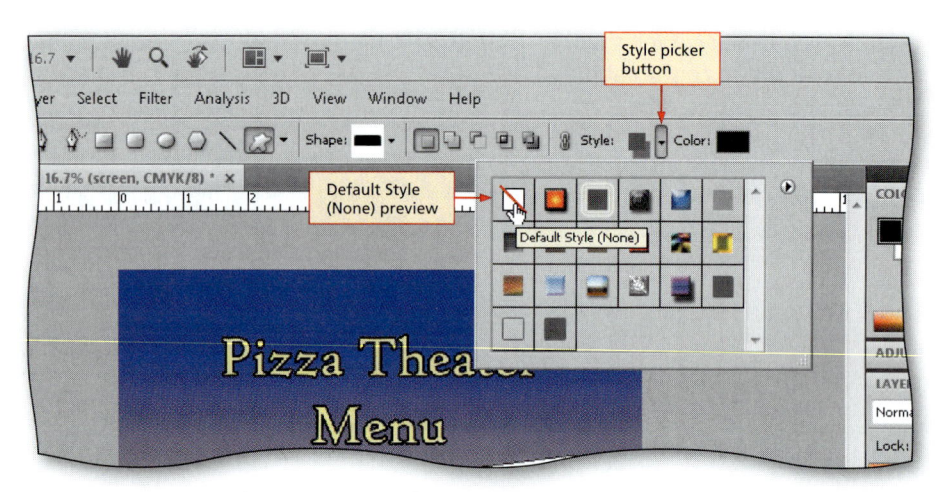

Figure 4–50

BTW

Pop-Up Panels
On some options bars, clicking a button will cause a pop-up panel to appear, similar to the one in Figure 4–50. These pop-up panels may contain buttons, boxes, sliders, lists, and a menu button for more choices.

To Create and Transform the Shape Layer

The following steps draw the custom shape in the document window and transform it to look like the screen housing.

1 In the document window, drag the shape to be approximately 3.75 inches wide and .25 inches tall.

2 Press CTRL+T to display the bounding box.

3 Right-click the shape and then click Rotate 180 on the context menu to invert the shape.

4 On the options bar, type –7 in the Set rotation box.

5 Drag the new shape to a location at the top of the white screen (Figure 4–51).

6 Press the ENTER key to commit the transformation. If necessary, press the V key to access the Move tool and then reposition the shape layer in the document window.

Figure 4–51

To Set Layer Properties

The following steps name the layer and set its identification color.

1. Double-click the name, Shape 1, in the Layers panel. Type `screen housing` to replace the name and press the ENTER key.

2. Right-click the visibility icon, and then click Orange in the list to change the layer's identification color.

To Create the Projector Layer

Now you must add a projector and pizza to the menu cover, dragging from one window to another. You also will create a new layer and use the Polygonal Lasso tool to create a projection light between the projector and the screen. The following steps open the file, Projector, arrange the document windows, and drag a copy from one window to the other, to add the projector to the menu cover.

1. Open the Projector file from the Chapter04 folder of the Data Files for Students, or a location specified by your instructor.

2. Change the magnification to 16.67%, if necessary, to view the entire image.

3. Click the Arrange Documents button, and then click the first 2 Up button to display the windows beside each other.

4. Use the Move tool to drag the projector image and drop it in the Menu Cover window.

5. In the Menu Cover window, drag the projector to the left margin approximately .5 inches above the text as shown in Figure 4–52.

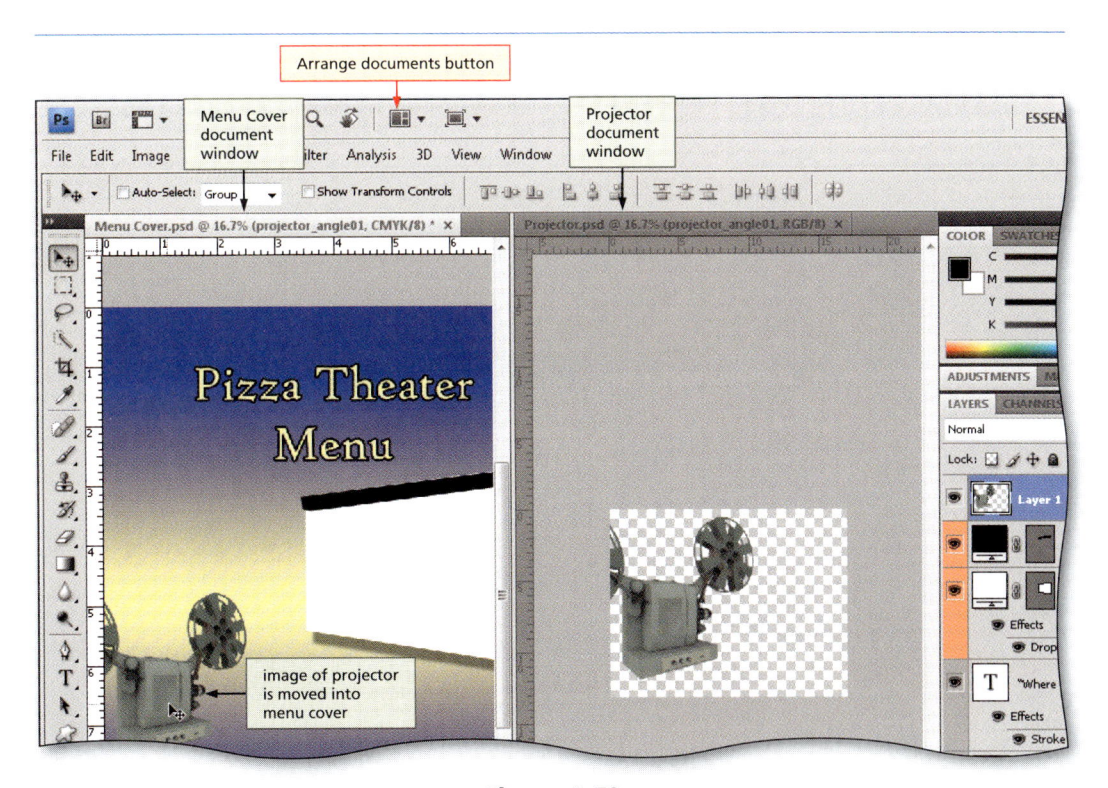

Figure 4–52

To Close the Projector Window

Because you are finished with the Projector file, you close it in the following step.

1 Click the Close button on the Projector document window title bar. If Photoshop displays a dialog box asking if you want to save the changes, click the No button.

To Set Layer Properties

The following steps name the layer and set its identification color.

1 Rename the new layer, projector.

2 Change the layer's identification color to Violet.

To Create the Pizza Layer

The following steps open the file, Pizza, arrange the document windows, and drag a copy from one window to the other to add the pizza to the screen.

1 Open the Pizza file from the Chapter04 folder of the Data Files for Students, or a location specified by your instructor.

2 Change the magnification to 33.33%, if necessary, to view the entire image.

3 Click the Arrange Documents button, and then click the first 2 Up button to display the windows beside each other.

4 Use the Move tool to drag the pizza image and drop it in the Menu Cover window.

5 In the Menu Cover window, scroll as necessary to display the entire white screen shape and then drag the pizza to the center of the white screen, as shown in Figure 4–53.

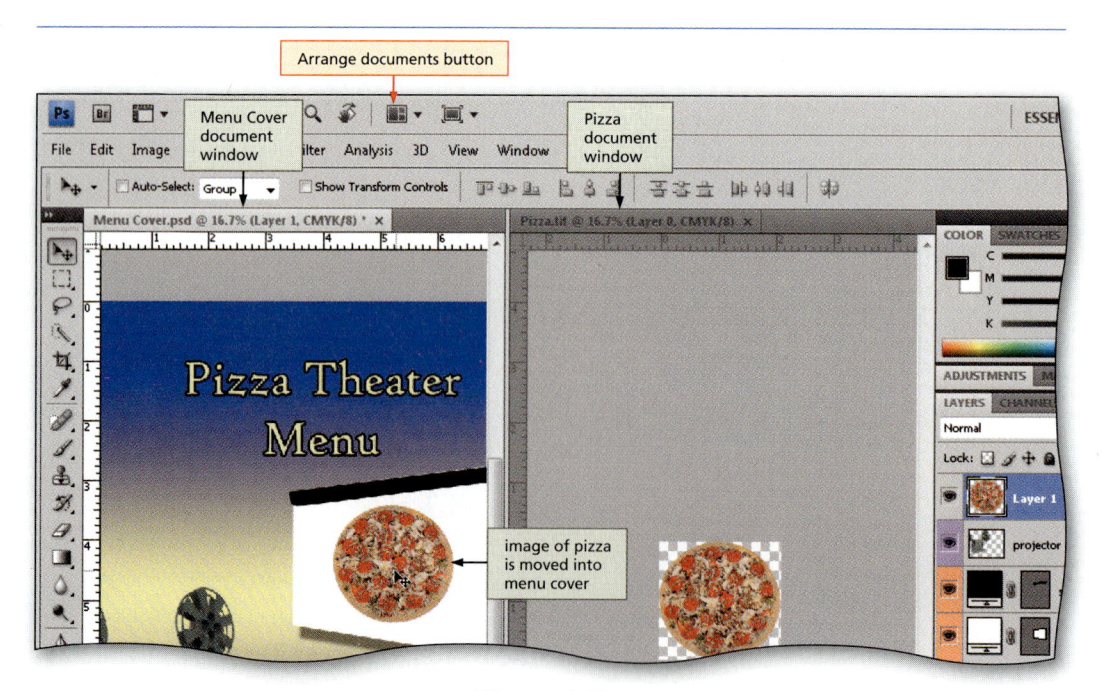

Figure 4–53

To Close the Pizza Window

Because you are finished with the Pizza file, you close it in the following step.

1. Close the Pizza document window. If Photoshop displays a dialog box asking if you want to save the changes, click the No button.

To Set Layer Properties

The following steps name the layer and set its identification color.

1. Rename the new layer, Pizza.
2. Change the layer's identification color to Red.

To Save the File

Because you have added new images and created a screen, you should save the file again before using the Paint Bucket tool.

1. Press CTRL+S to save the Menu Cover file with the same name.

The Paint Bucket Tool

The Paint Bucket tool fills adjacent, similar pixels with color. To use the Paint Bucket tool you select it on the Tools panel and then click in the document window. Recall that the Paint Bucket tool is displayed on the same context menu as the Gradient tool. The Paint Bucket options bar displays choices for fine-tuning the use of the Paint Bucket tool (Figure 4–54). By default, the Paint Bucket tool uses the foreground color as its fill color, but you also can choose from a predefined pattern when filling. The Fill Mode, Opacity, and Tolerance boxes work the same way as they do for the Magic Wand tool and the Eraser tools. Recall that higher tolerance values fill a wider range of colors. The Contiguous check box allows you to fill all adjacent pixels of the same color within the tolerance.

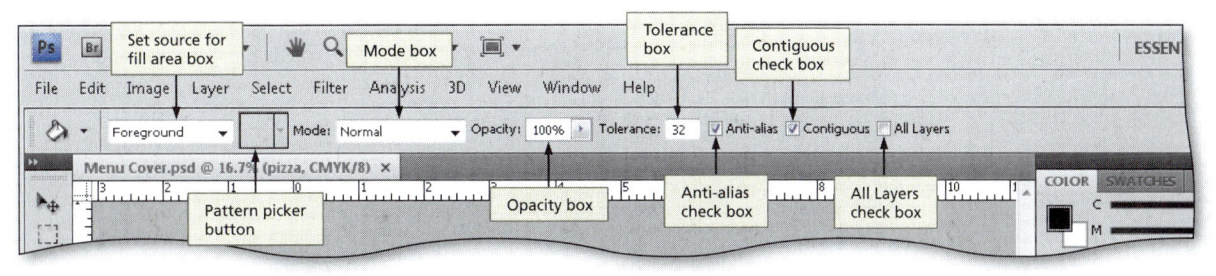

Figure 4–54

PS 280 Photoshop Chapter 4 Drawing and Painting with Color

The Paint Bucket tool mouse pointer displays a paint bucket. The tip of the paint coming out of the bucket is the fill location.

To create a graphic that simulates a projection light coming out of the projector, first you will create a new layer on the menu cover. Then you will draw a polygonal selection. After editing the foreground color, you will fill the selection using the Paint Bucket tool.

To Create a New Layer

The following steps create a new layer for the light projection. Painting on a new layer is a non-destructive way to edit color, rather than painting on an existing layer, possibly destroying other pixels of color.

1
- Press SHIFT+CTRL+N to open the New Layer dialog box.
- Type `light projection` in the Name box.
- Click the Color box arrow and then click Orange in the list (Figure 4–55).

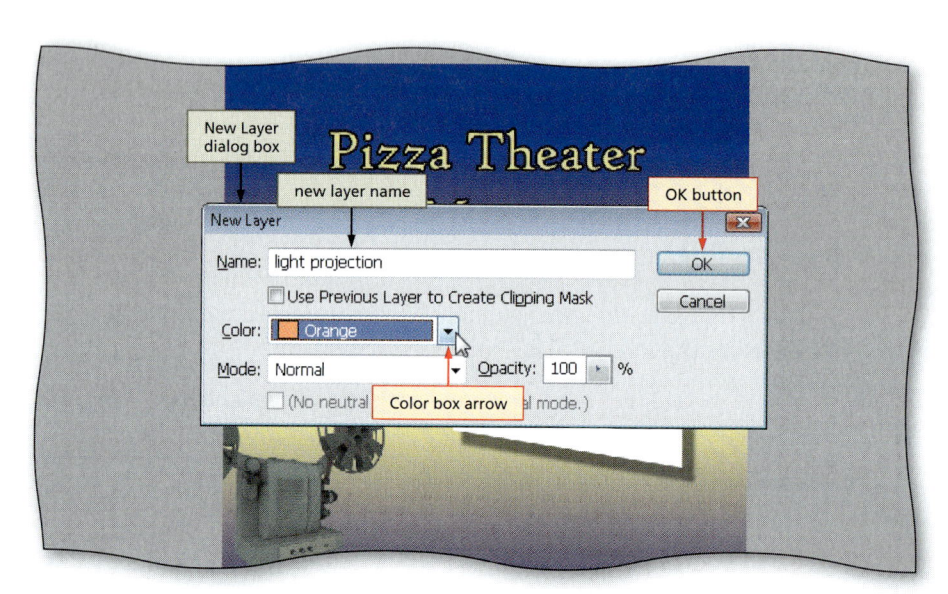

Figure 4–55

2
- Click the OK button to create the new, empty layer.
- In the Layers panel, drag the light projection layer to a location below the projector layer (Figure 4–56).

Q&A | Why do I need to move the layer?
The light projector will need to appear behind the projector's upper reel.

Other Ways
1. On Layer menu, point to New, click Layer, choose settings

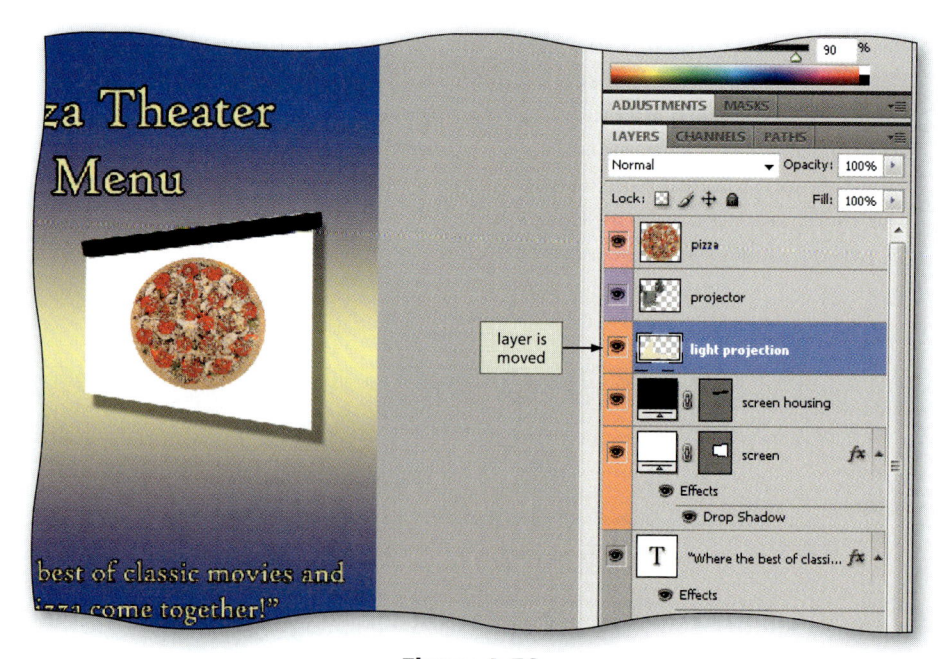

Figure 4–56

To Create a Polygonal Selection

Recall that the Shape options bar can be used to create polygonal shapes; however, shapes that are selected from the Shape options bar must have sides of equal length. In the following steps, you will use the Polygonal Lasso tool to create a customized selection marquee tailored to the area between the projector and the screen.

1

- On the Tools panel, right-click the current lasso tool and then click Polygonal Lasso Tool to choose it from the context menu.

- Click the top corner of the projector lens to begin the lasso. Click the upper-left corner of the white screen to draw the first side of the polygon marquee. Zoom as necessary (Figure 4–57).

Figure 4–57

2

- Click the bottom-left corner of the white screen, and then click the bottom-right corner of the white screen, to continue creating sides.

- Click the bottom corner of the projector lens and then double-click to complete the lasso. Do not click or press any other keys (Figure 4–58).

Figure 4–58

PS 282 Photoshop Chapter 4 Drawing and Painting with Color

Plan Ahead	**Choose colors purposefully.** Choose two or three colors that fit with your client's colors or match a color that already exists in an image in your layout. Limiting the number of colors creates a stronger brand or identity. The main color should be the one that viewers will remember when they look away. Colors two and three should either contrast or complement the main color to balance the design. Complementary colors create gray, white, or black when mixed in proper proportions, or those found opposite one another on a standard color wheel.

Editing Default Colors

The default color scheme of black over white is a good starting point for most editing techniques in the document window. There are times, however, when you need to change the default colors. Previously you used the Eyedropper tool to select a color from the document window itself, creating consistency in color. Another way to change the default color is to use the Color Stop dialog box that appears when you click either the Set foreground color button or the Set background color button on the Tools panel. Recall that the various color selection dialog boxes are all very similar in Photoshop, using color number boxes, a color bar, or a color panel to select colors.

To Edit the Foreground Color

To choose a color to use with the Paint Bucket tool, you will edit the foreground color in the following steps.

1

- On the Tools panel, click the Set foreground color button to display the Color Picker dialog box (Figure 4–59).

🔍 Experiment

- Drag the color slider and click various colors to watch the color panel and the color boxes change value.

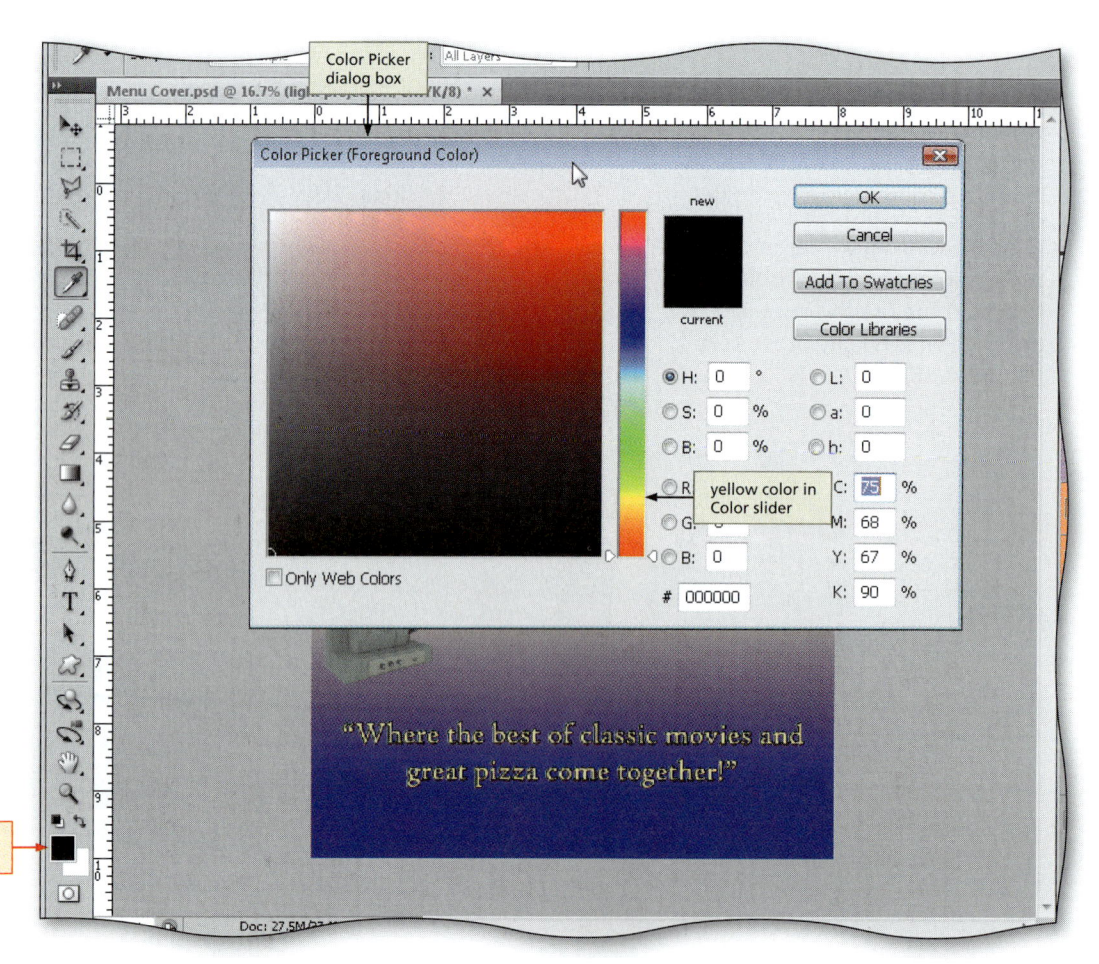

Figure 4–59

2
- Scroll in the Color Slider as necessary to display yellow.
- Click a yellow color in the Color Slider to display shades of yellow in the color panel.
- Click a pale yellow color at the top of the color field, or enter the CMYK colors of 2, 1, 27, and 0 in the color boxes (Figure 4–60).

3
- Click the OK button to close the Color Picker dialog box.

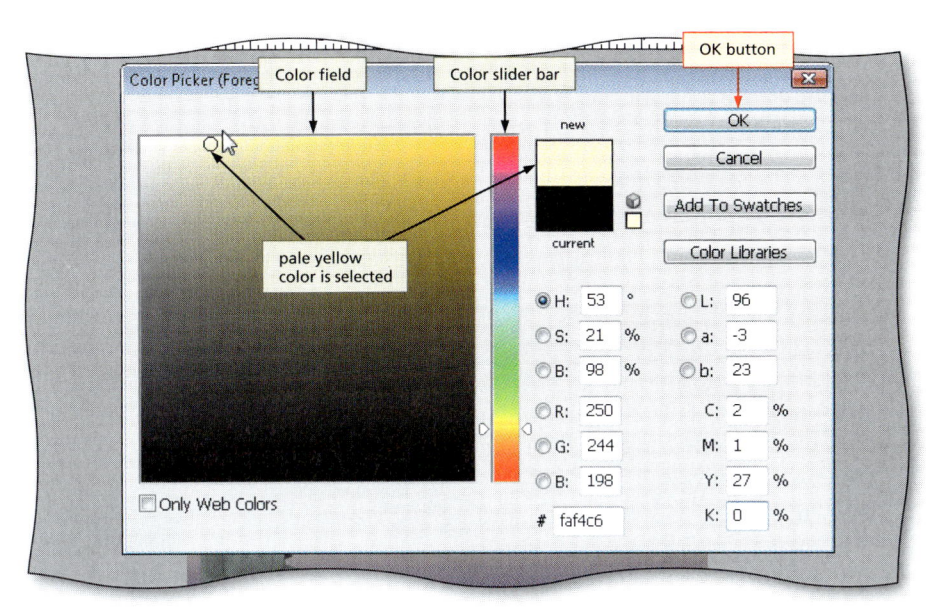

Figure 4–60

To Fill Using the Paint Bucket Tool

The following steps use the Paint Bucket tool to fill the lasso selection with the pale yellow color to simulate light from a projector.

1
- Press the G key to access the Gradient or Paint Bucket Tool.
- On the Tools panel, right-click the current tool button to display the context menu (Figure 4–61).

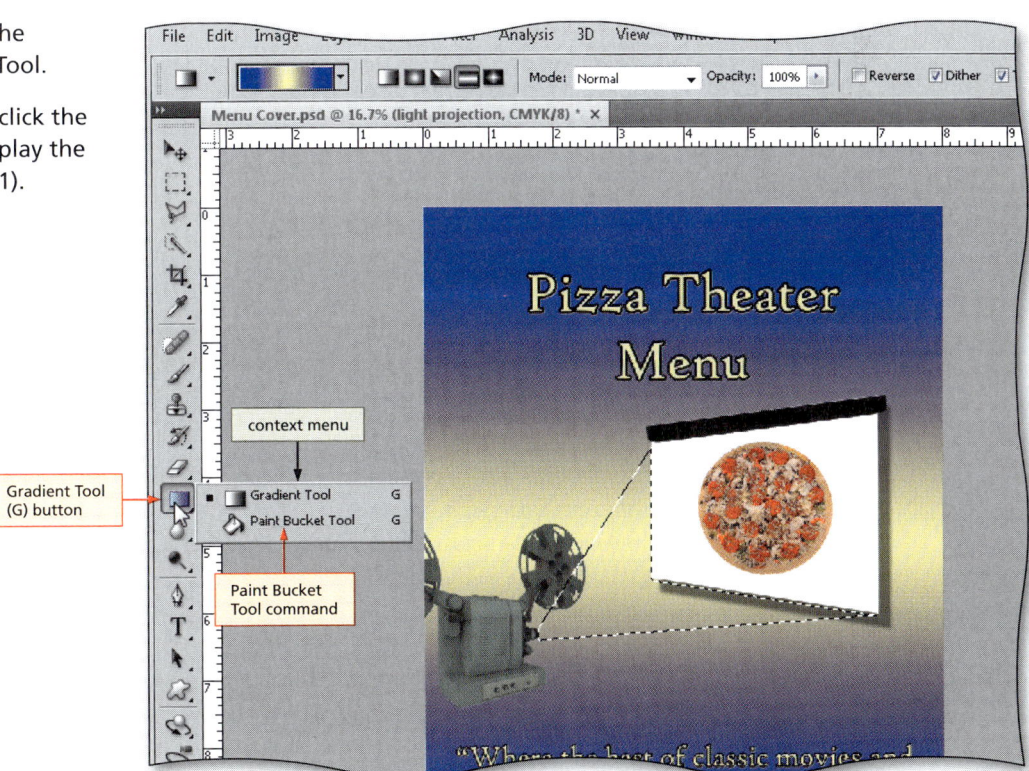

Figure 4–61

2

- Click Paint Bucket Tool to select it.
- Click inside the selection to fill it (Figure 4–62).
- Press CTRL+D to remove the selection marquee.

Experiment

- Drag the light projection layer to various locations in the Layers panel and see how it changes the document window. Drag it above the projector layer and then drag it below the projector layer. Notice how higher layers in the Layers panel appear in front on the document window.

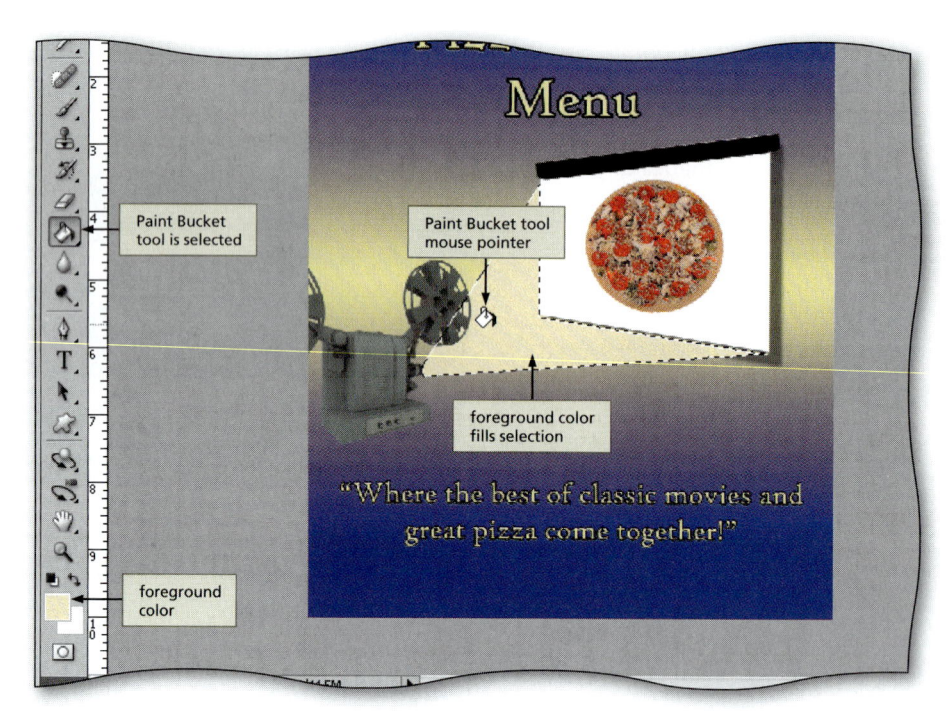

Figure 4–62

Plan Ahead	**Design your brush strokes.** When choosing a brush tip, keep in mind the basic shape of your brush strokes or marks. Use the Brushes panel to choose a Brush Preset or Brush Tip shape. Then adjust settings for the beginning, middle, and end of the brush stroke, especially if you do not have a pressure sensitive pen or drawing tablet. For the beginning, choose an appropriate tip, color, shape, rotation, hardness, spacing, and diameter. For the middle of the stroke, set the shape dynamics, such as pen pressure and tilt, texture, flow, brush edge, distortion, noise, and scattering. For the end of the brush stroke, set the fading.

Painting with Brushes

The painting tools change the color of pixels in an image. As you have seen, the Gradient tool and the Paint Bucket tool are used to fill large areas with color. The Pencil and Brush tools work like their traditional counterparts, applying color with strokes. The Color Replacement tool and History Brush tool modify the existing colors in the image. By specifying how each tool applies or modifies the color, you can create an endless number of possibilities. You can apply color gradually, with soft or hard edges, with small or large brush tips, with various brush dynamics and blending properties, as well as by using brushes of different shapes. You even can simulate spraying paint with an airbrush.

In the next section, you will create the screen hardware using the Brush tool. First, you will restore the default colors and then create a new layer for the screen hardware. Next, you will select the Brush tool, choose a Brush preset, and finally draw the pieces of hardware.

To Reset the Default Colors

The following step resets the default colors.

1. Press the D key to choose the default colors. If the Tools panel does not display black over white, press the X key to switch background and foreground colors.

To Create a New Layer

The following steps create a new layer on which to draw the screen hardware.

1. Press SHIFT+CTRL+N to create a new layer.
2. When the New Layer dialog box is displayed, type screen hardware for the name.
3. Click the Color box arrow and then click Orange to change the layer's identification color.
4. Click the OK button to close the New Layer dialog box and display the new layer on the Layers panel (Figure 4–63).

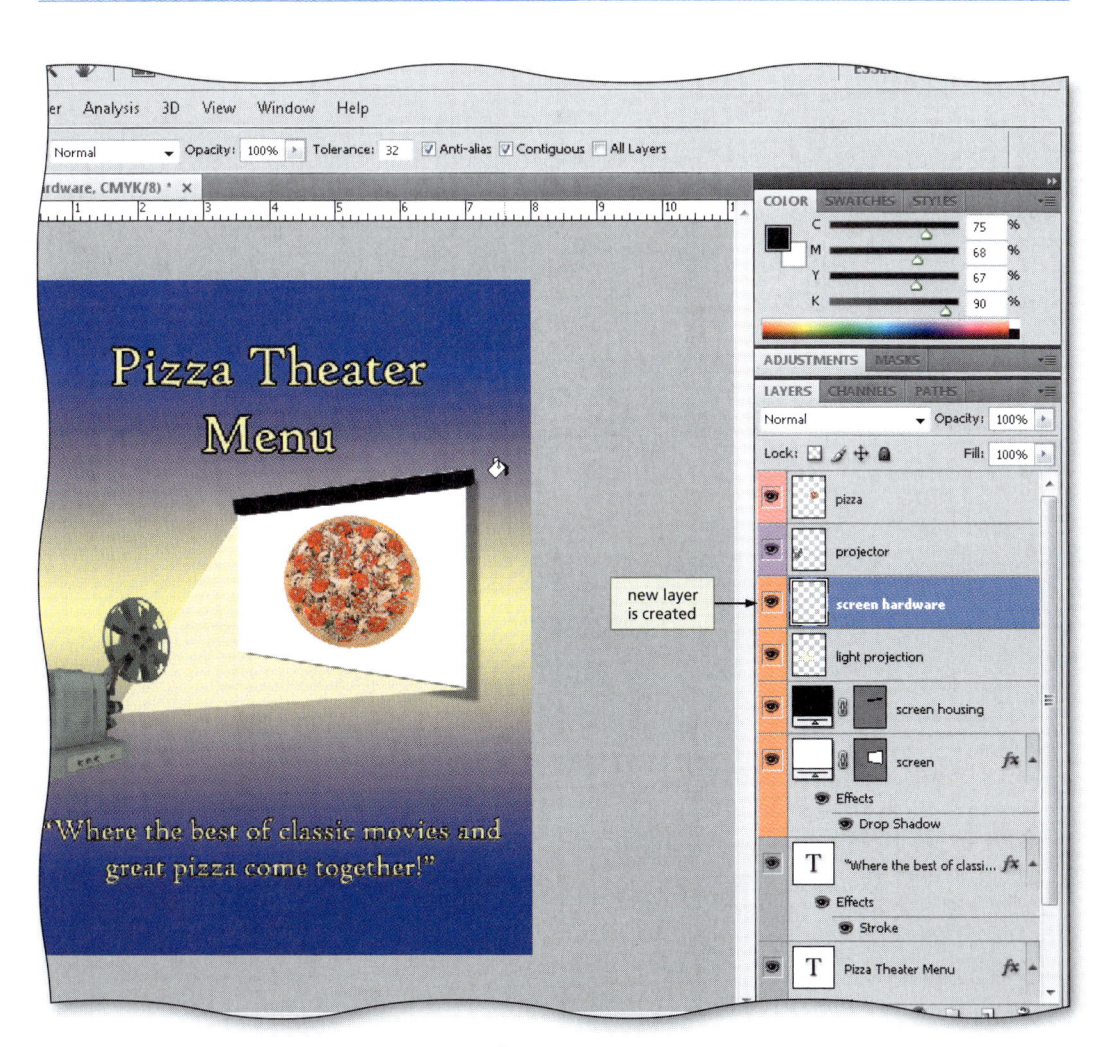

Figure 4–63

The Brush Tool

The Brush tool paints the current foreground color on an image with strokes of color as you drag. When you click the Brush Tool (B) button on the Tools panel, the Brush options bar is displayed (Figure 4–64).

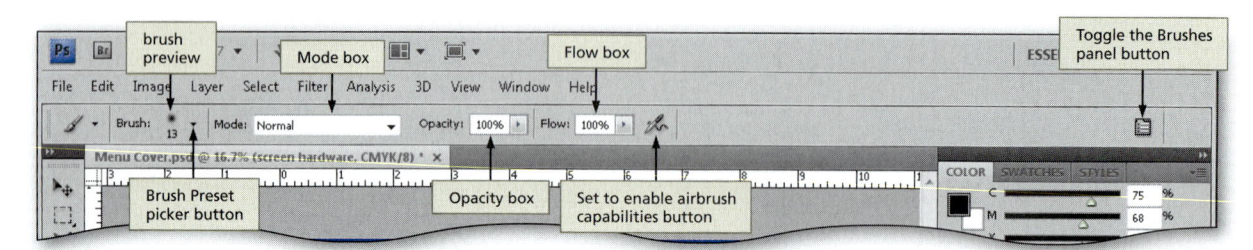

Figure 4–64

Similar to the Gradient and Shape pickers, the Brush Preset picker button displays the current set of brush tips and settings such as brush size and hardness. The Mode box arrow displays Brush blending modes when clicked, and the Opacity box allows you to specify the degree of transparency. Entering a value in the Flow box specifies how quickly the paint is applied. A lower number applies paint more slowly. The airbrush button enables airbrush capabilities. On the right side of the options bar is a button to show and hide the Brushes panel.

Accessed from the Brush tool's context menu, the Pencil and Color Replacement tools are related closely to the Brush tool. The only difference between the Pencil and Brush tools is that the Brush tool paints with an anti-aliased or smooth edge, and the Pencil tool draws with an aliased or rough edge. The Color Replacement tool replaces specific colors when you paint over a targeted color with a corrective color. The Color Replacement tool does not work with Bitmap or Indexed color modes.

To Select the Brush Tool

The following steps select the Brush tool on the Tools panel.

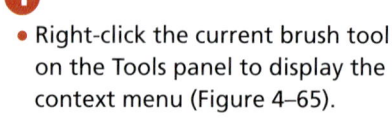

1
- Right-click the current brush tool on the Tools panel to display the context menu (Figure 4–65).

2
- Click Brush Tool in the list to select it.

Other Ways
1. Press B

Figure 4–65

To Use the Brush Preset Picker

You will use the Brush Preset picker in the following steps to choose a brush stroke with a diameter of 19 pixels to draw the screen hangers and the handle. Photoshop uses a percentage value, called **hardness**, to denote how solid the edge of the brush stroke is displayed. The brush stroke for the parts of the screen will have a hardness level of 100%. Once you choose a diameter and hardness setting, and later a brush tip, the Brush Preset picker button displays an icon with a visual representation or preview of the brush on the options bar. As you draw with the Brush tool, the strokes appear with those settings in the selected foreground color.

1

- On the Brush options bar, click the Brush Preset picker button to display the Brush picker panel.
- In the list of displayed brushes, click the Hard Round 19 pixels brush to select it (Figure 4–66).

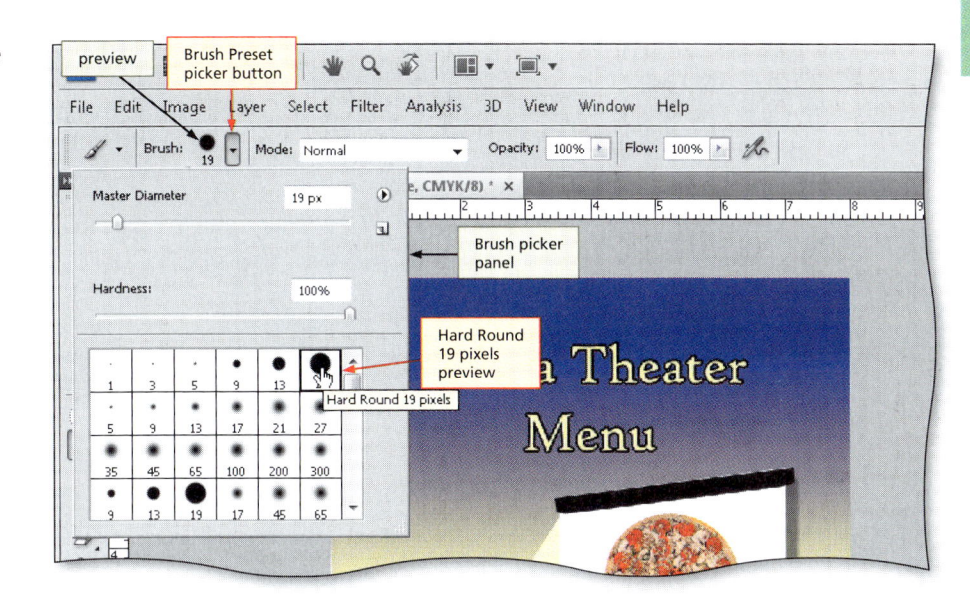

Figure 4–66

To Draw Using the Brush Tool

The following steps use the Brush tool to draw the screen hangers. If you create a brush stroke that is incorrect, press CTRL+Z and draw again.

1

- With the screen hardware layer still selected, drag a small c shape at the top-left corner of the screen housing (Figure 4–67).

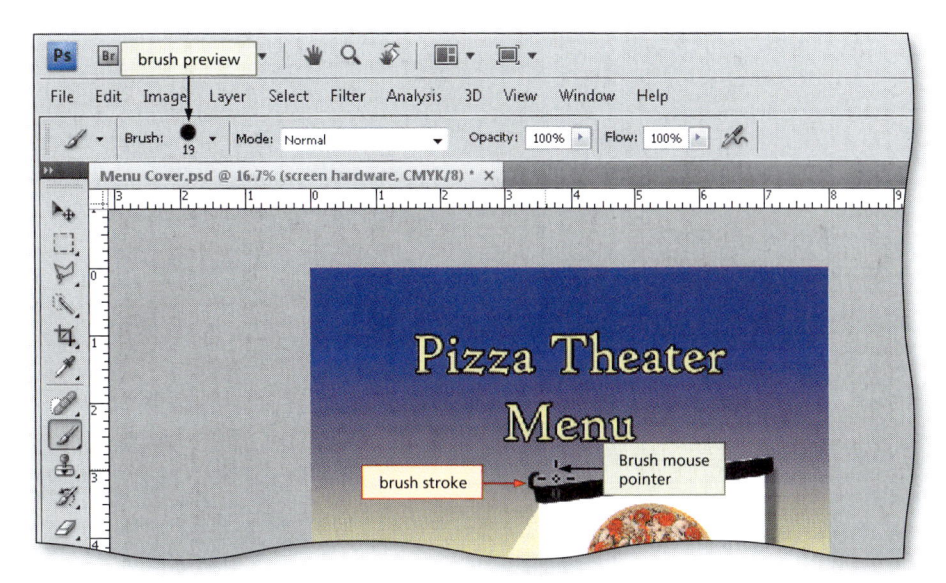

Figure 4–67

2

- Draw another small c shape at the top-right corner of the screen housing (Figure 4–68).

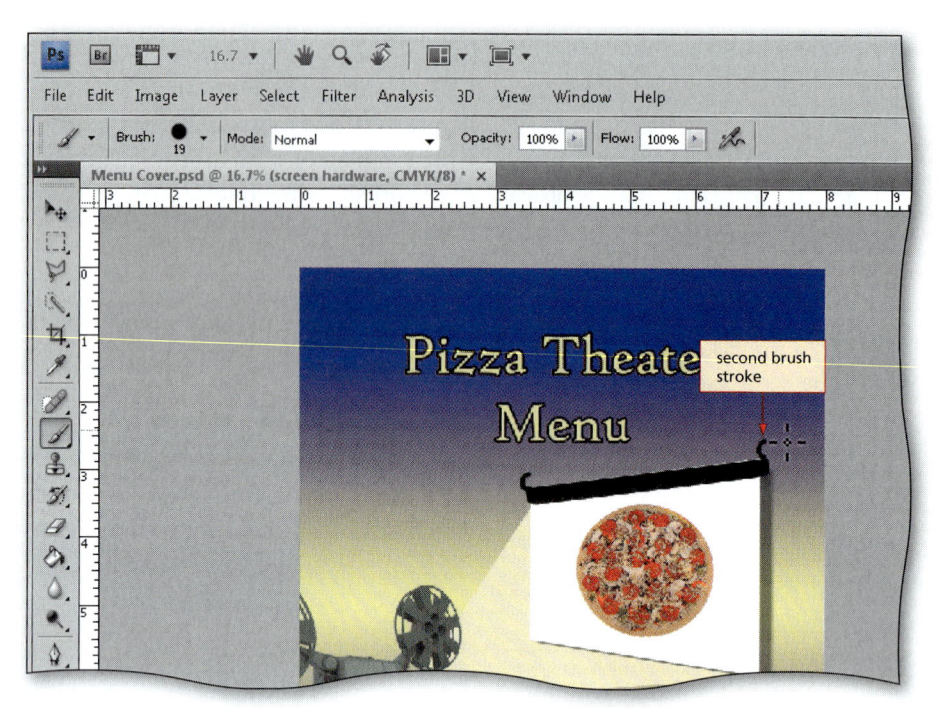

Figure 4–68

To Draw Straight Lines with the Brush Tool

You will use the Brush tool to draw the screen pull attached at the bottom of the screen. To draw straight lines with exact corners you will click and SHIFT+click with the Brush tool, which connects the color. Alternatively, you can press the SHIFT key while dragging to draw straight lines, freehand. Remember that if you make a mistake while creating the brush strokes, you can click Undo on the Edit menu, press CTRL+Z to undo, or click a previous state in the History panel, and then begin again.

1

- Change the magnification to 50%.
- With the screen hardware layer still selected, click at the bottom of the white screen, just left of center to start the brush stroke.
- Move rather than drag, the mouse pointer slightly down to position the corner of the screen pull (Figure 4–69).

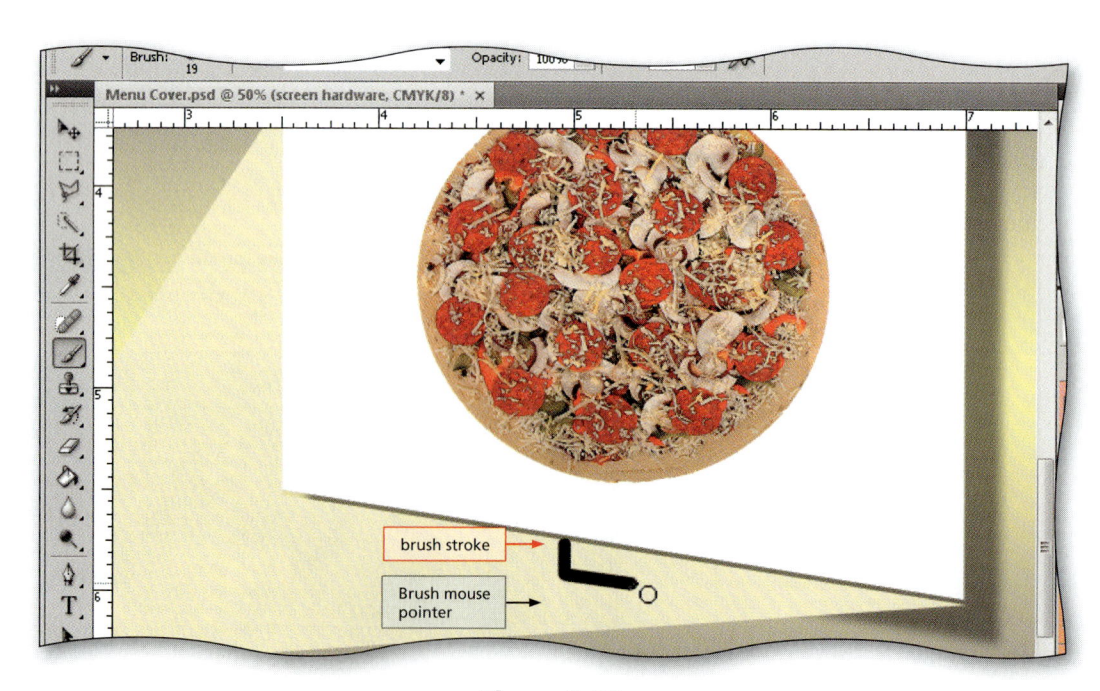

Figure 4–69

②
- SHIFT+click to connect the two locations with a brush stroke (Figure 4–70).

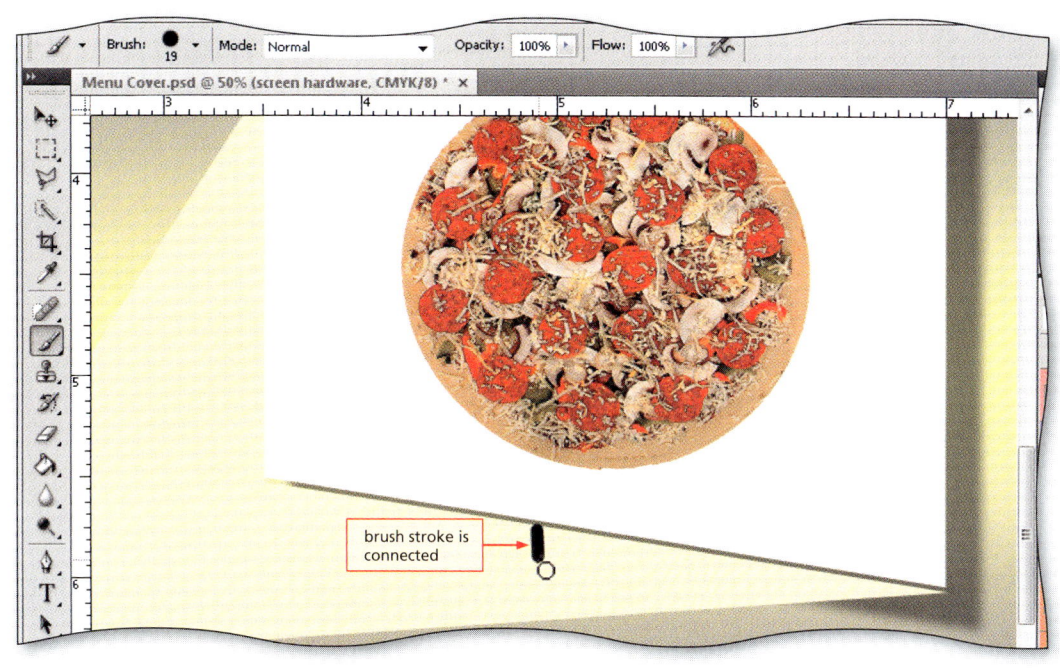

Figure 4–70

③
- Move, rather than drag, the mouse pointer to the right approximately .5 inches to position the other corner of the screen pull. The position should be slightly lower than the previous click to align with the slanted edge of the white screen.
- SHIFT+click to connect the brush stroke (Figure 4–71).

Figure 4–71

4
- Move rather than drag, the mouse pointer up to the edge of the white screen to position the final brush stroke.
- SHIFT+click to finish the screen handle (Figure 4–72).

5
- Zoom to 16.67%.

handle is complete

Figure 4–72

BTW

Graphics Tablet
Dragging, without using the shift key, creates strokes of color that may include corners, curves, and arcs. Graphic designers who create many free-hand brush strokes sometimes use a **graphics tablet**, which is an input device that uses a stylus, or specialized mouse, to draw on a tablet surface.

To Create a New Layer

The following steps create a new layer on which to draw the final star graphics for the menu cover.

1. Press SHIFT+CTRL+N to create a new layer.
2. When the New Layer dialog box is displayed, type stars for the name.
3. Click the Color box arrow and then click Yellow to change the layer's identification color.
4. Click the OK button to close the New Layer dialog box and display the new layer on the Layers panel.

To Choose the Yellow Text Color

In preparation for painting stars on the menu cover, the following steps use the Eyedropper tool to sample the yellow text color.

1. Press the I key to activate the Eyedropper tool.
2. Click the yellow color in the Pizza Theater Menu text to assign it to the foreground color.

The Brushes Panel

Recall that clicking the Brush Picker button displays a small panel with presets, diameter, and hardness settings. The Brushes panel (Figure 4–73) displays even more settings including brush tips, painting characteristics, angles, and spacing, among others. To display the Brushes panel, you can click the Toggle the Brushes panel button on the Brush options bar, click Brushes on the Window menu, or press the F5 key. Once the Brushes panel is open, you can click the Brushes panel menu button, to display a list of available commands, thumbnail sizes, and sets of brushes that can replaced or be appended to the current list.

BTW

Brush Preset Previews
When you click the Brush Preset picker button, your previews might appear as thumbnails, as lists, or as text only. You can choose the preview style on the Brush Preset Picker menu.

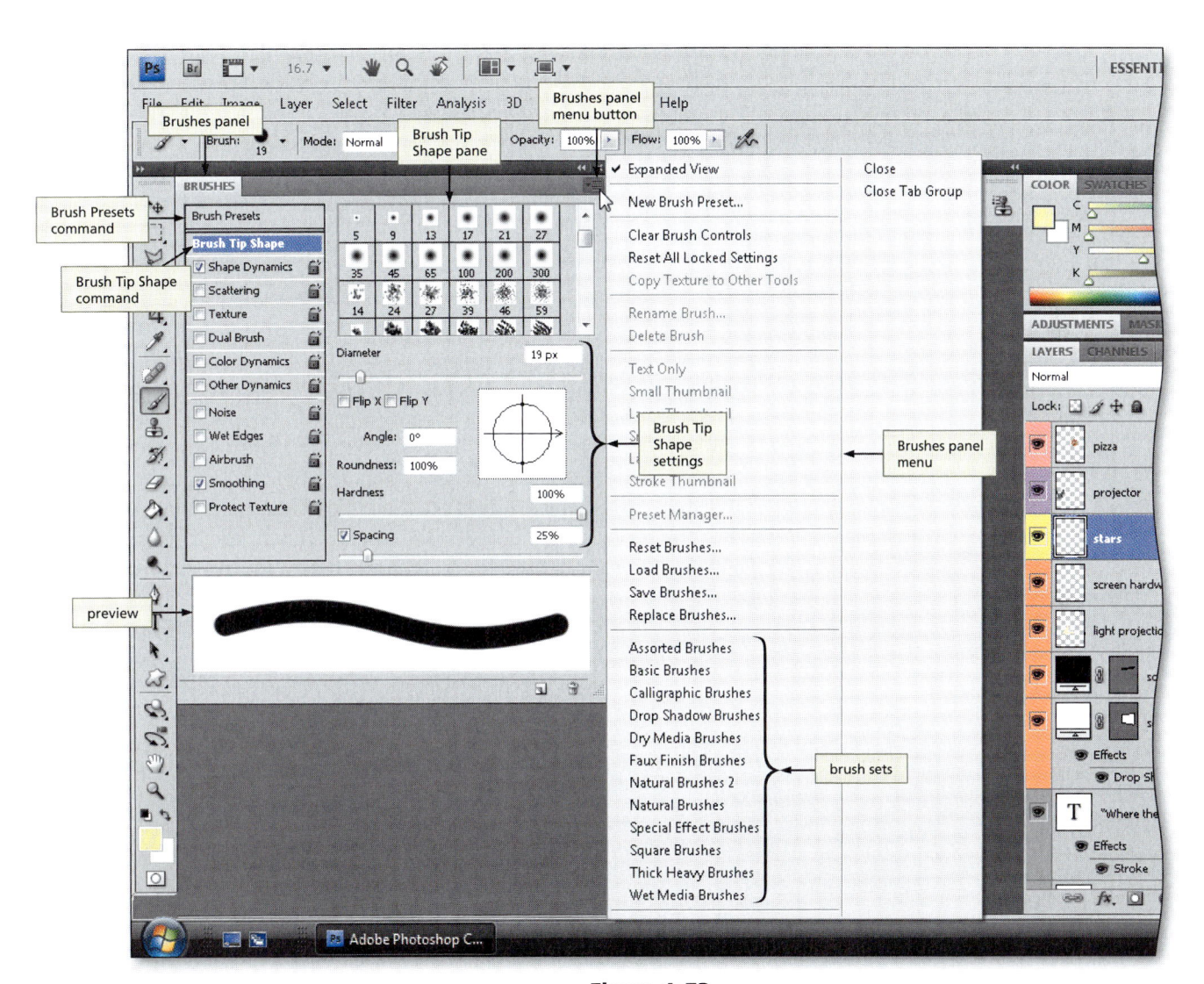

Figure 4–73

BTW

The Preset Manager
The Preset Manager helps you manage the libraries of preset brushes, gradients, styles, custom shapes, patterns, and other tools. Use it to change the current set of preset items or create new libraries. The Preset Manager lists new presets all in one place for easy access. To use the Preset Manager, click Preset Manager on the Edit menu.

BTW

Quick Reference
For a table that lists how to complete the tasks covered in this book using the mouse, shortcut menu, and keyboard, see the Quick Reference Summary at the back of this book or visit the Photoshop CS4 Quick Reference Web page (scsite.com/pscs4//qr).

A **preset brush tip** has specific characteristics such as size, shape, and hardness. When you use the Brush tool, the tip creates the shape that paints in the document window. In addition to the basic brush tips, Photoshop offers 11 other libraries of brush tips that you can append to the panel. If you change the size, shape, or hardness of a preset brush, the change is temporary; the next time you choose that tip, the brush goes back to its original settings. If you use a certain brush tip and characteristics often, you might use the Save command on the Brushes panel menu, which saves your settings as a preset. The Brushes panel displays two different panes. The Brush Presets pane is accessed by clicking Brush Presets on the left side of the Brushes panel. That pane displays a list of preset brushes similar to those in the Brush Preset picker panel. The Brush Tip Shape pane displays the preset brush tips, but also allows you to customize the brush. For example, you can set the **diameter**, which scales the size of the brush tip. The **flip boxes** change the direction of the brush tip on the specified axis. For example, a brush tip that displays a leaf image with the stem down would display the leaf with the stem up if the Flip X check box were checked. The Angle box allows you to enter degrees of flat rotation. Positive numbers rotate the brush tip counterclockwise; negative numbers rotate the brush tip clockwise. For example, a brush tip of a raindrop with the pointed end straight up would point left if rotated 90 degrees. The **Roundness** percentage specifies the ratio between the brush's short and long axes. Adjusting the roundness makes the brush tip appear to rotate on its vertical axis in a 3D fashion. A value of 100% indicates a full view or circular brush tip. A value of 0% indicates a sideways view or linear brush tip. Values between 0% and 100% represent partial view or elliptical brush tips. For example, a star brush tip set at 50% roundness creates a star that is tipped backward from the top. The **Spacing** slider controls the distance between the brush marks in a stroke. The lower the percentage, the closer together the brush tips are displayed within the stroke. For example, a snowflake brush tip set at 1% spacing would display a snowflake shape connected to another snowflake shape. Higher percentages — up to 1000% — space the brush tips farther apart as you drag. For example, a spacing value of 200% would create snowflakes all across the brush stroke with some space in between each one. When the Spacing check box is deselected, the speed of the cursor determines the spacing.

Solid brush tips have a hardness setting that indicates the amount of anti-aliasing for the Brush tool. The higher the percentage, the cleaner the edge appears.

Brush Options

Brush options are displayed as check boxes in the Brushes panel. When you choose an option, settings specific to that dynamic appear on the right pane of the Brushes panel. Table 4–3 displays some of the options not previously mentioned, along with their settings and descriptions.

Table 4–3 Brush Shape Options

Option	Setting	Description
Shape Dynamic	Jitter	specifies how the size, angle, or roundness of brush marks vary in a stroke
	Fade	fades the size of brush marks between the initial diameter and the minimum diameter in the specified number of steps
	Pen Pressure, Pen Tilt, Stylus Wheel, Rotation	available only with graphic tablets — varies the size of brush marks between the initial diameter and the minimum diameter based on the pen pressure, pen tilt, position of the pen thumbwheel, or rotation of the pen
Scattering	Scatter	specifies how brush marks are distributed in a stroke — if Both Axes is selected, brush marks are distributed in a radial direction; if Both Axes is deselected, brush marks are distributed perpendicular to the stroke path
	Count	specifies the number of brush marks applied at each spacing interval

Table 4–3 Brush Shape Options (continued)

Option	Setting	Description
Texture	Invert	used for patterns — inverts the high and low points in the texture based on the tones in the pattern
	Scale	specifies the scale of the pattern
	Depth	specifies how deeply the paint penetrates into the texture
Dual Brush	Mode	sets a blending mode to use when combining brush marks from the primary tip and the dual tip
Color Dynamics	Hue, Saturation, Brightness, Purity	specifies a percentage by which the hue, saturation, or brightness of the paint can vary in a stroke
Other Dynamics	Flow	specifies how the flow of paint varies in a brush stroke
Noise		adds additional randomness to individual brush tips
Wet Edges		causes paint to build up along the edges of the brush stroke, creating a watercolor effect
Airbrush		applies gradual tones to an image, simulating traditional airbrush techniques
Smoothing		produces smoother curves in brush strokes
Protect Texture		applies the same pattern and scale to all brush presets that have a texture

BTW

Brush Sets
While Photoshop contains more than one hundred brush tips, grouped by category, from which you may choose, sometimes you might want a unique or distinctive brush that is not available in Photoshop. In that case, you can purchase the design or create it from scratch. Brush tip files have the extension abr and are readily available for purchase on the Web.

To Display the Brushes Panel

The specific brush tip for the menu cover is not on the default list. Neither is it included in any of the brush tip sets that you can append. Therefore, in the next steps you will use the Brushes panel to load a new retro star brush tip from the Data Files for Students, and then use it to paint stars on the menu cover.

1
- Press the B key to select the Brush tool.
- Press the F5 key to display the Brushes panel.
- Click Brush Tip Shape to display the Brush Tip Shape pane (Figure 4–74).

Other Ways
1. On Window menu, click Brushes, click Brush Tip Shape
2. On Brush options bar, click Toggle the Brushes panel button, click Brush Tip Shape

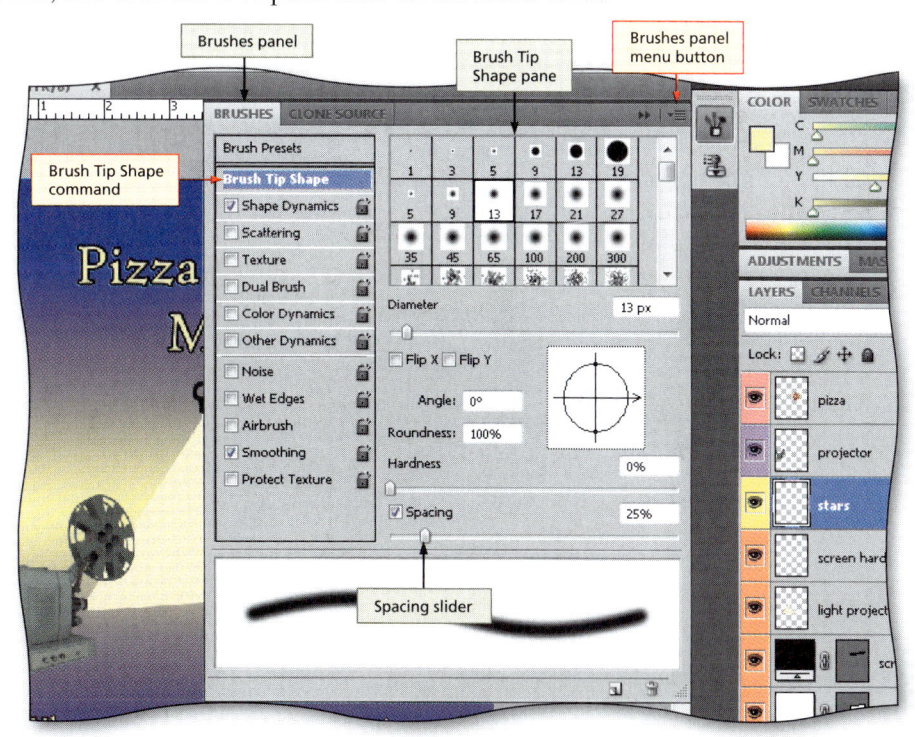

Figure 4–74

Photoshop Chapter 4 Drawing and Painting with Color

To Append a New Brush Set to the Brushes Panel

The Retro_Star brush set is included in the Data Files for Students. You can access the Data Files for Students on the DVD that accompanies this book. See the inside back cover of this book for instructions on downloading the Data Files for Students, or contact your instructor for information about accessing the required files. In the following steps, you will append the Retro_Star brush set to the panel set.

1
- Click the Brushes panel menu button to display the menu (Figure 4–75).

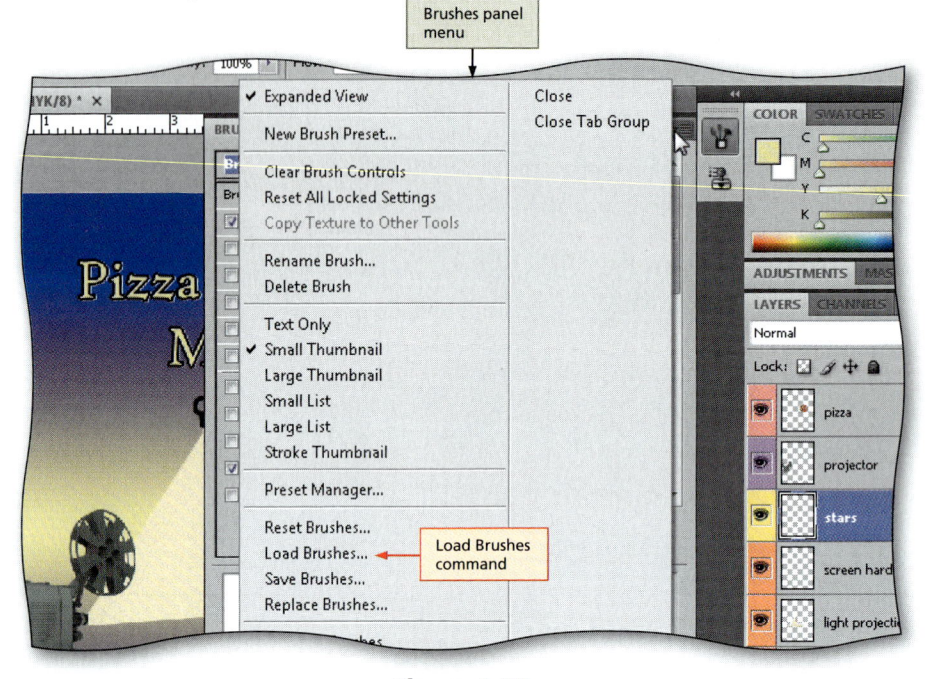

Figure 4–75

2
- Click Load Brushes to display the Load dialog box.
- Click the Look in box arrow and then navigate to the Data Files for Students. Double-click the folder named Chapter04 to open it (Figure 4–76).

3
- Double-click the file, Retro_Star.abr to load the new brush set.

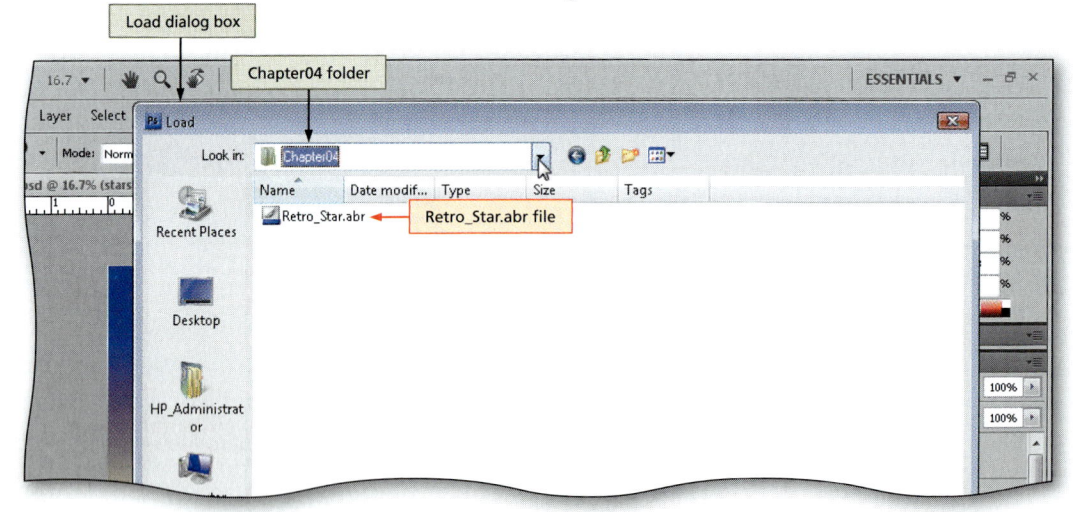

Figure 4–76

To Select the Brush Tip and Settings

To select a brush tip, the following steps click the tip preview in the Brush Tip Shape pane and adjust the settings.

1
- Scroll as necessary to display the preview of a new brush tip, 50s_Star, size 64.
- Click the preview of the new brush tip to select it.
- Drag the Diameter slider to 160px.
- Drag the Spacing slider to 1000% to display only one star (Figure 4–77).

Experiment
- Drag the slider and angle arrow to watch how the preview changes. When finished, reset the Angle to 0 and change the settings as noted above.

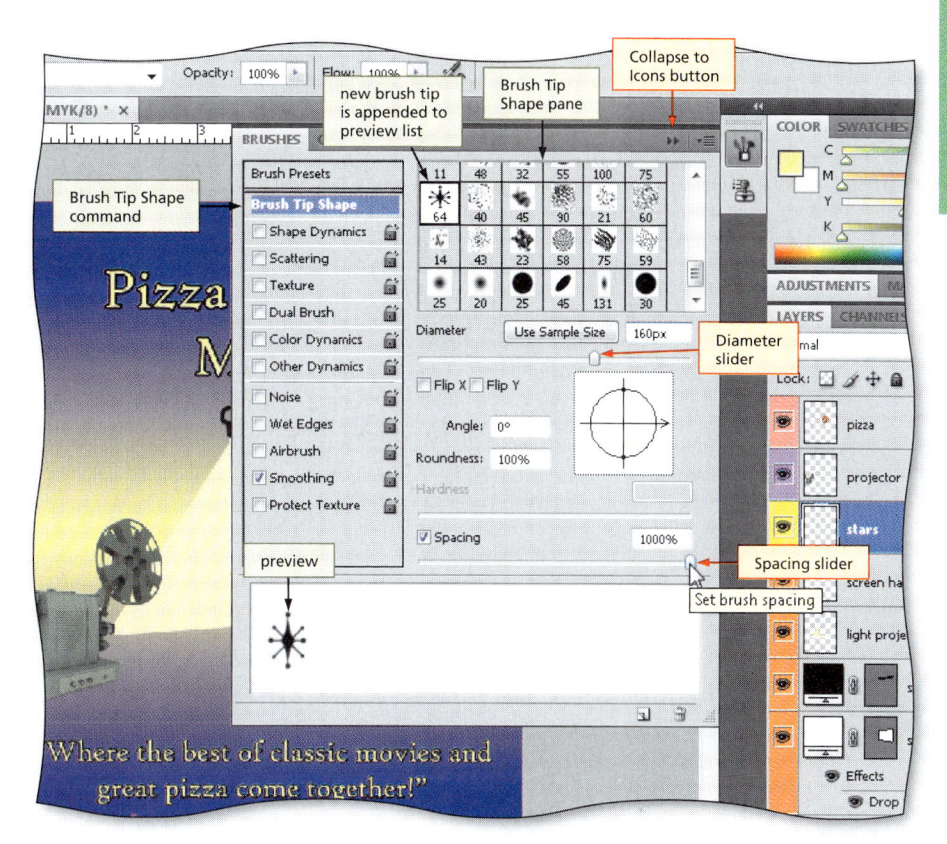

Figure 4–77

To Paint Using the 50s_Star Brush Tip

1
- Click the Collapse to Icons button on the Brushes panel title bar to collapse the panel.
- With the stars layer still selected, click the upper-left corner of the document window to create a star.
- Move the mouse pointer to view the star (Figure 4–78).

Figure 4–78

2

- Click other places across the top of the menu cover to create a random pattern.

- Click various places across the bottom of the menu cover to create a random pattern (Figure 4–79).

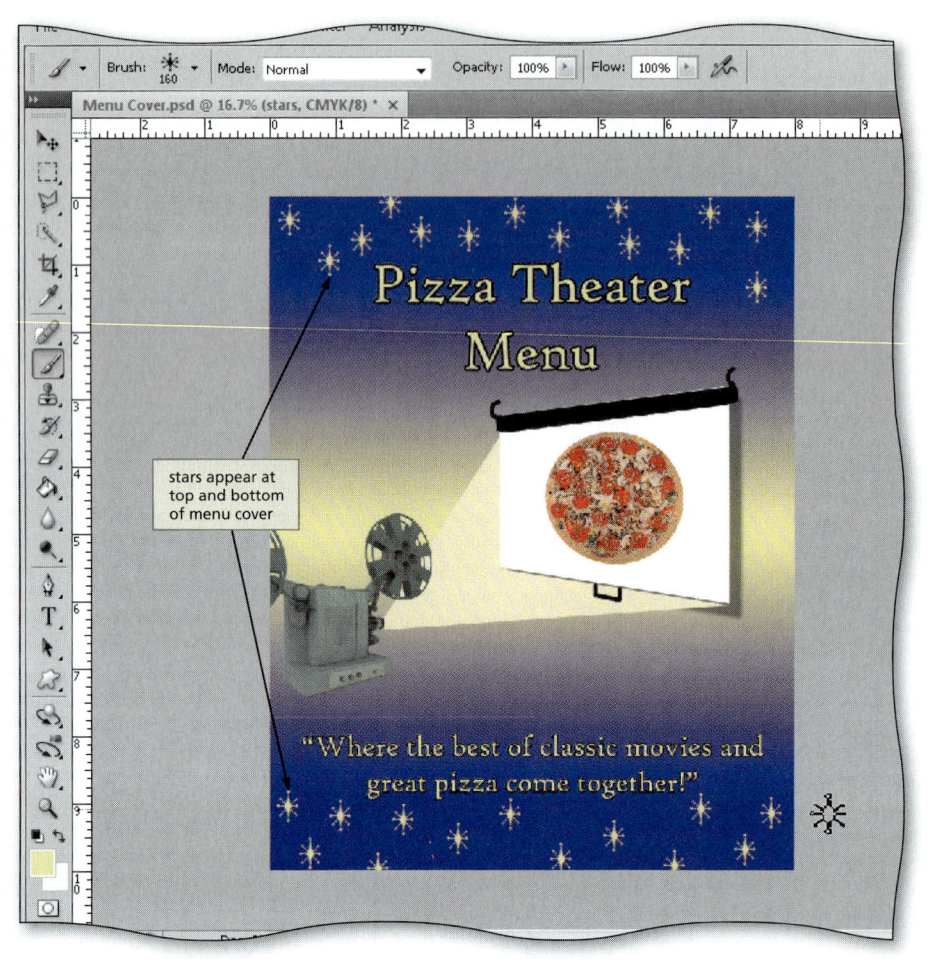

Figure 4–79

BTW

The Use Sample Size Button
When selecting brush tip shapes on the Brushes panel, if you change the diameter of a brush tip, Photoshop might display a Use Sample Size button. The Use Sample Size button allows you to reset the brush tip back to its default size.

Finishing the Menu Cover

The final graphic for the menu cover is made up of brush strokes that simulate heat coming off the pizza. First, you will create a new layer and sample a dark red color from the pizza. Then you will append the Assorted Brushes to the Brushes panel. After changing the Brush Tip Shape settings, you will draw the heat waves in the document window.

To Create a New Layer

The following steps create a new layer on which to draw the heat wave.

1. Press SHIFT+CTRL+N to create a new layer.

2. Rename the new layer, heat.

3. Change the heat layer's identification color to red.

4. Click the OK button to close the New Layer dialog box and display the new layer on the Layers panel.

To Sample a Red Color

The following steps sample a color from the pizza to use in the heat waves.

1. Press the I key to activate the Eyedropper tool.
2. Zoom as necessary and click a dark red color in the pizza to assign a new foreground color.

To Append Assorted Brushes

The following steps append the Assorted Brushes to the Brushes panel.

1. Press the B key to select the Brush tool.
2. Press the F5 key to redisplay the Brushes panel.
3. Click the Brushes panel menu button and then click Assorted Brushes to select the group.
4. Click the Append button in the Photoshop dialog box confirming your choice.

Select a Brush Tip and Settings for the Heat Wave

The following steps select a brush tip for the heat waves.

1. In the Brush Tip Shape pane of the Brushes panel, scroll down to display Ornament 3, size 41 and click the preview to select it.
2. Drag the Diameter slider to 200 pixels to enlarge the brush tip.
3. Drag the Angle arrow to approximately –110 degrees to place the brush tip on its side.
4. Drag the Spacing slider to 800% to space the heat waves apart.
5. In the document window, type 25 in the magnification box on the status bar and then press the ENTER key.
6. Scroll to display the white screen, while keeping the Brushes panel open (Figure 4–80 on the next page).

BTW

Dual Brushes
A dual brush uses two tips to create brush marks. For example, a solid border, circle brush tip used as the primary tip could be dressed up with a secondary feather tip for a customized look of a feathered circle. For the primary tip, you set a regular brush tip shape. For the second brush tip click Dual Brushes and choose the desired settings.

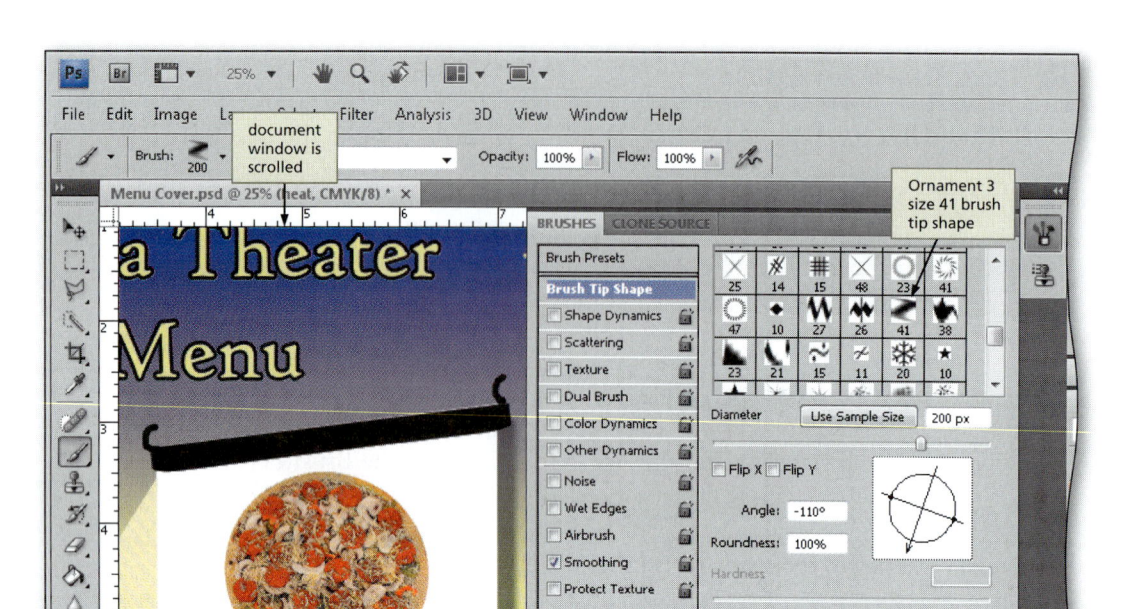

PS 298 **Photoshop Chapter 4** Drawing and Painting with Color

Figure 4–80

To Use the Ornament Brush Tip

1
- Click twice to the left of the pizza to create two strokes, as shown in Figure 4–81.

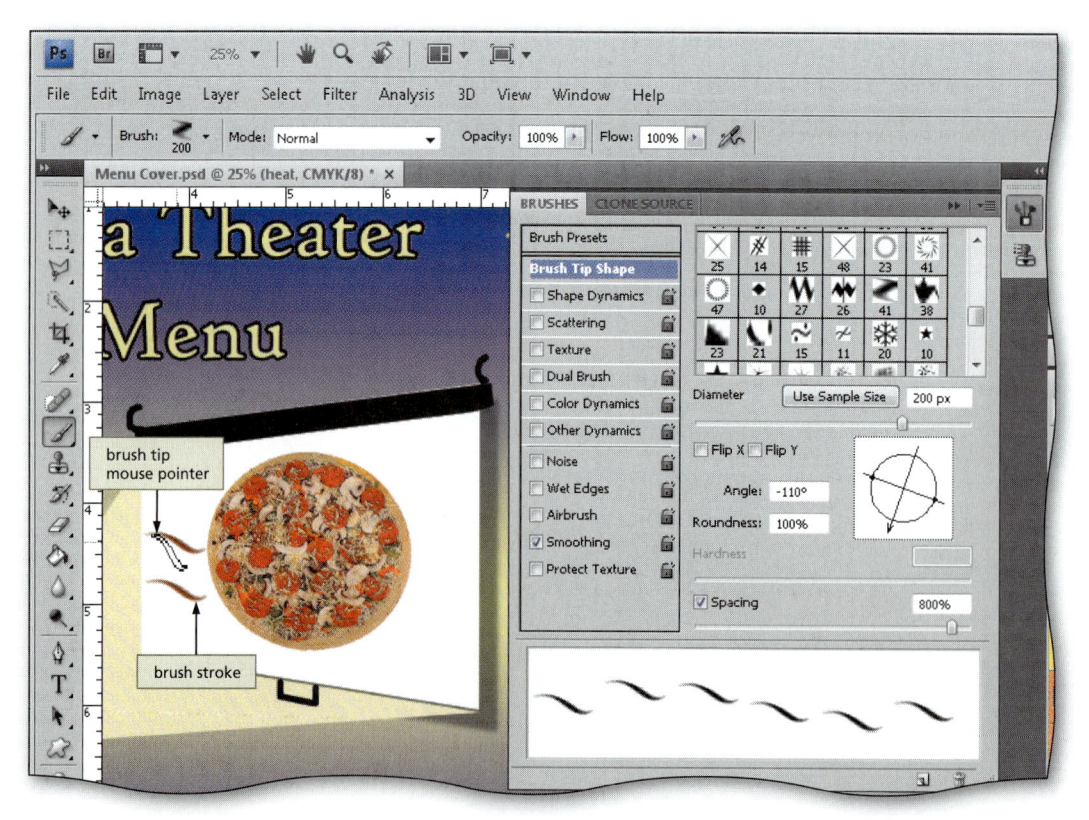

Figure 4–81

2

- On the Brushes panel, change the angle to approximately −130 degrees and drag two strokes at the upper-left corner of the pizza (Figure 4–82).

Q&A Should I click or drag to create these brush strokes?

You can do it either way. Dragging creates new strokes spaced evenly apart. You might have more control over the placement by clicking.

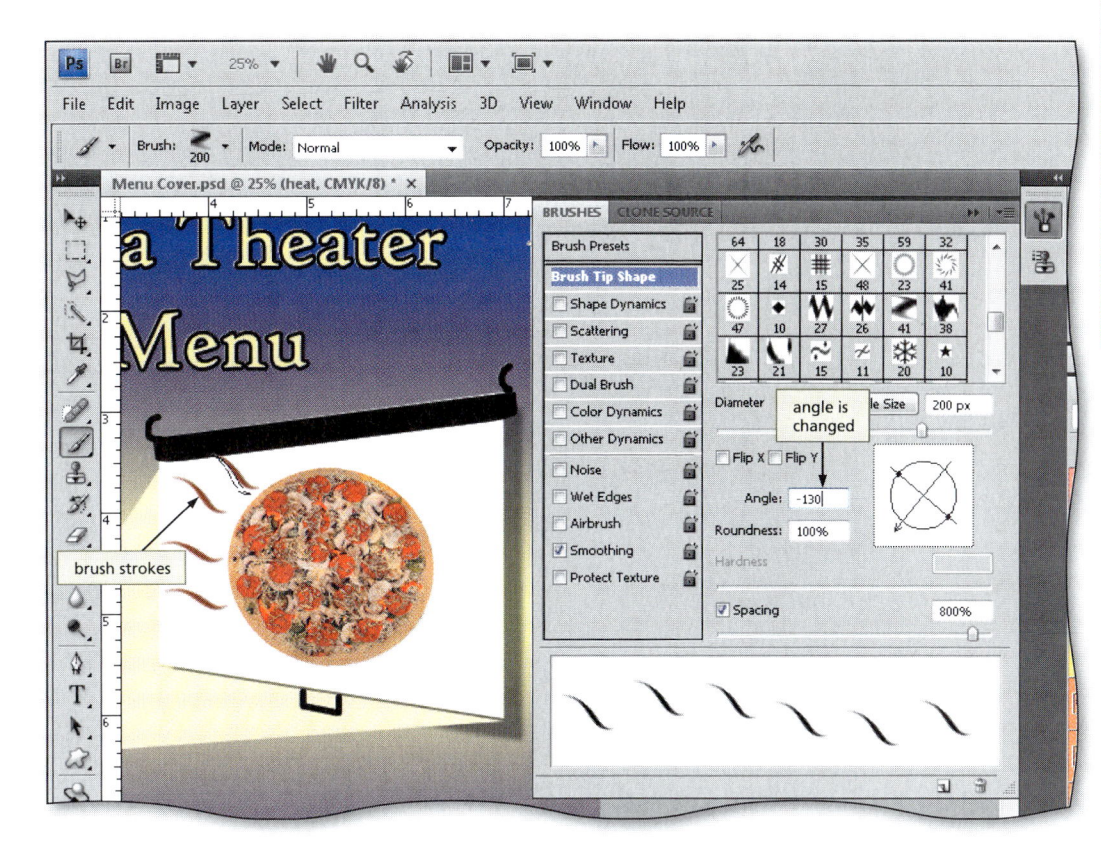

Figure 4–82

3

- Continue changing the angle by approximately 20 degrees and then click to create each stroke around the top and right sides of the pizza (Figure 4–83).

4

- Press the F5 key to minimize the Brushes panel.

Figure 4–83

> **BTW**
>
> **Photoshop Help**
> The best way to become familiar with Photoshop Help is to use it. Appendix D includes detailed information about Photoshop Help and exercises that will help you gain confidence in using it.

To Save the File

The menu cover is complete. You will save the file with the name Menu Cover with Layers in the PSD format.

1 Press SHIFT+CTRL+S and save the file with the name, Menu Cover with Layers.

To Flatten and Save the File

The following steps flatten the image and save it as a TIFF file.

1 On the Layer menu, click the Flatten Image command.

2 Press SHIFT+CTRL+S and save the file with the name Menu Cover for Printing, in the TIFF format.

To Close the Document Window and Quit Photoshop

The final step is to close the document window and quit Photoshop.

1 Click the Close button on the Application bar to close the document window and quit Photoshop.

Chapter Summary

You used many tools and panels as you created the menu cover in this chapter. You started a new file from scratch and used the Gradient tool to add two colors blended together. You created a shape and added a drop shadow for the screen, and a custom shape created the screen housing. You used the type tool to add text and then stroked it. You added images of a projector and a pizza, and painted a light projection. You selected a brush and drew the screen hardware, and then appended one new brush tip to create stars and another to create heat waves. Finally, you flattened the image and saved the file.

The items listed below include all the new Photoshop skills you have learned in this chapter:

1. Create a Photoshop File from Scratch (PS 247)
2. Change the Color Panel (PS 250)
3. Create a Gradient (PS 253)
4. Select a Gradient Preset (PS 255)
5. Select a Stop Color (PS 256)
6. Draw the Gradient (PS 258)
7. Use the Eyedropper Tool (PS 260)
8. Select the Horizontal Type Tool (PS 262)
9. Set Font Options (PS 262)
10. Insert Text (PS 264)
11. Stroke the Text (PS 266)
12. Create a Shape (PS 270)
13. Skew a Shape (PS 271)
14. Add a Drop Shadow (PS 272)
15. Add New Shapes Using the Shape Picker (PS 274)
16. Create a New Layer (PS 280)
17. Create a Polygonal Selection (PS 281)
18. Edit the Foreground Color (PS 282)
19. Fill Using the Paint Bucket Tool (PS 283)
20. Select the Brush Tool (PS 286)
21. Use the Brush Preset Picker (PS 287)
22. Draw Using the Brush Tool (PS 287)
23. Draw Straight Lines with the Brush Tool (PS 288)
24. Display the Brushes Panel (PS 293)
25. Append a New Brush Set to the Brushes Panel (PS 294)
26. Select the Brush Tip and Settings (PS 295)
27. Paint Using the 50s_Star Brush Tip (PS 295)
28. Use the Ornament Brush Tip (PS 298)

Learn It Online

Test your knowledge of chapter content and key terms.

Instructions: To complete the Learn It Online exercises, start your browser, click the Address bar, and then enter the Web address `scsite.com/pscs4/learn`. When the Photoshop CS4 Learn It Online page is displayed, click the link for the exercise you want to complete and then read the instructions.

Chapter Reinforcement TF, MC, and SA
A series of true/false, multiple choice, and short answer questions that test your knowledge of the chapter content.

Flash Cards
An interactive learning environment where you identify chapter key terms associated with displayed definitions.

Practice Test
A series of multiple choice questions that test your knowledge of chapter content and key terms.

Who Wants To Be a Computer Genius?
An interactive game that challenges your knowledge of chapter content in the style of a television quiz show.

Wheel of Terms
An interactive game that challenges your knowledge of chapter key terms in the style of the television show *Wheel of Fortune*.

Crossword Puzzle Challenge
A crossword puzzle that challenges your knowledge of key terms presented in the chapter.

Apply Your Knowledge

Reinforce the skills and apply the concepts you learned in this chapter.

Creating a Book Cover

Instructions: Start Photoshop and perform the customization steps found on pages PS 7 through PS 9. Open the Apply 4-1 Book Cover file from the Chapter04 folder of the Data Files for Students. You can access the Data Files for Students on the DVD that accompanies this book. See the inside back cover of this book for instructions on downloading the Data Files for Students, or contact your instructor for information about accessing the required files.

The purpose of this exercise is to create a composite photo by adding a gradient and custom shape to create a graphic similar to the one shown in Figure 4–84.

Figure 4–84

Continued >

Apply Your Knowledge *continued*

Perform the following tasks:
1. Use the Save As command to save the image on your USB flash drive as a PSD file, with the file name Apply 4-1 Book Cover Edited. Hide the text layers.
2. Select the Gradient tool. On the options bar, click the Gradient Editor box. Double-click the left Color Stop button to display the Select stop color dialog box. Click a yellow color on the color bar and then on the color field. Repeat the process to select a light orange or peach color for the right Color Stop button. If other Color Stop buttons are displayed, click them and then click the Delete button in the Gradient Editor dialog box. When you are finished, click the OK button.
3. Drag from the upper-left to the lower-right to create the gradient.
4. Open the file named Apply 4-1 Rose from the Chapter 04 folder of the Data Files for Students or from a location specified by your instructor. Use the Arrange Documents button to display the windows side by side. Use the Move tool to drag the rose into the Book Cover document window. Close the Rose document window. If necessary, press CTRL+T and then scale the rose to match the size in Figure 4–84 on the previous page and reposition it. Press the ENTER key to commit the transformation. Name the layer, rose.
5. Use the Magic Eraser tool to erase the black background from the rose layer.
6. On the Tools panel, click the current shape tool. On the Shape options bar, click the Custom Shape Tool button. Click the Custom shape picker. When the pop-up panel is displayed, click the menu button. Click Nature in the list. Append the shapes. Scroll as necessary, and then click the Raindrop shape.
7. On the Tools panel, double-click the Set foreground color button to access the Color Picker (Foreground Color) dialog box. Click in the color slider to choose blue, and then click a light blue in the color field. Click the OK button.
8. Drag in the document window several times, with varying lengths, to create the raindrops similar to those shown in Figure 4–84. Each raindrop will create its own layer.
9. Click the visibility icon next to both text layers.
10. Save the file again, and then flatten the image.
11. Save the flattened file with the name Apply 4-1 Book Cover Complete in the TIF format. Submit the file in the format specified by your instructor.

Extend Your Knowledge

Extend the skills you learned in this chapter and experiment with new skills. You may need to use Help to complete the assignment.

Creating a Promotional Movie Poster

Instructions: Start Photoshop and perform the customization steps found on pages PS 7 through PS 9. Open the Extend 4-1 Movie Poster file from the Chapter04 folder of the Data Files for Students. See the inside back cover of this book for instruction on downloading the Data Files for Students, or contact your instructor for information about accessing the required files. The purpose of this exercise is to create a composite photo with various components, similar to Figure 4–85, and to create both a PSD and TIF version of the final composition.

Figure 4–85

1. Save the image on your USB flash drive as a PSD file, with the file name Extend 4-1 Movie Poster Edited.
2. Create a gradient at the top of the photo:
    a. Create a new layer named, sky.
    b. With the new layer selected, use the Rectangular Marquee tool to create a selection that includes the top half of the canvas, down to the horizon line in the photo.
    c. Select the Gradient tool and its Linear Gradient style. Click the Gradient Editor box to display the Gradient Editor dialog box. Click the left stop button and sample a dark blue in the photo. Click the right stop button and sample a light blue from the photo. (*Hint*: You may have to drag the dialog boxes out of the way to sample the colors.) Close the Gradient Editor dialog box.
    d. Shift+drag from the top of the selection to the bottom of the section to create a linear gradient.
3. Create a gradient at the bottom of the photo:
    a. Create a new layer and name it footer.
    b. With the new layer selected, use the Rectangular marquee to create a selection that includes the bottom two inches of the photo.
    c. Select the Gradient tool and its Linear Gradient style. Click the Gradient Editor box to display the Gradient Editor. Choose the second preset, named Foreground to Transparent. Close the Gradient Editor dialog box.
    d. SHIFT+drag from the bottom of the selection to the top of the section to create a linear gradient.
4. Insert placeholder text:
    a. Open the Extend 4-1 Movie Text file and arrange the two document windows side by side.
    b. Use the Move tool to drag the text into the Extend 4-1 Movie Poster Edited file and position it in the lower part of the photo as shown in Figure 4–85.
    c. Close the Extend 4-1 Movie Text file.
5. Insert movie rating text:
    a. Open the Extend 4-1 Movie Rating file and arrange the two document windows side by side.
    b. Use the Move tool to drag the rating into the Extend 4-1 Movie Poster Edited file and position it below the placeholder text as shown in Figure 4–85.
    c. Close the Extend 4-1 Movie Rating file.

Continued >

Extend Your Knowledge *continued*

6. Create movie title text:

   a. Select the Horizontal Text tool. Choose a Serif font like Trajan Pro or Garamond. Set the font size to 100 and select a light shade for the color. Drag a text box across the top of the canvas. Type `The Big City` in the text box.

   b. On the Layers panel, use the Add a layer style button to add a stroke to the title using a dark blue or green color sampled from the photo.

7. Create movie subtitle text:

   a. Using the Horizontal Text tool again, with the same font, set the font size to 30. Drag a text box below the title and to the right. Type `A MOVIE ABOUT THE CITY` in the text box.

8. Add the movie reel image:

   a. Use Photoshop Help to read about the Place command. Click File on the menu bar and then click Place. Browse to the file named Extend 4-1 Movie Reel and select it. Click the Place button and then position the movie reel image as shown in Figure 4–85 on the previous page. Press the ENTER key to finish the place.

9. Save the file again and then flatten the image.

10. Press SHIFT+CTRL+S to open the Save As dialog box. Type `Extend 4-1 Movie Poster Complete` in the Name box. Click the Format box arrow and then click TIF in the list. Click the Save button. When Photoshop displays the TIFF Options dialog box, click the OK button to finish saving the file.

11. Submit the file in the format specified by your instructor.

Make It Right

Analyze a project and correct all errors and/or improve the design.

Correcting a Cell Phone Ad

Instructions: Start Photoshop and perform the customization steps found on pages PS 7 through PS 9. Open the Make It Right 4-1 Cell Phone file from the Chapter 04 folder of the Data Files for Students. You can access the Data Files for Students on the DVD that accompanies this book. See the inside back cover of this book for instructions on downloading the Data Files for Students, or contact your instructor for information about accessing the required files.

The file contains an ad for the Super Chrome 2000 cell phone (Figure 4–86). The client thinks that it is too bland. You are to improve the look of the ad with gradients and brushes.

Figure 4–86

1. On the violet background layer, create a radial gradient with shades of purple, from the upper right to the lower left, so the radial appears around the cell phone.
2. Add a radial gradient with shades of green from left to right to the shape in the green layer.
3. Add a radial gradient with shades of blue from top to bottom to the shape in the blue layer.
4. On the Layers panel, CTRL+click the super chrome layer thumbnail to select its content. Apply the Chrome preset gradient in a linear style from top to bottom.
5. Repeat Step 4 for the 2000 layer.
6. For a final touch, use the Add a layer style button to add a bevel and a drop shadow to help set the text layers apart from the blue background. Use the default settings for both layer styles.
7. Save the file as Make It Right 4-1 Cell Phone Edited.

In the Lab

Design and/or create a project using the guidelines, concepts, and skills presented in this chapter. Labs are listed in order of increasing difficulty.

Lab 1: Creating an Advertisement Using Gradients and Shapes

Problem: A friend of your father's owns a small golf course on the edge of town. He has heard of your study of Photoshop and would like you to create an advertisement for him. He plans to place the color ad in a regional golfing magazine, therefore he wants a high resolution, CMYK file to submit to the publisher. The owner has a file with the appropriate text copy, an image of a golf ball, and an image of a golfer. You need to put it all together, adding a gradient background and inserting a shape. A sample solution is shown in Figure 4–87 on the next page.

Continued >

In the Lab *continued*

Instructions: Perform the following tasks:

1. Start Photoshop. Set the default workspace, default colors, and reset all tools.

2. Open the file Lab 4-1 Golf Outing from the Chapter04 folder of the Data Files for Students. You can access the Data Files for Students on the DVD that accompanies this book. See the inside back cover of this book for instructions on downloading the Data Files for Students, or contact your instructor for information about accessing the required files.

3. Click the Save As command on the File menu. Browse to your USB flash drive storage device. Click the Save button. If Photoshop displays a format Options dialog box, click the OK button.

Figure 4–87

4. In the Layers panel, click the visibility icons to hide all text layers. Click the Background layer to select it, if necessary.

5. Press the G key to activate the Gradient tool. If the Paint Bucket tool is active, press SHIFT+G to toggle to the Gradient tool.

6. On the Gradient options bar, click the Linear Gradient button and then click the Gradient Editor box. When Photoshop displays the Gradient Editor dialog box, click the Foreground to Background preset. Click the Gradient Type box arrow and then click Solid. Double-click the Smoothness box and then type 100.

7. Below the color bar, double-click the left Color Stop button. When the Select stop color dialog box is displayed, click light blue in the color panel. Click the OK button.

8. Below the color bar, double-click the right Color Stop button. When the Select stop color dialog box is displayed, click light yellow in the color panel. Click the OK button.

9. Below the center of the color bar, double-click to create a new Color Stop button. When the Select stop color dialog box is displayed, choose a light orange color. Click the OK button.

10. Drag the orange Color Stop button slightly to the right until the gradient smoothly transitions from one color to another, similar to that shown in Figure 4–87. Adjust any Color Midpoint diamonds as necessary.

11. Click the OK button in the Gradient Editor dialog box. Draw a gradient by dragging from the upper-right corner of the page in the document window to the lower-left corner. (*Hint:* If you do not like the result and want to redo the gradient, press CTRL+Z to undo the step and then repeat Steps 6 through 11.)

12. In the Layers panel, display the text layers.

13. Press CTRL+O and then navigate to the file named Lab 4-1 Golfer. Open the file.
14. Use the Arrange Documents button to display the windows side by side. In the Lab 4-1 Golfer document window, press CTRL+A to select the entire image. Use the Move tool to drag the image to the Lab 4-1 Golf Outing document window. Position the golfer as shown in Figure 4–87.
15. Close the Lab 4-1 Golfer document window. In the Layers panel, rename the new layer.
16. Press CTRL+O and then navigate to the file named Lab 4-1 Golf Ball. Open the file.
17. In the Lab 4-1 Golf Ball document window, press CTRL+A to select the entire image. Press CTRL+C to copy the image. Select the Lab 4-1 Golf Outing document window and then press CTRL+V to paste the image. Close the Lab 4-1 Golf Ball document window. Position the golf ball as shown in Figure 4–87.
18. Increase the magnification as necessary in the Lab 4-1 Golf Outing document window. Press the E key to access the current Eraser tool. Use the Magic Eraser tool to erase the blue areas around the golf ball.
19. Resize the golf ball to make it smaller by pressing CTRL+T to display the bounding box. SHIFT+drag a corner sizing handle and then press the ENTER key. Rename the new layer, golf ball.
20. Press the U key to access the shape tools. On the Shape options bar, click the Shape Layers button to select it, if necessary. Click the Custom Shape Tool button.
21. On the Shape options bar, click the Custom Shape picker. When the pop-up panel is displayed, click the menu button and then click Web in the list. When Photoshop asks if you want to replace or append the shapes, click the Append button. When the new shapes are displayed, scroll as necessary and double-click the Time shape.
22. On the Shape options bar, click the Color box. When the Color Picker dialog box is displayed, select a Light Gray color. Click the OK button.
23. In the document window, SHIFT+drag to create a clock in the lower-right portion of the image, similar to the one shown in Figure 4–87. On the Layers panel, drag the Opacity slider to make the appearance of the clock more subtle. Rename the layer, clock. A border may appear around the edges of the clock. It will disappear when you flatten the image.
24. On the File menu, click Save.
25. On the Layer menu, click Flatten Image. Save the flattened image as `Lab 4-1 Golf Outing Complete` in the TIFF format.
26. Quit Photoshop. E-mail the file as an attachment to your instructor.

In the Lab

Lab 2: Creating a Web Graphic from Scratch

Problem: A planetarium is holding a contest to choose a Web graphic to advertise its new exhibit. The winning promotional piece will represent themes related to the search for life in deep space. The winner of the contest will receive $500 and a family membership to the planetarium. You decide to enter. Using a gradient, a shape, and brush strokes, you create a piece that symbolizes the planets, the sky, motion, searching, and life. A sample image is displayed in Figure 4–88 on the next page.

Continued >

In the Lab *continued*

Instructions: Perform the following tasks:
1. Start Photoshop. Set the default workspace and reset all tools.
2. Click New on the File menu. When the New dialog box is displayed, use the following settings:

   Name: Lab 4-2 Planetarium Graphic

   Width: 8 inches

   Height: 8 inches

   Resolution: 300 pixels/inch

   Color Mode: RGB Color, 8 bit

   Background Contents: White
3. Save the file on your storage device in the PSD format.
4. Select the Gradient tool. On the Gradient options bar, click the Gradient Editor box arrow and then double-click the Chrome gradient.

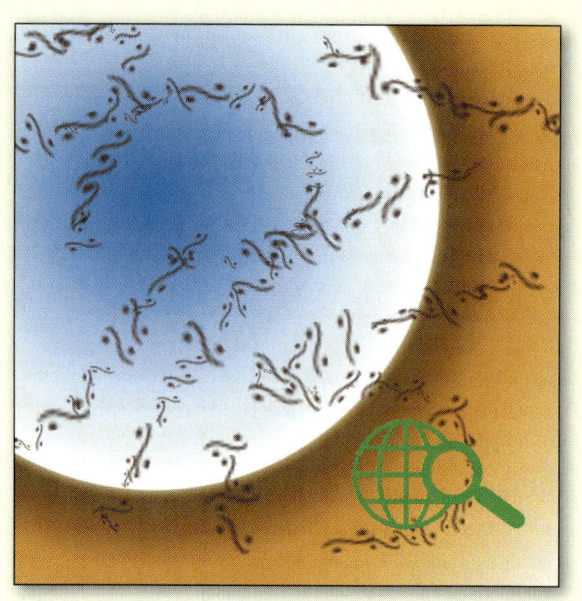

Figure 4–88

5. On the options bar, click the Radial Gradient button, and then drag from the upper-left corner to the lower-right corner.
6. Select the Eyedropper tool and sample the darkest brown color in the Chrome gradient. In the Color panel, if a warning triangle displays, click the square next to it to select a gamut color.
7. Select the Brush tool. Display the Brushes panel and then click the panel menu button. On the panel menu, click Assorted Brushes and append the brushes.
8. Click the Brush Tip Shape button. Scroll as necessary and then click the Ornament 7 size 15 brush tip. Click the Shape Dynamics check box so it displays a check mark. Set the Diameter to 200 pixels, and the Spacing to 150%. Press the F5 key to return the Brushes panel to the dock of collapsed panels. Drag with short strokes, randomly in the image, at different angles. Your design does not have to match the one in Figure 4–88.
9. Click the Set foreground color button on the Tools panel. When Photoshop displays the Color Picker (Foreground Color) dialog box, click the Only Web Colors check box so it displays a check mark. Click green in the color slider and then click an appropriate green color in the color field. Click the OK button.
10. Select the Shape tool. On the Shape options bar, click the Shape layers button to select it, if necessary. Click the Custom Shape Tool button. Click the Custom Shape picker, and then click the shape menu button on the pop-up panel. On the menu, click Web. When Photoshop asks if you want to replace or append, click the Append button. Scroll as necessary and then select the World Wide Web Search Shape.
11. In the document window, SHIFT+drag to add the sphere and magnifying glass in the lower-right corner. Move the sphere and magnifying glass if necessary.
12. Assign an appropriate name and identification color to the new layer you created.
13. Save the file again and then flatten the image.
14. Press SHIFT+CTRL+S to access the Save As dialog box. In the File name box, type Lab 4-2 Planetarium Graphic Complete as the name. Save the file using the TIF format.
15. For extra credit, create a simple Web page and display your image. Send your instructor a copy of the image as an e-mail attachment or send the URL.

In the Lab

Lab 3: Creating a Flyer

Problem: Your local bowling alley has asked you to create a simple image with the words, Bowl-O-Rama above a colorful bowling ball. The address should appear below the bowling ball. A sample image is displayed in Figure 4–89.

Figure 4–89

Instructions: Perform the following tasks: Start Photoshop. Set the default workspace and reset all tools. Create a new Photoshop file named Lab 4-3 Bowling Flyer and save it to your USB flash drive storage device. The new file should be approximately 8.5 inches wide by 5.5 inches high. Choose a mid-level resolution and use RGB, 8 bit for the color mode.

Create a background layer containing a radial gradient with shades of purple. Drag in the canvas from the middle to the upper-right corner. Create a selection that includes the lower half of the canvas and create a second linear gradient as shown in Figure 4–89. (*Hint*: The Reverse check box on the options bar should not display a check mark.) Create a new layer named shadow and draw a large circle in the middle of the canvas. (*Hint*: Use the Elliptical Marquee tool and the SHIFT key.) Add a radial gradient using the Foreground to Transparent preset.

In a new layer, Use a Shape tool to create the bowling ball. (*Hint*: On the options bar, click the Style picker and then click the Nebula preset.) Adjust the opacity of the bowling ball. Create the finger holes on the bowling ball. (*Hint*: Reset the default colors to black over white.)

Create the upper text using the appropriate tool, a typeface similar to Cooper Std, and a large size font. (*Hint*: Warp the text using the Arc style from within the Warp Text dialog box.) Add the lower text. Create the stars in their own layer using an appropriate brush to randomly make a star pattern across the top of the background.

Save the image again, flatten it, and then save it in the TIF format with the file name, Lab 4-3 Bowling Flyer Complete. Submit it in the format specified by your instructor.

Cases and Places

Apply your creative thinking and problem-solving skills to design and implement a solution.

• Easier   •• More Difficult

• 1: Create a Sign with Shapes

Create a sign to place on the paper recycling box in your computer lab. Start with a blank page that is 8.5 inches by 11 inches. Choose a shape tool and then click the Custom Shape Tool button on the Shape options bar. Click the Shape box. When the shapes are displayed, click Shape Preset picker menu button and then click Symbols in the list. Click to Append the Symbols to the current set. Scroll to display the recycling logo and click it. Drag to create a recycling logo that fills the page, leaving a 1-inch margin on each side. Select a dark blue color from the Swatches panel and then use the Paint Bucket tool to color the logo. If you are asked to rasterize the layer, click the OK button. Find a graphic of a piece of paper with something printed on it. Drag a copy to the middle of the recycling logo. Print the sign on a color printer.

• 2: Color a Photo

Scan in a black-and-white photo and open it in Photoshop. Print a copy of the photo. Use the Magic Wand tool to select portions of clothing, buildings, sky, grass, or walls. Double-click the Set foreground color button on the Tools panel, and then select a color using the Color Picker (Foreground Color) dialog box. Use the Paint Bucket tool to fill the selections with color. Save the colorized version of the photo with a different name. Print the colorized version. Turn in both the before and after printouts to your instructor.

•• 3: Think About Shapes and Brushes

Look through newspapers and magazines to find graphics of images that were created from scratch rather than from photos. For example, you might see a drawing of a book shape, a car, or an activity. Find three different examples and write a paragraph on each, describing how the graphic might be recreated using shapes and brushes. In your description, include the shapes, transformations, brush strokes, shadows, and settings that you might use. If directed by your instructor, recreate one of the graphics using Photoshop.

•• 4: Redesign a School Logo

Make It Personal

Ask your instructor for a digital copy of your school's logo. Start a new document from scratch and create a background gradient using one of the Gradient buttons other than Linear. Open the logo file and drag a copy into the new document. Include at least four different strokes or shapes from the concepts presented in this chapter, such as a color change, brush strokes, shapes, or drawing with the Pen tool.

•• 5: Create a Special Effects Storyboard

Working Together

Your team is in charge of special effects for a small movie production company. You need to plan a storyboard of special effects for an upcoming action movie. Together, decide on a theme for your movie. Each member should bring a real digital or electronic image to use in the storyboard. As you did when adding heat lines to the menu cover, use painting and drawing tools to add at least four of the following special effects to each of the real images: flames, lightning bolts, explosions, tattoos, a change of eye color, jet streams, rocket flares, spider webs, sunbursts, or some other effect of your choosing.

5 Enhancing and Repairing Photos

Objectives

You will have mastered the material in this chapter when you can:

- Discuss technical tips for digital cameras and scanners
- Repair documents with aging damage
- Make level corrections for contrast
- Sharpen images with the Unsharp Mask
- Correct small blemishes using the Spot Healing Brush tool
- Correct tears and scratches using the Healing Brush tool
- Retouch images using the Patch tool
- Correct red-eye
- Use the Dodge and Burn tools
- Remove or correct angle and perspective distortions
- Enhance a photo using the Blur tool

5 Enhancing and Repairing Photos

Introduction

Repairing and enhancing photos is an important skill for people such as graphic designers, restoration experts, and professional photographers. It is a useful skill for the amateur photographer as well. Many families have old photographs that have been damaged over time, and most people have taken a red-eye photo, a photo that is too light or dark, or one in which the subject is tilted. Freelance photographers, genealogists, family historians, and proud parents all use Photoshop to restore, correct, and improve their photographs.

It is impossible to make every photo look perfect, however. Graphics-related professionals know that a camera lacks the flexibility to rival reality — the tonal range of color is too small. The large number of colors visible to human eyes is a spectrum that cannot be completely reproduced by cameras or digital creations. Therefore, enhancing and repairing photos is both an art and a science. Using the digital tools available in Photoshop, you can employ technology to make reparative and restorative changes. Artistically, you need a strong sense of color and design sensibility.

Restoring original documents is a highly skilled art. It takes education, research, and years of practice. When dealing with documents of great value, or when dealing with materials in advanced stages of deterioration, a professional conservator or restoration service should be consulted. Many restorers, however, choose to renovate or repair original documents using digital copies. If the document can be scanned or photographed, the original does not have to be disturbed. Photoshop has many tools to help repair and enhance documents.

Project — Enhancing and Repairing Photos

Chapter 5 uses Photoshop to enhance and repair several photographs and documents. In preparation for the centennial anniversary of a landmark schoolhouse, an old report card needs to be restored for easier reading. An old photo of the first schoolmaster is damaged by wrinkles and defects. A photo of a teacher and student needs to be enhanced by repairing light damage. A photo of the schoolhouse itself needs a perspective correction. A picture of a recent student visitor needs to have the red-eye removed. Finally, another photo is enhanced to show motion. The before and after photos are illustrated in Figure 5–1.

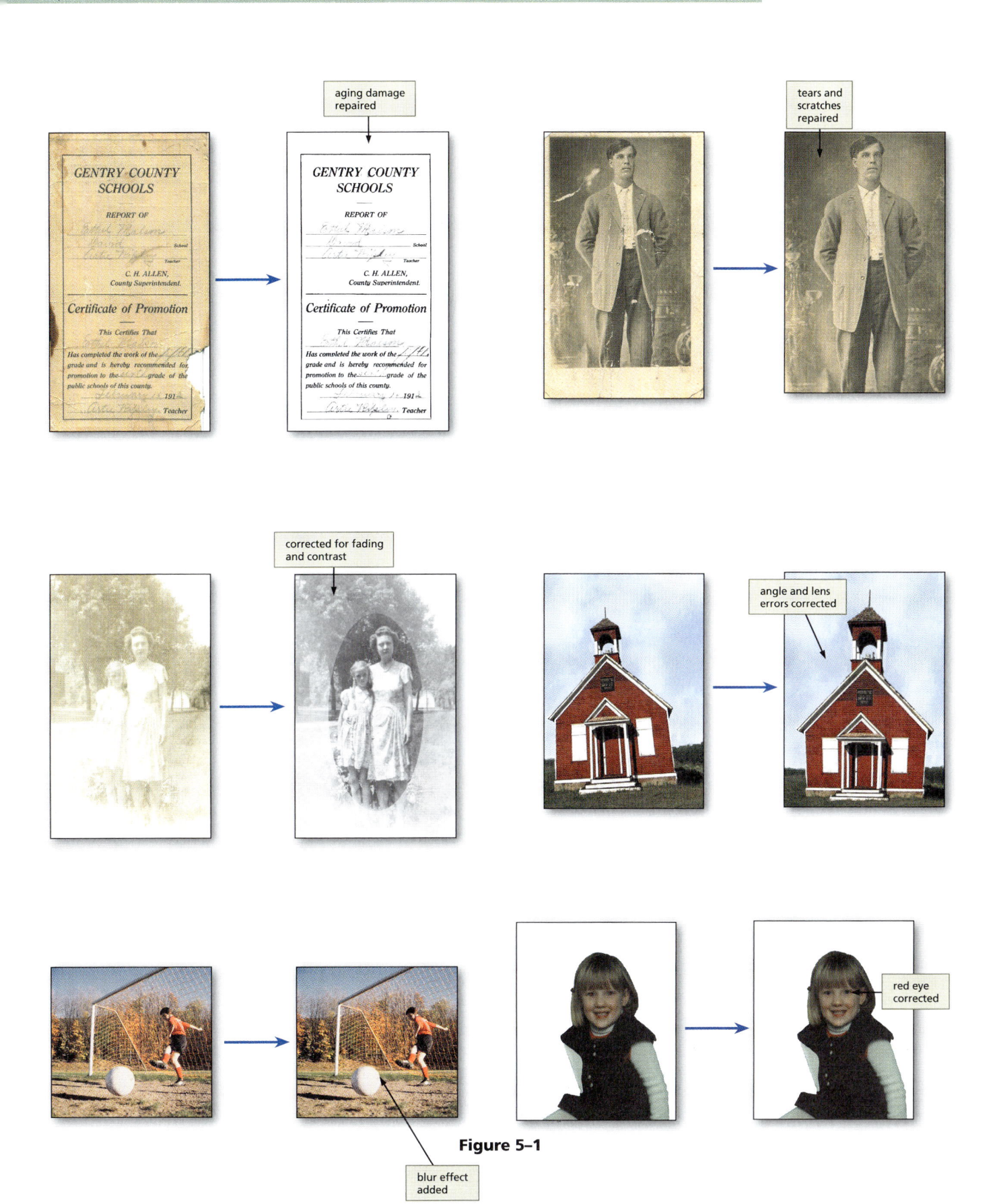

Help
Adobe **Photoshop CS4**

aging damage repaired

tears and scratches repaired

corrected for fading and contrast

angle and lens errors corrected

Figure 5–1

blur effect added

red eye corrected

PS 313

Overview

As you read this chapter, you will learn how to enhance and repair the images shown in Figure 5–1 on the previous page by performing these general tasks:

- Remove yellowing.
- Sharpen images.
- Restore missing portions of a document.
- Repair tears and blemishes.
- Correct red-eye.
- Fix light and dark spots in a photo.
- Create a vignette.
- Correct lens errors and distortions.
- Use blurring for artistic effect.

Plan Ahead

General Project Guidelines

When editing a photo, the actions you perform and decisions you make will affect the appearance and characteristics of the finished product. As you edit photos, such as the ones shown in Figure 5–1, you should follow these general guidelines:

1. **Create a high-resolution digital image**. When repairing a printed photo or document, the scanning technique is the most important step in enhancing and repairing the image. Scan using the highest resolution possible with the correct settings. Other image sources may include digital cameras and graphics from the Web. Always work on a copy of the original scan, or create a corrections layer.

2. **Sharpen images and retouch as necessary.** Sharpening images that have been scanned creates more recognizable edges and improves the overall look of the image. Retouching includes erasing, cloning, and correcting light and dark spots.

3. **Heal specific defects.** Remove defects such as yellowing, blemishes, tears, and red-eye to improve legibility and clarity. Restoration professionals attempt to recreate the original look and feel of old documents and photos.

4. **Correct lens errors.** The final touch is to correct any lens errors. You can correct distortion, angles, blurs, vignetting, perspective errors, keystone distortions, barrel distortions, chromatic aberrations, and scaling.

When necessary, more specific details concerning the above guidelines are presented at appropriate points in the chapter. The chapter also will identify the actions performed and decisions made regarding these guidelines during the creation of the edited photos shown in Figure 5–1.

Gathering Images

Recall that there are a variety of ways that pictures and documents can be imported into Photoshop. Pictures taken using old photograph-generating devices, such as tintypes, daguerreotypes, and stereographic cameras, as well as those taken with film and instant print cameras, must be scanned using a digital scanner. Many photo-processing services will digitize any type of film onto a photo CD or DVD. Modern digital cameras use simple software to transfer pictures directly into computer systems. Documents and personal papers can be scanned in as images; or, if they are typewritten and easily legible, some scanners can produce digital text files. However, no matter how you generate the image, creating a high-quality, high-resolution copy is an important step in enhancing and repairing photos and documents.

> **Create a high-resolution digital image.**
> You may acquire images from a variety of sources:
>
> - Scanners: Considerations that affect the outcome of a scanned image include color, size, and resolution settings of the scanner and the desired file type. When converting an original image to a digital copy, some loss of resolution is inevitable, so you should try to minimize that loss by using correct scanner settings.
> - Digital cameras and cell phones: Images can be transferred directly from a digital camera's storage medium to a file or imported into Photoshop, avoiding any loss of resolution. Use the highest possible image file settings. Cell phone images can be e-mailed as well.
> - Web: Images downloaded from the Web or sent by e-mail sometimes need enhancement or repair. Make sure you have the legal rights to use the image.

Plan Ahead

Scanners

A **scanner** is a peripheral hardware device that scans photos, documents, or even 3D objects, in an optical manner, converting the result to a digital image. Table 5–1 displays some simple tips about using digital scanners that will produce better results. In addition, you should review your scanner documentation carefully.

Table 5–1 Scanner Tips

Issue	Tip
File Type and Mode	Most scanners have a setting related to the type of file you are selecting. Scanners make automatic anti-aliasing adjustments and tonal changes based on the file type you choose. Use the closest possible settings to your original. For example, if you have a text-only document, do not use a setting related to color photos; use the black-and-white, or grayscale, setting.
Multiple Scans	Do not assume that your first scan is the one you will use. Try scanning with various file types, settings, and at different sizes. Look at a black-and-white scan even if color was your first choice. Keep in mind your final use of the image.
Placement	Place the photo in the upper-left corner of the scanner bed. Align the long side of the original with the long side of the scanner. Use the scanner's preview capability so that the scanner will determine the size and location of the photograph. Use scanner settings to select the exact size rather than the entire scanner bed when possible. After a preview scan, if available, a scaling feature, such as Scale to Fit page, will produce a bigger copy.
Quality	Always choose the best resolution when scanning an image for use in Photoshop, keeping in mind that an image with higher resolution requires more disk space to store and may be slower to edit and print. Image resolution is a compromise between image quality and file size.
Resolution	The scanner's resolution is a measure of how many dots per inch are scanned. Higher-resolution images can reproduce greater detail and subtler color transitions than lower-resolution images because of the density of the pixels in the images. High-quality images often look good at any print size.
Shading	To maintain the background shading, especially in color, select a setting related to text with pictures rather than just text. A text-only setting can create a picture area that appears as a solid black rectangle.
Size	Use the largest original you can. For instance, an 8 × 10-inch photo will produce a higher quality 24-inch poster than a 4 × 6-inch photo. Only use a reduced or enlarged setting when absolutely necessary. Keep in mind that when you print a copy, most printers need at least 1/4-inch margin. A printed copy produced from a scan may lose its edges if the original is the exact size as the paper.
Text	Most scanners have a text or drawing setting, which is appropriate only if your original contains only black-and-white areas, text, or other solid areas, such as signatures, clip art, line drawings, maps, or blueprints. If you use this setting for a photograph or picture that also contains gray areas, the result may be unsatisfactory.
Tone	If the copy appears too light or too dark, or just appears as solid black, make sure that you have selected the correct file type for the original you are using. Look for darken and lighten settings that might be adjusted.

Digital Cameras

The advent of digital cameras and cell phones with cameras has reduced dramatically the need for the intermediate step of scanning. Images can be transferred directly from the camera's storage medium to a file or imported directly into Photoshop. A digital camera's resolution is measured in megapixels, or millions of dots per inch. It is not uncommon for a digital camera to create photos with eight or more megapixels. Figure 5–2a displays a photo taken at 8 megapixels. Figure 5–2b displays the same image taken at 2 megapixels. Notice the finer details and brighter colors produced by more megapixels. Certain digital cameras export images using Windows Image Acquisition (WIA) support. When you use WIA, Photoshop works with Windows and your digital camera or scanner software to import images directly into Photoshop.

(a) 8 megapixels

(b) 2 megapixels

Figure 5–2

BTW

Camera Raw Files
Working with camera raw files allows maximum control for settings such as white balance, tonal range, contrast, color saturation, and sharpening, similar to how photo processors try to fix photos taken by traditional film, reprocessing the negative with different shades and tints. Photoshop displays a special dialog box when working with camera raw photos.

Table 5–2 displays some simple tips about digital cameras that will produce better results when working with Photoshop. Again, carefully review your camera's documentation.

Table 5–2 Digital Camera Tips

Issue	Tip
File Type	If possible, set the camera to save files in its own raw file format. The Adobe Web site, www.adobe.com, has a list of cameras supported by Photoshop.
Quality	Use high-capacity memory cards and higher megapixel counts to take more images at a much higher resolution. Use the highest quality compression setting as well.
Storage	Copy images from the camera to a storage device before editing them in Photoshop. Adobe Bridge can read from most media cards, or you can use the software that comes with your camera.
Lighting and Speed	Experiment with the correlation between light and shutter speeds. Most of the newer digital cameras can take many pictures in a short amount of time, avoiding the shutter lag problem — the delay that occurs between pressing the shutter release button and the actual moment the picture is taken.
Balance	Changing your white balance setting from auto to cloudy when shooting outdoors creates a filtered, richer color, increasing the reds and yellows.
Filters	If possible, use a polarizing filter for landscapes and outdoor shooting. It reduces glare and unwanted reflections. Polarized shots have richer, more saturated colors, especially in the sky. You also can use sunglasses in front of the lens to reduce glare. When shooting through glass, use an infinity focus setting.

Table 5–2 Digital Camera Tips (*continued*)	
Issue	**Tip**
Flash	When shooting pictures of people or detailed subjects, use the flash — even outdoors. If available, use the camera's fill flash or flash on mode. That way, the camera exposes the background first and then adds just enough light to illuminate your subject. Keep in mind that most flash mechanisms only have a range of approximately 10 feet.
Settings	When possible, use a plain background, look at your subject in a straight, level manner, and move in as close as possible. Consider the rule of thirds when taking photographs. For busy backgrounds, if your camera has a focus lock feature, center the subject and push the shutter button halfway down to focus on the subject. Then move the camera horizontally or vertically away from the center before pressing the shutter button all the way down.
Motion	For moving objects use a fast shutter speed.

> **BTW**
>
> **EPS**
> The EPS (Encapsulated PostScript) file format is best used for print, because it is printer device-independent and delivers the best output at any size or resolution. PostScript printers contain a built-in interpreter that executes PostScript instructions with the ability to handle the complex text and graphics typical in graphic design and desktop publishing.

Web Graphics

A vast source of images and documents can be found on the Web. The advantage in using Web graphics is the fact that the pictures and documents already are digitized, so you do not have to manipulate or scan them; neither do you lose any resolution when transferring them to your computer system. The disadvantage of using Web graphics is in ownership. You must obtain permission to use images you download from the Web unless the image is free and unrestricted. You need to scrutinize carefully any Web sites that advertise free graphics. Some cannot be used for business purposes, for reproductions, or for resale. Some illegitimate sites that advertise free downloads also may embed spyware on your system.

Starting and Customizing Photoshop

The following steps start Photoshop and reset the default workspace, tools, colors, and Layer panel options.

To Start Photoshop

The following steps, which assume Windows Vista is running, start Photoshop based on a typical installation.

1. Click the Start button on the Windows Vista taskbar and then click All Programs to display the All Programs list.

2. Click Adobe Design Premium CS4, or your version of the Adobe suite, in the All Programs list, and then click Adobe Photoshop CS4 to start Photoshop.

3. Maximize the Photoshop window, if necessary.

To Reset the Workspace

The following step uses the Workspace switcher to select the Essentials workspace.

1. On the Photoshop Application bar, click the Workspace switcher and then click Essentials to restore the workspace to its default settings.

To Reset the Tools and the Options Bar

The following steps select the Rectangular Marquee tool and reset all tool settings in the options bar.

1. Activate the Rectangular Marquee Tool (M) button on the Tools panel.
2. Change the Tools panel to one column, if necessary.
3. Right-click the Rectangular Marquee tool icon on the options bar to display the context menu, click Reset All Tools, and then click the OK button in the resulting dialog box.

To Reset the Default Colors

The following step resets the default colors.

1. On the Tools panel, click the Default Foreground and Background Colors (D) button to reset the default colors of black and white. If black is not the foreground color, press the X key to reverse the colors.

To Reset the Layers Panel

The following steps reset the Layers panel to make the thumbnails match the figures shown in this book.

1. Click the Layers panel menu button and then click Panel Options on the list to display the Layers Panel Options dialog box.
2. Click the option button for the smallest of the thumbnail sizes.
3. If necessary, click the Layer Bounds option button to select it.
4. Click the OK button.

Restoring Documents

BTW
Photo Fading
Exposure to light is the main factor causing photos printed using ink jet printers to fade. Humidity, temperature, and ozone levels also can cause photos to fade. The better the quality of the ink and paper you use, the less tendency it has to fade.

Antique documents, such as licenses, records, letters, and other forms of paper, have some unique aging features that photographs typically do not have. Common document paper is an organic substance composed of cellulose plant fibers that will deteriorate faster than professional photo paper. While some paper used before the year 1900 was very strong and durable, much of it was not. Rapid deterioration results from the use of production acids that break down the fibers, weakening the paper. Acid deterioration commonly is accompanied by a yellow discoloration due to the alum-resin sizing agents. High temperatures and moisture compound the problem. Even now, unless the paper is designated as acid-free, archival quality, or permanent, its expected useful life is less than 50 years.

Other types of damage include dry and brittle creases caused by folding or rolling documents; brown spots due to water stains or fungus, called **foxing**; brown edges due to airborne pollutants; the fading of colors due to light damage; as well as mold, bacteria, improper storage, and deterioration caused by animal or insect damage. Handwritten portions of documents are particularly vulnerable. Ink and pencil exposed to significant amounts of sunlight can fade dramatically.

Repairing damage using the Photoshop restoration tools can require some trial and error. Many of the tools work in similar ways, and you might find it more intuitive to use one tool rather than another. It also is possible that in correcting one error, you create another. In this case, use CTRL+Z to undo the last step, or work your way back through the History panel. The effectiveness or obviousness of a repair is subjective, so be willing to experiment to achieve the desired results. The more you work with the Photoshop repair tools, the more proficient you will be with them.

To Open the Report Card File

The first image you will edit is the yellowed report card. The report card has discoloration, foxing, torn edges, crease damage, and fading. To repair the photo, several restorative techniques will be employed. The following steps open the scanned image from the Data Files for Students. Your instructor may designate a different location for the file.

1. Open the Report Card file from the Chapter05 folder of the Data Files for Students, or a location specified by your instructor.

2. Change the magnification to 25%, if necessary, to view the entire image (Figure 5–3).

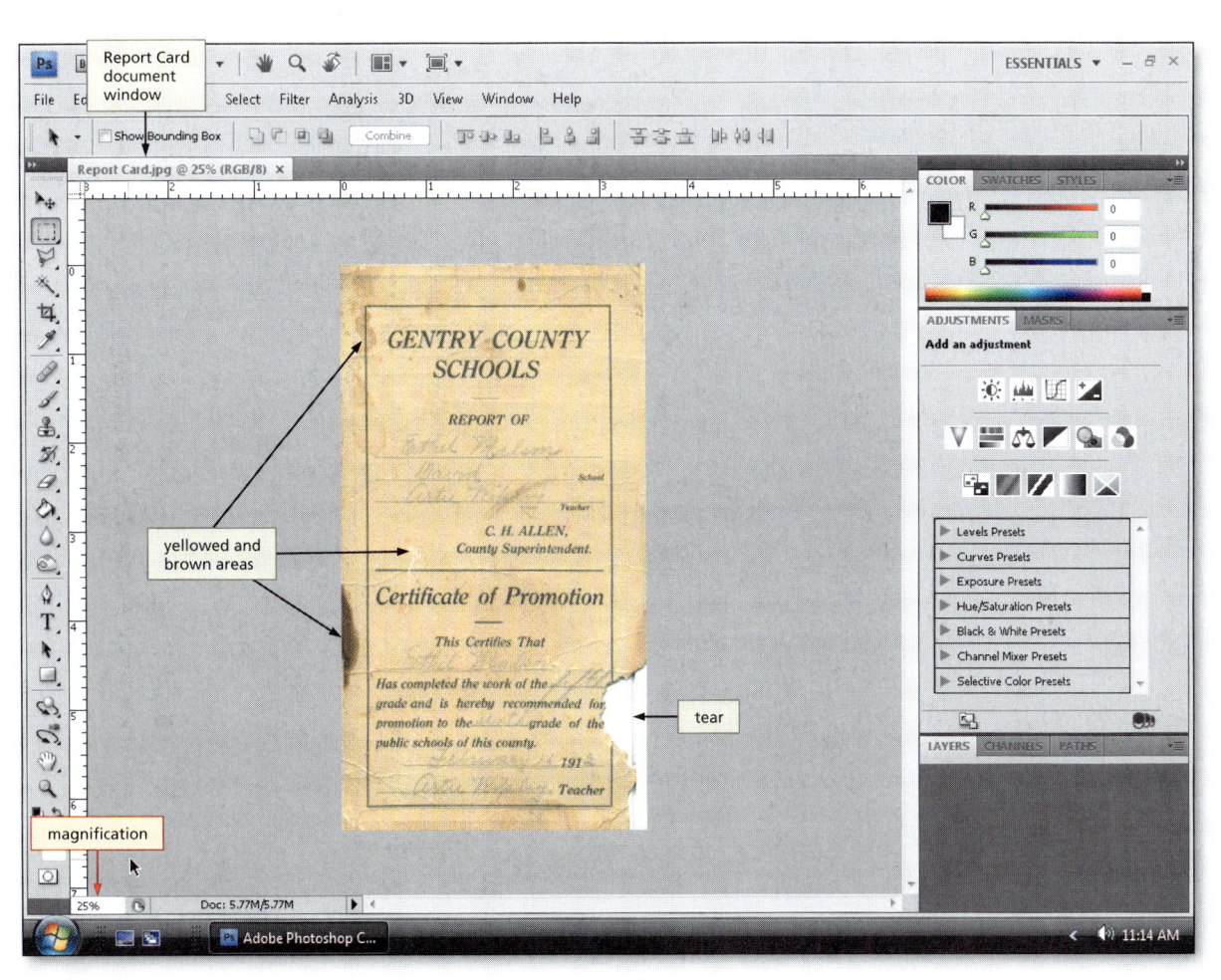

Figure 5–3

BTW

Restorations
For severely damaged documents, professional restorers and researchers now are using dehumidification and freezing techniques for water damage, fiber-optic light to illuminate hidden text covered by paper binding or strong fungus, and ultraviolet fluorescence to recover faded, burned, or even erased text.

To Save the File in the PSD Format

The following steps save the file in the PSD format.

1. With your USB flash drive connected to one of the computer's USB ports, click File on the menu bar to display the File menu, and then click Save As to display the Save As dialog box.

2. In the file name text box, type Report Card Repaired to rename the file. Do not press the ENTER key after typing the file name.

3. Click the Save in box arrow, and then click UDISK 2.0 (F:), or the location associated with your USB flash drive, in the list. If you want to create a folder for the photos in Chapter 5, click the Create New Folder button. Then when the new folder is displayed, type a chapter name, such as Chapter05, and press the ENTER key.

4. Click the Format button to display the list of available file formats and then click Photoshop (*.PSD, *.PDD) in the list, if necessary.

5. Click the Save button in the Save As dialog box to save the file. If Photoshop displays a dialog box, click the OK button.

To Correct Yellowed Portions of the Document

The following steps begin the document repair by removing all yellow and brown from the image by converting it to grayscale mode. Grayscale mode uses different shades of gray in an image. When Photoshop converts an image with color to grayscale, it discards all color information in the original image. The luminosity of the original pixels is represented by shades of gray in the converted pixels.

1
- Click Image on the menu bar, then point to Mode to display the Mode submenu (Figure 5–4).

🔍 **Experiment**
- Click various color modes and watch how the image changes. Press CTRL+Z to undo each one.

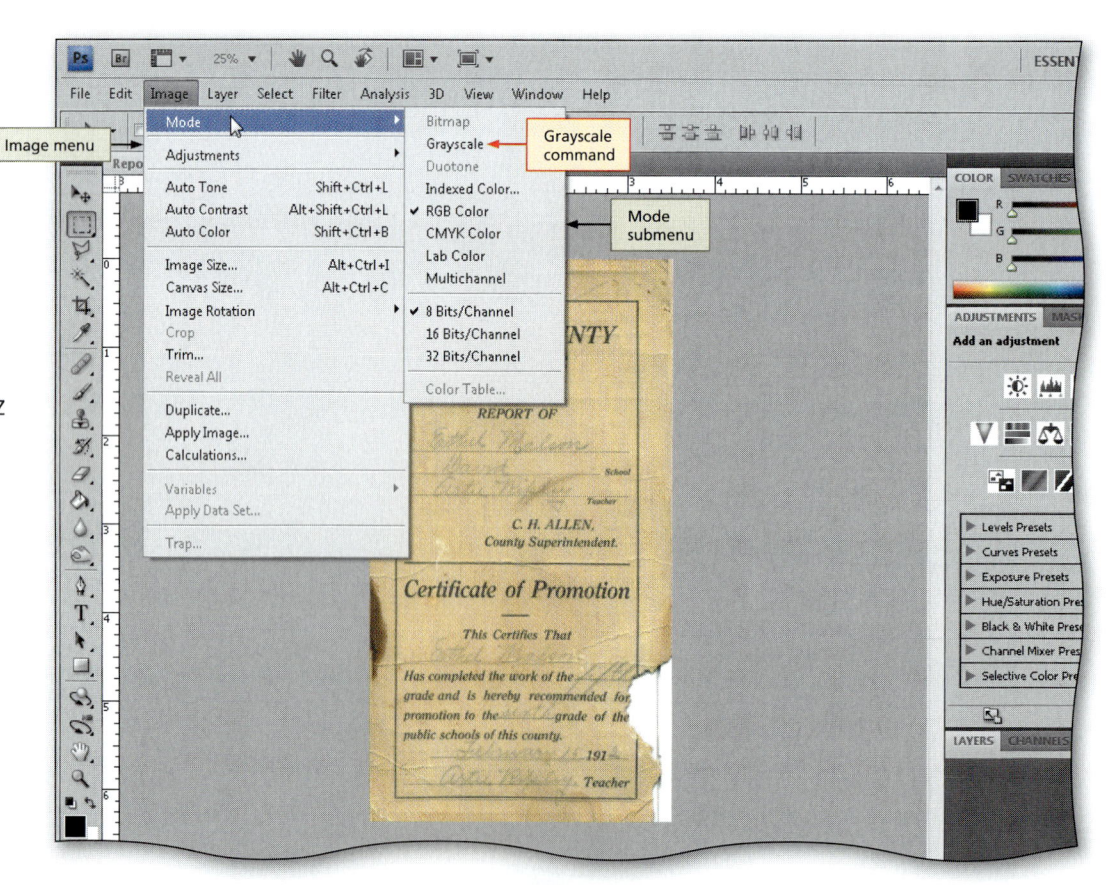

Figure 5–4

❷
- Click Grayscale to remove all color. When Photoshop asks if you want to discard all color information, click the Discard button (Figure 5–5).

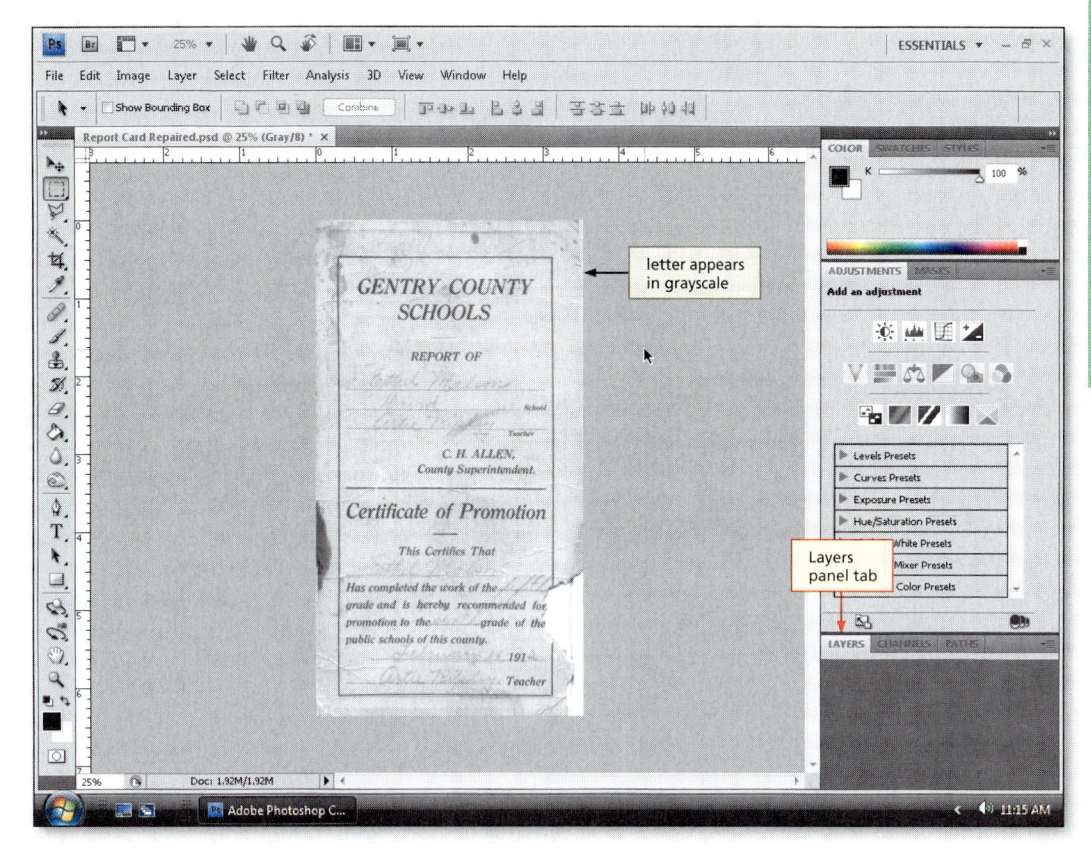

Figure 5–5

Blending Modes

Recall that Blending modes define how an object interacts with other objects. In previous chapters you have used a blending mode such as opacity to edit a layer's transparency. The Mode box appears in the options bar of many tools, as well as on several panels in Photoshop. Typically, it displays a list of blending modes to change how pixels in the image are affected by a color. The default value is Normal, which sometimes is called the **threshold**. Each blending mode works differently depending on the tool. For example, if you select the Gradient tool, the blending mode changes how the gradient colors the pixels as the colors change from one shade to another. The combination of these blending modes with the other settings on the options bar creates an almost infinite number of possibilities.

Experimenting with the blending modes can give you a better feel for how they work. Photoshop Help has sample images of each of the blending modes. Table 5–3 on the next page describes some of the blending modes. As you look through the list, keep in mind that the **base color** is the original color in the image. The **blend color** is the color being applied with the painting or editing tool. The **result color** is the color resulting from the blend. Not all of the blending modes appear on every Mode list.

> **BTW**
>
> **Blending Modes**
> Not all modes are available to every color event. The burn-based or darkening blending modes are more appropriate for applying a gradient over another image or layer. Other blending modes result in solid white or black unless the opacity setting is changed. The dodge-based or lightening blending modes — hard, vivid, and linear — react differently for colors on either side of the 50% gray threshold.

Table 5–3 Blending Modes	
Blending Mode	**Description**
Normal	paints each pixel to make it the result color
Dissolve	used in conjunction with opacity to paint each pixel randomly with the result color
Behind	paints each pixel in the transparent part of a layer — the Transparency check box must be deselected
Darken	the result color becomes the darker of either the base or blend color — pixels lighter than the blend color are replaced, and pixels darker than the blend color do not change
Multiply	multiplies the base color by the blend color, resulting in a darker color
Color Burn	darkens the base color to reflect the blend color by increasing the contrast
Linear Burn	darkens the base color to reflect the blend color by decreasing the brightness
Darker Color	the result color is the lower value of the base or blend colors
Lighten	the result color becomes the lighter of either the base or blend color — pixels darker than the blend color are replaced, and pixels lighter than the blend color do not change
Screen	multiplies the inverse of the blend and base colors, resulting in a lighter color
Color Dodge	brightens the base color to reflect the blend color by decreasing the contrast
Linear Dodge (Add)	brightens the base color to reflect the blend color by increasing the brightness
Lighter Color	the result color is the higher value of the base or blend colors
Overlay	preserves the highlights and shadows of the base color, as it is mixed with the blend color to reflect the lightness or darkness of the base color
Soft Light	darkens or lightens the colors depending on the blend color — the effect is similar to shining a diffused spotlight on the image
Hard Light	multiplies or screens the colors depending on the blend color — the effect is similar to shining a harsh spotlight on the image
Vivid Light	burns or dodges the colors by increasing or decreasing the contrast depending on the blend color
Linear Light	burns or dodges the colors by decreasing or increasing the brightness depending on the blend color
Pin Light	replaces the colors depending on the blend color, creating a special effect
Hard Mix	changes all pixels to primary colors by adjusting the RGB values
Difference	looks at the color information in each channel and subtracts either the blend color from the base color, or the base color from the blend color, depending on which has the greater brightness value; blending with white inverts the base color values; blending with black produces no change
Exclusion	creates an effect similar to, but lower in contrast than, the Difference blending mode
Hue	creates a result color with the luminance and saturation of the base color, and the hue of the blend color
Saturation	creates a result color with the luminance and hue of the base color, and the saturation of the blend color
Color	creates a result color with the luminance of the base color, and the hue and saturation of the blend color
Luminosity	creates a result color with the hue and saturation of the base color and the luminance of the blend color

To Set the Blending Mode

In the following steps, the Background layer is renamed corrections and the blending mode is changed to Lighten in the Layers panel.

1
- Zoom to 25% magnification, if necessary.
- Double-click the Layers tab to display the Layers panel, if necessary (Figure 5–5 on PS 321).
- Double-click the Background layer to display the New Layer dialog box.
- Type `corrections` in the Name text box.
- Click the Mode box arrow to display the list (Figure 5–6).

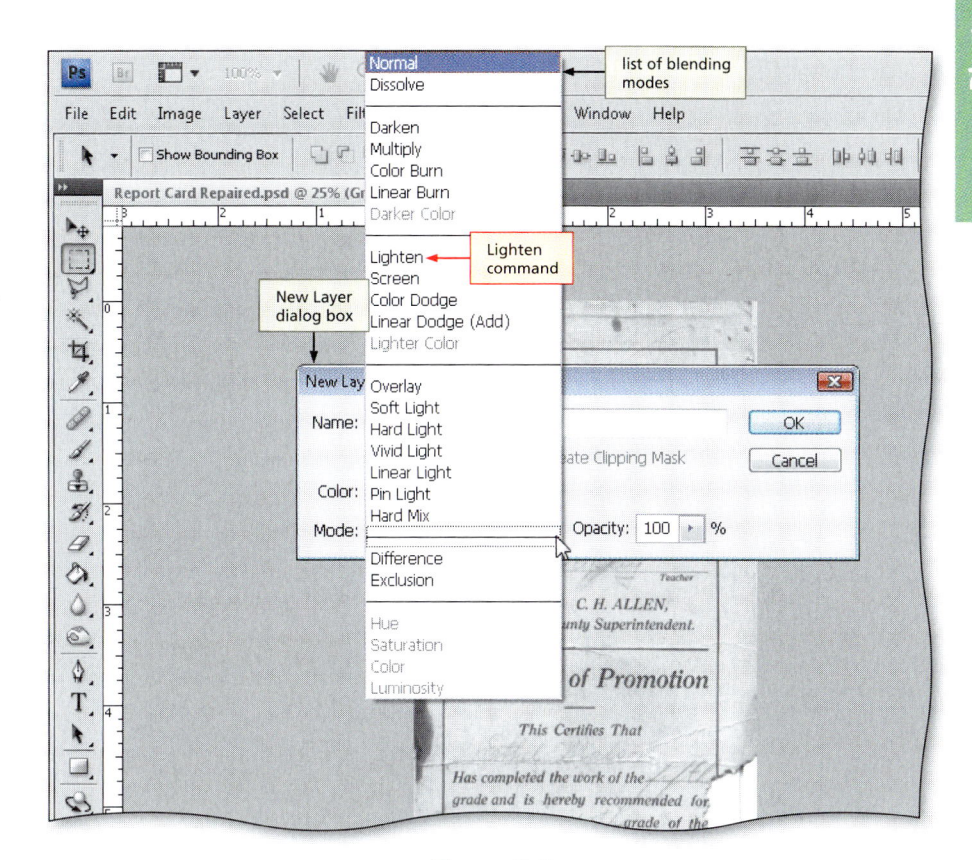

Figure 5–6

2
- Click Lighten to set the layer's blending mode to Lighten (Figure 5–7).

Q&A Why did I choose the Lighten blending mode?

The Lighten blending mode will help later when you repair the foxing and stains in the image. The repair result will become a lighter version of either the existing (base) color or the brush (blend) color — pixels darker than the blend color will be replaced, and pixels lighter than the existing color will not change.

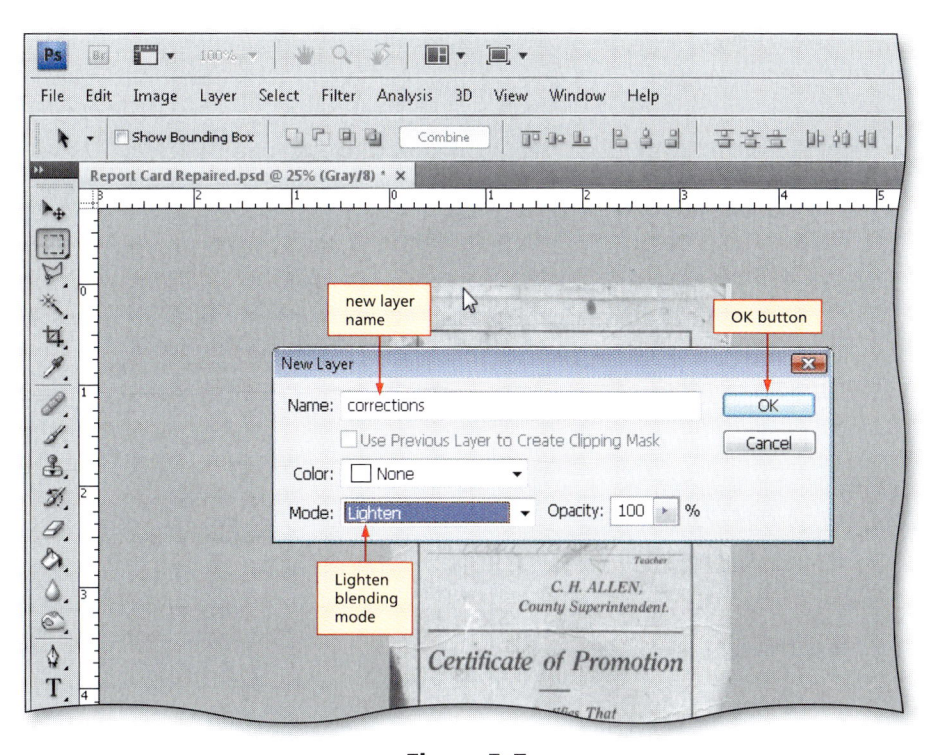

Figure 5–7

3

- Click the OK button to close the New Layer dialog box.
- On the Layers panel, click the Lock transparent pixels button (Figure 5–8).

Q&A What does the Lock transparent pixels button do?

It confines editing to the opaque portions of the layer, so when you erase, you erase to the background color, rather than to transparency.

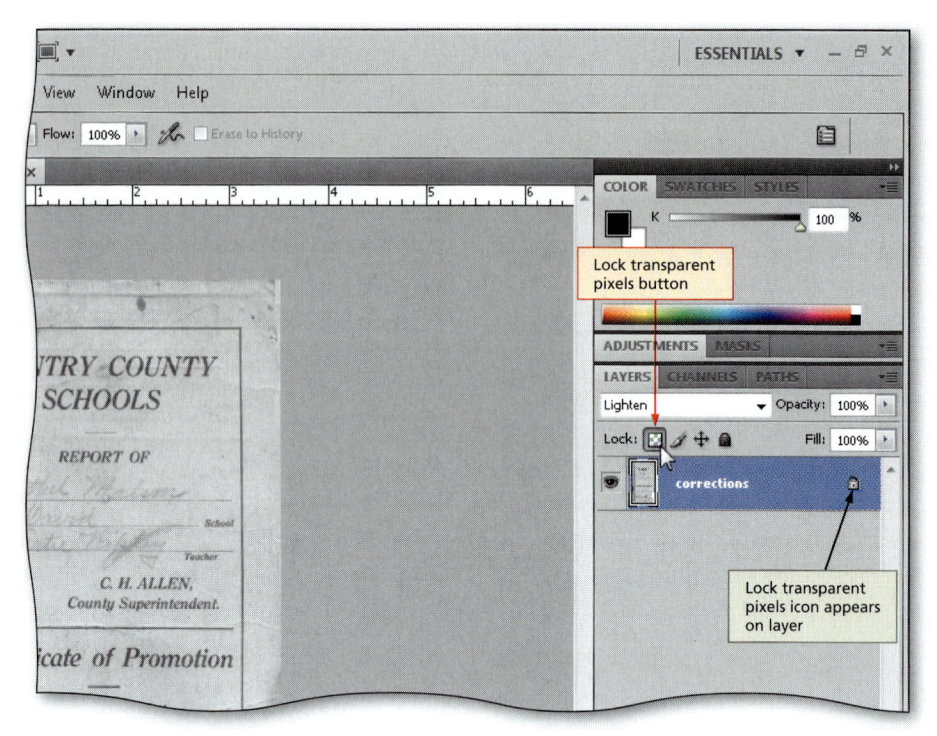

Figure 5–8

To Set Levels

After converting to grayscale and setting the blending mode in a corrections layer, the next step is to adjust the levels to correct the tonal range and contrast. Recall from Chapter 3 that the Levels dialog box allows you to adjust the intensity levels of shadows, midtones, and highlights. The following steps adjust black, gray, and white in the document.

1

- Press CTRL+L to display the Levels dialog box (Figure 5–9).

🔍 **Experiment**

- Drag the black, gray, and white level sliders and watch how the document changes.

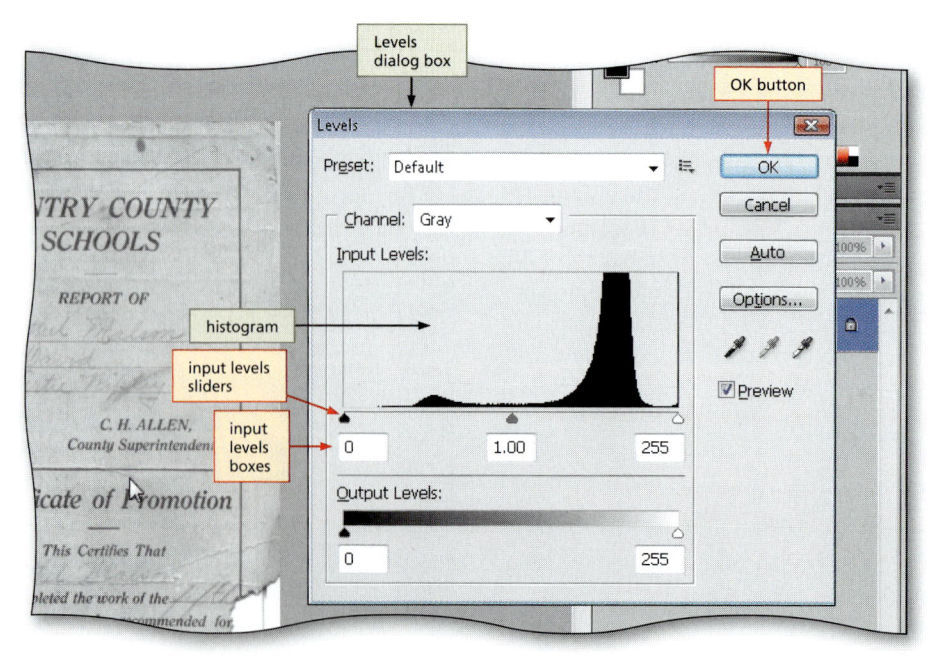

Figure 5–9

②
- Type `39` in the first input levels box to adjust the black levels. Type `0.85` in the second input levels box to adjust the gray or midtones. Type `210` in the third box to adjust the white levels. (Figure 5–10).

③
- Click the OK button in the Levels dialog box to apply the changes.

Q&A

Is this Levels dialog box the same as Levels on the Adjustments panel?

Yes. The shortcut key merely opens the Levels settings in a dialog box and then automatically applies it to the current layer.

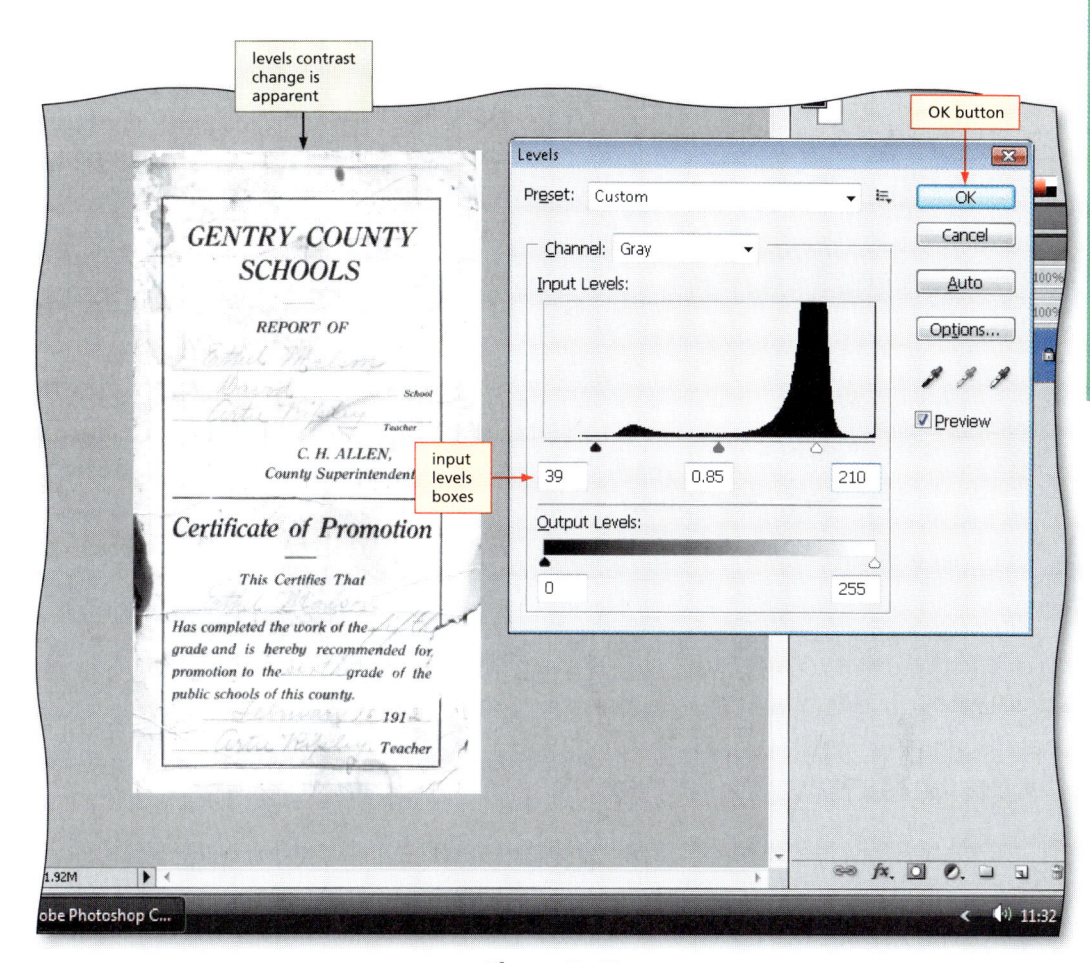

Figure 5–10

Other Ways
1. On Image menu, point to Adjustments, click Levels, drag sliders, click OK

Sharpen images and retouch as necessary.
Sharpening enhances the edges of all objects in an image. Here are a few tips when sharpening:

- Use a copy of the digital file or create a corrections layer so you will have the flexibility of making changes later. In color images, set the blending mode of the layer to Luminosity to prevent color shifts along edges.
- If you need to make other edits such as reducing image noise, do so before sharpening.
- Sharpen your image multiple times in small amounts. Sharpen to correct capture blur, then sharpen after colorization and resizing.
- Adjust sharpening to fit the output media. If you have a Background layer, compare it against the corrections layer as you sharpen.

Plan Ahead

BTW

Tonal Range
Most images look best when they utilize the full tonal range of dark to light that can be displayed on the screen or in print. It often is best to make sure the histogram extends all the way from black to white. Images that do not extend to fill the entire tonal range often look washed out.

Sharpening Images

The Unsharp Mask is a filter used to sharpen images. When you **sharpen**, you emphasize the transitions between light and dark objects in your image. The Unsharp Mask works by evaluating the contrast between adjacent pixels and increasing that contrast based on your settings. While Photoshop has a Sharpen command and a Sharpen More command, the Unsharp Mask command is more versatile because it allows you to sharpen with more

BTW

Color Photos
Moving the Levels sliders to the edge of the histogram can clip the subtle shadows and highlights in a color photo, causing the image to lose its soft light or mood. Color photos are more prone to user levels errors than are black-and-white images.

precision, including settings for amount, radius, and threshold. The way you adjust these settings depends primarily on the image content, and secondarily on the resolution and output purpose. Close subjects with soft details need adjusting in different ways from distant subjects with fine details. While changing these settings is somewhat subjective and depends on your point of view, there are some general guidelines.

The Amount value specifies how much of the sharpening effect to apply to the image. By dragging the slider or entering an amount, you can preview the results. It is a good practice to keep the amount below 300. More than that tends to create a halo effect.

The Radius setting specifies the width of the sharpened edge, measured in pixels. Larger values will sharpen surrounding pixels. A good rule is to start with a radius value of 2 and then reduce the radius if the image has fine, crisp details. Raise it if the image has soft details.

The Threshold setting specifies how different the sharpened pixels must be from the surrounding area before they are considered edge pixels and sharpened by the filter. For example, a threshold of 4 affects all pixels that have tonal values that differ by a value of 4 or more. A value of 0 sharpens all pixels in the image.

Many graphic artists set the radius first, the threshold second, and then the amount. That way, the width and edge are specified before the sharpening effect is applied, allowing the amount value to be more flexible. Additionally, sharpening at magnifications from 50% to 100% gives you a better feel for the final result.

To Apply the Unsharp Mask Filter

The following steps apply the Unsharp Mask filter to improve the appearance of the report card.

1
- Click Filter on the menu bar and then point to Sharpen to display the Sharpen submenu (Figure 5–11).

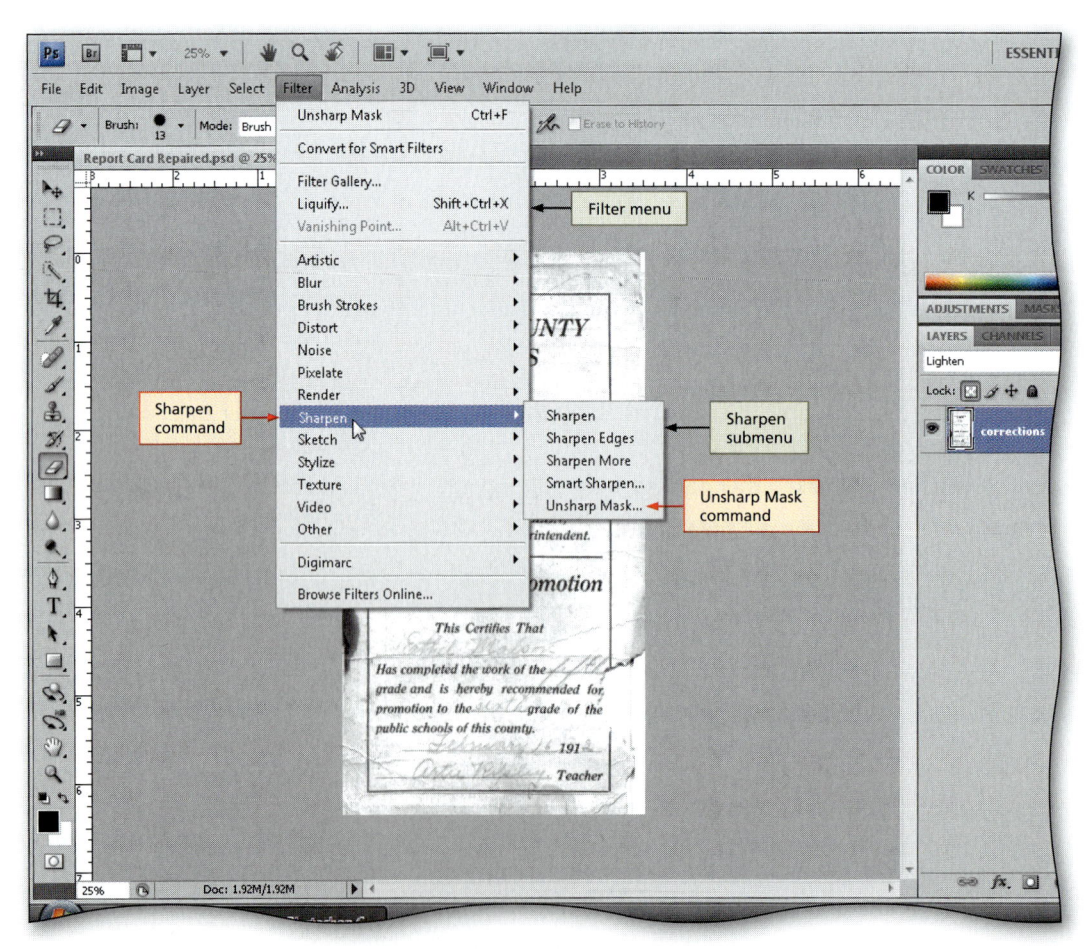

Figure 5–11

2

- Click Unsharp Mask to display the Unsharp Mask dialog box.
- Drag in the preview until the student name appears.
- Type 4 in the Radius box to specify a width of 4 pixels.
- Type 20 in the Threshold box to specify how different the pixels must be from their surroundings in order to become an edge.
- Drag the Amount slider until the image is displayed more clearly, as shown in Figure 5–12.

3

- Click the OK button to close the Unsharp Mask dialog box.

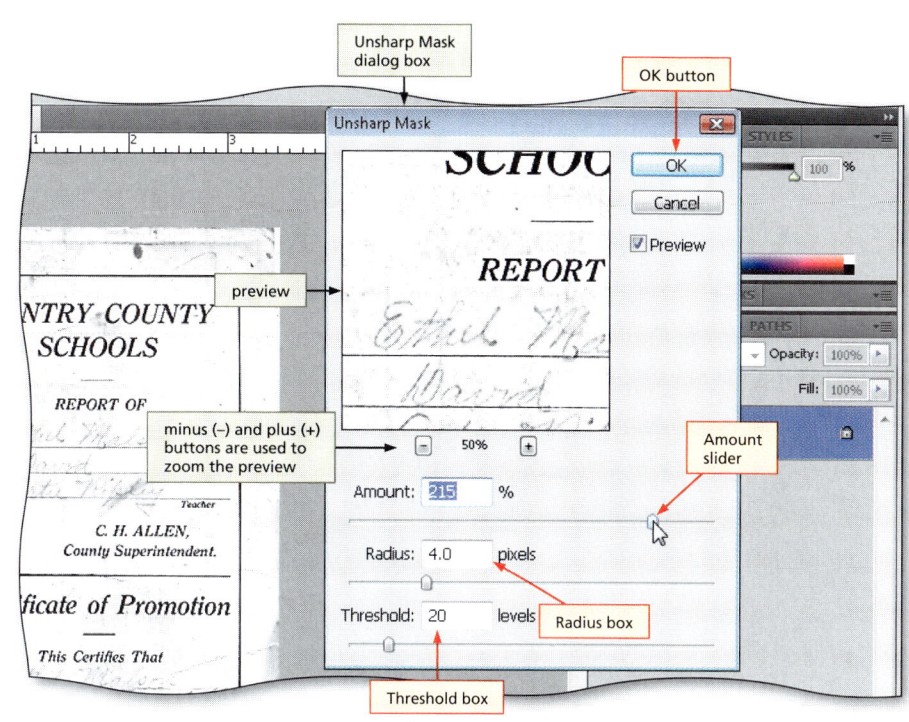

Figure 5–12

To Recreate Missing Portions of the Document

Sometimes you may want to leave the obvious flaws in a document for people to see; however, many graphic artists try to create a copy that looks as close as possible to the way the original document looked. In those cases, it is necessary to recreate missing portions. Notice that on the report card, a portion is missing. The following steps recreate the edge.

1

- On the Tools panel, select the Rectangular Marquee tool.
- Drag a rectangle on the right side of the image from the edge to just inside the black line border (Figure 5–13).

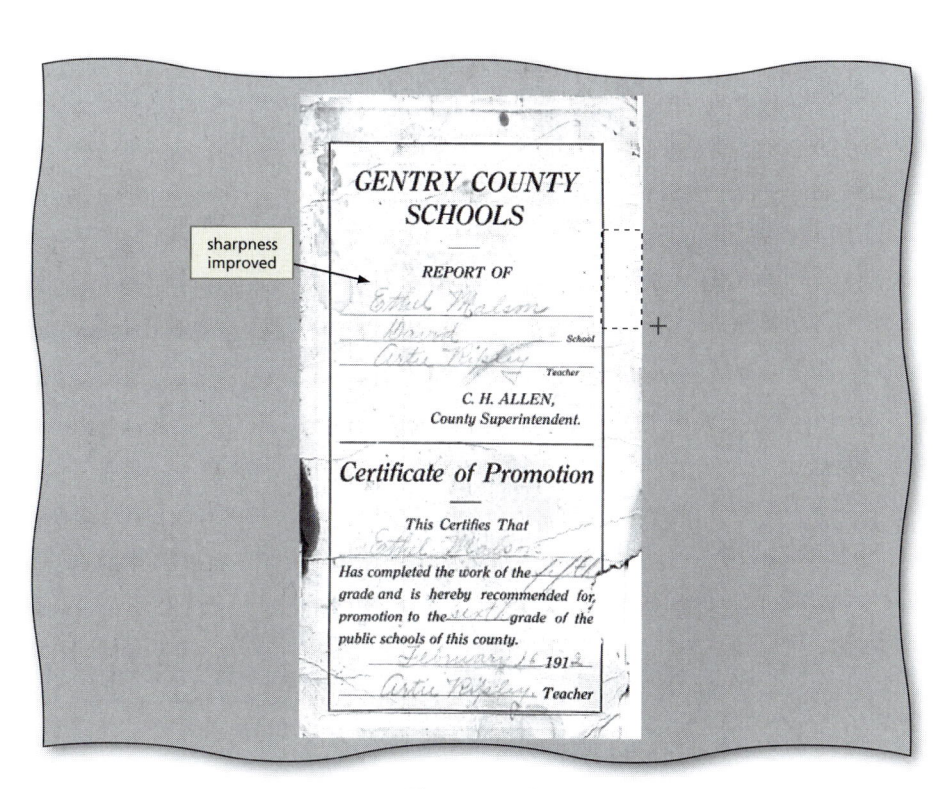

Figure 5–13

PS 328 Photoshop Chapter 5 Enhancing and Repairing Photos

2
- Press the V key to access the Move tool. SHIFT+ALT+drag the selection to the lower part of the image (Figure 5–14).

Q&A Why should I use the SHIFT and ALT keys while I drag?

The ALT key creates a duplicate copy. The SHIFT key keeps the duplicate moving in a straight line.

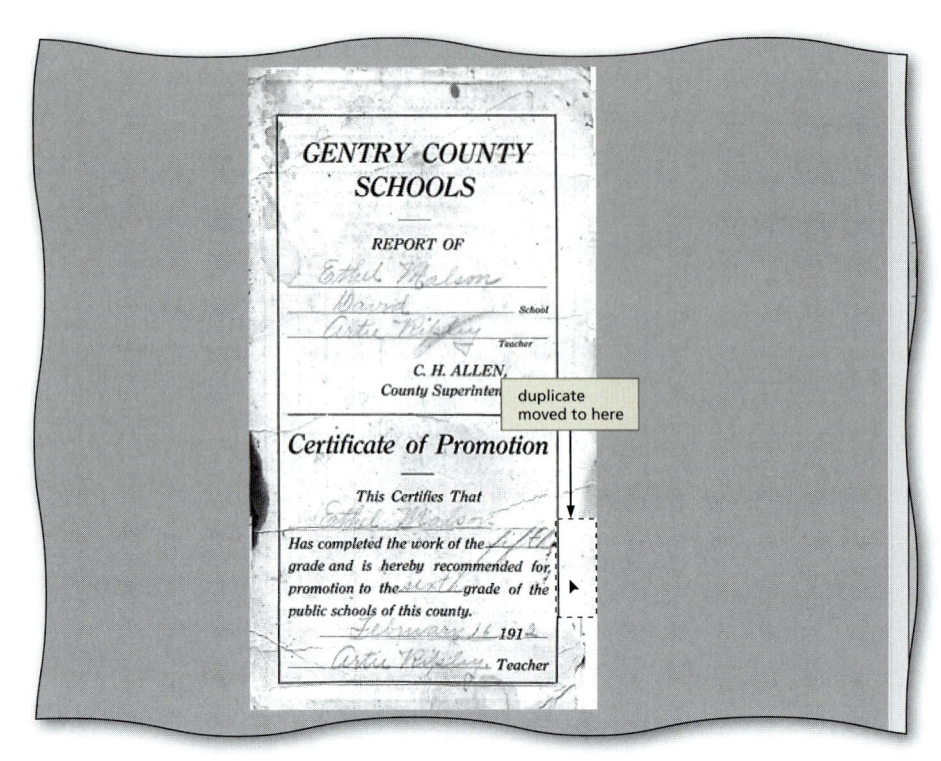

Figure 5–14

3
- Repeat Step 2 as necessary to repair the entire right edge (Figure 5–15).

4
- Press CTRL+D to deselect.

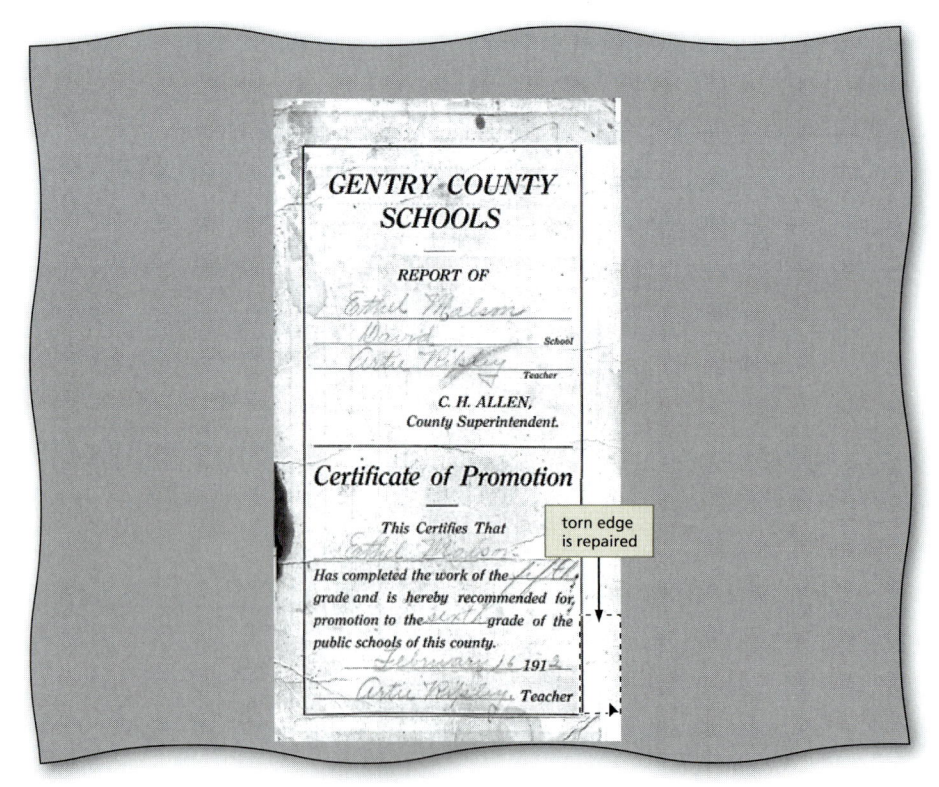

Figure 5–15

To Use the Eraser Tool

Finally, the dark spots in the document will be cleaned using the Eraser tool in the following step.

1
- On the Tools panel, right-click the current eraser tool, and then click Eraser Tool to select it.

- Use the LEFT BRACKET ([ ) or RIGHT BRACKET ( ]) keys to adjust the size of the eraser brush. With short strokes, drag through remaining gray areas that are not part of the print or handwriting itself. If you make a mistake, press CTRL+Z. Zoom and scroll as necessary.

- When you are finished, zoom out to display the entire document (Figure 5–16).

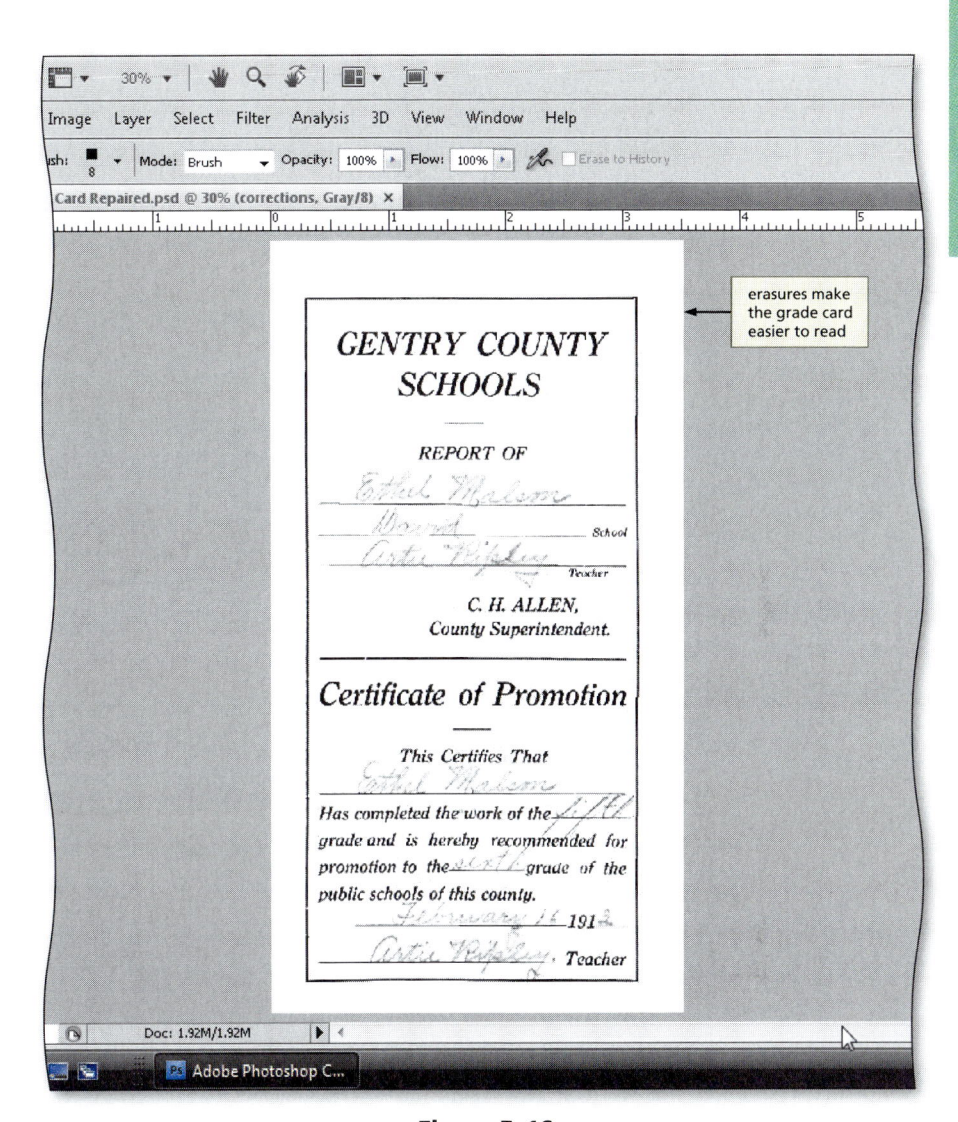

Figure 5–16

Other Ways
1. Press E, drag dark spots

To Save and Close the File

1 Press CTRL+S to save the file again.

2 Press CTRL+W to close the file without quitting Photoshop.

Plan Ahead

Heal specific defects.
Defects in photos and documents that are not related to user or lens errors may include the following:

- physical tears, ragged edges, or missing portions
- fading due to exposure to light
- light or dark spots due to aging
- foxing and yellowing due to paper construction and age
- creasing due to folding
- natural aging of paper

It is helpful to make a list of the specific repairs you plan to apply. Create a corrections layer so you can use portions, textures, and colors from the original document for the repairs. Repair smaller areas first. Consider making separate layers for each large repair. Do not be afraid to experiment until the repair is perfect.

Retouching Tools

Sometimes photos are damaged or worn from excessive use, age, physical damage, or improper storage. Photoshop has several **retouching tools** that help you touch up spots, tears, wrinkles, and scratches. The retouching tools are organized in the middle of the Tools panel. Table 5–4 lists some of the tools and their usage. Each of the retouching tools will be explained further as it is used.

Table 5–4 Retouching Tools

Tool	Use	Button
Blur tool	blurs small portions of the image	
Burn tool	darkens areas in an image	
Dodge tool	lightens areas in an image	
Healing Brush tool	removes and repairs imperfections by first taking a sample from another place in the image and then painting to match the texture, lighting, transparency, and shading of the sampled pixels to the pixels being healed	
Patch tool	repairs imperfections in a selected area of an image by copying a sample or pattern taken from another part of the image — commonly used for larger areas and does not allow brush size selection as with the Healing Brush tool	
Red Eye tool	removes the red tint from all contiguous cells	
Sharpen tool	sharpens small portions of an image	
Smudge tool	simulates the effect you see when you drag a finger through wet paint	
Sponge tool	changes the color saturation of an area	
Spot Healing Brush tool	removes blemishes and imperfections by sampling pixels around the spot and then paints with matching texture, lighting, transparency, and shading	

The first set of retouching tools includes four healing or restoration tools to correct imperfections in photos and images. The Spot Healing Brush tool, the Healing Brush tool, the Patch tool, and the Red Eye tool are used to make specific kinds of repairs to blemishes, tears, holes, and red-eye problems.

To Open and Crop the Schoolmaster Image

The first photo you will edit will be a damaged picture of one of the early schoolmasters of the county. The following steps open and crop the photo.

1 Open the file named Schoolmaster from the Chapter05 folder of the Data Files for Students, or from a location specified by your instructor. If necessary, change the magnification to display the entire image.

2 To remove the excess border, click the Crop Tool (C) button on the Tools panel and then, in the photo itself, drag from the upper-left corner to the lower-right corner. Press the ENTER key to crop the image (Figure 5–17).

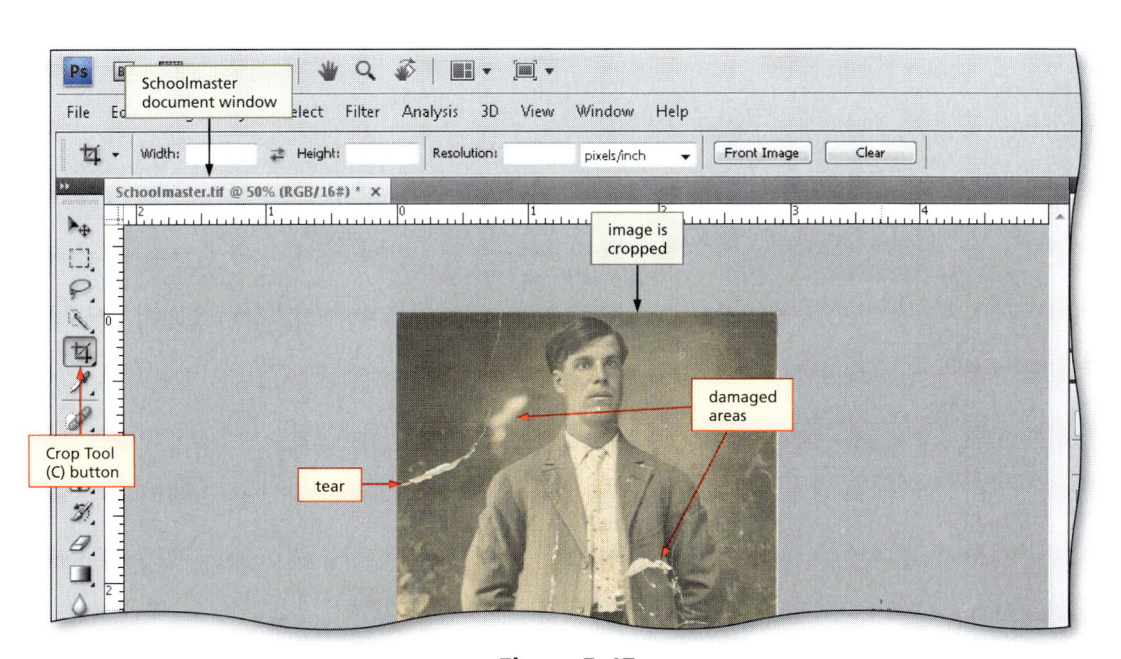

Figure 5–17

The Spot Healing Brush Tool

The Spot Healing Brush tool removes blemishes and imperfections by sampling pixels around the spot. Photoshop then paints in the image with matching texture, lighting, transparency, and shading. Recall that sampling occurs when Photoshop stores the pixel values of a selected spot or area. The Spot Healing Brush Tool options bar contains settings for the blending mode of the repair and the sampling methods (Figure 5–18).

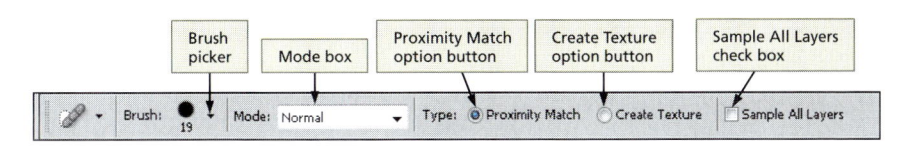

Figure 5–18

BTW

Duplicating Layers
The Duplicate Layer command creates a copy of the background on a new layer in the Layers panel. The Layer From Background command changes the Background layer itself, unlocking it for additional kinds of editing such as the application of blending modes and erasing to transparency.

To Duplicate a Layer for Corrections

In the Schoolmaster photo, many spots and tears need fixing. It is a good practice to create a layer for the corrections as shown in the following steps. The Duplicate Layer command creates an exact copy on which you can make changes, allowing you to review more easily the before and after images. The following steps create a duplicate layer.

1
- Right-click the Background layer in the Layers panel. When the context menu is displayed, click Duplicate Layer to display the Duplicate Layer dialog box (Figure 5–19).

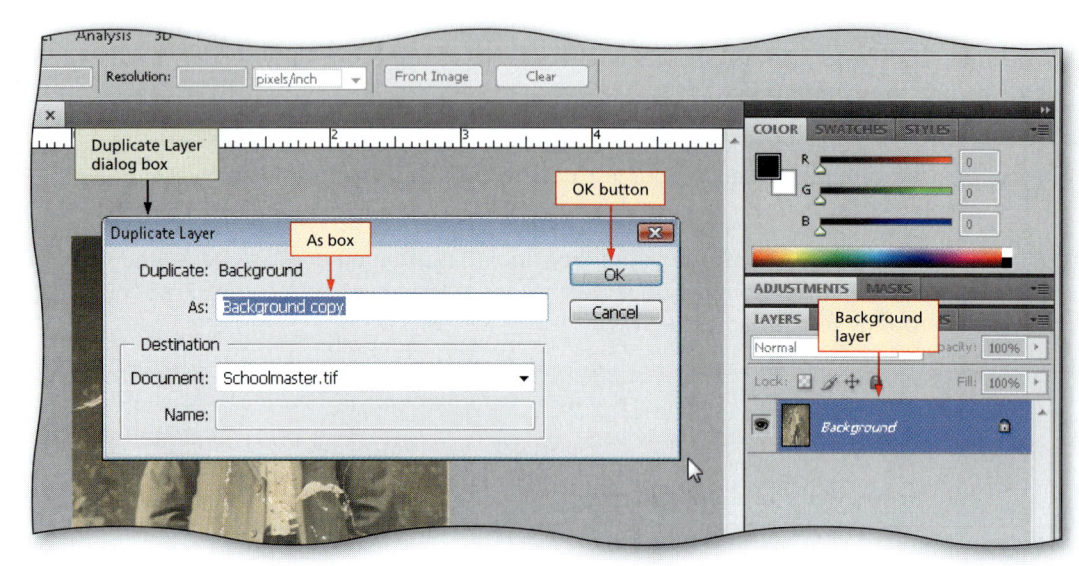

Figure 5–19

2
- Type `corrections` in the As box and then click the OK button.
- Zoom to 100% magnification and scroll to display the man's face (Figure 5–20).

Other Ways
1. Click Layers panel menu button, click Duplicate Layer
2. On Layer menu, click Duplicate Layer

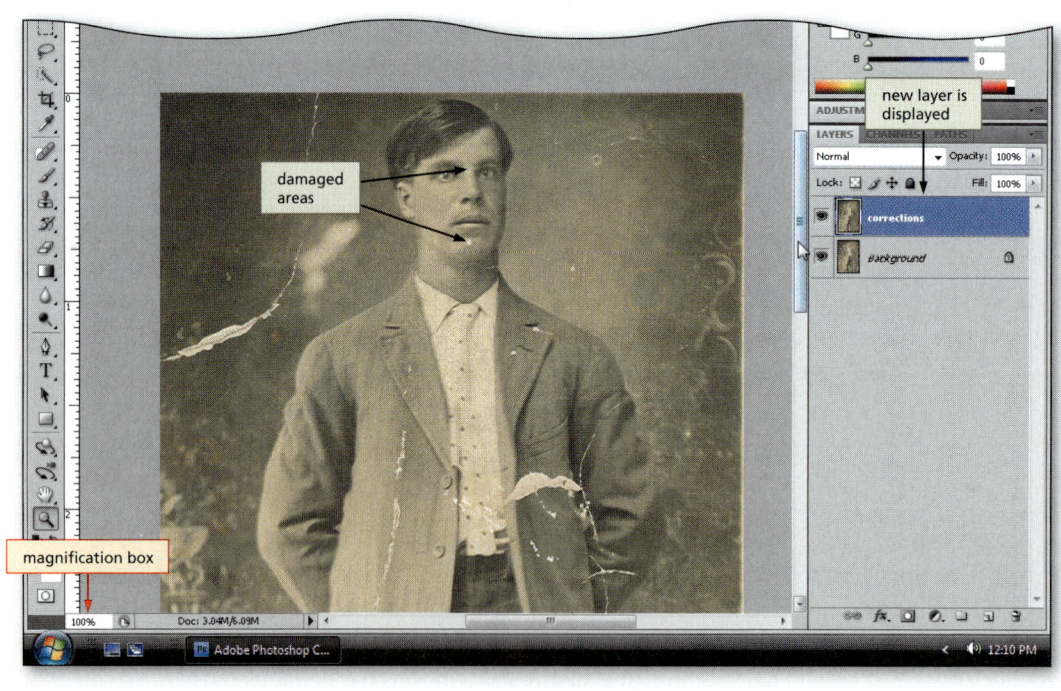

Figure 5–20

To Repair Damage with the Spot Healing Brush Tool

The following steps use the Spot Healing Brush tool to fix several small damaged spots on the face. When using the Spot Healing Brush tool, it is important to use the smallest possible brush tip so that the sample comes from the area directly adjacent to the imperfection.

1
- Right-click the current healing tool on the Tools panel and then click Spot Healing Brush Tool in the list.
- If necessary on the options bar, click the Mode box arrow, and then click Normal.
- Click the Proximity Match option button, if necessary, to select it.
- Move the mouse pointer into the document window and point to the white spot on the chin. Press the LEFT BRACKET ([ ) key or the RIGHT BRACKET ( ]) key until the brush tip is just slightly larger than the spot (Figure 5–21).

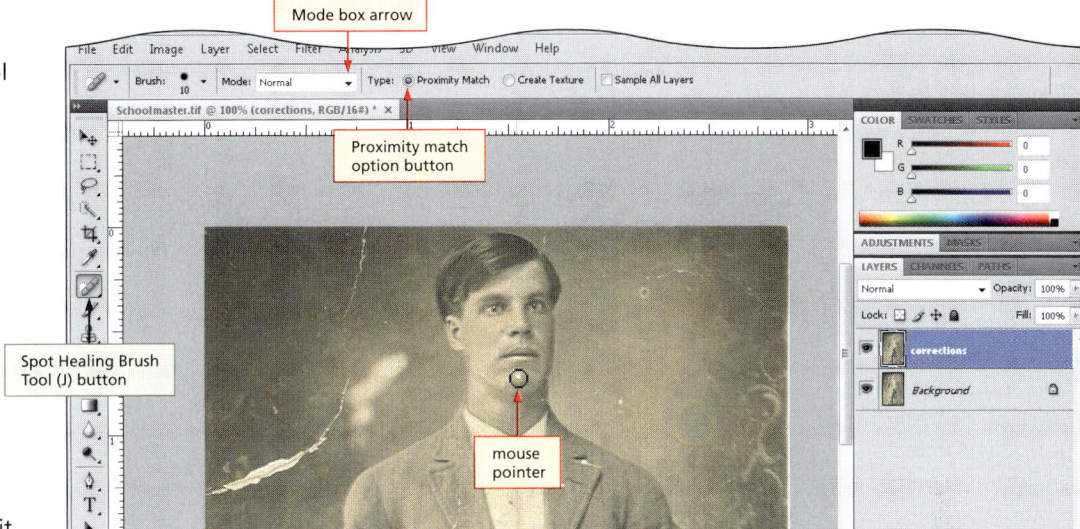

Figure 5–21

2
- Click the spot and then move the mouse pointer away to view the results (Figure 5–22).

Q&A Why does my correction look different?

The size or position of your mouse pointer may have been different, or the color settings on your monitor may be slightly different. If you do not like the result, press CTRL+Z and then try it again.

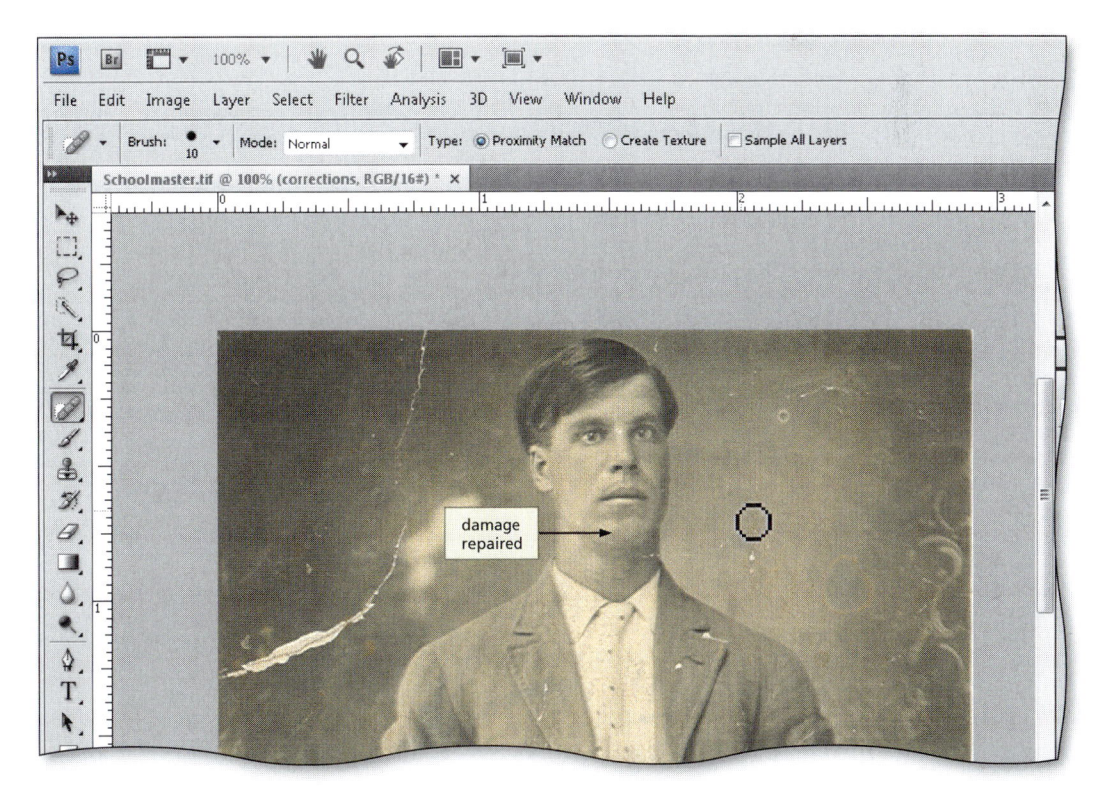

Figure 5–22

PS 334 Photoshop Chapter 5 Enhancing and Repairing Photos

3

- Move the mouse pointer to the spot between the eyes. Press the LEFT BRACKET ([ ) key to reduce the size of the brush tip. Click the spot and then move the mouse pointer away to view the results (Figure 5–23).

🔍 **Experiment**

- Try fixing a large spot in the photo. Notice that the larger the correction, the poorer the quality, as the Spot Healing brush is better suited for small imperfections. Press CTRL+Z to undo the unwanted correction.

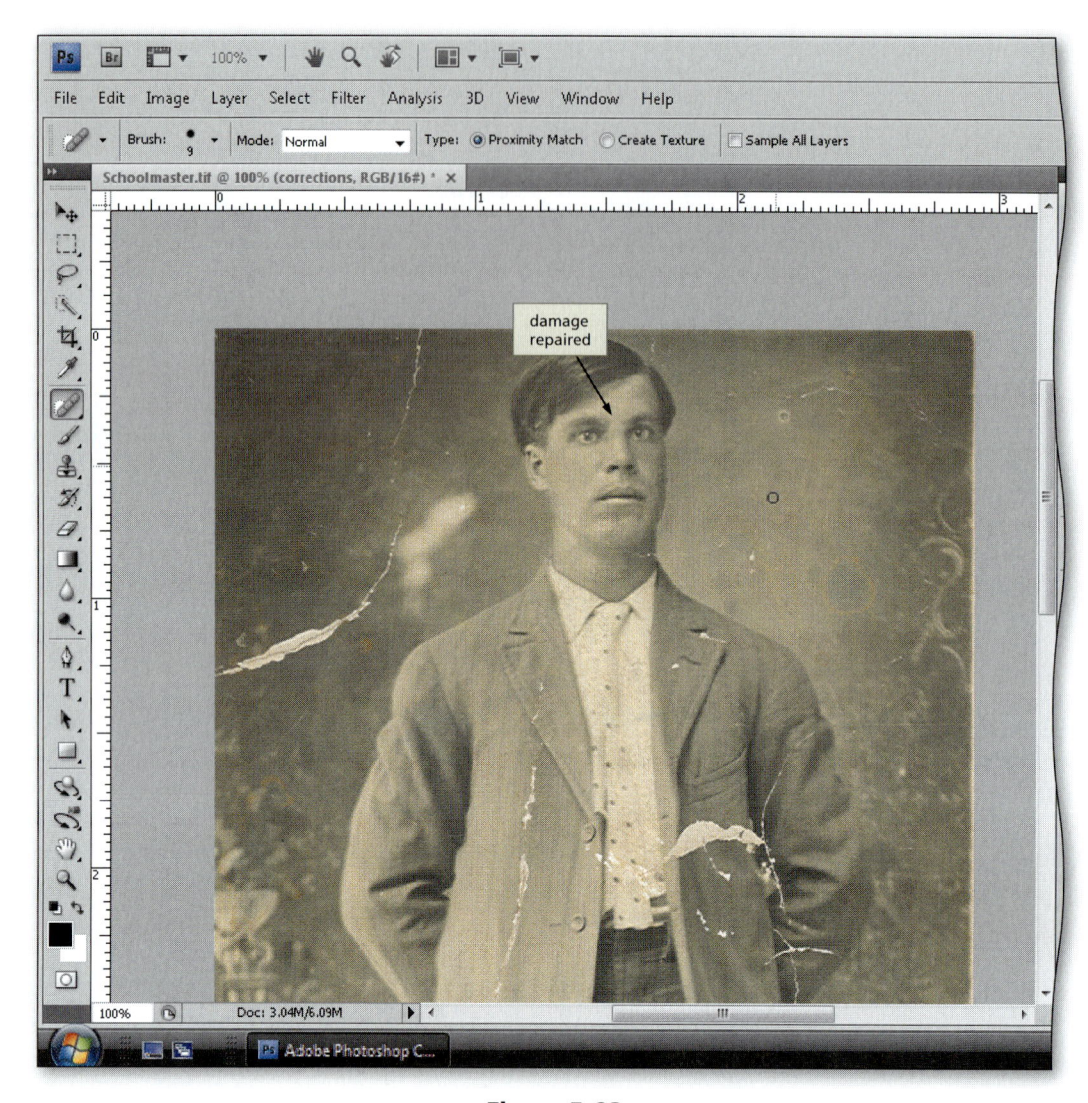

Figure 5–23

4

- Repeat Step 3 for other spots on the face and neck.

Q&A What if I make a repair that does not look good?

You can press CTRL+Z, to undo your most recent repair. Pressing CTRL+ALT+Z steps back through your recent steps. Or you can display the History panel and click a previous state. Then, you can try the repair again.

Other Ways

1. Press J or SHIFT+J, adjust brush size, click imperfection

The Healing Brush Tool

The Healing Brush tool is better suited for larger areas such as tears or wrinkles. While the Spot Healing Brush tool samples the surrounding pixels automatically, the Healing Brush tool requires you to choose the sampled (source) area, as you did with the Clone tool. When using the Healing Brush tool, the Brush Preset picker allows you to set specific characteristics of the brush, including the use of a tablet pen. The Mode box allows you to choose one of several blending modes, or choose to replace the pixels to preserve the grain and texture at the edges of the brush stroke. Additionally, the Healing Brush tool options bar has an Aligned setting to sample pixels continuously without losing the current sampling point, even if you release the mouse button (Figure 5–24).

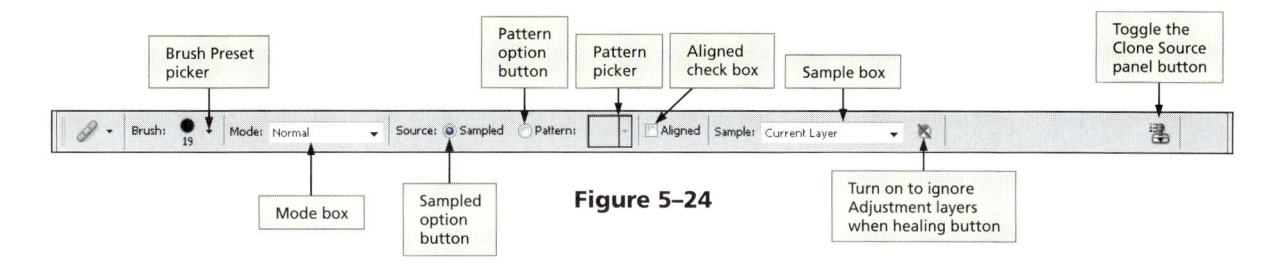

Figure 5–24

To Sample and Paint with the Healing Brush Tool

The following steps use the Healing Brush tool to fix the tears and damage in the upper-left corner of the photo.

1

- Scroll to display the upper-left corner of the photo.
- If necessary, press CTRL+R to view the rulers.
- Right-click the Spot Healing Brush Tool (J) button to display the context menu (Figure 5–25).

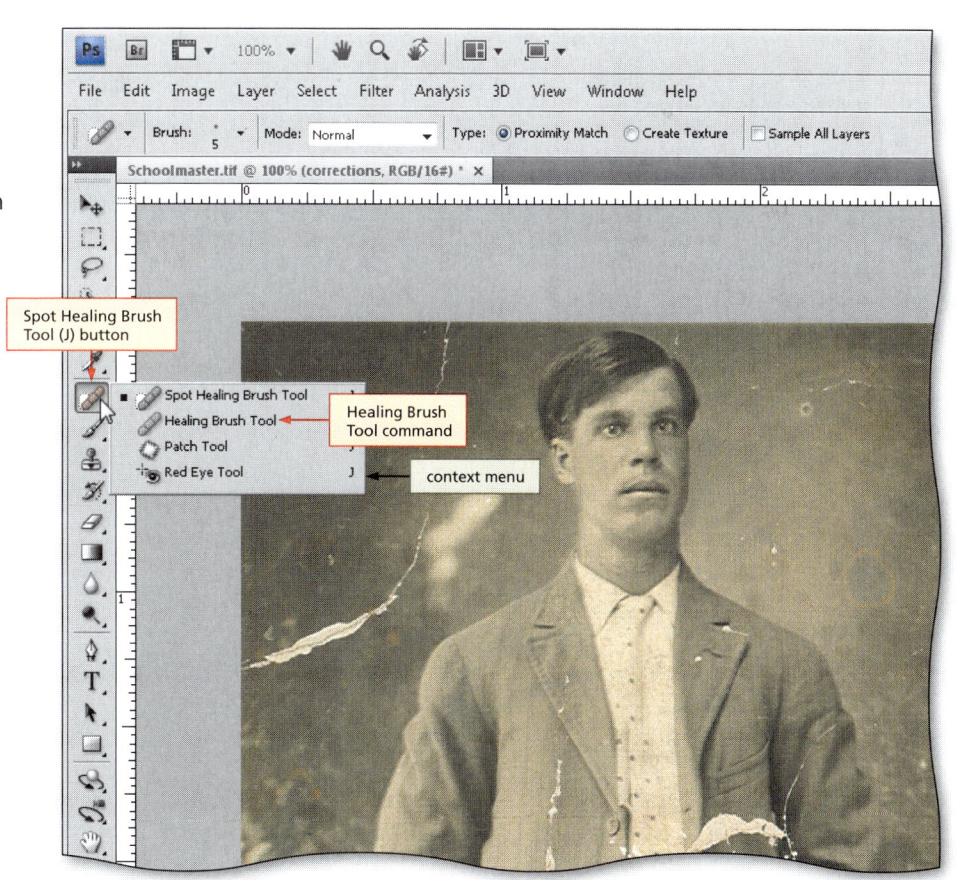

Figure 5–25

2

- Click Healing Brush Tool in the list.
- If necessary, click the Sampled option button on the options bar to select it.
- Click the Aligned check box so it displays a check mark.
- Click the Brush picker button on the options bar to display the settings.
- In the Diameter box, type 19 to set the brush size, if necessary.
- Click the Size box arrow, and then click Off in the list (Figure 5–26).

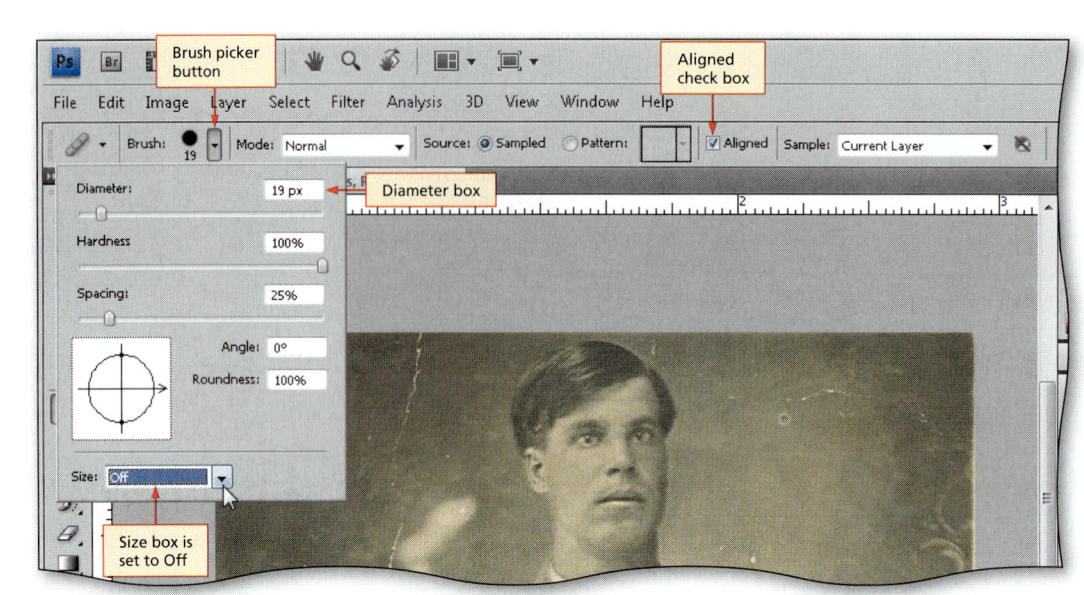

Figure 5–26

Q&A Why should I turn the size off?

The Size box allows you to specify if you will be using pen pressure or mouse wheel to change the size of the healing brush mouse pointer. Because you changed the diameter of the brush size manually, you do not have to rely on the other methods.

3

- To sample the pixels, ALT+click to the right of the upper tear.
- Drag from the top of the tear down, approximately .5 inches to repair the damage (Figure 5–27).

Q&A What is the difference between the Healing Brush tool and the Clone tool?

The Healing Brush tool does not create an exact copy. It samples the texture, color, and grain of the source and then applies that to the destination, matching the destination surrounding pixels as much as possible.

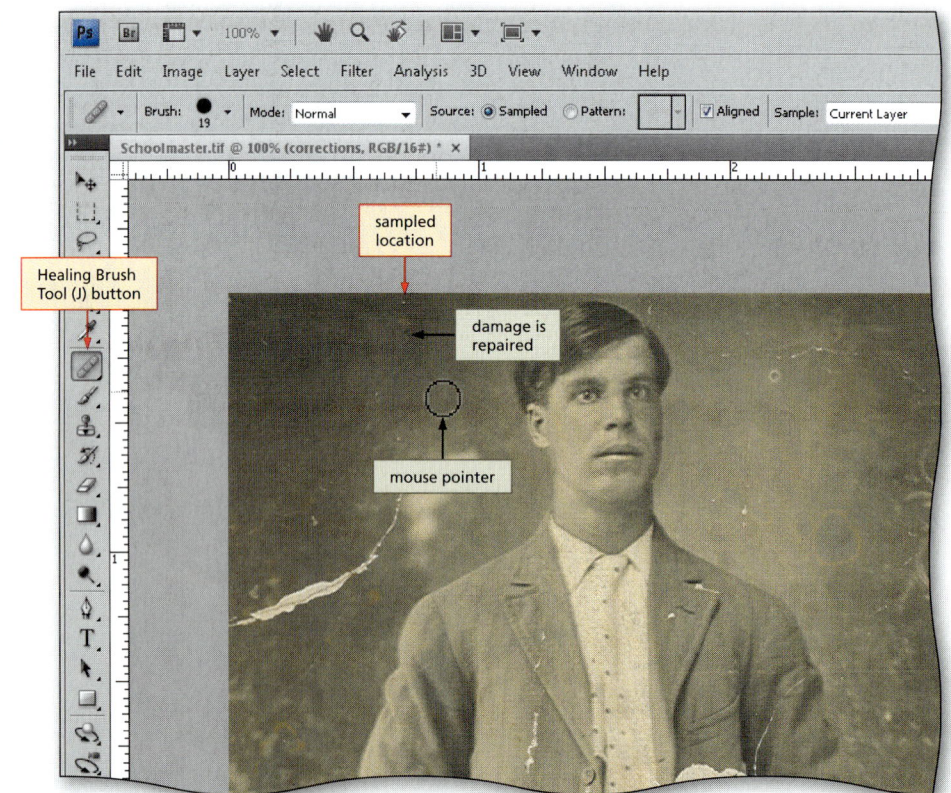

Figure 5–27

4

- ALT+click below the tear at the left margin to sample.
- On the options bar, click the Mode box arrow, and then click Replace in the list.
- Drag from left to right, using short strokes to correct the tear. Resample as necessary to match color and grain (Figure 5–28).

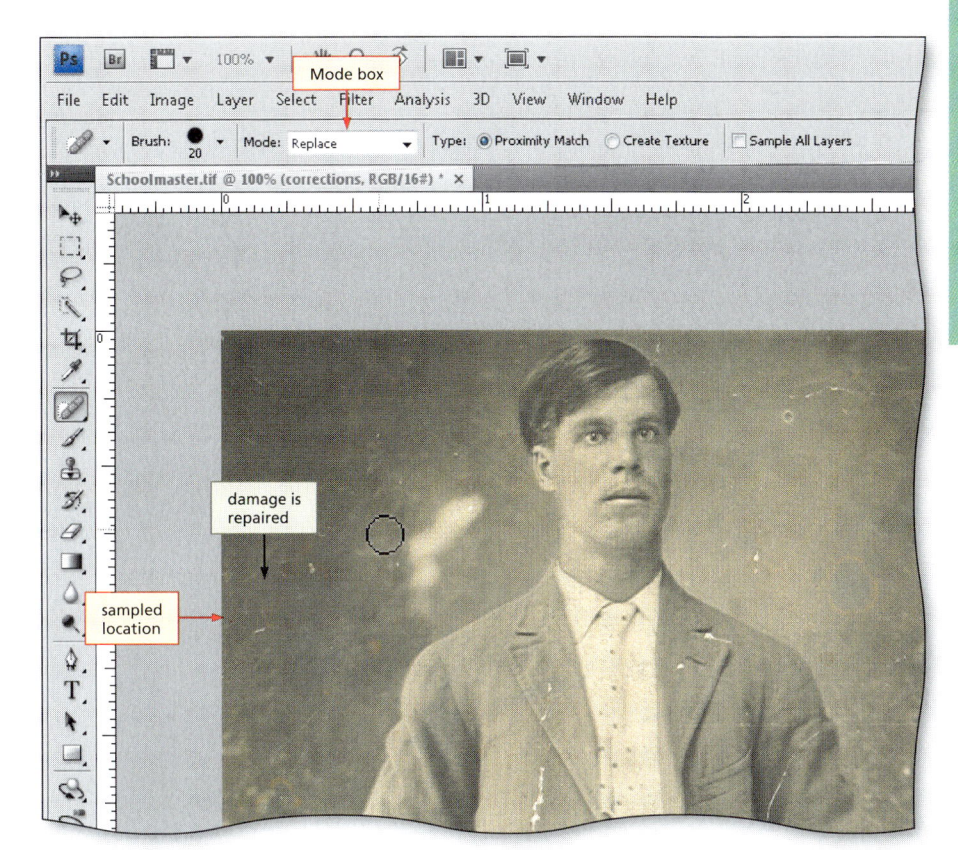

Figure 5–28

Other Ways

1. Press J or SHIFT+J, ALT+click sample, drag flawed areas

The Patch Tool

The Patch tool lets you repair imperfections within a selected area using pixels from another area or by using a pattern. The Patch tool is more than just a copy-and-paste mechanism, however. Like the Healing Brush tool, the Patch tool matches the texture, shading, and lighting of the pixels. When repairing with pixels from the image, select a small area to produce the best results. The Patch tool can sample pixels from the same image, from a different image, or from a chosen pattern. The Patch tool options bar displays settings for the source and destination of the patch, as well as options to adjust the selection or use a pattern to make the patch repair (Figure 5–29).

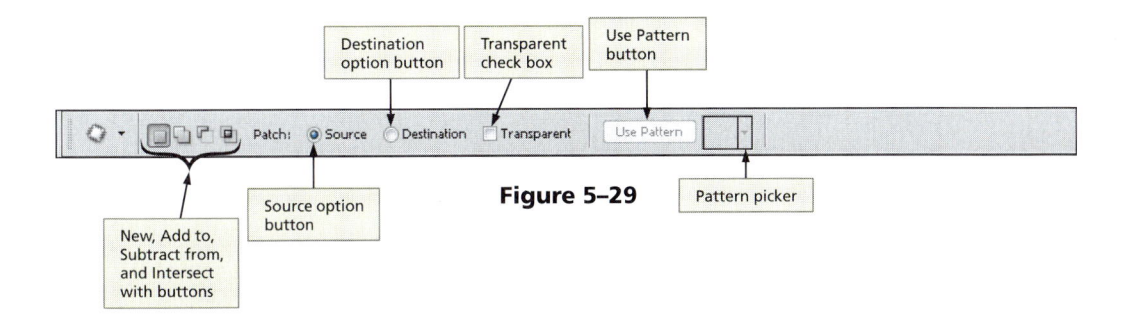

Figure 5–29

To Patch Areas

The following steps use the Patch tool to patch the light area to the left of the man's head.

1

- Right-click the Spot Healing Brush Tool (J) button, and then click Patch Tool in the list.
- If necessary, click the Source option button on the Patch tool options bar to select it.
- Move the mouse pointer to an area above the light spot, near the man's head to display the Patch tool mouse pointer (Figure 5–30).

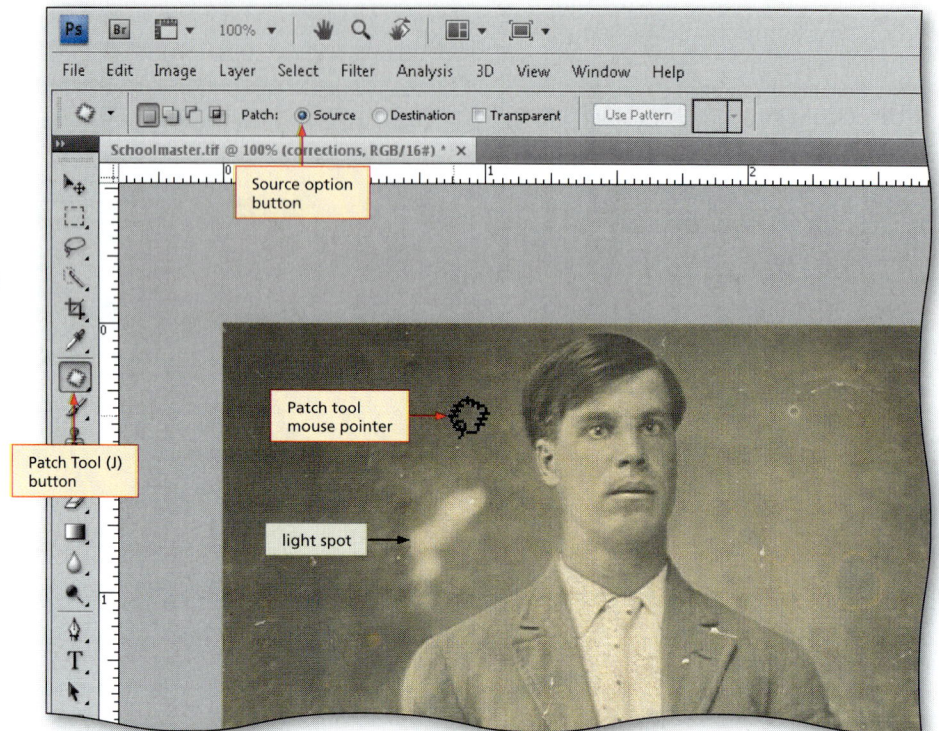

Figure 5–30

2

- Drag an area above the light spot, to create a marquee, approximately as big as the light spot. Do not include the light spot in the selection (Figure 5–31).

Q&A Do I have to click Source first, before I draw the marquee?

Actually, you can do it either way — draw the marquee first and then click Source, or vice versa.

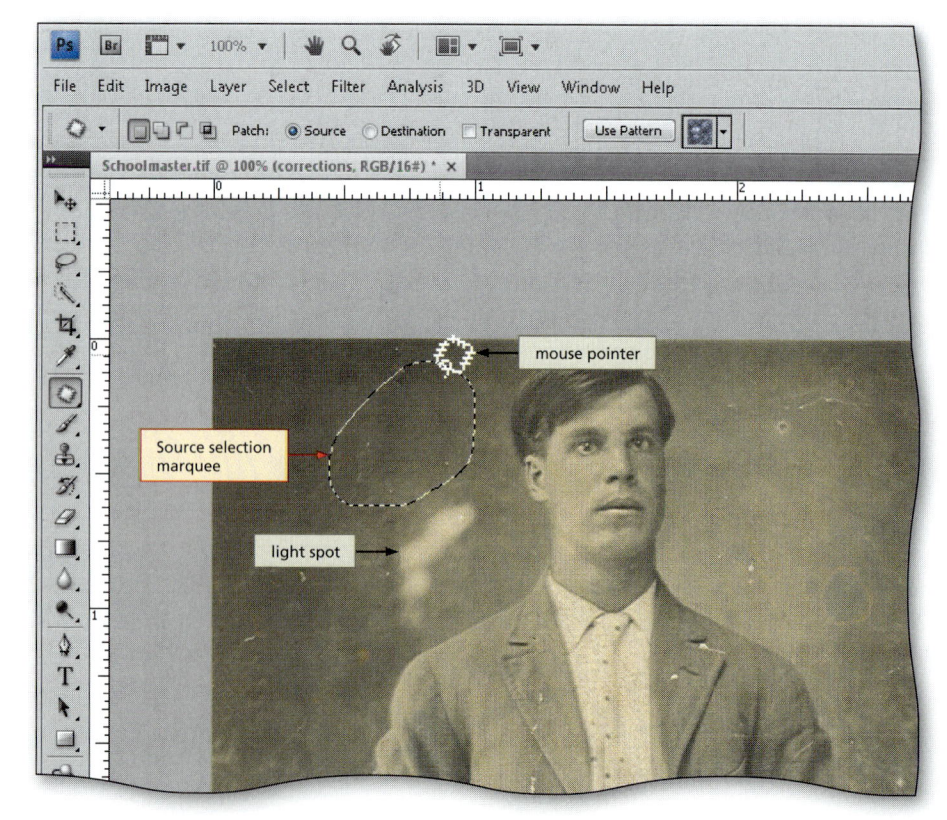

Figure 5–31

3
- On the Patch options bar, click the Destination option button.
- Drag the selection to cover the light spot.
- Press CTRL+D to remove the selection and display the patch (Figure 5–32).

Q&A What is the difference between the Patch tool and the Healing Brush tool?

They are very similar, but the Patch tool is intended for larger areas of correction. Both tools apply tonal characteristics of the sampled source to the area of the flaw.

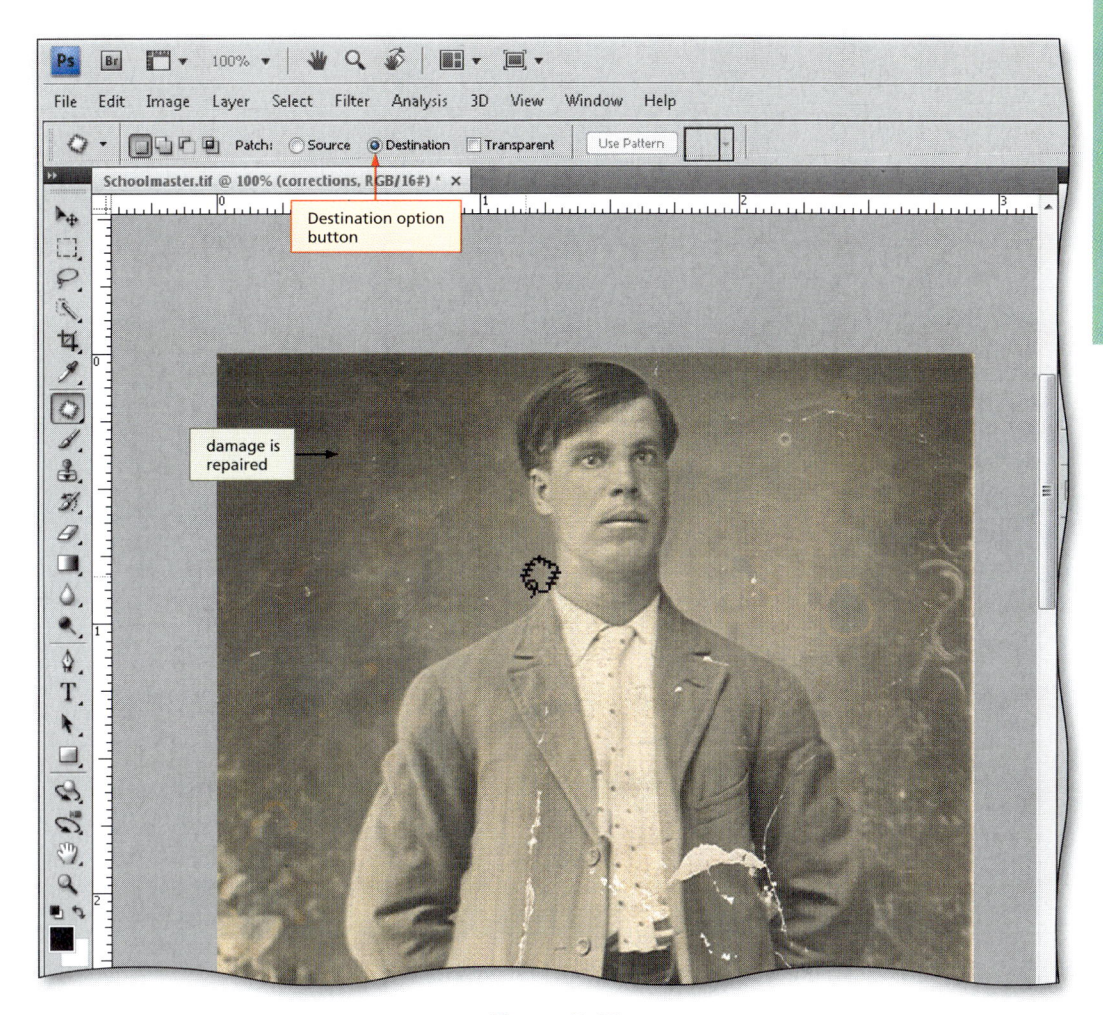

Figure 5–32

Other Ways
1. Press J or SHIFT+J, click Source, drag area, click Destination, drag area

To Repair Other Damage

The final steps illustrate how to repair other damaged areas in the photo. If you make a repair that does not look good, press CTRL+Z, and then try again. Zoom and scroll as necessary.

1 Right-click the Patch Tool (J) button and then click Spot Healing Brush Tool in the list.

2 Choose a very small damaged area in the photo. Adjust the brush size to be just larger than the damage. Click with the Spot Healing Brush tool to repair the damage.

3 Right-click the Spot Healing Tool (J) button, and then click Healing Brush Tool in the list.

4 Choose a larger damaged area in the photo. ALT+click close to the damage. Drag with short strokes to repair the damage.

5 Repeat the steps as necessary to fix other damaged areas and then zoom to display the entire image (Figure 5–33 on the next page).

BTW

TIFs and JPGs
Some file resolution is lost through compression when saving JPG edits in Photoshop. Saving JPG files in the TIF format allows for the exchange of files between applications and across computer platforms. TIF is a flexible format supported by virtually all paint, image editing, and page layout applications. However, TIF files are larger in size.

Figure 5–33

To View the Corrections

The following step compares the original layer with the corrections layer.

1
- On the Layers panel, click the visibility icon in the corrections layer to view the original image before corrections (Figure 5–34)
- Click the visibility icon again to view the corrections.

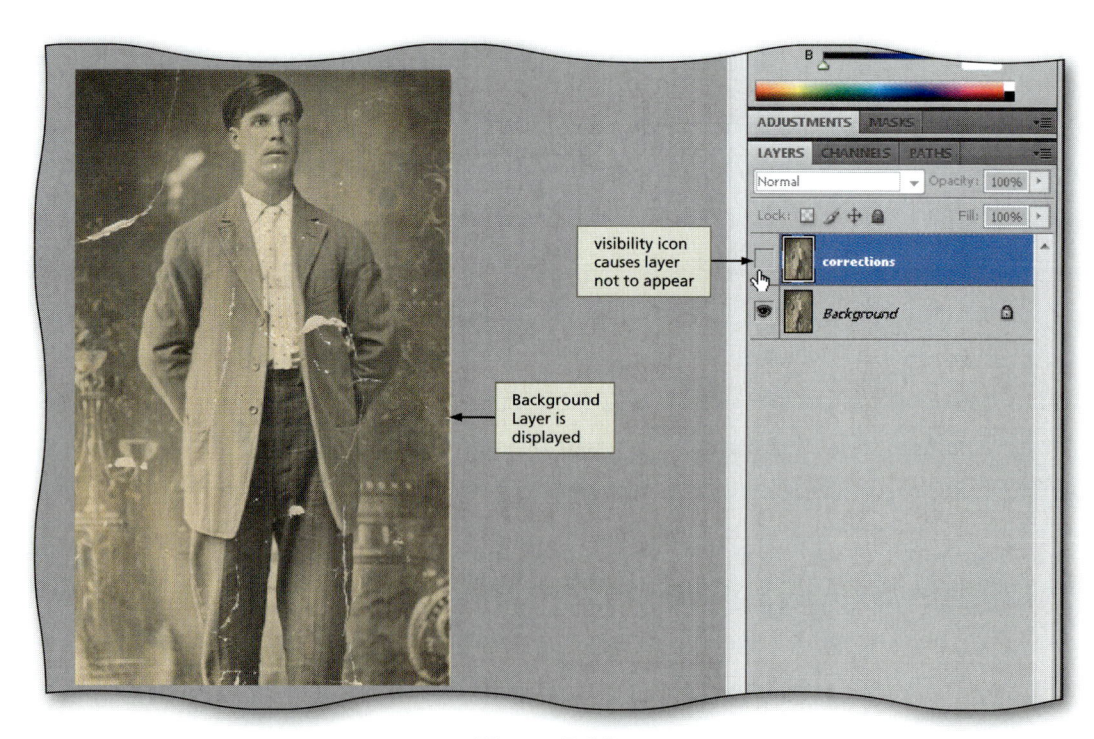

Figure 5–34

To Save and Close the Schoolmaster File

The final steps are to save and close the Schoolmaster file. During the process, Photoshop will ask if you want to save the layers. Clicking the OK button will increase the file size but will retain your edit layers. If you wish to flatten the layers, click Flatten Image on the Layer menu and then save the file.

1. With your USB flash drive connected to one of the computer's USB ports, click File on the menu bar and then Save As.

2. When the Save As dialog box is displayed, type `Schoolmaster Repaired` in the File name text box. Do not press the ENTER key.

3. Click the Save in box arrow and then click UDISK (F:), or the location associated with your USB flash drive, in the list, if necessary.

4. Click the Save button. When Photoshop displays the TIFF Options dialog box, click the OK button. When Photoshop displays a warning message about increased file size, click the OK button.

5. Click the Close button on the Schoolmaster Repaired document window title bar to close the file.

To Open the Girl Image

The next photo is of a more recent child who visited the schoolhouse. The photo with a red-eye problem is opened in the following steps.

1. Open the file named Girl from the Chapter05 folder of the Data Files for Students, or from a location specified by your instructor.

2. If necessary, change the magnification to 25% (Figure 5–35).

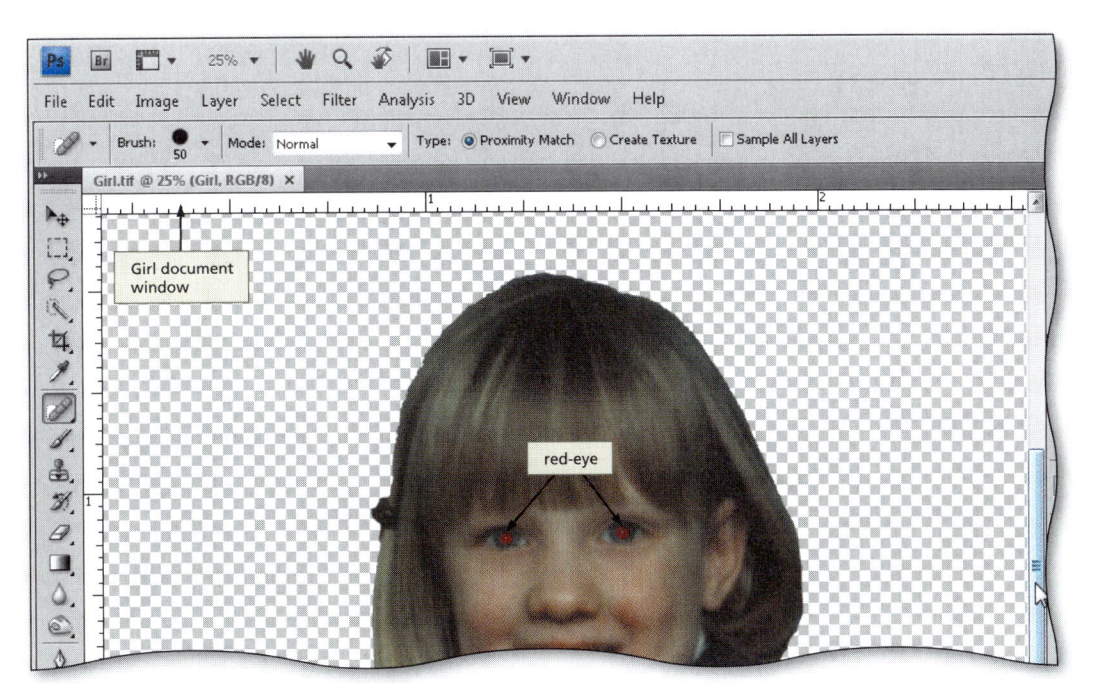

Figure 5–35

BTW

Quick Reference
For a table that lists how to complete the tasks covered in this book using the mouse, shortcut menu, and keyboard, see the Quick Reference Summary at the back of this book or visit the Photoshop CS4 Quick Reference Web page (scsite.com/pscs4//qr).

The Red Eye Tool

In photographs, **red-eye** is when the pupils of the subject's eyes appear red. Red-eye is caused in flash photography where the flash of a camera is bright enough to cause a reflection off the retina. The red color comes from the blood vessels in the eye. Red-eye can be avoided by moving the flash farther away from the lens or by using a more modern camera that has a red-eye reduction feature. In those cameras, the flash goes off twice — once before the picture is taken and then again to take the picture. The first flash causes the pupils to contract, which significantly reduces the red-eye.

Red-eye can be corrected in Photoshop using a specialized tool designed specifically for this problem. The Red Eye tool removes red-eye in flash photos by recoloring all contiguous red pixels. The Red Eye options bar has settings to change the pupil size and the darken amount. The Red Eye tool can be used only on photos in the RGB and Lab color formats. It does not work with CMYK color mode.

The Red Eye tool options bar displays options for the pupil size and percentage of darkening (Figure 5–36). The labels are scrubby sliders.

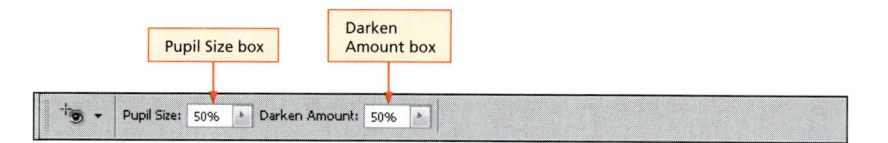

Figure 5–36

To Correct Red-Eye

The following steps remove the red-eye from the photo.

1
- On the Tools panel, right-click the current healing tool button and then click Red Eye Tool in the list.
- On the options bar, drag the Darken Amount scrubby slider to 25%.
- Move the mouse pointer to the girl's eye on the left to display the crosshair mouse pointer (Figure 5–37).

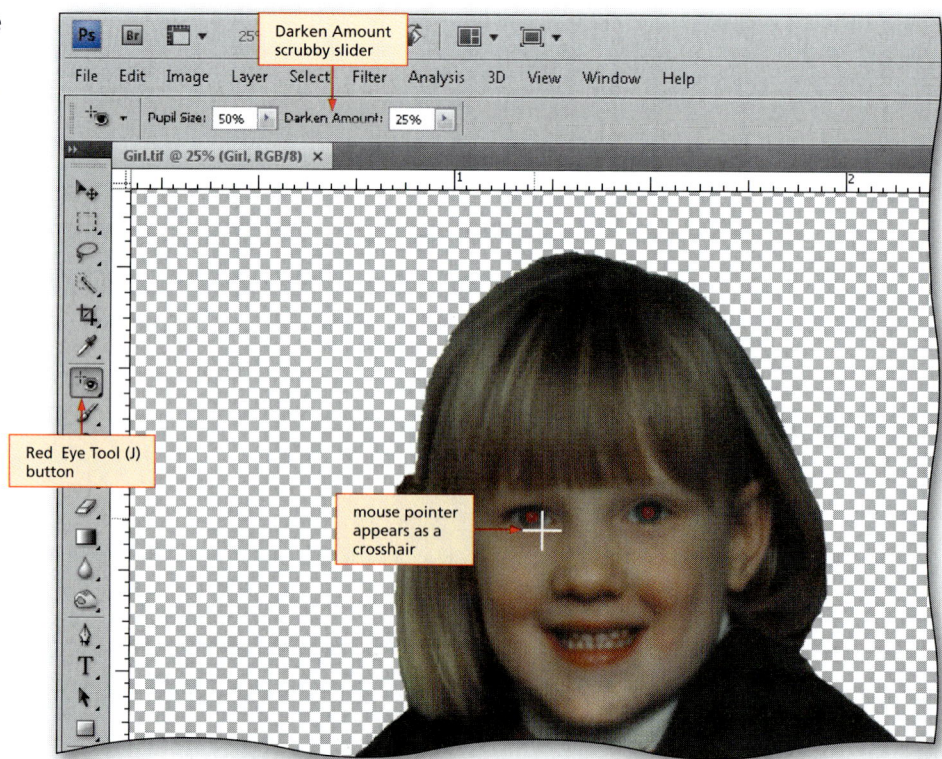

Figure 5–37

2
- Click the red portion of the eye to remove the red-eye. Move the mouse pointer to view the result (Figure 5–38).

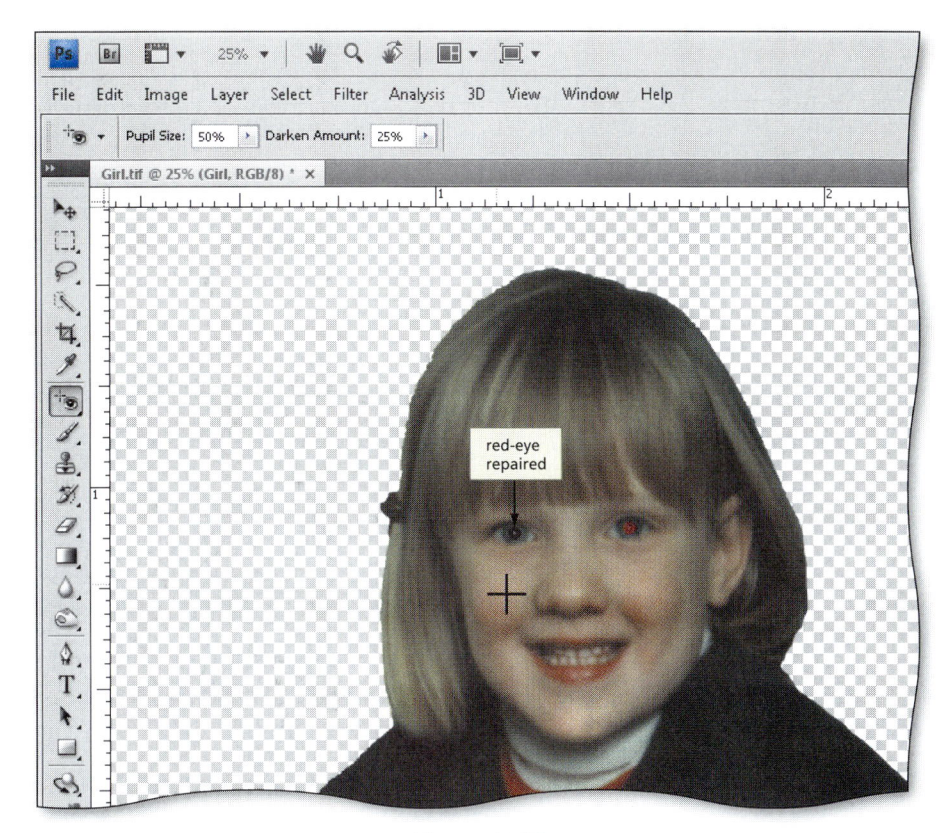

Figure 5–38

3
- Click the other eye to fix the red-eye problem (Figure 5–39).

Other Ways
1. Press SHIFT+J until Red Eye tool is active, click red-eye

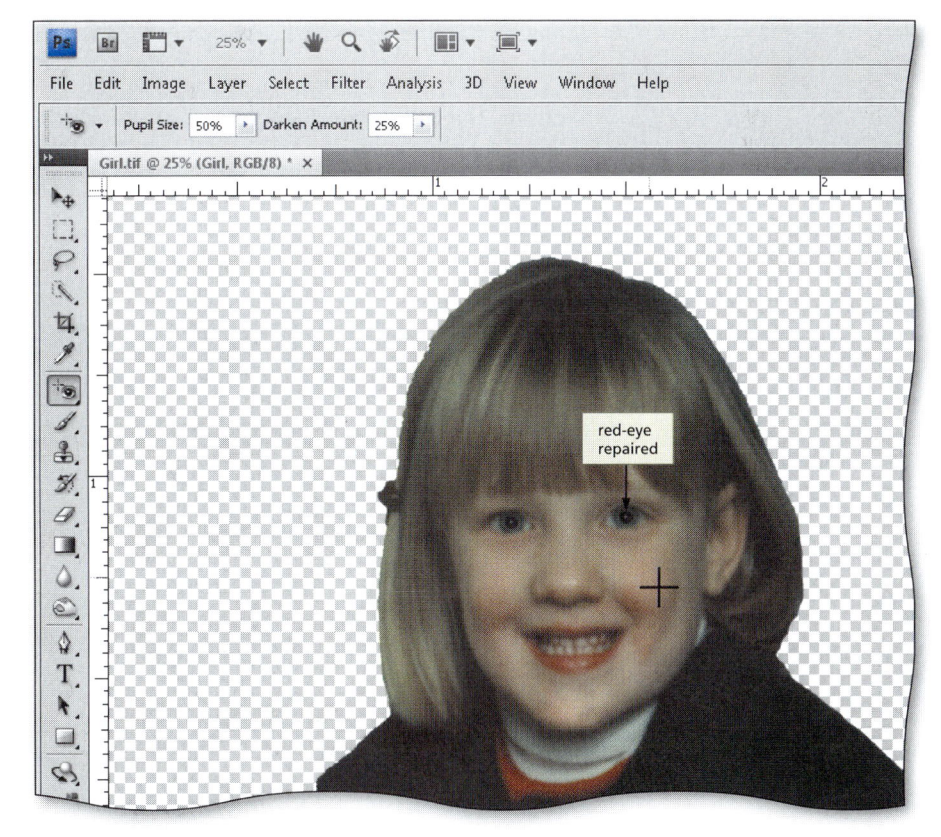

Figure 5–39

To Save the Girl File

The final steps are to save and close the Girl file.

1. With your USB flash drive connected to one of the computer's USB ports, click File on the menu bar and then Save As.

2. When the Save As dialog box is displayed, type `Girl Repaired` in the File name text box. Do not press the ENTER key.

3. Click the Save in box arrow and then click UDISK (F:), or the location associated with your USB flash drive, in the list.

4. Click the Save button. When Photoshop displays the TIFF Options dialog box, click the OK button. If Photoshop asks to include layers, click the OK button.

5. Click the Close button on the Girl Repaired document window title bar to close the file.

To Open a Photo and Remove Yellowing

> **BTW**
>
> **Photoshop Help**
> The best way to become familiar with Photoshop Help is to use it. Appendix D includes detailed information about Photoshop Help and exercises that will help you gain confidence in using it.

The next photo to repair is the Teacher and Student file. This scanned photo from the 1940s has light damage and needs adjustment. The following steps open the file, change the color mode to grayscale, and create a corrections layer.

1. Open the file named Teacher and Student from the Chapter05 folder of the Data Files for Students, or from a location specified by your instructor. If necessary, change the magnification to 50%.

2. On the Image menu, point to Mode and then click Grayscale. If Photoshop displays a message asking whether discard color information, click the Discard button.

3. On the Layers panel, right-click the Background layer and then click Duplicate Layer to display the Duplicate Layer dialog box.

4. Type `corrections` in the As box and then click the OK button to create the new layer (Figure 5–40).

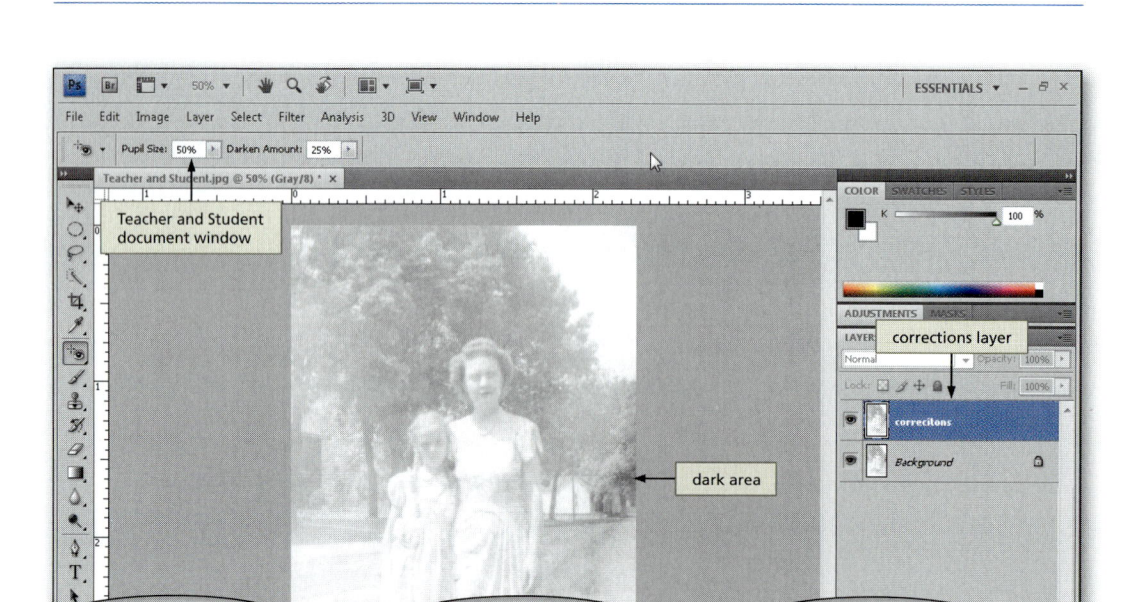

Figure 5–40

The Dodge, Burn, and Sponge Tools

The Dodge tool is used to lighten areas of an image. The Burn tool does just the opposite; it darkens areas of an image. Both tools are based on a technique of traditional photography, regulating exposure on specific areas of a print. Photographers reduce exposure to lighten an isolated area on the print, which is called **dodging**. Increasing the exposure to darken areas on a print is called **burning**. Another tool, the Sponge tool subtly changes the color saturation of an area. In Grayscale mode, the tool increases or decreases contrast by moving gray levels away from or toward the middle gray.

An Exposure box on the options bar allows you to specify a percentage of dodging or burning. The default value is 50%. A higher percentage in the Exposure box increases the effect, while a lower percentage reduces it (Figure 5–41). The Dodge, Burn, and Sponge tools have similar options bars.

> **BTW**
>
> **Exposure**
> **Exposure** refers to the amount of light allowed in during the process of taking a photograph. If exposed too long, the photograph will be washed out. If exposed too short, the photograph will appear too dark. A light meter can be used to measure the light and set an ideal exposure rate.

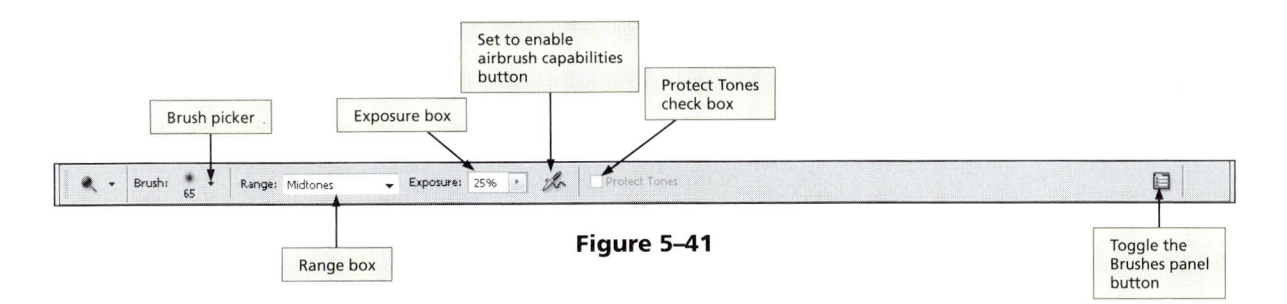

Figure 5–41

To Lighten Using the Dodge Tool

The following step fixes some problem areas in the Teacher and Student photo. Part of the photo is too dark, and another portion has light damage.

1
- Click the Dodge Tool (O) button on the Tools panel.
- On the options bar, type 25 in the Exposure box.
- Using short strokes and adjusting the brush size using the bracket keys, drag through the darker portions of the image on the right to lighten them (Figure 5–42).

Experiment
- Using the Dodge tool, click in the same spot in the photograph until the area becomes too light. Then undo the dodge using History panel.

Figure 5–42

Vignetting

Vignetting is a reduction of an image's brightness at the edges compared to the center. Vignetting usually is an unintended effect, such as the halo effect that occurs when photographing a projection screen or other light source against a dark background, but sometimes it is used as a creative effect to draw attention to the center of the image. Special camera filters and post-processing procedures can create a vignette, but you also can create it using Photoshop.

> **BTW**
>
> **Colorization of Old Photos**
> Before the advent of color film, black and white photos were often colorized by painting directly on the photographic prints with special paints or inks. The original photo of the Teacher and Student was hand tinted with blue sky.

To Create an Oval for the Vignette

The following steps create an oval in preparation for creating the vignette.

1. Right-click the current marquee tool button and then click Elliptical Marquee Tool on the context menu.

2. Drag an oval over the center portion of the image, approximately 3 inches long. While dragging, press and hold the spacebar key to reposition the marquee (Figure 5–43).

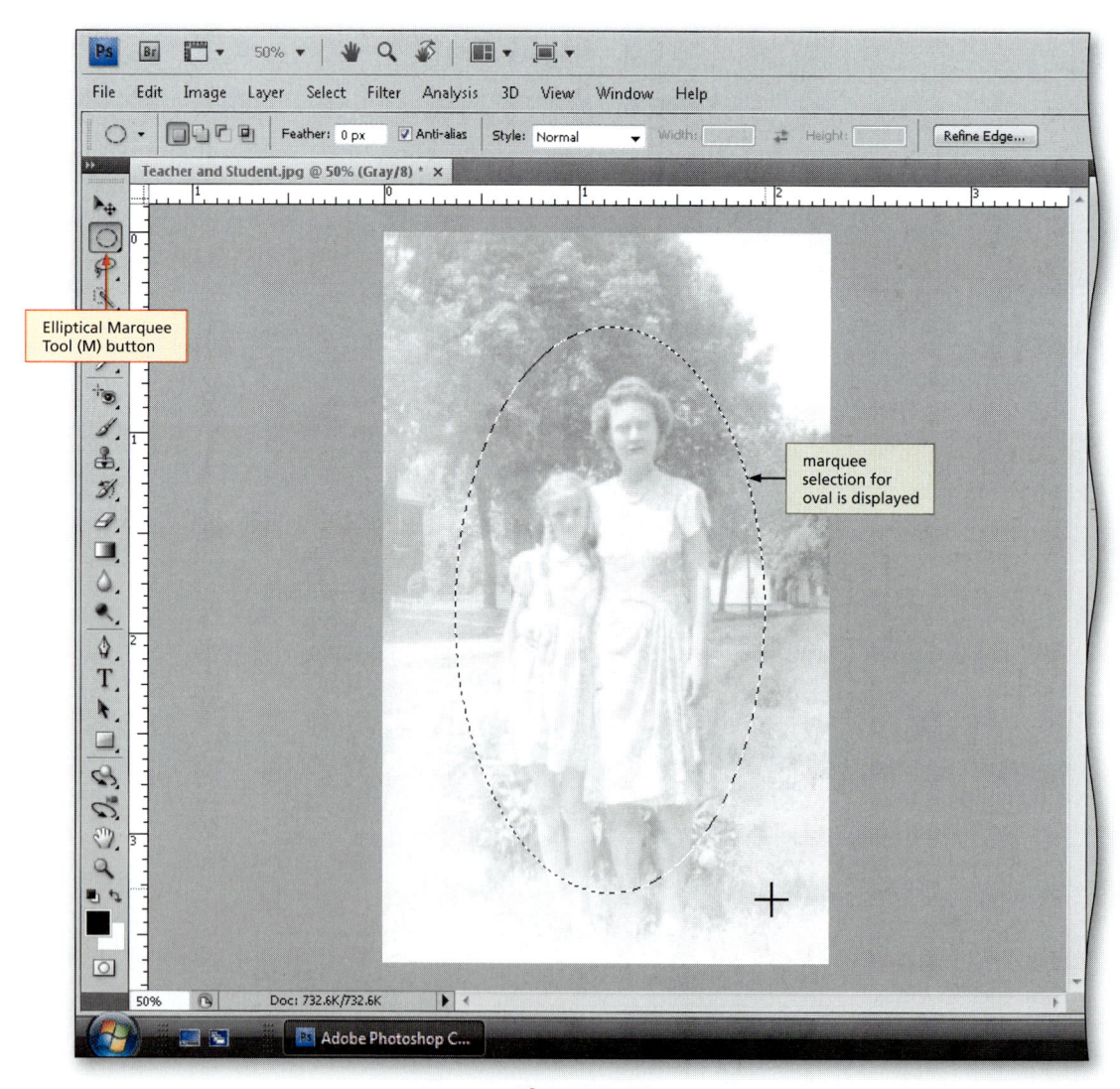

Figure 5–43

To Darken Using the Burn Tool

The following steps use the Burn tool to darken the oval, creating the vignette effect. Burning will enhance the details in the features and clothing of the teacher and student.

1
- Right-click the Dodge Tool (O) button and then click Burn Tool in the context menu.
- Use the right-bracket (]) key to enlarge the size of the brush to be slightly greater than the oval.
- Click several times to burn the image, enhancing the details of the photo (Figure 5–44).

2
- Press CTRL+D to deselect. Press the M key to return to the current Marquee tool.

Figure 5–44

To View the Corrections

The following steps view the corrections and compare them to the original.

1 On the Layers panel, click the visibility icon in the corrections layer to view the original image before corrections.

2 Click the visibility icon again to view the corrections.

To Save and Close the Teacher and Student File

With the corrections complete, the steps below save the image and close the Teacher and Student file. Because the image contains layers, Photoshop will offer the TIFF format automatically in the Save dialog box.

1. Save the Teacher and Student file as Teacher and Student Repaired in the Chapter05 folder on your USB flash drive.

2. When Photoshop displays the TIFF Options dialog box, click the OK button. When Photoshop asks to include layers, click the OK button.

3. Close the Teacher and Student Repaired document window.

Plan Ahead

Correct lens errors.
While modern digital cameras help you correct many user and lighting errors, some **lens correction** is necessary from time to time. If you have a photo that has lens errors, correct these errors after making any color, sharpening, cropping, or healing corrections.

Lens Correction Tools

Many kinds of photographic errors can be corrected in Photoshop. The most common mistakes include lens flaws, focus errors, distortions, unintended angle errors, and perspective errors. Every photographer has made an error from time to time. The next series of steps uses the Lens Correction filter to fix some of the lens flaws, distortions, and errors in the Schoolhouse photo. You can try different settings before committing them permanently to the image. Table 5–5 describes some typical errors and correction methods using the Lens Correction filter.

Table 5–5 Kinds of Distortions

Type of Error	Description	Correction Method
Angle error	an image is crooked or tilted in the photograph	rotate image
Barrel distortion	a lens defect that causes straight lines to bow out toward the edges of the image	decrease the barrel effect by negatively removing distortion
Chromatic aberration	appears as a color fringe along the edges of objects caused by the lens focusing on different colors of light	increase or decrease the red/cyan fringe or blue/yellow fringe in different planes
Keystone distortion	wider top or bottom effect that occurs when an object is photographed from an angle or perspective	correct vertical and/or horizontal perspective error
Pincushion distortion	a lens defect that causes straight lines to bend inward	decrease the pincushion effect by positively removing distortion
Vignette distortion	a defect where the edges, especially the corners, of an image are darker than the center	lighten or darken the amount of color at the four corners based on a midpoint in the image

You also can use the Lens Correction filter to rotate an image or fix image perspective caused by vertical or horizontal camera tilt. The filter's image grid makes these adjustments easier and more accurate than using the Transform command.

Angle and Perspective Errors

While the Crop tool and warp grids can be used to transform and correct the perspective in an image, the Lens Correction dialog box has the added advantages of very precise measurements and other ways to correct errors. This is useful particularly when working with photos that contain keystone distortion. Keystone distortion in perspective occurs when an object is photographed from an angle. For example, if you take a picture of a tall building from ground level, the edges of the building appear closer to each other at the top than they do at the bottom. Keystone distortions can be corrected by changing the vertical or horizontal perspective in the photo. Angle errors occur when the camera is tilted to the left or right, making objects in the photo appear slanted.

After correcting keystone and angle errors, it is sometimes necessary to scale the image to regain any edges that were clipped by the correction. You also might need to fill in transparent edges created by changing the angle. The Lens Correction dialog box (Figure 5–45) has boxes, sliders, and buttons, for correcting the distortions and repairing collateral damage created by the correction.

BTW

Focal Length
Some camera lenses cause defects because of the focal length or the f-stop used. You can set the Photoshop Lens Correction filter with settings based on the camera, lens, and focal length used to take the image.

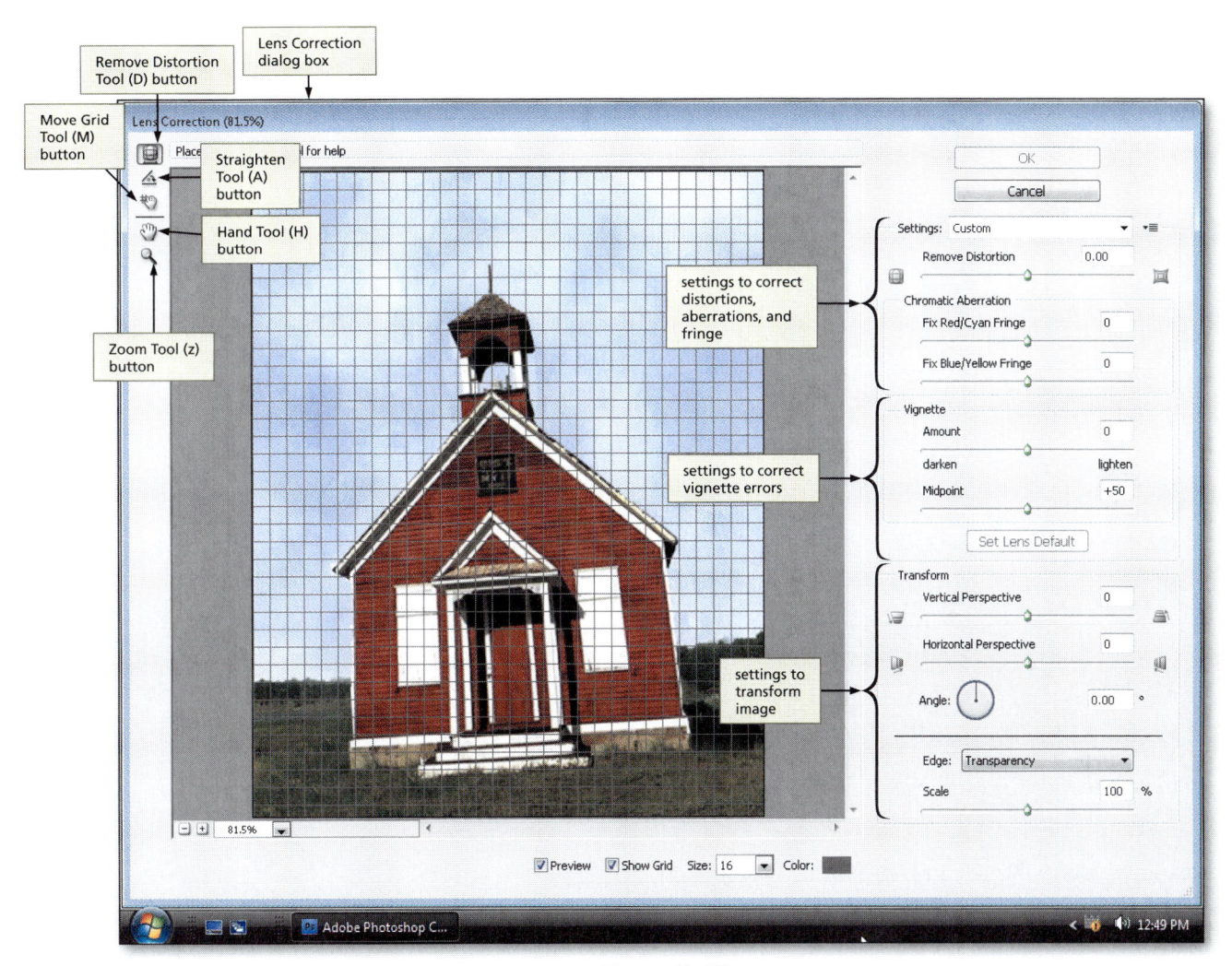

Figure 5–45

BTW

The Lens Correction Dialog Box
The Remove Distortion Tool (D) button corrects barrel and pincushion distortions. The Move Grid Tool (M) button is used to drag the grid lines to any position to help align edges within the image. The Hand Tool (H) button moves or scrolls images that are more than 100% magnified.

To Open the Schoolhouse Image

The following steps open the file named Schoolhouse image.

1. Open the file named Schoolhouse from the Chapter05 folder of the Data Files for Students, or from a location specified by your instructor.

2. If necessary, change the magnification to 81.5% (Figure 5–46).

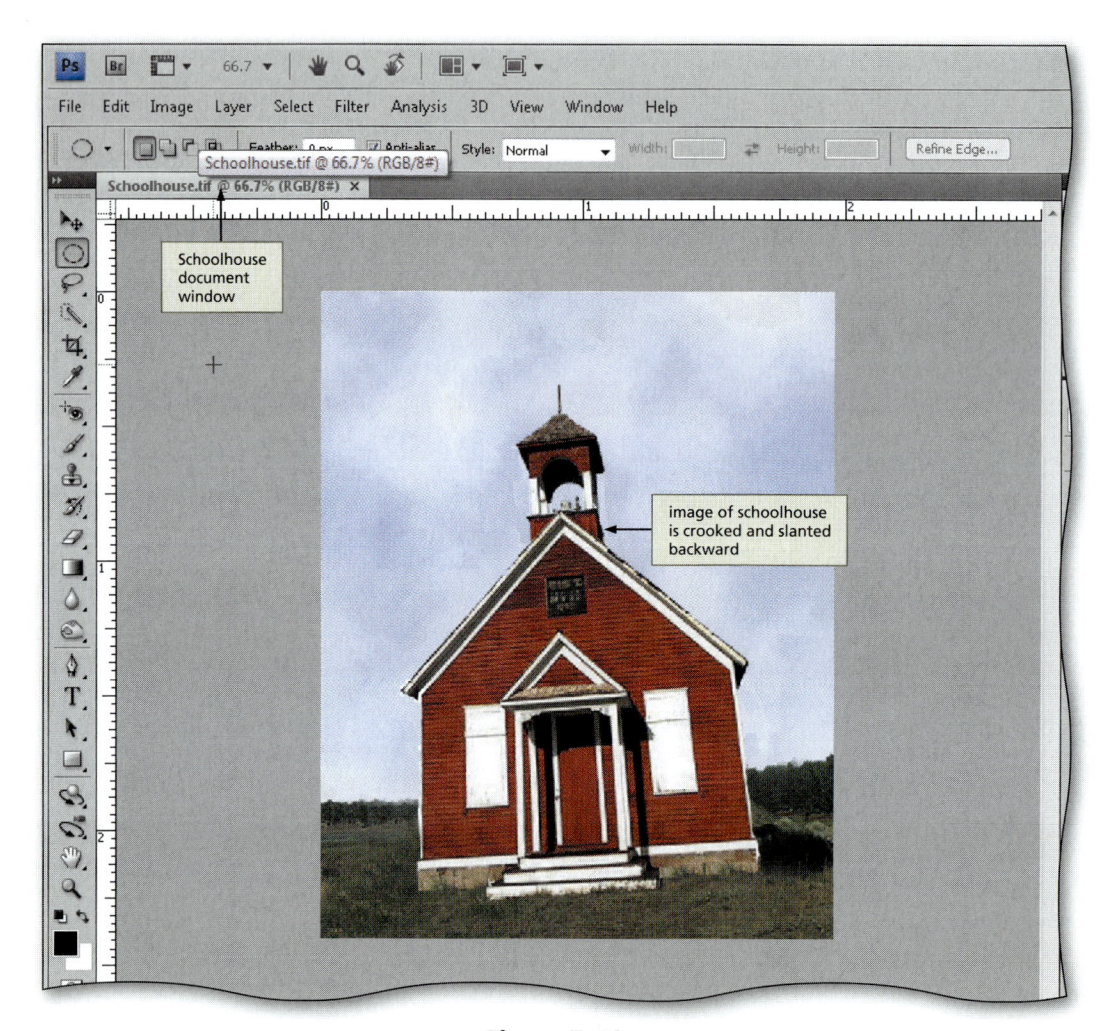

Figure 5–46

To Correct Angle and Perspective Errors

To straighten the photo and correct the angle distortion, the following steps use the Lens Correction dialog box.

1
- Click Filter on the menu bar and then point to Distort to display the Distort submenu (Figure 5–47).

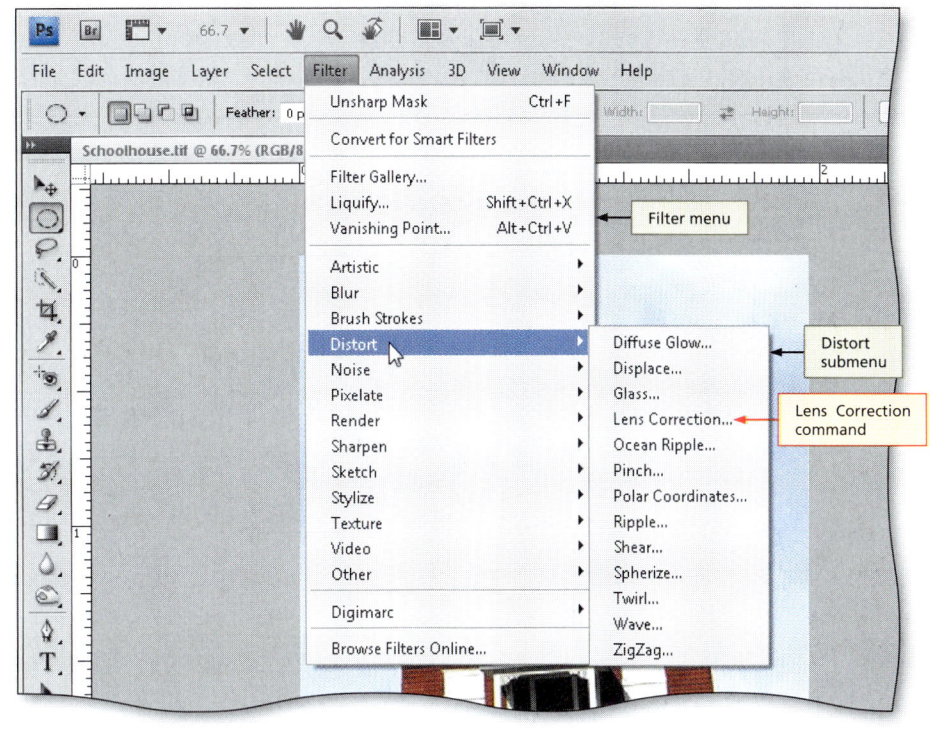

Figure 5–47

2
- Click Lens Correction on the Distort submenu to display the Lens Correction dialog box (Figure 5–48).

  Experiment
- Turn on or manipulate grid lines that are displayed in the image preview using the settings at the bottom of the dialog box.

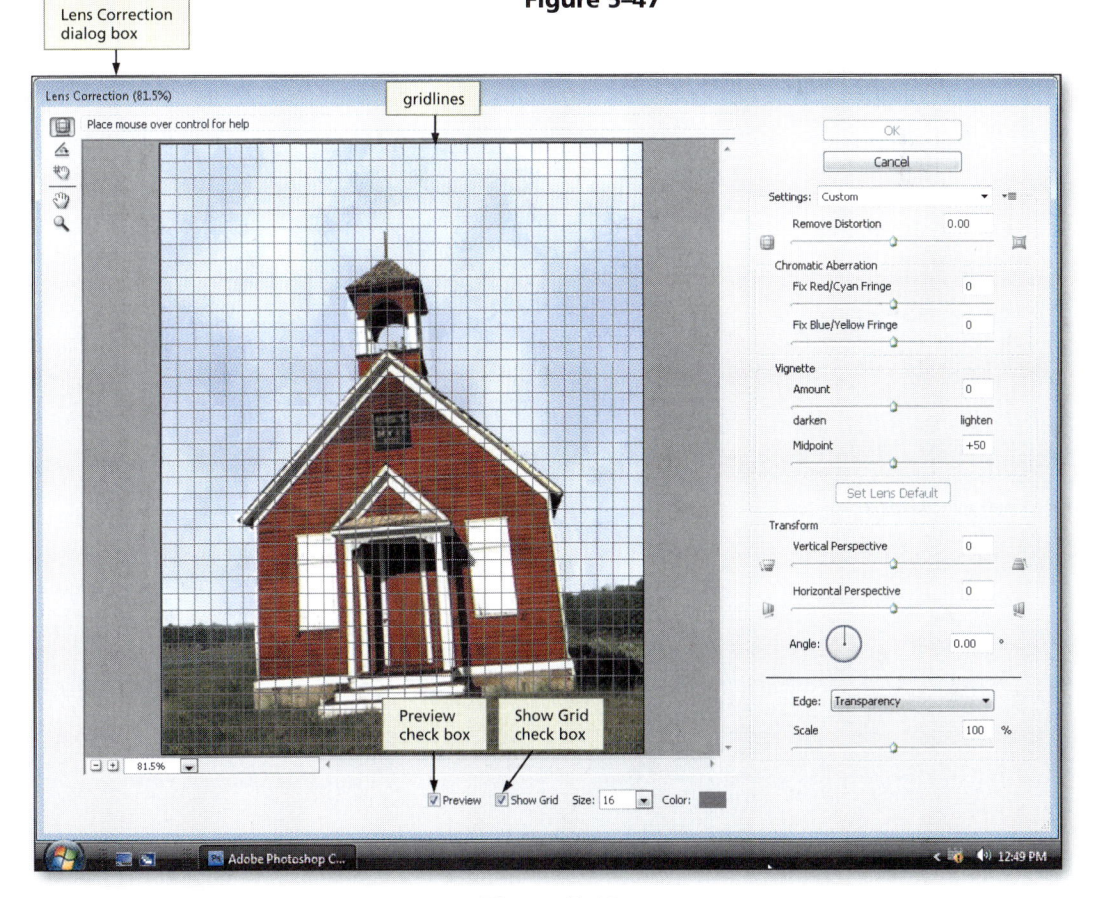

Figure 5–48

3

- Double-click the Vertical Perspective box and type –75 to remove the keystone distortion (Figure 5–49).

Q&A | How do negative values affect the vertical perspective?

A negative value in the Vertical Perspective box brings the top of the picture closer, such as when shooting up from the base of a tall building.

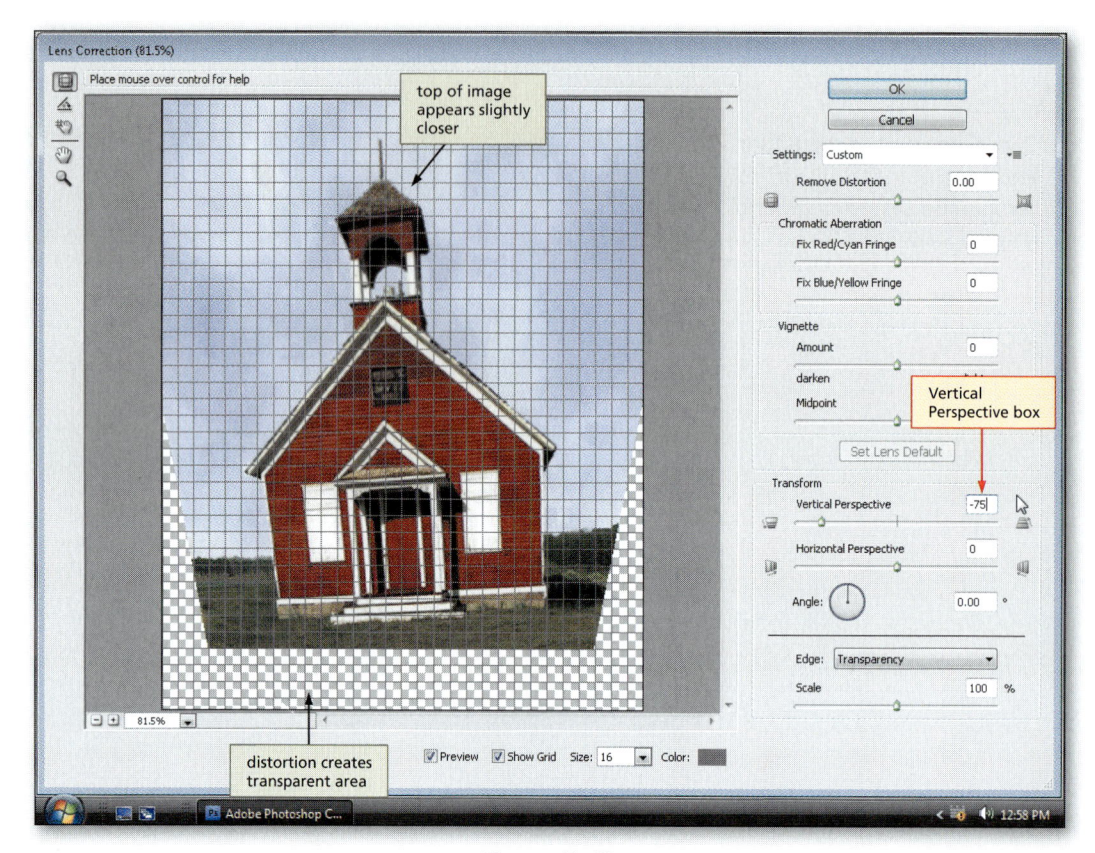

Figure 5–49

4

- Double-click the Horizontal Perspective box. Type –5 to adjust the slight left-to-right distortion (Figure 5–50).

Q&A | How do negative values affect the horizontal perspective?

A negative value in the Horizontal Perspective box brings the left side of the picture closer.

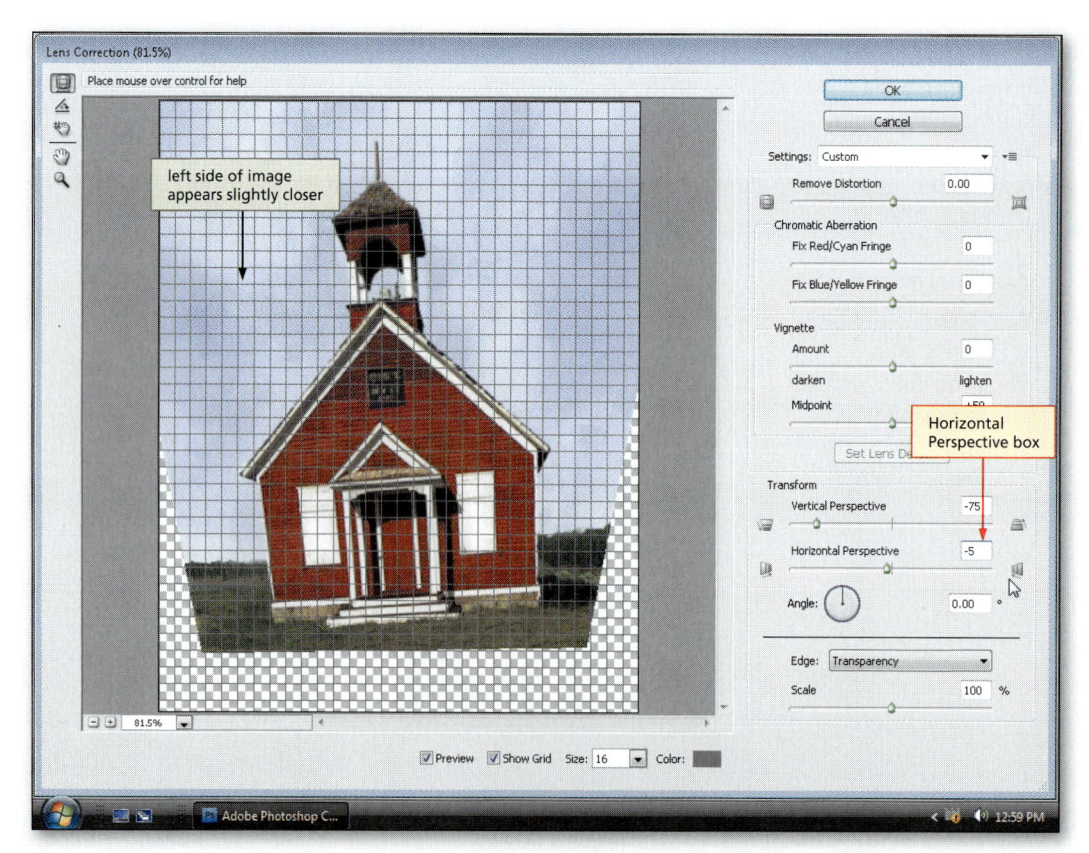

Figure 5–50

5
- Click the Straighten Tool (A) button on the Lens Correction dialog box.
- Drag a line from the top of the belfry down to the grass, passing through the center of the doorway (Figure 5–51).

Q&A Could I use the Angle icon to align the building?

The angle can be adjusted by dragging the Angle icon. The angle is based on 360 degrees. Acceptable values run from 1 to 359 with counterclockwise rotation.

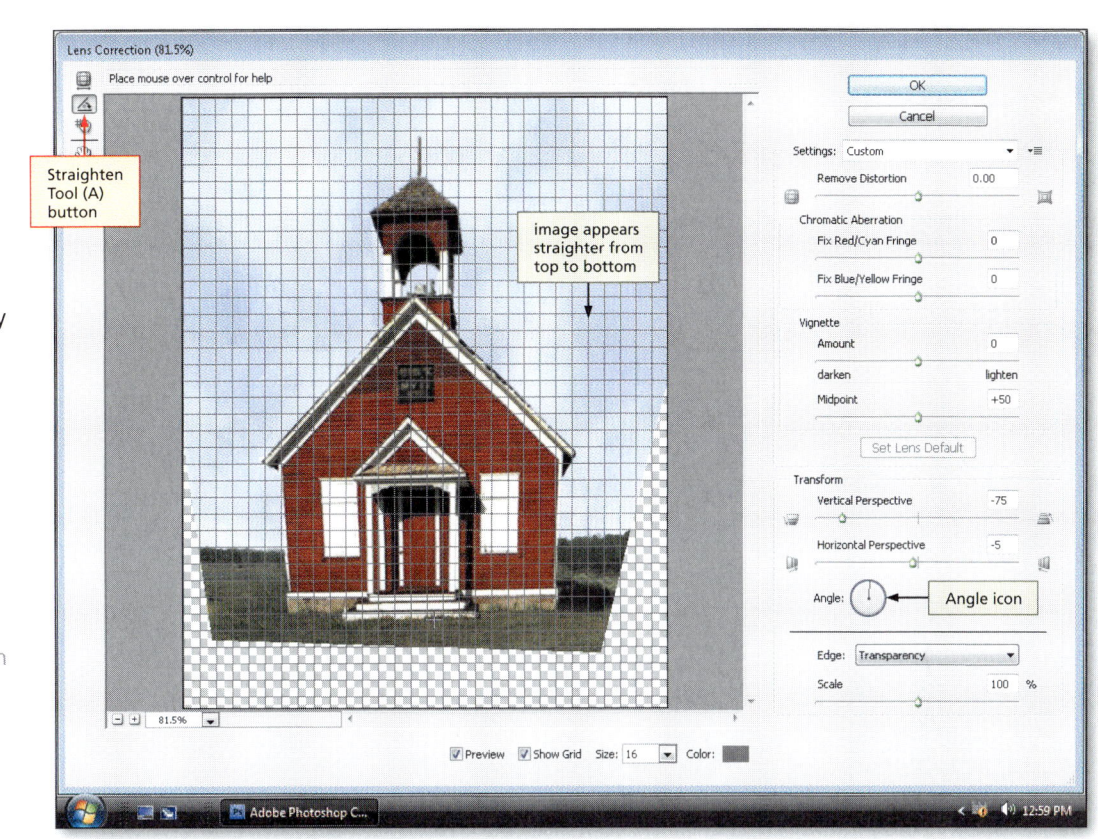

Figure 5–51

6
- Drag a line along the top of the foundation of the schoolhouse, from left to right, to straighten the image (Figure 5–52).

🔍 **Experiment**
- Drag at different angles and watch the image change. When you are finished, drag in the image in a straight line, left to right and top to bottom.

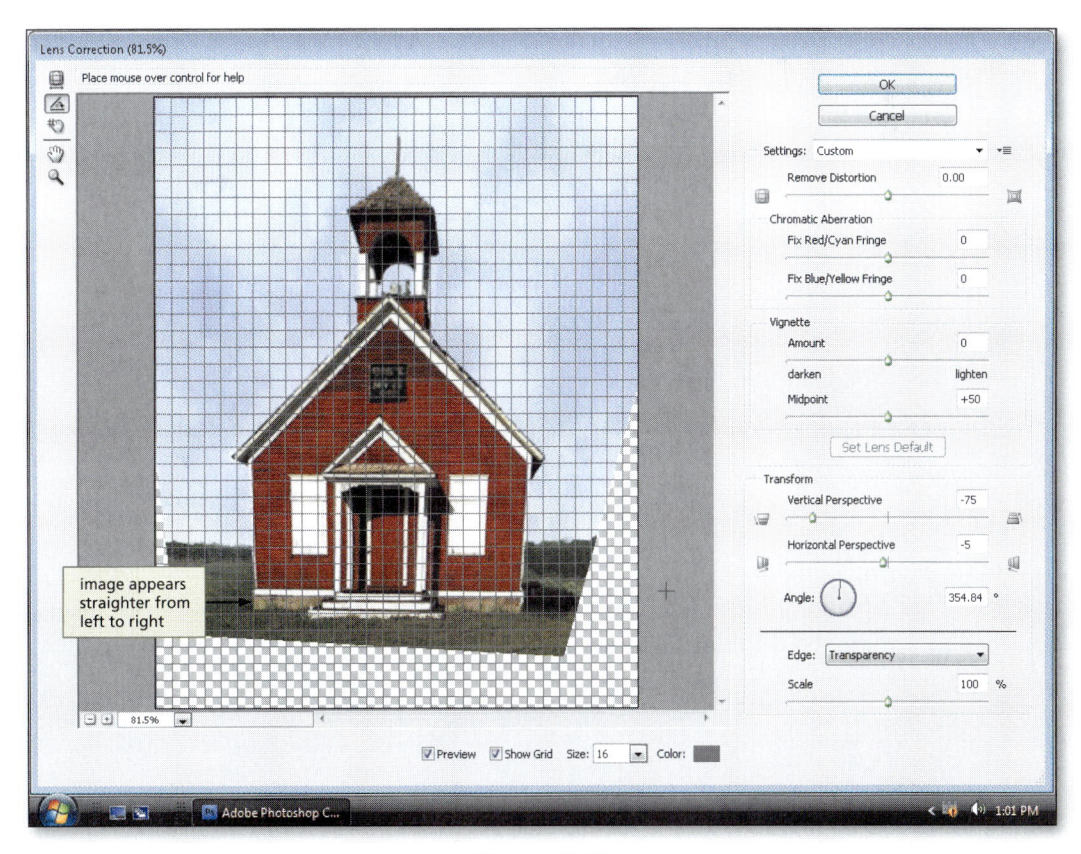

Figure 5–52

PS 354 **Photoshop Chapter 5** Enhancing and Repairing Photos

7
- Click the Edge box arrow and then click Edge Extension in the list to fill the transparent pixels in the image with matching textures (Figure 5–53).

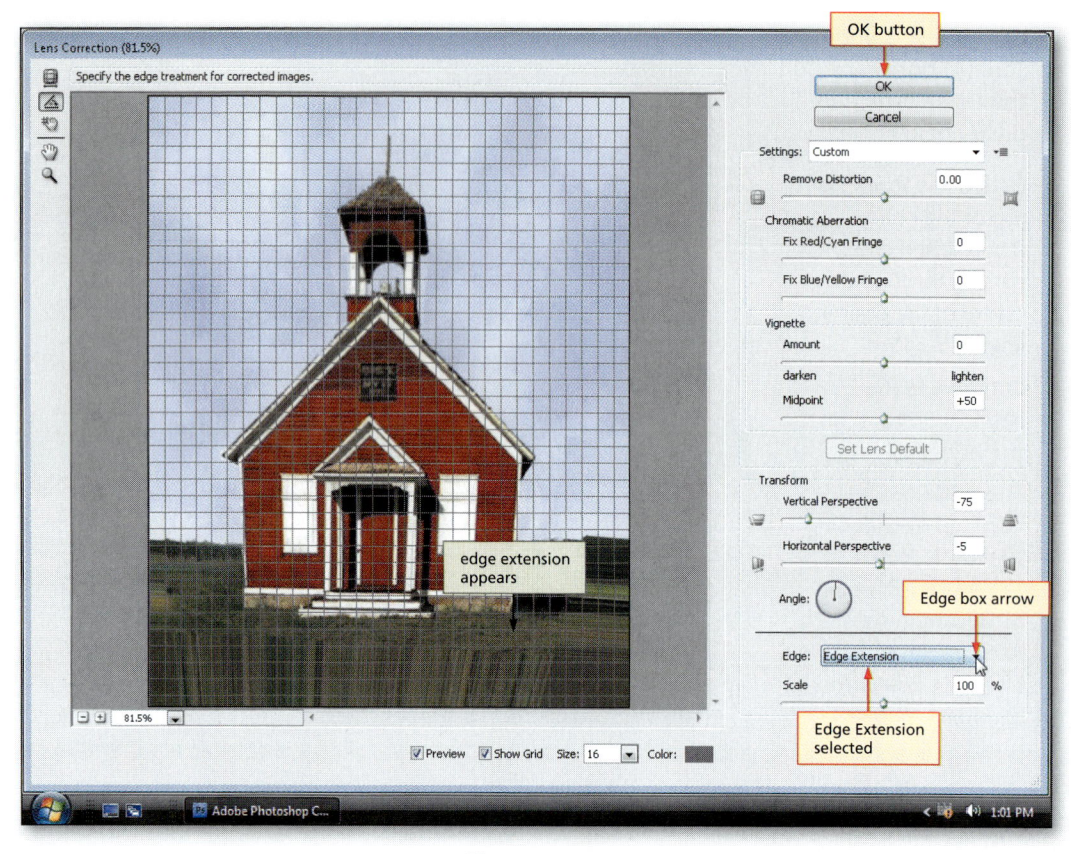

Figure 5–53

8
- Click the OK button to close the Lens Distortion dialog box (Figure 5–54).

Figure 5–54

To Crop the Image

With the image distortion corrected, the following steps crop the edited image.

1. Press the C key to access the Crop tool.
2. In the image, move the mouse pointer to the lower-right portion of the grass that is still in focus.
3. Drag to the upper-left corner of the image just far enough to include the grass that is still in focus to the left of the schoolhouse. If necessary, use the sizing handles to adjust the selected area.
4. Press the ENTER key to crop the image (Figure 5–55).

BTW

Extending Edges
Because the angle distortion corrections created some transparent areas along the edge of the photo, extend the edges after a lens correction for an image with square corners. The extension does not look good, but filling in the transparent areas allows you to crop to the maximum usable area.

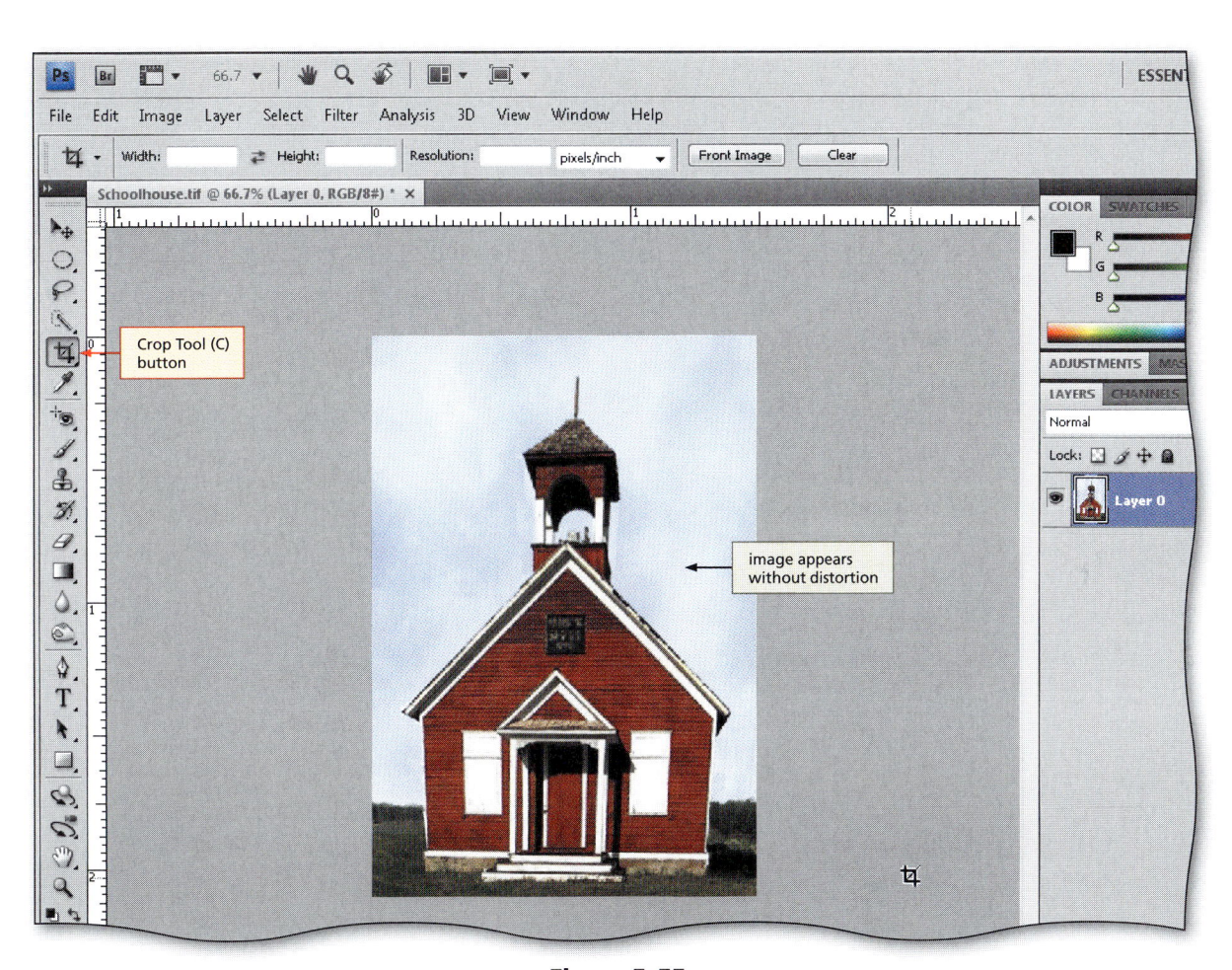

Figure 5–55

To Save the Image

In the next steps, the image is saved and minimized.

1. Save the Schoolhouse image as Schoolhouse Repaired in Chapter05 folder of your USB flash drive
2. When Photoshop displays the TIFF options dialog box, click the OK button.
3. Close the Schoolhouse Repaired document window.

BTW

Vanishing Point
For photographs with several planes and angles, correcting perspective errors can be tricky. On the Filter menu, the Vanishing Point command lets you specify the planes in the photo. Photoshop remembers the perspective of the plane, resulting in properly scaled and oriented, more realistic-looking pictures.

The Blur, Sharpen, and Smudge Tools

A final set of tools used to help enhance, restore, and create special effects include the Blur, Sharpen, and Smudge tools.

The Blur tool softens hard edges or reduces detail in an image when you drag in the selection or image, by decreasing the color contrast between consecutive pixels. The Blur tool is used for very subtle changes in small areas. If you are working on a high-resolution image, then the effect of the Blur tool can be very slight; zooming in on a portion of the photo helps you notice the effect. The options bar includes settings for brush size, mode, and strength.

The Sharpen tool is the opposite of the Blur tool. It increases contrast along edges to add sharpness. The more you paint over an area with the tool, the greater the sharpen effect. The Smudge tool simulates the effect you see when you drag a finger through wet paint. The tool picks up color where the stroke begins and pushes it in the direction you drag. The effect is much like finger painting.

To Open the Boy Image

BTW

Sharpen Tool
While the Sharpen filter's Unsharp Mask provides an overall sharpening of the focus in an image, the Sharpen tool works more like the Blur tool — the effect is more apparent when you zoom in and use it with small portions of the image. The options bar includes settings for brush size, mode, and strength.

You will use the Blur tool to enhance the motion in a picture of a young boy playing soccer outside the schoolhouse, opened in the following steps.

1. Open the file named Boy from the Chapter05 folder of the Data Files for Students, or from a location specified by your instructor.

2. If necessary, change the magnification to 50% and scroll to display the soccer ball, as shown in Figure 5–56.

Figure 5–56

To Create a Corrections Layer

The steps that follow duplicate the Background layer to create a corrections layer.

1. Right-click the Background layer on the Layers panel to display the context menu.
2. Click Duplicate Layer to display the Duplicate Layer dialog box.
3. Type `corrections` in the As box and then click the OK button to create the new layer (Figure 5–57).

Figure 5–57

To Blur

The following steps use the Blur tool to enhance the motion in the Boy image.

1
- On the Tools panel, right-click the Blur Tool button to display the context menu (Figure 5–58).

Figure 5–58

2
- Click Blur Tool to select it.
- Click the Brush picker button on the Blur tool options bar to display the selection panel. (Figure 5–59).

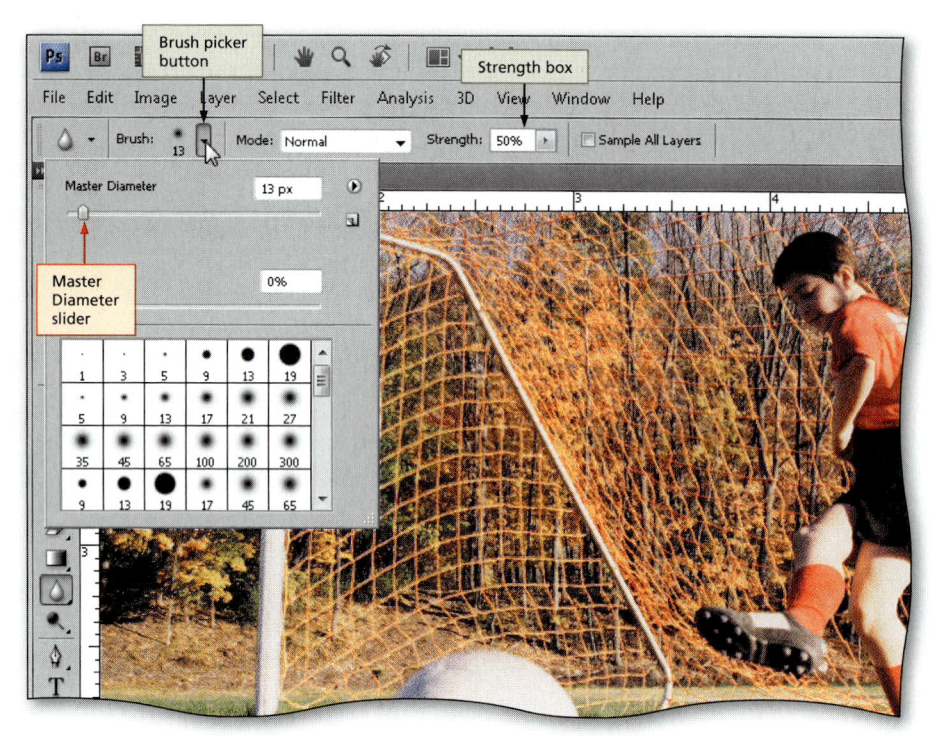

Figure 5–59

3
- Drag the Master Diameter slider to 80 px to increase the size of the Blur tool mouse pointer.
- Drag the Strength scrubby slider to 100% to increase the strength of the blur.
- Move the mouse pointer into the image (Figure 5–60).

Figure 5–60

4
- Drag over the upper-right quadrant of the edge of the soccer ball several times to create a blur (Figure 5–61).

  🔍 **Experiment**

- Experiment with blurring other portions of the photo to show motion, including the boy's foot.

Figure 5–61

To Compare the Layers

The steps that follow compare the corrections to the original.

1 On the Layers panel, click the visibility icon in the corrections layer to view the original image before blurring.

2 Click the visibility icon again to view the blur.

To Save the Boy File

The final steps are to save and close the Boy file.

1 With your USB flash drive connected to one of the computer's USB ports, click File on the menu bar and then Save As.

2 When the Save As dialog box is displayed, type Boy Enhanced in the File name text box. Do not press the ENTER key.

3 Click the Save in box arrow and then click UDISK (F:), or the location associated with your USB flash drive, in the list.

4 Click the Save button.

5 Click the Close button on the Boy Enhanced document window title bar to close the file.

BTW

Smudge Tool
On the Smudge tool options bar, the Smudge tool's Strength setting modifies the power of the smudge. Setting the Strength to 100%, erases nearly all of the existing color. A Strength setting of 15% will give the appearance of trying to smudge dried paint. The Finger Painting check box mimics dipping your finger in the paint color before performing the smudge.

Chapter Summary

To repair and enhance photos, you used healing tools, tools that repaired damage, tools to straighten and align, and tools to create an artistic effect. You first edited a yellowed document, patched a tear, and used the Unsharp Mask tool to bring it into better focus. You then repaired scratches and damage to a black-and-white photo. You removed the red-eye from a color photo of a child. Next, you repaired light damage to an old picture of a teacher and student and added a vignetting effect. You opened a schoolhouse photo that had keystone and angle distortion, which you corrected using the Lens Correction dialog box. Finally, you used the Blur tool to enhance the motion in a photo.

The items listed below include all the new Photoshop skills you have learned in this chapter:

1. Correct Yellowed Portions of the Document (PS 320)
2. Set the Blending Mode (PS 323)
3. Set Levels (PS 324)
4. Apply the Unsharp Mask Filter (PS 326)
5. Recreate Missing Portions of the Document (PS 327)
6. Use the Eraser Tool (PS 329)
7. Duplicate a Layer for Corrections (PS 332)
8. Repair Damage with the Spot Healing Brush Tool (PS 333)
9. Sample and Paint with the Healing Brush Tool (PS 335)
10. Patch Areas (PS 338)
11. View the Corrections (PS 340)
12. Correct Red-Eye (PS 342)
13. Lighten Using the Dodge Tool (PS 345)
14. Darken Using the Burn Tool (PS 347)
15. Correct Angle and Perspective Errors (PS 351)
16. Blur (PS 357)

Learn It Online

Test your knowledge of chapter content and key terms.

Instructions: To complete the Learn It Online exercises, start your browser, click the Address bar, and then enter the Web address `scsite.com/pscs4/learn`. When the Photoshop CS4 Learn It Online page is displayed, click the link for the exercise you want to complete and then read the instructions.

Chapter Reinforcement TF, MC, and SA
A series of true/false, multiple choice, and short answer questions that test your knowledge of the chapter content.

Flash Cards
An interactive learning environment where you identify chapter key terms associated with displayed definitions.

Practice Test
A series of multiple choice questions that test your knowledge of chapter content and key terms.

Who Wants To Be a Computer Genius?
An interactive game that challenges your knowledge of chapter content in the style of a television quiz show.

Wheel of Terms
An interactive game that challenges your knowledge of chapter key terms in the style of the television show *Wheel of Fortune*.

Crossword Puzzle Challenge
A crossword puzzle that challenges your knowledge of key terms presented in the chapter.

Apply Your Knowledge

Reinforce the skills and apply the concepts you learned in this chapter.

Enhancing a Photo for the Web

Instructions: Start Photoshop and perform the customization steps found on pages PS 7 through PS 9. Open the Apply 5-1 Antique file from the Chapter05 folder of the Data Files for Students. You can access the Data Files for Students on the DVD that accompanies this book. See the inside back cover of this book for instructions on downloading the Data Files for Students, or contact your instructor for information about accessing the required files.

The purpose of this exercise is to repair a photo of an antique typewriter and enhance it for use on an auction Web site. The edited photo is shown in Figure 5–62.

1. Use the Save As command to save the image on your USB flash drive as a PSD file, with the file name, Apply 5-1 Antique Enhanced.
2. In the Layers panel, right-click the Background layer and then click Duplicate Layer on the shortcut menu.
3. In the Duplicate Layer dialog box, type Corrections in the As box, and then click the OK button.
4. With the Corrections layer selected, click Filter on the menu bar, point to Distort, and then click Lens Correction.
5. When the Lens Correction dialog box is displayed, edit the following settings:
   a. To adjust the barrel distortion, type 15 in the Remove Distortion box.
   b. To straighten the photo, type 358 in the Angle box.
   c. To correct the keystone distortion, type 50 in the Vertical Perspective box.
   d. To adjust the scale and remove transparent areas in the photo, type 123 in the Scale box.
6. Click the OK button in the Lens Correction dialog box.
7. Click Filter on the menu bar, point to Sharpen, and then click Unsharp Mask. When the Unsharp Mask dialog box is displayed, edit the following settings:
   a. Type 4 in the Threshold box.
   b. Type 1 in the Radius box.
   c. Type 50 in the Amount box.
8. Click the OK button in the Unsharp Mask dialog box.
9. On the Tools panel, right-click the current healing tool button and then click Spot Healing Brush Tool in the list. Use the Spot Healing Brush tool to correct the damaged area on the wall to the right of the typewriter. Zoom as needed. Remember to adjust the brush size to be only slightly larger than the damaged area.
10. Experiment with the healing tools to correct flaws in the white baseboard and remove the small red ball to the left of the table.
11. Right-click the Spot Healing Brush tool and then click Healing Brush Tool in the list. On the options bar, click the Mode box arrow and then click Replace.

Figure 5–62

12. ALT+click a light area in the floor and then, using short strokes, drag through the darker areas in the floor. Resample as necessary.
13. To remove the electrical cord in the photo:
    a. Click the Clone Stamp tool.
    b. ALT+click the floor at the bottom of the photo just inside the left leg of the table. Drag from left to right through the parts of the electrical cord that are visible on the floor.
    c. ALT+click below the table at the top of the baseboard, close to the left leg of the table. Drag from left to right through the parts of the electrical cord and outlet that are visible on the baseboard.
14. Press CTRL+S to save the file again. If Photoshop displays an options dialog box, click the OK button.
15. Click File on the menu bar and then click the Save for Web & Devices command. When the Save for Web & Devices dialog box is displayed, click the 4-Up tab, if necessary, and then click the best preview for your system. Click the Save button. When the Save Optimized As dialog box is displayed, save the image on your USB flash drive. Photoshop will fill in the name, Apply-5-1-Antique-Enhanced, and the file type for you.
16. Submit this assignment in the format specified by your instructor.

Extend Your Knowledge

Extend the skills you learned in this chapter and experiment with new skills. You may need to use Help to complete the assignment.

Creating a Moving Automobile Photo

Instructions: Start Photoshop and perform the customization steps found on pages PS 7 through PS 9. Open the Extend 5-1 Auto file from the Chapter05 folder of the Data Files for Students. See the inside back cover of this book for instructions on downloading the Data Files for Students, or contact your instructor for information on accessing the required files.. The purpose of this exercise is to edit a photograph of parked automobile and make it look like it is in motion, creating both PSD and TIF versions of the final image. Many times it is impossible to take an action photo of an automobile or other subject traveling at a high speed. This technique will show how to take an existing still photo and make it appear to be moving, as in Figure 5–63.

Figure 5–63

Perform the following tasks:

1. Start Photoshop. Set the default workspace, default colors, and reset all tools.
2. Save the image on your USB flash drive as a PSD file, with the file name Extend 5-1 Auto Complete.
3. To separate the foreground from the background:
    a. Create a selection marquee around the entire car to separate it from the background.
    b. Press CTRL+J or use the Layer via Copy command to place a copy of the automobile on a new layer and assign the layer an appropriate name.
4. To create an illusion of speed in the background:
    a. Select the background layer. Click Filter on the menu bar, point to Blur and then click Motion Blur to display the Motion Blur dialog box. (*Hint:* You might want to read about Blur filters in Photoshop Help.)
    b. When the Motion Blur dialog box appears, experiment with the Angle and Distance settings until you are satisfied with the results. Close the Motion Blur dialog box.
5. To create an illusion of wheel spin:
    a. Select the automobile layer and then create a selection marquee around the front wheel.
    b. Add a Radial Blur to the wheel by clicking Filter on the menu bar. Click Blur on the Filter submenu, then click Radial Blur to display the Radial Blur dialog box. Select the Spin Blur Method. Experiment with the Amount and Quality settings. When you are satisfied with the effect, close the Radial Blur dialog box and deselect the wheel.
    c. Select the back wheel and then apply the same Radial Blur setting used for the front wheel by pressing CTRL+F to repeat the filter. Deselect the back wheel.
6. To tint the windshield and side windows:
    a. With the automobile layer still active, create a selection marquee around the windshield. Use the Add to selection button to add the side windows to the selection.
    b. Press CTRL+J or use the Layer via Copy command to create a new layer. Assign the layer an appropriate name.
    c. Press CTRL+L to display the Levels dialog box.
    d. Drag the white Output Levels slider to the left until the windows look tinted.
    e. Click OK to close the dialog box.
7. Save the file again. Flatten the image.
8. Save the image as Extend 5-1 Auto Complete in the TIFF format. If Photoshop displays a dialog box, click the OK button.
9. Submit the assignment in the format specified by your instructor.
10. Quit Photoshop.

Make It Right

Analyze a project and correct all errors and/or improve the design.

Altering a Tattoo Photo

Instructions: Start Photoshop and perform the customization steps found on pages PS 7 through PS 9. Open the Make It Right 5-1 Tattoo file from the Chapter05 folder of the Data Files for Students. See the inside back cover of this book for instructions on downloading the Data Files for Students, or contact your instructor for information on accessing the required files.

The manager of the local tattoo parlor wants to display a tattoo design, the ever-popular Mom Heart design, on a person's arm, but he does not have a photo. Using the shop's photo of another tattoo on someone's arm, as shown in Figure 5–64, you are to create the requested image.

Perform the following tasks:
This Photoshop file contains the original photo with the old tattoo. Make a copy of the background by dragging the background layer to the Layers panel status bar and dropping on the Create a new layer button. Hide the Background layer. Using the Patch Tool, remove the old tattoo by replacing it with clean skin. (*Hint:* You might want to patch small portions and overlap sections to achieve a satisfactory result.)

Open the Make It Right 5-1 Mom Tattoo image and drag it to the current window. Close the Make It Right 5-1 Mom Tattoo document window. Scale the new layer to an appropriate size and place it in the upper arm area. Change the blending mode of this layer to Multiply to remove the white regions. Try other blending modes to see which ones work the best. (*Hint:* Reduce the opacity of the new layer to improve the blending characteristics.)

Use the smudge tool with a low strength to slightly smudge the edges and make the ink appear to be a bit blurry, like a real tattoo. Save the image as Make It Right 5-1 Tattoo Edited in the PSD file format and in the TIFF format. Submit the TIFF file to your instructor.

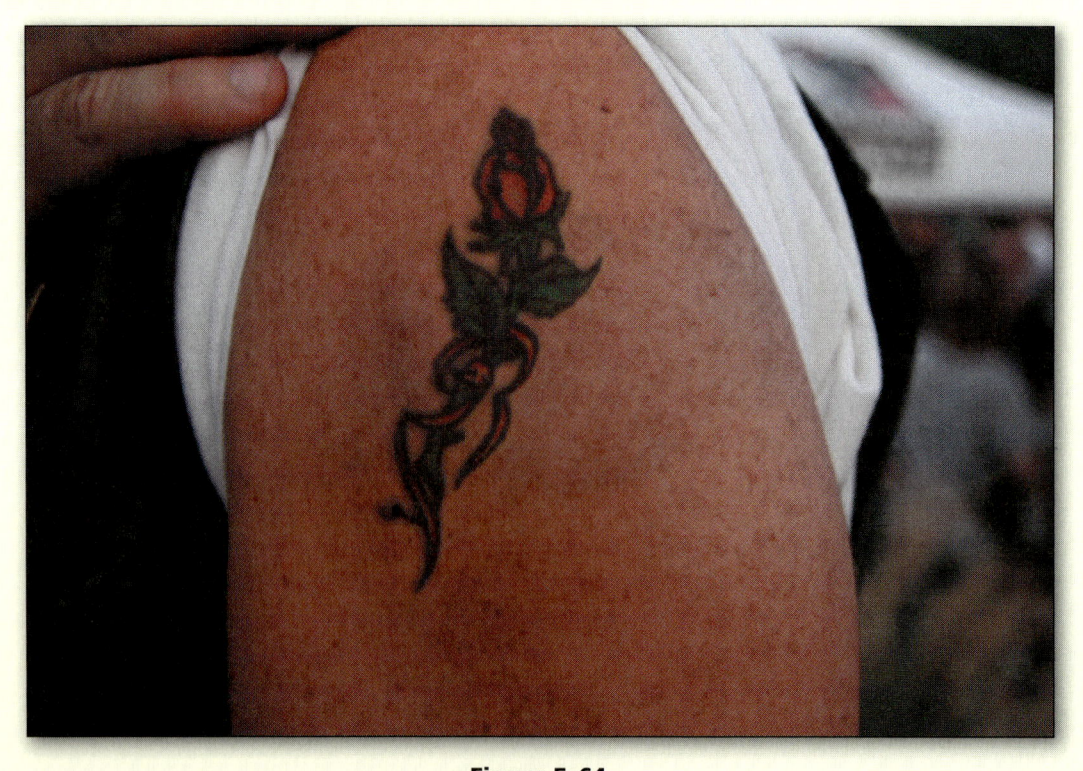

Figure 5–64

In the Lab

Design and/or create a publication using the guidelines, concepts, and skills presented in this chapter. Labs are listed in order of increasing difficulty.

Lab 1: Repairing Blemishes and Red-Eye

Problem: You would like to fix a photo of your niece and print several copies. The photo has several blemishes and a red-eye problem. You also would like to remove the date that was embedded when the photo was taken with a digital camera. The repaired photo is shown in Figure 5–65.

Instructions: Perform the following tasks:

1. Start Photoshop. Set the Default Workspace and then reset all tools. Reset the previews in the Layers panel and then reset the default colors.

2. Open the file Lab 5-1 Baby from the Chapter05 folder of the Data Files for Students. See the inside back cover of this book for instructions on downloading the Data Files for Students, or contact your instructor for information on accessing the required files.

3. Click the Save As command on the File menu. Type `Lab 5-1 Baby Repaired` as the file name. Save the file in the PSD format on your USB flash drive.

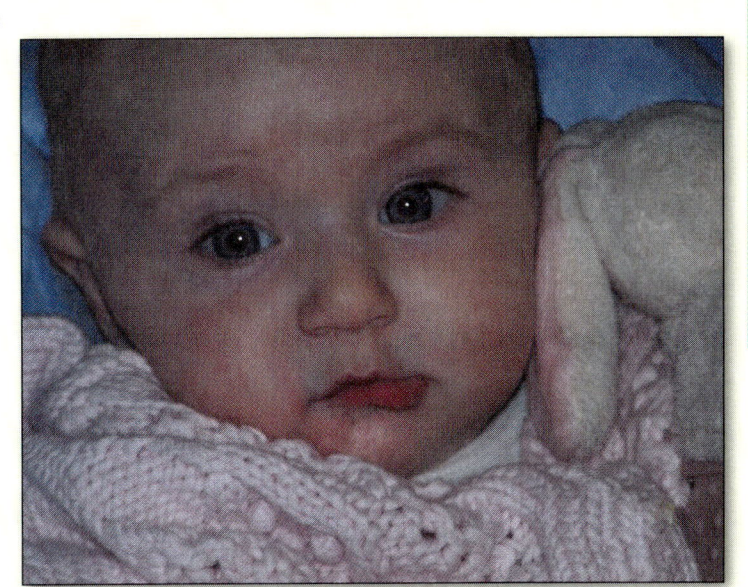

Figure 5–65

4. Duplicate the Background layer and name it corrections. Hide the Background layer.

5. Select the Spot Healing Brush tool. On the options bar, click Proximity Match. Change the size of the brush to be slightly larger than the blemish. Fix the small blemishes on the baby's face.

6. Use the healing tools to fix reflections from the flash on the baby's nose, lips, and chin. If you make a bad correction, press CTRL+Z and then decrease your brush size before trying again.

7. Select the Spot Healing Brush tool. On the options bar, click Create Texture. Move the mouse pointer to the baby's chin. Increase the brush size to include the larger blemish. Click the blemish.

8. To remove the date from the lower-right corner, select the Healing Brush tool. On the options bar, click the Mode box arrow and then click Replace. Adjust the brush size to be just larger than an individual number in the date. ALT+click below the left side of the date. Drag across the date.

9. Select the Red Eye tool. On the options bar, change the Pupil Size to 40%. Change the Darken Amount to 45%. In the image, click each eye.

10. Make any other adjustments you feel are necessary. Turn off and on the visibility of the corrections and Background layers to notice the difference between the original and the corrections.

11. Save the image again. Flatten the layers. If Photoshop displays a dialog box asking to discard hidden layers, click the OK button. Save the image with the file name Lab 5-1 Baby Final in the TIFF format, and then print a copy for your instructor.

PS 366 Photoshop Chapter 5 Enhancing and Repairing Photos

In the Lab

Lab 2: Altering a Building Photo

Problem: A local apartment complex needs to create a flyer to publicize improvements that have been made to one of the units. The only photo available shows a building with graffiti. To make matters worse, this photo shows an old apartment building with only three windows, and all the new ones have four. You will need to lighten the photo, clean up the graffiti from the bricks, and make another window. Because the photo is at an angle, the Clone Stamp tool will not work very well. After your edits, the photo should appear as shown in Figure 5–66.

Instructions: Perform the following tasks:

1. Start Photoshop. Set the Default Workspace and then reset all tools. Reset the previews in the Layers panel and then reset the default colors.
2. Open the Lab 5-2 Graffiti file from the Chapter05 folder of the Data Files for Students. See the inside back cover of this book for instructions on downloading the Data Files for Students, or contact your instructor for information on accessing the required files.
3. Save the file on your USB flash drive storage device as Lab 5-2 Graffiti Repaired in the PSD format.

Figure 5–66

4. Create a corrections layer and fix the levels in the photograph. In the Levels dialog box, drag the black, midtone, and white Input Levels sliders to 14, 1.45 and 238, respectively. Close the Levels dialog box.
5. To create a correction that is in perspective, click Filter on the menu bar, then click Vanishing Point to display the Vanishing Point dialog box. (*Hint:* Read the BTW information about the Vanishing Point filter on page PS 355.)
6. Press the Z key to access the Zoom tool and then ALT+click to zoom out. If necessary, click the Edit Plane tool. Drag the corners of the grid to align with the corners of the building.
7. Press the S key to access the Stamp tool, which acts as a perspective-oriented clone tool. On the options bar, change the Diameter to 200, the Hardness to 50, and the Opacity to 100.
8. Using the cloning technique you learned in Chapter 3, ALT+click to establish a clone source point and slowly paint over the graffiti, resampling as necessary. Use the left bracket ([ ) and right bracket ( ]) keys as necessary to change the size of the brush. Zoom as necessary. If you make an error, close the dialog box and start again with Step 5.
9. Press the M key to switch to the Marquee Tool. Drag a marquee selection around the upper window. ALT+drag a copy of the window to the newly repaired blank area.
10. Close the Vanishing Point dialog box and save the image again.
11. Flatten the layers. Save a copy of the image as Lab 5-2 Graffiti for Print in the EPS format. If Photoshop displays a dialog box about saving options, click the OK button. Submit the assignment in the format specified by your instructor.

In the Lab

Lab 3: Fixing Distortions

Problem: On your recent trip to Germany with the international exchange program, you took a picture of a famous cathedral in Berlin. When you got home, you realized that it was slightly out of perspective and slanted. It had been a cloudy day and the photo is dark. Before preparing a slide show for your fellow students and family, you want to enhance the photo. The upper-right side of the photo should be brought closer, and the building's base should be leveled. The details of the cathedral also might be improved with sharpening and lightening. After your repairs, the photo should appear as shown in Figure 5–67.

Figure 5–67

Instructions: Perform the following tasks:
Start Photoshop and perform the customization steps found on pages PS 7 through PS 9. Open the file Lab 5-3 Cathedral and save it as Lab 5-3 Cathedral Repaired.psd on your USB flash drive storage device.

Duplicate the Background layer and name it, corrections. With the corrections layer selected, open the Lens Correction dialog box and change the vertical perspective to –43; change the horizontal perspective to 23. (*Hint*: Because the picture was taken at a significant angle, the correction will not make the face of the building perfectly flat.) Change the angle to 359 to correct the slant, change the edge to Edge Extension, and change the scale to 90% to display the top of the cathedral. Make any other changes that you feel would help the photo, and then click the OK button in the Lens Correction dialog box. Crop the photo to include only the sidewalk and building. (*Hint*: Cars will still be visible in the cropped version.)

Open the Unsharp Mask dialog box, set the Radius to 1.3, and set the Threshold to 30. Slide the Amount slider until the image is sharpened to your satisfaction. Select the Dodge tool and increase the brush size to cover the entire image. Click the Range box arrow and then click Shadows in the list to adjust the darker portions of the photo. Type 30 in the Exposure box, click the Set to enable airbrush capabilities button, move the mouse pointer into the image, and click.

Make any other adjustments you feel necessary. Save the image again. Flatten the layers. Save a copy of the image as Lab 5-3 Cathedral for Print. Use the EPS format, selecting Photoshop EPS (*.EPS) in the Format box. If Photoshop displays a dialog box about saving options, click the OK button. If possible, print the image on a PostScript printer.

Cases and Places

Apply your creative thinking and problem-solving skills to design and implement a solution.

• Easier   •• More Difficult

• 1: Correct Defects in a Photo

You are tracing your family history back to the 1800s in England. You found a photo that has a crease across the bottom and some light areas. Start Photoshop and then reset all the defaults. Open the Case 5-1 Family History photo that is located in the Chapter05 folder of the Data Files for Students. Crop the border. Save the photo in the PSD format on your USB flash drive storage device as Case 5-1 Family History Repaired. Create a layer named Corrections. Use the Healing Brush tool to repair the crease across the bottom. Use the Patch tool or the Burn tool to correct the light area. Save the photo again.

•• 2: Repair Tears

Your grandmother's favorite photo of your mother has a tear on the edge. You decide to fix it for her. Start Photoshop and then reset all the defaults. Open the Case 5-2 Girl With Carriage photo that is located in the Chapter05 folder of the Data Files for Students. Use the Polygonal Lasso tool to outline the torn corner. On the Layer menu, point to New and then click Layer via Cut. Hide the Background layer. Select the new layer. Delete any white that appears in the new layer. Redisplay the background image and move the layer closer to the rest of the picture. When you have the best match (the tear will not fit exactly), flatten the image. Use the Healing Brush tool to repair any remnants of the tear. Crop the original white border. Save the photo in the PSD format on your USB flash drive storage device.

•• 3: Evaluate Printed Photos

Find a color photo, taken with a digital camera, that came out too dark. Open it in Photoshop. Convert it to the CMYK color mode. Use the Dodge tool to lighten it. Use the Unsharp Mask command to sharpen the image. Use the Lens Correction dialog box to correct any distortion. Save the file in the TIF format and print it on a desktop printer. Save the file in the EPS format and, if possible, print it on a PostScript printer. Write a paragraph describing the differences between the two printouts. List specific changes in the photo that look better in EPS print. Turn in the paragraph and both photos to your instructor.

•• 4: Scan and Import a Photo

Make It Personal

Find a print photo in need of repair. With your computer system attached to a scanner, place the photo in the upper-left corner of the scanner bed. Start Photoshop and reset all the defaults. On the File menu, point to the Import command, and then click your scanner in the list of devices. When your scanner's dialog box is displayed, choose the highest resolution with the most colors. Save the scan. Scan the image again in black and white. Save the scan. Choose the better of the two scans and repair any damage. Print your best effort.

•• 5: Create an Orientation Postcard

Working Together

Your team is in charge of creating a postcard to remind incoming students and their parents of the upcoming school orientation. Gather photos of students having fun on campus and several campus buildings. As a group, choose the best photos. One at a time, open each of the images in Photoshop. Correct all damaged areas, distortions, and flaws. Save each of the repaired images. Create a CMYK formatted, 5.5 × 4.25-inch blank canvas. At a group meeting, decide on a background for your postcard that uses an artistic effect such as smudging. Import the best photos and superimpose and fade them as necessary. Create appropriate text using your school colors, or colors that are highly visible, for the type color.

6 Creating Color Channels and Actions

Objectives

You will have mastered the material in this chapter when you can:

- View channel color separations
- Use the Channels panel to create alpha channels
- Describe different methods of converting an image to black and white
- Create a master image
- Create black-and-white, sepia, and duotone versions of an image
- Create a logo with warped text
- Create a new action set
- Record, save, edit, and play back an action
- Convert an RGB image to LAB color and then to CMYK
- List prepress activities
- Print color separations
- Resize and resample images

6 Creating Color Channels and Actions

Introduction

Photographers and graphic artists routinely create different versions of the same image. Creating a master version, along with versions for the Web, for black-and-white advertising media, for color separations and tints, and for various color modes and sizes, enables maximum repurposing. Multiple versions of photos are used commonly in advertising, photo cataloging, and on photo Web sites. Portrait studios produce and sell a wide assortment of special effect portraits, which require a variety of image versions. Creating a reusable logo adds to the flexibility for business publications.

Another timesaving tool is the ability to record your steps as you work in Photoshop and play them back when needed. The saved recording, a Photoshop action, is a powerful automation device. Tasks that you perform repeatedly, such as adding a logo to each publication, can be recorded and then played back with a single keystroke.

You will learn about channels, color changes, actions, resizing, and resampling as you work through this chapter.

Project — Candy Shop Advertising

Chapter 6 uses Photoshop to edit a photograph for a store called The Sweet Spot that sells candy, cookies, and nuts, among other sweets. First, you will remove the background and create a floating image piece of artwork that can be dropped into other backgrounds and page layout applications. Second, a black-and-white version of the photo will be created for newspaper placement. Sepia and tinted versions will offer the store variety and styling such as retro or filtered special effects. A company logo will be designed with an automated placement action. Finally, an image with exact size and resolution requirements will be created for an advertisement insert. The ad, complete with graphics and text, will be converted to the CMYK color model and printed with color separations. The images are shown in Figure 6–1.

Figure 6–1

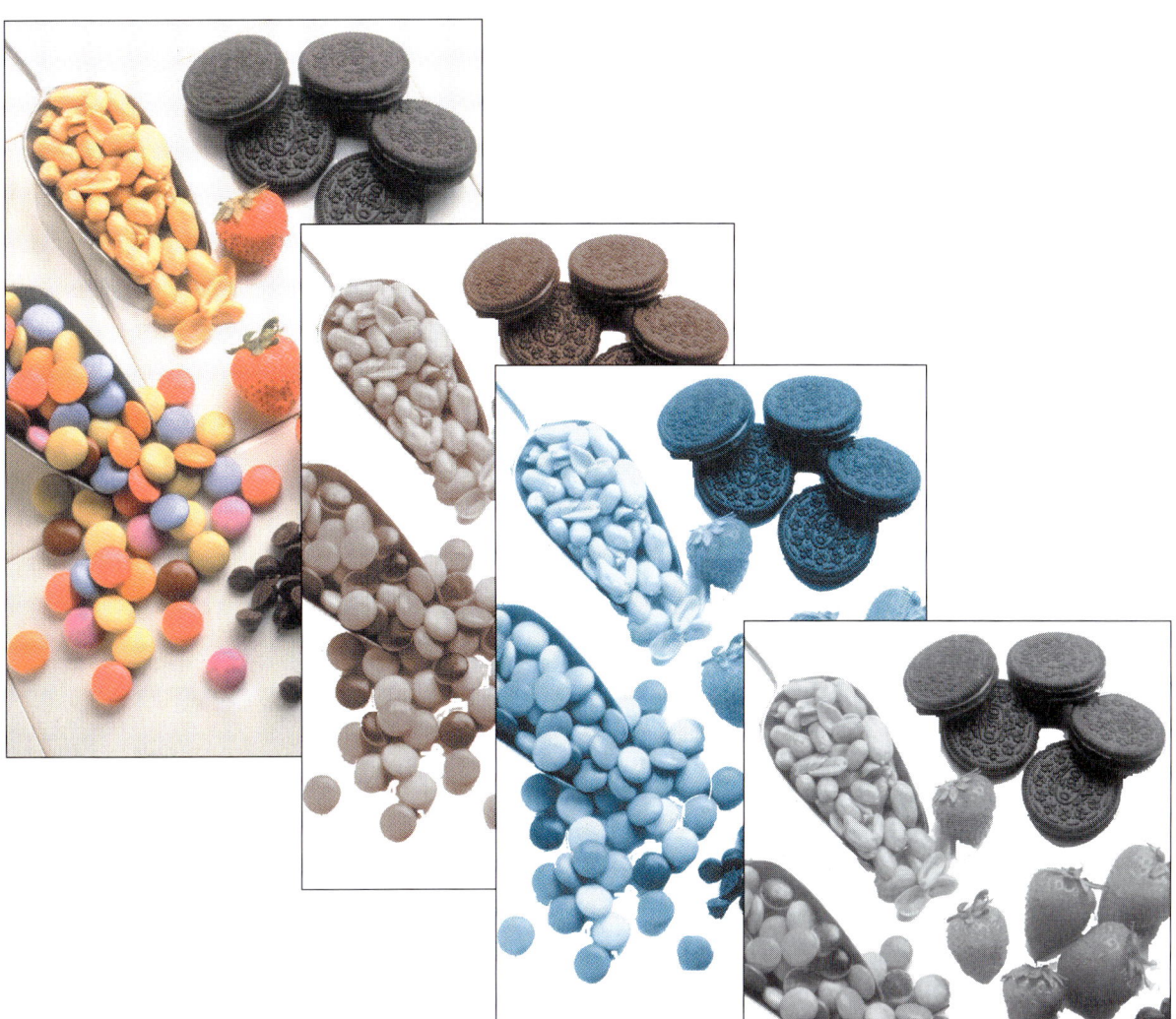

Overview

As you read this chapter, you will learn how to create the images shown in Figure 6–1 on the previous page by performing these general tasks:

- Add an alpha channel.
- Remove the background to create a floating image.
- Recolor images to produce black and white, sepia, and duotones.
- Create a logo.
- Use action sets.
- Record and play back an action.
- Resample and resize an image.
- Print color separations.

Plan Ahead

General Project Guidelines
When editing a photo, the actions you perform and decisions you make will affect the appearance and characteristics of the finished product. As you edit photos, such as the ones shown in Figure 6–1, you should follow these general guidelines:

1. **Plan your versions.** Always start with a high-quality photo and create a master image. Anticipate all the ways the image might be used or repurposed. Consider client needs as you create versions such as color, floating images, black and white, tints, and color modes.

2. **Choose the best tool for the job.** As you make decisions about how to edit your image, look at various ways to accomplish the same task. For example, compare using a simple delete command versus an alpha channel mask. Ask yourself if you will need to use the selection again. Is the background extensively complicated? If you are considering a black-and-white version, decide whether a simple grayscale will be as effective as an adjustment layer where you can fine-tune the contrast.

3. **Record actions for repetitive tasks.** If you or your client have specialized, repetitive tasks that you perform several times a week, consider recording an action. This playback feature will not only save time, it will create identical edits. Actions can give users flexibility by pausing for user decisions at critical points or by waiting for dialog box responses.

When necessary, more specific details concerning the above guidelines are presented at appropriate points in the chapter. The chapter also will identify the actions performed and decisions made regarding these guidelines during the creation of the edited photos shown in Figure 6–1.

Starting and Customizing Photoshop

The following steps start Photoshop and reset the default workspace, tools, colors, and Layer panel options.

To Start Photoshop

The following steps, which assume Windows Vista is running, start Photoshop based on a typical installation.

1 Click the Start button on the Windows Vista taskbar and then click All Programs to display the All Programs list.

2 Click Adobe Design Premium CS4 and then click Photoshop CS4, or your version of the Adobe suite in the All Programs list, to start Photoshop.

3 Maximize the Photoshop window, if necessary.

To Reset the Workspace

The following step uses the Workspace switcher to select the Essentials workspace.

1 Click the Workspace switcher and then click Essentials to restore the workspace to its default settings.

To Reset the Tools and the Options Bar

The following steps select the Rectangular Marquee tool and reset all tool settings in the options bar.

1 Activate the Rectangular Marquee Tool (M) button on the Tools panel.

2 Change the Tools panel to one column, if necessary.

3 Right-click the Rectangular Marquee tool icon on the options bar to display the context menu, click Reset All Tools, and then click the OK button if necessary.

To Reset the Default Colors

The following step resets the default colors.

1 On the Tools panel, click the Default Foreground and Background Colors (D) button to reset the default colors of black and white. If black is not the foreground color, press the X key to reverse the colors.

To Reset the Layers Panel

The following steps reset the Layers panel to make the thumbnails match the figures shown in this book.

1 Click the Layers panel menu button and then click Panel Options on the list to display the Layers Panel Options dialog box.

2 Click the option button for the smallest of the thumbnail sizes.

3 If necessary, click the Layer Bounds option button to select it.

4 Click the OK button.

To Open a Photo

The following steps open the Sweets photo from the Data Files for Students. Your instructor may designate a different location for the file.

1 Open the Sweets file from the Chapter06 folder of the Data Files for Students, or a location specified by your instructor.

2 Change the magnification to 16.67%, if necessary, to view the entire image. If rulers do not appear, press CTRL+R to display them (Figure 6–2).

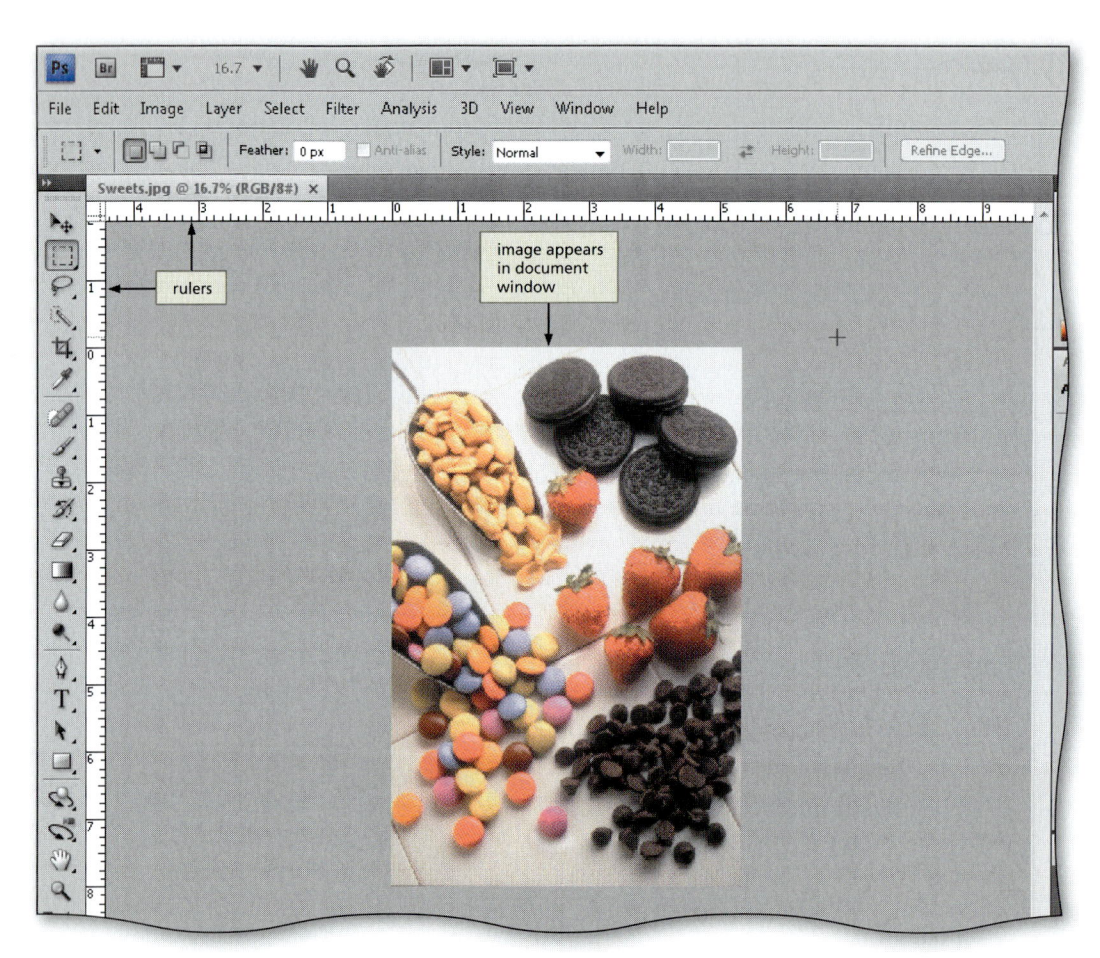

Figure 6–2

To Save the File in the PSD Format

When creating multiple versions of an image, you should create a master copy in PSD format. That way, new versions can be created from an original that remains unchanged. Recall that PSD is the only format that supports all Photoshop features. The following steps save the file in the PSD format using the Save As command.

1 With your USB flash drive connected to one of the computer's USB ports, click File on the menu bar to display the File menu, and then click Save As to display the Save As dialog box.

2 In the File name box, type Sweets Master to rename the file. Do not press the ENTER key after typing the file name.

3. Click the Save in box arrow and then click UDISK 2.0 (F:), or the location associated with your USB flash drive, in the list. If you want to create a folder for the photos in Chapter 6, click the Create New Folder button. Then when the new folder is displayed, type a chapter name, such as Chapter06, and press the ENTER key.

4. Click the Format button to display the list of available file formats and then click Photoshop (*.PSD, *.PDD) in the list, if necessary.

5. Click the Save button in the Save As dialog box to save the file. If Photoshop displays a dialog box, click the OK button.

To Create an Edits Layer

The following steps create an edits layer on top of the Background layer.

1. Double-click the Layers panel tab to display the Layers panel, if necessary.

2. Right-click the Background layer and then click Duplicate Layer on the shortcut menu.

3. When the Duplicate Layer dialog box is displayed, type `edits` in the As box, and then click the OK button.

4. Click the visibility icon for the Background layer to hide it (Figure 6–3).

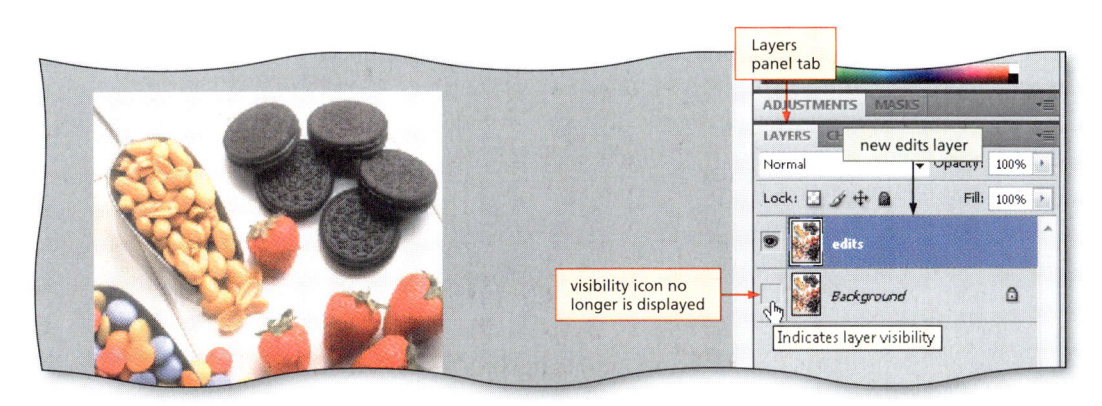

Figure 6–3

Plan Ahead

Plan your versions.
Once you create a master image, plan for possible uses and versions. If you are creating a photo for a client or business, consider all the ways the image could be repurposed. **Repurposing** is the concept of using all or part of a photo for something other than its original purpose. Ask yourself these questions:

- Might the image need to be used with and without its background?
- Will the image be used in more than one medium, such as Web, newspaper, posters, flyers, etc.?
- Might you need both a color and black-and-white version?
- Would special tints, such as sepia or duotones, extend the possibilities for the image?
- Could you use all or part of the photo in another composite image?
- Can you save money by performing some prepress activities yourself?
- How will you organize your versions for maximum shelf life?

Using Channels

The first version of the photo will be a floating image without a background. **Floating images** have a transparent background so they can be placed in front of other pictures. There are many ways to remove a background, including the ones you have used before, such as the Eraser tool, layer masks, or editing selections. Another way to isolate the background is to use Photoshop channels.

As you learned in previous chapters, digital images are made of many pixels, or tiny dots, each of which represents an abstract sample of color. Pixels use combinations of primary colors, or pigments. A **primary color** is one that cannot be created by mixing other colors in the gamut of a given color space. Traditionally, the colors red, yellow, and blue are considered primary colors. Those colors, however, are not the same hues as the red, yellow, and blue used on most computer monitors. Many modern computer applications and hardware devices use the primary additive colors of red, green, and blue, and the primary subtractive colors of magenta, yellow, and cyan. Recall that additive colors involve light emitted directly from a source. Subtractive colors absorb some wavelengths of light and reflect others. The two color modes, RGB and CMYK, are based respectively on the additive and subtractive primary colors.

Each of the primary colors creates a channel in Photoshop. In an image, a **channel** is all of the pixels of the same color, identified using the color modes. An image from a digital camera will have a red, green, and blue channel, while a printed image will have a cyan, magenta, yellow, and black channel. Channels are used in Photoshop to separate and store information about an image's colors so that users can manipulate them. Traditionally, color separations referred to the process of separating image colors into individual films or pattern plates of cyan, magenta, yellow, and black in preparation for printing. Photoshop takes that process one step further by automatically creating the color separation anytime you convert to the CMYK color mode.

Channels are created automatically when you open a new image. The color mode determines the number of color channels created. By default, bitmap, grayscale, duotone, and indexed-color images have one channel; RGB and LAB images have three, plus a composite; and CMYK images have four plus a composite. You can add specialized channels to all image types except bitmap images.

In addition to the default color channels, extra channels, called alpha channels, are used for storing and editing selections as masks; and spot color channels can be added to incorporate spot color plates for printing. A spot color plate is an extra part of the separation printing process that applies a single color to areas of the artwork.

> **BTW**
> **Saving Channels**
> As long as you save a file in a format supporting color modes, the normal color channels are preserved. Alpha channels are saved only when using the PSD, PDF, PICT, Pixar, TIF, PNG, or camera raw formats.

The Channels Panel

The Channels panel (Figure 6–4) is used to create and manage channels. The panel lists all channels in the image — the composite channel first, then each individual color channel, followed by any spot color channels, and finally any alpha channels. As in the Layers panel, the Channels panel displays a visibility icon followed by a thumbnail of each channel's contents. The visibility icon is useful for viewing specific colors in the document window or to see how edits might affect a specific color.

> **BTW**
> **Thumbnails**
> Viewing thumbnails is a convenient way of tracking channel contents; however, turning off the display of thumbnails can improve performance. To resize or hide channel thumbnails, choose Panel Options from the Channels panel menu. Click a thumbnail size to adjust the size of the display, or click None, to turn off the display of thumbnails.

Using Channels **PS 377**

Figure 6–4

When you select one specific channel, it is displayed in grayscale in the document window by default. If more than one channel is selected, the document window displays the color combinations.

The Channels panel menu displays commands to create new channels, change the color overlay, or set other channel options.

To View Channels

The following steps open the Channels panel and view individual channels. As you view each channel, the channel color will appear almost white; other colors will appear in shades of gray.

1
- Click the Channels panel tab to access the Channels panel (Figure 6–5).

Experiment
- One at a time, click each of the channels. As you view each channel, look for strong contrast between the lightest and darkest colors in the image.

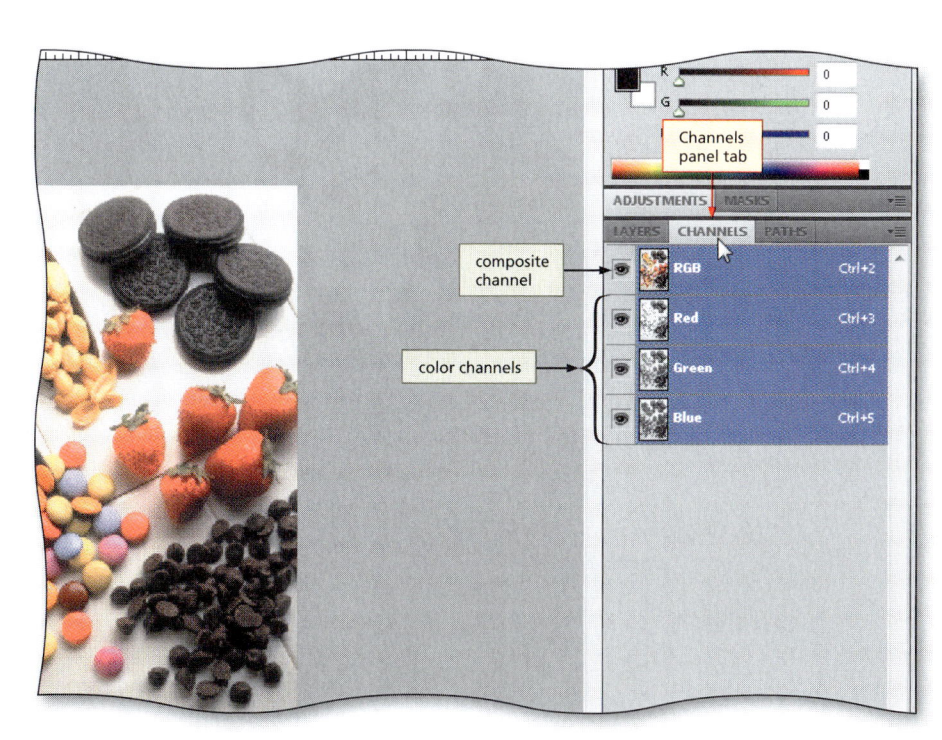

Figure 6–5

PS 378 Photoshop Chapter 6 Creating Color Channels and Actions

2
- Click the Red channel to display it. Do not click the thumbnail (Figure 6–6).

Q&A Why does the Red channel appear in gray?

Photoshop takes all of the pixels that are red and creates a grayscale image of those pixels, called a channel. Channels are created in grayscale to provide the most contrast possible for editing purposes.

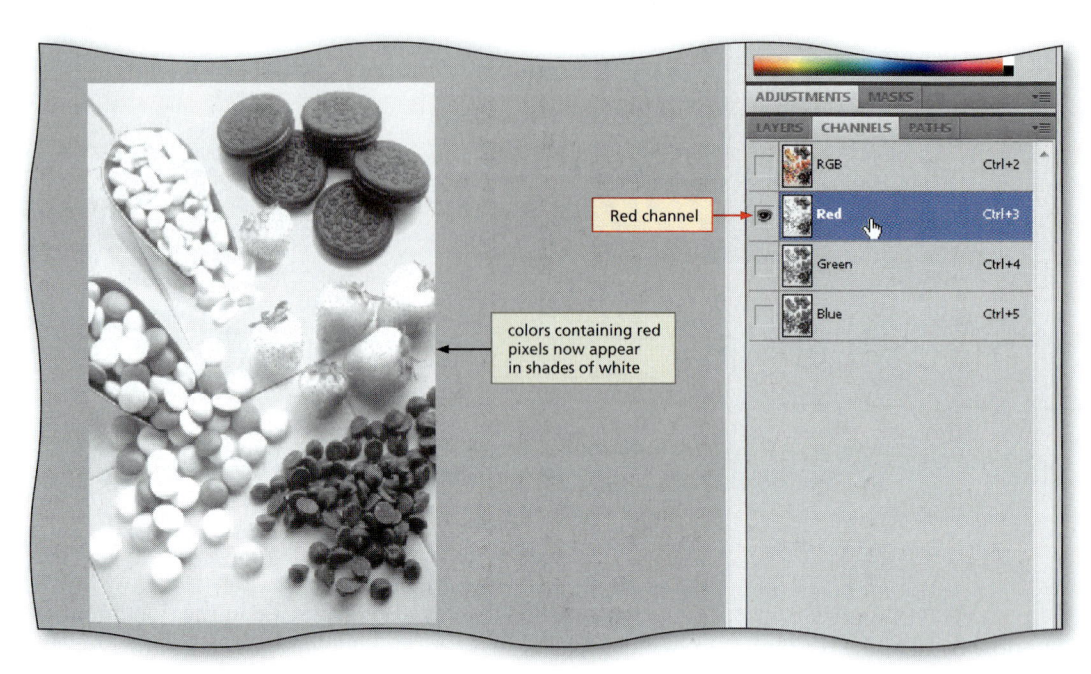

Figure 6–6

3
- Because the Blue channel contains the most contrast, click the Blue channel (Figure 6–7).

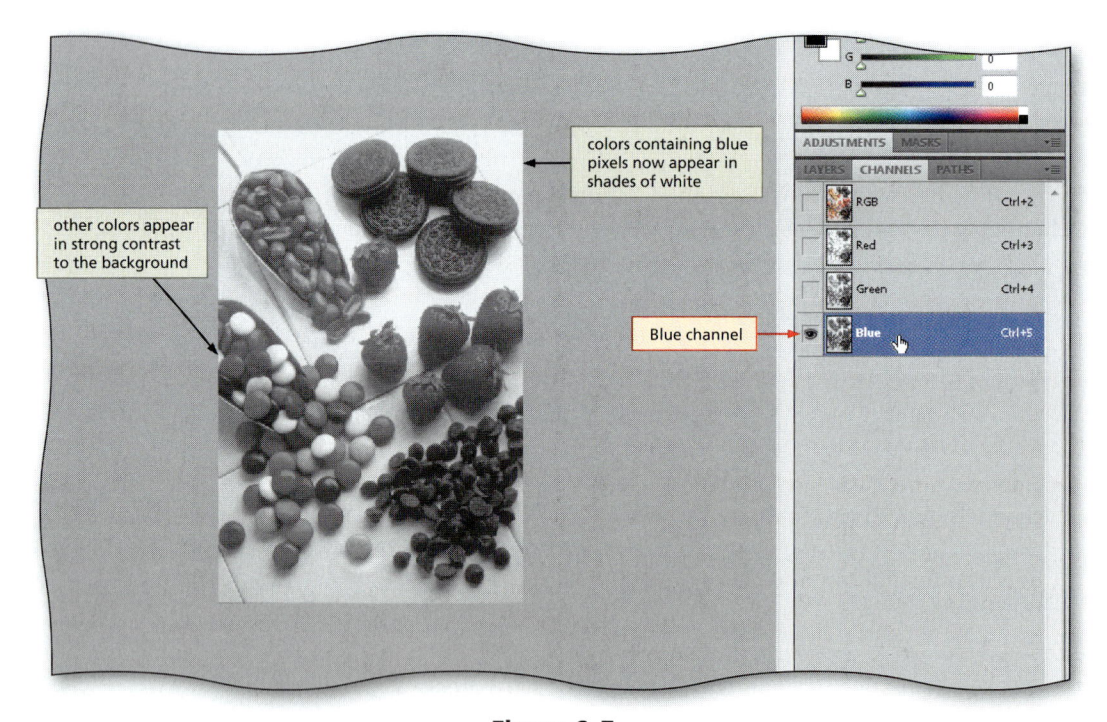

Figure 6–7

Other Ways

1. To display composite, press CTRL+~
2. To display first channel, press CTRL+1
3. To display second channel, press CTRL+2
4. To display third channel, press CTRL+3

To Select Using a Channel

The first goal in editing the Sweets Master image is to remove the background to create a floating image that can be repurposed. Recall that removing the background in an image involves isolating it in a selection area and then deleting it. When you have a solid background, it is easy to select and delete. But often, the background is busy or shaded, requiring more creative steps to remove it. Variegated colors, such as shades of green in grassy areas or blue in sky areas, may be hard to delete as they appear behind, between, and around other objects. In a channel, those kinds of backgrounds appear as a single color; thus, they are isolated and selected easily.

In the Blue channel, you will use the Magic Wand tool to select as much of the background as possible, in the following steps.

1

- With the Blue channel still selected, right-click the Quick Selection tool and then click Magic Wand Tool on the context menu.

- On the options bar, click the Add to selection button. Type 15 in the Tolerance box. Make sure the Anti-alias and Contiguous check boxes are selected (Figure 6–8).

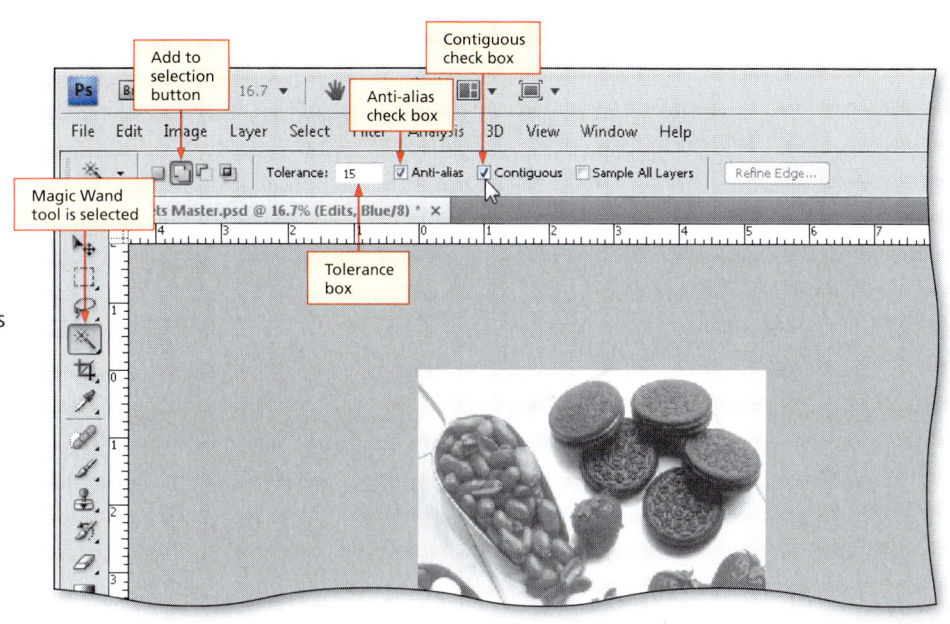

Figure 6–8

2

- Click the background in all the areas around the sweets and the scoops. If a click adds too much to the selection, press CTRL+Z and click again. (Figure 6–9).

Q&A Could I have used the Magic Eraser tool to erase the background?

Yes, you could have, but the selection of the background would not be saved, and further editing might be tedious to get a clean look.

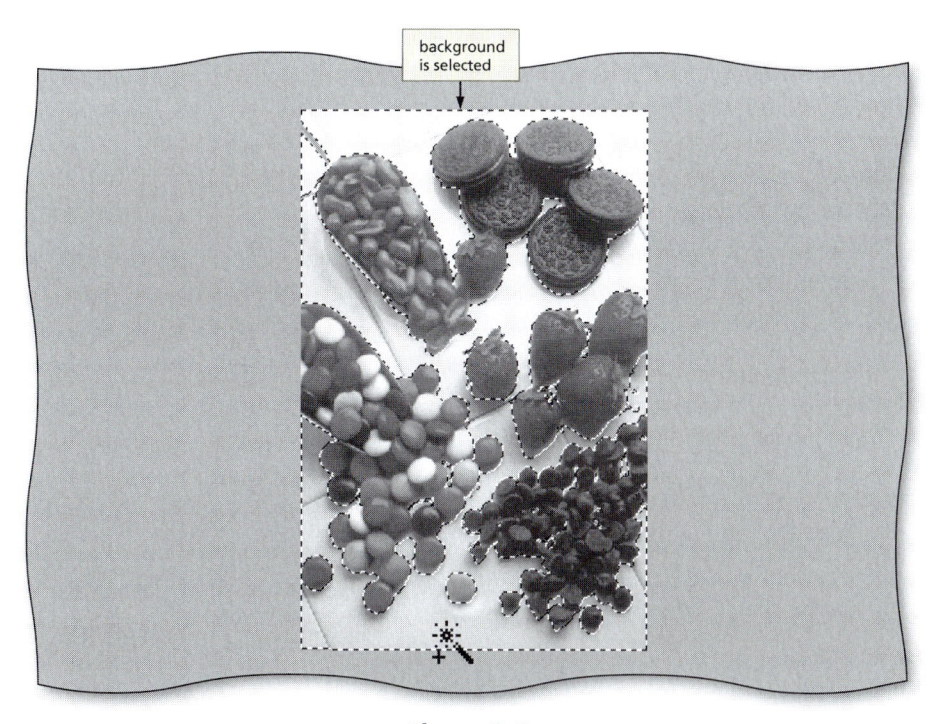

Figure 6–9

BTW

Displaying Color Channels
When you display one channel at a time, by default it displays in grayscale. If you want to make the channels appear in color, click Edit on the menu bar, point to Preferences, and then click Interface. Click the Show Channels in Color check box to select it.

Alpha Channels

When you create a new channel, by default it becomes an alpha channel. An **alpha channel**, or **alpha channel mask**, is a special channel that saves and loads selection marquees. It is similar to a new layer or layer mask in that it is used to edit or mask parts of an image. Alpha channel masking can be performed on the background layer, whereas masks created using the Layers panel cannot. Alpha channels represent selections and exist independently of any particular layer — for that reason, storing selections as alpha channels creates more permanent masks than layer masks. You can reuse the stored selections or even load them into another image. The Channel Options command on the panel menu allows you to name the alpha channel and adjust settings related to editing.

Most commonly, alpha channels are used to isolate and protect areas of an image as you apply color changes, filters, or other effects to the rest of the image. Additionally, alpha channels are used for complex image editing, such as gradually applying color or filter effects to an image. For instance, viewing an alpha channel and the composite channel together allows you to see how changes made in the alpha channel relate to the entire image. When you display an alpha channel at the same time as a color channel, the alpha channel appears as a transparent color overlay in the document window.

To Create an Alpha Channel

When making an alpha channel, you can create the channel first and then paint the selected area, or you can select the area first and then create the channel. The following step creates an alpha channel where the background of the image already has been selected. You will use the Save selection as channel button on the Channels status bar to create an alpha channel with colored overlay and adjustable opacity. You can edit the channel using any painting tool, or modify it with a filter.

1
- With the Blue channel still selected in the Channels panel, click the Save selection as channel button to create an alpha channel.

- Click the visibility icon next to the Alpha 1 channel to display its color overlay (Figure 6–10).

Experiment
- Double-click the Alpha 1 channel thumbnail and view the name, color, and opacity settings. Click the OK button to close the dialog box.

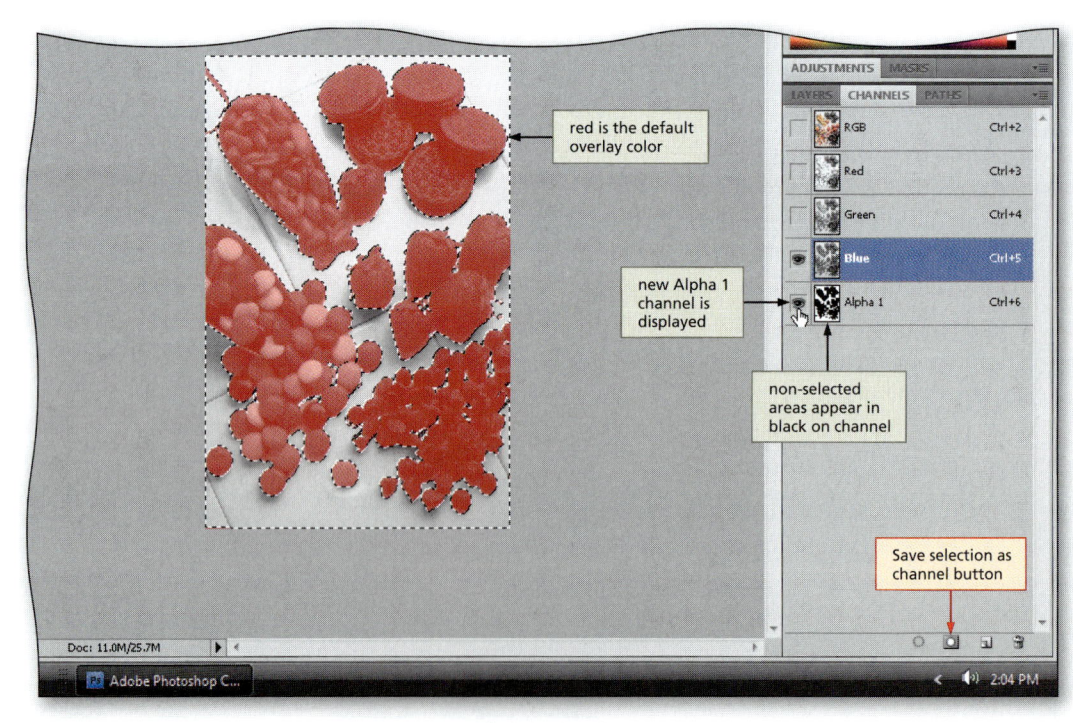

Figure 6–10

Other Ways
1. On Channel panel status bar, ALT+click the Create new Channel button
2. On Channels panel menu, click New Channel, edit settings

To Select More of the Background

The color overlay may reveal other areas of the background that were not included in the previous selection. Any missed areas will appear in light pink in the color overlay. The next step adds those areas to the selection.

1 Click any light pink areas that may remain around the edges of the food. If a click adds too much to the selection, press CTRL+Z and click again in a slightly different spot (Figure 6–11).

BTW

Alpha Masks and Opacity
Neither the Color setting nor the Opacity setting has any effect on how an alpha channel mask works. Those settings only change the mask color that appears in the document window when another channel is selected. Some Photoshop users change the color and opacity to make the mask more easily visible against the other colors in the image.

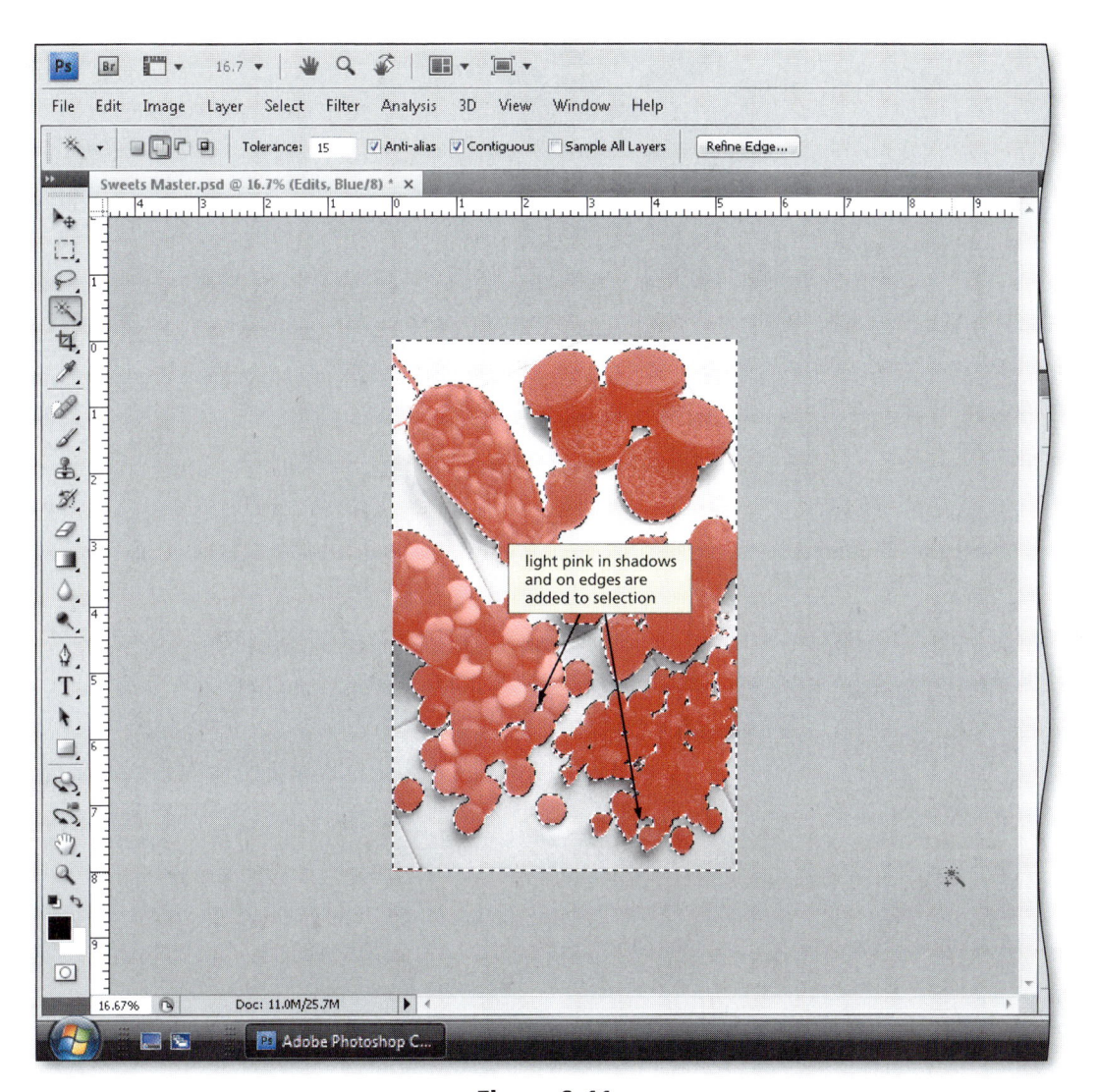

Figure 6–11

To Edit the Alpha Channel

Finally, to fine-tune the selection, you will edit the alpha channel itself. Recall that masks are displayed in black on the Layers panel; to add to the mask, you paint with black. Alpha channels are just the opposite; they use white to mask. In the steps that follow, you will paint any remaining background with white to mask the background fully.

1
- Click the visibility icon beside the Blue channel to remove it.
- If necessary, click the Alpha 1 channel to select it.
- Press CTRL+D to remove the selection and reveal fine border areas (Figure 6–12).

Q&A My foreground and background colors are not the same. Did I do something wrong?

The colors may have been changed inadvertently. Change the foreground color to white and the background color to white on the Tools panel.

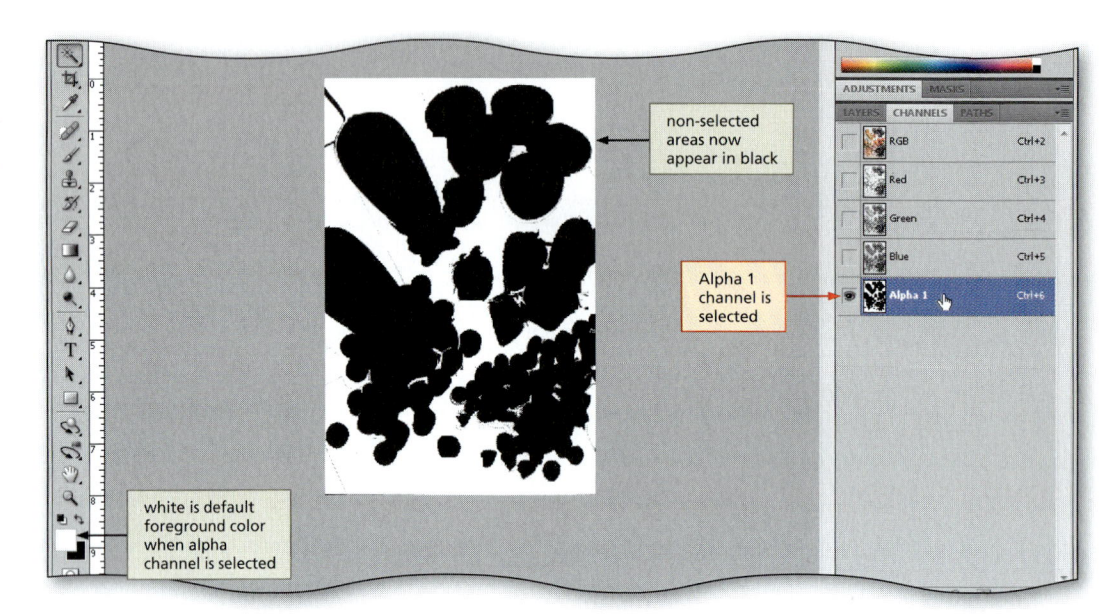

Figure 6–12

2
- Press B to access the Brush tool and then click the Brush Preset picker to display the panel.
- Drag the Hardness slider to 100% to create a brush with strong edges (Figure 6–13).

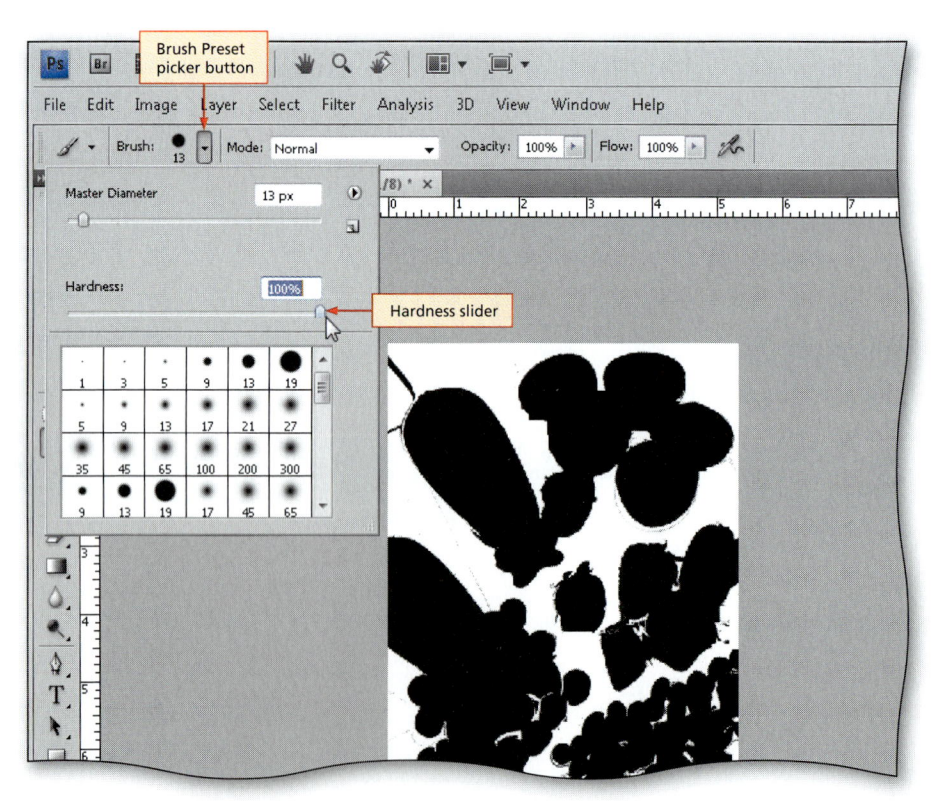

Figure 6–13

3
- Click the Brush Preset picker again to close the panel.
- In the document window, paint with white around the edges of the objects to create clean borders. Change the brush size using the bracket keys, as necessary.
- Paint over any background that may remain.
- If some of the sweets are white, press the X key to change the brush to black, and then paint them (Figure 6–14).

Q&A How can I tell which part is the background and which part is the candy?

You can click the RGB composite channel to view the image in color and then click back on the Alpha channel to identify the remaining background.

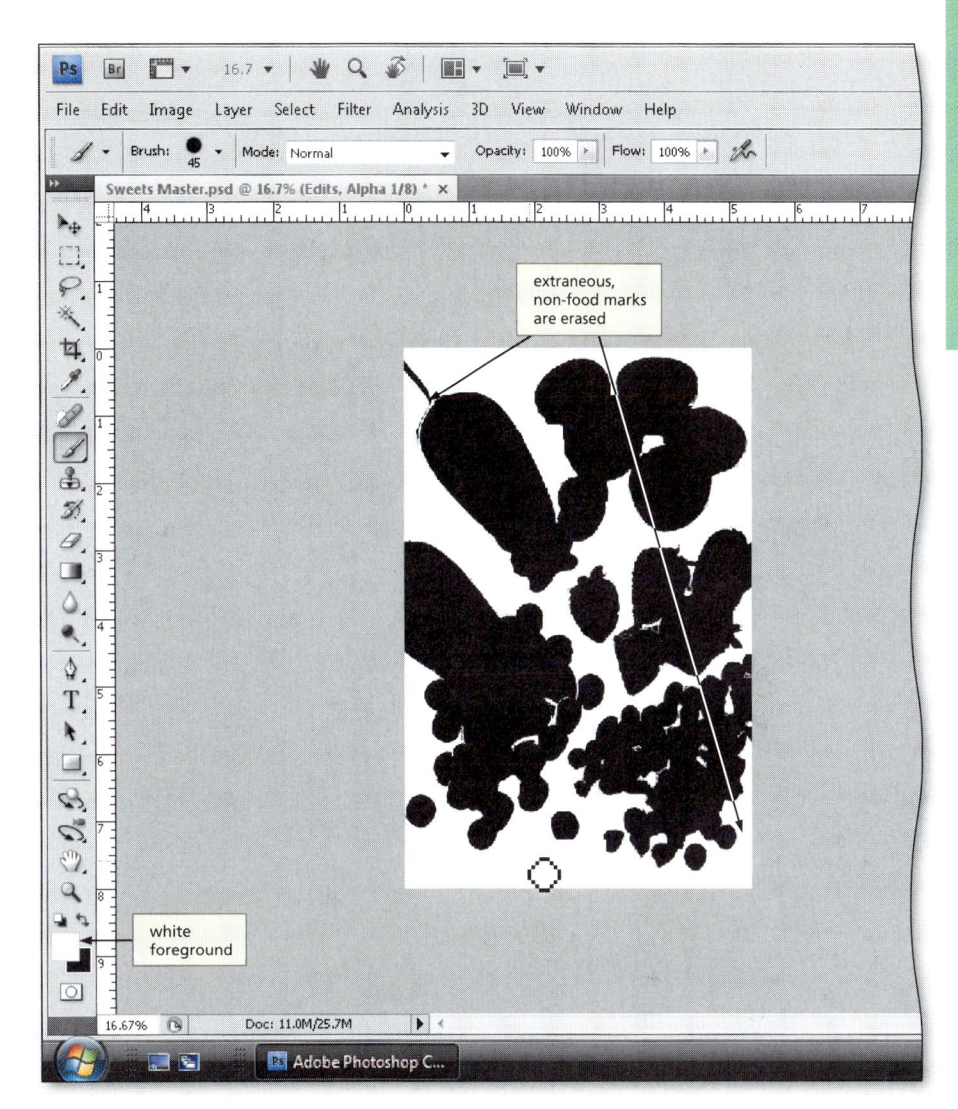

Figure 6–14

To Delete a Background Using an Alpha Channel

The final step in creating the floating image is to delete the background using the alpha channel. The background is represented by the white area in the alpha channel. Selecting the white area and then viewing the composite creates a clean selection border in the image around all of the background, as shown in the steps on the next page. The deleted background becomes transparent in the floating image, ready for the customer to drop in a new background or use the floating image in other artwork.

PS 384 Photoshop Chapter 6 Creating Color Channels and Actions

❶
- Press the W key to access the Magic Wand tool.
- On the options bar, remove the check mark in the Contiguous check box.
- Click the white area (Figure 6–15).

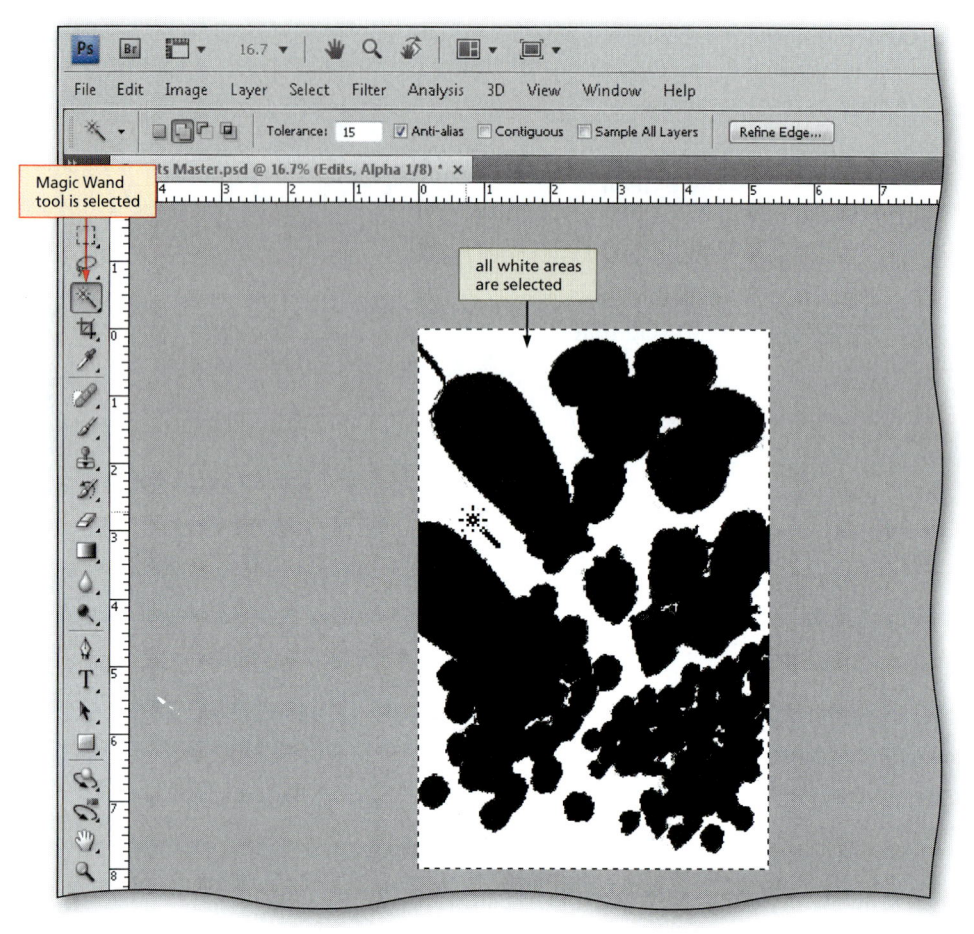

Figure 6–15

❷
- On the Channels panel, click the RGB composite channel.
- Press the DELETE key to delete the selection.
- Press CTRL+D to deselect (Figure 6–16).

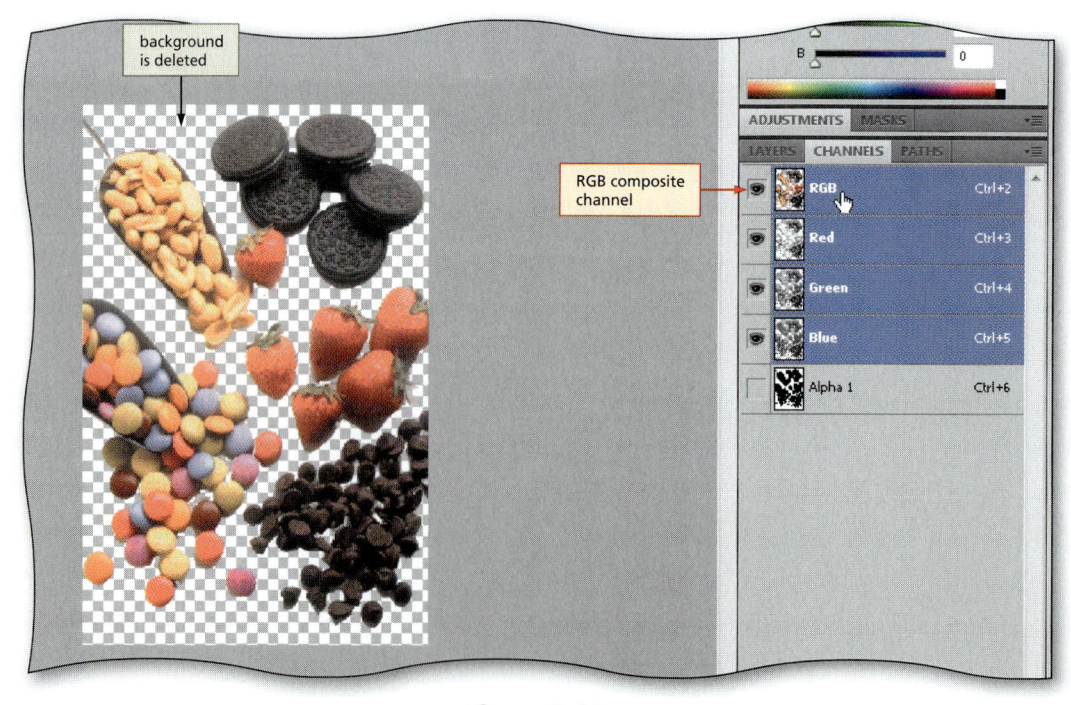

Figure 6–16

To Save the Floating Image

The floating image is complete. The next steps save the file.

1. Press SHIFT+CTRL+S to open the Save As dialog box.

2. Type `Sweets Floating` to enter the file name.

3. Click the Save button to save the image. If Photoshop displays a dialog box, click the OK button.

> **Plan Ahead**
>
> **Choose the best tool for the job.**
> With so many ways to accomplish the same or similar tasks, sometimes it is hard to decide which tool to use. While using the tool with which you are most familiar may save you time, the result might not be as satisfactory as you could achieve with a different tool. Look through the various tools related to your task and experiment with the settings. For example, there are five Healing Brush tools, more than 20 adjustments on the Adjustment panel, two menus with adjustment commands, countless ways to select, copy, move, and delete, and many more. Unless your image is just a quick mock-up or sketch, choose the tool that gives you the most flexibility and settings. Also, do not forget the detail edits. Consider adjustments and color toning among the most important edits you can perform.

Color Toning and Conversions

Color toning is the process of changing or intensifying the color of a photograph after it has been processed by the camera. In traditional photography, toning was a darkroom technique that changed the black colors in a black-and-white photograph to a chosen color, such as sepia or blue. In digital photography, toning includes a variety of techniques, including converting to black and white, creating duotones or split tones, and adding tints.

Many of the color toning adjustments are located on the Adjustments panel, but some are available only through the menu system. Most of the tools work in the same way — they map or plot an existing range of pixel values to a new range of values. The main difference is the amount of control each tool provides. For example, the various color adjustment commands on the Image menu alter the pixels in the current layer. Another way to adjust color is to use an adjustment layer created using the Layer menu. This approach allows you to experiment with color and tonal adjustments first, before committing them to the image. Using an adjustment layer adds to the file size of the image, however; it also demands more random access memory (RAM) from your computer. Another way to access adjustments is to use the New Adjustment Layer submenu on the Layers menu. The difference is that when you access the settings using the menu system, Photoshop opens a dialog box allowing you to name and color the layer as you create it. You fine tune the settings using the Adjustments panel either way.

Table 6–1 on the next page displays color adjustment commands that are not located on the Adjustments panel and therefore must be accessed through the menu system.

> **BTW**
>
> **Spot Color Channel**
> Another special channel in Photoshop is the **spot color channel**, added to specify additional printing plates for printing with spot color inks. This option lets you simulate the density of the printed spot color. A value of 100% simulates an ink that completely covers the inks beneath; 0% simulates a transparent ink that completely reveals the inks beneath. To create a spot color channel, CTRL+click the Create new channel button.

BTW

Converting to Black and White
Another way to change to black and white is by converting the image to the LAB Color mode, creating a layer from the Lightness channel. Creating layers from channels offers you more control over contrast than some other conversion methods. It also offers you the flexibility of being able to change aspects of the conversion at anytime in the future. Many design professionals prefer to use channels when converting to black and white because it permits precise control of shades, levels, and the conversion process.

Table 6–1 Menu-Only Color Adjustment Commands

Command	Purpose	Menu Access
Desaturate	produces a grayscale image but leaves the image in the same color mode	Image | Adjustments
Equalize	redistributes the brightness values of all pixels, so they represent the entire range of brightness levels more evenly	Image | Adjustments
Match Color	matches the color across selections, layers, or photos as well as adjusting luminance, color range, and color casts in an image	Image | Adjustments
Replace Color	replaces specified colors in an image with new color values	Image | Adjustments
Shadow/Highlight	lightens or darkens based on surrounding pixels to correct photos with strong backlighting or other lighting errors	Image | Adjustments
Variations	adjusts the color balance, contrast, and saturation of an image using thumbnail samples	Image | Adjustments

Black and White

Recall that converting a color image to the grayscale mode on the Image Mode submenu is one way to discard color information from the pixels in the image. If you change the color mode to LAB Color, a Lightness channel also creates a black-and-white image. Several settings on the Adjustments panel can be used to create a black-and-white or grayscale image. Additionally, some graphic artists create two adjustments layers, one for black and one for white, to emulate the film and filter process of traditional photography.

First, you will use the Desaturate command to view the image in grayscale; then you will undo and use the Black and White settings on the Adjustments panel.

To Desaturate

The steps that follow use the Desaturate command on the Adjustments submenu to produce a grayscale image.

1
- On the Image menu, point to Adjustments to display the submenu (Figure 6–17).

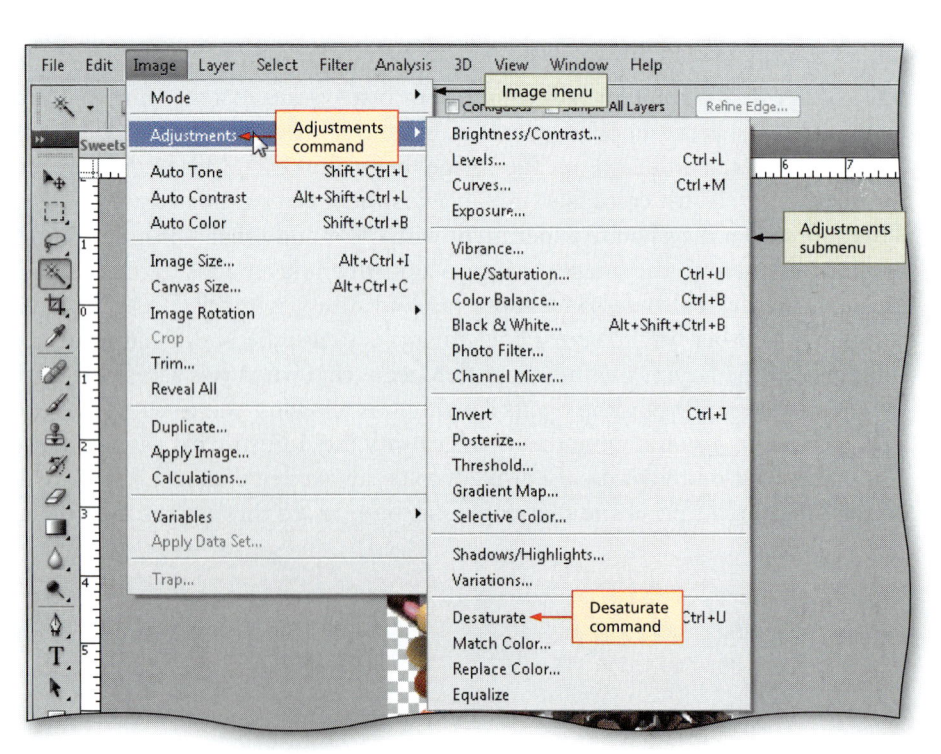

Figure 6–17

2
- Click Desaturate to produce a grayscale image (Figure 6–18).

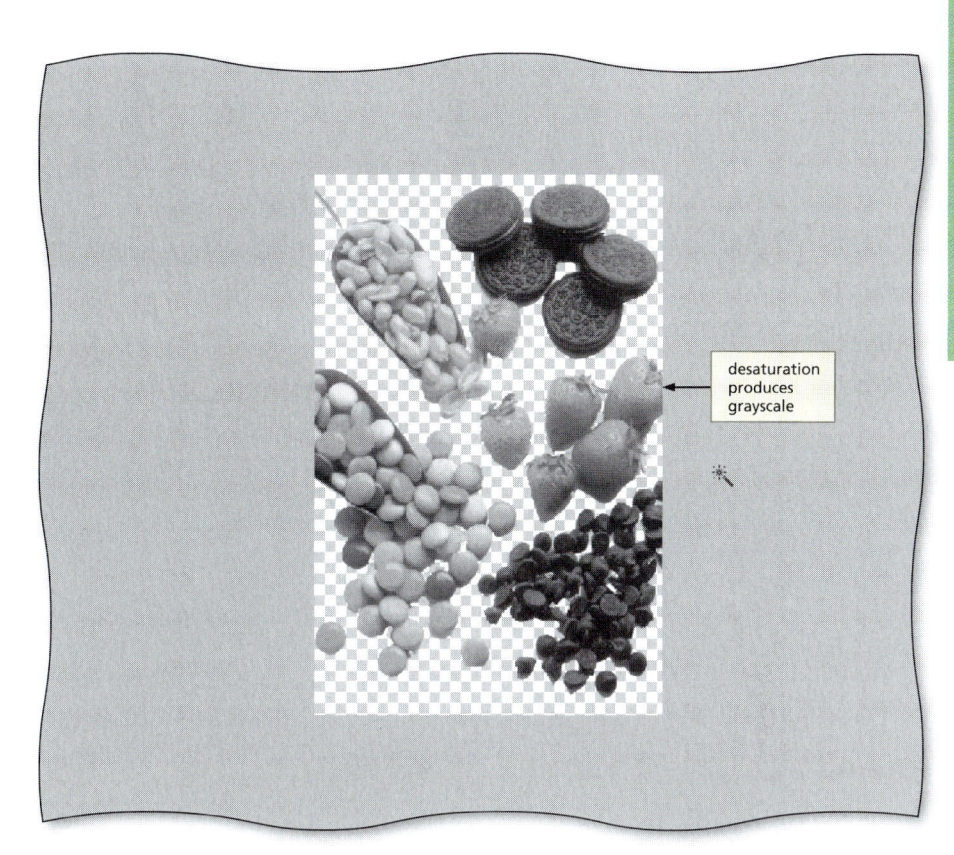

Figure 6–18

desaturation produces grayscale

Other Ways
1. Press SHIFT+CTRL+U

To Undo the Desaturate Command

While the Desaturate command is appropriate for technical illustrations or when you want to neutralize or de-emphasize a background, it leaves the image in the same color mode, usually rendering a flat, uninspiring version compared to other methods. Therefore, the following step undoes the Desaturate command.

1 Press CTRL+Z to undo.

To Create a Black-and-White Adjustment

The Adjustments panel and its Black & White settings allow you to customize the shades of gray in the document window itself. By customizing the shades, you can create more diversity among the various shaded candies. For example, all the candies in the scoop are displayed in similar shades of gray. By adjusting a channel, the black-and-white version will appear with more variety. In the steps on the next page, all the blue candy will be adjusted to a darker shade of gray.

PS 388 Photoshop Chapter 6 Creating Color Channels and Actions

1
- Double-click the Adjustments tab to display the Adjustments panel (Figure 6–19).

Desaturation undone

Adjustments panel

Black & White icon

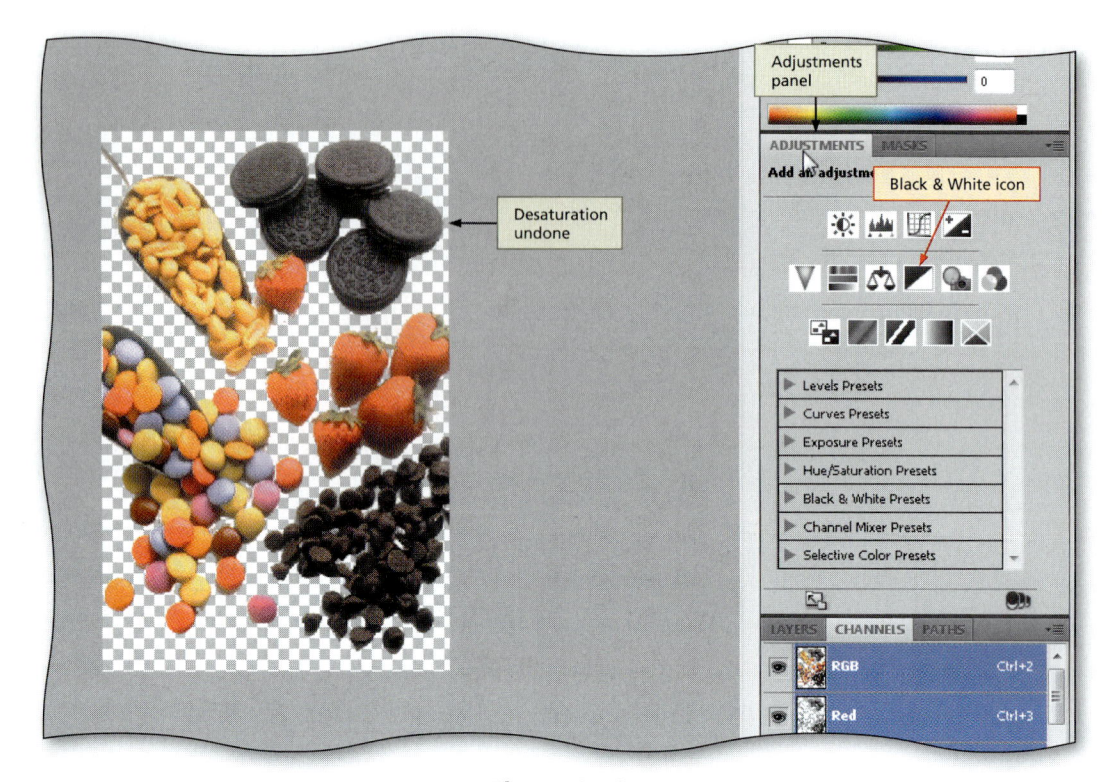

Figure 6–19

2
- Click the Black & White icon in the Adjustments panel to display the settings.

- In the Adjustments panel status bar, click the Clip to layer button to create an adjustments layer.

- Click the Modify a slider button to enable color changes in the document itself, and then move the mouse pointer into the document window and position it over a piece of candy that used to be blue, as shown in Figure 6–20.

mouse pointer

Black & White settings

Modify a slider button

Clip to layer button

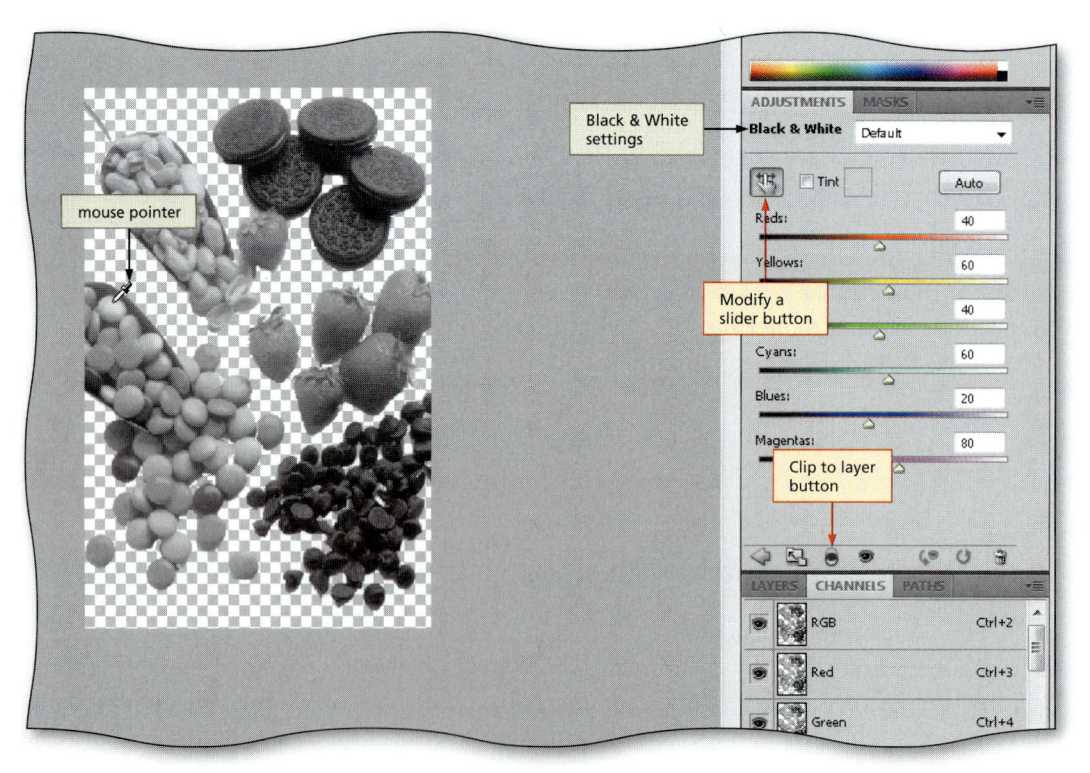

Figure 6–20

3

- Drag to the left to increase the contrast in the blue parts of the image (Figure 6–21).

Experiment

- Experiment with other pieces of candy and drag in both directions.

4

- In the Adjustments panel status bar, click the Return to adjustment list button to close the Black & White settings on the Adjustments panel.

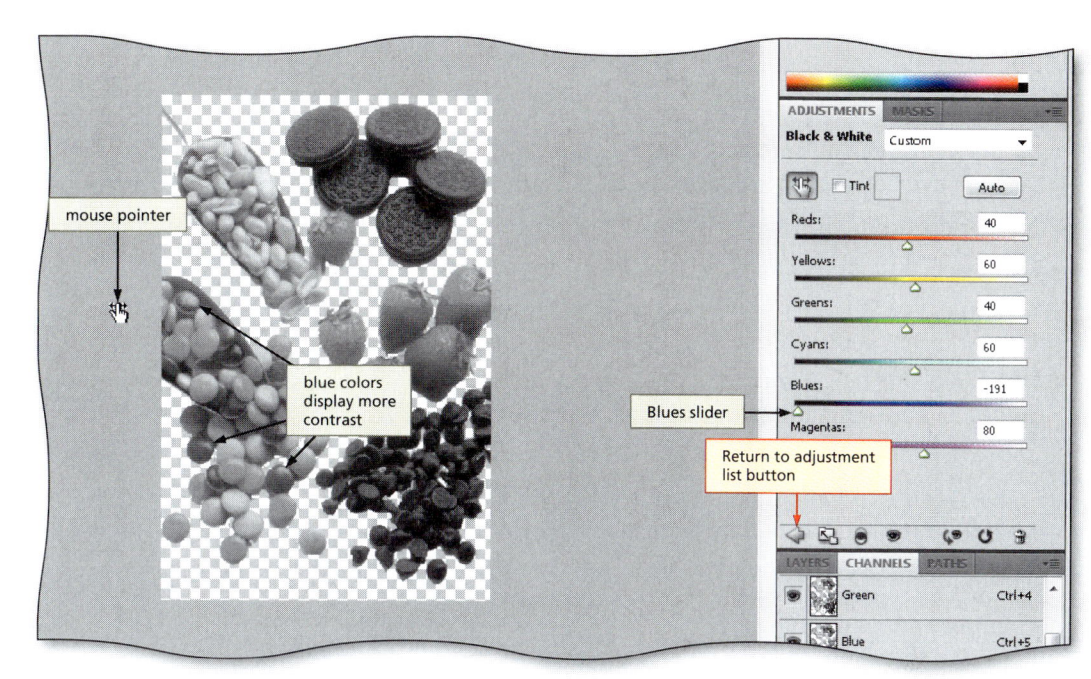

Figure 6–21

Q&A Could I have used the sliders on the Adjustments panel to make the changes?

Yes, the sliders work the same way on the panel as they do in the document window.

To Save the Black-and-White Image

The black-and-white image is complete. The next steps save the file.

1. Press SHIFT+CTRL+S to open the Save As dialog box.
2. Type `Sweets Black and White` to enter the file name.
3. Click the Save button to save the image. If Photoshop displays a dialog box, click the OK button.

Other Ways

1. On Image menu, point to Adjustment, click Black & White, change settings
2. On Layer menu, point to New Adjustment Layer, click Black & White, change settings
3. Press ALT+SHIFT+CTRL+B, change settings

Sepia

Sepia is a color toning technique resulting in a reddish-brown tint. Originally created through a pigmenting process for preservation of photos, it has become a popular kind of tinting to emulate older photos or for special effects. As with black-and-white conversions, Photoshop has many ways to create a sepia tone, including tints, channel mixing, selective coloring, filters, and processing raw data from a digital camera.

BTW **The Channel Mixer**
The Channel Mixer creates high-quality images by choosing the percentages from each color channel. It lends itself more toward artistic expression than for tasks related to simple restoration or technical graphics. Artists use the Channel Mixer to create a variety of tints, pastels, infrareds, and sepia tones.

To Create a Sepia Image Using Selective Color

The following steps create a sepia color using the Selective Color settings on the Adjustments panel.

1

- On the Adjustments panel, click the Selective Color icon to display its settings.
- Click the Clip to layer button on the status bar to create an adjustment layer.
- Click the Colors box arrow to display its list (Figure 6–22).

Q&A Where is the Selective Color icon?

In the previous steps, you clicked the Return to Adjustment button on the Adjustments panel status bar, which redisplays the main Adjustment panel and its icons. The Selective Color icon is the last one in the third row of icons.

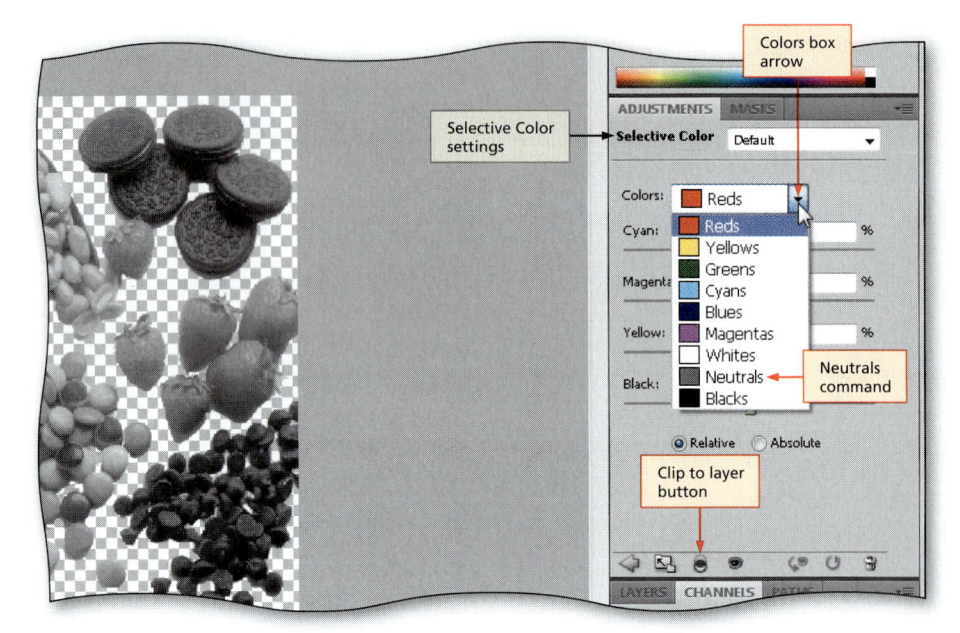

Figure 6–22

2

- Click Neutrals to adjust the neutral colors in the image.
- Drag the Cyan slider to –53. Drag the Magenta slider to –31. Drag the Yellow slider to –18. Drag the Black slider to the right until a warm brown color is attained (Figure 6–23).

Q&A What do the Relative and Absolute option buttons do?

If you select the Relative option button, the percentage of change is multiplied by the current color. If you select the Absolute option button, the percentage of change is added to the current color.

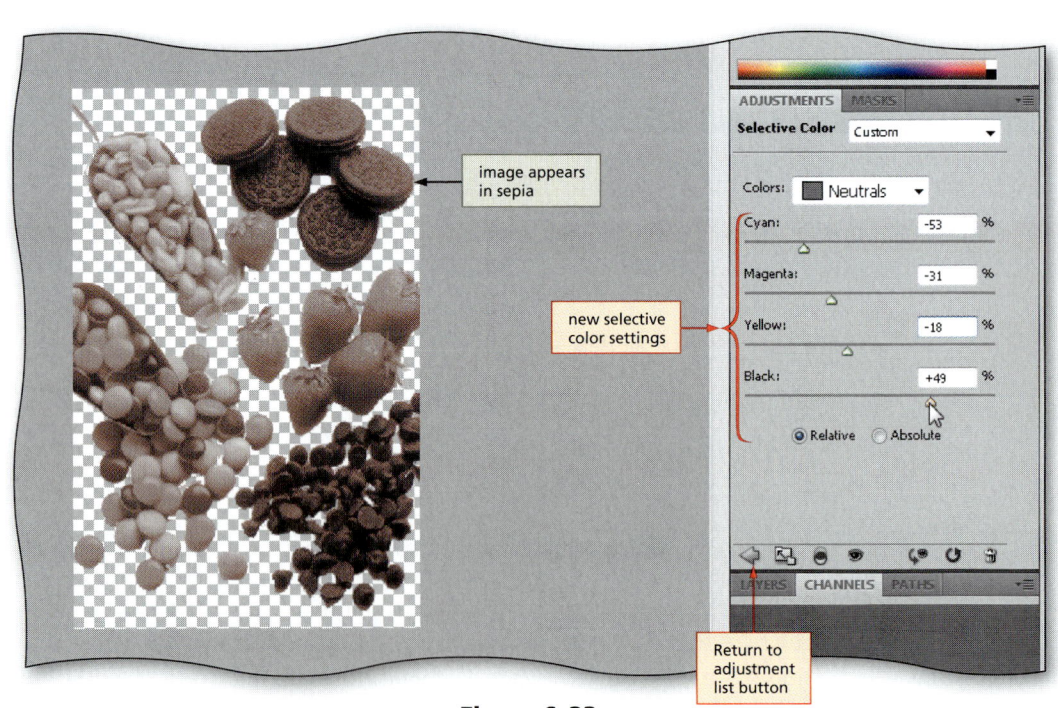

Figure 6–23

3

- In the Adjustments panel status bar, click the Return to adjustment list button.

To Save the Sepia Image

The sepia image is complete. The next steps save the file.

1. Press SHIFT+CTRL+S to open the Save As dialog box.

2. Type `Sweets Sepia` to enter the file name.

3. Click the Save button to save the image. If Photoshop displays a dialog box, click the OK button.

Duotone

Duotone is a generic term for a variety of grayscale images printed with the addition of one, two, three, or four inks. In these images, colored inks, rather than different shades of gray, are used to reproduce tinted grays, increasing the tonal range of a grayscale image. Although a grayscale image displays up to 256 shades of gray, a printing press can reproduce only about 50 shades. For this reason, a grayscale image printed with only black ink can look significantly coarser than the same image on the screen. Printing with two, three, or four inks, each reproducing up to 50 levels of gray, produces an image with a slight tint and a wider dynamic range.

Because duotones affect only the gray levels, they contain only one channel; however, you can manipulate a wide range of tint using the Duotone Options dialog box.

BTW

PANTONE
Duotones are ideal for two-color print jobs with a spot color such as a PANTONE color used for accent. The Pantone color matching system is a standardized color reproduction system in which users and printing professionals can make sure colors match without direct contact with one another.

To Convert an Image to Duotone

Because duotone requires a completely grayscale image, you will convert the current image to grayscale and then to duotone.

1.
- On the Image menu, point to Mode and then click Grayscale.

- When Photoshop asks to discard adjustment layers, click the OK button.

- When Photoshop asks to discard color information, click the Discard button (Figure 6–24).

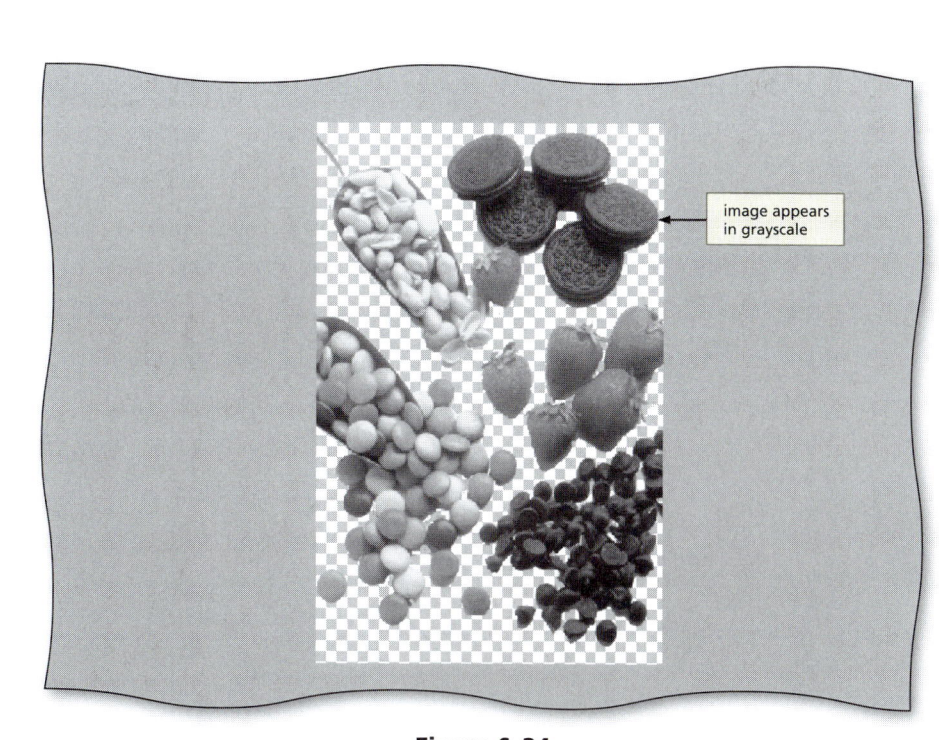

image appears in grayscale

Figure 6–24

PS 392 **Photoshop Chapter 6** Creating Color Channels and Actions

2

- On the Image menu, point to Mode and then click Duotone to display the Duotone Options dialog box. Click the Preview check box to preview the image, if necessary.

- Drag the title bar of the dialog box to the right to view the image (Figure 6–25).

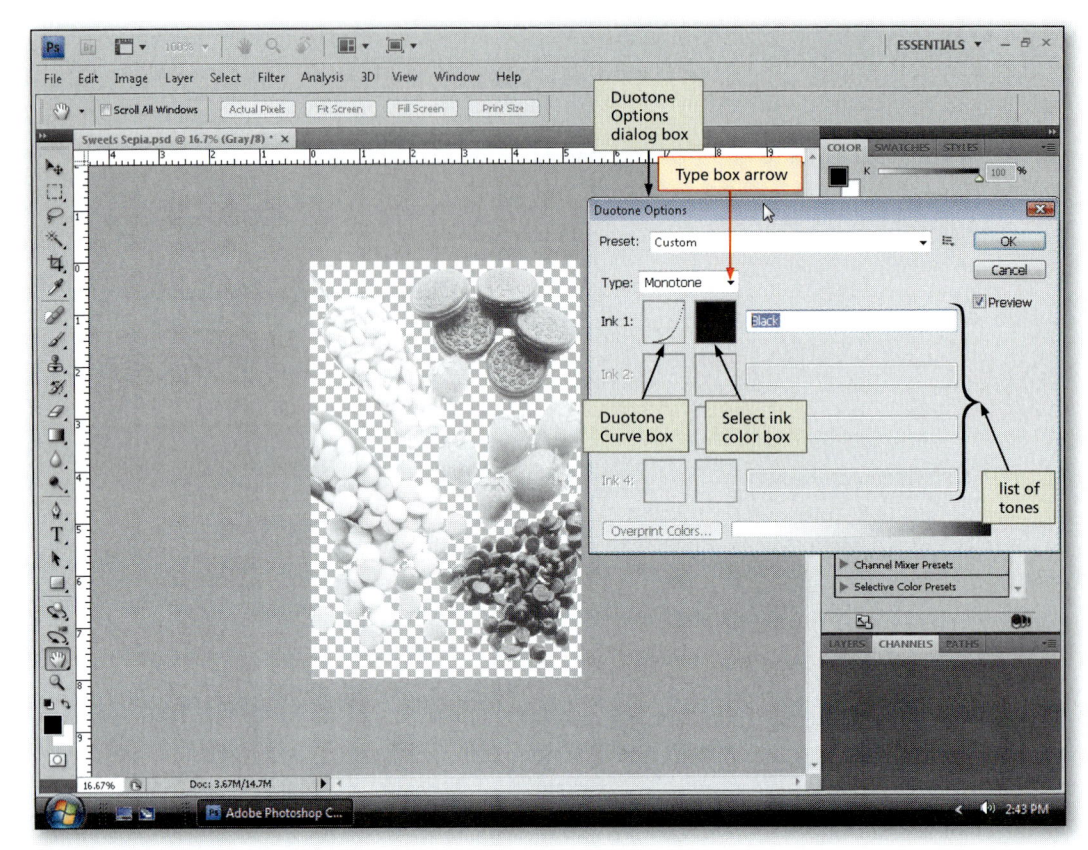

Figure 6–25

3

- Click the Type box arrow to display its list (Figure 6–26).

Q&A What do the two boxes in front of the Black tone represent?

The first box is the curve that indicates how the color is spread across the image. The second box is the color itself. Clicking either box allows you to adjust the settings.

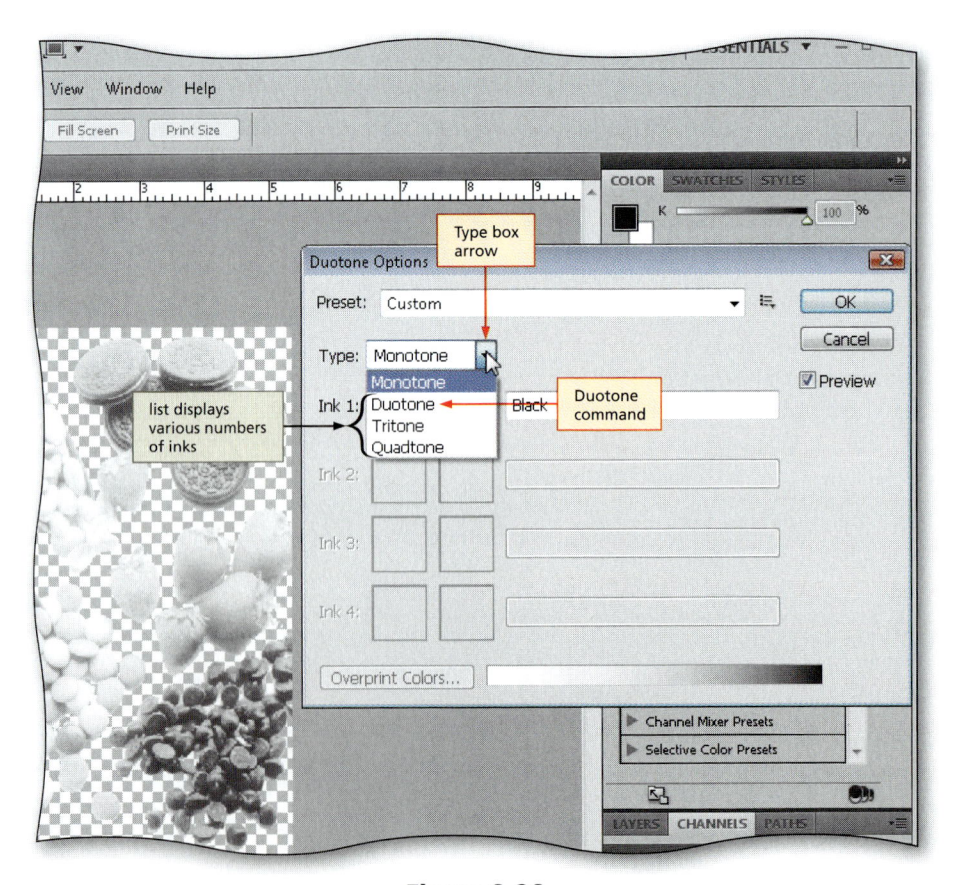

Figure 6–26

Color Toning and Conversions **PS** 393

4
- Click Duotone to add one color to the original black (Figure 6–27).

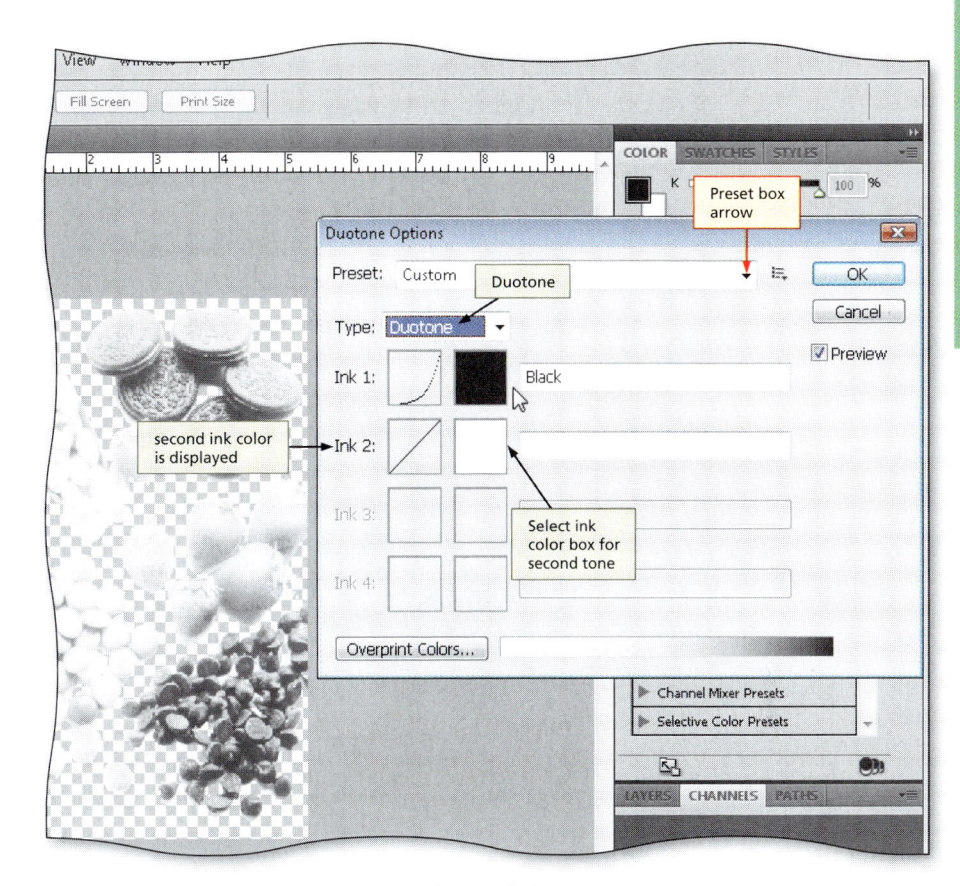

Figure 6–27

5
- To specify the second color, click the Preset box arrow to display its list (Figure 6–28).

Q&A | Could I just choose the color using the Select an ink color box?
Yes, but the Preset box list includes standard colors that print shops and service bureaus can match easily.

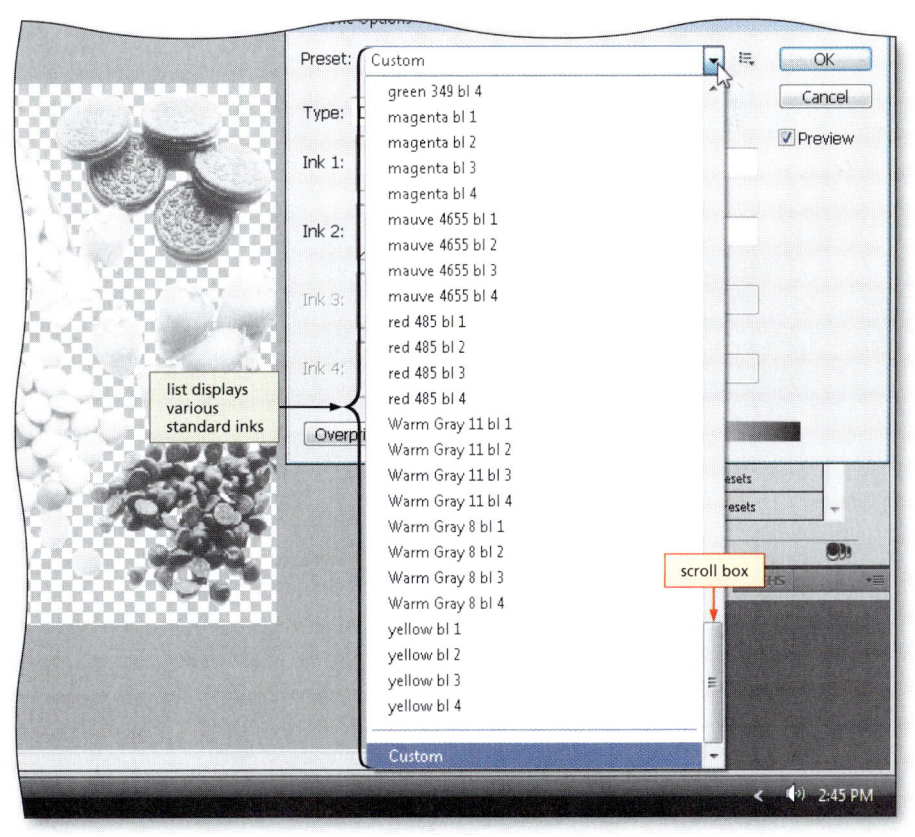

Figure 6–28

6
- Scroll as necessary and then click cyan bl 1 to select a blue duotone (Figure 6–29).

7
- Click the OK button to close the Duotone Options dialog box.

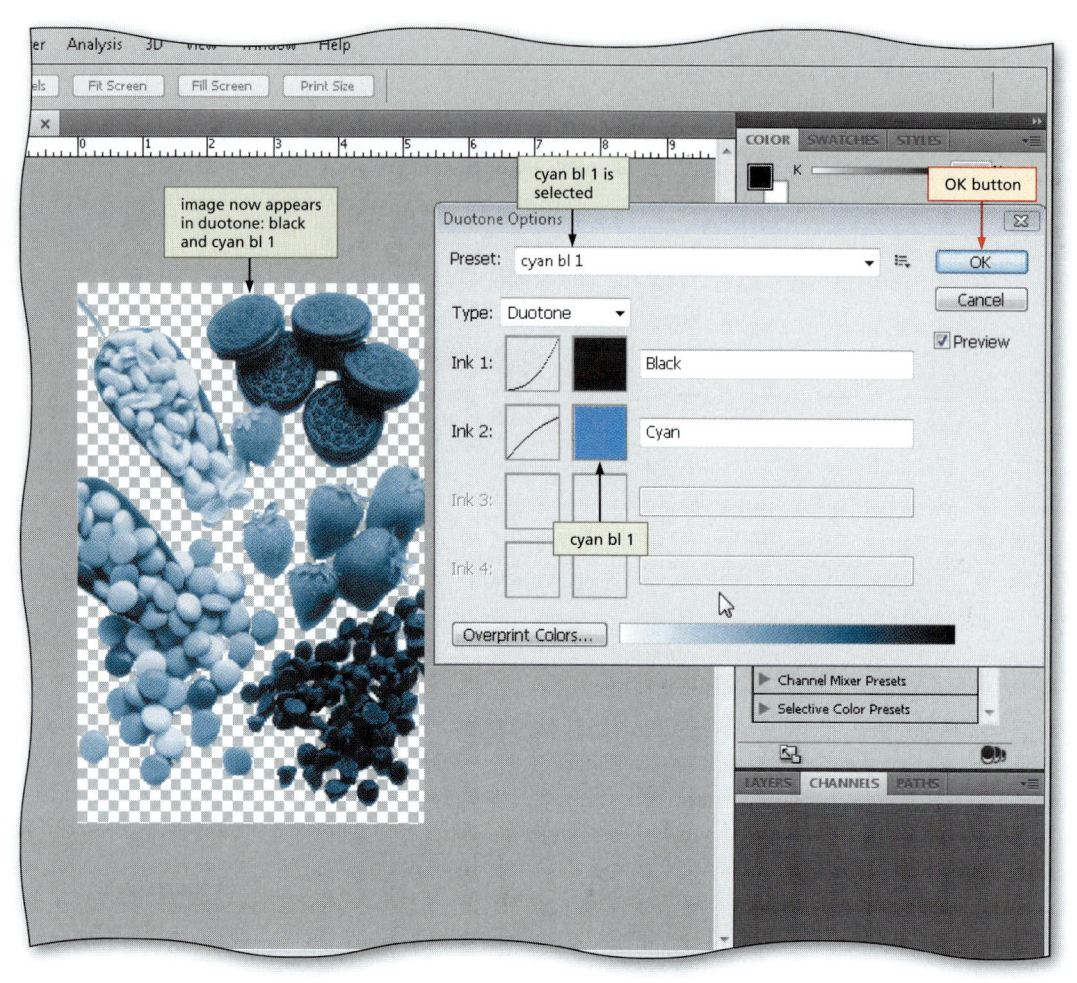

Figure 6–29

To Save the Duotone Image

The duotone image is complete. The next steps save the file.

1 Press SHIFT+CTRL+S to open the Save As dialog box.

2 Type `Sweets Duotone` to enter the file name.

3 Click the Save button to save the image. If Photoshop displays a dialog box, click the OK button.

To Close the File

Because you are finished with the color conversions, you will close the file in the following step.

1 Click the Close button on the Sweets Duotone document window tab.

Logos

A **logo** is an emblem or a symbol that a company uses to identify or brand itself. Customers remember effective logos and associate the company with the product. Popular logos include those for soft drinks, fast food restaurants, sports teams or franchises, and trendy clothing.

The logo created for The Sweet Spot candy store includes a white candy bag, warped text, and a lollipop. The logo will be updated to include color embellishment using a Photoshop action.

To Create a Blank Transparent Canvas

The following steps create a transparent canvas to begin the company logo.

1. Press CTRL+N to open the New dialog box.
2. Type `Sweets Logo` in the Name box.
3. Click the Width unit box and then click inches in the list, if necessary.
4. Type `2` in the Width box and type `2` in the Height box, if necessary.
5. Type `300` in the Resolution box, if necessary.
6. Click the Color Mode box arrow and then click CMYK Color in the list.
7. Click the Background Contents box arrow and then click Transparent in the list (Figure 6–30).
8. Click the OK button to create the blank canvas.

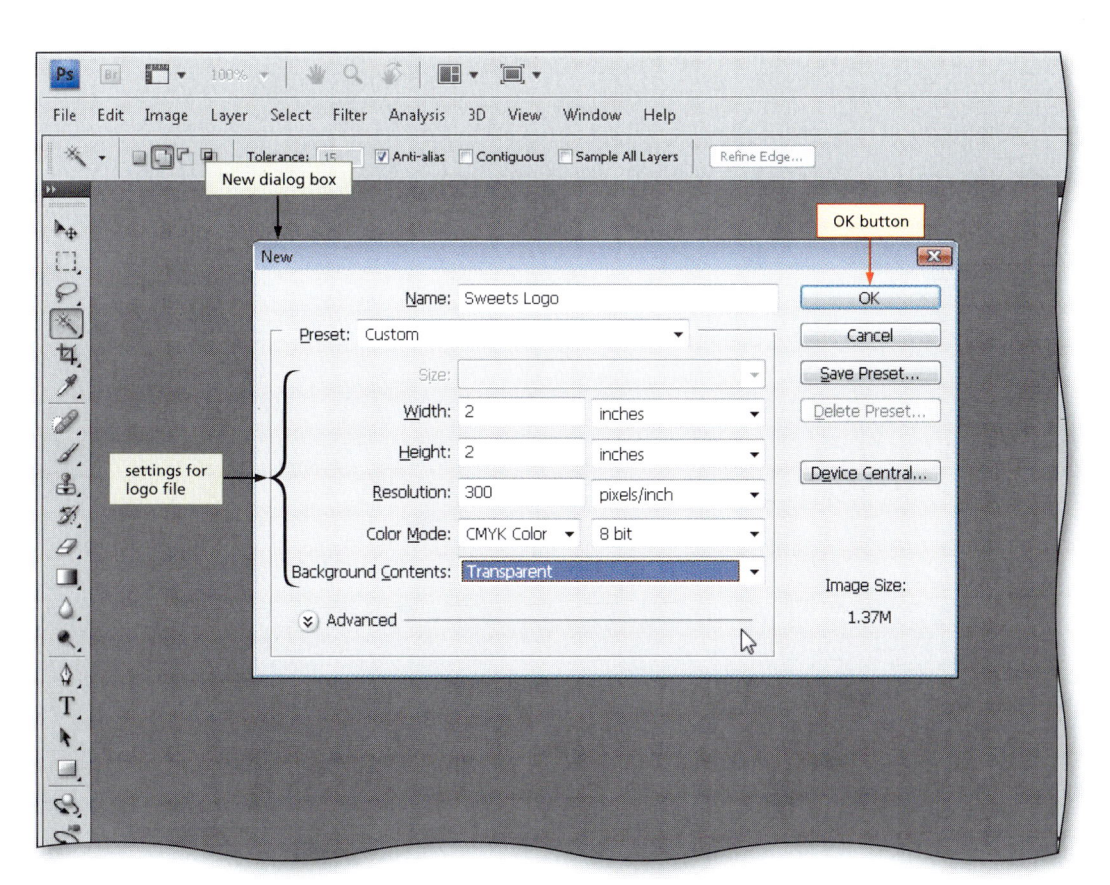

Figure 6–30

To Save the Logo File

The following steps save the file in the PSD format using the Save As command. Because it was named in the New dialog box, Photoshop automatically fills in the file name for you.

1. Press SHIFT+CTRL+S to open the Save As dialog box.

2. Click the Save button in the Save As dialog box to save the file. If Photoshop displays a dialog box, click the OK button.

To Add an Image to the Logo

The following steps add a white paper bag to the blank canvas.

1. Open the file Bag from the Chapter06 folder of the Data Files for Students. Change the magnification to 66.67%, if necessary.

2. Arrange the document windows side by side, using the Arrange Documents button.

3. Use the Move tool to drag the bag image from the Bag document window to the Sweets Logo document window.

4. Use the Move tool to position the bag in the center of the image.

5. Close the Bag document window (Figure 6–31).

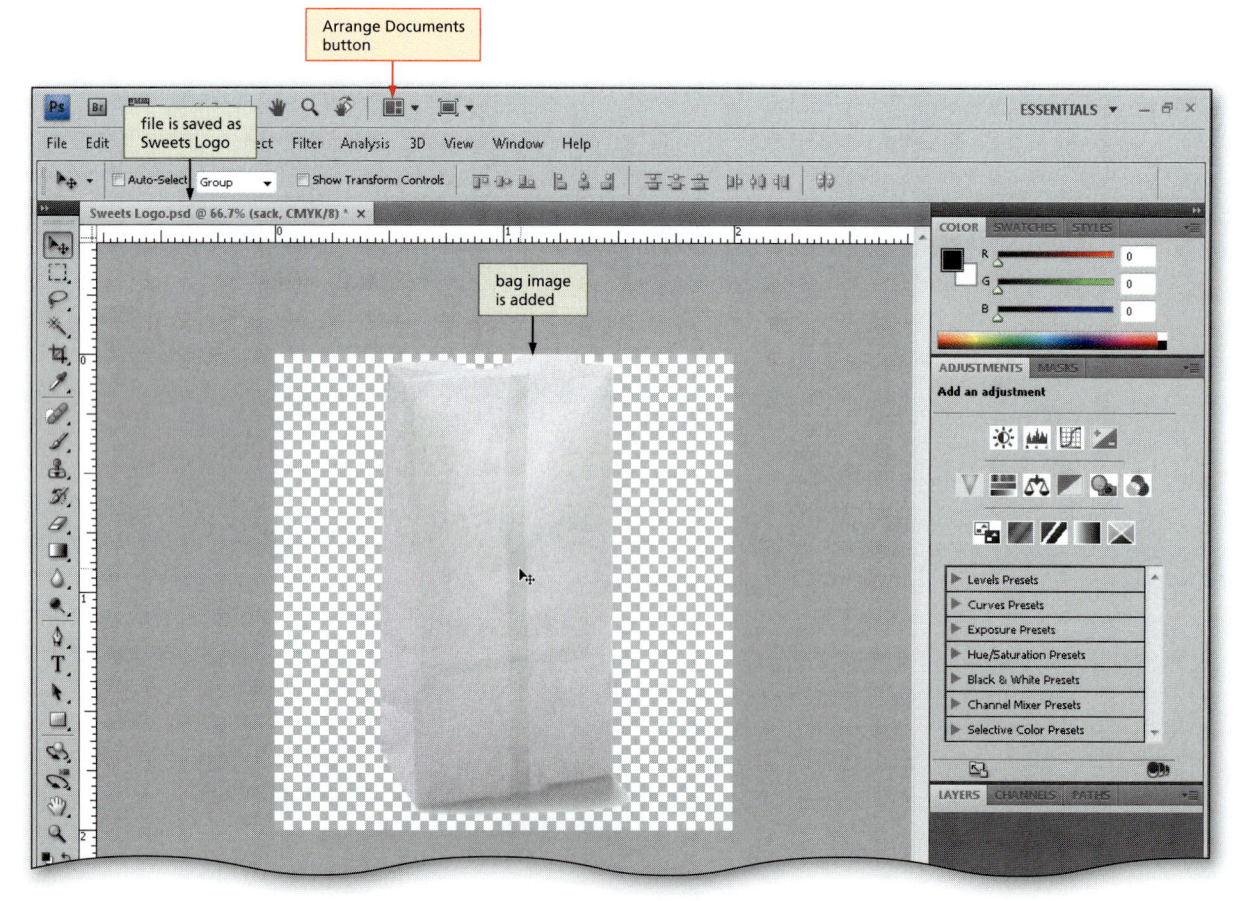

Figure 6–31

To Add Another Image to the Logo

The following steps add a lollipop to the logo.

1. Open the file Lollipop from the Chapter06 folder of the Data Files for Students.
2. Arrange the document windows side by side.
3. Drag the lollipop image from the Lollipop document window to the Sweets Logo document window.
4. Use the Move tool to position the lollipop to either side of the bag.
5. Close the Lollipop document window (Figure 6–32).

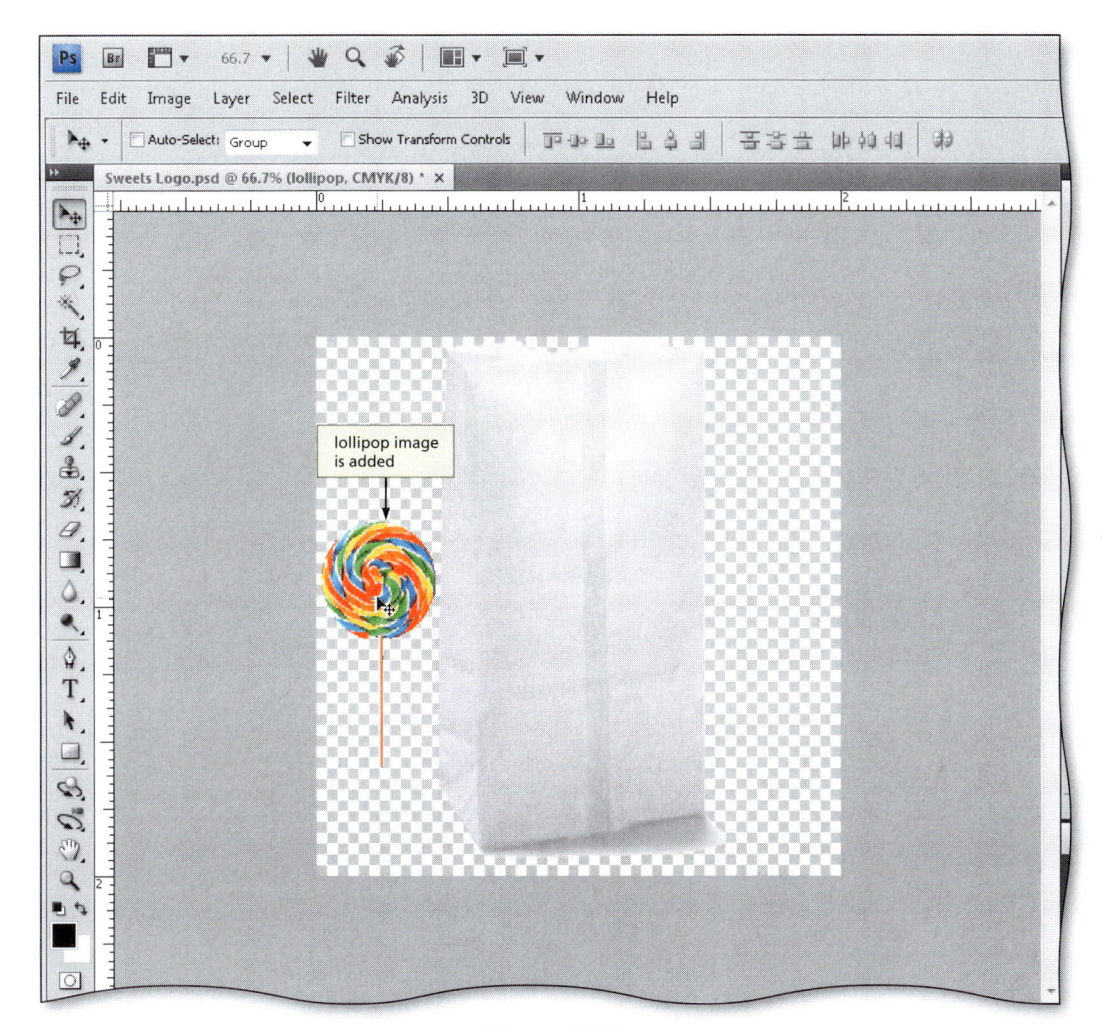

Figure 6–32

To Choose a Foreground Color

The following steps choose a red color from the lollipop to use as the foreground color.

1. Press the I key to access the Eyedropper tool.
2. Click a red color in the lollipop.

To Warp Text

One way to make your text eye-catching is to use the Warp Text dialog box. Photoshop has 15 different warp styles, each with adjustable settings, to create an endless number of possibilities for warped text. The next steps create warped text for the logo.

1
- Press the T key to access the type tool.
- Drag a large text box over the bag that approximately fills the bag.
- On the options bar, choose the Perpetua font, using the bold font style.
- Type 28 in the font size box and click the Left align text button, if necessary (Figure 6–33).

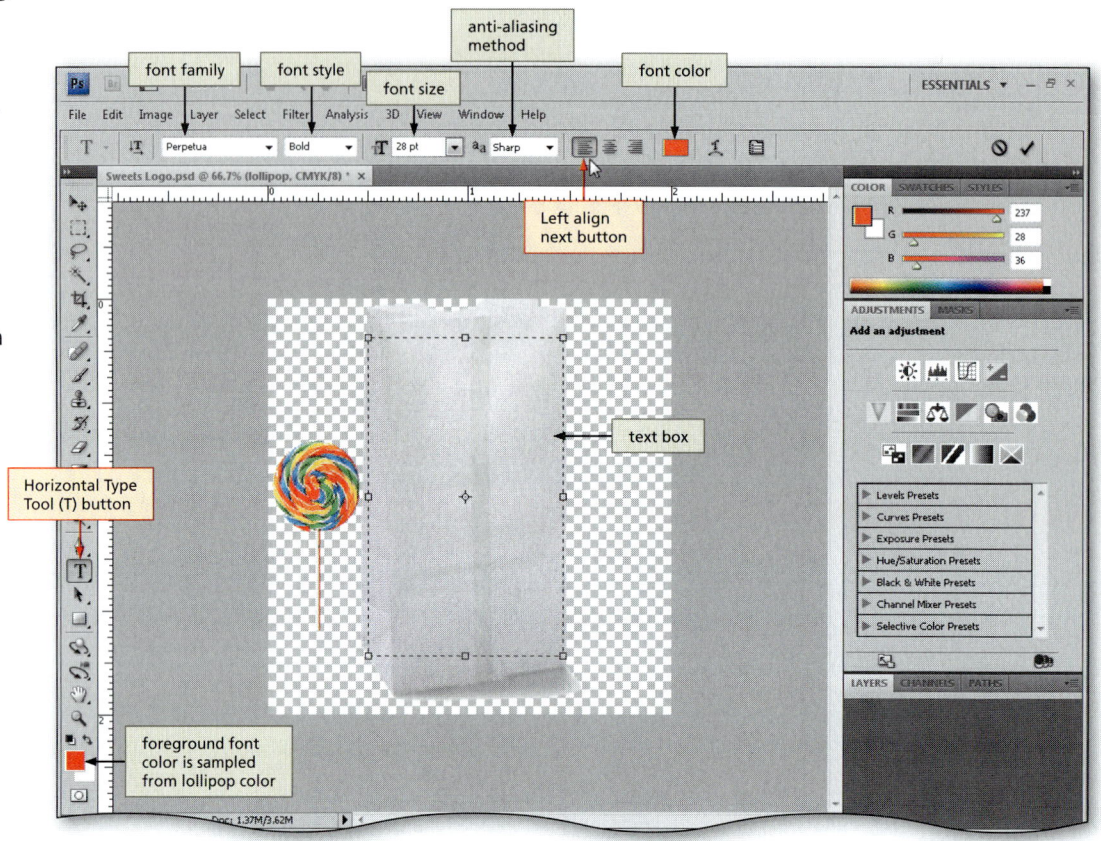

Figure 6–33

2
- Type The and press the ENTER key. Type Sweet and press the ENTER key. Type Spot to complete the text (Figure 6–34).

Q&A My text wrapped strangely. Did I do something wrong?

Your text box may not have been large enough. Press the ESC key and drag a bigger box

Figure 6–34

3

- On the options bar, click the Create warped text button to display the Warp Text dialog box.
- Drag the dialog box title bar to move the dialog box to the side if necessary, so the text is fully visible.
- Click the Style box arrow to display its list (Figure 6–35).

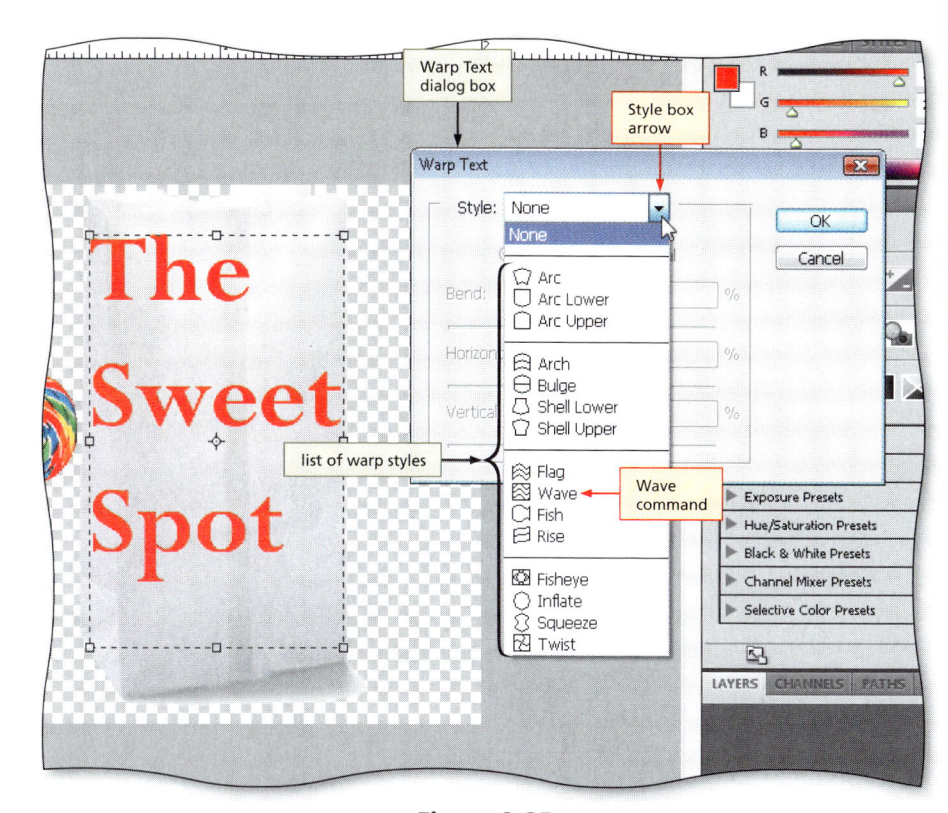

Figure 6–35

4

- Click Wave to select a wavy style.
- Drag the Bend slider to 25 to warp the text slightly (Figure 6–36).

Experiment

- Drag the Horizontal Distortion and Vertical Distortion sliders to both the right and left, watching how they affect the text box. When finished, return both sliders to the 0 value.

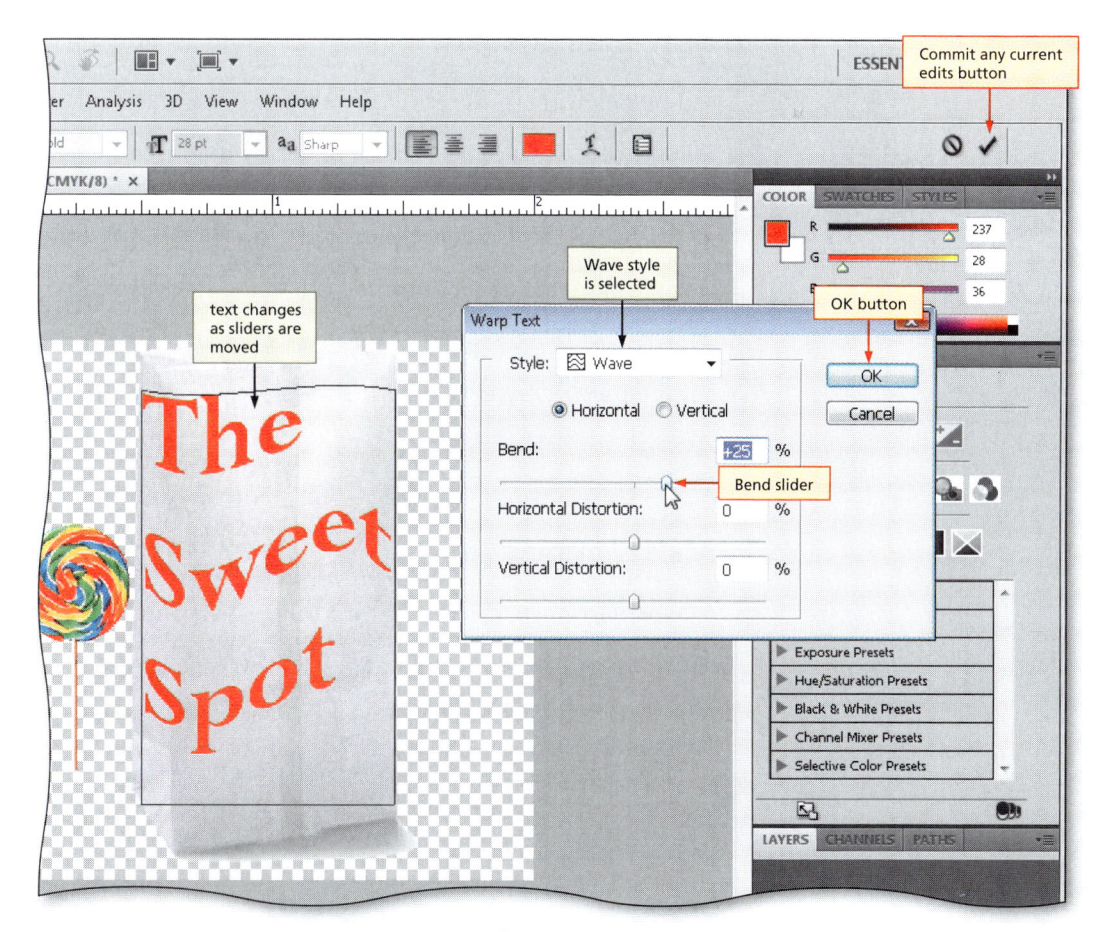

Figure 6–36

5
- Click the OK button to close the Warp Text dialog box.
- Click the Commit any current edits button on the options bar to close the text box (Figure 6–37).

text is warped

Figure 6–37

To Move the Lollipop

The following steps move the lollipop to a location over the letter o in the text.

1 Double-click the Layers panel tab to display the Layers panel.

2 On the Layers panel, drag the lollipop layer above the text layer, so it will appear in front of the text in the document window.

3 Use the Move tool to move the lollipop so the candy portion covers the letter, o, in the text.

4 Press CTRL+T to display the bounding box and scale the lollipop as necessary.

5 Press the ENTER key to commit the transformation (Figure 6–38).

To Merge and Save

The following steps merge the visible layers and then save the logo again.

1 Press SHIFT+CTRL+E to merge the visible layers.

2 Press CTRL+S to save the file.

lollipop is moved and scaled

Figure 6–38

Plan Ahead

Record actions for repetitive tasks.
If you or your client performs the same Photoshop tasks repeatedly, record the keystrokes for quick playback using an action. When creating and saving an action, the general workflow is as follows:

1. Practice the action and write down the steps.
2. Create a new action set, or select one you have previously created.
3. Create a new action, giving it a name and keyboard shortcut.
4. Click the Record button.
5. Carefully proceed through the steps of your task.
6. Click the Stop button.
7. Turn on dialog boxes and then edit stop points as necessary.
8. Save the set as an atn file for use in other documents.

If you make a mistake while recording the action, the best plan may be to stop the recording and begin again. If you decide to edit an action, you can double-click an individual step in the Actions panel and then change its settings. To omit a recorded step during playback, click the Toggle item on/off box in the left column of the Actions panel.

Actions

An **action** is an automation task that stores a series of commands and keystrokes for repeated use later. For example, because of the large number of pixels generated by digital cameras, Photoshop typically imports those photos with very large document dimensions. If you use a digital camera often, you could save the resize process as an action. Then, each time you edit a photo from your camera, you could use a single command to play the action and perform the steps again. You can create your own actions, download sample actions from the Web, or use predefined actions that come with Photoshop.

BTW

Droplets
The Droplet command automation feature converts an action into a standalone program with its own icon. Dragging a file icon onto the Droplet icon will start Photoshop and perform the action on the image. Droplets are cross-platform and transferable. Most graphic intensive publications — from yearbooks to church directories — use droplets to standardize size and resolution of photos.

BTW

Modal Icons
Each step in an action can have its own modality, which means that the action will stop at every dialog box. You might want the playback to stop at certain points to allow user decisions, while at other steps, you might want to mandate the settings. If an action set contains steps with mixed modalities, the modal icon beside the action set will be displayed in red. If all steps are modal, the modal icon will be displayed in black.

An action is created in a manner similar to that of a tape or video recorder. The steps are recorded as they happen and then saved in a location on your system. The next time you need it, the action can be loaded and played back. Action recording and playback steps are not recorded as states on the History panel. Actions are comparable to macros or functions in other software applications. Photoshop records nearly all commands and tools used in the Photoshop window; it will not record steps performed in other windows.

Actions might include **stops**, or places in the series of steps that pause during playback, waiting for the user to perform a task, such as choosing a brush size. Actions also might include **modal** controls that stop to let you enter values in a dialog box while playing an action. If there are no modal controls in an action, you can choose not to display the various dialog boxes. When you toggle them off, the playback runs through the steps seamlessly, without any visible dialog boxes.

The Actions Panel

The Actions panel helps you manage actions you have created and those predefined actions that come with Photoshop (Figure 6–39). Each time you create a new action, it is added to the panel. An **action set** is an organizational folder that includes multiple actions, and can be opened or expanded by clicking the triangle to the left of the action set.

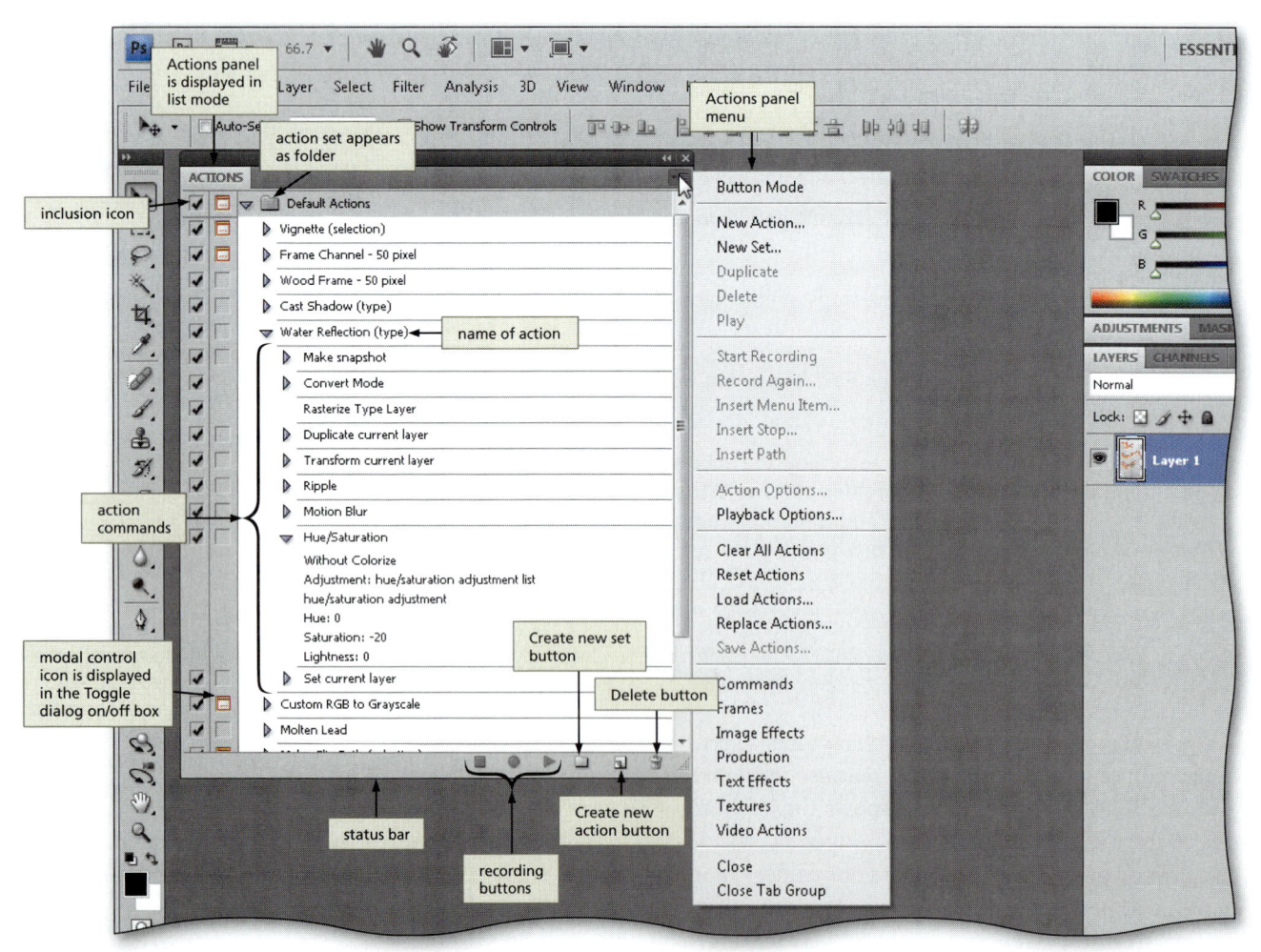

Figure 6–39

In Figure 6–39, the Default Actions set is expanded to display the predefined actions. The Water Reflection action is expanded to display the individual commands. On the left, a column of check marks indicates each command's inclusion in the action. Photoshop allows you to exclude specific commands during playback if you wish. The second column indicates whether the action is modal. Enabling the modal control creates an action generic enough to work with any image, pausing to allow the user to make adjustments. To enable modal controls, click the Toggle dialog on/off box on the Actions panel. On the panel's status bar are tape recorder-style buttons for stop, record, and play, as well as buttons to create sets and actions. The Actions panel menu displays commands to manage actions, set options, and load new sets of predefined actions. Action sets can be saved independently for use in other images. A saved action displays a file extension of atn. In the Save Action dialog box, Photoshop opens the folder where it stores other atn files by default.

The Actions panel can be displayed in two modes. The list mode, shown in Figure 6–39, allows you to make more choices about selecting, editing, playing, and managing your actions. The button mode, shown in Figure 6–40, is used for quick playbacks. To switch modes, choose the command from the Actions panel menu.

BTW

Actions with Prerequisites
If you see parentheses after the action name, the action only works at certain times. For example, if the word, Type, is in parentheses, you must have a text box selected. If the word, Selection, is in parentheses, the action will work only if you have a current selection marquee.

BTW

Photoshop Actions
Many Photoshop actions use a beginning step of making a snapshot in the History panel. That way, you can see what the image looked like before the changes were made.

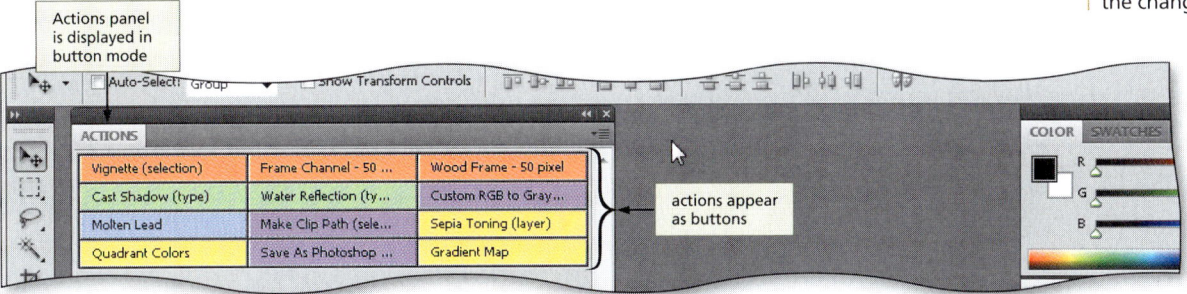

Figure 6–40

To Display the Actions Panel

The following step displays the Actions panel.

1
- Click Window on the menu bar and then click Actions to display the Actions panel (Figure 6–41).

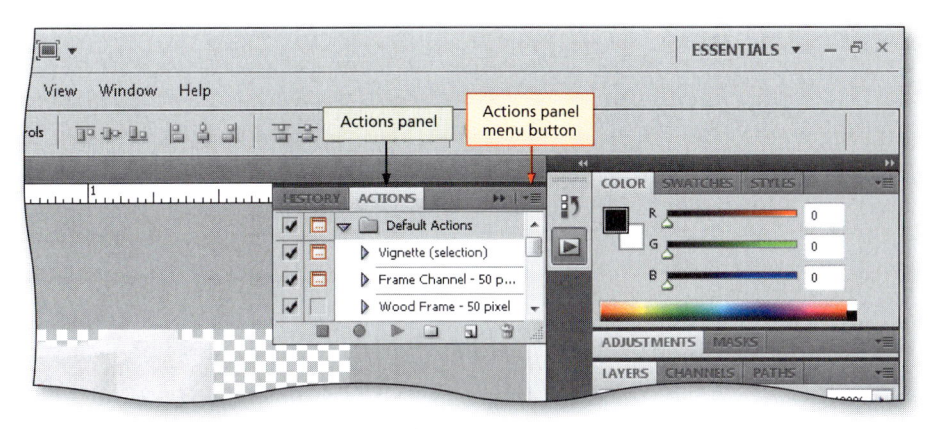

Figure 6–41

Other Ways
1. Press ALT+F9

To Append Action Sets

The Actions menu contains a default set that provides 12 different actions. In addition to the Default Actions set, seven other sets are available on the panel menu. In the following steps, you will append one of those sets to the list in the Actions panel.

1
- Click the Actions panel menu button to display the menu (Figure 6–42).

Q&A What does the Load Actions command do?

It opens a dialog box so you can navigate to the location of an action set. Any actions or action sets not saved previously with the image must be loaded.

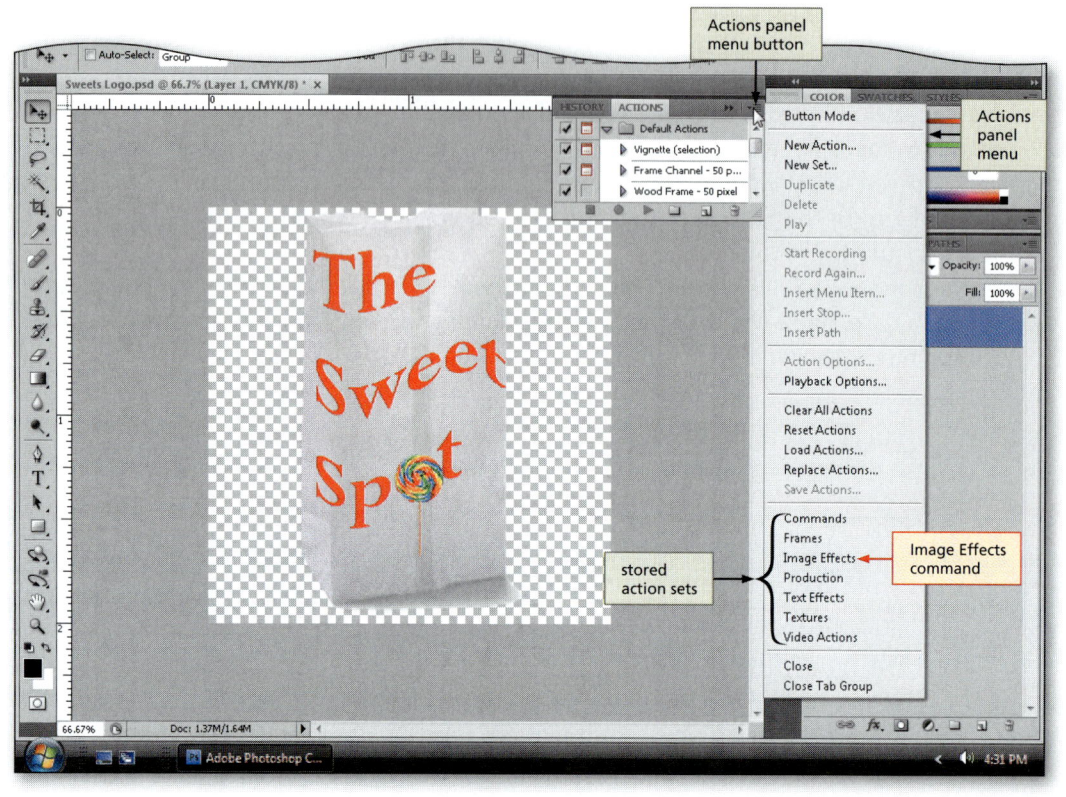

Figure 6–42

2
- Click Image Effects to choose the action set.
- Scroll in the panel to display the Image Effects set and click the Soft Posterize action (Figure 6–43).

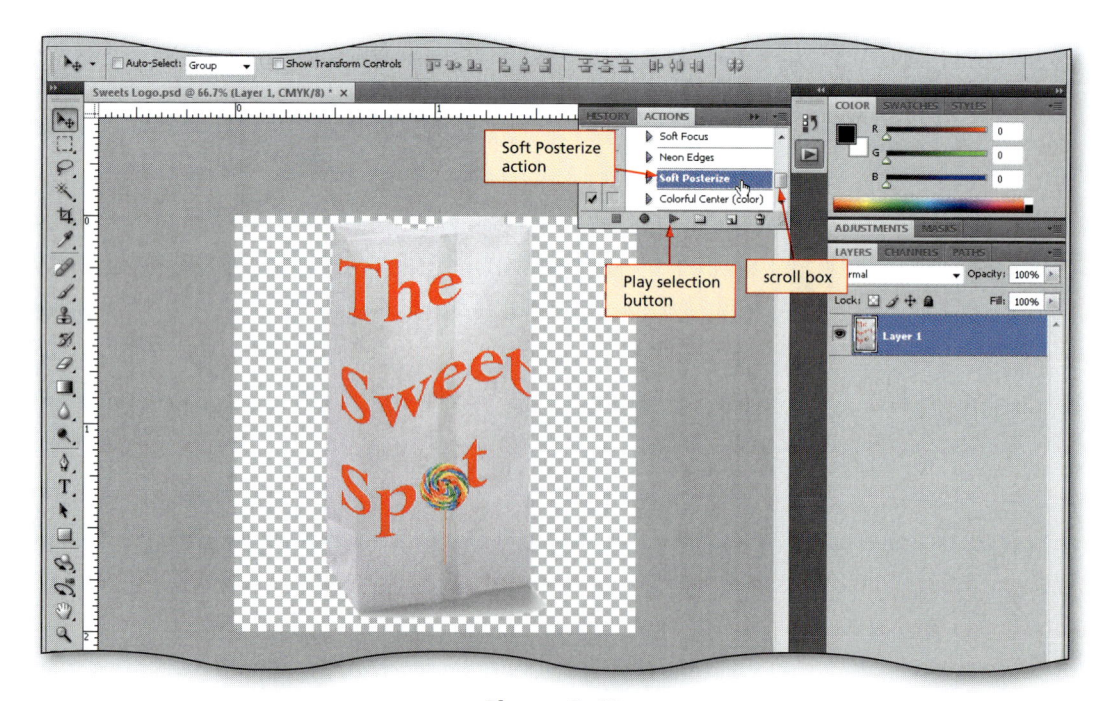

Figure 6–43

To Play an Action

To play an action, you click the Play selection button on the Actions panel status bar. In the step that follows, the Soft Posterize action is played to create a pink shade that enhances the Sweets Logo image. This Photoshop action uses a filter to blur the color in an image and then darken it for a hazy effect. The action frequently is used to present the impression of a dream or to soften wedding photos. Later in this chapter, you will create a custom action.

1
- Click the Play selection button on the Actions panel status bar to play the action (Figure 6–44).

Q&A What are the right-pointing triangles on the Actions panel?

If you click a right-pointing triangle, Photoshop displays setting changes, if any, that are related to each command.

Figure 6–44

To Save the Logo Again

The logo image is complete. The next steps save and close the file.

1 Press CTRL+S to save the logo again. If Photoshop displays a dialog box, click the OK button.

2 Click the Close button on the document window tab.

BTW

Storing Actions
On most systems, the location of stored actions is C:\Program Files\Adobe\Adobe Photoshop CS4\Presets\Photoshop Actions. If you are working in a lab setting, however, you should browse to your storage device in the Save Action dialog box and then save your action set.

Organizing Actions
You can organize sets of actions for different types of work, such as online publishing or print publishing, and then transfer sets to other computers. Normally, user-defined action sets are stored with the file in which they are created. You can save your sets and actions to a separate actions file, however, so you can recover them if the file in which they were created is destroyed.

Creating Actions
You must be careful when you record actions that involve selecting a named layer. When you play back the action in a different file, Photoshop will look for that layer. If the named layer does not exist in the file, the action will not function correctly.

Automate Commands
Actions are not the only way to automate processes. The Automate submenu on the File menu has several ways to automate tasks, including crop and straighten, creating a droplet, and photomerge, among others.

To Create a New Document

In preparation for recording a new action, you will create a blank canvas for The Sweet Spot's advertising flyer, as shown in the following steps.

1. Press CTRL+N to open the New dialog box.
2. Type `Sweets Advertisement` in the Name box.
3. Click the Width unit box and then click inches in the list, if necessary.
4. Type `9` in the Width box and type `6.5` in the Height box.
5. Type `300` in the Resolution box.
6. Click the Color Mode box arrow and then click RGB Color in the list.
7. Click the Background Contents box arrow and then click White in the list (Figure 6–45).
8. Click the OK button to create the blank canvas. Change the magnification to 16.67% if necessary.

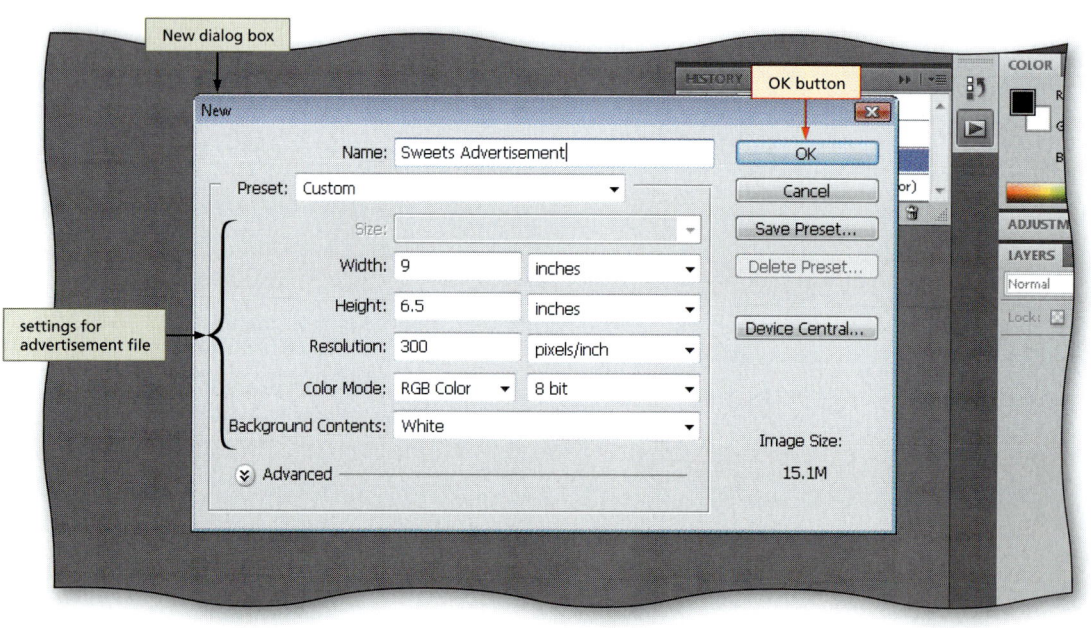

Figure 6–45

Actions **PS 407**

To Create a New Action Set

The following steps create a new action set named Personal Actions in the Sweets Master file.

1

- On the Actions panel status bar, click the Create new set button to display the New Set dialog box.

- Type `Sweet Spot Actions` in the Name box to name the action set (Figure 6–46).

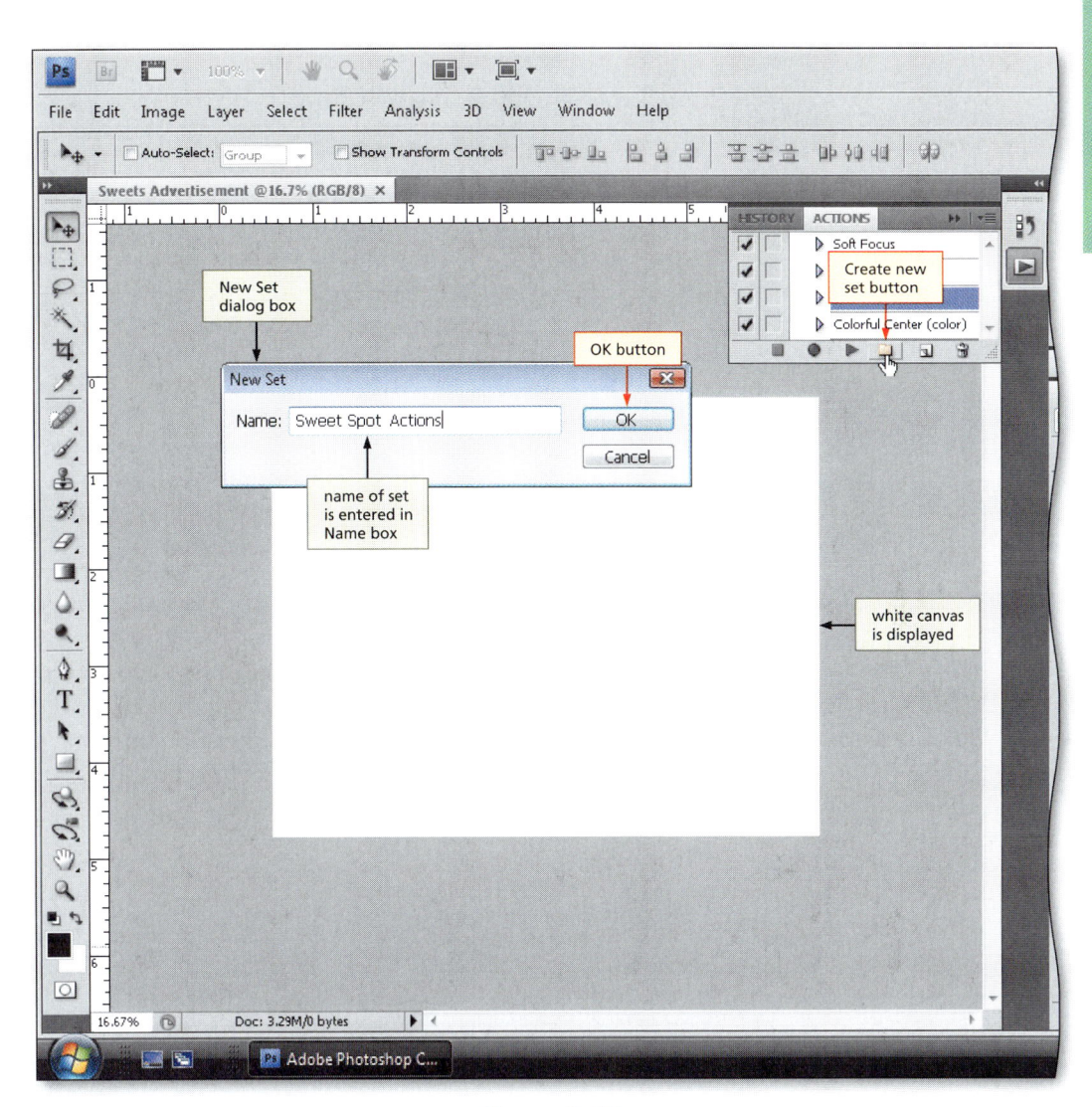

Figure 6–46

2

- Click the OK button to create the action and have it appear on the Actions panel (Figure 6–47).

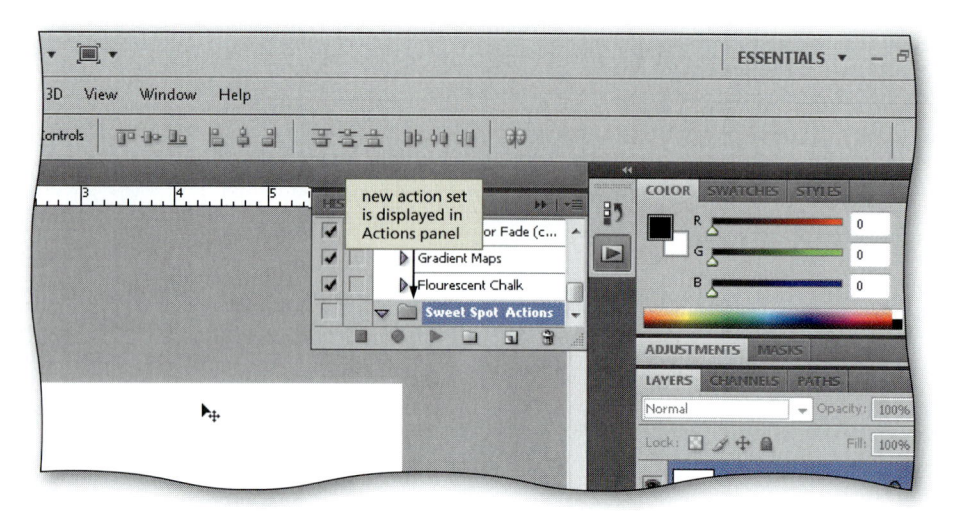

Figure 6–47

> **Other Ways**
> 1. On Actions panel menu, click New Set

To Create a New Action

When you click the Create new action button, the New Action dialog box is displayed. The New Action dialog box allows you to name your action, position it within a set, assign a function key, and choose a display color for the action in the panel. After editing the settings, a Record button begins the process, as explained in the next series of steps.

1

- On the Actions panel status bar, click the Create new action button to display the New Action dialog box.

- Type `Place Logo` in the Name box to name the action.

- Click the Function Key box arrow and then click F11 in the list to assign a function key to the action.

- Click the Color box arrow and then click Red in the list to assign a color. Do not close the dialog box (Figure 6–48).

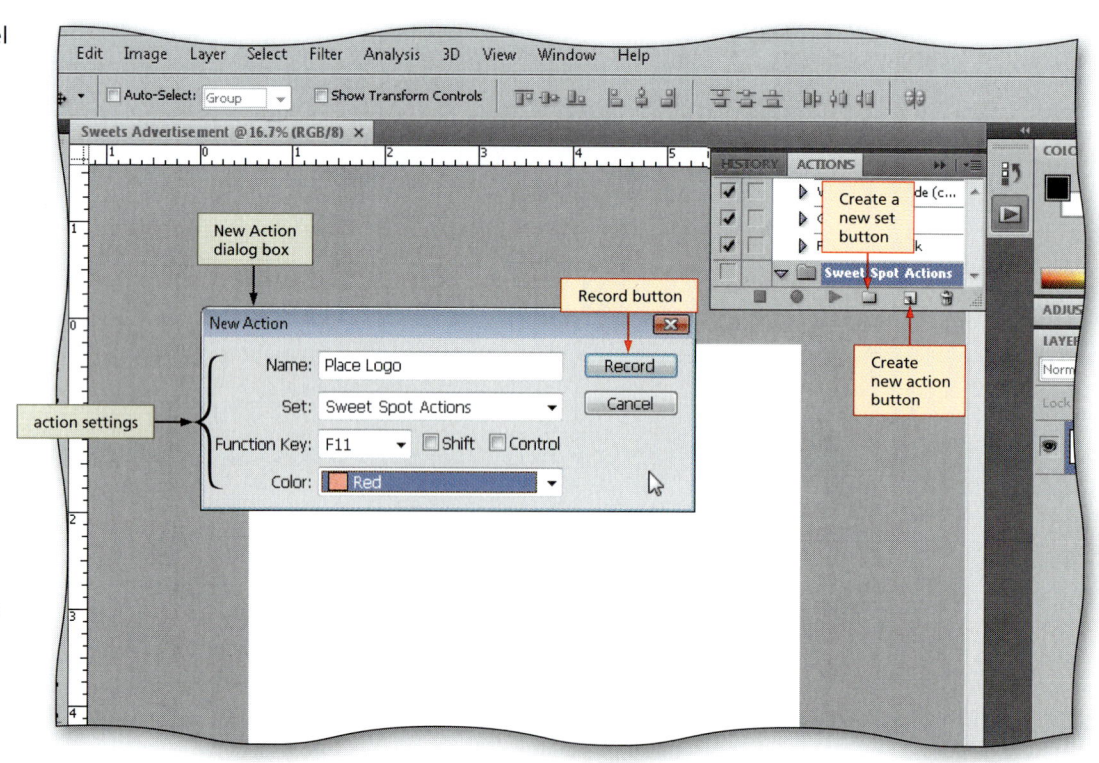

Figure 6–48

To Record an Action

The next steps record an action that places the company logo on any publication.

1
- In the New Action dialog box, click the Record button to close the dialog box and begin recording keystrokes (Figure 6–49).

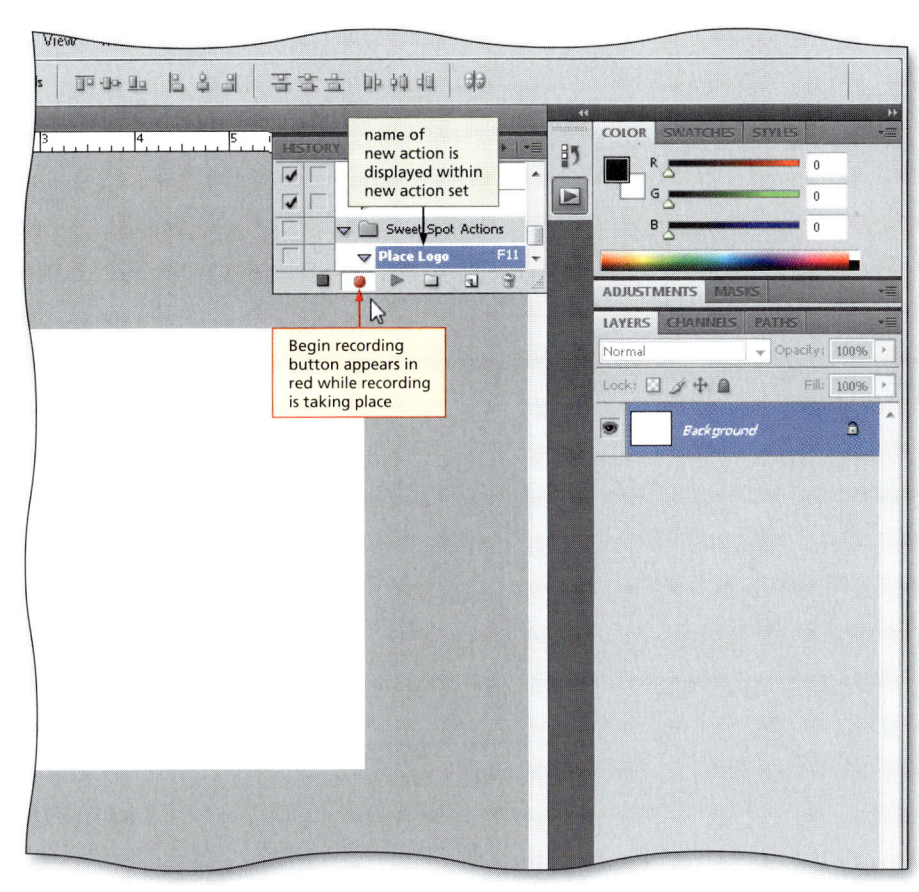

Figure 6–49

2
- Click File on the menu bar to display the File menu and to record the first keystroke (Figure 6–50).

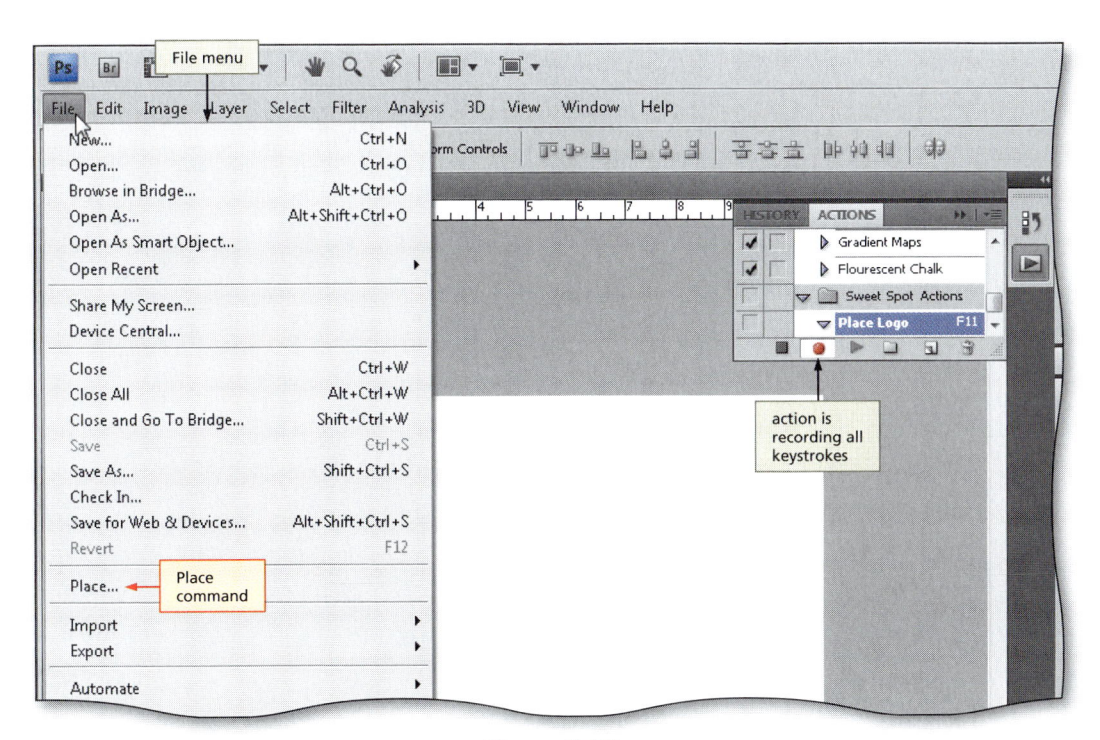

Figure 6–50

3

- Click Place to open the Place dialog box and to record the second keystroke (Figure 6–51).

Q&A What if I make a mistake while recording an action?

If you click inadvertently while creating an action, you can press CTRL+Z to cancel the recording and then start over.

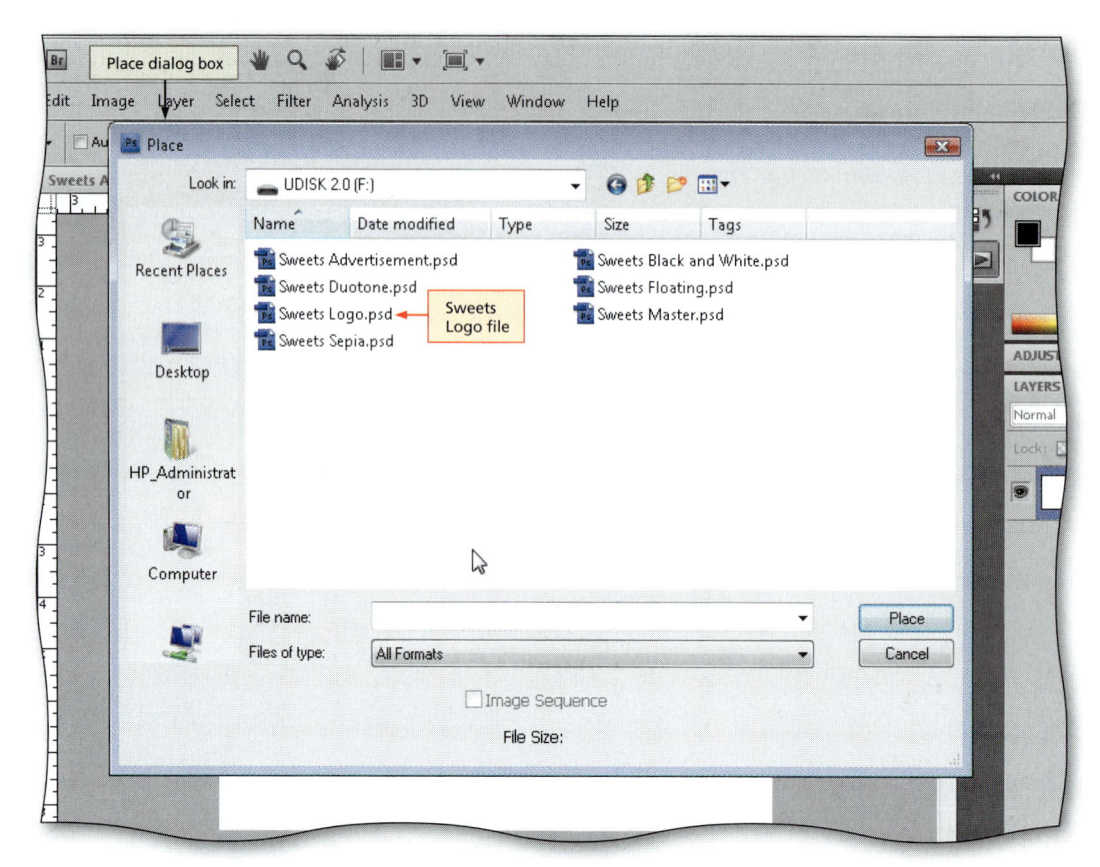

Figure 6–51

4

- Double-click the Sweets Logo file name to place it in the document window and to record the third keystroke (Figure 6–52).

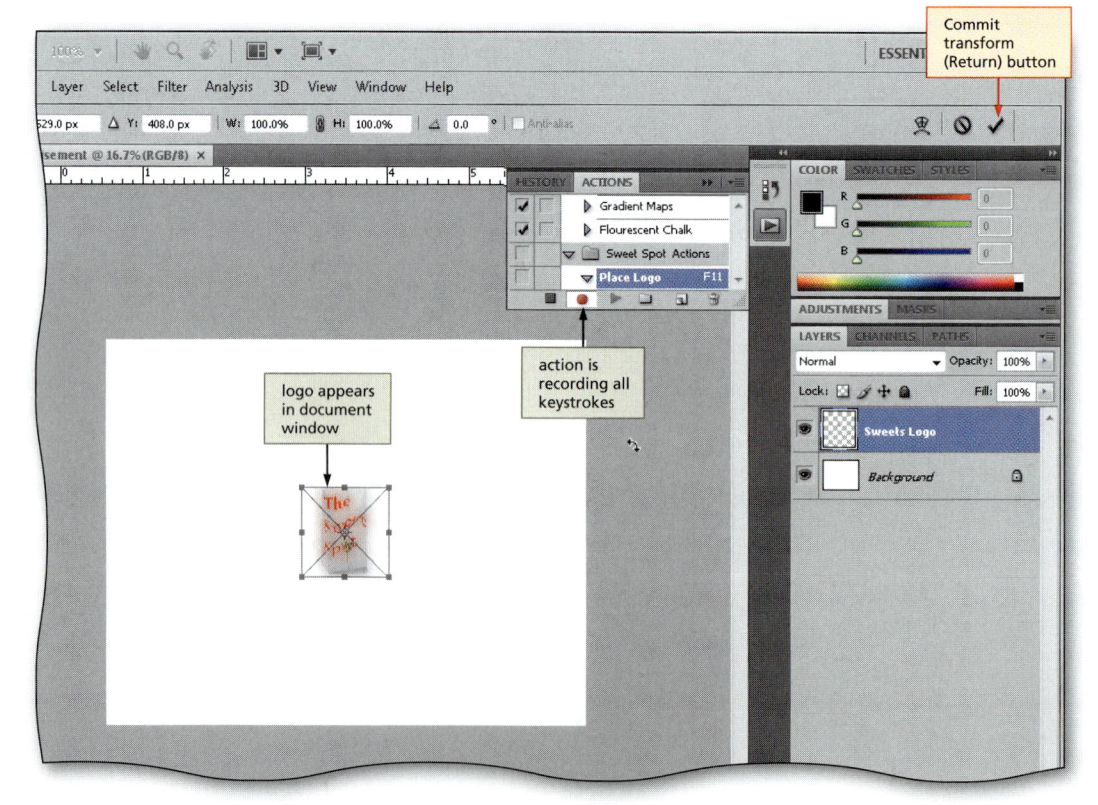

Figure 6–52

Actions **PS** 411

5
- Click the Commit transform (Return) button on the options bar to commit the placement and to record the fourth keystroke (Figure 6–53).

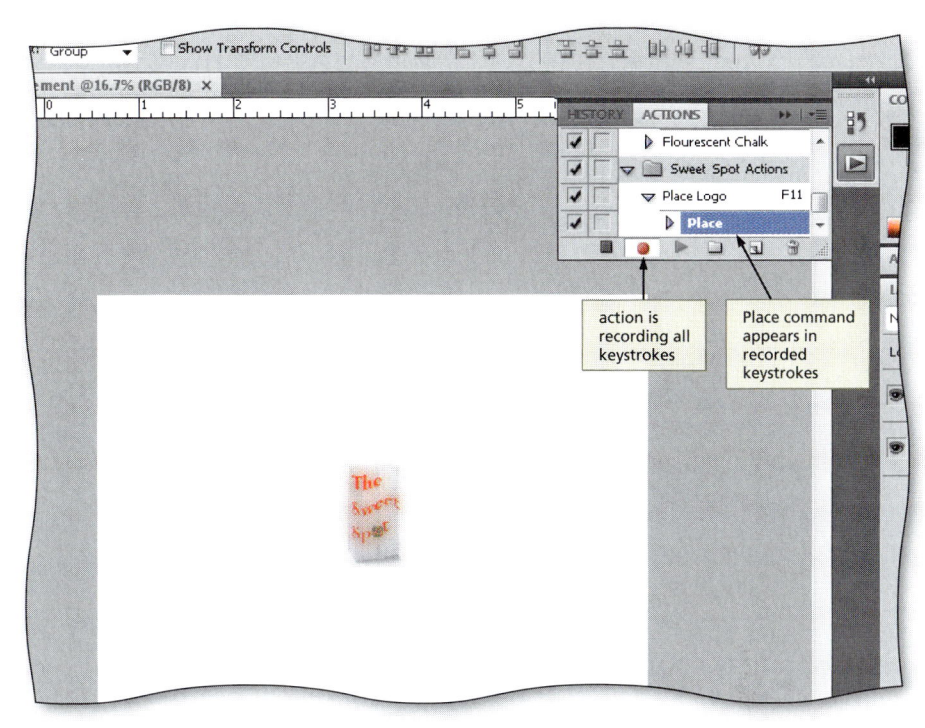

Figure 6–53

6
- Click the Stop playing/recording button to stop the recording (Figure 6–54).

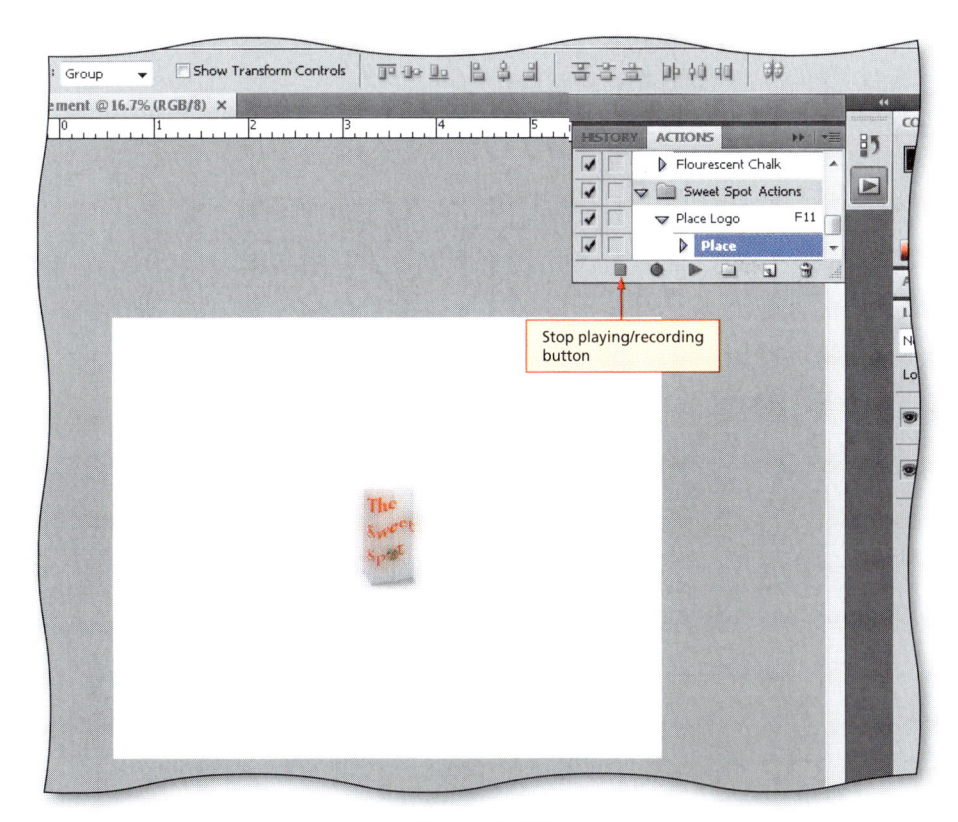

Figure 6–54

Other Ways
1. On Actions panel menu, click Start/Stop Recording

To Test the Action

To test the action, the following step deletes the logo and then play back the action using the function key to confirm that it works.

1

- With the logo layer selected, press the DELETE key.
- Press the F11 key to play the action and redisplay the logo.

To Save an Action Set

The following steps save a new action set using the Actions panel menu.

1

- On the Actions panel, click the Sweet Spot Actions set.
- Click the Actions panel menu button to display the menu (Figure 6–55).

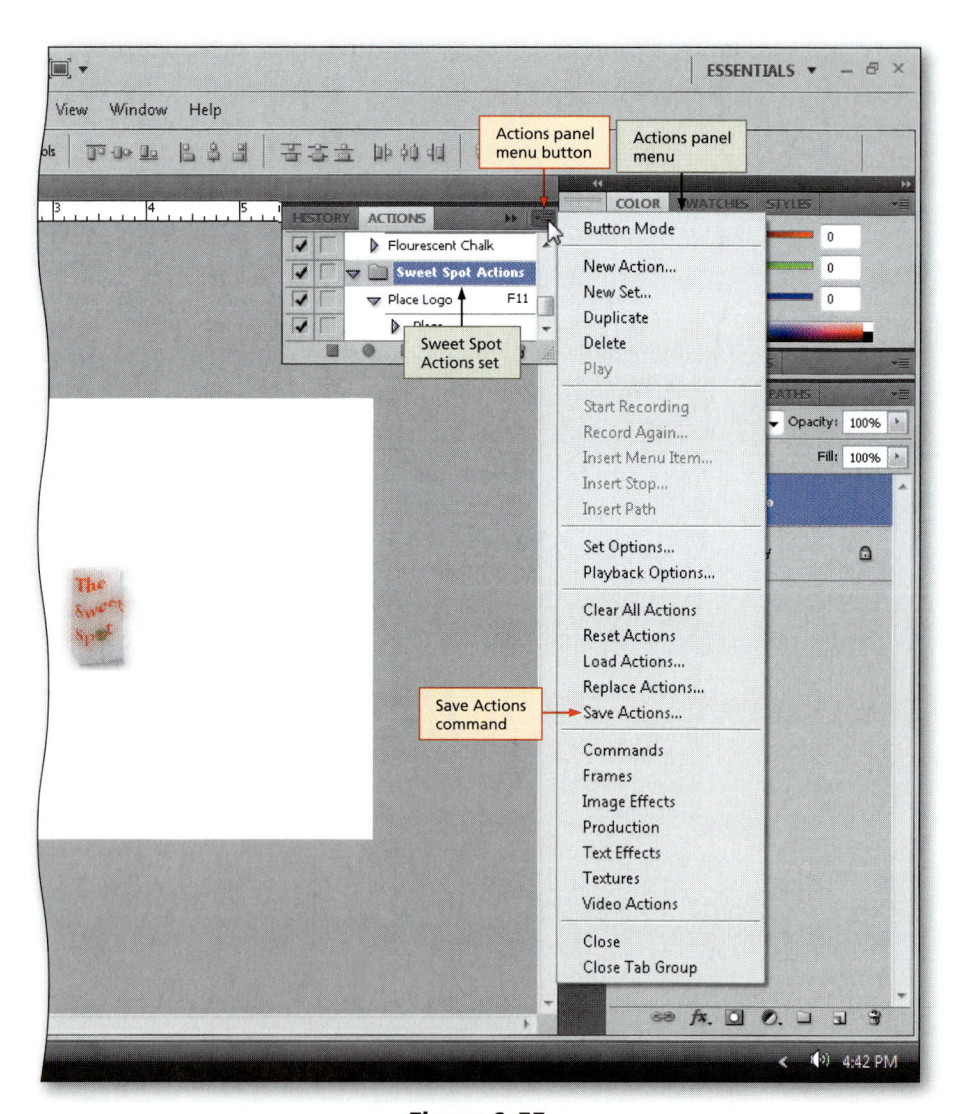

Figure 6–55

2
- With your USB flash drive connected to one of the computer's USB ports, click Save Actions.

- When the Save dialog box is displayed, click the Save in box arrow and then click UDISK 2.0 (F:), or the location associated with your USB flash drive, in the list (Figure 6–56).

Q&A
Could I save the action set in the Actions folder with the installed Photoshop actions?

You could; however, saving on a personal storage device keeps lab installation actions unchanged for other students.

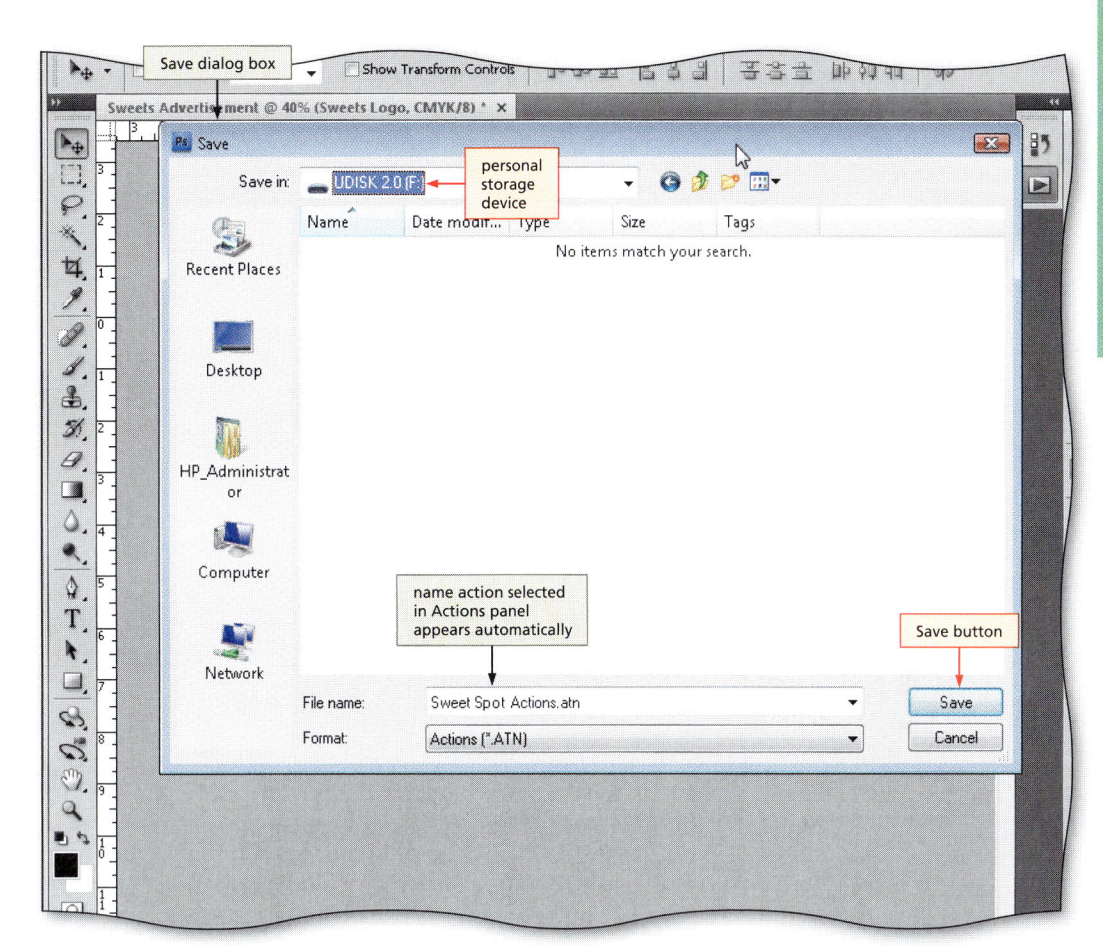

3
- Click the Save button.

Figure 6–56

Completing the Advertisement

To complete the advertisement, you will create a colored rectangle shape for the background and move the layer behind the logo. You then will add the floating image. Finally, you will create text for the advertisement.

To Create a Background Rectangle

The following steps use the Shape tool to create a background.

1. Press the I key to access the Eyedropper tool. Sample a pink color from the logo.
2. Press the U key to access the Shape tool. On the Shapes options bar, click the Rectangle Tool button, if necessary.
3. Drag a rectangle that is slightly smaller than the white canvas.
4. On the Layers panel, drag the logo layer above the rectangle layer.
5. Press the V key to access the Move tool. Drag the logo to the left about one inch from the margin.

BTW

Editing Actions
Other edits that you can perform on the recorded steps include deselecting some check boxes, dragging a command to the Delete button on the status bar to remove it permanently, and setting playback options on the Actions panel menu.

BTW

Stop Actions
After recording an action, you can delete image-specific steps and then insert an action stop using the panel menu. You can even include a reminder message. When the action is played back, it will pause — so users can create their own brush stroke, for example — and then continue with the action.

To Insert and Scale the Floating Image

The following steps insert the floating image into the advertisement. Because images taken with digital cameras typically are very large, to incorporate as many pixels as possible, you will have to scale the image to fit in the advertisement.

1. Press CTRL+O to display the Open dialog box. Double-click the Sweets Floating image to open it.

2. Use the Arrange Documents button to arrange the windows side by side.

3. Drag the floating image from the Sweets Floating window to the Sweets Advertisement window. The image will be very large in that window.

4. Close the Sweets Floating document window.

5. Press CTRL+T to transform the selection. Scale the image as necessary to fit within the advertisement canvas.

6. Press the ENTER key to apply the transformation. Drag the image to a location on the right of the advertisement.

To Create Text

The final steps are to create three text areas for the advertisement.

1. Press T to access the Horizontal Type tool. On the options bar, choose the Harrington font, Regular, size 32, with a Strong anti-aliasing method. If the font color is not black, click the Color box on the options bar, and choose black.

2. Drag a text box beginning at the upper-left corner of the pink rectangle, approximately 3.5 inches wide and 1 inch tall.

BTW

Photoshop Help
The best way to become familiar with Photoshop Help is to use it. Appendix D includes detailed information about Photoshop Help and exercises that will help you gain confidence in using it.

3. Type `The Sweet Spot` to enter the text. On the options bar, click the Commit any current edits button to close the text box.

4. Deselect The Sweet Spot text box.

5. Drag a second text box beginning just below the previous text and slightly right. Make the text box 2 inches wide and 1.5 inches tall so it fits above the logo. On the options bar, change the font size to 18.

6. Type `has fresh fruit and candy bouquets for every occasion! Call, stop by, or visit our Web site.` and then click the Commit any current edits button to close the text box.

7. Drag a third text box below the logo that extends to the bottom margin and right approximately 2.5 inches.

8. Type the address, phone, and URL, as shown in Figure 6–57. Adjust the magnification as necessary.

Preparing for Four-Color Processing **PS 415**

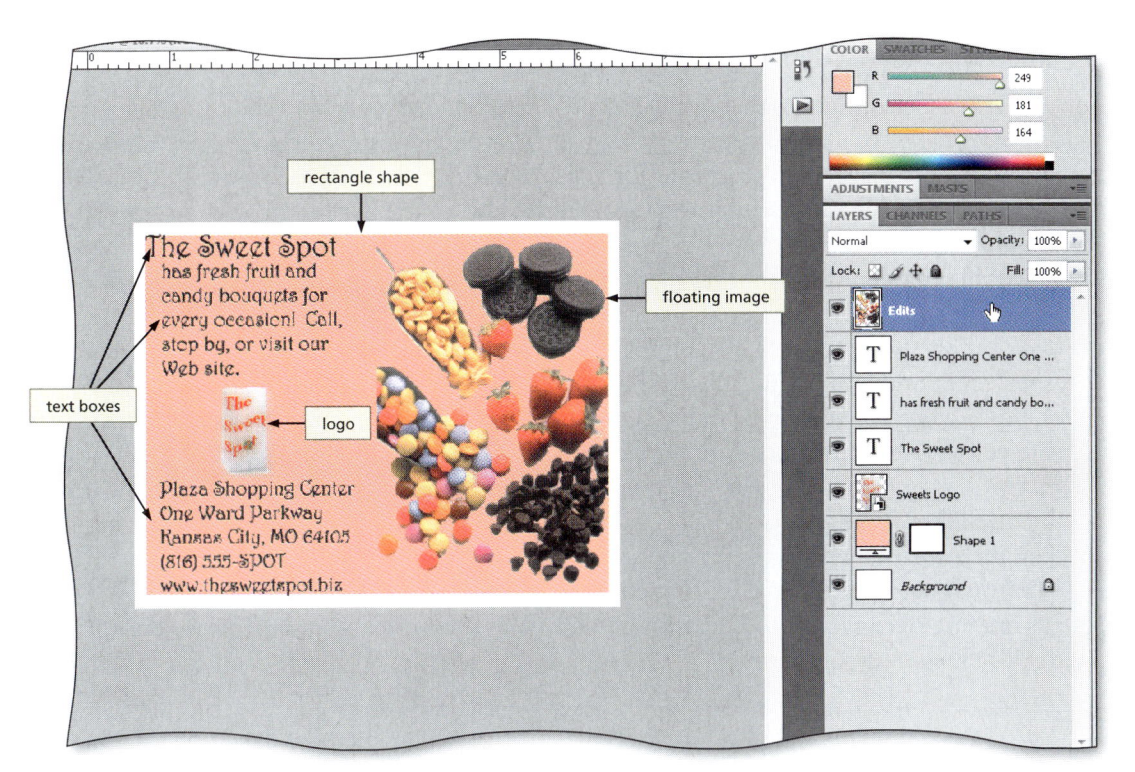

Figure 6–57

To Save the Advertisement

Because you have made many changes, the next steps save the file.

1. Press SHIFT+CTRL+S to open the Save As dialog box.

2. Type `Sweets Advertisement` to enter the file name.

3. Click the Save button to save the image. If Photoshop displays a dialog box, click the OK button.

> **BTW**
>
> **Service Bureaus**
> A **service bureau** is a business that offers data processing, color proofing, and online services.

Preparing for Four-Color Processing

Most digital cameras create an RGB file. While that is fine for online viewing and Web graphics, many traditional full-color printing presses can print only four colors: cyan, magenta, yellow, and black (CMYK). Other colors in the spectrum are simulated using various combinations of those colors. When you plan to print a photo professionally, you may have to convert it from one color model to the other. The sweets image was taken with a digital camera and uses the RGB color model. The Sweet Spot wants a professional color print of the advertisement. The service bureau has specified the Trumatch 4-color matching system that uses the CMYK color model.

Photoshop allows you to convert directly from RGB to CMYK; however, using the intermediary LAB color mode gives you more flexibility in color changes and contrast.

BTW

Color Models vs. Color Modes
A color model is a numeric representation of the colors in digital images. A color mode determines which color model is used to display and print the image. A mode is based on a model.

Using LAB Color

LAB Color is an internationally accepted color mode that defines colors mathematically using a lightness or luminance setting, and two color or chromatic channels — an A-axis color for colors from magenta to green, and a B-axis color for colors from yellow to blue. The LAB Color mode, which tries to emulate the colors viewable by the human eye, incorporates all the colors in the RGB and CMYK color spectrums, and often is used as an intermediary when converting from one format to another.

In Figure 6–58, the LAB color space is represented by the color spectrum. The black outline represents RGB's color space. The white outline represents CMYK's color space. RGB and CMYK are subsets, but they also are slanted in the color spectrum. For example, when converting from RGB to CMYK, you lose some of the blue's intensity but gain yellow. Reds and greens are better in RGB; cyans (blues) and magentas are better in CMYK, as you would suspect. Contrast, a result of how bright the white is and how dark the black is, is represented poorly in CMYK. The printer cannot make white any brighter than the paper on which it is printed. A solid black does not exist in CMYK on a display monitor. Therefore, when adjusting color and contrast during a conversion, it is appropriate to convert it to LAB Color, make your adjustments, and then convert it to CMYK.

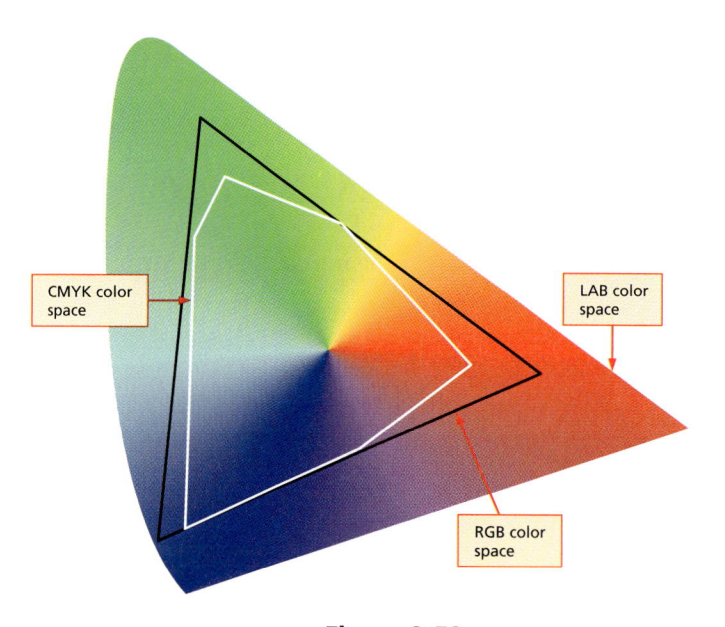

Figure 6–58

The LAB Color mode calculates each color description, rather than generating it from a combination, as is the case for RGB. Because RGB colors are combinations of colors, they may look different on different devices. For example, a row of televisions in a department store displaying the same program will look different because different television manufacturers combine red, green, and blue in slightly different ways. Working with LAB colors usually provides colors that are more consistent across platforms.

The LAB Color mode is independent of the type of device or media, and may be used for either display or printing. Many photo CD images use LAB colors where the luminance and color values are edited independently.

To Convert to LAB Color

The LAB Color mode will be used in the conversion process for the advertisement. Converting to LAB color rasterizes or changes vector-based text layers to pixel based images. The conversion process also merges the layers. The following steps convert to LAB color.

1
- Click Image on the menu bar, point to Mode, and then click Lab Color to begin the conversion and display the warning dialog box about rasterizing (Figure 6–59).

2
- Click the Rasterize button.
- When Photoshop displays a message about flattening layers, click the Flatten button.

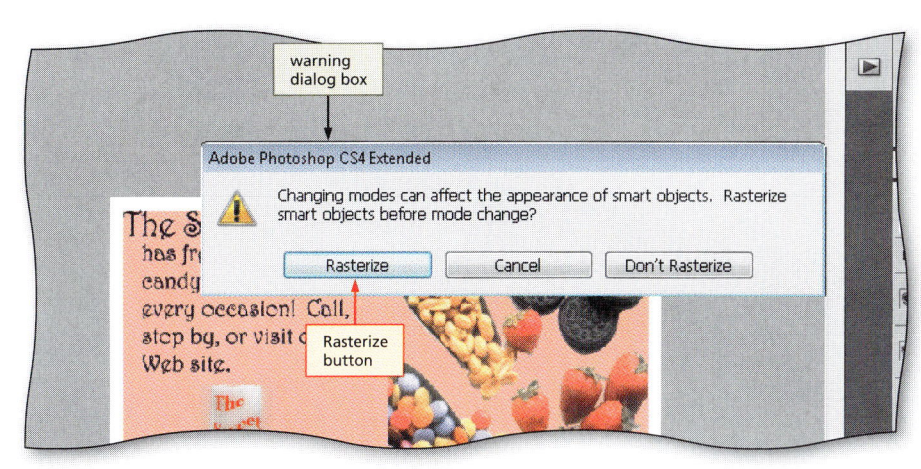

Figure 6–59

To Convert to CMYK

The final conversion will be to CMYK so size, color, and tonal changes can be applied before printing.

1 In the Channels panel, click the Lab channel.

2 Click Image on the menu bar, point to Mode, and then click CMYK Color. If Photoshop displays a dialog box, click the OK button.

To Save the Advertisement

After the conversion to LAB and the conversion to CMYK, it is a good idea to save the file again.

1 Press CTRL+S to save the file. If Photoshop displays a dialog box, click the OK button.

BTW

JPEG Artifacts
Sometimes, when converting from RGB to LAB color, a JPEG image will leave behind some small blotches of irregular color, called **artifacts**, because of the compression method involved. Sharpening the image will remove those kinds of artifacts.

BTW

Adjusting LAB Colors
Other adjustments that can be performed on the intermediary LAB color include filtering out noise or artifacts, applying spot color and alpha channels, or applying a varnish or tint to the image.

Resizing, Resampling, and Interpolation

Recall that you used the Image Size dialog box to resize an image in an earlier chapter. Resizing an image can reduce the image quality. For example, when you resize an image to larger dimensions, the image may lose some detail and sharpness because Photoshop has to add or stretch pixels. When you make an image smaller, some pixels must be reduced or discarded and cannot be recovered once the image is saved. That is why you should always work with a copy of the original image, in case you do not like the changes.

BTW

Quick Reference
For a table that lists how to complete the tasks covered in this book using the mouse, shortcut menu, and keyboard, see the Quick Reference Summary at the back of this book or visit the Photoshop CS4 Quick Reference Web page (scsite.com/pscs4//qr).

BTW

Scale Styles
If your image has layers with styles applied to them, select Scale Styles in the Image Size dialog box to scale the effects in the resized image. This option is available only if you select the Constrain Proportions check box.

BTW

Resampling
In the General Preferences dialog box, you can specify which default interpolation method to use whenever you resample images using the Image Size or transformation commands. The Image Size command also lets you specify an interpolation method other than the default.

Changing the document size, or physical size, of photos is one of the most common tasks in digital imagery, as is changing the file size, or number of required bytes to store the image.

Photoshop allows you to make the interpolation, resampling, and sizing changes, yourself. **Interpolation** is the mathematical process of adding or subtracting pixels in an image, either to enlarge or reduce the size. Once the location of the interpolated pixels is determined, Photoshop uses a **resampling method** that assigns a new color value to pixels by taking a sample of the surrounding ones. Before you resample, however, it is important to check with your lab or service bureau, as some services automatically resample and resize at the time of printing. In those cases, retaining as much digital data as possible is the best choice. On the other hand, if a digital image must have a specific resolution and a specific size, then resampling may be warranted.

If you **downsample**, or decrease the number of pixels, information is deleted from the image. Downsampling reduces image data by representing a group of pixels with a single pixel. For instance, if an image needs to be reduced by 50 percent, Photoshop will have to destroy half of the pixels. If during the destruction, black-and-white pixels come next to each other, both pixels are changed using a complex calculation to produce a smoother tonal gradation of gray. The disadvantage of downsampling is the loss of data, or **lossiness**.

If you **upsample**, or increase the number of pixels, Photoshop assigns a new color to the added pixels based on an average interpolation. For example, if an image needs to be enlarged, the interpolation notes where a new pixel should be added. If that new pixel falls at the edge of a yellow insignia on a red sweater, the new pixel would be orange. Photoshop samples the two colors and averages the color values. At the pixel level, it would be hard to notice orange in the finished product; but it is something to keep in mind when upsampling. Remember that Photoshop cannot insert detailed information that was not captured from the original image. Photos will start to look softer, with less detail, as they are enlarged.

Table 6–2 lists the five interpolation methods offered by Photoshop; however, other interpolation methods can be downloaded from the Web.

Table 6–2 Photoshop Interpolation Methods

Interpolation Method	Description
Bicubic (best for smooth gradients)	a slow, but precise, interpolation method based on an examination of the values of surrounding pixels — applies more complex calculations to produce smoother tonal gradations
Bicubic Sharper (best for reduction)	a bicubic interpolation method that works well for reducing images with enhanced sharpening while maintaining details
Bicubic Smoother (best for enlargement)	an interpolation method that works well for enlarging images with smoother results than bicubic alone
Bilinear	an interpolation method that produces medium-quality results by averaging the color values to produce new pixels
Nearest Neighbor (preserve hard edges)	a fast interpolation method that produces a smaller file size but may become jagged when scaling as it tries to preserve hard edges

No matter what resampling method you choose, it may introduce artifacts, or changed pixels, that do not look good and were not in the original image. Blurs or halos may be introduced. Jagged edges may appear when upsampling, and moiré patterns may appear when downsampling. A **moiré pattern** is an alternating of blurred and clear areas, forming thin stripes or dots on the screen. Table 6–3 describes some of the problems.

Table 6–3 Resampling Problems

Problem	Description	Possible Solution	Sample
Aliasing	jagged edges or moiré patterns	Set anti-aliasing options (during down-scaling)	
Blur	a loss of image sharpness, more visible at higher magnifications	Use the Unsharp Mask filter	
Halos	appears as a halo around edges — while a small amount may improve the perceived sharpness, a high amount does not look good	Use Defringe matting	

The Image Size Dialog Box

Recall that Photoshop uses the Image Size dialog box to make choices about the number of pixels, the document size, and the resampling method. Each setting in the Image Size dialog box makes a difference in the resulting type of file and document. Table 6–4 displays the settings and their effects. When resampling, pixels are added or subtracted during resizing. Without resampling, you are stretching or compressing the existing pixels by changing the resolution.

Table 6–4 Image Size Dialog Box Settings

Setting	Unit Of Measurement	Effect With Resampling	Effect Without Resampling
Pixel Dimensions	percent or pixels	The document size is adjusted in proportion to pixel dimensions, but the resolution does not change.	The pixel dimensions remain the same, but the resolution value changes to represent what the image can provide at that size.
Document Size	percent, inches, centimeters, millimeters, points, picas, or columns	The pixels are adjusted in proportion to document size, but the resolution does not change.	The pixel dimensions remain the same, but the resolution value changes to represent what the image can provide at that size.
Resolution	pixels per inch or pixels per centimeter	The pixel dimensions change and the document size remains the same.	The document size changes and the pixel dimensions remain the same.

If you make changes in the Image Size dialog box and wish to go back to the original dimensions or resolution, press and hold the ALT key before closing the dialog box. The Cancel button will change to a Reset button.

To Resize a File with Resampling

The current dimensions of the Sweets Advertisement image are approximately 7 inches wide by 5 inches tall. The advertisement for the insert should be a half-page ad measuring approximately 5.5 inches wide. In addition, the printing service has specified a file resolution of 300 pixels per inch for best print results. The steps on the next page resize the file with resampling, which means the pixels will be downsampled using the Bicubic Sharper method because it works well for reducing images while maintaining details.

1

- Click Image on the menu bar, and then click Image Size to display the Image Size dialog box.
- Click the Resample Image check box to select it, if necessary.
- Click the Constrain Proportions check box to select it, if necessary.
- Click the Resample Image box arrow to display the interpolation methods (Figure 6–60).

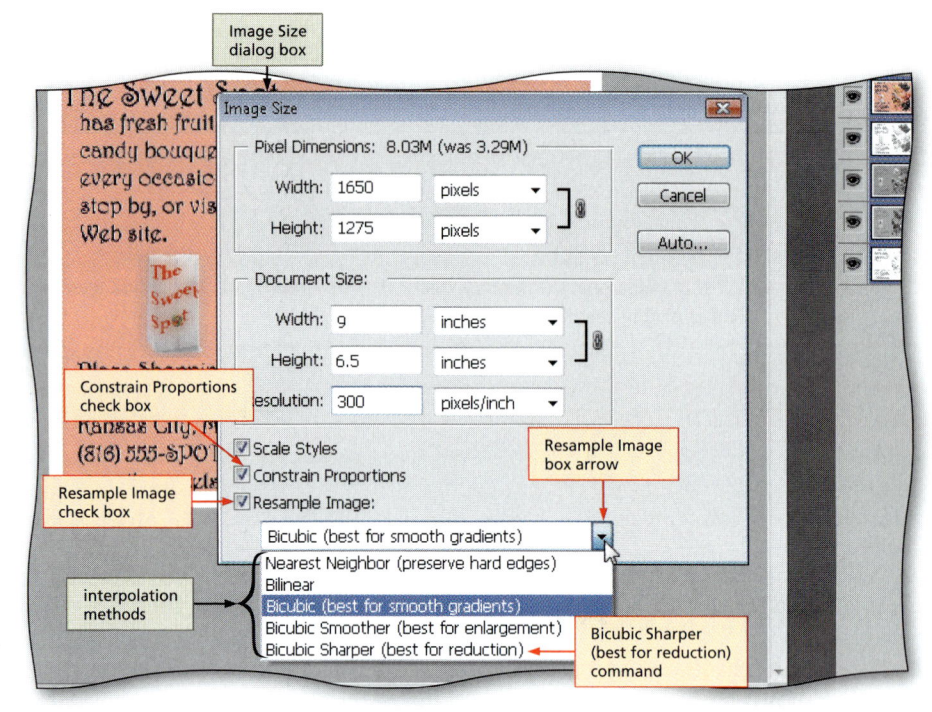

Figure 6–60

2

- Click Bicubic Sharper (best for reduction).
- If necessary, click the Width unit box arrow in the Document Size area and then click inches in the list.
- Type 5.5 in the Width box.
- Type 300 in the Resolution box, if necessary (Figure 6–61).

Q&A Should I enter a height value?

No, the Height value was completed automatically because Constrain Proportions was selected. Your height might differ. The Pixel Dimensions settings also are adjusted.

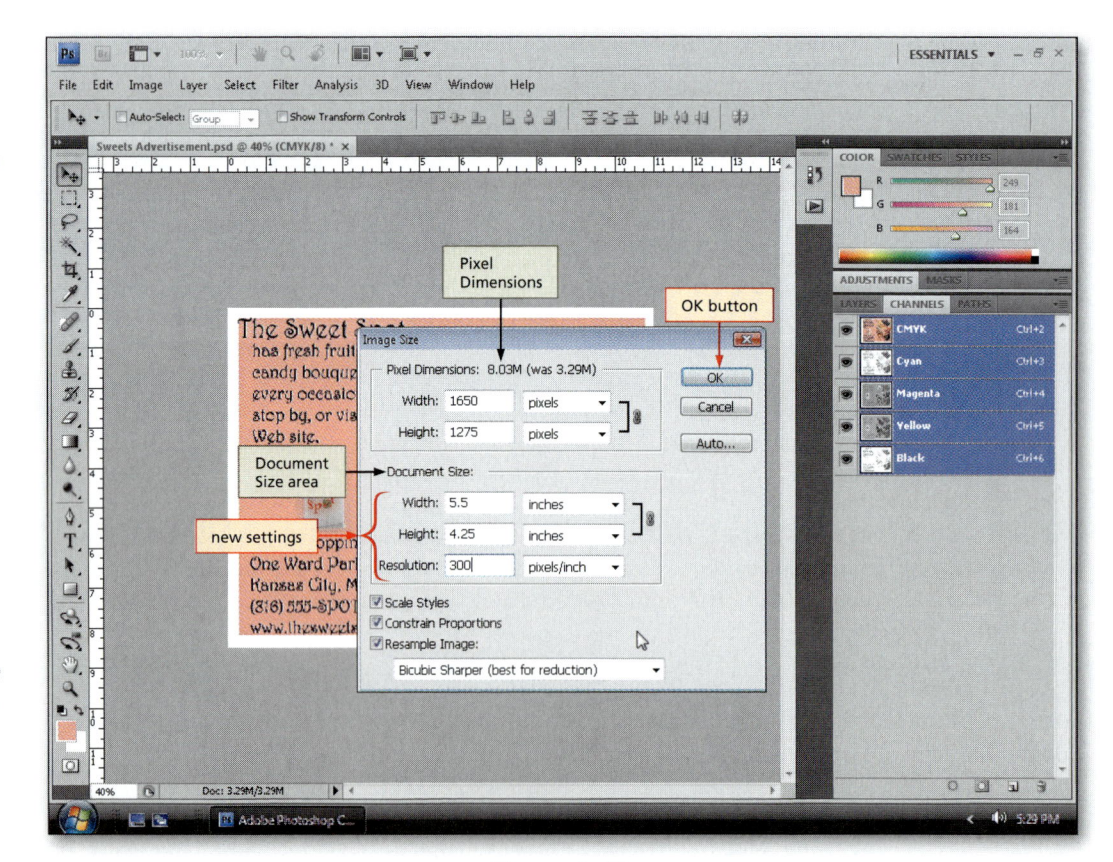

Figure 6–61

3

- Click the OK button to close the dialog box and apply the settings.
- Change the magnification of the document window, if necessary.

Printing Color Separations

Graphic professionals sometimes use print shops, labs, or service bureaus for their advanced printing needs. Service bureaus typically use image setters to create high quality prints. An **image setter** is a high-resolution output device that can transfer electronic files directly to photosensitive paper, plates, or film. While many service bureaus can resize and edit color at the time of printing, you save both time and money by performing these prepress tasks ahead of time in Photoshop. **Prepress tasks** are the various printing-related services performed before ink actually is put on the printed page.

When preparing your image for prepress, and working with CMYK images or images with spot color, you can print each color channel as a separate page. Photoshop also has a Split Channels command on the Channels panel menu that will split the channels into separate document windows for view and adjusting, if desired. Different service bureaus and labs require different kinds of submissions that are highly printer dependent. Even when supplying a composite for reference by the service bureau, you might want to print color separations for proofing purposes. Separations help you see if your composite file will separate correctly and help you catch other mistakes that might not be apparent by looking at the composite. The following steps print color separations.

> **BTW**
>
> **Printing**
> The Photoshop Print dialog box displays many choices for printing locations, scaled versions, and page setup. If you want to print the color separations in landscape mode, click the Page Setup button, click the Layout tab, click the Orientation box arrow, and then click Landscape.

To Print Color Separations

1
- Ready the printer attached to your system.
- Click File on the menu bar and then click Print to display the Print dialog box.
- Click the Color Handling box arrow to display its list (Figure 6–62).

2
- Click Separations in the list.
- Click the Print button to display your printer-dependent Print dialog box.
- Click the Print button or the appropriate button for your printer.

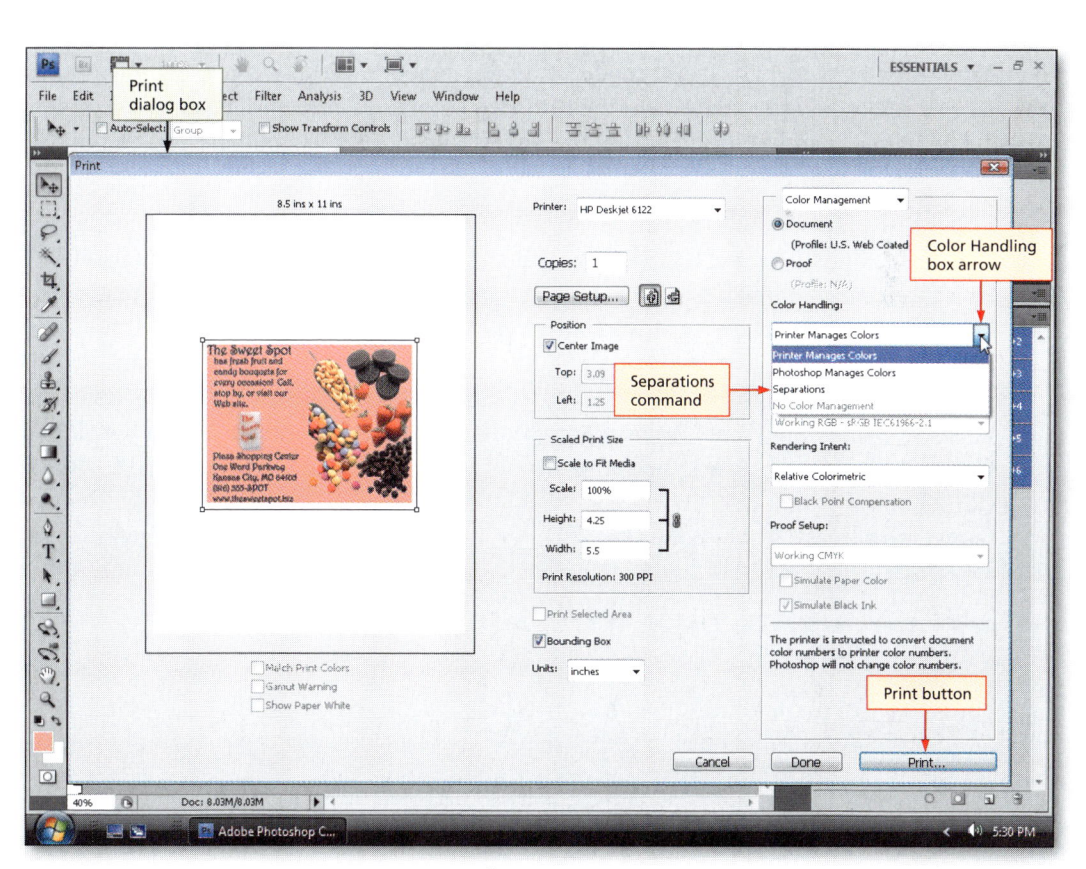

Figure 6–62

> **BTW**
>
> **Printing Versions**
> Printing a version with resampling and without resampling allows you to understand the difference visually.

To Save and Close the Four-Color Version

The following steps save and close the four-color version.

1 Press CTRL+S.

2 Click the Close button on the document window title bar.

To Quit Photoshop

The chapter is complete. The final step is to quit Photoshop.

1 Click the Close button on the right side of the Photoshop title bar.

Chapter Summary

In this chapter, you used a master copy of an image as the basis for creating four new versions. First, you created a floating image with the background removed by using an alpha channel. You learned various ways to create black-and-white, sepia, and duotone images. Then you created a logo with warped text and used an action to embellish it. You recorded an action to place the logo whenever you need it in a publication. Finally, for the version of the image used for an advertisement insert, you placed the logo, imported the floating image, and created additional text. You converted the image to LAB Color mode, and then converted it to CMYK color. Among the prepress activities, you resized and resampled the image, and then printed color separations.

The items listed below include all the new Photoshop skills you have learned in this chapter:

1. View Channels (PS 377)
2. Select Using a Channel (PS 379)
3. Create an Alpha Channel (PS 380)
4. Edit the Alpha Channel (PS 382)
5. Delete a Background Using an Alpha Channel (PS 383)
6. Desaturate (PS 386)
7. Create a Black-and-White Adjustment (PS 387)
8. Create a Sepia Image Using Selective Color (PS 390)
9. Convert an Image to Duotone (PS 391)
10. Warp Text (PS 398)
11. Display the Actions Panel (PS 403)
12. Append Action Sets (PS 404)
13. Play an Action (PS 405)
14. Create a New Action Set (PS 407)
15. Create a New Action (PS 408)
16. Record an Action (PS 409)
17. Test the Action (PS 412)
18. Save an Action Set (PS 412)
19. Convert to LAB Color (PS 417)
20. Resize a File with Resampling (PS 419)
21. Print Color Separations (PS 421)

Learn It Online

Test your knowledge of chapter content and key terms.

Instructions: To complete the Learn It Online exercises, start your browser, click the Address bar, and then enter the Web address scsite.com/pscs4/learn. When the Photoshop CS4 Learn It Online page is displayed, click the link for the exercise you want to complete and then read the instructions.

Chapter Reinforcement TF, MC, and SA
A series of true/false, multiple choice, and short answer questions that test your knowledge of the chapter content.

Flash Cards
An interactive learning environment where you identify chapter key terms associated with displayed definitions.

Practice Test
A series of multiple choice questions that test your knowledge of chapter content and key terms.

Who Wants To Be a Computer Genius?
An interactive game that challenges your knowledge of chapter content in the style of a television quiz show.

Wheel of Terms
An interactive game that challenges your knowledge of chapter key terms in the style of the television show *Wheel of Fortune*.

Crossword Puzzle Challenge
A crossword puzzle that challenges your knowledge of key terms presented in the chapter.

Apply Your Knowledge

Reinforce the skills and apply the concepts you learned in this chapter.

Creating an Alpha Channel

Instructions: Start Photoshop and perform the customization steps found on pages PS 7 through PS 9. Open the Apply 6-1 Fruit file from the Chapter06 folder of the Data Files for Students. You can access the Data Files for Students on the DVD that accompanies this book. See the inside back cover of this book for instructions on downloading the Data Files for Students, or contact your instructor for information about accessing the required files.

You will edit the file to create an alpha channel, removing a background. You are to remove the background, make tonal adjustments, and then add the text to create the photo shown in Figure 6–63 on the next page.

Continued >

PS 424 Photoshop Chapter 6 Creating Color Channels and Actions

Apply Your Knowledge continued

Figure 6–63

Perform the following tasks:

1. On the File menu, click Save As. Save the image on your USB flash drive as a PSD file, with the file name Apply 6-1 Fruit Edited.

2. On the Layers panel, right-click the Background layer and then click Duplicate Layer. Name the new layer, edits. Select only the edits layer, and hide the Background layer by clicking its visibility icon.

3. Click the Channels panel and then, one at a time, view each channel independent of the others. Decide which channel has the most contrast to facilitate removing the background.

4. First, to select the background so only it is visible:

    a. Use the Magic Wand tool with a Tolerance setting of 20. Click many times to select the different shades of color in the background. You will not be able to select everything.

    b. If some of the fruit or bowl becomes selected, select the Elliptical Marquee tool. On the options bar, click the Subtract from selection button. Carefully select the fruit or bowl, which will remove it from the background selection.

    c. Select the Rectangular Marquee tool. On the options bar, click the Add to selection button. Carefully draw large rectangles on the four edges of the photo to add the remaining pixels to the section. Do not include the fruit or bowls. If some of the plant becomes selected, you will remove it in the next step.

5. Next, to create the alpha channel:
   a. On the Channels panel, select the channel with the most contrast.
   b. Click the Save selection as channel button on the Channels panel status bar. Press CTRL+D to deselect.
   c. Select the new channel. With black as the foreground color, use the Brush tool to paint with black any areas of the fruit, bowls, or plant that are not black. Use the bracket keys to change the size of the brush as necessary.
   d. Select the Eraser tool and erase any remaining background spots, so only the fruit, bowls, and plant are black.
6. To delete the background:
   a. Select the Magic Wand tool and then click the white area.
   b. In the Channels panel, click the RGB composite channel, and then press the DELETE key.
   c. Press CTRL+D to deselect. If some areas of background remain, select the alpha channel, make the channel with the highest contrast visible, and then paint them with white.
7. Save the document.
8. Using the Layer menu, flatten the image. Discard any hidden layers.
9. On the Image menu, point to Mode and then click Lab Color to convert the image. On the Channels panel, access the Lightness channel. On the Adjustments panel, access the settings for Levels. Drag both the black and white sliders toward the middle until a strong contrast is displayed. Click the composite channel and verify your adjustments. If you do not like the changes, click the previous state on the History panel and try again.
10. Convert the image to CMYK and click the OK button in each of the resulting dialog boxes, if necessary. Click Image on the menu bar, point to Adjustments, and then click Channel Mixer. Select the Black channel and drag the Black slider to the left until the avocados are lighter. Make any other Channel Mixer changes that cause the colors to look more vivid. Close the Channel Mixer dialog box.
11. To create the text:
    a. Click the Horizontal Type Tool (T) button on the Tools panel.
    b. On the options bar, choose the Harlow Solid Italic font, or a similar font on your system, using Figure 6–63 as a guide. Choose a font size of 100. Choose Smooth in the list of anti-aliasing methods. Choose a gray font color. Your alignment may be different if you use a different font.
    c. Drag a text box that cover the canvas, leaving .25 inches at the top and right margins.
    d. On the options bar, click the Right align text button. Type Have you and then press the ENTER key twice.
    e. Click the Left align text button. Type eaten and then press the ENTER key three times.
    f. Click the Right align text button. Type your five today? to complete the text.
    g. On the options bar, click the Commit any current edits button.
12. Save the image with the name Apply 6-1 Fruit Complete.
13. To resize the image for printing on a desktop printer:
    a. On the Image menu, click Image Size.
    b. Click the Resample Image check box to deselect it.
    c. Type 9 in the Width box.
    d. Click the OK button.
14. Ready your printer. Print color separations in Landscape mode and turn them in to your instructor.
15. Quit Photoshop without saving the resized file.

Extend Your Knowledge

Extend the skills you learned in this chapter and experiment with new skills. You may need to use Help to complete the assignment.

Adding Spot Colors to a Print

Instructions: Start Photoshop and perform the customization steps found on pages PS 7 through PS 9. Open the Extend 6-1 Spot Color file from the Chapter06 folder of the Data Files for Students. See the inside back cover of this book for instructions on downloading the Data Files for Students, or contact your instructor for information about accessing the required files. The purpose of this exercise is to add two spot colors to a four-color travel flyer. The two inks are PANTONE shades, not contained in the standard CMYK range. The file contains two extra channels with saved text selections that will be loaded and recolored. The final edited photo is displayed in Figure 6–64.

Figure 6–64

Perform the following tasks:
1. Press SHIFT+CTRL+S to save the image on your USB flash drive as a PSD file, with the file name Extend 6-1 Spot Color Complete.
2. To convert the image from RGB mode to CMYK mode:
   a. Point to Mode on the Image menu, then click CMYK Color.
   b. When Photoshop displays a dialog box, click the Don't Merge button, and then click the OK button to accept any default settings.
3. Click the Channels panel tab to activate the panel.
4. Click Select on the menu bar and then click Load Selection to open the Load Selection dialog box. (*Hint:* read the topic, Save and Load Selections, in Photoshop Help.)

5. Click the Channel box arrow, click the Saint Basil's Cathedral channel, and then click the OK button to load the first text channel and display the selection marquee in the document window.
6. Click the Channels panel menu button and then click New Spot Channel to open the New Spot Channel dialog box.
7. Type 100 in the Solidity box and click the color box to access a color selection dialog box. If the Select Spot Color dialog box appears, click the Color Libraries button to display the Color Libraries dialog box.
8. Click the Book box arrow and then click PANTONE metallic coated in the list. Scroll in the color bar and select an appropriate color.
9. Click the OK button to close the Color Libraries dialog box. Click the OK button again to close the New Spot Channel dialog box.
10. Repeat Steps 4 through 9 for the World Wide Travel, Inc channel. Choose a color from the PANTONE pastel coated colors.
11. Save the image again.
12. Use the SAVE AS command to save a copy of the file as Extend 6-1 Spot Color Complete in the Photoshop DCS 2.0 (*.EPS) in the format, which saves the file in a format that contains the extra spot channels.
13. Submit the assignment in the format specified by your instructor.

Make It Right

Analyze a project and correct all errors and/or improve the design.

Fixing a Grainy Photo Using Channels

Instructions: Start Photoshop and perform the customization steps found on pages PS 7 through PS 9. Open the Make It Right 6-1 Grainy file from the Data Files for Students and save it as Make It Right 6-1 Grainy Edited in the PSD file format.

You have a poor quality photo of an image that you need for a brochure. Because the ISO settings on your camera were set too high, there is a lot of visual noise in the pixels, which makes the image appear grainy. You will use channels to fix the problem.

Perform the following tasks:
Access the Channels panel and click each color channel one at a time. Notice that the Red and Green channels appear fine but the Blue channel is full of noise and pixilation. With the Blue channel selected, click the visibility icon next to the RGB master channel. On the menu bar, click Filter, point to Blur, and then click Gaussian Blur to open the Gaussian Blur dialog box (Figure 6–65 on the next page). Adjust the Radius, blurring the Blue channel to reduce some of the noise in the photo. On the menu bar, click Filter, point to Noise, and then click Reduce Noise. Adjust the settings to reduce the noise and pixilation further. When you are happy with the outcome, save the file and turn it in to your instructor.

Continued >

Make It Right *continued*

Figure 6–65

In the Lab

Design and/or create a publication using the guidelines, concepts, and skills presented in this chapter. Labs are listed in order of increasing difficulty.

Lab 1: Creating a Frost Effect Using Channels

Problem: You need a photo of a field with an early frost on the ground for a collage, but it is in the middle of the summer and everything is green. You will use your knowledge of channels to make the grass and trees look as though they have frost on them. The finished product is displayed in Figure 6–66.

Figure 6–66

Instructions: Perform the following tasks:
1. Start Photoshop. Perform the customization steps found on pages PS 7 through PS 9.
2. Open the file Lab 6-1 Green Grass from the Chapter06 folder of the Data Files for Students. You can access the Data Files for Students on the DVD that accompanies this book. See the inside back cover of this book for instructions on downloading the Data Files for Students, or contact your instructor for information about accessing the required files.
3. Save the file as Lab 6-1 White Frost. Browse to your USB flash drive storage device. Click the Save button. If Photoshop displays a dialog box, click the OK button.
4. If necessary, double-click the Layers panel tab to display the layers. Right-click the Background layer and then click Duplicate Layer on the context menu. Name the new layer, frost.
5. At the top of the Layers panel, click the Blending Mode box arrow and then click Lighten.
6. Double-click the Adjustments panel tab to access the Adjustments panel. Click the Channel Mixer icon to display its settings. (*Hint:* the Channel Mixer icon is the last one in the second row.)
   a. Click the Monochrome check box to select it.
   b. Type 200 in the Red box.
   c. Type 100 in the Green box.
   d. Type –74 in the Blue box.
   e. Type 0 in the Contrast box, if necessary.
7. Double-click the Layers panel tab and then select the Background layer.
8. To select the sky:
   a. Click the Channels panel tab to access the Channels panel.
   b. Notice that an alpha channel has been created previously, and named, sky. Click the sky channel.
   c. Click the Load channel as selection button on the status bar.
   d. Click the RGB channel to return to the composite.
9. To load the channel and create the sky layer:
   a. Click the Layers panel tab.
   b. On the menu bar, click Select and then click Load Selection to display the Load Selection dialog box.
   c. Click the Channel box arrow and then click sky in the list, if necessary.
   d. Click the OK button to close the Load Selection dialog box and to display the selection marquee in the document window.
   e. Press CTRL+J to create a new layer. Name the layer, sky.
   f. On the Layers panel, drag the new sky layer above the others.
10. Save the file again.
11. Flatten the image and then save the file in the JPEG format and submit it to your instructor as directed.

In the Lab

Lab 2: Using Predefined Actions

Problem: Your cousin wants you to use her senior picture to create an invitation to a graduation open house. You decide to investigate Photoshop's predefined actions to look for a specialized frame that you can apply to the photo. The finished product is displayed in Figure 6–67 on the next page.

Continued >

In the Lab continued

Figure 6–67

Instructions:
1. Start Photoshop. Perform the customization steps found on pages PS 7 through PS 9.
2. Open the file Lab 6-2 Senior Picture from the Chapter06 folder of the Data Files for Students. You can access the Data Files for Students on the DVD that accompanies this book. See the inside back cover of this book for instructions on downloading the Data Files for Students, or contact your instructor for information about accessing the required files.
3. Click the Save As command on the File menu. Type `Lab 6-2 Invitation` as the file name. Browse to your USB flash drive storage device. Click the Save button. If Photoshop displays a dialog box, click the OK button.
4. Select the Elliptical Marquee tool. On the options bar, click the New selection button if necessary. Drag a large selection that encompasses the face and neck of the girl. Without clicking anywhere else, drag the selection to center it. Some of the selection may overlap the top and bottom edges.
5. Press ALT+F9 to display the Actions panel. If the Frames action set is not listed, click the panel menu button, and then click Frames. If necessary, click the right pointing triangle of the Frames action set to display the actions stored in the set. Scroll down and click the Vignette (selection) action.
6. Click the Play selection button on the Actions panel status bar. When the action pauses to request a feather selection, type 5 in the Feather Radius box, if necessary. Click the OK button.
7. When the action is complete, close the Actions panel. On the Layers panel, select the layer of the vignette itself and then select the Move tool. In the document window, drag the vignette to the right.
8. Select the Magic Wand tool on the Tools panel. On the options bar, click the Add to selection button, if necessary. In the document window, click to select the white areas around the vignette. Use the Color panel to choose an off-white or beige color. Use the Paint Bucket tool to fill the white areas with the color.

9. Click the Horizontal Type Tool (T) button on the Tools panel.
10. To adjust the text settings:
    a. On the options bar, select the Lucida Handwriting font family or a similar font.
    b. Set the font style to Italic.
    c. Set the font size to 60.
    d. Set the anti-aliasing method to Smooth.
    e. Click the Center text button. Choose a black font color.
11. Drag a text box that fills the left side of the image. In the text box, type `You are invited to Lindsey's open house, Saturday, June 6th, 2010, 1:00-4:00 p.m.`, pressing the ENTER key as necessary to create the lines shown in Figure 6–67. When you are finished, click the Commit any current edits button on the options bar. Use the Move tool to adjust the placement of the text box if needed.
12. When you are finished, use the Flatten Image command to flatten all of the layers into the background. Save the flattened image.
13. E-mail your instructor with the Lab 6-2 Invitation file as an attachment, or see your instructor for another way to submit this assignment.

In the Lab

Lab 3: Creating an Attention Getter

Problem: Your summer job is working with a Girl Scout Day Camp center whose theme is exploration. You have taken a picture of two Brownies who just visited the face-painting booth. You are to edit their photo and place it in a moon scene backdrop, creating a picture they can send to their grandmother. The edited photo is shown Figure 6–68.

Instructions: Perform the following tasks: Start Photoshop. Perform the customization steps found on pages PS 7 through PS 9. Open the Lab 6-3 Brownies photo from the Chapter 06 folder of the Data Files for Students. You can access the Data Files for Students on the DVD that accompanies this book. See the inside back cover of this book for instructions on downloading the Data Files for Students, or contact your instructor for information about accessing the required files. Select the background and create an alpha channel. Delete the background and edit as necessary to display only the girls. Open the file named Lab 6-3 Moon. Arrange the documents side by side and then use the Move tool to drag the moon image into the Lab 6-3 Brownies document window. Adjust and scale the layers as necessary. Use the Adjustments panel to adjust the levels and contrast so the girls match the moon scene. Create a Warped text box with white lettering, as shown in Figure 6–68. Save the file as Lab 6-3 Brownies on the Moon in the PSD format.

Figure 6–68

Cases and Places

Apply your creative thinking and problem-solving skills to design and implement a solution.

• Easier   •• More Difficult

• 1: Create a Sepia Tone Image

A wedding planner wants to use a picture of a tulip on her business cards. The tulip is in full color, but her business cards are going to use brown spot color on ivory paper. Open the Case 6-1 Tulip image that is located in the Chapter06 folder. Save the image on your storage device with the name Case 6-1 Tulip Edited. Use an alpha channel to remove the background. Flatten the image. Convert the image to grayscale and then convert the image to duotone. When the Duotone dialog box is displayed, double-click the Color Picker and choose a sepia color. Type sepia in the Name box. Click the OK button. Convert the image to CMYK color. Save the image again and then print a copy.

• 2: Create Multiple Versions

Choose a digital photo that you have recently taken. Open it in Photoshop and then save it with the name Case 6-2 Master Copy. Create an Edits layer. Use the techniques learned in this chapter to create three versions of the photo: one in black and white, one with background images removed, and one in CMYK Color mode. Choose one of the three versions and then add a decorative shape with text. Print all three versions.

•• 3: Apply an Action

Open any image in Photoshop. On the Actions panel, click the panel menu button. Choose one of the stored action sets, such as Image Effects. When the stored action set is displayed on the Actions panel, if necessary open the set to display the actions. On a piece of paper, write down the name of the first action. Click the Play recording button. On the paper, write a short description of what happened to the photo. If the action does not play, try to figure out why. For example, if the action has the word selection in parentheses, you first must make a selection before playing the action. After writing down your description, open the action itself by clicking the right-pointing triangle. Scroll through the steps in the panel and compare that to your description. On the History panel, click the original file thumbnail and then choose another action to play. Repeat the process until you have tried five different actions. Turn in your paper to your instructor.

•• 4: Create an Actions Set

Make It Personal

Your school wants to use its name and address in many pieces of artwork, such as the banner at the top of their Web page, on stationery, on promotional pieces, and on a student resume template. Create an Actions set named Personal Actions. Record a new action named School Address, which displays a text box with the school's name and address. Use an Arial font with a font size of 14. Choose a font color that matches one of your school colors. Save the Personal Actions atn file on your storage device. Open one of your previous Photoshop assignments, load the action set if necessary, and then play back the action.

•• 5: Evaluate Tonal Adjustments

Working Together

Graphic designers who have art skills, and those who can make tonal and color adjustments, are in demand in the marketplace. To practice these skills, your instructor has divided you into teams for a group project. Ask each member of your team to bring in a digital picture of his or her choice. As a group, examine the pictures and select the one that needs the most color correction. Distribute a copy to each member, by e-mail or on a class Web server. Then, individually have each member make color adjustments using the Channel Mixer and other tools on the Adjustments submenu. Choose the photo with the best tonal adjustments and submit it to your instructor.

Appendix A
Project Planning Guidelines

Using Project Planning Guidelines

The process of communicating specific information to others is a learned, rational skill. Computers and software, especially Adobe Photoshop CS4, can help you develop ideas and present detailed information to a particular audience.

Using Adobe Photoshop CS4, you can edit photos and create original graphics. Computer hardware and productivity software, such as Adobe Photoshop CS4, reduces much of the laborious work of drafting and revising projects. Some design professionals use sketch pads or storyboards, others compose directly on the computer, and others have developed unique strategies that work for their own particular thinking and artistic styles.

No matter what method you use to plan a project, follow specific guidelines to arrive at a final product that presents an image or images clearly and effectively (Figure A–1). Use some aspects of these guidelines every time you undertake a project, and others as needed in specific instances. For example, in determining content for a project, you may decide an original graphic would communicate the idea more effectively than an existing photo. If so, you would create this graphical element from scratch.

Determine the Project's Purpose

Begin by clearly defining why you are undertaking this assignment. For example, you may want to correct camera errors and adjust image flaws. Or you may want to create a graphic for a specific publishing or marketing purpose. Once you clearly understand the purpose of your task, begin to draft ideas of how best to communicate this information.

Analyze Your Audience

Learn about the people who will use, analyze, or view your work. Where are they employed? What are their educational backgrounds? What are their expectations? What questions do they have? Design experts suggest drawing a mental picture of these people or finding photographs of people who fit this profile so that you can develop a project with the audience in mind.

PROJECT PLANNING GUIDELINES

1. DETERMINE THE PROJECT'S PURPOSE
Why are you undertaking the project?

2. ANALYZE YOUR AUDIENCE
Who are the people who will use your work?

3. GATHER POSSIBLE CONTENT
What graphics exist, and in what forms?

4. DETERMINE WHAT CONTENT TO PRESENT TO YOUR AUDIENCE
What image will communicate the project's purpose to your audience in the most effective manner?

Figure A–1

By knowing your audience members, you can tailor a project to meet their interests and needs. You will not present them with information they already possess, and you will not omit the information they need to know.

Example: Your assignment is to raise the profile of your college's nursing program in the community. How much does the audience know about your college and the nursing curriculum? What are the admission requirements? How many of the applicants admitted complete the program? What percent pass the state nursing boards?

Gather Possible Content

Rarely are you in a position to develop all the material for a project. Typically, you would begin by gathering existing images and photos, or designing new graphics based on information that may reside in spreadsheets or databases. Design work for clients often must align with and adhere to existing marketing campaigns or publicity materials. Web sites, pamphlets, magazine and newspaper articles, and books could provide insights of how others have approached your topic. Personal interviews often provide perspectives not available by any other means. Consider video and audio clips as potential sources for material that might complement or support the factual data you uncover. Make sure you have all legal rights to any photographs you may use.

Determine What Content to Present to Your Audience

Experienced designers recommend writing three or four major ideas you want an audience member to remember after viewing your project. It also is helpful to envision your project's endpoint, the key fact or universal theme that you wish to emphasize. All project elements should lead to this ending point.

As you make content decisions, you also need to think about other factors. Presentation of the project content is an important consideration. For example, will your brochure be printed on thick, colored paper or transparencies? Will your photo be viewed in a classroom with excellent lighting and a bright projector, or will it be viewed on a notebook computer monitor? Determine relevant time factors, such as the length of time to develop the project, how long editors will spend reviewing your project, or the amount of time allocated for presenting your designs to the customer. Your project will need to accommodate all of these constraints.

Decide whether a graphic, photograph, or artistic element can express or emphasize a particular concept. The right hemisphere of the brain processes images by attaching an emotion to them, so in the long run, audience members are more apt to recall themes from graphics rather than those from the text.

Finally, review your project to make sure the theme still easily is identifiable and has been emphasized successfully. Is the focal point clear and presented without distraction? Does the project satisfy the requirements?

Summary

When creating a project, it is beneficial to follow some basic guidelines from the outset. By taking some time at the beginning of the process to determine the project's purpose, analyze the audience, gather possible content, and determine what content to present to the audience, you can produce a project that is informative, relevant, and effective.

Appendix B
Graphic Design Overview

Understanding Design Principles

Understanding a few basic design principles can catapult you to the next level of digital artistry. Beyond knowing how to use software, a graphic designer must know how to create effective and readable layouts no matter what the product type. In this Appendix you will learn the design principles, color theory, typography, and other technical knowledge required to create usable and successful graphic designs.

    A major goal in graphic design work, whether for print or Web page layout, is to guide the viewer's eyes toward some key point. Another major goal of design work is to convey a certain emotion — a project can have the effect of making the viewer feel relaxed, energetic, hungry, hopeful, or even anxious. By implementing a few basic principles of design, you can control your viewers' physical focus so they look where you want them to look as you steer them toward a desired emotion. Design principles typically include the following:

- Balance
- Contrast
- Dominance
- Proximity
- Repetition
- Closure
- Continuance
- Negative space
- Unity

Balance

Visual elements can be **balanced** within a design, just as items may be balanced on either side of a scale. Unbalanced designs can cause viewers to feel anxious or uncomfortable, or even like they are falling sideways out of their seats. Balance may be achieved symmetrically or asymmetrically. Symmetrical balance mirrors a visual element to achieve equilibrium (Figure B–1). Asymmetrical balance can be achieved by balancing a small, dark element with a large, light element (Figure B–2) or balancing one large element with several smaller elements (Figure B–3).

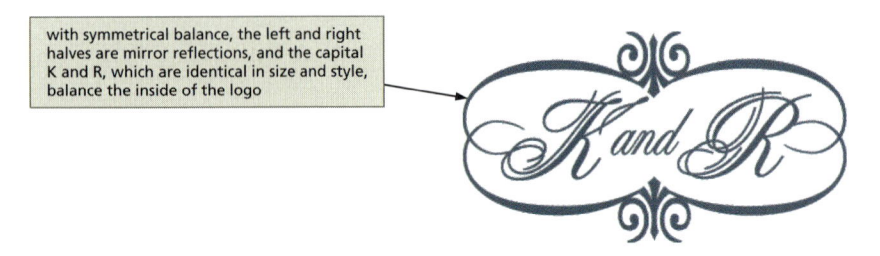

with symmetrical balance, the left and right halves are mirror reflections, and the capital K and R, which are identical in size and style, balance the inside of the logo

Figure B–1

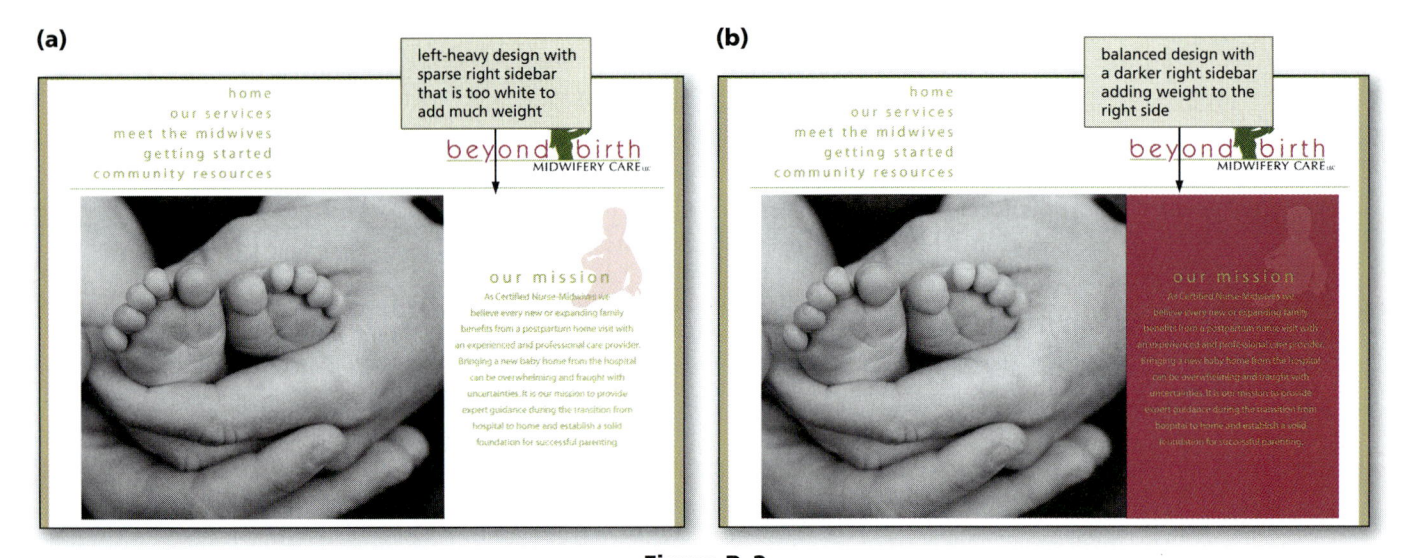

(a) left-heavy design with sparse right sidebar that is too white to add much weight

(b) balanced design with a darker right sidebar adding weight to the right side

Figure B–2

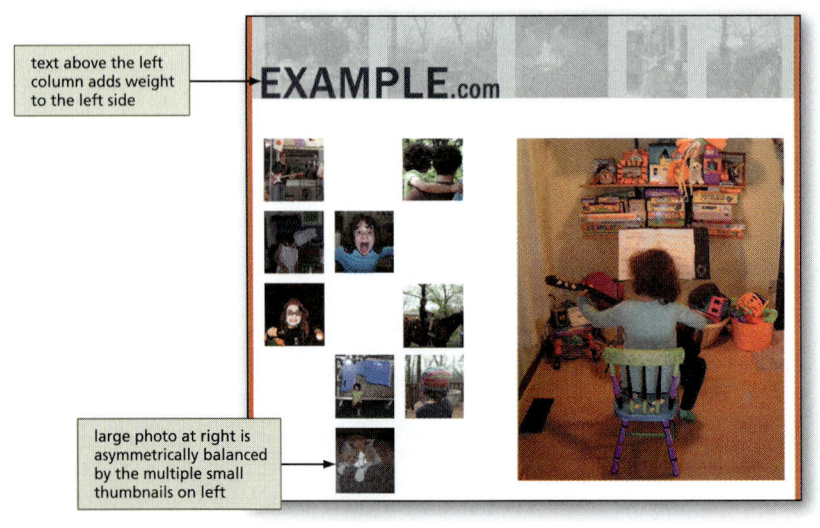

text above the left column adds weight to the left side

large photo at right is asymmetrically balanced by the multiple small thumbnails on left

Figure B–3

Contrast

Contrast describes the visual differences between elements; it adds variety to a design and helps to draw the viewer's focus. Differences in color, scale, quantity, or other characteristics of visual elements help to achieve contrast. The element that is different from the others draws the viewer's attention. In Figure B–4, the word, Projects, in white, contrasts against the other words on the page, and the viewer's eye is drawn to that word.

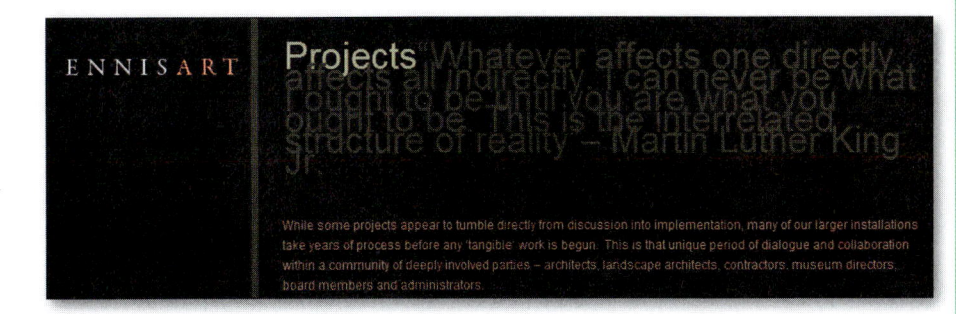

Figure B–4

Dominance

Dominance is a critical principle in controlling viewer focus. The dominant element in a design is the one to which a viewer's eyes and attention usually move first. An element's position within a design or its contrast to other elements can establish dominance. If you want your viewer to focus on a certain area of your design or on a specific design element, make it dominant, like the words, Comedy Night, in the poster shown in Figure B–5.

Figure B–5

Proximity

Proximity describes the relative space between elements. Related elements should be close to each other. Headings should be close to their related paragraph text, and product names should be close to their photos and prices. As shown in Figure B–6, when related items are not within close proximity of each other, the viewer may not know the items are related. When elements are too close, the design looks cluttered and text can become difficult to read. Strive for balance in your proximity.

Figure B–6

BTW

Natural Repetition Repetition occurs naturally in the petals around a flower, patterns on snakeskin, and polygons on turtle shells.

Repetition

Repeating a visual element helps to tie a design together. **Repetition** of color, shape, texture, and other characteristics can help to unify your design, create patterns, or impart a sense of movement (Figure B–7). Most Web sites repeat a design theme across all the pages so users know they are on the same site as they navigate from page to page. Repeated colors and layouts help to unify the overall Web site design.

Figure B–7

Closure

Not everything in a design must be composed of solid lines. Composing objects from small parts and spaces allows a design to breathe and creates visual interest. Under the concept of **closure**, the human brain will fill in the blanks to close or complete the object (Figure B–8).

Continuance

Once a viewer's eyes start to move across a page, they tend to keep moving — and you can exploit this **continuance** to guide their eyes exactly where you want to guide them. A dominant object can capture the viewer's initial focus, and diagonal lines within that dominant object can guide the viewer's eyes toward the focal point of your design (Figure B–9).

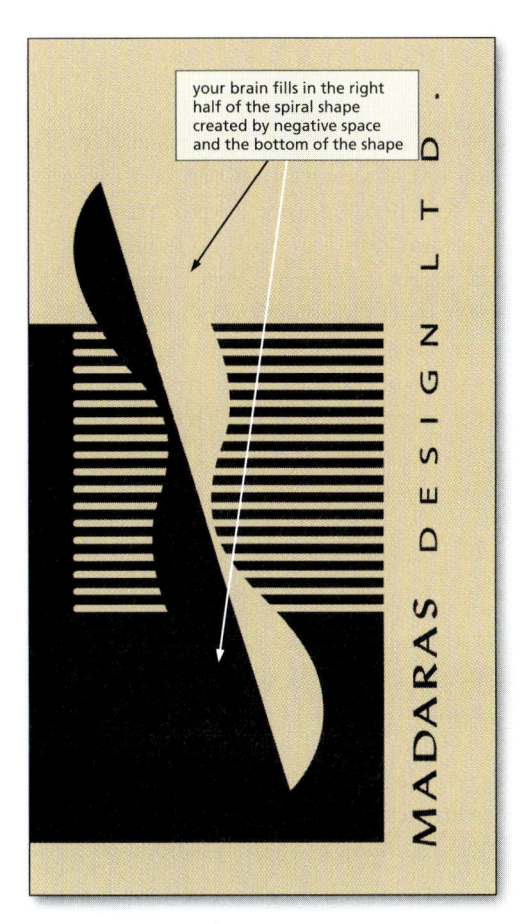

Figure B–8

Figure B–9

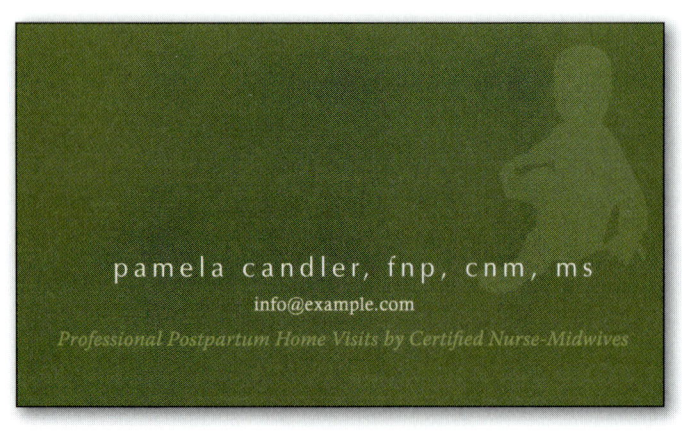

Negative Space

Negative space refers to the space in your design that does not contain information, or the space between elements. For example, the space between heading and paragraph text or the space between a logo and the company name, as shown in Figure B–10, is negative space. Without negative space, your design will feel cluttered, and viewers will have difficulty identifying on the focal point. Note that negative space, also called **white space**, does not literally translate to "white space," as negative space does not have to be white (Figure B–10).

Figure B–10

Unity

> **BTW**
> **Unity**
> Unity is not limited to elements in a specific piece of work; it can apply to multiple pieces. For example, a business card, Web site, letterhead, and product packaging that feature a similar color and style can help unify a business's identity.

Unity refers to the concept that all elements within a design work well together to form a whole. The individual images, textures, text, and negative space join together to create a single unified message or meaning. Unity can be created by applying a combination of basic design principles. Balanced elements alone do not produce a visually appealing design. The same is true for elements with appropriate proximity and negative space, good contrast, or clear dominance. No single design principle is responsible for a pleasing design. Instead, the combination of these principles creates a single unified design. Without unity, a design degrades into chaos and loses meaning. Of course, that is not a bad thing if chaos is the intentional message.

Layout Grids

> **BTW**
> **Dominant Object Placement**
> Placing an object at a certain location within a grid, such as the intersection of thirds or slightly above and to the right of center, helps to establish dominance.

A graphic designer needs to know where to place elements within a document or Web page. The use of grids makes it easy to align objects to each other and can help with balance and proximity. There are many standard grids that can be applied to Web page layouts or print layouts for standard paper sizes. One very popular grid system uses thirds, which is derived from the golden ratio.

Rule of Thirds and Golden Ratio The rule of thirds specifies that splitting a segment into thirds produces an aesthetically pleasing ratio. The rule of thirds is derived from a more complex mathematical concept called the golden ratio, which specifies segment ratios of long segment divided by short segment equal to about 1.618 — which is close enough to the rule of thirds that designers typically apply the rule of thirds rather than break out their slide rulers (Figure B–11).

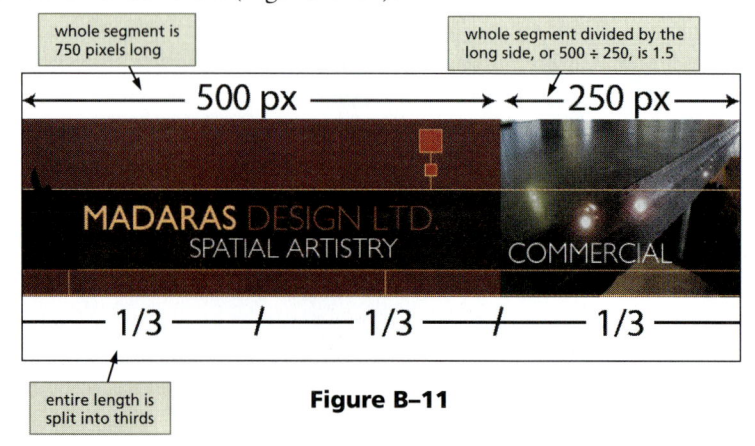

Figure B–11

Color Theory

Color can have a profound effect on the overall message a design conveys. Certain colors evoke specific emotions, and the way colors are combined can make the difference between readable copy and copy that is unable to be read.

Color Properties

Before you begin to work with color, it is important to understand the properties of color, which include hue, saturation, shade, tint, and value.

Hue refers to the tone, or actual color, such as red, yellow, or blue. Many color theorists interpret hue to mean pure color. A pure color, or hue, can be modified to create color variations. A basic color wheel, shown in Figure B–12, displays hue.

Saturation refers to the intensity of a color. As hues become less saturated, they create muted tones and pastels as they approach gray. As hues become more saturated, they appear very bright (Figure B–13).

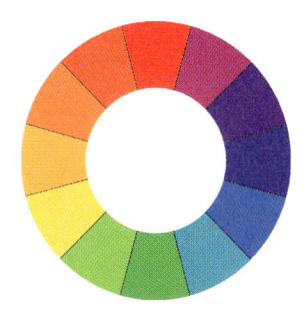

Figure B–12

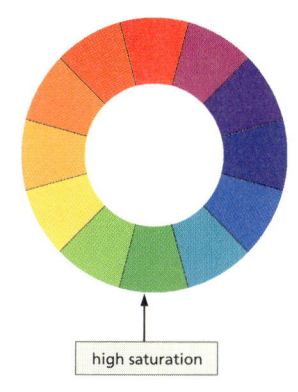

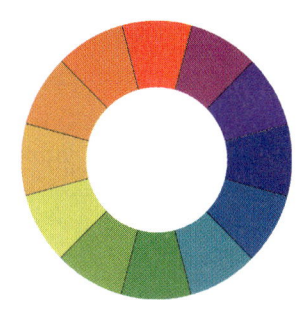

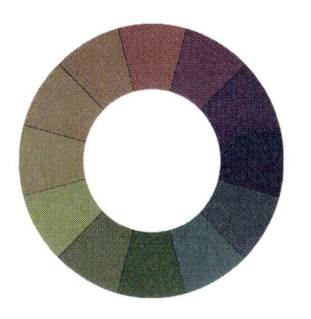

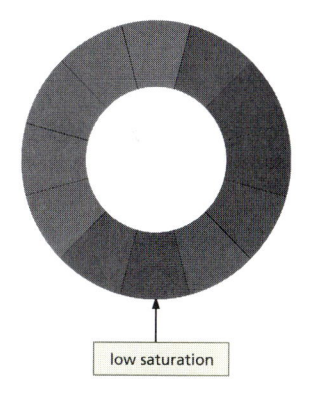

high saturation

Figure B–13

low saturation

Desaturated colors can produce mellow tones and evoke calm feelings (Figure B–14). Oversaturated colors can produce almost neon colors and cause excitement (Figure B–15). Sometimes it is appropriate to use very bright colors, such as in a picture book for children or a high-energy advertisement for a sports drink. Other times, bright, saturated colors produce the wrong feeling for your work.

desaturated hues can have a calming effect

Figure B–14

oversaturated hues can be hard on the eyes

Figure B–15

Figure B–16

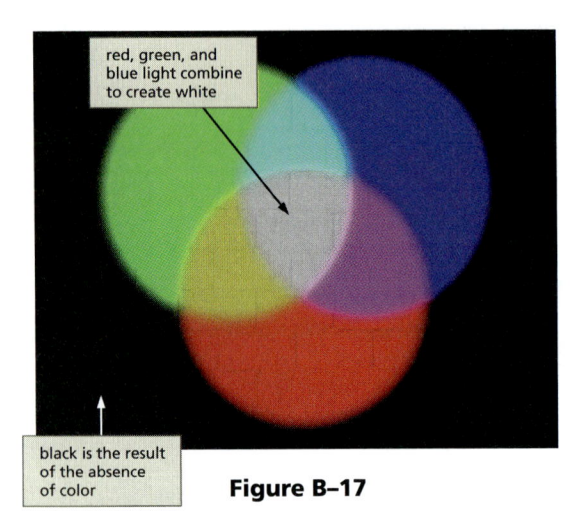

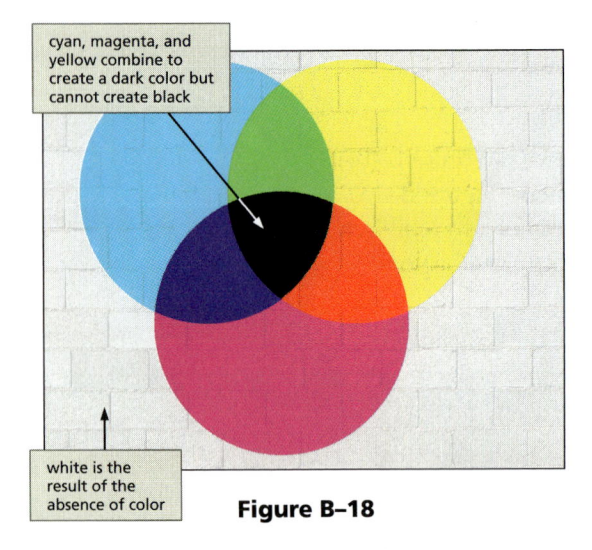

A **shade** is a mixture of a hue and black, producing a darker color. A **tint** is a mixture of a hue and white, producing a lighter color. A color's **value** describes its overall lightness or darkness. A tint has a higher value, while a shade has a lower value (Figure B–16). Mixing a hue with its shades, tints, and variations of saturation can lead to very harmonious color combinations.

Color Models

A color model describes the way in which colors combine to create other colors. The most commonly used color models are RGB, CMYK, and LAB. Each model has its strengths and weaknesses, and each is appropriate for a specific type of work.

The **RGB** color model mixes red, green, and blue light to create other colors. Computer monitors and TV screens use the RGB color model. All images used on a Web site must use the RGB color model because few Web browsers can display CMYK images. RGB is an additive color model, meaning colored light combines (light waves are added) to create other colors. The absence of all color in the RGB model results in black. As colored light is added, white is created, as shown in Figure B–17. RGB is also device dependent, because the colors you see depend on the viewing device. Different computer screens will display colors in the same photograph differently due to variances in the manufacturing process — and even component wear over time. Do not waste your time trying to get your Web site to display the same exact colors consistently from computer to computer. It is not possible.

Figure B–17

The **CMYK** color model mixes physical cyan, magenta, yellow, and black pigments (such as ink) to create other colors, and is used in color printing. CMYK is a subtractive color model. The absence of all color in the CMYK model results in white light, and, as colored pigment is added, light wavelengths are absorbed or subtracted, creating color (Figure B–18). Cyan, magenta, and yellow alone cannot create black; thus, the need for pure black in the CMYK model.

Unlike RGB and CMYK, which combine individual well-defined colors, the **LAB** color model combines levels of lightness with two color channels, a and b. One color channel ranges from green to magenta, while the other includes blue through yellow. By combining color ranges with lightness values, LAB is able to closely approximate the true human perception of

Figure B–18

BTW | LAB
LAB is sometimes written as L*a*b for lightness, color channel a, and color channel b.

color and thus is able to produce more colors than either RGB or CMYK. This makes it an ideal color model for photographers wanting to have access to every possible color in a photograph. LAB typically is used during photographic retouching and color correction. The image then is converted to RGB or CMYK for use with electronic media or print.

Psychological Considerations of Color

Colors can evoke both positive and negative emotions from people, and the influence of a color can differ between individuals and cultures. While the effect of color on people is not an exact science, there are some generalities.

White often is associated with cleanliness, purity, and hope. Doctors and brides in most Western cultures wear white. However, white is associated with death and mourning attire in some Eastern cultures. White is the most popular background color and offers great contrast for highly readable dark text.

Black often is used to represent evil, death, or mourning, but also mystery, intelligence, elegance, and power. Black text on a white background is the easiest to read.

Red is used in Western cultures to signify love, passion, and comfort — but also is used to represent sin, hell, and danger. Use dark reds to imply indulgence or fine living and brownish reds for designs dealing with Thanksgiving, harvest, or the fall season in general.

Green symbolizes many positives such as growth, tranquility, luck, money, and health, but it also symbolizes jealousy. Green can have a calming effect.

Blue often is cited as the favorite color by men. Like green, it evokes feelings of calmness and serenity. Blue implies authority, stability, loyalty, and confidence. However, it is one of the least appetizing colors, as there are few naturally blue foods. It also is associated with sadness and bad luck, as evidenced in blues music or phrases like "I've got the blues."

Yellow generally makes people happy. It is a highly visible and active color. However, too much yellow can lead to frustration and eye fatigue. Babies cry more in yellow rooms. Avoid using yellow as a page background and use it instead in smaller areas to draw attention.

Print Considerations for Color

The printing process cannot reproduce every color. Gamut refers to the range of printable colors and colors that cannot be printed are said to be *out of gamut*. If an out of gamut color exists in your document, the printer you are using will simply get as close to it as it can — but it will not be exact. Depending on the printer you have installed, the actual color produced can vary. Photoshop identifies out of gamut colors in the Color Picker with a small icon. If your document contains out of gamut colors, you have two options: change or replace the out of gamut color with one that is in gamut; or accept that the final print may not be exactly what you expected.

Web Considerations for Color

When working with color for the Web, the most important thing to remember is that colors will appear differently on different computers. Web sites look similar, but not exactly the same, from computer to computer. Years ago, Web designers used only the **Web-safe** colors, which was a set of 216 colors that supposedly appear the same on all monitors. This was due to the limitations of video subsystems at the time, as computer monitors could display only 256 specific colors. Microsoft Windows supported 256 specific colors, and Apple Macintosh supported a different 256 colors. Of the two sets, 216 were the same across both platforms; these 216 became the Web-safe palette. However, designers soon realized that only 22 of those 216 were truly the same between Windows and Macintosh; this subset was called the **really Web-safe** colors.

Photoshop displays a warning in the Color Picker for non–Web-safe colors. Modern computers (as well as cell phone browsers) can display millions of distinct colors, so limiting yourself to 216 Web-safe colors is no longer a necessity. In fact, it is extremely limiting, because the 216 Web-safe colors are generally very bright or very dark with few choices for pastels or saturation and value variances. Most designers do not use Web-safe colors for their designs.

> **BTW**
>
> **Using Web-Safe Colors**
> Use Web-safe colors if you know the site will be viewed on ancient computer systems; otherwise, allow yourself the full spectrum with the understanding the colors will vary slightly from computer to computer.

[gray looks lighter against maroon background]

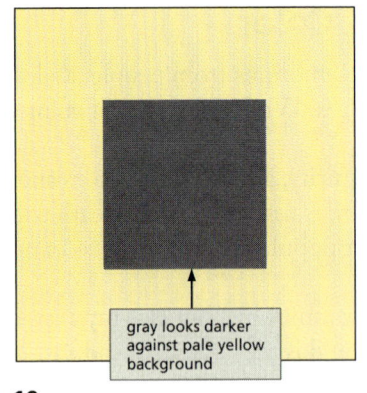

[gray looks darker against pale yellow background]

Figure B–19

Relativity

A color's relative lightness/darkness value can appear different depending on what other color neighbors it. The gray block in Figure B–22 looks lighter when against the dark red background and darker when against the light yellow background. Keep this in mind as you choose background/foreground relationships. A certain hue (or tint or shade) might look great when it is by itself, but you may not be so fond of it when used in close proximity to another certain color.

Color Schemes and Matching

Choosing colors that work well together and enforce the design's message can be difficult but worth the effort. The color scheme can make or break a design. Successful color matching requires an understanding of **color schemes**, which simply describes an organized method of matching colors based on their positions on a color wheel.

Figure B–12 on page APP 9 displayed a color wheel. While there are various color wheel models, the most popular uses the primary colors red, blue, and yellow (Figure B–20). Primary colors combine to create the secondary colors green, orange, and purple (Figure B–20). A primary and a secondary color combine to create a tertiary (third level) color (Figure B–20). More complex color wheels can include gradients to show varying saturation, tints, and shades (Figure B–21).

primary colors   **secondary colors**   **tertiary colors**

Figure B–20

saturation   **tints**   **shades**

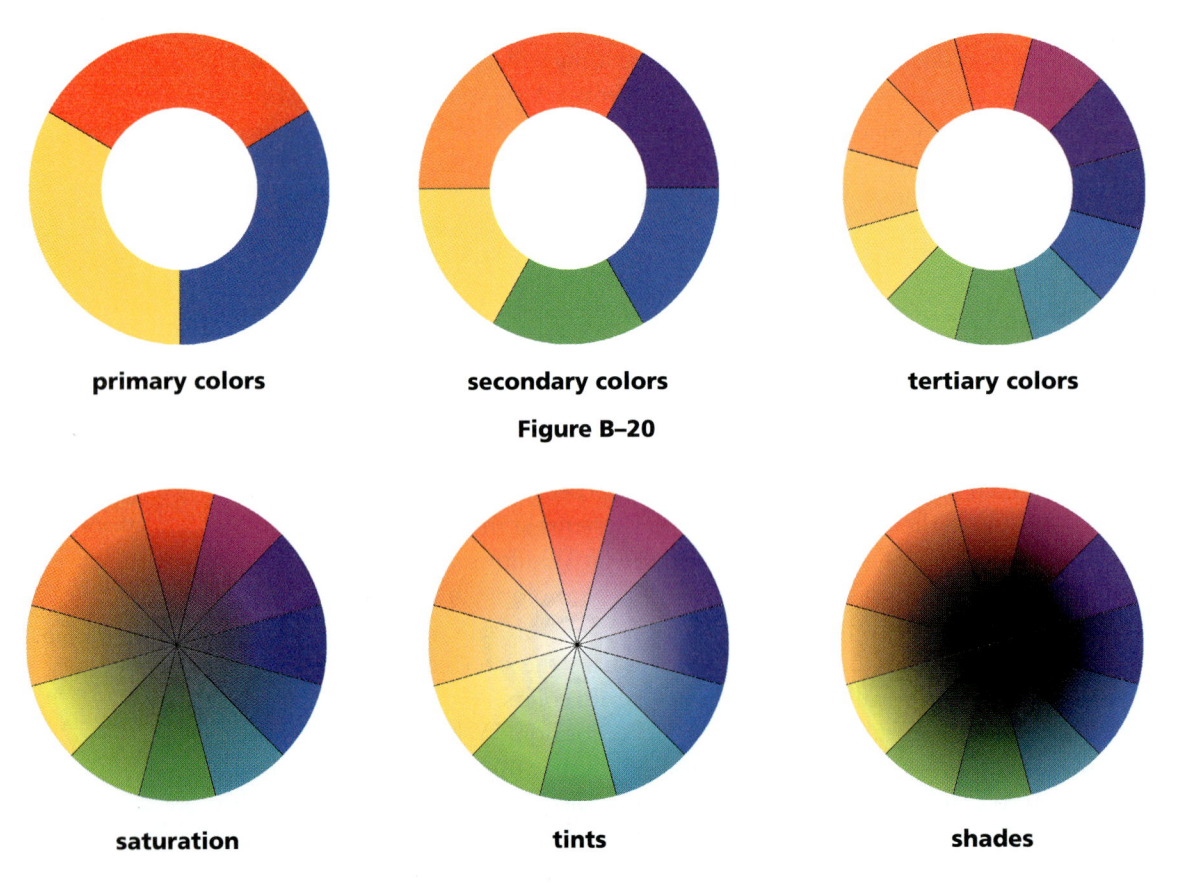

Figure B–21

Color Schemes A **monochromatic** color scheme is one that uses a single hue with a variety of shades and tints (Figure B–22). This is an easy color scheme to create. While a monochromatic color scheme can appear soothing, the lack of hue variance can leave it looking a bit boring.

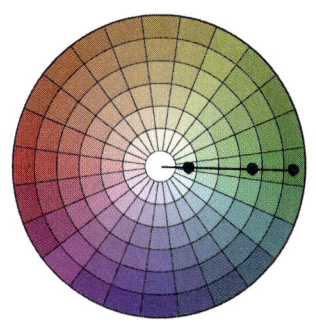

Figure B–22

A **complementary** color scheme uses colors directly across from each other on the color wheel. Their high contrast can look vibrant but also can be hard on the eyes. Avoid using complementary pairs in a foreground/background relationship, as shown in Figure B–23. Adjusting the saturation or substituting tints and shades makes this color scheme more workable.

BTW

Color Scheme Web Sites
Stand-alone color scheme software programs are available for purchase, but Adobe offers a free online service at kuler.adobe.com that lets you browse color schemes created by other users, modify them, and create and save your own.

bright complementary colors do not work well in a foreground/background relationship

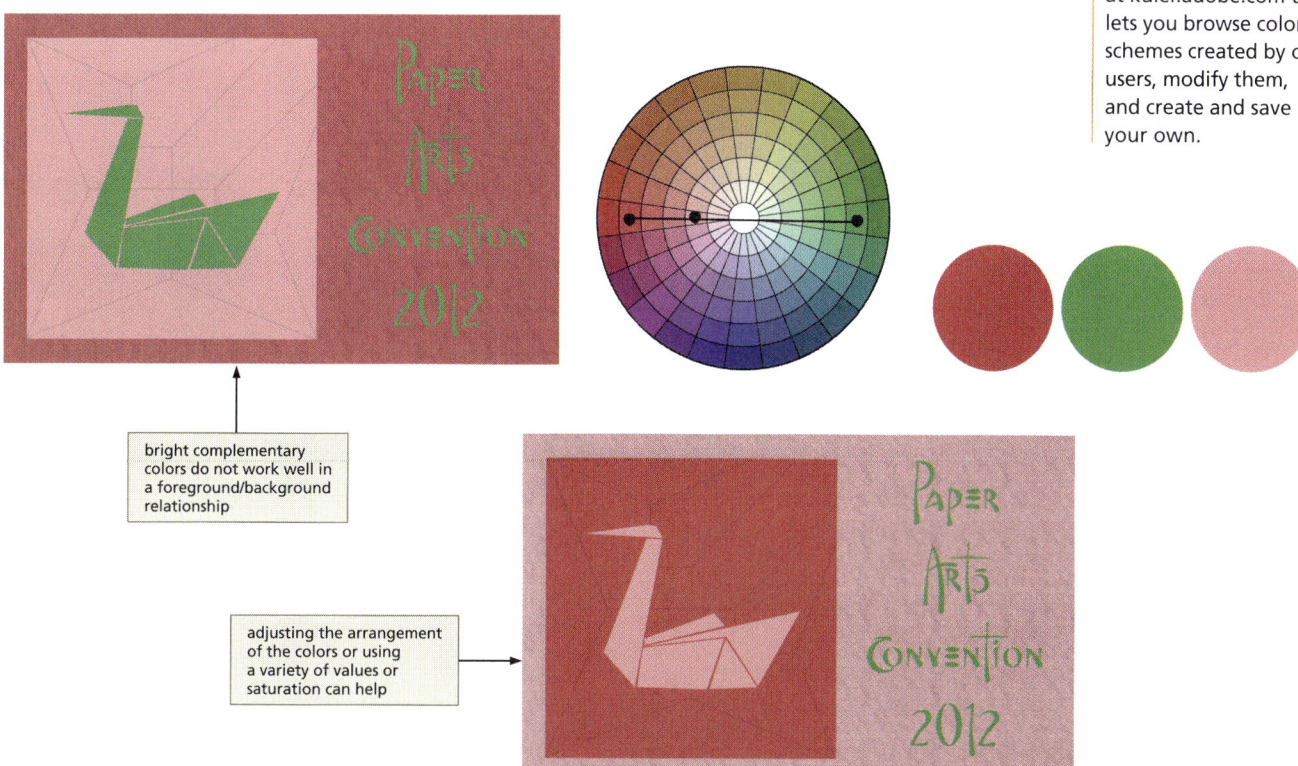

adjusting the arrangement of the colors or using a variety of values or saturation can help

Figure B–23

An **analogous** color scheme uses colors next to each other on the color wheel. This color scheme is generally very appealing and evokes positive feelings (Figure B–24). Be careful not to choose colors that are too far apart. A very wide range of analogous colors can appear mismatched.

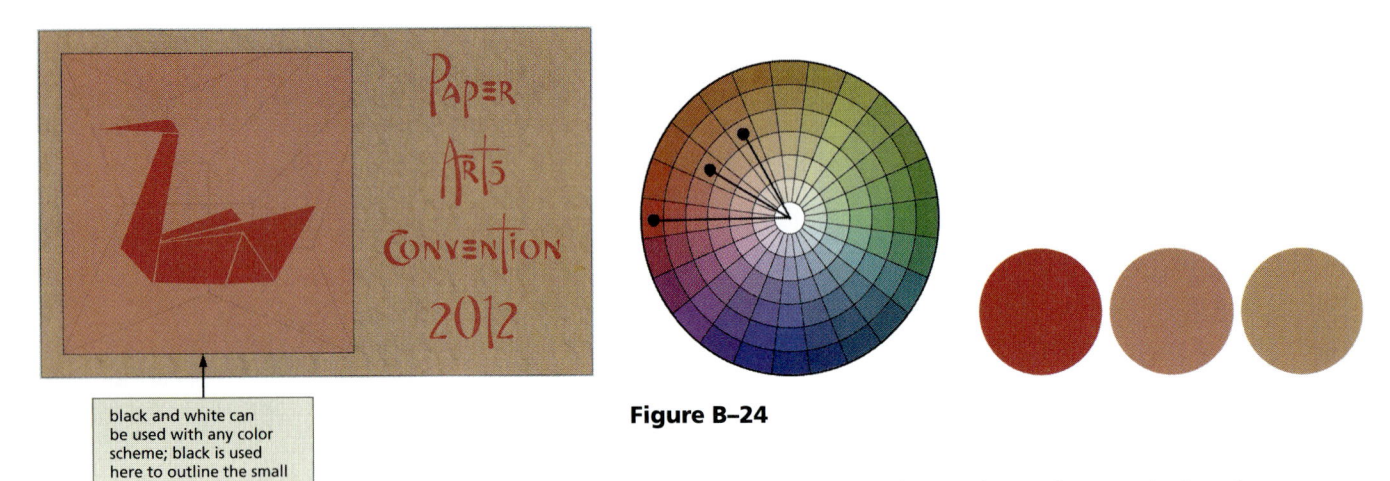

black and white can be used with any color scheme; black is used here to outline the small square to provide better contrast

Figure B–24

The **split-complementary** scheme uses a base color and, instead of its direct complement, the two colors on either side of its complement (Figure B–25). This scheme offers a lot of hue variance, and therefore excitement. However, if all the hues are overly saturated, split-complementary colors can be very harsh. Try keeping one hue saturated and use tints, shades, or desaturated colors for the rest of the scheme.

Figure B–25

Other color schemes such as triadic, tetradic, neutral, and an infinite number of custom schemes also exist. Using a color matching resource such as software or a Web site is a good way to help you get started choosing colors and allows you to experiment to see what you and your client like.

Typography

Typography is the art of working with text. Perhaps the two most important factors for graphic designers to address when working with text are visual appeal and readability. A dull text heading will not entice viewers to read the rest of the advertisement, but a beautiful text heading can be useless if it is not readable (Figure B–26).

Figure B–26

Readability

Readability is the measurement of how comfortable or easy it is for readers to read the text. Many factors contribute to overall readability. Commonly accepted readability factors include the following:

- Large text passages written in lowercase are easier to read than long text passages in uppercase.
- Regular text is easier to read than italicized text.
- Black text on a white background is easier to read than white text on a black background.
- Legibility affects readability.
- Line length, letterforms, and appearance all influence readability.

Before learning the details of readability, you must understand some type basics. A **font** is a set of characters of a specific family, size, and style. For example, the description Times New Roman, 11 points, italic is a font. What most people consider a font is actually a **typeface** (Times New Roman, in this example). A font represents only a single specific size and style within a family, while a typeface is a set or family of one or more fonts.

Legibility refers to the ease with which a reader can determine what a letter actually is. If readers cannot figure out the letter, they cannot read the text, resulting in low readability and failed message delivery. The difference between legibility and readability is subtle. Figure B–27 shows the Fontasia typeface with letters that are difficult to read. It says, "Fishing is fun."

Line length refers to the physical length of a line of text. When lines are too long, the reader's eyes can get lost trying to go all the way back to the left side of the page to find the next line. There is no conclusive magic number for how long a line of text should be. Optimal line lengths differ for adults and children, and for people with dyslexia and without. The best choices for line length differ based on the media of the message; printed newspapers, books, text on a Web site, and the subject lines in an e-mail message all require different line lengths. Some studies recommend line lengths based on physical lengths in inches, while other studies recommend a maximum number of characters per line. However, many designers follow the guideline that line lengths should not exceed 70 characters (about two-and-a-half alphabets' worth of characters).

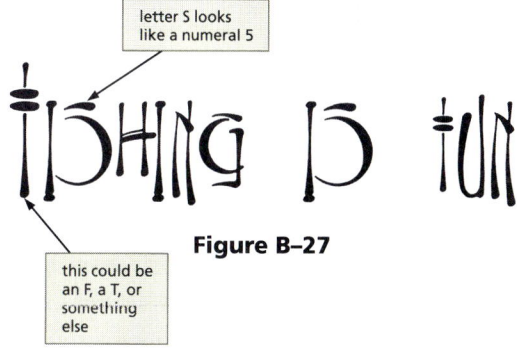

Figure B–27

> **BTW**
>
> **DON'T YELL**
> Not only is typing in all uppercase difficult to read, but it connotes yelling at your reader.

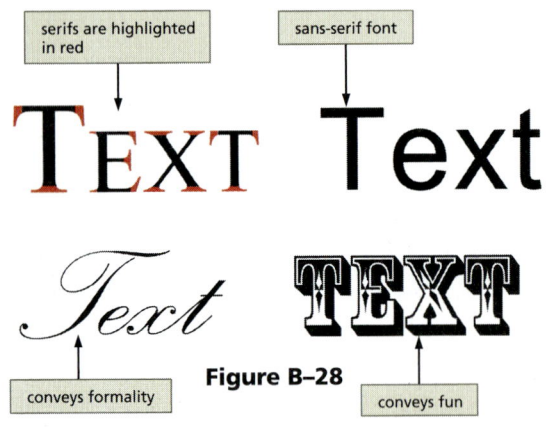

Typeface Categories

Typefaces are organized into several categories, including serif, sans-serif, script, and display. Serif fonts include additional appendages, while sans-serif fonts do not (Figure B–28). It is generally accepted that large passages of serif text in print are easy to read, while sans-serif text is easier to read on a Web page. Because headlines are typically small, either serif or sans-serif is appropriate. Varying the headline typeface style from the body copy typeface style is an effective method of adding some visual excitement to an otherwise dull page of text. Script fonts look like handwriting, and display fonts are decorative.

In addition to differences in readability, the choice of a serif, sans-serif, or other font can help to create an emotion much like the selection of a color scheme. Wedding invitations often use a script font to signify elegance, while headlines using display fonts can grab a reader's attention. The same phrase written in different typefaces can have different implications (Figure B–29). Similarly, differences in the size, weight (boldness), or spacing of a font also can influence emotion or meaning (Figure B–30).

Figure B–28

Figure B–29

Figure B–30

Designing for Web vs. Print

Graphic designers must be aware of subtle differences in how print and Web projects are created and perceived when designing for these media. While many design principles are common to both, it takes a different mindset to successfully create a design for either medium. Print designs are static, as the layout never varies from print to print (though differences in color may appear due to inconsistencies with the printer or printing press). Web designs morph, depending on the device used to view them. Some print designers struggle with the device dependency and fluidity of Web page designs. Some Web designers unnecessarily concern themselves about accommodating fluid or shifting content when designing a print advertisement.

Device Dependency and Fluidity

The main differences between print and Web design are related to device dependency and fluidity. Web pages are **device dependent**, meaning that the appearance of the page varies depending on the device (computer, cell phone, or PDA) on which they are viewed (Figure B–31). Discrepancies in monitor color calibration, screen resolution, and browser window size can affect how a Web page appears to the viewer. Colors can change, objects can shift, and text can wrap to a new line on different words from one device to another. In comparison, a newspaper or magazine looks the same no matter where it is purchased or where it is read.

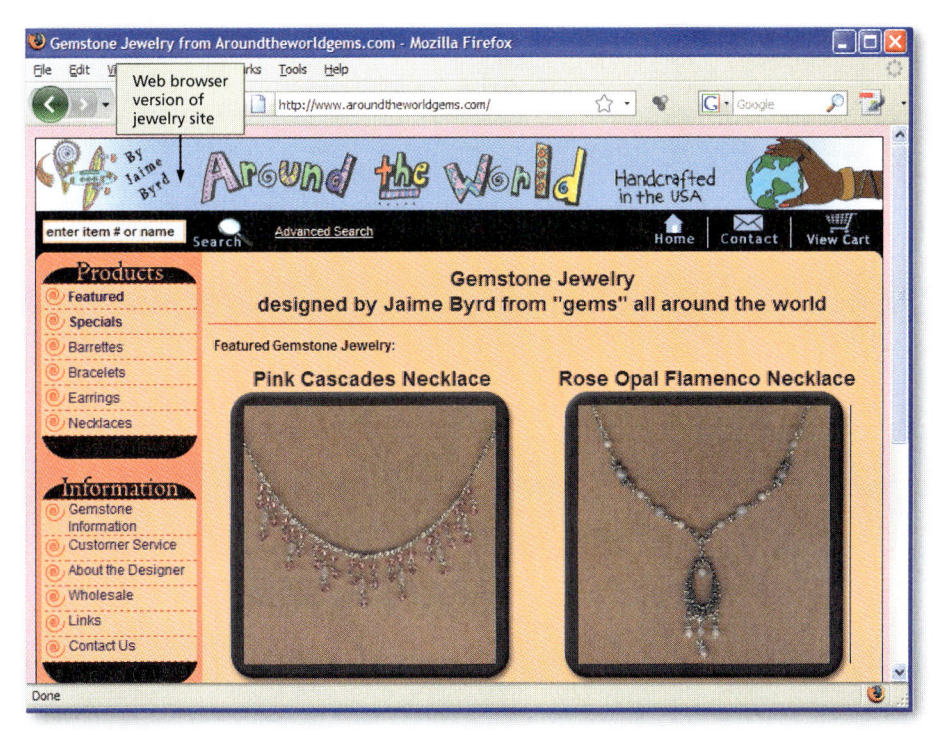

Figure B–31

Pixels, Dimensions, and Resolution

A pixel is the smallest element of a digital image. Magnifying an image reveals the individual pixels (Figure B–32). A pixel, unlike an inch or centimeter, is not an absolute measurement. The physical size of a pixel can change depending on resolution.

As you learned in Chapter 1, resolution refers to the number of pixels displayed on a computer screen. More pixels means greater detail. When referring to an image file, the phrase, document dimensions, is used to describe the number of pixels in the file. For example, an image may have the dimensions of 450 × 337, meaning it contains 450 pixels across and 337 pixels vertically, for a total of 151,650 pixels. File size is directly related to pixel dimension. The more pixels there are in a document, the larger the file size.

When used to describe an image file, the word, resolution, also is used to describe the printed output. The print resolution is given in pixels per inch (PPI); for example, 72 PPI or 300 PPI. PPI is a linear measurement: 72 PPI means that, when printed, the output will contain 72 pixels across every linear inch. If the document dimensions were 450 × 337, those 450 horizontal pixels would print in groups of 72 PPI, resulting in a printout just over six inches wide (Figure B–33 on the following page). If the resolution, but not the dimensions, was increased to 300 PPI, then those same 450 pixels would print in groups of 300 per inch, producing a final output about 1.5 inches wide.

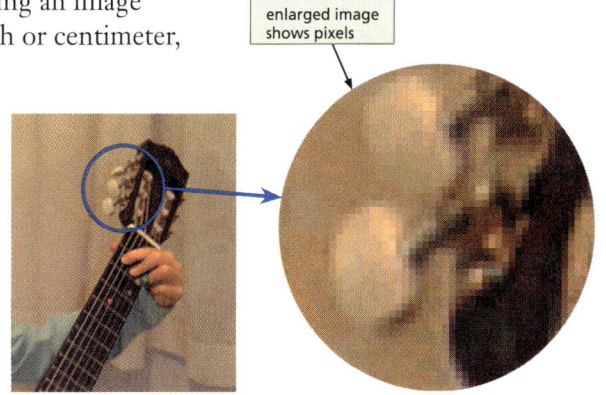

Figure B–32

Figure B–33

Key points to remember when working with resolution are:

- A pixel is not a static measurement. Pixels change in size. They get smaller or larger to fill an inch as defined in the PPI setting.
- Changing the resolution of an image file has no effect on the file size. It affects the physical size of the printed output.
- Changing the document dimensions does affect the file size.

When printing documents, printers create each individual pixel with a group of microscopic dots of ink (or toner or other pigment). The number of dots a printer can generate is measured in dots per inch (DPI). People sometimes incorrectly use the term DPI when they really mean PPI. A printer with a resolution of 2400 DPI means it can squeeze 2400 dots of ink (not pixels) into a single inch. The more dots used to create a pixel, the truer color each pixel can have — resulting in a higher quality print.

A common misconception related to creating image files is that all graphics for use on the Web should be created at a resolution of 72 PPI. However, because PPI affects the output of printing only, the PPI setting has no effect on the screen display of an image.

It is common practice to save Web images at 72 PPI, not because it optimizes images for the Web, but because the 72 DPI Myth so widely is believed, saving Web images at 72 PPI simply is very common.

> **BTW — Resolution and Print Quality**
> The higher the resolution, the smaller the pixels and the printout, and the better the quality.

> **BTW — PPI and Printing**
> An image with the dimensions of 800 x 600 at 72 PPI will look exactly the same on screen as the same image at 300 PPI. In fact, the file sizes will be identical. There will only be a difference when printed. For Web images, you can save them at 0 PPI, and they would work just as well, and have the same file size, as if you saved them at 1200 PPI. However, when printed, they will differ.

Working as a Graphic Designer

The business world offers many opportunities for people with creativity and an eye for design. From automotive design to fashion to advertising, the need for talented graphic artists is vast. Many industry experts believe there are generally three levels of professionals working in the graphics field: graphic artists, graphic designers, and people who own graphics editing/design software.

Graphic artists typically receive extensive schooling as art majors and know a lot about design principles and art history. However, schooling does not necessarily mean formal education in a school environment. A graphic artist can be self-educated. The key to the "artist" designation revolves around a personal need to creatively express oneself beyond that of producing commercial work for hire. While graphic artists work with software, they typically also produce art with more traditional media such as paints, pencils, fiber, metals, or other physical materials. Graphic artists may hold the same job as a graphic designer, but very often graphic artists will create and sell their own original artwork. This personal drive to create and the resulting independent production of original artwork is what distinguishes graphic artists from graphic designers.

The line separating graphic artists from graphic designers is a fine one. A **graphic designer** often is knowledgeable about design principles and may possess a wealth of information about art history, but not all graphic designers are graphic artists. They usually create design products for others, such as brochures, advertisements, or Web sites, using software, but do not create their own original works.

The third category of graphic designers includes people who own and use graphics design software for various purposes. This category, **software owners**, is not a true graphic design designation. Simply owning a copy of Photoshop or knowing how to use a certain software program does not make you a graphic artist/designer. Whereas artists and designers understand principles of design, effective use of color, and possess a certain degree of artistic ability or raw talent, design amateurs rely on the power of the software to help them create projects. Of course, it is possible for an amateur to become a professional designer or artist — but doing so requires education and training, not just purchasing a software suite.

Jobs in Graphic Design

An understanding of design principles and software skills opens the door to many opportunities in the professional graphics industry. Jobs for graphic designers range from freelance work and self-employment to full-time careers with advertising agencies, Web design firms, print houses, software companies, or the marketing team within an organization such as a school or commercial or nonprofit business. Perhaps the most important questions to ask yourself when considering a job in this field are:

- Do I want to work for myself or for someone else?
- Am I truly an artist? Am I creative? Or do I simply follow direction well, understand basic design principles, and know how to use graphics software?
- What is my preferred medium — physical (print) or electronic (Web, software interface)?

Once you have secured a position in the graphics field, you will be assigned projects that will call on your design skills and other abilities.

Design Projects

A successful project always begins with solid planning. Proper planning helps you to stay focused and reduces the potential for wasted time and money — both yours and your client's. A project plan must specify the following aspects of the project:

- Scope of design work
- Roles and responsibilities of designer and client
- Expectations and specifications for final product, including time frame

When you and your client agree on the scope of the work and are clear on what the final product should look like, you as the designer know exactly what it is you need to produce. It is better to take the time to plan a project before sitting down with Photoshop, so you have a good idea of what to do once you start the software.

Client and Designer Roles

Both the client and the designer have specific jobs. Defining and agreeing on these roles is crucial for the success of the collaboration.

Simply put, the client must clearly communicate his or her expectations. Clients often need help articulating their wants and needs, and the designer must be able to help draw this information from the client. Additionally, the client must be available to provide feedback when the designer offers a draft for feedback or proofing. A client's responsibilities include the following:

- Clearly communicate the needs of the project
- Provide timely and constructive feedback
- Trust the designer's expertise
- Pay the bills on time

Aside from the obvious (creating the product), the designer also is responsible for making sure the client knows their own responsibilities and avoids poor design choices. Sometimes, a client will request something that is just bad — like certain colors that do not work well together or make text unreadable. The designer is responsible for respectfully steering the client away from the bad options and toward a better alternative.

In a highly competitive job market, you must determine what sets you apart from your competition. A potential client might choose one designer over another not because one is a better or more creative artist, but simply because they like the other designer more.

Customer service is part of your job, as well. Treat your client and your client's time and money with respect, be personable, and appreciate your client, and you will have more to offer than your competitors will. In addition to meeting the responsibilities previously defined, you should do the following:

- Be on time to meetings
- Meet or beat your deadlines so you don't submit work late

- Treat your clients and their time and money with respect
- Be able to explain your design choices
- Ensure adherence to copyright law

Defining the Project

As a designer, you must understand you are acting in the role of a hired hand — not an artist with complete creative control. You are being hired to create what your client wants, not what you necessarily prefer. While you need to educate your client as to best practices in design, ultimately the client is paying the bill, so they have the final word when it comes to making decisions.

Specifying Project Details

Project details should be discussed with the client and agreed upon before any design work begins. One detail to consider is what the client needs for files. For example, does the client require a 300 PPI TIF file or a layered Photoshop file? How will the files be delivered? Will they be sent by e-mail, burned to a CD and mailed, or downloaded from a Web site or FTP server? Additionally, a timeline of deliverables should be stated. A first draft of the design should be sent to the client for approval by a certain date, and pending timely client feedback, the final version should be delivered by the project deadline. The client may have a desired time frame, and the designer must be able to deliver the work within that time frame. Sometimes a compromise must be reached.

Collecting Materials

Existing materials help to speed up the design process. If you are hired to create a Web site or brochure, ask your client for copies of their existing promotional materials, such as a business card, letterhead, or logo. Ask your client what they like and dislike about these materials and if the product you are creating should be stylistically similar. This approach can prevent you from going down the wrong path, inadvertently creating something the client does not like. Additionally, you will need to collect any photographs your client has earmarked for the project.

Next, you must gather other assets for the project; specifically, high-quality artwork and photographs.

Original Artwork If you have the raw artistic ability or own quality camera equipment, you can create your own original artwork or take your own photographs if you are a professional-level photographer. You can outsource some of this work to professional artists or photographers — just be sure to get your client's approval for the cost. Your other option is to use stock art.

Stock Art Stock art includes existing artwork and photographs that can be licensed for use. The cost of a single picture can range from zero to several thousand dollars, depending on the source and license restrictions. Realistically, you should expect to pay between $5 and $40 for each print-quality digital file if you cannot find free sources.

Stock art is commercially available from many companies, most with a Web presence — meaning you can download images or purchase whole collections of stock art on CD or DVD from a Web site. Thousands of companies sell commercial stock art online. Some of the most popular resources are fotosearch.com, corbis.com, and gettyimages.com.

BTW

Photos on CD
If possible, get photos and images on a CD. Many times a collection of photographs and other materials are too large to send by e-mail, and even if they are successfully sent, e-mails accidentally get deleted. Having all the materials on CD also guarantees you always have a backup of the original files as you modify copies with Photoshop or other software.

BTW

Public Domain vs. Commercial Stock Art
Public domain stock art sites can be difficult to use because they do not have the funding for the more intuitive style of interface found on the commercial sites. You can often find exactly what you want in the public domain. However, sometimes it is worth the $5 to more easily find exactly what you want on a commercial Web site.

When searching for stock art, be sure to seek out **royalty-free images**. Images that are royalty free can be reused without paying additional fees. For example, you could spend $100 to purchase an image that is not royalty free and use it on a Web site. If you want to use the same image in a brochure or another client's Web site, you might have to pay another fee to reuse the image. Royalty free means that once the initial payment is made, there are no re-usage fees.

If you do not want to pay anything for your images, look into finding **public domain** artwork or photographs. Images in the public domain are completely free to use. The only trick is finding quality artwork in the public domain. Whereas commercial stock art Web sites typically have millions of high-quality images from which to choose, public domain stock art Web sites often have far fewer choices. Public domain stock art sites include Flickr, Morgue File, and Uncle Sam's Photos.

Other Licenses There are usage licenses allowing free unrestricted use of images, audio, video, text, and other content similar to that of the public domain. These licenses include Copyleft, Creative Commons, education use, fair use, GNU general public license, and open source. The definitions of these alternative licenses read like a law book, but it is helpful to recognize the names. Laws related to these licenses allow for limited use of copyright-protected material without requiring the permission of the copyright owner. If you find images or other content offered as one of these alternatives, there is a good chance it will be completely free to use.

Whatever the source for your images, be sure to read the license and usage rights and restrictions carefully. No matter your source for artwork, you need to document its origin. The documentation serves two important purposes. First, it provides a record of the image's origin in case you need to get additional similar artwork. Second, it provides peace of mind should you or your client ever face legal action for copyright infringement. The documentation does not have to be fancy; it can simply be a list of where an image is used in a project and where that image was acquired.

Summary

Successful design uses the principles of balance, contrast, dominance, proximity, repetition, closure, continuance, negative space, and unity. The properties of color include hue, saturation, shade, tint, and value. Color models include RGB for Web images, CMYK for images you intend to print, and LAB for access to the largest color space possible when working with digital photographs. Adherence to Web-safe colors is unnecessary. Colors can have emotional implications and should be used in harmony with neighboring colors. Color schemes include monochrome, complementary, analogous, and split-complementary.

Typeface selections can affect text readability, as can line lengths. Typefaces are organized into several categories, including serif, sans-serif, script, and display. The same Web site can look different from one monitor or computer to another.

Pixels per inch (PPI) determines the number of pixels printed per inch and affects the printed size of an image only, not how it appears onscreen or its file size. Higher PPI settings produce better quality printouts but have no effect on how an image appears onscreen. Dots per inch (DPI) refers to printer capabilities and defines how many microscopic dots of ink a printer can print in a linear inch. Pixel dimensions, not image resolution, affect how large an image appears on-screen and the size of a file.

Working in graphic design can incorporate a range of creative roles; working with clients in a design role requires specifying project expectations and the responsibilities of both designer and client.

Appendix C
Changing Screen Resolution and Editing Preferences

This appendix explains how to change the screen resolution in Windows Vista to the resolution used in this book. It also describes how to customize the Photoshop window by setting preferences and resetting user changes.

Screen Resolution

Screen resolution indicates the number of pixels (dots) that the computer uses to display the graphics, text, and background you see on the screen. The screen resolution usually is stated as the product of two numbers, such as 1024 × 768. That resolution results in a display of 1,024 distinct pixels on each of 768 lines, or about 786,432 pixels. The figures in this book were created using a screen resolution of 1024 × 768.

To Change Screen Resolution

The following steps change your screen's resolution to 1024 × 768 pixels. Your computer already may be set to 1024 × 768 or some other resolution.

1
- If necessary, minimize all programs so that the Windows Vista desktop is displayed.
- Right-click the Windows Vista desktop to display the desktop shortcut menu (Figure C–1).

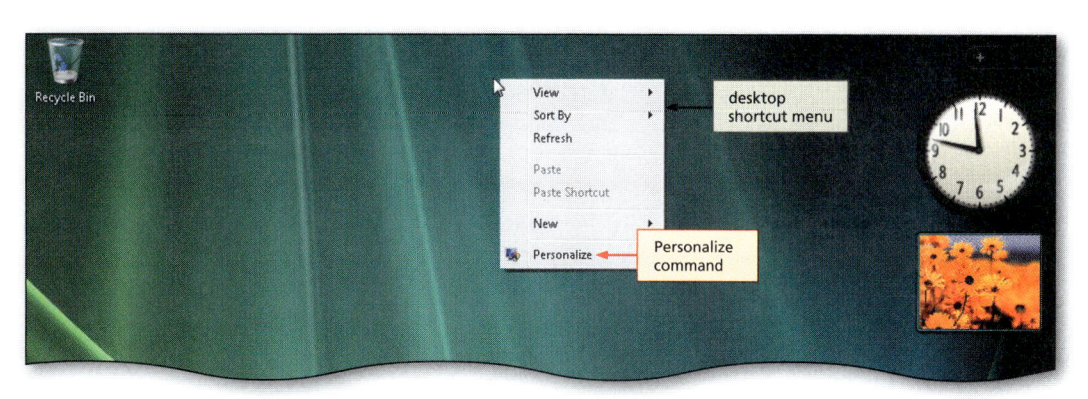

Figure C–1

2

- Click Personalize on the shortcut menu to open the Personalization window (Figure C–2).

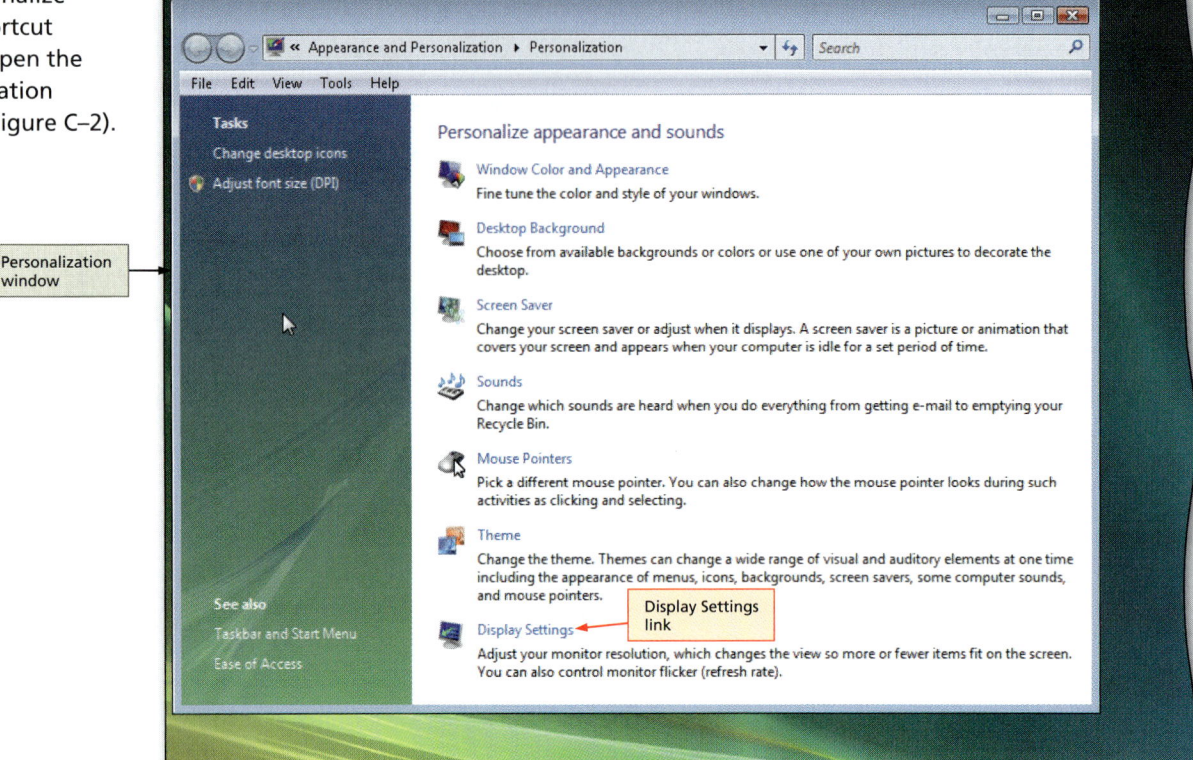

Figure C–2

3

- Click Display Settings in the Personalization window to display the Display Settings dialog box (Figure C–3).

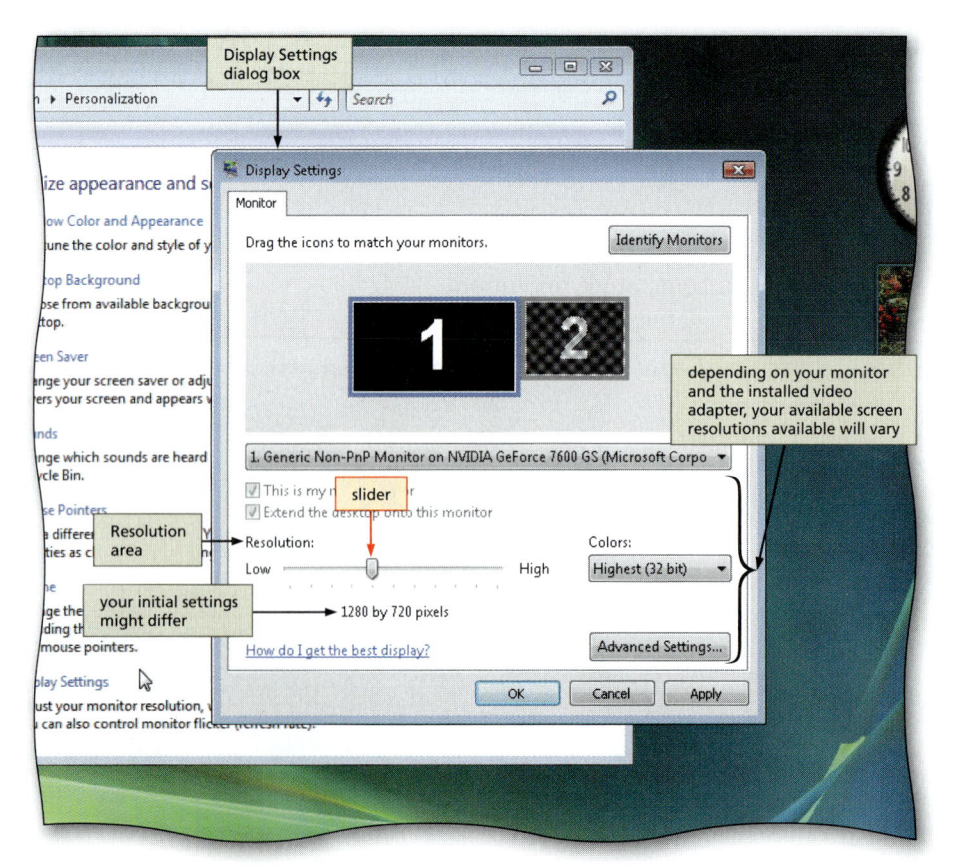

Figure C–3

4
- Drag the slider in the Resolution area so that the screen resolution changes to 1024 by 768, if necessary (Figure C–4).

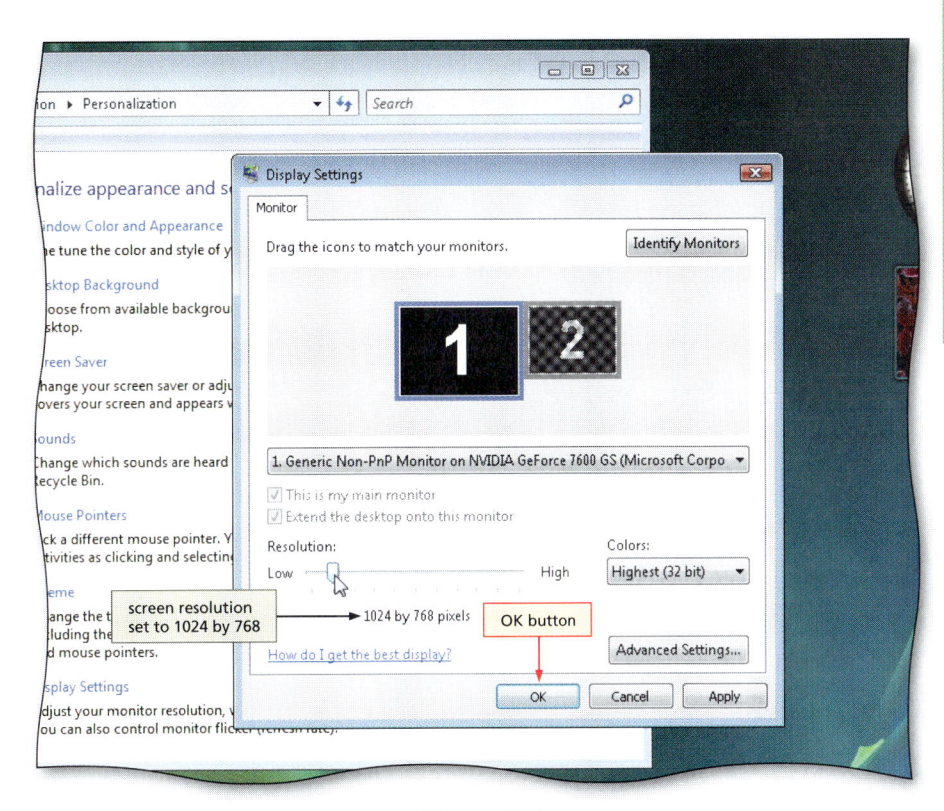

Figure C–4

5
- Click the OK button to change the screen resolution (Figure C–5).

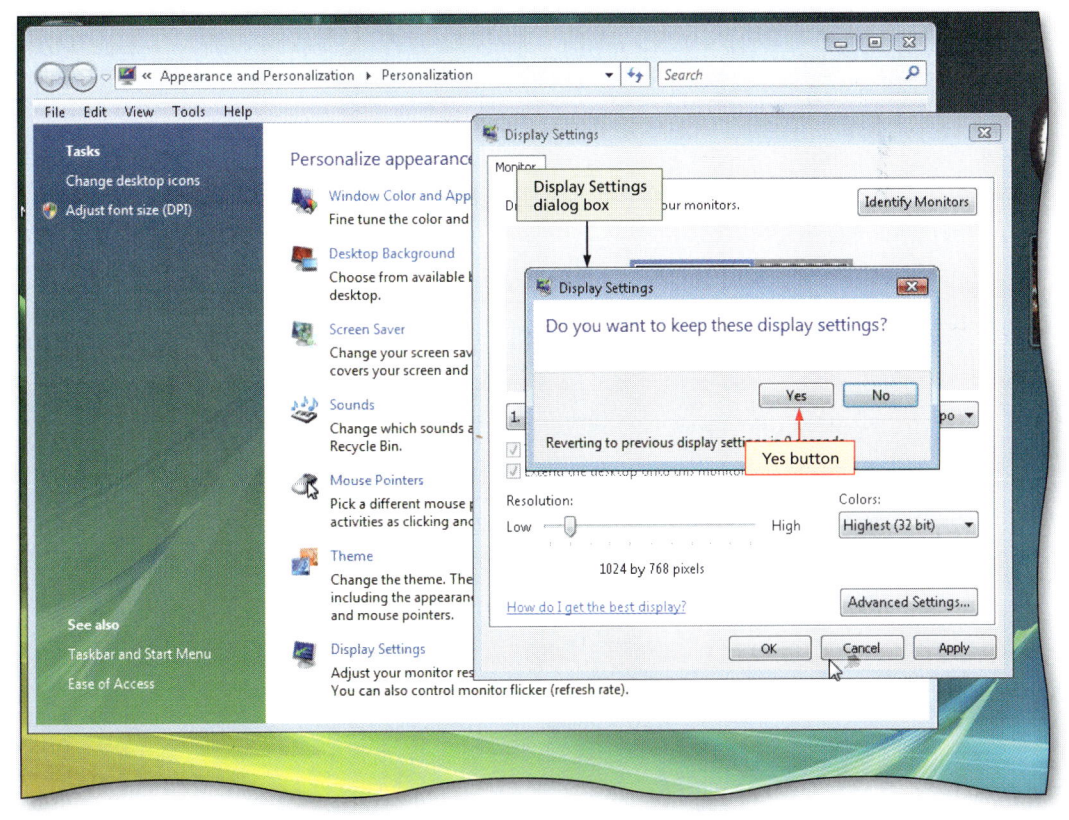

Figure C–5

APP 26 Appendix C Changing Screen Resolution and Editing Preferences

6
- Click the Yes button to accept the changes (Figure C–6).

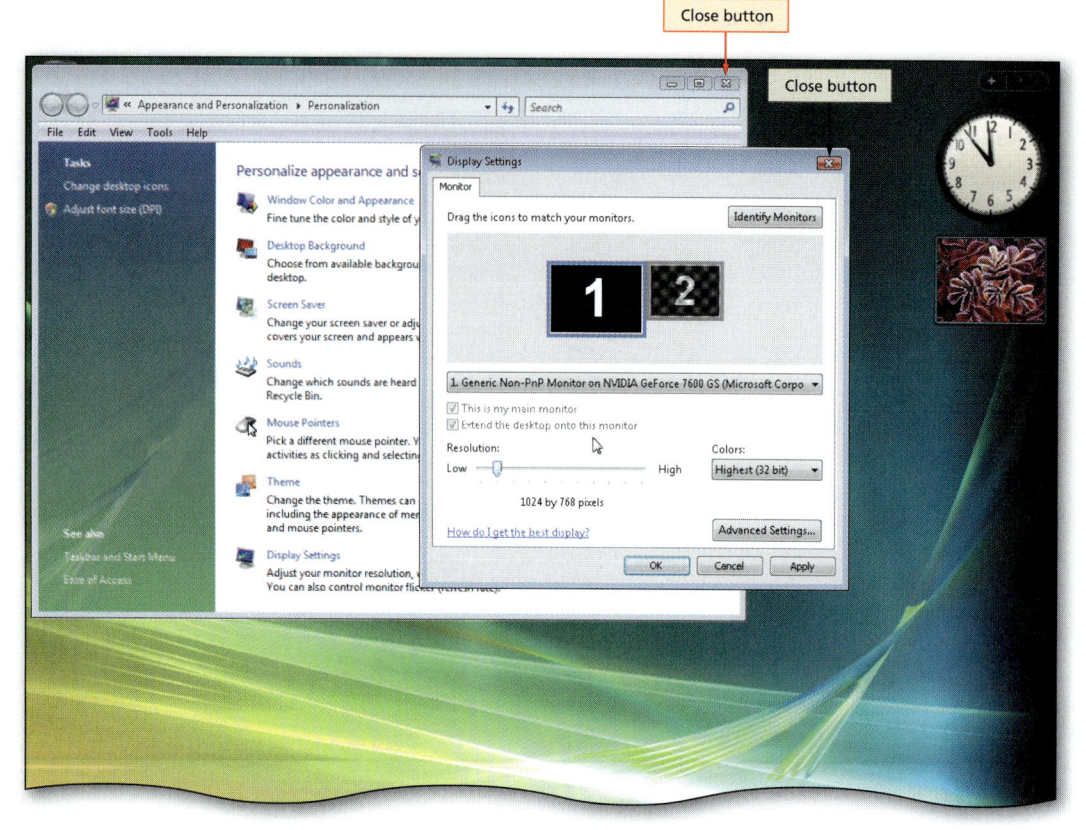

Figure C–6

7
- Click the Close button in the Display Settings dialog box.
- Click the Close button in the Personalization window to close the window (Figure C–7).

Figure C–7

Editing Photoshop Preferences

In Chapter 1, you learned how to start Photoshop and reset the default workspace, select the default tool, and reset all tools to their default settings. There are other preferences and settings you can edit to customize the Photoshop workspace and maximize your efficiency.

Editing General Preferences

General preferences include how Photoshop displays and stores your work. For example, you can change how many states are saved in the History panel, change the number of files shown on the Open Recent menu, or reset the display and cursors.

BTW

Screen Resolutions
When you increase the screen resolution, Windows displays more information on the screen, but the information decreases in size. The reverse also is true; as you decrease the screen resolution, Windows displays less information on the screen, but the information increases in size.

To Edit General Preferences

In the following steps, you will traverse through several Preferences dialog boxes to reset values and change preferences. You can access this set of dialog boxes by pressing CTRL+K or by clicking Preferences on the Edit menu.

1

- Start Photoshop CS4 for your system.
- Press CTRL+K to display the Preferences dialog box.
- Make sure your Options check boxes are selected as shown in Figure C–8.
- Click the Reset All Warning Dialogs button, so your dialog boxes will match the ones in this book.
- When Photoshop displays a Preferences dialog box, click the OK button.

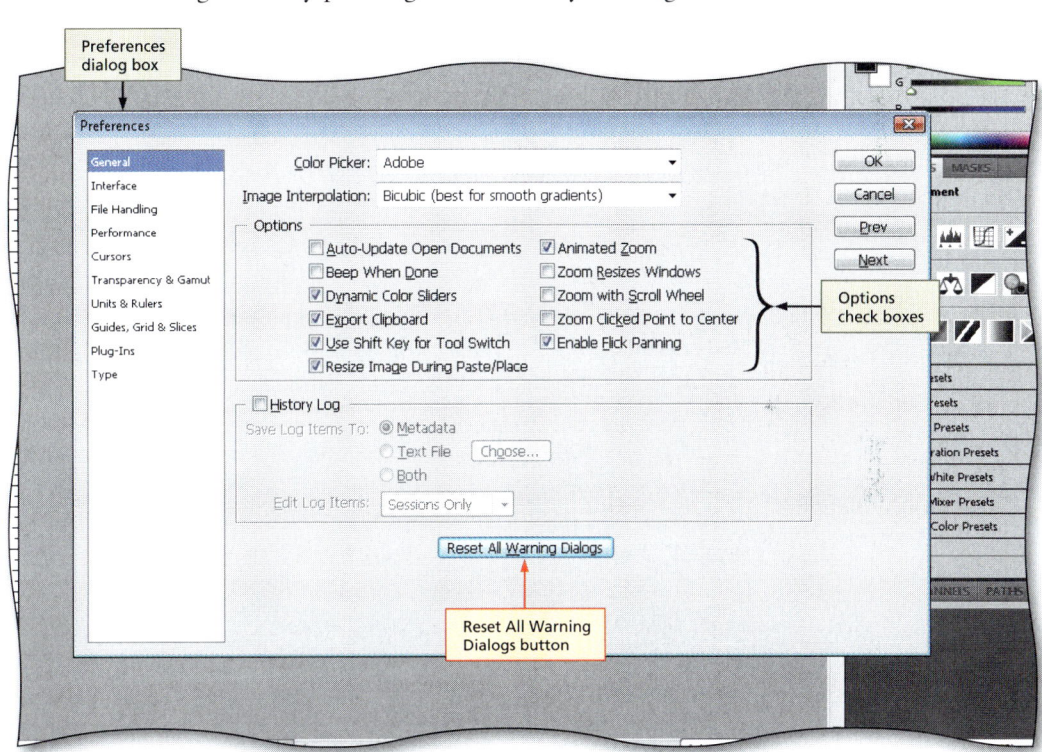

Figure C–8

2

- Click File Handling in the list of Preferences.

- Click the File Extension box arrow and then click Use Lower Case in the list, so Photoshop will use lowercase letters when saving.

- Make sure your check boxes are selected as shown in Figure C–9.

- Click the Maximize PSD and PSB File Compatibility box arrow and then click Ask in order for Photoshop to ask about saving files in PSD format.

- Type 10 in the Recent file list contains box, if necessary, to specify that Photoshop will display the last 10 files.

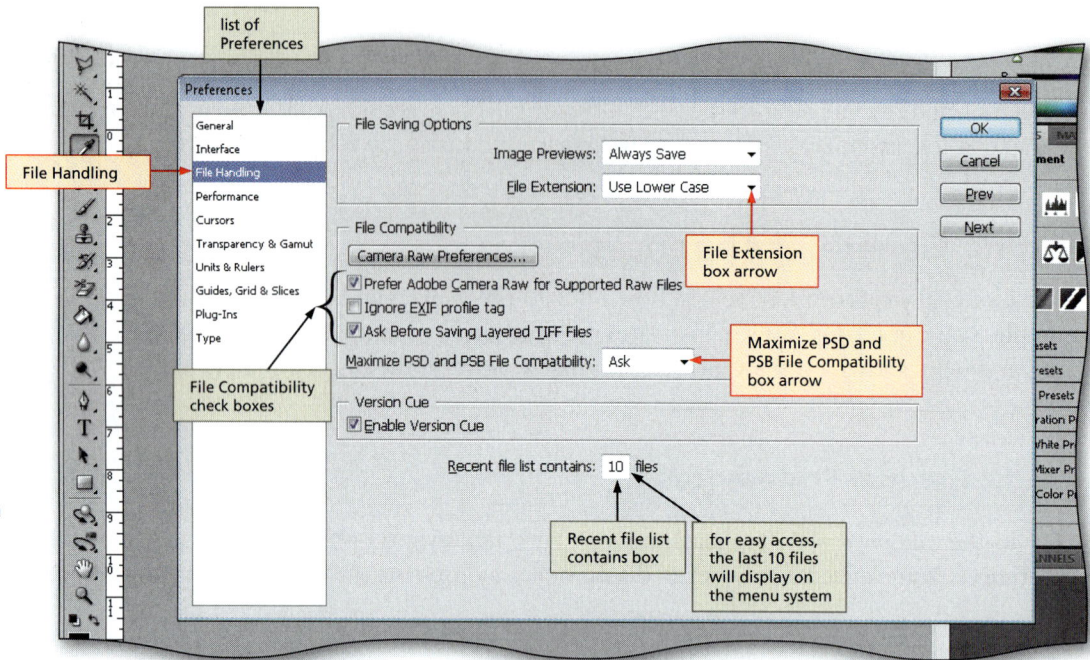

Figure C–9

3

- Click Performance in the list of Preferences.

- When the Preferences dialog box is displayed, if necessary, type 20 in the History States box, so Photoshop will allow you to back up through the last 20 steps of any editing session (Figure C–10).

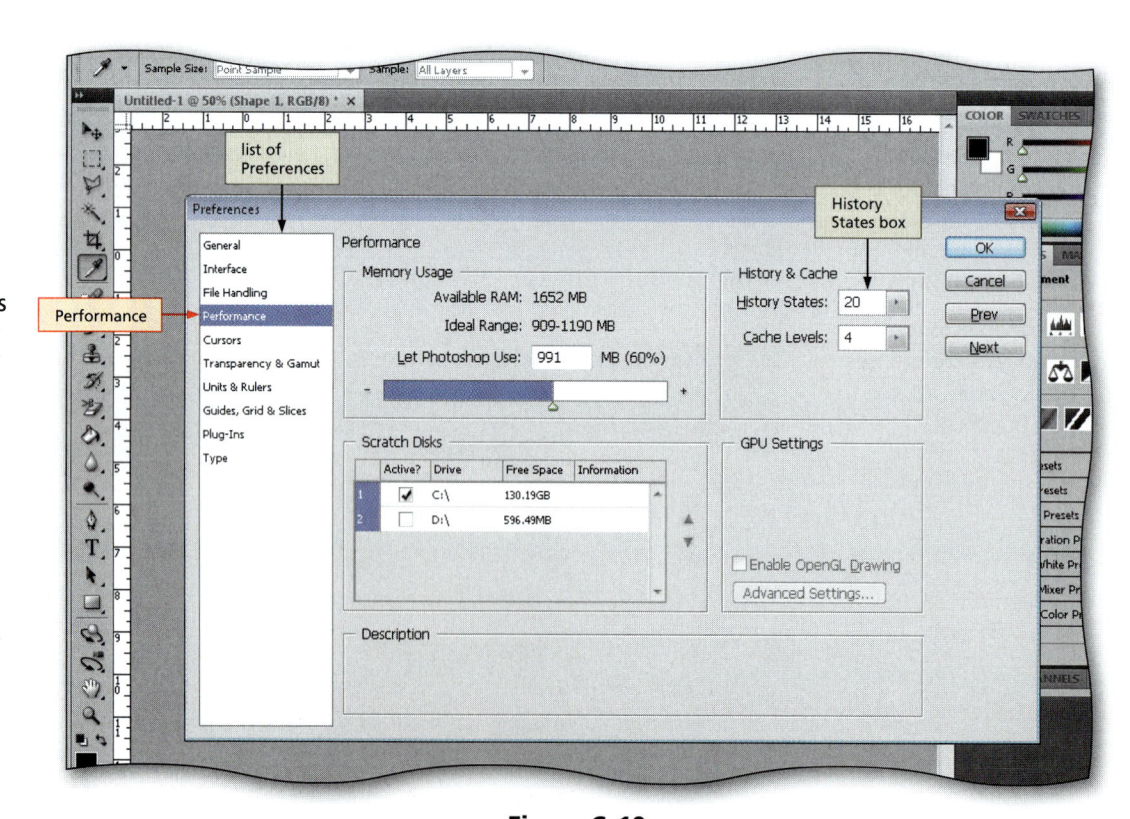

Figure C–10

4
- Click Cursors in the list of Preferences.
- If necessary, select Normal Brush Tip in the Painting Cursors area and Standard in the Other Cursors area, to reset those options back to their default values (Figure C–11).

5
- When you are finished, click the OK button.

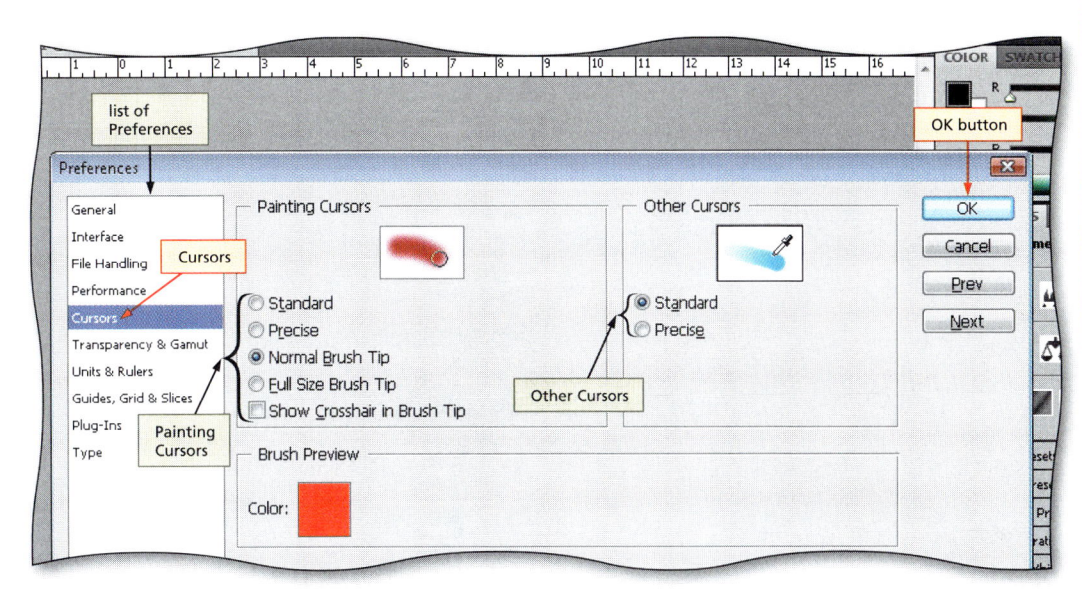

Figure C–11

The Preferences dialog boxes contain a variety of settings that can be changed to suit individual needs and styles. The Reset All Warning Dialogs button in Figure C–8 on page APP 27 especially is useful to display the dialog boxes if someone has turned them off by clicking the Don't show again check box.

In Figure C–11, **Normal Brush Tip** causes the mouse pointer outline to correspond to approximately 50 percent of the area that the tool will affect. This option shows the pixels that would be most visibly affected. It is easier to work with Normal Brush Tip than **Full Size Brush Tip**, especially when using larger brushes. A **Standard painting cursor** displays mouse pointers as tool icons; a **Precise painting cursor** displays the mouse pointer as a crosshair.

Menu Command Preferences

Photoshop allows users to customize both the application menus and the panel menus in several ways. You can hide commands that you seldom use. You can set colors on the menu structure to highlight or organize your favorite commands. Or, you can let Photoshop organize your menus with color based on functionality. If changes have been made to the menu structure, you can reset the menus back to their default states.

Hiding and Showing Menu Commands

If there are menu commands that you seldom use, you can hide them to access other commands more quickly. A **hidden command** is a menu command that does not appear currently on a menu. If menu commands have been hidden, a Show All Menu Items command will be displayed at the bottom of the menu list. When you click the Show All Menu Items command or press and hold the CTRL key as you click the menu name, Photoshop displays all menu commands, including hidden ones.

Other Ways
1. On Edit menu, point to Preferences, click General, select individual preferences

Changing Preferences
If there is one particular setting you wish to change, you can open that specific Preferences dialog box from the menu. For example, if you want to change the color of a ruler guide, you can point to Preferences on the Edit menu and then click Guides, Grid & Slices on the Preferences submenu to go directly to those settings and make your edits.

Resetting Preferences
To restore all preferences to their default settings, you can press and hold ALT+CTRL+SHIFT as you start Photoshop, which causes the system to prompt that you are about to delete the current settings.

To Hide and Show Menu Commands

The following steps hide a menu command and then redisplay it.

1
- Click Edit on the menu bar, and then click Menus to display the Keyboard Shortcuts and Menus dialog box (Figure C–12).

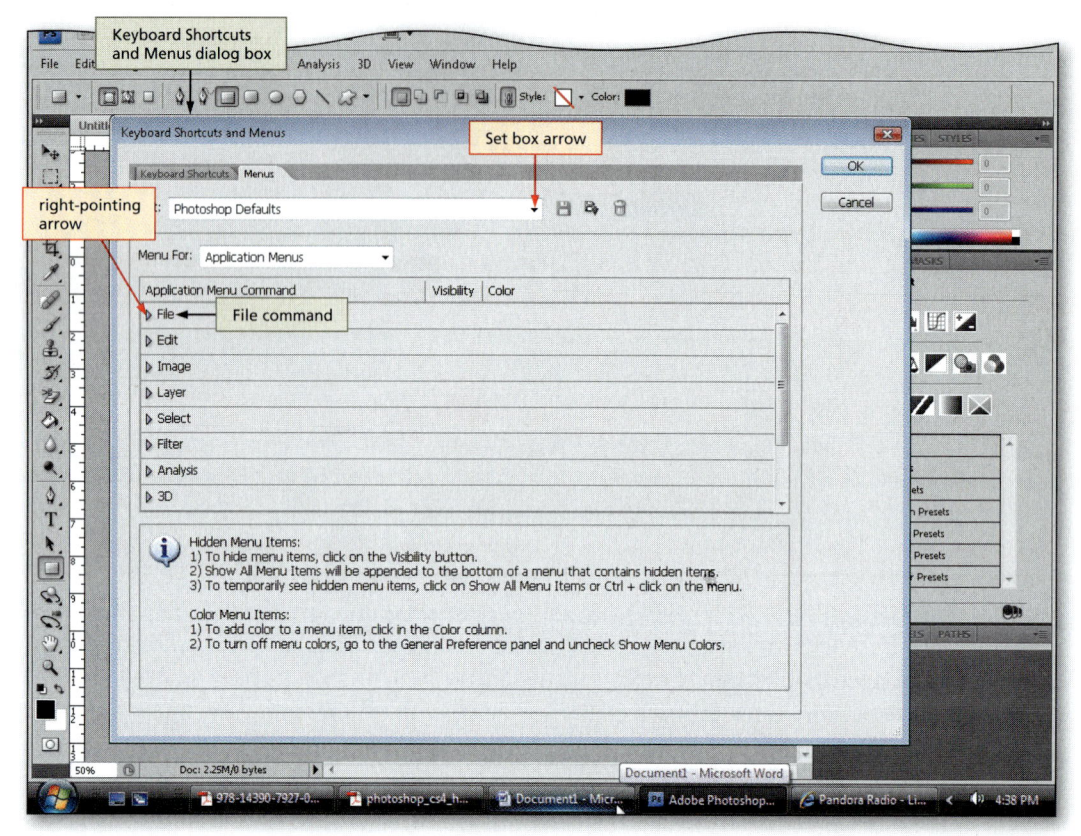

Figure C–12

2
- If necessary, click the Set box arrow and then click Photoshop Defaults.
- Click the right-pointing arrow next to the word File to display the File commands (Figure C–13).

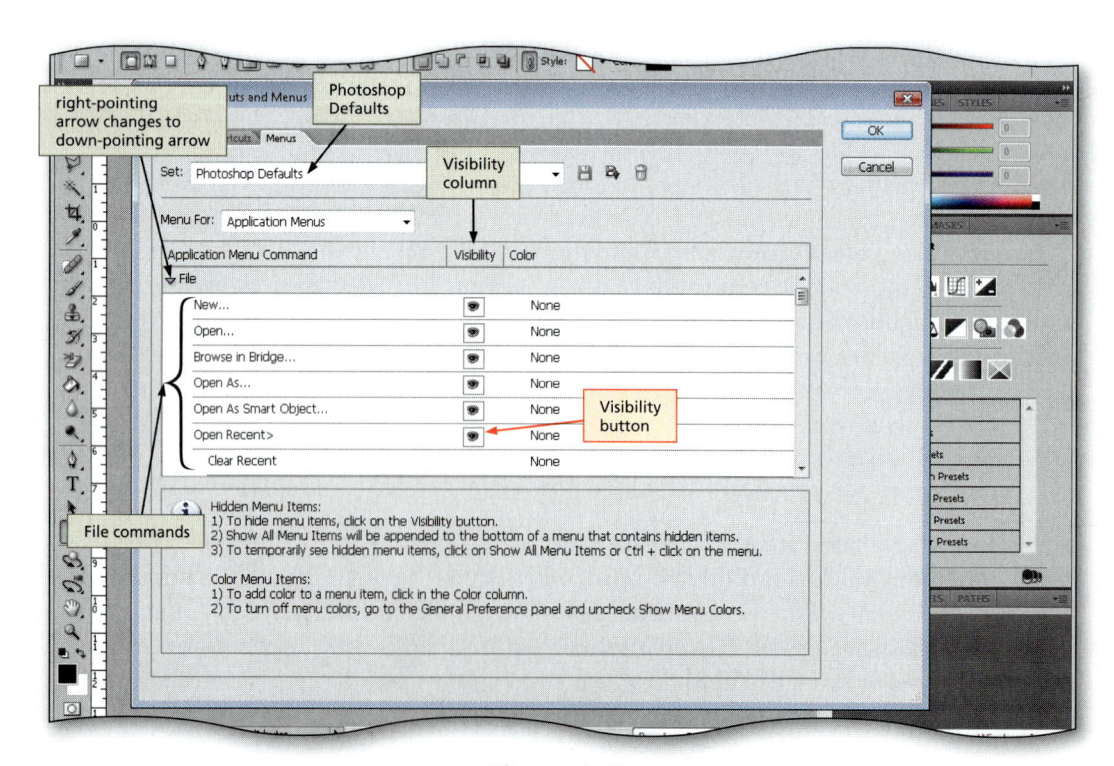

Figure C–13

3

- In the Visibility column, click the Visibility button next to the Open Recent command so it no longer is displayed (Figure C–14).

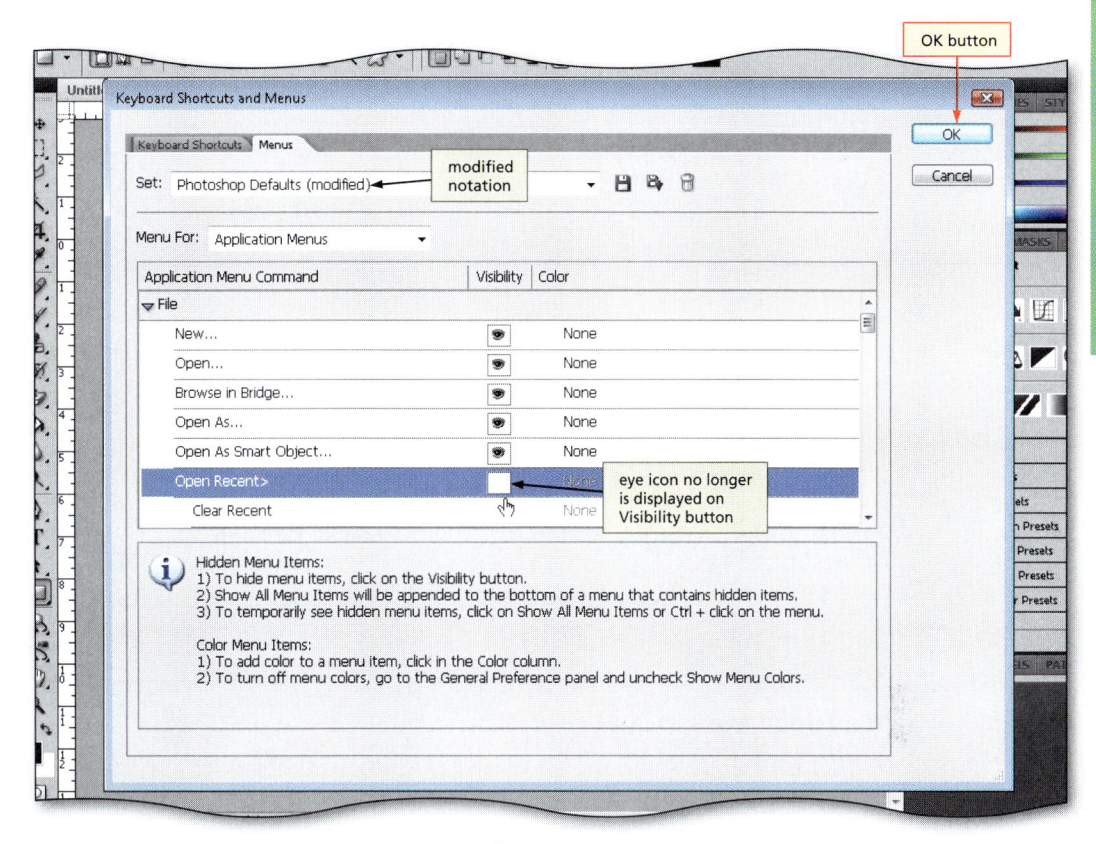

Figure C–14

4

- Click the OK button in the Keyboard Shortcuts and Menus dialog box to close the dialog box.
- Click File on the menu bar to display the file menu (Figure C–15).

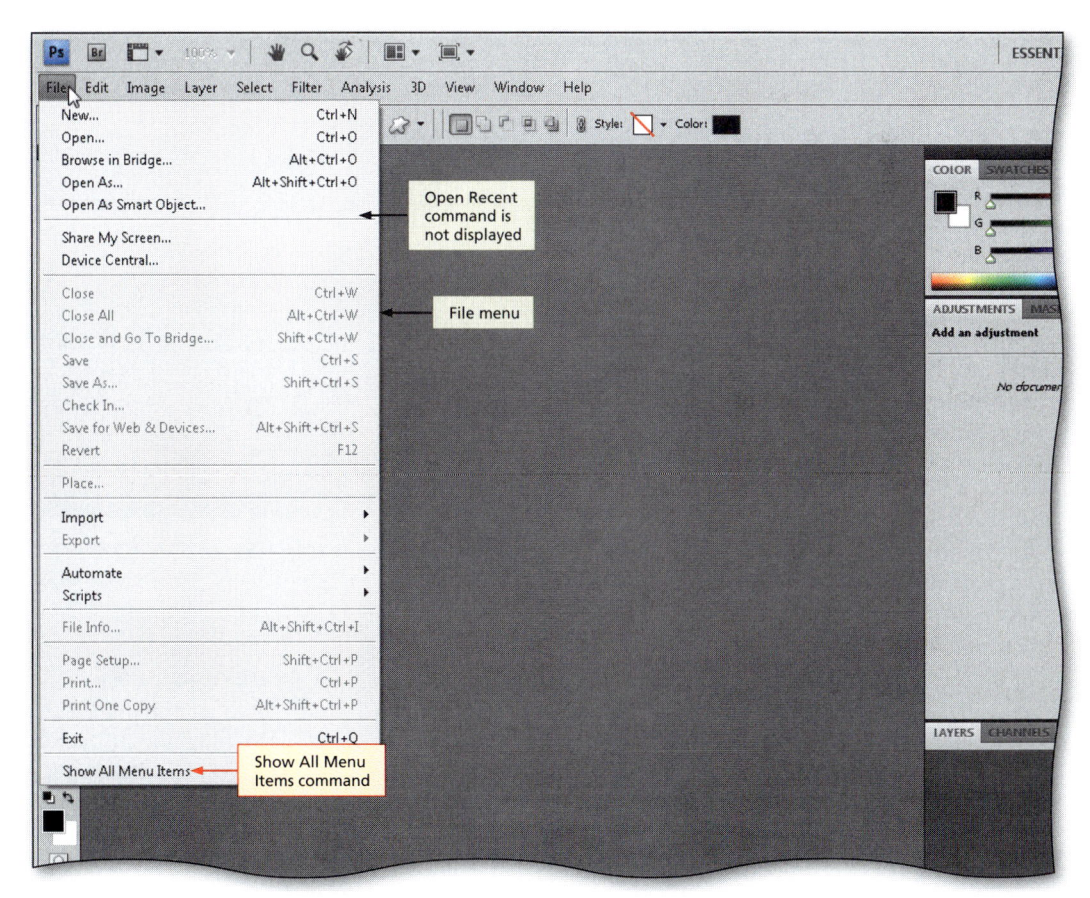

Figure C–15

APP 32 Appendix C Changing Screen Resolution and Editing Preferences

5
- On the File menu, click Show All Menu Items to redisplay the command that you hid in Step 3 (Figure C–16).

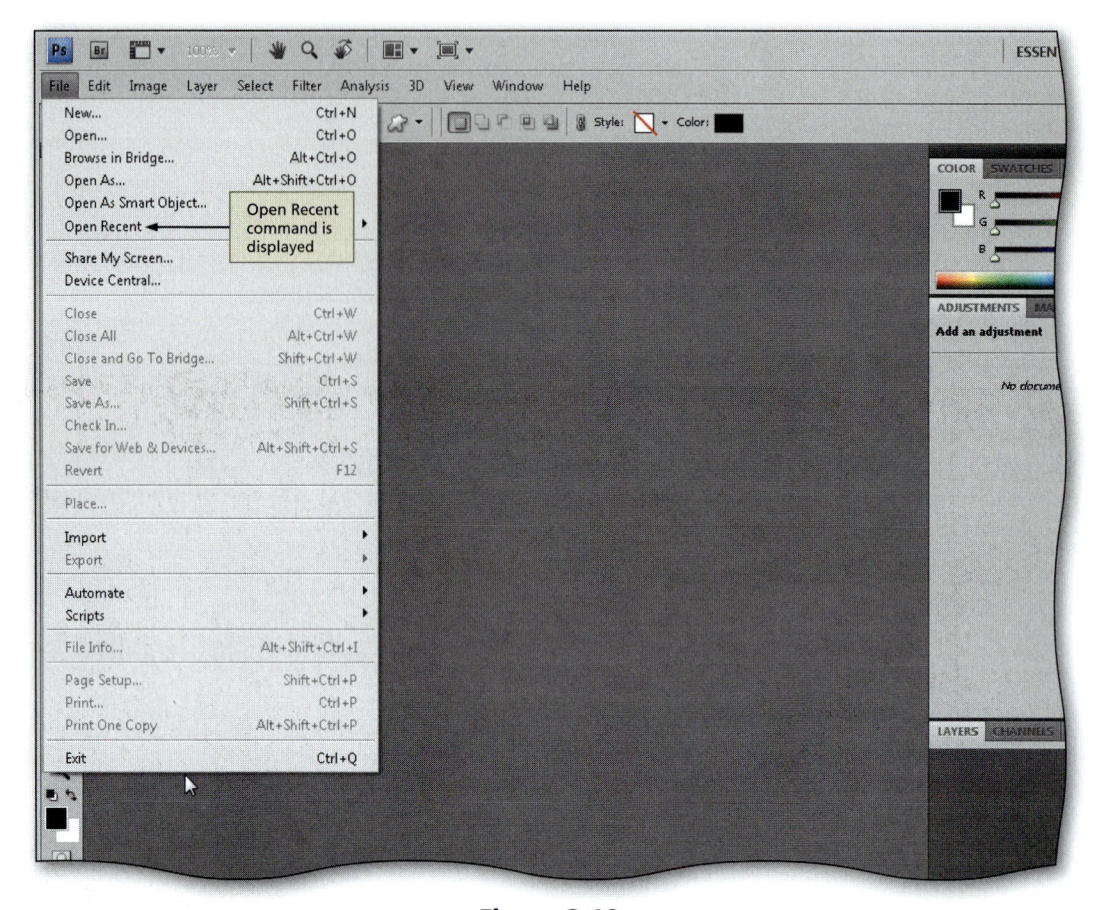

Figure C–16

6
- Click Edit on the menu bar and then click Menus to display the Keyboard Shortcuts and Menus dialog box again.

- If necessary, click the right-pointing arrow next to the word File to display its list.

- Click the Visibility button next to the Open Recent command so it again is displayed (Figure C–17).

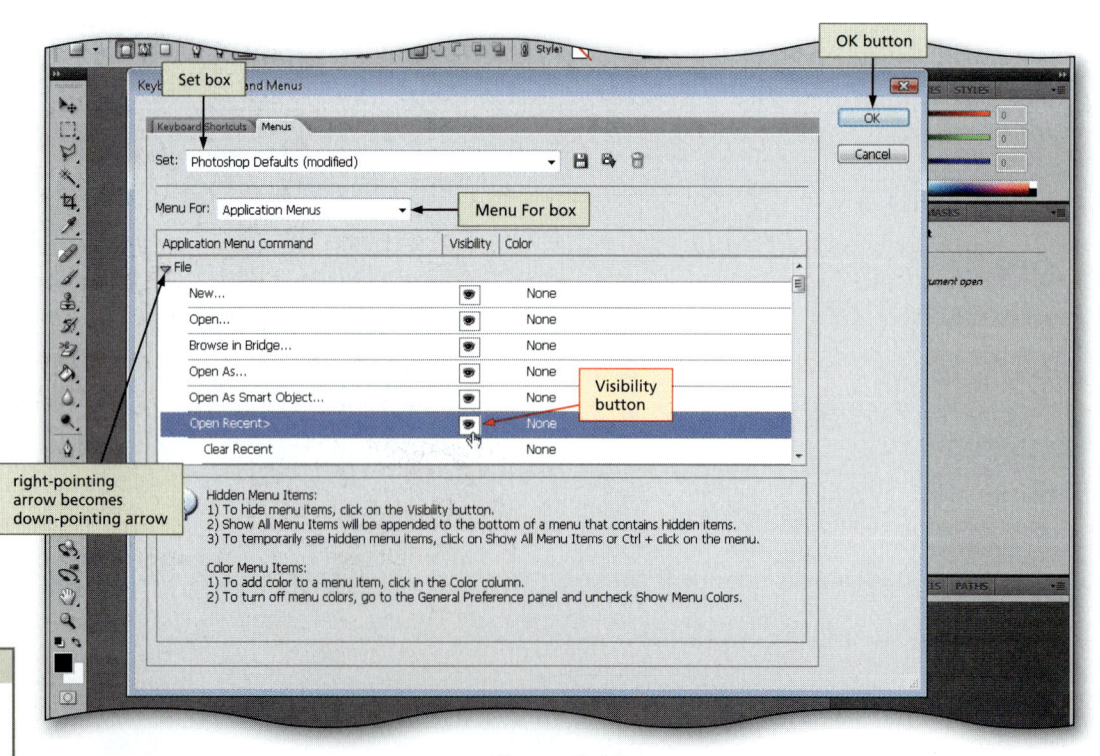

Figure C–17

Other Ways

1. On Window menu, point to Workspace, click Keyboard Shortcuts & Menus
2. Press ALT+SHIFT+CTRL+M

To Add Color to Menu Commands

You can add color to your menu commands to help you find them easily or to organize them into groups based on personal preferences. The following steps change the color of the Open and Open As commands.

1
- With the Keyboard Shortcuts and Menus dialog box still displayed, click the word, None, in the row associated with the Open command to display a list of colors (Figure C–18).

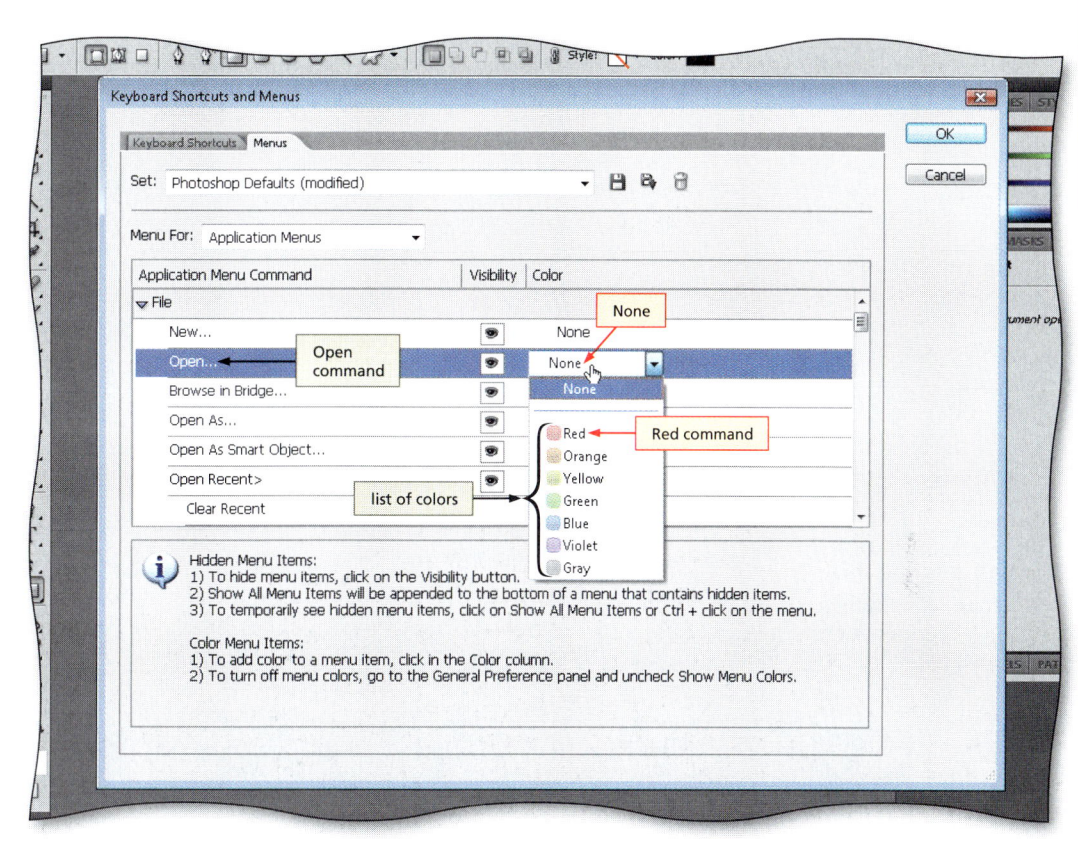

Figure C–18

2
- Click Red in the list to select a red color for the Open command.
- Click the word, None, in the row associated with the Open As command, and then click Red in the list to select a red color for the Open As command (Figure C–19).

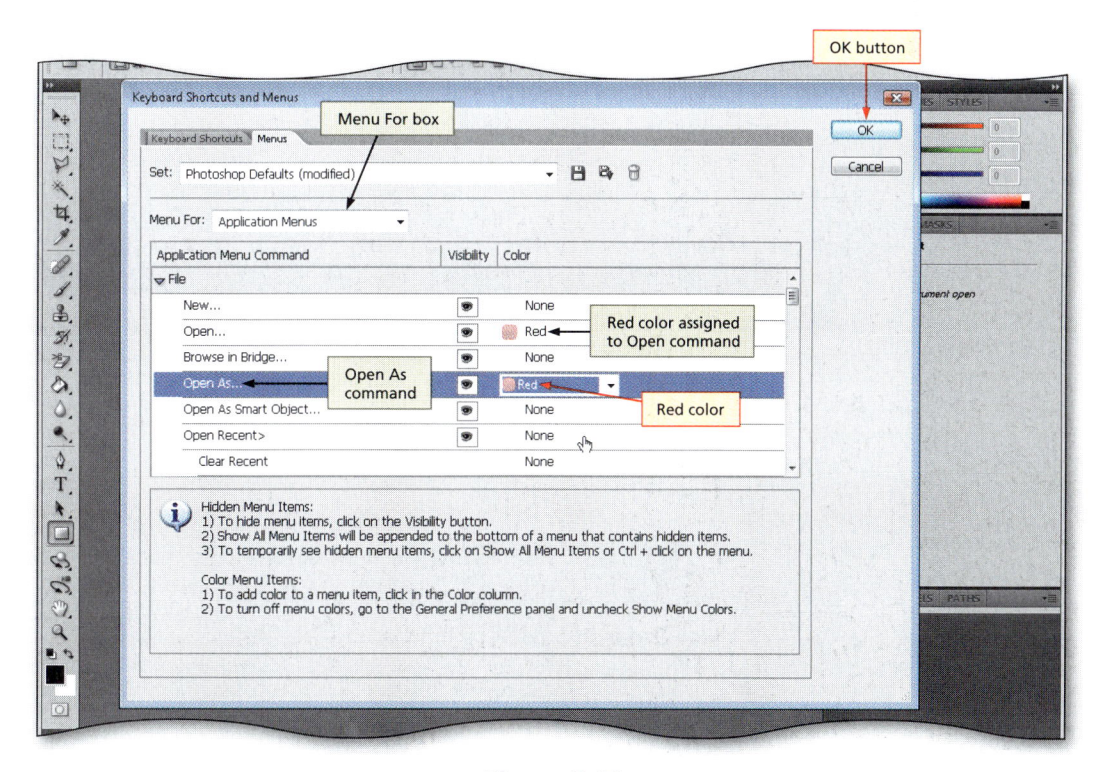

Figure C–19

3
- Click the OK button to close the Keyboard Shortcuts and Menus dialog box.
- Click File on the Photoshop menu bar to display the new color settings (Figure C–20).

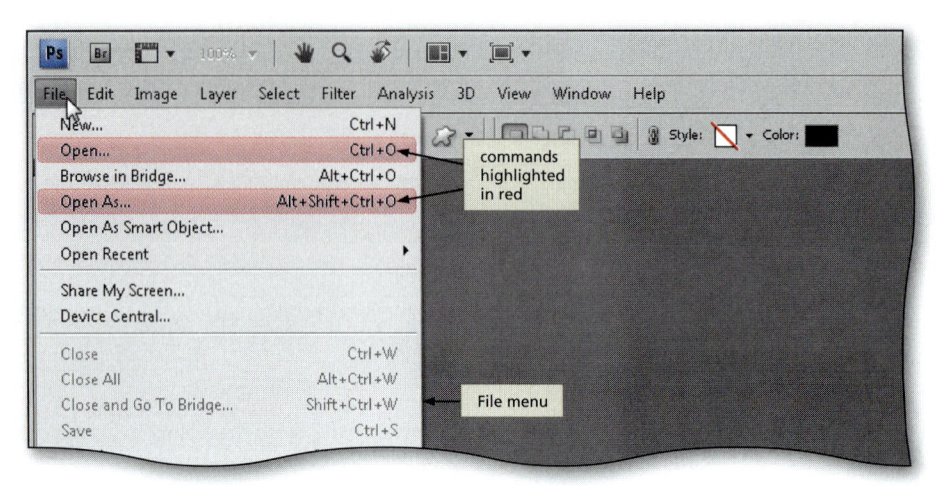

Figure C–20

BTW

Menu Box
The Menu For box (Figure C–18) allows you to set options for Applications Menus or Panel Menus.

The Set box (Figure C–21) lists four sets of stored menu commands: Photoshop Defaults, Basic, What's New in CS4, and Photoshop Defaults (modified), which you created in the previous steps. Choosing a set causes Photoshop to display related commands with color. For example, if you choose What's New in CS4, the commands on all menus that are new will appear in blue.

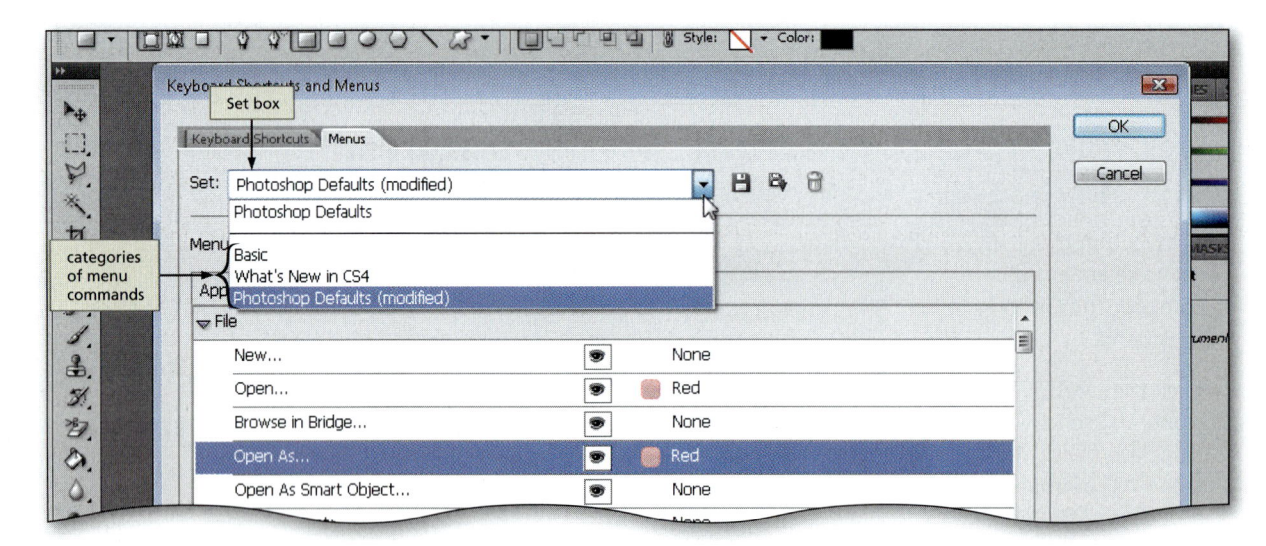

Figure C–21

To Reset the Menus

The following steps reset the menus, removing the red color from the Open commands.

1 Click Edit on the menu bar and then click Menus to display the Keyboard Shortcuts and Menus dialog box.

2 Click the Set box arrow and then click Photoshop Defaults in the list.

Menu Command Preferences **APP 35**

③ When Photoshop asks if you want to save the previous modifications, click the No button.

④ Click the OK button to close the Keyboard Shortcuts and Menus dialog box.

Resetting the Panels, Keyboard Shortcuts, and Menus

A **tool preset** is a way to store settings from the options bar. Besides the default settings for each tool, Photoshop contains tool presets for many of the tools that automatically change the options bar. For example, the Crop tool contains a preset to crop for a 5 × 7 photo. You can load other tool presets, edit current presets, or create new presets.

In a lab situation, if you notice that some tools are not working they way they are supposed to, or some presets are missing, someone may have changed the settings. The following steps reload all of the default tool presets.

To Reset Tool Presets

①
- On the options bar, click the Tool Preset picker and then click the menu button to display the Tool Preset menu (Figure C–22).

②
- Click Reset Tool Presets.
- If Photoshop displays a dialog box, click the OK button to reload all of the default tool presets.

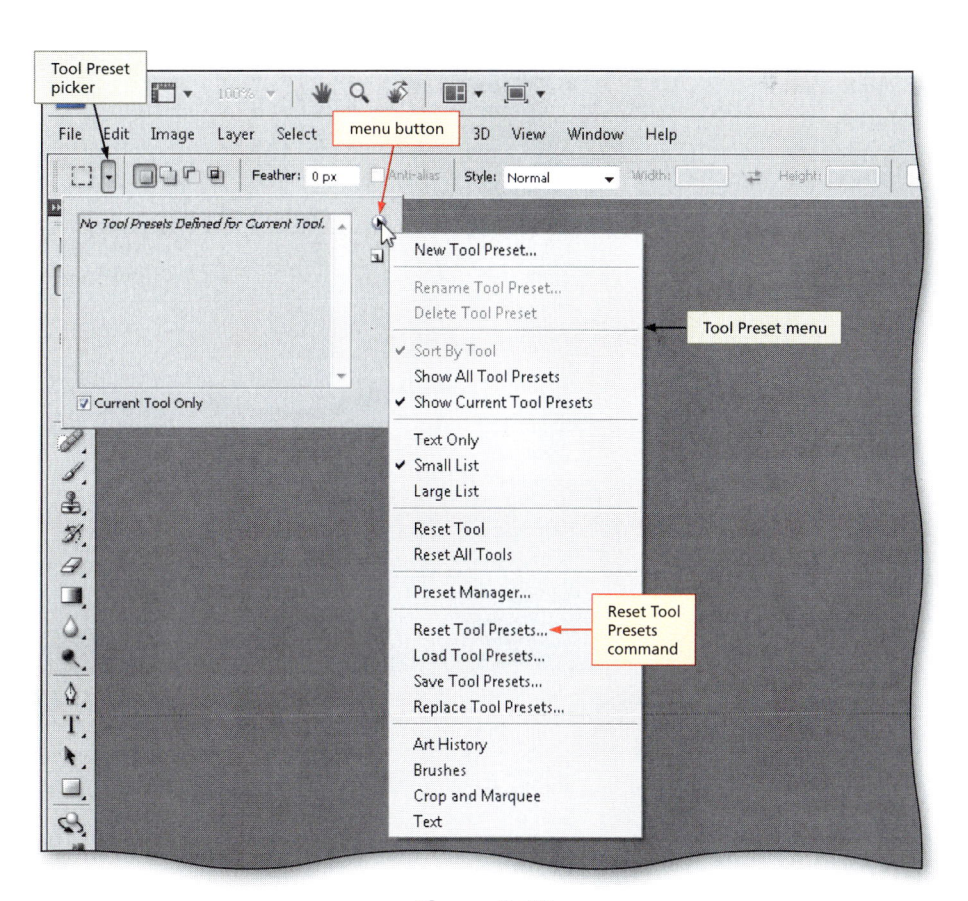

Figure C–22

> **Other Ways**
> 1. From any panel menu, click Reset Tool Presets, click OK

Resetting Panel Components

Many panels, including the Brushes, Swatches, and Styles panels, display preset samples with preset shapes, colors, and sizes. A few options bars, including the Gradient and Shape options bars, as well as the Contours box in the Layer Style dialog box, also display similar components — all of which may need to be reset at some time.

You can reset these presets using the Preset Manager, or each panel menu.

To Reset the Brushes

One of the most used tools in Photoshop is the Brush tool. Users make many choices in the Brushes panel and options bar that carry over from one session to another. In order to begin with a clean set of brushes and the default settings, the following steps clear the brush controls and reset the brush tips.

1
- Press the B key to activate the Brush tool. Press the F5 key to display the Brushes panel.
- Click the Brushes panel menu button to display the menu (Figure C–23).

2
- Click Clear Brush Controls.
- Click the Brushes panel menu button again, and then click Reset Brushes.
- When Photoshop asks if you want to use the default brushes, click the OK button.

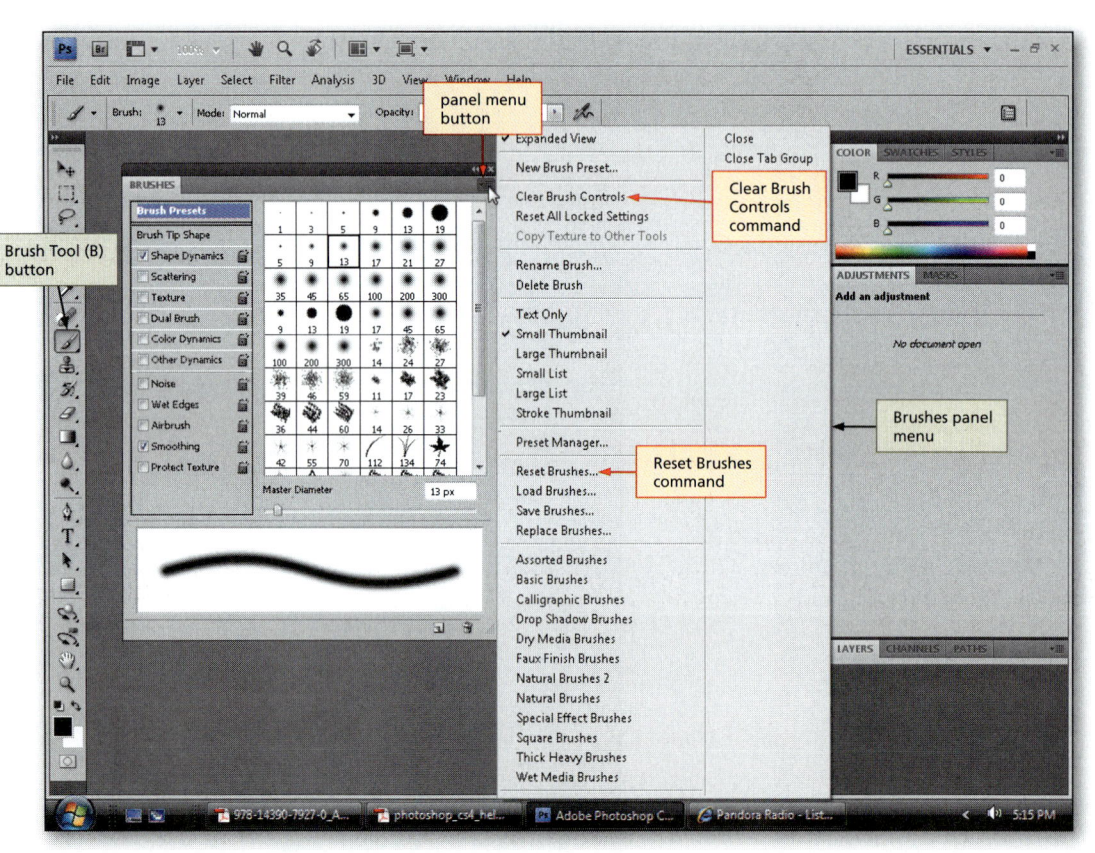

Figure C–23

Other Ways

1. On Brush options bar, click Toggle Brushes Panel, click panel menu button, click Reset Brushes

Changing Preferences

Changing the Color and Style of Guides, Grid, and Slices

Instructions: You would like to use some different colors and styles for grids and guides because the current colors are very similar to the colors in your image, making them hard to see. You decide to change the color and style preferences on your system as described in the following steps.

1. Start Photoshop CS4.
2. On the Edit menu, point to Preferences, and then click Guides, Grid, & Slices.
3. When the Preferences dialog box is displayed, change the Color and Style settings as shown in Figure C–24.

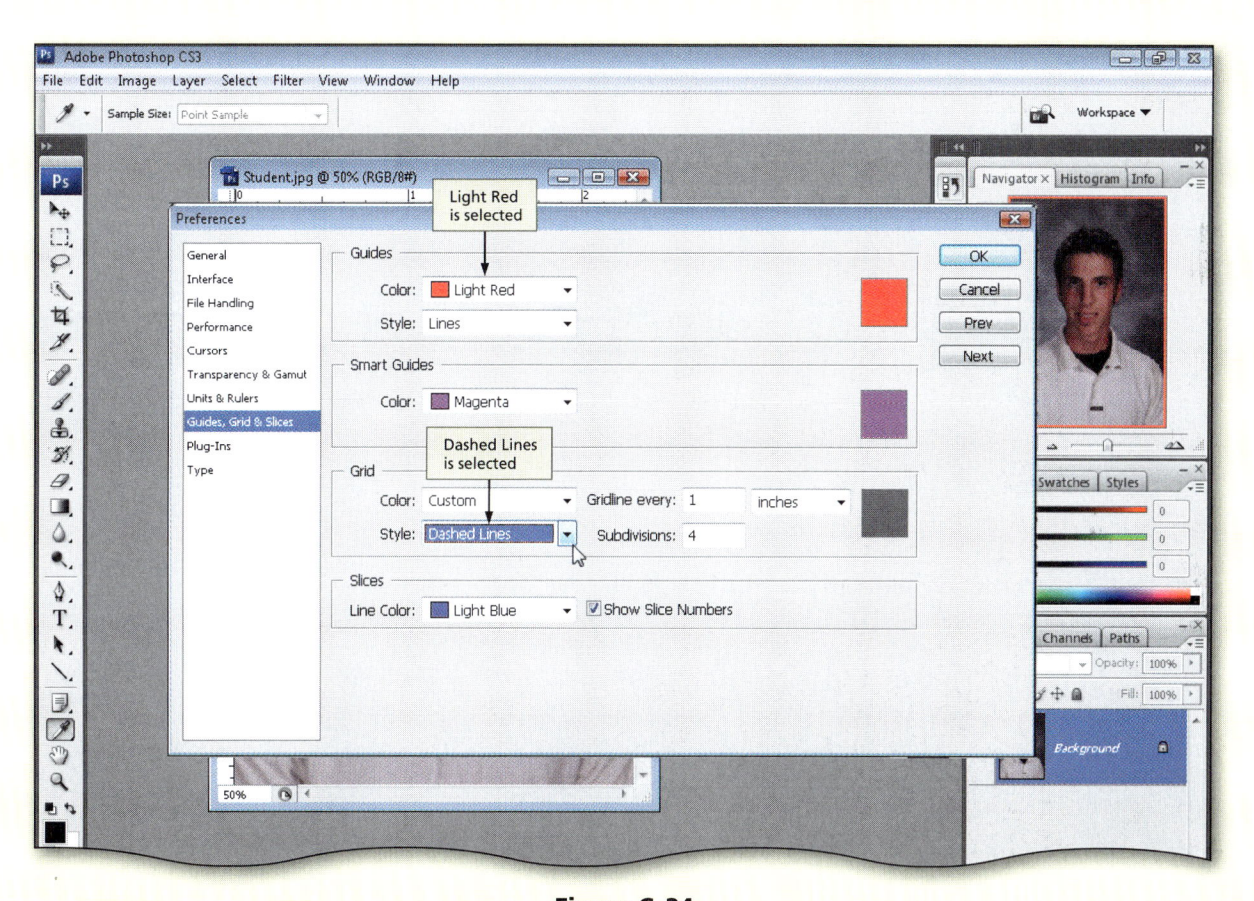

Figure C–24

4. Click the OK button.
5. Open any image file you have saved on your system and drag a guide from the horizontal ruler. Note the Light Red colored line.
6. On the View menu, point to Show, and then click Grid. Note the grid with dashed gray lines.
7. To clear the guides, on the View menu, click Clear Guides.
8. To hide the grid, on the View menu, point to Show and then click Grid.
9. To reset the colors and styles, either change the guide color back to Cyan and the grid style back to Lines, or quit Photoshop and then restart Photoshop while pressing ALT+CTRL+SHIFT. If Photoshop asks if you wish to delete the previous settings, click the Yes button.

Resetting Styles

Instructions: Someone has loaded many styles into the style box, making it difficult to find the common styles you are used to. You decide to reset the styles using the following steps.

1. Start Photoshop CS4.
2. On the Edit menu, click Preset Manager to display the Preset Manager dialog box.
3. Click the Preset Type box arrow to display the Preset list, and then click Styles in the list (Figure C–25).
4. Click the Preset Manager menu button to display a list of commands about the Styles Presets. Click Reset Styles in the list.
5. When Photoshop asks if you want to replace the styles with the default set, click the OK button.
6. Click the Done button to close the Preset Manager dialog box.
7. Quit Photoshop.

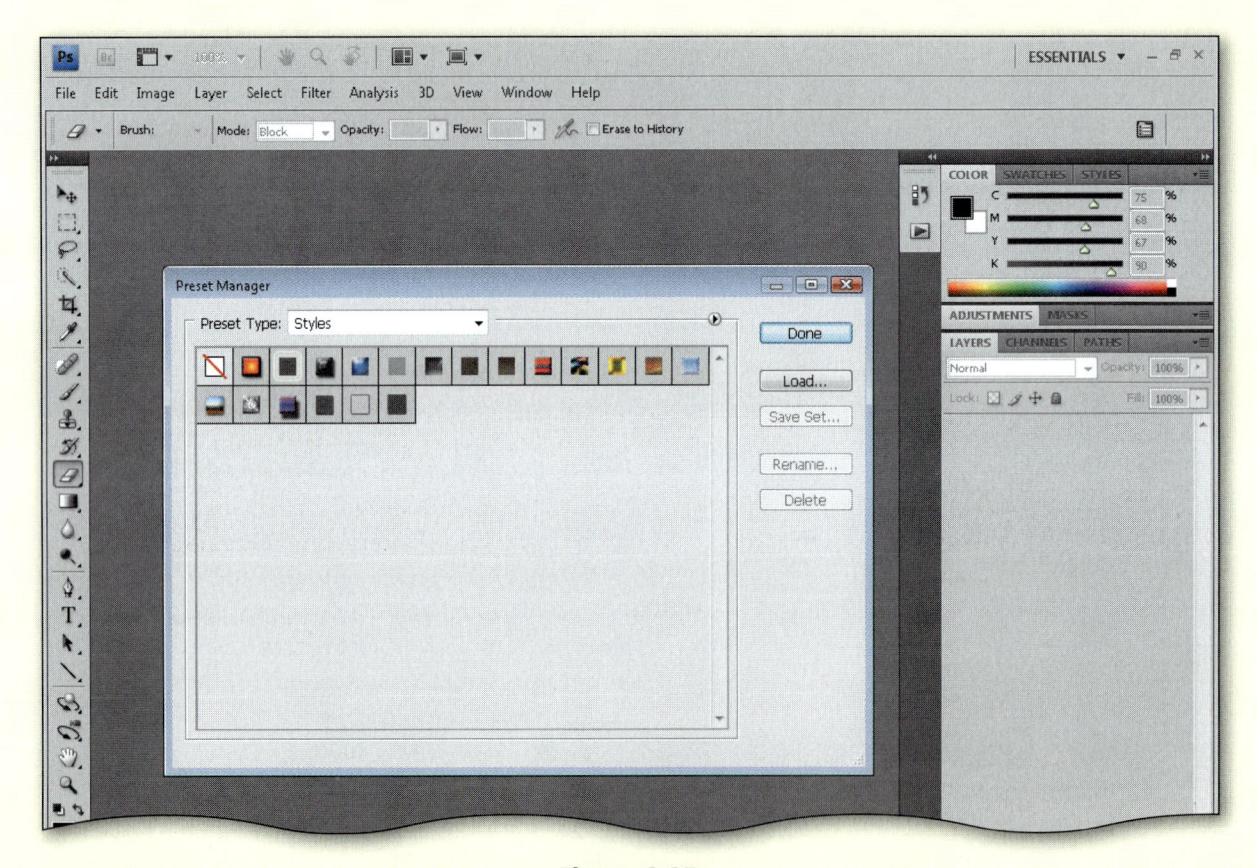

Figure C–25

Searching the Web

Instructions: You want to learn more about optimizing Photoshop settings and your computer system's memory by setting preferences for file size, history states, and cached views. Perform a Web search by using the Google search engine at google.com (or any major search engine) to display and print three Web pages that pertain to optimizing Photoshop CS4. On each printout, highlight something new that you learned by reading the Web page.

Appendix D
Using Photoshop Help

This appendix shows you how to use Photoshop Help. At anytime, whether you are accessing Photoshop currently or not, there are ways to interact with Photoshop Help and display information on any Photoshop topic. The help system is a complete reference manual at your fingertips.

Photoshop Help

Photoshop Help documentation for Photoshop CS4 is available in several formats, as shown in Figure D–1 on the next page. The first format is a Web-based help system that was introduced in Chapter 1. If you press the F1 key or choose Photoshop Help on the Help menu, the Adobe: Photoshop Support Center appears in your default browser. You then can click the link for Photoshop Help (web) and use the Web page to search for help topics. You must be connected to the Web to use this form of Photoshop Help.

A second form of Photoshop Help is available as a PDF file. Again, pressing the F1 key or choosing Photoshop Help on the Help menu opens the Adobe: Photoshop Support Center page on the Web. Then, you can click the Photoshop Help PDF (printable) link to open a searchable help documentation in book format. You can save the Photoshop Help PDF file on your storage device, or continue to use it on the Web.

The Photoshop Help PDF file also is packaged with Photoshop if you purchase the software on a DVD. To view the documentation, open the Documents folder on the installation or content DVD for your software, and then double-click Photoshop Help. If you prefer to view documentation in print form, you can print the Photoshop Help PDF file.

The Photoshop Support Center Web page also contains many other kinds of assistance including tutorials and videos. Photoshop Help on the Web displays two main panes. The left pane displays a navigation system. The right pane displays help information on the selected topic. Photoshop Help PDF displays a chapter navigation system on the left, and pages from Photoshop Help documentation on the right.

Searching for Help Using Words and Phrases

The quickest way to navigate Photoshop Help on the Web is through the **Search box** in the upper-right corner of the Photoshop Help Web page. Here you can type words, such as *layer mask*, *hue*, or *file formats*; or you can type phrases, such as *preview a Web graphic*, or *drawing with the Pen tool*. Photoshop Help responds by displaying search results with a list of topics you can click.

Here are some tips regarding the words or phrases you enter to initiate a search:

1. Check the spelling of the word or phrase.
2. Keep your search specific, with fewer than seven words, to return the most accurate results.
3. If you search using a specific phrase, such as *shape tool*, put quotation marks around the phrase — the search returns only those topics containing all words in the phrase.
4. If a search term does not yield the desired results, try using a synonym, such as Web instead of Internet.

APP 40 Appendix D Using Photoshop Help

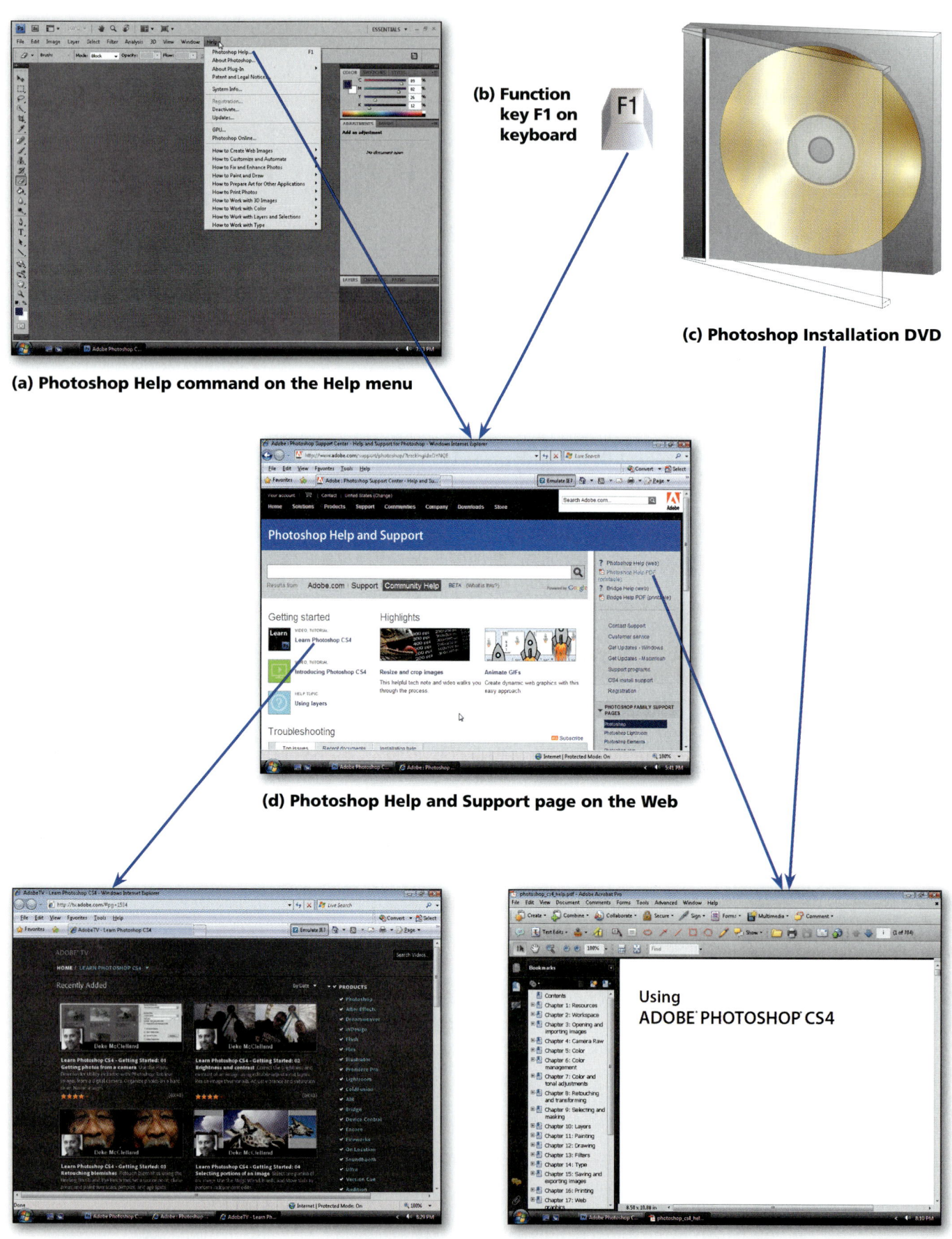

(a) Photoshop Help command on the Help menu

(b) Function key F1 on keyboard

(c) Photoshop Installation DVD

(d) Photoshop Help and Support page on the Web

(e) Videos and Tutorials

(f) Photoshop Help in PDF format

Figure D–1

To Obtain Help Using the Search Box

The following steps show how to open Adobe Help and use the Search box to obtain useful information by entering the keywords, ruler origin.

1

- With Photoshop running on your system, press the F1 key on the keyboard to display the Adobe: Photoshop Support Center (Figure D–2).

- When the Adobe Help Viewer 1.1 window is displayed, double-click the title bar to maximize the window, if necessary.

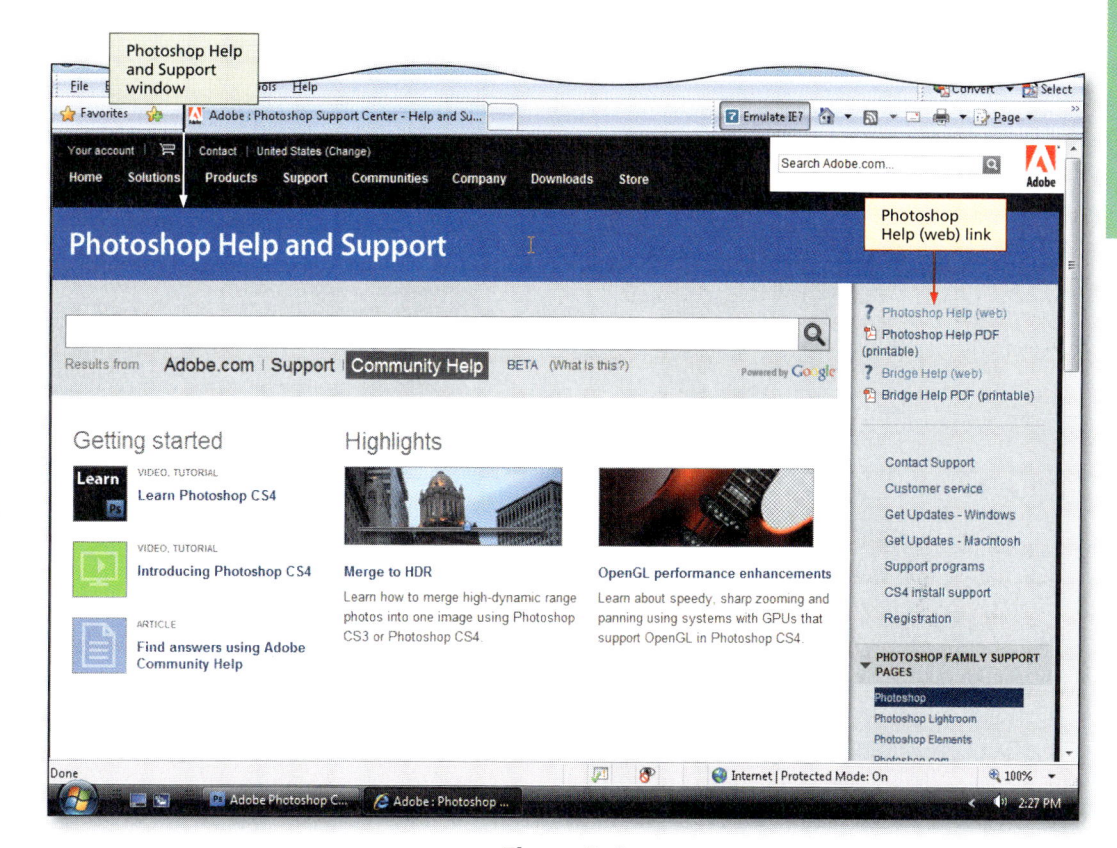

Figure D–2

2

- In the list of links on the right, click the Photoshop Help (web) link to display the Using Adobe Photoshop CS4 window (Figure D–3).

Q&A Can I use the links on the left?

Yes, the Web site displays two main panes. The left pane displays a navigation system. The right pane displays help information on the selected topic.

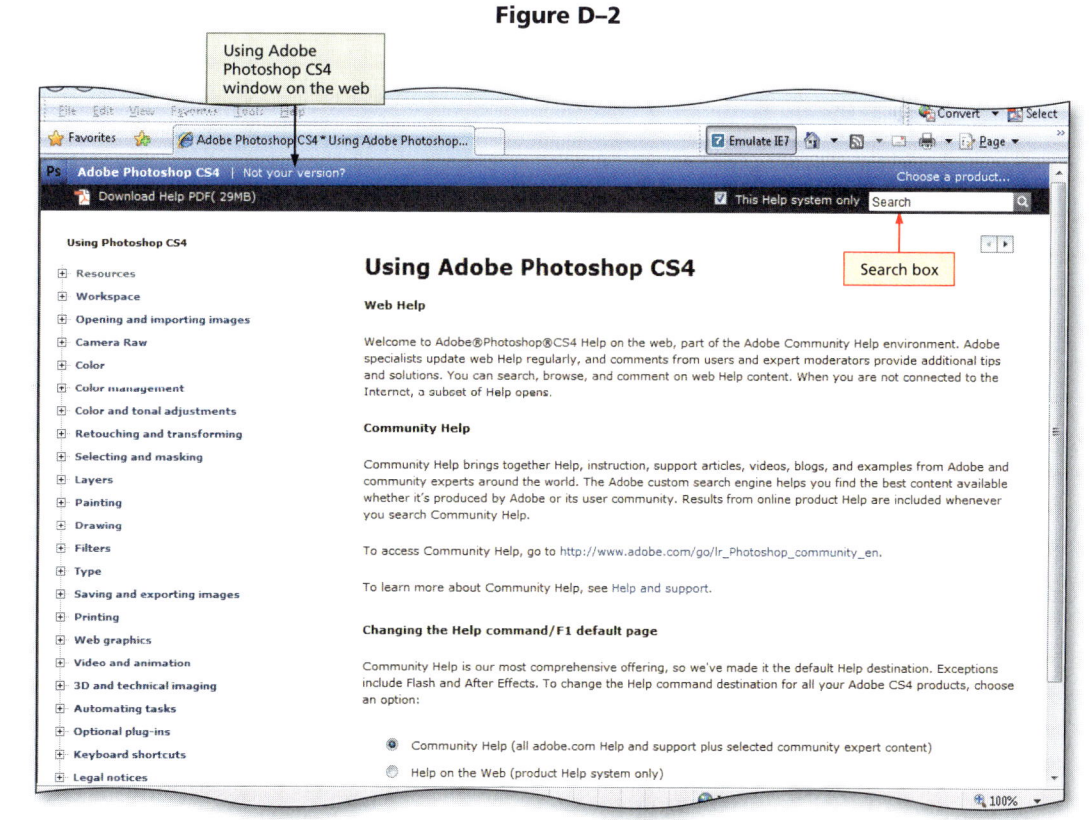

Figure D–3

APP 42 Appendix D Using Photoshop Help

3
- Click the Search box in the upper-right corner of the window, type ruler origin and then press the ENTER key to display the search results (Figure D–4).

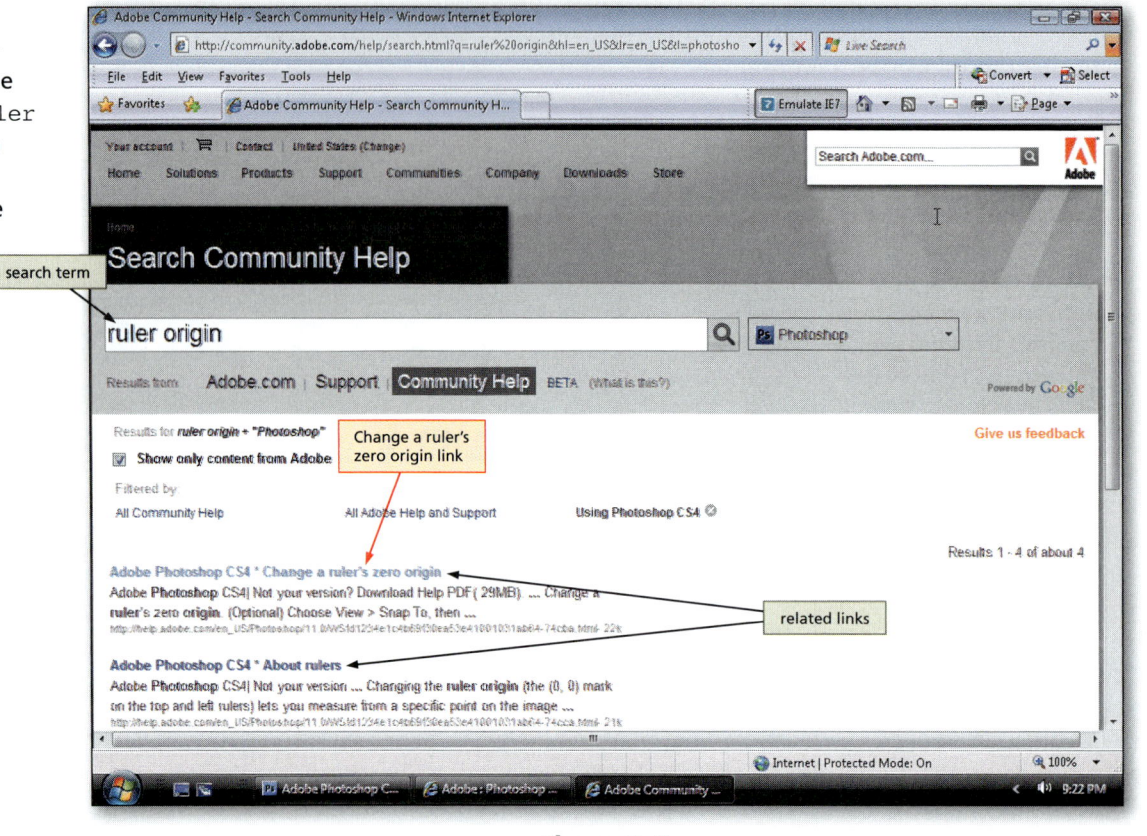

Figure D–4

4
- Click the link, Change a ruler's zero origin, to display information about the topic (Figure D–5).

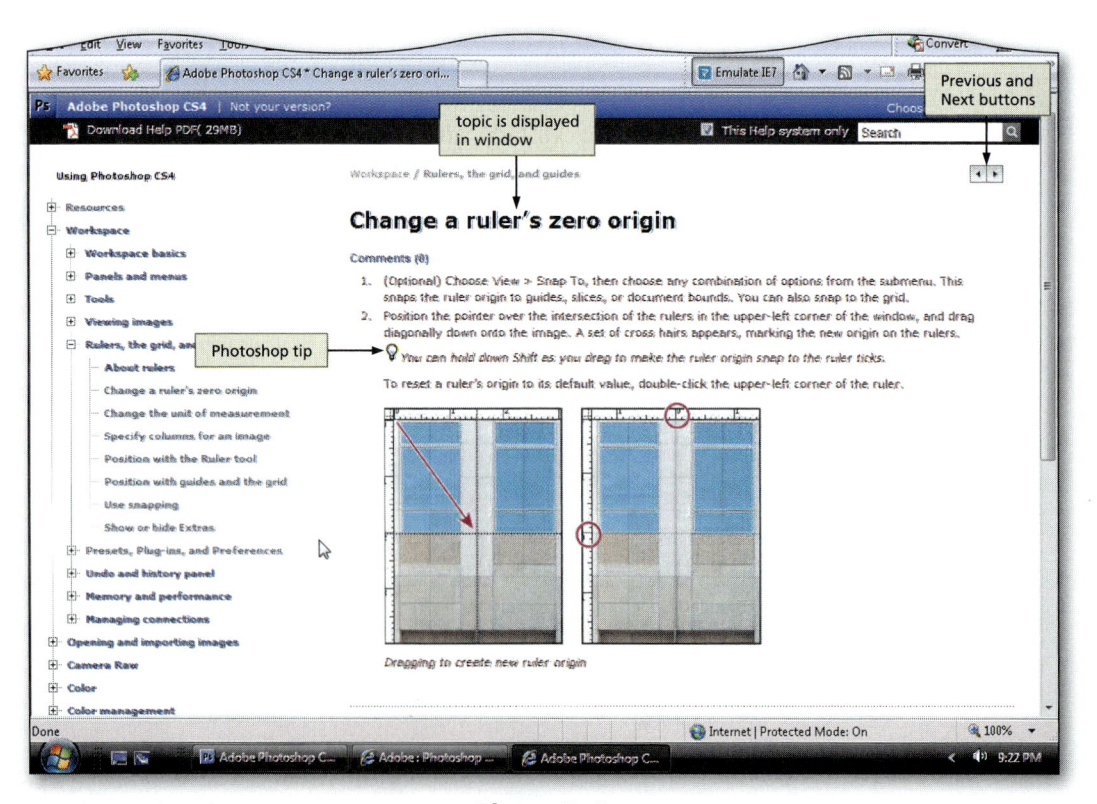

Figure D–5

On the right, Photoshop Help displays information about the topic, instructions, and a graphic. A light bulb icon indicates a Photoshop tip.

If none of the topics presents the information you want, you can refine the search by entering another word or phrase in the Search box.

As you click topics on the left, Adobe Help displays new pages of information. Adobe Help remembers the topics you visited and allows you to redisplay the pages visited during a session by clicking the Previous and Next buttons (Figure D–5 on page APP 42).

Using the Topics List

The Topics List is similar to a table of contents in a book. To use the Topics List, click any plus sign on the left side of Photoshop Help to display subtopics as shown in the following steps.

To Use the Topics List

The following steps use the Topics List to look up information about layers.

1

- In the Photoshop Help window, scroll down and then click the plus sign next to the word, Layers, and then click the plus sign next to the words, Layer basics, to expand the list of topics (Figure D–6).

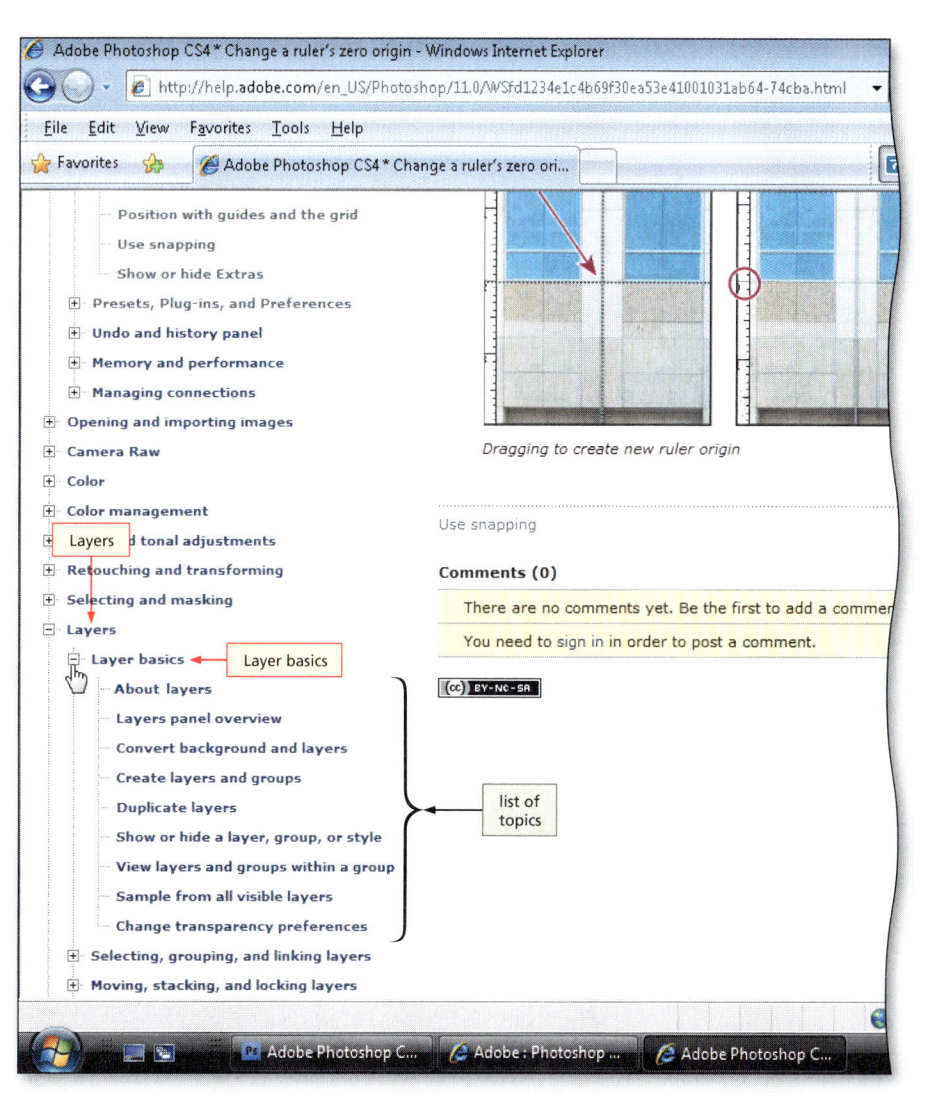

Figure D–6

2

- Click About layers to display information about Photoshop layers (Figure D–7).

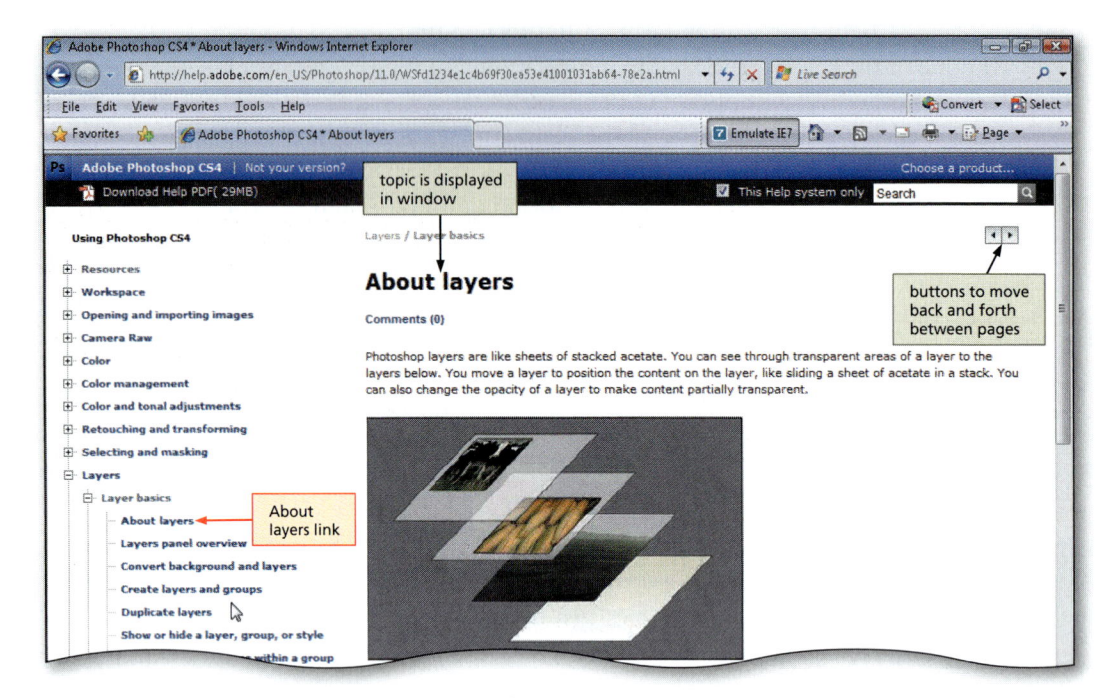

Figure D–7

To View a Video

Using Photoshop Help on the Web, you can view online videos and tutorials, as done in the following steps.

1

- With the topic, About Layers, displayed on the right side of the Photoshop Help window, scroll down to the lower portion of the page (Figure D–8).

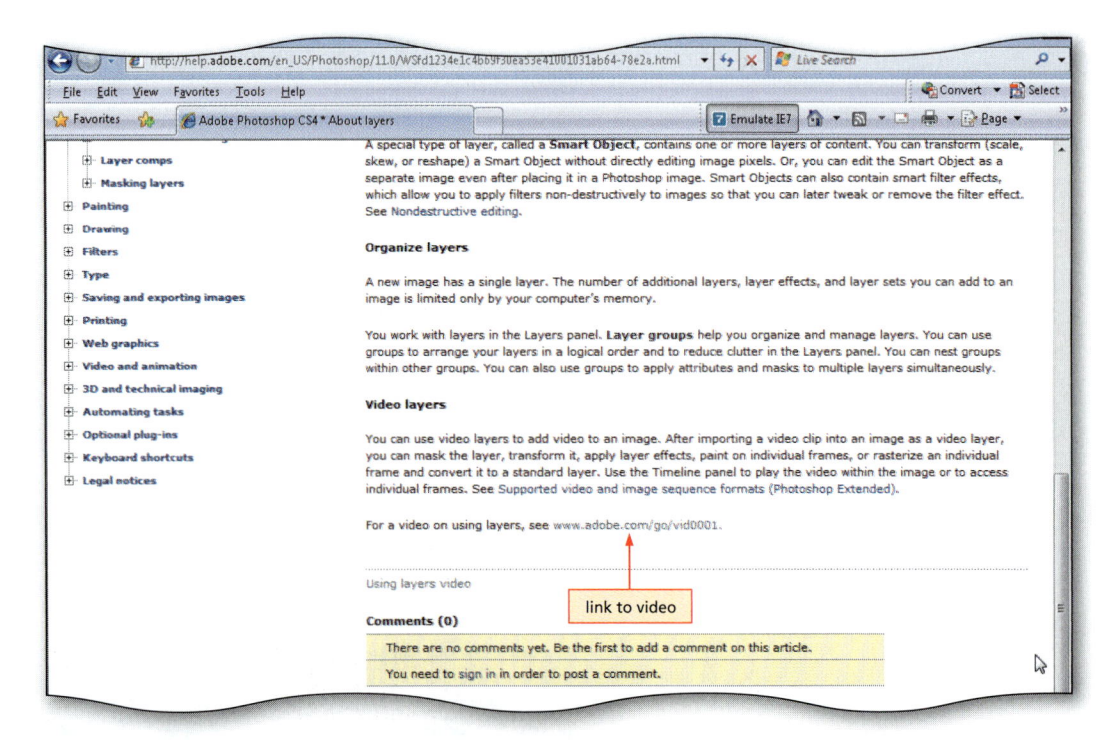

Figure D–8

Using Photoshop Help PDF **APP 45**

2
- Click the link www.adobe.com/go/vid0001 to start a video about creating layers (Figure D–9).

3
- When the video is finished playing, click the video window Close button to close the window.

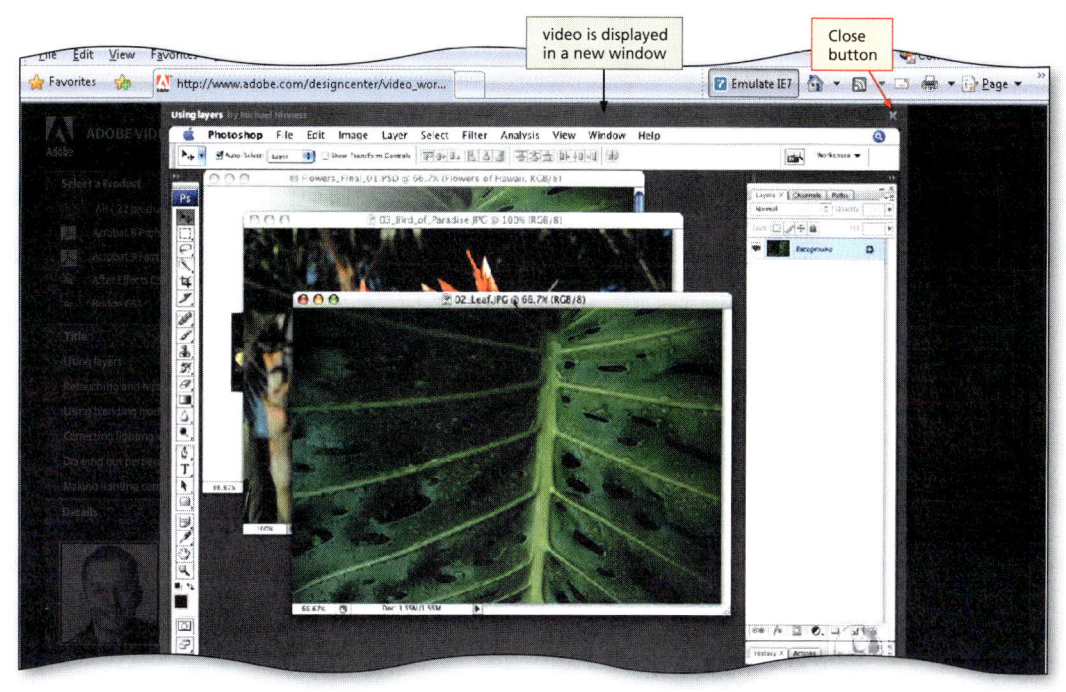

Figure D–9

Using Photoshop Help PDF

Photoshop Help PDF is complete documentation for using Photoshop CS4. The PDF file is organized into 22 chapters with a table of contents and an index like a regular book. You can access Photoshop Help PDF by clicking the link on the Adobe: Photoshop Support Center Web page or by opening the file from the installation DVD.

To Open Photoshop Help PDF

The following steps open the Photoshop Help PDF file from the Adobe: Photoshop Support Center Web page. You will use Adobe Acrobat to view the documentation.

1
- If necessary, click the Adobe: Photoshop Support Center button on the task bar. If you previously closed the brower page, open Photoshop, and press the F1 key to display the Adobe: Photoshop Support Center Web page (Figure D–10).

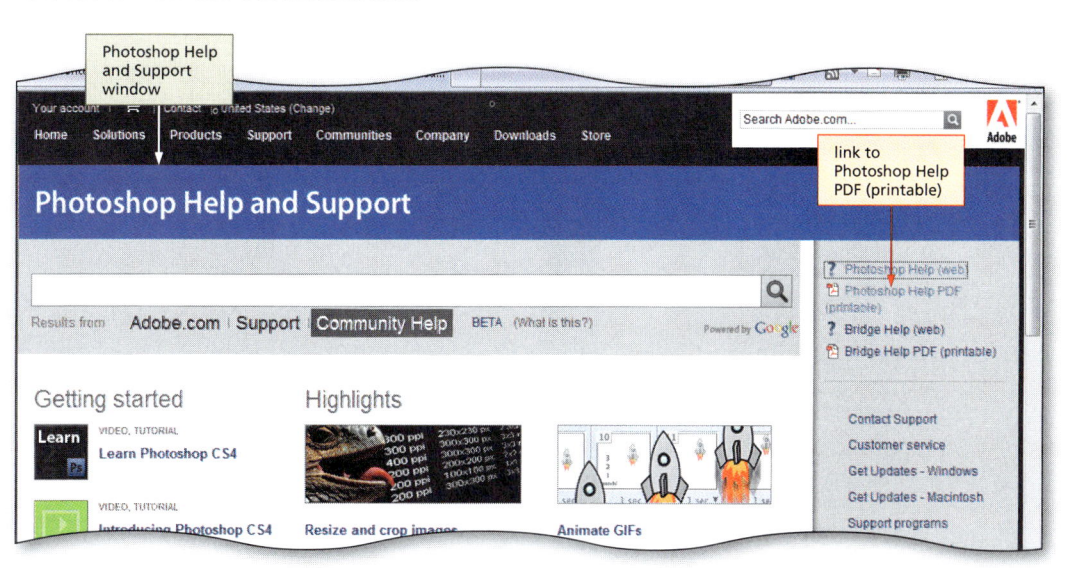

Figure D–10

2

- Click the link, Photoshop Help PDF (printable) in the upper-right corner of the window, to open the Using Adobe Photoshop CS4 documentation.

- Double-click the title bar, if necessary, to maximize the window (Figure D–11).

Q&A
The file would not open because I don't have Adobe Acrobat on my system.

See your instructor for ways to access the file.

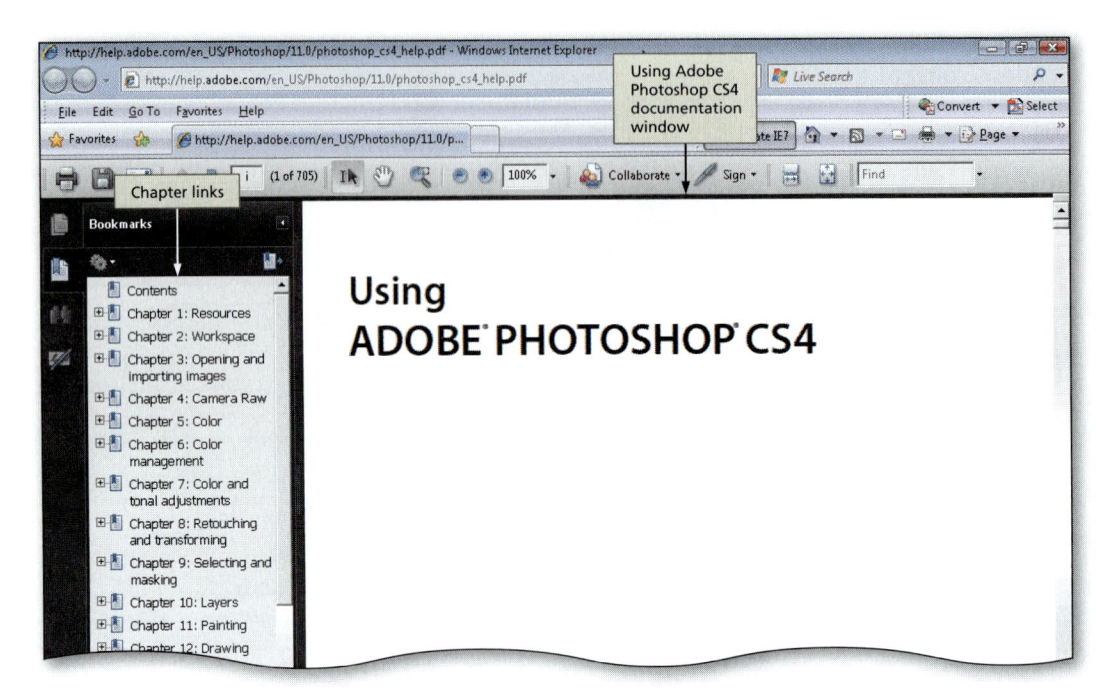

Figure D–11

To Navigate the Documentation by Chapter

The following steps use the left pane of the documentation window to find information related to color.

1

- With the Photoshop Help PDF file still displayed, click the plus sign next to the words Chapter 5: Color, and then click the plus sign next to the words About color to display the topics (Figure D–12).

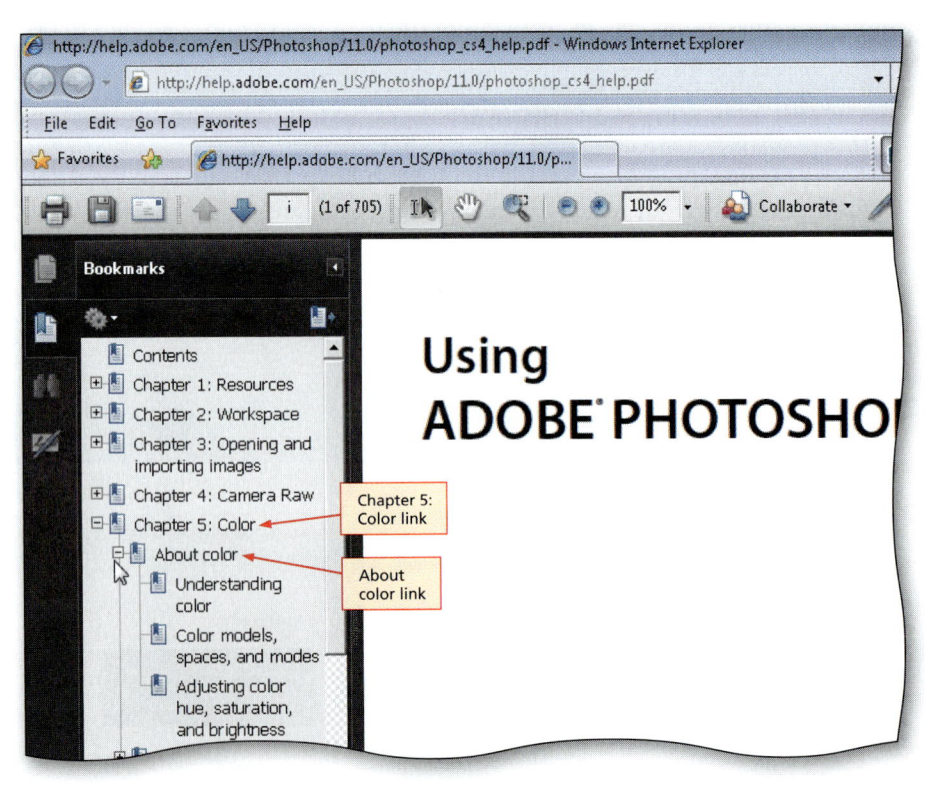

Figure D–12

2

- Click the words, Understanding color to display the information on the right side of the window (Figure D–13).

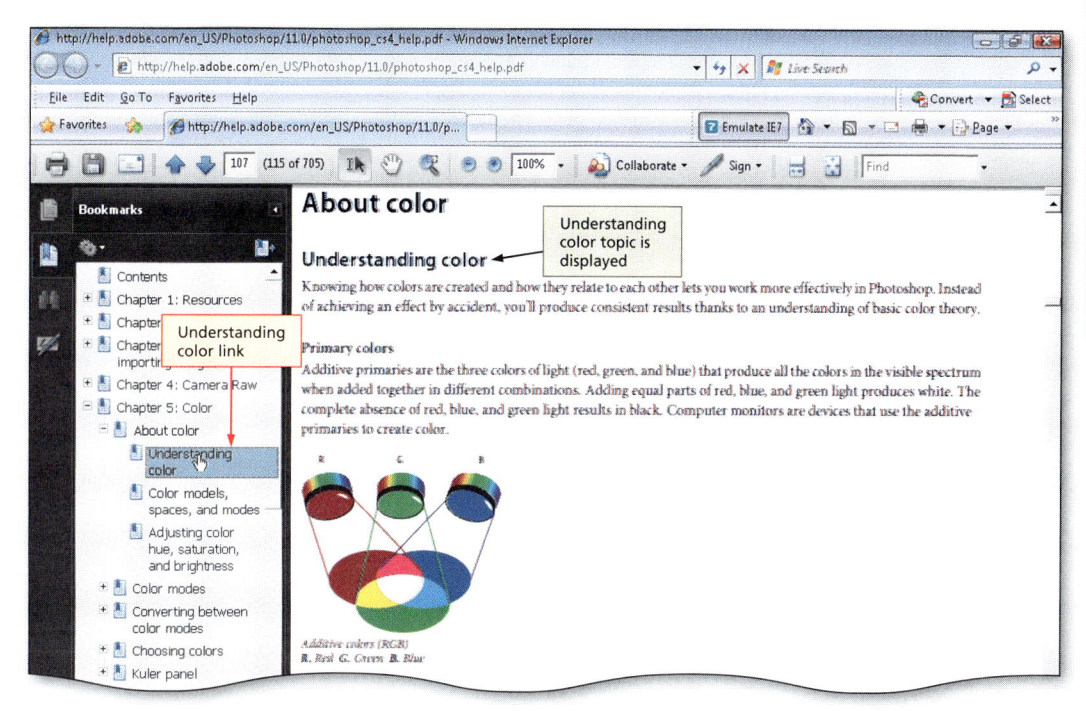

Figure D–13

To Use the Find Box

The following steps search the documentation information about the topic, retouch and transform, using the Adobe Acrobat Find box.

1

- With the Photoshop Help PDF file still displayed, click the Find box in the Adobe Acrobat toolbar and then type `retouch and transform`. Press the ENTER key to search for the terms (Figure D–14).

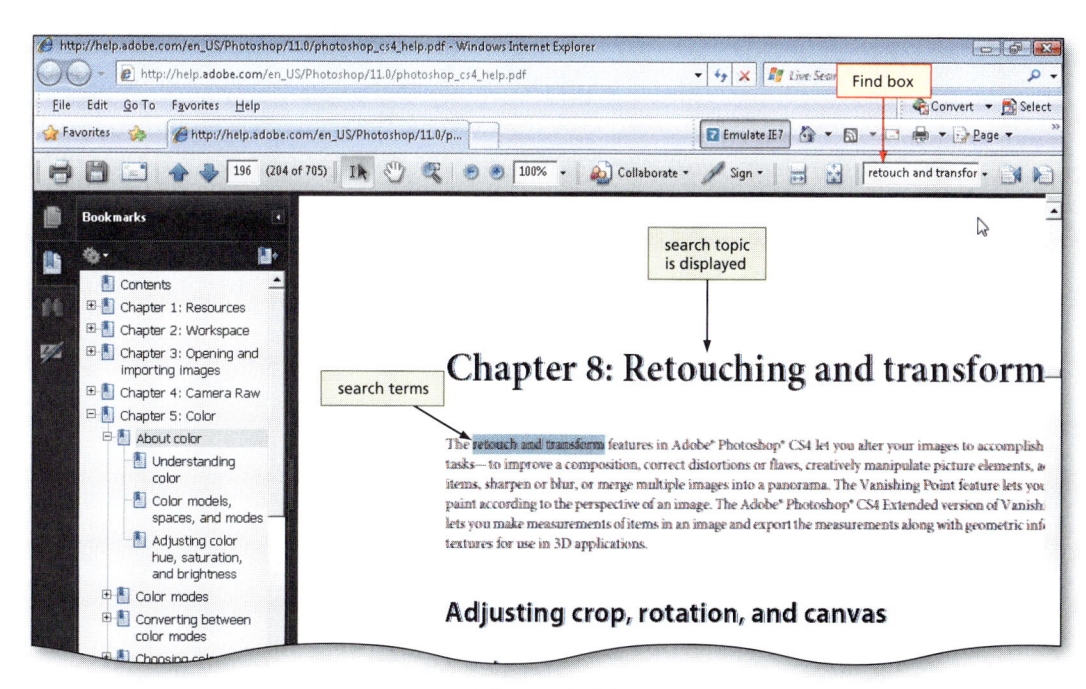

Figure D–14

Use Help

1: Using Adobe Help on the Web

Instructions: Perform the following tasks using Photoshop Help on the Web.

1. Type `pencil tool` in the Search box to obtain help on using the Pencil tool.
2. When the topics are displayed, click Paint with the Brush tool or Pencil tool.
3. One at a time, click two additional links and print the information. Hand in the printouts to your instructor. Use the Back to previous page and Forward to next page buttons to return to the original page.
4. Use the Search box to search for information on alignment. Click the Automatically align image layers topic in the search results. Read and print the information. One at a time, click the links on the page and print the information for any new page that is displayed.
5. Search for a topic that is of interest to you and take a survey or add a comment. Print the page and hand in the printout to your instructor. (Adding a comment may require you to register with Adobe. See your instructor for more details if you do not have an Adobe account issued with your software.)
6. In a browser, navigate to the Web page at www.adobe.com/designcenter/tutorials and then click the link for Photoshop. Navigate to a tutorial of your choice and follow the directions. Write three paragraphs describing your experience, including how easy or difficult it was to follow the tutorial and what you learned. Turn in the paragraphs to your instructor.
7. Close the browser window.

Use Help

2: Using Adobe Help PDF Documentation

Instructions: Use the Photoshop Help PDF to understand the topics better and answer the questions listed below. Answer the questions on your own paper, or hand in the printed Help information to your instructor.

1. Use the Photoshop Help PDF documentation to find help on snapping. Use the Search box, and enter `use snapping` as the term. Click the search result entitled, Use snapping and print the page. Hand in the printouts to your instructor.
2. Use the Photoshop Help PDF documentation and navigate to Chapter 12: Drawing. Click the plus sign next to Drawing Shapes. One at a time, click each link and print the page. Hand in the printouts to your instructor.

Appendix E
Using Adobe Bridge CS4

This appendix shows you how to use Adobe Bridge CS4. Adobe Bridge is a file exploration tool similar to Windows Explorer, but with added functionality related to images. Adobe Bridge replaces previous file browsing techniques, and now is the control center for the Adobe Creative Suite. Bridge is used to organize, browse, and locate the assets you need to create content for print, the Web, and mobile devices with drag-and-drop functionality.

Adobe Bridge

You can access Adobe Bridge from Photoshop or from the Windows Vista Start menu. Adobe Bridge can run independently from Photoshop as a stand-alone program.

To Start Bridge Using Windows

The following steps start Adobe Bridge from the Windows Vista Start menu.

1
- Click the Start button on the Windows taskbar and then click All Programs at the bottom of the left pane on the Start menu to display the All Programs submenu (Figure E–1).

Figure E–1

2

- Click Adobe Bridge CS4 in the list. When the Adobe Bridge window is displayed, double-click its title bar to maximize the window, if necessary (Figure E-2).

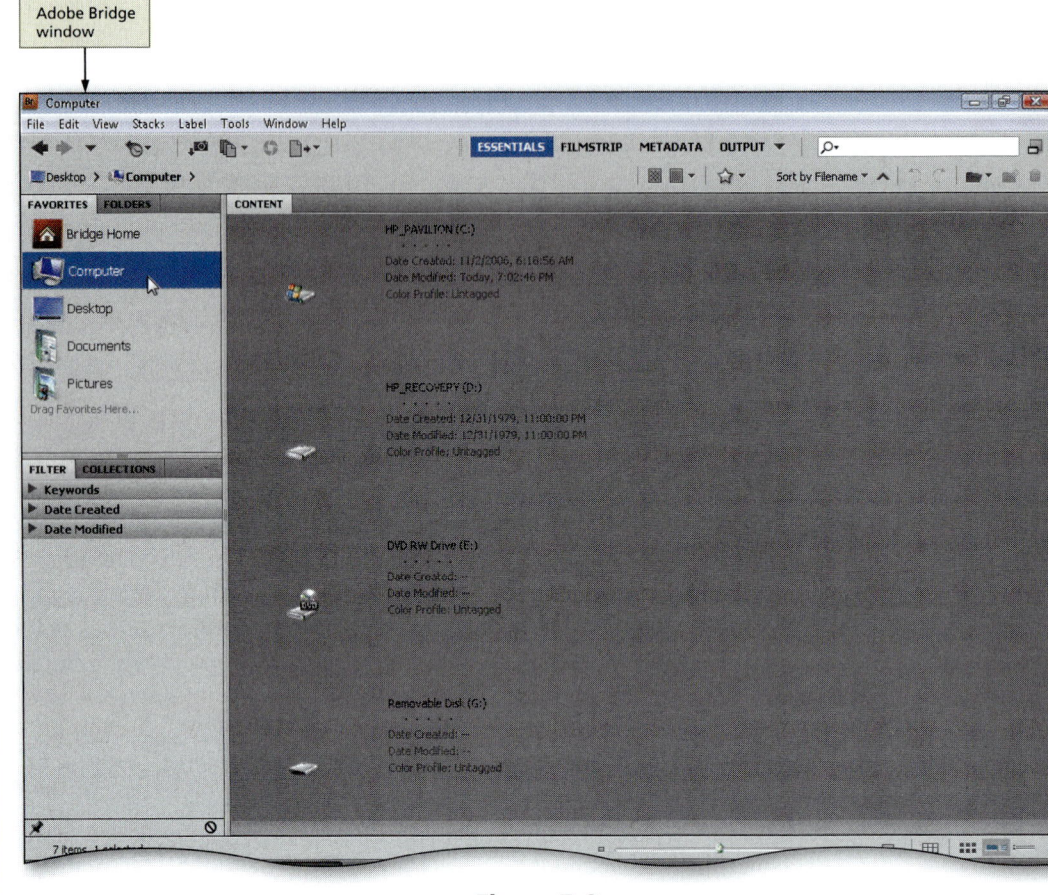

Figure E–2

Other Ways

1. In Photoshop, click File on menu bar, click Browse
2. In Photoshop, click Go To Bridge button on options bar
3. Press ATL+CTRL+O

To Reset the Workspace

To make your installation of Adobe Bridge match the figures in this book, you will reset the workspace to its default settings in the following steps.

1

- Click Window on the menu bar, and then point to Workspace to display the Workspace submenu (Figure E–3).

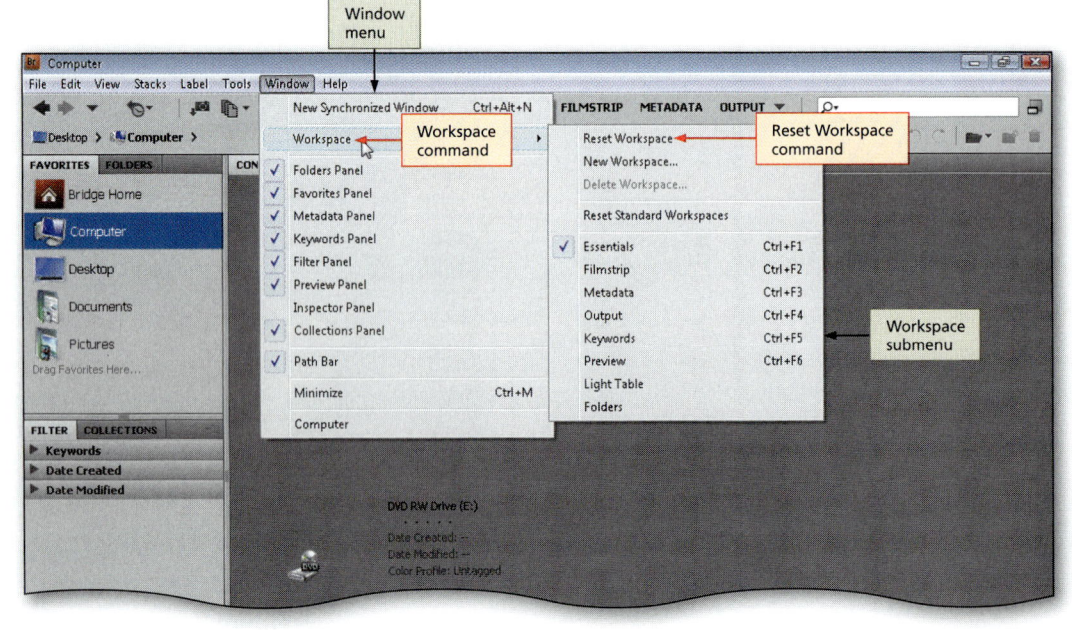

Figure E–3

2

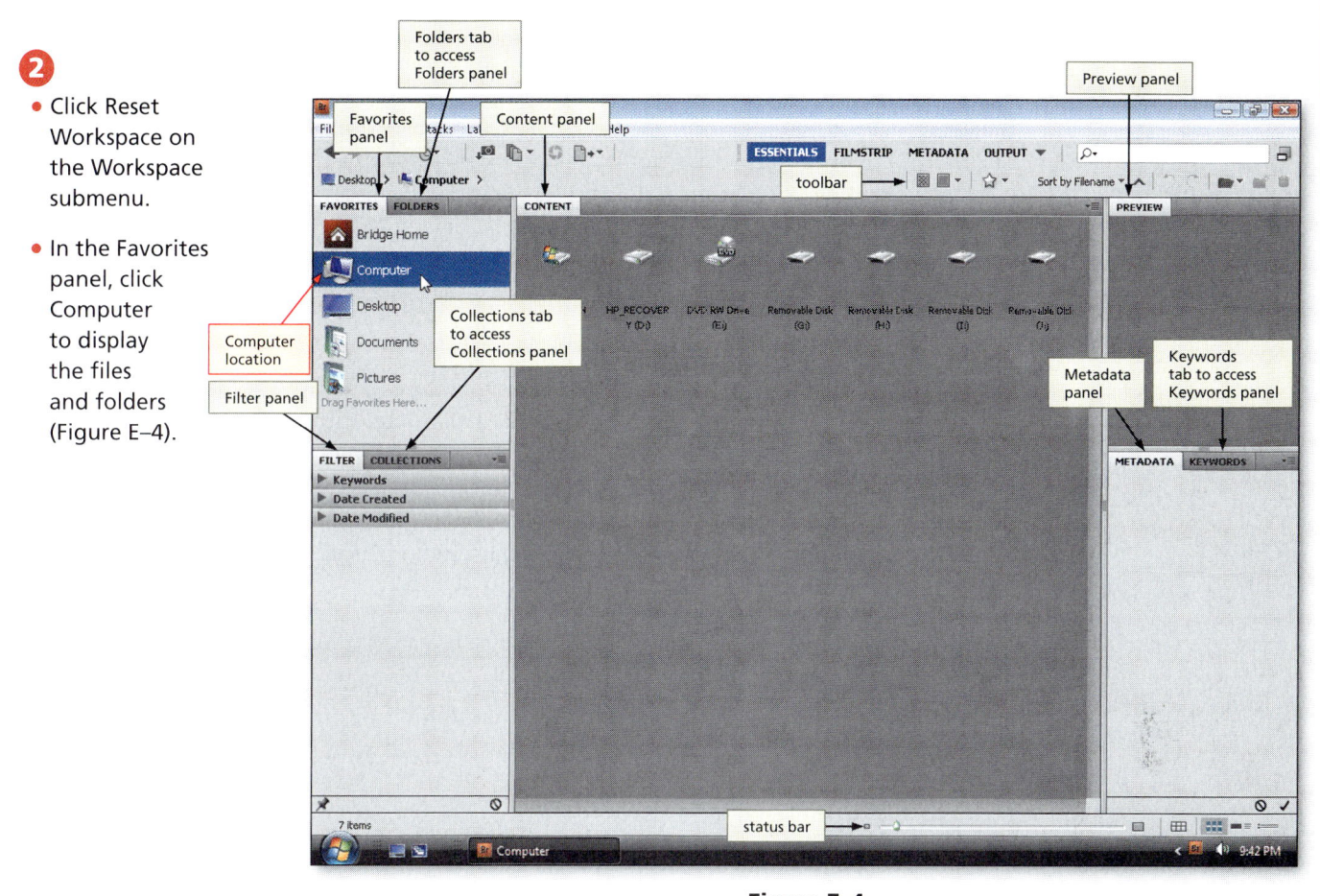

- Click Reset Workspace on the Workspace submenu.

- In the Favorites panel, click Computer to display the files and folders (Figure E–4).

Figure E–4

Other Ways

1. Press CTRL+F1

The Adobe Bridge Window

The parts of the Adobe Bridge window are displayed in Figure E–4. The window is divided into panels and includes a toolbar and status bar.

The Panels

Several panels are displayed in the Bridge workspace in default view. To select a panel, click its tab. You can change the location of the panels by dragging their tabs. You can enlarge or reduce the size of the panels by dragging their borders. Some panels include buttons and menus to help you organize displayed information.

Favorites Panel The **Favorites panel** allows quick access to common locations and folders, as well as access to other Adobe applications. Click a location to display its contents in the Content panel. If you click an application name, Windows will launch or open the application.

Folders Panel The **Folders panel** shows the folder hierarchy in a display similar to that of Windows Explorer. Users click the plus sign to expand folders and the minus sign to collapse them.

Content Panel The **Content panel** is displayed in a large pane in the center of the Adobe Bridge window. The content panel includes a view of each file and folder, its name, the creation date, and other information about each item. The Content panel is used to select files and open folders. To select a file, click it. To open a folder, double-click it. You can change how the Content panel is displayed on the Bridge status bar.

Preview Panel The **Preview panel** displays a preview of the selected file that is usually larger than the thumbnail displayed in the Content panel. If the panel is resized, the preview also is resized.

Filter Panel The **Filter panel** is displayed in the lower-left region of the Adobe Bridge window. The Filter panel includes four categories of criteria used to filter or control which files display in the Content panel. The categories are File Type, Keywords, Date Created, and Date Modified. The criteria items include metadata that is generated dynamically depending on the file type. For example, if the Content panel displays images, the criteria include camera data. If the Content panel displays audio files, the criteria include artist, album genre, and so on.

Collections Panel The **Collections panel** is displayed in the lower-left region of the Adobe Bridge window. **Collections** are a way to group photos in one place for easy viewing, even if the images are located in different folders or on different hard drives. The Collections panel allows you to create and display previously created collections, by identifying files or by saving previous searches.

Metadata Panel The **Metadata panel** contains metadata information for the selected file. Recall that metadata is information about the file including properties, camera data, creation and modification data, and other pieces of information. If multiple files are selected, shared data is listed such as keywords, date created, and exposure settings.

Keywords Panel The **Keywords panel** allows you to assign keywords using categories designed by Bridge, or you can create new ones. The keywords help you organize and search your images.

Toolbars and Buttons

Bridge displays several toolbars and sets of buttons to help you work more efficiently (Figure E–5).

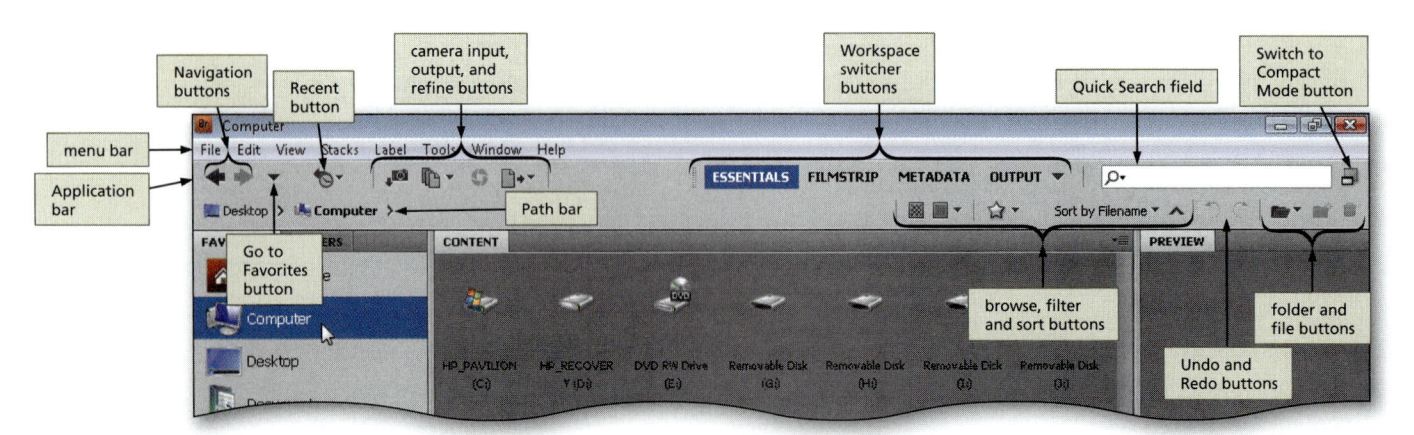

Figure E–5

Menu Bar The menu bar is displayed at the top of the Bridge window and contains commands specific to Bridge.

Application Bar Below the menu bar is the Application bar, which includes the navigation buttons, file retrieval and output buttons, buttons for switching workspaces, and other buttons to search for files.

Look In Box To the right of the Navigation buttons is the Look In box. When you click the box arrow, Bridge displays the current folder's hierarchy, as well as favorite and recent folders. To the right of the Look In box is a Go up button to move up in the file hierarchy.

Path Bar The path bar displays the path for the current file. On the right side of the Path bar are shortcut buttons to help you work with your files. Browse, Filter, and Sort buttons change the display in the Content panel. The Create a new folder button inserts a new folder in the current location. The rotate buttons are active when an image file is selected in the Content panel. The Delete item button deletes the selected item.

Status Bar At the bottom of the Bridge window, the status bar displays information and contains buttons (Figure E–6). On the left side of the status bar is information regarding the number of items in the current location and how many files are selected, if any. On the right side of the status bar, the Thumbnail slider sets the size of the thumbnails. To the right of the slider are four buttons used to change the display of the Content panel, including the Click to lock thumbnail grid button, the View contents as thumbnail button, the View contents as details button, and the View contents as list button.

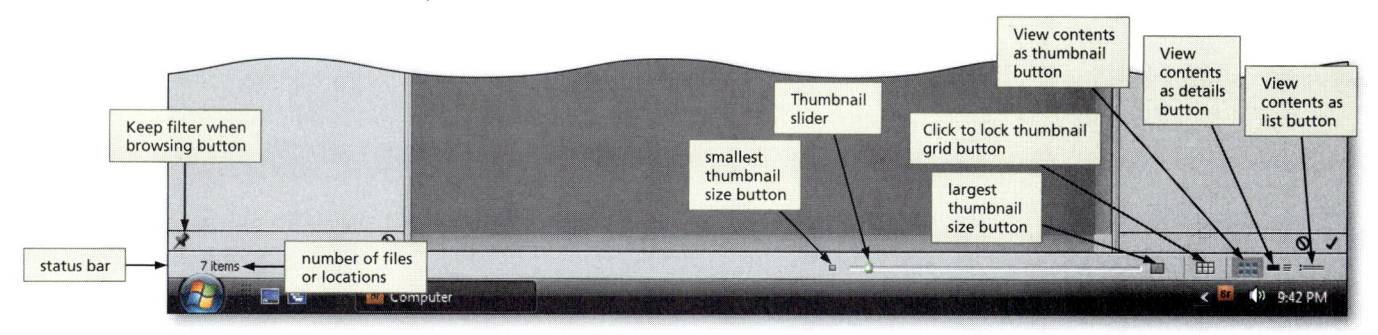

Figure E–6

Bridge Navigation and File Viewing

The advantages of using Bridge to navigate through the files and folders on your computer system include an interface that looks the same in all folders, the ability to see the images quickly, and the ease with which you can open the files in Photoshop or other image editing software. Besides the four kinds of displays represented by the Workspace switcher buttons on the right side of the status bar, Bridge offers several other configurations or layouts of the workspace accessible by clicking Workspace submenu on the Window menu (Figure E–3 on page APP 50).

To Navigate and View Files Using Bridge

The following steps navigate to a DVD to view files. Your instructor might specify a different location for these files. You then will use the Workspace switcher buttons to view the Content panel in different styles.

1

- Insert the DVD that accompanies this book into your DVD drive.

- After a few seconds, if Windows displays a dialog box, click its Close button.

- In the Content panel, double-click the DVD icon associated with your DVD drive.

- When the folders and files of the DVD are displayed, double-click the Chapter01 folder to display the files (Figure E–7).

- One at a time, click each of the workspace buttons on the options bar and note how the Content panel changes.

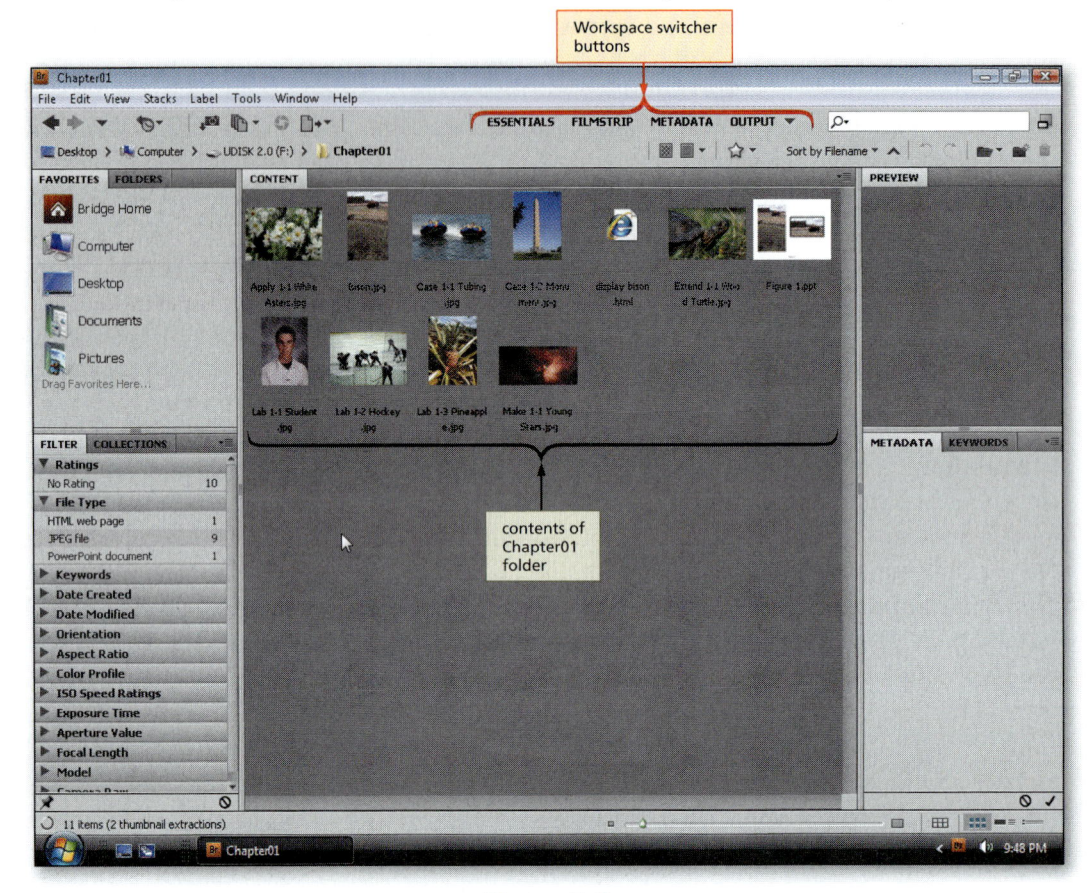

Figure E–7

2

- Press CTRL+F1 to return to the Essentials workspace.

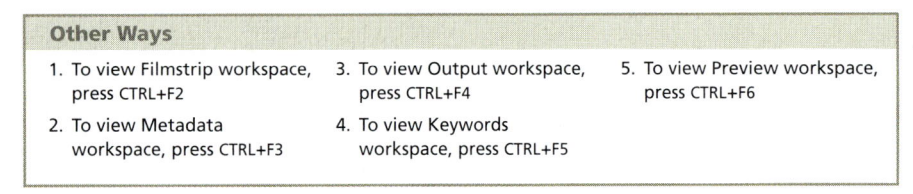

Other Ways		
1. To view Filmstrip workspace, press CTRL+F2	3. To view Output workspace, press CTRL+F4	5. To view Preview workspace, press CTRL+F6
2. To view Metadata workspace, press CTRL+F3	4. To view Keywords workspace, press CTRL+F5	

BTW

Duplicating Files
Bridge also offers a Duplicate command on the Edit menu (Figure E–8) that makes a copy in the same folder. Bridge renames the second file with the word Copy appended to the file name.

Managing Files

If you want to move a file to a folder that currently is displayed in the Content panel, you can drag and drop the file. The right-drag option is not available. If you want to copy a file, you can choose Copy on the Edit menu, navigate to the new folder and then choose Paste on the Edit menu. At anytime you can press the DELETE key to delete a file or folder, or right-click and then click Delete on the shortcut menu. To rename a photo in Bridge, right-click the file and then click Rename. Type the new name.

To Copy a File

The following steps copy a file from a DVD to a USB flash drive using Bridge.

1
- With the Chapter01 folder contents still displaying in the Content panel, click the Case 1-1 Tubing thumbnail to select it.
- Click Edit on the menu bar to display the Edit menu (Figure E–8).

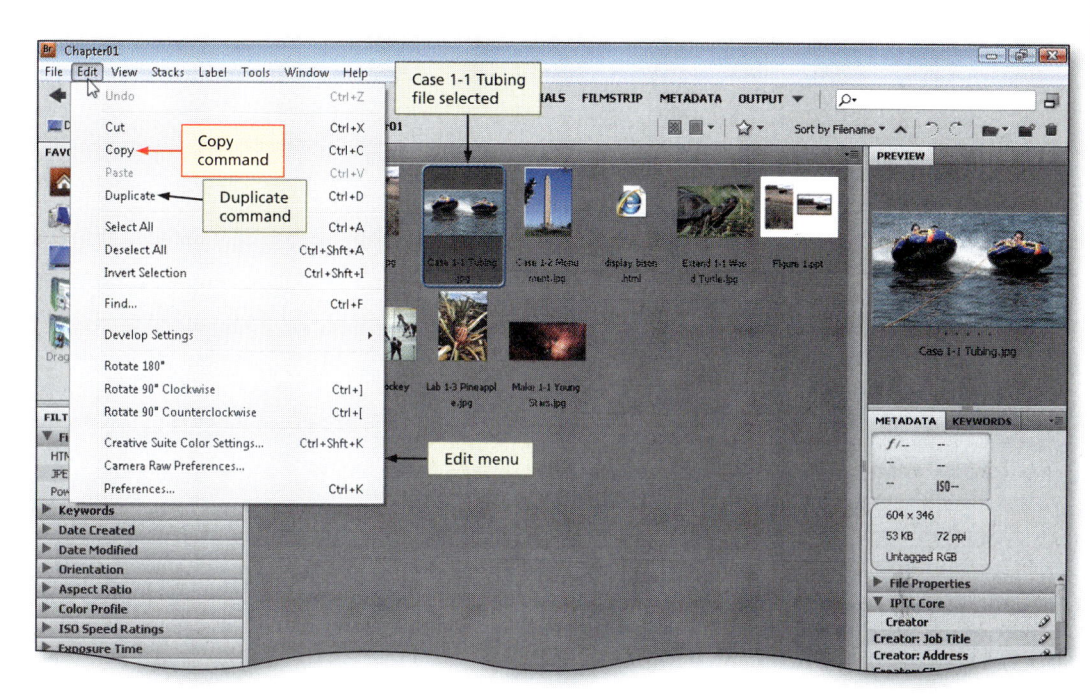

Figure E–8

2
- Click Copy on the Edit menu.
- In the Favorites panel, click Computer.
- When the Computer locations are displayed in the Content panel, double-click drive F or the drive associated with your USB flash drive.

3
- Click Edit on the menu bar, and then click Paste to display the copy in its new location (Figure E–9).

Other Ways
1. To copy, press CTRL+C
2. To paste, press CTRL+V

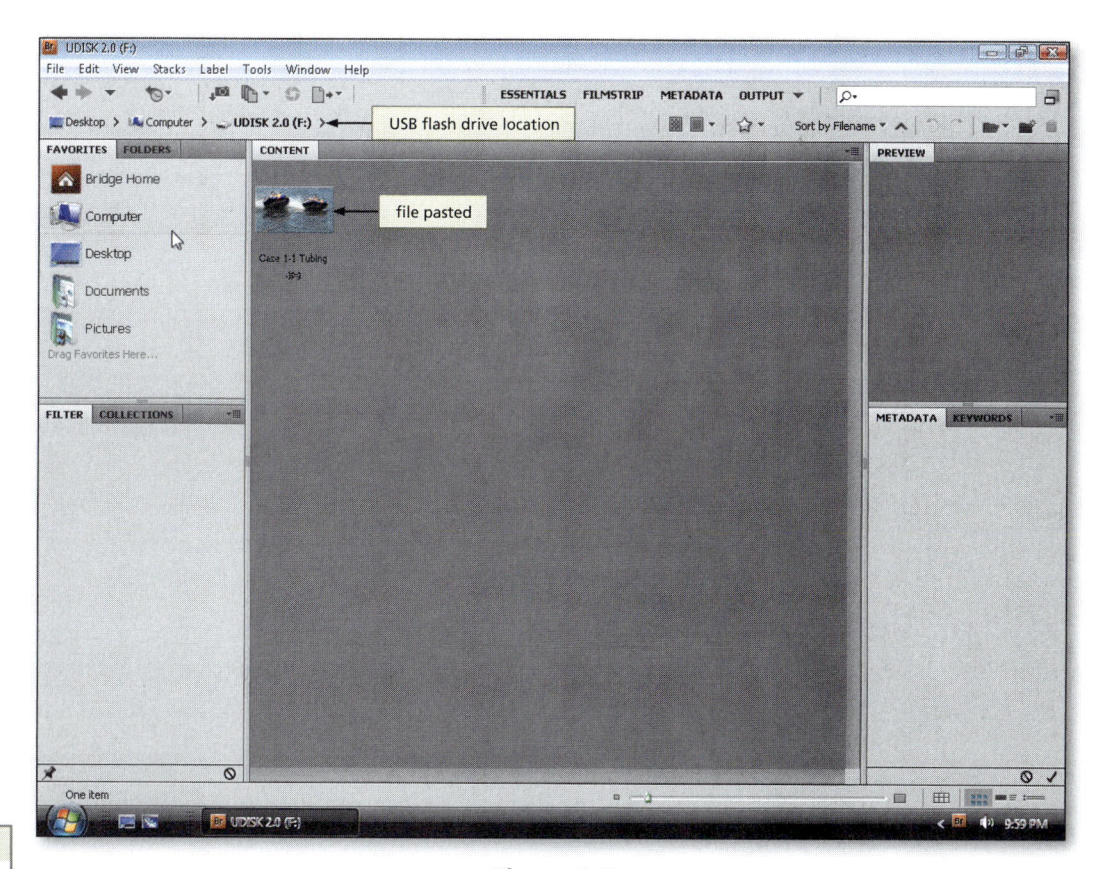

Figure E–9

Metadata

BTW

Metadata
This extended set of metadata is particularly useful for large businesses, such as the newspaper industry, which contracts with many photographers and must maintain photo history.

BTW

Metadata Panel Menu
The Metadata panel menu button displays options to change the font size of the fields in the panel, options to set preferences, and ways to find and add new fields. For example, if your digital camera records global positioning system (GPS) information, you can use the menu to append that data to the digital photos.

A popular use for Bridge allows you to assign metadata to files. Metadata, such as information about the file, author, resolution, color space, and copyright, is used for searching and categorizing photos. You can utilize metadata to streamline your workflow and organize your files.

Metadata is divided into categories, depending on the type of software you are using and the selected files. The category **File Properties** includes things like file type, creation date, dimensions, and color mode. **IPTC Core** stands for International Press Telecommunications Council, which is data used to identify transmitted text and images, such as data describing the image or the location of a photo. **Camera Data (Exif)** refers to the Exchangeable Image File Format, a standard for storing interchange information in image files, especially those using JPEG compression. Most digital cameras now use the EXIF format. The standardization of IPTC and EXIF encourages interoperability between imaging devices. Other categories may include Audio, Video, Fonts, Camera Raw and Version Cue, among others. You can see a list of all the metadata categories and their definitions by using Bridge Help.

To Assign and View Metadata

The Metadata Focus workspace makes it easier to assign or enter metadata for photos. In the Metadata panel, you can click the pencil icon to select fields of metadata, or you can move through the fields by pressing the TAB key. The following steps enter description and location information for the selected file.

1
- Click the Case 1-1 Tubing thumbnail to select it.

- In the Metadata panel, if necessary, click the right-pointing arrow next to IPTC Core to display its fields. Scroll down to the Description field (Figure E–10).

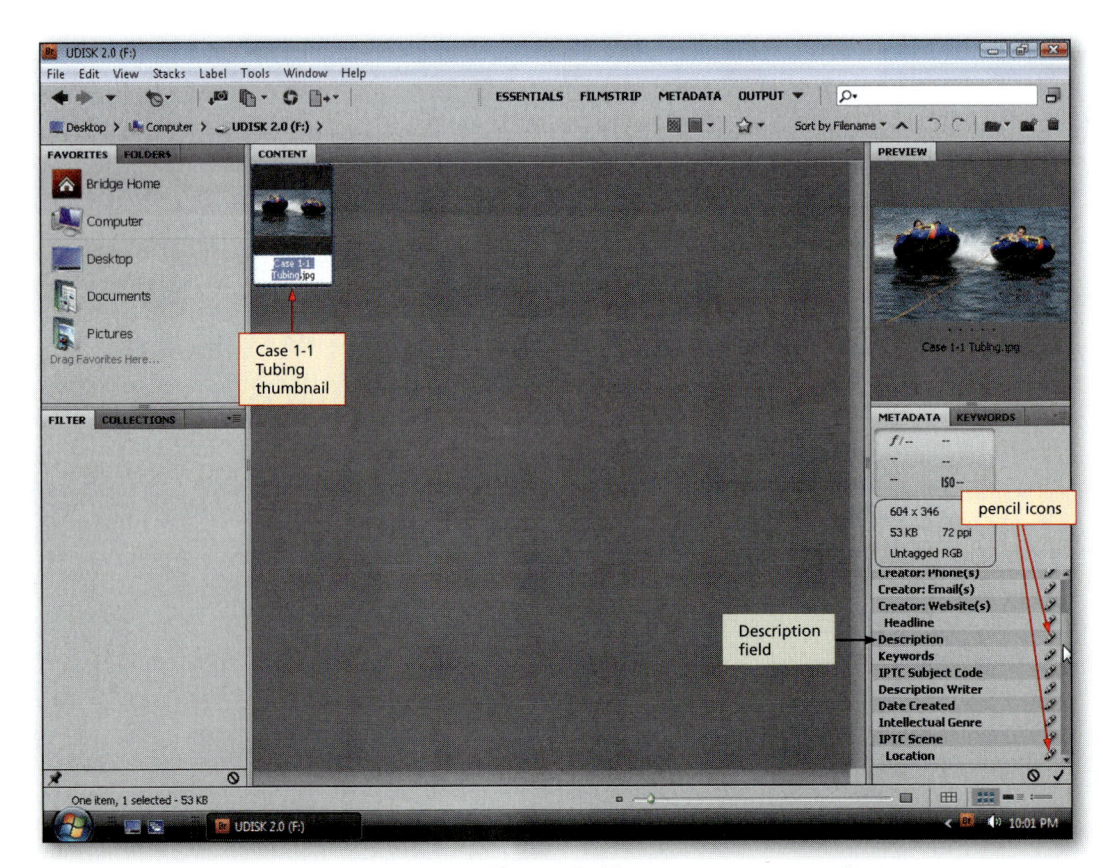

Figure E–10

2

- Click the pencil icon to the right of the Description field. Type `Tubing Adventure` as the description.

- Scroll as needed and then click the pencil icon to the right of the Location field. Type `Raccoon Lake` as the location.

- Press the TAB key, Type `Rockville` as the city.

- Press the TAB key. Type `Indiana` as the state (Figure E–11).

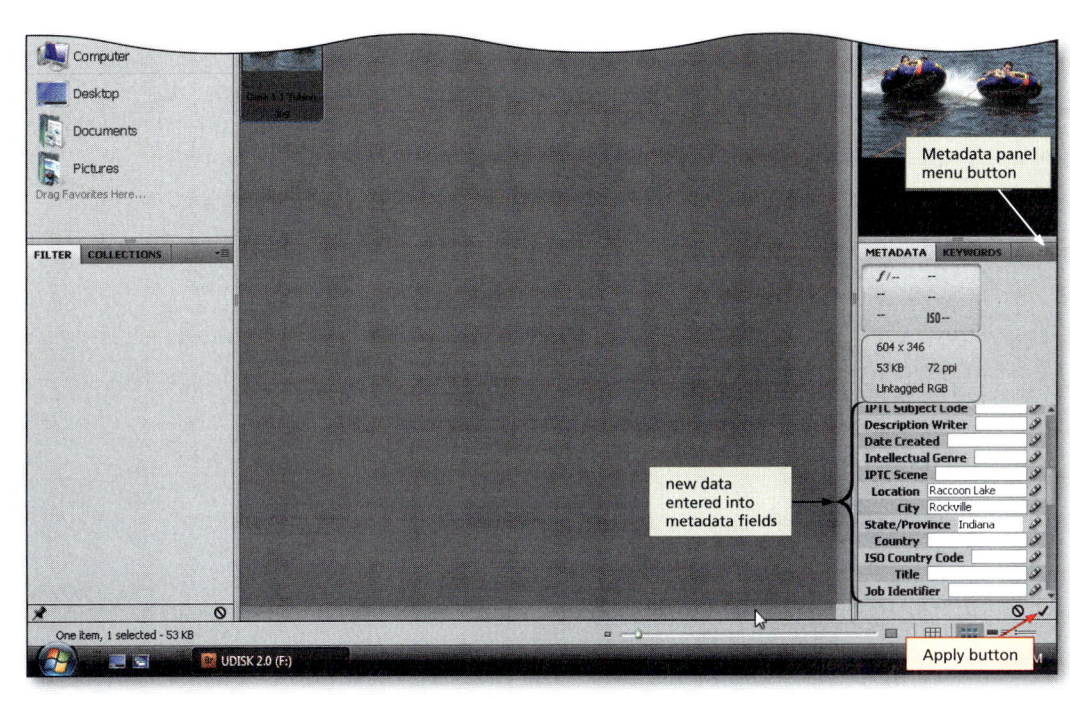

Figure E–11

3

- Click the Apply button at the bottom of the Metadata panel to assign the metadata to the photo.

- Click File on the menu bar and then click File Info to display the Case 1-1 Tubing.jpg dialog box (Figure E–12).

- Click the OK button to close the dialog box.

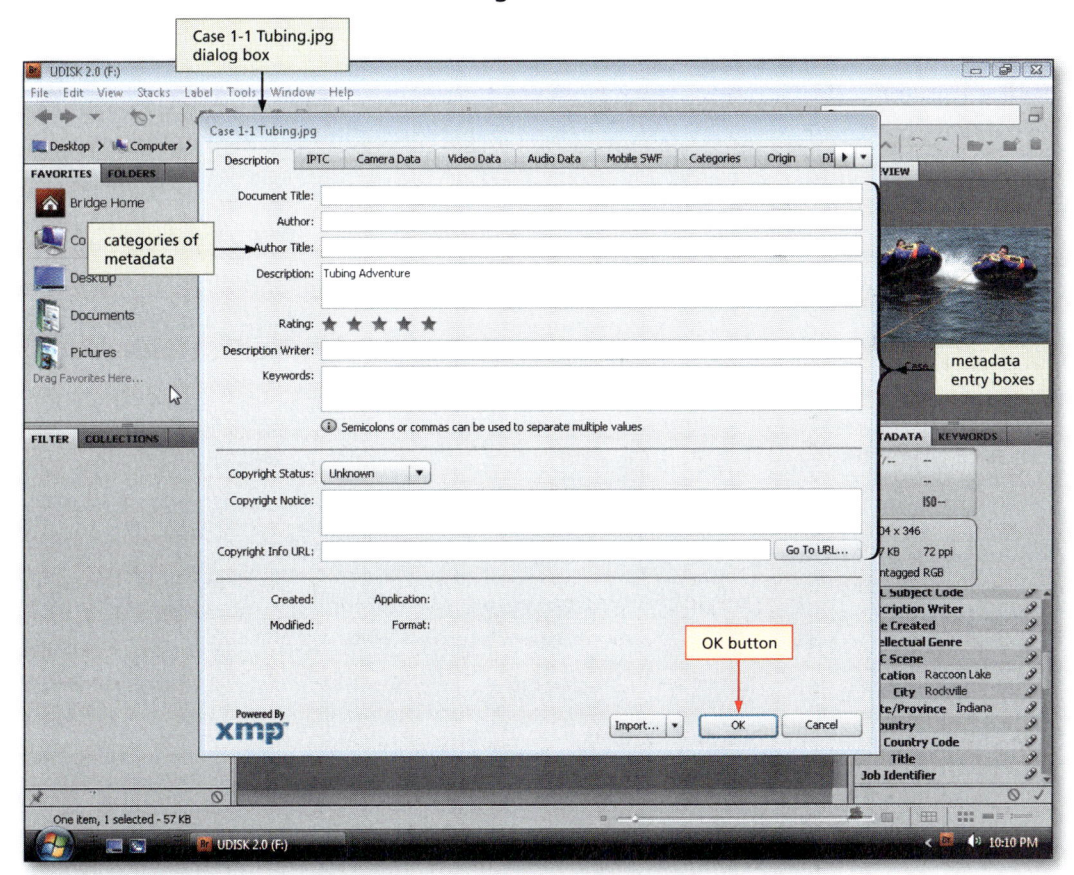

Figure E–12

Other Ways
1. Press CTRL+F4, enter data

To Enter a New Keyword

The Keywords panel lets you create and apply Bridge **keywords** to files. Keywords can be organized into categories called **sets**. Using keywords and sets, you identify and search for files based on their content. To assign keywords, you click the box to the left of the keyword in the Keywords panel, as shown in the following steps.

1
- With the Case 1-1 Tubing image still selected, click the Keywords tab.
- Scroll down to display the keyword set named, Places.
- Right-click the word, Places, to display the context menu (Figure E–13).

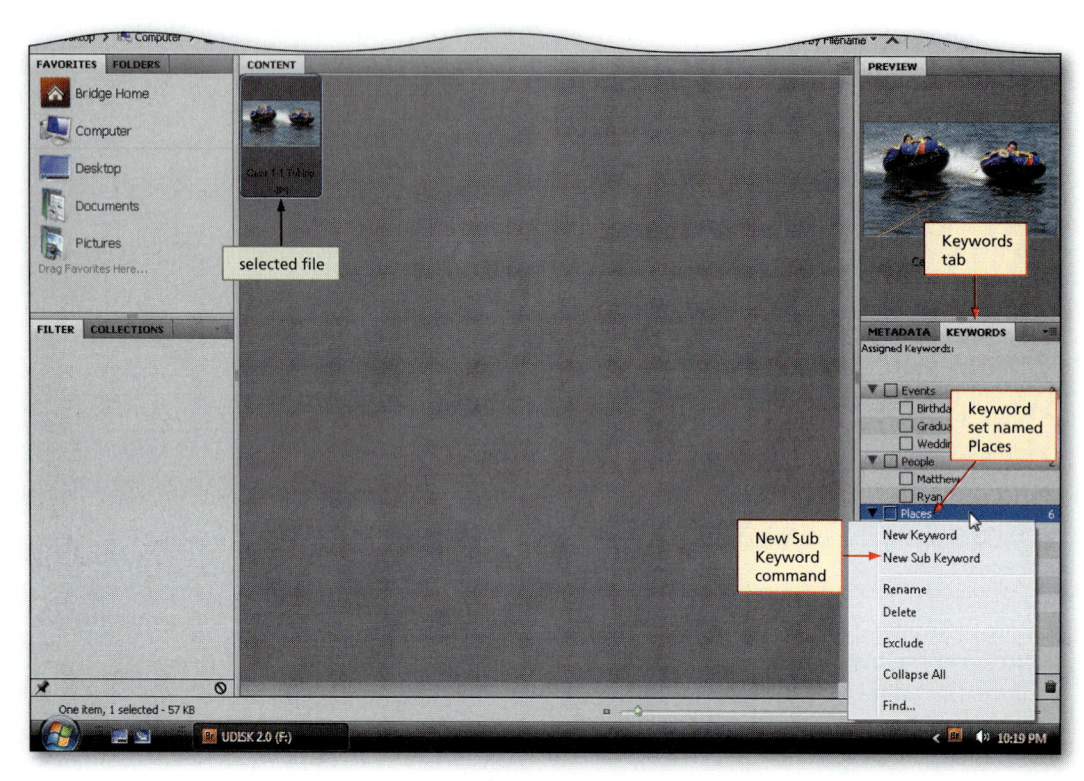

Figure E–13

2
- Click New Sub Keyword on the context menu.
- When the new field is displayed in the Keywords panel, type Indiana and then press the ENTER key to create the new item in Places.
- Click the check box to the left of Indiana to assign an Indiana keyword to the picture (Figure E–14).

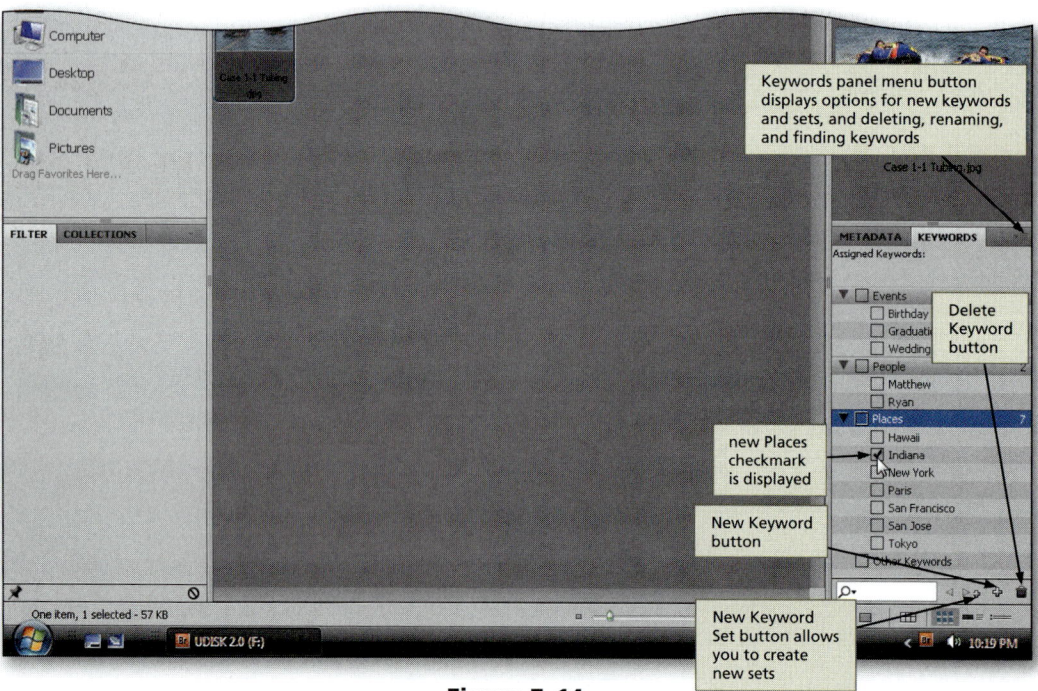

Figure E–14

To Rate a Photo

A rating system from zero stars to five stars is available in Bridge to rate your images and photos. A rating system helps you organize and flag your favorite, or best, files. Many photographers transfer their digital photos from a camera into Bridge and then look back through them, rating and grouping the photos. You can rate a photo using the Label menu or using shortcut keys. Once the photo is rated, stars are displayed below or above the file name depending on the workspace view. To change a rating, click Label on the menu bar and then either increase or decrease the rating. To remove all stars, click Label on the menu bar and then click No Rating. In some views, you can change a rating by clicking stars or dots that display below the thumbnail. You can remove the rating by clicking left of the stars.

The following steps add a rating to a photo file in Bridge.

1
- With the Case 1-1 Tubing image still selected in the Content panel, press CTRL+3 to assign a three star rating (Figure E–15).

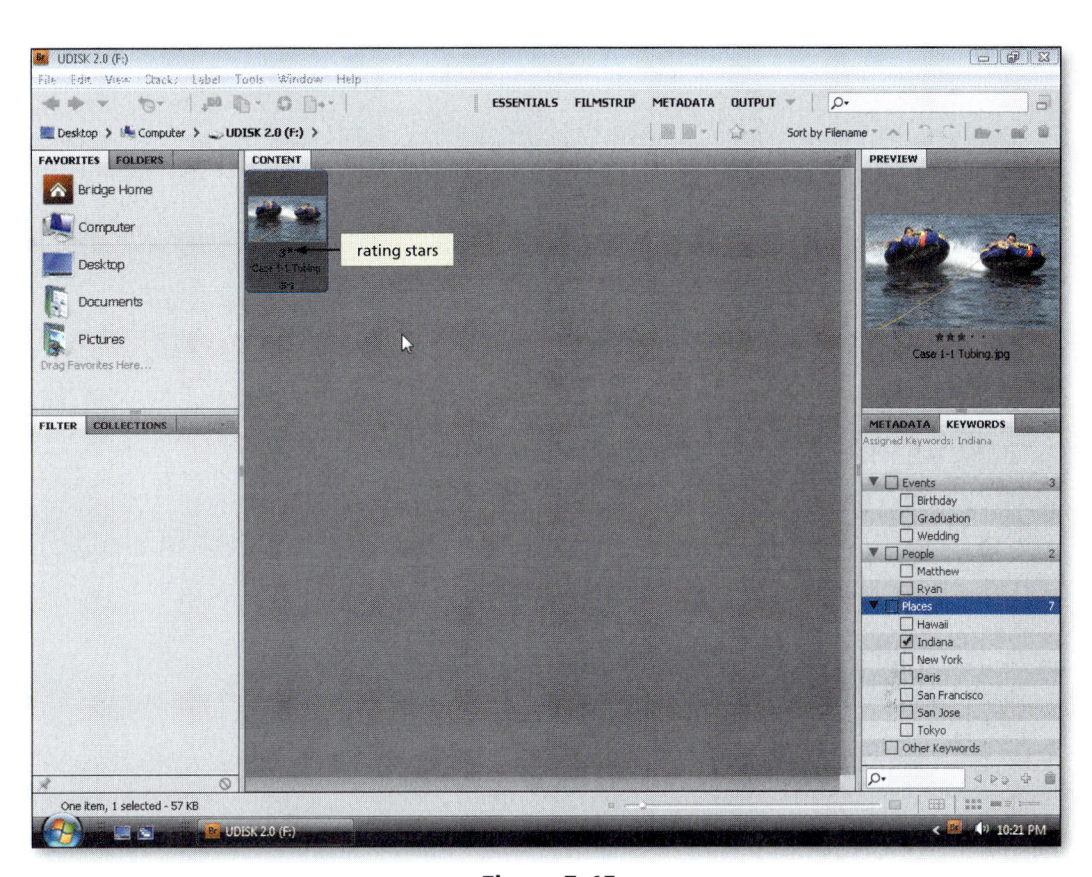

Figure E–15

Other Ways
1. On Label menu, select desired rating

To Label a Photo with Color-Coding

Another way to group photos in Bridge is to use a color-coding system. Bridge provides five colors with which users can label or group their photos. Each color has a category keyword that can be used to group photos. Keywords such as Approved, Second, or Review are used in photojournalism to indicate the status of the photo for future usage. Some companies use the colors for sorting and selecting only. The following steps add a green color indicating approval to the Case 1-1 Tubing image using the menu system. Shortcut keys also are available for labeling photos with color-coding.

1

- With the Case 1-1 Tubing image still selected in the Content panel, click Label on the menu bar to display the Label menu (Figure E–16).

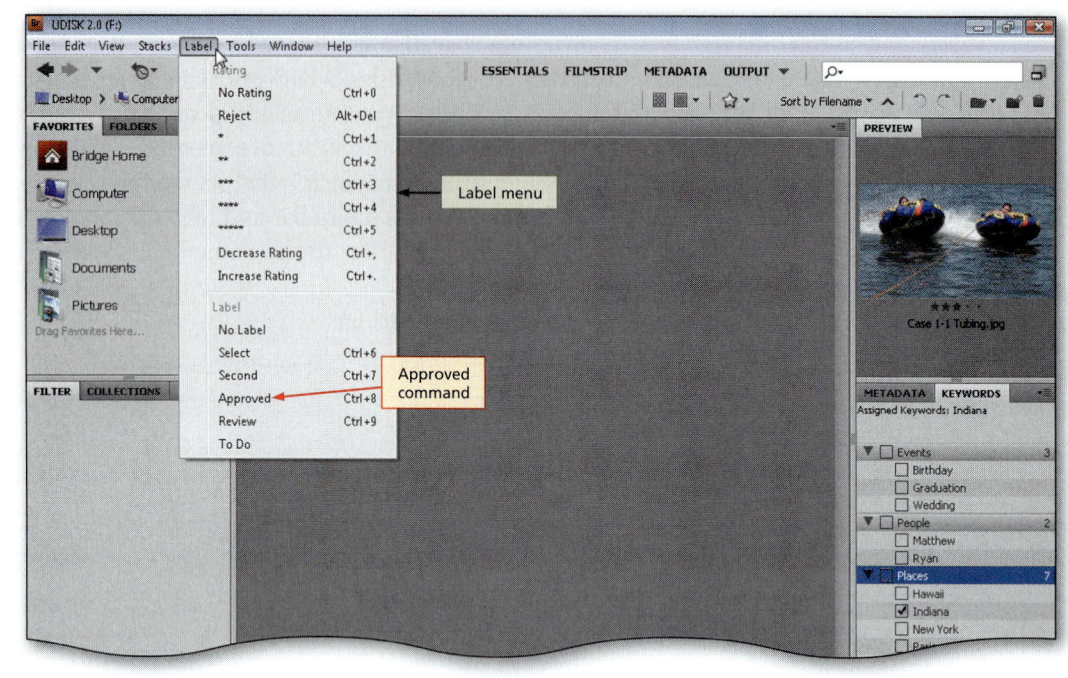

Figure E–16

2

- Click Approved.
- If Bridge displays a dialog box, click its OK button to apply the color (Figure E–17).

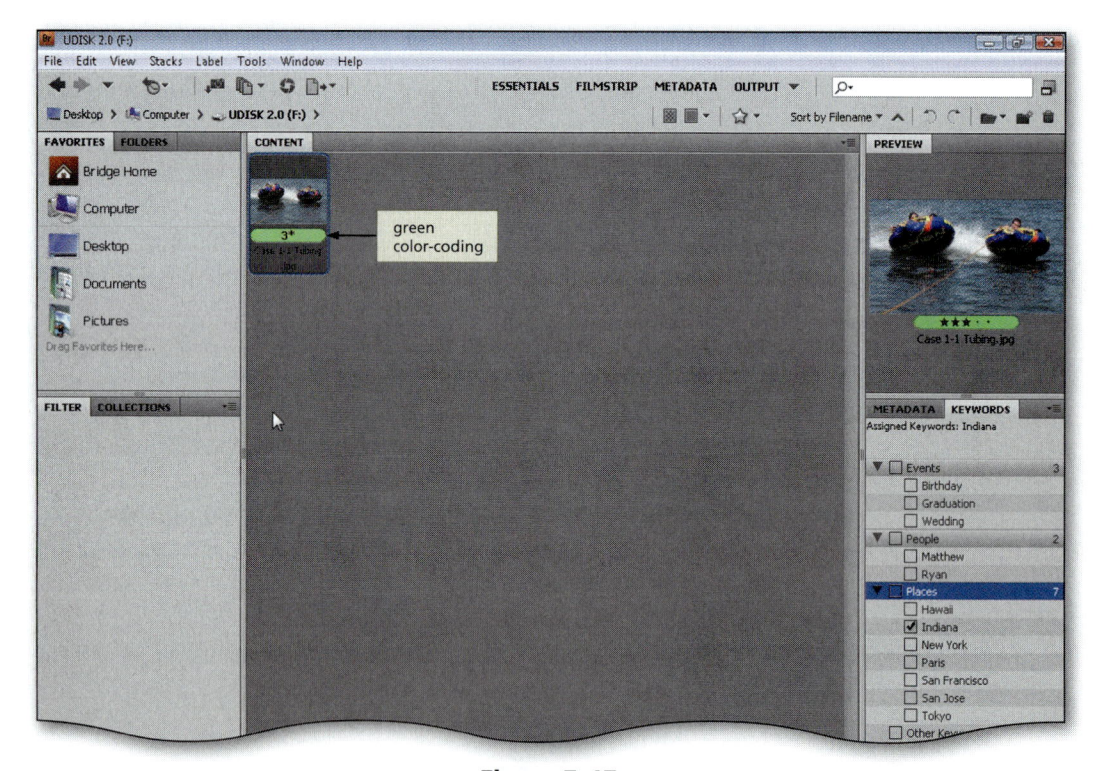

Figure E–17

Other Ways

1. Press CTRL+8

Searching Bridge

Searching is a powerful tool in Adobe Bridge, especially as the number of stored image files increases on your computer system. It is a good idea to enter keywords, or metadata, for every image file you store, to make searching more efficient. Without Adobe Bridge and the search tool, you would have to view all files as filmstrips in Windows, and then look at them a screen at a time until you found what you wanted.

> **BTW**
>
> **Saving Ratings**
> Color coding and ratings are permanent only when photos have embedded extensible markup platform (XMP) storage space. Otherwise, the colors and ratings are stored in your system's cached memory.

Using the Find Command

In Bridge, you can enter the kind of data or field that you want to search, parameters for that field, and the text you are looking for using the Find command. For example, you could search for all files with a rating of three stars or better, for files less than one megabyte in size, or files that begin with the letter m.

To Use the Find Command

The Find dialog box displays many boxes and buttons to help you search effectively. In the following steps, you will look for all files with metadata that includes the word Indiana.

1
- Click Edit on the menu bar, and then click Find to display the Find dialog box (Figure E–18).

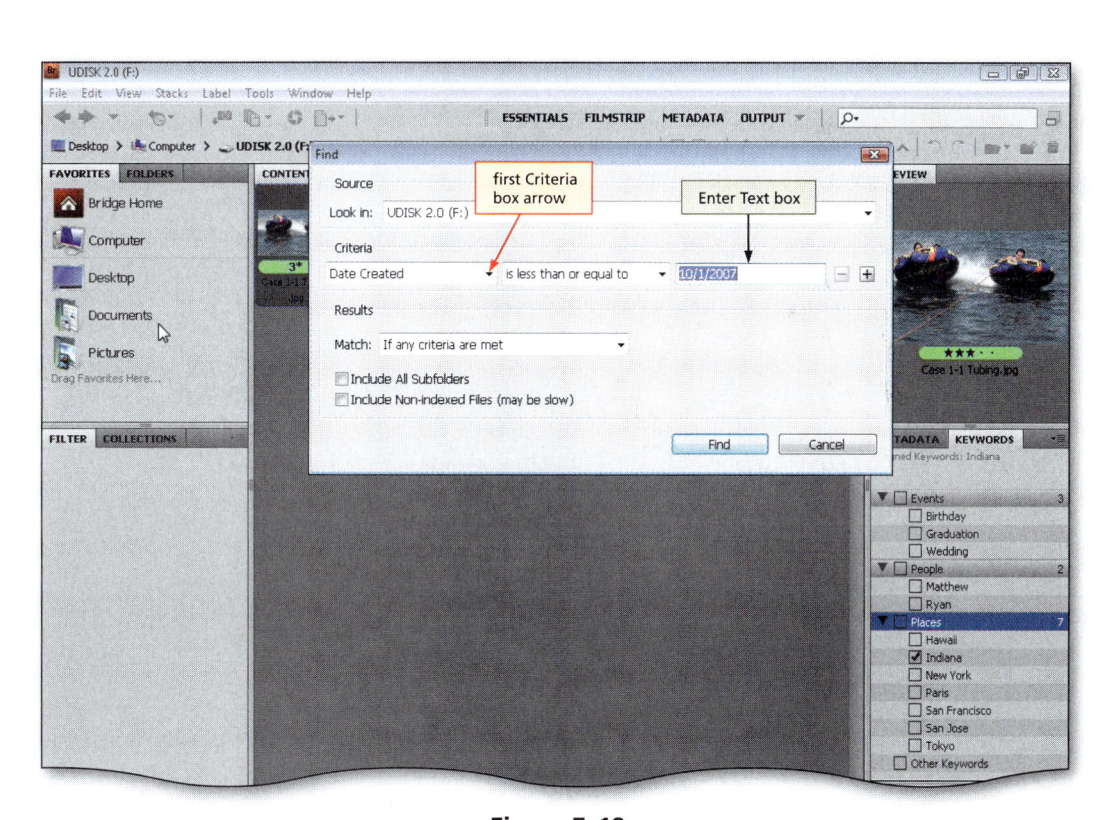

Figure E–18

APP 62 Appendix E Using Adobe Bridge CS4

2
- Click the first Criteria box arrow, and then click All Metadata at the bottom of the criteria list.
- Press the TAB key twice, and then type `Indiana` in the Enter Text box to enter the criteria (Figure E–19).

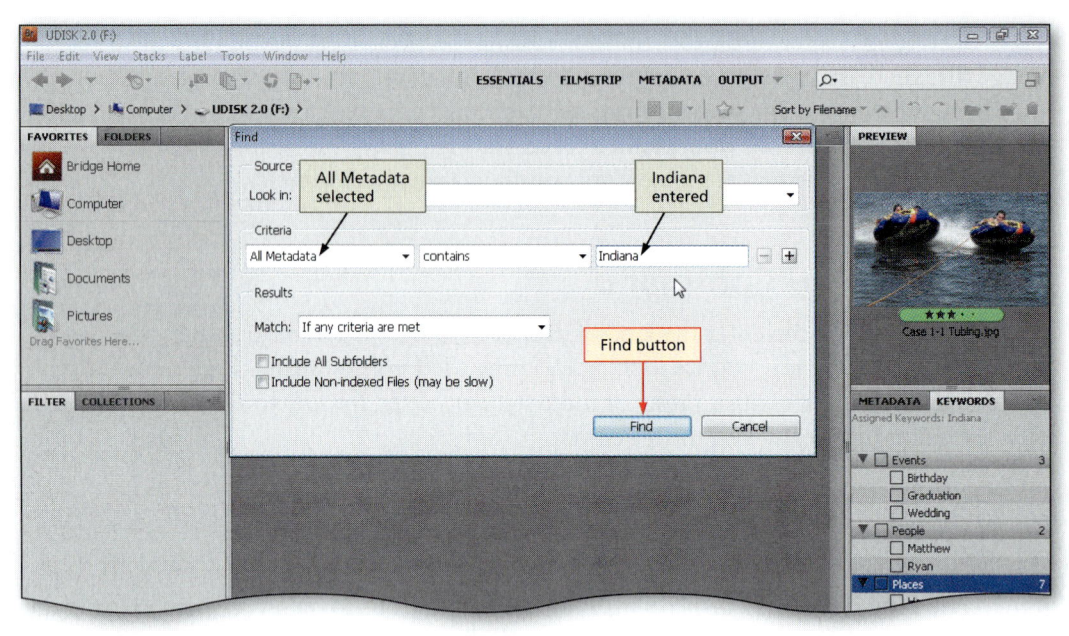

Figure E–19

3
- Click the Find button to display all files that have the word, Indiana, in any part of their metadata (Figure E–20).
- Click the Cancel button in the Search title bar.

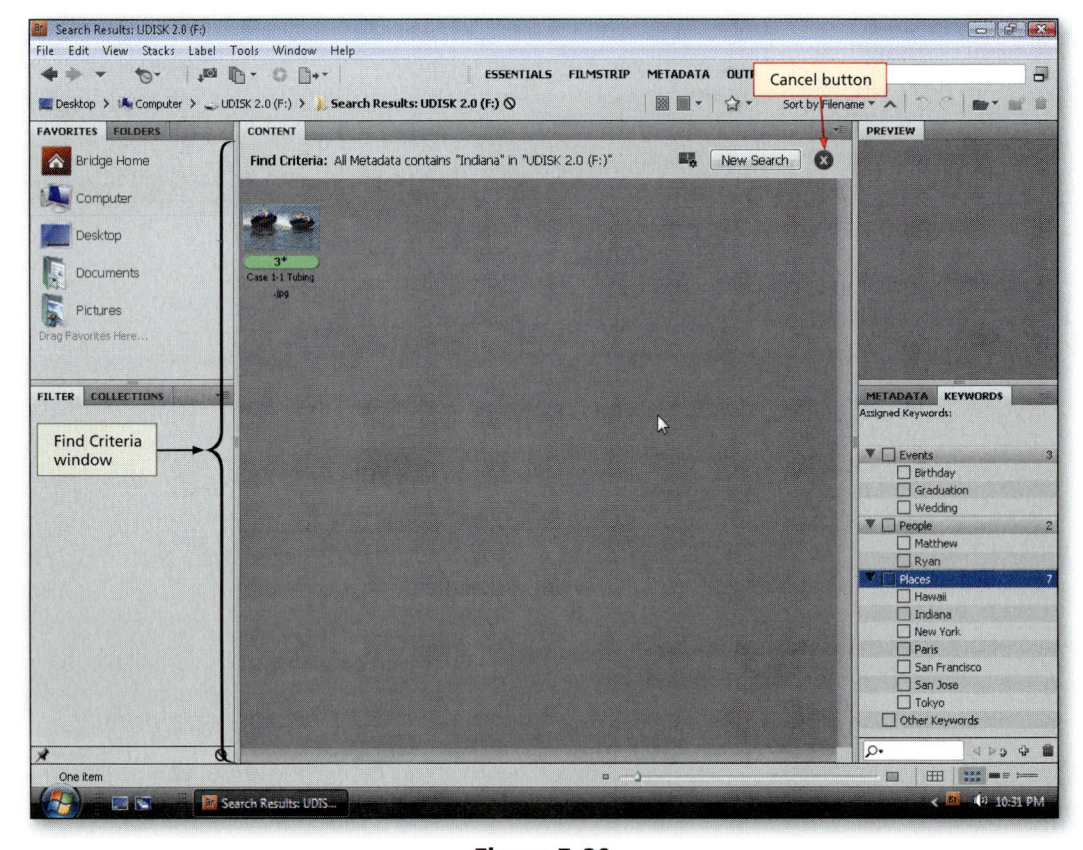

Figure E–20

Other Ways
1. Press CTRL+F

The plus sign to the right of the search boxes in the Find dialog box allows you to search multiple fields. When you click the plus sign, a second line of search boxes is displayed. For example, if you needed to find photos that were created last winter from your vacation in the Rockies, you could search for the date in the first line of boxes, click the plus button, and then enter the keyword to narrow your search even further in the second line of boxes (Figure E–21). When clicked, the Match box arrow allows you to match any or all criteria.

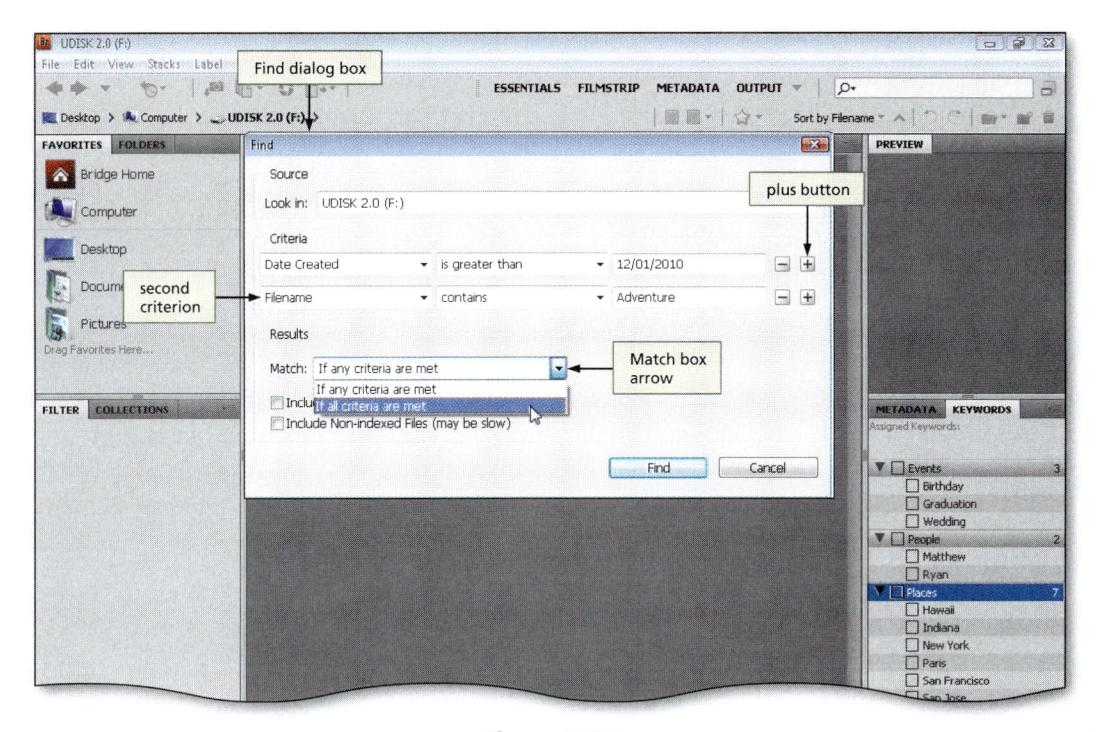

Figure E–21

Bridge offers you a way to save common searches as a **collection** for use later. For example, if you were working for a grocery wholesaler who stores many files for artwork in advertising, searching for pictures related to dairy products would be a common search. Looking through folders of images for pictures of milk or cheese would be very time consuming. Bridge then offers to name the search and store it. To display stored collections, click Collections in the Favorites panel. Then to perform the search again, double-click the collection. With metadata and collection searches, Bridge saves a lot of time.

To Close the Search Results Window and Quit Bridge

The final step closes the Find Criteria window, which quits Adobe Bridge.

1 Click the Cancel button in the Find Criteria window.

Using Bridge

1: Assigning Metadata

Instructions: You would like to assign metadata to some of the photos you worked on in previous chapters in this book. The photos can be found on the DVD containing the Data Files for Students that accompanies this book, or your instructor may direct you to a different location. You will copy the photos from the DVD to a local storage device and then assign metadata using Adobe Bridge.

1. Insert the DVD that accompanies this book or see your instructor for the location of the data files.
2. Start Adobe Bridge on your system. When the Adobe Bridge window is displayed, on the Favorites tab, click Computer. In the Content panel, double-click the DVD that accompanies this book, or navigate to the location specified by your instructor.
3. Right-click the Chapter01 folder, and then click Copy on the shortcut menu.
4. Using the Favorites tab, click Computer, and then navigate to your USB flash drive or other storage location.
5. On the Edit menu, click Paste. After a few moments, the Chapter01 folder will appear in the right pane. Double-click the folder to open it. If necessary, click the Default button on the Bridge status bar.
6. Click the first photo. In the Metadata pane, scroll down and click Description. In the description box, enter a short description of the picture. Click Description Writer. Enter your name.
7. With the first photo still selected, click the Keywords tab. When the Adobe Bridge dialog box appears, click Apply to apply the changes you just made in the Metadata pane. On the Keywords tab, click to place a check mark next to any keywords that apply to the photo.
8. Scroll to the bottom of the keywords list. If there is not an Other Keywords category, create one by right-clicking on the empty space below the last keyword, clicking New Keyword Set on the shortcut menu, and typing `Other Keywords` when the words Untitled Set are displayed. Right-click the Other Keywords category and then click New Keyword on the shortcut menu. When the words Untitled Keyword are displayed, type a new keyword relating to the selected photo.
9. Repeat Steps 6 through 8 for each photo in the right pane of the Adobe Bridge window.

Using Bridge

2: Rating and Categorizing Photos

Instructions: You would like to rate and categorize some of the photos you worked on in previous chapters in this book. The photos can be found on the DVD that accompanies this book, or your instructor may direct you to a different location.

1. If you did not perform exercise 1, Assigning Metadata, perform steps 1 through 5 from Exercise 1 to copy images to your storage location.
2. With the photos from the Chapter01 folder displayed in the right pane of the Adobe Bridge window, click the first photo. Rate the photo on a scale from 1 to 5 with 1 being the worst photo in the group and 5 being the best photo in the group. On the Label menu, click the number of stars that corresponds to your rating. Repeat the process for each of the photos in the folder.
3. Click the first photo again to select it. Click Label on the menu bar. Choose a label setting, such as Approved. Repeat the process for each of the photos in the folder, choosing different label settings.
4. Choose your favorite photo in the folder and right-click the image. Click Add to Favorites on the shortcut menu.
5. Consult with at least three other members of your class to compare your ratings.

Quick Reference Summary

In Adobe Photoshop CS4, you can accomplish a task or activate a tool in a number of ways. The following table provides a quick reference to each task and tool presented in this textbook. The first column identifies the task or tool. The second column indicates the page number on which the task or tool is discussed in the book. The subsequent three columns list the different ways the task or tool in column one can be carried out or activated.

Adobe Photoshop CS4 Quick Reference Summary

Tool or Task	Page Number	Mouse	Menu	Keyboard Shortcut
Actions Panel	PS 404		Window	Actions	ALT+F9
Add Drop Shadow	PS 213	Add a layer style button	Layer	Layer Style	Drop Shadow	
Add Layer Mask	PS 197	Add layer mask button		
Add to Selection	PS 87	Add to selection button		SHIFT+DRAG
Adjustment Layer	PS 210	Clip to layer button	Layer	New Adjustment Layer	
Adjustments Panel	PS 209		Window	Adjustments	
Alpha Channels	PS 380	Create new channel button		ALT+click
Angle Distortion	PS 351	Drag angle icon	Filter	Distort	Lens Correction	
Arrange Document Windows	PS 177	Arrange Documents button	Window	Arrange	
Assign Layer Properties	PS 179	Right-click layer	click Layer Properties	Layer	Layer Properties	
Auto-Align Layers	PS 90	Auto-Align Layers button	Edit	Auto-Align Layers	
Background Eraser Tool	PS 185	Background Eraser Tool (E) button		E
Black and White Adjustment	PS 388	Adjustments panel	Black & White icon	Image	Adjustments	Black & White	ALT+SHIFT+CTRL+B
Blur Tool	PS 357	Blur Tool button		
Bridge, Adobe	PS 61	Launch Bridge button	File	Browse in Bridge	ALT+CTRL+O
Brightness/Contrast	PS 212	Adjustments panel	Brightness/Contrast icon	Layer	New Adjustment Layer	Brightness/Contrast	
Brush Preset Picker	PS 287	Brush Preset picker button		
Brush Tool	PS 286	Brush Tool button		B
Burn Tool	PS 347	Burn Tool (O) button		O
Change Default Foreground and Background Colors	PS 164	Default Foreground/Background Colors button		D
Change Opacity	PS 206	Drag Opacity slider		
Change Screen Mode	PS 31	Screen Mode button	View	Screen Mode	F
Channel, Create	PS 380	Create new channel button		

Adobe Photoshop CS4 Quick Reference Summary (continued)

Tool or Task	Page Number	Mouse	Menu	Keyboard Shortcut
Channels, View	PS 378	Visibility icon		CTR+1
Choose Download Speed	PS 55	Select download speed button		
Clone Source Panel	PS 220		Window | Clone Source	
Clone Stamp Tool	PS 220	Clone Stamp Tool (S) button		S
Close Bridge	PS 63	Close button	File | Exit	CTRL+Q
Close File	PS 51	Close button	File | Close	CTRL+W or CTRL+F4
Clouds Filter	PS 216		Filter | Render | Clouds	
Collapse Panel	PS 29	Collapse to Icons button		
Color a Layer	PS 173	Right-click visibility area | click color		
Color Balance	PS 251		Image | Adjustments | Color Balance	
Color Layer	PS 173	Right-click layer | click Layer Properties		
Color Panel	PS 250		Window | Color	F6
Commit Change	PS 98	Commit transform (Return) button		ENTER
Composite Channel, View	PS 377	Visibility icon		CTR+—
Consolidate Windows	PS 195	Right-click document window tab | click Consolidate All to Here or click Arrange Documents | click Consolidate All button		
Convert Color Mode	PS 386		Image | Mode	
Copy	PS 94		Edit | Copy	CTRL+C or F3
Copy Layer Style	PS 216	Right-click layer | click Copy Layer Style		
Create Keyboard Shortcuts	PS 143		Edit | Keyboard Shortcuts	ALT+SHIFT+CTRL+K
Create Layer	PS 171, PS 172, PS 176, PS 178, PS 182	Drag image into document window	Layer | New Layer	SHIFT+CTRL+N
Create New Action Set	PS 407	Create new set button	Actions panel menu button | New Set	
Create PDF	PS 138		File | Save As, choose PDF Format or File | Print, choose PDF printer	
Crop	PS 37	Crop Tool (C) button	Image | Crop	C
Default Foreground/Background Colors	PS 285	Default Foreground/Background Colors (D) button		D
Desaturate	PS 387		Image | Adjustments | Desaturate	SHIFT+CTRL+U
Deselect	PS 46	Click document window	Select | Deselect	CTRL+D
Distort	PS 96	Enter rotation percentage or drag outside of bounding box	Edit | Transform | Distort	
Dodge Tool	PS 345	Dodge Tool (O) button		O
Drop Shadow	PS 272	Add a layer style button	Layer | Layer Style | Drop Shadow	
Duplicate Layer (Group)	PS 205		Layer | Duplicate Layer (Group)	
Duplicate Selection	PS 94		Edit | Copy	ALT+DRAG
Edit Menus	APP 30		Edit | Menus	ALT+SHIFT+CTRL+M
Edit Preferences	APP 27		Edit | Preferences | General	CTRL+K
Elliptical Marquee	PS 86	Elliptical Marquee Tool (M) button		M

Adobe Photoshop CS4 Quick Reference Summary (continued)

Tool or Task	Page Number	Mouse	Menu	Keyboard Shortcut
Eraser Tool	PS 185, PS 189	Eraser Tool (E) button		E
Exit	PS 63	Close button	File	Exit	CTRL+Q
Eyedropper Tool	PS 260	Eyedropper Tool (I) button		I
Fill	PS 44		Edit	Fill	SHIFT+F5
Flatten Image	PS 225	Right-click layer	click Flatten Image	Layer	Flatten Image	
Flip Horizontal	PS 96, PS 99	Right-click selection	click Flip Horizontal	Edit	Transform	Flip Horizontal	
Flip Vertical	PS 96	Right-click selection	click Flip Vertical	Edit	Transform	Flip Vertical	
Free Transform	PS 96		Edit	Free Transform	CTRL+T
Gradient Tool	PS 253	Gradient Tool (G) button		G
Grid, Hide or Show	PS 109	View Extras button	Show Grid	View	Show	Grid	CTRL+'
Grow	PS 133		Select	Grow	
Guides, Create	PS 110	Drag from ruler	View	New Guide	
Guides, Hide or Show	PS 108	View Extras button	Show Guides	View	Show	Guides	CTRL+;
Hand Tool	PS 30	Hand Tool (H) button or Hand Tool button		H
Healing Brush Tool	PS 335	Healing Brush Tool (J) button		J
Hide Layer	PS 174	Indicates layer visibility button	Layer	Hide Layers	
History Panel	PS 115		Window	History	
Horizontal Type Tool	PS 262	Horizontal Type Tool (T) button		T
Hue/Saturation	PS 210	Adjustments panel	Hue/Saturation icon	Layer	New Adjustment Layer	Hue/Saturation	CTRL+U
Keyboard Shortcuts	PS 142		Edit	Keyboard Shortcuts	ALT+SHIFT+CTRL+K
Lasso Tool	PS 120	Lasso Tool (L) button		L
Layer Mask, Add	PS 197	Add layer mask button		
Layer Mask, Reveal All	PS 199		Layer	Layer Mask	Reveal All	
Layer Properties	PS 179		Layer	Layer Properties	
Layer Style, Add	PS 214	Add a layer style button	Layer	Layer Style	
Layer via Cut	PS 172	Right-click selection	click Layer via Cut	Layer	New	Layer via Cut	SHIFT+CTRL+J
Layers Panel, Set Options	PS 169	Right-click layer thumbnail	Layer panel menu	Panel Options	
Levels, Adjust	PS 209	Adjustments panel	Levels icon	Image	Adjustments	Levels	CTRL+L
Load Actions	PS 404		Actions panel menu button	Load Actions	
Magic Eraser Tool	PS 185, PS 186	Magic Eraser Tool (E) button		E
Magic Wand Tool	PS 122	Magic Wand Tool (W) button		W
Magnetic Lasso Tool	PS 123	Magnetic Lasso Tool (L) button		L
Masks Panel	PS 202		Window	Masks	
Modify Border	PS 42		Select	Modify	Border	
Modify Smooth	PS 43		Select	Modify	Smooth	
Move Tool	PS 91	Move Tool (V) button		V
Name Layer	PS 173	Double-click layer name		
Navigator Panel	PS 28		Window	Navigator	
Open Bridge	PS 61	Launch Bridge button	File	Browse in Bridge	
Open File	PS 10	Right-click file	Open With	Adobe Photoshop CS4	File	Open	CTRL+O

Adobe Photoshop CS4 Quick Reference Summary (continued)

Tool or Task	Page Number	Mouse	Menu	Keyboard Shortcut
Open Second Image	PS 176		File | Open	CTRL+O
Paint Bucket Tool	PS 283	Paint Bucket Tool (G) button		G
Paste	PS 127		Edit | Paste	CTRL+V or F4
Patch Tool	PS 338	Patch Tool (J) button		J
Pattern Stamp Tool	PS 219	Pattern Stamp Tool (S) button		S
Photoshop Help	PS 64		Help | Photoshop Help	F1
Play Action	PS 405	Play selection button	Actions panel menu | Play	
Polygonal Lasso Tool	PS 128	Polygonal Lasso Tool (L) button		L
Print	PS 50		File | Print	CTRL+P
Print Color Separations	PS 421		File | Print | Color Handling box arrow	
Print One Copy	PS 50		File | Print One Copy	ALT+SHIFT+CTRL+P
Quick Selection Tool	PS 113	Quick Selection Tool (W) button		W
Quit Photoshop	PS 66	Close button	File | Exit	CTRL+Q
Record Action	PS 409	Create new action button	Actions Panel menu button | Start/Stop Recording	
Rectangular Marquee	PS 86	Rectangular Marquee Tool (M) button		M
Red Eye Tool	PS 342	Red Eye Tool (J) button		J
Refine Edge	PS 117	Refine Edge button or right-click selection | click Refine Edge	Select | Refine Edge	ALT+CTRL+R
Resample	PS 431		Image | Size	
Reset All Tools	PS 8	Right-click tool icon on options bar | click Reset All Tools	Tool Presets panel menu | Reset All Tools or right-click tool button on options bar	
Reset Options Bar	PS 8	Right-click Rectangular Marquee | Reset All Tools		
Resize Document Window	PS 82	Drag document window tab | drag sizing handle		
Resize Image	PS 47		Image | Image Size	ALT+CTRL+I
Restore Default Workspace	PS 7	Workspace Switcher	Window | Workspace | Essentials (Default)	
Rotate	PS 96	Enter degree rotation on options bar	Edit | Transform | Rotate	
Rotate 180°	PS 96	Enter degree rotation on options bar	Edit | Transform | Rotate 180°	
Rotate 90° CCW	PS 96	Enter degree rotation on options bar	Edit | Transform | Rotate 90° CCW	
Rotate 90° CW	PS 96	Enter degree rotation on options bar	Edit | Transform | Rotate 90° CW	
Save a File	PS 20		File | Save	CTRL+S
Save Action Set	PS 412		Actions panel menu | Save Actions	
Save As	PS 20		File | Save As	SHIFT+CTRL+S
Save For Web & Devices	PS 66		File | Save for Web & Devices	ALT+SHIFT+CTRL+S
Scale	PS 98	Enter height and width values on options bar or right-click selection | click Scale	Edit | Transform | Scale	SHIFT+DRAG CORNER SIZING HANDLE
Select All	PS 40		Select | All	CTRL+A
Set Default Workspace	PS 7	Workspace Switcher | Essentials	Window | Workspace | Essentials (Default)	
Shape Tool	PS 270	Shape Tool (U) button		U

Adobe Photoshop CS4 Quick Reference Summary (continued)

Tool or Task	Page Number	Mouse	Menu	Keyboard Shortcut
Show Layers	PS 174	Indicates layer visibility button	Layer | Show Layers	
Show Rulers	PS 33	View Extras button | Show Rulers	View | Rulers	CTRL+R
Single Column Marquee	PS 86	Single Column Marquee Tool button		
Single Row Marquee	PS 86	Single Row Marquee Tool button		
Skew	PS 96	Right-click bounding box | click Skew	Edit | Transform | Skew	
Smart Object	PS 180		Layers panel menu button | Convert to Smart Object or Layer | Smart Objects	
Snap	PS 108, PS 122	Drag selection near guide	View | Snap	SHIFT+CTRL+;
Snapshot	PS 106	Create new snapshot button	History panel menu button | New Snapshot	
Spot Healing Brush Tool	PS 333	Spot Healing Brush Tool (J) button		J
Step Backward in History	PS 107	Click state in History panel	History panel menu | Step Backward	CTRL+ALT+Z
Step Forward in History	PS 107	Click state in History panel	History panel menu | Step Forward	CTRL+SHIFT+Z
Stop Recording	PS 412	Stop Playing/Recording button	Actions panel menu | Stop Recording	
Subtract from Selection	PS 87	Subtract from selection button or right-click selection | click Subtract from selection		ALT+DRAG
Switch Between Background and Foreground Colors	PS 199	Switch Between Background and Foreground Colors (X) button		X
Thumbnail, Change Size	PS 169	Right-click thumbnail | select size	Layers panel menu button | Panel Options	
Transform Perspective	PS 96	Right-click bounding box | click Skew	Edit | Transform | Perspective	
Undo/Redo	PS 36, PS 115	Click previous state in History panel	Edit | Undo/Redo	CTRL+Z
Unsharp Mask	PS 326		Filter | Sharpen | Unsharp Mask	
Warp	PS 101	Warp button on Transform options bar, or right-click selection | click Warp	Edit | Transform | Warp	
Zoom In	PS 25	Zoom In button	View | Zoom In	CTRL++ or CTRL+=
Zoom Out	PS 26	Zoom Out button	View | Zoom Out	CTRL+−
Zoom Tool	PS 25	Zoom Tool (Z) button		Z
Zoomify	PS 52		File | Export | Zoomify	

Index

Note: Page numbers in boldface indicate key terms.

( ) (parentheses), PS 403

A

action(s)
  described, **PS 401–402**
  editing, PS 413
  organizing, PS 406
  overview, PS 401–415
  playing, PS 405
  recording, PS 409–411
  sets, PS 404, PS 407–408, PS 412–413
  stopping, PS 414
  storing, PS 405
  testing, PS 412
Actions panel, PS 402–415
Actual Pixels button, PS 24, PS 30
adjustment layers, **PS 205–208**
Adjustments panel, PS 209–212, PS 385, PS 387–391
Adobe Bridge. *See* Bridge (Adobe)
Adobe Design Premium CS4, PS 5, PS 81
Adobe Photoshop Support Center, PS 63–64
advertisements
  creating, PS 78–158, PS 370–422
  described, **PS 78**
  file formats and, PS 79, PS 137
  Web use of, PS 137
advertising piece, **PS 78**. *See also* advertisements
All Programs list, PS 5, PS 81
Angle Radius icon, PS 216
annotation area, **PS 55**
Anti-alias check box, PS 93, PS 186–197
anti-aliasing, **PS 87–88**, PS 93, PS 186–197, PS 263
Application bar, **PS 12–13**, PS 30
Auto-Enhance check box, PS 113
Auto-Select check box, PS 90

B

background color(s). *See also* color
  color channels and, PS 381–384
  described, **PS 250–251**
  gradients and, PS 255
  selecting, PS 259–261
Background Eraser tool, PS 185, PS 191–193
Background layer. *See also* layers
  described, **PS 167**
  hiding, PS 174
backgrounds. *See also* background color; Background layer
  color channels and, **PS 381–384**
  deleting, PS 383–384
  for logos, PS 413
balance, principle of, **APP 4**
bit depth, **PS 245**, PS 247
bitmap files, **PS 19**
black-and-white images, PS 385–389
blended borders, PS 39–40. *See also* borders
blending modes, PS 43–45, PS 206, PS 321–325
Blur tool, PS 330, PS 356–359
border(s)
  blended, PS 39–40
  creating, PS 39–40
  described, **PS 39–40**
  feathering and, PS 87
Border command, PS 41, PS 42–43
Border Selection dialog box, PS 42
bounding boxes, **PS 95**
boy image, PS 356–359
Bridge (Adobe)
  described, **APP 49–64**, PS 60–63
  keywords, APP 58, PS 60
  panels, APP 51–53
  viewing files with, PS 61–62
Brightness/Contrast adjustment, PS 208, PS 211–213
brush(es)
  appending, PS 297
  dual, **PS 297**
  options, PS 292–296
  overview, PS 284–300
  presets, PS 287, **PS 291–292**
  resetting, APP 36
  strokes, designing, PS 284
Brush Preset picker, PS 287
Brush tool, APP 36, PS 382–383
  described, **PS 286–290**
  drawing with, PS 287–289
Brushes panel, **PS 292–296**
Burn tool, PS 330, PS 345, PS 347
burning, **PS 345**

C

candy shop advertisement, PS 370–422. *See also* advertisements
canvas, blank, creating, PS 395
Channel Mixer, PS 389–390
channels. *See* color channels
Channels panel, PS 376–385
Character panel, PS 6
clipboard, PS 119
clips, **PS 207**
Clone Source panel, PS 218–219
Clone Stamp tool, PS 218–224
Clone tool, PS 335–336
Close button, PS 10, PS 15, PS 28, PS 51, PS 59
closure, principle of, **APP 7**
CLUT (color lookup table), PS 245
CMS (color management system), **PS 245**
CMYK color model
  choosing, PS 251
  color channels and, PS 376, PS 415–417
  color separations and, PS 421
  creating files from scratch and, PS 247–250
  described, **APP 10**, PS 219, PS 245
  gradients and, PS 251, 256–258
  Red Eye tool and, PS 242

IND 1

color. *See also* background color; color channels; foreground color
  adding, to menu commands, APP 33–34
  base, **PS 321**
  blend, PS 321
  Clone Stamp tool and, PS 219
  -coding images, APP 59–60
  contrast, **PS 120**
  default settings, PS 91, PS 164, PS 282–283, PS 285
  depth, PS 245
  design tips for, PS 282
  eraser tools and, PS 191
  fills and, PS 43–46
  four-color process, **PS 245**, PS 415–416, PS 422
  grids and, APP 37, PS 112
  guides and, APP 37, PS 112
  layers and, PS 173–174
  Magic Wand tool and, PS 92
  matching, **APP 12**
  models, **APP 10**, PS 219, PS 416, PS 244–245
  modes, **PS 244–245**, PS 416
  Move tool and, PS 91
  optimizing images and, PS 56, PS 57–58
  palettes, APP 11
  printing, APP 11, PS 421–422
  relativity, APP 12
  result, PS 321
  schemes, **APP 12–14**
  separations, PS 421–422
  spot, **PS 385**
  theory, APP 9–10
  toning, **PS 385–386**
  value of, APP 10
  Web-safe, **APP 11**, PS 56, PS 256
color channel(s)
  alpha, **PS 380–384**
  creating, PS 380
  described, **PS 376**
  displaying, PS 380
  editing, PS 382–383
  masks, **PS 380–381**
  overview, PS 370–432
  primary, **PS 376**
  sampling, PS 259–261
  saving, **PS 376**
  viewing, PS 377–378
Color panel, **PS 250–251**
Color Replacement tool, PS 286
colorcast, **PS 252**
colorization, of old photos, PS 346
committing changes, **PS 97**
Community Help, PS 63. *See also* help
composite images
  creating, PS 162–171
  described, **PS 160**
  flattening, **PS 224–227**
composition techniques, PS 162
compression, of images, PS 339
consumers, target, PS 80
context menus, **PS 8–9**. *See also* menus
context-sensitivity, **PS 8**
Contiguous check box, PS 92
continuance, principle of, APP 7
Contract command, PS 41
Contract/Expand slider, PS 116, PS 117
contrast, principle of, **APP 5**. *See also* Brightness/Contrast adjustment
Contrast slider, PS 116
Control panel, PS 6, **PS 14**. *See also* options bar
Copy command, PS 119, PS 127
Create New Folder button, PS 22
Crop command, PS 35
Crop tool, PS 36, PS 37–38, PS 349, PS 355
cropping images, PS 34, **PS 35–39**, PS 136–137
customizing Photoshop, PS 81–82
Cut command, PS 127
cutting and pasting, PS 119, **PS 127**

D

Desaturate command, PS 386–386
deselecting, use of the term, **PS 46**
design principles, **APP 3–22**, PS 4, PS 34
Device Central window, PS 56
device dependency, **APP 16**
diameters, of brush tips, PS 292
digital cameras, PS 315, **PS 316–317**
digital images, use of the term, **PS 2**
display area, **PS 16**
Distort command, PS 96
dithering, **PS 53**
document window
  described, **PS 15**
  tab, **PS 15–16**
documents, recreating missing portions of, PS 327–328
Dodge tool, PS 330, PS 345
dodging, PS 330, **PS 345**
dominance, principle of, **APP 5**
download speed, for optimized images, PS 55
downsampling images, **PS 418**
DPI (dots per inch), APP 19
drop shadows
  described, **PS 272**
  for shapes, PS 272–274
Droplet command, PS 401
duotone images, **PS 391–394**. *See also* grayscale images
Duplicate Layer command, PS 331, PS 344
DVDs (digital video disks), opening photos from, PS 10–11, PS 82–83, PS 165

E

edges, extending, after a lens correction, PS 355
Edit menu
  Copy command, PS 119, PS 127
  Cut command, PS 127
  Fill command, PS 44
  Paste command, PS 119, PS 127
  Preferences command, PS 112
  Transform command, PS 95–96
  Undo command, PS 36, PS 288
Elliptical Marquee tool, PS 87–88
e-mail attachments, PS 137

EPS (Encapsulated PostScript) files, **PS 19**, PS 317
Equalize command, PS 386
eraser tools, **PS 185–196**, PS 329
Essentials (default) workspace, PS 6, PS 7
Expand command, PS 41, PS 52
exposure, **PS 345**
extras, displaying, PS 112
Eyedropper tool, PS 259–261, PS 290

F

Feather command, PS 41
Feather slider, PS 116
feathering, **PS 87**
file(s). See also file formats; file names
  compression, PS 339
  copying, APP 55
  creating, PS 244–249
  displaying multiple, PS 176–180
  flattening, PS 36
  recreating missing portions of, PS 327–328
  size of, APP 17–19, PS 48, PS 56
file formats. See also specific file formats
  advertisements and, PS 79, PS 137
  described, **PS 18–19**
  portability and, PS 79, PS 137
File menu
  Export command, PS 52
  New command, PS 247
  Open As command, APP 33–34
  Open command, APP 33–34, PS 10–12
  Print command, PS 138–139
  Print One Copy command, PS 49–50
  Save As command, PS 20–23, PS 49
  Save command, PS 46–47
file name(s). See also file formats
  character limits, PS 21
  extensions, **PS 18–19**

saving photos and, PS 46–47, PS 49
  tips for choosing, PS 21
Fill command, PS 44
Fill dialog box, PS 44–45
Fill Screen button, PS 24, PS 30
fills, PS 43–46, PS 206
Find dialog box, APP 61–63
Fit Screen button, PS 24, PS 30
flash drives
  saving images to, PS 20–23, PS 49, PS 60, PS 84–85, PS 140–141, PS 166–167
  viewing images on, PS 62–63
flattening files, PS 36
fluidity, **APP 16–17**
flip boxes, **PS 292**
Flip Horizontal command, PS 96, PS 99–100
Flip Vertical command, PS 96
floating images, **PS 376**
focal length, PS 349
folders, creating, PS 22, PS 166
font(s). See also text
  described, **APP 15**
  sans-serif, **PS 261**
  serif, **PS 261**
  setting, PS 262–263
foreground color, PS 250–251, PS 282–283, PS 397
four-color process, **PS 245**, PS 415–416, PS 422
foxing, **PS 318–320**, PS 330
free transform, **PS 96**
Full Size Brush Tip, **APP 29**

G

gamma (midtones), **PS 208**
gamut
  described, **PS 245**
  mapping, **PS 245**
  out of, **PS 245**
GIF (Graphics Interchange Format) files, **PS 19**, PS 52, PS 57–58
girl image, PS 341–344
golden ratio, APP 8, PS 36, PS 37

Google, APP 38–39
gradient(s)
  creating, PS 253
  described, **PS 251**
  drawing, PS 258
  fills, **PS 251–258**
  noise, **PS 254**
  overview, PS 251–254
  presets, PS 254–255
  selecting stop colors and, PS 256–257
  solid, **PS 254**
  styles, **PS 252**
Gradient Editor, **PS 252–258**
Gradient tool, PS 251–254, PS 321
graphic(s)
  artists, **APP 19**
  designers, **APP 19–20**
graphics tablet, **PS 290**
grayscale images. See also duotone images
  described, **PS 196**
  layer masks and, PS 196–200
  repairing images and, PS 320–321
grid(s)
  color, PS 112
  described, **PS 108–111**
  design principles and, APP 8
  displaying, PS 108–110
  hiding, PS 110
  preferences, APP 37
gripper bar, PS 13, **PS 14**
Grow command, PS 131–134
guide(s)
  color, PS 112
  creating, PS 110–111
  described, **PS 108–111**
  manipulating, PS 108
  preferences, APP 37
  snapping images to, PS 122–123

H

hard copy, **PS 49**. See also printing
Hand tool, PS 13, **PS 30**
hardness values, **PS 287**
Healing Brush tool, PS 330, PS 335–337

help
  accessing, PS 64
  Adobe Photoshop Support Center, PS 63–64
  overview, APP 39–48, PS 63–66
  Search box, APP 39–45, **PS 65–66**
  Topics list, APP 43–45
hidden commands, APP 29–32, **PS 14**
highlights, **PS 208**
histograms, **PS 208**
History button, PS 104
History panel
  collapsing, PS 107–108
  described, **PS 103–108**
  displaying, PS 105, PS 142–147
  Duplicate states and, PS 119
  reviewing edits with, PS 36
  snapshots, PS 204
  undo feature and, PS 115
History Brush tool, PS 224
horizon line, **PS 81**
Horizontal Type tool, PS 262–265
HTML (HyperText Markup Language), **PS 52**, PS 58, PS 59
hue and saturation adjustments, **APP 9**, PS 208, PS 210–211

I

icons
  double-clicking, PS 6
  modal, **PS 402**
image setters, **PS 421**
Image Size area, PS 56
Image Size dialog box, PS 48, PS 419–420
interpolation, **PS 47–49**, PS 417–419

J

JPEG (Joint Photographic Experts Group) files
  artifacts, PS 417
  described, **PS 19**
  resolution and, PS 339

K

keyboard shortcuts. *See* shortcut keys
Keyboard Shortcuts and Menus dialog box, PS 144–148
keywords, APP 58, PS 60

L

LAB color, PS 386, PS 415–417
  described, **APP 10**, PS 245
  Red Eye tool and, PS 242
landmark schoolhouse image, PS 312–314
landscape design project, PS 160–239
Lasso tool, PS 88, PS 119, **PS 120–121**
Launch Bridge button, PS 12–13, PS 61
layer(s)
  adjustments, **PS 205–208**
  arranging, PS 168
  compositions, **PS 203–204**
  creating composite images with, PS 167–239
  deleting, PS 176
  described, **PS 90**, PS 160
  dragging selections to create, PS 180–185
  duplicating, PS 331–332, PS 344
  eraser tools and, PS 185–196
  groups, PS 176
  hiding/showing, PS 174–175
  locking, PS 167
  masks, **PS 196–205**
  moving, PS 171
  naming, PS 173–174
  opaque, PS 160, PS 206
  positioning, PS 178, PS 193, PS 200, PS 203
  properties, PS 179–180, PS 183, PS 203–205
  resizing, PS 200, PS 203
  styles, **PS 213–216**
  transparent, PS 160, PS 191
  working with, PS 159–239
Layer Comps panel, PS 204
Layer Panel Options dialog box, PS 169–171
Layer Properties dialog box, PS 173–174
Layer Style dialog box, PS 272–273
Layers panel
  described, **PS 167–171**, PS 175, PS 179–180, PS 215
  layer properties and, PS 258
  resetting, PS 246
layout
  described, **PS 80**
  perspective and, PS 80–81
  planning, PS 251
legibility, **APP 15**
Lens Correction filter, PS 348–355
level adjustments, PS 208–210
Levels dialog box, PS 208–210, PS 324–325
licenses, APP 21–22
Lighten blending mode, PS 322–324
line(s)
  drawing straight, PS 288–289
  length, **APP 15**
linked layer masks, **PS 197**
logos, PS 395–415

M

Macintosh (Apple), APP 11
Magic Eraser tool, **PS 185–187**
Magic Wand tool, PS 88, **PS 92–95**, PS 120, PS 122, PS 132, PS 379, PS 384
Magnetic Lasso tool, PS 88, PS 119–120, PS 123–125
magnification. *See also* zooming
  described, **PS 16**
  status bar and, PS 16
marching ants. *See* marquees
marquee tools, **PS 83–89**
marquees, **PS 40**, PS 83–89
Masks panel, PS 200–205
master images, creating, PS 374–375
Match Color command, PS 386
Maximize button, PS 81
memory, PS 19. *See also* RAM (random-access memory)
menu(s)
  bar, **PS 13–14**

command preferences, APP 29–38
context, **PS 8–9**
resetting, APP 34–36
menu cover project, 241–300
message area
  described, **PS 16**
  magnification box and, PS 16
metadata, **APP 56–57**, PS 60
Microsoft Windows. *See* Windows (Microsoft)
midtones (gamma), **PS 208**
Minimize button, PS 15
modal icons, **PS 402**
Modify submenu, PS 41, PS 42–43
moiré patterns, **PS 418**
monitor resolution, **APP 23–26**, PS 5, PS 81
montage, **PS 160**
mouse
  cursors, preferences for, APP 29
  pointers, minus signs next to, PS 93
Move tool, PS 90–94, PS 114, PS 118, PS 126, PS 131, PS 133–135, PS 396

N

Navigator panel, **PS 27–29**
negative space, principle of, **APP 8**
New Action dialog box, PS 408–409
New dialog box, PS 395, PS 406
New Layer dialog box, PS 285, PS 324
Normal Brush Tip, **APP 29**

O

opacity
  color channels and, PS 381
  described, **PS 43**
  layers and, PS 160, PS 206
  shapes and, PS 273
Open As command, APP 33–34
Open command, APP 33–34, PS 10–12
Open dialog box, PS 10–11, PS 51, PS 82

opening images, PS 10–12, PS 51, PS 82–83, PS 165
optimization, PS 52–60
options bar. *See also* Control panel
  described, **PS 14**
  docking/floating, **PS 14**
  resetting, PS 8–9, PS 82, PS 164

P

Paint Bucket tool, PS 279–284
palettes, PS 12. *See also* panels
panel(s)
  arranging, PS 17
  collapsed, PS 16
  described, **PS 12**, PS 16–18
  expanded, PS 16
  groups, **PS 16**
  list of, PS 18
  minimized, PS 16
  resetting, APP 35–36
  stacking, PS 17
Panel Options command, PS 28
Panel Options dialog box, PS 28
PANTONE color, PS 391
Paragraph panel, PS 6
parentheses, PS 403
Paste command, PS 119, PS 127
Patch tool, PS 330, 337–341
patterns
  moiré, **PS 418**
  use of the term, **PS 219**
PDD (Photoshop Deluxe) format, **PS 23**
PDF (Portable Document Format) files
  closing, PS 141
  creating, PS 138–142
  described, **PS 19**
  file extensions for, PS 19
  with help information, APP 45–48
  portability of, PS 79, PS 137
  viewing, PS 141
Pencil tool, PS 286
perspective
  described, **PS 80–81**
  gradients and, PS 251
  shapes and, PS 268, PS 271–272

Perspective command, PS 96
photograph, use of the term, **PS 2**
pixel(s)
  depth, **PS 245**
  described, **APP 17**, PS 40
  eraser tools and, PS 186
  marquee tools and, PS 86
  per centimeter, **PS 244–245**
  per inch (PPI), APP 17–19, PS 244–245
  primary colors and, PS 376
  resizing images and, PS 418–420
Polygonal Lasso tool, **PS 120**, PS 127–131, PS 281
polygons, PS 269, PS 281–282
pop-up panels, PS 276
post-processing, **PS 34**. *See also* editing photos
postcard(s)
  borders, PS 39–40
  described, **PS 3**
  cropping, PS 35–39
  described, **PS 3**
  editing, PS 3–76
  finding appropriate images for, PS 9
  optimizing, for Web use, PS 52–60
  printing, PS 49–52
ppi (pixels per inch), **APP 17–19**, PS 244–245
Precise painting cursor, **APP 29**
preference(s)
  grid, PS 112
  guide, PS 112
  setting, APP 27–38, PS 112
Preferences command, PS 112
Preferences dialog box, APP 27–38
prepress tasks, **PS 421**
Preset area, PS 56
Preset Manager, PS 292
Preview button, PS 59
previewing images, PS 53–54, PS 59
Print button, PS 140
Print command, PS 138–139
Print dialog box, PS 49–51, PS 52, PS 138, PS 421

Print One Copy command,
    PS 49–50, PS 52
printing
  color, APP 11, PS 421–422
  design principles and, APP 16
  orientation, PS 139
  overview, PS 49–52
  resolution, APP 19
  TIFF images, PS 227
printouts, **PS 49**. *See also* printing
project guidelines
  for advertisements, PS 79,
    PS 370–422
  for editing images, PS 4, PS 314
  for landscape design projects,
    PS 162
  for menu covers, PS 244
  overview, APP 1–2
  for repairing photos, PS 314
proximity, principle of, **APP 6**
proxy view area, PS 27
PSD (Photoshop Document) files
  described, **PS 19**
  file extensions for, PS 19
  saving photos and, PS 19–23,
    PS 166–167, PS 300, PS 320,
    PS 374–375
  when to use, PS 137
public-domain images, **APP 22**

Q

Quick Selection tool, PS 112–115,
    PS 132
quitting Photoshop, PS 66, PS 148,
    PS 227

R

Radius slider, PS 116
RAM (random access memory),
    PS 385. *See also* memory
raster images, **PS 226**
rating systems, for images,
    APP 59–60
RAW files, **PS 19**, PS 316
really-Web safe colors, **APP 11**

Rectangular Marquee tool, PS 39,
    PS 82, PS 85–86, PS 88–89,
    PS 327
Red Eye tool, PS 330, PS 342–344
red-eye, **PS 342**. *See also* Red
    Eye tool
reference points, **PS 95**
Refine Edge dialog box, PS 115–119,
    PS 125, PS 131
render filters, **PS 216–218**
repetition, principle of, **APP 6**
Replace Color command, PS 386
report card image, PS 312–330
resampling, **PS 47–49**, PS 417–420
Reset All Tools option, PS 9, PS 82
Resize Windows To Fit check box,
    PS 24
resizing images, **PS 34**, PS 47–49,
    PS 56, PS 58, PS 417–419
resolution
  design principles and, APP 17–19
  image, APP 17–19, PS 40,
    PS 47–49, PS 248, PS 315,
    PS 339
  lost, through compression, PS 339
  printing and, APP 19
  scanners and, PS 315
  screen, APP 23–26, PS 5, PS 81
retouching tools, **PS 330–331**
RGB (red-green-blue) color model
  color channels and, PS 376,
    PS 385, PS 415–416
  described, **APP 10**, PS 219,
    PS 245
  gradients and, PS 251, 256–258
  Red Eye tool and, PS 242
Rotate command, PS 96
Rotate scrubby slider, PS 126
rotating photos, PS 34
roundness settings, **PS 292**
royalty-free images, **APP 22**
readability, **APP 15**
rule of thirds, APP 8, PS 34–35,
    PS 37
ruler(s)
  cropping images and, PS 38
  described, **PS 33–34**

displaying, PS 33–34
guides and, PS 33, PS 110–111
viewing, PS 83

S

Sample Radius box, PS 43
samples, use of the term, **PS 218**
Save As command, PS 20–23,
    PS 49
Save As dialog box, PS 19, PS 21,
    PS 49, PS 83–85, PS 166,
    PS 249
Save button, PS 19, PS 23, PS 49
Save command, PS 46–47
Save For Web & Devices
    command, PS 52–60
Save Optimized As dialog box,
    PS 60
Save PDF File As dialog box,
    PS 140–142
saving images
  described, **PS 10**, PS 84–85
  file names and, PS 46–47, PS 49
  to Flash drives, PS 20–23, PS 49,
    PS 60, PS 84–85, PS 140–141,
    PS 166–167
  layers and, PS 224
  overview, PS 19–23
  in PSD format, PS 19–23,
    PS 166–167, PS 300, PS 320,
    PS 374–375
  shortcut keys for, PS 137
  for use on the Web, PS 52–60
Scale command, PS 96
Scale to Fit feature, PS 138
scanners, **PS 315**
schoolhouse image, PS 350–355
schoolmaster image, PS 331–341
screen mode(s)
  changing, PS 31–32
  described, **PS 31**
  full, **PS 31–32**
  standard, **PS 31**
Screen Mode button, PS 13, PS 31
screen resolution, **APP 23–26**,
    PS 5, PS 81

Scroll All Windows check box, PS 30
scroll bars, **PS 16**
scrubby sliders, **PS 97**
Search box, APP 39–45, **PS 65–66**
Select Stop Color dialog box, PS 256–259
selection(s)
  creating layers by dragging, PS 180–185
  deleting, PS 90
  deselecting, PS 46, PS 103
  duplicating, PS 90, 94–95, PS 100, PS 135–136
  filling, PS 43–46
  flipping, PS 96, **PS 99–100**
  inverse, **PS 88**
  layer masks, **PS 200–201**
  making, PS 40–41
  modifying, PS 41
  moving, PS 114, PS 126
  nudging, PS 90
  resizing, PS 97
  rotating, PS 96–97, PS 126
  scaling, **PS 98–100**
  transformation commands and, PS 95–103
  warping, PS 96, PS 101–102
sepia images, **PS 389–391**
shades, **APP 10**
Shadow/Highlight command, PS 386
shadows, **PS 208**
shape(s)
  creating/transforming, PS 276
  described, **PS 268**
  layers, **PS 269**
  modes, PS 269
  overview, PS 268–279
  Paint Bucket tool and, PS 281
  skewing, PS 271–272
Shape tool, PS 268–279, PS 413
Sharpen tool, PS 330, PS 356–359
sharpening images, **PS 325–330**, PS 356–359
shortcut keys
  creating, PS 142–147

default settings, PS 147–148
  described, **PS 142–148**
  deselecting selections with, PS 103
  moving selections with, PS 126
  quitting Photoshop with, PS 148
  removing white space with, PS 131
  resetting, APP 35–36
  saving images with, PS 137
  testing, PS 146
  zooming with, PS 123, PS 126, PS 132
shortcut menus. *See* context menus
Show Grids command, PS 109
Show Guides command, PS 33
Show Transform Controls check box, PS 90, PS 95
Similar command, PS 131
Single Column Marquee tool, PS 86
Single Row Marquee tool, PS 86
Skew command, PS 96, PS 118–119
slices, APP 37
smart objects, PS 180
Smooth command, PS 41, PS 43
Smooth slider, PS 116
smoothness settings, **PS 254–255**, PS 293
Smudge tool, PS 330, PS 356–359
snapping, **PS 108**
snapshots, **PS 106**
Spacing slider, **PS 292**
Sponge tool, PS 330, PS 345
spot color channel, **PS 385**
Spot Healing tool, PS 330–334, PS 338, PS 339
stacking order, of layers, PS 171
Standard painting cursor, **APP 29**
starting Photoshop, **PS 5–6**, PS 81–82, PS 163
states, **PS 103**. *See also* History panel
status bar, **PS 16**
stock images, APP 21–22, PS 178
stop(s)
  actions and, **PS 402**
  color, PS 254–259

storyboards
  described, **PS 81**
  duplications and, PS 95
strokes
  described, **PS 266**
  text, PS 261, **PS 266–269**
style(s)
  layers and, PS 205
  resetting, APP 38
Styles panel, PS 6
stylus, PS 290
submenus, **PS 13–14**

T

tab groups, **PS 16**
text. *See also* fonts
  color, PS 290
  inserting, PS 261–265
  strokes, PS 261, **PS 266–269**
  styles, PS 261
  warping, PS 398–400
threshold, **PS 321**
thumbnails
  Adobe Bridge and, PS 60–63
  advertisements and, PS 81
  color channels and, PS 376
  layers and, PS 169–171
TIFF (Tagged Image File Format) files, PS 19, **PS 226–227**
  resolution and, PS 339
  saving, PS 300
title bars, **PS 15–16**
toggles, **PS 10**
tolerance levels, PS 186
tonal
  adjustments, to layers, **PS 205**
  range, PS 325
tool(s). *See also* specific tools
  choosing the correct, PS 84
  described, **PS 14**
  expandable, PS 14
  presets, **APP 35**
  selecting, PS 14
tool icon, PS 13, PS 14
Tool Preset picker, PS 24, PS 30, PS 86–87

Tools panel, PS 14–15, PS 24
  help, PS 65–66
  settings, PS 8, PS 82, PS 164
Topics list, APP 43–45
Transform command, PS 95–96
Transform Options bar, PS 96
transformation commands, PS 95–103
Trim command, PS 35
tints, **APP 10**
tutorials, APP 44–45
typeface, **APP 15–16**
typography, **APP 15**
Typography workspace, PS 6

U

undo feature, PS 36, PS 115, PS 185, PS 288
unity, principle of, **APP 8**
Unsharp Mask filter, PS 325–327, PS 356
upsampling images, **PS 418**

V

vanishing points, PS 355
Variations command, PS 386
vector objects, **PS 268**. *See also* shapes
videos, in Photoshop Help, APP 44–45
viewing images, PS 24–26, PS 61–62, PS 112
vignettes, **PS 87**, PS 346–347, PS 348
viruses, PS 137

W

Warp command, PS 96, PS 101–102
Warp Text dialog box, PS 398–400
Webmasters, PS 137
white space
  importance of, PS 81
  removing, PS 122, PS 131, PS 132
WIA (Windows Image Acquisition) support, PS 315
windows, consolidating/arranging, PS 176–178, PS 195–196
Windows (Microsoft)
  color palettes and, APP 11
  Explorer, PS 60
  opening Bridge with, PS 62
  starting Photoshop with, PS 5–6
workspace
  customizing, PS 6–10
  default (Essentials workspace), PS 6, PS 7
  described, **PS 6**, PS 12–19
  resetting, APP 50–51, PS 82, PS 163
Workspace switcher, **PS 7**, PS 12–13, PS 82, PS 146
World Wide Web
  design principles and, APP 16
  downloading images from, PS 315, PS 317
  optimizing photos for, PS 52–60
  -safe colors, **APP 11**, PS 56, PS 256
  searches, APP 38–39

Y

yellowing, from light damage, PS 344–345

Z

Zoom All Windows check box, PS 24
Zoom Slider, PS 27
Zoom tool, PS 24–26, PS 126
Zoomify command, PS 52
zooming. *See also* magnification
  described, **PS 24–26**
  with the Navigator Panel, PS 27–29
  shortcut keys, PS 123

Photo Credits

Ch 1 Fig 1–1: National Park Service, Bison in Upper Geyser Basin; J Schmidt, 1977; Fig 1–87: National Park Service, Indiana Dunes National Lakeshore; Fig 1–88: John J. Mosesso/NBII.Gov; Fig 1–89: NASA/JPL-Caltech/Harvard-Smithsonian CFA; Fig 1–90: Fred Starks; Fig 1–92, Case and Places 1: Katie Starks; Cases and Places 2: Jeffrey Olson Sgt. Floyd Monument Sioux City Iowa; **Ch 2** Fig 2–1, 2-91, 2-92, Cases and Places 1, Cases and Places 2: Fred Starks; **Ch 3** Fig 3–1, Fig 3–83, Fig 3–84, Fig 3–85, Fig 3–86: Fred Starks; Fig 3–87, Fig 3–88: Kevin Marshall; **Ch 4** Figure 4–1, pizza: Fred Starks; Figure 4–1, projector: Kevin Marshall; Figure 4–85, shoreline: Kevin Marshall; Figure 4–85, movie reel: Kevin Marshall; Figure 4–86, cell phone: Kevin Marshall; **Ch 5** Figure 5–1, Soccer boy: Jupiterimages; Figure 5–63: Kevin Marshall; Figure 5–64: Kevin Marshall; Figure 5–66: Kevin Marshall; Figure 5–67: Fred Starks; **Ch 6** Figure 6–1, candy and snacks: Jupiterimages; Figure 6–64: Kevin Marshall; Figure 6–65: Kevin Marshall; Figure 6–66: Kevin Marshall; Figure 6–68, moon image: NASA